VISUAL BASIC 4
HOW-TO

THE DEFINITIVE VISUAL BASIC 4 PROBLEM-SOLVER

Zane Thomas, Karl Peterson,
Constance Petersen, James Shields,
Stuart Greenberg, Mitchell Waite

WAITE
GROUP
PRESS™

Corte Madera, CA

PUBLISHER Mitchell Waite
EDITOR-IN-CHIEF Charles Drucker
ACQUISITIONS EDITOR Jill Pisoni
EDITORIAL DIRECTOR John Crudo
MANAGING EDITOR Kurt Stephan
TECHNICAL REVIEWER Steve Peschka
COPY EDITOR Carol Henry
PRODUCTION DIRECTOR Julianne Ososke
PRODUCTION MANAGER Cecile Kaufman
PRODUCTION TRAFFIC COORDINATOR Ingrid Owen
DESIGNER Karen Johnston
PRODUCTION Lumina Design, Tom Debolski
ILLUSTRATIONS Pat Rogondino
COVER DESIGN Sestina Quarequio
COVER ILLUSTRATION Robert Burger

Printed in the United States of America
   96 97   •   10 9 8 7 6 5 4

Library of Congress Cataloging-in-Publication Data

Visual Basic 4 how-To / Zane Thomas... [et al.].
        p. cm.
     Rev. ed. of: Visual Basic how-To / Zane Thomas, Robert Arnson,
   Mitchell Waite. c1993.
     Includes index.
     ISBN 1-57169-001-8
        1. BASIC (Computer program language) 2. Microsoft Visual BASIC.
   I. Thomas, Zane. II. Thomas, Zane. Visual Basic how-To.
   QA76.73.B3V55 1995
   005.26--dc20
                                                                95-9521
                                                                CIP

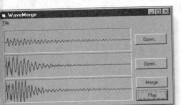

Figure 4-9-1 WaveMerge with RINGOUT.WAV and DING.WAV merged

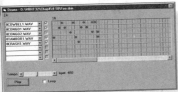

Figure 4-10-1 The Drum Machine

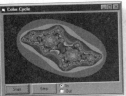

Figure 5-1-1 The CYCLECLR project

Figure 5-2-2 The READDIB project

Figure 5-8-1 Spaceship on a moving background

Figure 5-9-1 Space game in action

Figure 6-1-1 Program Manager Browser in action

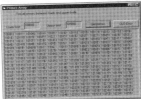

Figure 6-2-1 The PRIMES program, running

Figure 6-3-1 The Object Viewer showing its stuff

Figure 6-4-1 The document assembler in action

Figure 7-1-1 SPOOL.VBP in action

Figure 7-2-1 INI File Editor running

Figure 7-3-1 GETHWND project in action

Figure 7-4-1 The GETHANDL project in action

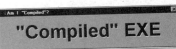

Figure 7-5-1 VBEXE32.EXE when executed

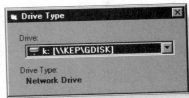

Figure 7-6-1 The DRIVETYP project

Figure 7-7-1 FEXIST in action

Figure 7-8-1 FILEDT showing the date/time stamp of WIN.INI

SAMPLE SCREENS FROM VISUAL BASIC 4 HOW-TO

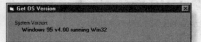

Figure 7-10-1 GETOSVER's display

Figure 7-9-1 Executable File Icon Viewer in action

Figure 8-1-2 The SelectAddress form during design

Figure 8-2-1 Multiple database selections in action on the Select Cities form

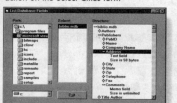

Figure 8-3-1 Displaying Access database tables and fields

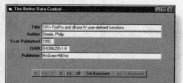

Figure 8-4-1 The DataCtl project

Figure 8-5-1 Field displays in action on the Display Database Fields form

Figure 8-6-1 The DBCreate project

Figure 8-8-1 The Soundex project in action

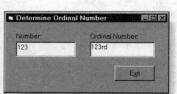

Figure 9-1-1 The ordinal number calculator in action

Figure 9-2-1 The Make an Anniversary Message project in action

Figure 9-3-1 The WallPaper program, running

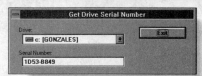

Figure 9-4-1 Schedule of dates in action

Figure 9-5-1 The CFiles demonstration project in action

Figure 9-6-1 The Bugger program in action

Figure 9-6-3 BugPad displaying sample debugging output

Figure 9-7-1 The Parser in action

Figure 9-8-1 The HiLo form, demonstrating boundary conditions

DEDICATION

Zane Thomas: To my wife Deborah, and my children Zachary, Chelsea, and Alexander.

Karl Peterson: To my wife Ann and our sons Cole and Tyler, without whose incredible support my contributions to this book would not have been possible. It has caused a lot of missed family time that can never be recaptured, but will be made up for with a vengeance in the near future.

Constance Petersen: To Lynn, love of my life, for keeping me steady. To Nic, for keeping me honest. To Daniel, for keeping me dreaming. To Zac, for keeping me laughing. To Steff, always in my memories, for keeping me caring.

James Shields: To Mom, for always being there. To Malcolm, for making Mom happy. To Penny, with hope.

Stuart Greenberg: To Andrew Fluegelman, for talking me into buying my first PC and helping me start writing about them. I know that somehow he'll see this. To Mom, Dad, Bob, and Mela, for loving their resident computer geek. And to Grandma Hannah, for her constant desire to see her grandson's name in print.

Mitchell Waite: To Lubani—the road to Hana was long, but so worth it. To Nick—your furry face makes my day.

Message from the
Publisher

WELCOME TO OUR NERVOUS SYSTEM

Some people say that the World Wide Web is a graphical extension of the information superhighway, just a network of humans and machines sending each other long lists of the equivalent of digital junk mail.

I think it is much more than that. To me the Web is nothing less than the nervous system of the entire planet—not just a collection of computer brains connected together, but more like a billion silicon neurons entangled and recirculating electro-chemical signals of information and data, each contributing to the birth of another CPU and another Web site.

Think of each person's hard disk connected at once to every other hard disk on earth, driven by human navigators searching like Columbus for the New World. Seen this way the Web is more of a super entity, a growing, living thing, controlled by the universal human will to expand, to be more. Yet unlike a purposeful business plan with rigid rules, the Web expands in a nonlinear, unpredictable, creative way that echoes natural evolution.

We created our Web site not just to extend the reach of our computer book products but to be part of this synaptic neural network, to experience, like a nerve in the body, the flow of ideas and then to pass those ideas up the food chain of the mind. Your mind. Even more, we wanted to pump some of our own creative juices into this rich wine of technology.

TASTE OUR DIGITAL WINE

And so we ask you to taste our wine by visiting the body of our business. Begin by understanding the metaphor we have created for our Web site—a universal learning center, situated in outer space in the form of a space station. A place where you can journey to study any topic from the convenience of your own screen. Right now we are focusing on computer topics, but the stars are the limit on the Web.

If you are interested in discussing this Web site, or finding out more about the Waite Group, please send me email with your comments and I will be happy to respond. Being a programmer myself, I love to talk about technology and find out what our readers are looking for.

Sincerely,

Mitchell Waite

Mitchell Waite, C.E.O. and Publisher

200 Tamal Plaza
Corte Madera CA 94925
415 924 2575
415 924 2576 fax

Internet email:
mwaite@waite.com

CompuServe email:
75146,3515

Website:
http://www.waite.com/waite

CREATING THE HIGHEST QUALITY COMPUTER BOOKS IN THE INDUSTRY

Waite Group Press
Waite Group New Media

Come Visit
WAITE.COM
Waite Group Press
World Wide Web Site

Now find all the latest information on Waite Group books at our new Web site, **http://www.waite.com/waite.** You'll find an online catalog where you can examine and order any title, review upcoming books, and send email to our authors and editors. Our ftp site has all you need to update your book: the latest program listings, errata sheets, most recent versions of Fractint, POV Ray, Polyray, DMorph, and all the programs featured in our books. So download, talk to us, ask questions, on **http://www.waite.com/waite.**

The New Arrivals Room has all our new books listed by month. Just click for a description, Index, Table of Contents, and links to authors.

The Backlist Room has all our books listed alphabetically.

The People Room is where you'll interact with Waite Group employees.

Links to Cyberspace get you in touch with other computer book publishers and other interesting Web sites.

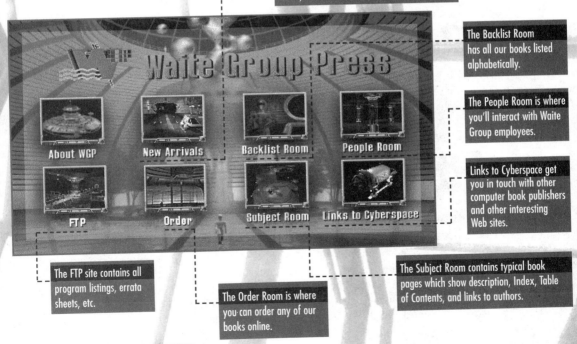

The FTP site contains all program listings, errata sheets, etc.

The Order Room is where you can order any of our books online.

The Subject Room contains typical book pages which show description, Index, Table of Contents, and links to authors.

ABOUT THE AUTHORS

Zane Thomas

Zane began programming in the mid-'70s on a 6800 microprocessor with a whopping 512 (there really is no K here!) bytes. After a few months he dropped his pursuit of a degree in molecular biology and started programming full time. He soon found himself at Alpha Microsystems, one of the many startup companies that blossomed during the beginning of the personal computer revolution. Since then he has programmed using a number of processors, operating systems, and languages.

Zane lives in the state of Washington with his wife and three children. He and his wife Deborah are active in environmental issues in the Pacific Northwest.

Karl Peterson

Karl is a senior technical transportation planner for a regional planning agency located in Vancouver, WA. His roles include geographic information system analysis, custom cartography and other computer graphics work, system and network administration, as well as custom in-house programming projects. In his "spare" time, he also keeps busy as a contributing editor writing articles and columns for Visual Basic Programmer's Journal (VBPJ), and serves on its Technical Review Board. Online, Karl has been designated by Microsoft as one of its Product Support Service's Most Valuable Professionals (MVP) for his contributions to the MSBASIC forum. He's also a section leader in VBPJ's CompuServe forum, and has been selected by CompuServe to participate in its Support Professionals (CSP) program.

Having used various flavors of BASIC since 1976, he'll readily admit to being a "Basic-bigot" through-and-through.

Constance Petersen

Constance lives and works in Atlanta. A software developer for 20 years, she has worked for large corporations and as an independent consultant. She takes hands-on responsibility for all aspects of software development, keeping the focus on ease of use and user satisfaction. In recent years, Constance has taken up knitting—knitting together custom applications, that is. She currently knits with Microsoft's Visual Basic, Access, and Word; WexTech's Doc-To-Help; Shapeware's Visio; and an ever-expanding set of VBXs and OCXs.

She also enjoys nature photography and camping in the north Georgia mountains with her friends, her husband Lynn Torkelson, and their three boys, Nic, Daniel, and Zac.

James Shields

James has been involved with computers in one fashion or another since he was six. Currently he spends most of his time developing Windows components (custom controls). He is the founder of Mabry Software, Inc., a Seattle-based company specializing in Windows programming tools and components.

Stuart Greenberg

Stuart earned his B.S. in computer science in 1976 and spent several years as a mainframe database programmer. He learned the inner workings of personal computers during the "hobby days" by building various components from kits. From 1988 through 1993, as senior programmer for *PC Magazine* Labs, Stuart redesigned the user interface and several test programs for *PC Magazine's* widely distributed Hardware Benchmark Series. He is also the author of Scriptware, a popular word processor for TV and movie scriptwriters.

   He currently runs a consulting business specializing in Visual Basic and Access from his Long Island home. Besides writing applications, Stuart is a frequent contributor to *VB Tech Journal* magazine. In his not-too-frequent off hours, Stuart can be found biking through the neighboring farmland and seen, both on and off the stage, at local comedy clubs.

Mitchell Waite

Mitchell is President and CEO of The Waite Group, developer and publisher of innovative computer books and learning systems. He is an experienced programmer fluent in a variety of computer languages, including Visual Basic, C, Pascal, BASIC, Assembly, and HyperTalk. He wrote his first computer book in 1976, and is co-author of many best-selling computer books, including *The Waite Group's C Primer Plus*, *Microsoft QuickC Programming*, *Microsoft QuickBASIC Bible*, *The Waite Group's Master C*, and *Visual Basic How-To, Second Edition*.

CONTENTS

TABLE OF CONTENTS

ACKNOWLEDGMENTS

How did he put up with all of us? We may never understand exactly how he did it, but we wish to acknowledge—with much thanks and admiration—Kurt Stephan, our managing editor. He prodded, pushed, and kept us going with more patience and kindness than, at times, we deserved. We also want to thank Jill Pisoni for bringing us together, getting us focused, and keeping us connected with Microsoft. Thank you also to Cecile Kaufman and her excellent production department at Waite Group Press, as well as the myriad of folks behind the scenes at WGP who helped with the zillion tasks involved in bringing this book and CD-ROM to you.

We were fortunate to get William Storage's help with Chapter 6 (Object Linking and Embedding). Bill is incredibly knowledgeable about object-oriented programming (OOP) and the object-linking and embedding (OLE) technology that is clearly the future of Windows. Bill was a key contributor to the Visual Basic 4.0 Technical Beta. When Bill spoke about OOP and OLE and their implementation in VB4, Microsoft *listened*. And we're quite certain VB4 is a better tool because of it.

Thanks, too, to Steve Peschka, our technical reviewer. He plowed through reams of code, and gave us great suggestions for making it better and more understandable. We also want to express our gratitude to Carol Henry, our copy/content editor. She clarified, simplified, and removed much of the techno-speak—and even more importantly, helped us speak with one voice.

Also, a major thank you is owed to the Microsoft developers who created Visual Basic 4. Special thanks go to Chris Dias and several other very knowledgeable folks who supported us through the trials and tribulations of beta testing as we were writing this book. Those were certainly days *none* of us will soon forget!

Last, but certainly not least, we owe a debt of gratitude to Mitch Waite, our co-author and our publisher. He jumped on the class file bandwagon right away, and he made sure none of us were left behind. When you read Chapter One, you'll see that he's making sure you're not left behind either!

FOREWORD

I first became acquainted with the Waite Group while inside a U.S. Air Force C-130 transport plane. I was a member of a "first in/last out" combat communications team. After the plane hit an air pocket, dropping a quick 4,000 feet and leaving my stomach on the ceiling, I decided there had to be an easier way to make a living. I had just picked up a recommended Waite Group programming book. As the C-130 continued to bounce its way to our destination, I popped open my "portable" Kaypro computer and went at it. It was during those 12 long hours (and two bouncing air refuelings) that I learned how to program assembly language under the modern CP/M operating system. Fortunately, I lived through all of it, including assembly language. Since that fun flight, I have relied on Waite Group publications to keep my programming knowledge up to date.

The Waite Group has been producing some of the finest computer books on the market for over 10 years. Waite Group Press books have consistently been packed with tons of useful information while being some of the most readable and approachable programming books available. With this all-new *Visual Basic 4 How-To*, Mitch Waite and crew have done it again. Far from just giving a different slant on the basic user manuals, this book retains the successful question-and-answer format to provide in-depth information on a wide range of topics. The authors have taken the time to think as developers do and provide the information developers will surely be asking for. The book has something for everyone. There are little things, like correctly determing a drive type, that will have you smiling at the "fit-n-finish" within your VB application. Then there are big items such as the MsgHook custom control, which will allow you to intercept Windows system messages that are sent to any control. This control can add an incredible amount of flexibility to your applications as well as giving you another powerful tool for those late-night debug sessions.

Visual Basic version 4 is an exciting release for all of us at Microsoft. From making it possible to build your own class modules to giving complete access to the Jet 3.0 database engine, Visual Basic 4 gives the experienced programmer more power to create compelling and robust applications. Yet a new programmer will find Visual Basic even easier to use than before. It is designed to make Windows programming accessible to an even wider audience of programmers.

The book you hold in your hands represents the best way to dive in, have some fun, and become an excellent Visual Basic programmer. We are proud of the work the Waite Group has done in the area of Visual Basic programming. I can think of no better investment for programmers of all experience levels than a Waite Group Press publication. Thank you for purchasing Microsoft's Visual Basic, and good luck with your programming adventures. You are in great hands with Waite Group Press. If you're ever in a C-130, fasten your seat belt and ask for a window seat!

Best of luck,

Rick Segal
Director, Strategic Relations
Microsoft Corporation

INTRODUCTION

Microsoft Visual Basic 4.0 is the classy new release of Visual Basic. We'll introduce you to it here. Then we'll tell you what this book, *Visual Basic 4 How-To,* is all about and how to make the best use of it. We'll explain what's in the book and what's on the CD-ROM. Finally, we'll tell you how to load and run, browse, install, and use the projects on the CD, how to install the system files, and how to register the custom controls.

About Visual Basic 4

Creates Great Windows Applications

You probably already know that Visual Basic is a great tool for creating robust and useful Windows applications. Its productivity-enhancing tools for graphical user interface (GUI) development are highly regarded throughout the industry. Visual Basic allows you to create databases and front-end applications for most popular database formats. Its object linking and embedding (OLE) features allow you to use the functionality provided by other applications, including Microsoft Word for Windows, Microsoft Excel, and Visio. Its ability to access the Windows API and other dynamic link libraries (DLLs) makes it an extremely flexible and open development language.

Comes in Three Flavors

There are three editions of Visual Basic 4.0. With the Standard Edition you can create 32-bit applications for Windows NT (starting with version 3.51) and Windows 95. You can create both 16-bit and 32-bit applications with the Professional Edition, which includes everything in the Standard Edition along with additional custom controls and the Crystal Report Writer. The Enterprise Edition provides the tools you'll need to create robust client/server applications in an enterprise environment. It includes all the features of the Professional Edition along with an automation manager, a component manager, a set of database management tools, and Visual SourceSafe, a project-oriented version control system.

Includes Many New Features

Visual Basic, Applications Edition, version 2.0 (VBA 2.0) is the new language engine in Visual Basic. It's compatible with earlier versions of Visual Basic, as well as VBA 1.0, the language engine in Microsoft Excel 5.0 and Microsoft Project 4.0. This new language engine makes it easier to program OLE Automation objects and to exchange code with other applications that support OLE Automation. OLE Automation has been enhanced in Visual Basic 4.0. Now you can create both in-process and out-of-process OLE Automation Servers, and you can negotiate menus and provide in-place editing of OLE application objects. Visual Basic 4.0's new class modules allow you to create reusable objects, with their own properties and methods, and assemble them into an object model. You can also create your own collections, built using Visual Basic's new Collection object.

In the enhanced development environment, a right mouse click will pop up context-sensitive menus for forms, controls, and code. You can attach add-ins for source code control and other features. If you have the Professional Edition, you can even create your own add-ins. Forms have become full-fledged objects, with their own public and private property procedures, methods, and events. A new Object Browser lets you cut and paste from a hierarchical display of all the classes, properties, and methods available to your application from Visual Basic and other OLE components. Conditional compilation allows you to selectively build 16-bit and 32-bit versions of your application from one code base. Long filenames are supported in the 32-bit version of Visual Basic 4.0. And new custom controls let you add a Windows 95 look and feel to your 32-bit applications.

DBList, DBCombo, and DBGrid are new data-bound controls. The OLE container control is also data-bound. The Microsoft Jet database engine is upgraded to 2.5 (16-bit) and 3.0 (32-bit). You use the new Data Access Objects (DAO) programming model for cascading updates and deletes, programmatic access to referential integrity, and improved speed for many queries. You can also establish and modify security settings in a Microsoft Access database. With Jet 3.0 you can replicate a database and direct- manipulate it from within Visual Basic code.

The Enterprise Edition provides Remote Automation so you can create shared, reusable OLE Automation components on a network. A number of tools assist client/server development, including tools to catalog, install and configure components, and to manage source code access. You can use Remote Data Objects (RDO) and the Remote Data Control (RDC) to access any ODBC data source, without using a local query processor. This technique promises significantly higher performance and more flexibility when accessing remote client/server database engines such as Microsoft SQL Server and Oracle.

About This Book
Takes Visual Basic to its Limits

Following in the footsteps of the Visual Basic How-To, Second Edition, this all-new book has a plethora of tips, tricks, and techniques for taking Visual Basic 4.0 to its ultimate limits. You'll learn, for example, to create splitter bars, rollup tools, and animated splash screens. You'll build a game, full of explosive sound and animation. You'll use object-oriented class files to build in-process and out-of-process OLE automation servers. How to create Quicken-like combo boxes, multiselect lookup tables, and sound-alike searches are just some of the database tricks you'll learn. In addition, there are details on how to extract icons from executable files, write debugging information to the Windows Notepad, and even recursively search an entire disk or directory tree.

Uses Windows APIs Extensively

Visual Basic has some great new commands that make the Windows Application Program Interface (API) routines a bit less necessary. Did you know, for example, about the new PaintPicture method? We'll show you how to use it, in place of the BitBlt Windows API function, to perform a wide variety of bit operations for speedy graphics. But we've still found occasion to use dozens of Windows API calls in our How-Tos. We'll show you how to use Windows APIs to send messages to forms and controls, make another application the parent of your program, and change the Windows Wallpaper. We'll even show you how to determine which operating system is running, quite a complex feat now that the choice of Windows operating systems is so varied!

Provides 32-bit and 16-bit Code

And speaking of Windows operating systems, we've focused our graphics on Windows 95 and our discussion on 32-bit issues. Nevertheless, a large number of the projects can be compiled into either 16-bit or 32-bit code. Many of these make use of Visual Basic 4.0's new conditional compilation features, allowing them to be compiled with either the 16-bit or the 32-bit Visual Basic compiler. Our use of Windows APIs made that a necessity—the Declare statements for every API have changed in 32-bit Windows, and most parameters that were integer are now long. Don't worry; by the time you finish this book, adjusting the Declares from 16-bit to 32-bit will be a piece of cake. A few projects (those that don't rely on Windows API commands) can be compiled unchanged in either environment. For yet another set of How-Tos, we felt that enabling both 16-bit and 32-bit in one project would get in the way of what we wanted to illustrate. In those cases, we created and explained a 32-bit-only version for the book. Often, though, we were also able to include a 16-bit version of the project on the CD.

Question and Answer Format

Don't worry, we wouldn't consider changing the format that worked so well in the best-selling *Visual Basic How-To, Second Edition.* You'll find questions and answers arranged by categories: Visual Basic 4.0 class fundamentals, forms, controls, sounds, graphics, object linking and embedding (OLE), system services, database, tips and tricks. Each How-To contains a program solution with complete construction details. All the code, bitmaps, icons, forms, OCXs, and DLLs are contained on the enclosed CD.

Free Custom Controls and DLLs

You probably would have been quite satisfied just to get a book that's chock-full of example projects, covering a wide variety of tips, tricks, and techniques. Well, you might have been, but we weren't! So the bundled CD also contains a number of free custom controls and DLLs. The custom controls are all OCXs, and we're providing

16-bit and 32-bit versions of each. There's a MsgHook custom control, MSGHOO16.OCX and MSGHOO32.OCX, that lets you intercept Windows messages sent to any control. You'll see it used, for example, to intercept a "Done" message sent by the Multimedia subsystem in Windows.

Additionally, there's a FireEvent custom control, FIREVE16.OCX and FIREVE32.OCX, that allows you to fire events within your application from the outside via OLE Automation. It's used, for example, to keep a Sprite bouncing within a boundary box by creating an event when the Sprite approaches the boundary.

Also, you get a HiTime custom control, HITIME16.OCX and HITIME32.OCX, that lets you set values as small as 1 millisecond for the timer interval, then it fires events every millisecond. The Visual Basic Timer lets you set millisecond values for the Interval property, but actually only uses multiples of 55 milliseconds. In one How-To, for example, the HiTime custom control is used to control the drum beats in a multitrack drum machine.

We are also including WinG, Microsoft's powerful and fast new graphics API. WinG is a set of DLLs, written and distributed for free by Microsoft. And we're providing some free WinG Helper DLLs (WINGHELP.DLL and WINGEX32.DLL) to provide functions for copying bitmaps with and without transparency. In Chapter 5, Graphics, you'll see WinG and the Helper DLLs used to animate sprites over a fast, smoothly scrolling background. Finally, WAVEMIX.DLL is included, also written and distributed for free by Microsoft. It makes it possible to play up to eight wavefiles simultaneously. In Chapter 4, Sound, you'll see how we've encapsulated it in a class file that you'll find easy to use in your own applications.

Expected Level of Reader

This book is for you, no matter what your level of expertise with Visual Basic. We've marked each How-To with a complexity level: Easy, Intermediate, or Advanced. If a How-To is marked Easy, it should be quick and simple to follow. Try these first if you're just starting out with Visual Basic. The ones marked Intermediate will be a bit longer, and will often use a few simple Windows API commands. If you're more experienced using Visual Basic, you'll want check these out. If you're very comfortable in Visual Basic and want to see it and the Windows API really get a workout, check out some of the Advanced-complexity How-Tos.

What You Need to Use This Book

In order to use this book, you'll need a computer running Windows 3.1, Windows for Workgroups, Windows 95, or Windows NT 3.51. And, of course, you'll need Visual Basic 4.0. Most of the projects will run with the Standard Edition of Visual Basic 4.0. A few, particularly in Chapter 8, Database, require the Professional Edition. A few of the projects will run also in Visual Basic 3.0, and these are noted in the book. You'll get the most good out of the book if you're running a 32-bit version of Windows (95 or NT 3.51). But as we've noted above, many of the projects will compile successfully with both the 16-bit and the 32-bit versions of Visual Basic. You'll need to have either the Professional or Enterprise Edition of Visual Basic 4.0 in order to compile 16-bit versions of the code.

How This Book is Organized

This book is divided into 9 chapters as follows:

Chapter 1: Visual Basic 4 Class Fundamentals

This chapter introduces Visual Basic 4.0's classes, properties, and objects. It will prepare you for the extensive use of these object-oriented techniques throughout the rest of the book. It starts by showing how to set up the simplest of classes, which it compares to a regular procedure or module. Step by step, the How-Tos in this chapter will show you how to add private and public variables, methods, and properties to your classes. You'll learn how to provide output from your class to a variety of objects, including the debug window, a form, and a picture control. Along the way you will learn how Visual Basic's implementation of classes compares to a true OOP language such as C++. Since Visual Basic 4.0 classes lack an event property, we've provided the FIREVENTS.OCX control to help create class events. In the final How-To, you'll build an intelligent sprite object. You'll program properties, methods, and events for your sprite that will allow you to create a simple demo that bounces sprite-shaped "balls" around on a picture.

Chapter 2: Forms

This chapter makes use of more than 30 Windows API functions and subroutines in a variety of techniques you can use to add sophistication to your forms. You'll learn how to display animated and dynamic information on a splash screen while your application loads. You'll find out how to use a new feature of Visual Basic 4.0 to create animated cursors. You'll learn techniques to turn plain-vanilla forms into slick widgets just like those used in commercial applications. For example, you'll learn to a create rollup tool (similar to those used in CorelDRAW!), drag a captionless form (such as the Windows 3.1 Clock), and make a floating toolbar with a mini-title bar (like Visual Basic's toolbar). You'll learn to make MDI forms more sophisticated by painting an interesting background on an MDI parent form, and by saving and restoring the positions of MDI child forms. You'll gain new control over the Windows desktop, learning to place a minimized icon on the desktop wherever you want it positioned, and learn to automatically reposition and resize controls to fit their containers. Finally, thanks to the new object-oriented nature of Visual Basic 4.0, forms have become fully functioning objects, with public and private properties and methods. In the last How-To, you'll learn to take advantage of this to make your forms more modular and much more reusable. Specifically, you'll discover how to start and terminate a reusable form using the new form properties and methods.

Chapter 3: Controls

Visual Basic 4.0 provides an incredible array of controls, allowing you to create great Windows applications just by dragging and dropping controls onto forms and setting their properties at design time. But no matter how much you can do this way, you'll make the controls in your application even smarter with a bit of code. This chapter is all about showing you how to make the controls in your programs more sophisticated using Visual Basic code and the Windows API. You'll learn to support dragging an item from one list box and dropping it (where you want it inserted) in another list box. You'll learn to make a more flexible PictureBox that can shrink, stretch, and scroll the picture it contains. You'll find out how to add undo to an edit box, automatic dropdown to a combo box, and a horizontal scroll bar to a list box. You'll learn to go beyond the capabilities of Visual Basic 4.0's 3D setting in the new Appearance property, using 3D effects to show which control has the focus, and adding more flexible 3D effects to all controls. Looking for more? You'll also find out how to create a splitter bar for text, clear a multiselect list box with a single call, use long values with scroll bars, guarantee fixed width font availability on any machine, and build your own toolbar without using a VBX or OCX. This chapter will even unlock the secret of LostFocus, a mystery that has baffled many a Visual Basic programmer. You'll learn to use LostFocus correctly for data validation no matter what the user does to trigger the lost focus.

Chapter 4: Sounds

This chapter is all about adding sound to your Visual Basic programs. You'll learn to read and write Resource Interchange Format Files (RIFF). RIFF files are used to store wave-audio data, palettes, AVI files, and many other types of multimedia data. You'll also learn to create, read, and write Multimedia Memory files—files that hold the key to getting good performance in your multimedia programs. You'll learn to use the Windows MCI command string interface to access virtually anything that can be done with the Multimedia subsystem in Windows. We've provided the free WAVEMIX.DLL, and use it in a project that lets you play up to eight wavefiles at once. As you explore ways to use wavefiles in your programs, you'll learn to display wavefiles, play them using low-level API calls, change their volume, and even merge them. Class files are used throughout this chapter to make it easy for you to add sound to your own programs. Everything comes together in the final project, which shows how to make a drum machine. It provides some interesting graphical effects and digital drum sounds that you can use in your own projects.

Chapter 5: Graphics

In this chapter you'll learn how to create a number of wonderful special effects with graphics. In the first How-To, you'll learn about color palettes, as you begin to build a color palette class and add methods for cycling colors in a fractal image. Moving on, you'll learn to create, read, and display information in Device Independent Bitmap (DIB) files, the format used in almost all Windows .BMP files. In subsequent How-Tos you'll learn to fill backgrounds with a smooth transition of colors, similar to what is often used in setup programs. You'll find out how to change background colors without repainting the form, and how to fade text titles in and out. Other How-Tos provide techniques to create the effect of moving into a tunnel, to display twinkling stars in a night sky, and to fade from one picture to another as you might do with a pair of slide projectors. Moving on, you'll learn to use WinG, a set of DLLs that Microsoft distributes for free, which provide high-performance, device-independent graphics capabilities. With the aid of WinG you'll learn to create animated sprites, those irregularly shaped bitmaps that move across a background without flickering. You'll also use WinG to create a fast, smoothly scrolling background, as well as a number of ray-traced frames to create a realistic-looking spaceship that you can fly around the scrolling universe. You'll put it all together in the final How To, creating a shoot'em-up space game with enemy ships that explode in balls of flame when hit. No game would be complete without sound effects: a continuous background music track, laser sounds, and explosive sounds—all of which you'll incorporate in this game.

Chapter 6: Object Linking and Embedding

Visual Basic 4.0's new OLE automation features allow you to create in-process and out-of-process OLE automation servers. Just as in version 3.0, with Visual Basic 4.0 you can control OLE automation servers. Now, not only can you control those available in other programs such as Visio and Word for Windows 6.0, but you can also control those you create yourself with Visual Basic 4.0. In one How-To, you'll learn to create an in-process OLE automation server that can perform long running background operations while your program continues other processing. You'll also create a utility for viewing OLE application objects. Along the way you'll learn how to activate the objects in-place and how to negotiate the OLE object's menus with your own application menus. In the final How-To, you'll learn to create an OLE automation server that facilitates communications between applications—cleanly and without resorting to Dynamic Data Exchange (DDE) custom controls or API functions. But DDE isn't dead yet. The only way to control many useful programs is still through DDE. The Windows 3.1 Program Manager, for example, offers a DDE interface which is also supported by Windows for Workgroups 3.11, Windows 95, and Windows NT. Using DDE to communicate with the Program Manager, this chapter's first How-To creates a useful utility to browse Program Manager's groups and items. Another How-To uses both DDE and OLE Automation to assemble a document in Word for Windows using data provided by a Visual Basic program.

Chapter 7: System Services

This chapter will show you how to harness the power of more than two dozen API functions and subroutines to incorporate a variety of Windows system services in your programs. You'll learn to use API calls to submit a file directly to the print spooler, store and retrieve information in .INI files, and get the windows handle of another application when you have little information about it. You'll also learn how to determine whether your application is compiled or running in the Visual Basic design environment. In other How-Tos, you'll learn techniques to determine a drive type, check for a file's existence, set a file's date and time, detect which operating system is running, and extract and view icons embedded in executable files.

Chapter 8: Database

This chapter scratches the surface of Visual Basic 4.0's database enhancements. These enhancements provide access to new versions of the Jet database engine (version 2.5 for 16-bit applications, and version 3.0 for 32-bit applications) along with a new interface to data access objects DAO. You'll encapsulate logic in a class file to create a Quicken-style Combo Box from a text box and the new DBList control. You'll learn how to make multiple selections from a lookup table using a technique that combines the data control, DAO code, and an ordinary ListBox. You'll also learn to use the new, object-oriented Data Definition Language (DDL) to extract the definitions of tables and fields from an Access database. Navigating through your database is covered in a couple of other How-Tos, where you'll learn to build a better data control and to display values from any database. Other techniques covered include creating a database based on definition information in a text file, importing text records into the new database, and finding incorrectly spelled names in a database. This last technique uses the Soundex algorithm to help find not only misspelled, but also sound-alike and similarly spelled words.

Chapter 9: Tips and Tricks

This chapter provides a variety of tips and tricks you'll find useful in your Visual Basic programs. You'll learn how to return an ordinal number for any number, compute the difference in years between two dates, and combine the techniques in special anniversary messages to commemorate weddings, birthdays, and years on the job. You'll learn to generate dates in a series— useful for scheduling meetings, for example. Other tips and tricks include setting the Windows Wallpaper from your Visual Basic code and using the Windows Notepad to capture debugging information remotely from an installed version of your program. You'll learn the power of recursive programming in a How-To that searches an entire disk or directory tree for desired files and directories. In the last two How-Tos of this book, you'll find some general-purpose routines to parse a string into separate elements and to manipulate bits, bytes, words, and double words.

About the CD-ROM
Packed with Projects, Classes, and Controls

The included CD-ROM is packed with all the files you'll need to run the 80 projects in this book. Actually, there are more than 80 projects on the CD. Most projects will run in either the 16-bit or the 32-bit version of Visual Basic 4.0, often using conditional compilation. In some cases we've provided separate 16-bit and 32-bit versions, which brings the project count in at well over 80. Note that a handful of projects are written to run only in the 32-bit version of Visual Basic.

You'll find that the projects on the CD are organized by Chapter and How-To. There's a folder for each Chapter and, within each Chapter, a folder for each How-To. In the How-To folder, you'll find the Visual Basic Project file and all the Forms, Classes, and General modules needed to run the project. If the project also uses a custom control or dynamic link library unique to this book, it will be available in another folder. More about that coming up next!

The CD is also loaded with reusable class files—45 to be exact! As you work through the projects in this book, you can expect to find a few class modules (or more than a few) that you'll want to drop into your own projects and reuse. And we expect you'll feel the same way about reusing the general modules, custom controls, and dynamic link libraries (DLLs). We've made it easy by organizing them into an additional set of folders. We've gathered up all the class modules (.CLS), general modules (.BAS), custom controls (.OCX) and dynamic link libraries (.DLL) into their own folders. The class modules are all together in a folder called CLASSES, the general modules are in a folder called MODULES, and the OCXs and DLLs are in a folder called SYSTEM.

Ready to Load and Run in Visual Basic 4.0

Most of the projects are ready to run direct from the CD, without any preparation on your part. You can just start Visual Basic, open a Project file (.VBP), and run it. But be aware that if you load and run a project from the CD without copying it to your hard drive, you won't be able to save changes. Some How-To's may attempt to write to the project folder in order to demonstrate a concept. Of course, this will result in a run-time error, and you'll need to copy these projects to your hard drive to get them to run successfully.

Having said all this, if you've got the disk space for it (about 17MB), the best way to use the CD is to just to copy everything to your hard drive. Using the Windows 95 Explorer or your Windows File Manager, you can easily drag the VB4HOWTO folder from the CD to your hard drive. Or if you want to conserve on disk space, drag a How-To folder to your hard drive when you're ready for it, as you work through the How-To in the book. Note that the files on the CD are all marked Read-only. When you copy them to your CD, you'll want to remove the Read-only attribute so you can change them as needed. If you're using the Windows 95 Explorer, it's easy to highlight all the files, click the right mouse button to view their properties, and uncheck the Read-only property. The Read Me file on the CD provides information about other ways to copy the files and remove the Read-only attribute.

Installing the System Files

Before you run a project that uses a custom control or dynamic link library, you'll need to copy it to your Window's System folder. You only need to do this once, of course, before you use it for the first time. The simplest method may be just to copy all the custom controls and dynamic link libraries at once, using the Window 95 Explorer or the Windows File Manager. First highlight the files in the SYSTEM folder on the CD, then drag them all to your Windows System folder.

Where exactly you need to place them will depend on which operating system(s) you're using. If you're using either Windows NT or Windows 95, drag all of them to the System folder located in your Windows folder. If you're dual booting NT and Windows 3.x, drag the 16-bit files to your \WINDOWS\SYSTEM directory, and the 32-bit files to your \WINDOWS\SYSTEM32 directory. If you're dual booting Windows 95 and Windows 3.x, drag the 16-bit files to your Windows 3.x \WINDOWS\SYSTEM directory, and drag all of the system files to the System folder located in your Windows folder. If you're running Windows 3.x only, drag the 16-bit files to your \WINDOWS\SYSTEM directory. The following table shows which system files are 16-bit and which are 32-bit.

16-BIT SYSTEM FILES	32-BIT SYSTEM FILES
FIREVE16.OCX	FIREVE32.OCX
MSGHOO16.OCX	MSGHOO32.OCX
WAVEMIX.DLL	WAVMIX32.DLL
WINGHELP.DLL	WINGEX32.DLL
HITIME1.VBX	HITIME32.OCX
HITIME.LIC	

After you copy the System files to your hard drive, you'll need to register the custom controls. The easiest way to do this is to open Visual Basic and choose Custom Controls from the Tools menu. From this dialog, press the Browse button, highlight each of the OCX files in turn, and press OK. The selected OCX will register itself with your system. When you finish, you should see them listed with your other Custom Controls. You may now check and uncheck the references to include and exclude them from your projects. Of course, only the 32-bit OCXs will load into the 32-bit version of Visual Basic, and only the 16-bit OCXs and VBXs will load into the 16-bit version of Visual Basic.

For the Final Word, Read the Read Me!

You'll find a Read Me file at the root level of the CD-ROM. Please read it first to review your installation options and for some alternative ways to copy files and remove their Read-only attributes. The Read Me file will also identify which How-To's include only 32-bit code. As of this writing, they are: 2-6, 3-10, 7-1, 7-2, 7-3, 7-4, 7-6, 7-8, 7-10, and 9-3. We needed to make some minor code changes to a few projects after the book had gone to print. In each of those projects' folders, you'll find a README.TXT file describing the changes that were made.

1

CLASS FUNDAMENTALS

1

CLASS FUNDAMENTALS

How do I...

Before you can take advantage of Visual Basic 4.0's new features, you need to learn how to use classes. Why? Because classes make it possible to finally create reusable component-based software: functions built around classes. Reusable components in Visual Basic 4.0 "take on" the abilities of third-party controls. In fact, Visual Basic 4.0 classes are designed to make objects, and since controls are objects, you can think of a class as having all the features of a control.

There are a few differences. First, Visual Basic 4.0 class-based objects do not yet come with a convenient property interface such as controls have. You have to write that yourself. Second, Visual Basic 4.0 classes are not yet as advanced as objects built in C++. Class implementation in Visual Basic 4.0 will occasionally have you pulling your hair out. For example, events, Interclass communications, automatic inheritance, and several other features have been omitted. But the clever programmers here at Waite Group Press University have come up with a few tricks that will help you get around some of these weaknesses. In fact, a few tricks will have you bragging to your C++ friends that you have replaced these missing features with third-party controls.

This chapter will help teach you about using classes. It's not an exhaustive tutorial, and it's not a set of How-To's that cover a wide range of interesting topics like the other chapters of the book. As a Visual Basic programmer coming from Visual Basic 3.0, you will find Visual Basic 4.0's classes the major hurdle to overcome.

Of course, you can ignore classes and build your Visual Basic 4.0 programs as you have always built them in 3.0, using modules, global definitions, and good commenting. However, you will be missing the major beauty of classes—a new and exciting way of looking at your programs in terms of properties, and methods that makes programming much more powerful and fun. Class-based programming forces you to really think about what you are doing before you start doing it. *By using classes, you also gain the ability to protect your methods and properties—so that you can make future changes and the calling programs will not break.*

In this chapter, five How-To's, numbers 1.1 to 1.5, are designed to be studied sequentially. Each teaches you a little about a class. The first shows you how to make a class that's just like any other Basic module. Then you learn how to add a private property, a private method, multiple properties; and finally how to output from a class. The sixth and last How-To shows you how to use all the ideas in the first five How-To's to make a Sprite object.

1.1 Set Up the World's Most Simple Class

Visual Basic 4.0's classes, properties, and objects are new and powerful, but most beginners to 4.0 are not OOP experts and will find them confusing. This How-To will show how to set up a simple class with the minimum of features. It defines a class and compares it to a regular procedure or module. We will set up a class that generates a series of numbers, and has one public variable and one public method.

1.2 Add a Private Property to My Simple Class

The real power of classes is in their ability to offer private variables. This How-To will show how to make a single variable private, so it is only accessible inside the class. We will learn to use the new Visual Basic 4.0 Let keyword to define our property. Then we will see the Property Let statement do validity checking on our variable.

1.3 Add a Private Method to My Simple Class

Methods inside the classes can also be made public or private. This How-To will make a public method into a private one, which will let you reap the power of protected methods.

1.4 Add More Properties to My Simple Class

The beauty of classes becomes apparent when you look at them as property-based objects. In this How-To we will add more properties to the number generator, such as the ability to control the step size between values generated, as well as whether even, odd, or all numbers are generated. We will also see how to spruce up our number generator's interface using the new Auto3D property of the form, which gives it a 3D grayscale look.

1.5 Output to a PictureBox from My Simple Class

In How-To's 1.1–1.4, our number generator sent its output to the debug window with debug.print. This How-To shows how to output to a form or picture control from inside the class. You will see that you can easily tell your class what to output to by passing a PictureBox or form object to the class with the "as object" declaration.

1.6 Make a Flexible Class-Based Sprite Object

In this How-To we will show you all the features of classes at work in a practical project that builds an intelligent Sprite object: an object that acts like a Visual Basic control, that is programmed through its properties, and that has methods and events you can program. Along the way you will learn Microsoft's particular implementation of classes in comparison to a true OOP language such as C++. Our simple demo will bounce six Sprite-shaped "balls" around on a Picture. You'll learn about designing a real-world project using classes, and end up with something that you can put to work in many projects. To make your classes even more useful we will provide you with a custom control called Firevents. It's a fully functional OLE Custom Control, and you'll find it on the CD that comes with this book. (You are welcome, of course, to use FIREVENTS.OCX in your programs.) Since classes lack an event property, we will use the FIREVENTS.OCX control to give our Sprites the ability to create an event when the Sprite crosses a "boundary box."

Note About Appearance Property

Forms, buttons, check boxes, and most objects, except scroll bars, have an Appearance property. This property defaults to 3D. It also can be set to Flat. All the properties in this book use the default 3D Appearance property.

1.1 How do I...
Set Up the World's Most Simple Class?

COMPLEXITY: EASY
COMPATIBILITY: VB4 ONLY

Problem

Visual Basic 4.0's classes, properties, and objects are new and powerful. But I am not a C++ or OOP expert, so they confuse me. The manuals are not much help, either. I want to know how to set up a simple class with a minimum of features. I want to know what makes a class a class and how it compares to a regular procedure or module.

Technique

In this example we set up a class that generates a series of numbers and displays them in the debug window using debug.print (see Figure 1-1-1). The class will be named cGen and will have one public variable and one public method. It is not a good example of the value of classes, because it has no protection of its variables and methods (Private is not used). Also, since they are like globals, these variables can be freely altered externally . . . in How-To 1.2 we will see how to make our class more robust and protected by using Private variables.

Steps

Open and run GEN1.VBP. Bring the debug window to the front and arrange so it is underneath the form. Then click on the Generate button and note the resulting sequence of numbers.

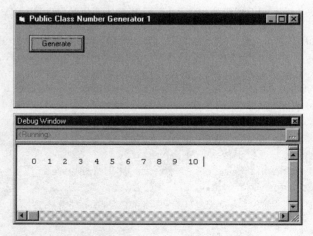

Figure 1-1-1 The Gen1 project and its output

1. Create a new project named GEN1.VBP. Create a new form with the objects and properties in Table 1-1-1 and save it as FORM1.FRM. Your form should look like Figure 1-1-1.

2. Use the Insert Class Module menu item to add a new class to your project. Use the Project window to open your new class module, and then use the Properties window to set the module's name to cGen. Also, be sure that the Creatable property is set to True.

Table 1-1-1 Objects and properties for Form1

OBJECT	PROPERTY	SETTING
Form	Name	Form1
	Caption	Public Class Number Generator 1
CommandButton	Caption	"Generate"
	Name	Command1

3. Add the following code to the General section of cGen:

```
' FIRST CLASSY
' This is a bad example of a class but it helps understand it.
' Variables and methods are all public; anyone can muck with them.
' There is no checking to see if values are permissible.

' Limit sets maximum number generated
'
Public Limit As Integer

Public Sub GenerateNums()
    Debug.Print
    For i = 0 To Limit
        Debug.Print i;
    Next i
End Sub
```

4. Add the following code to the Command button. This code sets up a New object from our number generator class, sets a value to the Limit property, and calls the method in our class, GenerateNums.

```
' Declare an object of class cGen
'
Dim GenObj As cGen


Private Sub Command1_Click()          ' when user clicks
    Set GenObj = New cGen             ' create a new cGen object
    GenObj.Limit = 10                 ' set Limit property to 10
    GenObj.GenerateNums               ' call the GenerateNums method
End Sub
```

How It Works

This How-To demonstrates how a simple class is made, its syntax, and how a single property of it is accessed. The class computes a series of numbers using a FOR NEXT loop. The maximum limit for the loop comes from a public property called Limit. Because Limit is a public property, any external program can access and change it. The method for computing the numbers is called GenerateNums and is a public method, so it, too, can be called by any external routine.

Comments

At this point, there is not much difference between cGen and a subroutine call in a module or BAS file.

1.2 How do I...
Add a Private Property to My Simple Class?

COMPLEXITY: EASY
COMPATIBILITY: VB4 ONLY

Problem

I understand from How-To 1.1 how to set up a class with public properties, and that it is much like making up a custom subroutine in a module. But I know the real power of classes is in their ability to offer private variables. How do I make the Limit variable private, so it's only accessible inside my class?

Technique

To make a property in our little class private, we use the Private keyword when we first define the variable. And we use the new-to-4.0 Let keyword to define our property. In this How-To we modify the public property from the Gen1 project and make it private, so that we can control the behavior of the variable in our actual method. We are shielding our variables. We let people modify the variable Limit, but internally we use a new variable called m_Limit (m_ means member from the C++ language). The external/internal variable naming is handled by Visual Basic's Property Let statement. In the body of the Property Let, the program will pass the external value to our internal value.

Later we will see that it is in the Property Let statement that we do validity checking on the variable.

Steps

Open and run GEN2.VBP. Bring the debug window to the front and arrange so it is underneath the form. Then click on Generate and note the resulting sequence of numbers.

1. Create a new project named GEN2.VBP. Create a new form with the objects and properties in Table 1-2-1 and save it as FORM1.FRM. Your form should look like Figure 1-1-1 in How-To 1.1.

2. Use the Insert Class Module menu item to add a new class to your project. Use the project window to open your new class module, and then use the properties window to set the module's name to cGen. Also, be sure that the Creatable property is set to True.

Table 1-2-1 Objects and properties for Form1

OBJECT	PROPERTY	SETTING
Form	Name	Form1
	Caption	Private Number Generator 2
CommandButton	Caption	"Generate"
	Name	Command1

3. Add the following code to the General section of cGen. What is different about this code is that the previous public property, Limit, has been replaced with its own internal private variable called m_Limit.

```
' SECOND CLASSY
' Now we make the Limit variable private
' This requires the Let Statement

' Change Public to Private
'
Private m_Limit As Integer

Public Sub GenerateNums()
    Debug.Print
    For i = 0 To m_Limit
        Debug.Print i;
    Next i
End Sub

' Note code allows changing private property
'
Public Property Let Limit(n As Integer)
    m_Limit = n
End Property
```

4. The following code is unchanged from the previous How-To. This code sets up a New object from our number generator class which we call GenObj, sets a value to the Limit property, and calls the method in our class, GenerateNums.

```
Dim GenObj As cGen

Private Sub Command1_Click()      ' when user clicks
    Set GenObj = New cGen         ' create a new cGen object
    GenObj.Limit = 10             ' set Limit property to 10
    GenObj.GenerateNums           ' call the GenerateNums method
End Sub
```

How It Works

The key to making a private property is in this code:

```
Private m_Limit As Integer

Public Property Let Limit(n As Integer)
    m_Limit = n
End Property
```

Here the private declaration sets up the internal variable m_Limit as our new variable to represent Limit. (The m_ means that the variable is a member variable.) The member variable "shadows" the property that external programs will access. No external program can change or redefine m_Limit. Next, the Limit property is defined as a public property, meaning external programs can change it. The keyword Let is used to define a writable property. (A readable property is set with the Get keyword.)

In this case we are setting Limit to be the property name. The statement

```
GenObj.Limit = 3
```

will pass 3 as the value of n when the statement is executed. The subprocedure serves to pass the value of n to the internal variable m_Limit. Thus, the public Property Let statement has exposed the internal variable so it can be accessed. This allows us to do things inside of the Let property statement. In our example we simply pass the value of Limit directly through to m_Limit. We can at any time alter the way Limit affects m_Limit.

Comments

You have protected the Limit property so no one can alter what happens when Limit is used. In How-To 1.3 you'll see how to make the method private too.

1.3 How do I...
Add a Private Method to My Simple Class?

COMPLEXITY: EASY
COMPATIBILITY: VB4 ONLY

Problem

I want to make sure that the methods in my class can also profit from class protection features. How do I do that?

Technique

Make the current public method private, and then add a new public method with a different name. External programs can call this public method, which in turn it passes its parameters on to the internal private method. A private method is exposed in the same manner as the private variable Limit in How-To 1.2.

Steps

Open and run GEN3.VBP. Bring the debug window to the front and arrange it so it is underneath the form. Then click on Generate and note the resulting sequence of numbers that are generated.

1. Create a new project named GEN3.VBP. Create a new form with the objects and properties in Table 1-3-1 and save it as FORM1.FRM. Your form should look like Figure 1-1-1 in How-To 1.1.

2. Use the Insert Class Module menu item to add a new class to your project. Use the project window to open your new class module, and then use the properties window to set the module's name to cGen. Also, be sure that the Creatable property is set to True.

Table 1-3-1 Objects and properties for Form1

OBJECT	PROPERTY	SETTING
Form	Name	Form1
	Caption	Private Method Num Generator 3
CommandButton	Caption	"Generate"
	Name	Command1

3. Add the following code to the General section of cGen:

```
' THIRD CLASSY
' To make a private method we have to change names in the
' subroutine, and rename our subroutine to private
```

Continued on next page

Continued from previous page

```
' Add a Public subroutine so external programs can indirectly
' call this internal private routine.
' Now no one can interfere with the internals of our private method

Private m_Limit As Integer ' maximum N generated

'
' This has been renamed as a Private sub
'
Private Sub GenerateNums()
    Debug.Print
    For i = 0 To m_Limit
        Debug.Print i;
    Next i
End Sub

'
' the m_Limit Write Property
'
Public Property Let Limit(n As Integer)
    m_Limit = n
End Property

'
' This sets up the name Generate to call our function GenerateNums
'
Public Sub Generate()
    GenerateNums
End Sub
```

4. The only difference between the code in step 3 and that of How-To 1.2 is that the name of the method in our class has been changed to Generate. The name GenerateNums is the class internal name and is now protected from being called.

```
Dim GenObj As cGen   ' declare an object of class cGen

Private Sub Command1_Click() 'when user clicks
    Set GenObj = New cGen     'create a new cGen object
    GenObj.Limit = 10         'set Limit property to 10
    GenObj.Generate           'Note we now call the Generate method
End Sub
```

How It Works

The key to making a method private is to wrap it in a protective procedure and give it a new name:

```
Public Sub Generate()
    GenerateNums
End Sub
```

Because the GenerateNums function is inside a subprocedure, you can easily modify the private method, without worrying about it being called directly.

Comments

Now that you have a private class, How-To 1.4 will show how to add more properties.

1.4 How do I...
Add More Properties to My Simple Class?

COMPLEXITY: EASY
COMPATIBILITY: VB4 ONLY

Problem

I want to add more properties to my number generator, such as the ability to control the step size between values generated, as well as whether even, odd, or all numbers are generated. How do I control properties like these, and what do I have to do to my code to get them to work? And is there any way to spruce up the number generator's interface?

Technique

It's easy to add more properties to the number generator. You use a collection of public Property Let statements to set up private variables so they can be accessed (written to) by an external program. And while we are improving the little number generator's actions, we'll show how to give our interface a modern, 3D grayscale look.

Steps

Open and run GEN4.VBP. Bring the debug window to the front and arrange it so it is underneath the form. Then click on Generate and note the resulting sequence of numbers. Next, select an ODD, EVEN, or ALL option for the sequence of numbers. Click on Generate and see how the sequence changes. Change the step size scroll bar and note its effect on the series.

1. Create a new project named GEN4.VBP. Create a new form with the objects and properties in Table 1-4-1 and save it as FORM1.FRM. Set the Form's Auto3D property to True. This will make most of the controls take on a 3D grayscale appearance. Your form should look like Figure 1-4-1.

2. Use the Insert Class Module menu item to add a new class to your project. Use the project window to open your new class module, and then use the properties window to set the module's name to cGen. Also, be sure that the Creatable property is set to True.

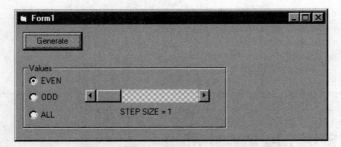

Figure 1-4-1 The Gen4 Project with more controlled variables

Table 1-4-1 Objects and properties for Form1

OBJECT	PROPERTY	SETTING
Form	Name	Form1
	Caption	Private Method Num Generator 4
	Auto3D	True
CommandButton	Caption	Generate
	Name	Command1
OptionButton	Caption	EVEN
	Index	0
OptionButton	Caption	ODD
	Index	1
OptionButton	Caption	ALL
	Index	2
HorizontalScroll	Name	Hscroll1
	Max	4
	Min	1
	Value	1
Label	Name	Label1
	Text	Step Size
Frame	Name	Frame1
	Caption	Values

3. Add the following code to the General section of cGen. The new private variable m_Step controls the increment between numbers, and m_Kind controls whether the number generator generates even, odd, or all the numbers.

```
Private m_Limit As Integer    ' maximum N generated
Private m_Step As Integer     ' increment between numbers
Private m_Kind As Integer     ' ALL, EVEN, or ODD
'
```

```
' Generate numbers from 0 to m_Limit
'
Private Sub GenerateNums()
    Select Case m_Kind
        Case ALL
            For i = 0 To m_Limit Step m_Step
                Debug.Print i;
            Next i
        Case ODD
            For i = 0 To m_Limit Step m_Step
                If i Mod 2 = 1 Then Debug.Print i;
            Next i
        Case EVEN
            For i = 0 To m_Limit Step m_Step
                If i Mod 2 = 0 Then Debug.Print i;
            Next i
    End Select
    Debug.Print
End Sub
```

4. Add the following code to the General section of cGen. The public method Generate calls the private sub GenerateNums. The public writable properties are created with the Property Let statement, which passes the parameters that come from the public subroutine call to the private variables.

```
' --------------------------------------------------------
' Public Methods
' --------------------------------------------------------
Public Sub Generate()         'Makes our number generator public
    GenerateNums
End Sub


' --------------------------------------------------------
' Public Write Properties
' --------------------------------------------------------
Public Property Let Limit(n As Integer)
    m_Limit = n                ' Exposes the var m_Limit
End Property

Public Property Let Step(n As Integer)
    m_Step = n                 ' Exposes the var m_Step
End Property

Public Property Let Kind(n As Integer)
    m_Kind = n                 ' Exposes the var m_Kind
End Property
```

5. Add the following code to the General section of Form1. This declares the object GenObj to be an instance of the class cGen.

```
Dim GenObj As cGen   ' declare an object of class cGen
```

6. Add the following code to the Command1 button on Form1. This routine creates the new GenObj, sets up the public properties, and then makes the subroutine call to GenObj.Generate.

```
Public Sub Command1_Click() 'when user clicks
    Dim i As Integer
    Set GenObj = New cGen
    GenObj.Limit = 20
    GenObj.Step = HScroll1.Value
    For i = 0 To 2
        If Option1(i).Value = True Then
            GenObj.Kind = i
        End If
    Next
    GenObj.Generate                    ' call the Generate method
End Sub
```

7. Add the following code to the Form_Load section of Form1. This puts the value of the horizontal scroll bar into the label when the project is first started, so we can read the bar's value.

```
Private Sub Form_Load()
    Label1.Caption = "STEP SIZE = " + CStr(HScroll1.Value)
End Sub
```

8. Add the following code to the horizontal scroll bar's Change event. This changes the value displayed in the step size label.

```
Private Sub HScroll1_Change()
    Label1.Caption = "STEP SIZE = " + CStr(HScroll1.Value)
End Sub
```

9. Use the Insert Class Module menu item to insert a new module into your project. Add the following code to it. This holds the values of the global public constants for the m_Kind property.

```
Public Const EVEN As Integer = 0
Public Const ODD As Integer = 1
Public Const ALL As Integer = 2
```

How It Works

We have simply extended the idea of wrapping the private variables in protective code. For example:

```
Public Property Let Kind(n As Integer)
    m_Kind = n
End Property
```

Here is the code for reading a property and passing it to a method:

```
GenObj.Step = HScroll1.Value
```

Consider this sequence:

```
For i = 0 To 2
   If Option1(i).Value = True Then
        GenObj.Kind = i
   End If
Next
```

This code simply scans the values of the option buttons looking for one that is selected. When it is found the public property GenOjb.Kind is assigned the number 0, 1, or 2.

Comments

The only thing missing from our program now is producing output to a real picture control. We'll do that in the next How-To, and learn about passing objects to classes.

1.5 How do I...
Output to a PictureBox from My Simple Class?

COMPLEXITY: EASY
COMPATIBILITY: VB4 ONLY

Problem

How-To 1.4 just outputs to the debug window with debug.print. What about outputting to a form or picture control from inside my class? I don't want to use names like Form1.Print inside my class, since that defeats the whole purpose of general-purpose classes. Shouldn't I be able to tell my class what control to send output to when I call its methods?

Technique

You can easily tell your class the target for its output by passing an output object to the class. You do this with the "as object" declaration. Create a new class member called m_Canvas. This variable is defined in Visual Basic 4.0 as being of the type object. We then use the Property Set statement to make the name Canvas a property of the cGen class. This way we can have statements such as GenObj.Canvas = Picture1, where Picture1 is the name of a PictureBox on our Form, and GenObj is an instance of the class cGen.

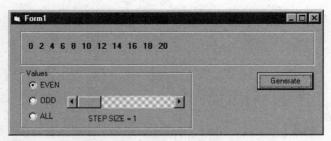

Figure 1-5-1 The Gen5 Project with more controlled variables

Steps

Open and run GEN5.VBP. Bring the debug window to the front and arrange so it is underneath the form. Then click on Generate and note the resulting sequence of numbers. Next, select an ODD, EVEN, or ALL option for the sequence of numbers. Click on Generate and see how the sequence changes. Change the step size scroll bar and note its effect on the series.

1. Create a new project named GEN5.VBP. Create a new form with the objects and properties in Table 1-5-1 and save it as FORM1.FRM. Your form should look like Figure 1-5-1.

2. Use the Insert Class Module menu item to add a new class to your project. Use the project window to open your new class module, and then use the properties window to set the module's name to cGen. Also, be sure that the Creatable property is set to True.

Table 1-5-1 Objects and properties for Form1

OBJECT	PROPERTY	SETTING
Form	Name	Form1
	Caption	Private Method Num Generator 5
	Appearance	1-3D
CommandButton	Caption	Generate
	Name	Command1
OptionButton	Caption	EVEN
	Index	0
OptionButton	Caption	ODD
	Index	1
OptionButton	Caption	ALL
	Index	2
HorizontalScroll	Name	Hscroll1

OBJECT	PROPERTY	SETTING
	Max	4
	Min	1
	Value	1
Label	Name	Label1
	Text	Step Size
Frame	Name	Frame1
	Caption	Values
Frame	Name	Frame2
	Caption	""
PictureBox	Name	Picture1

3. Add the following code to the General section of cGen. The debug.print output has been changed so the output is directed at the PictureBox object. *The code in bold is different from that in How-To 1.4.*

```
Private m_Limit As Integer   ' maximum N generated
Private m_Step As Integer    ' increment between numbers
Private m_Kind As Integer    ' ALL, EVEN, or ODD
'
Private m_Canvas As Object        ' new output object

Private Sub GenerateNums()        ' generates numbers up to a limit
    m_Canvas.Cls                  ' clears the form
    m_Canvas.Font.Bold = True     ' sets font to bold on form
    Select Case m_Kind
        Case ALL
            For i = 0 To m_Limit Step m_Step
                m_Canvas.Print i;         ' replace debug.print
            Next i
        Case ODD
            For i = 0 To m_Limit Step m_Step
                If i Mod 2 = 1 Then m_Canvas.Print i;
            Next i
        Case EVEN
            For i = 0 To m_Limit Step m_Step
                If i Mod 2 = 0 Then m_Canvas.Print i;
            Next i
    End Select
End Sub
```

4. Add the following code to the General section of cGen. This is identical to the code in How-To 1.4. The public method Generate calls the private sub GenerateNums. The public writable properties are created with the Property Let statement, which pass the parameters that come from the public subroutine call to the private variables.

```
' -----------------------------------------------------------
' Public Methods
' -----------------------------------------------------------
Public Sub Generate()          'Makes our number generator public
    GenerateNums
End Sub

' -----------------------------------------------------------
' Public Write Properties
' -----------------------------------------------------------
Public Property Let Limit(n As Integer)
    m_Limit = n                'Exposes the var m_Limit
End Property

Public Property Let Step(n As Integer)
    m_Step = n                 'Exposes the var m_Step
End Property

Public Property Let Kind(n As Integer)
    m_Kind = n                 'Exposes the var m_Kind
End Property
```

5. Add the following code to the General Section of cGen. This code sets up the ability for our class to receive a control as a parameter, and is therefore for writing information to the class. In this sense, Set and Let are similar. We must use another Set in the Form_Load to initialize Canvas to Picture1.

```
' -----------------------------------------------------------
' Property Write Properties (Property Set)
' -----------------------------------------------------------

Public Property Set Canvas(aControl As Object)
    Set m_Canvas = aControl
End Property
```

6. Add the following code to the General section of Form1. This declares the object GenObj to be an instance of the class cGen.

```
Dim GenObj As cGen  ' declare an object of class cGen
```

7. Add the following code to the Command1 button on Form1. This routine creates the new GenObj, sets up the public properties, and makes the subroutine call to GenObj.Generate. The code is almost identical to the code in How-To 1.4, except that we set the Canvas property of the GenObj instance to be a Picture control.

```
Public Sub Command1_Click()            'when user clicks
    Dim i As Integer
    Set GenObj = New cGen
    Set GenObj.Canvas = Picture1   ' select Picture to draw to
    GenObj.Limit = 20
    GenObj.Step = HScroll1.Value
```

```
    For i = 0 To 2
        If Option1(i).Value = True Then
            GenObj.Kind = i
        End If
    Next
    GenObj.Generate                        ' call the Generate method
End Sub
```

8. Add the following code to the Form_Load section of Form1. This puts the value of the horizontal scroll bar into the label when the project is first started, so we can read the bar's value.

```
Private Sub Form_Load()
    Label1.Caption = "STEP SIZE = " + CStr(HScroll1.Value)
End Sub
```

9. Add the following code to the horizontal scroll bar's Change event. This changes the value displayed in the step size label.

```
Private Sub HScroll1_Change()
    Label1.Caption = "STEP SIZE = " + CStr(HScroll1.Value)
End Sub
```

10. Use the Insert Module menu item to insert a new module called Module1 into your project. Add the following code to it. This holds the values of the global public constants for the m_Kind property.

```
Public Const EVEN As Integer = 0
Public Const ODD As Integer = 1
Public Const ALL As Integer = 2
```

How It Works

The code in this project works almost identically to the code in the previous How-To. The main difference is that we set up a new private variable in our class. This code declares a private instance of an "object" called m_Canvas. This object can be a control, such as a PictureBox, Label, Form, or even another class. In our case, we want to define a PictureBox control.

```
Private m_Canvas As Object    ' new output object
```

In our Form_Load we can easily access the properties of the PictureBox:

```
m_Canvas.Cls                  ' clears the form
m_Canvas.Font.Bold = True     ' sets font to bold on form
```

and print into the PictureBox:

```
m_Canvas.Print i;             ' replace debug.print
```

Comments

If you have read the last five How-To's and understood them, you are ready to take the plunge and build a real application that utilizes classes and object-oriented programming.

1.6 How do I...
Make a Flexible Class-Based Sprite Object?

COMPLEXITY: EASY
COMPATIBILITY: VB4 ONLY

Problem

I'd like to make an intelligent Sprite object that acts like a Visual Basic control, is programmed through its properties, and has methods and events I can master. I think I can do this with a class, but I am not sure how. I would like to see all the ways a class in Visual Basic works, as well as a brief and honest appraisal of Microsoft's implementation of classes in comparison to a true OOP language, such as C++.

Technique

In How-To's 1.1–1.5 we learned about classes by making a number generator. Beyond exposing you to the power of property-based classes, the ideas in these first How-To's can be extended to a broader phenomena: moving objects on the screen. The numbers that represent a moving object's X and Y locations in space are easily generated by a simple number generator not unlike the one we just made. In this How-To we demonstrate how to build a Sprite class and use it to make a demo that bounces six Sprite-shaped "balls" around on a PictureBox (see Figure 1-6-1). The number of Sprites we manipulate is unlimited: We just make new ones using the New object statement. We'll draw the balls into a PictureBox, and it will sit on top of a Frame control. The form's Appearance property will be set to 1=3D, so the frame and all the controls are in the 3D style.

Here you'll learn about designing a real-world project using classes, and end up with something that you can put to work in other projects. This project uses most of the powerful features of VB4's classes, objects, and custom controls. The beauty of these class-based Sprites is that they act just like controls—they are property driven and therefore a lot easier to use than the typical subroutine calls from pre-OOP days. You read and write their properties. You call their methods. When you start thinking about your programs in terms of objects, you will begin to see a transformation of the way your ideas are expressed in code. Our Sprite is a semi-intelligent object that can move itself around on the screen, responding to simple commands from your form-based calling program. You can tell a Sprite to start out in a location, move in a certain direction and at a certain speed, and let you know when it has reached a given location, such as a wall or another object.

Our Sprite consists of a VB4 class called CSprite, which will inherit the properties of a very simple class called CPoint. This project shows much of the power (and some weaknesses) of classes, including the requirement that we "fake" inheritance, passing objects to functions, protection, properties, initialization, and termination. You'll learn about how to design a class, how to decide what should be a property and what should be a method, and, probably most important, when to use a Property Get or a Property Let.

The Missing Ingredient: Adding Events to Classes with FIREVENTS.OCX

You get another "bonus" control in this How-To (see Figure 1-6-2). Unlike typical objects in Visual Basic (such as buttons and list boxes), class-based objects in Visual Basic 4.0 can't create their own events. You can see how this would limit a control—imagine a command button without a Click event, or a scroll bar without a Change event. In C++, objects can create the equivalent of any kind of event via a message and the message can be sent from any place in an object's layers, but implementation of classes in VB4 has left events out of the code.

A Sprite object needs some way to communicate with the world outside it. Using global variables won't work because all the public and private features would be lost. Not to be daunted, after playing hours of Doom II, we turned to our custom-control guru in the Pacific forests of Washington, who in a fortnight spun us a custom control called Firevents. It's a fully functional OLE Custom Control, and is provided on the CD that comes with this book—all ready to use in your programs.

We will use the FIREVENTS.OCX control to give our Sprite the ability to create an event when the Sprite crosses a "boundary box." The boundary box will be a set

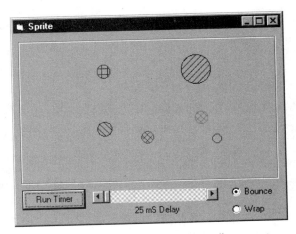

Figure 1-6-1 The Sprite Bouncing Ball project is simple yet powerful

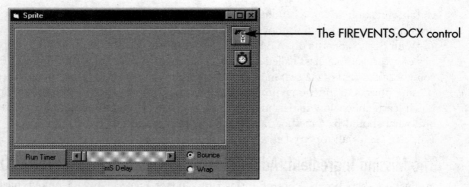
The FIREVENTS.OCX control

Figure 1-6-2 Our Firevents Custom Control—don't start a class without one

of values that define the top, bottom, left, and right sides of an area within which the Sprite must stay. With some work you could even use Firevents to tell when one Sprite collides with another, or use an event to know when we hit a paddle or a certain brick.

Tutorial

We will start by defining what a Sprite should be and do. Keep in mind that in defining a class you are building a living, breathing, object—the more you see it that way, the easier it will be to design your class structure. By defining a Sprite in a general way, you can do a better job defining the type of class you will need.

Here is what our Sprite should do for us:

➤ Draw and erase itself on the screen and have a location

➤ Be capable of motion and have a velocity

➤ Draw itself as a picture or graphic

➤ Have a radius (if it's a circle), a color, and a fill

➤ Know when it has passed beyond the edges of a bounding box

➤ Be an element of an array of Sprites, so multiple Sprites can be manipulated with an index (e.g., we can use sprite(index) for accessing a Sprite)

➤ Have a Tick method that, when called, triggers the Sprite to update its location based on the setting of its location and velocity properties, then erase and redraw itself; that way all Sprites can be updated the same way and at roughly the same instance

If we set up a Sprite this way, we will have a very simple and elegant design.

Designing the CPoint Class

The goal of object-oriented programming is to organize the most general properties and methods to the lowest-level class. Then you build more levels of abstraction around that class, inheriting its features in the next class up the hierarchy. In the case of a Sprite, the most primitive event is that of a point moving in two-dimensional space. What is needed for such a class?

➤ A location for the point; call it X and Y.

➤ A velocity for the point. A velocity can be represented several ways, as a directional angle and a number representing the velocity in that direction, or as two numbers. We will use two numbers, one the X velocity, Xv, and the other the Y velocity, Yv.

We need to make some important plans about these four point variables. We will turn all the variables to properties whose values can be read using Property Get. We will only allow the velocity values Xv and Yv to be writable, using the Property Let statement to control these values. The values of the point location, X and Y, will NOT be writable properties. Why not?

We want to make sure that our object moves in the right way. If we allowed X or Y to be changed externally to our class, it would be possible for the calling program to change only one and not the other of these values. This would introduce uncertainty as to how the X and Y inputs will be presented to our CPoint class. What we need when designing movement algorithms is to let the class control the moving of a point internally; we only supply the starting location and the velocity of the point. By letting our CPoint class do the moving and updating of the point location X and Y, the movement is predictable. We can only change the location of a point through calling a routine, which will always find known values waiting for it.

In addition two methods are needed in the CPoint class: MoveTo and Step. The MoveTo method takes an X and a Y value and moves the point to that location. The Step method takes the Xv and Yv velocity properties you have set and adds them to the current X and Y position, creating a new position for X and Y. Figure 1-6-3

Figure 1-6-3 The CPoint class has four properties and two methods

Note to Propeller and Beanie Heads

Visual Basic 4.0 does not offer true inheritance. You have to do some tricks to set up the code properly so the inheritance works. In the C++ world, the word inheritance usually indicates that there is an "is-a" relationship between one object and another (Class A "is-a" kind of class B). C++ aficionados also speak of a "has-a" type of relationship (Class A "has-a" class B). Our VB program here is using a "has-a" relationship (CSprite "has-a" CPoint). We are, however, creating the effect of an "is-a" relationship by simply passing things through from CSprite to CPoint.

The line between is-a and has-a is somewhat unclear, and it would be easy to argue that a Sprite has a point because a point is a handle for things that a Sprite does. It is also valid to take the course we have taken—namely, defining a moving point in space and then "deriving" a new class that has some specialized behavior.

shows a way to visualize the CPoint class. Note that there is no drawing in this CPoint class; we are saving that for a better class.

Designing the Sprite Class

Now we are ready to design our Sprite class (see Figure 1-6-4). First you will note that the Sprite class has the same four variables and two methods found in the CPoint class: X, Y, Xv, Yv, Draw and MoveTo. These are "inherited" properties and methods, and show how a class can take on the features of a class it inherits.

The Radius property we set up tells how large a radius our Sprite's circle should be when it's drawn. We set up Top, Bottom, Right, and Left properties in the CSprite class that define a boundary box that all Sprites are confined to. FillStyle and FillColor properties mimic similar properties on a Form—they control the fill and type color of the Sprite. This process of using similar properties is another idea in OOP design. By itself, a class is not a real physical object like a button, so we need to give it some kind of surface to draw on. We need to give our class a control such as a PictureBox or a Form. (We will use a PictureBox.) The actual object we will draw to is controlled via a Canvas property we will give the CSprite class. This feature shows off how to pass an object to a class. Finally, we will need a simple integer property called ID_Done to hold the number of the Sprite that caused a boundary crossing event. Our actual event property is controlled by a reference to a CSprite property called Sink. We'll use a Property Set command to let external programs use this property.

Now let's look at the methods for our Sprite class. The MoveTo and Step methods were inherited from the CPoint class. The most important method of the Sprite class will be a Draw and Remove method, which takes the point location, paints something for us to see, and erases it. In this How-To we will simply draw circles, (in

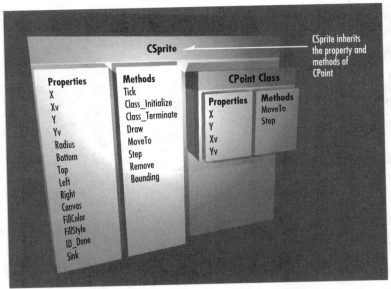

Figure 1-6-4 The Sprite class has 14 properties and 8 methods

subsequent How-To's we will see how to draw bitmaps). If we wanted to get more sophisticated we would perhaps create a general-purpose Draw class that could be used in other programs easily. However, for brevity, we will stick with a simple function call.

We set up a method called Bounding, which checks to see if our Sprite is inside or outside a bounding box. If it's outside, the Bounding method creates an event that our calling program will detect and respond to. The Tick method is a special method. When called, it calls Remove to erase the last Sprite that was drawn, calls Step to move the Sprite, and finally calls Draw to paint the Sprite on the screen. Finally, we set up a Class_Initialize and Class_Terminate method, which sets up our CPoint object when the Form is started, then destroys the object when the program is stopped. We destroy objects by setting them to Nothing, a new keyword in VB4.

The Form-Calling Program

Now we are ready to rumble. Figure 1-6-5 shows a diagram of the Form and its methods and properties. The Circle method belongs to the Form. However, we will be using Circle in the CSprite class as an inherited property of Canvas, which in our case is the Picture1 control. Thus we will use syntax such as this:

```
m_Canvas.Circle (X, Y), m_Radius, m_FillColor
```

to tell the CSprite class to draw a circle of a certain Radius, with a certain FillColor.

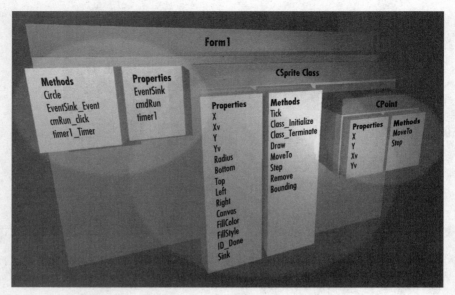

Figure 1-6-5 The Form contains the Sprite class

The cmdRun_click method contains a short amount of code for controlling the Sprite. A Timer contains the loop that calls the Tick routine, which causes all the Sprites to get updated.

```
For i = 0 To PLAYERS
     Sprite(i).Tick
     DoEvents
Next
```

DoEvents makes sure the rest of Windows gets some processing time. Sprite(i).Tick calls the Tick method for Sprite(0) to Sprite(PLAYERS).

The EventSink_Event method is where we go when an event is triggered in the CSprite class. The property belongs to the object EventSink, which is a Custom Control provided with this book.

Now that you have a good idea of how the classes for CSprite and CPoint are organized, let's build the project and see how the code is written to implement these features.

Steps

Open and run SPRITE.VBP. Click on the Run button. Six Sprites are created on the PictureBox, each a circle shape and each filled with a random color and style, from solid to hatched with different lines. The Sprites will bounce off the imaginary walls of a 320x200 pixel-bounding box. If you click on the Wrap option button, you will see the Sprites reappear at the other side of the screen. The horizontal scroll bar controls the interval for the timer. The default is 1 ms, and you can slow it down to 200 ms. Thus we control how often the Tick method is called and the movement speed of the entire group. Click on the Stop button, and click again. A new set of random circles will start bouncing or wrapping, depending on how you have the WrapBounce property set.

Table 1-6-1 Objects and properties for Form1

OBJECT	PROPERTY	SETTING
Form	Caption	"Sprite"
	Name	Form1
	Appearance	1-3D
	ScaleMode	0-User
	ScaleWidth	320
	ScaleHeight	200
Frame	Name	Frame1
	Caption	"" (none)
Picture	Name	Picture1
	BackColor	&H00C0C0C0
	BorderStyle	0 - None
CommandButton	Caption	"Run"
	Name	Command1
Timer	Name	Timer1
	Interval	25
HorizontalScroll	Name	Hscroll1
	Min	25
	Max	200
OptionButton	Name	Option1
	Value	True
	Caption	Bounce
OptionButton	Name	Option2
	Value	False
	Caption	Wrap
Label	Name	Label1
	Caption	mS Delay
EventSink	Name	EventSink1
CPoint	Name	CPoint
	Creatable	True
CSprite	Name	CSprite
	Creatable	True

Create the CPoint Class

1. We will begin this project at the bottom, where the most primitive class is made. From the Insert menu, choose the Class Module object to insert it into your project. Name it CPoint and set its Creatable Property to True. Put the following code inside the CPoint class:

```
Option Explicit
' m_X and m_Y are the location of the point and are passed to CPoint
' m_Xv and m_Yv are properties for the X and Y velocity
' MoveTo locates the points to a new location
' Step moves the point according to the X and Y velocity

Private m_X As Single
Private m_Y As Single
Private m_Xv As Single
Private m_Yv As Single

' MoveTo moves the point based on the valu of X and Y passed
Public Sub MoveTo(X As Single, Y As Single)
    m_X = X
    m_Y = Y
End Sub

' Step moves the point based on the value of the X and Y velocity
Public Sub Step()
    m_X = m_X + m_Xv
    m_Y = m_Y + m_Yv
End Sub

' make a property for X velocity
Public Property Let Xv(n As Single)
    m_Xv = n
End Property

' make a property for Y velocity
Public Property Let Yv(n As Single)
    m_Yv = n
End Property

' in order to find out the value of X and Y we need to make them
' read only variables with Get
Public Property Get X() As Single
    X = m_X
End Property

Public Property Get Y() As Single
    Y = m_Y
End Property

' in order to find out the value of Xv and Yv we need to provide
' a Get
Public Property Get Xv() As Single
    Xv = m_Xv
```

```
End Property

Public Property Get Yv() As Single
    Yv = m_Yv
End Property
```

Create the CSprite Class

2. Now create the CSprite class and inherit the properties and methods of the CPoint class. From the Insert menu, choose Class Module. Insert it into your project and name it CSprite. Set its Creatable property to True and put the following code inside:

```
Option Explicit
' -------------------------------------------------------------
'   CSprite Private Variables
' -------------------------------------------------------------

Private m_point As CPoint
Private m_Canvas As Object
Private m_Radius As Single
Private m_FillColor As Long
Private m_FillStyle As Integer
Private m_Top, m_Bottom, m_Right, m_Left As Single
Private m_Sink As Control
Private m_ID_Done As Integer


' -------------------------------------------------------------
'   CSprite Private Methods
' -------------------------------------------------------------

' the Initialize method
Private Sub Class_Initialize()
    Set m_point = New CPoint
End Sub

' the Terminate method
Private Sub Class_Terminate()
    Set m_point = Nothing
End Sub


' -------------------------------------------------------------
'   CSprite Public Methods
' -------------------------------------------------------------

' the Tick method
Public Sub Tick()
    Remove
    Step
    Bounding
    Draw
End Sub
```

Continued on next page

Continued from previous page

```vb
' the MoveTo method
Public Sub MoveTo(X As Single, Y As Single)
    m_point.MoveTo X, Y
End Sub


' the Step method
Public Sub Step()
    m_point.Step
End Sub


' the Draw method
Public Sub Draw()
    m_Canvas.FillStyle = m_FillStyle
    m_Canvas.FillColor = m_FillColor
    m_Canvas.Circle (X, Y), m_Radius, m_FillColor
End Sub


' the Remove method
Public Sub Remove()
    m_Canvas.FillStyle = 0
    m_Canvas.FillColor = m_Canvas.BackColor
    m_Canvas.Circle (X, Y), m_Radius, m_Canvas.BackColor
End Sub


' the Bounding method fires event if we hit a wall
Public Sub Bounding()
    If m_point.Y > m_Top Then
        m_Sink.FireEvent m_ID_Done, "BOTTOM"
    End If
    If m_point.Y < m_Bottom Then
        m_Sink.FireEvent m_ID_Done, "TOP"
    End If
    If m_point.X > m_Right Then
        m_Sink.FireEvent m_ID_Done, "RIGHT"
    End If
    If m_point.X < m_Left Then
        m_Sink.FireEvent m_ID_Done, "LEFT"
    End If
End Sub



' --------------------------------------------------------------------
'   CSprite Public Read and Write Properties
' --------------------------------------------------------------------

' the X read property
Public Property Get X() As Single
    X = m_point.X
End Property


' the Y read property
Public Property Get Y() As Single
    Y = m_point.Y
End Property
```

```vb
' the Top Write Property
Public Property Let Top(n As Single)
    m_Top = n
End Property

' the Bottom Write Property
Public Property Let Bottom(n As Single)
    m_Bottom = n
End Property

' the Left Write Property
Public Property Let Left(n As Single)
    m_Left = n
End Property

' the Right Write Property
Public Property Let Right(n As Single)
    m_Right = n
End Property

' the FillStyle Write Property
Public Property Let FillStyle(n As Integer)
    m_FillStyle = n
End Property

'the FillColor Write Property
Public Property Let FillColor(n As Long)
    m_FillColor = n
End Property

' the Radius Write property
Public Property Let Radius(n As Single)
    m_Radius = n
End Property

' the Xv Write property
Public Property Let Xv(n As Single)
    m_point.Xv = n
End Property

' the Xv read property
Public Property Get Xv() As Single
    Xv = m_point.Xv
End Property

' the Yv Write property
Public Property Let Yv(n As Single)
    m_point.Yv = n
End Property

' the Yv read property
Public Property Get Yv() As Single
    Yv = m_point.Yv
End Property
```

Continued on next page

Continued from previous page

```
' the ID_Done Write Property
Public Property Let ID_Done(n As Integer)
    m_ID_Done = n
End Property


' -----------------------------------------------------------------
'   CSprite Public Reference Properties
' -----------------------------------------------------------------

' the m_Canvas property reference
Public Property Set canvas(aControl As Object)
    Set m_Canvas = aControl
End Property

' the Sink Property Reference
Public Property Set Sink(anEventSink As Control)
    Set m_Sink = anEventSink
End Property
```

3. From the Insert menu, insert a Module into your project named MODULE1.BAS, and put the following code inside it:

```
Public Const XMAX = 320
Public Const XMIN = 20
Public Const YMAX = 200
Public Const YMIN = 20
Public Const PLAYERS = 3
Public Const WRAP = 0
Public Const BOUNCE = 1
```

The Form

4. Add the following code to the General section of the Form. The two Dim statements declare that we are going to be creating an array of objects of type CSprite, called Sprite. This is a very powerful statement and is the basis of what makes using classes so innovative.

```
Dim Sprite(PLAYERS) As CSprite
Dim Reflection As Integer

Private Sub Form_Load()
    Randomize
    Option1_Click (0)
    Picture1.ScaleMode = 3    ' Switch to Pixel mode
    Dim i As Integer
    For i = 0 To PLAYERS
        Set Sprite(i) = New CSprite
        Set Sprite(i).canvas = Picture1
        Sprite(i).Top = YMAX
        Sprite(i).Bottom = YMIN
        Sprite(i).Left = XMIN
        Sprite(i).Right = XMAX
        Sprite(i).MoveTo Rnd * XMAX, Rnd * YMAX
```

```
        Sprite(i).Xv = Rnd * 5
        Sprite(i).Yv = Rnd * -5
        Sprite(i).Radius = (Rnd * 25) + 5
        Sprite(i).FillColor = QBColor(Rnd * 15)
        Sprite(i).FillStyle = Rnd * 7
        Set Sprite(i).Sink = EventSink1
        Sprite(i).ID_Done = i
    Next
End Sub
```

5. Add the following code to the cmdRun button. This accomplishes the same set of things as the routines in the Form1_Load procedure, each time the Run button is pressed. The caption of the Run button is adjusted to reflect its state.

```
' This sets up random values for the sprite and enables the tick timer
Private Sub cmdRun_Click()
    If cmdRun.Caption = "Run Timer" Then
      For i = 0 To PLAYERS
          Sprite(i).MoveTo Rnd * XMAX, Rnd * YMAX
          Sprite(i).Xv = 1 + (Rnd * 20)
          Sprite(i).Yv = -1 + (Rnd * -15)
          Sprite(i).Radius = (Rnd * 15) + 5
          Sprite(i).FillColor = QBColor(Rnd * 14)
          Sprite(i).FillStyle = Rnd * 7
          Sprite(i).Top = YMAX
          Sprite(i).Bottom = YMIN
          Sprite(i).Left = XMIN
          Sprite(i).Right = XMAX
    Next
          cmdRun.Caption = "Stop Timer"
          Picture1.Cls
          Timer1.Enabled = True
      Else
          cmdRun.Caption = "Run Timer"
          Timer1.Enabled = False
      End If
End Sub
```

6. Put the following code in the HScroll_Change procedure of the Hscroll1 control:

```
Private Sub HScroll1_Change()
    Timer1.Interval = HScroll1.Value
    Label1.Caption = Str(HScroll1.Value) + " mS Delay"
End Sub
```

This sets the timer's interval to a value between 1 and 200 whenever the horizontal scroll bar is moved. We don't have to worry about readjusting the Sprite class while it's running. Nothing gets done until there is a click.

7. Put the following code in the Option1_Click procedure of the Option1() button. This sets the variable Reflection to be either the value of BOUNCE (0) or WRAP (1), both of which are public constants declared in MODULE1.BAS.

```
Private Sub Option1_Click(Index As Integer)
    If Index = 0 Then Reflection = BOUNCE
    If Index = 1 Then Reflection = WRAP
End Sub
```

8. Put the following code in the Timer1_Timer procedure of the Timer1 control:

```
Private Sub Timer1_Timer()
' this is the main tick counter that forces our sprites to all move
For i = 0 To PLAYERS
    Sprite(i).Tick
    DoEvents
Next
End Sub
```

This calls the Sprite array elements one at a time, and calls the Tick method for each Sprite. Since they are objects, the Tick method for Sprite(0) is different from the one for Sprite(1). Each Sprite's properties are private to that Sprite.

9. Add the following code to the General section of Form1:

```
' we come here when a sprite hits a wall
Private Sub EventSink1_Event(ByVal EventNumber As Long, EventData As
Variant)
    If Reflection = BOUNCE Then
    Select Case EventData
        Case "BOTTOM"
            Sprite(EventNumber).Yv = -Sprite(EventNumber).Yv
        Case "TOP"
            Sprite(EventNumber).Yv = -Sprite(EventNumber).Yv
        Case "LEFT"
            Sprite(EventNumber).Xv = -Sprite(EventNumber).Xv
        Case "RIGHT"
            Sprite(EventNumber).Xv = -Sprite(EventNumber).Xv
    End Select
    Else
        Select Case EventData
        Case "BOTTOM"
            Sprite(EventNumber).MoveTo Sprite(EventNumber).X, YMIN
        Case "TOP"
            Sprite(EventNumber).MoveTo Sprite(EventNumber).X, YMAX
        Case "LEFT"
            Sprite(EventNumber).MoveTo XMAX, Sprite(EventNumber).Y
        Case "RIGHT"
            Sprite(EventNumber).MoveTo XMIN, Sprite(EventNumber).Y
    End Select
    End If
End Sub
```

How It Works

The Sprite class contains a lot of features. Let's learn them one at a time. Consider this How-To your first course on classes.

The CPoint Class

Study this code carefully, for it demonstrates most of the secrets of using classes. The properties we want to assign to CPoint require that we first declare them, and that is done in the beginning of the module, with

```
Private m_X As Single
Private m_Y As Single
Private m_Xv As Single
Private m_Yv As Single
```

This defines four names as single precision floating-point private variables. Because they are private, no other program outside the scope of the class can change them. If you try to do that, your program will report an error when it tries to compile. Thus you are avoiding potential variable-leakage bugs.

To turn a variable into a property, we decide first if we want to be able to write or set the property, read the property, or both. In our program, we wish to set the value of the Xv and Yv velocities. We arrange this via the Property Let statement:

```
Public Property Let Xv(n As Single)
    m_Xv = n
End Property
```

Here we simply make a public property called X. When X is passed to the CPoint class as a value, it is passed as the parameter n. Then it is assigned to the internal private variable of the CPoint class, m_Xv. To get a better idea of how to use Let, Get, and Set, see Table 1-6-2.

Table 1-6-2 How to use Property Let, Get, and Set

IF PROPERTY IS...	USE THIS...
Writable	Property Let
Readable	Property Get
An object	Property Set

Now we want to set up the variables X, Y, Xv, and Yv so their values can be "read" by an external program. We can see in Table 1-6-2 that for Readable, we need the Property Get procedure.

```
Public Property Get X() As Single
    X = m_X
End Property
```

This code sets up the variable X so that its value can be read by the external program. The routine does nothing more than tell the calling code that if the variable X is accessed, the routine will set X to the value of the internal variable m_X.

We need some methods to finish our CPoint class. Here is the simple code for locating the point to a starting location:

```
Public Sub MoveTo(X As Single, Y As Single)
    m_X = X
    m_Y = Y
End Sub
```

and the code to call MoveTo would look like this:

```
Sprite(n).MoveTo X, Y
```

All the work to move the point occurs in this tiny Step procedure that simply adds the value of the velocity to the current location and makes that the new location.

```
Public Sub Step()
    m_X = m_X + m_Xv
    m_Y = m_Y + m_Yv
End Sub
```

The CSprite's Class Private Parts

Here is how the CSprite Class works.

The code in the CSprite class starts by defining a set of private variables that will be used for properties. These give you an idea of what is important in the program.

```
Private m_point As CPoint
Private m_Canvas As Object
Private m_Radius As Single
Private m_FillColor As Long
Private m_FillStyle As Integer
Private m_Top, m_Bottom, m_Right, m_Left As Single
Private m_Sink As Control
Private m_ID_Done As Integer
```

Pass-Through of Properties

```
Private m_point As CPoint
```

The statement tells our CSprite class to inherit all the properties and methods of the CPoint class. That means the CSprite class can access the X, Y, Xv, and Yv properties of the CPoint class and offer them to the program calling the CSprite class. The only catch is that in order to allow the CSprite class to inherit the CPoint properties, VB code is required in CSprite to "pass through" the properties of CPoint.

Take, for example, the CPoint properties Xv and Yv. We want our calling program to be able to write these, so we need to allow it to pass its values on to the CPoint class variables. The Property Let statement can be used to set this up, as follows:

```
' the Xv Write property
Public Property Let Xv(n As Single)
    m_point.Xv = n
End Property

' the Yv Write property
Public Property Let Yv(n As Single)
    m_point.Yv = n
End Property
```

Here, whenever the calling program makes a reference to Xv, such as CSprite(0).Xv = 4, the value of Xv will be passed to m_point.Xv, the property name for Xv inside of CPoint. The same goes for Yv.

That takes care of setting or writing the value for Xv and Yv, but what if we want to read the values of Xv and Yv at some later time? We do that with the Property Get statement, as follows:

```
' the Xv read property
Public Property Get Xv() As Single
    Xv = m_point.Xv
End Property

' the Yv read property
Public Property Get Yv() As Single
    Yv = m_point.Yv
End Property
```

In this code, whenever the Sprite.Xv property is accessed, the code sets Xv to the value contained in the CPoint's Xv property.

The Sink Property

Another distinct new property to examine is the m_Sink private variable for the Sink property. The Sink control receives, or sinks, events. Note there is no "is-a" relationship between a Sprite and a Firevents, but is a "has-a" relationship. The code needed in VB4 is essentially a Property Set that sets a reference to the FIREVENTS.OCX control.

```
' the Sink Property Reference
Public Property Set Sink(anEventSink As Control)
    Set m_Sink = anEventSink
End Property
```

Public Methods

The next section of code includes the public methods of the Sprite class. Study each of these methods to see how they work.

The Initialization method is set up so that when the CSprite object is created for the first time, it creates an object of type CPoint and assigns it to the property m_point. When we terminate the class, we must remove the object by setting it to Nothing with the Terminate method.

The Public methods for the CSprite class are grouped together, so they are easy to examine and follow. Notable here is the simplicity of the Tick method:

```
' the Tick method
Public Sub Tick()
    Remove
    Step
    Bounding
    Draw
End Sub
```

All we do when we get a Tick call is erase the old circle, move the circle's point, check if it has hit the edge of its bounding box, and then draw it. What could be simpler?

Pass-Through Methods

How do we use the MoveTo method since it also is inside the CPoint class? The variable m_point is the object that we wish to actually move, and it has a MoveTo method. We call the Sprite MoveTo with something like Sprite(n).MoveTo X, Y; therefore, we need a way to translate this into the MoveTo method that is in our CPoint class. The following code does that. Essentially we have translated the Sprite's MoveTo, to access the Point's MoveTo. This is necessary because VB4 still lacks the power of real OOP.

```
' the MoveTo method
Public Sub MoveTo(X As Single, Y As Single)
    m_point.MoveTo X, Y
End Sub
```

The Draw and Remove procedures are straightforward and easy to understand.

The Bounding Box and the Event

The Bounding method uses our FIREVENTS.OCX control. We do a call to Bounding every time we receive a Tick method call.

```
' the Bounding method fires event if we hit a wall
Public Sub Bounding()
    If m_point.Y > m_Top Then
        m_Sink.FireEvent m_ID_Done, "BOTTOM"
    End If
    If m_point.Y < m_Bottom Then
        m_Sink.FireEvent m_ID_Done, "TOP"
    End If
```

```
    If m_point.X > m_Right Then
        m_Sink.FireEvent m_ID_Done, "RIGHT"
    End If
    If m_point.X < m_Left Then
        m_Sink.FireEvent m_ID_Done, "LEFT"
    End If
End Sub
```

The routine examines the four bounding properties of the Sprite's bounding box, and determines if any X,Y pair has exceeded one of those boundaries. If a boundary is crossed, the m_Sink.FireEvent method is called, and two parameters are returned to the calling program. The value m_ID_Done contains the number representing the Sprite as it was created—e.g., 0, 1, 2, 3 for our program. The second parameter contains the name of the boundary that was crossed. Both these values are returned to the event sink in the Form, and used to decide what to do with the event.

The Canvas Property Set

Take a look at the code for the canvas property:

```
' the m_Canvas property reference
Public Property Set canvas(aControl As Object)
    Set m_Canvas = aControl
End Property
```

When the calling program says Sprite(n).Canvas = Picture1, for example, this code will pass Picture1 through a Control and use it to set the private variable m_Canvas. Our internal drawing program will use this to determine where to draw its circle object.

The Form

The two Dim statements declare that we are going to be creating an array of objects of type CSprite, called Sprite. This is a very powerful statement. The Form1_Load loops through the array of Sprite objects, from 0 to PLAYERS, which is set to 3 in a MODULE1.BAS. Each Sprite object must be created with the statement:

```
Set Sprite(i) = New CSprite
```

The rest of the statements simply set the properties that we have designed for our class. The Canvas property is assigned to each Sprite; the point parameters are set up; and the Radius, FillColor, and FillStyle are all set to random values. The most interesting statement is

```
Set Sprite(i).Sink = EventSink1
```

which sets up each Sprite so it inherits the properties of the EventSink custom control on the form.

The EventSink Call

We come to this simple, dual Select Case statement whenever there is an event from our CSprite class. In the statement:

```
Private Sub EventSink1_Event(ByVal EventNumber As Long, EventData As
Variant)
```

the variable EventNumber is returned to identify what event control caused the event. We will pass it the Sprite's ID_Done value, which is set in the Form1_Load to be the same as the array number for the Sprite. So Sprite(0) returns 0 for m_ID_Done. The parameter EventDate is passed as a variant, meaning it can be anything. We will pass it a value that represents where the Sprite crossed, so it will be the value of the public constant BOTTOM, TOP, RIGHT, or LEFT. The Select Case statement uses this value to decide what to do when that particular wall is crossed. The Reflection variable tells the event routine what to do (bounce the balls or wrap them). That is it!

Comments

The Sprite class we have created contains all the important properties and methods you need to move an object around on the screen and can be thought of as a default Sprite class. In its default mode, it draws circles on its canvas. We may in the future want to create a new kind of Sprite, one that moves a Picture object instead of painting a circle on the canvas, for instance. To do this we would inherit all methods and properties from CSprite for a new kind of Sprite called, perhaps, CPicSprite. If we wanted to just move Picture Controls, we would not need to use the Draw method, and so we would modify the CPicSprite code to move Pictures.

Why not just make a new class that is a modified version of CSprite instead of faking inheritance (which we now know requires all those ugly pass-through statements)? Because, if we go for inheritance, we are using the component approach to software. When later we improve the CSprite or CPoint code, the improvements will automatically work for progams using CSprite, so CPicSprite would instantly be updated.

2

FORMS

2

FORMS

How do I...

Forms are the most fundamental building blocks of Visual Basic — it is impossible to program in Visual Basic without a working knowledge of them. This chapter contains a number of techniques you can use to make your programs more versatile and to give them the polished look that users expect in Windows programs. You will learn how to display a *splash screen* while your program loads, how to paint the background of an MDI parent form, how to create toolbars just like Visual Basic's, and much more. You will also learn how to use form properties and methods to pass variables to forms and retrieve the return values, a capability that has been missing in previous versions of Visual Basic.

To accomplish their magic most of the techniques in this chapter use one or more Windows API calls. The various How-To's will show you how to use the following Windows API calls:

WINDOWS API	HOW-TO'S
BitBlt	2.5
CreateEllipticRgn	2.5
CreatePen	2.5
CreateSolidBrush	2.5
DeleteObject	2.5
FindWindow	2.7
FillRect	2.5
FillRgn	2.5
GetActiveWindow	2.4
GetClassName	2.7
GetClientRect	2.5
GetCursorPos	2.4, 2.7
GetDC	2.5
GetPrivateProfileString	2.6
GetSysColor	2.4
GetSystemMetrics	2.2, 2.4
GetWindow	2.5, 2.7
InflateRect	2.5
MoveWindow	2.7
Rectangle	2.5
ReleaseCapture	2.3, 2.4
ReleaseDC	2.5
ScreenToClient	2.4
SelectObject	2.5
SendMessage	2.2, 2.3, 2.4
SetWindowWord	2.1, 2.2
StretchBlt	2.6
TextOut	2.5
WritePrivateProfileString	2.6

2.1 Start an Application with a Splash Screen

Commercial-quality applications almost always display a splash screen while the application loads. Splash screens usually provide information about the program, such as its name and version. It is especially important that you display a splash screen for a program that takes a long time to load so that the user knows something is happening. This How-To will show you everything you need to know to display interesting and informative information on a splash screen while your application loads.

2.2 Include Rollup Tools in My Application

Toolbars and other useful widgets can be helpful to your program's users. These toolbars and other control-oriented windows aren't very useful, however, if they aren't easily accessible. So it is desirable to display them during the time you might want them used. However, displaying a few of these screen aids can really clutter up the screen and make it difficult to find the thing you're actually trying to work on! Some applications, such as CorelDRAW, have implemented what is called a rollup window, which can be "rolled up" so that it takes very little screen space. When the user selects the tool it drops down so that it can be used. How-To 2.2 will show you how to add rollup tools to your applications.

2.3 Allow Dragging of a Captionless Form

There are times when you want to make a simple applet that doesn't really need much screen space, or even a caption. You can easily remove a form's title bar—but then there is no way for the user to move the form around on the screen. This How-To will demonstrate how to allow the user to drag a captionless form on the screen, so it can be positioned in a convienient spot.

2.4 Make a Floating Toolbar with a Mini-Title Bar

If you've ever wanted to make a toolbar like the one you use in Visual Basic, this project is for you. The techniques in How-To 2.4 let you build a perfect imitation of Visual Basic's toolbar, complete with a miniature toolbar and control box.

2.5 Paint an Interesting Background on an MDI Parent Form

Visual Basic 4.0 lets you set the background color of an MDI parent form, but this small improvement over VB3 still falls significantly short of what programmers usually need to display on an MDI parent form, including company logos and other information.

In this How-To you will learn not just how to display information on an MDI form, but a number of interesting graphics techniques, as well.

2.6 Save and Restore Window Positions

Few things are more annoying to a user than to have carefully arranged a window in an MDI application—only to find that the window settings are totally gone the next time the application is run. This How-To will show you an easy way to keep track of MDI child window settings, using an INI file and a couple of Windows API calls.

2.7 Position an Icon at a Given Location

Normally, Windows takes care of positioning a program's minimized-program icon. However, there are times when you might want to position a program's icon yourself. For instance, you could move an icon to the lower-right corner of the screen and make it blink to get attention. But Visual Basic generates an error if you try to use the Move method when a form is minimized. In How-To 2.7 you will learn how to use the Window API function MoveWindow, instead, to move an icon on the screen.

2.8 Create an Animated Cursor

It's boring seeing the same old hourglass displayed every time a program is working on a lengthy operation. In this How-To you will learn how to use a new feature of Visual Basic 4.0 to create animated cursors. You can now easily create an animated hourglass with flowing sand that flips over when all the sand has run to the bottom of the hourglass.

2.9 Automatically Resize Controls

Professional-looking Windows programs reposition and resize controls when the size of a window changes. There is at least one custom control available to add this capability to Visual Basic programs, but this control doesn't always do exactly what you'd like it to do. In How-To 2.9 you will learn how to create a class module that will automatically resize a group of controls on a form. Using the class module, called Cstretch, you can create different groupings of controls and customize the resize behavior of each group. And, best of all, since the Cstretch class is written entirely in Visual Basic, you can customize to meet special project requirements.

2.10 Pass Variables to and Return Variables from a Form

Visual Basic 4.0 has finally overcome a major obstacle to making modular programs. Beginning with VB4, a form can have Properties and Methods, just like an OLE automation server. This makes it much easier to copy forms and reuse them in multiple projects, because no global variables are required to pass start-up arguments to a form, and global variables are no longer required to retrieve return results from a form. How-To 2.10 will show how to start-up and terminate a reusable form using VB4's new form properties and methods.

2.1 How do I...
Start an Application with a Splash Screen?

COMPLEXITY: EASY
COMPATIBILITY: VB4 ONLY

Problem

I like the way Visual Basic, Word for Windows, and other commercial applications start with a splash screen. It adds polish and gives the user something to look at while the program loads. How can I incorporate a splash screen into my Visual Basic application?

Technique

This How-To builds the Splash screen as a borderless form, eliminating the control box, title bar, and min/max buttons. First the Load event of the Startup form displays the Splash screen and pauses for impact. Then it makes the Startup form appear underneath the Splash screen. To keep the Splash screen on top of the Startup form, the Load event uses a Windows API subroutine that makes the Startup form the parent of the Splash screen. The Load event also regularly updates the Splash screen with information about its progress. While waiting for the application to finish loading, the user can also watch the visible parts of the Startup form gradually fill with information.

Displaying the Startup form before Load is done with its work means the user could begin triggering form and control events before the form is ready to be used. To prevent this, the Startup form is disabled from user input until the Load event is complete.

Steps

Open and run SPLASH.VBP. While the application is loading, it will look something like Figure 2-1-1. You'll see the Splash screen appear briefly by itself before the Startup form appears underneath it. If you watch the Startup form carefully, you'll see a list box and a combo box fill with values. Notice that the Splash screen shows progress in several ways. Its progress bar fills with color and reports the percent complete. There is a spinning arrow and a regularly updated status message (e.g., "Load in Progress - Filling Check Boxes"). To confirm that the Startup form won't react to user-triggered events as it's loading, click on the form while the Splash screen is still visible.

1. Create a new project called SPLASH.VBP, and create a new form called START-UP.FRM. Place the controls on the form as shown in Figure 2-1-2. Then set all the properties listed in Table 2-1-1.

49

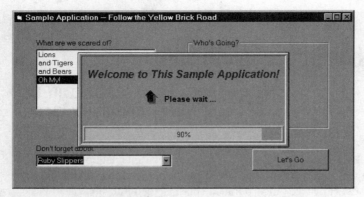

Figure 2-1-1 The Splash screen in action above the Startup form

Table 2-1-1 STARTUP.FRM objects and properties

OBJECT	PROPERTY	SETTING
Form	Name	Startup
	Caption	"Sample Application — Follow the Yellow Brick Road"
CommandButton	Name	Command1
	Caption	"Let's Go"
Frame	Name	Frame1
	Caption	"Who's Going?"
CheckBox	Name Caption	"Check1"
CheckBox	Name Caption	"Check2"
CheckBox	Name Caption	"Check3"
CheckBox	Name Caption	"Check4"
ComboBox	Name	Combo1
ListBox	Name	List1
Label	Name	Label1
	AutoSize	-1 'True
	BackStyle	0 'Transparent
	Caption	"What are we scared of?"
Label	Name	Label2
	AutoSize	-1 'True
	BackStyle	0 'Transparent
	Caption	"Don't forget about:"

2. Create another new form called SPLASH.FRM. Place the controls on the form as shown in Figure 2-1-3. Then set all the properties listed in Table 2-1-2.

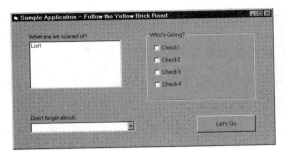

Figure 2-1-2 The Startup form during design

Figure 2-1-3 The Splash screen during design

Table 2-1-2 SPLASH.FRM objects and properties

OBJECT	PROPERTY	SETTING
Form	Name	Splash
	BorderStyle	0 'None
	Caption	"Splash Form"
	ControlBox	0 'False
	MaxButton	0 'False
	BackStyle	0 'Transparent
	MinButton	0 'False
SSPanel	Name	SSPanel2
	Bevelwidth	2 - Raised
Form	Name	Splash
	Bevelinner	1 - Inset
	Borderwidth	3
	Outline	-1 'True
Label	Name	Label1
	Alignment	2 'Center
	AutoSize	-1 'True
	BackStyle	0 'Transparent
	Caption	"Label1"
	Font.Name	"Arial"
	Font.Style	"Regular"
	Font.Size	8
Label	Name	Label2
	Alignment	2 'Center
	BackStyle	0 'Transparent
	Caption	"Welcome to This Sample Application!"
	Font.Name	"Arial"

Continued on next page

Continued from previous page

OBJECT	PROPERTY	SETTING
	Font.Style	"Regular"
	Font.Size	8
	Font.Name	"Arial"
	Font.Style	"Bold Italic"
	Font.Size	12
	ForeColor	&H000000FF& (Red)
Label	Name	Label3
	AutoSize	-1 'True
	BackStyle	0 'Transparent
	Caption	"Please wait ..."
	Font.Name	"Arial"
	Font.Style	"Bold"
	Font.Size	9
	ForeColor	&H00FF0000& (Blue)
Image	Name	Animate
SSPanel	Name	SSPanel1
	Caption	"SSPanel1"
	Borderwidth	2 - Raised
	Bevelinner	1 - Inset
	Floodtype	1 - Left to Right
	Floodcolor	&H0000FFFF& (Yellow)

3. Place the following code at the beginning of the STARTUP.FRM module. This subroutine is used in the Form_Load event procedure every time it needs to simulate doing extended work in a real application.

```
Option Explicit

Sub DoWorkUnits(NbrWorkUnits As Integer)
    Dim i As Integer
'
' Wait .2 seconds and advance the Splash screen animation picture
' one time for each simulated unit of work.
'
    i = 0
    Do While i < NbrWorkUnits
        Call Wait(0.2)
        Call Splash.AdvanceSplashAnimation
        i = i + 1
    Loop
End Sub
```

4. Place the following code in the Startup.Form_Load event procedure, to display the Splash screen while filling the Startup form with information. By showing the

Startup form behind the Splash screen, the user can see its progress as it fills with information. This makes the apparent load time quicker.

```
Private Sub Form_Load()
'
' Prepare and show the Splash screen.
'
    MousePointer = vbHourglass
    Splash.Label1 = ""
    Call Splash.AdvanceSplashAnimation
    Call CenterForm(Splash)
    Splash.Show
'
' Prepare the Startup form, disabling it and putting the
' Splash screen on top. Allow the Splash screen to show
' for a second before showing the Startup form behind it.
' Wait another second before continuing.
'
    Splash.SSPanel1.FloodPercent = 0
    Startup.Enabled = False
    Call CenterForm(Startup)
    Dim RtnCode As Integer
    RtnCode = SetWindowWord(Splash.hWnd, _
                    GWW_HWNDPARENT, _
                    Startup.hWnd)
Call Wait(1)
    Startup.Visible = True
    Call Wait(1)
'
' Continue with units of work (filling the list box, some
' check boxes, and a combo box). Call the DoWorkUnits routine
' to simulate the extra time it might take a real application
' to do a lot of work.
'
' Fill the list box.
    Splash.Label1 = "Load in Progress — Filling List Box"
    List1.AddItem "Lions"
    Call DoWorkUnits(2)
    Splash.SSPanel1.FloodPercent _
                = Splash.SSPanel1.FloodPercent + (100 * (2 / 20))
    List1.AddItem "and Tigers"
    Call DoWorkUnits(2)
    Splash.SSPanel1.FloodPercent _
                = Splash.SSPanel1.FloodPercent + (100 * (2 / 20))
    List1.AddItem "and Bears"
    Call DoWorkUnits(2)
    Splash.SSPanel1.FloodPercent _
                = Splash.SSPanel1.FloodPercent + (100 * (2 / 20))
    List1.AddItem "Oh My!"
    List1.Selected(List1.NewIndex) = True
    Call DoWorkUnits(2)
    Splash.SSPanel1.FloodPercent _
                = Splash.SSPanel1.FloodPercent + (100 * (2 / 20))
'
```

Continued on next page

53

Continued from previous page

```
' Label and check the check boxes.
    Splash.Label1 = "Load in Progress - Filling Check Boxes"
    Check1.Caption = "Dorothy"
    Check1 = vbChecked
    Call DoWorkUnits(1)
    Splash.SSPanel1.FloodPercent _
                    = Splash.SSPanel1.FloodPercent + (100 * (1 / 20))
    Check2.Caption = "Scarecrow"
    Check2 = vbChecked
    Call DoWorkUnits(1)
    Splash.SSPanel1.FloodPercent _
                    = Splash.SSPanel1.FloodPercent + (100 * (1 / 20))
    Check3.Caption = "Tin Man"
    Check3 = vbChecked
    Call DoWorkUnits(1)
    Splash.SSPanel1.FloodPercent _
                    = Splash.SSPanel1.FloodPercent + (100 * (1 / 20))
    Check4.Caption = "Lion"
    Check4 = vbChecked
    Call DoWorkUnits(1)
    Splash.SSPanel1.FloodPercent _
                    = Splash.SSPanel1.FloodPercent + (100 * (1 / 20))
'
' Fill Combo box.
    Splash.Label1 = "Load in Progress - Updating Combo List"
    Combo1.AddItem "Toto"
    Call DoWorkUnits(1)
    Splash.SSPanel1.FloodPercent _
                    = Splash.SSPanel1.FloodPercent + (100 * (1 / 20))
    Combo1.AddItem "Tornado"
    Call DoWorkUnits(1)
    Splash.SSPanel1.FloodPercent _
                    = Splash.SSPanel1.FloodPercent + (100 * (1 / 20))
    Combo1.AddItem "Wicked Witch of the West"
    Call DoWorkUnits(1)
    Splash.SSPanel1.FloodPercent _
                    = Splash.SSPanel1.FloodPercent + (100 * (1 / 20))
    Combo1.AddItem "Horse of a Different Color"
    Call DoWorkUnits(1)
    Splash.SSPanel1.FloodPercent _
                    = Splash.SSPanel1.FloodPercent + (100 * (1 / 20))
    Combo1.AddItem "Ruby Slippers"
    Call DoWorkUnits(1)
    Splash.SSPanel1.FloodPercent _
                    = Splash.SSPanel1.FloodPercent + (100 * (1 / 20))
    Combo1.AddItem "Kansas"
    Call DoWorkUnits(1)
    Splash.SSPanel1.FloodPercent _
                    = Splash.SSPanel1.FloodPercent + (100 * (1 / 20))
    Combo1.Text = "Ruby Slippers"
    Combo1.SelStart = 0
    Combo1.SelLength = Len(Combo1.Text)
'
' Update the Splash screen to show that the Startup form is ready
' to go. Then wait 3 seconds before unloading it.
'
```

```
    Splash.Label1 = ""
    Call DoWorkUnits(2)
    Splash.Label3 = "Thanks for waiting."
    Splash.Label1 = "P.S., you're not in Kansas anymore!"
    Splash.SSPanel1.FloodPercent _
                    = Splash.SSPanel1.FloodPercent + (100 * (2 / 20))

    Call Wait(3)
    Unload Splash
'
' Change the Startup form's caption to give one more visual clue that
' everything is ready. Then enable it and give it the focus.
'
    Startup.Caption = "Sample Application - We're Off to See the Wizard"
    Startup.Enabled = True
    Startup.SetFocus
    MousePointer = vbDefault
End Sub
```

5. Place the following code in the Startup.Command1_Click event procedure to end the program:

```
Private Sub Command1_Click()
    End
End Sub
```

6. Place the following code at the beginning of the SPLASH.FRM module. This subroutine is used to indicate action in the Startup form by animating a picture on the Splash screen. In this How-To, the animated picture is a spinning arrow.

```
Option Explicit

Sub AdvanceSplashAnimation()
    Static AnimatePic As Integer
'
' Animate spinning picture by showing the right picture the first
' time. After that iterate through, showing down, left, and top
' pictures before starting over on the right picture.
'
' 1=Right Picture, 2=Down Picture, 3=Left Picture, 4=Top Picture
'
    If IsEmpty (Animate.Picture) Then
        AnimatePic = 1
    Else
        If AnimatePic < 4 Then
            AnimatePic = AnimatePic + 1
        Else
            AnimatePic = 1
        End If
    End If
'
' Show the selected picture.
'
    Dim PicPath As String
    PicPath = App.Path & (IIF(Right$ (App.Path, 1) <> "\", "\", "")
```

Continued on next page

Continued from previous page

```
    Select Case AnimatePic
        Case 1
            Animate.Picture _
                    = LoadPicture(PicPath & "ARW04RT.ICO)
        Case 2
            Animate.Picture _
                    = LoadPicture(PicPath & "ARWT04DN.ICO)
        Case 3
            Animate.Picture _
                    = LoadPicture(PicPath & "ARWT04LT.ICO)
        Case 4
            Animate.Picture _
                    = LoadPicture(PicPath & "ARWT04UP.ICO)
    End Select
End Sub
```

7. Place the following code at the beginning of the GENERAL.BAS module. The declaration enables a Windows API function that is used to keep the Splash screen on top of the Startup form while it is loading. The CenterForm subroutine is used to center both the Startup form and the Splash screen. The Wait subroutine waits for a specified number of seconds, which can be fractional. It includes a DoEvents to allow other processing to continue while the calling routine waits.

```
Option Explicit

Global Const GWW_HWNDPARENT = (-8)

Declare Function SetWindowWord Lib "User" _
                                (ByVal hWnd As Integer, _
                                 ByVal nIndex As Integer, _
                                 ByVal wNewWord As Integer) _
                    As Integer

Sub CenterForm(AnyForm As Form)
'
'Center the form
'
    If AnyForm.WindowState = 0 Then
        AnyForm.Top = (Screen.Height - AnyForm.Height) / 2
        AnyForm.Left = (Screen.Width - AnyForm.Width) / 2
    End If
End Sub

Sub Wait(WaitSeconds As Single)
'
' Wait for specified number of seconds, but allow other
' processing to continue
'
    Dim StartTime As Single
    StartTime = Timer
    Do While Timer < StartTime + WaitSeconds
        DoEvents
    Loop
End Sub
```

How It Works

To show off the Splash, this How-To makes use of a routine called DoWorkUnits. You tell DoWorkUnits how many units of work it should do, and it simulates the time it would take for a real application to do that work in its Load event. For each unit of work, DoWorkUnits waits two-tenths of a second before advancing the Splash screen's animated arrow to the next picture. A real program's Load event would just advance the Splash screen's animated arrow each time it finished a small chunk of work.

New in Visual Basic 4.0 is the ability to call a form's public procedures from outside the form. You'll see this in action as the Startup form module's DoWorkUnits subroutine calls the Splash form module's AdvanceSplashAnimation subroutine.

After showing the Splash screen and before displaying the Startup form, the Startup Load event procedure needs to make the Startup form the parent window of the Splash screen. This allows the Splash screen to stay on top after the Startup form becomes visible. To do this, the Load event procedure calls a Windows API function, SetWindowWord. It passes the window handles of both the Splash form and the Startup form, along with a parameter that directs the new parent assignment.

Comments

You'll need to be careful when you use the SetWindowWord API function to change a form's parent window. If you unload the new parent form before restoring the child form's original parent window, a general protection fault (GPF) will occur. To avoid this, save the value returned by the SetWindowWord function when you first set the new parent. That value is the handle to the child window's original parent window. Then, in the Unload event procedure for the new parent, you can do another SetWindowWord to restore the child form's parent window to its original state. In this How-To, it's not necessary to add this code, because the child window (the Splash screen) is unloaded before its new parent window (the Startup form).

2.2 How do I...
Include Rollup Tools in My Application?

COMPLEXITY: INTERMEDIATE
COMPATIBILITY: VB3 OR VB4

Problem

I would like to mimic the functionality provided by CorelDRAW's rollup windows. These windows are a convenient alternative to dialog boxes for obtaining information from the user.

Because a rollup window stays open even after the selected options are applied, the user can make adjustments and try various options without having to keep reopening a dialog box. The window can be rolled up, hiding its controls when not in use. With a single click, the window rolls open and is instantly available. The user can close it by double-clicking the system control box on the title bar or by selecting Close from the control box's drop-down menu. The drop-down menu also provides options for arranging one or all rollup windows off to the side and out of the way of the drawing.

Technique

This How-To uses an MDI Main form and a Child form to simulate CorelDRAW's drawing environment. It creates a rollup tool that mimics the look of a rollup window in CorelDRAW. The Rollup Tool form provides some sample controls that let you adjust the color of the Child form's background.

The Rollup Tool form has a narrower-than-normal title bar. The title bar includes a system control box to the left and a rollup button to the right. The look of the title bar cannot be achieved directly with form properties in Visual Basic, so this How-To shows a way to create the look with image controls and a label on a captionless form. Visual Basic's ability to display popup menus anywhere is employed to mimic the look of a real control box's drop-down menu.

Because the rollup tool is captionless, it cannot be dragged in the normal way. The Windows API comes to the rescue. The form is dragged using the technique covered in How-To 2.3, and kept on top of the other forms by applying the splash screen technique covered in How-To 2.1.

The Windows API also provides some assistance with aligning the rollup tool out of the way in the upper-right corner of the Main form. With the GetSystemMetrics API function, it provides system metrics for sizes of the standard Windows title bar, menu bar, frame, and border. These metrics enable a precise alignment of the rollup tool (similar to CorelDRAW's Arrange and Arrange All capabilities).

Steps

Open and run ROLLUP.VBP. Choose Color Changer Tool from the Rollup Tools menu, and notice that My Rollup Tool loads into the top-right corner of the Main form. Click on the rollup tool's right button (the one labeled with a down arrow), and you'll see the tool roll down to reveal its other controls. While it's rolled down, try previewing the color choices and applying them to the Color Me child form. Also try undoing the color changes. Figure 2-2-1 shows the rollup tool in action.

Click the down-arrow button repeatedly to toggle between rolled up and rolled down, and notice that the button has a 3D look—that is, it looks depressed when you click and hold the mouse down on it. Also notice that the arrow on the button changes to indicate the next action. The arrow points up when the tool is rolled down and the next button action will be to roll it up. It points down when the tool is rolled up and the next button action will be to roll it down. You can drag the rollup tool around whether it's rolled up or down.

Now click once on the system control box. You'll see a drop-down menu with two choices, Align and Close. Selecting Align causes the rollup tool to realign in the

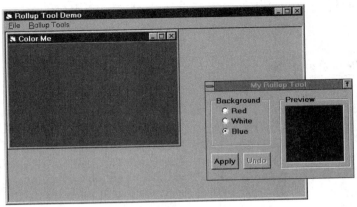

Figure 2-2-1 The rollup tool in action, changing the background color of the child form

top-right corner of the Main form after the rollup has been dragged to another spot. Selecting Close unloads the rollup tool. You can open it again from the main form's menu. Notice the check mark next to the Color Changer Tool menu item. The check mark appears when the rollup tool is loaded and disappears when it's unloaded.

1. Create a new project called ROLLUP.VBP. Choose MDI Form from the Insert menu, and save the form as MDIROLL.FRM. Set the form and menu properties listed in Table 2-2-1.

Table 2-2-1 MDIROLL.FRM form and menu properties

OBJECT	PROPERTY	SETTING
Form	Name	MainForm
	Caption	"Rollup Tool Demo"
Menu	Name	mnuFile
	Caption	"&File"
	Index	0
Menu	Name	mnuExit
	Caption	"E&xit"
Menu	Name	mnuRollupTools
	Caption	"&Rollup Tools"
	Index	1
Menu	Name	mnuColorChanger
	Caption	"&Color Changer Tool"

2. Create another new form called CHILD.FRM. Set the properties listed in Table 2-2-2.

Table 2-2-2 CHILD.FRM form properties

OBJECT	PROPERTY	SETTING
Form	Name	ChildForm
	Caption	"Color Me"
	MDIChild	-1 'True

3. Create another new form called ROLLUP.FRM. Place controls on the form as shown in Figure 2-2-2. Then set all the properties listed in Table 2-2-3.

Table 2-2-3 ROLLUP.FRM objects and properties

OBJECT	PROPERTY	SETTING
Form	Name	RollupForm
	BorderStyle	0 'None
	Caption	"RollupForm"
	ControlBox	"False"
	MaxButton	"False"
	MinButton	"False"
Frame	Name	BackgroundFrame
	Caption	"Background"
OptionButton	Name	ColorOption
	Caption	"Red"
	Index	0
OptionButton	Name	ColorOption
	Caption	"White"
	Index	1
OptionButton	Name	ColorOption
	Caption	"Blue"
	Index	2
Frame	Name	PreviewFrame
	Caption	"Preview"
PictureBox	Name	ColorPicture
	BackColor	&H000000FF&
CommandButton	Name	DoCommand

OBJECT	PROPERTY	SETTING
	Caption	"Apply"
	Index	0
CommandButton	Name	DoCommand
	Caption	"Undo"
	Index	1
PictureBox	Name	RollupControlBox
	AutoSize	-1 'True
	Appearance	0 'Flat
	BorderStyle	0 'None
	Picture	"CNTLBOX.BMP
Label	Name	RollupTitle
	Alignment	2 'Center
	Appearance	0 'Flat
	BorderStyle	1 'Fixed Single
	Caption	"My Rollup Tool"
PictureBox	Name	RollButton
	AutoSize	-1 'True
	BorderStyle	0 'None
	Picture	"RDWNUP.BMP"
Shape	Name	RollupFormShape
	Shape	0 'Rectangular

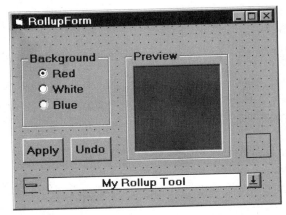

Figure 2-2-2 The Rollup form during design

4. Create another new form called CNTRLBOX.FRM, and set its properties as shown in Table 2-2-4.

Table 2-2-4 CNTRLBOX.FRM form properties

OBJECT	PROPERTY	SETTING
Form	Name	ControlBoxForm
	Caption	"Control Box"
	Visible	0 'False
Menu	Name	mnuPop
	Caption	"&Pop"
	Index	0
Menu	Name	mpAlign
	Caption	"&Align"
	Index	0
Menu	Name	mpHyphen
	Caption	"-"
	Menu	mpClose
	Caption	"&Close"
	Index	1

5. Place the following code at the beginning of the module MDIROLL.FRM, to display the Child form sized to one half the width of its parent:

```
Option Explicit

Private Sub MDIForm_Load()
    '
    ' Set the MDI Child to half the width of it's parent
    ' and show it.
    '
    ChildForm.Width = MainForm.Width / 2
    ChildForm.Show
End Sub
```

6. Place the following code in the MainForm.mnuExitClick event procedure, to unload all the forms and end the program:

```
Private Sub mnuExit_Click()
    '
    ' Unload all forms and end.
    '
    Unload ControlBoxForm
    Unload RollupForm
    Unload MainForm
    End
End Sub
```

7. Place the following code in the MainForm.mnuColorChanger_Click event procedure to load and unload the Rollup Tool from the menu:

```
Private Sub mnuColorChanger_Click()
    '
    ' Toggle between Color Changer Rollup Tool showing and
    ' not loaded. Indicate status with check next to menu item.
    '
    If mnuColorChanger.Checked Then
        Unload RollupForm
        mnuColorChanger.Checked = False
    Else
        RollupForm.Show
        mnuColorChanger.Checked = True
    End If
    '
    ' Return focus to Child form.
    '
    ChildForm.SetFocus
End Sub
```

8. Place the following code at the beginning of the ROLLUP.FRM module:

```
Option Explicit

Dim RolledDown As Boolean
Const ApplyColor As Integer = 0
Const UndoColor As Integer = 1
```

9. Place the following code in the RollupForm.Form_Load event procedure to apply and undo the Child form's back color:

```
Private Sub DoCommand_Click(Index As Integer)
    '
    ' Save the old BackColor of the Child form before applying
    ' new color. Restore the old BackColor when Undo button is
    ' clicked.
    '
    Static OldBackColor
    If Index = ApplyColor Then
        OldBackColor = ChildForm.BackColor
        ChildForm.BackColor = ColorPicture.BackColor
        DoCommand(ApplyColor).Enabled = False
        DoCommand(UndoColor).Enabled = True
    Else 'Index = UndoColor
        ChildForm.BackColor = OldBackColor
        DoCommand(ApplyColor).Enabled = True
        DoCommand(UndoColor).Enabled = False
    End If
    '
    ' Return focus to Child form.
    '
    ChildForm.SetFocus
End Sub
```

10. Place the following code in the RollupForm.Form_Load event procedure to align and size the controls and form appropriately. This event procedure also enables and disables the Rollup Tool buttons, consistent with the Child form's back color. Finally, it places the Rollup Tool in the top right corner of the MainForm, set to stay On Top.

```
Private Sub Form_Load()
    '
    ' Initialize rolled down state of rollup tool.
    '
    RolledDown = False
    '
    ' Align rollup tool controls across top of form to mimic
    ' Windows control box, title bar, and roll up/down button'
    '
    RollupControlBox.Top = 0
    RollupTitle.Top = 0
    RollButton.Top = 0
    RollupControlBox.Left = 0
    RollupTitle.Left = RollupControlBox.Width
    RollButton.Left = RollupControlBox.Width + RollupTitle.Width
    RollupTitle.Height = RollupControlBox.Height
    '
    ' Set Fore and Back Colors to simulate inactive title bar.
    '
    RollupTitle.BackColor = vbInactiveTitleBar
    RollupTitle.ForeColor = vbInactiveCaptionText
    '
    ' Size rollup tool form to fit exactly to the size of the
    ' simulated control box, tool bar, and roll up/down button.
    '
    Me.Width = RollupControlBox.Width _
                        + RollupTitle.Width _
                        + RollButton.Width
    Me.Height = RollupControlBox.Height
    '
    ' Size graphic to simulate border around edge of form.
    '
    RollupFormShape.Top = 0
    RollupFormShape.Left = 0
    RollupFormShape.Height = 2100
    RollupFormShape.Width = Me.Width
    '
    ' Trigger ColorOption event to make sure Apply/Undo button is
    ' enabled/disabled based on current BackColor of Child form.
    '
    Call ColorOption_Click(0)
    '
    ' Place Rollup form snugly into top right corner of Main form.
    '
    Call AlignRollupInMain(Me, MainForm)
    '
    ' Make Rollup Tool form stay on top of Main form.
    '
```

```
      Call SetWindowWord(Me.hWnd, SWW_HPARENT, MainForm.hWnd)
End Sub
```

11. Create the following event procedures. They are needed so that when the form and these controls are clicked with the mouse, focus immediately returns to the Child form.

```
Private Sub Form_MouseDown(Button As Integer, _
                           Shift As Integer, _
                           X As Single, _
                           Y As Single)

    '
    ' Return focus to Child form.
    '
    ChildForm.SetFocus
End Sub

Private Sub BackgroundFrame_MouseDown(Button As Integer, _
                                      Shift As Integer, _
                                      X As Single, _
                                      Y As Single)

    '
    ' Return focus to Child form.
    '
    ChildForm.SetFocus
End Sub

Private Sub PreviewFrame_Click()

    '
    ' Return focus to Child form.
    '
    ChildForm.SetFocus
End Sub

Private Sub ColorPicture_Click()

    '
    ' Return focus to Child form.
    '
    ChildForm.SetFocus
End Sub
```

12. Place the following code in the RollupForm.ColorOption_Click event procedure to preview the selected color and to enable and disable the Rollup Tool buttons, consistent with the Child form's back color:

```
Private Sub ColorOption_Click(Index As Integer)

    Const SelectedRed As Integer = 0
    Const SelectedWhite As Integer = 1
    Const SelectedBlue As Integer = 2
    '
    ' Show the selected color in the Preview frame's picture box.
    '
```

Continued on next page

Continued from previous page

```
    Select Case Index
        Case SelectedRed
            ColorPicture.BackColor = vbRed
        Case SelectedWhite
            ColorPicture.BackColor = vbWhite
        Case SelectedBlue
            ColorPicture.BackColor = vbBlue
    End Select
    '
    ' Disable apply button if selected color = current BackColor of
    ' Child form. Enable Apply and disable Undo buttons if a different
    ' color has been selected to be applied.
    '
    If ColorPicture.BackColor = ChildForm.BackColor Then
        DoCommand(ApplyColor).Enabled = False
    Else
        DoCommand(ApplyColor).Enabled = True
        DoCommand(UndoColor).Enabled = False
    End If
    '
    ' Return focus to Child form.
    '
    ChildForm.SetFocus
End Sub
```

13. Place the following code in the RollupForm.RollButton_Click event procedure to roll up the Rollup Tool when it is down, and to roll it down when it is up:

```
Private Sub RollButton_Click()
    '
    ' RolledDown is a toggle. When the rollup tool is down, roll
    ' it up. Otherwise roll it down. In either case toggle the
    ' RolledDown value.
    '
    If RolledDown Then
        Me.Height = RollupControlBox.Height
        RolledDown = False
    Else
        Me.Height = 2100
        RolledDown = True
    End If
    '
    ' Return focus to Child form.
    '
    ChildForm.SetFocus
End Sub
```

14. Place the following code in the RollupForm.RollButton_MouseDown event procedure to display a depressed RollButton picture with an arrow pointing in the direction the Tool will roll:

```
Private Sub RollButton_MouseDown(Button As Integer, _
                                 Shift As Integer, _
```

```
                               X As Single, _
                               Y As Single)
    '
    ' This event is triggered when pressing down on Roll button.
    ' If Rollup Tool form is rolled down, change button to depressed
    ' arrow pointing up. If form is rolled up, change button to
    ' depressed arrow pointing down.
    '
    If RolledDown Then
        RollButton.Picture = LoadPicture(App.Path & "\rupdwn.bmp")
    Else
        RollButton.Picture = LoadPicture(App.Path & "\rdwndwn.bmp")
    End If
End Sub
```

15. Place the following code in the RollupForm.RollButton_MouseUp event procedure to display a released RollButton picture with an arrow pointing in the direction the Tool will roll:

```
Private Sub RollButton_MouseUp(Button As Integer, _
                               Shift As Integer, _
                               X As Single, _
                               Y As Single)
    '
    ' This event is triggered when releasing Roll button.
    ' If Rollup Tool form is rolled down, change button to
    ' undepressed arrow pointing up. If form is rolled up,
    ' change button to undepressed arrow pointing down.
    '
    If RolledDown Then
        RollButton.Picture = LoadPicture(App.Path & "\rdwnup.bmp")
    Else
        RollButton.Picture = LoadPicture(App.Path & "\rupup.bmp")
    End If
End Sub
```

16. Create the following two RollupForm.RollControlBox event procedures to display the ControlBox menu when it's clicked and to unload the Rollup Tool when its Control Box is double-clicked:

```
Private Sub RollupControlBox_Click()
    '
    ' The ControlBox form is used only to provide a popup menu
    ' for the RollupControlBox. Here the menu is displayed just
    ' below the RollupControlBox and left aligned even with the
    ' left of the Rollup form. The left mouse button is active.
    '
    PopupMenu ControlBoxForm.mnuPop(0), _
              vbPopupMenuLeftAlign Or vbPopupMenuLeftButton, _
              0, _
              RollupControlBox.Height
End Sub
```

Continued on next page

67

Continued from previous page

```
Private Sub RollupControlBox_DblClick()
    '
    ' When the RollupControlBox is double-clicked, unload the
    ' Rollup form and uncheck the ColorChanger menu item.
    '
    Unload RollupForm
    MainForm.mnuColorChanger.Checked = False
End Sub
```

17. Place the following code in the RollupForm.RollupTitle_MouseDown event procedure to simulate an active form title bar when the mouse is pressed down on the Title Bar. The code also tells Windows to drag the form as the user moves the mouse, a technique described in more detail in How-To 2.3.

```
Private Sub RollupTitle_MouseDown(Button As Integer, _
                                  Shift As Integer, _
                                  X As Single, _
                                  Y As Single)
    '
    ' When left mouse button is pressed on RollupTitle, change
    ' Rollup Title colors to active and drag Rollup form.
    ' Return colors to inactive when done dragging.
    '
    Dim RtnCode As Long
    If Button And vbLeftButton Then
        RollupTitle.BackColor = vbActiveTitleBar
        RollupTitle.ForeColor = vbTitleBarText
        ReleaseCapture
        RtnCode = SendMessage(Me.hWnd, _
                              WM_NCLBUTTONDOWN, _
                              HTCAPTION, _
                              0&)
        RollupTitle.BackColor = vbInactiveTitleBar
        RollupTitle.ForeColor = vbInactiveCaptionText
    End If
    '
    ' Return focus to Child form.
    '
    ChildForm.SetFocus
End Sub
```

18. Place the following code in the CNTRLBOX.FRM module to align the Rollup Tool in the top right corner of the MainForm when the ControlBox Align menu item is clicked:

```
Private Sub mpAlign_Click(Index As Integer)
    '
    ' Place Rollup form snugly into top-right corner of Main form.
    '
    Call AlignRollupInMain(RollupForm, MainForm)
    '
    ' Return focus to Child form.
    '
```

```
    ChildForm.SetFocus
End Sub

Private Sub mpClose_Click(Index As Integer)
    '
    ' Unload Rollup form and uncheck Main form's ColorChanger
    ' menu item.
    '
    Unload RollupForm
    MainForm.mnuColorChanger.Checked = False
End Sub
```

19. Place the following code at the beginning of the ROLLUP.BAS module to provide
    the Windows API functions needed to align and move the Rollup Tool:

```
'Windows messages, for use with SendMessage
Global Const WM_NCLBUTTONDOWN = &ha1

'Used to fool Windows that it's in the title bar
Global Const HTCAPTION = 2

'GetSystemMetrics constants
Global Const SM_CXFRAME = 32
Global Const SM_CXBORDER = 5
Global Const SM_CYFRAME = 33
Global Const SM_CYCAPTION = 4
Global Const SM_CYMENU = 15
Global Const SM_CYBORDER = 6

'SetWindowWord constant
Global Const SWW_HPARENT = -8


If Win32 Then
    Declare Function SendMessage Lib "user32" _
        Alias "SendMessageA" _
            (ByVal hWnd As Long, _
            ByVal wMsg As Long, _
            ByVal wParam As Long, _
            lParam As Any) _
        As Long
    Declare Function GetSystemMetrics Lib "user32" _
            (ByVal nIndex As Long) _
        As Long
    Declare Sub SetWindowWord Lib "user32" _
            (ByVal hWnd As Long, _
            ByVal nCmd As Long, _
            ByVal nVal As Long)
    Declare Sub ReleaseCapture Lib "User" ()
Else
    Declare Function SendMessage Lib "User" _
            (ByVal hWnd As Integer, _
            ByVal wMsg As Integer, _
            ByVal wParam As Integer, _
            lParam As Any) _
        As Long
```

Continued on next page

Continued from previous page

```
    Declare Function GetSystemMetrics Lib "User" _
            (ByVal nIndex As Integer) _
            As Integer
    Declare Sub SetWindowWord Lib "User" _
            (ByVal hWnd As Integer, _
            ByVal nCmd As Integer, _
            ByVal nVal As Integer)
    Declare Sub ReleaseCapture Lib "User" ()
End If
```

20. Place the following subroutine in the ROLLUP.BAS module to align a form inside the top and right edge of another:

```
Sub AlignRollupInMain(AnyRollup As Form, AnyMain As Form)
    '
    ' Align top of rollup form to fit just below main form's
    ' frame, caption and menu. Align right edge of rollup form
    ' to line up with inside frame of right edge of main form.
    '
    AnyRollup.Top = AnyMain.Top _
        + GetSystemMetrics(SM_CYFRAME) * Screen.TwipsPerPixelY _
        + GetSystemMetrics(SM_CYCAPTION) * Screen.TwipsPerPixelY _
        + GetSystemMetrics(SM_CYMENU) * Screen.TwipsPerPixelY _
        + GetSystemMetrics(SM_CYBORDER) * Screen.TwipsPerPixelY _
    AnyRollup.Left = AnyMain.Left _
        + MainForm.Width _
        - RollupForm.Width _
        - GetSystemMetrics(SM_CXFRAME) * Screen.TwipsPerPixelX _
        - GetSystemMetrics(SM_CXBORDER) * Screen.TwipsPerPixelX _
End Sub
```

How It Works

Creating a narrow title bar with only Control Box and an up/down arrow button is key to making a rollup tool that looks like a CorelDRAW rollup window. Windows 3.1 does not offer this style option for title bars, so we use picture boxes and a label to create the look.

The rolluptool title bar may or may not appear narrow in Windows 95. Its appearance will be measured against the height of the other forms' active title bars which are user controllable settings in Windows 95. The graphics for the control box and arrow buttons have been sized to be exactly identical in height. And they have been designed to create the look of a solid title bar when sandwiched around a label with a fixed single border. A rectangular graphic is sized exactly to the size of the rolled-down Rollup Tool form. This provides a narrow border of black around the light-gray form, so it won't "disappear" into a gray-colored desktop or other application.

The Rollup form is made captionless as described in How-To 2-3. This allows the title bar controls to be placed at the very top of the form. A mouse pressed down on the title bar label triggers drag by using the Windows API subroutine, Release-Capture, and the API function SendMessage (See How-To 2.3 for specifics). The RollupForm stays on top of the Main form and its child form by using the Windows API subroutine SetWindowWord. How-To 2.1 explains this technique.

The Rollup form's Load event and the Align menu Click event both call a common subroutine, AlignRollupInMain. The subroutine uses the Windows API function, GetSystemMetrics, to get the sizes of the normal frame, caption bar, border, and menu bar. The sizes will vary depending on the Windows desktop definition for each system. Converting the measurements to twips standardizes the calculations. It aligns the top of the rollup tool below the top of the Main form's frame, caption bar, border, and menu bar. And it aligns the right edge of the Rollup Tool next to the inside edge of the Main form's right frame and border.

A double-click on the system control box picture closes the rollup tool, providing the feel of a real system control box. A single click triggers the PopupMenu method, which makes the menu appear just below the control box picture, imitating a real system control box menu. The menu is defined on a separate ControlBox form, because the Rollup form cannot remain captionless if it has a menu bar. Four pictures are used to simulate a button that appears pushed. The pictures are of two up-arrow buttons (one up and the other depressed) and two down-arrow buttons (one up and the other depressed). These pictures are cycled in and out depending on whether or not the mouse is down on the picture box and whether the tool is rolled up or down.

Comments

In an application with more than one rollup tool, an Align All control box menu option could add the functionality of CorelDRAW's Arrange All option. The Visual Basic 4.0 "For each item in collection" code construct could be used to align each rollup tool in a collection of like forms. The code could stack them, each one underneath the prior one, in the top-right corner of the Main form.

2.3 How do I...
Allow Dragging of a Captionless Form?

COMPLEXITY: EASY
COMPATIBILITY: VB3 OR VB4

Problem

How can I allow my users to drag a form that doesn't have a title bar, just like the Windows Clock applet?

Technique

The typical answer to this question involves capturing all mouse movements, drawing the drag outline directly on the screen's device context, and then manually moving the form when the user releases the mouse button. That's a lot of code—prone to failure. There is a much easier method: you convince Windows that the pointer was on a title bar when the user pressed the mouse button. This technique uses the

SendMessage API to send the application the same message it would normally receive if there were a title bar.

Steps

Open and run DRAG.VBP. You will see a window that looks much like the Windows Clock applet. To move it, press and hold the left mouse button anywhere over the form, drag it to its new location, and release the mouse. Figure 2-3-1 shows how the form will appear while being dragged. Resizing the window also resizes the fonts used to display the time and date. To exit, press (**ALT**)-(**F4**) or click the right mouse button anywhere on the form.

1. Create a new project called DRAG.VBP. Create a new form with the objects and properties shown in Table 2-3-1 and save it as DRAG.FRM. To create a Visual Basic form without a title bar, the settings shown for Caption, ControlBox, MinButton, and MaxButton must all be as shown. Otherwise, the form will have the standard title bar.

Table 2-3-1 DRAG.FRM objects and properties

OBJECT	PROPERTY	SETTING
Form	Name	Drag
	Appearance	1 - 3D
	AutoRedraw	True
	BackColor	&H8000000F&
	Caption	"" (none)
	ControlBox	False
	FontName	Arial
	MaxButton	False
	MinButton	False
Timer	Name	Timer1
	Enabled	True
	Interval	500

Figure 2-3-1 Dragging the captionless form

2. Insert the following code in the Declarations section of the form. The two API functions declared are used to fool Windows into dragging the window automatically. The Constants are used with SendMessage.

```
Option Explicit

#If Win16 Then
    '
    ' Win16 API declarations required
    '
    Private Declare Sub ReleaseCapture Lib "User" ()
    Private Declare Function SendMessage Lib "User" (ByVal hWnd As ⇒
            Integer, ByVal wMsg As Integer, ByVal wParam As Integer, ByVal ⇒
            lParam As Any) As Long
#ElseIf Win32 Then
    '
    ' Win32 API declarations required
    '
    Private Declare Sub ReleaseCapture Lib "user32" ()
    Private Declare Function SendMessage Lib "user32" Alias "SendMessageA" ⇒
            (ByVal hWnd As Long, ByVal wMsg As Long, ByVal wParam ⇒
            As Long, lParam As Any) As Long
#End If
'
' Constants to use with SendMessage
' Same for both Win16/Win32
'
Const WM_NCLBUTTONDOWN = &HA1
Const HTCAPTION = 2
```

3. To re-create the Clock display, place a subroutine called UpdateClock in the Declarations section of the form, containing the following code. Call this routine every time the Timer1_Timer event fires. UpdateClock formats and positions the current date and time strings. Setting AutoRedraw to True prevents unsightly flashing during the updates.

```
Sub Timer1_Timer ()
    '
    ' As it says
    '
    UpdateClock
End Sub

Sub UpdateClock ()
    Dim dt$
    '
    ' Display date
    '
    Cls
    dt$ = Format$(Now, "long date")
    CurrentX = (ScaleWidth - TextWidth(dt$)) \ 2
    CurrentY = ScaleHeight \ 2 + TextHeight(dt$) \ 4
    Print dt$
```

Continued on next page

Continued from previous page

```
    '
    ' Display time in font twice as large
    '
    FontSize = 2 * FontSize
    dt$ = Format$(Now, "long time")
    CurrentX = (ScaleWidth - TextWidth(dt$)) \ 2
    CurrentY = ScaleHeight \ 2 - TextHeight(dt$)
    Print dt$
    FontSize = FontSize / 2
End Sub
```

4. Insert the following code in the Form_Resize event, and create the subroutine SizeDateFont. SizeDateFont chooses a new FontSize when the user resizes the form. The assumption is that the largest font desired for the date display is 36 points. Keep in mind that the time display is twice as large as the date display. The new size is chosen by reducing the FontSize one point at a time until the date string fits nicely.

```
Sub Form_Resize ()
    '
    ' Clean up the display
    '
    Me.Cls
    Me.Refresh
    '
    ' Choose new font size for time display
    '
    SizeDateFont
    UpdateClock
End Sub

Sub SizeDateFont ()
    '
    ' Initialize some temp vars and largest fontsize desired
    '
    Dim d$
    d$ = Format$(Now, "long date")
    FontSize = 36
    '
    ' Size date string so that it's no more than 75% as wide,
    '
    Do While TextWidth(d$) > ScaleWidth * .75
       FontSize = FontSize - 1
    Loop
    '
    ' and 25% as tall as client space
    '
    Do While TextHeight(d$) > ScaleHeight \ 4 And FontSize > 6
       FontSize = FontSize - 1
    Loop
End Sub
```

5. Insert the following code into Form_Load, to center the form on screen:

```
Sub Form_Load ()
    '
    ' Center form on screen
    '
    Move (Screen.Width - Me.Width) \ 2, (Screen.Height - Me.Height) \ 2
End Sub
```

6. Insert the following code into Form_KeyDown, to allow customary hotkey exit from the applet:

```
Sub Form_KeyDown (KeyCode As Integer, Shift As Integer)
    '
    ' Provide normal shutdown method, Alt-F4
    '
    If (Shift And 4) And KeyCode = 115 Then End
End Sub
```

7. Finally, insert the following code in the Form_MouseDown event. Here, Windows is told to take over the task of dragging the window as the user moves the mouse. Notice that there is no difference in how the API calls are made, whether running under Win16 or Win32. While this is often not the case, in this situation no changes are required.

```
Sub Form_MouseDown (Button As Integer, Shift As Integer, X As Single, ⇒
                    Y As Single)
    Dim nRet&
    '
    ' This is the heart of the solution.
    '
    If Button And 1 Then
        '
        ' Left button is down
        ' VB calls SetCapture with every MouseDown, undo that
        ' Send message that initiates Windows dragging effect
        '
        ReleaseCapture
        nRet = SendMessage(Me.hWnd, WM_NCLBUTTONDOWN, HTCAPTION, 0&)
    ElseIf Button And 2 Then
        '
        ' Right button is down
        ' Let user exit
        '
        If MsgBox("Do you want to Exit?", 292) = 6 Then
            End
        End If
    End If
End Sub
```

8. Optionally, place the following code into the Form_DblClick event. This toggles display of the title bar on and off when the user double-clicks anywhere on the form. It's designed to maintain the same position and size on screen even when a resize is necessitated by adding or removing the title bar. The call to DoEvents

allows the revealed windows the opportunity to repaint themselves after the Main form is hidden. Otherwise, a distracting remnant may be left in these areas. Try commenting out DoEvents to observe this behavior. You will notice that the screen window, or wallpaper, does repaint immediately, because Windows is aware that our form has been hidden. Windows posts a repaint message to other affected windows, but there is no opportunity given to act upon it without our insertion of DoEvents.

```
Sub Form_DblClick ()
    '
    ' Toggle Caption On/Off with each DblClick
    '
    Dim oldHeight%, oldTop%
    Screen.MousePointer = vbHourglass
    Hide
        DoEvents
        oldHeight = Height
        oldTop = Top
        If Len(Caption) Then
            Me.Caption = ""
        Else
            Me.Caption = "Drag Demo"
        End If
        Move Me.Left, oldTop, Me.Width, oldHeight
    Show
    Screen.MousePointer = vbDefault
End Sub
```

How It Works

Most of the code in this applet is used to display the date and time in a manner similar to Windows Clock. Two Windows API functions solve the problem of allowing the user to drag the captionless form. Called in the Form_MouseDown event, these functions convince Windows to do what it normally does if there were a title bar. This program demonstrates how simple it can be to allow your application to work in both 16- and 32-bit versions of Visual Basic. In this case, all that was required was to conditionally compile the API declarations. The actual use of these functions turned out to be identical, so no conditional execution was necessary.

For this trick to work, the first task is to unlock Visual Basic's grip on the mouse pointer. Every time the user presses a mouse button in the client space of a form or control, Visual Basic calls SetCapture so that it receives notification of all mouse movements. Normally, ReleaseCapture would be called when the user releases the mouse button. Since the goal is for Windows, not Visual Basic, to be processing all mouse movement messages, this applet must call ReleaseCapture before dragging begins.

When the user presses the left mouse button on the title bar, Windows sends the WM_NCLBUTTONDOWN message, with HTCAPTION as wParam, to an application. Visual Basic passes this message on to its default window procedure, which in turn passes it back to Windows, and Windows then manages the dragging. When the user releases the left mouse button, the form is actually moved by Windows. The trick is that the sequence of events is initiated in the Form_MouseDown event, rather than by Windows. Now, the whole form is considered a title bar!

One interesting note is that the lParam parameter to SendMessage is ignored in this case. Normally, this parameter would contain the X,Y screen coordinates of the mouse pointer. Since these coordinates are not critical to this function, a long zero (0&) can be safely passed instead.

Comments

A title bar will result if you define a menu on your form, even if the menu is invisible or disabled. Setting ControlBox to False removes the system menu. So, you must decide how to offer the user choices typically presented in menus. This applet uses a message box on the right MouseDown to query if the user wants to exit. If your captionless form is part of a larger application, you could add menus at the end of another form's top-level menu. These could be used as PopupMenus, triggered by a right mouse click. If the captionless form is the only visible form in your application, and you need PopupMenus, you must load an invisible form to contain the menus.

Using the technique presented in this How-To, you can easily support dragging a form using areas other than the title bar. Another potential use of this method would be to create a form with a mini-title bar, similar to the toolbox in Visual Basic. In fact, How-To 2.4 will do just that!

2.4 How do I...
Make a Floating Toolbar with a Mini-Title Bar?

COMPLEXITY: ADVANCED
COMPATIBILITY: VB3 OR VB4

Problem

I need to develop a floating toolbar using a mini-title bar, like Visual Basic or Microsoft Word. I don't necessarily want it to float over everything as Windows Clock does, but I want it to always be visible when the user is working in my application. How can I make it float over just my Main form?

Technique

This project completely replaces the built-in functionality Windows normally provides, as there are no native methods for producing nonstandard title bars. (This means all screen drawing and mouse and menu handling must be performed by our applications.) The Main form assumes ownership of the toolbar form so that the toolbar will float over it. Optionally, the toolbar form may be made topmost to float above all windows. A variety of powerful API functions are used to achieve these capabilities.

Steps

Open and run FLOAT.VBP. Select Toolbar from the Demo menu, or press (CTRL)-(T) to show the toolbar. The toolbar supports dragging with the title bar; a control menu accessible via either the mouse or (ALT)-(SPACEBAR); system colors depending on active status; and it floats above the main form. Figure 2-4-1 illustrates the appearance of this project at run time. The principal emphasis of this How-To is to demonstrate various window-handling methods; therefore, to reduce confusion, there are no actual tools on the toolbar.

Try clicking back and forth between the Main form and the toolbar. Notice how the title bar repaints to reflect its active status. Activate another application and notice that the same behavior occurs. From the toolbar's control menu, select Always on Top; then activate another application to see how the toolbar now floats above all windows. Drag the toolbar around, or try selecting Move from its control menu to allow keyboard repositioning. Close the toolbar with one of four methods: double-clicking on the control box, pressing (ALT)-(SPACEBAR)-(C) on the keyboard, pressing (ALT)-(F4), or selecting Close from the control menu with the mouse.

Create FLOATDEC.BAS

1. Add the following declarations and definitions to the Declarations section of a new module called FLOATDEC.BAS. This module holds all global definitions that

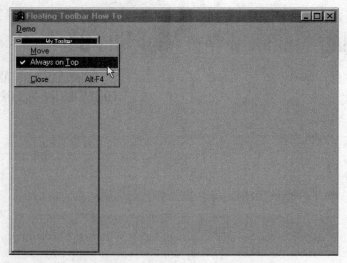

Figure 2-4-1 Floating toolbar project at run time, showing custom control menu

(possibly) need to be accessible to all forms and modules. To allow this project to work in both 16- and 32-bit versions of Visual Basic, one structure and all the API declarations are conditionally included. All constants are the same in both environments.

```
Option Explicit
'
' Type declaration used to get mouse coordinates
'
#If Win16 Then
    Type POINTAPI
        x As Integer
        y As Integer
    End Type
#ElseIf Win32 Then
    Type POINTAPI
        x As Long
        y As Long
    End Type
#End If
'
' Form Caption Colors
'
Public Const COLOR_ACTIVECAPTION = 2
Public Const COLOR_INACTIVECAPTION = 3
Public Const COLOR_CAPTIONTEXT = 9
Public Const COLOR_INACTIVECAPTIONTEXT = 19
'
' SysCommand, wParam Constants for use with SendMessage
'
Public Const SC_MOVE = &HF010
Public Const SC_CLOSE = &HF060
'
' Windows messages, for use with SendMessage
'
Public Const WM_NCLBUTTONDOWN = &HA1
Public Const WM_SYSCOMMAND = &H112
'
' Windows messages for MsgHook to catch
'
Public Const WM_ACTIVATEAPP = &H1C
Public Const WM_SYSCOLORCHANGE = &H15
'
' Used to fool Windows that the mouse is in the title bar
'
Public Const HTCAPTION = 2
'
' SetWindowWord constant
'
Public Const SWW_HPARENT = -8
'
' GetSystemMetrics constants
'
Public Const SM_CXBORDER = 5
```

Continued on next page

Continued from previous page

```
Public Const SM_CYBORDER = 6
Public Const SM_CXFRAME = 32
Public Const SM_CYFRAME = 33
'
' SetWindowPos() hwndInsertAfter values
'
Public Const HWND_TOP = 0
Public Const HWND_BOTTOM = 1
Public Const HWND_TOPMOST = -1
Public Const HWND_NOTOPMOST = -2
'
' SetWindowPos Flags
'
Public Const SWP_NOSIZE = &H1
Public Const SWP_NOMOVE = &H2
'
' API Declarations
'
#If Win16 Then
    Declare Function GetSysColor Lib "User" (ByVal nIndex As Integer) ⇒
            As Long
    Declare Function GetSystemMetrics Lib "User" (ByVal nIndex As ⇒
            Integer) As Integer
    Declare Function SendMessage Lib "User" (ByVal hWnd As Integer, ⇒
            ByVal wMsg As Integer, ByVal wParam As Integer, lParam As Any) As Long
    Declare Function GetActiveWindow Lib "User" () As Integer
    Declare Sub GetCursorPos Lib "User" (lpPoint As POINTAPI)
    Declare Sub ScreenToClient Lib "User" (ByVal hWnd As Integer, ⇒
            lpPoint As POINTAPI)
    Declare Sub ReleaseCapture Lib "User" ()
    Declare Sub SetWindowWord Lib "User" (ByVal hWnd As Integer, ByVal ⇒
            nCmd As Integer, ByVal nVal As Integer)
    Declare Sub SetWindowPos Lib "User" (ByVal hWnd As Integer, ByVal ⇒
            hWndInsertAfter As Integer, ByVal x As Integer, ByVal y As Integer, ⇒
            ByVal cx As Integer, ByVal cy As Integer, ByVal wFlags As Integer)
#ElseIf Win32 Then
    Declare Function GetSysColor Lib "user32" (ByVal nIndex As Long) ⇒
            As Long
    Declare Function GetSystemMetrics Lib "user32" (ByVal nIndex ⇒
            As Long) As Long
    Declare Function SendMessage Lib "user32" Alias "SendMessageA" ⇒
            (ByVal hWnd As Long, ByVal wMsg As Long, ByVal wParam As Integer, ⇒
            ByVal lParam As Long) As Long
    Declare Function GetActiveWindow Lib "user32" () As Long
    Declare Function GetCursorPos Lib "user32" (lpPoint As POINTAPI) ⇒
            As Long
    Declare Function ScreenToClient Lib "user32" (ByVal hWnd As Long, ⇒
            lpPoint As POINTAPI) As Long
    Declare Function ReleaseCapture Lib "user32" () As Long
    Declare Function SetWindowWord Lib "user32" (ByVal hWnd As Long, ⇒
            ByVal nIndex As Long, ByVal wNewWord As Long) As Long
    Declare Function SetWindowPos Lib "user32" (ByVal hWnd As Long, ⇒
            ByVal hWndInsertAfter As Long, ByVal x As Long, ByVal y As Long, ⇒
            ByVal cx As Long, ByVal cy As Long, ByVal wFlags As Long) As Long
#End If
'
```

```
' Menu constants
'
Public Const mmDemo = 0
Public Const mmPopup = 1
Public Const mfToolbox = 0
Public Const mfExit = 2
Public Const mpMove = 0
Public Const mpOnTop = 1
Public Const mpClose = 3
```

Create FRMMAIN.FRM

2. Create a new project called FLOAT.VBP, and a new form with the properties listed in Table 2-4-1.

Table 2-4-1 Floating toolbar project's FRMMAIN.FRM properties

OBJECT	PROPERTY	SETTING
Form	Name	frmMain
	Caption	"Floating Toolbar How-To"

3. Create a menu for the form, as shown in Table 2-4-2, using the Menu Design window. Note that the Popup menu, frmMain.mMain(1) has Visible set to False. This is the menu that will be used as a PopupMenu in lieu of a real control menu on the toolbar form. It must be on separate form, since the presence of a menu will force Windows to draw a normal title bar. (ALT)-(F4) cannot be assigned as a hotkey for Visual Basic menus, because it is reserved by the system as the default Close hotkey. So, while designing the PopupMenu, add the text "Alt-F4" to the caption, paying attention to the spacing so that it looks good.

Table 2-4-2 FRMMAIN.FRM's menu settings

CAPTION		NAME	INDEX	VISIBLE
&Demo		mMain	0	True
&Toolbar		mDemo	0	True
-		mDemo	1	True
E&xit		mDemo	2	True
Popup		mMain	1	False
&Move		mPopup	0	True
Always on &Top		mPopup	1	True
-		mPopup	2	True
&Close	Alt-F4	mPopup	3	True

4. Add the following code to frmMain's Form_Load procedure. This centers the main form on the screen and sets the caption for the toolbar. The toolbar is invisibly loaded and positioned in the upper-left corner of frmMain's client space.

```
Private Sub Form_Load()
    '
    ' Center form on screen
    '
    Move (Screen.Width - Width) \ 2, (Screen.Height - Height) \ 2
    '
    ' Load floating toolbar (invisibly)
    ' Set caption using custom property
    ' Position toolbar
    '
    frmTool.Kaption = "My Toolbar"
    frmTool.Left = Me.Left _
                + GetSystemMetrics(SM_CXFRAME) _
                * Screen.TwipsPerPixelX
    frmTool.Top = Me.Top _
                + (Me.Height - Me.ScaleHeight) _
                - (GetSystemMetrics(SM_CXFRAME) _
                * Screen.TwipsPerPixelX)
    frmTool.Height = Me.ScaleHeight
End Sub
```

5. Make sure the toolbar gets unloaded when the Main form does, as the application ends.

```
Sub Form_Unload(Cancel As Integer)
    '
    ' Make sure to also unload the toolbox!
    '
    Unload frmTool
End Sub
```

6. Add the following menu-handling code to the mDemo_Click event. The visibility of the toolbar is set to match the status of its menu item.

```
Private Sub mDemo_Click(Index As Integer)
    '
    ' Use checkmark to indicate if toolbar is visible
    ' Set visibility of toolbar based on check mark
    '
    Select Case Index
        Case mfToolbox
            mDemo(mfToolbox).Checked = Not mDemo(mfToolbox).Checked
            frmTool.Visible = mDemo(mfToolbox).Checked
        Case mfExit
            Unload Me
    End Select
End Sub
```

7. Add the following code to the mPopup_Click event. This is where all menu handling for the toolbar's control menu will take place.

```
Private Sub mPopup_Click(Index As Integer)
    '
    ' Popup menu handler for floating toolbox
    '
    Select Case Index
        '
        ' Tell Windows to initiate keyboard drag
        '
        Case mpMove
            Dim nRet&
            nRet& = SendMessage(frmTool.hWnd, WM_SYSCOMMAND, SC_MOVE, 0)
        '
        ' Toggle toolbox to float above all windows
        '
        Case mpOnTop
            mPopup(mpOnTop).Checked = Not mPopup(mpOnTop).Checked
            frmTool.OnTop = mPopup(mpOnTop).Checked
        '
        ' Hide toolbox by calling ToggleToolbar "method"
        '
        Case mpClose
            frmMain.ToggleToolbar
    End Select
End Sub
```

8. Provide a public method to frmMain that toggles the toolbar's visibility by entering the following code. Routines in other forms and modules may call this method to turn the toolbar on or off.

```
Public Sub ToggleToolbar()
    '
    ' Provide a generic "method" for toggling toolbar.
    ' Call the menu click event from here in case menu changes.
    '
    mDemo_Click (mfToolbox)
End Sub
```

Create FRMTOOL.FRM

9. Create a new form with the objects and properties listed in Table 2-4-3 and save it as FRMTOOL.FRM.

Table 2-4-3 Objects and properties on FRMTOOL.FRM

OBJECT	PROPERTY	SETTING
Form	Name	frmTool
	Appearance	1 - 3D

Continued on next page

Continued from previous page

OBJECT	PROPERTY	SETTING
	BorderStyle	5 - Sizable ToolWindow
	Caption	""
	ControlBox	False
	KeyPreview	True
	MaxButton	False
	MinButton	False
	ScaleMode	3 - Pixel
	Visible	False
MsgHook	Name	MsgHook1

10. Place the following code in the Declarations section. Declare several tracking variables to hold the current colors frmTool will use when repainting its title bar. Set aside a private string to hold the form's custom Caption property, a Boolean for its OnTop property, and declare two constants to make forthcoming code more readable.

```
Option Explicit
'
'Form level variables to track caption colors
'
Private CaptionBack As Long
Private CaptionText As Long
'
' Form level string to hold Caption property
'
Private m_Caption As String
'
' Form level variable to store OnTop property
'
Private m_OnTop As Boolean
'
' Toolbar size constants for comparisons
'
Private Const TITLE_HEIGHT = 8   'Height of title bar in pixels
Private Const CTRLBOXWIDTH = 10  'Width of control box in pixels
```

11. Add the following code to frmTool's Form_Load event. The call to SetWindowWord establishes frmMain's ownership over frmTool. This is also where the MsgHook custom control must be initialized and a default font chosen to be used in the caption text.

```
Private Sub Form_Load()
    '
    ' Make float above *just* the main form, not all windows
    ' Form *must* use PIXELS as scalemode for mouse routines to work
    '
    Call SetWindowWord(Me.hWnd, SWW_HPARENT, frmMain.hWnd)
```

```
ScaleMode = vbPixels
'
' Initialize MsgHook control to catch application activations
' and changes to WIN.INI (for caption color).
'
With MsgHook1
   .HwndHook = Me.hWnd
   .Message(WM_ACTIVATEAPP) = True
   .Message(WM_SYSCOLORCHANGE) = True
End With
'
' Set font attributes
'
With Me.Font
   .Name = "Arial"
   .Size = 6
   .Weight = 400
End With
End Sub
```

12. Add the following two routines to handle activation and deactivation of the toolbar. Although these events only support focus shifts within a Visual Basic application, MsgHook will be used to expand their usefulness.

```
Private Sub Form_Activate()
   '
   ' Repaint title bar with "active" color
   '
   CaptionBack = GetSysColor(COLOR_ACTIVECAPTION)
   CaptionText = GetSysColor(COLOR_CAPTIONTEXT)
   Refresh
End Sub

Private Sub Form_Deactivate()
   '
   'Repaint title bar with "non-active" color
   '
   CaptionBack = GetSysColor(COLOR_INACTIVECAPTION)
   CaptionText = GetSysColor(COLOR_INACTIVECAPTIONTEXT)
   Refresh
End Sub
```

13. Place the following code in the MsgHook1_Message event. This event will fire whenever one of the desired messages arrives. The two messages of interest to this form concern the need to repaint. WM_ACTIVATEAPP is sent to all top-level windows whenever focus shifts among applications, and must be used to prevent our mini-title bar from retaining its active color when that form isn't active. WM_SYSCOLORCHANGE is watched in case the Windows system colors change, which would require a title bar repaint. Following our processing of either message, MsgHook's InvokeWindowProc method is called to allow the original window procedure for the form to receive the message as well.

The MsgHook custom control has been written as two separate OCXs. MsgHoo16.OCX is for use in 16-bit Visual Basic, and MsgHoo32.OCX is for 32-bit Visual Basic. Both have the same usage, so conditional compilation is not required to use this control with this example. Additionally, they both place the same GUID in the registry, so there is no need to maintain parallel forms for Win16 and Win32.

```
Private Sub MsgHook1_Message(ByVal msg As Long, ByVal wp As Long, _
                            ByVal lp As Long, result As Long)
    Select Case msg
        Case WM_ACTIVATEAPP
            '
            ' Catch whenever this application is deactivated.
            ' Make sure that minititle bar is colored properly.
            ' If user clicks on toolbar when it's "Always on Top",
            ' set main form to be next below topmost window layer.
            '
            Print "WM_ACTIVATEAPP", wp
            If wp = 0 Then
                Form_Deactivate
            Else
                If GetActiveWindow() = Me.hWnd Then
                    Call SetWindowPos(frmMain.hWnd, HWND_TOP, 0, 0, 0, 0, _
                                      SWP_NOSIZE Or SWP_NOMOVE)
                Form_Activate
                End If
            End If

        Case WM_SYSCOLORCHANGE
            '
            ' Repaint using new system colors if those change.
            '
            If GetActiveWindow() = Me.hWnd Then
                CaptionBack = GetSysColor(COLOR_ACTIVECAPTION)
                CaptionText = GetSysColor(COLOR_CAPTIONTEXT)
            Else
                CaptionBack = GetSysColor(COLOR_INACTIVECAPTION)
                CaptionText = GetSysColor(COLOR_INACTIVECAPTIONTEXT)
            End If
            Refresh
    End Select
    '
    ' Allow original window procedure to process message,
    ' and generate return result.
    '
    result = MsgHook1.InvokeWindowProc(msg, wp, lp)
End Sub
```

14. Place the following code in frmTool's Form_Repaint event. This is where this project takes over Window's normal role and paints its own title bar complete with caption text. Saving and restoring the form's ScaleMode is simply good style, and allows this procedure to be cut into a common module and used with other forms without regard to their ScaleMode. This routine alone will make you appreciate all the work Windows normally does for us!

```
Private Sub Form_Paint()
    '
    ' Store old ScaleMode (makes routine less dependent
    ' on "knowing" about this form).
    '
    Dim oldScale As Integer
    oldScale = Me.ScaleMode
    Me.ScaleMode = vbPixels
    '
    ' Proceed with painting individual elements of titlebar.
    '
    'Paint title bar background
        Me.Line (0, -1)-Step(Me.Width, 9), CaptionBack, BF
    'Horizontal line under title bar
        Me.Line (0, 8)-Step(Me.ScaleWidth, 0), QBColor(0)
    'Vertical line beteen control menu and 'caption' area
        Me.Line (10, 0)-Step(0, 8), QBColor(0)
    'Background for control menu
        Me.Line (0, 0)-Step(9, 7), QBColor(7), BF
    'Box for bar in control menu
        Me.Line (2, 2)-Step(5, 2), QBColor(0), B
    'Line inside bar in control menu
        Me.Line (3, 3)-Step(4, 0), QBColor(15)
    'Horizontal shadow on bar in control menu
        Me.Line (3, 5)-Step(5, 0), QBColor(8)
    'Vertical shadow on bar in control menu
        Me.Line (8, 3)-Step(0, 3), QBColor(8)
    'Caption text
        Dim WorkingWidth As Integer
        WorkingWidth = Me.ScaleWidth - CTRLBOXWIDTH
        If TextWidth(m_Caption) > WorkingWidth Then
            Me.CurrentX = CTRLBOXWIDTH + 1
        Else
            Me.CurrentX = (WorkingWidth - Me.TextWidth(m_Caption)) \ 2 _
                        + CTRLBOXWIDTH
        End If
        Me.CurrentY = -1
        Me.ForeColor = CaptionText
        Print m_Caption;
    '
    ' Restore ScaleMode
    '
    Me.ScaleMode = oldScale
End Sub
```

15. Mouse and menu handling are next on the agenda. Place the following code in the Form_MouseDown event. Here we manually initiate dragging if the user presses the mouse button in the title bar area outside the control menu box. Otherwise, the popup from frmMain is displayed.

```
Private Sub Form_MouseDown(Button As Integer, Shift As Integer, _
                           X As Single, Y As Single)
    '
    'Check if click is in "non-client" area
    '
```

Continued on next page

Continued from previous page

```
    If Button = vbLeftButton And Y < TITLE_HEIGHT Then
        If X < CTRLBOXWIDTH Then
            '
            ' Control box, show menu
            '
            PopupMenu frmMain.mMain(mmPopup), 0, -1, TITLE_HEIGHT
        Else
            '
            ' Title bar, allow Windows to process dragging
            '
            ReleaseCapture
            Call SendMessage(Me.hWnd, WM_NCLBUTTONDOWN, HTCAPTION, 0&)
        End If
    End If
End Sub
```

16. Add the following code to the Form_DblClick event, to support closure of the toolbar by double-clicking on the control menu box. Since the toolbar's visibility is tied to its menu choice being checked on frmMain, call the frmMain method ToggleToolbar to close the toolbar. This keeps everything in sync.

```
Private Sub Form_DblClick()
    '
    ' Get coords of mouse relative to form
    '
    Dim pt As POINTAPI
    GetCursorPos pt
    ScreenToClient Me.hWnd, pt
    '
    'Check if in ControlBox
    '
    If pt.X < CTRLBOXWIDTH And pt.Y < TITLE_HEIGHT Then
        frmMain.ToggleToolbar
    End If
End Sub
```

17. Add the following code to Form_KeyDown, to provide keyboard support for standard Windows interaction with the control menu.

```
Private Sub Form_KeyDown(KeyCode As Integer, Shift As Integer)
    '
    ' Dropdown "system" menu if user presses Alt-Space.
    ' Initiate Close if user presses Alt-F4.
    '
    If (Shift And vbAltMask) Then
        Select Case KeyCode
            Case vbKeySpace
                DoEvents      'Required to avoid Beep!
                PopupMenu frmMain.mMain(mmPopup), vbPopupMenuRightButton, _
                                          -1, TITLE_HEIGHT
            Case vbKeyF4
                frmMain.ToggleToolbar
                KeyCode = 0   'Eat keystroke
        End Select
```

```
        End If
End Sub
```

18. Microsoft recommends resetting ownership of forms on which you've called SetWindowWord to change ownership. It appears that this is not a valid concern, but in case that changes in the future, place the following code into the Form_Unload event:

```
Private Sub Form_Unload(Cancel As Integer)
    '
    ' Clear parent-child relationship for safety.
    ' This is recommended, but perhaps not neccessary.
    '
    Call SetWindowWord(Me.hWnd, SWW_HPARENT, 0)
End Sub
```

19. To provide an interface for outside forms and modules to alter the caption of the toolbar, add the following pair of Property procedures to frmTool. Since Caption is an existing member of the Form object class, an alternate name is required.

```
Public Property Let Kaption(NewCaption As Variant)
    m_Caption = CStr(NewCaption)
End Property

Public Property Get Kaption() As Variant
    Kaption = m_Caption
End Property
```

20. The reaction to a user's menu choices occurs in another form, so there needs to be a public interface to the code that makes the toolbar float above all windows (be "Always on Top"). Place the following pair of Property procedures in frmTool, allowing other forms and modules to set or retrieve the OnTop status of the toolbar:

```
Public Property Let OnTop(SetOnTop As Boolean)
    '
    ' Set/Unset toolbox to float above all windows
    '
    If SetOnTop Then
        Call SetWindowPos(Me.hWnd, HWND_TOPMOST, 0, 0, 0, 0, _
                        SWP_NOSIZE Or SWP_NOMOVE)
    Else
        Call SetWindowPos(Me.hWnd, HWND_NOTOPMOST, 0, 0, 0, 0, _
                        SWP_NOSIZE Or SWP_NOMOVE)
    End If
    m_OnTop = SetOnTop
End Property

Public Property Get OnTop() As Boolean
    '
    ' Return current status
    '
```

Continued on next page

Continued from previous page

```
    OnTop = m_OnTop
End Property
```

How It Works

This project demonstrates an intricate balance of calling the appropriate API calls at the right time to emulate the work Windows normally does behind the scenes. The Main form takes "ownership" of the toolbar, forcing it to always be at least one position above the Main form in the master window list. This is the preferred method for floating one form above another in your project. Even when focus is on the other form, the owned form (a virtual child) will float at a higher level.

Beginning with Windows 3.1, the concept of two window layers is supported. By calling another API, SetWindowPos, the toolbar can be forced into the topmost of the two layers. The Main form remains in the layer occupied by all "normal" windows. The topmost layer also supports a stacking order, and multiple windows in the topmost layer may be swapped in order by activation. Under Windows 95 and Windows NT, it's sometimes required to actually be running from an EXE in order to observe the "Always On Top" effect.

Painting the title bar is handled internally with a series of graphics methods executed every time the toolbar's Form_Repaint event fires. This sequence of methods may be edited to create virtually any kind of title bar imaginable. To maintain consistency with the current system, the GetSysColor API is called whenever necessary to capture the colors in use by Windows. These color references have to be updated whenever the form is activated or deactivated, but not just as Visual Basic defines those terms! The custom control, MsgHook, is used to capture the focus shifts to or from other running applications—an event that Visual Basic still does not support. To ensure the current system colors are always the ones we use, MsgHook is also used to alert us whenever the user changes these settings.

The dragging logic used in this project is the same as that used in How-To 2.3. The principal difference here is the obvious restriction of the title bar area to the title bar we're drawing on screen, whereas the other project used the whole form as a virtual title bar.

To create a form suitable for drawing our own title bar, there are several restrictions imposed by Visual Basic. The form may not have a ControlBox, MinButton, MaxButton, Caption, or any defined menus. The restriction on menus means that the popup menu used must be defined on another form (in this case, the Main form). Some gymnastics are imposed by this design. Code that should be modularized, or kept together, must now be kept apart. Code in frmMain sends a WM_SYSCOMMAND message with SC_MOVE as wParam to initiate the Windows' keyboard window-moving logic. Unfortunately we must use frmTool's hWnd. With the introduction of Property procedures in Visual Basic 4.0, the other instance of code in one form regularly altering another form can be handled much more cleanly. OnTop is set up as a custom property of frmTool, and can be set or have its value retrieved like any other built-in property.

By setting KeyPreview to True on frmTool, the form itself can intercept and act on any keystrokes commonly used by Windows for menu access. When catching (ALT)-(F4), make sure to set the KeyCode back to 0 if you hide or unload the toolbar. Failure to do so will pass the key-combination along to frmMain, causing the application to shut down. When the user requests the control menu with (ALT)-(SPACEBAR), use vbPopupMenuRightButton in the Flags argument to PopupMenu. This prevents the menu from rolling right back up, and allows the user to select a menu item with the arrow keys.

Comments

It adds a very nice touch to float toolbars over other forms within your application. Depending on the nature of the application, your users may appreciate being able to set the toolbar to float not only over related forms, but over all windows. This How-To shows you how to do both. Also, other valid reasons may exist for altering the "standard" appearance of title bars, and one method has been presented. A number of very powerful API functions to implement the capabilities required are used and worth further exploration. Keep in mind, however, that Windows 95 will offer the user much greater control over the appearance of individual graphic elements—two of which will be title bar height and font. Although this technique works in Windows 95, it is best suited to Windows 3.x or Windows NT, since considerable alterations of the drawing routine would be required to deal with all the possibilities.

Other than the Property procedures and public form procedures, this project can be easily translated to Visual Basic 3.0. A slight reworking will be required to compensate for the new capabilities of Visual Basic 4.0. For example, the custom properties will need to be declared as Global variables for easy retrieval. The OnTop property and the ToggleToolbar method procedures would need to be moved to code modules to make them publicly accessible.

2.5 How do I...
Paint an Interesting Background on an MDI Parent Form?

COMPLEXITY: DIFFICULT
COMPATIBILITY: VB3 OR VB4

Problem

With Visual Basic 3.0, I was limited to using the systemwide color for my MDIForm backgrounds. Now Visual Basic 4.0 allows me to set a solid background color. But what I really want to do is decorate it a little more elaborately—for example, center or maybe tile my company logo across the background. How can I use graphics like this to add zip to my application?

Technique

Since Visual Basic's graphics methods are not applicable to MDIForms, this project uses Windows graphic device interface (GDI) calls to paint a variety of backgrounds in the client space of the Main form. The first trick to this technique is capturing the necessary window handle, or hWnd, which opens all the power of Windows API to our project. The window we're interested in is called the client space, where the children "live." In fact, this is quite easy, because the client space is the first child of the Main form. Even with the hWnd, however, there still needs to be a trigger mechanism to repaint the background. For this, the client space itself can be subclassed, with the MsgHook custom control that comes with this book.

When an iconized child form is dragged by the user, you need to repaint the background once to maintain consistency with normal MDI behavior. To do so, MDI children forms also need to be subclassed. If this step is not taken, the image of the icon's old position remains until the user drops the icon in its new location.

A code module will be developed, which supplies a variety of different background styles. Each uses a slightly different approach by taking advantage of a variety of GDI function calls. This project will give you a taste of the substantial power available when going directly to Windows for graphics methods.

Steps

Open and run MDIDRAW.VBP. You will notice right away that this project is very different. The background of the Main form has a tiled pattern, as shown in Figure 2-5-1. Move or resize the child or parent form, and watch how the background is instantly repainted. From the Window menu, you can add additional children or arrange the children. The Background menu offers a choice of seven different back-

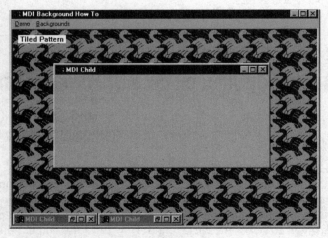

Figure 2-5-1 The MDIDRAW project at run time

ground styles. Try them all and observe the impact of the various graphics methods on the speed of repaints.

This project will use two form files and one code module:

➤ An MDIForm as the main startup form (MDIDRAW.FRM)

➤ A regular form, instances of which will be the MDI children (MDICHILD.FRM)

➤ A code module to contain routines used to paint MDI backgrounds (MDI-GRAFX.BAS)

Create MDIDRAW.FRM

1. Create a new project and name it MDIDRAW.VBP. From the Insert menu, select MDI Form and name it frmMain. Set this as your startup form in the dialog for the Tools - Project Options menu. Create the objects and set their properties as listed in Table 2-5-1, and save it as MDIDRAW.FRM. Since only controls that have the Align property may be directly placed on an MDIForm, Picture0 is used as a container for the remainder of the listed controls. When you've finished designing it, this form should appear similar to that in Figure 2-5-2.

Table 2-5-1 Objects and properties for frmMain

OBJECT	PROPERTY	SETTING
MDIForm	Name	frmMain
	AutoShowChildren	False
	Caption	"MDI Background How To"
PictureBox	Name	Picture0
	Align	1 - Align Top
	Visible	False
PictureBox	Name	Picture1
	AutoRedraw	True
	BorderStyle	0 - None
	Picture	(Bitmap) 'ECLIPSE.BMP
	Visible	False
PictureBox	Name	Picture2
	AutoRedraw	True
	BorderStyle	0 - None
	Picture	(Bitmap) 'ESCHER.BMP
	Visible	False
MsgHook	Name	MsgHook1

2. Create a menu for the MDIForm, using the Menu Design window, with the properties shown in Table 2-5-2.

Table 2-5-2 MDI background menu

CAPTION	NAME	INDEX
&Demo	mMain	0
E&xit	mExit	
&Background	mMain	1
&Solid	mBack	0
&Tiled BMP	mBack	1
&Gradient	mBack	2
Tunnel&1	mBack	3
Tunnel&2	mBack	4
Centered &BMP	mBack	5
St&retched BMP	mBack	6
&Warped BMP	mBack	7

3. Place the following code in the Declarations section of frmMain:

```
Option Explicit
'
' Highest numbered background supported
'
Const BackHighest = 7
'
' Variable to track current background style
'
Private mdiBackStyle As Integer
```

Figure 2-5-2 MDIDRAW.FRM at design time

4. Place the following code into the MDIForm_Load event. The Main form is first sized to be approximately 640x480, then centered on screen. The MsgHook custom control is initialized to watch the client space window for several messages, and the parent and several child forms are shown.

```
Private Sub MDIForm_Load()
    '
    ' Position form on screen, use 640x480 as target dimension
    '
    Dim newWidth As Integer
    Dim newHeight As Integer
    newWidth = 640 * Screen.TwipsPerPixelX
    If Screen.Height > 480 * Screen.TwipsPerPixelY Then
        newHeight = 480 * Screen.TwipsPerPixelY
    Else
        newHeight = 0.9 * Screen.Height
    End If
    Me.Move (Screen.Width - newWidth) \ 2, _
            (Screen.Height - newHeight) \ 2, _
            newWidth, newHeight

    ' Set up MsgHook control
    '
    MsgHook1.HwndHook = (GetWindow(Me.hWnd, GW_CHILD))
    MsgHook1.Message(WM_PAINT) = True
    MsgHook1.Message(WM_ERASEBKGND) = True
    '
    ' Set BackStyle to something interesting
    '
    Me.BackStyle = 1
    '
    ' Show main MDIForm and 3 children
    '
    Show
    Dim X As New frmChild
    Dim Y As New frmChild
    Dim Z As New frmChild
    X.Show
    Y.Show
    Z.Show
End Sub
```

5. Create a pair of property procedures to assign and retrieve the BackStyle of frmMain. These allow other modules to set or reference frmMain.BackStyle, so that control isn't restricted to within this form. Assigning a value to frmMain.BackStyle is all that is necessary to flip among the available patterns. Whenever this property is set, the Background menu is updated to reflect the current state, and the client space repaint is initiated.

```
Public Property Let BackStyle(Which As Integer)
    '
    ' Make sure passed value is in range
```

Continued on next page

Continued from previous page

```
    ' Store for future reference, update menu, and repaint
    '
    If Which >= 0 And Which <= BackHighest Then
        Dim i As Integer
        For i = 0 To BackHighest
            mBack(i).Checked = False
        Next i
        mBack(Which).Checked = True
        mdiBackStyle = Which
        If Me.Visible = True And Me.WindowState <> vbMinimized Then
            Me.MdiPaint
        End If
    End If
End Property

Public Property Get BackStyle() As Integer
    '
    ' Return current BackStyle
    '
    BackStyle = mdiBackStyle
End Property
```

6. Add the following code to the appropriate menu event procedures. Note that changing the frmMain.BackStyle property is all that's required to update the background according to the user's choice.

```
Private Sub mExit_Click()
    '
    ' User clicked Exit on menu
    '
    Unload Me
End Sub

Private Sub mBack_Click(Index As Integer)
    '
    ' Set BackStyle property, initiate repaint
    '
    Me.BackStyle = Index
End Sub
```

7. Place the following code in the MsgHook1_Message event. This is where the real action occurs. When the WM_PAINT message is received by the client space window, the custom Paint method is invoked.

```
Private Sub MsgHook1_Message(ByVal Msg As Long, _
            ByVal wp As Long, ByVal lp As Long, result As Long)
    Static Busy As Integer
    Const mhPassToVB = 0
    Const mhHideFromVB = 1
    '
    ' We got the message we need to repaint the background.
    ' Must avoid recursion with certain painting methods!
    '
```

```
        If Busy Then Exit Sub
        Busy = True
            Select Case Msg
                '
                ' This is the message we've been waiting for!
                ' Call the custom MdiPaint method, then invoke
                ' the original window procedure.
                '
                Case WM_PAINT
                    Me.MdiPaint
                    result = MsgHook1.InvokeWindowProc(Msg, wp, lp)
                '
                ' By hiding this message from VB, and returning a
                ' non-zero tells Windows that we'll handle the erase.
                '
                Case WM_ERASEBKGND
                    result = 1
            End Select
        Busy = False
    End Sub
```

8. Place the following code in the MDIForm_Resize event. Unfortunately, Windows isn't always convinced that a given window needs to be repainted—especially when the window is reduced in size. To overcome Window's reluctance to issue a repaint when the form is shrunk, the new size needs to be compared to the old size. In practical use, this only needs to be checked for certain types of backgrounds. If the background you've chosen centers something, or sizes a graphic to fit, then you need to react in this manner.

```
Private Sub MDIForm_Resize()
    Static LastState%, LastWidth%, LastHeight%
    '
    ' Ensure a repaint if form had been maximized,
    ' or it was reduced in size. .  If Windows doesn't
    ' feel it's neccessary, the required messages
    ' aren't always passed.
    '
    If LastState = vbMaximized _
        Or Me.Width < LastWidth _
        Or Me.Height < LastHeight Then
        Me.MdiPaint
    End If '
    ' Store new size
    '
    LastState = WindowState
    LastWidth = Me.Width
    LastHeight = Me.Height
End Sub
```

9. Finally, place the following code in the custom method MdiPaint. This is declared as a public routine so it can be called from outside modules, similar to a

Form.Refresh method. Here, the appropriate routine is called based on the current setting of the BackStyle property.

```
Public Sub MdiPaint()
    '
    ' Our new MdiPaint method chooses one of several available
    ' subroutines to do the actual painting.
    '
    Select Case Me.BackStyle
        '
        ' Solid background ñ effectively reproduces BackColor property
        ' Also useful to set background color when centering a bitmap
        '
        Case 0
            mdiPaintSolid (Me.hWnd), &H400000
            mdiTextOut (Me.hWnd), " Solid Fill ", 10, 10
        '
        ' Tile a bitmap across background
        '
        Case 1
            mdiBitBltTiled (Picture1.hWnd), (Picture1.hDC), (Me.hWnd)
            mdiTextOut (Me.hWnd), " Tiled Pattern ", 10, 10
        '
        ' Paint a shaded blue to black gradient background
        '
        Case 2
            mdiPaintGradient (Me.hWnd)
            mdiTextOut (Me.hWnd), " Gradient Fill, Style 1 ", 10, 10
        '
        ' Paint a "tunnel" gradient using rectangles
        '
        Case 3
            mdiPaintTunnel1 (Me.hWnd)
            mdiTextOut (Me.hWnd), " Gradient Fill, Style 2 ", 10, 10
        '
        ' Paint a "tunnel" gradient using elipses
        '
        Case 4
            mdiPaintTunnel2 (Me.hWnd)
            mdiTextOut (Me.hWnd), " Gradient Fill, Style 3 ", 10, 10
        '
        ' Center a bitmap on a complimentary background shade
        '
        Case 5
            mdiPaintSolid (Me.hWnd), 0&
            mdiBitBltCentered (Picture2.hWnd), (Picture2.hDC), (Me.hWnd)
            mdiTextOut (Me.hWnd), " Centered Bitmap ", 10, 10
        '
        ' Stretch a bitmap proportionately to fit the constraining
        ' dimension of the background
        '
        Case 6
            mdiPaintSolid (Me.hWnd), 0&
            mdiStretchBlt (Picture2.hWnd), (Picture2.hDC), (Me.hWnd), True
```

```
        mdiTextOut (Me.hWnd), " Stretched (Proportionally) Bitmap ", 10, 10
    '
    ' Stretch a bitmap to fit the background dimensions
    '
    Case 7
        mdiStretchBlt (Picture2.hWnd), (Picture2.hDC), (Me.hWnd), False
        mdiTextOut (Me.hWnd), " Stretched (Non-Proportionally) Bitmap ", 10, 10
  End Select
End Sub
```

Create MDICHILD.FRM

10. Create a new form with the objects and properties shown in Table 2-5-3, and save it as MDICHILD.FRM.

Table 2-5-3 Objects and properties for frmChild

OBJECT	PROPERTY	SETTING
Form	Name	frmChild
	Caption	"MDI Child"
	MDIChild	True
MsgHook	Name	MsgHook1

11. Place the following code in frmChild's Form_Load event. A frmMain.MdiPaint method needs to be invoked whenever the icon begins to drag. The MsgHook custom control will watch the Windows message stream and react to the appropriate messages. This code is not strictly necessary in Windows 95, which uses a different metaphor for minimized MDI children. But, it does improve the display in either Windows 3.x or Windows NT.

```
Private Sub Form_Load()
    '
    ' Set up MsgHook control to watch for icon movement
    '
    MsgHook1.HwndHook = Me.hWnd
    MsgHook1.Message(WM_QUERYDRAGICON) = True
    MsgHook1.Message(WM_WINDOWPOSCHANGED) = True
End Sub
```

12. Place the following code in frmChild's MsgHook1_Message event. When the user begins dragging an icon, several WM_WINDOWPOSCHANGED messages are fired. However, the background of the MDIForm needs to be repainted the first time only. So, a flag is set when the WM_QUERYDRAGICON message is received, and used to decide whether to issue a MdiPaint when WM_WINDOW-POSCHANGED messages are received.

```
Private Sub MsgHook1_Message(ByVal Msg As Long, _
        ByVal wp As Long, ByVal lp As Long, result As Long)
```

Continued on next page

Continued from previous page

```
'
' Repaint background so we don't leave a ghost
' Use WM_QUERYDRAGICON followed by WM_WINDOWPOSCHANGED
' to trigger repaint
'
Static MovingIcon%
Select Case Msg
   Case WM_QUERYDRAGICON
      MovingIcon = True
   Case WM_WINDOWPOSCHANGED
      If MovingIcon Then
         frmMain.MdiPaint
         MovingIcon = False
      End If
End Select
'
' Allow default window processing to occur.
'
result = MsgHook1.InvokeWindowProc(Msg, wp, lp)
End Sub
```

13. Place the following code in the Form_QueryUnload event of frmChild. Since the purpose of this project is to demonstrate the various triggers for repainting the MDIForm background, it would serve no purpose to allow the child forms to be unloaded prior to application termination.

```
Private Sub Form_QueryUnload(Cancel As Integer, UnloadMode As Integer)
   '
   ' Leave the form there so demonstration is complete
   '
   If UnloadMode = vbFormControlMenu Then
      Beep
      Cancel = True
   End If
End Sub
```

Create MDIGRAFX.BAS

14. Create a new code module and save it as MDIGRAFX.BAS. Place the following code in the Declarations section. This module contains the seven examples of different ways to paint the MDIForm's background. A variety of GDI calls are employed to give you a taste of what's possible.

```
Option Explicit
'
' API structure definition for Rectangle
'
Public Type RECT
   Left As Long
   Top As Long
   Right As Long
   Bottom As Long
End Type
```

```
'
' API structure definition for Point
'
Public Type POINTAPI
    X As Long
    Y As Long
End Type
'
' API structure definition for Brush
'
Public Type LOGBRUSH
    lbStyle As Long
    lbColor As Long
    lbHatch As Long
End Type
'
' API structure definition for Pen
'
Public Type LOGPEN
    lopnStyle As Long
    lopnWidth As POINTAPI
    lopnColor As Long
End Type
'
' API function declarations
'
Public Declare Function GetWindow Lib "user32" (ByVal hWnd As Long,
    ByVal wCmd As Long) As Long
Public Declare Sub GetClientRect Lib "user32" (ByVal hWnd As Long,
                                               lpRect As RECT)
Public Declare Function GetDC Lib "user32" (ByVal hWnd As Long) As Long
Public Declare Function ReleaseDC Lib "user32" (ByVal hWnd As Long,
    ByVal hDC As Long) As Long
Public Declare Function SelectObject Lib "gdi32" (ByVal hDC As Long,
    ByVal hObject As Long) As Long
Public Declare Function DeleteObject Lib "gdi32" (ByVal hObject
                                                  As Long) As Long
Public Declare Function CreateSolidBrush Lib "gdi32" (ByVal crColor
                                                      As Long) As Long
Public Declare Function CreatePen Lib "gdi32" (ByVal nPenStyle
    As Long, ByVal nWidth As Long, ByVal crColor As Long) As Long
Public Declare Function CreateEllipticRgn Lib "gdi32" (ByVal X1
    As Long, ByVal Y1 As Long, ByVal X2 As Long, ByVal Y2 As Long) As Long
Public Declare Sub InflateRect Lib "user32" (lpRect As RECT, ByVal X As Long,
                                             ByVal Y As Long)
Public Declare Function BitBlt Lib "gdi32" (ByVal hDestDC As Long,
    ByVal X As Long, ByVal Y As Long, ByVal nWidth As Long, ByVal nHeight
    As Long, ByVal hSrcDC As Long, ByVal XSrc As Long, ByVal YSrc
    As Long, ByVal dwRop As Long) As Long
Public Declare Function StretchBlt Lib "gdi32" (ByVal hDC As Long,
    ByVal X As Long, ByVal Y As Long, ByVal nWidth
    As Long, ByVal nHeight As Long, ByVal hSrcDC As Long, ByVal XSrc
    As Long, ByVal YSrc As Long, ByVal nSrcWidth As Long,
    ByVal nSrcHeight As Long,ByVal dwRop As Long) As Long
```

Continued on next page

Continued from previous page

```
Public Declare Function Rectangle Lib "gdi32" (ByVal hDC As Long,
    ByVal X1 As Long, ByVal Y1 As Long, ByVal X2 As Long, ByVal Y2
    As Long) As Long
Public Declare Function FillRect Lib "user32" (ByVal hDC As Long,
    lpRect As RECT, ByVal hBrush As Long) As Long
Public Declare Function FillRgn Lib "gdi32" (ByVal hDC As Long,
    ByVal hRgn As Long, ByVal hBrush As Long) As Long
Public Declare Function TextOut Lib "gdi32" Alias "TextOutA"
    (ByVal hDC As Long, ByVal X As Long, ByVal Y As Long, ByVal lpString
    As String, ByVal nCount As Long) As Long
'
' Raster-op for Blt's
'
Public Const SRCCOPY = &HCC0020
'
' Pen Style constant
'
Public Const PS_SOLID = 0
```

15. Also, place the following API constant declarations in the Declarations section of MDIGRAFX.BAS. These constants are used throughout the project, and therefore are declared globally.

```
'
' Windows messages watched for by MsgHook
'
Public Const WM_ERASEBKGND = &H14
Public Const WM_PAINT = &HF
Public Const WM_QUERYDRAGICON = &H37
Public Const WM_WINDOWPOSCHANGED = &H47
'
' Constant used with GetWindow() to obtain handle
' to MDIForm's client space
'
Public Const GW_CHILD = 5
'
```

16. Create a new subroutine called mdiPaintSolid and place the following code in it. Pass the MDIForm.hWnd, and the color to paint the background. This subroutine is included primarily to demonstrate the work that Visual Basic 4.0 does for you when you set the backcolor of an MDIForm. Of course, Visual Basic 3.0 didn't offer this capability at all, so this routine would still be useful in that environment. As is the case in all the routines in this module, it is critical that the retrieved device context is properly released and all created objects (pens and brushes) are deleted. Failure to do so will cause rapid depletion of system resources, and an inevitable crash.

```
Public Sub mdiPaintSolid(hWndParent As Long, FillColor As Long)
    Dim cWnd As Long
    Dim cDC As Long
    Dim nRet As Long
    Dim cRect As RECT
```

```
Dim NewBrush As Long
Dim OldBrush As Long
Dim NewPen As Long
Dim OldPen As Long
'
' Get DC to client space (assumes we're drawing
' onto an MDI client space)
'
cWnd = GetWindow(hWndParent, GW_CHILD)
cDC = GetDC(cWnd)
'
' Create new brush and pen and select them in
'
NewBrush = CreateSolidBrush(FillColor)
OldBrush = SelectObject(cDC, NewBrush)
NewPen = CreatePen(PS_SOLID, 1, FillColor)
OldPen = SelectObject(cDC, NewPen)
'
' Get target dimensions and paint it.The Rectangle function uses
' the current pen and brush selected into the DC
'
Call GetClientRect(cWnd, cRect)
nRet = Rectangle(cDC, cRect.Left, cRect.Top, cRect.Right, cRect.Bottom)
'
' Select old brush and pen back in
' Delete new brush and pen objects
' Release DC (very important!)
'
nRet = SelectObject(cDC, OldBrush)
nRet = DeleteObject(NewBrush)
nRet = SelectObject(cDC, OldPen)
nRet = DeleteObject(NewPen)
nRet = ReleaseDC(cWnd, cDC)
End Sub
```

17. Create a new subroutine called mdiBitBltTiled and place the following code in it. Pass it the source hWnd, source hDC, and the destination MDIForm.hWnd. By determining the dimensions of the source and destination rectangles, loops can be set up to tile the source bitmap across the destination. The BitBlt GDI function is extremely fast, and the painting pattern used is virtually unnoticeable on relatively fast machines. Performance will be on a par with screen repaints when Windows is using tiled wallpaper.

```
Public Sub mdiBitBltTiled(sWnd As Long, sDC As Long, dWnd As Long)
    Dim nRet As Long
    Dim cDC As Long
    Dim cWnd As Long
    Dim dX As Long
    Dim dY As Long
    Dim Rows As Integer
    Dim Cols As Integer
    Dim i As Integer
    Dim j As Integer
```

Continued on next page

Continued from previous page

```
    Dim sR As RECT
    Dim dR As RECT
    '
    ' Get DC to client space (assumes we're Blt'ing
    ' onto an MDI client space)
    '
    cWnd = GetWindow(dWnd, GW_CHILD)
    cDC = GetDC(cWnd)
    '
    ' Get source and destination rectangles
    '
    Call GetClientRect(sWnd, sR)
    Call GetClientRect(cWnd, dR)
    '
    ' Calc parameters
    '
    Rows = dR.Right \ sR.Right
    Cols = dR.Bottom \ sR.Bottom
    '
    ' Spray out across destination
    '
    For i = 0 To Rows
        dX = i * sR.Right
        For j = 0 To Cols
            dY = j * sR.Bottom
            nRet = BitBlt(cDC, dX, dY, sR.Right, sR.Bottom, _
                          sDC, 0, 0, SRCCOPY)
        Next j
    Next i
    '
    ' and clean up
    '
    nRet = ReleaseDC(cWnd, cDC)
End Sub
```

18. Create a new subroutine called mdiPaintGradient and place the following code in it. Pass it the destination MDIForm.hWnd, and the background will have a blue-to-black gradient painted in it. The module has two other routines, mdiPaintTunnel1 and mdiPaintTunnel2, that are very similar but produce slightly different effects. This routine uses 64 shades, ranging from blue to black, to fill 64 rectangles in the destination.

```
Public Sub mdiPaintGradient(hWndParent As Long)
    Const Shades% = 64
    Dim cWnd As Long
    Dim cDC As Long
    Dim nRet As Long
    Dim FillBoxHeight As Integer
    Dim NewBrush As Long
    Dim i As Integer
    Dim cRect As RECT
    Static fRect(1 To Shades) As RECT
    '
    ' Get DC to client space (assumes we're drawing
```

```
' onto an MDI client space)
'
cWnd = GetWindow(hWndParent, GW_CHILD)
cDC = GetDC(cWnd)
'
' Set up a structure of rectangles for fills
'
Call GetClientRect(cWnd, cRect)
FillBoxHeight = cRect.Bottom \ Shades
For i = 1 To Shades
    fRect(i).Left = cRect.Left
    fRect(i).Right = cRect.Right
    fRect(i).Top = (i - 1) * FillBoxHeight
    fRect(i).Bottom = fRect(i).Top + FillBoxHeight
Next i
'
' Make up for slop on last one
'
fRect(Shades).Bottom = cRect.Bottom
'
' Fill-it-up!
'
For i = Shades - 1 To 0 Step -1
    NewBrush = CreateSolidBrush(RGB(0, 0, (i + 1) * 4 - 1))
    nRet = FillRect(cDC, fRect(Shades - i), NewBrush)
    nRet = DeleteObject(NewBrush)
Next i
'
' and clean up
'
nRet = ReleaseDC(cWnd, cDC)
End Sub
```

19. Create a new subroutine called mdiPaintTunnel1 and place the following code in it. Pass it the destination MDIForm.hWnd, and the background will have a red-to-black series of fading rectangles painted in it. This routine also uses the FillRect GDI call, but introduces the InflateRect GDI call. InflateRect is a wonderfully quick way to alter the dimensions and location of a rectangle by a given factor.

```
Public Sub mdiPaintTunnel1(hWndParent As Long)
    Const Shades% = 64
    Dim cWnd As Long
    Dim cDC As Long
    Dim nRet As Long
    Dim i As Integer
    Dim dX As Long
    Dim dY As Long
    Dim NewBrush As Long
    Dim cRect As RECT
    '
    ' Get DC to client space (assumes we're drawing
    ' onto an MDI client space)
    '
```

Continued on next page

Continued from previous page

```
    cWnd = GetWindow(hWndParent, GW_CHILD)
    cDC = GetDC(cWnd)
    '
    ' Get target dimensions and calculate shrinkage factors
    '
    Call GetClientRect(cWnd, cRect)
    dX = cRect.Right / Shades \ 2
    dY = cRect.Bottom / Shades \ 2
    '
    ' Fill-it-up!
    '
    For i = Shades - 1 To 0 Step -1
        NewBrush = CreateSolidBrush(RGB((i + 1) * 4 - 1, 0, 0))
        nRet = FillRect(cDC, cRect, NewBrush)
        nRet = DeleteObject(NewBrush)
        InflateRect cRect, -dX, -dY
    Next i
    '
    ' and clean up
    '
    nRet = ReleaseDC(cWnd, cDC)
End Sub
```

20. Add another similar routine, mdiPaintTunnel2, to the MDIGRAFX.BAS module. This one uses a series of elliptical regions rather than rectangles to create its effect. Note that this sort of effect does cause a significant performance penalty even on the fastest machines, and that filling an elliptical region is quite a bit slower than FillRect. Another potential problem with regions is that they tend to be one of the first GDI objects to fall prey to low system resources. When this happens, the general symptom is a failure on the call to create the region, sometimes occuring at a level as early as 30% free system resources. This is principally a concern when running under Win16 environments. No error checking is employed here, as such failure will not cause any problems other than incorrect painting on the form.

```
Public Sub mdiPaintTunnel2(hWndParent As Long)
    Const Shades% = 32
    Dim cWnd As Long
    Dim cDC As Long
    Dim nRet As Long
    Dim i As Integer
    Dim dX As Long
    Dim dY As Long
    Dim NewBrush As Long
    Dim eRgn As Long
    Dim cRect As RECT
    '
    ' Get DC to client space (assumes we're drawing
    ' onto an MDI client space)
    '
    cWnd = GetWindow(hWndParent, GW_CHILD)
    cDC = GetDC(cWnd)
    '
```

```
' Get target dimensions and calculate shrinkage factors
'
Call GetClientRect(cWnd, cRect)
dX = cRect.Right / Shades / 2
dY = cRect.Bottom / Shades / 2
'
' Fill background with solid green
'
NewBrush = CreateSolidBrush(RGB(0, 255, 0))
nRet = FillRect(cDC, cRect, NewBrush)
nRet = DeleteObject(NewBrush)
'
' Fill-it-up!Shades from Green to Black
'
For i = Shades - 1 To 0 Step -1
    NewBrush = CreateSolidBrush(RGB(0, (i + 1) * 8 - 8, 0))
    eRgn = CreateEllipticRgn(cRect.Left, cRect.Top, cRect.Right, ⇒
      cRect.Bottom)
    nRet = FillRgn(cDC, eRgn, NewBrush)
    nRet = DeleteObject(NewBrush)
    nRet = DeleteObject(eRgn)
    Call InflateRect(cRect, -dX, -dY)
Next i
'
' and clean up
'
nRet = ReleaseDC(cWnd, cDC)
End Sub
```

21. Create a new subroutine called mdiBitBltCentered and place the following code
    in it. Pass it the source hWnd, source hDC, and the destination MDIForm.hWnd.
    The destination will have the source centered within it. Performance of this
    routine will be on a par with repaints of the screen background when Windows is
    using centered wallpaper.

```
Public Sub mdiBitBltCentered(sWnd As Long, sDC As Long, dWnd As Long)
    Dim nRet As Long
    Dim cDC As Long
    Dim cWnd As Long
    Dim dX As Long
    Dim dY As Long
    Dim sR As RECT
    Dim dR As RECT
    '
    ' Get DC to client space (assumes we're Blt'ing
    ' onto an MDI client space)
    '
    cWnd = GetWindow(dWnd, GW_CHILD)
    cDC = GetDC(cWnd)
    '
    ' Get source and destination rectangles
    '
    Call GetClientRect(sWnd, sR)
    Call GetClientRect(cWnd, dR)
```

Continued on next page

Continued from previous page

```
    '
    ' Calc parameters
    '
    dX = (dR.Right - sR.Right) \ 2
    dY = (dR.Bottom - sR.Bottom) \ 2
    '
    ' Do the BitBlt and clean up
    '
    nRet = BitBlt(cDC, dX, dY, sR.Right, sR.Bottom, _
                  sDC, 0, 0, SRCCOPY)
    nRet = ReleaseDC(cWnd, cDC)
End Sub
```

22. Create a new subroutine called mdiStretchBlt and place the following code in it. Pass it the source hWnd, source hDC, and the destination MDIForm.hWnd. The source will be stretched, either proportionally or non proportionally, to fit the destination. The StretchBlt GDI call is not nearly as fast as BitBlt, as you'll see when trying this effect.

```
Public Sub mdiStretchBlt(sWnd As Long, sDC As Long, dWnd As Long,
Proportional As Boolean)
    Dim nRet As Long
    Dim cDC As Long
    Dim cWnd As Long
    Dim sR As RECT
    Dim dR As RECT
    Dim factor As Single
    Dim dX As Long
    Dim dY As Long
    '
    ' Get DC to client space (assumes we're Blt'ing
    ' onto an MDI client space)
    '
    cWnd = GetWindow(dWnd, GW_CHILD)
    cDC = GetDC(cWnd)
    '
    ' Get source and destination rectangles
    '
    Call GetClientRect(sWnd, sR)
    Call GetClientRect(cWnd, dR)
    '
    ' Alter destination if proportional to respect constraining
    ' dimension
    '
    If Proportional Then
       If dR.Bottom / sR.Bottom < dR.Right / sR.Right Then
          'Height is constraining dimension
          factor! = dR.Bottom / sR.Bottom
          dX = (dR.Right - (factor! * sR.Right)) \ -2
       Else
          'Width is constraining dimension
          factor! = dR.Right / sR.Right
          dY = (dR.Bottom - (factor! * sR.Bottom)) \ -2
       End If
```

```
        InflateRect dR, dX, dY
    End If
    '
    ' Stretch out across destination and clean up
    '
    nRet = StretchBlt(cDC, dR.Left, dR.Top, CLng(dR.Right - dR.Left), _
                      CLng(dR.Bottom - dR.Top), sDC, 0&, 0&, _
                      sR.Right, sR.Bottom, SRCCOPY)
    nRet = ReleaseDC(cWnd, cDC)
End Sub
```

23. Finally, create a new subroutine called mdiTextOut and place the following code in it. Pass it the destination MDIForm.hWnd, a text string, and X,Y coordinates for the text to be output at that location in the MDI client space. You are encouraged to play with this routine to enable it to use more interesting fonts. As written, it's using the default font for a window of this class, which eliminates dependencies on fonts available on a given system, but can be rather boring.

```
Public Sub mdiTextOut(dWnd As Long, Text$, dX As Long, dY As Long)
    Dim nRet As Long
    Dim cWnd As Long
    Dim cDC As Long
    '
    ' Get DC to client space (assumes we're drawing
    ' onto an MDI client space)
    '
    cWnd = GetWindow(dWnd, GW_CHILD)
    cDC = GetDC(cWnd)
    '
    ' Place text at location passed in call and clean up
    '
    nRet = TextOut(cDC, dX, dY, Text$, Len(Text$))
    nRet = ReleaseDC(cWnd, cDC)
End Sub
```

How It Works

There are several key elements to the functioning of this How-To. First and foremost is acquiring the window handle, or hWnd, to the MDIForm's client space. Knowing the relationship of the client space to its form provides the answer. The client space is the first child of the MDIForm (in a different sense than that of MDI children). A quick call to GetWindow, passing the handle to the MDIForm and the constant GW_CHILD, returns this first child's handle.

The trickier element is determining when to apply graphics methods to the client space. Visual Basic 4.0 still does not support the trapping of user-defined window messages. Until it does, the only option for adding this capability is to use a custom control. This is called subclassing, because intercepting messages headed for a given window and altering the response that Visual Basic would normally provide, adds new properties to a previously defined windows class. That is, in all aspects except where specific intervention is called for, the Window class behaves just as it otherwise would. But where additional functionality is required, the subclassing comes into play.

For regular, non-MDIForms, Visual Basic itself intercepts the WM_PAINT message and fires the event Form_Paint. For MDIForms, on the other hand, the creators of Visual Basic have decided programmers don't need to react to this message. But, to place graphics into an MDIForm's client space, this is not the case. So, the MsgHook custom controls (MSGHOO16.OCX and MSGHOO32.OCX) that comes with this book are employed here to allow the application to react appropriately whenever Windows notifies it.

The various graphic methods offered are but a small sampling of what is possible when using Windows GDI functions rather than Visual Basic's graphics methods. In this case, GDI calls were required, because Visual Basic doesn't support its own graphics methods on MDIForms. As you have seen, there are distinct performance penalties associated with the use of certain GDI methods. Usage must be considered in light of how often the methods will be called and in what context. The two "tunnel" methods are probably not suited for the background of a form that will need to be repainted often.

Comments

With just a little reworking, the methods employed here are fully capable of being used in Visual Basic 3.0. The only restrictions would be where new features of Visual Basic 4.0 provide somewhat greater flexibility, and these are easily worked around. Remember that Visual Basic 4.0 now offers a BackColor property for MDIForms, the preferred route if you only want to paint the background in a distinct color.

2.6 How do I...
Save and Restore Window Positions?

COMPLEXITY: EASY
COMPATIBILITY: VB4 ONLY

Problem

I've used many programs that save their position from one run to another. I really like the way I can set the position of the window and the program will "remember" it. How can I get my program to save its position?

Technique

WINPOS uses a class called CWinPos to save and restore the position of its form. CWinPos uses the INI file API function calls to keep its data in your program's INI file. The Left, Top, Width, and Height properties are all stored in one entry in your program's INI file. All that's required is a little string formatting when writing, and a little parsing when reading.

Steps

Open and run WINPOS.VBP. The form will show you the current size and position of the window, and you will see a form similar to that shown in Figure 2-6-1. Reposition and resize the window; then double-click on the system menu to exit. Restart the program, and notice that the size and position are retained.

1. Create a new project named WINPOS.VBP. Use the Insert Class Module menu item to add a new class module to the project. Set the new class's Name property to CWinPos, and add the following code to the General section of CWinPos:

```
Option Explicit
'
' Declare registration database functions
'
Const HKEY_LOCAL_MACHINE = &H80000002
Const REG_SZ = 1
Private Declare Function RegCloseKey Lib "advapi32.dll" (ByVal hKey
        As Long) As Long
Private Declare Function RegCreateKey Lib "advapi32.dll" Alias
        "RegCreateKeyA" _
        (ByVal hKey As Long, ByVal lpSubKey As String, phkResult As Long)
        As Long
Private Declare Function RegOpenKey Lib "advapi32.dll" Alias
        "RegOpenKeyA" _
        (ByVal hKey As Long, ByVal lpSubKey As String, phkResult As Long)
        As Long
Private Declare Function RegQueryValue Lib "advapi32.dll" Alias
        "RegQueryValueA" _
        (ByVal hKey As Long, ByVal lpSubKey As String, ByVal lpValue As String, _
        lpcbValue As Long) As Long
Private Declare Function RegSetValue Lib "advapi32.dll" Alias
        "RegSetValueA" _
        (ByVal hKey As Long, ByVal lpSubKey As String, ByVal dwType As Long, _
        ByVal lpData As String, ByVal cbData As Long) As Long
```

2. Add the following code to the General section of CWinPos. The private SetValue function sets one of the Left, Top, Width, or Height properties of the form object

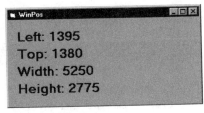

Figure 2-6-1 The WINPOS project

passed in. The value set is determined by the Index parameter. This function is used by the RestoreForm method, to be added next.

```
'
' sets individual value for form value 0 is left,
' 1 is top, 2 is width, 3 is height. This function
' allows us to loop through string w/o specialized
' code
'
Private Sub SetValue(CurForm As Object, I As Integer, _
      Value As Single)
   Select Case I
      Case 0
         CurForm.Left = Value

      Case 1
         CurForm.Top = Value

      Case 2
         CurForm.Width = Value

      Case 3
         CurForm.Height = Value

      End Select
End Sub
```

3. Add the following code to the General section of CWinPos. This function gets the size and position information about the current form from the INI file. If it exists, this function cycles through the elements (numbers) in the string retrieved and passes them to SetValue() to set CurForm's properties.

```
'
' restores form to previous position and size. Retrieves
' size and pos information from the app's INI file in section
' specified by Entry
'
Public Sub RestoreForm(CurForm As Object, AppName As String, Entry As String)
   Dim I As Integer
   Dim Index As Integer
   Dim Value As String
   Dim KeyName As String
   Dim KeyValue As String
   Dim KeyHandle As Long
   Dim KeyValueLength As Long
   Dim Ret As Long
   '
   ' initialize string with enough space to receive data
   ' otherwise, GPF will occur
   '
   Value = Space(512)
   '
   ' get previous size and position information from the INI file
   '
```

```
KeyName = "WGP\" & AppName & "\Form Position"
KeyValue = Space(512)
KeyValueLength = Len(KeyValue)

Ret = RegOpenKey(HKEY_LOCAL_MACHINE, "SOFTWARE", KeyHandle)
If Ret <> 0 Then
    Exit Sub
End If

Ret = RegQueryValue(KeyHandle, KeyName, KeyValue, KeyValueLength)
If Ret <> 0 Then
    Ret = RegCloseKey(KeyHandle)
    Exit Sub
End If

Ret = RegCloseKey(KeyHandle)
Value = Trim(Left(KeyValue, KeyValueLength))
'
' start at beginning of properties to set
'
Index = 0
'
' loop through all four properties, while there is
' data to set
'
Do While (Index < 4) And (Len(Value) > 0)
    '
    ' get position of next space (our delimiter)
    '
    I = InStr(Value, " ")
    '
    ' if there are no spaces, this is the last element
    '
    If (I <= 0) Then
        '
        ' set the value for this element
        '
        SetValue CurForm, Index, Val(Value)
        '
        ' ensure we don't loop again
        '
        Value = ""
    Else
        '
        ' set the value for this element
        '
        SetValue CurForm, Index, Val(Left(Value, I - 1))
        '
        ' remove current element from the front of the string
        ' thus, setting the string up for the next loop
        '
        Value = Trim(Mid(Value, I + 1))
    End If
    '
    ' move to next element
```

Continued on next page

Continued from previous page

```
            '
            Index = Index + 1
    Loop
End Sub
```

4. Add the following subroutine to the General section of CWinPos. This function writes the current form's size and position information to the application's INI file. It writes this information to the section and entry defined by AppName and Entry.

```
'
' save size and position information to app's INI file to the
' section and entry specified by AppName and Entry.
'
Public Sub SaveForm(CurForm As Object, AppName As String, Entry As String)
    Dim KeyName As String
    Dim KeyValue As String
    Dim KeyHandle As Long
    Dim Ret As Long
    '
    ' write size/pos info to the registry, using the format
    ' Entry=Left Top Width Height
    '
    KeyName = "WGP\" & AppName & "\Form Position"
    KeyValue = CurForm.Left & " " & CurForm.TOP & " " & CurForm.Width & ⇒
        " " & CurForm.Height

    Ret = RegCreateKey(HKEY_LOCAL_MACHINE, "SOFTWARE", KeyHandle)
    If Ret <> 0 Then
        Exit Sub
    End If

    Ret = RegSetValue(KeyHandle, KeyName, REG_SZ, KeyValue, Len(KeyValue))
    Ret = RegCloseKey(KeyHandle)
End Sub
```

5. Select Form1; then create objects and set their properties as shown in Table 2-6-1.

Table 2-6-1 Objects, properties, and settings for Form1

OBJECT	PROPERTY	SETTING
Form	Name	WinPos
	Height	2400
	Width	5400
	Caption	"Window Size and Position"
Timer	Name	Timer1
	Interval	100
	Left	120

OBJECT	PROPERTY	SETTING
	Top	2520
	Enabled	0 ' False
Label	Name	lblLeft
	FontSize	18
	Left	240
	Top	240
	Width	5000
Label	Name	lblTop
	FontSize	18
	Left	240
	Top	720
	Width	5000
Label	Name	lblWidth
	FontSize	18
	Left	240
	Top	1200
	Width	5000
Label	Name	lblHeight
	FontSize	18
	Left	240
	Top	1680
	Width	5000

6. Add the following code to the General declarations section of Form1.

```
Option Explicit
'
' create new instance of class which saves
' restores items
'
Dim CWinPos As New CWinPos
'
' keep track of last position of form, since VB
' does not offer a Move event
'
Dim LastLeft As Single
Dim LastTop As Single
```

7. Add the following code to Form1's Form_Load subroutine. This routine first restores the window using the size and position information saved in the program's INI file, if any. It does this by using the RestoreForm method from the CWinPos class. Next, Form_Load sets the LastLeft and LastTop variables to -1. This ensures that the values are different from the actual Left and Top values for

the form. This means that the next time Timer1_Timer is called, the Left and Top values in lblLeft and lblTop will be updated. Finally, Timer1 is enabled and then immediately "fired." The timer event code is called immediately, to make sure that the Left and Top values are displayed quickly.

```
Private Sub Form_Load()
    '
    ' restore windows size and position using the
    ' cWinPos class
    '
    CWinPos.RestoreForm Me, "WinPos", "Form Position"
    '
    ' ensure values are initially different
    ' for the timer procedure
    '
    LastLeft = -1
    LastTop = -1
    '
    ' start the timer
    '
    Timer1.Enabled = True
    '
    ' call the timer procedure once to ensure values
    ' are shown on screen
    '
    Timer1_Timer
End Sub
```

8. Add the following code to the Resize event routine of Form1. This code puts the Width and Height properties of the form into the lblWidth and lblHeight labels.

```
Private Sub Form_Resize()
    '
    ' when the size of the form changes, set labels
    ' to display the size information
    '
    lblWidth = "Width: " & Me.Width
    lblHeight = "Height: " & Me.Height
End Sub
```

9. Add the following code to Form1's Unload event subroutine. This is where the form's size and position get saved. This subroutine uses the SaveForm method in the CWinPos class to save the information to the application's INI file.

```
Private Sub Form_Unload(Cancel As Integer)
    CWinPos.SaveForm Me, "WinPos", "Form Position"
End Sub
```

10. Add the following code to Timer1's Timer event procedure. This routine ensures that the current position information is displayed to the user. Since VB4 doesn't have a Move event for forms, we have to use a timer (set to go off every 100 milliseconds). The LastLeft and LastTop variables are used to make sure the labels (lblLeft and lblTop) are only updated when necessary.

```
Private Sub Timer1_Timer()
    '
    ' check for window movement,
    '
    If (Me.Left <> LastLeft) And (Me.Top <> LastTop) Then
        '
        ' if window has moved, set captions
        ' for position labels
        '
        lblLeft = "Left: " & Me.Left
        lblTop = "Top: " & Me.Top
    End If
End Sub
```

How It Works

WINPOS relies on the functions/methods provided by the CWinPos class. When the program calls SaveForm, the form's Left, Top, Width, and Height properties are all put into a string (separated by spaces), and then written to the application's INI file.

When the program calls the CWinPos RestoreForm (presumably on startup), it reads the string from the INI file, unpacks the size and position information, and then sets the properties.

CWinPos can be placed in any program and used to save and restore the position of any of the forms in your project. Remember to use a different Entry name for each form.

Comments

This How-To demonstrates saving window size and position information. You can extend the techniques shown here to include other information that you may wish to save from one execution of your program to another (such as the configuration of a toolbar; which windows are showing and which aren't; etc.).

2.7 How do I...
Position an Icon at a Given Location?

COMPLEXITY: EASY
COMPATIBILITY: VB3 OR VB4

Problem

I'm writing an add-on utility for another application. I'd like my icon to always be positioned in the upper-right corner of the screen when its form is minimized. But setting the Top or Left properties or attempting the Move method on a minimized form all generate a Visual Basic error. Is there an API call that will allow me to move my icon where I want it?

Technique

You can use the MoveWindow API to move an icon just as you would a normal-sized window. This turns out to be such an easy How-To that we have decided to have some fun with it. Some years ago, there was a shareware program that loaded itself as an icon. Whenever the user moved the cursor near the icon, it would scoot away, effectively preventing the user from ever catching it. It was fun to start it up on a coworker's machine and watch them try figuring out how to get rid of it. The only possible method was through Task Manager, but most people never thought of that. Let's re-create this functionality to show how to position an icon.

One limitation of Visual Basic we'll need to overcome is that minimized forms don't receive mouse events. The other is that Visual Basic offers no event whatsoever for the caption window that appears below an icon. To clear these hurdles, we'll use our old subclassing friend, the MsgHook custom control that's included with this book. It can be set to intercept messages destined for the icon and its caption, which can be interpreted to meet the needs of this little applet.

Another thing to be aware of is that the whole concept of an icon has been radically changed in Windows 95. In essence, icons no longer exist as we know them. However, by setting the correct set of properties, an "icon" of sorts can be achieved in Windows 95. It will appear similar to a minimized child window in an MDI application, but will be lacking the actual icon image. Although this demonstration will indeed work in Windows 95, it is truly designed for the older interface used in Windows NT.

Steps

Open and run CATCHME.VBP. In Windows NT, an icon of a not-so-smiley face will show up somewhere along the bottom of the screen. In Windows 95, a minimized titlebar should appear right above the taskbar. Try catching up to the icon with your mouse cursor. No matter what you try, it just runs away from you. If you don't blink, you might notice that it sort of smiles each time it escapes. Try switching to it with either (ALT)-(F4) or through Task Manager. Nothing will happen. Only by selecting End Task in Task Manager (if it's an EXE), or pressing the Stop button (if you're running from the environment) can you exercise some control over CATCHME. To create CATCHME, perform the following steps:

1. Create a new project called CATCHME.VBP, with the objects and properties as listed in Table 2-7-1. Save it as CATCHME.FRM. The form should look something like Figure 2-7-1. As one step in the defense against the user resizing the form while it's an icon, ControlBox, MaxButton, and MinButton are all set to false. To achieve the icon effect in Windows 95, the BorderStyle is set to Fixed Dialog. Two image controls hold the icons that alternate back and forth as the iconic form scoots away from the cursor. Once again, the MsgHook subclassing controls provided with this book, MSGHOO16.OCX and MSGHOO32.OCX, are employed to extend the range of "events" Visual Basic's can respond to. MsgHook

Figure 2-7-1 CATCHME.FRM
appearance at design time

is set up as the first element (0) in a control array, so another can be loaded at run time. Both the icon and its caption will need to be subclassed, watching for messages related to mouse movements and menu selections.

Table 2-7-1 CATCHME.FRM Objects and properties

OBJECT	PROPERTY	SETTING
Form	Name	Form1
	BorderStyle	3 - Fixed Dialog
	Caption	"Can't Catch Me!"
	ControlBox	False
	Icon	(Icon) 'FACE01.ICO
	MaxButton	False
	MinButton	False
	WindowState	1 - Minimized
Image	Name	Image1
Picture	(Icon) 'FACE01.ICO	
Image	Name	Image2
	Picture	(Icon) 'FACE03.ICO
MsgHook	Name	MsgHook
	Index	0

2. Insert the following code into the Form_Load event of Form1. The form needs to actually be visible before values can be assigned to the MsgHook controls, since the caption window that "lives" below the icon (in Windows NT only) won't actually exist until the icon is first shown. The first MsgHook control is set to watch the icon itself by using the form's hWnd. Another instance of MsgHook is loaded and set to watch the caption window, using a special function that will be described shortly. Since the hWnd property is read-only, it must be passed ByVal to the function that retrieves the caption window's handle. This is accomplished by enclosing it in an additional set of parentheses.

```
Private Sub Form_Load()
    '
    ' Show before assiging MsgHook values because
    ' caption window won't exist otherwise.
```

Continued on next page

Continued from previous page

```
'
    Me.Show
    '
    ' Assign first MsgHook to watch icon for certain messages
    ' Assign second MsgHook to watch caption for same messages
    '
    Msghook(0).HwndHook = Me.hwnd
    Msghook(0).Message(WM_SYSCOMMAND) = True
    Msghook(0).Message(WM_SETCURSOR) = True
    Load Msghook(1)
    Msghook(1).HwndHook = GetCaptionHandle((Me.hwnd))
    Msghook(1).Message(WM_SYSCOMMAND) = True
    Msghook(1).Message(WM_SETCURSOR) = True
    '
    ' Center images on form so animation works in Win95.
    '
    Image1.Move (Me.ScaleWidth - Image1.Width) \ 2, (Me.ScaleHeight - ⇒
        Image1.Height) \ 2
    Image2.Move (Me.ScaleWidth - Image2.Width) \ 2, (Me.ScaleHeight - ⇒
        Image2.Height) \ 2
    Image1.Visible = True
    Image2.Visible = False
End Sub
```

3. Insert the following code into the MsgHook_Message event, to watch for two specific Windows messages. WM_SYSCOMMAND indicates that a control menu event has just happened. In this case, the most likely cause would be Task Manager or (ALT)-(TAB) trying to activate the icon. By intercepting WM_SYSCOMMAND, the form can be prevented from reacting to it. The WM_SETCURSOR is sent to a window whenever the mouse has moved within it. This message is used as a trigger to make the icon jump away from the cursor. Recursion is prevented by setting a flag before beginning the scooting process. After the icon has been moved, a short little loop pauses to flash a smile at the user for 1/10 of a second.

```
Private Sub Msghook_Message(index As Integer, ByVal msg As Long, ⇒
ByVal wp As Long, ByVal lp As Long, result As Long)
    Dim MovePending As Integer
    Dim Elapsed As Double
    '
    ' Decide what to do based on which message is received.
    ' WM_SYSCOMMAND says user has somehow triggered a menu action
    ' WM_SETCURSOR means the cursor has encroached over the window
    '
    Select Case msg
        Case WM_SYSCOMMAND
            '
            ' Windows uses the four low order bits of wParam internally,
            ' so turn them off.
            ' Don't allow user interaction with the control menu.
            ' Most likely this was triggered through TaskMan.
            '
            wp = wp And &HFFF0
```

```
            If wp = SC_SIZE Or wp = SC_RESTORE Or wp = SC_MOVE Then
                'Action = MH_EATMESSAGE
                result = 0
            End If
        Case WM_SETCURSOR
            '
            ' Avoid recursion into this by setting a flag before proceeding.
            ' Set smiley face icon and refresh it.
            ' Scoot icon away from cursor then wait 2/10 second before
            ' restoring original icon.
            '
            If Not MovePending Then
                MovePending = True
                    result = Msghook(index).InvokeWindowProc(msg, wp, lp)
                    If Me.WindowState = vbMinimized Then
                        Me.Icon = Me.Image2
                        Me.Refresh
                    Else
                        Me.Image2.Visible = True
                    End If
                    ScootAway Me
                    Elapsed = Timer + 0.2
                    Do While Elapsed > Timer
                        DoEvents
                    Loop
                    If Me.WindowState = vbMinimized Then
                        Me.Icon = Me.Image1
                    Else
                        Me.Image2.Visible = False
                    End If
                MovePending = False
            End If
    End Select
End Sub
```

4. Add a new code module to the project. Select Module on the Insert menu, allow
it to keep its default name Module1, and save it as CATCHME.BAS. Insert the
following code in the Declarations section of Module1. These declarations,
definitions, and constants are used by the subroutines and function in this
module. Note that this module was created so it could be used with either the
16- or 32-bit versions of Visual Basic 4.0. API function declarations and one API
structure require conditional compilation.

```
Option Explicit
#If Win16 Then
    '
    ' API point data structure
    '
    Type POINTAPI
        x As Integer
        y As Integer
    End Type
    '
    ' Win16 API call declarations
```

Continued on next page

Continued from previous page

```
    '
    Declare Sub GetCursorPos Lib "User" (lpPoint As POINTAPI)
    Declare Sub MoveWindow Lib "User" (ByVal hwnd As Integer, ⇒
            ByVal x As Integer, ByVal y As Integer, ByVal nWidth As Integer, ⇒
            ByVal nHeight As Integer, ByVal bRepaint As Integer)
    Declare Function FindWindow Lib "User" (ByVal lpClassName As Any, ⇒
            ByVal lpWindowName As Any) As Integer
    Declare Function GetWindow Lib "User" (ByVal hwnd As Integer, ⇒
            ByVal wCmd As Integer) As Integer
    Declare Function GetParent Lib "User" (ByVal hwnd As Integer) ⇒
            As Integer
    Declare Function GetClassName Lib "User" (ByVal hwnd As Integer, ⇒
            ByVal lpClassName As String, ByVal nMaxCount As Integer) As Integer
#ElseIf Win32 Then
    '
    ' API point data structure
    '
    Type POINTAPI
        x As Long
        y As Long
    End Type
    '
    ' Win32 API call declarations
    '
    Declare Function GetCursorPos Lib "user32" (lpPoint As POINTAPI) ⇒
            As Long
    Declare Function MoveWindow Lib "user32" (ByVal hwnd As Long, ⇒
            ByVal x As Long, ByVal y As Long, ByVal nWidth As Long, ⇒
            ByVal nHeight As Long, ByVal bRepaint As Long) As Long
    Declare Function FindWindow Lib "user32" Alias "FindWindowA" ⇒
            (ByVal lpClassName As String, ByVal lpWindowName As String) As Long
    Declare Function GetParent Lib "user32" (ByVal hwnd As Long) As Long
    Declare Function GetClassName Lib "user32" Alias "GetClassNameA" ⇒
            (ByVal hwnd As Long, ByVal lpClassName As String, ⇒
            ByVal nMaxCount As Long) As Long
    Declare Function GetWindow Lib "user32" (ByVal hwnd As Long, ⇒
            ByVal wCmd As Long) As Long
#End If
'
' Public Constants used by GetWindow
'
Public Const GW_HWNDFIRST = 0
Public Const GW_HWNDNEXT = 2
'
' System menu command values to intercept
' These can't be passed on to VB!
'
Public Const SC_SIZE = &HF000
Public Const SC_MOVE = &HF010
Public Const SC_RESTORE = &HF120
'
' Public Constants used by MsgHook
' These are what we watch for
'
Public Const WM_SYSCOMMAND = &H112
Public Const WM_SETCURSOR = &H20
```

5. Create a function called GetCaptionHandle in Module1, and place the following code in it. This is a generic routine to retrieve the passed icon's caption window handle. It relies on the unique classname assigned to all such windows under Windows 3.x and Windows NT 3.x, but will need to be tested in new versions of Windows as they become available. To find the caption window, GetCaptionHandle "walks" the list of top-level windows looking for the child of the window passed in as a parameter. Then its classname is retrieved and compared to the "magic" value of "#32772" which is the classname assigned to all caption windows. If both these criteria are met, the correct handle has been found, and the function can exit.

Note how the function's declaration, as well as the local variable's allocation, are performed conditionally depending on whether the 16- or 32-bit version of Visual Basic is being used. The remainder of the function is written so that it doesn't matter whether it's Win16 or Win32. Coding in this manner will allow you to reduce the amount of parallel code that must be maintained for different operating systems.

```
#If Win16 Then
Public Function GetCaptionHandle(ParentWnd As Integer) As Integer
    Dim hCapWnd As Integer
    Dim nRet As Integer
#ElseIf Win32 Then
Public Function GetCaptionHandle(ParentWnd As Long) As Long
    Dim hCapWnd As Long
    Dim nRet As Long
#End If
    Dim Buffer As String
    '
    ' Get first window in Windows master list
    '
    hCapWnd = GetWindow(ParentWnd, GW_HWNDFIRST)
    '
    ' Check every top-level window
    '
    Do While hCapWnd <> 0
        '
        ' The caption window is a child of the icon
        ' Check to see if returned window has this relation
        ' with the passed window (the icon)
        '
        If GetParent(hCapWnd) = ParentWnd Then
            '
            ' If we have a child, make sure it's a Caption.
            ' Under Windows 3.x and NT, caption windows always have the
            ' classname "#32772". . Will always fail in Win95.
            '
            Buffer$ = Space$(128)
            nRet = GetClassName(hCapWnd, Buffer$, Len(Buffer$))
            Buffer$ = Left$(Buffer$, nRet)
            If Buffer$ = "#32772" Then
                GetCaptionHandle = hCapWnd
```

Continued on next page

Continued from previous page

```
            Exit Function
        End If
    End If
    '
    ' Get the next task list item in the master list.
    '
    hCapWnd = GetWindow(hCapWnd, GW_HWNDNEXT)
    Loop
End Function
```

6. Next comes the real workhorse of this project. Create a new subroutine in
   Module1 called ScootAway and place the following code in it. As complicated as
   it may at first appear, this routine is really very simple. First it calculates the center point of the icon and gets the position of the cursor, both in screen coordinates. Then a series of comparisons are made to determine from which direction
   the cursor is approaching and appropriate offsets are applied to the centroid. If
   the new centroid is almost off screen, it's wrapped to the other edge. The new top
   and left positions are calculated, and a call is made to the routine that moves it.

```
Public Sub ScootAway(Frm As Form)
    Static BeenHere As Integer
    Static tppX As Integer
    Static tppY As Integer
    Static HalfX As Integer
    Static HalfY As Integer
    Static Centroid As POINTAPI
    Static CursorPos As POINTAPI
    Dim xOffset As Integer
    Dim yOffset As Integer
    Const Offset% = 32
    '
    ' Need to initialize a few static vars the first time here
    ' For performance reasons, it's best to just calc these once
    '
    If Not BeenHere Then
        tppX = Screen.TwipsPerPixelX
        tppY = Screen.TwipsPerPixelY
        HalfX = Frm.Width \ tppX \ 2
        HalfY = Frm.Height \ tppY \ 2
        BeenHere = True
    End If
    '
    ' Calc the center point of the icon, and
    ' get the position of the cursor.
    '
    Centroid.x = (Frm.Left \ tppX) + HalfX
    Centroid.y = (Frm.TOP \ tppY) + HalfY
    Call GetCursorPos(CursorPos)
    '
    ' Figure out what direction the cursor is approaching from,
    ' and set new offsets appropriately.
    '
    If CursorPos.y < Centroid.y Then        'approaching from top
```

```
      If CursorPos.x < Centroid.x Then          'from left
         xOffset = Offset
         yOffset = Offset
      ElseIf CursorPos.x > Centroid.x Then    'from right
         xOffset = -Offset
         yOffset = Offset
      ElseIf CursorPos.x = Centroid.x Then    'from above
         xOffset = 0
         yOffset = Offset
      End If
   ElseIf CursorPos.y > Centroid.y Then 'approaching from below
      If CursorPos.x < Centroid.x Then          'from left
         xOffset = Offset
         yOffset = -Offset
      ElseIf CursorPos.x > Centroid.x Then    'from right
         xOffset = -Offset
         yOffset = -Offset
      ElseIf CursorPos.x = Centroid.x Then    'from below
         xOffset = 0
         yOffset = -Offset
      End If
   ElseIf CursorPos.y = Centroid.y Then    'approaching from side
      If CursorPos.x < Centroid.x Then          'from left
         xOffset = Offset
         yOffset = 0
      ElseIf CursorPos.x > Centroid.x Then    'from right
         xOffset = -Offset
         yOffset = 0
      ElseIf CursorPos.x = Centroid.x Then    'from exact center
         xOffset = Offset
         yOffset = Offset
      End If
   End If
End If
'
' Calc point where center of icon should move to
'
Centroid.x = Centroid.x + xOffset
Centroid.y = Centroid.y + yOffset
'
' Apply a little screen wrap logic on left and right
'
If Centroid.x <= HalfX Then
   Centroid.x = Screen.Width \ tppX - HalfX
ElseIf Centroid.x >= Screen.Width \ tppX - HalfX Then
   Centroid.x = HalfX
End If
'
' Apply a little screen wrap logic on top and bottom
'
If Centroid.y <= HalfY Then
   Centroid.y = Screen.Height \ tppY - HalfY
ElseIf Centroid.y >= Screen.Height \ tppY - HalfY Then
   Centroid.y = HalfY
End If
'
```

Continued on next page

Continued from previous page

```
' Calc new Left and Top positions for icon
'
Centroid.x = Centroid.x - HalfX
Centroid.y = Centroid.y - HalfY
'
' Call routine to reposition icon
'
MoveIcon Frm, CInt(Centroid.x), CInt(Centroid.y)
End Sub
```

7. Now we're ready to get back to the original question! Add a new subroutine called MoveIcon to Module1. This routine calls the MoveWindow API to reposition the icon at the coordinates calculated in ScootAway. Caption windows generally seem wedded to icons, but calling MoveWindow on an icon clearly shows that they are indeed distinct windows. Single-stepping through this routine, you'll notice that after the MoveWindow call, the caption window is no longer directly below the icon. The solution is to force the caption to redraw itself. The easiest way to accomplish this is to assign its current value back into itself.

```
Private Sub MoveIcon(Frm As Form, iLeft As Integer, iTop As Integer)
    '
    ' This is where the "work" is done
    ' Pass the Left and Top positions in *pixels*
    ' The Caption must be reset for it to move too
    '
    Call MoveWindow(Frm.hWnd, iLeft, iTop, _
                    Frm.Width \ Screen.TwipsPerPixelX, _
                    Frm.Height \ Screen.TwipsPerPixelY, True)
    Frm.Caption = Frm.Caption
End Sub
```

How It Works

The key to this project is overcoming the lack of mouse messages for minimized forms. MsgHook comes to the rescue again. It's set up to intercept two specific messages from the stream of messages Windows sends to the application. As the mouse approaches either the icon or its caption, the ScootAway function is called to calculate a direction and distance to jump away from the cursor. To position an icon, all that's required is a call to the MoveWindow API, and a refresh of the caption. Remember, once this application is compiled, the only way to get rid of it is to select End Task from the Task Manager. See how long it takes your coworkers, kids, or spouse to figure it out!

Comments

Even though this project was a fun one, there is one important thing to keep in mind: Icons as we know them are destined for obscurity as Windows evolves. The GetCaptionHandle function relies on a hard-coded classname for caption windows, which may well change in the future. Any time this sort of trickery is resorted to, it's likely that something will change, forcing you to find another workaround. In the meantime, enjoy!

2.8 How do I...
Create an Animated Cursor?

COMPLEXITY: EASY
COMPATIBILITY: VB4 ONLY

Problem

I like the way CorelDRAW displays an hourglass with the sand flowing from the top chamber to the bottom, and rotating when the top is empty. Can I have my cursor do this during a long process?

Technique

Visual Basic 4.0 offers the new property MouseIcon for setting a custom icon into any object's MousePointer. By setting the MousePointer property to vbCustom, you induce this change. To incorporate animation, simply rotate through a series of icons.

Steps

Open and run ANIPTR.VBP. Press the command button once to start the animation sequence, and again to stop it. The command button toggles a timer, which rotates through a series of six icons. This project sets the custom MouseIcon for the entire form.

1. Create a new project called ANIPTR.VBP with the objects and properties listed in Table 2-8-1. Save it as ANIPTR.FRM. The form should look something like Figure 2-8-1.

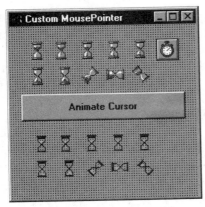

Figure 2-8-1 The animated cursor
Main form at design time

Table 2-8-1 Objects and properties for animated cursor project

OBJECT	PROPERTY	SETTING
Form	Name	Form1
	Caption	"Custom MousePointer"
Image	Name	imgPtr
	Index	0
	Picture	("Icon") ' HOUR01.ICO
	Visible	False
Image	Name	imgPtr
	Index	1
	Picture	("Icon") ' HOUR02.ICO
	Visible	False
Image	Name	imgPtr
	Index	2
	Picture	("Icon") ' HOUR03.ICO
	Visible	False
Image	Name	imgPtr
	Index	3
	Picture	("Icon") ' HOUR04.ICO
	Visible	False
Image	Name	imgPtr
	Index	4
	Picture	("Icon") ' HOUR05.ICO
	Visible	False
Image	Name	imgPtr
	Index	5
	Picture	("Icon") ' HOUR06.ICO
	Visible	False
Image	Name	imgPtr
	Index	6
	Picture	("Icon") ' HOUR07.ICO
	Visible	False
Image	Name	imgPtr
	Index	7
	Picture	("Icon") ' HOUR08.ICO
	Visible	False
Image	Name	imgPtr
	Index	8
	Picture	("Icon") ' HOUR09.ICO
	Visible	False

OBJECT	PROPERTY	SETTING
Image	Name	imgPtr
	Index	9
	Picture	("Icon") ' HOUR10.ICO
	Visible	False
Image	Name	imgPtr
	Index	10
	Picture	("Icon") ' HOUR01M.ICO
	Visible	False
Image	Name	imgPtr
	Index	11
	Picture	("Icon") ' HOUR02M.ICO
	Visible	False
Image	Name	imgPtr
	Index	12
	Picture	("Icon") ' HOUR03M.ICO
	Visible	False
Image	Name	imgPtr
	Index	13
	Picture	("Icon") ' HOUR04M.ICO
	Visible	False
Image	Name	imgPtr
	Index	14
	Picture	("Icon") ' HOUR05M.ICO
	Visible	False
Image	Name	imgPtr
	Index	15
	Picture	("Icon") ' HOUR06M.ICO
	Visible	False
Image	Name	imgPtr
	Index	16
	Picture	("Icon") ' HOUR07M.ICO
	Visible	False
Image	Name	imgPtr
	Index	17
	Picture	("Icon") ' HOUR08M.ICO
	Visible	False
Image	Name	imgPtr
	Index	18
	Picture	("Icon") ' HOUR09M.ICO

Continued on next page

129

Continued from previous page

OBJECT	PROPERTY	SETTING
	Visible	False
Image	Name	imgPtr
	Index	19
	Picture	("Icon") ' HOUR10M.ICO
	Visible	False
Timer	Name	Timer1
	Enabled	False
	Interval	200
CommandButton	Name	Command1
	Caption	"Animate Cursor"

2. Place the following code in the declarations section of Form1:

```
Option Explicit
'
' Index variable to track current cell in animation
'
    Private CustomPtr As Integer
```

3. Place the following code in the Click event for Command1:

```
Private Sub Command1_Click()
    If Not Timer1.Enabled Then
        '
        ' Turn on animation if Timer isn't enabled.
        '
        Timer1.Enabled = True
        Me.MousePointer = vbCustom
        Command1.Caption = "Stop Cursor Animation"
    Else
        '
        ' Turn off animation if Timer is enabled.
        ' Reset MouseIcon and index to position 0.
        '
        Timer1.Enabled = False
        Me.MousePointer = vbDefault
        Command1.Caption = "Animate Cursor"
        CustomPtr = 0
        Me.MouseIcon = imgPtr(CustomPtr)
    End If
End Sub
```

4. Do the actual animation when the timer fires by placing the following code in the Timer1_Timer event. Figure 2-8-2 captures one cell in the animation sequence.

```
Private Sub Timer1_Timer()
    '
```

```
   ' Set MouseIcon to current index, and increment
   ' index (looping back if neccessary).
   ' Use cursors designed for B&W if Win16, or
   ' full color cursors in Win32.
   '
   #If Win16 Then
       Me.MouseIcon = imgPtr(CustomPtr + 10)
   #ElseIf Win32 Then
       Me.MouseIcon = imgPtr(CustomPtr)
   #End If
   CustomPtr = (CustomPtr + 1) Mod 10
End Sub
```

How It Works

In this project, we animate the cursor by rotating it though a series of prepared images. Each update is triggered by a timer event. One method of performing a long task is to divide it up into smaller "chunks" of work. The routine doing the actual work maintains the state of progress (working or ready to work) and the actual progress of the process when it's working. Such an algorithm is called a state machine. Typically, state machines are driven by a timer, to allow the system time for other tasks in a cooperative multitasking environment. This allows smooth functioning of the entire system. In addition to calling the work process, a call to a cursor animation routine will tell the user that the program is truly still working.

Comments

The 32-bit version of Visual Basic 4.0 supports the use of full-color cursors, while the 16-bit version does not. For this reason, two sets of custom cursors were incorporated, each designed to look as good as possible depending on whether it was to be displayed in full color or monochrome. Note that even though the cursors designed for monochrome use color within, only black is displayed when displayed as a custom MouseIcon. Areas defined as "Screen" color in an icon editor will display whatever is beneath the cursor, but everything else will be black.

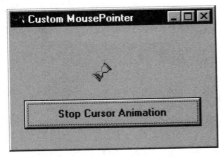

Figure 2-8-2 Animated cursor at run time

Another important point is that the center pixel of the icon will become the hot-spot for the MousePointer. Using this project, move the cursor up toward the title bar while it's animated. Notice that it changes back to an arrow as the center of the hourglass passes the division between the client space and the title bar (or crosses the border on either side).

2.9 How do I...
Automatically Resize Controls?

COMPLEXITY: INTERMEDIATE
COMPATIBILITY: VB4

Problem

I've got a form in which I want the controls to adjust when the form is resized. I've seen other programs do this, but I can't seem to get it to happen easily. How can I get the controls on my forms to resize automatically?

Technique

STRETCH performs this feat by using CStretch, a class that handles all of the resizing for the form. CStretch takes a container object (usually a form) and a list of the objects/controls in the container that need to be automatically resized and reposi-tioned. When the client container gets resized, it calls the Stretch method of Cstretch. This goes through the list of child objects and recomputes the position of each.

Because it is implemented as a class, multiple instances can be created to handle multiple containers. Multiple containers should fire the Stretch method in order of containment. In other words, the Stretch method for a form should be fired first, then the Stretch method for any containers on the form, and so forth.

Steps

Open and run STRETCH.VBP. The form (Figure 2-9-1) is a sample database entry form. It has a couple of check boxes that control the mode of stretching.

Figure 2-9-1 The STRETCH project

1. Create a new project named STRETCH.VBP. Use the Insert Class Module menu item to add a new Class module to the project. Set the new class's Name property to CStretch, and set the Creatable and Public properties to True. Then add the following code to the General section of Cstretch (this code declares the member variables for the class).

```
Option Explicit
'
' these variables define the current size of the form
' we're supporting
'
Private m_Initialized As Boolean
Private m_Mode As Integer
Private m_Width As Single
Private m_Height As Single
Private m_Client As Object
Private m_ChildObjects() As Object
```

2. Add the following code to the General section of CStretch. This is the initialization subroutine for the CStretch class. It sets the default stretch mode to both horizontal and vertical stretching, clears the width and height variables, and ensures that the class is flagged as uninitialized.

```
Private Sub Class_Initialize()
    '
    ' default to stretching both horz and vert
    '
    m_Mode = 3
    '
    ' ensure first pass through stretch routine
    ' initializes Width and Height
    '
    m_Width = -1
    m_Height = -1
    '
    ' flag to tell us if we have a valid client object
    '
    m_Initialized = False
End Sub
```

3. Add the following code to the General section of CStretch. This function returns the current setting of the stretch mode to the program.

```
Property Get Mode() As Integer
    '
    ' get current stretch mode flags
    '
    Mode = m_Mode
End Property
```

4. Add the following code to the General section of CStretch. This function sets the current stretch mode of the CStretch class.

```
Property Let Mode(NewMode As Integer)
    '
    ' set new stretch mode flags
    '
    m_Mode = NewMode
End Property
```

5. Add the following subroutine to the General section of CStretch. This function passes the current client object back to the program.

```
Property Get Client() As Object
    '
    ' get the current client object
    '
    Client = m_Client
End Property
```

6. Add the following subroutine to the General section of CStretch. This function gets the current client object from the project and sets up the class for servicing the client. The list of child objects is cleared, the initialized flag is set to True, and the current size of the client is retrieved for use when the client changes size.

```
Property Set Client(NewClient As Object)
    '
    ' set the new client object
    '
    Set m_Client = NewClient
    '
    ' clear any children from the child object list
    '
    ReDim m_ChildObjects(0 To 0)
    '
    ' set intialized flag to true, we now have a valid
    ' client object
    '
    m_Initialized = True
    '
    ' get current width and height of client object,
    ' for use next time we're stretched
    '
    m_Width = m_Client.Width
    m_Height = m_Client.Height
End Property
```

7. Add the following subroutine to the General section of CStretch. This function sets up the list of child objects. It can take either an array of objects or a single object. If something that's not an object is passed in, the function aborts. Otherwise, this function resizes the internal array of children. Then it scans through the array of objects passed in and copies them to the internal array.

```
Public Sub  AddChildren(ChildObject As Variant)
    Dim I As Integer
```

```
Dim LowerBound As Integer
Dim UpperBound As Integer
'
' if the item passed in is not an object, abort
'
If (VarType(ChildObject) And 9) = 0 And _
        Not IsObject(ChildObject) Then
    Exit Sub
End If
'
' special case for a single object
'
If (VarType(ChildObject) And 8192) = 0 Then
    '
    ' resize array and put the new child in it
    '
    ReDim m_ChildObjects(1 To 1)
    Set m_ChildObjects(1) = ChildObject
Else
    '
    ' get bounds of child array
    '
    LowerBound = LBound(ChildObject)
    UpperBound = UBound(ChildObject)
    '
    ' resize array of children to keep object
    '
    ReDim m_ChildObjects(1 To (UpperBound - LowerBound + 1))
    '
    ' loop through array and get our own copies
    ' of the objects
    '
    For I = LowerBound To UpperBound
        Set m_ChildObjects(I - LowerBound + 1) = ChildObject(I)
    Next I
    End If
End Property
```

8. Add the following subroutine to the General section of CStretch. This function does the actual resizing/repositioning work. It first checks to see if the client has been set or if the stretch mode is set to None. If either of these cases is True, the function aborts. It also ensures that the height and width have been set. Then it computes the factors, both horizontally and vertically, by which the client has been stretched. It uses these factors and traverses the list of child objects passed into the class by the Children property. Each child object is repositioned/resized using the Move method only if there has been a change in its position. This is done to reduce the amount of repainting.

Labels are handled specially by this class. Labels will not be resized to smaller than the minimum size required to display their text.

```
Public Sub Stretch()
    Dim NewLeft As Single
```

Continued on next page

Continued from previous page

```
Dim NewTop As Single
Dim NewWidth As Single
Dim NewHeight As Single
Dim LowerBound As Integer
Dim UpperBound As Integer
Dim I As Integer
Dim S As Single
Dim DeltaX As Single
Dim DeltaY As Single
Dim SaveFont As Object
'
' if we have no valid client object yet, abort
'
If Not m_Initialized Or Not m_Mode Then
    Exit Sub
End If
'
' if the current height and width are uninitialized,
' set them and exit
'
If (m_Width = -1) Or (m_Height = -1) Then
    m_Width = m_Client.Width
    m_Height = m_Client.Height
    Exit Sub
End If
'
' get factor to resize horizontally by
'
If m_Client.Width = m_Width Then
    DeltaX = 1
Else
    DeltaX = m_Client.Width / m_Width
End If
'
' get factor to resize vertically by
'
If (m_Client.Height = m_Height) Then
    DeltaY = 1
Else
    DeltaY = m_Client.Height / m_Height
End If
'
' set class Height and Width variables to
' current height and width
'
m_Width = m_Client.Width
m_Height = m_Client.Height
'
' get bounds of children list
'
LowerBound = LBound(m_ChildObjects)
UpperBound = UBound(m_ChildObjects)
'
' if there are no children, abort
'
```

```
If (LowerBound = 0) And (UpperBound = 0) Then
    Exit Sub
End If
'
' loop through all children
'
For I = LowerBound To UpperBound
    '
    ' get current size of child object
    '
    NewLeft = m_ChildObjects(I).Left
    NewTop = m_ChildObjects(I).Top
    NewWidth = m_ChildObjects(I).Width
    NewHeight = m_ChildObjects(I).Height
    '
    ' if horizontal resizing is turned on, and we
    ' have a change in the width of the client
    '
    If (m_Mode And 2) And (DeltaX <> 1) Then
        '
        ' scale the position of the child
        '
        NewLeft = NewLeft * DeltaX
        '
        ' if the child is not a label, scale the width
        '
        If Not (TypeOf m_ChildObjects(I) Is Label) Then
            NewWidth = NewWidth * DeltaX
        Else
            '
            ' if the child is a label, save the current
            ' font. labels have no TextWidth method, so
            ' we're forced to use the client's
            '
            Set SaveFont = m_Client.Font
            Set m_Client.Font = m_ChildObjects(I).Font
            '
            ' compute the minimum width using the label's font
            '
            S = m_Client.TextWidth(m_ChildObjects(I).Caption)
            '
            ' if the new height is greater than the minimum
            ' height, use it
            '
            If NewWidth * DeltaX >= S Then
                NewWidth = NewWidth * DeltaX
            End If
            '
            ' restore the client's font
            '
            Set m_Client.Font = SaveFont
        End If
    End If
    '
```

Continued on next page

Continued from previous page

```
      ' if vertical resizing is turned on, and we
      ' have a change in the height of the client
      '
      If (m_Mode And 1) And (DeltaY <> 1) Then
          '
          ' scale the position of the child
          '
          NewTop = NewTop * DeltaY
          '
          ' if the child is not a label, scale the height
          '
          If Not (TypeOf m_ChildObjects(I) Is Label) Then
              NewHeight = NewHeight * DeltaY
          Else
              '
              ' if the child is a label, save the current
              ' font. labels have no TextWidth method, so
              ' we're forced to use the client's
              '
              Set SaveFont = m_Client.Font
              Set m_Client.Font = m_ChildObjects(I).Font
              '
              ' compute the minimum height using the label's font
              '
              S = m_Client.TextHeight(m_ChildObjects(I).Caption)
              '
              ' if the new width is greater than the minimum
              ' width, use it
              '
              If NewHeight * DeltaY >= S Then
                  NewHeight = NewHeight * DeltaY
              End If
              '
              ' restore the client's font
              '
              Set m_Client.Font = SaveFont
          End If
      End If
      '
      ' if the size or position has changed, set it
      '
      If (NewLeft <> m_ChildObjects(I).Left) Or _
          (NewTop <> m_ChildObjects(I).Top) Or _
          (NewWidth <> m_ChildObjects(I).Width) Or _
          (NewHeight <> m_ChildObjects(I).Height) Then
          m_ChildObjects(I).Move NewLeft, NewTop, NewWidth, NewHeight
      End If
    Next I
End Sub
```

9. Select Form1; then create objects and set their properties as shown in Table 2-9-1.

Table 2-9-1 Objects, properties, and settings for Form1

OBJECT	PROPERTY	SETTING
Form1	Caption	"Stretch"
	Height	3060
	Width	8775
Frame	Name	Frame1
Object	Property	Setting
	Caption	"Stretch Mode"
	Height	1215
	Left	6240
	Top	1200
	Width	2175
CommandButton	Name	Command1
	Caption	"OK"
	Default	True
	Height	375
	Left	6960
	Top	240
	Width	1335
CommandButton	Name	Command2
	Cancel	True
	Caption	"Cancel"
	Height	375
	Left	6960
	Top	720
	Width	1335
TextBox	Name	Text1
	Height	285
	Left	1560
	Top	240
	Width	4455
TextBox	Name	Text2
	Height	285
	Left	1560
	Top	720
	Width	4455
TextBox	Name	Text3
	Height	285
	Left	1560
	Top	1200

Continued on next page

Continued from previous page

OBJECT	PROPERTY	SETTING
	Width	4455
TextBox	Name	Text4
	Height	285
	Left	1560
	Top	1680
	Width	615
TextBox	Name	Text5
	Height	285
	Left	4320
	Top	1680
	Width	1695
Label	Name	Label1
	Alignment	Right Justify
	Caption	"Name:"
	Height	255
	Left	120
	Top	240
	Width	1335
Label	Name	Label2
	Alignment	Right Justify
	Caption	"Address:"
	Height	255
	Left	240
	Top	720
	Width	1215
Label	Name	Label3
	Alignment	Right Justify
	Caption	"City:"
	Height	255
	Left	240
	Top	1200
	Width	1215
Label	Name	Label4
	Alignment	Right Justify
	Caption	"State:"
	Height	255
	Left	240
	Top	1680
	Width	1215

OBJECT	PROPERTY	SETTING
Label	Name	Label5
	Alignment	Right Justify
	Caption	"Zip Code:"
	Height	255
	Left	3000
	Top	1680
	Width	1215

10. Select Frame1; then create objects in it and set their properties as shown in Table 2-9-2.

Table 2-9-2 Objects, properties, and settings for Frame1

OBJECT	PROPERTY	SETTING
CheckBox	Name	Check1
	Alignment	Right Justify
	Caption	"Stretch Vertical"
	Height	255
	Left	120
	Top	720
	Width	1935
CheckBox	Name	Check2
	Alignment	Right Justify
	Caption	"Stretch Horizontal"
	Height	255
	Left	120
	Top	360
	Value	Checked
	Width	1935

11. Add the following code to the General declarations section of Form1:

```
Option Explicit
'
' define new stretch object, to handle control moves
'
Dim Stretch As New CStretch
Dim StretchFrame As New CStretch
'
' list of objects to resize/move when form size is changed
'
Dim StretchObjects() As Object
```

12. Add the following code to the General section of Form1. This code is used by the Check1 and Check2 click events. It sets the proper mode for stretching (horizontal and/or vertical).

```
Private Sub SetStretchMode()
   Dim NewMode As Integer
   '
   ' if user wants to stretch vertically
   '
   If Check1.Value Then
      '
      ' set the new mode
      '
      NewMode = 1
   Else
      NewMode = 0
   End If
   '
   ' if user wants to stretch vertically
   '
   If Check2.Value Then
      '
      ' add horizontal bit
      '
      NewMode = NewMode Or 2
   End If
   '
   ' set new stretch mode in class
   '
   Stretch.Mode = NewMode
   StretchFrame.Mode = NewMode
End Sub
```

13. Add the following code to the Click event subroutine for Check1. This subroutine makes sure that the stretch mode is set correctly.

```
Private Sub Check1_Click()
   '
   ' set new stretch mode
   '
   SetStretchMode
End Sub
```

14. Add the following code to the Click event subroutine for Check2. This subroutine makes sure that the stretch mode is set correctly.

```
Private Sub Check2_Click()
   '
   ' set new stretch mode
   '
   SetStretchMode
End Sub
```

15. Add the following code to Form1's Form_Load subroutine. This function first sets the stretch mode to Horizontal only. Then, it registers the current form with

CStretch. It fills an array with the list of objects that CStretch should handle. Finally, it registers the list of controls with CStretch.

```
Private Sub Form_Load()
    '
    ' stretch horizontally
    '
    Stretch.Mode = 2
    '
    ' stretch the current form
    '
    Set Stretch.Client = Me
    '
    ' make list of controls to stretch
    '
    ReDim StretchObjects(1 To 13)
    Set StretchObjects(1) = Label1
    Set StretchObjects(2) = Label2
    Set StretchObjects(3) = Label3
    Set StretchObjects(4) = Label4
    Set StretchObjects(5) = Label5
    Set StretchObjects(6) = Text1
    Set StretchObjects(7) = Text2
    Set StretchObjects(8) = Text3
    Set StretchObjects(9) = Text4
    Set StretchObjects(10) = Text5
    Set StretchObjects(11) = Command1
    Set StretchObjects(12) = Command2
    Set StretchObjects(13) = Frame1
    '
    ' tell stretch class which controls to stretch
    '
    Stretch.AddChildren StretchObjects
    '
    ' Setup stretch for frame
    ' stretch horizontally
    '
    StretchFrame.Mode = 2
    '
    ' stretch the frame
    '
    Set StretchFrame.Client = Frame1
    '
    ' make list of controls to stretch
    '
    ReDim StretchObjects(1 To 2)
    Set StretchObjects(1) = Check1
    Set StretchObjects(2) = Check2
    '
    ' tell stretch class which controls to stretch
    '
    StretchFrame.AddChildren StretchObjects
End Sub
```

16. Add the following code to the Resize event routine of Form1. This code uses the Stretch method of the CStretch class to resize and reposition the controls on the form.

```
Private Sub Form_Resize()
    '
    ' resize/move controls when the form size is changed
    '
    Stretch.Stretch
    StretchFrame.Stretch
End Sub
```

Figure 2-9-2 shows the results of the form after resizing.

How It Works

STRETCH relies on the functionality provided by the CStretch class. CStretch provides two methods: AddChildren and Stretch. It also has two properties: Client and Mode. Client should be set with the container object whose children you wish to automatically resize. Mode defines how CStretch resizes and repositions the child objects (0 for no resizing, 1 for vertical resizing, 2 for horizontal resizing, and 3 for both horizontal and vertical).

Select which objects to stretch by making a list of objects and passing it to the AddChildren method.

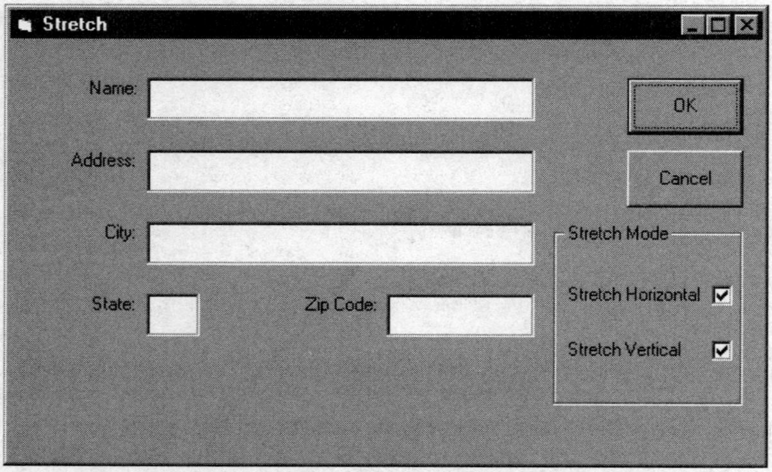

Figure 2-9-2 Form after the STRETCH project is run

When the form is resized, the program invokes CStretch's Stretch method. CStretch then scans the list of children and resizes/repositions them according to the current setting of Mode.

Comments

This How-To demonstrates how to automatically resize and reposition controls when the window is resized. The technique can also be used to handle frames and other containers. Just set the frame as the client of CStretch, and fill the child array with the controls that are in the frame. This can even be extended to make a simple splitter-window scheme.

You should enforce a minimum size for the client. Using this code, if the client is sized extremely small, the controls will not arrange properly when the client grows again.

2.10 How do I...

Pass Variables to and Return Variables from a Form?

COMPLEXITY: EASY

COMPATIBILITY: VB4 ONLY

Problem

How can I pass parameters into a form, so that it can use internal logic to customize its behavior and appearance? I'd also like to have the form return values after it's been dismissed. In Visual Basic 3.0, I had to maintain parallel code modules, and do a delicate dance to force the form to set itself up properly and then retrieve whatever data the user had entered. Is there a better way to do this in Visual Basic 4.0?

Technique

One of the perennial "flame war" topics on CompuServe and at other gatherings of Visual Basic programmers has always been the "proper" place to put code—in the form, or a code module, or a combination of both, and if in both, where the split is defined. If a form property were set before the form was loaded, even a property as innocuous as the Tag or Caption, that action would trigger the Form_Load event. The newly set property would not take effect until Form_Load had completed, so there was no way to use the new property value to determine how to proceed.

In Visual Basic 4.0, there are several new features that may finally put this issue to rest. The Form_Initialize event will be triggered when the first reference to the form is made. However, Form_Load won't fire until the form is explicitly loaded or shown. The key to this new technique is the availability of public form properties and methods, which allow data to be passed in and retrieved from an unloaded form.

Steps

Open and run LOADFRM.VBP. You will be see a file-selection dialog containing a list box of all the directories and files in your Windows directory. Select any list box entry and click either the OK or Cancel button. The routine that called the dialog retrieves your selection (or lack thereof) and reports the results. You'll be given as many chances to try different selection methods as you'd care to make.

Create the Dialog

1. Create a new project called LOADFRM.VBP. On a new form, create the objects and properties as listed in Table 2-10-1. Save it as LOADFRM.FRM. The form should look something like Figure 2-10-1.

Table 2-10-1 LOADFRM.FRM objects and properties

OBJECT	PROPERTY	SETTING
Form	Name	frmFilePick
	Appearance	1 - 3D
Label	Name	Label1
	AutoSize	True
	Left	240
	Top	210
ListBox	Name	lstPick
	Height	3735
	Left	240
	Top	480
	Width	4125
CommandButton	Name	cmdOK
	Caption	OK
	Default	True
	Height	375
	Left	675
	Top	4365
	Width	1335
CommandButton	Name	cmdCancel
	Caption	Cancel
	Cancel	True
	Height	375
	Left	2475
	Top	4365
	Width	1335

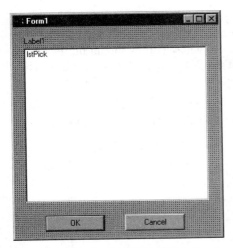

Figure 2-10-1 LOADFRM.FRM at design time

2. Insert the following code in the declarations section of frmFilePick. This declares a private data type used to store data associated with the form. Another new feature of Visual Basic 4.0 is the ability to include user-defined types (UDT's) within a form module.

```
Option Explicit
'
' Store passed and accessible data in a UDT variable
'
Private Type ControlSetupData
    cap     As String
    path    As String
    lab1    As String
    file    As String
End Type
Private m_cntls As ControlSetupData
```

3. Insert the following code in the Form_Initialize event of frmFilePick. This sets fairly benign values into the private data type stored in this form.

```
Private Sub Form_Initialize()
    '
    ' Assign innocuous values to initialize setup data
    '
    m_cntls.cap = "Make a Selection"
    m_cntls.path = ""
    m_cntls.lab1 = "Choose From:"
    m_cntls.file = ""
End Sub
```

4. Insert the following code in a new public procedure called SetData. This method is used to pass parameters to the form, prior to loading and showing it. The only required parameter is ShowPath, the directory whose entries should fill the list-box. Optionally, captions for the form and the listbox may also be passed in. The new function IsMissing is used to determine whether the optional parameters were actually received.

```
Public Sub SetData(ShowPath, Optional CaptionForm, Optional CaptionList)
    '
    ' Require path be passed in, but allow captions optionally.
    '
    m_cntls.path = Trim(ShowPath)
    If Right(m_cntls.path, 1)  "\" Then
        m_cntls.path = m_cntls.path + "\"
    End If
    If Not IsMissing(CaptionForm) Then
        m_cntls.cap = Trim(CaptionForm)
    End If
    If Not IsMissing(CaptionList) Then
        m_cntls.lab1 = Trim(CaptionList)
    End If
End Sub
```

5. Insert the following code in a new public procedure called GetData. This method is used to return values on demand to the calling routine.

```
Public Sub GetData(FileReturn, PathReturn)
    '
    ' Return requested information
    '
    FileReturn = m_cntls.file
    PathReturn = m_cntls.path
End Sub
```

6. Insert the following code in the Form_Load event of frmFilePick:

```
Private Sub Form_Load()
    '
    ' Center form on screen
    '
    Me.Move (Screen.Width - Me.Width) \ 2, (Screen.Height - Me.Height) \ 2
    '
    ' Set stored captions in place
    '
    Caption = m_cntls.cap
    Label1 = m_cntls.lab1
    '
    ' Fill lstPick with all the files and directories as requested
    '
    FillPickList
End Sub
```

7. Insert the following code in a new procedure called FillPickList. This routine searches for all the directories, then all the files, in the path that was passed in as a parameter.

```
Private Sub FillPickList()
    Dim Spec As String
    '
    ' Fill listbox with all directories in passed directory
    ' Ignore dot entries, "." and ".."
    '
    Spec = Dir(m_cntls.path & "*.*", vbDirectory)
    Do While Len(Spec)
        If InStr(Spec, ".") <> 1 Then
            If GetAttr(m_cntls.path & Spec) And vbDirectory Then
                lstPick.AddItem UCase(Spec)
            End If
        End If
        Spec = Dir
    Loop
    '
    ' Fill listbox with all files in passed directory
    '
    Spec = Dir(m_cntls.path & "*.*", vbNormal)
    Do While Len(Spec)
        lstPick.AddItem LCase(Spec)
        Spec = Dir
    Loop
End Sub
```

8. Insert the following code in the command-button click events. If the user clicks on OK and a file is selected, it will be stored in the appropriate member of the private UDT. Otherwise, a null string is stored to indicate no selection was made. At this point, it is safe to unload the form. Unloading a form does not destroy any data that is stored at the module level within it. To completely clear a form from memory, it needs to be set to Nothing.

```
Private Sub cmdOK_Click()
    '
    ' User pressed OK or Enter
    ' Return highlighted file, if any
    '
    If lstPick.ListIndex Then
        m_cntls.file = lstPick
    Else
        m_cntls.file = ""
    End If
    Unload Me
End Sub

Private Sub cmdCancel_Click()
    '
    ' User pressed Cancel or Escape ñ bail out
```

Continued on next page

Continued from previous page

```
    '
    m_cntls.file = ""
    Unload Me
End Sub
```

9. Insert the following code in the lstPick_DblClick event, to allow the user to select a file by simply double-clicking on it:

```
Private Sub lstPick_DblClick()
    '
    ' Allow selection via double-click
    '
    cmdOK_Click
End Sub
```

Create a Calling Module

10. Create a new code module by selecting Module from the Insert menu. Create a Sub Main in it, and insert the following code. Select Sub Main as the Startup Form in the Project Options dialog (loaded from the Tools menu). This routine sets up a short loop, passing parameters each time through to a new instance of frmFilePick, before showing it to gather user input. Notice that named parameters are used to pass the values to the form, and that they are not passed in the same order as declared in the form itself. After the user dismisses the form, the required values are retrieved directly from the form and it is destroyed. Each time through the loop, the user is presented with the choice made, and asked if they want to make another.

```
Sub Main()
    Dim RetFile As String
    Dim RetPath As String
    Dim msg As String
    Dim nRet As Integer
    '
    ' Loop until user quits
    '
    Do
        '
        ' Create new instance of frmFilePick
        '
        Dim Pick As New frmFilePick
        '
        ' Replace Environ("windir") with App.Path or another
        ' location, if preferred.
        '
        RetPath = Environ("windir")
        '
        ' Pass named parameters into new instance of frmFilePick,
        ' then show new form modally.
        '
        Call Pick.SetData(CaptionForm:="Listing of " & RetPath, _
```

```
                        CaptionList:="Select a File or Directory:", _
                        ShowPath:=RetPath)
    Pick.Show vbModal
    '
    ' Retrieve data from Pick and destroy it.
    '
    Call Pick.GetData(RetFile, RetPath)
    Set Pick = Nothing
    '
    ' Show we really did get data back from Pick
    '
    If Len(RetFile) Then
        If GetAttr(RetPath & RetFile) And vbDirectory Then
            msg = "You picked directory: " & RetFile
        Else
            msg = "You picked file: " & RetFile
        End If
    Else
        msg = "You didn't choose a file or directory."
    End If
    msg = msg & Chr(13) & "Pick another?"
    If MsgBox(msg, vbYesNo, "Results") = vbNo Then
        Exit Do
    End If
    Loop
End Sub
```

How It Works

To use this technique, you need not start your projects from a Sub Main rather than a normal startup form. The same basic steps can be used in any routine of any form or module:

➤ Declare a new instance of the dialog form.

➤ Pass parameters to the form using one of its methods, or assign values to the form's public properties.

➤ Show the form modally.

➤ Retrieve the return values from the form via either a method or reading the form's public properties.

➤ Destroy the new instance.

In this project, when Sub Main makes the call to Pick.SetData, the Form_Initialize event is immediately fired. As that event finishes, entry is made into the SetData routine. Another approach that may be taken to loading data into a form would be to assign values to the form's properties prior to showing it. At this point, the Form_Load event has not yet fired. SetData stores the values that are passed to it. (An interesting side note is that two of the three parameters are optional.) These values are then available for use when Form_Load is fired by the Show method performed on it in Sub Main.

After the user makes a selection, the form is internally unloaded. It's important to remember at this point that the data within the form is not destroyed by unloading it. Rather, the only way to totally remove a form and its data from memory is to set it to Nothing. Since this form was loaded modally, when it is subsequently unloaded control is returned to Sub Main. The stored values can now be retrieved, and the form destroyed.

Comments

It will be interesting to see how this new technique is accepted by a community that has argued over workarounds for the same purpose since the release of Visual Basic 1. There will no doubt be a collective sigh of relief now that this is supported; others may still argue that separation of code from forms must be maintained. But one thing is certain—the dividing line is shifting! It is no longer necessary to have a related code module in order to pass values to and return values from an independent dialog form.

3

CONTROLS

3

CONTROLS

How do I...

The standard controls that come with Visual Basic give you a solid start for building applications. However, in almost every application you will want to do some things that are not directly supported by Visual Basic, or not supported at all by the underlying Windows controls.

This chapter contains a number of techniques you can use to access the more subtle functionality in VB's custom controls, as well as some that show you how to add completely new functionality to existing controls. You will learn how to add great 3D effects to all your controls, how to create a scroll bar that isn't restricted to values less than 65536, how to create powerful, professional-looking toolbars, and much more.

A number of the How-To's in this chapter create class modules that you can use over and over again in your applications. In fact, many of these class modules are used to enhance How-To's you'll study in subsequent chapters.

Many of the techniques in this chapter use one or more Windows API calls to accomplish their magic. You will see the following Windows API calls at work:

WINDOWS API	HOW-TO'S
BitBlt	3.10
CreateCompatibleDC	3.10
DeleteDC	3.10
DeleteObject	3.14
GetObject	3.10
GetStockObject	3.14
SelectObject	3.10
SendMessage	3.5, 3.6, 3.7, 3.9, 3.14
SetParent	3.10

3.1 Drag, Drop, and Insert Items into a List Box

One popular and convenient feature of Windows programs is the ability to drag something from one list to another. Often the position where an item is dropped into the target list is important. Visual Basic doesn't provide a way to know this position, so this How-To demonstrates a simple technique for building ordered drag-and-drop lists.

3.2 Make a More Flexible PictureBox

Visual Basic provides only one option for displaying a picture in a PictureBox: the AutoSize option. When it is set to True, the PictureBox grows or shrinks to accommodate the size of the picture. Set to False, a large picture is truncated in the PictureBox. However, when viewing graphics it is nice to be able to shrink or stretch images so that they completely fill some area. In this How-To you'll learn a handy way to accomplish automatic scaling of Picture controls, as well as a convenient way to scroll pictures when they are not "sized to fit."

3.3 Indicate Focus Using 3D Effects

This How-To will demonstrate an interesting technique for indicating which control has the focus. Instead of reversing foreground/background colors, or using stark visual effects, this project alters a control's 3D effect when it has focus: it appears to pop out of the screen.

3.4 Add the 3D Effects Microsoft Forgot

Visual Basic 4.0 added the handy new Auto3D property for forms. Setting Auto3D to True causes 3D effects to be drawn around certain controls. Unfortunately, Auto3D does not work on all controls (for instance, PictureBoxes and scroll bars), and you cannot control the width of the 3D border or whether the effect is depressed or raised.

This How-To will build a powerful class module, CBorder3D, which you can use in your projects to add 3D effects to any control you choose. Also, with the CBorder3D class you can choose from several different types of 3D effects. And, best of all, the project is written using Visual Basic alone so you will be able to easily modify it to add special effects of your own.

3.5 Support All the Edit Functions for Text Boxes

Edit boxes don't support all the common edit functions for text boxes. Cut, Copy, Paste, and Delete are easily accomplished with Visual Basic alone, but there's no support for Undo. This How-To will demonstrate an easy technique you can use to add this important capability to your program's edit boxes.

3.6 Create a More Powerful ComboBox

Visual Basic handles the basics when it comes to ComboBoxes, but you may want to add a few things. When you tab into a drop-down ComboBox, it would be convenient for the list to automatically drop open. Also, it would be helpful to be able to revert back to the original value in the text box after (ESC) is pressed.

In this How-To a new Class module will be developed, which comprises all of the functionality listed above, and more.

3.7 Add a Horizontal Scroll Bar to a List Box

Visual Basic puts a vertical scroll bar in a list box whenever the number of items exceed's the height of the box, but it doesn't provide a horizontal scroll bar when the width of one or more items exceeds the width of the list box. In this project you'll develop and use a handy class module that can be used to add a horizontal scroll bar to any list box.

3.8 Make a Splitter Bar between Two Text Windows

Splitter bars are a handy way to allow users to see more than one part of a document at a time. Despite their common use in Windows applications, Visual Basic does not support them directly. Luckily, there is an easy way, as shown in this project, to make a splitter bar using a picture control and two text boxes.

3.9 Clear a Multiselect List Box in One Call

In this How-To you'll learn an API trick that quickly clears a multiselect list box. (Using Visual Basic alone, the best you can do is clear each selection, one at a time.)

3.10 Build My Own Toolbar with PictureBoxes

Toolbars are as common as command buttons in today's Windows programs. A number of toolbar VBXs and OCXs are available, and although they all have interesting and useful features, you will seldom find one that just fits all of your application's requirements.

In this How-To you will see how to build two class modules, CToolButton and CToolBar, which can be used to create a toolbar that rivals (or betters!) commercially available toolbars. Best of all, the code is VB through-and-through, so when you need something special on your toolbar you'll be able to add it to the CToolBar Class.

3.11 Use LostFocus Correctly for Data Validation

Visual Basic is not always intuitive in the order in which it fires events. For instance, when the user clicks a scroll bar on a form, the scroll bar Change event will fire before the LostFocus event for the control that had focus at the time. This is just one of the many LostFocus mysteries explored in this How-To. Followers of the CIS MSBASIC forum may recall the infamous Lost Focus and Son of Lost Focus threads. Many hundreds of often heated messages from these threads are distilled in this How-To's discussion into concise and interesting techniques that you can use to perform field-level validation. Everything is clearly explained without recourse to quantum mechanics, not even once. (Followers of the Lost Focus saga will know what I mean!)

3.12 Create a Multiselect Drag-and-Drop File Dialog

It is often necessary to allow users to work with many files at once. Using a common dialog to do this is a problem because it won't accept multiple files. This How-To shows a way to build a file open dialog box that allows drag-and-drop operations to select a number of files.

3.13 Use Long Values with Scroll Bars

Often, a project will need to use values greater than those within the short integer range for scroll bar properties. This How-To provides a way to extend the default range Visual Basic provides for scroll bars.

3.14 Guarantee Fixed-Width Font Availability

The proportional-width fonts on most Windows computers are poor at displaying (and saving to file) tables that need precise alignment because they require extensive formatting routines. Formatting fixed-width fonts is easy; however, there's no guarantee a user will have the specfic font you used on his or her machine. This How-To shows a way to create file output with fixed-width screen fonts that are guaranteed on all Windows machines.

3.1 How do I...
Drag, Drop, and Insert Items into a List Box?

COMPLEXITY: INTERMEDIATE
COMPATIBILITY: VB3 AND VB4

Problem

Sometimes my users need to select from one list of items to build another, sequenced in the order they want. For example, they might choose items in a "Stuff to Do" list, placing the items *in the desired order* into a "Do Today" list. I'd like let to the users drag and drop between list boxes, but Visual Basic doesn't directly identify the target position of an item before it is dropped.

Technique

The MouseDown, DragOver, and DragDrop methods can be used to copy items from one list box to another. The trick here is to devise a way to calculate where in the list the mouse is pointing as it drags an item over a list box. Then, as the item is dragged over the target list, the point of insertion can be shown by highlighting the target list item directly under the item being dragged. When the item is dropped into the target list, the newly inserted item can be highlighted.

Steps

Open and run INSERT.VBP. Use the left mouse button to scroll the source list. Hold down Shift and click and hold the left mouse button to drag the selected source item to the target list. Then drop the copy of the source item into the target list. Repeat the drag-and-drop several times, varying the source item and the point of insertion into the target list. Figure 3-1-1 shows this in action.

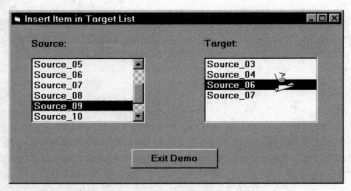

Figure 3-1-1 Drag and drop in action in the INSERT.VBP project

Notice what happens when you drop the item into an empty space after the last item in the list, and what happens when the list fills up and you want to insert an item at the end. Finally, notice that when you Shift-click on an item in the source list, the mouse changes to a hand holding a document. When you drag the mouse over the target list, it changes to a hand dropping a document. But when you drag over any other part of the form, the mouse pointer changes to the No Drop symbol. If you drop the source item anywhere but over the target list, the mouse pointer changes back to the normal arrow and nothing else happens.

1. Create a new project called INSERT.VBP. Create a form with controls as shown in Figure 3-1-2, and set objects and properties as shown in Table 3-1-1. Add Option Explicit to the general declarations section, and save the form as INSERT.FRM.

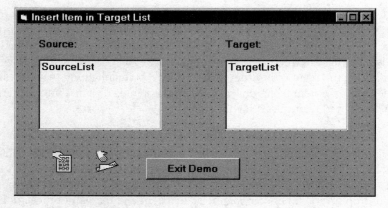

Figure 3-1-2 The design of the InsertItemForm

Table 3-1-1 INSERT.FRM form and menu properties

OBJECT	PROPERTY	SETTING
Form	Name	InsertItemForm
	Caption	"Insert Item in Target List"
Label	Name	Label1
	Caption	"****Source:"
Label	Name	Label2
	Caption	"Target:"
Listbox	Name	SourceList
Listbox	Name	TargetList
Image	DragImage	DRAG01XX.BMP
	Visible	0 'False
Image	DropImage	DROP01XX.BMP
	Visible	0 'False
Commandbutton	Name	ExitDemo
	Caption	"Exit Demo"

2. Place the following code in the Form_Load event procedure to fill the SourceList list box and highlight its first item:

```
Private Sub Form_Load()
    Dim ItemIndex As Integer
    Dim strNumber As String
    '
    ' Load 12 sample values into source list. Highlight first
    ' item in source list.
    '
    For ItemIndex = 1 To 12
        strNumber = Format(ItemIndex, "00")
        SourceList.AddItem "Source_" & strNumber
    Next ItemIndex
    SourceList.ListIndex = 0
End Sub
```

3. Place the following code in the SourceList_MouseDown event procedure to initiate dragging when the (SHIFT) key and left mouse button are pressed:

```
Private Sub SourceList_MouseDown(Button As Integer, _
                          Shift As Integer, _
                          X As Single, Y As Single)

    '
    ' If list is not empty and Shift key is pressed and Left mouse
    ' button is pressed, then set drag icon and begin dragging.
    '
    If SourceList.ListCount > 0 Then
        If Button = vbLeftButton And Shift = vbShiftMask Then
            SourceList.DragIcon = DragImage.Picture
```

Continued on next page

Continued from previous page

```
        SourceList.Drag vbBeginDrag
      End If
    End If
End Sub
```

4. Place the following code in the Form_DragOver event procedure to change the mouse pointer to a No Drop image when dragging out of the SourceList list box:

```
Private Sub Form_DragOver(source As Control, _
                          X As Single, Y As Single, _
                          State As Integer)
    '
    ' Drag is initiated only from the SourceList. As soon as the
    ' mouse leaves the source list and is dragged over the form,
    ' remove the DragIcon image and change the MousePointer to
    ' NoDrop.
    '
    MousePointer = vbNoDrop
    SourceList.DragIcon = Nothing
End Sub
```

5. Place the following code in the TargetList_DragOver event procedure to display the Drop picture, highlighting the item in the TargetList list box which the mouse is over:

```
Private Sub TargetList_DragOver(source As Control, _
                                X As Single, Y As Single, _
                                State As Integer)
    Dim BoxColumnHeight As Long
    Dim BoxIndex As Integer
    Dim OverIndex As Integer
    '
    ' This is where the item will be dropped, so set the drag
    ' icon to the drop picture.
    '
    SourceList.DragIcon = DropImage.Picture
    '
    ' Use height of one column in box to determine which column
    ' in the visible box the mouse is over. Add that to the index
    ' of the item in the top of the box to determine the index
    ' of the actual item the mouse is over.
    '
    BoxColumnHeight = TextHeight("A ")
    BoxIndex = Y \ BoxColumnHeight
    OverIndex = TargetList.TopIndex + BoxIndex
    '
    ' Highlight index that mouse is over, if any.
    '
    If OverIndex < TargetList.ListCount Then
        TargetList.ListIndex = OverIndex
    Else
        TargetList.ListIndex = -1
    End If
End Sub
```

6. To change the mouse pointer back to its default image, place the following code in these DragDrop event procedures: SourceList, Label1, Label2, ExitDemo, and Form.

```
Private Sub SourceList_DragDrop(source As Control, _
                            X As Single, Y As Single)

    '
    ' Wherever drop occurs, change MousePointer back to Default.
    '
    MousePointer = vbDefault
End Sub

Private Sub Label1_DragDrop(source As Control, _
                            X As Single, Y As Single)

    '
    ' Wherever drop occurs, change MousePointer back to Default.
    '
    MousePointer = vbDefault
End Sub

Private Sub Label2_DragDrop(source As Control, _
                            X As Single, Y As Single)

    '
    ' Wherever drop occurs, change MousePointer back to Default.
    '
    MousePointer = vbDefault
End Sub

Private Sub ExitDemo_DragDrop(source As Control, _
                            X As Single, Y As Single)

    '
    ' Wherever drop occurs, change MousePointer back to Default.
    '
    MousePointer = vbDefault
End Sub

Private Sub Form_DragDrop(source As Control, _
                            X As Single, Y As Single)

    '
    ' Wherever drop occurs, change MousePointer back to Default.
    '
    MousePointer = vbDefault
End Sub
```

7. Place the following code in the TargetList_DragDrop event procedure to insert the selected SourceList item into the TargetList list box:

```
Private Sub TargetList_DragDrop(source As Control, _
                            X As Single, Y As Single)

    Dim BoxColumnHeight As Long
    Dim BoxIndex As Integer
    Dim OverIndex As Integer
    Dim InsertIndex As Integer
    Dim BoxMaxColumns As Integer
```

Continued on next page

Continued from previous page

```
    Dim Response As Integer
    Dim InsertWhereMsg As String
    '
    ' Wherever drop occurs, change MousePointer back to Default.
    '
    MousePointer = vbDefault
    '
    ' Use height of one column in box to determine which column
    ' in the visible box the mouse is over. Add that to the index
    ' of the item in the top of the box to determine the index
    ' of the actual item the mouse is over.
    '
    BoxColumnHeight = TextHeight("A ")
    BoxIndex = Y \ BoxColumnHeight
    OverIndex = TargetList.TopIndex + BoxIndex
    '
    ' If the item to be inserted is being dropped past the end of
    ' the list, insert it at the end, otherwise insert it right
    ' before the item it's over. If it's over the last item in the
    ' list and there's no room for the user to place it past the
    ' last item in the list, ask the user whether to insert it
    ' before or after the last item in the list.
    '
    InsertIndex = IIf(OverIndex > TargetList.ListCount, _
                        TargetList.ListCount, OverIndex)
    BoxMaxColumns = TargetList.Height \ BoxColumnHeight
    If InsertIndex = (TargetList.ListCount - 1) Then
        If TargetList.ListCount >= BoxMaxColumns Then
            InsertWhereMsg _
                = "Yes to Insert After Last Item InList"
            InsertWhereMsg = InsertWhereMsg & Chr$(13)
            InsertWhereMsg = InsertWhereMsg _
                & "No to Insert Before Last Item In Target List"
            Response = MsgBox(InsertWhereMsg, vbYesNo, "What to Do?")
            If Response = vbYes Then
                InsertIndex = InsertIndex + 1
            End If
        End If
    End If
    TargetList.AddItem source.List(source.ListIndex), InsertIndex
    TargetList.ListIndex = InsertIndex
End Sub
```

8. Place the following code in the ExitDemo_Click event procedure to end the program:

```
Private Sub ExitDemo_Click()
    End
End Sub
```

How It Works

This example uses the AddItem method to add a sample list of items into the source list. It lets you drag an item from one list box into another, and the item will be inserted directly into the list at the point where it is dropped. List boxes respond to a click on an item by highlighting the item and setting its ListIndex property to correspond to that item's position in the list. This response means we can scroll the list by pressing the left mouse button and dragging through the list. Because dragging with the left mouse button means scroll the list, we need to provide the user with a different way to drag the item from the source list to the target list. With the drag mode set to manual at design time, the SourceList's MouseDown event procedure begins the drag when the user holds down the Shift key and presses the left mouse button.

When the drag begins, DragIcon is set to the image of a hand holding a piece of paper. As the mouse is dragged out of the source list and over the form, the DragIcon is set to nothing and the MousePointer is set to the No Drop image. Then when the mouse is dragged over the target list, the DragIcon is set to the image of a hand dropping a piece of paper. Whenever the mouse is released, drag mode ends and the MousePointer is returned to its default. All of this works in concert to present the user with a clear, graphical representation of what can be expected from this program's drag and drop operation.

Where Am I in the Target List?

Now let's focus on the target list box and examine how to identify which item, if any, the mouse is currently over during the DragOver event.

Visual Basic provides a couple of clues to get us started. The run-time property called TextHeight allows us to calculate the height of one column in the box (BoxColumnHeight). And it dynamically tells us the X and Y coordinates of the mouse pointer as it drags over the list box. These coordinates are passed as arguments to the DragOver event procedure. Dividing the Y coordinate by the box column height tells us which column (relative to 0) the mouse is currently being dragged over (BoxIndex).

But if we have to scroll to see all the items in the target list, the box index won't match the item index. Visual Basic comes to the rescue with the TopIndex property. TopIndex is the index of the item currently displayed at the top of the list box (relative to 0). We can calculate OverIndex as the sum of TopIndex and BoxIndex.

Now we just need to handle the possibility that the mouse may be beyond the end of the items in the list, over an empty area of the box. We use the ListCount property to determine the index of the last item in the list. This provides the information we need to highlight dynamically each item over which the mouse moves as it drags across the list box. We turn off highlighting by setting the ListIndex property to -1 when OverIndex is greater than the last item in the list. Otherwise, we highlight by setting the ListIndex property to OverIndex.

Inserting into the Target List

The TargetList object's DragDrop event makes use of the same calculations as its Drag Over event to determine which item, if any, the mouse is over when the item is dropped. We need to specify an index in order for the AddItem method to *insert* the item in the desired position. If the mouse is over an empty area beyond the last item in the list, we simply set the point of insertion (InsertIndex) to one more than the index of the last item in the list. If the mouse is over an item in the list, we can set the point of insertion to the item the mouse is over (OverIndex). We must also allow for the possibility that the list box is full. When the user drags to the last item in list box, we'll need to ask if they want to insert the new item before or after the last item.

In any case, after adding the item to the list, there's one last thing to do: set the ListIndex property to the value of the insertion index. This causes the inserted item to be highlighted in the list.

Comments

If this were a real application, we would not use the message box to ask the user where to insert the item. The Yes and No buttons are not clear enough. We would customize a form to provide button choices labeled Before and After.

3.2 How do I...
Make a More Flexible PictureBox?

COMPLEXITY: INTERMEDIATE
COMPATIBILITY: VB4 ONLY

Problem

Visual Basic provides only one option for displaying a picture in a PictureBox, the AutoSize option. With AutoSize set to True, the PictureBox grows or shrinks to accommodate the size of the picture. Set to False, a large picture is truncated in the PictureBox. These behaviors rarely meet my needs. Is there a way to keep the PictureBox a fixed size and have the picture compress or stretch to fit? That's what I'm usually looking for, and I want it to happen without distorting the picture so it looks unnatural. I'd like to see the true size and proportions of the picture in the PictureBox, and be able to scroll the picture when necessary to see all of it, rendered in accurate size and proportion.

Technique

A class file, which we'll call CPicBox, provides a clean way to generalize the additional code that is needed to achieve these new PictureBox capabilities.

CPicBox uses two PictureBox controls, a horizontal scroll bar and a vertical scroll bar, to work its magic. It needs the name of a picture to load, and the desired viewing option. The calling program requires minimal code to provide these to CPicBox, and CPicBox takes care of the rest. It paints the picture into the container, appropriate to the selected viewing option and size of the picture, and it displays either or both of the scroll bars when needed.

Steps

Open and run PICBOX.VBP. Try out each of the pictures that come with this How-To to see what happens with small, wide, tall, and big pictures. Notice how the tall and wide pictures are significantly distorted when the picture is sized to fit. Also watch how each scroll bar appears only when needed for the true size of the picture. Figure 3-2-1 shows the form in action.

1. Create a new project called PICBOX.VBP. Create a form with controls as shown in Figure 3-2-2. Set form objects and properties as shown in Table 3-2-1, and save the form as PICBOX.FRM.

Figure 3-2-1 The PICBOX form in action

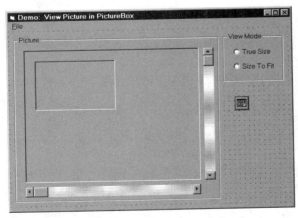

Figure 3-2-2 Arrangement of controls for the PICBOX.VBP project

Table 3-2-1 PICBOX.FRM form properties

OBJECT	PROPERTY	SETTING
Form	Name	PicBoxForm
	Caption	"Demo: View Picture in PictureBox"
	ScaleMode	3 'Pixel
Frame	Name	PictureFrame
	Caption	"Picture"
PictureBox	Name	Picture1
	ScaleMode	3 'Pixel
PictureBox	Name	Picture2
	ScaleMode	3 'Pixel
HScrollBar	Name	HScroll1
	LargeChange	10
	Max	100
	Min	1
	Value	0
	Visible	0 'False
VScrollBar	Name	VScroll1
	LargeChange	10
	Max	100
	Min	1
	Value	0
	Visible	0 'False
Frame	Name	OptFrame
	Caption	"View Mode"
OptionButton	Name	ViewOpt
	Caption	"Size To Fit"
	Index	1
OptionButton	Name	ViewOpt
	Caption	"True Size"
	Index	0
CommonDialog	Name	CommonDialog1
Menu	Name	FileMenu
	Caption	"&File"
Menu	Name	FileOpenCmd
	Caption	"&Open"
Menu	Name	sep
	Caption	"-"
Menu	Name	ExitCmd
	Caption	"E&xit"

2. Place the following code at the beginning of the PICBOX.FRM. This defines an object variable called CPic1 which is based on CPicBox, a class object that adds flexibility to the Visual Basic PictureBox. The code also defines constant values for sizing images in the PictureBox.

```
Option Explicit
'
' Values for how to fit image in PictureBox.
'
Const cTrueSize As Integer = 0
Const cSizePicToFit As Integer = 1
'
' CPicBox class object is a smarter PictureBox.
'
Dim CPic1 As New CPicBox
```

3. Place the following code in the Form_Load event procedure. This code centers the form and hides the trick PictureBox contained in the main PictureBox by moving its top-left corner to the bottom-right corner of the main PictureBox. The subroutine also initializes the CPicBox class container, Picture, Hscroll, and Vscroll objects. It defaults the viewing mode for our smart PictureBox to True Size.

```
Private Sub Form_Load()
    '
    ' Center the form and hide Picture2 which is contained in
    ' Picture1 by moving it to the bottom right of Picture1.
    '
    Move (Screen.Width - Width) \ 2, (Screen.Height - Height) \ 2
    Picture2.Move Picture1.Width, Picture1.Left
    '
    ' Set the control components of the CPicBox class for CPic1.
    '
    Set CPic1.Container = Picture1
    Set CPic1.Picture = Picture2
    Set CPic1.HScroll = HScroll1
    Set CPic1.VScroll = VScroll1
    '
    ' Start out with the PictureBox viewing choice set to
    ' TrueSize. This triggers the ViewOpt_Click event procedure.
    '
    ViewOpt(cTrueSize) = True
End Sub
```

4. Place the following code in the ViewOpt_Click event procedure. This procedure sets the viewing mode for the sample PictureBox. When the viewing mode is set to True Size, the full size of the picture can be viewed in the PictureBox, with either or both scroll bars available as needed to see the whole thing. When the

viewing mode is set to Size to Fit, the selected picture is stretched or compressed as needed to fit into the exact size of the PictureBox.

```
Private Sub ViewOpt_Click(Index As Integer)
    '
    ' Set the current PictureBox viewing choice for CPic1.
    '
    CPic1.ViewMode = Index
End Sub
```

5. Place the following code in the VScroll1_Change event procedure. This procedure triggers a subroutine in the CPicBox class file that handles adjustment of the PictureBox image based on the new vertical scroll bar value.

```
Private Sub VScroll1_Change()
    '
    ' Let CPic1's class file know the vertical scroll value has
    ' changed.
    '
    CPic1.VScroll_Change
End Sub
```

6. Place the following code in the HScroll1_Change event procedure. This procedure triggers a subroutine in the CPicBox class file that handles adjustment of the PictureBox image based on the new horizontal scroll bar value.

```
Private Sub HScroll1_Change()
    '
    ' Let CPic1's class file know the horizontal scroll value has
    ' changed.
    '
    CPic1.HScroll_Change
End Sub
```

7. Place the following code in the FileOpenCmd_Click event procedure to support selection of an image via the File Open command. This procedure displays the File Open common dialog box with filter and file name ready to select a bitmap file type. If any error occurs, including the primary error condition, the procedure skips sending the filename to the CPicBox class file and clicks the Cancel button on the File Open dialog box.

```
Private Sub FileOpenCmd_Click()
    '
    ' Provide ShowOpen common dialog so user can select a picture
    ' for viewing.
    '
    On Error Resume Next
    CommonDialog1.CancelError = True
    CommonDialog1.Filter = "*.BMP"
    CommonDialog1.FileName = "*.BMP"
    CommonDialog1.ShowOpen
    If Err.Number = 0 Then
```

```
      CPic1.PicFileName = CommonDialog1.FileName
   End If
End Sub
```

8. Place the following code in the ExitCmd_Click event procedure, to support exiting the program from the menu bar:

```
Private Sub ExitCmd_Click()
   '
   ' Exit the program.
   '
   End
End Sub
```

9. Use the Insert Class menu item to create a new class module and save it as PICBOX.CLS. Name it CPicBox, and put the following code at the beginning of the file. This code sets constant values for the two types of PictureBox view modes supported by the CPicBox class. It also defines each of the class property variables.

```
Option Explicit
'
' Valid values for ViewMode.
'
Const cTrueSize As Integer = 0
Const cSizePicToFit As Integer = 1
'
' These variables define the CPicBox class file and options.
'
Private m_Initialized As Boolean
Private m_Container As Object
Private m_HScroll As Object
Private m_VScroll As Object
Private m_Picture As Object
Private m_PicFileName As String
Private m_ViewMode As Integer
```

10. Continue by adding the following code to the General section of CPicBox. This code sets variables needed to perform the PaintPicture method, to paint some or all of the selected picture into the PictureBox container.

```
'
' Container size variables.
'
Private m_CWidth As Integer
Private m_CHeight As Integer
'
' Picture position and size variables.
'
Private m_PLeft As Integer
Private m_PTop As Integer
Private m_PWidth As Integer
Private m_PHeight As Integer
'
```

Continued on next page

Continued from previous page

```
' PaintPicture Destination size variables.
'
Private m_DWidth As Integer
Private m_DHeight As Integer
'
' PaintPicture Source position and size variables.
'
Private m_SLeft As Integer
Private m_STop As Integer
Private m_SWidth As Integer
Private m_SHeight As Integer
```

11. Add the following code to the General section of CPicBox. The Set Container subroutine gets and stores the current container object from the calling program, making sure it is of the PictureBox control type. This subroutine saves the PictureBox width and height, which will be used in subsequent calculations to improve processing speed. It also performs the CheckObjectsSet subroutine that sets an initialized flag to True when all necessary components have been set by the calling program.

```
Public Property Set Container(NewContainer As Object)
    '
    ' Set the new Container object which must be a PictureBox.
    ' Save its position and size in variables for speedier
    ' processing. Check if all objects have been set (i.e., all
    ' required initialization done).
    '
    If TypeOf NewContainer Is PictureBox Then
        Set m_Container = NewContainer
        m_CWidth = m_Container.ScaleWidth
        m_CHeight = m_Container.ScaleHeight
        If Not m_Initialized then CheckObjectsSet
    Else
        MsgBox NewContainer.Name _
            & " is not a PictureBox. Cannot make it a new" _
            & " container. Ignored.", , "CPicBox Class Error"
    End If
End Property
```

12. Add the following code to the General section of CPicBox. The Get Container subroutine allows the calling program to read the current value of the Container property.

```
Public Property Get Container() As Object
    '
    ' Return the current container object.
    '
    Set Container = m_Container
End Property
```

13. Add the following code to the General section of CPicBox. The Set Picture subroutine gets and stores the current picture object from the calling program,

making sure it is of the PictureBox control type. The subroutine sets AutoSize to True so the PictureBox can size to fit any picture that gets loaded. The PictureBox initial width and height are saved, for use in subsequent calculations to improve processing speed. Set Picture also performs the CheckObjectsSet subroutine that sets an initialized flag to True when all necessary components have been set by the calling program.

```
Public Property Set Picture(NewPicture As Object)
    '
    ' Set the new Picture object which must be a PictureBox. Set
    ' AutoSize to True to allow it to resize with each new picture
    ' it's loaded with. Set variables for its size for speedier
    ' processing. Check if all objects have been set (i.e., all
    ' required initialization done).
    '
    If TypeOf NewPicture Is PictureBox Then
        Set m_Picture = NewPicture
        m_Picture.AutoSize = True
        m_PWidth = m_Picture.Width
        m_PHeight = m_Picture.Height
        If Not m_Initialized then CheckObjectsSet
    Else
        MsgBox NewPicture.Name _
            & " is not a PictureBox." _
            & " Cannot make it a new viewable picture." _
            & " Ignored.", , "CPicBox Class Error"
    End If
End Property
```

14. Add the following code to the General section of CPicBox. The Get Picture subroutine allows the calling program to read the current value of the Picture property.

```
Public Property Get Picture() As Object
    '
    ' Return the current Picture object.
    '
    Set Picture = m_Picture
End Property
```

15. Add the following code to the General section of CPicBox. The Let PicFileName subroutine gets and stores the current picture filename, loads the Picture object that AutoSizes, and updates variables for the picture's new width and height. After checking if initialization is done, the subroutine clears the container and performs a routine to paint the new picture into the container.

```
Public Property Let PicFileName(NewPicFileName As String)
    '
    ' Get a new PicFileName and, if it's valid, load it into
    ' the Picture object. Update variables for the new Width
    ' and Height for speedier processing. Check if all objects
    ' have been set (i.e., all required initialization done).
    ' Then clear the container and repaint it with new picture.
```

Continued on next page

Continued from previous page

```
    '
    On Error Resume Next
    m_Picture.Picture = LoadPicture(NewPicFileName)
    If Err.Number = 0 Then
        m_PicFileName = NewPicFileName
        m_PWidth = m_Picture.ScaleWidth
        m_PHeight = m_Picture.ScaleHeight
        If Not m_Initialized then CheckObjectsSet
        m_Container.Cls
        PaintContainerWithPic
    Else
        MsgBox NewPicFileName & " is not a valid format.", _
            , "CPicBox Class Error"
    End If
End Property
```

16. Add the following code to the General section of CPicBox. The Get PicFileName subroutine allows the calling program to read the current value of the PicFileName property.

```
Public Property Get PicFileName() As String
    '
    ' Return the current PicFileName.
    '
    PicFileName = m_PicFileName
End Property
```

17. Add the following code to the General section of CPicBox. The Set HScroll subroutine gets and stores the current HScroll object from the calling program, making sure it is a horizontal scroll bar control type. The subroutine also performs the CheckObjectsSet subroutine that sets an initialized flag to True when all necessary components have been set by the calling program.

```
Public Property Set HScroll(NewHScroll As Object)
    '
    ' Set the new horizontal scroll object which must be a
    ' horizontal scroll bar control. Check if all objects have
    ' been set (i.e., all required initialization done).
    '
    '
    If TypeOf NewHScroll Is HScrollBar Then
        Set m_HScroll = NewHScroll
        If Not m_Initialized then CheckObjectsSet
    Else
        MsgBox NewHScroll.Name _
                & " is not an HScrollBar." _
                & " Ignored.", , "CPicBox Class Error"
    End If
End Property
```

18. Add the following code to the General section of CPicBox. The Get HScroll subroutine allows the calling program to read the current value of the HScroll property.

```
Public Property Get HScroll() As Object
    '
    ' Return the current horizontal scroll bar object.
    '
    Set HScroll = m_HScroll
End Property
```

19. Add the following code to the General section of CPicBox. The Set VScroll sub-routine gets and stores the current VScroll object from the calling program, making sure it is a vertical scroll bar control type. The subroutine also performs the CheckObjectsSet subroutine that sets an initialized flag to True when all necessary components have been set by the calling program.

```
Public Property Set VScroll(NewVScroll As Object)
    '
    ' Set the new vertical scroll object which must be a vertical
    ' scroll bar control. Check if all objects have been set
    ' (i.e., all required initialization done).
    '
    If TypeOf NewVScroll Is VScrollBar Then
        Set m_VScroll = NewVScroll
        If Not m_Initialized then CheckObjectsSet
    Else
        MsgBox NewVScroll.Name _
                & " is not an VScrollBar." _
                & " Ignored.", , "CPicBox Class Error"
    End If
End Property
```

20. Add the following code to the General section of CPicBox. The Get VScroll subroutine allows the calling program to read the current value of the VScroll property.

```
Public Property Get VScroll() As Object
    '
    ' Return the current vertical scroll bar object.
    '
    Set VScroll = m_VScroll
End Property
```

21. Add the following code to the General section of CPicBox. The Let ViewMode subroutine gets and stores the current view mode for the picture. After checking if initialization is done, the subroutine clears the container and performs a routine to paint the new picture into the container.

```
Public Property Let ViewMode(NewViewMode As Integer)
    '
    ' Set the new viewing mode (true size or size to fit). Check
    ' if all objects have been set (i.e., all required
    ' initialization done).
    '
    m_ViewMode = NewViewMode
    If Not m_Initialized then CheckObjectsSet
```

Continued on next page

Continued from previous page

```
    '
    ' Whenever a new viewing mode is set, clear the container and
    ' repaint it with the current picture.
    '
    m_Container.Cls
    PaintContainerWithPic
End Property
```

22. Add the following code to the General section of CPicBox. The Get ViewMode subroutine allows the calling program to read the current value of the ViewMode property.

```
Public Property Get ViewMode() As Integer
    '
    ' Return the current viewing mode (true size or size to fit).
    '
    ViewMode = m_ViewMode

End Property
```

23. Add the following subroutine to the General section of CPicBox. The CheckObjectsSet subroutine checks if all necessary class file components have been set by the calling program. When they are, it sets the initialized flag to True.

```
Private Sub CheckObjectsSet()
    '
    ' When all the control components are established, set the
    ' initialized flag to true.
    '
    On Error Resume Next
    If TypeOf m_Container Is PictureBox _
    And TypeOf m_Picture Is PictureBox _
    And TypeOf m_HScroll Is HScrollBar _
    And TypeOf m_VScroll Is VScrollBar _
    And (m_ViewMode = 0 Or m_ViewMode = 1) _
    And m_PicFileName<>"" Then
        If Err.Number = 0 Then
            m_Initialized = True
        End If
    End If
End Sub
```

24. Add the following subroutine to the General section of CPicBox. Assuming all components have been set, the Paint Container with the subroutine paints the picture into the container. If the selected viewing mode is Size to Fit, the PaintPicture method is used to paint the entire image into the entire container. PaintPicture takes care of compressing or stretching the picture as needed to fit. If the selected viewing mode is True Size, the calculations get a bit more complicated—but the upshot is that a section of the picture equal to the size of the container gets painted into the container. If it's smaller than the container, the entire picture is painted. Where the picture width and/or height exceed the container, the scroll bar settings are used to determine proportionately what slice of the picture to paint.

```
Private Sub PaintContainerWithPic()
    '
    ' Don't try to paint picture into container until all
    ' components have been established.
    '
    If m_Initialized<>True Then
        Exit Sub
    End If
    '
    ' Paint picture into container, sized to fit.
    '
    If m_ViewMode = cSizePicToFit Then
        '
        ' Paint picture into entire container, stretching or
        ' compressing it, if necessary, to fit.
        '
        m_Container.PaintPicture m_Picture.Picture, _
            0, 0, m_CWidth, m_CHeight
        m_HScroll.Visible = False
        m_VScroll.Visible = False
    '
    ' Paint picture into container at true size, showing as much
    ' as is possible given the size of the container.
    '
    Else 'm_ViewMode = cTrueSize
        '
        ' If picture is wider than container, calculate where to
        ' start painting from the left by multiplying a point in
        ' the valid range by the percent scrolled. Width of
        ' painting should fill container.
        '
        If m_PWidth > m_CWidth Then
            m_DWidth = m_CWidth
            m_SLeft = (m_PWidth - m_CWidth) _
                      * (m_HScroll.Value / m_HScroll.Max)
            m_SWidth = m_CWidth
            m_HScroll.Visible = True
        '
        ' If picture is not wider than container, paint beginning
        ' from left most point in picture for width of picture.
        '
        Else
            m_DWidth = m_PWidth
            m_SLeft = 0
            m_SWidth = m_PWidth
            m_HScroll.Visible = False
        End If
        '
        ' If picture is taller than container, calculate where to
        ' start painting from the top by multiplying a point in the
        ' valid range by the percent scrolled. Height of painting
        ' should fill container.
        '
        If m_PHeight > m_CHeight Then
            m_DHeight = m_CHeight
```

Continued on next page

177

Continued from previous page

```
            m_STop = (m_PHeight - m_CHeight) _
                     (m_VScroll.Value / m_VScroll.Max)
            m_SHeight = m_CHeight
            m_VScroll.Visible = True
        '
        ' If picture is not taller than container, paint beginning
        ' from topmost point in picture for height of picture.
        '
        Else
            m_DHeight = m_PHeight
            m_STop = 0
            m_SHeight = m_PHeight
            m_VScroll.Visible = False
        End If
        '
        ' Do the actual paint for variables set based on ViewMode
        ' set to true size.
        '
        m_Container.PaintPicture m_Picture.Picture, _
            0, 0, m_DWidth, m_DHeight, _
            m_SLeft, m_STop, m_SWidth, m_SHeight
    End If
End Sub
```

25. Add the following subroutines to the General section of CPicBox. The VScroll_Change and HScroll_Change subroutines cause a new slice of the picture to be painted into the CPicBox container whenever scrolling movement is recorded. Note that a horizontal scroll bar is visible only when the width of the picture exceeds the width of the container. Likewise, a vertical scroll bar is visible only when the height of the picture exceeds the height of the container.

```
Public Sub VScroll_Change()
    '
    ' Whenever the vertical scroll bar records a change, repaint
    ' the picture.
    '
    PaintContainerWithPic
End Sub

Public Sub HScroll_Change()
    '
    ' Whenever the horizontal scroll bar records a change, repaint
    ' the picture.
    '
    PaintContainerWithPic
End Sub
```

How It Works

To work its magic, CPicBox needs two PictureBoxes. One is visible and is painted with the whole picture or a portion of the picture for display. The second PictureBox is contained within the first, but it's hidden by moving its top-left corner to the bottom-right corner of the container PictureBox. The second PictureBox stores the entire picture and is the source for the picture when it needs to be painted or repainted into the container. Both horizontal and vertical scroll bars are needed; they are made visible when the picture is larger than the container and scrolling is used to see it all.

The calling program passes these four controls to the CPicBox class file. It also passes a view mode, indicating whether the picture should be shown in its entirety or sized to fit the PictureBox. Last but not least, the calling program passes the fully qualified file name of the picture to be displayed.

With all the components in hand, the class file paints all or a portion of the picture into the container. The PaintPicture method is key to making this work. It's new to Visual Basic 4.0 and provides some of the capabilities of the Windows API functions, BitBlt and StretchBlt. Horizontal and vertical scroll percents are taken into account when determining the exact segment of the picture to paint when its width or height exceeds the container size.

Comments

CPicBox provides a handy way to encapsulate PictureBox controls and provides the functionality that they do usually have. You could enhance the CPicBox class in a number of ways. For instance, you might add methods such as Edit, Copy, and Paste so that it would be easy to use the Clipboard with objects from the CPicBox class.

3.3 How do I...
Indicate Focus Using 3D Effects?

COMPLEXITY: EASY
COMPATIBILITY: VB3 OR VB4

Problem

I'd like to somehow call attention to the active text box on my data entry forms, but not with the gaudy effects I've seen in some applications. Rather than reversing the foreground and background colors, I'm looking for something a little more elegant and a lot less distracting. Is there some sort of 3D effect I could use?

Technique

The current style for text boxes and most other controls is a "sunken" (or depressed) 3D appearance. To draw more attention to the text box with focus, a common technique is to raise it while leaving the other boxes sunken. This project will show you a simple way to do that by drawing the desired effect directly on the form. Once you see how easy it is to add 3D effects this way, you will be tempted to modify these routines to use for all such work, rather than relying on custom controls.

Steps

Open and run FOCUS3D.VBP. A form with eight text boxes arranged in an array appears. Tab among them, or use the mouse to change focus. Notice the raised effect that the current (active) control assumes, as shown in Figure 3-3-1. Press the Quit button to exit.

1. Create a new project called FOCUS3D.VBP. Create a new form with the objects and properties listed in Table 3-3-1. Save it as FOCUS3D.FRM. The position and sizing of the text boxes isn't important; the idea is to use a control array and position the array in a sequential pattern.

Table 3-3-1 Objects and properties of FOCUS3D.FRM

OBJECT	PROPERTY	SETTING
Form	Name	Form1
	Appearance	1 - 3D
	AutoRedraw	False
	Caption	"3-D Focus Tracking"
TextBox	Name	Text1
	Index	0
	TabIndex	0
TextBox	Name	Text1
	Index	1
	TabIndex	1
TextBox	Name	Text1
	Index	2
	TabIndex	2
TextBox	Name	Text1
	Index	3
	TabIndex	3
TextBox	Name	Text1
	Index	4
	TabIndex	4
TextBox	Name	Text1
	Index	5
	TabIndex	5
TextBox	Name	Text1
	Index	6
	TabIndex	6
TextBox	Name	Text1
	Index	7

OBJECT	PROPERTY	SETTING
	TabIndex	7
CommandButton	Name	Command1
	Cancel	True
	Caption	Quit
	TabIndex	8

2. Using the Insert Module menu, add a code module to the project. Assign its Name property as Cheap3D, and save it as CHEAP3D.BAS. Insert the following code in the Declarations section of Cheap3D:

```
Option Explicit
'
' Private variables to store TwipsPerPixel for both
' X and Y dimensions rather than repeatedly reference
' the Screen object.
'
Private tppX As Integer
Private tppY As Integer
```

3. In Cheap3D, create a public subroutine called Initialize and insert the following code in it. Although Visual Basic 4.0 now supports an Initialize event for forms and class modules, it does not yet provide that support for code modules. This Cheap3D routine must be the first one called when the module is loaded. It's used to store the value for TwipsPerPixel in both dimensions for future reference. (Avoiding repeated reference to object properties is a classic optimization technique.)

```
Public Sub Initialize()
    '
    ' Store TwipsPerPixel for both X & Y to save time later
    '
    tppX = Screen.TwipsPerPixelX
    tppY = Screen.TwipsPerPixelY
End Sub
```

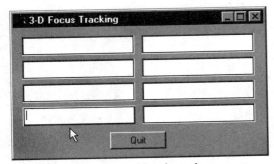

Figure 3-3-1 A raised border indicates text box with focus

4. In Cheap3D, create a public subroutine called Raised and insert the following code in it. A raised 3D border is drawn around the control that's passed to this routine. There are a number of little optimizations used here. First, the routine is declared as Static to preserve the local variables between calls. Their previous values are not reused, but this avoids having to allocate and deallocate space for them with every call. The second optimization is to reference properties of the passed control only once, by assigning them to local variables. Every reference to a control property takes more time than a similar reference to a variable.

```
Public Static Sub Raised(Cntl As Control)
    Dim pX1 As Integer
    Dim pY1 As Integer
    Dim pX2 As Integer
    Dim pY2 As Integer
    '
    ' Access properties just once, and set aside
    '
    pX1 = Cntl.Left - tppX
    pX2 = pX1 + Cntl.Width + tppX
    pY1 = Cntl.Top - tppY
    pY2 = pY1 + Cntl.Height + tppY
    '
    ' Draw shadow around control
    '
    Cntl.Parent.Line (pX1, pY1)-(pX2, pY2), vb3DShadow, B
    '
    ' Add one pixel to length of highlights, and
    ' Draw highlight along top and left edges.
    '
    Cntl.Parent.Line (pX1, pY1)-(pX2 + tppX, pY1), vb3DHighLight
    Cntl.Parent.Line (pX1, pY1)-(pX1, pY2 + tppY), vb3DHighLight
End Sub
```

5. In Cheap3D, create a public subroutine called Sunken and insert the following code in it. This routine is almost identical to Raised, except that it draws the more typical sunken border around the control that's passed into it.

```
Public Static Sub Sunken(Cntl As Control)
    Dim pX1 As Integer
    Dim pY1 As Integer
    Dim pX2 As Integer
    Dim pY2 As Integer
    '
    ' Access properties just once, and set aside
    '
    pX1 = Cntl.Left - tppX
    pX2 = pX1 + Cntl.Width + tppX
    pY1 = Cntl.Top - tppY
    pY2 = pY1 + Cntl.Height + tppY
    '
    ' Draw shadow around control
    '
    Cntl.Parent.Line (pX1, pY1)-(pX2, pY2), vb3DShadow, B
```

```
'
' Add one pixel to length of highlights, and
' Draw highlight along bottom and right edges.
'
    Cntl.Parent.Line (pX2, pY1)-(pX2, pY2 + tppY), vb3DHighLight
    Cntl.Parent.Line (pX1, pY2)-(pX2 + tppX, pY2), vb3DHighLight
End Sub
```

6. Insert the following code in the Initialize event of Form1. This event, which is fired before the Form_Load event, is used to also initialize the Cheap3D module.

```
Private Sub Form_Initialize()
    '
    ' Initialize the 3D module
    '
    Cheap3D.Initialize
End Sub
```

7. Insert the following code in the Text1_GotFocus event of Form1. One quick call to the Cheap3D.Raised method is all that's required to give the current control a unique raised appearance.

```
Private Sub Text1_GotFocus(Index As Integer)
    '
    ' Highlight this control by reversing the
    ' default 3D look -- raise it.
    '
    Cheap3D.Raised Text1(Index)
End Sub
```

8. Insert the following code in the Text1_LostFocus event of Form1. The text box must be returned to its default state when it loses focus to another control.

```
Private Sub Text1_LostFocus(Index As Integer)
    '
    ' Return control to default 3D appearance -- sunken
    '
    Cheap3D.Sunken Text1(Index)
End Sub
```

9. Insert the following code in the Form_Paint event of Form1. The custom 3D look that's been painted on the form with Cheap3D will need refreshing whenever the form itself needs to be refreshed. Here, the ActiveControl is checked to see whether it's a text box and should therefore be raised. Any number of tests may be applied, depending on the circumstances of different projects. If DoEvents isn't called before the Cheap3D method, the form doesn't take the opportunity to refresh its Auto3D effects, but rather waits until Cheap3D is done—which nullifies the effect we're after.

```
Private Sub Form_Paint()
    '
    ' See if the current control is one that should
    ' be highlighted by raising it.
    '
```

Continued on next page

Continued from previous page

```
    If TypeOf Me.ActiveControl Is text box Then
        '
        ' Allow the Auto3D to do its "stuff", then
        ' raise the current control.
        '
        DoEvents
        Cheap3D.Raised Me.ActiveControl
    End If
End Sub
```

10. Insert the following code in the Command1_Click event of Form1. This is used to terminate the project.

```
Private Sub Command1_Click()
    Unload Me
End Sub
```

11. Insert the following code in the Text1_KeyPress event of Form1. Though not in fact related to this specific technique, this is a slick way to allow the user an additional option in moving among text boxes. Whenever (ENTER) is pressed, (TAB) is substituted for it.

```
Private Sub Text1_KeyPress(Index As Integer, KeyAscii As Integer)
    '
    ' Allow user to move between text boxes with Enter
    ' in addition to Tab.
    '
    If KeyAscii = vbKeyReturn Then
        KeyAscii = 0
        SendKeys "{Tab}"
    End If
End Sub
```

How It Works

One of the nicer new interface touches added in Visual Basic 4.0 is the Auto3D property for forms. By setting this property to True, most of the standard controls assume the sunken 3D appearance. Taking advantage of this new feature, this project offers another option for calling attention to the current control. Whenever one of the "data entry" controls on the form receives focus, a raised 3D border is drawn around it. When it loses focus, the default sunken border is drawn. The custom effect must be reapplied whenever the form needs to be refreshed.

To use this method with Visual Basic 3.0, you will need to draw both types of effects. The Form_Paint event could cycle through the Controls collection, drawing a sunken border around each and then drawing only the raised border around only the ActiveControl. Of course, the new built-in constants would also need to be replaced with the appropriate values.

Comments

Reversing the 3D effect is a more subtle way to call attention to the active control. The methods presented in this project can be expanded to offer nearly any imaginable 3D effect—without the resource consumption a custom control would introduce.

3.4 How do I...
Add the 3D Effects Microsoft Forgot?

COMPLEXITY: INTERMEDIATE
COMPATIBILITY: VB4 ONLY

Problem

I like the 3D effects the new Appearance property Visual Basic gives to forms and controls, but I need more. For one thing, not all the controls are supported; and those that are supported have only one style. I'd like to be able to selectively add or remove the 3D properties for controls, have a variety of styles such as sunken and raised, add 3D effects around the edge of my forms, or even draw my own 3D frames. What's the easiest way to do this?

Technique

This How-To develops the CBorder3D class module and then demonstrates some of the many wonderful effects it offers. Other examples of its use will be scattered through the remainder of the book. The CBorder3D object will support a wide variety of properties, as well as a method that is useful for achieving many interesting border effects around your controls, forms, or just about anywhere. Though CBorder3D exposes a total of 15 properties, at its simplest it requires as few as two properties to be set. All effects are produced with native Visual Basic graphic methods and are fully encapsulated within the class module.

The name of the demonstration project is Cheap3D. (This name isn't meant to reflect on the value of the class module, but to suggest its potential savings!) When 3D effects are achieved through the use of a DLL or VBX/OCX, system resources can disappear at an alarming rate. With the CBorder3D class, the impact on system resources is next to nil since only Visual Basic code is used to create 3D effects. Also, there will be no impact on your wallet, since you won't have to buy a custom control.

Steps

Open and run CHEAP3D.VBP. The main form has its Appearance property set to True, and contains at least one of every standard control that ships with Visual Basic 4.0. Most of the controls have been left entirely in their default states, which would include having their Appearance property also set to 3D when supported. As shown in Figure 3-4-1, the scroll bars and the labels don't display any 3D effects.

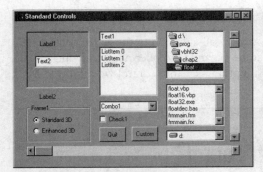

Figure 3-4-1 Default 3D Appearance effects offered by Visual Basic 4.0

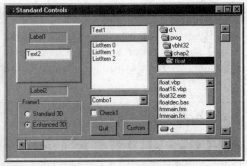

Figure 3-4-2 Enhanced 3D standard effects offered by CBorder3D

Select the Enhanced 3D option button. Now, the labels appear sunken (depressed) into their background, the scroll bars have the same sunken appearance as the other controls, the PictureBox has a wide raised border, and the form itself has an interesting double border. These effects are illustrated in Figure 3-4-2.

Press the Custom command button. A new form (Figure 3-4-3) appears. Here you can experiment a little with the custom 3D effects offered by CBorder3D. Two CBorder3D objects are employed by the form Custom 3D Effects. One is initially set to be drawn just within the edge of the form; the second is set to be just within the PictureBox that contains the command buttons. Both use the settings indicated by the controls on this form.

Experiment with the custom styles: Framed, Double, and Within. Of the three, only Within draws within the coordinates set in the text box. The other two, Framed and Double, draw around the coordinates. Select either the Framed or Double option buttons; the border around the form disappears and the one within the PictureBox is now outside it. Try adjusting the Top, Left, Width, or Height properties to bring the form border object within view. The framed custom style is identical in appearance to Visual Basic's Frame control, so it is unaffected by the border and bevel properties.

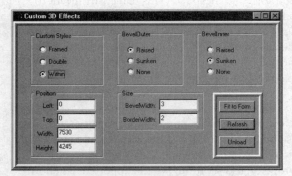

Figure 3-4-3 3D custom effects offered by CBorder3D

Creating the CBorder3D Class Module

1. Create a new project named CHEAP3D.VBP. Use the Insert Class Module menu item to add a new class module, name it CBorder3D, and save it as CBORDR3D.CLS.

2. Add the following code to the General section of CBorder3D. The first list of constants, which represent the various styles supported by CBorder3D, should be pasted into the Declarations section of any project with which you intend to use this class module. Several module-level variables are declared to save time later, as graphics of this sort need to operate as fast as possible. Finally, a list of variables is declared to store the many properties of CBorder3D.

```
Option Explicit
'
' Styles supported by CBorder3D
' Copy these constants into form module
'
Private Const StyleNone = 0
Private Const StyleSunken = 1
Private Const StyleRaised = 2
Private Const StyleFramed = 3
Private Const StyleDouble = 4
Private Const StyleWithin = 5
Private Const StyleCustomFramed = 6
Private Const StyleCustomDouble = 7
Private Const StyleCustomWithin = 8
'
' Variables used to hold TwipsPerPixel values
' Screen object only accessed once
'
Private tppX As Integer
Private tppY As Integer
'
' Variables used to hold drawing coordinates
' Object properties only accessed once per Refresh
' Declared here to save time allocating and deallocating
'
Private pX1 As Integer
Private pY1 As Integer
Private pX2 As Integer
Private pY2 As Integer
'
' Member variables to hold class properties
'
Private m_Client As Object
Private m_Canvas As Object
Private m_Style3D As Integer
Private m_BevelInner As Integer
Private m_BevelOuter As Integer
Private m_BevelWidth As Integer
Private m_BorderWidth As Integer
Private m_Left As Integer
```

Continued on next page

Continued from previous page

```
Private m_Top As Integer
Private m_Width As Integer
Private m_Height As Integer
Private m_Highlight As Long
Private m_Shadow As Long
Private m_Background As Long
Private m_ActOnNone As Boolean
```

3. Insert the following code in the Class_Initialize event of CBorder3D. More often than not, the default ScaleMode of Twips will be in effect, so all calculations assume that setting. CBorder3D sets the ScaleMode to Twips before drawing, and resets ScaleMode to its previous value when finished. For that reason, and to avoid repeatedly reading the Screen object's properties, the constant values for TwipsPerPixel in both X and Y are stored as the class is initialized. The remaining code sets the default values for the exposed properties. See Table 3-4-1 for a summary of properties.

```
'======================================================
' Initialize
'======================================================
Private Sub Class_Initialize()
    '
    ' Store TwipsPerPixel for both X & Y to save time later
    '
    tppX = Screen.TwipsPerPixelX
    tppY = Screen.TwipsPerPixelY
    '
    ' Set default property values
    '
    Set m_Client = Nothing
    Set m_Canvas = Nothing
    m_Style3D = StyleNone
    m_BevelInner = StyleNone
    m_BevelOuter = StyleRaised
    m_BevelWidth = 3
    m_BorderWidth = 2
    m_Left = 0
    m_Top = 0
    m_Width = 0
    m_Height = 0
    m_Highlight = vb3DHighLight
    m_Shadow = vb3DShadow
    m_Background = vb3DFace
    m_ActOnNone = False
End Sub
```

Table 3-4-1 Summary of CBorder3D properties

NAME	TYPE	COMMENTS
Client	Object	For standard styles, the object around which to draw a 3D border.
Canvas	Object	The object on which to draw. Assumed to be Client.Parent if not set, and Client is a control.

NAME	TYPE	COMMENTS
Style3D	Integer	1 of the 9 styles offered, summarized in Table 3-4-2. Range: 0—8.
BevelInner	Integer	Style of inner bevel. Range: 0—2, same constants as Style3D.
BevelOuter	Integer	Style of outer bevel. Range: 0—2, same constants as Style3D.
BevelWidth	Integer	Width in pixels of bevels.
BorderWidth	Integer	Width in pixels between bevels.
Left	Integer	Left coordinate used for custom styles. Uses Twips.
Top	Integer	Top coordinate used for custom styles. Uses Twips.
Width	Integer	Width of custom styles. Uses Twips.
Height	Integer	Height of custom styles. Uses Twips.
Highlight	Long	Color used for 3D highlights.
Shadow	Long	Color used for 3D shadows.
Background	Long	Color used for 3D backgrounds.
ActOnNone	Boolean	Determines if StyleNone should be acted upon. Used to remove the Appearance effect Visual Basic asserts.

4. Add the following pair of property procedures to CBorder3D to set and retrieve the Client property. For the standard styles, the Client is the control around which you wish to place a 3D effect. The Client property is unused with the custom styles.

```
'=======================================================
' Properties
'=======================================================
Public Property Set Client(obj As Object)
    '
    ' Store control or form to draw around
    '
    Set m_Client = obj
End Property

Public Property Get Client() As Object
    '
    ' Return control or form
    '
    Set Client = m_Client
End Property
```

5. Add the following pair of property procedures to CBorder3D to set and retrieve the Canvas property. This is the control or form upon which the drawing takes place, and requires support for the ScaleMode property and the Line method. It is not always necessary to set ScaleMode, as it can often be inferred. If the Client property is set, but the Canvas property isn't, the Client.Parent object is used as

the Canvas for all the standard styles except StyleWithin. In that case, the Client itself will be used as the Canvas if this property is not set. Of course, for the custom styles, a Canvas is required. When the Client is contained within another control that supports Visual Basic's graphics methods, such as a PictureBox, the Canvas object must be set to that container because Client.Parent always returns the control's parent form.

```
Public Property Set Canvas(obj As Object)
    '
    ' Store control or form to draw on
    '
    Set m_Canvas = obj
End Property

Public Property Get Canvas() As Object
    '
    ' Return control or form
    '
    Set Canvas = m_Canvas
End Property
```

6. Add the following pair of property procedures to CBorder3D to set and retrieve the Style3D property. There are a total of nine supported styles for this property; see Table 3-4-2 for a complete summary. Later in these steps, Table 3-4-3 shows which properties are required, optional, or not useful for each of the nine styles.

```
Public Property Let Style3D(NewVal As Integer)
    '
    ' Store value for Style3D property if in legal range
    '
    If (NewVal >= StyleNone) And _
        (NewVal <= StyleCustomWithin) Then
            m_Style3D = NewVal
    End If
End Property

Public Property Get Style3D() As Integer
    '
    ' Return value for Style3D property
    '
    Style3D = m_Style3D
End Property
```

Table 3-4-2 Styles supported by Style3D property

STYLE	DESCRIPTION
StyleNone	No action taken unless ActOnNone property is True. Then border one pixel wide is drawn around control using background color. Also used to indicate no bevel for either the BevelInner or BevelOuter properties.
StyleSunken	Draws border one pixel wide around control; imparts standard sunken 3D appearance. Also used to indicate bevel type for either the BevelInner or BevelOuter properties.

STYLE	DESCRIPTION
StyleRaised	Draws border one pixel wide around control; imparts a raised 3D appearance.
	Also used to indicate bevel type for either the BevelInner or BevelOuter properties.
StyleFramed	Draws border two pixels wide around control; emulating the appearance of Visual Basic's Frame
	control when Appearance is set to 3D.
StyleDouble	Draws a double border around a control. Relies on the values of BevelInner, BevelOuter, and
	BorderWidth to determine appearance.
StyleWithin	Draws a double border within the edges of a control or form. Relies on the values of BevelInner,
	BevelOuter, and BorderWidth to determine appearance.
StyleCustomFramed	Draws a border two pixels wide around the rectangle defined by the Top, Left, Width, and
	Height properties. Appearance emulates Visual Basic's frame control when Appearance is set to 3D.
StyleCustomDouble	Draws a double border around the rectangle defined by the Top, Left, Width, and Height
	properties. Relies on the values of BevelInner, BevelOuter, and BorderWidth to determine appearance.
StyleCustomWithin	Draws a double border within the rectangle defined by the Top, Left, Width, and Height properties.
	Relies on the values of BevelInner, BevelOuter, and BorderWidth to determine appearance.

7. Add the following pair of property procedures to CBorder3D, to set and retrieve the BevelInner property. This property determines the appearance of the inner bevel (raised, sunken, or none).

```
Public Property Let BevelInner(NewVal As Integer)
    '
    ' Store value for BevelInner property if in legal range
    '
    If (NewVal >= StyleNone) And _
        (NewVal <= StyleRaised) Then
        m_BevelInner = NewVal
    End If
End Property

Public Property Get BevelInner() As Integer
    '
    ' Return value for BevelInner property
    '
    BevelInner = m_BevelInner
End Property
```

8. Add the following pair of property procedures to CBorder3D, to set and retrieve the BevelOuter property. This property determines the appearance of the outer bevel (raised, sunken, or none).

```
Public Property Let BevelOuter(NewVal As Integer)
    '
    ' Store value for BevelOuter property if in legal range
    '
    If (NewVal >= StyleNone) And _
        (NewVal <= StyleRaised) Then
        m_BevelOuter = NewVal
```

Continued on next page

Continued from previous page

```
    End If
End Property

Public Property Get BevelOuter() As Integer
    '
    ' Return value for BevelOuter property
    '
    BevelOuter = m_BevelOuter
End Property
```

9. Add the following pair of property procedures to CBorder3D, to set and retrieve the BevelWidth property. This property determines the width *in pixels* of both the inner and outer bevels.

```
Public Property Let BevelWidth(NewVal As Integer)
    '
    ' Store value for BevelWidth property if positive
    '
    If NewVal > 0 Then
        m_BevelWidth = NewVal
    End If
End Property

Public Property Get BevelWidth() As Integer
    '
    ' Return value for BevelWidth property
    '
    BevelWidth = m_BevelWidth
End Property
```

10. Add the following pair of property procedures to CBorder3D, to set and retrieve the BorderWidth property. This property determines the width *in pixels* between the inner and outer bevels.

```
Public Property Let BorderWidth(NewVal As Integer)
    '
    ' Store value for BorderWidth property if positive
    '
    If NewVal >= 0 Then
        m_BorderWidth = NewVal
    End If
End Property

Public Property Get BorderWidth() As Integer
    '
    ' Return value for BorderWidth property
    '
    BorderWidth = m_BorderWidth
End Property
```

11. Add the following four pairs of property procedures to CBorder3D, to set and retrieve the Left, Top, Width, and Height properties. These properties determine the rectangle around or within which the custom styles draw. For the drawing routines to function correctly, values *must* be expressed in Twips.

```
Public Property Let Left(NewVal As Integer)
    '
    ' Store value for Left property of Custom style
    ' Must be expressed in Twips for drawing to work!
    '
    m_Left = NewVal
End Property

Public Property Get Left() As Integer
    '
    ' Return value for Left property
    '
    Left = m_Left
End Property

Public Property Let Top(NewVal As Integer)
    '
    ' Store value for Top property of Custom style
    ' Must be expressed in Twips for drawing to work!
    '
    m_Top = NewVal
End Property

Public Property Get Top() As Integer
    '
    ' Return value for Top property
    '
    Top = m_Top
End Property

Public Property Let Width(NewVal As Integer)
    '
    ' Store value for Width property of Custom style
    ' Must be expressed in Twips for drawing to work!
    '
    m_Width = NewVal
End Property

Public Property Get Width() As Integer
    '
    ' Return value for Width property
    '
    Width = m_Width
End Property

Public Property Let Height(NewVal As Integer)
    '
    ' Store value for Height property of Custom style
    ' Must be expressed in Twips for drawing to work!
    '
    m_Height = NewVal
End Property

Public Property Get Height() As Integer
    '
```

Continued on next page

Continued from previous page

```
' Return value for Height property
'
Height = m_Height
End Property
```

12. Add the following three pairs of property procedures to CBorder3D, to set and retrieve the Highlight, Shadow, and Background properties. These refer to the colors used to paint the 3D effects. Visual Basic defines a series of constants to which CBorder3D defaults, but if you want to devise a custom color scheme, change these properties.

```
Public Property Let Highlight(NewVal As Long)
    '
    ' Store value for Highlight color property
    '
    m_Highlight = NewVal
End Property

Public Property Get Highlight() As Long
    '
    ' Return value for Highlight color property
    '
    Highlight = m_Highlight
End Property

Public Property Let Shadow(NewVal As Long)
    '
    ' Store value for Shadow color property
    '
    m_Shadow = NewVal
End Property

Public Property Get Shadow() As Long
    '
    ' Return value for Shadow color property
    '
    Shadow = m_Shadow
End Property

Public Property Let Background(NewVal As Long)
    '
    ' Store value for Background color property
    '
    m_Background = NewVal
End Property

Public Property Get Background() As Long
    '
    ' Return value for Background color property
    '
    Background = m_Background
End Property
```

Table 3-4-3 Which properties work with which styles?

↑ = Required
↔ = Optional
↓ = Not Useful

Properties	StyleNone	StyleSunken	StyleRaised	StyleFramed	StyleDouble	StyleWithin	StyleCustomFramed	StyleCustomDouble	StyleCustomWithin
Client	↑	↑	↑	↑	↑	↑	↓	↓	↓
Canvas	↔	↔	↔	↔	↔	↔	↑	↑	↑
Style3D	↑	↑	↑	↑	↑	↑	↑	↑	↑
BevelInner	↓	↓	↓	↓	↔	↔	↓	↔	↔
BevelOuter	↓	↓	↓	↓	↔	↔	↓	↔	↔
BevelWidth	↓	↓	↓	↓	↔	↔	↓	↔	↔
BorderWidth	↓	↓	↓	↓	↔	↔	↔	↔	↓
Left	↓	↓	↓	↓	↓	↓	↑	↑	↑
Top	↓	↓	↓	↓	↓	↓	↑	↑	↑
Width	↓	↓	↓	↓	↓	↓	↑	↑	↑
Height	↓	↓	↓	↓	↓	↓	↑	↑	↑
Highlight	↔	↔	↔	↔	↔	↔	↔	↔	↔
Shadow	↔	↔	↔	↔	↔	↔	↔	↔	↔
Background	↔	↔	↔	↔	↔	↔	↔	↔	↔
ActOnNone	↔	↓	↓	↓	↓	↓	↓	↓	↓

13. Add the following property procedure to CBorder3D to set and retrieve the ActOnNone property. When this property is False and the Style3D property is set to StyleNone, no action is taken when the CBorder3D object is refreshed. If this property is set to True, however, and the Style3D property is set to StyleNone, a one-pixel-wide rectangle is drawn around the Client control. This is useful if you want to temporarily override, or "turn off," the 3D effects that Visual Basic places on the controls it supports.

```
Public Property Let ActOnNone(NewVal As Boolean)
    '
    ' Store value for ActOnNone property.
    ' If True, then StyleNone is drawn as a box
    ' using the Background color. If False, then
    ' Refresh is ignored.
    '
    m_ActOnNone = NewVal
End Property

Public Property Get ActOnNone() As Boolean
    '
    ' Return value for ActOnNone property
    '
    ActOnNone = m_ActOnNone
End Property
```

14. Add the following public Refresh procedure; this is CBorder3D's only method. If the Canvas property isn't set, an attempt is made to determine the logical object to draw on given the Style3D property. If neither the Client nor Canvas properties are set, or no logical Canvas can be determined, an error is raised. The ScaleMode property of the Canvas object is then set to Twips. The original ScaleMode is stored so that it can be reset after drawing is complete. The appropriate private drawing routine is then called to do the actual work.

```vb
'========================================================
' Public Method
'========================================================
Public Sub Refresh()
    Dim ResetMode As Integer
    '
    ' Make sure there's a canvas to draw on
    ' Use parent form as default for simple styles
    ' Use client if style is within
    '
    If (m_Canvas Is Nothing) Then
        If (m_Client Is Nothing) Then
            Err.Raise Number:=vbObjectError + 1024, _
                      Source:="CHugeScroll", _
                      Description:="Canvas and/or Client Properties not set."
        ElseIf m_Style3D <= StyleFramed Then
            Set m_Canvas = m_Client.Parent
        ElseIf m_Style3D = StyleWithin Then
            Set m_Canvas = m_Client
        Else
            Err.Raise Number:=vbObjectError + 1025, _
                      Source:="CHugeScroll", _
                      Description:="Canvas Property ambiguous."
        End If
    End If
    '
    ' Store Canvas.ScaleMode and reset to Twips
    '
    ResetMode = m_Canvas.ScaleMode
    m_Canvas.ScaleMode = vbTwips
    '
    ' Draw desired effect
    '
    Select Case m_Style3D
        Case StyleNone
            If m_ActOnNone Then DrawNone
        Case StyleSunken
            DrawSunken
        Case StyleRaised
            DrawRaised
        Case StyleFramed, StyleCustomFramed
            DrawFramed
        Case StyleDouble, StyleCustomDouble
            DrawDouble
```

```
      Case StyleWithin, StyleCustomWithin
          DrawWithin
   End Select
   '
   ' Restore previous Canvas.ScaleMode
   '
   m_Canvas.ScaleMode = ResetMode
End Sub
```

15. Add a private routine called DrawNone to CBorder3D, and insert the following code in it. If the Style3D is StyleNone, and the ActOnNone property is True, this routine draws a rectangle around the Client control in the background color.

```
'========================================================
' Private Support Routines
'========================================================
Private Sub DrawNone()
   '
   ' Access properties just once, and set aside
   '
   pX1 = m_Client.Left - tppX
   pX2 = pX1 + m_Client.Width + tppX
   pY1 = m_Client.Top - tppY
   pY2 = pY1 + m_Client.Height + tppY
   '
   ' Draw box around control in background color
   '
   m_Canvas.Line (pX1, pY1)-(pX2, pY2), m_Background, B
End Sub
```

16. Add a private routine called DrawSunken to CBorder3D, and insert the following code in it. This is called when Style3D is StyleSunken, and draws the classic sunken 3D border around the Client control.

```
Private Sub DrawSunken()
   '
   ' Access properties just once, and set aside
   '
   pX1 = m_Client.Left - tppX
   pX2 = pX1 + m_Client.Width + tppX
   pY1 = m_Client.Top - tppY
   pY2 = pY1 + m_Client.Height + tppY
   '
   ' Draw shadow around control
   '
   m_Canvas.Line (pX1, pY1)-(pX2, pY2), m_Shadow, B
   '
   ' Add one pixel to length of highlights, and
   ' Draw highlight along bottom and right edges.
   '
   m_Canvas.Line (pX2, pY1)-(pX2, pY2 + tppY), m_Highlight
   m_Canvas.Line (pX1, pY2)-(pX2 + tppX, pY2), m_Highlight
End Sub
```

17. Add a private routine called DrawRaised to CBorder3D, and insert the following code in it. This is called when Style3D is StyleRaised, and draws the reverse of the classic sunken 3D border around the Client control.

```
Private Sub DrawRaised()
    '
    ' Access properties just once, and set aside
    '
    pX1 = m_Client.Left - tppX
    pX2 = pX1 + m_Client.Width + tppX
    pY1 = m_Client.Top - tppY
    pY2 = pY1 + m_Client.Height + tppY
    '
    ' Draw shadow around control
    '
    m_Canvas.Line (pX1, pY1)-(pX2, pY2), m_Shadow, B
    '
    ' Add one pixel to length of highlights, and
    ' Draw highlight along top and left edges.
    '
    m_Canvas.Line (pX1, pY1)-(pX2 + tppX, pY1), m_Highlight
    m_Canvas.Line (pX1, pY1)-(pX1, pY2 + tppY), m_Highlight
End Sub
```

18. Add a private routine called DrawFramed to CBorder3D, and insert the following code in it. This is called when Style3D is either StyleFramed or StyleCustomFramed, and draws a frame similar to Visual Basic's Frame control around the Client control or the rectangle defined by the Top, Left, Width, and Height properties.

```
Private Sub DrawFramed()
    '
    ' Access properties just once, and set aside.
    ' Extend it up and to the left two pixels.
    ' Either use Client coords for simple outlines,
    ' or property coords for custom outlines.
    '
    If m_Style3D = StyleCustomFramed Then
        pX1 = m_Left - tppX * 2
        pY1 = m_Top - tppY * 2
        pX2 = pX1 + m_Width + tppX * 2
        pY2 = pY1 + m_Height + tppY * 2
    Else 'm_Style3D = StyleFramed
        pX1 = m_Client.Left - tppX * 2
        pY1 = m_Client.Top - tppY * 2
        pX2 = pX1 + m_Client.Width + tppX * 2
        pY2 = pY1 + m_Client.Height + tppY * 2
    End If
    '
    ' Draw shadow around control or custom area
    '
    m_Canvas.Line (pX1, pY1)-(pX2, pY2), m_Shadow, B
    '
    ' Draw highlight around control or custom area
```

```
' by shifting down and to right one pixel
'
m_Canvas.Line (pX1 + tppX, pY1 + tppY)-(pX2 + tppX, pY2 + tppY),⇒
           m_Highlight, B
End Sub
```

19. Add a private routine called DrawDouble to CBorder3D, and insert the following code in it. Called when Style3D is either StyleDouble or StyleCustomDouble, this routine calculates the width in pixels of the double border, and inflates the rectangle used to define it. It then calls a routine that calls another series of routines which do the actual drawing based on the settings for the BevelInner and BevelOuter properties.

```
Private Sub DrawDouble()
    '
    ' Calculate FrameWidth of border
    '
    Dim FrameWidth As Integer
    If (m_BevelInner <> StyleNone) And _
       (m_BevelOuter <> StyleNone) Then
        FrameWidth = m_BorderWidth + m_BevelWidth * 2
    Else
        FrameWidth = m_BevelWidth
    End If
    '
    ' Access properties just once, and set aside.
    ' Either use Client coords for simple outlines,
    ' or property coords for custom outlines.
    '
    If m_Style3D = StyleCustomDouble Then
        pX1 = m_Left - (FrameWidth * tppX)
        pY1 = m_Top - (FrameWidth * tppY)
        pX2 = m_Width + (FrameWidth * tppX * 2) + pX1 - tppX
        pY2 = m_Height + (FrameWidth * tppY * 2) + pY1 - tppY
    Else 'm_Style3D = StyleDouble
        pX1 = m_Client.Left - (FrameWidth * tppX)
        pY1 = m_Client.Top - (FrameWidth * tppY)
        pX2 = m_Client.Width + (FrameWidth * tppX * 2) + pX1 - tppX
        pY2 = m_Client.Height + (FrameWidth * tppY * 2) + pY1 - tppY
    End If
    '
    ' Call routine that calls routine(s) that do actual drawing
    '
    DrawDblBorder
End Sub
```

20. Add a private routine called DrawWithin to CBorder3D, and insert the following code in it. Called when Style3D is either StyleWithin or StyleCustomWithin, this routine calculates the width in pixels of the double border, and deflates the rectangle used to define it. It then calls a routine that calls another series of routines which do the actual drawing based on the settings for the BevelInner and BevelOuter properties.

```
Private Sub DrawWithin()
    '
    ' Access properties just once, and set aside
    ' Either use Client coords for simple outlines,
    ' or property coords for custom outlines.
    '
    If m_Style3D = StyleCustomWithin Then
        pX1 = m_Left
        pY1 = m_Top
        pX2 = pX1 + m_Width - tppX
        pY2 = pY1 + m_Height - tppY
    Else 'm_Style = StyleWithin
        pX1 = 0
        pY1 = 0
        pX2 = m_Client.ScaleWidth - tppX
        pY2 = m_Client.ScaleHeight - tppY
    End If
    '
    ' Call routine that calls routine(s) that do actual drawing
    '
    DrawDblBorder
End Sub
```

21. Add a private routine called DrawDblBorder to CBorder3D, and insert the follow-
    ing code in it. Called by both DrawDouble and DrawWithin, this routine
    determines whether to call the routines that draw the raised or sunken borders,
    based on the settings for the BevelInner and BevelOuter properties. If both bevels
    are being used, the rectangle is deflated, to pass to the routine that draws the
    inner bevel.

```
Private Sub DrawDblBorder()
    '
    ' Draw outer border
    '
    If m_BevelOuter = StyleRaised Then
        DrawDblRaised
    ElseIf m_BevelOuter = StyleSunken Then
        DrawDblSunken
    ElseIf m_BevelOuter = StyleNone Then
        '
        ' No outer border was specified, so use inner border instead,
        ' then exit sub
        '
        If m_BevelInner = StyleRaised Then
            DrawDblRaised
        ElseIf m_BevelInner = StyleSunken Then
            DrawDblSunken
        End If
        Exit Sub
    End If
    '
    ' Adjust coordinates for inner border
    '
```

```
    pX1 = pX1 + (m_BevelWidth * tppX) + (m_BorderWidth * tppX)
    pY1 = pY1 + (m_BevelWidth * tppY) + (m_BorderWidth * tppY)
    pX2 = pX2 - (m_BevelWidth * tppX) - (m_BorderWidth * tppX)
    pY2 = pY2 - (m_BevelWidth * tppX) - (m_BorderWidth * tppX)
    '
    ' Draw inner border
    '
    If m_BevelInner = StyleRaised Then
        DrawDblRaised
    ElseIf m_BevelInner = StyleSunken Then
        DrawDblSunken
    End If
End Sub
```

22. Add this pair of private routines, DrawDblSunken and DrawDblRaised, to CBorder3D, and insert the following code in them. These are called by DrawDblBorder, as appropriate, based on the settings for the BevelInner and BevelOuter properties.

```
Private Sub DrawDblSunken()
    Dim i As Integer
    For i = 0 To m_BevelWidth - 1
        '
        ' Draw bottom and right lines -- highlighted
        '
        m_Canvas.Line (pX1 + i * tppX, pY2 - i * tppY)-(pX2 - i * tppX,
                pY2 - i * tppY), m_Highlight
        m_Canvas.Line (pX2 - i * tppX, pY1 + i * tppY)-(pX2 - i * tppX,
                pY2 - i * tppY + tppY), m_Highlight

        ' Draw top and left lines -- shadowed
        '
        m_Canvas.Line (pX1 + i * tppX, pY1 + i * tppY)-(pX2 - i * tppX,
                pY1 + i * tppY), m_Shadow
        m_Canvas.Line (pX1 + i * tppX, pY1 + i * tppY)-(pX1 + i * tppX,
                pY2 - i * tppY), m_Shadow
    Next i
End Sub

Private Sub DrawDblRaised()
    Dim i As Integer
    For i = 0 To m_BevelWidth - 1
        '
        ' Draw top and left lines -- highlighted
        '
        m_Canvas.Line (pX1 + i * tppX, pY1 + i * tppY)-(pX2 - i * tppX,
                pY1 + i * tppY), m_Highlight
        m_Canvas.Line (pX1 + i * tppX, pY1 + i * tppY)-(pX1 + i * tppX,
                pY2 - i * tppY), m_Highlight

        ' Draw bottom and right lines -- shadowed
        '
        m_Canvas.Line (pX1 + i * tppX, pY2 - i * tppY)-(pX2 - i * tppX,
                pY2 - i * tppY), m_Shadow
```

Continued on next page

Continued from previous page

```
        m_Canvas.Line (pX2 - i * tppX, pY1 + i * tppY)-(pX2 - i * tppX,
                       pY2 - i * tppY + tppY), m_Shadow
    Next i
End Sub
```

Building a Test Project to Use the Standard Styles of CBorder3D

This project will use two forms. The first demonstrates how CBorder3D can add attractive 3D effects to the controls that Microsoft neglected to support. It also draws a double border just within the edges of the form. The second form allows you to play a little at adjusting the properties of two CBorder3D objects.

23. Add a new form to your project, name it frmCheap3D, and save it as CHEAP3D.FRM. Place at least one of each of the standard Visual Basic controls on it, and set their properties as listed in Table 3-4-4. Within Frame1 and Picture1, place controls and set their properties as listed in Table 3-4-5. For this demonstration, very few of the default properties need be altered, and position and size are inconsequential. The idea is just to get as many controls onto the form as are available.

Table 3-4-4 Objects and their properties on frmCheap3D

OBJECT	PROPERTY	SETTING
Form	Name	frmCheap3D
	Appearance	1 - 3D
	Caption	"Standard Controls"
PictureBox	Name	Picture1
	BorderStyle	1 - Fixed Single
text box	Name	Text1
ListBox	Name	List1
ComboBox	Name	Combo1
DirListBox	Name	Dir1
FileListBox	Name	File1
DriveListBox	Name	Drive1
VScrollBar	Name	VScroll1
HScrollBar	Name	HScroll1
CheckBox	Name	Check1
Frame	Name	Frame1
Label	Name	Label2
CommandButton	Name	Command1
	Caption	"Quit"
CommandButton	Name	Command2
	Caption	"Custom"

Table 3-4-5 Objects and their properties contained by Frame1 and Picture1

OBJECT	PROPERTY	SETTING	CONTAINER
OptionButton	Name	Option1	Frame1
	Caption	"Standard 3D"	
	Index	0	
OptionButton	Name	Option1	Frame1
	Caption	"Enhanced 3D"	
	Index	1	
text box	Name	Text2	Picture1
Label	Name	Label1	Picture1

24. Insert the following code in the Declarations section of frmCheap3D. The style constants supported by CBorder3D are copied into this form for easy reference and readability. Also, an array of CBorder3D objects is dimensioned to set up a variety of borders.

```
Option Explicit
'
' Option state constants
'
Const Std3d = 0
Const Enh3d = 1
'
' 3D styles supported be CBorder3D
'
Const StyleNone = 0
Const StyleSunken = 1
Const StyleRaised = 2
Const StyleFramed = 3
Const StyleDouble = 4
Const StyleWithin = 5
Const StyleCustomFramed = 6
Const StyleCustomDouble = 7
Const StyleCustomWithin = 8
'
' Array of CBorder3D objects for special effects
'
Private Obj3D(0 To 5) As New CBorder3D
```

25. Insert the following code in the Form_Initialize event of frmCheap3D. Here, the required properties for all CBorder3D objects are set. Notice that using the standard styles is a very simple task.

```
Private Sub Form_Initialize()
    '
    ' Initialize CBorder3D object for Label on Picture box
    '
    Set Obj3D(0).Client = Label1
    Set Obj3D(0).Canvas = Picture1
```

Continued on next page

Continued from previous page

```
    Obj3D(0).Style3D = StyleSunken
    '
    ' Initialize CBorder3D object for Label on Form
    '
    Set Obj3D(1).Client = Label2
    Obj3D(1).Style3D = StyleSunken
    '
    ' Initialize CBorder3D object for VScroll on Form
    '
    Set Obj3D(2).Client = VScroll1
    Obj3D(2).Style3D = StyleSunken
    '
    ' Initialize CBorder3D object for HScroll on Form
    '
    Set Obj3D(3).Client = HScroll1
    Obj3D(3).Style3D = StyleSunken
    '
    ' Initialize CBorder3D object for Picture box on Form
    '
    Set Obj3D(4).Client = Picture1
    Set Obj3D(4).Canvas = Me
    Obj3D(4).Style3D = StyleDouble
    Obj3D(4).BevelOuter = StyleRaised
    Obj3D(4).BevelInner = StyleNone
    Obj3D(4).BevelWidth = 3
    '
    ' Initialize CBorder3D object for Form
    '
    Set Obj3D(5).Client = Me
    Set Obj3D(5).Canvas = Me
    Obj3D(5).Style3D = StyleWithin
    Obj3D(5).BevelOuter = StyleSunken
    Obj3D(5).BevelInner = StyleNone
    Obj3D(5).BevelWidth = 3
    Obj3D(5).BorderWidth = 2
End Sub
```

26. Insert the following code in the Form_Load event of frmCheap3D, to add a few items to the demo listbox and position the form on screen.

```
Private Sub Form_Load()
    '
    ' Add some data to listbox
    '
    List1.AddItem "ListItem 0"
    List1.AddItem "ListItem 1"
    List1.AddItem "ListItem 2"
    '
    ' Position form in upper left quadrant
    '
    Me.Left = Screen.Height \ 8
    Me.Top = Screen.Height \ 8
End Sub
```

27. Insert the following code in the Form_Paint event of frmCheap3D. If the Enhanced 3D option button is not selected, the objects are ignored.

```
Private Sub Form_Paint()
   Dim i As Integer
   '
   ' If in "enhanced" mode refresh all the custom objects
   '
   If Option1(Enh3d) Then
      Picture1.Cls
      For i = LBound(Obj3D) To UBound(Obj3D)
         Obj3D(i).Refresh
      Next i
   End If
End Sub
```

28. Add the following pair of event procedures to support the two command buttons. If the user clicks the first button, the form is unloaded. If the user clicks the second command, another form is loaded modally to demonstrate some of the custom functionality of CBorder3D.

```
Private Sub Command1_Click()
   '
   ' End the project
   '
   Unload Me
End Sub

Private Sub Command2_Click()
   '
   ' Load and show custom styles form
   '
   frmCustom3D.Show vbModal
   Set frmCustom3D = Nothing
End Sub
```

29. Insert the following code in the Form_Resize and Option1_Click events of frmCheap3D. These events force a redraw of all the 3D effects, if they're turned on. When the 3D option is toggled, so is the BorderStyle for the Picture box.

```
Private Sub Form_Resize()
   '
   ' Remove remnants of old custom border around edge
   '
   Me.Cls
   Me.Refresh
End Sub

Private Sub Option1_Click(Index As Integer)
   '
   ' Set Picture control's BorderStyle appropriately
   '
```

Continued on next page

Continued from previous page

```
    Picture1.BorderStyle = (Index + 1) Mod 2
    '
    ' Show effects user picked
    '
    Me.Refresh
End Sub
```

Experimenting with the Custom Styles of CBorder3D

30. Add another new form to your project, name it frmCustom3D, and save it as CUSTOM3D.FRM. Place the controls listed in Table 3-4-6 directly on the form, and set their properties as listed. Using Table 3-4-7 as a guide, place the listed controls within their proper containers, and set their properties appropriately.

Table 3-4-6 Objects and properties on frmCustom3D

OBJECT	PROPERTY	SETTING
Form	Name	frmCustom3D
	Appearance	1 - 3D
	Caption	"Custom 3D Effects"
Frame	Name	Frame1
	Caption	"Custom Styles"
Frame	Name	Frame1
	Caption	"Position"
Frame	Name	Frame1
	Caption	"BevelOuter"
Frame	Name	Frame1
	Caption	"BevelInner"
Frame	Name	Frame1
	Caption	"Size"
PictureBox	Name	Picture1
	BorderStyle	0 - None

Table 3-4-7 Objects and their properties contained by other controls on frmCustom3D

OBJECT	PROPERTY	SETTING	CONTAINER
OptionButton	Name	optCustom	Frame1
	Caption	"Framed"	
	Index	0	
OptionButton	Name	optCustom	Frame1
	Caption	"Double"	
	Index	1	
OptionButton	Name	optCustom	Frame1
	Caption	"Within"	

OBJECT	PROPERTY	SETTING	CONTAINER
	Index	2	
	Value	True	
text box	Name	txtSize	Frame2
	Index	0	
	Text	"txtSize(0)"	
text box	Name	txtSize	Frame2
	Index	1	
	Text	"txtSize(1)"	
text box	Name	txtSize	Frame2
	Index	2	
	Text	"txtSize(2)"	
text box	Name	txtSize	Frame2
	Index	3	
	Text	"txtSize(3)"	
Label	Name	lblSize	Frame2
	Caption	"Left:"	
	Index	0	
Label	Name	lblSize	Frame2
	Caption	"Top:"	
	Index	1	
Label	Name	lblSize	Frame2
	Caption	"Width:"	
	Index	2	
Label	Name	lblSize	Frame2
	Caption	"Height:"	
	Index	3	
OptionButton	Name	optOuter	Frame3
	Caption	"Raised"	
	Index	0	
	Value	True	
OptionButton	Name	optOuter	Frame3
	Caption	"Sunken"	
	Index	1	
OptionButton	Name	optOuter	Frame3
	Caption	"None"	
	Index	2	
OptionButton	Name	optOuter	Frame4
	Caption	"Raised"	
	Index	0	

Continued on next page

Continued from previous page

OBJECT	PROPERTY	SETTING	CONTAINER
OptionButton	Name	optOuter	Frame4
	Caption	"Sunken"	
	Index	1	
	Value	True	
OptionButton	Name	optOuter	Frame4
	Caption	"None"	
	Index	2	
text box	Name	txtSize	Frame5
	Index	4	
	Text	"txtSize(4)"	
text box	Name	txtSize	Frame5
	Index	5	
	Text	"txtSize(5)"	
Label	Name	lblSize	Frame5
	Caption	"BevelWidth:"	
	Index	4	
Label	Name	lblSize	Frame5
	Caption	"BorderWidth:"	
	Index	4	
CommandButton	Name	Command1	Picture1
	Caption	"Refresh"	
	Default	True	
CommandButton	Name	Command2	Picture1
	Cancel	True	
	Caption	"Unload"	
CommandButton	Name	Command3	Picture1
	Caption	"Fit to Form"	

31. Insert the following code in the Declarations section of frmCustom3D. Again, the supported constants from CBorder3D are pasted in to allow for easy reference and readability. Several more constants are defined to cycle through the control arrays, and two CBorder3D objects are declared.

```
Option Explicit
'
' 3D styles supported be CBorder3D
'
Const StyleNone = 0
Const StyleSunken = 1
Const StyleRaised = 2
Const StyleFramed = 3
Const StyleDouble = 4
Const StyleWithin = 5
```

```
Const StyleCustomFramed = 6
Const StyleCustomDouble = 7
Const StyleCustomWithin = 8
'
' Index to text box array
'
Const tLeft = 0
Const tTop = 1
Const tWidth = 2
Const tHeight = 3
Const tBevel = 4
Const tBorder = 5
'
' Indexes to option button arrays
'
Const oFramed = 0
Const oDouble = 1
Const oWithin = 2
Const oRaised = 0
Const oSunken = 1
Const oNone = 3
'
' CBorder3D objects for special effects
'
Private Obj3D1 As New CBorder3D
Private Obj3D2 As New CBorder3D
```

32. Insert the following code in the Form_Load event of frmCustom3D. Two
    CBorder3D objects are used with this form: Obj3D1 will initially be set to draw
    along the edges of the form, and Obj3D2 will follow the edges of the PictureBox.
    Here the Canvas property for two CBorder3D objects is set to the form and the
    PictureBox. Some startup properties for the form's border object are placed into
    the text controls; the remaining startup properties were placed into the option
    buttons at design time. The border objects will be refreshed each time the form
    itself is.

```
Private Sub Form_Load()
    '
    ' Initialize 3D objects
    '
    Set Obj3D1.Canvas = Me
    Set Obj3D2.Canvas = Picture1
    '
    ' Set text boxes to startup properties
    '
    txtSize(tLeft) = 0
    txtSize(tTop) = 0
    txtSize(tWidth) = Me.ScaleWidth
    txtSize(tHeight) = Me.ScaleHeight
    txtSize(tBevel) = 3
    txtSize(tBorder) = 2
    '
    ' Position form in lower right quadrant
    '
```

Continued on next page

Continued from previous page

```
    Me.Left = Screen.Width - Screen.Height \ 8 - Me.Width
    Me.Top = Screen.Height - Screen.Height \ 8 - Me.Height
End Sub
```

33. Insert the following code in the Form_Paint event of frmCustom3D. This calls the routine that reads what properties the user desires for the custom 3D border objects. Then the Refresh method of each object is triggered.

```
Private Sub Form_Paint()
    '
    ' Call routine to reset properties as user input
    '
    SetProperties
    '
    ' Refresh the 3D objects
    '
    Picture1.Cls
    Obj3D1.Refresh
    Obj3D2.Refresh
End Sub
```

34. Add a new private routine called SetProperties to frmCustom3D. This routine is called whenever the form repaints. It retrieves the values the user has entered into the various text boxes, sets these values into the properties of the Obj3D1, and applies the selected option buttons to both Obj3D1 and Obj3D2. (This may seem complicated, but it would never be this involved in an actual application. This demo is designed to allow almost complete control over Obj3D1, and limited control over Obj3D2, so there's a lot happening.)

```
Private Sub SetProperties()
    '
    ' Most properties can be read right out of
    ' text boxes.
    '
    Obj3D1.Top = Val(txtSize(tTop))
    Obj3D1.Left = Val(txtSize(tLeft))
    Obj3D1.BevelWidth = Val(txtSize(tBevel))
    Obj3D1.BorderWidth = Val(txtSize(tBorder))
    Obj3D1.Width = Val(txtSize(tWidth))
    Obj3D1.Height = Val(txtSize(tHeight))
    '
    ' Set inner bevel type
    '
    If optInner(oRaised) Then
        Obj3D1.BevelInner = StyleRaised
        Obj3D2.BevelInner = StyleRaised
    ElseIf optInner(oSunken) Then
        Obj3D1.BevelInner = StyleSunken
        Obj3D2.BevelInner = StyleSunken
    Else
        Obj3D1.BevelInner = StyleNone
        Obj3D2.BevelInner = StyleNone
    End If
    '
```

```
' Set outer bevel type
'
If optOuter(oRaised) Then
    Obj3D1.BevelOuter = StyleRaised
    Obj3D2.BevelOuter = StyleRaised
ElseIf optOuter(oSunken) Then
    Obj3D1.BevelOuter = StyleSunken
    Obj3D2.BevelOuter = StyleSunken
Else
    Obj3D1.BevelOuter = StyleNone
    Obj3D2.BevelOuter = StyleNone
End If
'
' Set custom style type
'
If optCustom(oFramed) Then
    Obj3D1.Style3D = StyleCustomFramed
    Obj3D2.Style3D = StyleCustomFramed
ElseIf optCustom(oDouble) Then
    Obj3D1.Style3D = StyleCustomDouble
    Obj3D2.Style3D = StyleCustomDouble
ElseIf optCustom(oWithin) Then
    Obj3D1.Style3D = StyleCustomWithin
    Obj3D2.Style3D = StyleCustomWithin
End If
'
' Adjust settings for second 3D object
'
If optCustom(oWithin) Then
    Set Obj3D2.Canvas = Picture1
    Obj3D2.Top = 0
    Obj3D2.Left = 0
    Obj3D2.Width = Picture1.ScaleWidth
    Obj3D2.Height = Picture1.ScaleHeight
Else
    Set Obj3D2.Canvas = Me
    Obj3D2.Top = Picture1.Top
    Obj3D2.Left = Picture1.Left
    Obj3D2.Width = Picture1.Width
    Obj3D2.Height = Picture1.Height
End If
End Sub
```

35. Insert the following code in the Command3_Click event of frmCustom3D. This
    event resets the values in the text boxes, so that Obj3D1 will be sized to fit the
    form with the next refresh.

```
Private Sub Command3_Click()
    '
    ' Set new values to fit 3D object to form,
    ' then repaint
    '
    txtSize(tLeft) = "0"
    txtSize(tTop) = "0"
```

Continued on next page

Continued from previous page

```
    txtSize(tWidth) = Format(Me.ScaleWidth)
    txtSize(tHeight) = Format(Me.ScaleHeight)
    optCustom(oWithin) = True
    Me.Refresh
End Sub
```

36. Insert the following code in the Command1_Click and Command2_Click events of frmCustom3D. The first event forces a refresh of the form and its custom 3D border objects, and the second unloads the form and returns control to frmCheap3D.

```
Private Sub Command1_Click()
    '
    ' Repaint according to user input.
    ' This button has Default=True so user can
    ' press Enter any time to see new settings.
    '
    Me.Refresh
End Sub

Private Sub Command2_Click()
    '
    ' Unload this form and return to main form
    '
    Unload Me
End Sub
```

37. Insert the following code in the optCustom_Click, optInner_Click, and optOuter_Click events of frmCustom3D. Each time an option is chosen in one of these groups, the form and the custom 3D border objects are refreshed.

```
Private Sub optCustom_Click(Index As Integer)
    '
    ' Repaint immediately to give user feedback
    ' on new custom style
    '
    Me.Refresh
End Sub

Private Sub optInner_Click(Index As Integer)
    '
    ' Repaint immediately to give user feedback
    ' on new inner bevel type
    '
    Me.Refresh
End Sub

Private Sub optOuter_Click(Index As Integer)
    '
    ' Repaint immediately to give user feedback
    ' on new outer bevel type
    '
    Me.Refresh
End Sub
```

How It Works

The CBorder3D class module exposes an interface to a somewhat involved set of drawing routines that provide the popular 3D appearance used by today's Windows interfaces. These same effects can be achieved by using custom controls, but those can consume resources at an alarming rate and also add to the distribution size of your application. By drawing the effects directly on the form or control, not only are resources conserved, but the programmer can be in charge of exactly what sort of effects are created.

Few steps are required to use one of CBorder3D's standard styles. You declare a new instance of the object and assign its Client property to a control on your form, set the Style3D property to the desired effect, and then, whenever necessary, execute the border object's Refresh method. Refresh calls a series of routines that first determine the current coordinates for drawing, and then do the actual drawing. Visual Basic graphics methods are used to draw directly on the Canvas object. To draw one of the standard effects usually takes only two or three calls to the Line method of the Canvas object. A box is drawn around the control in the shadow color; then two lines are drawn along the appropriate sides using the highlight color.

Using the custom styles is only slightly more complicated. These styles aren't restricted to bounding a control or form. In fact, the Client property has no meaning, and only the Canvas object is referred to. By setting the Top, Left, Width, and Height properties of the border object, you define the rectangle that's used to draw the effect. Wide borders or bevels are drawn with a series of one-pixel wide lines to give the corner effects. The coordinates for the outermost rectangle are calculated, and with each pass the rectangle is deflated by one pixel on each side.

Visual Basic now offers intrinsic constants for the classic 3D colors, which are used as defaults for the various drawing methods (you are free to experiment with alternative color schemes, as well). A rich set of 15 properties and 9 drawing styles are offered. Generally, one object will be permanently assigned for each border required, and the same effect is refreshed whenever required.

Comments

Hopefully, this class module is but a springboard for you to develop many interesting techniques. CBorder3D certainly offers quite a variety, but you will undoubtedly think of more as time goes on and standards evolve. One possible extension would be to use the GDI functions Windows provides, to extend the drawing capability to any control, not just those that support Visual Basic's graphics methods. This demonstration only scratches the surface of what's possible using CBorder3D, and more examples are scattered throughout the remainder of the book.

3.5 How do I...
Support All the Edit Functions for Text Boxes?

COMPLEXITY: EASY
COMPATIBILITY: VB3 OR VB4

Problem

I'd like to support all the common edit functions for text boxes on my form, using both menu access and the standard shortcut keys. I can do Cut, Copy, Paste, and Delete with Visual Basic alone, but there's no support for Undo. Is there an API call that solves this for me?

Technique

The SendMessage API function can be used to support all the editing functionality you're accustomed to in other text editors, such as Notepad. The native edit controls that Visual Basic programmers know as text boxes support the messages we're all accustomed to using: WM_CUT, WM_COPY, WM_PASTE, and WM_CLEAR. Also, SendMessage is useful for determining whether some functions are possible based on the current state of a control, and to find out if a text box has been modified by the user. There are a few other functions, however, that Visual Basic doesn't support: WM_UNDO, EM_CANUNDO, EM_GETMODIFY, and EM_SETMODIFY.

This How-To uses all but the last of these to expand editing support to include all the functionality users are accustomed to, by wrapping all the calls into a single routine called by the user's menu choices. In addition, the Edit menu is enhanced to be "smart"; only valid options are enabled whenever the menu is dropped down. This is done with one API call to determine whether the user's last action can be undone while the remainder of the Edit menu choices are enabled based on information Visual Basic provides, such as the type of active control and the length of selected text.

Steps

Open and run EDITME.VBP. A copy of your AUTOEXEC.BAT file is loaded into the main text box to provide some data to play with, as shown in Figure 3-5-1. You can perform any editing function from the keyboard or through the menus. For example, highlight an area of text, press (DELETE), and then go the Edit menu and select Undo to bring the text back. Notice that the menu is context sensitive. If there's no text highlighted, Cut, Copy, and Paste are not enabled. If there's no text in the Clipboard, Paste is not enabled. And if you haven't done any editing at all, Undo is not enabled. To quit, select Exit from the Demo menu.

1. Create a new project called EDITME.VBP. Create a new form with the objects and properties listed in Table 3-5-1. The position of the text box is not important, because it is sized to fit at run time.

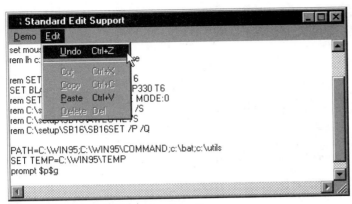

Figure 3-5-1 EditMe project in action

Table 3-5-1 Properties and objects for frmEdit

OBJECT	PROPERTY	SETTING
Form	Name	frmEdit
	Caption	"Standard Edit Support"
text box	Name	Text1
	BorderStyle	0 - None
	MultiLine	True
	Scrollbars	3 - Both

2. Use the Menu Design window to create a menu for frmEdit with the items listed in Table 3-5-2.

Table 3-5-2 Menu settings for frmEdit

CONTROL NAME	INDEX	CAPTION	SHORTCUT KEY
mMain	0	"&Demo	
mLoad		"&Load AUTOEXEC"	
mBar		"-"	
mExit		"E&xit"	
mMain	1	"&Edit"	
mEdit	0	"&Undo"	Ctrl-Z
mEdit	1	"-"	
mEdit	2	"Cu&t"	Ctrl-X
mEdit	3	"&Copy"	Ctrl-C
mEdit	4	"&Paste"	Ctrl-V
mEdit	5	"&Delete"	Del

215

3. Insert the following code in the Declarations section of frmEdit. Notice that most of the constants are the same for Win16 and Win32, but that two vary, thus requiring conditional compilation. Of course, the API declaration for SendMessage also necessitates using conditionals.

```
Option Explicit
'
' Windows API call used to control text box
'
#If Win16 Then
    Private Declare Function SendMessage Lib "User" (ByVal hWnd ⇒
            As Integer, ByVal wMsg As Integer, ByVal wParam As Integer, ⇒
            lParam As Any) As Long
#ElseIf Win32 Then
    Private Declare Function SendMessage Lib "user32" Alias "SendMessageA" ⇒
            (ByVal hWnd As Long, ByVal wMsg As Long, ByVal wParam As Long, ⇒
            lParam As Any) As Long
#End If
'
' Edit Control Messages
'
Const WM_CUT = &H300
Const WM_COPY = &H301
Const WM_PASTE = &H302
Const WM_CLEAR = &H303
Const WM_UNDO = &H304
#If Win16 Then
    Const EM_CANUNDO = &H416        'WM_USER + 22
    Const EM_GETMODIFY = &H408      'WM_USER + 8
#ElseIf Win32 Then
    Const EM_CANUNDO = &HC6
    Const EM_GETMODIFY = &HB8
#End If
'
' Edit menu array constants
'
Const mUndo = 0
Const mCut = 2
Const mCopy = 3
Const mPaste = 4
Const mDelete = 5
```

4. Insert the following code in the Form_Resize event. This allows the text box to be resized to fit the form whenever the form is resized.

```
Private Sub Form_Resize()
    '
    ' Size edit area to fit form
    '
    Text1.Move 0, 0, Me.ScaleWidth, Me.ScaleHeight
End Sub
```

5. Insert the following code in the Form_Load event. This calls the menu event that loads AUTOEXEC.BAT into the edit control.

```
Private Sub Form_Load()
    '
    ' Load some data
    '
    mLoad_Click
End Sub
```

6. Insert the following code into the mLoad_Click event. Without regard to errors, this routine attempts to load a copy of AUTOEXEC.BAT into the edit control, so there's some data on which to try the editing functions. If a user again selects this menu item and the data has been changed, a prompt about whether to proceed will appear.

```
Private Sub mLoad_Click()
    Dim Proceed As Integer
    '
    ' See if user has changed the text, and if so
    ' prompt before loading new copy.
    '
    Proceed = vbYes
    If SendMessage(Text1.hWnd, EM_GETMODIFY, 0, 0&) Then
        Proceed = MsgBox("Text has been modified" _
                        & Chr$(13) & "Continue?", _
                        vbYesNo, "Warning")
    End If
    If Proceed = vbYes Then
        '
        ' Load AUTOEXEC.BAT (if exists) into text box
        '
        On Error Resume Next
            Open "c:\autoexec.bat" For Binary As #1
            Text1.Text = Input(LOF(1), 1)
            Close #1
        On Error GoTo 0
    End If
End Sub
```

7. Insert the following code in the mExit_Click event.

```
Private Sub mExit_Click()
    Unload Me
End Sub
```

8. Insert the following code in the mMain_Click event. This will be triggered whenever the user attempts to drop down one of the top-level menus. If the Edit menu is selected, a generic routine is called that determines available edit functions based on the current state of the system.

```
Private Sub mMain_Click(Index As Integer)
    Const mDemo = 0
    Const mEdit = 1
    '
    ' If Edit menu is dropped down, set available choices
    '
```

Continued on next page

Continued from previous page

```
    If Index = mEdit Then
        EditMenuToggle
    End If
End Sub
```

9. Create a private subroutine called EditMenuToggle, and insert the following code in it. SendMessage is used to query whether the active text box can have its last editing operation undone. The length of the currently selected text is used to toggle Cut, Copy, and Paste availability; if there's nothing selected, these functions need not be available. The Clipboard object is queried to see if it contains text, which would enable Paste. If the active control is not a text box, all the editing options are disabled.

```
Private Sub EditMenuToggle()
    If TypeOf Me.ActiveControl Is text box Then
        '
        ' Determine if last edit can be undone
        '
        Me.mEdit(mUndo).Enabled = SendMessage(Me.ActiveControl.hWnd, ⇒
            EM_CANUNDO, 0, 0&)
        '
        ' See if there's anything to cut, copy, or delete
        '
        Me.mEdit(mCut).Enabled = Me.ActiveControl.SelLength
        Me.mEdit(mCopy).Enabled = Me.ActiveControl.SelLength
        Me.mEdit(mDelete).Enabled = Me.ActiveControl.SelLength
        '
        ' See if there's anything to paste
        '
        Me.mEdit(mPaste) = Clipboard.GetFormat(vbCFText)
    Else
        '
        ' If active control is not a text box then disable all
        '
        Me.mEdit(mUndo).Enabled = False
        Me.mEdit(mCut).Enabled = False
        Me.mEdit(mCopy).Enabled = False
        Me.mEdit(mPaste).Enabled = False
        Me.mEdit(mDelete).Enabled = False
    End If
End Sub
```

10. Insert the following code in the mEdit_Click event. Based on the index passed in, a request is made to a generic function that performs the appropriate edit function. Remember, if a given choice is invalid, the EditMenuToggle routine would have already prevented that item from being selected.

```
Private Sub mEdit_Click(Index As Integer)
    '
    ' Call generic routine to perform requested action.
    ' Same routine could be called from a toolbar event.
    '
```

```
   Select Case Index
      Case mUndo
         EditPerform WM_UNDO
      Case mCut
         EditPerform WM_CUT
      Case mCopy
         EditPerform WM_COPY
      Case mPaste
         EditPerform WM_PASTE
      Case mDelete
         EditPerform WM_CLEAR
   End Select
End Sub
```

11. Create a private subroutine called EditPerform, and insert the following code in it. This is just a simple wrapper routine around the SendMessage API function that does all the work. EditPerform has been separated into its own routine to facilitate calling from multiple events, such as both menu and toolbar.

```
Private Sub EditPerform(EditFunction As Integer)
   '
   ' A "wrapper" function for SendMessage
   ' Requests function passed in EditFunction
   ' Beeps if active control is not a text box
   '
   If TypeOf Me.ActiveControl Is text box Then
      Call SendMessage(Me.ActiveControl.hWnd, EditFunction, 0, 0&)
   Else
      Beep
   End If
End Sub
```

How It Works

Rather than using Visual Basic to handle the editing functions that are possible, all support is provided with the SendMessage API. This considerably reduces the program's complexity—especially for operations such as Cut and Paste which would have to perform string manipulation on the text box contents. SendMessage also opens up methods not available natively under Visual Basic, such as Undo.

Visual Basic subclasses the common edit control for its text boxes. The editing functionality is "built in" to this control and typically accessed with SendMessage. To provide an Undo capability, our project first checks whether an undo is possible given the current state of the text box, by sending it EM_CANUNDO. (If there have been no edits, the API cannot provide an undo.) To perform the undo, WM_UNDO is sent to the text box.

Another intrinsic capability of edit controls that Visual Basic doesn't support is the modify flag. This flag is set when the contents of the edit control change, and cleared whenever the WM_SETTEXT message is received (which is how Visual Basic assigns text to a text box). This can be emulated in Visual Basic by setting a module-level flag for each text box whenever its Change event is fired. Why bother if this information is provided for the asking? The mLoad_Click event checks the value of this API-provided modify flag as an example of how the user might be prompted to save before loading new data.

The generic routines EditMenuToggle and EditPerform check what type of control the ActiveControl is, and react accordingly. These routines could easily be plugged into any application and would work just as well on any number of text boxes. Because the ActiveControl property is used, be careful of what toolbar controls you choose. If a toolbar button receives focus when it's clicked, then these routines can't be as generic, and you'll be forced to track the last active text box. The SSRibbon control that is part of THREED.OCX (available with Visual Basic Professional Edition) doesn't accept focus when clicked, and for that reason makes an excellent choice for toolbar buttons. Image controls are another possibility.

One interesting aspect of text boxes and the standard editing shortcut keys is that text boxes normally support the shortcut keys without any additional effort in a project's code. However, if the stardard shortcut keys are assigned to menu items in the Menu Design window, this intrinsic support is eliminated and must be provided within the project.

Comments

This project will work equally well in either Visual Basic 3.0 or 4.0. It adds capabilities not natively supported by Visual Basic, extending the range of editing functionality to what is typical in other applications. Although only one text box is demonstrated here, any number of text boxes can be supported by the same routines. If you plan to use a toolbar with these routines, make sure the buttons are of the type that don't receive focus.

3.6 How do I...
Create a More Powerful ComboBox?

COMPLEXITY: INTERMEDIATE
COMPATIBILITY: VB4 ONLY

Problem

Visual Basic handles the basics when it comes to ComboBoxes, but I'd like to soup mine up a bit. When I tab into a drop-down ComboBox, I want it to automatically drop open. When I pick an item in the list or enter some new text and then change my mind, I want the item to revert to the original value in the text box when I press (ESC). When I enter a new item, I'd like it to be automatically selected. Also, I want to be able to specify an optional limit on the number of characters that can be entered in the text box portion of the ComboBox.

Technique

A class module is definitely the way to go for adding all these options and hiding the code complexity needed to provide a souped-up ComboBox. A class module can offer properties for the box to drop open upon entry, and to limit the number of characters entered in the text edit portion of the ComboBox. A class can have methods for GotFocus, KeyPress, and LostFocus that may be accessed whenever Visual Basic fires corresponding events in the calling program. It can also provide methods for AddItem, RemoveItem, and Clear, which may be substituted for the intrinsic Visual Basic ComboBox methods.

We can use the SendMessage Windows API function to send messages to the ComboBox. One message can be sent to limit the number of text characters that may be entered, and another to drop open the ComboBox. With a KeyPress or KeyDown event, we can send to the class file any character entered in the ComboBox, and we can hide the work involved in dealing with these characters. A number of factors must be taken into account programmatically: Is text entry allowed? Is it to be limited? Have we exceeded the limit? Did the user press (ESC)? Which style ComboBox is involved? All complexity can be hidden and made reusable by encapsulating it in a class file.

Steps

Open and run COMBO.VBP, and try out the three ComboBox styles. Add items, remove items, and clear the list. See what happens when you press (ESC) after clicking an item in a Dropdown List style control. Also see what happens when you press (ESC) after beginning to type text into a Dropdown or Simple Combo style control. Try out all of the text entry options, as well, on these styles. Set the automatic drop-down option, and tab into the two drop-down style ComboBoxes. Figure 3-6-1 shows the form in action.

1. Create a new project called COMBO.VBP. Select Form1, arrange the objects as shown in Figure 3-6-2, and set their properties as shown in Table 3-6-1. Save the form as COMBO.FRM. Three ComboBox objects are added to the form, each with a different style: Dropdown Combo, Simple Combo, and Dropdown List. This is necessary because the ComboBox Style property cannot be changed at runtime.

Table 3-6-1 COMBO.FRM form properties

OBJECT	PROPERTY	SETTING
Form	Name	ComboForm
	Caption	"Combo Widget Sampler"
Frame	Name	ComboStyleFrame
	Caption	"Combo Style"

Continued on next page

Continued from previous page

OBJECT	PROPERTY	SETTING
OptionButton	Name	ComboStyleOpt
	Caption	"Drop Down"
	Index	0
OptionButton	Name	ComboStyleOpt
	Caption	"Simple"
	Index	1
OptionButton	Name	ComboStyleOpt
	Caption	"List"
	Index	2
Frame	Name	AutoDropDownFrame
	Caption	"Auto Drop Down"
OptionButton	Name	ShowDDOpt
	Caption	"Yes"
	Index	1
OptionButton	Name	ShowDDOpt
	Caption	"No"
	Index	0
Frame	Name	TextEntryFrame
	Caption	"Text Entry"
Frame	Name	AcceptTextFrame
	Caption	"Accept Text"
OptionButton	Name	AcceptTextOpt
	Caption	"Yes"
	Index	1
OptionButton	Name	AcceptTextOpt
	Caption	"No"
	Index	0
Frame	Name	LimitEntryFrame
	Caption	"Limit Entry"
OptionButton	Name	LimitEntryOpt
	Caption	"Limit to 5"
	Index	1
OptionButton	Name	LimitEntryOpt
	Caption	"No Limit"
	Index	0
Frame	Name	SampleComboFrame
	Caption	"Sample Combo Box"
ComboBox	Name	Combo1
	Index	0

OBJECT	PROPERTY	SETTING
	Style	0 'Dropdown Combo
	Visible	0 'False
ComboBox	Name	Combo1
	Index	1
	Style	1 'Simple Combo
	Visible	0 'False
ComboBox	Name	Combo1
	Index	2
	Style	2 'Dropdown List
	Visible	0 'False
CommandButton	Name	Command1
	Caption	"Add Item"
	Index	0
CommandButton	Name	Command1
	Caption	"Remove Item"
	Index	1
CommandButton	Name	Command1
	Caption	"Clear List"
	Index	2
CommandButton	Name	Command1
	Caption	"Exit"
	Index	3

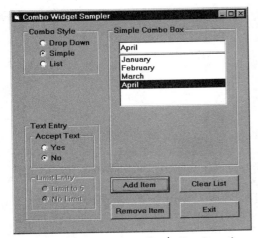

Figure 3-6-1 A smart ComboBox in action in the COMBO.VBP project

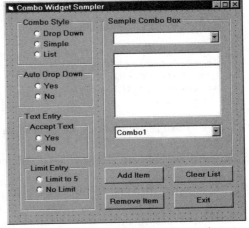

Figure 3-6-2 COMBO.FRM during design

2. Place the following code at the beginning of the COMBO.FRM. This defines an array of three object variables called MyCombo, which are based on CCombo, a class object that brings additional power to the Visual Basic ComboBox. The code also defines an index for the active ComboBox.

```
Option Explicit
Private MyCombo(2) As CCombo
Private ActiveIndex As Integer
```

3. Place the following code in the Form_Load event procedure. This subroutine establishes each Combo1 control as the client object of a new MyCombo class object. It also lines up each of the Combo1 controls in one spot on the form and sets default options. One of the default options establishes the visible ComboBox to be the one with the Dropdown Combo style.

```
Private Sub Form_Load()
    '
    ' Center the form and align optional combobox controls at the
    ' same position on the form. Only one is used at a time.
    '
    Move (Screen.Width - Width) \ 2, (Screen.Height - Height) \ 2
    Combo1(1).Top = Combo1(0).Top
    Combo1(2).Top = Combo1(0).Top
    '
    ' Create an instance of the CCombo class for each sample
    ' combobox.
    '
    Set MyCombo(0) = New CCombo
    Set MyCombo(0).Client = Combo1(0)
    Set MyCombo(1) = New CCombo
    Set MyCombo(1).Client = Combo1(1)
    Set MyCombo(2) = New CCombo
    Set MyCombo(2).Client = Combo1(2)
    '
    ' Set default startup options.
    '
    ComboStyleOpt(0) = True
    ShowDDOpt(0) = True
    LimitEntryOpt(0) = True
    AcceptTextOpt(0) = True
End Sub
```

4. Place the following code in the ComboStyleOpt_Click event procedure. This procedure sets the user's choice of styles for the sample ComboBox, making the other ComboBoxes invisible. When the user selects either the Dropdown or the Simple Combo style, the text entry options become available. When the user selects either the Dropdown Combo or the Dropdown List style, the automatic dropdown option becomes available. No matter what the choice, this procedure reinitializes the other options and clears the ComboBox.

```
Private Sub ComboStyleOpt_Click(Index As Integer)
    '
    ' The combobox style can only be set at design time, so for
    ' this sample we keep 3 comboboxes, one of each style, and
    ' make the appropriate one visible depending on the style
    ' choice. Other choices are made visible when applicable to
    ' the style just selected.
    '
    Select Case Index
        Case 0
            SampleComboFrame.Caption = "Drop Down Combo Box"
            AutoDropDownFrame.Visible = True
            TextEntryFrame.Visible = True
            Combo1(1).Visible = False
            Combo1(2).Visible = False
            Combo1(0).Visible = True
        Case 1
            SampleComboFrame.Caption = "Simple Combo Box"
            AutoDropDownFrame.Visible = False
            TextEntryFrame.Visible = True
            Combo1(0).Visible = False
            Combo1(2).Visible = False
            Combo1(1).Visible = True
        Case 2
            SampleComboFrame.Caption = "Drop Down List Box"
            AutoDropDownFrame.Visible = True
            TextEntryFrame.Visible = False
            Combo1(0).Visible = False
            Combo1(1).Visible = False
            Combo1(2).Visible = True
    End Select
    '
    ' Reinitialize options and clear out list when a different
    ' combobox style is chosen.
    '
    ShowDDOpt(0) = True
    LimitEntryOpt(0) = True
    AcceptTextOpt(0) = True
    Command1(2) = True
    '
    ' Save the index of the combobox that's now visible.
    '
    ActiveIndex = Index
```

5. Place the following code in the ShowDDOpt_Click event procedure, to set a property of the active MyCombo object. This property indicates the user choice of whether to drop down a Dropdown Combo or Dropdown List ComboBox automatically upon entry (i.e., when it gets the focus).

```
Private Sub ShowDDOpt_Click(Index As Integer)
    '
    ' Set CCombo drop down option based on user choice.
    '
    MyCombo(ActiveIndex).ShowDropDown = CBool(Index)
End Sub
```

6. Place the following code in the AcceptTextOpt_Click event procedure, to set a property of the active MyCombo object. This property indicates the user choice of whether or not to accept input in the text-entry portion of a Dropdown or Simple Combo ComboBox. Note that the Dropdown List ComboBox by design does not allow text entry. If the choice is to allow text entry, the limit entry options are enabled.

```
Private Sub AcceptTextOpt_Click(Index As Integer)
    '
    ' Provide example options to enable or disable text entry.
    ' If text entry is disabled, don't get provide option to
    ' limit length of text entry.
    '
    MyCombo(ActiveIndex).EnableTextEntry = CBool(Index)
    If Index = 1 Then
        LimitEntryFrame.Enabled = True
        LimitEntryOpt(0).Enabled = True
        LimitEntryOpt(1).Enabled = True
        LimitEntryOpt(0) = True
        LimitEntryOpt(1) = False
    Else
        LimitEntryFrame.Enabled = False
        LimitEntryOpt(0).Enabled = False
        LimitEntryOpt(1).Enabled = False
    End If
End Sub
```

7. Place the following code in the LimitEntryOpt_Click event procedure, to set a property of the active MyCombo object. This property indicates the user's choice for the amount of text allowed in the text-entry portion of a Dropdown or a Simple ComboBox. Five is used in this example. When Unlimited is selected, 2048 is used (the maximum entry length for a ComboBox).

```
Private Sub LimitEntryOpt_Click(Index As Integer)
    '
    ' Provide example options to limit text entry either to 5
    ' characters or unlimited (2048 is max for combo text).
    '
    If Index = 1 Then
        MyCombo(ActiveIndex).MaxEntryLength = 5
    Else
        MyCombo(ActiveIndex).MaxEntryLength = 2048
    End If
End Sub
```

8. Place the following code in the Combo1_GotFocus event procedure. This subroutine simply triggers the GotFocus procedure in the CCombo class file.

```
Private Sub Combo1_GotFocus(Index As Integer)
    '
    ' Trigger CCombo GotFocus function.
    '
```

```
    MyCombo(Index).GotFocus
End Sub
```

9. Place the following code in the Combo1_KeyPress event procedure. This subroutine triggers the KeyPress procedure in the CCombo class file, passing it the key that was pressed.

```
Private Sub Combo1_KeyPress(Index As Integer, _
                        KeyAscii As Integer)
    '
    ' Trigger CCombo KeyPress function. This event does not
    ' get triggered when the style is 2 (drop down list).
    '
    MyCombo(Index).KeyPress KeyAscii
End Sub
```

10. Place the following code in the Combo1_KeyDown event procedure. When the active ComboBox has the Dropdown List style, this subroutine triggers the KeyPress procedure in the CCombo class file, passing it the key that was pressed. This event procedure is necessary because no KeyPress event is triggered for the Dropdown List style.

```
Private Sub Combo1_KeyDown(Index As Integer, _
                    KeyCode As Integer, Shift As Integer)
    '
    ' If style is 2 (drop down list), trigger CCombo KeyPress
    ' function. The keypress event does not get triggered when
    ' the style is 2 (drop down list).
    '
    If Index = 2 Then MyCombo(Index).KeyPress KeyCode
End Sub
```

11. Place the following code in the Combo1_LostFocus event procedure. This subroutine simply triggers the LostFocus procedure in the CCombo class file.

```
Private Sub Combo1_LostFocus(Index As Integer)
    '
    ' Trigger CCombo lost focus function.
    '
    MyCombo(Index).LostFocus
End Sub
```

12. Place the following code in the Command1_Click event procedure. This code demonstrates the behavior of the CCombo class when an item is added or removed and when the client list box is cleared. Of course, these behaviors will vary based on the options set and passed as properties to the CCombo class.

```
Private Sub Command1_Click(Index As Integer)
    Static DaysOfWeek As String
    Static ItemNbr As Integer
    Dim MonthName As String
```

Continued on next page

227

Continued from previous page

```
    Select Case Index
        '
        ' Trigger CCombo AddItem function, passing it the next
        ' month of the year.
        '
        Case 0
            ItemNbr = (ItemNbr + 1) Mod 12
            MonthName = Format(CDate(ItemNbr & "/1"), "mmmm")
            MyCombo(ActiveIndex).AddItem MonthName
        '
        ' Trigger CCombo RemoveItem, passing it the item to remove.
        '
        Case 1
            If Combo1(ActiveIndex).ListCount > 0 Then
                MyCombo(ActiveIndex).RemoveItem _
                    Combo1(ActiveIndex).ListIndex
            End If
        '
        ' Trigger CCombo ClearItem.
        '
        Case 2
            ItemNbr = 0
            MyCombo(ActiveIndex).Clear
        '
        ' End the program.
        '
        Case 3
            End
    End Select
End Sub
```

13. Use the Insert Class menu item to create a new class module, and save it as COMBO.CLS. Name it CCombo, and put the following code at the beginning of the file. This code defines each of the class property variables and other class file variables. It also defines the SendMessage Windows API function and associated constants that will be used to send messages to the client ComboBox control, to drop down the ComboBox (upon entry) and to limit the number of characters, if any, that are allowed.

```
Option Explicit
'
' SendMessage function and constants used in this class file.
'
Const WM_USER = &h400
Const CB_SHOWDROPDOWN = (WM_USER + 15)
Const CB_LIMITTEXT = (WM_USER + 1)
#If WIN32 Then
    Private Declare Function SendMessage Lib "user 32"_
        Alias "SendMessageA"_
        (ByVal hwnd As Long, ByVal wMsg As Long,_
        ByVal wParam As Integer, ByVal lParam As Long)_
    As Long
#Else
    Private Declare Function SendMessage Lib "user" _
```

```
        (ByVal hWnd As Integer, ByVal wMsg As Integer, _
         ByVal wParam As Integer, lParam As Any) _
    As Long
#End If
'
' These variables define the combobox class file and options.
'
Private m_Initialized As Boolean
Private m_Client As Object
Private m_ShowDropDown As Boolean
Private m_EnableTextEntry As Boolean
Private m_MaxEntryLength As Integer
'
' These variables support saving and restoring the text entry.
'
Private NewTextEntered As Boolean
Private OriginalText As String
```

14. Add the following code to the Initialization section of CCombo. This is the initialization subroutine for the CCombo class. It sets the default values for all the variables, and flags the class as uninitialized.

```
Private Sub Class_Initialize()
    '
    ' Initialize variables.
    '
    m_ShowDropDown = False
    m_EnableTextEntry = False
    m_MaxEntryLength = 0
    m_Initialized = False
    NewTextEntered = False
    OriginalText = ""
End Sub
```

15. Add the following code to the General section of CCombo. The Set client subroutine gets and stores the current client object from the calling program, making sure it is of the ComboBox control type. It also sets the initialized flag to True. The Get client subroutine allows the calling program to reference the current Client value.

```
Public Property Set Client(NewClient As Object)
    '
    ' Set the new client object which must be a ComboBox.
    '
    If TypeOf NewClient Is ComboBox Then
        Set m_Client = NewClient
        m_Initialized = True
    Else
        MsgBox NewClient.Name _
                & " is not a ComboBox. Cannot make it a new client." _
                & " Ignored.", , "ListBox Class Error"
    End If
End Property
```

Continued on next page

Continued from previous page

```
Public Property Get Client() As Object
    '
    ' Return the current client object.
    '
    Set Client = m_Client
End Property
```

16. Add the following code to the General section of CCombo. The Let ShowDropDown subroutine gets the current drop-down mode from the calling program. The Get ShowDropDown subroutine returns the current drop-down mode to the calling program.

```
Public Property Let ShowDropDown(NewShowDropDown As Boolean)
    '
    ' Set current choice of whether or not to drop down a drop
    ' down combo or list style combobox when it gets the focus.
    '
    m_ShowDropDown = NewShowDropDown
End Property

Public Property Get ShowDropDown() As Boolean
    '
    ' Return current choice of whether or not to drop down a drop
    ' down combo or list style combobox when it gets the focus.
    '
    ShowDropDown = m_ShowDropDown
End Property
```

17. Add the following code to the General section of CCombo. The Let EnableTextEntry subroutine retrieves from the calling program the current choice of whether or not to permit text entry. The Get EnableTextEntry subroutine returns that option to the calling program.

```
Public Property Let EnableTextEntry(NewEnableTextEntry As Boolean)
    '
    ' Set current choice of whether or not to permit text entry in
    ' a drop down combo or simple combo style combobox.
    '
    m_EnableTextEntry = NewEnableTextEntry
End Property

Public Property Get EnableTextEntry() As Boolean
    '
    ' Set current choice of whether or not to permit text entry in
    ' a drop down combo or simple combo style combobox.
    '
    EnableTextEntry = m_EnableTextEntry
End Property
```

18. Add the following code to the General section of CCombo. The Let MaxEntryLength subroutine retrieves and stores the desired maximum length for text entry. It limits the maximum value to 2048 (maximum text-entry length for a VB4 ComboBox).

The Get MaxEntryLength subroutine returns the current maximum value to the calling program.

```
Public Property Let MaxEntryLength(NewMaxEntryLength As Integer)
    '
    ' Set the max text entry length which cannot exceed 2048 in
    ' a combobox.
    '
    If NewMaxEntryLength > 2048 Then
        m_MaxEntryLength = 2048
    Else
        m_MaxEntryLength = NewMaxEntryLength
    End If
    Dim rCode As Long
    rCode = SendMessage(m_Client.hWnd, CB_LIMITTEXT, m_MaxEntryLength, 0)
End Property

Public Property Get MaxEntryLength() As Integer
    '
    ' Return the current max text entry length.
    '
        MaxEntryLength = m_MaxEntryLength
End Property
```

19. Add the following subroutine to the General section of CCombo. This subroutine provides the GotFocus method for the Client ComboBox and will generally be called from that ComboBox's GotFocus event procedure. For all ComboBox styles, it saves the original text in the ComboBox and sets a flag to indicate that new text has not yet been input. This is needed so that the original text can be restored if the user presses (ESC) before leaving the ComboBox. The subroutine also automatically drops down the Client ComboBox when appropriate for the style and current setting of the ShowDropDown property. Dropping down the ComboBox is a simple matter of sending the appropriate message to the Client control's window handle.

```
Public Sub GotFocus()
    '
    ' Save the original text and reset NewTextEntered variable.
    '
    OriginalText = m_Client.Text
    NewTextEntered = False
    '
    ' For drop down combo and list styles, set the combobox to
    ' drop down when it gets the focus if that is the option
    ' set for this combobox.
    '
    If m_Client.Style = 1 Then Exit Sub
    Dim rCode As Long
    If m_ShowDropDown Then
        rCode = SendMessage(m_Client.hWnd, CB_SHOWDROPDOWN, 1, 0)
    End If
End Sub
```

20. Add the following subroutine to the General section of CCombo. This subroutine provides the KeyPress method for the Client ComboBox and will generally be called from that ComboBox's KeyPress event procedure for DropDown and Simple Combo styles, which allow a KeyPress event. When the Client ComboBox is of the DropDown List style, this subroutine can be called from the KeyDown event procedure, because this style does not accept text entry and thus does not trigger a KeyPress event. This subroutine ensures that, when the (ESC) is pressed, the original text is restored to any style ComboBox. For other keypresses, when the text entry option is turned on, the flag is set to indicate new text has been entered. When the text entry option is turned off, it rejects the keypress (KeyAscii = 0) and beeps.

```
Public Sub KeyPress(KeyAscii As Integer)
    '
    ' If the escape key is pressed, return the text entry to its
    ' original value. Otherwise if text entry is permissible, set
    ' a flag to indicate this. If not permissible, "swallow" the
    ' text and beep.
    '
    If KeyAscii = vbKeyEscape Then
        m_Client.Text = OriginalText
        NewTextEntered = False
    Else
        If m_Client.Style  2 Then
            If m_EnableTextEntry Then
                NewTextEntered = True
            Else
                KeyAscii = 0
                Beep
            End If
        End If
    End If
End Sub
```

21. Add the following subroutine to the General section of CCombo. This code provides the LostFocus method for the Client ComboBox and will generally be called from that ComboBox's LostFocus event procedure. When text entry is allowed and new text has been entered, the text is added as a new item into the Client ComboBox.

```
Public Sub LostFocus()
    '
    ' For drop down and simple combo styles (styles where text
    ' entry is an option), if new text was entered, add it as a
    ' new item in the list.
    '
    If m_Client.Style = 2 Then Exit Sub
    If m_EnableTextEntry Then
        If NewTextEntered = True Then
            AddItem m_Client.Text
        End If
```

```
    End If
End Sub
```

22. Add the following subroutine to the General section of CCombo. First, the
    RemoveItemIndex is used to remove the desired item from the Client ComboBox.
    Then the next item in the list, if there is one, is highlighted; otherwise, the previ-
    ous item in the list is highlighted.

```
Public Sub RemoveItem(RemoveItemIndex As Integer)
    '
    ' Remove the item and highlight the one below it in the list
    ' or if there is none below, the one above it in the list.
    '
    m_Client.RemoveItem RemoveItemIndex
    If RemoveItemIndex > m_Client.ListCount - 1 Then
        m_Client.ListIndex = m_Client.ListCount - 1
    Else
        m_Client.ListIndex = RemoveItemIndex
    End If
End Sub
```

23. Add the following subroutine to the General section of CListBox. This subroutine
    simply clears the list of items in the Client ComboBox.

```
Public Sub Clear()
    '
    ' Clear the list of items.
    '
    m_Client.Clear
End Sub
```

How It Works

The project in this How-To combines powerful new ComboBox features into a CCombo
class. A ComboBox is set as the Client of the CCombo class. A ShowDropDown property provides an option for whether to open a drop-down style ComboBox upon entry
(i.e. when the ComboBox gets the focus by tabbing into it or clicking on it). An
EnableTextEntry option defines whether any text entry is allowed a ComboBox.
When text entry is enabled, it can be further controlled through a new
MaxEntryLength property. This allows a limit to be set for the number of characters
entered. Whenever a selection or text entry is started, it's considered "polite" to provide an undo capability. Pressing the (ESC) key is a standard way to communicate the
need to undo a selection or text entry, and our smart CCombo class knows how to
be polite.

When the option is set to prevent all text entry from a ComboBox, a CCombo
class subroutine "swallows" any entered character by capturing it on a KeyPress event
and changing it to a KeyAscii value of 0. This makes the character disappear. When
the option is set to limit the text to a specified number of characters, a ComboBox
message for this purpose—the CB_LIMITTEXT message—is used. When the option

is set to drop down the ComboBox upon entry, another ComboBox message is called into play—the CB_SHOWDROPDOWN message.

Comments

How-To 8.1 provides a technique for creating a Quicken-style ComboBox using a text box and a ListBox. The CCombo class file developed for this project could be made even more powerful by augmenting it with How-To 8.1's functionality.

3.7 How do I...
Add a Horizontal Scroll Bar to a List Box?

COMPLEXITY: INTERMEDIATE
COMPATIBILITY: VB4 ONLY

Problem

Visual Basic puts a vertical scroll bar in my list box whenever the number of items exceeds the height of the box, but it doesn't provide a horizontal scroll bar when the width of one or more items exceeds the width of the list box. I usually want to be able to scroll to read the entire item in a list box. For the most flexibility, I'd like to be able to choose whether or not to have a horizontal scroll bar in the a list box. Also, sometimes I store additional information at the end of the list of items. I'd like to keep that information hidden, so I want the option of scrolling only to a certain maximum length, to be specified when needed.

Technique

This How-To performs all its horizontal scroll bar feats with the aid of the class module, CListBox, which handles the AddItem, RemoveItem, and Clear methods for the client list box.

The calling program defines the client list box to CListBox and provides values for a set of properties, including whether or not to show a horizontal scroll bar. If one is to be shown, the calling program sets a property option for adjusting the scrolling range either to the length of the longest item in the list or to a fixed width. A property is also set to indicate the width of the list box itself. When items are added and removed, when the list is cleared, and when any of the various properties changes, a CListBox subroutine again determines if a horizontal scroll bar is called for. If so, the scroll bar is displayed, with the appropriate scrolling width.

Steps

Open and run HSCROLL.VBP, and add several items. Then switch back and forth between showing and not showing a horizontal scroll bar, and watch what happens when the longest item exceeds the width of the ListBox. Try setting the scroll limit to 400 pixels and see how that affects the scrolling range. Also, examine what happens

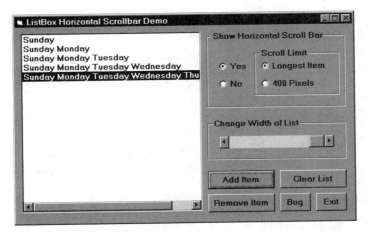

Figure 3-7-1 List Box with a horizontal scroll bar in
HSCROLL.FRM

when you remove items and when you clear the item list. Click on the Bug button to
see what happens when this sample application passes a non-list box object to the
class file that provides the horizontal scroll bar.

1. Create a new project called HSCROLL.VBP. Create a form with controls as shown
   in Figure 3-7-1, set form objects and properties as shown in Table 3-7-1, and
   save the form as HSCROLL.FRM.

Table 3-7-1 HSCROLL.FRM form properties

OBJECT	PROPERTY	SETTING
Form	Name	HScrollForm
	Caption	"ListBox Horizontal Scroll Bar Demo"
ListBox	Name	List1
Frame	Name	ShowHScrollFrame
	Caption	"Show Horizontal Scroll Bar"
OptionButton	Name	HScrollOpt
	Caption	"Yes"
	Index	1
OptionButton	Name	HScrollOpt
	Caption	"No"
	Index	0
Frame	Name	ScrollLimitFrame
	Caption	"Scroll Limit"
OptionButton	Name	ScrollLimitOpt
	Caption	"Longest Item"

Continued on next page

Continued from previous page

OBJECT	PROPERTY	SETTING
	Index	0
	Visible	0 'False
OptionButton	Name	ScrollLimitOpt
	Caption	"400 Pixels"
	Index	1
	Visible	0 'False
Frame	Name	ChgListWidthFrame
	Caption	"Change Width of List"
HScrollBar	Name	HScroll1
	LargeChange	50
	Max	300
	Min	50
	SmallChange	10
	Value	300
CommandButton	Name	Command1
	Caption	"Add Item"
	Index	0
CommandButton	Name	Command1
	Caption	"Remove Item"
	Index	1
CommandButton	Name	Command1
	Caption	"Clear List"
	Index	2
CommandButton	Name	Command1
	Caption	"Exit"
	Index	3
CommandButton	Name	Command1
	Caption	"Bug"
	Index	4

2. Place the following code at the beginning of the HSCROLL.FRM. This code ensures that all variables are coded explicitly, and it defines an object variable called MyList that is based on CListBox.

```
Option Explicit

Private MyList As New CListBox
```

3. Place the following code in the Form_Load event procedure. This establishes the List1 control as the client control for the MyList object and sets its initial width. It also sets the horizontal scroll option to True, which triggers the HScrollOpt_Click event.

```
Private Sub Form_Load()
    '
    ' Center the form, and establish List1 as the client for the
    ' MyList instance of the CListBox class object. Initialize
    ' MyList.Width and start out with the horizontal scroll bar
    ' option set on.
    '
    Move (Screen.Width - Width) \ 2, (Screen.Height - Height) \ 2
    Set MyList.Client = List1
    MyList.Width = HScroll1.Value
    HScrollOpt(1) = True
End Sub
```

4. Place the following code in the HScrollOpt_Click event procedure. This procedure sets a property of the MyList object, to indicate the user choice of whether to include a horizontal scroll bar. If a horizontal scroll bar is requested, the user is offered an additional option for establishing the range of the scroll bar.

```
Private Sub HScrollOpt_Click(Index As Integer)
    '
    ' Allow the user to enter a choice of whether or not to
    ' include a horizontal scroll bar and set the corresponding
    ' MyList property accordingly. If the user choses to include
    ' the horizontal scroll bar, make the scroll bar options
    ' visible, otherwise hide them.
    '
    MyList.HScroll = CBool(Index)
    If Index = 1 Then
        ScrollLimitOpt(0).Visible = True
        ScrollLimitOpt(0) = True
        ScrollLimitOpt(1).Visible = True
        ScrollLimitOpt(1) = False
        ScrollLimitFrame.Visible = True
    Else
        ScrollLimitOpt(0).Visible = False
        ScrollLimitOpt(1).Visible = False
        ScrollLimitFrame.Visible = False
    End If
End Sub
```

5. Place the following code in the ScrollLimitOpt_Click event procedure. This procedure sets a property for the MyList object, to indicate the user's choice of how far to scroll the list box.

```
Private Sub ScrollLimitOpt_Click(Index As Integer)
    '
    ' Allow the user to enter a choice of whether the horizontal
    ' scroll bar should be limited to scroll exactly 400 pixels or
    ' to scroll as far as is needed to show the longest item in
    ' the list.
    '
    If Index = 0 Then
```

Continued on next page

Continued from previous page

```
        MyList.HScrollWidth = 0
    Else
        MyList.HScrollWidth = 400
    End If
End Sub
```

6. Place the following code in the HScroll1_Change event procedure. The width is set as a property of the MyList object so that horizontal scroll calculations can account for the current width of the client list box.

```
Private Sub HScroll1_Change()
    '
    ' Changes to the HScroll1 control result in adjusting the
    ' width of the List1 control and its corresponding CListBox
    ' width property.
    '
    List1.Width = HScroll1.Value
    MyList.Width = HScroll1.Value
End Sub
```

7. Place the following code in the Command1_Click event procedure. This code determines the behavior of the CListBox class when an item is added or removed, when the client list box is cleared, and when the client is set to a control that's not a list box.

```
Private Sub Command1_Click(Index As Integer)
    Static DaysOfWeek As String
    Static ItemNbr As Integer
    Select Case Index
        '
        ' Trigger CListBox AddItem, passing it the next day of the
        ' week.
        '
        Case 0
            ItemNbr = (ItemNbr + 1) Mod 7
            If ItemNbr = 1 Then DaysOfWeek = ""
            DaysOfWeek = DaysOfWeek & Format(ItemNbr, "dddd") & " "
            MyList.AddItem DaysOfWeek
        '
        ' Trigger CListBox RemoveItem, passing it the item to remove.
        '
        Case 1
            If List1.ListCount > 0 Then
                MyList.RemoveItem List1.ListIndex
            End If
        '
        ' Trigger CListBox ClearItem.
        '
        Case 2
            ItemNbr = 0
            MyList.ClearListBox
        '
        ' End the program.
        '
```

```
      Case 3
         End
      '
      ' Trigger a bug by setting the CListBox Client property to
      ' a control that's not a ListBox.
      '
      Case 4
         Set MyList.Client = ChgListWidthFrame
   End Select
End Sub
```

8. Use the Insert Class menu item to create a new class module, and save it as CLISTBOX.CLS. Name it CListBox, and put the following code at the beginning of the file. This code defines each of the class property variables and other class file variables. It also defines the SendMessage Windows API function and associated constants that will be used to send a message to the client list box control to set and remove a horizontal scroll bar.

```
Option Explicit
'
' SendMessage function and constants used in this class file.
'
Const WM_USER = &h400
Const LB_SETHORIZONTALEXTENT = (WM_USER + 21)
#If Win32 Then
    Private Declare Function SendMessage Lib "user32"_
        Alias "SendMessageA"_
        (ByVal hwnd As Long, ByVal wMsg As Long,_
        ByVal wParam As Integer, ByVal lParam As Long)_
    As Long
    Private Declare Function SendMessage Lib "user" _
        (ByVal hWnd As Integer, ByVal wMsg As Integer, _
        ByVal wParam As Integer, lParam As Any) _
    As Long
#End If
'
' These variables define the listbox class file and options.
'
Private m_Initialized As Boolean
Private m_Client As Object
Private m_HScroll As Boolean
Private m_HScrollWidth As Integer
Private m_ListBoxWidth As Integer
'
' This variable keeps track of the longest item in the listbox.
'
Private LongestItemWidth As Integer
```

9. Add the following code to the Initialization section of CListBox. This is the initialization subroutine for the CListBox class. It sets the default mode for horizontal scrolling to False, sets the scroll and list box width variables to zero, and flags the class as uninitialized.

```
Private Sub Class_Initialize()
    '
    ' Set default values for variables.
    '
    m_HScroll = False
    m_HScrollWidth = 0
    m_ListBoxWidth = 0
    '
    ' Flag to tell if a valid control object has been identified.
    '
    m_Initialized = False
End Sub
```

10. Add the following code to the General section of CListBox. The Set Client sub-routine gets the current client object from the calling program, makes sure the client object is of the list box control type, and then sets the initialized flag to True.

```
Property Set Client(NewClient As Object)
    '
    ' Set the new client object which must be a ListBox.
    '
    If TypeOf NewClient Is ListBox Then
        Set m_Client = NewClient
        m_Initialized = True
    Else
        MsgBox NewClient.Name & _
        " is not a ListBox. Cannot make it a new client. Ignored.", _
        , "ListBox Class Error"
    End If
End Property
```

11. Add the following code to the General section of CListBox. The Get HScroll sub-routine returns the current client object to the calling program.

```
Property Get HScroll() As Boolean
    '
    ' Returns current choice to show or not show horizontal scroll
    ' bar.
    '
    HScroll = m_HScroll
End Property
```

12. Add the following code to the General section of CListBox. The Let HScroll sub-routine sets the mode for horizontal scrolling and executes the SetHScrollBar sub-routine to activate the new mode.

```
Property Let HScroll(NewHScroll As Boolean)
    '
    ' Set current choice to show or not show horizontal scroll
    ' bar and adjust scrollbar behavior accordingly.
    '
```

```
    m_HScroll = NewHScroll
    SetHScrollBar
End Property
```

13. Add the following code to the General section of CListBox. The Get HScroll subroutine returns the current horizontal scrolling mode to the calling program.

```
Property Get HScroll() As Boolean
    '
    ' Returns current choice to show or not show horizontal scroll
    ' bar.
    '
    HScroll = m_HScroll
End Property
```

14. Add the following code to the General section of CListBox. The Let HScrollWidth subroutine sets the horizontal scroll width variable and executes the SetHScrollBar subroutine to activate the new scroll width.

```
Property Let HScrollWidth(NewHScrollWidth As Integer)
    '
    ' Set current choice regarding width of scrollbar and adjust
    ' scrollbar behavior accordingly.
    '
    m_HScrollWidth = NewHScrollWidth
    SetHScrollBar
End Property
```

15. Add the following code to the General section of CListBox. The Get HScrollWidth subroutine returns the current horizontal scroll width to the calling program.

```
Property Get HScrollWidth() as Integer
    '
    ' Return current choice regarding width of scrollbar.
    '
    HScrollWidth = m_HScrollWidth
End Property
```

16. Add the following code to the General section of CListBox. The Let Width subroutine sets the list box width variable and executes the SetHScrollBar subroutine to activate the new list box width.

```
Property Let Width(NewListBoxWidth As Integer)
    '
    ' Set current choice regarding width of scrollbar and adjust
    ' scrollbar behavior accordingly.
    '
    m_ListBoxWidth = NewListBoxWidth
    SetHScrollBar
End Property
```

17. Add the following code to the General section of CListBox. The Get Width subroutine returns the current setting for the list box width to the calling program.

```
Property Get Width() As Integer
    '
    ' Return current setting for width of scrollbar.
    '
    Width = m_ListBoxWidth
End Property
```

18. Add the following subroutine to the General section of CListBox. The AddItem
method performs the primary function of adding the item to the list box, along
with the functions that make this a "smart" list box object. If the new item is
longer than the previously calculated longest item width, the length of the new
item is captured and the SetHScrollBar function is executed to take into account
the new length. The new item is also highlighted in the list.

```
Public Sub AddItem(NewItem As String)
    '
    ' Capture the width of the new item if it's wider than what
    ' has previously been saved. If the width is changed, adjust
    ' the scrollbar accordingly.
    '
    If m_Client.Parent.TextWidth(NewItem) > LongestItemWidth Then
        LongestItemWidth = m_Client.Parent.TextWidth(NewItem)
        SetHScrollBar
    End If
    '
    ' Add the new item to the end of the list and highlight it
    ' in the list.
    '
    m_Client.AddItem NewItem
    m_Client.ListIndex = (m_Client.ListCount - 1)
End Sub
```

19. Add the following subroutine to the General section of CListBox. The
RemoveItem method performs the primary function of removing the item from
the list box, along with additional functions that contribute to making this a
"smart" list box object. The subroutine highlights the next item in the list, if there
is one; otherwise, it highlights the previous item in the list. If the item being
removed is the longest item in the list, the length of the next longest item in the
list is determined, and the SetHScrollBar subroutine is executed to take into
account the new length.

```
Public Sub RemoveItem(RemoveItemIndex As Integer)
    Dim Iindex As Integer
    Dim RemoveItemWidth As Integer
    '
    ' Calculate the width of the item being removed before
    ' removing it from the listbox. Highlight the next item in
```

```
' the list if there is a next item. Otherwise highlight the
' previous item in the list if there is one.
'
RemoveItemWidth _
    = m_Client.Parent.TextWidth(m_Client.List(RemoveItemIndex))
m_Client.RemoveItem RemoveItemIndex
If RemoveItemIndex > m_Client.ListCount - 1 Then
    m_Client.ListIndex = m_Client.ListCount - 1
Else
    m_Client.ListIndex = RemoveItemIndex
End If
'
' If the item removed was the widest in the list, loop
' through the remaining items in the list to capture the
' width of the one that is now widest and then adjust the
' scrollbar accordingly.
'
If RemoveItemWidth = LongestItemWidth Then
    LongestItemWidth = 0
    For Iindex = 0 To m_Client.ListCount - 1
        If m_Client.Parent.TextWidth(m_Client.List(Iindex)) _
            > LongestItemWidth Then
            LongestItemWidth _
                = m_Client.Parent.TextWidth(m_Client.List(Iindex))
        End If
    Next Iindex
    SetHScrollBar
End If
End Sub
```

20. Add the following subroutine to the General section of CListBox. The ClearListBox method clears all items out of the list box object. Along with that, it resets the longest item width variable to 0 and performs the SetHScrollBar subroutine to reflect the empty list box.

```
Public Sub ClearListBox()
    '
    ' Reset the longest item width to 0 to reflect nothing in
    ' the list, and adjust the scrollbar accordingly (along with
    ' clearing the listbox).
    '
    LongestItemWidth = 0
    SetHScrollBar
    m_Client.Clear
End Sub
```

21. Add the following subroutine to the General section of CListBox. By now the name of this subroutine, SetHScrollBar, should be familiar to you, if not its functionality. That's because it's the same private subroutine executed by each of the other public methods and most of the other write properties in this class. This subroutine uses the current settings for the various class file variables to determine whether or not a horizontal scroll bar is needed, and if so, what the

scrolling width should be. Then it executes the SendMessage Windows API function to set or remove the horizontal scroll bar for the client object.

```
Private Sub SetHScrollBar()
    Dim rCode As Long
    '
    ' If the longest item in the listbox does not exceed the
    ' scrollbar width or if no scrollbar is desired, set the
    ' listbox so that it does not show a horizontal scrollbar and
    ' exit the subroutine.
    '
    If LongestItemWidth <= m_ListBoxWidth _
    Or m_HScroll = False Then
        rCode = SendMessage(m_Client.hWnd, _
            LB_SETHORIZONTALEXTENT, 0, 0)
        Exit Sub
    End If
    '
    ' If a scrollbar is desired and needed, set to scroll to show
    ' the longest item in the list or to a specific width depend-
    ' in on the current ScrollWidth choice.
    '
    If m_HScrollWidth = 0 Then
        rCode = SendMessage(m_Client.hWnd, _
            LB_SETHORIZONTALEXTENT, LongestItemWidth, 0)
    Else
        rCode = SendMessage(m_Client.hWnd, _
            LB_SETHORIZONTALEXTENT, m_HScrollWidth, 0)
    End If
End Sub
```

How It Works

The project in this How-To relies on the functionality of the CListBox class. HScroll defines whether a horizontal scroll bar is desired. When HScrollWidth is set to zero, the longest item's width is used to set the scrolling range; otherwise, the scrolling width is set to the width specified in HScrollWidth. If a scroll bar is desired, the width of the list box is compared to the desired scrolling range to determine if the scroll bar is needed. When any property value changes—including the width of the list box itself—and when the list of items in the list box changes, the scroll bar calculations must be redone.

To set or remove the horizontal scroll bar takes just one call to the SendMessage Windows API function. The call defines the list box window handle, the message to send (LB_SETHORIZONTALEXTENT), and the range to scroll (0 to turn off the scroll bar).

Comments

To keep it simple, CListBox supports only a simple form of the AddItem method; that is, it always inserts the item at the end of the list. The project could be enhanced to accept an insert index defining the point of insertion. When inserting an item anywhere in the list, the highlighted item would need to be calculated based on the new index rather than on the index of the last item in the list.

For added flexibility, highlighting the new item in the list could be turned into an option that the calling program could set. This would be especially handy for multiselect list boxes, where user input is needed to determine the appropriate selection.

3.8 How do I...
Make a Splitter Bar between Two Text Windows?

COMPLEXITY: EASY

COMPATIBILITY: VB3 OR VB4

Problem

I need to let my users work with two large, multiline text boxes at once. I'd like to offer an option similar to that in Visual Basic's editor: a splitter bar that can be dragged to change the proportion of the total window occupied by the top and bottom text boxes. Is there a simple way to do this?

Technique

This is a deceptively simple How-To that has several subtle considerations, but nothing tricky. The general idea is to have a PictureBox act as the splitter bar. When it's dragged and dropped on one of the text boxes, its position relative to the form is calculated. That allows a recalculation of the percentage allocated to each text box.

Steps

Open and run SPLIT.VBP. It's set to open with the bottom text box using all the space available on the form. Grab the splitter bar with the mouse, drag it downward midway on the form, and drop it. The splitter bar moves to where you dropped it, and the text boxes are resized to fill either side of it. Press the Data command button on the toolbar and your CONFIG.SYS and AUTOEXEC.BAT files will be loaded just to give you a sense of how this sort of control arrangement works with "live" data. Pressing (ALT)-(DOWN) arrow or (ALT)-(UP) arrow moves the splitter bar up and down, and pressing (F6) toggles between the two text boxes. The split window project is shown in action in Figure 3-8-1. Press the Quit command button to exit.

1. Create a new project called SPLIT.VBP. Create a new form named frmSplitTxt, and save it as SPLIT.FRM. Assign the objects and properties for this form as listed in Table 3-8-1. The form will look similar to Figure 3-8-2 when you've completed this step. Precise arrangement of the controls isn't required, as that will be handled at run time.

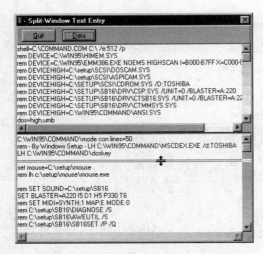

Figure 3-8-1 SPLIT.FRM at run time

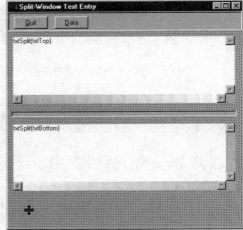

Figure 3-8-2 SPLIT.FRM at design time

Table 3-8-1 Objects and properties of SPLIT.FRM

OBJECT	PROPERTY	SETTING
Form	Name	frmSplitTxt
	Appearance	1 - 3D
	Caption	"Split-Window Text Entry"
	KeyPreview	True
text box	Name	txtSplit
	BorderStyle	0 - None
	Index	0
	MultiLine	True
	Scrollbars	3 - Both
	TabIndex	1
	Text	"txtSplit(txtTop)"
text box	Name	txtSplit
	BorderStyle	0 - None
	Index	1
	MultiLine	True
	Scrollbars	3 - Both
	TabIndex	0
	Text	"txtSplit(txtBottom)"
PictureBox	Name	picSplit
	BackColor	&H8000000F&
	BorderStyle	1 - Fixed Single
	DragMode	1 - Automatic

OBJECT	PROPERTY	SETTING
PictureBox	Name	picTool
	Align	1 - Align Top
	BackColor	&H8000000F&
CommandButton	Name	cmdQuit
	Caption	"&Quit"
	Cancel	True
	TabIndex	2
CommandButton	Name	cmdData
	Caption	"&Data"
	TabIndex	3
Image	Name	Image1
	Picture	(Icon) 'SPLITTER.ICO
	Visible	False

2. Insert the following code into the Declarations section of frmSplitTxt:

```
Option Explicit
'
' Store current percentage dedicated to top text box
'
Private m_Split As Integer
'
' Index constants for text boxes
'
Const txtTop = 0
Const txtBottom = 1
```

3. Insert the following code into the Form_Initialize event. You can use this to set the initial split to whatever percentage you desire. In this project, 0 percent is used, so the top text box is not seen at startup.

```
Private Sub Form_Initialize()
    '
    ' Set initial split to whatever size is desirable
    '
    m_Split = 0
End Sub
```

4. Insert the following code in the Form_Load event. This sets up the graphical properties of some of the controls. Using constants in Visual Basic 4.0 is much simpler than in previous versions. Notice how easy it is to set the background colors for several controls. Ever wondered if the BackColor property had any purpose on command buttons? It's actually quite useful if the button is on a background other than white. Setting a command button's BackColor property alters four pixels, one at each corner, providing a cleaner look. Another new feature of VB4 is the ability to set custom mouse pointers. Here, the icon stored in Image1 is assigned to the MouseIcon property of the splitter bar:

```
Private Sub Form_Load()
    '
    ' Color corner pixels of command buttons to match background
    '
    cmdExit.BackColor = vb3DFace
    cmdData.BackColor = vb3DFace
    '
    ' Set graphic attributes of toolbar picture box
    '
    picTool.BackColor = vb3DFace
    picTool.BorderStyle = vbBSNone
    picTool.DrawWidth = 2
    '
    ' Set splitter to be 5 pixels high, color it, and
    ' assign a custom mousepointer icon.
    '
    picSplit.Height = 5 * Screen.TwipsPerPixelY
    picSplit.BackColor = vb3DFace
    picSplit.MouseIcon = Image1.Picture
    picSplit.MousePointer = vbCustom
End Sub
```

5. Insert the following code in the Form_Resize event. This calls the routine that resizes all controls based on the current split factor, and then forces the toolbar to repaint itself with its Refresh method.

```
Private Sub Form_Resize()
    '
    ' Call routine that resizes all the controls,
    ' then repaint the toolbar.
    '
    ResizeControls
    picTool.Refresh
End Sub
```

6. Insert the following code in the txtSplit_DragDrop event. If the dropped control is the splitter bar, the Y coordinate that was passed in is converted to its position relative to the form's client space. Dividing this relative Y by the form's ScaleHeight, minus the toolbar's Height, gives the new percentage of the form to be occupied by the top text box. Then resizing the routine is called to act on this new split factor.

```
Private Sub txtSplit_DragDrop(Index As Integer, Source As Control, ⇒
        X As Single, Y As Single)
    Dim frmY As Integer
    '
    ' Was it the splitter bar that user dropped?
    '
    If Source Is picSplit Then
        '
        ' Calc the Y coordinate of drop relative to form
        '
        frmY = txtSplit(Index).Top + Y - picTool.Height
        '
```

```
        ' Calc new split and resize the controls
        '
        m_Split = (frmY / (Me.ScaleHeight - picTool.Height)) * 100
        ResizeControls
    End If
End Sub
```

7. Insert the following code into a new subroutine called ResizeControls. This is mostly just simple math. The important thing to remember is that all controls are accounted for. Adding a toolbar to the demo shows how its position must be considered when doing these calculations. One calculated dimension merits some examination, however. The splitter bar, picSplit, is sized to be three times the width of the interior of the form, and then centered horizontally. This allows the user to drag it from one side to the other, without ever seeing the ends. Because some of the intermediate numbers can get large, long integers were introduced to prevent numeric overflows in two locations.

```
Private Static Sub ResizeControls()
    Dim t1Top As Integer
    Dim t1Height As Integer
    Dim t2Top As Integer
    Dim t2Height As Integer
    Dim fWidth As Integer
    Dim fHeight As Integer
    Dim pHeight As Integer
    '
    ' It's faster to just access properties once
    '
    fWidth = Me.ScaleWidth
    fHeight = Me.ScaleHeight
    pHeight = picSplit.Height
    '
    ' Calc new top and height for the top text box
    '
    t1Top = picTool.Height
    t1Height = (m_Split * CLng(fHeight - t1Top - (pHeight \ 2))) \ 100
    '
    ' Calc new top and height for the bottom text box
    '
    t2Top = t1Top + t1Height + pHeight
    t2Height = fHeight - t2Top
    If t2Height < 0 Then t2Height = 0
    '
    ' Move splitter and text boxes
    '
    picSplit.Move -fWidth, t1Top + t1Height, fWidth * 3&
    txtSplit(txtTop).Move 0, t1Top, fWidth, t1Height
    txtSplit(txtBottom).Move 0, t2Top, fWidth, t2Height
End Sub
```

8. Insert the following code in the Form_KeyDown event. Since the Form.KeyPreview property is set to True, all keystrokes are first filtered through this event. If the user presses either (ALT)-(DOWN) arrow or (ALT)-(UP) arrow, the splitter bar will

move in the appropriate direction in increments of 2 percent regardless of what control is active.

```
Private Sub Form_KeyDown(KeyCode As Integer, Shift As Integer)
    '
    ' Allow use of Alt-Down or Alt-Up to move splitter bar
    ' Each press bumps the split up or down 2%
    '
    If Shift = vbAltMask Then
        If KeyCode = vbKeyDown Then
            If m_Split < 99 Then
                m_Split = m_Split + 2
            Else
                m_Split = 100
            End If
            ResizeControls
        ElseIf KeyCode = vbKeyUp Then
            If m_Split > 1 Then
                m_Split = m_Split - 2
            Else
                m_Split = 0
            End If
            ResizeControls
        End If
    End If
End Sub
```

9. Insert the following code in the txtSplit_KeyDown event. This watches for the
   F6 key, and jumps to the other text box if any of it is visible—that is, if the split
   isn't either 0 percent or 100 percent.

```
Private Sub txtSplit_KeyDown(Index As Integer, KeyCode As Integer, ⇒
    Shift As Integer)
    '
    ' Support F6 (like VB) to toggle between split windows.
    '
    If KeyCode = vbKeyF6 Then
        If m_Split > 0 And m_Split < 100 Then
            txtSplit((Index + 1) Mod 2).SetFocus
        End If
    End If
End Sub
```

10. Insert the following code in the picTool_Paint event. This draws the highlights
    and shadows around the edge of the PictureBox. If you have Visual Basic
    Professional Edition, to achieve the same effect you can use the Panel3D control
    that's part of THREED.OCX.

```
Private Static Sub picTool_Paint()
    Dim pX As Integer
    Dim pY As Integer
    '
    ' Access properties just once, and set aside
```

```
'
pX = picTool.Width - Screen.TwipsPerPixelX
pY = picTool.Height - Screen.TwipsPerPixelY
'
' Draw highlight and shadow on picture box
'
picTool.Cls
picTool.Line (0, 0)-(pX, pY), vb3DDKShadow, B
picTool.Line (0, 0)-(0, pY), vb3DHighLight
picTool.Line (0, 0)-(pX, 0), vb3DHighLight
End Sub
```

11. Having some data in the text boxes will help you observe the working of this project, so insert the following code in the cmdData_Click event. This routine loads the contents of your CONFIG.SYS and AUTOEXEC.BAT files into the two text boxes, ignoring errors in case these files don't exist on your system. One interesting feature of this routine is that it uses the fastest method possible to read the entire file into a text box with just one call.

```
Private Sub cmdData_Click()
    '
    ' For demo, just open two data files that are likely to
    ' be there. .  Use different files if these don't exist.
    ' Note method to read entire file in one call.
    '
    On Error Resume Next
        Open "c:\config.sys" For Binary As #1
        Me.txtSplit(txtTop).Text = Input(LOF(1), 1)
        Open "c:\autoexec.bat" For Binary As #2
        Me.txtSplit(txtBottom).Text = Input(LOF(2), 2)
        Close
    On Error GoTo 0
End Sub
```

12. Insert the following code in the cmdExit_Click event.

```
Private Sub cmdExit_Click()
    Unload Me
End Sub
```

How It Works

A module-level variable, m_Split, tracks the percentage of the available space consumed by the top text box. The bottom text box uses what remains. (Half the splitter bar's height is subtracted from both text box areas.) When the user drags the splitter bar to a new position or uses the keyboard shortcut, the ResizeControls subroutine performs all the calculations necessary and then executes the Move method on the two text boxes and the splitter bar.

If the splitter bar were the same width as the form, the user would see the ends of the bar when the mouse was moved at all sideways while dragging. To prevent this unsightliness, the splitter bar is sized to be three times the interior width of the form.

Even if the user grabs the splitter bar at one edge of the form and drags it to the other, the end of the bar will not become visible.

In several subroutines, certain control and form properties need to be accessed repeatedly. In situations such as these, it's much more efficient to read the property once into a variable and then use the variable in subsequent calculations—especially when properties must be referred to within a loop. In this project, these routines are called quite frequently and performance is critical. So efficiency is gained by declaring the entire procedures static in two cases. With this declaration, space for the local variables is allocated at startup rather than with each call to the routine.

Comments

This project will work equally well in Visual Basic 3.0, only with slight modifications. Earlier versions of Visual Basic didn't support custom mouse pointers, so you must use one of the built-in ones, such as the north-south sizing arrow. In VB3 you also must declare all the constants that are "built in" to our example, or use their numeric equivalents.

The split window is an agreeable method for presenting two similar data sets to a user, perhaps allowing comparison of two files. The same technique may be used to create a vertical splitter bar for windows such as those in File Manager. An outline of some type could be on the left, with members of the highlighted branch displayed on the right.

With the speed of today's computers, in projects of this type there is little to worry about with graphics performance. If you need to support older, slower hardware, however, there is another method to make the resizing less unsightly. Contain the two text boxes and the splitter bar within another PictureBox. Then set the visible property of this container to False before all the resizing begins, and make it visible again afterward. This cleaner transition technique also provides true speed benefits, as well. The disadvantage to using this method is that more system resources are consumed by the extra PictureBox.

3.9 How do I...
Clear a Multiselect List Box in One Call?

COMPLEXITY: EASY
COMPATIBILITY: VB4 ONLY

Problem

When I try to clear all of the selections in a multiselect list box, my code has to turn off the selection on each item in the list box, one at a time. This can be very slow if I have a lot of items in the list box. How can I do this quickly? Can I do it in one call?

Technique

The CLEARLST project uses the SendMessage API call to clear the list box. It sends a LB_SETSEL message, which tells a multiselect list box to change its selection(s).

LB_SETSEL takes two arguments. The first argument determines whether the items affected are selected or deselected. The second argument determines which items are affected. The second parameter can hold either an index for a specific item, or −1, which means all list items are affected. So CLEARLST sends the LB_SETSEL message to the list box with the Boolean set to False (to turn off the items) and the index set to −1 (to affect all items in the list).

Steps

Open and run CLEARLST.VBP. The form shows you a list of random words, similar to that shown in Figure 3-9-1. Select some of the items in the list box, and then click the Clear Selections button. Notice that all of the selections disappear at once.

Figure 3-9-1 The CLEARLST project

1. Create a new project named CLEARLST.VBP. Add the following code to the General section of Form1:

```
Option Explicit
'
' list box set selection
'
Const LB_SETSEL = &h185
'
' declare SendMessage() API call
'
Private Declare Function SendMessage Lib "User32" Alias "SendMessageA" ⇒
    (ByVal hWnd As Long, ByVal wMsg As Long, ByVal wParam As Integer, ⇒
    lParam As Any) As Long
```

2. Select Form1, and create objects and set their properties as shown in Table 3-9-1.

Table 3-9-1 Objects, properties, and settings for Form1

OBJECT	PROPERTY	SETTING
Form	Name	Form1
	Caption	"Clear List"
	Height	6300
	Left	1035
Command Button	Name	Command1
	Caption	"Clear Selections"
	Height	375
	Left	240
	Top	5280
	Width	2415
List Box	Name	List1
	Height	4905
	Left	240
	MultiSelect	1 'Simple
	Top	240
	Width	2415

3. Add the following code to Form1's Form_Load subroutine. This routine fills the list box with randomly generated lines of garbage words.

```
Private Sub Form_Load()
    Dim I As Integer ' index variable
    Dim J As Integer ' index variable
    Dim TempStr As String ' temp string '
    Dim NextSpace As Integer ' index for space in string
    '
    ' initialize random number generator
```

```
'
Randomize
'
' fill list with random items
'
For I = 1 To 30
    '
    ' clear temp string
    '
    TempStr = ""
    NextSpace = 0
    '
    ' generate random text
    '
    For J = 1 To 20
        '
        ' if first letter after space
        '
        If J = NextSpace + 1 Then
            '
            ' generate random upper case letter
            '
            TempStr = TempStr & Chr(65 + Int(Rnd * 26))
            '
            ' Determine time for next space
            '
            NextSpace = J + Int(Rnd * 6) + 1
        ' if time for a space
        ElseIf J = NextSpace Then
            '
            ' add a space
            '
            TempStr = TempStr & " "
        Else
            '
            ' generate random lower case letter
            '
            TempStr = TempStr & Chr(97 + Int(Rnd * 26))
        End If
    Next J
    '
    ' add random string to list
    '
    List1.AddItem TempStr
Next I
End Sub
```

4. Add the following code to the Click event routine of Command1. This code removes all selections from the list box.

```
Private Sub Command1_Click()
    '
    ' clear all selections in list box
    ' caution: only use this with multiselect
```

Continued on next page

Continued from previous page

```
' List boxes
'
    SendMessage List1.hWnd, LB_SETSEL, 0, _
        ByVal CLng(&hffff))
End Sub
```

How It Works

CLEARLST relies on the Windows API to do its work. It uses one of the list box messages: LB_SETSEL, which takes two parameters: the new selection value (True or False) and the list item's index.

   If the list index is set to −1, LB_SETSEL performs the selection/deselection on all of the items in the list. So CLEARLST tells the list box to turn off everything by setting the new value to False (0) and setting the index to −1.

Comments

This How-To demonstrates the technique for clearing a multiselect list box quickly. You can change the technique slightly to select all items in a multiselect list box, by setting the new value to True, rather than False. In the Command1_Click function, change the third parameter of the SendMessage call to 1 (rather than 0). Then run the program and push the button.

3.10 How do I...
Build My Own Toolbar with PictureBoxes?

COMPLEXITY: ADVANCED
COMPATIBILITY: VB4 ONLY

Problem

To make my application look professional, I want it to include a toolbar. I tried making one myself, and even tried a few of the toolbar VBXes. In all cases, they didn't behave quite the way a toolbar should. For instance, how do I create a toolbar that behaves like the ones found in applications such as Word and Excel?

Technique

The toolbar in this example is basically a PictureBox containing a few objects. The toolbar supports three things: buttons (CToolButton), separators (effectively, nothing), and controls (typically combo boxes).

   Controls that are placed on the toolbar handle their own events. Whenever the user does something (edits, clicks, etc.) in a box, the normal events are fired. Aside from where they are placed on the toolbar, objects are responsible for managing themselves.

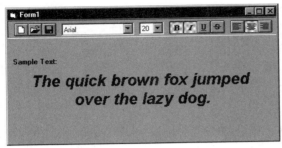

Figure 3-10-1 The TOOLBAR project

Buttons are handled differently. Each button has a unique ID number, much like a menu item's. The toolbar has special methods for adding and grouping its buttons on it. Buttons can act normally (like a command button), as a toggle button, or be in a group of buttons in which only one may be selected at any given time.

The buttons provided by CToolButton are only virtual buttons—bitmaps painted on the toolbar and made to look like buttons (normal, depressed, disabled, etc.). Since they're not real objects, the toolbar must tell the buttons when to repaint, as well as notify the buttons of any mouse events. In return, the buttons tell the toolbar if they've changed value. The toolbar uses this information to inform the program of what the user is doing.

Steps

Open and run TOOLBAR.VBP. You will see the program shown in Figure 3-10-1. Play with the buttons and combo boxes on the toolbar and watch the text change in reaction.

1. Create a new project named TOOLBAR.VBP. Select CFilePick, and add objects and properties with settings as shown in Table 3-10-1.

Table 3-10-1 Objects, properties, and settings for Form1

OBJECT	PROPERTY	SETTING
Form	Name	Form1
	Height	3555
	Left	1245
	Top	1425
	Width	6855
ComboBox	Name	cmbFontSize
	Height	300
	Left	2400
	Style	2 'Dropdown List

Continued on next page

Continued from previous page

OBJECT	PROPERTY	SETTING
	Top	240
	Width	615
ComboBox	Name	cmbFontName
	Height	300
	Left	240
	Sorted	-1 'True
	Style	2 'Dropdown List
	Top	240
	Width	1815
PictureBox	Name	Picture1
	BackColor	&H00C0C0C0&
	Height	630
	Left	120
	Top	120
	Width	6525
Label	Name	Label1
	Caption	"Sample Text:"
	Height	255
	Left	120
	Top	960
	Width	1815
Label	Name	lblSample
	Caption	"The quick brown fox jumped over the lazy dog."
	FontName	"Times New Roman"
	FontSize	10
	Height	1575
	Left	360
	Top	1320
	Width	6015

2. Add the following code to the General section of Form1. This code defines the button IDs that are used later.

```
Option Explicit
'
' define our toolbar
'
Dim TB As CToolBar
'
' button ID constants
'
Const BTN_NEW = 1
Const BTN_OPEN = 2
```

```
Const BTN_DISK = 3
Const BTN_BOLD = 4
Const BTN_ITAL = 5
Const BTN_UNDER = 6
Const BTN_STRIKE = 7
Const BTN_LEFT = 8
Const BTN_CENT = 9
Const BTN_RIGHT = 10
```

3. Add this function to the General section of Form1. This combo-box handler sets the name of the sample label's font when the font name's combo box changes.

```
Private Sub cmbFontName_Click()
    '
    ' when the font name combo changes, change the font
    ' name of the sample
    '
    lblSample.FontName = cmbFontName.Text
End Sub
```

4. Add this function to the General section of Form1. This combo-box handler sets the size of the sample label's font when the font size's combo box changes.

```
Private Sub cmbFontSize_Click()
    '
    ' when the font size combo changes, change the font
    ' size of the sample
    '
    lblSample.FontSize = Val(cmbFontSize.Text)
End Sub
```

5. Add this function to the General section of Form1. This function creates a new CToolBar object and then tells the new toolbar that its canvas (parent, home, etc.) is the PictureBox Picture1. Then the various buttons and the two combo boxes are added to the toolbar using CToolBar's AddButton, AddToggleButton, AddItem, and AddSeparator methods. The justification buttons are tied together like radio/option buttons using the Group method of CToolBar. Finally, the font name (cmbFontName) and font size (cmbFontSize) combo boxes are loaded up.

```
Private Sub Form_Load()
    '
    ' create new toolbar
    '
    Set TB = New CToolBar
    '
    ' make the picture box that toolbar's canvas
    '
    Set TB.Canvas = Picture1
    '
    ' allocate file manipulation buttons
    ' all normal buttons
    '
    TB.AddButton LoadPicture(App.Path & "\BTN_NEW.bmp"), BTN_NEW
```

Continued on next page

Continued from previous page

```
    TB.AddButton LoadPicture(App.Path & "\BTN_OPEN.bmp"), BTN_OPEN
    TB.AddButton LoadPicture(App.Path & "\BTN_DISK.bmp"), BTN_DISK
    '
    ' add font name combo box
    '
    TB.AddSeparator
    TB.AddItem cmbFontName
    '
    ' add font size combo box
    '
    TB.AddSeparator
    TB.AddItem cmbFontSize
    TB.AddSeparator
    '
    ' add font style toggle buttons
    '
    TB.AddToggleButton LoadPicture(App.Path & "\BTN_BOLD.bmp"), BTN_BOLD
    TB.AddToggleButton LoadPicture(App.Path & "\BTN_ITAL.bmp"), BTN_ITAL
    TB.AddToggleButton LoadPicture(App.Path & "\BTN_UNDE.bmp"), BTN_UNDER
    TB.AddToggleButton LoadPicture(App.Path & "\BTN_STRK.bmp"), BTN_STRIKE
    TB.AddSeparator
    '
    ' add label justification buttons
    '
    TB.AddButton LoadPicture(App.Path & "\BTN_LEFT.bmp"), BTN_LEFT
    TB.AddButton LoadPicture(App.Path & "\BTN_CENT.bmp"), BTN_CENT
    TB.AddButton LoadPicture(App.Path & "\BTN_RGHT.bmp"), BTN_RIGHT
    '
    ' make the justification buttons into a group
    '
    TB.Group BTN_LEFT, BTN_RIGHT
    '
    ' fill the font name combo box with common fonts
    '
    cmbFontName.AddItem "Arial"
    cmbFontName.AddItem "Courier New"
    cmbFontName.AddItem "Symbol"
    cmbFontName.AddItem "Times New Roman"
    cmbFontName.AddItem "Wingdings"
    '
    ' set the default to Times New Roman
    '
    cmbFontName.ListIndex = 3
    '
    ' fill the font size combo with values
    '
    cmbFontSize.AddItem "8"
    cmbFontSize.AddItem "9"
    cmbFontSize.AddItem "10"
    cmbFontSize.AddItem "12"
    cmbFontSize.AddItem "14"
    cmbFontSize.AddItem "16"
    cmbFontSize.AddItem "18"
    cmbFontSize.AddItem "20"
    cmbFontSize.AddItem "24"
    cmbFontSize.AddItem "36"
```

```
cmbFontSize.AddItem "48"
'
' set the default font size to 10
'
cmbFontSize.ListIndex = 2
End Sub
```

6. Add this function to the General section of Form1. This function ensures that the toolbar fills the upper part of the window. Since the PictureBox has a border around it, and the desired effect is to only have a single line below the toolbar, the PictureBox is positioned one pixel higher and to the left of the upper-left corner of the window. Also, it is made two pixels too wide. The resulting display is only a line between the toolbar and the rest of the window, and no extra lines above, to the right, or to the left of the toolbar.

```
Private Sub Form_Resize()
    '
    ' position picture box one pixel up and to the left
    ' of the upper left hand corner of the window
    '
    Picture1.Top = -Screen.TwipsPerPixelY
    Picture1.Left = -Screen.TwipsPerPixelX
    '
    ' set the width to 2 pixels wider, this
    ' makes a solid line below the bitmap and
    ' nothing else (top, left, or right)
    '
    Picture1.Width = Me.ScaleWidth + 2 * Screen.TwipsPerPixelX
End Sub
```

7. Add this function to the General section of Form1. This function deals with the IDs returned by the toolbar. IDs are returned only when something happens (a normal button is pressed and released, a toggle button changes state, or an option button is selected). Our sample toolbar reflects word processing capabilities, so this function's role is to turn on/off the bold, italic, underlining, and strikethrough attributes. These are turned on when the positive ID is returned by the toolbar, and off when the negative value is returned. Justification is handled merely by the selection of an ID. All of the other attributes are presumed to be turned off (since they are in an "option" button group).

```
Private Sub ToolBarHandle(ID As Integer)
    Select Case ID
        Case BTN_BOLD
            '
            ' set bold to true when bold button is pressed
            '
            lblSample.FontBold = True
        Case BTN_ITAL
            '
            ' set italic to true when bold button is pressed
            '
```

Continued on next page

Continued from previous page

```
                lblSample.FontItalic = True
        Case BTN_UNDER
            '
            ' set underline to true when bold button is pressed
            '
            lblSample.FontUnderline = True
        Case BTN_STRIKE
            '
            ' set strikethru to true when bold button is pressed
            '
            lblSample.FontStrikethru = True
        Case -BTN_BOLD
            '
            ' set bold to false when bold button is raised
            '
            lblSample.FontBold = False
        Case -BTN_ITAL
            '
            ' set italic to false when bold button is raised
            '
            lblSample.FontItalic = False
        Case -BTN_UNDER
            '
            ' set underline to false when bold button is raised
            '
            lblSample.FontUnderline = False
        Case -BTN_STRIKE
            '
            ' set strikethru to false when bold button is raised
            '
            lblSample.FontStrikethru = False
        Case BTN_LEFT
            '
            ' align left when BTN_LEFT is selected
            '
            lblSample.Alignment = 0
        Case BTN_CENT
            '
            ' align center when BTN_CENT is selected
            '
            lblSample.Alignment = 2
        Case BTN_RIGHT
            '
            ' align right when BTN_RIGHT is selected
            '
            lblSample.Alignment = 1
    End Select
End Sub
```

8. Put this function in the General section of Form1. It tells the toolbar when the mouse button is pressed down. The toolbar, in turn, designates whether this is something our program should be interested in, by returning an ID. This ID is passed to ToolBarHandle for processing. If no ID is passed, the toolbar returns zero (0).

```
Private Sub Picture1_MouseDown(button As Integer, Shift As _
       Integer, x As Single, y As Single)
    '
    ' tell toolbar about mouse down and then pass any
    ' ID off to ToolBarHandle (above)
    '
    If ( button = 1 ) Then
        ToolBarHandle (TB.MouseDown(x, y))
    End If
End Sub
```

9. Put this function in the General section of Form1. It tells the toolbar when the mouse button is released. The toolbar, in turn, designates whether this is something our program should be interested in, by returning an ID. This ID is passed to ToolBarHandle for processing. If no ID is passed, the toolbar returns zero (0).

```
Private Sub Picture1_MouseUp(button As Integer, Shift As Integer, _
       x As Single, y As Single)
    '
    ' tell toolbar about mouse up and then pass any
    ' ID off to ToolBarHandle (above)
    '
    If ( button = 1 ) Then
        ToolBarHandle (TB.MouseUp(x, y))
    End If
End Sub
```

10. Put this function in the General section of Form1. This function's job is to force the toolbar to repaint whenever the PictureBox does.

```
Private Sub Picture1_Paint()
    '
    ' redraw toolbar
    '
    TB.Show
End Sub
```

11. Use Class Module on the Insert menu to add a new class module. Change the name of this module to CToolButton in the properties window; then add the following code to the General section. This code defines the API calls employed, the bitmap structure used by the GetObject API call, and the storage for the properties of this class.

```
Option Explicit
'
' this is the VB equivalent of the BITMAP structure
'
Private Type Bitmap
    bmType As Long
    bmWidth As Long
    bmHeight As Long
    bmWidthBytes As Long
```

Continued on next page

Continued from previous page

```
    bmPlanes As Integer
    bmBitsPixel As Integer
    bmBits As Long
End Type
'
' private storage of properties
'
Private m_canvas   As Object
Private m_enabled As Boolean
Private m_faces    As Picture
Private m_fIgnoreNextUp As Boolean
Private m_height   As Single
Private m_left     As Single
Private m_mode     As Integer
Private m_top      As Single
Private m_value    As Boolean
Private m_visible  As Boolean
Private m_width    As Single
'
' declare API calls used
'
Private Declare Function BitBlt Lib "GDI32" (ByVal hDestDC As Long,⇒
        ByVal x As Long, ByVal y As Long, ByVal nWidth As Long, ⇒
        ByVal nHeight As Long, ByVal hSrcDC As Long, ByVal XSrc As Long, ⇒
        ByVal YSrc As Long, ByVal dwRop As Long) As Integer
Private Declare Function CreateCompatibleDC Lib "GDI32" (ByVal hDC ⇒
        As Long) As Long
Private Declare Function DeleteDC Lib "GDI32" (ByVal hDC As Long) ⇒
        As Long
Private Declare Function SelectObject Lib "GDI32" (ByVal hDC As Long, ⇒
        ByVal hObject As Long) As Long
Private Declare Function GetObject Lib "GDI32" Alias "GetObjectA" ⇒
        (ByVal hObject As Long, ByVal nCount As Long, lpObject As Any) ⇒
        As Long
'
' constant used in BitBlt call
'
Private Const SRCCOPY = &hcc0020
```

12. Put this code in the General section of CToolButton. This function positions the tool button (i.e., where it is supposed to paint itself).

```
Public Property Set Canvas(thing As Object)
    '
    ' get canvas object from caller
    '
    Set m_canvas = thing
End Property
```

13. Put this code in the General section of CToolButton. This function returns the tool button's canvas (parent, home, etc.).

```
Public Property Get Canvas() As Object
    '
```

```
' return current canvas to caller
'
    Set Canvas = m_canvas
End Property
```

14. Put this code in the General section of CToolButton. This function enables or disables the button. After setting the value, this function repaints the button to reflect the change.

```
Public Property Let Enabled(f As Boolean)
    '
    ' enable/disable button
    '
    m_enabled = f
    '
    ' repaint the button to reflect change
    '
    Show
End Property
```

15. Put this code in the General section of CToolButton. This function returns the enabled/disabled state of the button.

```
Public Property Get Enabled() As Boolean
    '
    ' return current enabled state to caller
    '
    Enabled = m_enabled
End Property
```

16. Put this code in the General section of CToolButton. This function sets the button faces, which are passed in as a picture (bitmap). The bitmap is presumed to contain four equal-sized button faces: the face in the upper-left corner is the enabled up face; the face in the upper-right corner is the enabled down face; the face in the lower-left corner is the disabled up face; and the face in the lower-right corner is the disabled down face. After saving the handle to the bitmap, the GetObject() API call is used to get the dimensions of the bitmap (in pixels). Those dimensions are then saved in the m_width and m_height properties as twips.

```
Public Property Set Faces(anImage As Object)
    Dim Bmp As Bitmap ' API BITMAP structure
    '
    ' save the bitmap
    '
    Set m_faces = anImage
    '
    ' get information about the bitmap to be used
    '
    Call GetObjectGDI(m_faces.Handle, 14&, Bmp)
    '
    ' set width and height of the button
    '
```

Continued on next page

Continued from previous page

```
    m_width = (Bmp.bmWidth / 2) * Screen.TwipsPerPixelX
    m_height = (Bmp.bmHeight / 2) * Screen.TwipsPerPixelY
End Property
```

17. Put this function in the General section of CToolButton. This function returns the picture currently in use by the button.

```
Public Property Get Faces() As Object
    '
    ' save picture that contains button faces
    '
    Set Faces = m_faces
End Property
```

18. Add this function to the General section of CToolButton. It sets the height of an individual button.

```
Public Property Let Height(h As Single)
    '
    ' change height
    '
    m_height = h
End Property
```

19. Add this function to the General section of CToolButton. It returns the height of the button.

```
Public Property Get Height() As Single
    '
    ' return button height to caller
    '
    Height = m_height
End Property
```

20. Add this function to the General section of CToolButton. It sets the horizontal position of the button on the canvas (in twips).

```
Public Property Let Left(l As Single)
    '
    ' set new horizontal position of button
    '
    m_left = l
End Property
```

21. Add this function to the General section of CToolButton. It returns the horizontal position of the button on the canvas (in twips).

```
Public Property Get Left() As Single
    '
    ' return horizontal position of button
    '
    Left = m_left
End Property
```

22. Add this function to the General section of CToolButton. This function sets the button's mode: Mode 0 is a normal button (user presses, it goes down; user releases, it goes up); mode 1 is toggle mode (each time the user clicks, it changes state, up or down); mode 2 is manual (only changeable through code).

```
Public Property Let Mode(m As Integer)
    '
    ' if the new mode is valid
    '
    If (m >= 0) And (m <= 2) Then
        '
        ' set the button mode (0 - normal,
        ' 1 - toggle, 2 - manual)
        '
        m_mode = m
    End If
End Property
```

23. Add this function to the General section of CToolButton. This function returns the current mode.

```
Public Property Get Mode() As Integer
    '
    ' return the current mode to the caller
    '
    Mode = m_mode
End Property
```

24. Put this function in the General section of CToolButton. It sets the vertical position of the button on its canvas.

```
Public Property Let Top(t As Single)
    '
    ' set the current vertical position
    '
    m_top = t
End Property
```

25. Put this function in the General section of CToolButton. It returns the vertical position of the button on its canvas.

```
Public Property Get Top() As Single
    '
    ' return the vertical position
    '
    Top = m_top
End Property
```

26. Put this function in the General section of CToolButton. It sets the current state of the button (up or down). After the state is set, it repaints the button to reflect the change.

```
Public Property Let Value(f As Boolean)
    '
    ' set the new state of the button
    '
    m_value = f
    '
    ' repaint button to reflect change
    '
    Show
End Property
```

27. Put this function in the General section of CToolButton. It returns the current state of the button (up or down).

```
Public Property Get Value() As Boolean
    '
    ' return the current button state
    '
    Value = m_value
End Property
```

28. Put this function in the General section of CToolButton. It sets the visibility of the button.

```
Public Property Let Visible(f As Boolean)
    '
    ' make control visible/invisible
    '
    m_visible = f
End Property
```

29. Put this function in the General section of CToolButton. It returns whether or not the button is visible.

```
Public Property Get Visible() As Boolean
    '
    ' return current visibility to caller
    '
    Visible = m_visible
End Property
```

30. Put this function in the General section of CToolButton. It sets the width (in twips) of the button.

```
Public Property Let Width(w As Single)
    '
    ' set the button's width
    '
    m_width = w
End Property
```

31. Put this function in the General section of CToolButton. It returns the width of the button (in twips).

```
Public Property Get Width() As Single
    '
    ' return the width of the button to the caller
    '
    Width = m_width
End Property
```

32. Add this code to the General section of CToolButton. This function determines whether or not a coordinate, passed in as x and y, is within the button.

```
Private Function MouseHit(x As Single, y As Single) As Boolean
    '
    ' this function checks to see if the click
    ' was on this button
    '
    ' if the button is invisible, no mouse hit
    '
    If (m_visible = False) Then
        MouseHit = False
    '
    ' if the click was vertically off, no mouse hit
    '
    ElseIf (y < m_top Or y >= m_top + m_height) Then
        MouseHit = False
    '
    ' if the click was horizontally off, no mouse hit
    '
    ElseIf (x < m_left Or x >= m_left + m_width) Then
        MouseHit = False
    Else
        '
        ' otherwise, we must've hit
        '
        MouseHit = True
    End If
End Function
```

33. Add this code to the General section of CToolButton. This function initializes the class. It enables the button, makes it a normal button, sets the initial position to up, and makes the button visible.

```
Private Sub Class_Initialize()
    '
    ' clear flag toggle flag
    '
    m_fIgnoreNextUp = False
    '
    ' button is initially enabled
    '
    m_enabled = True
    '
    ' normal button
    '
```

Continued on next page

Continued from previous page

```
    m_mode = 0
    '
    ' initial position is up
    '
    m_value = False
    '
    ' button is initially visible
    '
    m_visible = True
End Sub
```

34. Add this code to the General section of CToolButton. This function paints the button. If the button is visible, a new memory device context (DC) is created. Then the face's bitmap is brought into that DC. Next, the function computes the size and offset (in pixels) of the bitmap it wants. The offset is computed based on the Enabled and Value properties. Then BitBlt is used to copy the bitmap to the canvas. Lastly, some clean-up restores the DC to its original state and deletes it.

```
Public Sub Show()
    Dim p_left As Integer ' x position of button pixels
    Dim p_top As Integer ' y position of button pixels
    Dim p_width As Integer ' x size of button pixels
    Dim p_height As Integer ' y size of button pixels
    Dim srcdc As Integer ' hDC for button
    Dim oldbm As Integer ' saved bitmap handle
    Dim x As Integer ' x offset of face in button bitmap
    Dim y As Integer ' y offset of face in button bitmap
    '
    ' if the button is visible,
    '
    If m_visible Then
        '
        ' create new DC so we can BitBlt our button
        ' face to the screen
        '
        srcdc = CreateCompatibleDC(m_canvas.hDC)
        '
        ' select our face bitmap into the new DC
        ' and save the old bitmap
        '
        oldbm = SelectObject(srcdc, m_faces.Handle)
        '
        ' convert the size and position of the button
        ' from twips to pixels
        '
        p_left = m_left / Screen.TwipsPerPixelX
        p_width = m_width / Screen.TwipsPerPixelX
        p_top = m_top / Screen.TwipsPerPixelY
        p_height = m_height / Screen.TwipsPerPixelY
        '
        ' if enabled,
        '
        If m_enabled Then
            '
```

```
    ' use the enabled faces
    '
    y = 0
Else
    '
    ' otherwise, use the disabled faces
    '
    y = p_height
End If
'
' if the button is down,
'
If m_value Then
    '
    ' use the down faces
    '
    x = p_width
Else
    '
    ' otherwise, use the up faces
    '
    x = 0
End If
'
' copy the face from the new DC to the appropriate
' place on the canvas
'
BitBlt m_canvas.hDC, p_left, p_top, p_width, p_height, _
    srcdc, x, y, SRCCOPY
'
' restore the DC's old bitmap
'
SelectObject srcdc, oldbm
'
' delete the DC
'
DeleteDC srcdc
    End If
End Sub
```

35. Add this code to the General section of CToolButton. This function determines what to do when the mouse button is pressed. Nothing happens if the button is disabled or if the mouse click is not within the button (determined by MouseHit). When the button is enabled and the mouse is pressed within its borders, the button's action depends on the current mode.

➤ In mode 0 (normal), the button merely goes down and reports back to the caller that nothing has happened yet.

➤ If the mode is 1 (toggle) and the button is currently up, then the button is moved down, a flag is set to ignore the next mouse up, and the calling code is informed that the button is pressed down.

> If the mode is 2 (manual), the caller is informed that the mouse has been
> pressed, but there is no state (up/down) change.

```
Public Function MouseDown(x As Single, y As Single) As Integer
    Dim Result As Integer
    '
    ' default to no change of value
    '
    Result = 0
    '
    ' if the button is enabled and the mouse clicked
    ' in the button
    '
    If m_enabled And MouseHit(x, y) Then
        '
        ' behavior is determined by the mode of the button
        '
        Select Case m_mode
            Case 0 ' normal button
                '
                ' button is now down
                '
                m_value = True
            Case 1 ' toggle button
                If Not m_value Then
                    '
                    ' button is now down
                    '
                    m_value = True
                    '
                    ' don't pay attention to the next
                    ' mouse up
                    '
                    m_fIgnoreNextUp = True
                    '
                    ' button value has changed
                    '
                    Result = 1
                End If
            Case 2 ' manual button
                '
                ' always return a change
                '
                Result = 1
        End Select
        '
        ' repaint the button to reflect any changes
        '
        Show
    End If
    '
    ' return value to caller
    '
    MouseDown = Result
End Function
```

36. Add this code to the General section of CToolButton. This function determines what to do when the mouse button is released, based on the current mode of the button.

   ➤ If the button is in mode 0 (normal), then that button is raised (up). If the mouse up occurred within the button and the button is enabled, then the caller is informed that the button was clicked.

   ➤ If the button is in mode 1 (toggle), then nothing happens if that button is disabled, if the mouse press is not within that button (determined by MouseHit), if that button is already up, or if the Ignore Next Mouse Up flag is set. When none of these is true, then the button is raised and the calling program is informed of the raise by returning a –1 (as opposed to the normal 1).

   ➤ If the button is in mode 2 (manual), then the calling program receives notification that the raise occurred, but only if the button is enabled and the mouse up was within the button's borders.

```
Public Function MouseUp(x As Single, y As Single) As Integer
    Dim Result As Integer
    '
    ' default to no change of value
    '
    Result = 0
    '
    ' if this is a normal button, or if the button
    ' is enabled and the mouse clicked in the button
    '
    If m_enabled And MouseHit(x, y) Then
        '
        ' behavior is determined by the mode of the button
        '
        Select Case m_mode
            Case 0 ' normal button
                '
                ' button is now up
                '
                m_value = False
                '
                ' if the button is enabled and the
                ' up mouse was in the button, then
                ' return a value change
                '
                If m_enabled And MouseHit(x, y) Then
                    Result = 1
                End If
            Case 1
                '
                ' if the button is currently down, and
                ' we're supposed to pay attention to
                ' this mouse up
                '
```

Continued on next page

Continued from previous page

```
                If m_value And Not m_fIgnoreNextUp Then
                    '
                    ' button is now up
                    '
                    m_value = False
                    '
                    ' return the toggle button is now up
                    ' (indicated by a negative value)
                    '
                    Result = -1
                End If
                '
                ' pay attention to the next mouse up
                '
                m_fIgnoreNextUp = False
            Case 2 ' manual button
                '
                ' always return a change
                '
                Result = 1
        End Select
        '
        ' repaint the button to reflect any changes
        '
        Show
    End If
    '
    ' return value to caller
    '
    MouseUp = Result
End Function
```

37. Select Class Module from the Insert menu to add a new class module. Change the name of this module to CToolBar in the properties window, and add the following code to the General section of CToolBar:

```
Option Explicit
'
' information about a toolbar object
'
Private Type BarObject
    Item As Object
    ID As Integer
    Group As Integer
End Type
'
' define API calls used
'
Private Declare Function SetParent Lib "user32" (ByVal hwndChild As Long, ⇒
    ByVal hwndNewParent As Long) As Long
'
' private storage of properties
'
```

```
Private m_borderwidth        As Integer
Private m_buttons()          As BarObject
Private m_canvas             As Object
Private m_numbuttons         As Integer
Private m_separatorwidth     As Integer
```

38. Add this function to the General section of CToolBar, to initialize the toolbar. The toolbar starts out with no buttons, a vertical border width of 5 pixels, and a separator width (and left margin) of 10 pixels.

```
Private Sub Class_Initialize()
    '
    ' toolbar is initially empty
    '
    m_numbuttons = 0
    '
    ' vertical border is 5 pixels wide
    '
    m_borderwidth = 5
    '
    ' separator width is 10 pixels wide
    '
    m_separatorwidth = 10
End Sub
```

39. Add this function to the General section of CToolBar. It sets the current vertical border width.

```
Public Property Let BorderWidth(bw As Integer)
    '
    ' set new vertical border width
    '
    m_borderwidth = bw
    '
    ' recompute canvas size
    '
    ComputeCanvas
    '
    ' recompute item positions
    '
    ComputeItemPositions
End Property
```

40. Add this function to the General section of CToolBar. It returns the current vertical border width.

```
Public Property Get BorderWidth() As Integer
    '
    ' get current border width
    '
    BorderWidth = m_borderwidth
End Property
```

41. Add this function to the General section of CToolBar. It sets the toolbar's canvas.

```
Public Property Set Canvas(thing As Object)
    '
    ' set new canvas object (preferably a picture box)
    '
    Set m_canvas = thing
End Property
```

42. Add this function to the General section of CToolBar. It returns the toolbar's canvas.

```
Public Property Get Canvas() As Object
    '
    ' return canvas to caller
    '
    Set Canvas = m_canvas
End Property
```

43. Add this function to the General section of CToolBar. It sets the enabled property on all toolbar items that have the same ID as the one passed in. After the values are changed, the toolbar is redrawn.

```
Public Property Let Enabled(ID As Integer, e As Boolean)
    Dim Index As Integer ' index variable
    '
    ' cycle through all the buttons
    '
    For Index = 0 To m_numbuttons - 1
        '
        ' if this is a valid object and if its ID
        ' is the one we're interested in
        '
        If IsToolBarObject(Index) And (m_buttons(Index).ID = ID) Then
            '
            ' set the objects enabled property
            '
            m_buttons(Index).Item.Enabled = e
        End If
    Next Index
    '
    ' recompute canvas size
    '
    ComputeCanvas
    '
    ' recompute item positions
    '
    ComputeItemPositions
    '
    ' clear canvas
    '
    m_canvas.Cls
    '
    ' repaint all toolbar objects
    '
```

```
    Show
End Property
```

44. Add this function to the General section of CToolBar. It returns the enabled/disabled state of the first toolbar item that has the same ID number as the one passed in.

```
Public Property Get Enabled(ID As Integer) As Boolean
    Dim fEnabled As Boolean
    Dim Index As Integer
    '
    ' default return is false
    '
    fEnabled = False
    '
    ' cycle through all the buttons
    '
    For Index = 0 To m_numbuttons - 1
        '
        ' if this object has the ID we're interested in
        '
        If m_buttons(Index).ID = ID Then
            '
            ' and if it's a valid object
            '
            If IsToolBarObject(Index) Then
                '
                ' get the return value
                '
                fEnabled = m_buttons(Index).Item.Enabled
                '
                ' exit loop
                '
                Exit For
            End If
        End If
    Next Index
    '
    ' return value to caller
    '
    Enabled = fEnabled
End Property
```

45. Add this function to the General section of CToolBar. It sets the current separator width, which is also used as the left margin. This property is measured in pixels.

```
Public Property Let SeparatorWidth(sw As Integer)
    '
    ' set new separator width
    '
    m_separatorwidth = sw
    '
    ' recompute canvas size
    '
```

Continued on next page

Continued from previous page

```
    ComputeCanvas
    '
    ' recompute item positions
    '
    ComputeItemPositions
End Property
```

46. Add this function to the General section of CToolBar. It returns the current separator width.

```
Public Property Get SeparatorWidth() As Integer
    '
    ' return separator width to caller
    '
    SeparatorWidth = m_separatorwidth
End Property
```

47. Add this function to the General section of CToolBar. It sets the visible property on all toolbar items that have the same ID as the one passed in. After the values are changed, the toolbar is redrawn.

```
Public Property Let Visible(ID As Integer, v As Boolean)
    Dim Index As Integer
    '
    ' cycle through all the buttons
    '
    For Index = 0 To m_numbuttons - 1
        '
        ' if this is a valid object and if its ID
        ' is the one we're interested in
        '
        If IsToolBarObject(Index) And (m_buttons(Index).ID = ID) Then
            '
            ' set the object's visible property
            '
            m_buttons(Index).Item.Visible = v
        End If
    Next Index
    '
    ' recompute canvas size
    '
    ComputeCanvas
    '
    ' recompute item positions
    '
    ComputeItemPositions
    '
    ' clear canvas
    '
    m_canvas.Cls
    '
    ' repaint all toolbar objects
    '
    Show
End Property
```

48. Add this function to the General section of CToolBar. It returns the visible state of the first item that has the ID passed in.

```
Public Property Get Visible(ID As Integer) As Boolean
    Dim fVisible As Boolean
    Dim Index As Integer
    '
    ' default return is false
    '
    fVisible = False
    '
    ' cycle through all the buttons
    '
    For Index = 0 To m_numbuttons - 1
        '
        ' if this object has the ID we're interested in
        '
        If m_buttons(Index).ID = ID Then
            '
            ' and if it's a valid object
            '
            If IsToolBarObject(Index) Then
                '
                ' get the return value
                '
                fVisible = m_buttons(Index).Item.Visible
                '
                ' exit loop
                '
                Exit For
            End If
        End If
    Next Index
    '
    ' return value to caller
    '
    Visible = fVisible
End Property
```

49. Add this function to the General section of CToolBar. It returns whether or not a toolbar item is a valid object (i.e., not a separator).

```
Public Function IsToolBarObject(Index) As Boolean
    '
    ' if this is an invalid index, this is not a valid
    ' object
    '
    If (Index < 0) Or (Index >= m_numbuttons) Then
        IsToolBarObject = False
    '
    ' if this is a separator, not an object
    '
    ElseIf m_buttons(Index).ID = 0 Then
        IsToolBarObject = False
```

Continued on next page

Continued from previous page

```
    Else
        '
        ' otherwise, we have valid object
        '
        IsToolBarObject = True
    End If
End Function
```

50. Add this function to the General section of CToolBar. This function repositions and cycles through all the items in the toolbar. Tool buttons and other controls are centered vertically.

```
Private Sub ComputeItemPositions()
    Dim CurrentX As Single
    Dim I As Integer
    '
    ' initial position is separator width from the
    ' left edge. convert from pixels to twips
    '
    CurrentX = m_separatorwidth * Screen.TwipsPerPixelX
    '
    ' cycle through all buttons
    '
    For I = 0 To m_numbuttons - 1
        '
        ' if this is a separator, move the width
        ' of a separator
        '
        If m_buttons(I).ID = 0 Then
            CurrentX = CurrentX + (m_separatorwidth * _
                Screen.TwipsPerPixelX)
        Else
            '
            ' set the current position of the object
            '
            m_buttons(I).Item.Left = CurrentX
            '
            ' advance current position by the width
            ' of the current object
            '
            CurrentX = CurrentX + m_buttons(I).Item.Width - _
                Screen.TwipsPerPixelX
            '
            ' center the object vertically
            '
            m_buttons(I).Item.Top = (m_canvas.Height - _
                m_buttons(I).Item.Height - Screen.TwipsPerPixelY) / 2
        End If
    Next I
End Sub
```

51. Add this function to the General section of CToolBar. This function sets the height of the canvas. It finds the maximum height of all the toolbar items, and then computes the new canvas height based on the maximum height and the ver-

280

tical border width. If the size changes, all of the items are repositioned and the entire toolbar is redrawn.

```
Private Sub ComputeCanvas()
    Dim I As Integer
    Dim MaxHeight As Single
    '
    ' clear max height
    '
    MaxHeight = 0
    '
    ' cycle through all objects
    '
    For I = 0 To m_numbuttons - 1
        '
        ' if this is a valid object
        '
        If IsToolBarObject(I) Then
            '
            ' and its height is higher than the max
            '
            If m_buttons(I).Item.Height > MaxHeight Then
                ' set max height to current height
                MaxHeight = m_buttons(I).Item.Height
            End If
        End If
    Next I
    '
    ' if the canvas' height is not correct
    '
    If m_canvas.Height () MaxHeight + (2 * Screen.TwipsPerPixelY * _
        m_borderwidth) Then
        '
        ' resize the canvas
        '
        m_canvas.Height = MaxHeight + (2 * Screen.TwipsPerPixelY * _
            m_borderwidth)
        '
        ' repaint the canvas background
        '
        m_canvas.Cls
        '
        ' recompute item positions
        '
        ComputeItemPositions
        '
        ' repaint all objects
        '
        Show
    End If
End Sub
```

52. Add this function to the General section of CToolBar. This function appends a normal button to the end of the toolbar. It reallocates the array of toolbar items,

inserts a new CToolBar, sets the button's face to the picture passed in, and sets the current ID. Then, it recomputes the positions of all of the items and redraws the whole toolbar.

```
Public Function AddButton(Face As Object, ID As Integer) As Integer
    '
    ' if the ID number is invalid
    '
    If ID <= 0 Then
        '
        ' exit, returning an error
        '
        AddButton = -1
        Exit Function
    End If
    '
    ' expand the collection of objects to include this button
    '
    ReDim Preserve m_buttons(m_numbuttons)
    '
    ' set the object's ID
    '
    m_buttons(m_numbuttons).ID = ID
    '
    ' object is initially not in a group
    '
    m_buttons(m_numbuttons).Group = 0
    '
    ' get new button
    '
    Set m_buttons(m_numbuttons).Item = New CToolButton
    '
    ' set the button's face from picture passed in
    '
    Set m_buttons(m_numbuttons).Item.Faces = Face
    '
    ' set the button's canvas to the toolbar's canvas
    '
    Set m_buttons(m_numbuttons).Item.Canvas = m_canvas
    '
    ' increase button count
    '
    m_numbuttons = m_numbuttons + 1
    '
    ' recompute canvas size
    '
    ComputeCanvas
    '
    ' recompute item positions
    '
    ComputeItemPositions
    '
    ' show button
    '
    m_buttons(m_numbuttons - 1).Item.Show
    '
```

```
' return button index
'
   AddButton = m_numbuttons - 1
End Function
```

53. Add this function to the General section of CToolBar. This function appends a toggle button to the end of the toolbar. It reallocates the array of toolbar items, inserts a new CToolBar, sets the button's face to the picture passed in, and sets the current ID. Then, it recomputes the positions of all of the items and redraws the whole toolbar.

```
Public Function AddToggleButton(Face As Object, ID As Integer) As Integer
'
' if the ID number is invalid
'
If ID <= 0 Then
    '
    ' exit, returning an error
    '
    AddToggleButton = -1
    Exit Function
End If
'
' expand the collection of objects to include this button
'
ReDim Preserve m_buttons(m_numbuttons)
'
' set the object's ID
'
m_buttons(m_numbuttons).ID = ID
'
' object is not in a group, at first
'
m_buttons(m_numbuttons).Group = 0
'
' get new button
'
Set m_buttons(m_numbuttons).Item = New CToolButton
'
' set the button's face from picture passed in
'
Set m_buttons(m_numbuttons).Item.Faces = Face
'
' set the button's canvas to the toolbar's canvas
'
Set m_buttons(m_numbuttons).Item.Canvas = m_canvas
'
' button's mode is toggle
'
m_buttons(m_numbuttons).Item.Mode = 1
'
' increase button count
'
```

Continued on next page

Continued from previous page

```
    m_numbuttons = m_numbuttons + 1
    '
    ' recompute canvas size
    '
    ComputeCanvas
    '
    ' recompute item positions
    '
    ComputeItemPositions
    '
    ' show button
    '
    m_buttons(m_numbuttons - 1).Item.Show
    '
    ' return button index
    '
    AddToggleButton = m_numbuttons - 1
End Function
```

54. Add this next function to the General section of CToolBar, to append a control to the end of the toolbar. It reallocates the array of toolbar items, inserts the control, and sets the control's parent to the toolbar. Then it recomputes the positions of all the items and redraws the whole toolbar.

```
Public Function AddItem(Item As Object)
    ReDim Preserve m_buttons(m_numbuttons)
    '
    ' flag this as an object
    '
    m_buttons(m_numbuttons).ID = &h8000
    '
    ' set button object to object passed in
    '
    Set m_buttons(m_numbuttons).Item = Item
    '
    ' if the object is not a label or image
    '
    If Not ((TypeOf Item Is Label) Or (TypeOf Item Is Image)) Then
        '
        ' set the parent of the object to the
        ' toolbar's canvas
        '
        SetParent Item.hWnd, m_canvas.hWnd
    End If
    '
    ' increase button count
    '
    m_numbuttons = m_numbuttons + 1
    '
    ' recompute canvas size
    '
    ComputeCanvas
    '
    ' recompute item positions
```

```
ComputeItemPositions
    '
    ' return button index
    '
    AddItem = m_numbuttons - 1
End Function
```

55. Add this function to the General section of CToolBar. This function adds a separator (blank space) to the end of the toolbar. All it needs to do is reallocate the array of toolbar items, recompute the positions of all the items, and redraw the whole toolbar.

```
Public Function AddSeparator() As Integer
    ReDim Preserve m_buttons(m_numbuttons)
    '
    ' flag this as a separator
    '
    m_buttons(m_numbuttons).ID = 0
    '
    ' increase button count
    '
    m_numbuttons = m_numbuttons + 1
    '
    ' recompute item positions
    '
    ComputeItemPositions
    '
    ' return button index
    '
    AddSeparator = m_numbuttons - 1
End Function
```

56. Add this function to the General section of CToolBar. This function removes the item specified by Index from the toolbar. It shifts the array of toolbar items to remove the item specified, then reallocates the array of items, recomputes their positions, and redraws the entire toolbar.

```
Public Sub RemoveItem(Index As Integer)
    Dim I As Integer
    '
    ' if this is not a valid index
    '
    If (Index < 0) Or (Index >= m_numbuttons) Then
        '
        ' return, doing nothing
        '
        Exit Sub
    End If
    '
    ' if this is an object
    '
    If IsToolBarObject(Index) Then
        '
```

Continued on next page

Continued from previous page

```
        ' make it invisible
        '
        m_buttons(Index).Item.Visible = False
        '
        ' remove it
        '
        Set m_buttons(Index).Item = Nothing
    End If
    '
    ' adjust array of toolbar objects, removing
    ' item referenced by Index
    '
    For I = Index To m_numbuttons - 2
        m_buttons(I) = m_buttons(I + 1)
    Next I
    '
    ' decrease item count
    '
    m_numbuttons = m_numbuttons - 1
    '
    ' if there are still objects, re allocate array
    '
    If m_numbuttons () 0 Then
        ReDim Preserve m_buttons(m_numbuttons)
    End If
    '
    ' recompute canvas size
    '
    ComputeCanvas
    '
    ' recompute item positions
    '
    ComputeItemPositions
    '
    ' clear canvas
    '
    m_canvas.Cls
    '
    ' repaint all toolbar objects
    '
    Show
End Sub
```

57. To group the toolbuttons, add this function to the General section of CToolBar. It takes the start and stop IDs (as passed into AddButton) and cycles through all the buttons. Every button that has an ID between the start and stop ID (inclusive) is made part of the group. All of the buttons are set to be up, except the first one in the group, which is put down.

```
Public Sub Group(iStart As Integer, iStop As Integer)
    Dim GroupID As Integer
    Dim I As Integer
    '
    ' default group id is 1
    '
```

```
GroupID = 1
'
' scan through all buttons to determine unique group ID
'
For I = 0 To m_numbuttons - 1
    '
    ' if this is a valid object
    '
    If IsToolBarObject(I) Then
        '
        ' and if this is a CToolButton
        '
        If TypeOf m_buttons(I).Item Is CToolButton Then
            '
            ' and if the current GroupID is less than
            ' the buttons group ID
            '
            If GroupID <= m_buttons(I).Group Then
                '
                ' set the current group ID to
                ' one higher than the button's
                '
                GroupID = m_buttons(I).Group + 1
            End If
        End If
    End If
Next I
'
' cycle through all toolbar objects
'
For I = 0 To m_numbuttons - 1
    '
    ' if this is a valid object
    '
    If IsToolBarObject(I) Then
        '
        ' and if this is a CToolButton
        '
        If (TypeOf m_buttons(I).Item Is CToolButton) _
            And (m_buttons(I).ID >= iStart) _
            And (m_buttons(I).ID <= iStop) Then
            '
            ' set the first button down,
            ' all others up
            '
            If m_buttons(I).ID = iStart Then
                m_buttons(I).Item.Value = True
            Else
                m_buttons(I).Item.Value = False
            End If
            '
            ' set the group ID for the button
            '
            m_buttons(I).Group = GroupID
            '
```

Continued on next page

287

Continued from previous page

```
                    ' change the button's mode to manual
                    '
                    m_buttons(I).Item.Mode = 2
              End If
        End If
    Next I
End Sub
```

58. Add this function to the General section of CToolBar, to handle group button clicks. If the button pressed is already down, this function does nothing and exits. Otherwise, it sets the button that is pressed to be down, and all the other ones in the group up. Then it returns the clicked button's ID to the caller.

```
Private Function HandleGroup(Index, Group)
    Dim I As Integer
    '
    ' if the current button is down
    '
    If m_buttons(Index).Item.Value Then
        '
        ' no actions needed
        '
        HandleGroup = 0
        '
        ' get out
        '
        Exit Function
    End If
    '
    ' cycle through all the buttons
    '
    For I = 0 To m_numbuttons - 1
        '
        ' if the current button is in the group
        '
        If m_buttons(I).Group = Group Then
            '
            ' change the button's state to reflect
            ' mouse click
            '
            m_buttons(I).Item.Value = (I = Index)
        End If
    Next I
    '
    ' return button change
    '
    HandleGroup = m_buttons(Index).ID
End Function
```

59. Add this function to the General section of CToolBar, to handle the mouse-down event for the toolbar. It scans through all the toolbar items. If an item is a CToolButton, the MouseDown method is called for that button. Then, if the button is in a group, HandleGroup deals with the event. Otherwise, the function returns the button ID if the button has been clicked.

```
Public Function MouseDown(x As Single, y As Single) As Integer
    Dim I As Integer
    Dim ButtonID As Integer
    Dim ButtonStatus As Integer
    '
    ' default to no button pressed
    '
    ButtonID = 0
    '
    ' cycle through all the buttons
    '
    For I = 0 To m_numbuttons - 1
        '
        ' if this is a valid toolbar object
        '
        If IsToolBarObject(I) Then
            '
            ' and this is a tool button
            '
            If TypeOf m_buttons(I).Item Is CToolButton Then
                '
                ' try the mouse down for the current button
                '
                ButtonStatus = m_buttons(I).Item.MouseDown(x, y)
                '
                ' if the button reports being pressed, then...
                '
                If ButtonStatus Then
                    '
                    ' if the button is in a group
                    '
                    If m_buttons(I).Group Then
                        '
                        ' let HandleGroup deal with group
                        '
                        ButtonID = HandleGroup(I, m_buttons(I).Group)
                    Else
                        '
                        ' otherwise, return ID of button to caller
                        '
                        ButtonID = ButtonStatus * m_buttons(I).ID
                    End If
                    '
                    ' got a button, exit loop
                    '
                    Exit For
                End If
            End If
        End If
    Next I
    '
    ' return button's ID to caller
    '
    MouseDown = ButtonID
End Function
```

60. Add this function to the General section of CToolBar. It returns the current state of the button (up or down), and handles the mouse-up event for the toolbar. It scans through all the toolbar items. If an item is a CToolButton, the MouseUp method is called for that button. Then, if the button is not in a group, the function returns the button ID if the button has been clicked. If the button is a toggle button and it is going up, then button ID * −1 is returned.

```
Public Function MouseUp(x As Single, y As Single) As Integer
    Dim I As Integer
    Dim ButtonID As Integer
    Dim ButtonStatus As Integer
    '
    ' default to no button pressed
    '
    ButtonID = 0
    '
    ' cycle through all the buttons
    '
    For I = 0 To m_numbuttons - 1
        '
        ' if this is a valid toolbar object
        '
        If IsToolBarObject(I) Then
            '
            ' and this is a tool button
            '
            If TypeOf m_buttons(I).Item Is CToolButton Then
                '
                ' try the mouse down for the current button
                '
                ButtonStatus = m_buttons(I).Item.MouseUp(x, y)
                '
                ' if the button reports being pressed, then...
                '
                If ButtonStatus Then
                    '
                    ' if the button is not in a group
                    '
                    If m_buttons(I).Group = 0 Then
                        '
                        ' return ID of button to caller
                        '
                        ButtonID = ButtonStatus * m_buttons(I).ID
                    End If
                    '
                    ' got a button, exit loop
                    '
                    Exit For
                End If
            End If
        End If
    Next I
    '
    ' return button's ID to caller
    '
```

```
        MouseUp = ButtonID
End Function
```

61. Add this function to the General section of CToolBar, to redraw all the toolbar buttons. It cycles through all the toolbar items and forces a repaint of all the CToolButton objects.

```
Public Sub Show()
    Dim I As Integer
    '
    ' cycle through all objects
    '
    For I = 0 To m_numbuttons - 1
        '
        ' if this is a valid object
        '
        If IsToolBarObject(I) Then
            '
            ' and this is a CToolButton button
            '
            If TypeOf m_buttons(I).Item Is CToolButton Then
                '
                ' paint button
                '
                m_buttons(I).Item.Show
            End If
        End If
    Next I
End Sub
```

How It Works

This program works in layers. The program puts the toolbar on the PictureBox. Then the toolbar, which is handled by the CToolBar class, uses the CToolButton class to do most of its work.

To use the toolbar, the program first makes an instance of the toolbar. It then tells the toolbar to use the PictureBox as its canvas (the PictureBox is where the toolbar will appear). The program can place the PictureBox/toolbar wherever it likes; in this case, it is placed at the top of the form.

To get a line between the toolbar and the rest of the form, the PictureBox is given a border. When resized, the PictureBox is placed with its left, right, and top edges one pixel outside of the form. This way, only the bottom edge of the border is seen, giving the desired effect.

In this project we want font name and font size combo boxes, so those are created on the form at design time. Their size is set to what's desired on the toolbar, but their position is irrelevant, since the toolbar will move them to appropriate positions. These combo boxes are used to set the name and size of the font used in a label on the form. Their handling is done through normal events; all the toolbar does is place them on itself. Their values and defaults are loaded up during the form Load event.

The toolbar itself is also put together in the form's Load event subroutine. The new, open, and save buttons are loaded as normal buttons using the AddButton method of CToolButton. Then both combo boxes are added, loaded via the AddItem method. This method can load nearly any normal control. Image, Label, and other "graphical" controls do not work, because they are at a lower level in the window's z-order than a PictureBox. Next, the font style buttons are added. They're added as toggle buttons and used to turn the individual style elements on and off. Lastly, the alignment buttons (left, right, and center) are loaded onto the toolbar. These are grouped together, since only one of them can be used at any given time.

The toolbar class doesn't get the mouse and paint events directly, so it must be told about them in those event routines. The Paint event is handled by using CToolBar's Show method. This repaints the entire toolbar by using the Show methods of all of the CToolButton objects on the toolbar.

Mouse button events need a little more handling. MouseUp and MouseDown events are handled by methods of the same name; these methods require the X and Y coordinates of the mouse clicks. They return the ID number of a button whose state has changed: this is zero if no button has changed, and negative (i.e., −1 * the ID) if a toggle button has just risen (been turned off). This ID value is passed into a common subroutine (in the sample program, this is ToolBarHandle). This processing is handled by a Select Case statement at the program's level.

CToolBar

This is a class that creates a toolbar by placing simulated buttons (CToolButton) and real controls on itself and managing them. The toolbar is placed on a canvas. In the sample application this is a PictureBox, but whatever canvas is used, it needs to support the Cls method and have an hDC property.

Objects are appended to the toolbar through various methods—AddButton, AddToggleButton, AddItem, and AddSeparator—and removed using the RemoveItem method. Buttons can be set up as "option" button groups using the Group method.

The AddButton method adds a normal button. This method takes a picture with the button's faces in it and an ID number for the button. Typically, this ID number will be unique for the button.

AddToggleButton behaves very much like AddButton, except it adds a toggle button. Buttons like this are typically used to control the bold, italic, and other styles, or anything else that needs to be turned on or off.

AddItem adds an object (typically a control), and takes the control as its only parameter. The control is positioned automatically by the toolbar, but everything else needs to be handled in the parent form's code.

AddSeparator takes no parameters. It adds a blank space between items on the toolbar.

Group takes a pair of IDs. Every button on the toolbar (normal or toggle) whose ID is within those IDs (inclusive) is added to the group. The first button in the group is initially depressed. From then on, whenever any button in the group is pressed, all of the other buttons are raised. In effect, only one button within this group is ever down at any given time.

RemoveItem removes an item specified by an index passed to it.

Button presses are handled by the MouseUp and MouseDown methods. When these methods are called, the toolbar scans the list of buttons to find which one was clicked. Once the button is found, the next event depends on whether the button is in a group.

For the MouseDown method: if the button is in a group, then the button is lowered, all of the other buttons in that group are raised, and the ID of the lowered button is returned to the calling program. If the button is not in a group, then it behaves as defined initially. A normal button is lowered (handled by the CToolButton class) and nothing is returned to the user. A toggle button is lowered if it is currently up, and the ID is returned to the caller.

For the MouseUp method: nothing happens if the button is in a group. Buttons in a group only go up when another button is pressed. A normal button goes up, and the button's ID is returned to the caller. A toggle button rises, and the negative of the ID is returned to the caller.

Lastly, there's the Show method. This method repaints the entire toolbar.

CToolButton

This class handles a virtual button. CToolButton doesn't create an object, but merely paints itself on another object (called the button's canvas). The canvas must be the first thing set in the button.

The button paints itself using a bitmap that is given to it. The bitmap is presumed to have four equal-sized button pictures, one in each corner. The upper pictures are used when the button is enabled. The lower pictures are used when the button is disabled. The pictures on the left are for when the button is up, and the pictures on the right are for when the button is down.

Because the button isn't an object, it must get click notification from the object it's on. The canvas is responsible for passing MouseDown and MouseUp events to the button through events with the same name.

This class supports three different modes of operation: normal, toggle, and manual. In normal mode, the button goes down when there's a mouse-down event, and up when there is a mouse-up event. A normal button notifies the caller when the button goes up. With a toggle button, the button goes down when there's a mouse-down event and the button is currently up. The button returns a 1 to the caller when this happens. The button goes up when the button was already down and a mouse-up event occurs. The button returns a −1 to the caller when this happens.

In manual mode the button never moves by itself. It only changes by setting the Value property through code. This button always returns a hit to the caller for both mouse-up and mouse-down events.

The button paints itself by using the BitBlt API call to copy the appropriate portion of the button bitmap to the canvas.

Comments

The sample application only shows the toolbar in the upper portion of the client window. It can certainly be placed in other places, or even stacked as in Word 6.0. The toolbar class could even be extended to display vertically instead of horizontally. If extended even further to have a matrix of buttons, the toolbar could be put on a floating top-level window to create a floating toolbar.

3.11 How do I...
Use LostFocus Correctly for Data Validation?

COMPLEXITY: EASY
COMPATIBILITY: VB4 ONLY

Problem

The order in which Visual Basic events fire is not always intuitive. For instance, if the user clicks a scroll bar on my form, the scroll bar Change event will fire before the LostFocus event fires for the control that has focus at the time. Is there any way to more reliably use LostFocus for data validation in this case? I'd also like to add accelerator-key support for the buttons on my entry form, but those seem to interfere with the chain of events even further. Is the LostFocus event useless for field-level data validation?

Technique

This problem raises an assortment of questions. Do certain events occur out of the anticipated order? If so, can the order of execution in an application be arranged to accommodate this behavior? If the scroll bar's Change event has fired before performing validation on the previously active control, what happens when the validation routine finds a bad entry and focus must be reset to the original control?

To address these issues, first we must find methods to reset the scroll bar to its prior value, not act on the Change event, and return focus to the previous control. To achieve these goals, other methods will be derived that anticipate the disruption in the expected order of Visual Basic events, and reorganize program execution in response.

This How-To takes a slightly different approach than most others in this book. First, we will build a mini project demonstrating the problem. That project will progress through a series of alterations to correct the seemingly out-of-order chain of events. In the process, we'll discover good ways to track the order in which Visual Basic events are occurring, and how to observe this chain of events without thereby disturbing it. We want to avoid single-stepping through events, which can cause events that otherwise would have been fired to be missed, especially focus-related events.

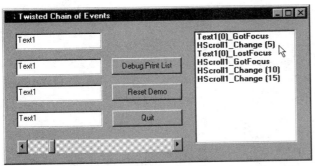

Figure 3-11-1 SoLF1 showing a twisted chain of events

Steps

Open and run SoLF1.VBP. Notice that the first text box has initial focus. Click several times on the scroll bar between the thumb and the right arrow, to cause a series of LargeChanges (see Figure 3-11-1). The mouse pointer is highlighting where the problems begin. Table 3-11-1 displays the actual sequence of Visual Basic events recorded in the list box, as compared to what would otherwise be anticipated.

Table 3-11-1 Expected versus actual order of events

EXPECTED EVENT	ACTUAL EVENT
Text1 (0)_GotFocus	Text1 (0)_GotFocus
Text1 (0)_LostFocus	HScroll1_Change (5)
HScroll1_GotFocus	Text1 (0)_LostFocus
HScroll1_Change (5)	HScroll1_GotFocus
HScroll1_Change (10)	HScroll1_Change (10)
HScroll1_Change (15)	HScroll1_Change (15)

In examining the problem, we will omit validation from the initial project. Rather, it will be a demonstration of the problem as it exists without any intervention. Press the Quit button to exit SoLF1.

To build this beginning project perform the following steps.

Analyzing the Problem

1. Create a new project called SoLF1.VBP. At this point, only Option Explicit and a few control array index constants are required in the Declarations section of Form1.

```
Option Explicit
'
' Index to command button array
'
```

Continued on next page

Continued from previous page

```
Const cmdDebug = 0
Const cmdReset = 1
Const cmdQuit = 2
```

2. Place objects and assign the properties listed in Table 3-11-2, and shown in Figure 3-11-2 on Form1. The exact positioning of the controls is unimportant. Save the form as SoLF1.FRM and the project as SoLF1.VBP.

Table 3-11-2 Objects and properties of SoLF1.FRM

OBJECT	PROPERTY	SETTING
Form	Name	Form1
	Caption	"Twisted Chain of Events"
text box	Name	Text1
	Index	0
	TabIndex	0
text box	Name	Text1
	Index	1
	TabIndex	1
text box	Name	Text1
	Index	2
	TabIndex	2
text box	Name	Text1
	Index	3
	TabIndex	3
HorizontalScrollbar	Name	HScroll1
	LargeChange	5
	Max	100
	Min	0
	SmallChange	1
	TabIndex	4
CommandButton	Name	Command1
	Caption	"Debug.Print List"
	Index	0
	TabIndex	7
CommandButton	Name	Command1
	Caption	"Reset Demo"
	Index	1
	TabIndex	6
CommandButton	Name	Command1
	Caption	"Quit"
	Index	2

OBJECT	PROPERTY	SETTING
	TabIndex	5
ListBox	Name	List1
	Font	MS Sans Serif Bold
	TabIndex	8

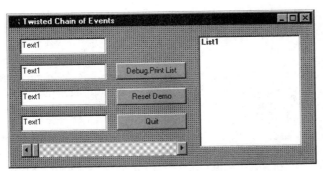

Figure 3-11-2 SoLF1.FRM at design time

3. Add the following code to the Command1_Click event. The first thing done by most of the events in this project is to report that they have been fired, by adding a line to the List1 list box. The three command buttons offer to copy the list box contents to the Debug window for longer-term reference, clear the list box and reset the demo, and exit the demo.

```
Private Sub Command1_Click(Index As Integer)
    Dim i As Integer
    '
    ' Indicate this event fired
    '
    List1.AddItem "Command1(" & Index & ")_Click"
    '
    ' Perform desired action
    '
    Select Case Index
        '
        ' Copy the entire listbox to the Debug window
        '
        Case cmdDebug
            Debug.Print String(25, "*")
            For i = 0 To List1.ListCount - 1
                Debug.Print List1.List(i)
            Next i
            Debug.Print String(25, "*")
        '
        ' Clear listbox, reset scrollbar, and send focus back to
```

Continued on next page

Continued from previous page

```
            ' first text box.
            '
        Case cmdReset
            List1.Clear
            HScroll1.Value = 0
            Text1(0).SetFocus
        '
        ' Exit demonstration
        '
        Case cmdQuit
            Unload Me
    End Select
End Sub
```

4. Add the following code to the events as indicated. At this point, we're only interested in determining the sequence of events. To do so without causing unintended events or missing anticipated events, each of the controls on the form adds a line to the list box whenever an event of interest is fired.

   Another frequently used method to track focus is direct output to the Debug window. That is less appropriate because this is a demonstration aimed specifically at uncovering this sort of information. Since our purpose is tracking Visual Basic's activities, it makes sense to include that output as a part of our form.

   Don't make the grievous mistake of using a MsgBox to indicate when events are fired. Because a MsgBox is itself a separate window, it plays havoc with focus issues. When a MsgBox is raised, focus is transferred from the active form to the default button on the MsgBox. Visual Basic MsgBoxes also have a tendency to "eat" other events that would normally have fired, as we'll see shortly. So it's unwise to use this seemingly intuitive method when tracking the Visual Basic chain of events.

```
Private Sub Command1_GotFocus(Index As Integer)
    List1.AddItem "Command1(" & Index & ")_GotFocus"
End Sub

Private Sub Command1_LostFocus(Index As Integer)
    If List1.ListCount Then
        '
        ' If demo is being reset, ignore this event
        '
        List1.AddItem "Command1(" & Index & ")_LostFocus"
    End If
End Sub

Private Sub HScroll1_Change()
    If List1.ListCount Then
        '
        ' If demo is being reset, ignore this event
        '
        List1.AddItem "HScroll1_Change (" & HScroll1.Value & ")"
    End If
End Sub
```

```
Private Sub HScroll1_GotFocus()
   List1.AddItem "HScroll1_GotFocus"
End Sub

Private Sub HScroll1_LostFocus()
   List1.AddItem "HScroll1_LostFocus"
End Sub

Private Sub List1_GotFocus()
   List1.AddItem "List1_GotFocus"
End Sub

Private Sub List1_LostFocus()
   List1.AddItem "List1_LostFocus"
End Sub

Private Sub Text1_GotFocus(Index As Integer)
   List1.AddItem "Text1(" & Index & ")_GotFocus"
End Sub

Private Sub Text1_LostFocus(Index As Integer)
   List1.AddItem "Text1(" & Index & ")_LostFocus"
End Sub
```

Adding Data Validation

5. Save SoLF1.FRM as SoLF2.FRM, and save SoLF1.VBP as SoLF2.VBP, using the Save File As and Save Project As menu items on Visual Basic's File menu. We need to determine some criteria to be used for data validation. To keep it simple, we'll require that the user enter the text box control array index plus one (1, 2, 3, 4, from top to bottom) in each text box before moving on to another control. Alter the Text1_LostFocus event's code as shown below, in order to alert the user if input isn't correct and then to reset focus back to the control with bad input.

```
Private Sub Text1_LostFocus(Index As Integer)
   List1.AddItem "Text1(" & Index & ")_LostFocus"
   '
   ' Clean up leading or trailing spaces
   '
   Text1(Index) = Trim(Text1(Index))
   '
   ' Test to see if input equals Index+1
   ' If not, alert the user and reset focus
   '
   If Text1(Index) <> CStr(Index + 1) Then
      MsgBox "Please enter: " & (Index + 1), , "Invalid Input"
      Text1(Index).SetFocus
   End If
End Sub
```

Run the project thus far (press (F5)). When the form comes up, before doing anything else press (TAB) to move from Text1(0) to Text1(1). Because we didn't

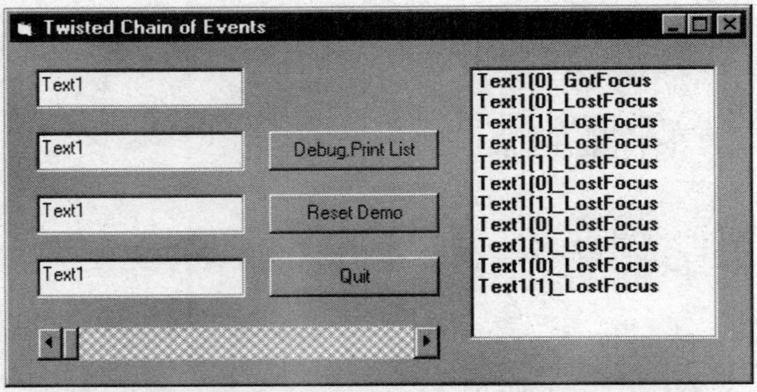

Figure 3-11-3 Infinite loop of LostFocus events when user tabs from one invalid entry to another

change the default Text property of Text1 when the form was designed, the current contents will not pass the validation test.

What happens next may confuse you. Consider that none of the text boxes have valid input. The user has tabbed from one to the next and up pops a MsgBox indicating bad input. But where does focus go when the MsgBox is dismissed? It goes to the second text box—but look at the listbox. There have been no Text1(1)_GotFocus events! What you are seeing is one of those instances where a MsgBox "consumes" a Visual Basic event. The Text1(1)_GotFocus event will not be fired with this sequence of instructions. Instead, the program is in an infinite loop, bouncing back and forth between LostFocus events for Text(0) and Text1(1), as shown in Figure 3-11-3. With each click on the MsgBox's OK button, another trip is taken through the data-validation scheme, and another invalid input is found. The only escape is to press (CTRL)-(BREAK) and then the Stop button on Visual Basic's toolbar.

6. Reverse the order of the MsgBox and SetFocus lines in the Text1_LostFocus event, so the If test appears is as shown below. Press (F5) to start the program; then immediately press (TAB) to trigger the data validation routine. All is well, now: Focus returned to Text1(0) before it had a chance to leave. Text1(1) never receives focus, and the MsgBox has no opportunity to interfere. Press the Quit button to exit.

```
Private Sub Text1_LostFocus(Index As Integer)
    List1.AddItem "Text1(" & Index & ")_LostFocus"
    '
    ' Clean up leading or trailing spaces
    '
    Text1(Index) = Trim(Text1(Index))
    '
    ' Test to see if input equals Index+1
```

```
' If not, alert the user and reset focus
'
If Text1(Index) <> CStr(Index + 1) Then
    Text1(Index).SetFocus
    MsgBox "Please enter: " & (Index + 1), , "Invalid Input"
End If
End Sub
```

7. Now we have another problem. The validation routine has no provision for the user's canceling input, and once again we need to make more alterations. Edit the Text1_LostFocus event, adding an If test that determines if the control grabbing the focus is the one that cancels the current operation. In this case, our Cancel button actually ends the application, but it's the same idea–in fact, all three command buttons can be considered equivalent to Cancel for the purpose of this demo. If the user is trying to cancel, the validation routine should be skipped, as they are obviously not interested in storing the results. Text1_LostFocus should now look as shown below, and the validation routine should be executing as expected in all but one instance, which we'll look at next.

```
Private Sub Text1_LostFocus(Index As Integer)
    List1.AddItem "Text1(" & Index & ")_LostFocus"
    '
    ' Since this is a validation routine, or would call one
    ' in a real application, we first need to determine if
    ' the user is attempting to cancel their input. For this
    ' demo, all buttons can be considered equivalent to Cancel.
    '
    If TypeOf Me.ActiveControl Is CommandButton Then
        Exit Sub
    End If
    '
    ' Clean up leading or trailing spaces
    '
    Text1(Index) = Trim(Text1(Index))
    '
    ' Test to see if input equals Index+1
    ' If not, reset focus and alert the user
    '
    If Text1(Index) <> Cstr(Index + 1) Then
        Text1(Index).SetFocus
        MsgBox "Please enter: " & (Index + 1), , "Invalid Input"
    End If
End Sub
```

Preserving the Scroll Bar's Value While Insuring Accurate Input

Clicking on the scroll bar with our present validation routines presents an interesting situation: the value of the scroll bar is altered, because its Change event is fired before the validation routines are. (There are no good explanations for this mysterious logic in Visual Basic, and the best we can do is cope with it.) Currently, the vali-

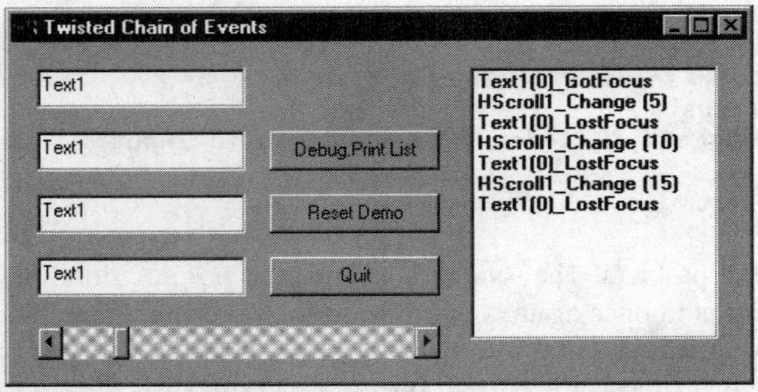

Figure 3-11-4 Scroll bar has advanced to Value=15, while text box still has invalid input

dation routine resets focus to the proper text box, and alerts the user of the problem therein. Figure 3-11-4 shows the project after several such iterations.

Consider a case where the scroll bar exists for the purpose of changing the record to be edited in a database browser utility. How should the scroll bar Change event react? Remember, when it is fired, the validation routine has not yet determined that there is bad input in the current record. There needs to be a method to ignore Change events when other data is invalid, and to reset the scroll bar's initial value so that subsequent clicks have the correct effect.

8. Save SoLF2.FRM as SoLF3.FRM, and save SoLF2.VBP as SoLF3.VBP, using the Save File As and Save Project As menu items on the File menu. We need a way to track the scroll bar's "real" value, so it can be reset when unwanted Change events occur. There are several ways to do this. A static variable in the Change event could be used, or the scroll bar's Tag property provides a built-in persistent data-storage area (if it's not being used for anything else). Since we have no other use for it in this demo, the Tag is a good choice. Add the following code to the Form_Load event to initialize the Tag property to whatever Value was assigned at design time.

```
Private Sub Form_Load()
    '
    ' Use the scrollbar's Tag property to store what should
    ' be its correct Value.
    '
    HScroll1.Tag = HScroll1.Value
End Sub
```

9. To determine whether a Change event should be acted upon or ignored, LostFocus-based data validation routines must be allowed to execute before proceeding with the core logic code of the Change event. Here, DoEvents comes to the rescue. By placing DoEvents near the top of the Change event, pending

events are allowed to fire. Afterward, it's a simple matter to decide whether to proceed with the Change event logic or to reset the scroll bar and bail out. By comparing the ActiveControl to HScroll1, we find out whether focus was transferred elsewhere during the DoEvents. If this is the case, then we restore the previous value from the Tag and exit the event.

```vb
Private Sub HScroll1_Change()
    '
    ' If demo is being reset, ignore this event,
    ' otherwise indicate this event fired
    '
    If List1.ListCount Then
        List1.AddItem "HScroll1_Change (" & HScroll1.Value & ")"
    Else
        Exit Sub
    End If
    '
    ' Allow validation routine(s) to do their thing
    '
    DoEvents
    '
    ' See if focus was transfered somewhere else, presumably due
    ' to bad input that was caught by a validation routine. If so,
    ' bail out of Change event after resetting Value.
    '
    If Not (Me.ActiveControl Is HScroll1) Then
        HScroll1.Value = Val(HScroll1.Tag)
        Exit Sub
    End If
    '
    ' Perform whatever other actions would normally be done in this
    ' event here. When done, store the new value in either the
    ' control's Tag property, or in a static variable.
    '
    HScroll1.Tag = HScroll1.Value
    '
    ' Indicate that complete event was executed
    '
    List1.AddItem "HScroll1_Change (Done!)"
End Sub
```

Table 3-11-3 shows the chain of events that occur if the first user action is to click on the gray area of the scroll bar, causing a LargeChange:

Table 3-11-3 Chain of events when scroll bar resets itself

EVENT	CAUSE
Text1(0)_GotFocus	Initial display of form
HScroll1_Change (5)	User click on the scroll bar
Text1(0)_LostFocus	DoEvents in HScroll1_Change
HScroll1_Change (0)	Resetting scroll bar value in HScroll1_Change

The first text box receives focus as the form is displayed. As shown in Table 3-11-3, clicking on the scroll bar fires the scroll bar Change event before the active control's LostFocus event fires. By placing DoEvents near the top of the Change, the tardy LostFocus is allowed to fire almost as if it were a procedure call from the Change event. But the most interesting aspect here is that the Change event has no knowledge of which event, if any, requires being called. DoEvents spins its spell, and the required work is carried out. Since the data was invalid, and focus was returned to the text box, another Change is precipitated when the scroll bar's value is reset to its previous value.

This sequence now introduces recursion into the picture—the Change event is, in effect, calling itself. Is this a potential problem? We see above that the Change event is being entered a second time while it's still executing the first instance. Is this acceptable since it's only going one level deep? In fact, the second instance of the Change event will be halted at the test for ActiveControl, so the code that would execute the Change logic in a legitimate event is never acted on in either instance.

What If You Don't Want a MsgBox?

There may be instances where a MsgBox is inappropriate for signalling bad entries. For example, your application may offer an "expert mode," where the user is capable of recognizing that if focus bounces back, a data error has occurred that needs correction. We saw in the first two projects (SoLF1 and SoLF2) that MsgBoxes can have unanticipated consequences in focus issues. Let's see what happens if the MsgBox in Text1_LostFocus is commented out.

10. Save SoLF3.FRM as SoLF4.FRM, and save SoLF3.VBP as SoLF4.VBP, using the Save File As and Save Project As items on the File menu. *Then save your work in other applications, or exit them, before going any further with this step.* Comment out the line in Text1_LostFocus that raises a MsgBox to alert the user to bad input. Press (F5) to run the project. Click and hold the left mouse button in the gray space between the thumb and the arrow of the scroll bar. Watch the list box, and you'll see the List1_Change event occurring nonstop. At this point, you can move the mouse away from the scroll bar, and the activity will most likely stop. But it may not. Repeat the click-and-hold over the scroll bar several times, and at some point the scroll bar will just start firing all on its own; the graphics in it may even become confused. The arrows may start painting in the gray area, for example. Table 3-11-4 illustrates the chain of events that is reported in the list box:

Table 3-11-4 Out-of-control scroll bar events

EVENT	COMMENT
Text1(0)_GotFocus	Initial form load
HScroll1_Change (5)	User presses mouse button down on scroll bar
Text1(0)_LostFocus	DoEvents in scroll bar Change event
HScroll1_GotFocus	MsgBox previously prevented this event!

EVENT	COMMENT
HScroll1_LostFocus	Validation removes focus from scroll bar
Text1(0)_GotFocus	Focus now clearly at text box
HScroll1_Change (0)	Change event resets scroll bar's Value
HScroll1_Change (5)	Beginning of "death spiral", because
HScroll1_Change (0)	user is still holding down mouse button,
HScroll1_Change (5)	. . .
HScroll1_Change (0)	. . .
HScroll1_Change (5)	. . .
HScroll1_Change (0)	and so on. . . until the mouse is released

The root of this problem is overstimulation. The user is ignoring the need to enter proper data in the text box and is instead bombarding the scroll bar with messages. The obvious answer then is to make further scroll bar input impossible. So we surround the line that invokes the recursion with statements that disable and re-enable the scroll bar, as shown in boldface in the following segment. With this code, there is no way for data validation to be missed, nor for it to otherwise interfere with the desired flow of events.

```
Private Sub HScroll1_Change()
'
' If demo is being reset, ignore this event,
' otherwise indicate this event fired.
' This block would *not* be used in a real app.
'
If List1.ListCount Then
    List1.AddItem "HScroll1_Change (" & HScroll1.Value & ")"
Else
    Exit Sub
End If
'
' Allow validation routine(s) to do their thing
'
DoEvents
'
' See if focus was transfered somewhere else, presumably due
' to bad input that was caught by a validation routine. If so,
' bail out of Change event after resetting Value. To prevent
' out-of-control mouse messages, disable the scrollbar before
' resetting its value.
'
If Not (Me.ActiveControl Is HScroll1) Then
    HScroll1.Enabled = False
        HScroll1.Value = Val(HScroll1.Tag)
    HScroll1.Enabled = True
    Exit Sub
End If
'
' Perform whatever other actions would normally be done in this
' event here. When done, store the new value in either the
```

Continued on next page

Continued from previous page

```
    ' control's Tag property, or in a static variable.
    '
    HScroll1.Tag = HScroll1.Value
    '
    ' Indicate that complete event was executed
    '
    List1.AddItem "HScroll1_Change (Done!)"
End Sub
```

Now, press (F5) to run the project again. Once again, hold the mouse button down over the scroll bar but don't release it. Notice the difference in the list box report of events. This time, all event processing is halted just as we want, as shown in Figure 3-11-5. The order of events has been altered slightly, but they're completely within a manageable realm.

Preventing a Validation Tug-of-War Between Text Boxes

The scroll bar is now working just fine. But try tabbing or clicking on the next text box. Now, focus bounces back and forth between the two text boxes at a furious pace. Once the list box is packed to capacity with event notifications, you'll get an error message that Visual Basic is "Out of Memory" (if you don't press (CTRL)-(BREAK) first). In this case, the MsgBox was doing us a favor by consuming other events. With the GotFocus earlier, MsgBox was "eating" the LostFocus for the newly active text box. Because focus was set back to the original control in the first control's LostFocus, the second control's GotFocus never fired. But focus did indeed transfer; Visual Basic just never had the opportunity to act on it because the active code never yielded.

When the first LostFocus event ends, focus is back at that control, and Visual Basic internally enters a GetMessage loop, which allows other Windows messages to be processed. At this point, it's recognized that the second control no longer has focus (a WM_KILLFOCUS message is received from Windows and processed), and Visual Basic fires its LostFocus event. This sets up an infinite loop, or tug-of-war, between the validation routines for the two text boxes. Neither has valid input, and both want to regain focus. Our task now is to convince the second text box that another control currently has precedence and to yield its validation efforts.

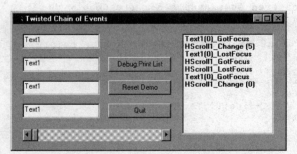

Figure 3-11-5 LostFocus under control with
SoLF4.VBP

Unfortunately, there are only two ways to prevent this sort of situation. If no data fields will ever be initialized to contain bad data, there is nothing to worry about. Although assuring valid data from the beginning is certainly the easiest solution, it is also the least feasible. When a field is to be initialized to blank and that is an invalid response, the remaining option is to set a flag when validation is currently in progress. If all validating text boxes on the form are in one control array, this flag can be a static variable within the LostFocus event itself. Another variation on this theme is to do all validation within one routine that's called from every LostFocus event. Otherwise, a form-level flag variable is required. We'll assume the worst and take that direction.

11. Save SoLF4.FRM as SoLF5.FRM, and save SoLF4.VBP as SoLF5.VBP, using the Save File As and Save Project As items on the File menu. Add the following dimension statement to the Declarations section of Form1. We'll use this flag to signal that a validation process is occurring, so that if another begins, it will know to defer.

```
'
' Flag variable to indicate validation in progress
'
Dim Validating As Boolean
```

12. Modify Text1_LostFocus as indicated by the code in boldface below. This checks the Validating flag to see if another process is already trying to keep order. If not, that flag is set and validation proceeds. If bad data is found, focus is reset back to the current instance of Text1. DoEvents is called to allow time for execution of the switched-to control's LostFocus event. This works because Visual Basic now has a chance to process waiting Windows messages. It finds a waiting WM_KILL-FOCUS message for the second text box, and fires that control's LostFocus event. If that text box contains bad initial data, the validation routine there will detect that Validating is True. Validation will not proceed with its own logic but instead will just allow focus to transfer back to where it started. At that point, execution returns to the original LostFocus event, and the Validating flag is cleared to end the process.

```
Private Sub Text1_LostFocus(Index As Integer)
    List1.AddItem "Text1(" & Index & ")_LostFocus"
    '
    ' Since this is a validation routine, or would call one
    ' in a real application, we first need to determine if
    ' the user is attempting to cancel their input. For this
    ' demo, all buttons can be considered equivalent to Cancel.
    '
    If TypeOf Me.ActiveControl Is CommandButton Then
        Exit Sub
    End If
    '
    ' Clean up leading or trailing spaces
    '
```

Continued on next page

Continued from previous page

```
    Text1(Index) = Trim(Text1(Index))
    '
    ' Don't proceed if currently validating another control
    '
    If Not Validating Then
        Validating = True
        '
        ' Test to see if input equals Index+1
        ' If not, reset focus and alert the user
        '
        If Text1(Index) <> CStr(Index + 1) Then
            Text1(Index).SetFocus
            ' MsgBox "Please enter: " & (Index + 1), , , "Invalid Input"
            '
            ' Allow previously active control's LostFocus to fire,
            ' since MsgBox is no longer preventing focus transfer.
            '
            DoEvents
        End If
        Validating = False
    End If
End Sub
```

Adding Accelerator Keys

So, you say you want to add accelerator keys to the command buttons or other controls? Let's give it a try.

13. Save SoLF5.FRM as SoLF6.FRM, and save SoLF5.VBP as SoLF6.VBP, using the Save File As and Save Project As items on the File menu. Modify the properties of the command buttons and add a new command button, as listed in Table 3-11-5.

Table 3-11-5 Modified objects and properties for SoLF6.VBP

OBJECT	PROPERTY	SETTING
CommandButton	Name	Command1
	Caption	"&Debug.Print List"
	Index	0
CommandButton	Name	Command1
	Caption	"&Reset Demo"
	Index	1
CommandButton	Name	Command1
	Caption	"&Quit"
	Index	2
CommandButton	Name	Command1
	Caption	"&Save"
	Index	3

14. Select Menu Editor from the Tools menu and add a menu to Form1 with the properties listed in Table 3-11-6.

Table 3-11-6 Menu properties for Form1 in SoLF6.VBP

CAPTION	NAME	SHORTCUT	SPECIAL
&File	mFile		
&Save	mSave	Ctrl-S	
E&xit	mExit		
&Expert	mExpert		
Use &MsgBox	mMsg	Ctrl-M	Checked = True

15. Add the following support routines for the new menu options:

```
Private Sub mExit_Click()
    Unload Me
End Sub

Private Sub mMsg_Click()
    '
    ' Toggle display of MsgBox if validation fails
    '
    mMsg.Checked = Not mMsg.Checked
End Sub

Private Sub mSave_Click()
    '
    ' Pretend that the data has been saved
    '
    MsgBox "Data has been saved!"
End Sub
```

16. Modify the Text1_LostFocus event so that only the Quit button is now ignored. If the user attempts to press any other command button, the data validation routine will execute. Also, include an If test that shows the MsgBox when that menu option has been checked. This would be similar to having an "expert mode" enabled or disabled.

```
Private Sub Text1_LostFocus(Index As Integer)
    List1.AddItem "Text1(" & Index & ")_LostFocus"
    '
    ' Since this is a validation routine, or would call one
    ' in a real application, we first need to determine if
    ' the user is attempting to cancel their input. For this
    ' demo, only the Quit button will represent Cancel.
    '
    If Me.ActiveControl Is Command1(cmdQuit) Then
        Exit Sub
    End If
    '
```

Continued on next page

Continued from previous page

```
    ' Clean up leading or trailing spaces
    '
    Text1(Index) = Trim(Text1(Index))
    '
    ' Don't proceed if currently validating another control
    '
    If Not Validating Then
        Validating = True
        '
        ' Test to see if input equals Index+1. If not, reset focus
        ' and alert the user if (mMsg.Checked = True).
        '
        If Text1(Index) <> CStr(Index + 1) Then
            Text1(Index).SetFocus
            If mMsg.Checked Then
                MsgBox "Please enter: " & (Index + 1), , "Invalid Input"
            End If
            '
            ' Allow previously active control's LostFocus to fire
            '
            DoEvents
        End If
        Validating = False
    End If
End Sub
```

Press (F5) to start running the project. Click the Debug.Print command button with the mouse. As expected, the Text1_LostFocus event is fired and a MsgBox indicates the input is bad. Dismiss the MsgBox, and all is well. Then press (ALT)-(D), the accelerator key for the Debug.Print command button.

Now you have stumbled upon another disruption in the expected chain of Visual Basic events. This time, the Command1(0)_Click event fires before the Text1_LostFocus event. In fact, it only gets worse (again) if the MsgBox is disabled. Bypass data validation by pressing (CTRL)-(M), or by toggling the check mark on that menu item to disable the MsgBox. Press (ALT)-(D) again. This time the chain of events as recorded in the list box is as shown in Table 3-11-7.

Table 3-11-7 Chain of events when accelerator key is pressed

EVENT	COMMENT
Command1(0)_Click	Accelerator key triggers Click before all else
Text1(0)_LostFocus	LostFocus trails behind
Command1(0)_GotFocus	Focus has been transferred
Command1(0)_LostFocus	Validation pulls focus back to Text1
Text1(0)_GotFocus	End of another twisted chain

Without the MsgBox, focus is actually transferred to the command button before returning to the text box. Of course, the Click event still occurs ahead of all others. Can the same sort of tricks as were used in the scroll bar's Change event be used with accelerator keys?

Preventing Accelerator Keys from Preempting Data Validation

17. Add a new private function called ValidationFailed, and insert the following code in it. This is a generic function that can be called from any event that needs to allow validation processing to complete before reacting to the core logic of the current event. As with the scroll bar example, DoEvents is first called to allow "missing" LostFocus events to be fired. Assuming that the associated LostFocus will reset focus back to the offending control if the input data is invalid, ValidationFailed will return True if the ActiveControl is no longer the one passed in.

```
Private Function ValidationFailed(Cntl As Control)
    '
    ' Allow validation routine(s) to do their thing
    '
    DoEvents
    '
    ' See if focus was transfered somewhere else, presumably due
    ' to bad input that was caught by a validation routine. If so,
    ' the control passed in will no longer be the ActiveControl.
    '
    If Me.ActiveControl Is Cntl Then
        ValidationFailed = False
    Else
        ValidationFailed = True
    End If
End Function
```

18. Modify the Command1_Click routine as shown below. Here, we selectively decide whether to proceed with the Click event. If the Quit button was pressed, execution will continue without regard to input validity. If either of the other buttons was pressed, a call is made to ValidationFailed. If that function returns True, the rest of the event is avoided with an Exit Sub. To confirm that this is happening, an additional list item is added at the end of the routine whenever execution falls through completely. Notice that support for the new Save button was added to the Select Case block, as well.

```
Private Sub Command1_Click(Index As Integer)
    Dim i As Integer
    '
    ' Indicate this event fired
    '
    List1.AddItem "Command1(" & Index & ")_Click"
    '
    ' We need to prevent continuation if the user pressed
    ' an accelerator key for other than the Quit button, and
    ' data validation routines have reset focus elsewhere.
    '
    If Index <> cmdQuit Then
        '
        ' Call generic routine which allows validation processing
```

Continued on next page

Continued from previous page

```
          ' to proceed, then checks to see if focus has transfered.
          '
          If ValidationFailed(Command1(Index)) Then
              Exit Sub
          End If
      End If
      '
      ' Perform desired action
      '
      Select Case Index
          '
          ' Copy the entire listbox to the Debug window
          '
          Case cmdDebug
              Debug.Print String(25, "*")
              For i = 0 To List1.ListCount - 1
                  Debug.Print List1.List(i)
              Next i
              Debug.Print String(25, "*")
          '
          ' Clear listbox, reset scrollbar, and send focus back to
          ' first text box.
          '
          Case cmdReset
              List1.Clear
              HScroll1.Value = 0
              Text1(0).SetFocus
          '
          ' Exit demonstration
          '
          Case cmdQuit
              Unload Me
          '
          ' Pretend the data has been saved
          '
          Case cmdSave
              MsgBox "Data has been saved!"
      End Select
      '
      ' Indicate this event exited normally
      '
      List1.AddItem "Command1(" & Index & ")_Click (Done!)"
End Sub
```

19. Using ValidationFailed, our original scroll bar Change event can be simplified, or at least made a little easier to read and maintain. Optionally, you can modify that routine as follows:

```
Private Sub HScroll1_Change()
      '
      ' If demo is being reset, ignore this event,
      ' otherwise indicate this event fired.
      ' This block would *not* be used in a real app.
      '
      If List1.ListCount Then
```

```
    List1.AddItem "HScroll1_Change (" & HScroll1.Value & ")"
Else
    Exit Sub
End If
'
' Call generic routine which allows validation routine(s) to
' do their thing, and returns True if validation failed.
'
If ValidationFailed(HScroll1) Then
    '
    ' Bail out of Change event after resetting Value. To prevent
    ' out-of-control mouse messages, disable the scrollbar before
    ' resetting its value.
    '
    HScroll1.Enabled = False
        HScroll1.Value = Val(HScroll1.Tag)
    HScroll1.Enabled = True
    Exit Sub
End If
'
' Perform whatever other actions would normally be done in this
' event here. When done, store the new value in either the
' control's Tag property, or in a static variable.
'
HScroll1.Tag = HScroll1.Value
'
' Indicate that complete event was executed
'
    List1.AddItem "HScroll1_Change (Done!)"
End Sub
```

Supporting Default and Cancel Properties

Suppose someone decides that this data entry form should also support the Default and Cancel properties for the Save and Quit buttons, respectively. What sort of modifications would be required? Actually, it's quite simple.

20. In Command1_Click, before testing for failed validation, explicitly set the focus (see boldface code below) to the clicked command button. Without this modification, if the user pressed Enter to signify Save, ValidationFailed would always return True. This is due to the design of these special Default and Cancel properties. Focus is never transferred when they are invoked. Instead, their entire accomplishment is the Click event of the associated command button. The code below defers if Quit is pressed, allowing the execution to fall through to the Select Case block where the form is unloaded. If any other button is pressed, pending validations are allowed to occur, and the button's actions are not carried out if validation fails.

```
'
' We need to prevent continuation if the user pressed
' an accelerator key for other than the Quit button, and
' data validation routines have reset focus elsewhere.
'
```

Continued on next page

Continued from previous page

```
If Index <> cmdQuit Then
    '
    ' Transfer focus in case the user pressed Enter or Escape.
    '
    Command1(Index).SetFocus
    '
    ' Call generic routine which allows validation processing
    ' to proceed, then checks to see if focus has transfered.
    '
    If ValidationFailed(Command1(Index)) Then
        Exit Sub
    End If
End If
```

Wouldn't Record-Level Validation Be Easier?

For all the data validation effort we've put into this form, there's still nothing to prevent a user from entering one valid response, leaving the remainder of the form invalid, and saving the record! This raises several questions. Is field-level validation the best choice, as in this demo, or record-level validation? It certainly seems easier to simply check every field immediately prior to saving the record, but the truth is that there is an absolute need to do both.

Though record-level validation is required as a final check for missing entries, field-level validation is required as a common courtesy to your users. They need immediate feedback or correction when invalid data has been entered. It is extremely frustrating to finish a long data-entry form, only to be returned to the beginning due to an incorrect entry—especially if later entries are affected by the earlier mistake.

This How-To has demonstrated that there's no simple way to ensure that your user hasn't skipped around and left default data in some of the entry areas before saving. If all the default data is valid, this won't be a problem. But often this isn't the case, as when the user leaves blank the Social Security number on a credit application. One possibility for validation is to track whether each control receives focus in a form-level array. Such a scheme would be considerably more work than a quick record-level validation routine, and it's far from being as fail-safe as checking each field one last time before saving the record.

"Ruthless control" over users is the antithesis of what Windows is all about. In older, character-based applications, the programmer did have absolute control over the order in which data was entered and accepted, and this approach was the norm. Today, the standards have changed. Users are accustomed to freedom of movement within dialog boxes, to picking and choosing the order in which they enter the required information. In the end, if missing information shall not be allowed, performing validity checking after each entry and before saving all entries is unavoidable.

How It Works

This How-To has demonstrated some of the most often tripped-over traps when using LostFocus for data validation purposes. There are times when Visual Basic fires its events in an order that is not immediately understandable and, seemingly, not as documented. Microsoft defends the behavior as "by design," but the varying sequences still present problems.

When certain events occur before a LostFocus, although intuitively they should occur after, the order of logical execution within an application can still be maintained. Often, a judicious call to DoEvents is all that's required. DoEvents will allow the firing of the "missing" LostFocus by allowing Visual Basic to process queued-up Windows messages, and any associated validation routines that LostFocus calls. If one of those validation routines resets focus to a control that had bad input, that focus shift can be detected in the original event and acted upon intelligently.

In most cases, when a validation routine has reset focus, the wayward event can simply be exited. There are times, as with the scroll bar, when further cleanup is required. Because the Value property of a scroll bar has already been updated before its Change event is fired, it must be reset to its original value when the application's validation rules dictate. Although this introduces recursion, it is only one level deep and doesn't pose much of a problem. A bigger problem with scroll bars is their tendency to get overstimulated by the mouse when the user has a heavy finger. To prevent this bad reaction to persistent users, disable the scroll bar before resetting its value, and then re-enable it.

When fields are initialized to invalid data, one validation routine triggers another competing validation and an infinite loop is entered. To solve this, either don't initialize with invalid data, or set a flag before resetting focus to a bad entry so that other validation routines know to defer. This alone is not enough, however. The second control's LostFocus event will not fire until the first one finishes—unless a DoEvents is inserted immediately after resetting focus. DoEvents lets the second LostFocus fire, detect that another validation routine is in progress, and then allow focus to transfer back to the first.

Accelerator keys can also cause events to fire out of order. With command buttons, the Click event will fire before GotFocus, which means it's also firing before the previously active control's LostFocus. A call to DoEvents allows the focus events to execute before proceeding with the logic of the button event. Determining the active control after the DoEvents indicates whether a validation routine has reset focus elsewhere. If so, bail out of the command button's Click event before any harm is done.

The Default and Cancel properties of command buttons can cause them to behave similarly to menu events. These settings will fire the command button's Click event when the user presses (ENTER) or (ESC), but neither setting transfers focus from the active control to the command button. Obviously, this can get in the way of validation efforts that rely on focus transfers. To get things back on track before letting the validation routines proceed, explicitly set focus to the command button. This allows the same logic as used for accelerator keys, in determining the active control after a DoEvents.

Although all output in the demonstration projects was directed at an on-screen list box, for "real" applications the best choice for tracking Visual Basic events is probably the Debug window. Also, for compiled applications, another option will be presented in How-To 9.6 using the Notepad applet in place of the Debug window.

With that technique, you could turn debugging output on remotely—at a client site, for example.

Comments

LostFocus events are naturals for field-level data validation. With the techniques presented in this How-To, you can feel confident that you won't miss the opportunity when it presents itself. If you run across other situations where LostFocus appears to be "missing" or out of order, this How-To also shows ways to track the flow of Visual Basic events and attempt to reorder execution back to its intuitive sequence.

3.12 How do I...
Create a Multiselect Drag-and-Drop File Dialog?

COMPLEXITY: INTERMEDIATE
COMPATIBILITY: VB4 ONLY

Problem

My users need to select and work with many files at once, not just a single file. I tried using a common dialog to do this, but I couldn't figure out how to make it accept multiple files. I often use drag-and-drop operations in my applications, so how can I build a file open dialog box that allows drag and drop to select a number of files?

Technique

FILEPIK2 (seen in Figure 3-12-1) displays a drag-and-drop file select dialog box (as shown in Figure 3-12-2) that allows the user to select multiple files. (Files may also be selected by double-clicking on them, but that's not the focus.)

In this case, VB's automatic drag-and-drop functionality is not adequate. It drags the entire control, not just part of it, so we have to manually start and handle drag-and-drop operations. In FILEPIK2, our drag-and-drop operation occurs just after the user presses the left mouse button in the file list box. The delay is slight, but still

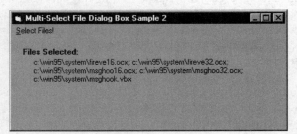

Figure 3-12-1 FILEPIK2's main screen

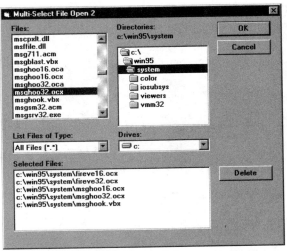

Figure 3-12-2 The drag-and-drop multiselect
file list dialog box

important, because it ensures that the drag-and-drop operation doesn't start if the
user is simply clicking.

As the user drags the file around the form, the mouse cursor changes to reflect
whether or not the file is allowed to drop in a particular spot. When the file is
dropped, the drag-and-drop operation is ended automatically by VB. If this occurs in
the selected files list box, the file is added.

Steps

1. Create a new project called FILEPIK2.VBP. Select Form1, and add objects and set
properties as shown in Table 3-12-1.

Table 3-12-1 Objects, properties, and settings for Form1

OBJECT	PROPERTY	SETTING
Form	Form	Form1
	Caption	"multiselect File Dialog Box Sample 2"
	Height	2640
	Left	1575
	Top	1455
	Width	5895
Label	Name	Label2
	Caption	"Files Selected:"
	Height	255

Continued on next page

Continued from previous page

OBJECT	PROPERTY	SETTING
	Left	240
	Top	240
	Width	1815
Label	Name	Label1
	Caption	"None"
	Height	1215
	Left	480
	Top	480
	Width	5055

2. Use the menu editor to add the menu shown in Table 3-12-2 to Form1.

Table 3-12-2 Menu for Form1

MENU NAME	CAPTION
MenuSelectFiles	"&Select Files!"

3. Add the following code to the General section of Form1:

```
Option Explicit
'
' make new instance of CFilePick2 form
'
Dim FP2 As New CFilePick2
```

4. Add this function to the General section of Form1:

```
Private Sub Form_Unload(Cancel As Integer)
    End
End Sub
```

5. Add the following code to the General section of Form1. This function brings up the multifile pick dialog box (CFilePick2). Then it takes the file list returned from FilePick and puts it in Label1. If the file list is empty, it displays "None."

```
Private Sub MenuSelectFiles_Click()
    '
    ' get files to play with
    '
    Label1.Caption = FP2.SelectFiles("Project Files _
        (*.VBP)|*.VBP|VB Files (*.FRM; *.VBP; *.FRX; _
        *.BAS)|*.FRM;*.VBP;*.FRX;*.BAS|All Files (*.*)|*.*")
    '
    ' if there are no files selected, say "None"
    '
    If Len(Label1.Caption) = 0 Then
        Label1.Caption = "None"
    End If
End Sub
```

6. Use the Insert Form menu item to add a new form to the project. Name the new form CFilePick2. Then select CFilePick2 and add objects and properties with settings as shown in Table 3-12-3.

Table 3-12-3 Objects, properties, and settings for CFilePick2

OBJECT	PROPERTY	SETTING
Form	Name	CFilePick2
	BorderStyle	3 'Fixed Double
	Caption	"Multi-Select File Open 2"
	Height	6285
	Left	1380
	LockControls	-1 'True
	MaxButton	0 'False
	MinButton	0 'False
	Top	1530
	Width	7095
Timer	Name	Timer1
	Enabled	0 'False
	Interval	200
	Left	5400
	Top	4920
PictureBox	Name	DragImage
	Height	495
	Left	5400
	Picture	"DRAG.ICO"
	Top	4320
	Visible	0 'False
	Width	495
CommandButton	Name	Command3
	Caption	"Delete"
	Height	375
	Left	5400
	Top	3840
	Width	1335
ListBox	Name	lstSelect
	Height	1785
	Left	240
	MultiSelect	2 'Extended
	Sorted	-1 'True
	Top	3840

Continued on next page

319

Continued from previous page

OBJECT	PROPERTY	SETTING
	Width	4935
ListBox	Name	lstPattern
	Height	1005
Object	Property	Setting
	Left	5400
	Top	2160
	Visible	0 'False
	Width	1335
FileListBox	Name	lstFile
	Height	2370
	Left	240
	Top	360
	Width	2415
CommandButton	Name	Command2
	Cancel	-1 'True
	Caption	"Cancel"
	Height	375
	Left	5400
	Top	600
	Width	1335
CommandButton	Name	Command1
	Caption	"OK"
	Default	-1 'True
	Height	375
	Left	5400
	Top	120
	Width	1335
ComboBox	Name	cmbPattern
	Height	300
	Left	240
	Style	2 'Dropdown List
	Top	3120
	Width	2415
DriveListBox	Name	lstDrive
	Height	315
	Left	2880
	Top	3120
	Width	2295
DirListBox	Name	lstDirectory

OBJECT	PROPERTY	SETTING
	Height	2055
	Left	2880
	Top	720
	Width	2295
Object	Property	Setting
Label	Name	Label3
	AutoSize	-1 'True
	Caption	"Selected Files:"
	Height	195
	Left	240
	Top	3600
	Width	1275
Label	Name	Label5
	AutoSize	-1 'True
	Caption	"List Files of Type:"
	Height	195
	Left	240
	Top	2880
	Width	1530
Label	Name	Label4
	AutoSize	-1 'True
	Caption	"Drives:"
	Height	195
	Left	2880
	Top	2880
	Width	615
Label	Name	lblDirectory
	Height	255
	Left	2880
	Top	360
	Width	2295
Label	Name	Label2
	AutoSize	-1 'True
	Caption	"Directories:"
	Height	195
	Left	2880
	Top	120
	Width	990
Label	Name	Label1

Continued on next page

Continued from previous page

OBJECT	PROPERTY	SETTING
	AutoSize	-1 'True
	Caption	"Files:"
	Height	195
	Left	240
	Top	120
	Width	465

7. Add the following code to the General Declarations section of CFilePick2. This function takes care of updating the file lists after a directory has changed.

```
Private Sub FileUpdate()
    '
    ' put the new path into the hidden file list
    '
    lstFile.Path = lstDirectory.Path
End Sub
```

8. Add the following code to the General Declarations section of CFilePick2. This function handles updating the directory paths and the file lists. It displays the current path by taking it from the directory list box and putting it into the directory label (lblDirectory). Then it updates the file lists by calling FileUpdate.

```
Private Sub DirectoryUpdate()
    '
    ' show the current directory to the user
    '
    lblDirectory = lstDirectory.Path
    '
    ' update the file lists
    '
    FileUpdate
End Sub
```

9. Add the following code to the General Declarations section of CFilePick2. This function handles changes in the pattern combo box. When the pattern changes, the function gets the actual pattern from the invisible pattern list box and places it into the Pattern property of the invisible file list box. Then it calls FileUpdate to reload the list of files.

```
Private Sub cmbPattern_Click()
    '
    ' set the pattern for the hidden file list from
    ' the hidden pattern list
    '
    lstFile.Pattern = lstPattern.List(cmbPattern.ListIndex)
    '
    ' update the file lists
    '
    FileUpdate
End Sub
```

10. Add the following code to the General Declarations section of CFilePick2. This function returns the mouse pointer to normal when files are dropped outside the selected files list.

```
Private Sub cmbPattern_DragDrop(Source As Control, X As Single, _
    Y As Single)
  MousePointer = vbDefault
End Sub
```

11. Add the following code to the General Declarations section of CFilePick2. This function causes the file dialog to exit by hiding itself.

```
Private Sub Command1_Click()
    '
    ' time to leave
    '
    Me.Hide
End Sub
```

12. Add the following code to the General Declarations section of CFilePick2. This function returns the mouse pointer to normal when files are dropped outside the selected files list.

```
Private Sub Command1_DragDrop(Source As Control, X As Single, _
    Y As Single)
  MousePointer = vbDefault
End Sub
```

13. Add the following code to the General Declarations section of CFilePick2. This is the handler for the Cancel button, and it clears all selections by clearing the visible file list box. Then it causes the file dialog to exit by hiding itself.

```
Private Sub Command2_Click()
    '
    ' clear selections
    '
    lstSelect.Clear
    '
    ' time to leave
    '
    Me.Hide
End Sub
```

14. Add the following code to the General Declarations section of CFilePick2. This function returns the mouse pointer to normal when files are dropped outside the selected files list.

```
Private Sub Command2_DragDrop(Source As Control, X As Single, _
    Y As Single)
    '
    ' return cursor to normal if file dropped here
    '
```

Continued on next page

Continued from previous page

```
    MousePointer = vbDefault
End Sub
```

15. Add the following code to the General Declarations section of CFilePick2. This function deletes files from the selected files list. It cycles through all the entries, deleting the ones that are selected.

```
Private Sub Command3_Click()
    Dim I As Integer
    '
    ' cycle through all the files in the selected
    ' list box
    '
    Do While I < (lstSelect.ListCount)
        '
        ' if the file is selected,
        '
        If lstSelect.Selected(I) Then
            '
            ' nuke it
            '
            lstSelect.RemoveItem I
        Else
            '
            ' otherwise, move on to the next
            '
            I = I + 1
        End If
    Loop
    '
    ' make sure we have a selection
    '
    If (lstSelect.ListIndex = -1) And (lstSelect.ListCount > 0) Then
        lstSelect.ListIndex = 0
    End If
    '
    ' put focus back on the selection window
    '
    lstSelect.SetFocus
End Sub
```

16. Add the following code to the General Declarations section of CFilePick2. This function returns the mouse pointer to normal when files are dropped outside the selected files list.

```
Private Sub Command3_DragDrop(Source As Control, X As Single, _
        Y As Single)
    '
    ' return cursor to normal if file dropped here
    '
    MousePointer = vbDefault
End Sub
```

17. Add the following code to the General Declarations section of CFilePick2. This function changes the mouse pointer to a "No" sign when the files are dragged over the form.

```
Private Sub Form_DragOver(Source As Control, X As Single, _
    Y As Single, State As Integer)
    '
    ' show user that files aren't supposed to
    ' be dropped here
    '
    MousePointer = vbNoDrop
    lstFile.DragIcon = Nothing
End Sub
```

18. Add the following code to the General Declarations section of CFilePick2. This function returns the mouse pointer to normal when files are dropped outside the selected files list.

```
Private Sub Label1_DragDrop(Source As Control, X As Single, _
    Y As Single)
    '
    ' return cursor to normal if file dropped here
    '
    MousePointer = vbDefault
End Sub
```

19. Add the following code to the General Declarations section of CFilePick2. This function returns the mouse pointer to normal when files are dropped outside the selected files list.

```
Private Sub Label2_DragDrop(Source As Control, X As Single, _
    Y As Single)
    '
    ' return cursor to normal if file dropped here
    '
    MousePointer = vbDefault
End Sub
```

20. Add the following code to the General Declarations section of CFilePick2. This function returns the mouse pointer to normal when files are dropped outside the selected files list.

```
Private Sub Label3_DragDrop(Source As Control, X As Single, _
    Y As Single)
    '
    ' return cursor to normal if file dropped here
    '
    MousePointer = vbDefault
End Sub
```

21. Add the following code to the General Declarations section of CFilePick2. This function returns the mouse pointer to normal when files are dropped outside the selected files list.

```
Private Sub Label4_DragDrop(Source As Control, X As Single, _
      Y As Single)
   '
   ' return cursor to normal if file dropped here
   '
   MousePointer = vbDefault
End Sub
```

22. Add the following code to the General Declarations section of CFilePick2. This function returns the mouse pointer to normal when files are dropped outside the selected files list.

```
Private Sub Label5_DragDrop(Source As Control, X As Single, _
      Y As Single)
   '
   ' return cursor to normal if file dropped here
   '
   MousePointer = vbDefault
End Sub
```

23. Add the following code to the General Declarations section of CFilePick2. This function returns the mouse pointer to normal when files are dropped outside the selected files list.

```
Private Sub lstDirectory_DragDrop(Source As Control, X As Single, _
      Y As Single)
   '
   ' return cursor to normal if file dropped here
   '
   MousePointer = vbDefault
End Sub
```

24. Add the following code to the General Declarations section of CFilePick2. This function handles changes in the drive combo box. It sets the new path of the directory list box to the path selected in the drive combo box. Then it calls DirectoryUpdate to update everything else.

```
Private Sub lstDrive_Change()
   '
   ' set the current path to the new drive
   '
   lstDirectory.Path = lstDrive.Drive
   '
   ' update the directories and file lists
   '
   DirectoryUpdate
End Sub
```

25. Add the following code to the General Declarations section of CFilePick2. This is the public entry point for the form and will be called by other forms, classes, etc. It loads the pattern combo box and the invisible pattern list box, it shows the form, and then it creates the list of files selected. This function takes one argument, the list of patterns allowed, in the format "Text|Pattern|Text|Pattern|...".

When this function first loads, it clears the pattern lists. Then it starts cycling through the patterns passed to it, adding each one to the pattern list and combo boxes. If no pattern is specified, it defaults to "All Files (*.*)" for the text and "*.*" for the pattern. Then it initializes everything else by selecting the first pattern, and calling DirectoryUpdate. Finally, it shows the form (modal). We don't get back to this code until one of the Me.Hide statements is executed from Command1_Click or Command2_Click (the OK and Cancel buttons). Once we do get back, a new list of files is generated. To do this, the selected file list (lstSelect) is scanned. All of the entries in this list are concatenated, separated by semicolons, and then returned to the caller.

```
Public Function SelectFiles(Patterns)
    Dim I As Integer ' offset of last item
    Dim IText As Integer ' offset of next text item
    Dim IPattern As Integer ' offset of next pattern item
    Dim TempStr As String ' temp string for files
    '
    ' set first index
    '
    I = 1
    '
    ' clear pattern lists
    '
    lstPattern.Clear
    cmbPattern.Clear
    '
    ' cycle while we have patterns
    '
    Do While (I <> 0) And (I < Len(Patterns))
        '
        ' get offset of end of text for pattern
        '
        IText = InStr(I, Patterns, "|")
        '
        ' if no text, we're done
        '
        If IText = 0 Then
            '
            ' get out of loop
            '
            Exit Do
        End If
        '
        ' get offset of end of pattern
        '
        IPattern = InStr(IText + 1, Patterns, "|")
        '
        ' add text for pattern to combo box
        '
        cmbPattern.AddItem Mid(Patterns, I, IText - I)
        '
        ' if there's no ending |
        '
```

Continued on next page

Continued from previous page

```
    If IPattern = 0 Then
        '
        ' add the rest of the string for the pattern
        '
        lstPattern.AddItem Mid(Patterns, IText + 1)
        '
        ' don't loop again
        '
        I = 0
    ElseIf IPattern - IText - 1 <= 0 Then
        '
        ' if pattern is empty, use *.* instead
        '
        lstPattern.AddItem "*.*"
        '
        ' starting point for next time around
        '
        I = IPattern + 1
    Else
        '
        ' add pattern to pattern list
        '
        lstPattern.AddItem Mid(Patterns, IText + 1, _
            IPattern - IText - 1)
        '
        ' starting point for next time around
        '
        I = IPattern + 1
    End If
Loop
'
' if nothing was added
'
If lstPattern.ListCount = 0 Then
    '
    ' add all files entry
    '
    lstPattern.AddItem "*.*"
    cmbPattern.AddItem "All Files (*.*)"
End If
'
' first pattern is the default
'
cmbPattern.ListIndex = 0
'
' update all of lists
'
DirectoryUpdate
'
' show form
'
Me.Show 1
'
' return file list
'
TempStr = ""
'
```

```
' if there are selections, loop through them
'
For I = 0 To lstSelect.ListCount - 1
    '
    ' separate files with semi-colons
    '
    If Len(TempStr) Then
        TempStr = TempStr & "; "
    End If
    '
    ' add file and its path to file list
    '
    TempStr = TempStr & lstSelect.List(I)
Next I
'
' return selected file list
'
SelectFiles = TempStr
End Function
```

26. Add the following code to the General Declarations section of CFilePick2, to handle changes in the directory list box. This function merely calls DirectoryUpdate to deal with the change.

```
Private Sub lstDirectory_Change()
    '
    ' update the directories and file lists
    '
    DirectoryUpdate
End Sub
```

27. Add the following code to the General Declarations section of CFilePick2, to handle changes in the directory list box. This function merely calls DirectoryUpdate to deal with the change.

```
Private Sub lstDirectory_Click()
    '
    ' update the directories and file lists
    '
    DirectoryUpdate
End Sub
```

28. Add the following code to the General Declarations section of CFilePick. This function takes a file, specified by Index, and adds it and the full path to the selected files list (lstSelect).

```
Private Sub TransferFile(Index As Integer)
    Dim DirStr As String
    Dim I As Integer
    '
    ' get the current path
    '
    DirStr = lblDirectory.Caption
```

Continued on next page

Continued from previous page

```
    '
    ' ensure there's a slash at the end
    '
    If Right(DirStr, 1) () "\" Then
        DirStr = DirStr & "\"
    End If
    '
    ' get the entire path and filename
    '
    DirStr = DirStr & lstFile.List(lstFile.ListIndex)
    '
    ' cycle through all of the currently
    ' selected files
    '
    For I = 0 To lstSelect.ListCount - 1
        '
        ' if this file is already selected
        '
        If lstSelect.List(I) = DirStr Then
            '
            ' move the list to it, and get out
            '
            lstSelect.ListIndex = I
            Exit Sub
        End If
    Next I
    '
    ' add the file name to the selected list
    '
    lstSelect.AddItem DirStr
    lstSelect.ListIndex = lstSelect.NewIndex
End Sub
```

29. Add the following code to the General Declarations section of CFilePick. This function moves a double-clicked file to the selected files list (lstSelect).

```
Private Sub lstFile_DblClick()
    '
    ' move file to selected list
    '
    TransferFile lstFile.ListIndex
End Sub
```

30. Add the following code to the General Declarations section of CFilePick2. This function returns the mouse pointer to normal when files are dropped outside the selected files list.

```
Private Sub lstFile_DragDrop(Source As Control, X As Single, _
    Y As Single)
    '
    ' return cursor to normal if file dropped here
    '
    MousePointer = vbDefault
End Sub
```

31. Add the following code to the General Declarations section of CFilePick2. This function starts the drop process. It first checks to see if a file is selected, and if so, enables the timer (which starts the drop when the Timer event fires).

```
Private Sub lstFile_MouseDown(Button As Integer, Shift As Integer, _
        X As Single, Y As Single)
    Dim I As Integer
    Dim NumSelected As Integer
    '
    ' cycle through all the files in the list
    '
    For I = 0 To lstFile.ListCount - 1
        '
        ' count the selected ones
        '
        If lstFile.Selected(I) Then
            NumSelected = NumSelected + 1
        End If
    Next I
    '
    ' if there are selected files and the left mouse
    ' button was used, enable the timer (which will
    ' start the drag in 200 milliseconds)
    '
    If (NumSelected > 0) And (Button = vbLeftButton) Then
        Timer1.Enabled = True
    End If
End Sub
```

32. Add the following code to the General Declarations section of CFilePick2. This disables the timer so that the drag-and-drop operation doesn't start if the user is merely clicking on the list.

```
Private Sub lstFile_MouseUp(Button As Integer, Shift As Integer, _
        X As Single, Y As Single)
    '
    ' if the mouse goes up, disable the timer so the
    ' drag doesn't start
    '
    Timer1.Enabled = False
End Sub
```

33. Add the following code to the General Declarations section of CFilePick2. This event handler is called when the file is dropped on the selected files list box (lstSelect). It transfers all selected files from the file list box to the selected files list box.

```
Private Sub lstSelect_DragDrop(Source As Control, X As Single, _
        Y As Single)
    Dim I As Integer
    '
    ' we just dropped a file, cycle through the file list
    '
```

Continued on next page

Continued from previous page

```
    For I = 0 To lstFile.ListCount - 1
        '
        ' copy any selected file(s) to the selected list
        '
        If lstFile.Selected(I) Then
            TransferFile I
        End If
    Next I
    '
    ' return the mouse pointer to normal
    '
    MousePointer = vbDefault
End Sub
```

34. Add the following code to the General Declarations section of CFilePick. This function changes the mouse pointer to the drag icon when there is a drag-and-drop operation going, and the cursor is over the selected files list box.

```
Private Sub lstSelect_DragOver(Source As Control, X As Single, _
    Y As Single, State As Integer)
    '
    ' since we're dragging over our target, make
    ' the mouse cursor a drag cursor
    '
    lstFile.DragIcon = DragImage.Picture
End Sub
```

35. Add the following code to the General Declarations section of CFilePick. The Timer event which fires 200 milliseconds after the user presses the mouse down on the files list box (lstFile), actually starts the drag-and-drop operation. It does this by setting the mouse cursor to the drag image and using the Drag method.

```
Private Sub Timer1_Timer()
    '
    ' time to start the drag and drop operation, set
    ' the cursor to a drag cursor
    '
    lstFile.DragIcon = DragImage.Picture
    '
    ' start the drag
    '
    lstFile.Drag vbBeginDrag
    '
    ' disable the timer
    '
    Timer1.Enabled = False
End Sub
```

How It Works

When the user chooses the Select Files! menu item, CFilePick!SelectFiles() is called. It displays a file open/select dialog box that behaves very much like the common file open dialog box, except that the user is allowed to select multiple files. The Visual

Basic built-in file list, directory list, and drive combo box are used to create the dialog box. When one of these is modified, the path and drive in the other two are updated to reflect the change.

Files get added to the selected files list when the user double-clicks on them or drags them from the files list box. Duplicate files are not added to the list. When the user presses OK, all of the files in the selected list are concatenated together and returned to the main program. When Cancel is pressed, a blank string is returned.

Comments

This file open dialog is useful in applications where users need to open multiple files that are spread across paths, drives, or even networks. The dialog also works well when the only input is "mouse" input, such as from a touch screen or a digitizing pad.

3.13 How do I...
Use Long Values with Scroll Bars?

COMPLEXITY: INTERMEDIATE
COMPATABILITY: VB4 ONLY

Problem

I need to use values greater than those within the short integer range for scroll bar properties in my project. Is there any way to extend the default range Visual Basic provides for scroll bars?

Technique

This project builds a custom class module that provides long values for several scroll bar properties. The class replaces the Value, Min, Max, SmallChange, and LargeChange default properties with new properties that use long rather than short integers. A new Change method is provided, which must be called whenever Visual Basic fires its intrinsic Change event. With the new Change method, the class properties are mathematically converted to a long value, and the real scroll bar is updated to visually reflect its new value. This project also employs the class module developed in How-To 3.4, to add 3D effects.

Steps

Open and run HGSCROLL.VBP. What you see will be similar to Figure 3-13-1. Initially, the new scroll bar object is set to a range of 0 to 10,000,000, with a LargeChange of 25,000 and a SmallChange of 1. Slide the horizontal scroll bar around, with all the methods provided by Windows—dragging the thumb, clicking on the end arrows, or clicking in the space between thumb and end arrows. The text

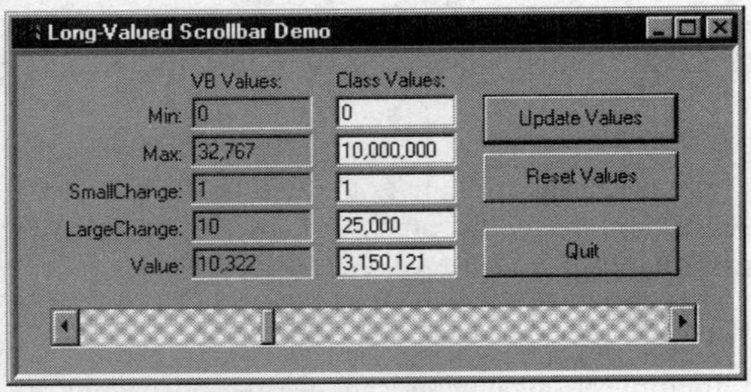

Figure 3-13-1 HGSCROLL in action

boxes will update the values for both the standard scroll bar which you are manipulating, and the CHugeScroll object.

The text boxes in the Class Values column are used to set new property values
for the "virtual" scroll bar. To adjust these properties, enter the new values and press
the Update Values button. Experiment with various settings. One of the more interesting values to try is reversing the Min and Max values. You'll find that CHugeScroll
reacts exactly as Visual Basic does in these cases: the direction of movement relative
to the scroll bar's value is reversed. Also, try setting all values within the short integer
range, to demonstrate that there is no need to revert to standard behavior as your
program needs change.

Building the CHugeScroll Class

1. Create a new project named HGSCROLL.VBP, and use Insert Class Module to add
   a new class module to the project. Name it CHugeScroll, and save it as
   CSCROLL.CLS. Add the following code to the General section of CHugeScroll.
   After the always-present Option Explicit are declarations for the member variables that track values for both the real and virtual scroll bar objects.

```
Option Explicit
'
' Variables to track virtual scrollbar properties.
'
Private m_Client As Object
Private m_Min As Long
Private m_Max As Long
Private m_SmallChange As Long
Private m_LargeChange As Long
Private m_Value As Long
'
' Variables to track real scrollbar properties.
'
Private m_vbValue As Integer
Private m_vbMin As Integer
Private m_vbMax As Integer
Private m_vbSmallChange As Integer
Private m_vbLargeChange As Integer
'
```

```
' Flag property to warn of possible recursion into
' real scrollbar's Change event.
'
Private m_Recursing As Boolean
```

2. Add the following pair of property procedures to CHugeScroll, to set and retrieve the Client property. Client is the scroll bar object whose functionality CHugeScroll replaces. First, we ascertain that a scroll bar was the object passed in; if not, an error is raised. Next, we adjust the real scroll bar's properties to offer a maximum range into which the virtual long property values can be mapped.

```
' ************************************************************
' Public Properties
' ************************************************************
Public Property Set Client(obj As Object)
    '
    ' Assign passed object to m_Client if appropriate type
    '
    If TypeOf obj Is HScrollBar Then
        Set m_Client = obj
    ElseIf TypeOf obj Is VScrollBar Then
        Set m_Client = obj
    Else
        Err.Clear
        Err.Raise Number:=vbObjectError + 1025, _
                  Source:="CHugeScroll", _
                  Description:="Client object must be a scrollbar."
    End If
    '
    ' Assign new value to intrinsic properties
    '
    If Not (m_Client Is Nothing) Then
        m_Client.Min = 0
        m_Client.Max = 32767
        m_Client.SmallChange = 1
        m_Client.LargeChange = 10
        m_Recursing = True
            m_Client.Value = 0
        m_Recursing = False
    End If
End Property

Public Property Get Client() As Object
    '
    ' Return m_Client object
    '
    Client = m_Client
End Property
```

3. CHugeScroll provides a fair number of properties. Add the following four pairs of property procedures to CHugeScroll, to provide support for setting and retrieving its virtual Min, Max, SmallChange, and LargeChange properties.

```vb
Public Property Let Max(NewVal As Long)
    '
    ' Assign Virtual Max property
    '
    m_Max = NewVal
End Property

Public Property Get Max() As Long
    '
    ' Return Virtual Max property
    '
    Max = m_Max
End Property

Public Property Let Min(NewVal As Long)
    '
    ' Assign Virtual Min property
    '
    m_Min = NewVal
End Property

Public Property Get Min() As Long
    '
    ' Return Virtual Min property
    '
    Min = m_Min
End Property

Public Property Let LargeChange(NewVal As Long)
    '
    ' Assign Virtual LargeChange property
    '
    m_LargeChange = NewVal
End Property

Public Property Get LargeChange() As Long
    '
    ' Return Virtual LargeChange property
    '
    LargeChange = m_LargeChange
End Property

Public Property Let SmallChange(NewVal As Long)
    '
    ' Assign Virtual SmallChange property
    '
    m_SmallChange = NewVal
End Property

Public Property Get SmallChange() As Long
    '
    ' Return Virtual SmallChange property
    '
    SmallChange = m_SmallChange
End Property
```

4. Add the following pair of property procedures to CHugeScroll, for support of the virtual Value property. This is where the interesting math begins! We check the new value to make sure it's within the legal range (Min <= NewVal <= Max); if not, it's adjusted to accommodate whichever extreme it exceeds. Next, the position of the thumb on the real scroll bar is calculated as a percentage of the virtual range. Then a new value for the real scroll bar is calculated by applying this percentage to the real range.

If the class's Min and Max properties are reversed (Min is greater than Max), the logic becomes fairly twisted. With standard scroll bars, Visual Basic "simply" reverses the direction in which the thumb moves when these properties are reversed. To support this same behavior in CHugeScroll, some of the calculations use Max when logic would dictate using Min, by creating temporary copies of the property values, and swapping them if Min is greater than Max.

```
Public Property Let Value(NewVal As Long)
    Dim VirtualRange As Long
    Dim RealRange As Long
    Dim Percent As Double
    Dim tmpMin As Long
    Dim tmpMax As Long
    '
    ' Cases where Virtual(Min>Max) need to be handled specially.
    ' Some calculations require swapped values.
    '
    If m_Min > m_Max Then
        tmpMin = m_Max
        tmpMax = m_Min
    Else
        tmpMin = m_Min
        tmpMax = m_Max
    End If
    '
    ' Get current values from real scrollbar
    '
    Call ReadRealValues
    '
    ' Rather than raise an error, correct out-of-range values
    '
    If NewVal < tmpMin Then
        NewVal = tmpMin
    ElseIf NewVal > tmpMax Then
        NewVal = tmpMax
    End If
    '
    ' Set Virtual value
    '
    m_Value = NewVal
    '
    ' Calculate Real value of scrollbar
    '
    VirtualRange = Abs(m_Max - m_Min)
    RealRange = Abs(m_vbMax - m_vbMin)
```

Continued on next page

Continued from previous page

```
    Percent = Abs(m_Value - tmpMin) / VirtualRange
    '
    ' If Virtual(Min>Max) then flip value
    '
    If m_Min <= m_Max Then
        m_vbValue = m_vbMin + (Percent * RealRange)
    Else
        m_vbValue = m_vbMax - (Percent * RealRange)
    End If
    '
    ' Update real scrollbar
    '
    Call UpdateRealValue
End Property

Public Property Get Value() As Long
    '
    ' Return Virtual value for scrollbar
    '
    Value = m_Value
End Property
```

5. As mentioned previously, changing the real scroll bar's Value property can cause Visual Basic's intrinsic Change event to fire. This can result in recursion or even infinite looping if we're not careful, since we'll need to change this value from within CHugeScroll. But, in order to alert CHugeScroll that the scroll bar's Value has changed, CHugeScroll must be called from Visual Basic's Change event. To prevent unchecked recursion, add the following read-only property procedure to CHugeScroll. The Recursing property can be set to True whenever CHugeScroll needs to alter the scroll bar's real Value property, and then immediately be set back to False. This property is checked within Visual Basic's Change event so that your application knows it was the user who triggered the Change.

```
Public Property Get Recursing() As Boolean
    '
    ' Let intrinsic Change event know not to act
    '
    Recursing = m_Recursing
End Property
```

6. In contrast to the numerous properties CHugeScroll provides, there is only one public method. Add the following code to a new public procedure called Change. (In a way, you might think of this method as an event. It's generally the first thing that needs to be called when the intrinsic Visual Basic Change event fires. We will see this demonstrated a little later when we build a form that tests this class module.)

   The Change method code is very similar to that in the Value property procedure. In fact, except for some very subtle differences, this method handles the user's sliding of the scroll bar thumb nearly identically to how the programmer alters the Value. The real difference is in how the Change method handles LargeChange and SmallChange adjustments. It first determines how much the real scroll bar changed, and then compares this to the real SmallChange and LargeChange values. If one of these match, the change is scaled to fit into the long scheme of the CHugeScroll object.

```
' *********************************************************
' Public Methods
' *********************************************************
Public Sub Change()
    Dim Delta As Long
    Dim VirtualRange As Long
    Dim RealRange As Long
    Dim Percent As Double
    Dim tmpMin As Long
    Dim tmpMax As Long
    '
    ' Calculate real change
    '
    Delta = m_Client.Value - m_vbValue
    '
    ' Cases where Virtual(Min>Max) need to be handled specially
    ' Most calculations can use swapped values.
    '
    If m_Min > m_Max Then
        tmpMin = m_Max
        tmpMax = m_Min
        Delta = -1 * Delta
    Else
        tmpMin = m_Min
        tmpMax = m_Max
    End If
    '
    ' Get current values from real scrollbar
    '
    Call ReadRealValues
    '
    ' See if Large or Small Change
    '
    If Abs(Delta) = m_vbLargeChange Or _
       Abs(Delta) = m_vbSmallChange Then
        '
        ' Adjust change to match virtual scaling
        '
        If Abs(Delta) = m_vbLargeChange Then
            Delta = Sgn(Delta) * m_LargeChange
        ElseIf Abs(Delta) = m_vbSmallChange Then
            Delta = Sgn(Delta) * m_SmallChange
        End If
        '
        ' Set virtual scale
        '
        m_Value = m_Value + Delta
        '
```

Continued on next page

Continued from previous page

```
        ' Check if out of bounds
        '
        If m_Value < tmpMin Then
            m_Value = tmpMin
        ElseIf m_Value > tmpMax Then
            m_Value = tmpMax
        End If
        '
        ' Calculate Real value of scrollbar
        '
        VirtualRange = Abs(m_Max - m_Min)
        RealRange = Abs(m_vbMax - m_vbMin)
        Percent = Abs(m_Value - tmpMin) / VirtualRange
        '
        ' If Virtual(Min>Max) then flip value
        '
        If m_Min <= m_Max Then
            m_vbValue = m_vbMin + (Percent * RealRange)
        Else
            m_vbValue = m_vbMax - (Percent * RealRange)
        End If

    Else
        '
        ' User moved thumb on scrollbar
        ' Calculate Virtual value of scrollbar
        '
        VirtualRange = Abs(m_Max - m_Min)
        RealRange = Abs(m_vbMax - m_vbMin)
        Percent = Abs(m_vbValue - m_vbMin) / RealRange
        '
        ' If Virtual(Min>Max) then flip value
        '
        If m_Min <= m_Max Then
            m_Value = tmpMin + (Percent * VirtualRange)
        Else
            m_Value = tmpMax - (Percent * VirtualRange)
        End If
    End If
    '
    ' Update real scrollbar
    '
    Call UpdateRealValue
End Sub
```

7. Insert the following code into a new private routine called ReadRealValues. Both the Value property procedure and the Change method procedure need to know some or all of the current values of the Client object. Although it is not recommended that a program change the native values of its scroll bars when using this module, in many cases it will work, and some degree of support is provided with this routine.

```
' *************************************************************
' Private Methods
' *************************************************************
Private Sub ReadRealValues()
    '
    ' Read current values from scrollbar
    '
    m_vbValue = m_Client.Value
    m_vbMin = m_Client.Min
    m_vbMax = m_Client.Max
    m_vbSmallChange = m_Client.SmallChange
    m_vbLargeChange = m_Client.LargeChange
End Sub
```

8. Insert the following code in a new routine called UpdateRealValue. Both the
   Value property procedure and the Change method procedure need to change the
   Value property of the Client object. This may cause a problem, because with
   the long range of the CHugeScroll class, the real value may calculate out to
   either the real Min or the real Max if the virtual Value is very close to the virtual
   Min or the virtual Max. In these cases, to allow further adjustment, a quick If test
   bumps the real Value up or down by one.

```
Private Sub UpdateRealValue()
    '
    ' This assures that if the virtual value is not quite
    ' to either the Min or Max that there's still room to
    ' adjust the slider.
    '
    If m_vbValue = m_vbMin Then
       If m_Value > m_Min Then
          m_vbValue = m_vbMin + 1
       End If
    ElseIf m_vbValue = m_vbMax Then
       If m_Value < m_Max Then
          m_vbValue = m_vbMax - 1
       End If
    End If
    '
    ' Update display. Note possible recursion!
    '
    m_Recursing = True
       m_Client.Value = m_vbValue
    m_Recursing = False
End Sub
```

Developing a Test Form for the CHugeScroll Class

9. Open the default Form1 form, add the objects listed in Table 3-13-1, and assign
   the listed properties. Save it as HGSCROLL.FRM. Note that none of the default
   properties is altered for the horizontal scroll bar. All you do is draw it on the
   form, and CHugeScroll takes care of the rest.

Table 3-13-1 Objects and their properties on HGSCROLL.FRM

OBJECT	PROPERTY	SETTING
Form	Name	Form1
	Caption	"Long-Valued Scrollbar Demo"
HorizontalScrollbar	Name	HScroll1
CommandButton	Name	cmdUpdate
	Caption	"Update Values"
	Default	True
CommandButton	Name	cmdReset
	Caption	"Reset Values"
CommandButton	Name	cmdQuit
	Cancel	True
	Caption	"Quit"
Label	Name	Label1
	Alignment	1 - Right Justified
	AutoSize	True
	Caption	"Min:"
	Index	0
	Left	1155
	Top	480
Label	Name	Label1
	Alignment	1 - Right Justified
	AutoSize	True
	Caption	"Max:"
	Index	1
	Left	1110
	Top	810
Label	Name	Label1
	Alignment	1 - Right Justified
	AutoSize	True
	Caption	"SmallChange:"
	Index	2
	Left	480
	Top	1140
Label	Name	Label1
	Alignment	1 - Right Justified
	AutoSize	True
	Caption	"LargeChange:"
	Index	3
	Left	450

OBJECT	PROPERTY	SETTING
	Top	1470
Label	Name	Label1
	Alignment	1 - Right Justified
	AutoSize	True
	Caption	"Value:"
	Index	4
	Left	1005
	Top	1800
Label	Name	Label2
	AutoSize	True
	Caption	"VB Values:"
	Index	0
	Left	1530
	Top	180
Label	Name	Label2
	AutoSize	True
	Caption	"Class Values:"
	Index	1
	Left	2760
	Top	180
text box	Name	txtVB
	Index	0
	Left	1530
	Locked	True
	Text	"txtVB(0)"
	Top	420
text box	Name	txtVB
	Index	1
	Left	1530
	Locked	True
	Text	"txtVB(1)"
	Top	750
text box	Name	txtVB
	Index	2
	Left	1530
	Locked	True
	Text	"txtVB(2)"
	Top	1080

Continued on next page

Continued from previous page

OBJECT	PROPERTY	SETTING
text box	Name	txtVB
	Index	3
	Left	1530
	Locked	True
	Text	"txtVB(3)"
	Top	1410
text box	Name	txtVB
	Index	4
	Left	1530
	Locked	True
	Text	"txtVB(4)"
	Top	1740
text box	Name	txtSB
	Index	0
	Left	2760
	Text	"txtSB(0)"
	Top	420
text box	Name	txtSB
	Index	1
	Left	2760
	Text	"txtSB(1)"
	Top	750
text box	Name	txtSB
	Index	2
	Left	2760
	Text	"txtSB(2)"
	Top	1080
text box	Name	txtSB
	Index	3
	Left	2760
	Text	"txtSB(3)"
	Top	1410
text box	Name	txtSB
	Index	4
	Left	2760
	Text	"txtSB(4)"
	Top	1740

10. Insert the following code in the Declarations section of HGSCROLL.FRM. An instance of the CHugeScroll object is declared, and an index to the label and text box control arrays is defined with constants.

```
Option Explicit
'
' Variable to use for virtual scrollbar
'
Private hsb As CHugeScroll
'
' Index to arrays of labels and text boxes
'
Const tMin = 0
Const tMax = 1
Const tSmC = 2
Const tLgC = 3
Const tVal = 4
'
' Formatting used to report values
'
Const fmt = "#,##0"
```

11. Add the following code to the Declarations section, as well. This declares two variables for the CBorder3D objects we'll use to dress up the run-time form, and imports the simple style constants from the CBorder3D class.

```
'
' Variables to hold CBorder3D objects
'
Private bdrForm As CBorder3D
Private bdrScroll As CBorder3D
'
' Styles supported by CBorder3D
'
Const StyleNone = 0
Const StyleSunken = 1
Const StyleRaised = 2
Const StyleFramed = 3
Const StyleDouble = 4
Const StyleWithin = 5
```

12. Add the following code to the Form_Load event of Form1. A new instance of the CHugeScroll class is created and assigned to the object variable hsb. Its Client property is set to the horizontal scroll bar. To enhance the form, the CBorder3D class is employed to draw an attractive double border within the form, and a sunken border around the scroll bar.

```
Private Sub Form_Load()
    '
    ' Create new instance of virtual scrollbar, and
    ' assign it to HScroll1.
    '
    Set hsb = New CHugeScroll
    Set hsb.Client = HScroll1
    '
    ' Set demo defaults and update display of values.
    '
    ResetScroll
```

Continued on next page

Continued from previous page

```
    UpdateLabels
    '
    ' Throw a few 3D effects in from CBorder3D
    ' bdrForm is a border around the form
    ' bdrScroll is a border around the scrollbar
    '
    Set bdrForm = New CBorder3D
    Set bdrForm.Client = Me
    bdrForm.Style3D = StyleWithin
    bdrForm.BevelOuter = StyleRaised
    bdrForm.BevelInner = StyleSunken
    Set bdrScroll = New CBorder3D
    Set bdrScroll.Client = HScroll1
    bdrScroll.Style3D = StyleSunken
End Sub
```

13. To Form 1, add a private routine called ResetScroll, and place the following code in it. This sets the default values for the demo, and resets them when the user requests.

```
Private Sub ResetScroll()
    '
    ' Set default values for this demo. Any may be used
    ' in other apps. All five properties are defined as
    ' Long.
    '
    hsb.Min = 0
    hsb.Max = 10000000          ' <- 10 Million!!!
    hsb.SmallChange = 1
    hsb.LargeChange = 25000
    hsb.Value = 0
End Sub
```

14. Add a private routine called UpdateLabels to Form1, and place the following code in it. This self-explanatory routine is employed whenever all or many of the text boxes need updating to reflect new values.

```
Private Sub UpdateLabels()
    '
    ' Retrieve property values from virtual scrollbar.
    '
    txtSB(tMin) = Format(hsb.Min, fmt)
    txtSB(tMax) = Format(hsb.Max, fmt)
    txtSB(tSmC) = Format(hsb.SmallChange, fmt)
    txtSB(tLgC) = Format(hsb.LargeChange, fmt)
    txtSB(tVal) = Format(hsb.Value, fmt)
    '
    ' Retrieve property values from real scrollbar.
    ' There is no need to set properties at design time,
    ' since they are reset in the CHugeScroll module
    ' when the Client property is set.
    '
    txtVB(tMin) = Format(HScroll1.Min, fmt)
    txtVB(tMax) = Format(HScroll1.Max, fmt)
```

```
   txtVB(tSmC) = Format(HScroll1.SmallChange, fmt)
   txtVB(tLgC) = Format(HScroll1.LargeChange, fmt)
   txtVB(tVal) = Format(HScroll1.Value, fmt)
End Sub
```

15. Insert the following code in the HScroll1_Change event. Whenever Visual Basic fires this event, the CHugeScroll Change method must be invoked. The issue of recursion must be handled for this event. Since CHugeScroll's Change method may alter the value of the Visual Basic scroll bar, thus triggering another Visual Basic Change event, the Recursing property is used to control whether the code is executed in this event.

```
Private Sub HScroll1_Change()
    '
    ' Since the Real Value of the VB scrollbar is often
    ' changed in the virtual Change event, recursion into
    ' this routine *absolutely* must be prevented!
    '
    If Not hsb.Recursing Then
        '
        ' Fire the virtual Change event!
        '
        hsb.Change
        '
        ' Perform (here) whatever other actions are required by
        ' the changing of this scrollbar. For this demo, only
        ' the display is updated.
        '
        txtSB(tVal) = Format(hsb.Value, fmt)
        txtVB(tVal) = Format(HScroll1.Value, fmt)
    End If
End Sub
```

16. Optionally, insert the following code in the HScroll1_Scroll event. This allows real-time tracking when the user drags the scroll bar's thumb. On slower machines, the Refresh method (which is commented out below) may be required to keep up with the action. Don't attempt to do too much in an event of this type, as its actions can be fired fast and furiously.

```
Private Sub HScroll1_Scroll()
    '
    ' The virtual Change event may be fired from VB's
    ' Scroll if a reaction is required as the user drags
    ' the scrollbar's thumb. Note that recursion is
    ' not a concern in this event.
    '
    hsb.Change
    txtSB(tVal) = Format(hsb.Value, fmt)
    txtVB(tVal) = Format(HScroll1.Value, fmt)
    'txtSB(tVal).Refresh
    'txtVB(tVal).Refresh
End Sub
```

17. Insert the following code in the button Click events, so that they perform the desired actions.

```
Private Sub cmdQuit_Click()
    Unload Me
End Sub

Private Sub cmdReset_Click()
    '
    ' Reset the virtual scrollbar to demo defaults.
    '
    ResetScroll
    UpdateLabels
End Sub

Private Sub cmdUpdate_Click()
    '
    ' Update virtual scrollbar properties to user
    ' input values.
    '
    UpdateScroll
    UpdateLabels
End Sub
```

18. To Form1, add a new procedure called UpdateScroll, and place the following code in it. This reads the values the user has entered in the text boxes and assigns them to the CHugeScroll object.

```
Private Sub UpdateScroll()
    '
    ' Set values that user input as new properties for
    ' virtual scrollbar. All five properties are defined
    ' as Long. Min and Max may be swapped.
    '
    hsb.Min = txtSB(tMin)
    hsb.Max = txtSB(tMax)
    hsb.SmallChange = txtSB(tSmC)
    hsb.LargeChange = txtSB(tLgC)
    hsb.Value = txtSB(tVal)
End Sub
```

19. Finally, add the following code to the Form_Paint and Form_Resize events, to keep the CBorder3D effects refreshed as needed.

```
Private Sub Form_Paint()
    '
    ' Refresh 3D effects from CBorder3D
    '
    Me.Cls
    bdrForm.Refresh
    bdrScroll.Refresh
End Sub
```

```
Private Sub Form_Resize()
    '
    ' Refresh the 3D effects
    '
    Me.Refresh
End Sub
```

How It Works

This How-To develops a new class module that supports the use of long integers for common properties of standard scroll bars. This is done by mapping the shorter default range into a new expanded range in the CHugeScroll class module. You can add this class module into any of your existing projects and immediately gain the ability to assign long integers to the Value, Min, Max, SmallChange, and LargeChange properties of your existing scroll bars, by simply setting them to the Client property of a new instance of the CHugeScroll class. Support is even included, through some mathematical gymnastics, for reversing the Min and Max properties.

To implement this new capability, add the CHugeScroll class module to your project. Declare an object variable of the CHugeScroll type, and set it equal to a New instance of that type. Set the Client property of the object variable to a scroll bar on your form, and set the remaining properties as desired. In the native scroll bar Change event, invoke the class's Change method. Be certain to prevent unwanted recursion or infinite loops by checking the class's Recursing property before invoking its Change method! There is no need to alter any default properties for native Visual Basic scroll bars, nor to refer to them during program execution. At run time, for best results refer only to the properties of the object variable.

Though it is possible to alter the property values for the Visual Basic scroll bar, we discourage you from doing it. The CHugeScroll class will generally work if you change the native Min and Max properties with one exception: strange results and even errors can occur if the Visual Basic Min is greater than the Visual Basic Max. Also, if the difference between Min and Max is less than the number of pixels of the scroll bar's length, unpredictable behavior may occur near the extremes of the scroll bar range. For these reasons, it's best to allow CHugeScroll to handle Min and Max property definition.

You'll also want to avoid altering the native SmallChange and LargeChange properties, for similar reasons. Keeping these values small, as CHugeScroll does, while keeping the native range large, makes it least likely that the user's dragging the thumb will be mistaken for either a SmallChange or LargeChange

Comments

By following the guidelines in this How-To, you will find the CHugeScroll class to be amazingly robust. A classic use for this sort of scroll bar would be to map the current position within a very large file in an editor-type application.

3.14 How do I...
Guarantee Fixed-Width Font Availability?

COMPLEXITY: INTERMEDIATE
COMPATIBILITY: VB4 ONLY

Problem

I have an application that displays and saves to file, tables that need precise alignment. I'd like to use the same routines to format the data for either display or file. But the proportional-width fonts on most Windows computers are a poor choice with this criteria, as they require extensive formatting routines to display an attractive table. Of course, the file output will use a fixed-width font, so formatting these is easy. There's no reliable choice of fixed-width screen fonts, however, that I can count on being installed on all Windows machines. Am I doomed to using proportional fonts, such as MS Sans Serif, and hoping the users haven't deleted them?

Technique

Windows provides Graphic Device Interface (GDI) objects known as "stock fonts"—some of which can be counted on to be always available. These are the fonts that Windows itself uses for such things as window captions, menu text, "DOS box" text, and dialog box text. This How-To develops a class module that will apply one of the predefined stock fonts to virtually any Visual Basic object that supports the hWnd property. The new class module, CStockFont, is a very simple example of how powerful the new Visual Basic 4.0 model can be. A new CStockFont object is declared, and two properties are set. The existing text, if any, is changed to the new font when the StockFont property is set.

Steps

Open and run SFONT.VBP. You are presented with a choice of the six stock fonts that Windows offers, with each option button's text displayed in the font it selects. When you choose a font, it changes the text on all controls but the option buttons and on the form itself. Uncheck the Use CStockFont check box, and the default font set in Visual Basic's Properties window is restored to the controls that are using the selected stock font. Figure 3-14-1 shows the project running with the sfSYSTEM_FIXED stock font selected. Figure 3-14-2 shows the default MS Sans Serif font being used throughout. Notice how nicely columns of data can be aligned in the list box at the bottom of the form.

Working with Stock Fonts

Stock fonts are GDI resources that are created when Windows starts up. The user has some control over which resource files are read, by changing entries in the WIN.INI and SYSTEM.INI files or in the system registry. Generally, however, this is not a good idea, because Windows and your video card manufacturer have already determined the optimal settings for these entries.

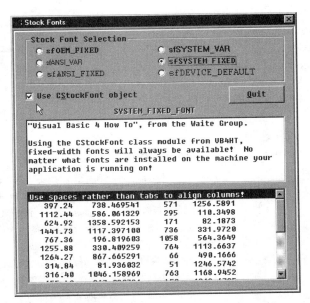

Figure 3-14-1 SFONT.VBP project in action, using the sfSYSTEM_FIXED stock font

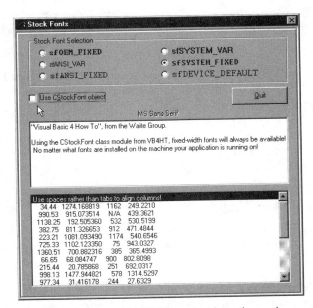

Figure 3-14-2 SFONT.VBP project in action, using default fonts

Six stock font objects are available for applications to retrieve and use. These are summarized in Table 3-14-1, which also lists the constants used by CStockFont and by GDI when referencing each object, and a brief description of what to expect from a given stock font. The most useful fonts for tables that require precise alignment are sfOEM_FIXED, sfANSI_FIXED, and sfSYSTEM_FIXED. Each of these has unique characteristics, and their use will be dictated primarily by individual taste.

Table 3-14-1 Stock fonts offered by CStockFont

CSTOCKFONT CONSTANTS	GDI CONSTANTS	DESCRIPTIONS
sfOEM_FIXED	OEM_FIXED_FONT	Fixed-width font using the OEM character set. For IBM computers and compatibles, the OEM font is based on the IBM PC character set. Commonly known as the terminal font.
sfANSI_VAR	ANSI_VAR_FONT	Variable-width font based on the Windows character set. Typically MS Sans Serif.
sfANSI_FIXED	ANSI_FIXED_FONT	Fixed-width font based on the Windows character set. Typically Courier.
sfSYSTEM_VAR	SYSTEM_FONT	Variable-width font based on the Windows character set. Used by the system to display window captions, menu text, and dialog box text. Always available.
sfSYSTEM_FIXED	SYSTEM_FIXED_FONT	Fixed-width font based on the Windows character set. Used prior to Windows 3.0 for captions, menus, and dialog text.
sfDEVICE_DEFAULT	DEVICE_DEFAULT_FONT	Font preferred by the device. May vary widely from device to device, depending on how the GDI font mapper interprets requests.

Rather than assigning stock fonts to an object's Font property, their use must be obtained via the API. A call to GetStockObject retrieves a handle to the chosen stock font, and SendMessage is used to tell a control or form to use it. From that point on, using Visual Basic's methods will work just as expected. You can print on forms or PictureBoxes, alter the contents of text boxes, add items to a list box, change the caption of command buttons, and just about anything else—except referring to the Font property. The Font property is not changed by this end-run past Visual Basic through the GDI.

Creating the CStockFont Class Module

1. Create a new project named SFONT.VBP, and use the Insert Class Module menu item to add a new class module to the project. Name the module CStockFont and save it as CSFONT.CLS.

2. Add the following code to the General section of CStockFont. Since the API definitions for stock font constants are not sequential, CStockFont exposes a translation scheme for font selection. By renumbering the offered fonts from 0 to 5, it's

much easier to loop through the available choices, or to use them with control arrays. Notice that very little is required to accommodate this class module to both 16- and 32-bit systems. Conditional compilation of the API declarations and the type definition of variables used within the class are the only items that vary. The constants used by Win16 and Win32 are identical.

```
Option Explicit
' '
' Win16/32 API calls required to use stock font objects
'
#If Win16 Then
    Private Declare Function GetStockObject Lib "GDI" (ByVal nIndex ⇒
        As Integer) As Integer
    Private Declare Function SendMessage Lib "User" (ByVal hWnd As Integer,⇒
        ByVal wMsg As Integer, ByVal wParam As Integer, ⇒
        lParam As Any) As Long
    Private Declare Function DeleteObject Lib "GDI" (ByVal hObject ⇒
        As Integer) As Integer
#Else
    Private Declare Function GetStockObject Lib "gdi32" (ByVal nIndex ⇒
        As Long) As Long
    Private Declare Function SendMessage Lib "user32" Alias "SendMessageA" ⇒
        (ByVal hWnd As Long, ByVal wMsg As Long, ByVal wParam ⇒
        As Long, lParam As Any) As Long
    Private Declare Function DeleteObject Lib "gdi32" (ByVal hObject ⇒
        As Long) As Long
#End If
'
' SendMessage constants for font messages
'
Private Const WM_SETFONT = &H30
Private Const WM_GETFONT = &H31
'
' API stock font identifier constants
'
Private Const OEM_FIXED_FONT = 10
Private Const ANSI_FIXED_FONT = 11
Private Const ANSI_VAR_FONT = 12
Private Const SYSTEM_FONT = 13
Private Const DEVICE_DEFAULT_FONT = 14
Private Const SYSTEM_FIXED_FONT = 16
'
' Class property constants -- copy these
' into modules that use this class
'
Private Const sfOEM_FIXED = 0
Private Const sfANSI_VAR = 1
Private Const sfANSI_FIXED = 2
Private Const sfSYSTEM_VAR = 3
Private Const sfSYSTEM_FIXED = 4
Private Const sfDEVICE_DEFAULT = 5
' '
' Variables to track class properties
'
```

Continued on next page

Continued from previous page

```
Private m_Client As Object
#If Win16 Then
    Private m_hWnd As Integer
    Private m_sFont As Integer
#ElseIf Win32 Then
    Private m_hWnd As Long
    Private m_sFont As Long
#End If
```

3. Insert the following code in the Class_Initialize event, which is fired whenever a new instance of the class is created. The event is used in CStockFont to set default values for the exposed properties.

```
' ***************************************************
' Initialization and Termination
' ***************************************************
Private Sub Class_Initialize()
    m_hWnd = 0
    m_sFont = SYSTEM_FIXED_FONT
End Sub
```

4. Add the following pair of property procedures to set and retrieve the class's Client property. The Client can be set to any Visual Basic control or form that supports the hWnd property; this is required in order to use SendMessage to communicate. If the passed object does not support the hWnd property, an error is raised. "Light" controls such as Labels don't support the hWnd property, as they're not really windows. Rather, Visual Basic draws these elements at run time. To emulate Labels with stock fonts, you must do what Visual Basic does—print them yourself, directly on the form.

```
' ***************************************************
' Properties
' ***************************************************
Public Property Set Client(NewObj As Object)
    '
    ' Use error trapping to test hWnd
    ' Passed object *must* have an hWnd!
    '
    On Error Resume Next
        m_hWnd = NewObj.hWnd
        If Err Then m_hWnd = 0
    On Error GoTo 0
    '
    ' Set Client property
    '
    If m_hWnd Then
        Set m_Client = NewObj
    Else
        Err.Raise Number:=vbObjectError + 1, _
                  Source:="CStockFont", _
                  Description:="Client object must support the hWnd property."
    End If
```

```
End Property

Public Property Get Client() As Object
    '
    ' Return client object
    '
    Set Client = m_Client
End Property
```

5. Add the following pair of property procedures to set and retrieve the StockFont property. Setting StockFont immediately resets the font in use by the Client object. As mentioned earlier, CStockFont uses a translation scheme for stock font numbers, so that they can be more conveniently numbered. This routine first converts the input value to its API equivalent. A call to GetStockObject retrieves a font handle (hFont), which is sent to the Client object in a WM_SETFONT message. Like all GDI objects, fonts must always be destroyed after use to avoid wasting system resources. Notice that no error checking is required in StockFont, because if a Client is not yet assigned, the m_hWnd variable will be still be 0. In this case, the message is simply sent into the ether.

```
Public Property Let StockFont(NewVal As Integer)
    #If Win16 Then
        Dim hFont As Integer
    #ElseIf Win32 Then
        Dim hFont As Long
    #End If
    '
    ' Store API constant in StockFont property
    ' Requires conversion from class constant
    '
    Select Case NewVal
        Case sfOEM_FIXED
            m_sFont = OEM_FIXED_FONT
        Case sfANSI_VAR
            m_sFont = ANSI_VAR_FONT
        Case sfANSI_FIXED
            m_sFont = ANSI_FIXED_FONT
        Case sfSYSTEM_VAR
            m_sFont = SYSTEM_FONT
        Case sfSYSTEM_FIXED
            m_sFont = SYSTEM_FIXED_FONT
        Case sfDEVICE_DEFAULT
            m_sFont = DEVICE_DEFAULT_FONT
    End Select
    '
    ' Select the stock font into the client text box
    ' Always use DeleteObject to clean up
    '
    hFont = GetStockObject(m_sFont)
    Call SendMessage(m_hWnd, WM_SETFONT, hFont, False)
    Call DeleteObject(hFont)
End Property
```

Continued on next page

Continued from previous page

```
Public Property Get StockFont() As Integer
    '
    ' Return StockFont property
    ' Requires conversion from the stored API constant
    '
    Select Case m_sFont
        Case OEM_FIXED_FONT
            StockFont = sfOEM_FIXED
        Case ANSI_FIXED_FONT
            StockFont = sfANSI_FIXED
        Case ANSI_VAR_FONT
            StockFont = sfANSI_VAR
        Case SYSTEM_FONT
            StockFont = sfSYSTEM_VAR
        Case DEVICE_DEFAULT_FONT
            StockFont = sfDEVICE_DEFAULT
        Case SYSTEM_FIXED_FONT
            StockFont = sfSYSTEM_FIXED
    End Select
End Property
```

Creating a Test Project for CStockFont

6. Open the default Form1. Place the objects listed in Table 3-14-2 on the form, and place the objects listed in Table 3-14-3 within Frame1, so that it appears similar to that in Figure 3-14-3. Assign the listed properties, and save it as SFONT.FRM. The form and all the controls should have their default fonts left in place, to demonstrate that it's not necessary to change these in order to use CStockFont.

Figure 3-14-3 SFONT.FRM at design time

Table 3-14-2 Objects and their properties on SFONT.FRM

OBJECT	PROPERTY	SETTING
Form	Name	Form1
	BorderStyle	3 - Fixed Double
	Caption	"Stock Fonts"
	Font	MS Sans Serif (default)
Frame	Name	Frame1
	Caption	"Stock Font Selection"
CheckBox	Name	Check1
	Caption	"Use C&StockFont object"
	Width	4500
CommandButton	Name	Command1
	Cancel	True
	Caption	"&Quit"
text box	Name	Text1
	MultiLine	True
ListBox	Name	List1
	IntegralHeight	False

Table 3-14-3 Objects and their properties contained within Frame1

OBJECT	PROPERTY	SETTING
OptionButton	Name	optFont
	Caption	"sfOEM_FIXED"
	Index	0
	Width	3000
	Value	True
OptionButton	Name	optFont
	Caption	"sfANSI_VAR"
	Index	1
	Width	3000
OptionButton	Name	optFont
	Caption	"sfANSI_FIXED"
	Index	2
	Width	3000
OptionButton	Name	optFont
	Caption	"sfSYSTEM_VAR"
	Index	3
	Width	3000
OptionButton	Name	optFont

Continued on next page

Continued from previous page

OBJECT	PROPERTY	SETTING
	Caption	"sfSYSTEM_FIXED"
	Index	4
	Width	3000
OptionButton	Name	optFont
	Caption	"sfDEVICE_DEFAULT"
	Index	5
	Width	3000

7. In the Declarations section of Form1, insert the constant definitions from the CStockFont class module. Declare a new collection to be used to store CStockFont objects for each of the controls that will need to be dynamically updated after the form is loaded. Declare an object variable of the Font type to hold a reference to the initial font assigned to the form. Declare an object variable of the type CBorder3D to dress the form up a little with some 3D effects, and import the constant definitions from the CBorder3D class module developed in How-To 3.4. (If you haven't already reviewed that project, you won't be hampered in understanding this one.)

```
Option Explicit
'
' Values allowed for StockFont property of CStockFont
'
Private Const sfOEM_FIXED = 0
Private Const sfANSI_VAR = 1
Private Const sfANSI_FIXED = 2
Private Const sfSYSTEM_VAR = 3
Private Const sfSYSTEM_FIXED = 4
Private Const sfDEVICE_DEFAULT = 5
'
' Collection to hold CStockFont objects
'
Private colSF As New Collection
'
' Variable to hold form's default font object
'
Private ttFont As Font
'
' Variable for 3D effects object
'
Private Obj3D As New CBorder3D
'
' Styles supported by CBorder3D
' Copy these constants into form module
'
Private Const StyleNone = 0
Private Const StyleSunken = 1
Private Const StyleRaised = 2
Private Const StyleFramed = 3
Private Const StyleDouble = 4
```

```
Private Const StyleWithin = 5
Private Const StyleCustomFramed = 6
Private Const StyleCustomDouble = 7
Private Const StyleCustomWithin = 8
```

8. In the Form_Initialize event of Form1, capture a copy of the default font object. In order to declare a variable of the type Font, you must make sure that your project references the Standard OLE Type library, by selecting References from the Tools menu and checking that item in the dialog.

```
Private Sub Form_Initialize()
    '
    ' Set aside copy of default font object
    '
    Set ttFont = Me.Font
End Sub
```

9. Insert the following code in the Form_Load event of Form1. Here, an array of new CStockFont objects is created, and the first element of it is used to set the appropriate stock font into each of the option buttons. This demonstrates how one CStockFont object may be used to set stock fonts into a series of controls, and is an appropriate technique for one-time settings. Next, each element of the CStockFont array is set to represent one of the controls whose font properties will be dynamically set in this demonstration. These are stored in a persistent collection for easy retrieval when the user selects a new font. This technique is more appropriate when you want to repeatedly change a number of object's fonts. To initiate the setting of fonts for new collection elements, the check box is then checked from code. Some sample text is loaded into the text box, and a demonstration of column alignment is prepared for the list box. Finally, the 3D object is initialized to draw a chiseled border around the edge of the form.

```
Private Sub Form_Load()
    Dim i As Integer
    Dim sfObj(0 To 5) As New CStockFont
    '
    ' Select matching stock font into option buttons
    '
    For i = sfOEM_FIXED To sfDEVICE_DEFAULT
        Set sfObj(0).Client = optFont(i)
        sfObj(0).StockFont = i
    Next i
    Set sfObj(0) = Nothing
    '
    ' Populate collection with CStockFont objects
    '
    Set sfObj(0).Client = Me
    Set sfObj(1).Client = Text1
    Set sfObj(2).Client = Command1
    Set sfObj(3).Client = Check1
    Set sfObj(4).Client = Frame1
```

Continued on next page

Continued from previous page

```
    Set sfObj(5).Client = List1
    For i = LBound(sfObj) To UBound(sfObj)
        colSF.Add sfObj(i)
        Set sfObj(i) = Nothing
    Next i
    '
    ' Turn on stock fonts for most controls
    '
    Check1 = vbChecked
    '
    ' Fill listbox and text box
    '
    Call FillListbox(List1)
    Call FillText box(Text1)
    '
    ' Setup some 3D border effects
    '
    Set Obj3D.Canvas = Me
    Obj3D.Style3D = StyleCustomWithin
    Obj3D.BevelInner = StyleRaised
    Obj3D.BevelOuter = StyleSunken
    Obj3D.BorderWidth = 0
    Obj3D.BevelWidth = 2
    Obj3D.Left = 0
    Obj3D.Top = 2 * Screen.TwipsPerPixelY
    Obj3D.Width = Me.ScaleWidth
    Obj3D.Height = Me.ScaleHeight - Obj3D.Top
    '
    ' Center form on screen
    '
    Me.Move (Screen.Width - Me.Width) \ 2, (Screen.Height - Me.Height) \ 2
End Sub
```

10. Both Check1_Click and optFont_Click place calls to the private routine SetStockFont.

```
Private Sub Check1_Click()
    Call SetStockFont
End Sub

Private Sub optFont_Click(Index As Integer)
    Call SetStockFont
End Sub
```

11. To Form1, add the private routine SetStockFont and place the following code in it. This is called whenever the check box is toggled, or when a different font option button is selected. If the check box is checked, the chosen stock font is selected into each of the elements within the collection of CStockFont objects. If the check box is unchecked, the original default font objects are reestablished in the objects associated with the controls and form. This demonstrates how setting up a collection of class objects can facilitate rapid changes of their properties. As

the routine concludes, the chosen font name is printed directly on the form with a call to PrintFontName, and for variety, the list box is refilled with new numbers.

```
Private Sub SetStockFont()
    Dim WhichFont As Integer
    Dim elem As Object
    '
    ' Update font used by most controls with
    ' either the custom stock font or its original
    ' font object.
    '
    If Check1 Then
        '
        ' Retrieve user's choice of stock fonts
        '
        WhichFont = GetStockFont()
        '
        ' Cycle through collection setting stock font
        '
        For Each elem In colSF
            elem.StockFont = WhichFont
        Next
    Else
        '
        ' Cycle through collection resetting each
        ' object's font object to the default.
        '
        For Each elem In colSF
            Set elem.Client.Font = ttFont
        Next
    End If
    '
    ' Print name of font used on form
    '
    Call PrintFontName
    '
    ' For variety, use new numbers in listbox each time
    '
    Call FillListbox(List1)
End Sub
```

12. To Form1, add the private function GetStockFont, and place the following code in it. Since the chosen index into the optFont option button array is needed in several routines, a separate function is used to cycle through that control array to determine which value to use.

```
Private Function GetStockFont() As Integer
    Dim i As Integer
    '
    ' Find which option button is selected, then
    ' set that font into most controls
    '
    For i = sfOEM_FIXED To sfDEVICE_DEFAULT
        If optFont(i) Then
```

Continued on next page

Continued from previous page

```
            GetStockFont = i
            Exit For
        End If
    Next i
End Function
```

13. To Form1, add the private routine PrintFontName and place the following code within it. This centers the name of the selected font over the text box. It demonstrates that all the usual printing methods are still available, even though the current font is not the one stored in the Font property of the form.

```
Private Sub PrintFontName()
    Dim fName As String
    Dim X As Integer
    Dim Y As Integer
    '
    ' Find string to use
    '
    If Check1 Then
        Select Case GetStockFont()
            Case sfOEM_FIXED
                fName = "OEM_FIXED_FONT"
            Case sfANSI_VAR
                fName = "ANSI_VAR_FONT"
            Case sfANSI_FIXED
                fName = "ANSI_FIXED_FONT"
            Case sfSYSTEM_VAR
                fName = "SYSTEM_FONT"
            Case sfSYSTEM_FIXED
                fName = "SYSTEM_FIXED_FONT"
            Case sfDEVICE_DEFAULT
                fName = "DEVICE_DEFAULT_FONT"
        End Select
    Else
        fName = ttFont.Name
    End If
    '
    ' Erase old printing
    '
    X = Text1.Left + Text1.Width
    Y = Text1.Top - Me.TextHeight(fName) * 2
    Me.Line (Text1.Left, Text1.Top)-(X, Y), vb3DFace, BF
    '
    ' Determine location to print centered over text box
    '
    X = Text1.Left + (Text1.Width - Me.TextWidth(fName)) \ 2
    Y = Text1.Top - Me.TextHeight(fName) * 1.25
    '
    ' First print using highlight color
    '
    CurrentX = X
    CurrentY = Y
    Me.ForeColor = vb3DHighLight
    Me.Print fName;
```

```
'
' Then print with a dark shadow color for 3D appearence.
' Offset up and to left by one pixel.
'
    CurrentX = X - Screen.TwipsPerPixelX
    CurrentY = Y - Screen.TwipsPerPixelY
    Me.ForeColor = vb3DDKShadow
    Me.Print fName;
End Sub
```

14. To Form1, add the private routine FillText box and place the following code in it. This is called when the form is first loaded, and fills the text box with some sample text to represent the result of using different stock fonts. Note the use of new constants supplied by the VBA typelib to insert carriage return/linefeed pairs.

```
Private Sub FillText box(Txt As text box)
    Dim data As String
    '
    ' Fill text box with short description of program
    '
    data = """"Visual Basic 4 How To"", from the Waite Group."

    data = data & vbCrLf & vbCrLf
    data = data & "Using the CStockFont class module from "
    data = data & "VB4HT, fixed-width fonts will always be "
    data = data & "available!  No matter what fonts are installed "
    data = data & "on the machine your application is running on!"
    Txt = data
End Sub
```

15. To Form1, add the private routine FillListbox and place the following code in it. This is called whenever a different font is chosen to offer variety in the list box's numeric display. A series of four columns is randomly generated to demonstrate how simple it is to format data of this sort when using fixed-width fonts.

```
Private Sub FillListbox(Lst As ListBox)
    Dim i As Integer
    Dim data As String
    '
    ' Fill the list with four formated columns of random numbers
    '
    Lst.Clear
    Lst.AddItem "Use spaces rather than tabs to align columns!"
    Randomize
    For i = 0 To 19
        data = LPad(Rnd * 1500, 2, 9)
        data = data & LPad(Rnd * 1500#, 6, 14)
        If Rnd * 1000 < 200 Then
            data = data & LPad("N/A", 0, 8)
        Else
            data = data & LPad(Rnd * 1500#, 0, 8)
        End If
        data = data & LPad(Rnd * 1500#, 4, 12)
```

Continued on next page

```
        Lst.AddItem data
    Next i
    Lst.ListIndex = 0
End Sub
```

16. Add the private function LPad to Form1, and place the following code in it. As parameters this function takes a number of any type, the number of output decimal digits, and the output width of the formatted string. Alternatively, a string may be passed in place of the value.

```
Private Function LPad(ValIn As Variant, nDec As Integer, WidthOut As
Integer) As String
    '
    ' Formatting function left pads with spaces, using specified
    ' number of decimal digits.
    '
    If IsNumeric(ValIn) Then
        If nDec > 0 Then
            LPad = Right(Space(WidthOut) & _
                    Format(ValIn, "0." & String(nDec, "0")), _
                    WidthOut)
        Else
            LPad = Right(Space(WidthOut) & Format(ValIn, "0"), WidthOut)
        End If
    Else
        LPad = Right(Space(WidthOut) & ValIn, WidthOut)
    End If
End Function
```

17. Insert the following code in the Form_Paint event of Form1. This refreshes the custom 3D border etched about the form, and repaints the font name over the text box.

```
Private Sub Form_Paint()
    '
    ' Refresh 3D border
    '
    Obj3D.Refresh
    '
    ' Repaint StockFont name above text box
    '
    Call PrintFontName
End Sub
```

18. Unload the form, ending the project, from the Command1_Click event.

```
Private Sub Command1_Click()
    Unload Me
End Sub
```

How It Works

The CStockFont class module provides an extremely simple interface for using Windows GDI stock font objects. By dimensioning a new instance of the CStockFont object and setting another window object into its Client property, the stage is set. To choose one of the six available stock fonts for the Client, set the class object's StockFont property to one of the defined constant values. For additional reading on the topic of stock fonts, see Microsoft Knowledge Base article Q10837, "A Discussion of Windows Fonts."

Since a number of the controls (and the form itself) have their fonts manipulated dynamically, a persistent collection of CStockFont objects is stored for easy reference. This collection can be cycled through using a For Each loop to either assign a new stock font or to restore the original default font object to each element.

This demo also takes advantage of another nice new property of list boxes, by setting IntegralHeight to False. Using this setting, list boxes are no longer resized so that fractional lines aren't displayed as font sizes change. In this way, you can be assured that the controls on your forms will appear exactly as you laid them out no matter which fonts are in use on other computers. You are also assured that if you resize a list box, perhaps in reaction to a user resizing your form, there will be no ugly gaps left if the space the list box was meant to occupy isn't an exact multiple of the font height it is using.

Comments

Windows' stock font objects provide a reliable resource for when you must guarantee the availability of a fixed-width font. These objects are useful for formatting columns of data that use only spaces as padding. Such a scheme allows the same procedures to be used for both screen and file output. Another potential use for stock font objects is to create your own custom MsgBox replacement object. Using the sfSYSTEM_VAR font, this replacement can be made to appear indistinguishable from the one that Windows provides.

4

SOUNDS

4

SOUNDS

How do I...

This chapter gets you well down the road toward developing a complete set of powerful class modules you can use for handling wavefiles (Microsoft.WAV files). Also, using the MCI Command String Interface shown in How-To 4.4, you can easily play MIDI files, AVI files, and more.

The collection of class modules (listed below) developed in the various How-To's of this chapter provide all the basic sound functionality you're likely to need in most of your applications. However, unlike custom controls, if you need more than what is provided in the class modules, you can always add more—since the code is 100 percent Visual Basic.

FILENAME	CLASS NAME	PURPOSE
CMMCHUNK.CLS	CMMChunkInfo	Used to encapsulate RIFF file chunks, used by CMmioFile
CMMIOFIL.CLS	CMmioFile	RIFF file I/O
CWAVEFIL.CLS	CWaveFile	Wavefile I/O
CWAVEEFF.CLS	CWaveEffects	Special effects for wavefiles
CWAVDSP.CLS	CWaveDisplay	Displays wavefiles
CWAVEOUT.CLS	CWaveOut	Uses low-level API functions to play wavefiles
CWAVEMIX.CLS	CWaveMix	Encapsulates WAVEMIX.DLL

Many of the techniques in this chapter use one or more Windows API calls to accomplish their magic. The various How-To's in this chapter will show you how to use the following Windows API calls:

WINDOWS API	HOW-TO'S
GlobalAlloc	4.6, 4.7
GlobalFree	4.6, 4.7
GlobalLock	4.6, 4.7
GlobalReAlloc	4.6
GlobalUnlock	4.6, 4.7
CopyMemory	4.1, 4.6, 4.7
mciGetErrorString	4.4
mciSendString	4.4
mmioAscend	4.1, 4.2, 4.3
mmioClose	4.1, 4.2, 4.3, 4.6
mmioCreateChunk	4.2, 4.3
mmioDescend	4.1, 4.3, 4.6
mmioOpen	4.1, 4.2, 4.3, 4.6
mmioRead	4.3, 4.6, 4.6
mmioSeek	4.3
mmioStringToFOURCC	4.3
mmioWrite	4.2, 4.3
waveOutClose	4.7
waveOutOpen	4.7
waveOutPrepareHeader	4.7
waveOutReset	4.7
waveOutWrite	4.7
waveOutUnprepare	4.7

4.1 Read RIFF Files

Wave-audio data, palettes, AVI files, and many other types of multimedia data are stored in Resource Interchange Format Files (RIFF). In this project you'll learn how to navigate in and read data from RIFF files. This How-To begins development of the first of many class modules used in Chapter 4.

4.2 Write RIFF Files

This How-To adds RIFF file-writing capabilites to the class modules developed in How-To 4.1, and shows you how to use the class modules to create your own RIFF files.

4.3 Use Multimedia Memory Files

Performance is an important issue in multimedia applications. A little-known secret of the Windows Multimedia extensions is the Multimedia Memory File. In this How-To you will learn how to create, read, and write these Memory Files.

4.4 Use the MCI Command String Interface

The Windows MCI Command String Interface provides easy access to virtually anything that can be done with the the Multimedia subsystem in Windows. This How-To will show you everything you need to know for using the powerful MCI Command String Interface in your Visual Basic applications.

4.5 Play Multiple Wavefiles Simultaneously

This How-To uses a really cool dll, WAVEMIX.DLL, to play up to eight wavefiles at once. As part of this project you will learn how to build a class module to handle wave channel allocation issues. The resulting class module, CWaveMix, hides all the details of WAVEMIX.DLL and provides a handy tool you can use in your applications.

4.6 Display a Wavefile

In this How-To you will explore the fundamentals of wavefiles. Some interesting techniques for using class modules are demonstrated, so if you're looking for new tricks to do with class modules, you won't want to miss this How-To.

4.7 Play Wavefiles Using Low-Level API Calls

If your application requires the utmost in precision wavefile handling, this is the How-To for you. A new class module, CWaveOut, will help get the absolute best control over wavefile output that can be obtained using Windows.

4.8 Change a Wavefile's Volume

This How-To adds another great trick to the bag of wavefile magic you get in Chapter 4. In addition to learning how to scale a wavefile's volume, you will also begin development of a new class module named CWaveEffects. Using the knowledge you gain in this How-To, you can easily add all sorts of special effects to wavefiles.

4.9 Merge Two Wavefiles

For some applications, wavefiles aren't merged for immediate use but rather for later use. A wavefile editor is an example of such an application. When you're authoring multimedia applications, there will be times when you really want to combine multiple wavefiles into a single wavefile. This How-To will add a new method named Merge to the CWaveEffects class developed in How-To 4.8. You will be able to add the ability to write wavefiles using techiniques shown in How-To's 4.2 and 4.3.

4.10 Make a Drum Machine

Of all the How-To's in this chapter, this one is the most fun to play with. It will develop a complete drum-track editor, with file save and load capabilities. The CWaveMix class module developed in How-To 4.5 is put to good use here. Some interesting graphical effects are demonstrated, as well. Included are some high-quality digital drum sounds that you can play with and use in your projects.

4.1 How do I...
Read RIFF Files?

COMPLEXITY: INTERMEDIATE
COMPATIBILITY: VB4 ONLY

Problem

Wave audio data, palettes, AVI files, and many other types of multimedia data are stored in Resource Interchange Format Files (RIFF). I'd like to be able to access this data from within my Visual Basic program, but VB doesn't provide the functions I need. How can I make my Visual Basic programs read RIFF files?

Technique

RIFF files are a flexible way to store and navigate large data files. Every RIFF file consists of one or more chunks. Each chunk contains the following fields:

➤ A four-character code that contains the chunk ID

➤ A 32-bit number that gives the size of the data field

➤ A data field

There are also two special chunk types: RIFF and LIST. Both RIFF and LIST chunks have an additional four-character code field which indentifies the type of the RIFF or LIST. These chunk types, and only these chunk types, are allowed to contain other chunks.

The first chunk in any RIFF file must be a RIFF chunk. All other chunks in a RIFF are either subchunks of the first chunk in the file (it's always a RIFF chunk!) or subchunks of subchunks. Figure 4-1-1 illustrates a RIFF chunk.

Anywhere in a RIFF file you would expect to encounter a chunk, you may find a LIST chunk or a subchunk of a LIST chunk. A LIST chunk provides a way to organize related chunks, and makes skipping over a group of chunks efficient because the LIST chunk gives the size of all of its subchunks. Figure 4-1-2 illustrates a LIST chunk.

The Multimedia subsystem of Windows provides special functions for navigating within the RIFF file chunks. The API function mmioDescend is used to descend into a chunk, and mmioAscend is used to ascend back out of a chunk. These functions

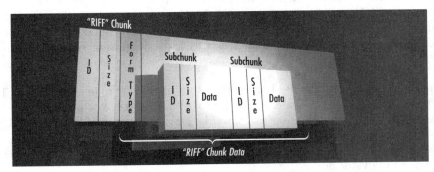

Figure 4-1-1 A simple RIFF file

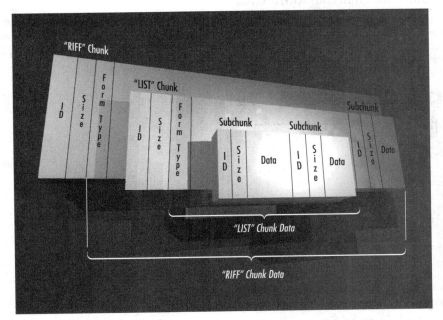

Figure 4-1-2 A LIST chunk

are much like the seek functions normally used with files, but they operate on chunks instead of on bytes or records.

In this How-To you will take the first step toward building a powerful set of class modules that can be used for multimedia programming. The RIFF reader you develop in this project requires two classes: CMMChunkInfo and CMmioFile.

CMMChunkInfo creates objects to store, access, and modify chunk information. A fairly simple class, CMMChunkInfo is used throughout many of the How-To's in this chapter, often aggregated inside other objects, and helps to hide some of the complexity of the more advanced projects.

The CMmioFile class provides easy access to the Multimedia file I/O functions. This class will be used throughout the chapter (but never without its friend CMMChunkInfo) for all sorts of things. In this How-To you will see a way to take those powerful but difficult to use API functions and hide them behind a class interface, so that even beginning programmers can use the Multimedia file functions.

Steps

Open and run RIFFREAD.VBP. Use the File Open menu item to open a wavefile. The chunks in the wavefile you selected are displayed in the list box. Open other wavefiles, and you will soon discover that wavefiles are all the same. What's worse, there's really not much to look at. For an example of an interesting RIFF file, locate and open an AVI file. Figure 4-1-3 shows RIFFREAD with the chunks from an AVI file displayed in the list box.

Create the CMMChunkInfo Class

1. Create a new project named RIFFREAD.VBP. Use the Insert Class Module menu item to add a new class to your project. Use the project window to open the new class module, and then use the properties window to set the module's name to CMMChunkInfo. Be sure that the Creatable property is set to True.

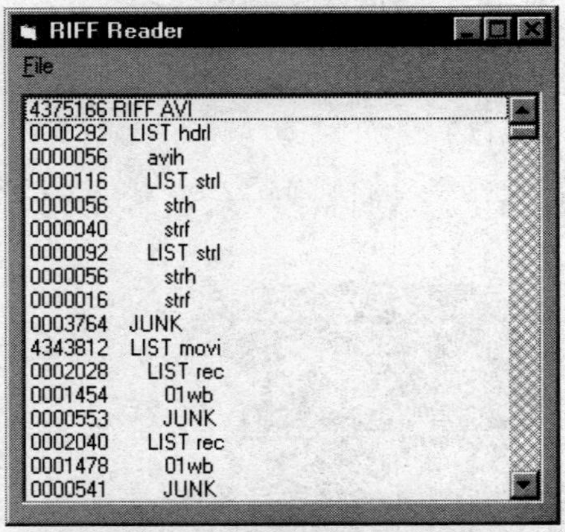

Figure 4-1-3 RIFFREAD displaying the chunks in an AVI file

2. Add the following code to the General section of CMMChunkInfo:

```
Option Explicit
'
' Windows API
'
Private Declare Sub CopyMemory Lib "KERNEL32" Alias "RtlMoveMemory" ⇒
        (dst As Any, src As Any, ByVal dwBytes As Long)
'
' Private instance of MMCKINFO, the user of this class
' is not allowed to directly manipulate the contents of
' of this structure
'
Private chunkInfo As MMCKINFO
```

3. Add the following pair of functions to the General section of CMMChunkInfo. These functions provide an interface to the ID property of CMMChunkInfo. The ID member of MMCKINFO is a long integer that is used to store four characters. The best way to manipulate chunk IDs in Visual Basic is to use four-character strings, so these two property routines convert long integer IDs to strings when you Get ID, and strings to a long integer when you need to set the value of a chunk ID. The Windows API function RtlMoveMemory (aliased as CopyMemory) is used to copy data between strings and the ckid field.

```
Public Property Get id() As String
    Dim S As String

    S = String(4, 0)
    CopyMemory ByVal S, chunkInfo.ckid, 4
    id = S
End Property

Public Property Let id(ckid As String)
    CopyMemory chunkInfo.ckid, ByVal ckid, 4
End Property
```

4. Add the following pair of functions to the General section of CMMChunkInfo. Like chunk IDs, chunk types are really long integer values. And like the Get ID and Let ID property routines, chunk types are converted for convenient use.

```
Public Property Get fccType() As String
    Dim S As String

    S = String$(4, 0)
    CopyMemory ByVal S, chunkInfo.fccType, 4
    fccType = S
End Property

Public Property Let fccType(anfcc As String)
    CopyMemory chunkInfo.fccType, ByVal anfcc, 4
End Property
```

5. Add the following pair of functions to the General section of CMMChunkInfo. The dwDataOffset field in MMCKINFO is the offset in bytes from the start of a chunk to the data portion of the chunk.

```
Public Property Get DataOffset() As Long
    '
    ' Get offset to chunk data
    '
    DataOffset = chunkInfo.dwDataOffset
End Property

Public Property Let DataOffset(dwOffset As Long)
    '
    ' Set offset to chunk data
    '
    chunkInfo.dwDataOffset = dwOffset
End Property
```

6. Add the following pair of functions to the General section of CMMChunkInfo. The cksize field in MMCKINFO contains the total number of bytes in a chunk. Cksize includes the size of both the chunk and its data.

```
Public Property Get Size() As Long
    '
    ' Get chunk size
    '
    Size = chunkInfo.cksize
End Property

Public Property Let Size(newSize As Long)
    '
    ' Assign chunk size
    '
    chunkInfo.cksize = newSize
End Property
```

7. Add the following pair of functions to the General section of CMMChunkInfo. As you will see later, it is sometimes necessary to pass the memory address of chunkInfo to a Windows API function. Visual Basic provides no direct way to do this, but the address of a string can be passed to a windows API function. So AsString returns a string that contains a copy of chunkInfo, and the address of that string is passed to API functions as a stand-in for chunkInfo. Also, some of the Windows API functions will modify one or more fields of chunkInfo's stand-in. When this happens, FromString can be used to update the contents of chunkInfo.

```
Public Function AsString() As String
    Dim result As String

    result = String(Len(chunkInfo), 0)
    CopyMemory ByVal result, chunkInfo, Len(chunkInfo)
```

```
        AsString = result
End Function

Public Sub FromString(newChunk As String)
    CopyMemory chunkInfo, ByVal newChunk, Len(chunkInfo)

End Sub
```

Create the CMmioFile Class

8. Now use Insert Class Module to create another class module, named CMmioFile, with its Creatable property set to True.

9. Add the following code to the General section of CMmioFile:

```
Option Explicit

'
' Private work variables
'
Private hmmio    As Long
```

10. This is where things start to get interesting. Add the following code to the General section of CMmioFile. The OpenFile function hides the details of using the API function mmioOpen from the casual programmer. OpenFile returns a Boolean to indicate success or failure on the file opening. The first parameter of OpenFile is simply the full filepath name of the file to be opened. The mode argument is used to specify what mode to use when opening the file. The mode constants (defined in WINMM32.BAS) and their meanings are shown in Table 4-1-1. The third and final argument to OpenFile (mminfo) is optional. In the READRIFF project you won't need to pass mminfo to OpenFile, but in later projects you will be using it for special kinds of file access.

```
Public Sub OpenFile(Filename As String, mode As Long, Optional mminfo ⇒
    As Variant)
    If (IsMissing(mminfo)) Then
        '
        ' Open as regular diskfile if no mmio data passed in
        '
        hmmio = mmioOpen(Filename, ByVal 0&, mode)
    Else
        '
        ' Some sort of special requirements ... use mminfo
        '
        hmmio = mmioOpen(Filename, ByVal CStr(mminfo), mode)
    End If
    '
    ' If the open failed raise an error
    '
    If (hmmio = 0&) Then
        Err.Raise _
            vbObjectError + 1, _
            "VBHT.CMmioFile", _
```

Continued on next page

Continued from previous page

```
                "Could not open " & Filename & "."
    End If
End Sub
```

Table 4-1-1 OpenFile modes

MODE CONSTANT	DESCRIPTION
MMIO_READ	Opens a file for reading only
MMIO_WRITE	Opens a file for writing only
MMIO_READWRITE	Opens a file for reading and writing
MMIO_CREATE	Creates a new file or truncates an existing file to zero length
MMIO_ALLOCBUF	Opens a file for buffered I/O

11. Add the following function to the General section of CMmioFile:

```
Public Function CloseFile() As Integer
    CloseFile = mmioClose(hmmio, 0)
End Function
```

12. Add the following code to the General section of CMmioFile. Descend is one of the two functions you will be using to navigate within RIFF files. The API function mmioDescend has an optional argument (ParentChunk) that is used when you are descending within a chunk: this argument is not used when there is no parent chunk (always the case for the first chunk in a file, the RIFF chunk). Here's where the AsString method comes into play. It would be ideal to be able to directly pass the chunkInfo variable from CMMChunkInfo objects into mmioDescend; unfortunately, Visual Basic won't let us do this. We have to work around this limitation by getting a copy of chunkInfo into a string and then passing the string to mmioDescend. Also, when chunkInfo needs to be modified, we have to copy the string back after we're done. Not pretty, but useable.

```
Public Function Descend(chunkInfo As CMMChunkInfo, flags As Integer, ⇒
    Optional ParentChunk As Variant) As Boolean
    Dim strChunkInfo As String
    Dim strParentChunk As String
    Dim result        As Integer
    '
    ' Bail if no file open
    '
    If (hmmio = 0) Then
        Descend = False
        Exit Function
    End If
    '
    ' Get string version of chunkInfo
    '
    strChunkInfo = chunkInfo.AsString()
    '
    ' Descend either into root or some parent chunk
```

```
'
If (Not IsMissing(ParentChunk)) Then
    strParentChunk = ParentChunk.AsString()
    result = mmioDescend(hmmio, ByVal strChunkInfo, ⇒
            ByVal strParentChunk, 0)
Else
    result = mmioDescend(hmmio, ByVal strChunkInfo, ByVal 0&, 0)
End If
'
' If no errors update chunkInfo and return True
'
If (result = 0) Then
    chunkInfo.FromString strChunkInfo
    Descend = True
Else
    Descend = False
End If
End Function
```

13. Add the following function to the General section of CMmioFile:

```
Public Function Ascend(chunkInfo As CMMChunkInfo) As Boolean
    Dim strChunkInfo As String
    Dim strParentChunk As String
    '
    ' Bail if there is no file
    '
    If (hmmio = 0) Then
        Ascend = False
        Exit Function
    End If
    '
    ' Get string version of chunkInfo
    '
    strChunkInfo = chunkInfo.AsString()
    '
    ' Do the Ascend and return result
    '
    If (mmioAscend(hmmio, ByVal strChunkInfo, 0) = 0) Then
        Ascend = True
    Else
        Ascend = False
    End If
End Function
```

14. Add the following functions to the Class section of CMmioFile. Class initialization and termination functions are one of the really useful programming tools introduced with Visual Basic 4.0. During initialization you can set variables to know states, allocate resouces, and so forth. Then, during termination, you can close open files, free resources, and clean up as needed. After you are accustomed to using these, you'll wonder how you ever got by without them.

```
Private Sub Class_Initialize()
    hmmio = 0
```

Continued on next page

Continued from previous page

```
End Sub

Private Sub Class_Terminate()
   Dim wRtn As Integer
   '
   ' Only close open files!
   '
   If (hmmio   0) Then
      wRtn = mmioClose(hmmio, 0)
   End If
End Sub
```

Create the Project

15. Select Form1, and add the controls and properties shown in Table 4-1-2 to the form.

Table 4-1-2 Objects and properties for Form1

OBJECT	PROPERTY	SETTING
Form		
	Caption	"RIFF Reader"
	Name	Form1
CommonDialog	FileTitle	"Open Riff File"
	Filter	"Wave (*.wav)|*.wav|Video (*.avi)|*.avi"
	Name	CommonDialog1
ListBox	Name	List1

16. Use the menu editor to add the items shown in Table 4-1-3 to Form1.

Table 4-1-3 Menu for Form1

MENU	CAPTION
FileMenu	"&File"
...FileOpen	"&Open..."
...FileSep1	"-"
...FileExit	"E&xit"

17. Add the following code to the General declaration section of Form1:

```
Option Explicit
'
' Used for padding strings
'
Const blanks = "                        "
```

18. Add the following code to the Resize event procedure of Form1:

```
Private Sub Form_Resize()
   Dim offset As Integer
```

```
'
' Resize list to fit window
'
offset = 5 * Screen.TwipsPerPixelX
List1.top = offset
List1.left = offset
List1.Width = Form1.ScaleWidth - 2 * offset
List1.Height = Form1.ScaleHeight - 2 * offset
End Sub
```

19. Add the following code to the FileOpen menu's Click event:

```
Private Sub FileOpen_Click()
    On Error Resume Next
    CommonDialog1.ShowOpen
    If (Err = 0) Then
        List1.Clear
        DisplayRiff CommonDialog1.Filename
    End If
End Sub
```

20. Add the following code to the FileExit menu's Click event:

```
Private Sub FileExit_Click()
    End
End Sub
```

21. Add the following subroutine to the General declarations section of Form1. This is where the action starts: FileOpen calls DisplayRiff after the user selects a file to display. After opening the file, the first chunk is descended into by calling GetNextChunk. If the call succeeds (valid RIFF file), then the DisplayChunk routine is called to display the contents of the chunk.

```
Private Sub DisplayRiff(fname As String)
    Dim wf  As New CMmioFile
    Dim fOk As Boolean
    Dim pi  As New CMMChunkInfo
    '
    ' This could take a while -- put up hourglass
    '
    Screen.MousePointer = 11
    On Error Resume Next
    wf.OpenFile fname, MMIO_READ
    If (Not Err) Then
        If (GetNextChunk(wf, pi)) Then
            DisplayChunk wf, pi
        End If
        wf.CloseFile
    Else
        MsgBox Err.Description
    End If
    Screen.MousePointer = 0
End Sub
```

22. Add the following subroutine to the General declarations section of Form1. RIFF files are recursively defined (chunks can contain lists, which can contain chunks) and so this function recursively descends into lists. As each chunk is found, its size, ID, and type are displayed in List1.

```
Private Sub DisplayChunk(wf As CMmioFile, pi As CMMChunkInfo)
    Dim ci          As New CMMChunkInfo
    Static indent As Integer
    '
    ' Display current chunk info
    '
    List1.AddItem Format(pi.Size, "0000000 ") + Left$(blanks, indent * 3) ⇒
        + pi.ID + " " + pi.fccType
    '
    ' Increase indent chunks at this level
    '
    indent = indent + 1
    '
    ' Loop as long as there are chunks to display
    '
    Do While GetNextChunk(wf, ci, pi) <> False
        If (ci.ID = "LIST") Then
            '
            ' Descent into LIST ... display LIST chunk
            '
            DisplayChunk wf, ci
        Else
            '
            ' Regular old chunk of some sort ... display info
            '
            List1.AddItem Format(ci.Size, "0000000 ") + Left$(blanks, ⇒
                indent * 3) + ci.ID + " " + ci.fccType
        End If
        Call wf.Ascend(ci)
    Loop
    indent = indent - 1
End Sub
```

23. Add the following function to the General declarations section of Form1:

```
Function GetNextChunk(wf As CMmioFile, chunkInfo As CMMChunkInfo, ⇒
        Optional parent As Variant) As Boolean
    '
    ' Invoke Descend method
    '
    GetNextChunk = wf.Descend(chunkInfo, 0, parent)
End Function
```

24. Add \VB4HT\MODULES\MMSYSTEM.BAS to your project. The MMSYSTEM.BAS file has constants and declarations for the Windows Multimedia System.

How It Works

The overwhelming majority of the work in this How-To revolves around building the core Multimedia I/O classes, CMMChunkInfo and CMmioFile. These classes are used together to provide a simple yet highly functional interface to the Multimedia file services.

Once the user selects a file, the DisplayRiff subroutine is called. In DisplayRiff a new instance of the CMmioFile class is created, using New CMmioFile, and then opened with the CMmioFile method, OpenFile. Next, GetNextChunk is called to descend into the first chunk, which must be a RIFF chunk (or the file is not a RIFF file).

The workhorse of this How-To is DisplayChunk. DisplayChunk begins by adding information to the list box about the current chunk. After incrementing indent, which determines the number of spaces preceding a chunk's listbox information, a loop is entered to display information about each chunk in the file. LIST chunks need special handling because they contain other chunks, and potentially other LIST chunks. DisplayChunk handles LIST chunks by calling itself! Then, after displaying information about the LIST chunk, the loop takes care of displaying the chunks contained in the list. And if yet another LIST chunk is encountered, DisplayChunk will be called again. Eventually, the end of either the RIFF or a LIST chunk is reached and DisplayChunk returns, perhaps to finish displaying some enclosing LIST chunk.

Comments

This How-To demonstrates some of the power of class modules. Hiding behind the simple interface seen by the user of CMmioFile are complex pointers, API calls, and all manner of unsavory details! As you will see in this chapter's other How-To's, containing complexity is not the only benefit you will realize from using class modules. Well-designed classes can be used over and over again, without ever having to look "behind the veil."

4.2 How do I...
Write RIFF Files?

COMPLEXITY: INTERMEDIATE
COMPATIBILITY: VB4 ONLY

Problem

Resource Interchange Format Files (RIFF) provide a convenient way to store various types of data, including WAVE data, MIDI data, palettes, and bitmaps. I'd like to be able to use RIFF files to organize multimedia-related data for my applications. Also, if I can write RIFF files using Visual Basic, I will be able to export Multimedia data for other applications such as wavefile editors. How can I write RIFF files using Visual Basic?

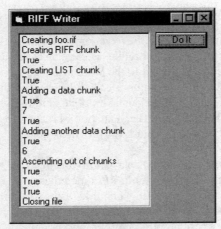

Figure 4-2-1 The RIFF Writer, after a successful completion

Technique

Writing RIFF files isn't difficult, once you have the right set of class modules. In this How-To you will build and use two class modules: CMMChunkInfo and CMmioFile. CMMChunkInfo provides properties and methods for creating and reading *chunks*, the fundamental building block of RIFF files. CMmioFile provides properties and methods you can use to open and read these files.

If you aren't familiar with RIFF files, you might want to look at How-To 4.1 before going ahead with this project.

Steps

Open and run the RIFFWRIT project. Click on the Do It command button, and the program's actions and results will be displayed in the list box on the form. Figure 4-2-1 shows RIFFWRIT after a successful completion.

1. Create a new project named RIFFWRIT.VBP. Use the File Add menu item to add CMMCHUNK.CLS from How-To 4.1 to your project. CMMCHUNK.CLS is used to encapsulate the Multimedia data structure MMCKINFO, which is required when working with RIFF files.

Create the CMmioFile Class

2. Now use the Insert Class Module menu item to create another class module, named CMmioFile, with its Creatable property set to True.

3. Add the following code to the General section of CMmioFile:

```
Option Explicit

'
' Private work variables
'
Private hmmio    As ILong
```

4. Now things start to get interesting. Add the following code to the General section of CMmioFile. The OpenFile function hides the details of using the API function mmioOpen from the casual programmer. OpenFile returns a Boolean to indicate success or failure on the file opening. The first parameter of OpenFile is simply the full filepath name of the file to be opened. The mode argument is used to specify what mode to use when opening the file. The mode constants (defined in WINMM32.BAS) and their meanings are shown in Table 4-2-1. The third and final argument to OpenFile (mminfo) is optional. In the READWRIT project you won't need to pass mminfo to OpenFile, but in later projects you will be using it for special kinds of file access.

```
Public Sub OpenFile(Filename As String, mode As Long, Optional mminfo ⇒
    As Variant)
    If (IsMissing(mminfo)) Then
        '
        ' Open as regular diskfile if no mmio data passed in
        '
        hmmio = mmioOpen(Filename, ByVal 0&, mode)
    Else
        '
        ' Some sort of special requirements ... use mminfo
        '
        hmmio = mmioOpen(Filename, ByVal CStr(mminfo), mode)
    End If
    '
    ' If the open failed raise an error
    '
    If (hmmio = 0&) Then
        Err.Raise _
            vbObjectError + 1, _
            "VBHT.CMmioFile", _
            "Could not open " & Filename & "."
    End If
End Sub
```

Table 4-2-1 OpenFile modes

MODE CONSTANT	DESCRIPTION
MMIO_READ	Opens a file for reading only
MMIO_WRITE	Opens a file for writing only
MMIO_READWRITE	Opens a file for reading and writing
MMIO_CREATE	Creates a new file or truncates an existing file
MMIO_ALLOCBUF	Opens a file for buffered I/O

5. Add the following function to the General section of CMmioFile:

```
Public Function CloseFile() As Integer
    CloseFile = mmioClose(hmmio, 0)
End Function
```

6. Add the following code to the General section of CMmioFile. WriteFile has two parameters: buffer and count. The buffer parameter is a Variant, so that it is possible to pass either a String or the address of a buffer. In this project, you will not be passing a Long as the buffer parameter, but it is useful to have this capability so that you can write data returned by API functions or data stored in buffers allocated with the API function GlobalAlloc. An exception is raised if neither a String nor a Long is passed to this function.

```
Public Function WriteFile(buffer As Variant, count As Long) As Long
    Dim s As String
    Dim l As Long
    '
    ' Bail if file not open
    '
    If (hmmio = 0) Then
        WriteFile = 0
        Exit Function
    End If
    '
    ' Use either a string or a long variable
    '
    Select Case VarType(buffer)
        Case vbString
            s = buffer
            WriteFile = mmioWrite(hmmio, ByVal s, count)
        Case vbLong
            l = buffer
            WriteFile = mmioWrite(hmmio, l, count)
        Case Else
            Err.Raise _
                vbObjectError + 1, _
                "VBHT.CMmioFile", _
                "Invalid buffer argument passed to WriteFile."
    End Select
End Function
```

7. Add the following code to the General section of CMmioFile. CreateChunk, as you might expect from its name, creates a chunk in a file. After checking to be sure there really is an open file to work with, the first order of business is to get the contents of the chunkInfo parameter into a useable form. ChunkInfo is an object variable, and Windows API functions don't expect to receive object variables as arguments, so the data embedded in the chunkInfo object are converted to a string, which can be passed to an API function. Finally, the API function mmioCreateChunk is called; if it succeeds, the modified chunk information is copied back to the chunkInfo object.

```
Public Function CreateChunk(chunkInfo As CMMChunkInfo, flags As Integer) ⇒
     As Boolean
   Dim strChunkInfo As String
   '
   ' Bail if no file opened
   '
   If (hmmio = 0) Then
       CreateChunk = False
       Exit Function
   End If
   '
   ' Get chunkInfo into a string
   '
   strChunkInfo = chunkInfo.AsString()
   '
   ' Create new chunk
   '
   If (mmioCreateChunk(hmmio, ByVal strChunkInfo, flags) = 0) Then
       '
       ' If create went well update chunkInfo
       '
       CreateChunk = True
       chunkInfo.FromString strChunkInfo
   Else
       CreateChunk = False
   End If
End Function
```

8. Add the following code to the General section of CMmioFile. The
mmioCreateChunk API function automatically descends into the newly created
chunk. You will use the Ascend function to back out of chunks you've created.
The chunkInfo structure tells the Multimedia file system what chunk to ascend
from. As with CreateChunk, it is necessary to convert the contents of the
chunkInfo structure to a string so that it can be passed to the mmioAscend API
function. After a successful call to mmioAscend, the string version of chunkInfo
is updated and must be copied back to the chunkInfo object.

```
Public Function Ascend(chunkInfo As CMMChunkInfo) As Boolean
   Dim strChunkInfo As String
   Dim strParentChunk As String
   '
   ' Bail if there is no file
   '
   If (hmmio = 0) Then
       Ascend = False
       Exit Function
   End If
   '
   ' Get string version of chunkInfo
   '
   strChunkInfo = chunkInfo.AsString()
   '
   ' Do the Ascend and return result
```

Continued on next page

Continued from previous page

```
    '
    If (mmioAscend(hmmio, ByVal strChunkInfo, 0) = 0) Then
        Ascend = True
    Else
        Ascend = False
    End If
End Function
```

9. Add the following function to the General section of CMmioFile. An object's Class_Initialize subroutine is called when the object is created. There's not much to do here, but it's always a good idea to make sure that an object's variables are correctly initialized.

```
Private Sub Class_Initialize()
    hmmio = 0
End Sub
```

10. Add the following function to the General section of CMmioFile. An object's Class_Terminate subroutine is called just before the object is destroyed. This is where you free resources, close open files, and so on.

```
Private Sub Class_Terminate()
    Dim wRtn As Integer
    '
    ' Only close open files!
    '
    If (hmmio <> 0) Then
        wRtn = mmioClose(hmmio, 0)
    End If
End Sub
```

Create the Project

11. Select Form1, and add the controls and properties shown in Table 4-2-2 to the form.

Table 4-2-2 Objects and properties for Form1

OBJECT	PROPERTY	SETTING
Form	Caption	"RIFF Writer"
	Name	Form1
ListBox	Name	List1
CommandButton	Caption	"Do It"
	Name	Command1

12. Add the following code to the General section of Form1:

```
Option Explicit
```

13. Add the following code to the Click event procedure of Form1. As you can see, creating a RIFF file is pretty easy once you have the right objects to work with!

```
Private Sub Command1_Click()
    Dim wf      As New CMmioFile
    Dim ci(3) As New CMMChunkInfo

    List1.Clear
    '
    ' Create file and RIFF chunk
    '
    List1.AddItem "Creating foo.rif"
    wf.OpenFile "foo.rif", MMIO_CREATE
    List1.AddItem "Creating RIFF chunk"
    ci(0).fccType = "VBHT"
    List1.AddItem wf.CreateChunk(ci(0), MMIO_CREATERIFF)
    '
    ' Create a LIST chunk
    '
    List1.AddItem "Creating LIST chunk"
    List1.AddItem wf.CreateChunk(ci(1), MMIO_CREATELIST)
    List1.AddItem "Adding a data chunk"
    '
    ' Add a data chunk
    '
    ci(2).ID = "data"
    List1.AddItem wf.CreateChunk(ci(2), 0)
    List1.AddItem wf.WriteFile("foo bar", 7)
    '
    ' Ascend out of first data chunk
    '
    List1.AddItem wf.Ascend(ci(2))
    '
    ' Add a second data chunk
    '
    List1.AddItem "Adding another data chunk"
    ci(2).ID = "more"
    List1.AddItem wf.CreateChunk(ci(2), 0)
    List1.AddItem wf.WriteFile("hooya!", 6)
    List1.AddItem "Ascending out of chunks"
    '
    ' Ascend out of data chunk
    '
    List1.AddItem wf.Ascend(ci(2))
    '
    ' Ascend out of LIST and RIFF chunks
    '
    List1.AddItem wf.Ascend(ci(1))
    List1.AddItem wf.Ascend(ci(0))
    '
    ' Close file
    '
    List1.AddItem "Closing file"
    wf.CloseFile
End Sub
```

How It Works

The bulk of the code for this project is in the two classes, CMMChunkInfo and CMmioFile. CMMChunkInfo is used to encapsulate MMCKINFO, a Multimedia data structure designed for C programmers. The CMMChunkInfo class also hides the data conversion processes from the programmer, making your work with chunks easier and less error prone.

The CMmioFile class is more complex than CMMChunkInfo, but it serves the same purpose: information hiding, and the containment of complexity.

The RIFF File

Before you can write to a RIFF file, you need to have one! After creating a new instance of the CMmioFile class with Dim wf As New CMmioFile, the file is created using the object's OpenFile method. The MMIO_CREATE flag passed to the OpenFile method tells the Multimedia system to either create a new file or truncate an existing one to zero length.

Every RIFF file has a RIFF chunk as its first chunk. You identify the type of RIFF file by setting the fccType member of a CMMChunkInfo object, before passing it to the CreateChunk member function. By setting the fccType member of ci(0) to VBHT, a VBHT RIFF file type is created. The MMIO_CREATERIFF flag passed to the CreateChunk member function tells the Multimedia file system to create a RIFF chunk; the chunk's ID is automatically set to RIFF.

You may have wondered about the array of CMMChunkInfo objects declared at the beginning of the Command1_Click subroutine. Creating chunks automatically causes a descent into the newly created chunk. Later, when it is necessary to ascend out of the chunks, you need to have saved information for each chunk that was descended into.

The LIST Chunk

Now that you have a RIFF file to work with you can begin adding chunks and data. The first chunk added by this project is a LIST chunk. Creating a LIST chunk is easily done, by simply invoking the CreateChunk method with MMIO_CREATELIST as the flag's argument. The Multimedia file system takes care of the rest.

Adding Chunks and Data to the LIST Chunk

An empty list isn't much fun, so a couple of data chunks are added to the LIST chunk. To add a data chunk, you first create a chunk and then write data to it (it really is that simple). Later, when you're reading the RIFF file, it's helpful to be able to locate certain chunks. The ID member of a CMMChunkInfo object lets you do this. You can assign any four-character string to the ID member, and it will be written to the file by CreateChunk. Later you can search the file for particular chunks, if required.

To write data to a chunk, you use CMmioFile's WriteFile member function. The first argument to WriteFile is either a string or an array of bytes. The second argument tells how many bytes to write. To avoid trouble, be sure to have at least as many bytes to write as indicated by the second argument. WriteFile is a fairly low-level facility; you can use it to write strings or arrays of bytes, but that's it. The Multimedia file system does not use Visual Basic variables. This isn't the end of the world, however, because you can always manage to copy Visual Basic variables to either a string or a byte array, and then write it to the file.

After you write data to a chunk, you use the Ascend member function to get out of the chunk. The Multimedia file system automatically sets the chunk's size field and returns the size in the chunk information structure. CMmioFile's Ascend member function copies the modified chunk information back to your CMMChunkInfo object.

Finishing Up

Once all of the chunks are created and data are written, you only need to Ascend out of each chunk, so that the Multimedia file system can set its size. This is why it was necessary to keep one instance of CMMChunkInfo for each level of chunk. The last thing to do is close the file using the CMmioFile CloseFile member function.

Comments

Multimedia files are a must if you want to exchange multimedia data with other programs. One shortcoming of RIFF files is that you cannot insert a chunk into the middle of a RIFF file. You can make the calls, but the result will be existing data being overwritten. Techniques from the upcoming How-To 4.3 can be used to make this problem a little easier to live with.

4.3 How do I...
Use Multimedia Memory Files?

COMPLEXITY: INTERMEDIATE
COMPATIBILITY: VB4 ONLY

Problem

I have written a wavefile editor using Visual Basic. One of the features of my program is the ability to cut and paste pieces of a file, or insert new pieces into a file. This requires copying a lot of data on the hard drive to either fill gaps or make room for new data. On small files this works fine, but on larger files it takes too much time to copy the data. I've read about Multimedia memory files, which let you treat a part of memory like a disk file. If I could use memory files in my program, the performance problem might be solved. How do I use Multimedia memory files in my Visual Basic programs?

Technique

Once you've learned how to read and write Multimedia files, as shown in How-To's 4.1 and 4.2, you're really close to having everything you need to create and use memory files. This project demonstrates the building of a CMemFile class that you can use in your programs. One outstanding feature of the CMemFile class is that you will need to change only the OpenFile calls in your program; an instance of CMemFile has the exact same properties and functions as the CMmioFile class.

Steps

Open and run MEMFILE.VBP, and you will see the form shown in Figure 4-3-1 displayed on your screen. Click on the Create Memory File command button (creating the memory file enables the other three buttons). You can then click on the Write to Memory File command button one or more times. After you have written some data to the memory file, click on the Copy to Disk File command button. This command creates a file named TESTFILE on your hard drive and copies the contents of the memory file to it. You can use the DOS TYPE command to display the contents of the file. When you have written the memory file and copied it to the hard drive, click on the Close Memory File command button.

Create the CMmioFile Class

1. Use the Insert Class menu item to add a new class module to your project, and name it CMmioFile.

2. Add the following code to the General declarations section of CMmioFile. The variable hmmio cannot be accessed by users of the CMmioFile class. It is private, to prevent incorrect values from being assigned to it.

```
Option Explicit
'
' Private work variables
'
Private hmmio    As Long
```

3. Add the following function to the General section of CMmioFile. The OpenFile function is also used in How-To 4.1 and is described in detail there. Unlike that

Figure 4-3-1 The
MEMFILE project when
first executed

project, however here you will be passing the optional argument mminfo to OpenFile. As you will see in the OpenFile function of CMemFile, mminfo can be used to tell the Multimedia file system that you want to create a memory file.

```
Public Sub OpenFile(Filename As String, mode As Long, Optional mminfo ⇒
    As Variant)
    If (IsMissing(mminfo)) Then
        '
        ' Open as regular diskfile if no mmio data passed in
        '
        hmmio = mmioOpen(Filename, ByVal 0&, mode)
    Else
        '
        ' Some sort of special requirements ... use mminfo
        '
        hmmio = mmioOpen(Filename, ByVal CStr(mminfo), mode)
    End If
    '
    ' If the open failed raise an error
    '
    If (hmmio = 0&) Then
        Err.Raise _
            vbObjectError + 1, _
            "VBHT.CMmioFile", _
            "Could not open " & Filename & "."
    End If
End Sub
```

4. Add the following function to the General section of CMmioFile. It isn't necessary to check to see if hmmio is valid here (as would be the case if a file were not opened), since mmioClose will check it for you and return an error if necessary.

```
Public Function CloseFile() As Integer
    CloseFile = mmioClose(hmmio, 0)
End Function
```

5. Add the following function to the General section of CMmioFile. SeekFile is used to set the position for subsequent reading or writing of a Multimedia file. Two parameters are required to specify the position of the read/write pointer for a file. The second parameter, position, describes how to use the first parameter, offset. Table 4-3-1 explains how offset is used for the possible values of position.

```
Public Function SeekFile(offset As Long, position As Integer) As Long
    '
    ' If the file isn't open return impossible value
    '
    If (hmmio = 0) Then
        SeekFile = -1
    Else
        SeekFile = mmioSeek(hmmio, offset, position)
    End If
End Function
```

Table 4-3-1 Use of the position parameter with SeekFile

POSITION	USE OF OFFSET
SEEK_SET	Positions the read/write pointer offset bytes from the beginning of the file.
SEEK_CUR	Positions the read/write pointer offset bytes from the current position. Offset may be either positive or negative. Positive values move the pointer forward in the file and negative values move the pointer backward.
SEEK_END	Positions the read/write pointer offset bytes before the end of the file.

6. Add the following function to the General section of CMmioFile. This ReadFile function is described in How-To 4.1.

```
Public Function ReadFile(buffer As Variant, count As Long) As Long
    Dim s As String
    Dim l As Long
    '
    ' Bail if file not open
    '
    If (hmmio = 0) Then
        ReadFile = 0
        Exit Function
    End If
    '
    ' Use either a string or a long variable
    '
    Select Case VarType(buffer)
        Case vbString
            s = buffer
            ReadFile = mmioRead(hmmio, ByVal s, count)
            buffer = s
        Case vbLong
            l = buffer
            ReadFile = mmioRead(hmmio, ByVal l, count)
        Case Else
            Err.Raise _
                vbObjectError + 1, _
                "VBHT.CMmioFile", _
                "Invalid buffer argument passed to ReadFile."
    End Select
End Function
```

7. Add the following function to the General section of CMmioFile. This WriteFile function is described in How-To 4.2.

```
Public Function WriteFile(buffer As Variant, count As Long) As Long
    Dim s As String
    Dim l As Long
    '
    ' Bail if file not open
    '
    If (hmmio = 0) Then
```

```
        WriteFile = 0
        Exit Function
     End If
     '
     ' Use either a string or a long variable
     '
     Select Case VarType(buffer)
        Case vbString
           s = buffer
           WriteFile = mmioWrite(hmmio, ByVal s, count)

        Case vbLong
           l = buffer
           WriteFile = mmioWrite(hmmio, l, count)
        Case Else
           Err.Raise _
              vbObjectError + 1, _
              "VBHT.CMmioFile", _
              "Invalid buffer argument passed to WriteFile."
     End Select
End Function
```

8. Add the following function to the Class section of CMmioFile. There's not much to do in the way of initialization, for instance, of CMmioFile, but it's always a good idea to make sure that variables are initialized correctly.

```
Private Sub Class_Initialize()
     hmmio = 0
End Sub
```

9. Add the following function to the Class section of CMmioFile. If there is an open file when an instance of CMmioFile is destroyed, the Class_Terminate function makes sure the file is closed. Programmers sometimes forget to do these things for themselves!

```
Private Sub Class_Terminate()
     '
     ' Only close open files!
     '
     If (hmmio <> 0) Then
        Call mmioClose(hmmio, 0)
     End If
End Sub
Create the CMemFile Class
```

10. Use the Insert Class menu item to create a new class module, and name it CMemFile. Add the following code to the General section of CMemFile. The variable mmioFile declared here is key to creating the CMemFile class. When you have one object as a private member of another object, you have inherited the interface and functionality of the member object. The ability to inherit methods and properties from objects is central to object-oriented programming. As you

will see below, this "inheritance through aggregation" makes it easy to build powerful class modules.

```
Option Explicit
'
' Windows API functions
'
Private Declare Sub CopyMemory Lib "KERNEL32" Alias "RtlMoveMemory" ⇒
    (dst As Any, src As Any, ByVal dwBytes As Long)
'
' Aggregated CMmioFile object
'
Private mmioFile As CMmioFile
```

11. Add the following code to the General section of CMemFile.

```
Public Sub OpenFile(Filename As String, mode As Integer, dwSize As Long, ⇒
    dwExpand As Long)
    Dim mminfo As MMIOINFO
    Dim hmmio  As Integer
    Dim temp   As String
    '
    ' Setup mminfo for a memory file
    '
    mminfo.fccIOProc = mmioStringToFOURCC(FOURCC_MEM, 0)
    mminfo.cchBuffer = dwSize
    mminfo.adwInfo(0) = dwExpand
    '
    ' Allocate a string to hold mminfo
    '
    temp = String(Len(mminfo), 0)
    '
    ' Copy mminfo to string
    '
    CopyMemory ByVal temp, mminfo, Len(mminfo)
    '
    ' Invoke OpenFile method ñ- may invoke Err.Raise
    '
    mmioFile.OpenFile Filename, mode Or MMIO_ALLOCBUF, temp
End Sub
```

The first thing to happen in the OpenFile method is the initialization of mminfo. The fccIOProc field of mminfo is set to a long integer containing the characters M, E, M, and a blank space. FOURCC_MEM is a string constant with MEM as its value, and the API function mmioStringToFOURCC converts it to a long integer.

This OpenFile subroutine has two parameters that are not present when you're using the CMmioFile class. The first extra parameter, dwSize, tells the Multimedia file system how much memory to allocate for your memory file when it is created. The second extra parameter, dwExpand, tells the Multimedia file system how many bytes to add to the memory file each time it needs to be expanded. If you pass a zero for dwExpand, the memory file will be of fixed length. Once the mminfo type is initialized, it is necessary to copy it to a string. (Visual Basic does not allow you to pass a user-defined type, like MMIOINFO, to an object's functions or subroutines.) So this function copies it to a string and passes the string instead.

Finally, the OpenFile function of the aggregated object, mmioFile, is called to open (or create) the memory file. An additional flag, MMIO_ALLOCBUF, is ORed with the calling code's mode flags so that the Multimedia system will allocate an internal buffer for the memory file.

12. Add the following functions to the General section of CMemFile. All of these functions have one purpose: to invoke functions of the aggregated class object, mmioFile. Here you can clearly see the benefit of inheriting the behavior of mmioFile. Not only does the CMemFile class have an interface identical to CMmioFile, but you don't have to do much work to achieve it.

```
Public Function CloseFile() As Integer
   CloseFile = mmioFile.CloseFile()
End Function

Public Function SeekFile(offset As Long, position As Integer) As Long
   SeekFile = mmioFile.SeekFile(offset, position)
End Function

Public Function ReadFile(buffer As Variant, count As Long) As Long
   ReadFile = mmioFile.ReadFile(buffer, count)
End Function

Public Function WriteFile(buffer As String, count As Long) As Long
   WriteFile = mmioFile.WriteFile(buffer, count)
End Function
```

13. Add the following code to the Class section of CMemFile. CMemFile's Class_Initialize subroutine is a little different from CMmioFile's. Instead of setting hmmio to zero, a new instance of CMmioFile is created, and it sets hmmio to zero as usual.

```
Private Sub Class_Initialize()
   Set mmioFile = New CMmioFile
End Sub



Private Sub Class_Terminate()
   Set mmioFile = Nothing
End Sub
```

14. Create a new project named MEMFILE.VBP. Add the objects and properties shown in Table 4-3-2 to Form1.

Table 4-3-2 Objects and properties for Form1

OBJECT	PROPERTY	SETTING
Form	Caption	"MEMFILE"
	Name	Form1
CommandButton	Caption	"Create Memory File"
	Index	0
	Name	Command1
CommandButton	Caption	"Write To Memory File"
	Index	1
	Name	Command1
CommandButton	Caption	"Copy To Disk File"
	Index	2
	Name	Command1
CommandButton	Caption	"Close Memory File"
	Index	3
	Name	Command1

15. Add the following code to the General declarations section of Form1. The second line declares memfile to be an object variable capable of holding an instance of the CMemFile class. After an instance of CMemFile is created, it is stored in memfile so that it can be used by the functions in Form1.

```
Option Explicit
'
' Variable declaration for a CMemFile object
'
Dim memfile As CMemFile
```

16. Add the following code to the Click event procedure of Command1. The command buttons for this How-To are a control array. The index of a command button is used to select the appropriate action when it is clicked. Command buttons with indexes 1 and 2 (write to memory file, and copy to disk file) simply call a function to perform the required work. Command buttons with indexes 0 and 3 (open and close memory file) ensure that command buttons are enabled and disabled as required by the current state of the program.

```
Private Sub Command1_Click(index As Integer)
    Dim s        As String
    Dim gotback  As Integer
    Dim size     As Long
    Dim i        As Integer

    Select Case index
        Case 0
```

```
    '
    ' Create memory file ... fix button enables
    '
    If (CreateMemFile() = True) Then
        Command1(0).Enabled = False
        For i = 1 To 3
            Command1(i).Enabled = True
        Next
    End If
Case 1
    '
    ' Write something to the memory file
    '
    WriteMemFile
Case 2
    '
    ' Copy memory file to disk file
    '
    CopyToDisk
Case 3
    '
    ' Close memory file ... fix button enables
    '
    CloseMemFile
    Command1(0).Enabled = True
    For i = 1 To 3
        Command1(i).Enabled = False
    Next
    End Select
End Sub
```

17. Add the following function to the General section of Form1. CreateMemFile first creates an instance of CMemFile and then uses the OpenFile method to create and open the memory file. The last two parameters passed to OpenFile specify that the memory file initially contains 8K, and that every time it becomes full, it should be expanded by 1K. If OpenFile fails, an error is displayed and False is returned; otherwise, True is returned.

```
Function CreateMemFile() As Boolean
    '
    ' Create memory file
    '
    Set memfile = New CMemFile
    On Error Resume Next
    memfile.OpenFile "testfile", MMIO_CREATE, 1024 * 8, 1024
    If (Err) Then
        MsgBox Err.Description
        CreateMemFile = False
    Else
        CreateMemFile = True
    End If
End Function
```

18. Add the following function to the General section of Form1. WriteMemFile simply creates a string and writes it to the memory file by invoking the WriteFile method.

```
Sub WriteMemFile()
    Dim s As String
    '
    ' Write a string to memmfile
    '
    s = "Contents of memory file. "
    Call memfile.WriteFile(s, Len(s))
End Sub
```

19. Add the following code to the General section of Form1:

```
Sub CopyToDisk()
    Dim diskfile    As New CMmioFile
    Dim size        As Long
    Dim s           As String
    '
    ' Open diskfile
    '
    Call diskfile.OpenFile("testfile", MMIO_CREATE)
    '
    ' Get size of memfile
    '
    size = memfile.SeekFile(0, SEEK_END)
    '
    ' Make string to use as buffer
    '
    s = String(size, 0)
    '
    ' Read contents of memfile
    '
    Call memfile.SeekFile(0, SEEK_SET)
    Call memfile.ReadFile(s, size)
    '
    ' Write contents of diskfile
    '
    Call diskfile.WriteFile(s, size)
    '
    ' Close diskfile
    '
    Call diskfile.CloseFile
End Sub
```

The CopyToDisk subroutine creates a file named TESTFILE on your hard drive and copies the current contents of the memory file to it. The SeekFile method of CMemFile is used to determine the number of bytes in the memory file. SeekFile returns a long integer, which gives the position of the read/write pointer in a file. By seeking to the end of the memory file (0 bytes from the end is the end), it is easy to determine the file's size. Next, a string of the correct size is allocated.

There's one last thing to do before reading from the memory file: the read/write pointer must be positioned to the start of the file. After SEEK_SET is used to move to the first byte of the file, ReadFile is invoked to copy the contents of the memory file to the previously allocated string. Finally, WriteFile is used to write the string to the hard drive file, and CloseFile finishes up.

20. Add the following function to the General declarations section of Form1. This function simply invokes the CloseFile method of CMemFile, which in turn invokes the CloseFile method of CMmioFile.

```
Sub CloseMemFile()
    '
    ' Close memory file
    '
    Call memfile.CloseFile
End Sub
```

How It Works

The first thing to do when running this project is click on the Open Memory File command button. This calls the CreateMemFile subroutine, where the power of building class modules becomes apparent. Disguised by the simplicity of invoking CMemFile's OpenFile method are a nested CMmioFile object, a Windows data structure, and a Windows API call.

Once you have a CMemFile object, you can access all of the methods you're accustomed to using with objects of the CMmioFile class. The WriteFile member function of CMemFile is identical to that of CMmioFile and, in fact, the call to CMemFile's WriteFile method results in a direct call to CMmioFile's WriteFile method. By initializing and using the CMmioFile object (mmiofile) in the CMemFile class, you avoid a lot of code duplication. This not only makes your program smaller, but makes maintenance easier, too. Changes to the CMmioFile class are automatically inherited by CMemFile class.

After clicking on the Write To Memory File command button you can use the Copy To Disk File command button to execute the CopyToDisk subroutine. CopyToDisk uses the methods of CMemFile and CMmioFile to create a copy of the memory file on your hard drive by first creating a file using CMmioFile's OpenFile method, and then using SeekFile, ReadFile, and WriteFile to get the job done. SeekFile determines the size of the memory file, so that a suitably sized string can be used to transfer data between the memory file and the disk file.

Finally, CloseFile is called to close the disk file. You may have noticed that it is not necessary to close the disk file, because when the diskfile object in CopyToDisk is detroyed as the subroutine exits, the CMmioFiles Class_Terminate subroutine will close the file if it is still open. It is preferable to close files explicitly, so that later reading of the code will be easier to interpret. There is little to confuse in this project, but in a more complex project it could be an issue whether the file was to be closed or left open. Adding clean-up code and checks such as that in Class_Terminate is a defensive programming technique, to prevent surprises if you forget something.

Comments

This How-To gives a simple demonstration of the power of building class modules. An instance of the CMmioFile class is used in CMemFile to inherit substantial functionality that otherwise would have required duplication of code, or modification of CMmioFile to call subroutines in a code module. The only drawback of inheriting another class's interface in this way is that you must duplicate the inherited object's methods and property procedures. In C++ this is done automatically. However, the advantages of inheritance far outweigh the inconvenience of writing a handful of "no-brainer" interface functions.

4.4 How do I...
Use the MCI Command String Interface?

COMPLEXITY: INTERMEDIATE
COMPATIBILITY: VB4 ONLY

Problem

I've read about the MCI Command String Interface in Microsoft's *Multimedia Programmer's Guide*. The MCI Command String Interface provides a powerful but easy-to-use way to work with Multimedia files such as wavefiles, MIDI files, and AVI files. I'd like to use the MCI Command String Interface in my programs. Can I do this from within Visual Basic programs?

Technique

The MCI Command String Interface is fairly easy to use in Visual Basic programs. With only two Windows API calls—mciSendString and mciGetErrorString—you can have access to all of the functionality and flexibility of the interface.

The mciSendString API function requires a string that specifies what action the multimedia subsystem should take. For instance, the following command strings can be used to open a wavefile and play it:

```
"open chimes.wav type waveaudio alias wavefile"
"play wavefile"
```

Unlike the simple high-level audio functions (such as sndPlaySound, which you can also use to open and play a wavefile), the MCI Command String Interface lets you control almost every parameter used with a particular multimedia device. For instance you can set the start position for a subsequent wavefile play command using the following command string:

```
"seek wavefile to" & Str(position)
```

There are far too many possible MCI commands to list and explain in this book. For that you need a copy of the Multimedia Programmer's Reference (or equivalent). In essence, each MCI device is required to support capability, close, info, open, and status commands. Most of these commands have additional arguments. For instance, the capability command accepts a number of arguments that you can use to determine a device's capabilities. Most MCI devices also support a number of other basic commands, including load, pause, play, record, resume, save, seek, set, status, and stop.

Steps

Open and run MCIPLAY.VBP. Use the program's File Open menu item to select a wavefile. The Play button on the form's toolbar will become enabled and the form will look like the one shown in Figure 4-4-1. When you click on the Play button, the wavefile starts playing and the Pause and Stop buttons are enabled. If you've opened a long file or if you move really fast, you can click on the Pause or Stop button before the file finishes playing. Any time the wavefile isn't playing, you can use the slider's thumb to set the position for the wavefile to start playing.

1. Create a new project named MCIPLAY.VBP. and use the File Add menu item to add the class files CTOOLBAR.CLS and CTOOLBUT.CLS to your project. These two files, which are in the VBHT\CLASSES subdirectory, were first introduced in How-To 3-10, in Chapter 3.

2. Add a new module named MCIPLAY.BAS to your project, and add the following code to it. Two MCI functions are declared, mciSendString and mciGetErrorString. These two functions (especially mciSendString) provide easy access to the substantial functionality available via the MCI Comand String Interface.

Figure 4-4-1 The MCI Wave Player

```
Declare Function mciGetErrorString Lib "winmm.dll" Alias "mciGetErrorStringA" ⇒
    (ByVal dwError As Long, ByVal lpstrBuffer As String, ⇒
    ByVal uLength As Long) As Long
Declare Function mciSendString Lib "winmm.dll" Alias "mciSendStringA" ⇒
    (ByVal lpstrCommand As String, ByVal lpstrReturnString As String, ⇒
    ByVal uReturnLength As Long, ByVal hwndCallback As Long) As Long
```

3. Add the following code to MCIPLAY.BAS. This SendMciCommand function provides a "wrapper" for the Windows API functions mciSendString and mciGetErrorString.

```
Function SendMciCommand(cmd As String, Result As String) As Integer
    Dim status As Integer
    '
    ' Assume success
    '
    SendMciCommand = 0
    '
    ' Create a buffer for the result string
    '
    Result = String$(256, 0)
    '
    ' Send the command and retrieve error message if the command
    ' fails
    '
    status = mciSendString(cmd, Result, Len(Result), Form1.hWnd)
    If (status <> 0) Then
        SendMciCommand = status
        status = mciGetErrorString(status, Result, Len(Result))
    End If
    '
    ' Return result or error string
    '
    Result = StripNull(Result)
End Function
```

4. Add the following function to MCIPLAY.BAS. Windows API functions sometimes require a buffer. In Visual Basic, one way to provide a buffer is to dimension a string large enough that Windows will not try to write outside of it. When Windows API functions return a string result in a buffer, the string is terminated with a CHR$(0) or simply a 0 byte. The StripNull function locates the end of a Windows-style string and returns a VB string containing only those characters that come before the 0 byte.

```
Function StripNull(from As String) As String
    Dim I As Integer

    I = InStr(from, Chr$(0))
    If (I  0) Then
        StripNull = Left$(from, I - 1)
    Else
        StripNull = from
    End If
End Function
```

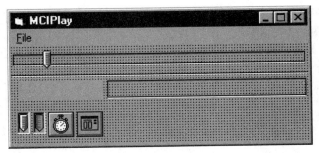

Figure 4-4-2 Positions of controls on Form1

5. Select Form1, and add the objects with properties and settings shown in Table 4-4-1. Positioning some of these controls, especially the Line1 controls, is a little tricky. The two Shape controls are used to create some basic frames, but they do not provide a 3D effect, so Line1(0), Line1(1), Line1(4), and Line1(5) are used to provide dark gray and white highlights, thus creating a 3D effect for the two Shape controls. The other two lines, Line1(2) and Line1(3), create a 3D separator between the top and bottom parts of the form. After you've got everything positioned, change the form's size until the Timer control is hidden and there are only a few pixels showing to the right of Shape2, as shown in Figure 4-4-2.

Table 4-4-1 Objects, properties, and settings for Form1

OBJECT	PROPERTY	SETTING
Form	AutoRedraw	-1 'True
	BackColor	&H00C0C0C0&
	BorderStyle	3 'Fixed Double
	Caption	"MCIPlay"
	Name	Form1
PictureBox	BackColor	&H00C0C0C0&
	BorderStyle	0 'None
	Name	Picture1
PictureBox	AutoSize	-1 'True
	Name	ThumbDn
	Picture	"THUMBDN.BMP"
	Visible	0 'False
PictureBox	AutoSize	-1 'True
	Name	ThumbUp
	Picture	"THUMBUP.BMP"
	Visible	0 'False
Timer	Name	Timer1

Continued on next page

Continued from previous page

OBJECT	PROPERTY	SETTING
CommonDialog	CancelError	-1 'True
	DefaultExt	"wav"
	DialogTitle	"Open Wave File"
	Filter	"Wave Files (*.wav)|*.wav|"
	Name	CommonDialog1
Label	BackStyle	0 'Transparent
	Name	Label1
Line	BorderColor	&H00808080&
	Index	0
	Name	Line1
Line	BorderColor	&H00FFFFFF&
	Index	1
	Name	Line1
Line	BorderColor	&H00000000&
	Index	2
	Name	Line1
Line	BorderColor	&H00FFFFFF&
	Index	3
	Name	Line1
Line	BorderColor	&H00808080&
	Index	4
	Name	Line1
Line	BorderColor	&H00FFFFFF&
	Index	5
	Name	Line1
Shape	Name	Shape1
Shape	Name	Shape2
Image	Name	Image1
	Picture	"THUMBUP.BMP"

6. Use the menu editor to add the menu described in Table 4-4-2 to Form1.

Table 4-4-2 Form1's menu

MENU NAME	CAPTION
FileMenu	"&File"
...FileOpen	"&Open..."
...FileSep1	"-"
...FileExit	"E&xit"

7. Add the following code to the General declarations section of Form1.

```
Option Explicit
'
' Set during Form_Load ... min and max horizontal
' positions for slider thumb
'
Dim thumbMaxX As Integer
Dim thumbMinX As Integer
'
' Set when a wavefile play finishes
'
Dim fRewind    As Boolean
'
' CToolBar object
'
Dim ToolBar As New CToolBar
'
' Loaded with wavefile length, used to compute thumb
' position
'
Dim wavefileLength As Long
'
' Toolbar button constants
'
Const BTN_PLAY = 1
Const BTN_PAUSE = 2
Const BTN_STOP = 3
```

8. Add the following code as Form1's Form_Load event procedure. The major part of Form_Load sets up a toolbar using the CToolBar class module. After the toolbar has been set up, the slider's thumb is positioned and the program is ready to open and play wavefiles.

```
Private Sub Form_Load()
    Dim i As Integer
    Dim AppPath As String
    '
    ' Make sure we can find the toolbar bitmap files
    '
    AppPath = App.Path
    '
    ' Set toolbar's visual surface
    '
    Set ToolBar.Canvas = Picture1
    '
    ' Set border width such the toolbuttons will be
    ' centered vertically
    '
    ToolBar.BorderWidth = ((Picture1.ScaleHeight \ Screen.TwipsPerPixelY) ⇒
        - 22) \ 2
    '
    ' Load instances of CToolButton
    '
```

Continued on next page

Continued from previous page

```
    ToolBar.AddButton LoadPicture(AppPath & "\BTN_PLAY.bmp"), BTN_PLAY
    ToolBar.AddButton LoadPicture(AppPath & "\BTN_PAUS.bmp"), BTN_PAUSE
    ToolBar.AddButton LoadPicture(AppPath & "\BTN_STOP.bmp"), BTN_STOP
    '
    ' Start with all of the buttons initially disabled
    '
    ToolBar.Enabled(BTN_PLAY) = False
    ToolBar.Enabled(BTN_PAUSE) = False
    ToolBar.Enabled(BTN_STOP) = False
    '
    ' Calculate min and max thumb positions
    '
    thumbMaxX = Shape1.Left + Shape1.Width - 1 - Image1.Width
    thumbMinX = Shape1.Left + 1
    '
    ' And finally, make sure the thumb is all the way to the left
    '
    Image1.Left = thumbMinX
End Sub
```

9. Add the following code as Form1's Form_Unload event procedure. It's important to ensure that the wave device is closed when the program exits. In Form_Unload, the wave device is unconditionally closed, and the error that occurs if the wave device has not been opened is ignored. It's easier to ignore the error here than it would be to keep track of whether or not the device was opened.

```
Private Sub Form_Unload(Cancel As Integer)
    Dim mciResult   As String
    '
    ' Close the wavefile (even if it's not open)
    '
    Call SendMciCommand("close wavefile", mciResult)
End Sub
```

10. Add the following subroutine to Form1. This ToolBarHandle routine is called by Picture1's MouseUp and MouseDown event procedures. The passed argument ID identifies the toolbar button affected at the time the mouse event was generated. The Select statement in this subroutine selects the correct code for the toolbar button that received the mouse event.

```
Private Sub ToolBarHandle(ID As Integer)
    Dim mciResult As String

    Select Case ID
       Case BTN_PLAY:
           '
           ' If we need to rewind after a play, do so
           '
           If (fRewind = True) Then
               '
               ' Rewind to start of wave file
               '
               Call SendMciCommand("seek wavefile to start", mciResult)
```

```
        Image1.Left = thumbMinX
    End If
    fRewind = False
    '
    ' Start playing the wave file
    '
    Call SendMciCommand("play wavefile", mciResult)
    '
    ' Turn on timer so slider thumb position will be
    ' updated
    '
    Timer1.Interval = 125
    Timer1.Enabled = True
    '
    ' Disable the Play button, enable Pause and Stop
    '
    ToolBar.Enabled(BTN_PLAY) = False
    ToolBar.Enabled(BTN_PAUSE) = True
    ToolBar.Enabled(BTN_STOP) = False
Case BTN_PAUSE:
    '
    ' Pause the wave file
    '
    Call SendMciCommand("pause wavefile", mciResult)
    '
    ' Suspend timer ... it's not needed while paused
    '
    Timer1.Enabled = False
    '
    ' Allow Play and Stop buttons now
    '
    ToolBar.Enabled(BTN_PLAY) = True
    ToolBar.Enabled(BTN_PAUSE) = False
    ToolBar.Enabled(BTN_STOP) = True
    '
    ' Set flag so we won't rewind if Play is pressed
    '
    fRewind = False
Case BTN_STOP:
    '
    ' Stop the wave file
    '
    Call SendMciCommand("stop wavefile", mciResult)
    '
    ' Rewind to start of wave file
    '
    Call SendMciCommand("seek wavefile to start", mciResult)
    fRewind = False
    '
    ' No need to update thumb position now
    '
    Timer1.Enabled = False
    '
    ' Reset slider position
    '
```

Continued on next page

Continued from previous page

```
            Image1.Left = Shape1.Left + 1
            '
            ' Enable Play, disable Pause and Stop
            '
            ToolBar.Enabled(BTN_PLAY) = True
            ToolBar.Enabled(BTN_PAUSE) = False
            ToolBar.Enabled(BTN_STOP) = False
    End Select
End Sub
```

11. Add the following code as Picture1's MouseDown event procedure. The CToolBar method MouseDown is called, but the return value (always zero) is ignored.

```
Private Sub Picture1_MouseDown(button As Integer, Shift As Integer, ⇒
      x As Single, y As Single)
    Call ToolBar.MouseDown(x, y)
End Sub
```

12. Add the following code as Picture1's MouseUp event procedure. When CToolBar's MouseUp method is called and the mouse pointer is over a toolbar object, the object's ID is returned from the MouseUp method. The ID is passed to ToolBarHandle, where the appropriate code is executed.

```
Private Sub Picture1_MouseUp(button As Integer, Shift As Integer, ⇒
      x As Single, y As Single)
    ToolBarHandle (ToolBar.MouseUp(x, y))
End Sub
```

13. Add the following code as Timer1's Timer event procedure. Timer1 is enabled whenever a wavefile is being played. Each time the Timer event is fired this routine checks the progress of the play and positions the slider's thumb to reflect the current playback position. Once MCI indicates that the end of the wavefile has been reached, the slider's thumb is forced all the way to the right and the timer is disabled.

```
Private Sub Timer1_Timer()
    Dim mciResult   As String
    Dim curpos      As Integer
    '
    ' Get the current wavefile positioni
    '
    Call SendMciCommand("status wavefile position", mciResult)
    curpos = Val(mciResult)
    '
    ' End of wavefile reached?
    '
    If (curpos = wavefileLength) Then
        '
        ' Yes make sure slider is all the way to the right
        '
        Image1.Left = thumbMaxX
        Timer1.Enabled = False
```

```
    '
    ' Ready to play again
    '
    ToolBar.Enabled(BTN_PLAY) = True
    ToolBar.Enabled(BTN_PAUSE) = False
    ToolBar.Enabled(BTN_STOP) = False
    fRewind = True
Else
    '
    ' Not done yet ... update slider position
    '
    Image1.Left = (Shape1.Width - Image1.Width) * curpos / wavefileLength
    End If
End Sub
```

14. Add the following code as Picture1's Paint event procedure. The CToolBar method Show takes care of painting the toolbar buttons.

```
Private Sub Picture1_Paint()
    ToolBar.Show
End Sub
```

15. Add the following code as Image1's MouseDown event procedure. The image is changed so that the thumb appears to be pressed.

```
Private Sub Image1_MouseDown(button As Integer, Shift As Integer, ⇒
    x As Single, y As Single)
    '
    ' Mouse down on thumb ... display thumb-down picture
    '
    Image1.Picture = ThumbDn.Picture
End Sub
```

16. Add the following code as Image1's MouseMove event procedure. When the left button is down over Image1 (button = 1) and there is a wavefile, then Image1 can be dragged back and forth across the area defined by Shape1. The basic idea here is to determine how far, and in what direction, the mouse pointer is from the vertical center-line of Image1. Then, after ensuring that Image1 cannot be moved outside of the slider area (defined by Shape1), Image1 is moved so that it is centered under the mouse's current location.

```
Private Sub Image1_MouseMove(button As Integer, Shift As Integer, ⇒
    x As Single, y As Single)
    Dim diff As Integer
    '
    ' We're tracking the mouse when mouseDown is True
    '
    If (button = 1 And wavefileLength > 0) Then
        '
        ' Find out how far off center the mouse is
        '
        diff = x - Image1.Width / 2
```

Continued on next page

Continued from previous page

```
          '
          ' Is the mouse to the right of center?
          '
          If (Image1.Width / 2 < x) Then
              '
              ' Yes, thumb all the way to the right?
              '
              If (Image1.Left + diff > thumbMaxX) Then
                  '
                  ' Yes ... stay there
                  '
                  Image1.Left = thumbMaxX
              Else
                  '
                  ' No ... get centered under the mouse
                  '
                  Image1.Left = Image1.Left + diff
              End If
          Else
              '
              ' Mouse has moved to the left of center
              ' make sure we don't go too far
              '
              If (Image1.Left + diff < thumbMinX) Then
                  Image1.Left = thumbMinX
              Else
                  Image1.Left = Image1.Left + diff
              End If
          End If
      End If
  End Sub
```

17. Add the following code as Image1's MouseUp event procedure:

```
Private Sub Image1_MouseUp(button As Integer, Shift As Integer, ⇒
    x As Single, y As Single)
  Dim mciResult     As String
  Dim position      As Long
  '
  ' Done tracking thumb ... reload thumb up bitmap
  '
  Image1.Picture = ThumbUp.Picture
  '
  ' Now seek to the corresponding place in our wave file
  '
  position = wavefileLength * (Image1.Left) \ Shape1.Width
  Call SendMciCommand("seek wavefile to" & Str(position), mciResult)
  '
  ' Don't rewind when play is clicked
  '
  fRewind = False
End Sub
```

When the MouseUp event is triggered for the slider's thumb (Image1), the first thing to do is provide feedback to the user. The thumb-up picture is displayed before anything else happens. Next, the wavefile's position is computed using the position of the thumb, and the command string "seek wavefile to" is used to reposition the wavefile's playback position. Finally, the fRewind flag is set to False. Normally a file plays to the end, and the fRewind flag is set so that when the play button is next pressed, the file will start playing again from the beginning. However, the user may use the slider to set a particular playback position. When this happens, it would be an error to rewind the file before playing it.

18. Add the following code as the FileOpen menu item's Click event procedure. Once the user selects a file name, the InitializeWaveFile routine is called.

```
Private Sub FileOpen_Click()
   Dim mciResult    As String
   '
   ' Close the previous file if any
   '
   If (CommonDialog1.filename <> "") Then
      Call SendMciCommand("close wavefile", mciResult)
   End If
   '
   ' Show the Open File dialog
   ' On Error Resume Next
   CommonDialog1.Action = 1
   '
   ' If no name specified go back to the previous name
   '
   If (Err) Then
      Exit Sub
   End If
   '
   ' Now if we've got a file then initialize things
   '
   InitializeWaveFile (CStr(CommonDialog1.filename))
End Sub
```

19. Add the following subroutine to Form1. This InitializeWaveFile function is called after the user has selected a wavefile to play.

```
Private Sub InitializeWaveFile(filename As String)
   Dim mciResult    As String
   Dim wRtn         As Integer
   Dim bytesInFile As Long
   '
   ' Open the wavefile
   '
   wRtn = SendMciCommand("open " & filename & " type waveaudio alias ⇒
      wavefile", mciResult)
   If (wRtn = 0) Then
      '
      ' Open worked ... set the time format to bytes
      '
      Call SendMciCommand("set wavefile time format bytes", mciResult)
```

Continued on next page

Continued from previous page

```
        Call SendMciCommand("status wavefile length", mciResult)
        bytesInFile = Val(mciResult)
        '
        '
        ' Now get the length of the wavefile in milliseconds
        '
        Call SendMciCommand("set wavefile time format milliseconds", ⇒
            mciResult)
        Call SendMciCommand("status wavefile length", mciResult)
        wavefileLength = Val(mciResult)
        '
        ' Put bytes and seconds in the status bar
        '
        Label1.Caption = Format(wavefileLength / 1000) & " seconds, " & ⇒
            Format(bytesInFile) & " bytes"
        '
        ' Enable play button
        '
        ToolBar.Enabled(BTN_PLAY) = True
    Else
        Label1.Caption = ""
        wavefileLength = 0
        ToolBar.Enabled(BTN_PLAY) = False
    End If
End Sub
```

The first task here is to open the wavefile using the "open FILENAME type waveaudio alias wavefile" command string.

Next, the command string "set wavefile time format bytes" is used to specify the units for the timing information. The command string "status wavefile length" returns the length of the wavefile expressed in the current timing units. So these two strings can get the number of bytes in a wavefile.

Next the timing format is switched to milliseconds, using the "set wavefile time format milliseconds" command string. Also, "status wavefile length" is used again, this time to return the number of milliseconds required to play the wavefile. The length in bytes and the time are both displayed in Label1.

20. Add the following code as the FileExit menu's Click event procedure. Unload is used so that Form_Unload will be called. Form_Unload makes sure the wave output device is closed.

```
Private Sub FileExit_Click()
    Unload Me
    End
End Sub
```

How It Works

During Form_Load, a toolbar is created and initialized, using the CToolBar class from How-To 3.10. Three buttons are created, for Play, Pause, and Stop.

When a file is loaded using the FileOpen menu item the Play button is enabled. A call to InitializeWaveFile reads the length in milliseconds and saves it in the variable wavefileLength. This variable is used in two ways. While a wavefile is playing, Timer1 is enabled; and each time a Timer event occurs, the current position of the wavefile is read and used together with wavefileLength to determine the progress of the play. The slider's thumb, Image1, is then moved so that it correctly indicates the current wavefile position. While a wavefile is *not* playing, moving the slider's thumb and then releasing the mouse button results in a change to the wavefile position to be used when play is started.

Playing the wavefile itself is pretty simple—a command string takes care of that. However, there is a small complication in deciding where to start the play. The fRewind flag is used to determine when a wavefile's position should be reset and when it should be left alone. After the form first loads, fRewind will be False. Later, after the user presses the Play button, play can be stopped in three different ways. The user can press the Stop or Pause button, or the wavefile may finish playing.

If the Stop button is pressed, fRewind is set to True. Thus, next time Play is pressed, the wavefile is rewound first. In two important cases, however, rewinding the file before playing it is not the correct thing to do. First, if the user drags the slider thumb after playing has ended (either by finishing or because the Stop button is pressed) then the thumb's (Image1's) MouseUp event procedure sets the fRewind flag to False. Also, when the Pause button is pressed, fRewind is set to False because the user will expect the wavefile to start replaying from the point at which it was paused.

Comments

This project shows how easy it is to use the MCI Command String Interface. You can handle most of the usual playback, and even some recording requirements, using command strings. There's also an attractive slider made from a Shape control, an Image control, and a couple of Lines. The slider is a perfect candidate for a class module—it wouldn't be too tough to take the basic idea and create a slider out of a single PictureBox control. And, of course, no project would be complete without making use of some previously written code. This project uses the CToolBar class from How-To 3.10.

4.5 How do I...
Play Multiple Wavefiles Simultaneously?

COMPLEXITY: ADVANCED
COMPATIBILITY: VB4 ONLY

Problem

I'm writing a program that needs to play more than one wavefile at a time. My program plays background wavefile music continuously and must also play various wavefiles for speech and sound effects—without disrupting the background music.

Most users only have one wave output device. How can I get around the "one wave-file at a time" limitation?

Technique

You're not alone; others have faced this same problem. You might try creating a memory file as demonstrated in How-To 4.3, mix the data from multiple wavefiles into the memory file, and then play that. But the performance results of this approach are inadequate for the real-time requirements of responding to user-generated events by playing waves.

Fortunately, the gnomes at Microsoft have written WAVEMIX.DLL, which makes it possible to play up to eight wavefiles simultaneously. WAVEMIX.DLL is written in C and assembler, and is efficient enough to mix eight wavefiles in real time on today's faster machines. Even on slower machines such as 486-SXs, it's possible to mix a few channels in real time using WAVEMIX.

In this How-To you learn how to develop a CWaveMix class and then use it to play up to eight wavefiles simultaneously.

Steps

Open and run WAVEMIX.VBP. Then use the File Load menu item to load wavefiles for two or more WAVEMIX channels. When you have selected a valid wavefile, its name appears in the text box that had focus when you used the File Load menu item, and the focus moves to the next text box. If you select an invalid file, an error message is displayed and focus returns to the text box that had focus when you used the File Load menu item. After you've loaded a few files, the program will look like Figure 4-5-1.

Try loading some other types of files to see how the error handling works. Once you've loaded some wavefiles, click on the Play command button, and the wavefiles are all played at the same time. After they have finished playing, click on the WMIX_CLEARQUEUE check box. Then click on the Play command button, and before the wavefiles have finished playing, click on Play again. The wavefiles will be

Figure 4-5-1 The WaveMix project with three wavefiles ready to play

restarted immediately. When WMIX_CLEARQUEUE is not checked, a channel's wavefile is queued and will not play until the previous wavefile finishes. When WMIX_CLEARQUEUE is checked, a request to play a channel's wavefile will immediately terminate any play in progress.

1. Create a new project named WAVEMIX.VBP, and use the Insert Module menu item to add a new module to the project. Name the module WAVEMIX.BAS and add the following code to it. The WAVEMIX dll supports eight channels. The constant MAX_WAVES can be used in your programs whenever you need to deal with the maximum number of wavefiles that can be mixed.

```
Option Explicit
'
' Maximum number of channels supported by wavemix
'
Global Const MAX_WAVES = 8
'
' Globals needed by CWaveMix
'
Global hWaveMix        As Integer
Global WaveChannelAllocated(MAX_WAVES) As Boolean
```

Instances of a class module cannot share data amongst themselves. This is somewhat of a shortcoming in VB4 requiring global variables whenever instances of a class need to share information. Having to create global variables to track a class's information violates the "black-box" principle and requires the programmer to add code to support a class.

Before you can use the other functions in WAVEMIX.DLL, you must first call WaveMixInit. However, it is an error to call WaveMixInit more than once. Also, WaveMixInit returns a handle (16-bit integer value) that each of the channels needs to know in order to call any of the other WAVEMIX functions. The global variable hWaveMix is used to store the handle returned by WaveMixInit. Since a valid handle returned by WaveMixInit will not be zero, CWaveMix's Class_Initialize procedure can check to see if hWaveMix is zero or not. If hWaveMix is zero, then WaveMixInit is called and the returned handle is stored in hWaveMix. So the first CWaveMix instance created will find hWaveMix to be zero, will initialize the dll, and will assign the handle to hWaveMix. Subsequent instances of CWaveMix will find hWaveMix to be non-zero and will simply use the handle.

In addition to keeping track of the session handle (hWaveMix), each instance of CWaveMix needs to determine which logical channel number to use. Logical channel numbers range from 0 to 7. The WaveChannelAllocated array is used to track which channels are in use. When a new CWaveMix instance is created, its Class_Initialize procedure scans the array, looking for an element containing False. If an unused channel (False) is found, then the element is set to True and the array index is used as the channel number.

2. Add the following code to WAVEMIX.BAS. A number of constants used by WAVEMIX.DLL are defined here.

```
'
' OpenChannel flags
'
Global Const WMIX_OPENSINGLE = 0
Global Const WMIX_OPENALL = 1
Global Const WMIX_OPENCOUNT = 2
'
' OpenWave flags
'
Global Const WMIX_FILE = 1
Global Const WMIX_RESOURCE = 2
Global Const WMIX_MEMORY = 4
'
' PlayWave flags
'
Global Const WMIX_QUEUEWAVE = 0
Global Const WMIX_CLEARQUEUE = 1
Global Const WMIX_USELRUCHANNEL = 2
Global Const WMIX_HIGHPRIORITY = 4
Global Const WMIX_WAIT = 8
```

3. Add the following declarations to CWaveMix. These data structures and API functions are used when calling functions in WAVEMIX.DLL.

```
'
Option Explicit
'

Private Type WAVEMIXINFO
    wSize As Integer
    bVersionMajor As String * 1
    bVersionMinor As String * 1
    szDate(12) As String
    dwFormats As Long
End Type

Private Type MIXCONFIG
    wSize As Integer
    dwFlagsLo As Integer
    dwFlagsHi As Integer
    wChannels As Integer
    wSamplingRate As Integer
End Type

Private Type MIXPLAYPARAMS
    wSize           As Integer
    hMixSessionLo As Integer
    hMixSessionHi As Integer
    iChannelLo      As Integer
    iChannelHi      As Integer
    lpMixWaveLo     As Integer
    lpMixWaveHi     As Integer
```

```
    hWndNotifyLo      As Integer
    hWndNotifyHi      As Integer
    dwFlagsLo         As Integer
    dwFlagsHi         As Integer
    wLoops            As Integer
End Type

Private Declare Function WaveMixInit Lib "WAVMIX32.DLL" _
    () As Long
Private Declare Function WaveMixConfigureInit Lib "WAVMIX32.DLL" _
    (lpConfig As MIXCONFIG) As Long
Private Declare Function WaveMixActivate Lib "WAVMIX32.DLL" _
    (ByVal hMixSession As Long, ByVal fActivate As Integer) As Long
Private Declare Function WaveMixOpenWave Lib "WAVMIX32.DLL" _
    (ByVal hMixSession As Long, szWaveFilename As Any, ⇒
        ByVal hInst As Long, ByVal dwFlags As Long) As Long
Private Declare Function WaveMixOpenChannel Lib "WAVMIX32.DLL" _
    (ByVal hMixSession As Long, ByVal iChannel As Long, ByVal dwFlags ⇒
        As Long) As Long
Private Declare Function WaveMixPlay Lib "WAVMIX32.DLL" _
    (lpMixPlayParams As Any) As Integer
Private Declare Function WaveMixFlushChannel Lib "WAVMIX32.DLL" _
    (ByVal hMixSession As Long, ByVal iChannel As Integer, ⇒
        ByVal dwFlags As Long) As Integer
Private Declare Function WaveMixCloseChannel Lib "WAVMIX32.DLL" _
    (ByVal hMixSession As Long, ByVal iChannel As Integer, ⇒
        ByVal dwFlags As Long) As Integer
Private Declare Function WaveMixFreeWave Lib "WAVMIX32.DLL" _
    (ByVal hMixSession As Long, ByVal lpMixWave As Long) As Integer
Private Declare Function WaveMixCloseSession Lib "WAVMIX32.DLL" _
    (ByVal hMixSession As Long) As Integer
Private Declare Sub WaveMixPump Lib "WAVMIX32.DLL" _
    ()
Private Declare Function WaveMixGetInfo Lib "WAVMIX32.DLL" _
    (lpWaveMixInfo As WAVEMIXINFO) As Integer
```

4. Add the following declarations to CWaveMix. The variable m_lpMixWave is used to hold a pointer returned from WaveMixOpenWave. This pointer is later passed to WaveMixPlay when it's time to play the wavefile opened by WaveMixOpenWave. The variable m_channel holds the channel number being used by an instance of CWaveMix. When m_channel is −1, there is no open channel for the instance containing m_channel.

```
Private m_lpMixWave      As Long
Private m_channel        As Integer

Private params      As MIXPLAYPARAMS
Private Function HiWord(ByVal l As Long) As Integer
    l = l \ &H10000

    HiWord = Val("&H" & Hex$(l))
End Function

Private Function LoWord(ByVal l As Long) As Integer
```

Continued on next page

419

Continued from previous page

```
    l = l And &HFFFF&

    LoWord = Val("&H" & Hex$(l))
End Function
```

5. Add the following Property Get procedure to CWaveMix. A channel can play a sound if it has been opened, and if a wavefile has been opened using CWaveMix's OpenWave subroutine.

```
Public Property Get IsPlayable() As Boolean
    '
    ' A channel is usable if it's open and it has a wave file
    '
    IsPlayable = (m_channel  -1) And (m_lpMixWave  0)
End Property
```

6. Add the following public subroutine to CWaveMix.

```
Public Sub OpenWave(fname As Variant, flags As Integer)
    '
    ' Can't do this if wave mixer not open
    '
    If (hWaveMix = 0) Then
        Err.Raise 32001, , "Wave mixer not open"
    End If
    '
    ' If a wave is already opened, close it
    '
    If (m_lpMixWave <> 0) Then
        Call WaveMixFreeWave(hWaveMix, m_lpMixWave)
    End If
    '
    ' Open wave file, raise error on failure
    '
If (VarType(fname) = vbString) Then
    m_lpMixWave = WaveMixOpenWave _
        (hWaveMix, ByVal CStr(fname), GetHInstance(), flags)
    Else
    m_lpMixWave = WaveMixOpenWave _
        (hWaveMix, ByVal CLng(fname), GetHInstance(), flags)
    End If    If (m_lpMixWave = 0&) Then
        Err.Raise 32002, , "Could not open wave file"
    End If
End Sub
```

Before a wavefile can be played by WAVEMIX.DLL, the file must first be prepared by calling WaveMixOpenWave. There are three possible values for the flag's argument: WMIX_FILE, WMIX_RESOURCE, and WMIX_MEMORY. The first argument to OpenWave, fname, is a Variant because there are three types of data required for the flag values. WMIX_FILE specifies that fname is a string containing the name of a disk file to open. WMIX_RESOURCE specifies that fname is an integer resource ID. And WMIX_MEMORY specifies a pointer to an MMIOINFO structure initialized with the following:

```
mmioInfo.pchBuffer = buffer
mmioInfo.cchBuffer= Len(buffer)
mmioInfo.fccIOProc=FOURCC_MEM
```

where *buffer* is the buffer of a memory file containing wavedata.

7. Add the following public subroutine to CWaveMix. This subroutine uses WaveMixFreeWave to free the wavefile currently used by an instance of CWaveMix. To change the file used by a channel, you can close the current file using CloseWave and then open a new wavefile using OpenWave.

```
Public Sub CloseWave()
    '
    ' Only close the wave if it's opened!
    '
    If (m_lpMixWave <> 0) Then
        Call WaveMixFreeWave(hWaveMix, m_lpMixWave)
        m_lpMixWave = 0
    End If
End Sub
```

8. Add the following public subroutine to CWaveMix. This OpenChannel routine has one argument, named flags, with two possible values: WMIX_OPENSINGLE and WMIX_ALL. WMIX_OPENSINGLE opens a single channel, and WMIX_ALL opens all channels.

```
Public Sub OpenChannel(flags As Integer)
    '
    ' Allocate a channel number
    '
    m_channel = GetChannel
    If (m_channel = -1) Then
        Err.Raise 32003, , "All channels in use"
    End If
    '
    ' Open channel, raise error on failure
    '
    If (WaveMixOpenChannel(hWaveMix, m_channel, flags)  0) Then
        m_channel = -1
        Err.Raise 32004, , "Could not open wave channel"
    End If
End Sub
```

9. Add the following public subroutine to CWaveMix. The flags argument can be either zero or WMIX_ALL. You can use WMIX_ALL to close all open channels, but be cautious with this option since it may close channels in use by other instances of CWaveMix and they will not know that their channel has been closed.

```
Public Sub CloseChannel(flags As Integer)
    '
    ' Close channel only if it's really open
    '
    If (m_channel <> -1) Then
        Call WaveMixCloseChannel(hWaveMix, m_channel, flags)
    End If
End Sub
```

10. Add the public subroutine PlayWave to CWaveMix.

```
Public Sub PlayWave(flags As Integer, loops As Integer, Optional hWndNotify)
If (IsMissing(loops)) Then
        loops = 0
    End If
    If (IsMissing(hWndNotify)) Then
        hWndNotify = 0
    End If

    '
    ' Fill in play params
    '
    params.wSize = Len(params)
    params.hMixSessionLo = LoWord(hWaveMix)
    params.hMixSessionHi = HiWord(hWaveMix)
    params.iChannelLo = m_channel
    params.iChannelHi = 0
    params.lpMixWaveLo = LoWord(m_lpMixWave)
    params.lpMixWaveHi = HiWord(m_lpMixWave)
    params.hWndNotifyLo = LoWord(hWndNotify)
    params.hWndNotifyHi = HiWord(hWndNotify)
    params.dwFlagsLo = LoWord(flags)
    params.dwFlagsHi = HiWord(flags)
    params.wLoops = loops
    '
    ' Play the wave
    '
    Call WaveMixPlay(params)
End Sub
```

PlayWave has two required arguments and one optional argument. The first argument, flags, has a number of possible values. It can have one or more bits set, as listed in Table 4-5-1. Loops, the second argument to PlayWave, can be used to cause a wavefile to be played more than once. A wavefile is played loops + 1 times; so setting loops to zero plays the file once, setting loops to 1 plays the file twice, and so on. The third argument, hWndNotify, is optional. If you pass a value for hWndNotify, it must be a valid window handle. When hWndNotify is non-zero, a MM_WOM_DONE will be sent to the window referenced by hWndNotify when the wavefile is finished playing. The constant MM_WOM_DONE is defined in MMSYSTEM.BAS.

Table 4-5-1 PlayWave Flag Bits

FLAG BIT	MEANING
WMIX_QUEUEWAVE	The wave will be placed on the specified channel and played after all waves that are currently waiting to play on that channel.
WMIX_CLEARQUEUE	This wave will preempt all waves currently playing on the specified channel. Notification messages will not be sent for any waves that get dumped. This message should not be combined with WMIX_QUEUEWAVE.
WMIX_HIGHPRIORITY	Play this wave immediately. This flag will interrupt the data buffered in the wave driver and remix the sound. If this flag is not set you may experience up to a half-second delay before sound is played.
WMIX_USELRUCHANNEL	The wave should be played on any available channel or played on the channel that was least recently used. This flag should be combined with WMIX_QUEUEWAVE or WMIX_CLEARQUEUE.

11. Add the following public subroutine to CWaveMix. During the initialization of a CWaveMix instance, Class_Initialize is called. Class_Initialize checks the global variable hWaveMix; if it is zero, the wave mixer is initialized.

```
Private Sub Class_Initialize()
    Dim config   As MIXCONFIG
    Dim wRtn As Integer
    '
    ' If this instance of CWaveMix is the first then
    ' initialize the wavemix dll
    '
    If (hWaveMix = 0) Then
    InitMixer
    End If
    '
    ' Initialize variables
    '
    m_lpMixWave = 0
    m_channel = -1
End Sub
```

12. Add the following private subroutine to CWaveMix. This InitMixer routine is called whenever the mixer needs to be initialized.

```
Private Sub InitMixer()
    Dim config   As MIXCONFIG
    Dim wRtn As Integer

    config.wSize = Len(config)
    config.dwFlags = 1
    config.wChannels = 2
    hWaveMix = WaveMixConfigureInit(config)
    wRtn = WaveMixActivate(hWaveMix, True)
    If (wRtn <> 0) Then
        MsgBox "Error activating wave mixer:" & Str(wRtn)
        Call WaveMixCloseSession(hWaveMix)
```

Continued on next page

Continued from previous page

```
        hWaveMix = 0
    End If
End Sub
```

13. Add the following public subroutine to CWaveMix. After calling WaveMixCloseChannel, CWaveMix's ReleaseChannel subroutine is called to make the current instance of CWaveMix's channel available for use by other instances of CWaveMix. Then WaveMixFreeWave is used to free the handle returned by WaveMixOpenWave. CWaveMix is an excellent example of how useful Class_Terminate subroutines can be. Whenever an instance of CWaveMix is destroyed, all of the resources it uses are freed. Not only does this make using a CWaveMix object easier—since you don't need to do any cleanup either before or after the object is destroyed—but it also protects against wasted resources.

```
Private Sub Class_Terminate()
    '
    ' Free channel if open
    '
    If (m_channel <> -1) Then
        Call WaveMixCloseChannel(hWaveMix, m_channel, 0)
        ReleaseChannel
    End If
    '
    ' Free wave file if allocated
    '
    If (m_lpMixWave <> 0) Then
        Call WaveMixFreeWave(hWaveMix, m_lpMixWave)
    End If
End Sub
```

14. Add the following private subroutine to CWaveMix. ReleaseChannel marks a channel as available by setting the channel's element in WaveChannelAllocated to False.

```
Private Sub ReleaseChannel()
    Dim i As Integer

    WaveChannelAllocated(m_channel) = False
    m_channel = -1
    For i = 0 To MAX_WAVES - 1
        If (WaveChannelAllocated(i) = True) Then
            Exit Sub
        End If
    Next
    '
    ' Last allocated channel has been released ... close session
    '
    WaveMixCloseSession (hWaveMix)
    hWaveMix = 0
End Sub
```

424

15. Add the following private function to CWaveMix. The GetChannel function first checks to see if the wave mixer needs to be reinitialized. As channels are released, ReleaseChannel determines if they have all been released, and if so, closes the wave mixer. It is possible that in some program you might like to close all channels and then reopen one or more of them. The check for hWaveMix = 0 will detect this situation and reinitialize the wave mixer. Next, GetChannel searches the WaveChannelAllocated array for a free channel, and returns the channel number if one is available; otherwise, −1 is returned.

```
Private Function GetChannel() As Integer
    Dim i As Integer
    '
    ' Check to make sure mixer doesn't need reinit ...
    ' this will happen whenever all channels are closed and
    ' then one is reopened.
    '
    If (hWaveMix = 0) Then
        InitMixer
    End If
    '
    ' Search for a free channel
    '
    For i = 0 To MAX_WAVES - 1
        If (WaveChannelAllocated(i) = False) Then
            GetChannel = i
            WaveChannelAllocated(i) = True
            Exit Function
        End If
    Next
    '
    ' All channels are in use
    '
    GetChannel = -1
End Function
```

16. Select Form1 and add the objects and properties with settings shown in Table 4-5-2.

Table 4-5-2 Objects, properties and settings for Form1

OBJECT	PROPERTY	SETTING
Form	Caption	"WaveMix"
	Name	Form1
CheckBox	Caption	"&WMIX_CLEARQUEUE"
	Name	Check1
	TabStop	0 'False
TextBox	Name	Text1
	TabIndex	1

Continued on next page

Continued from previous page

OBJECT	PROPERTY	SETTING
TextBox	Name	Text1
	TabIndex	2
TextBox	Name	Text1
	TabIndex	3
TextBox	Name	Text1
	TabIndex	4
TextBox	Name	Text1
	TabIndex	5
TextBox	Name	Text1
	TabIndex	6
TextBox	Name	Text1
	TabIndex	7
TextBox	Name	Text1
	TabIndex	8
CommandButton	Caption	"&Play"
	Name	Command1
	TabStop	0 'False
CommonDialog	CancelError	-1 'True
	DefaultExt	"wav"
	DialogTitle	"Load Wave File"
	Filter	"Wave (*.wav)|*.wav|"
	Name	CommonDialog1

17. Add the following code to the General declarations section of Form1:

```
Option Explicit
'
' Wave Channel Objects
'
Dim WaveThings(MAX_WAVES) As CWaveMix
'
' Used so that we know when to change a WaveThings
' wave file
'
Dim TextChanged(MAX_WAVES) As Boolean
Dim HasFocus As Integer
```

This CWaveMix object array, WaveThings, has enough elements to create a CWaveMix object for each possible mixer channel. There is also an array of Booleans called TextChanged, to keep track of changes to text box contents. It is important to know when a text box has changed, so that a channel's wavefile can be loaded. The HasFocus variable participates in the validation of text box contents, as you will see later in the Text1_GotFocus and Text1_LostFocus subroutines.

18. Add a Form_Load subroutine to Form1, including the code shown below. During form load, all eight wavemix channel objects are created using New CWaveMix, and the channels are opened using CWaveMix's OpenChannel method.

```
Private Sub Form_Load()
    Dim i As Integer
    '
    ' Create WaveThings and open a channel for each
    '
    For i = 0 To MAX_WAVES - 1
        Set WaveThings(i) = New CWaveMix
        WaveThings(i).OpenChannel WMIX_OPENSINGLE
    Next
End Sub
```

19. Add a Form_Unload subroutine to Form1, with the code shown below. When the form unloads, all of the CWaveMix objects are deleted by setting the WaveThings array elements to Nothing. When VB assigns some value to a variable that currently contains a reference to an object, the number of references to that object is decremented. When an object's reference count becomes zero, the object is destroyed.

```
Private Sub Form_Unload(Cancel As Integer)
    Dim i As Integer
    '
    ' Release WaveThings
    '
    For i = 0 To MAX_WAVES - 1
        Set WaveThings(i) = Nothing
    Next
End Sub
```

20. Add a FileLoad_Click subroutine to Form1, and include the following code:

```
Private Sub FileLoad_Click()
    '
    ' We need to control potential error conditions here
    '
    On Error Resume Next
    CommonDialog1.Action = 1
    If (Err) Then
        '
        ' User Canceled open dialog ... we're outta here
        '
        Exit Sub
    End If
    '
    ' Try opening the wave file
    '
    WaveThings(HasFocus).OpenWave CommonDialog1.FileName, WMIX_FILE
    If (Err) Then
        '
        ' Ouch, something's wrong with the wave file ... display
```

Continued on next page

Continued from previous page

```
    ' error and bail
    '
    MsgBox Err.Description
    Exit Sub
End If
'
' Wave file ok, put filename in text box
'
Text1(HasFocus).Text = CommonDialog1.FileName
'
' Display right-most characters
'
Text1(HasFocus).SelStart = Len(Text1(HasFocus).Text)
'
' Move focus to next text box
'
SendKeys "{TAB}"
End Sub
```

FileLoad_Click is called when the File Load menu item is selected, and when the user double-clicks on a text box. First we let the user select a file, with the CommonDialog control. CommonDialog1's CancelError is set to True, so an error will be generated if the user clicks on the dialog's Cancel command button. On Error Resume Next allows us to test for this condition after the dialog returns.

After the user selects a file, CWaveMix's OpenWave method is used to load it. Notice that the HasFocus variable is used here to load the wavefile into the correct channel. As you will see later, the code in Form1 prevents the user from selecting File Load when a text box does not have the focus. When a text box does have the focus, its index number is stored in HasFocus. If the user selects an invalid file, OpenWave generates an error (just as CommonDialog does). The CWaveMix class returns descriptions of errors in the Err object's Description property. When an error occurs during the OpenWave method, FileLoad displays the error description using MsgBox. If there are no errors (a wavefile is successfully loaded into a CWaveMix object), there are a few things to do to finish up.

First, the wavefile's name is loaded into the text box given by HasFocus. Next, the text box's insertion point is set to the end of the wavefile name, by setting SelStart equal to the wavefile name's length. This ensures that the rightmost characters in the string will be displayed and the user can see the wavefile name—even when the wavefile name includes a long path. Finally, SendKeys is used to Tab to the next text box, making it easy to load a number of wavefiles.

21. Add the following subroutine to Form1. When the FileExit menu item is clicked, Form1 unloads itself.

```
Private Sub FileExit_Click()
    Unload Me
End Sub
```

22. Add a Text1_GotFocus subroutine to Form1, and include the code shown below. Text1_GotFocus enables the FileLoad menu item and assigns to HasFocus the index of the text box receiving the focus.

```
Private Sub Text1_GotFocus(index As Integer)
    FileLoad.Enabled = True
    HasFocus = index
End Sub
```

23. Add a Text1_Change subroutine to Form1, and include the code shown below. Text1_Change records the fact that the contents of a text box have changed. Later, when the text box loses focus, the new wavefile will be loaded if TextChanged is True.

```
Private Sub Text1_Change(index As Integer)
    TextChanged(index) = True
End Sub
```

24. Add a Text1_KeyPress subroutine to Form1, include the code shown below. When the user presses the (ENTER) key, it is discarded (by setting keyascii equal to zero) and a Tab is sent to move the focus to the next text box. This makes it easy for the user to enter a number of wavefile names.

```
Private Sub Text1_KeyPress(index As Integer, keyascii As Integer)
    '
    ' Make <ENTER> act like <TAB>
    '
    If (keyascii = 13) Then
        SendKeys "{TAB}"
        keyascii = 0
    End If
End Sub
```

25. Add a Text1_DblClick subroutine to Form1, and include the code shown below. This subroutine provides an easy way to bring up the File Load dialog box.

```
Private Sub Text1_DblClick(index As Integer)
    FileLoad_Click
End Sub
```

26. Add a subroutine named Text1_LostFocus to Form1, and include the following code:

```
Private Sub Text1_LostFocus(index As Integer)
    '
    ' Leaving a textbox ... did the text change?
    '
    If (TextChanged(index)) Then
        '
        ' Yep, text changed ... try to open the wavefile
        '
```

Continued on next page

Continued from previous page

```
        On Error Resume Next
        If (Text 1 (index). Text <> "") Then
        WaveThings(index).OpenWave Text1(index).Text, WMIX_FILE
        End If
            If (Err) Then
            '
              ' Woops ... not a valid wave file
            '
            MsgBox Err.Description
            '
            ' Use <SHIFT><TAB> to move focus back to the
            ' textbox losing focus
            '
            SendKeys "+{TAB}"
        Else
            '
            ' Otherwise clear flag that indicates text has changed
            '
            TextChanged(index) = False
        End If
    End If
End Sub
```

If the text box losing focus hasn't changed, there isn't anything to do when it loses focus. However, when the text box has changed, the text box's Text property should contain a wavefile name. CWaveMix's OpenWave subroutine is then used to load the new wavefile. If the user selected an invalid file or entered an invalid file name, an error message is displayed, and SendKeys sends a (SHIFT)-(TAB) to return focus to the text box containing the erroneous file name. Once a useable file name is entered, the TextChanged element for the text box is set to False. This prevents unneeded reloading of wavefiles as the user Tabs among text boxes.

27. Add a Command1_Click event subroutine to Form1, and include the following code.

```
Private Sub Command1_Click()
    Dim i As Integer
    Dim f As Integer
    Dim c As Integer
    '
    ' Find highest numbered wave channel playable
    '
    c = -1
    For i = 0 To MAX_WAVES - 1
        If (WaveThings(i).IsPlayable) Then
            c = i
        End If
    Next
    If (c = -1) Then
        Exit Sub
    End If
    '
```

```
' Play all playable WaveThings
'
For i = 0 To c
    If (WaveThings(i).IsPlayable) Then
        '
        ' See if we want to clear the queue first or not
        '
        If (Check1.Value = 1) Then
            f = WMIX_CLEARQUEUE
        Else
            f = 0
        End If
        If (i   c) Then
            f = f Or WMIX_WAIT
        End If
        '
        ' Now queue/play the wave(s)
        '
        WaveThings(i).PlayWave f, 0
    End If
Next
End Sub
```

The first order of business in Command1_Click is to determine the highest-numbered channel that is going to be played. Bear in mind that the objective is to get all the selected wavefiles to play at the same time. Suppose each wavefile were simply queued for output (which starts output immediately on idle channels). It might happen that the user selects a very short wavefile followed by a very long wavefile. Then the short wavefile would start and finish playing before the longer wavefile was loaded. That's not the objective here. What we want is to get all the wavefiles to start playing simultaneously. WAVEMIX has a flag called WMIX_WAIT that is used for this, so the wave is queued but not started. To start a group of wavefiles playing all at the same time, you set the WMIX_WAIT flag for all files but the last one you're going to queue. When you queue a wavefile without the WMIX_WAIT flag set, all channels containing queued waves with WMIX_WAIT set are started.

28. Add a Command1_GotFocus event procedure to Form1, and include the code shown below. This subroutine disables the File Load menu item when the Play command button gets the focus. Later, when focus returns to a text box, the File Load menu item is re-enabled so that the user can select a file for the text box.

```
Private Sub Command1_GotFocus()
    FileLoad.Enabled = False
End Sub
```

How It Works

Three distinct activities take place in this project: initialization, wavefile selection, and wavefile playing. During Form_Load, each possible CWaveMix object is created, and its OpenChannel method is used to open a wave-mixer channel.

File selection presents a few problems. First, we want to make it as easy as possible for the user to select a group of wavefiles to play. By using the Text1_KeyPress routine to intercept keyboard characters, we can advance the focus to the next text box when the user presses Enter. Also, since the user will be using the File Load dialog to select files, the user's hand will be on the mouse after a file is selected for a text box. So having Text1's Double_Click event procedure pop up the File Load dialog facilitates loading several wavefiles without repeatedly moving the mouse pointer up to the menu bar. Nor is it necessary to use a keyboard accelerator, which would be inconvenient since the mouse is available after selecting from the File Load dialog.

When the focus shifts from one text box to the next, it's time to determine whether or not to load a wavefile. If the text box's contents have changed, the corresponding element in the TextChanged array will be True. Then OpenWave attempts to open the wavefile. If an error occurs, focus is returned to the text box, using SendKeys to send a (SHIFT)-(TAB) to Form1 so that the user can try again. Clearing a text box causes the call to OpenWave, as does any change to the text box's contents. Sending an empty string to OpenWave, on the other hand, does not cause an error, but simply frees a previously loaded wavefile. So, if the user has selected an unuseable (or nonexistent) file and then decides to abandon loading a wavefile for the currently selected text box, clearing the contents of the text box allows focus to move to another control.

The point of this exercise is, of course, to play a wavefile. When the user clicks on the Play button, CWaveMix's PlayWave method is used to queue all of the files for output. PlayWave has a number of flags for controlling the playing of the wavefile. In this project, the WMIX_CLEARQUEUE and WMIX_WAIT flags are used. WMIX_CLEARQUEUE aborts a play that is in progress on a channel. WMIX_WAIT is used to queue a number of channels without having any of them actually start playing. Inside Command1_Click's event procedure, all but one of the wavefiles are queued using WMIX_WAIT. Then the last wavefile is queued without the WMIX_WAIT flag, and all the wavefiles start playing simultaneously.

Comments

In addition to providing a useful class, CWaveMix, this How-To demonstrates a few user-friendly interface techniques. Entry of data into multiple text boxes is simplified by automatically moving the focus from one control to the next, and by providing a fast way to bring up the File Load dialog box for each text box. Also, by validating the contents of each text box when it loses focus, the user gets immediate feedback about errors, making it easier to understand why they occur and how to fix them.

4.6 How do I...
Display a Wavefile?

COMPLEXITY: ADVANCED
COMPATIBILITY: VB4 ONLY

Problem

I'd like to write a wavefile editor so that I can cut and paste sections of wavefiles, add special effects such as echo, change formats, and modify a wavefile's volume. In order to do all this, I need some way to display the wavefile. How can I do this using Visual Basic?

Technique

There are two parts to this problem: First, you need to be able to read wavefile data. Second, you need to understand the various wavefile formats and plot wavefile data on a form or control.

Windows stores wavedata in RIFF files (Resource Interchange Format File), and all Windows wavefiles are actually RIFF files. How-To 4.1 presented the fundamental techniques for reading a wavefile, and introduced some basic class modules for building a wavefile viewer. The CMMChunkInfo class is used to encapsulate data contained in a chunk (the fundamental RIFF data structure). Also introduced in How-To 4.1 was the CMmioFile class, which encapsulates the Windows API calls required to use RIFF files, thus facilitating reading of RIFF files. In this How-To, the CMmioFile class will be extended somewhat to provide additional functionality for displaying a wavefile (see Figure 4-6-1). And a new class module, CWaveFile, will be developed as a subclass of CMmioFile. You will see how building one class on top of another (subclassing) is a powerful way to use class modules.

The wavedata itself is fairly simple. It is usually produced by *sampling* the output of an analog-to-digital converter at some frequency. Common frequencies are 11.025,

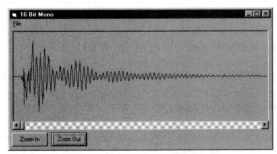

Figure 4-6-1 Displaying a wavefile

22.05, and 44.1 kHz. Each sample will use 1, 2, or 4 bytes; the number of bytes depends on the resolution of the converter (8 or 16 bits) and whether the recording is being done in stereo or mono. Figure 4-6-2 shows the data format in a wavefile for each of the four cases (8- or 16-bit, mono or stereo).

BYTE 0	BYTE 1	BYTE 2	BYTE 3
Sample 1	Sample 2	Sample 3	Sample 4
Channel 0	Channel 0	Channel 0	Channel 0

8-BIT MONO

BYTE 0	BYTE 1	BYTE 2	BYTE 3
Sample 1	Sample 1	Sample 2	Sample 2
Channel 0 (left)	Channel 1 (right)	Channel 0	Channel 1

8-BIT STEREO

BYTE 0	BYTE 1	BYTE 2	BYTE 3
Sample 1	Sample 1	Sample 2	Sample 2
Low-order byte	High-order byte	Low-order byte	High-order byte

16-BIT MONO

BYTE 0	BYTE 1	BYTE 2	BYTE 3
Sample 1	Sample 1	Sample 1	Sample 1
Channel 0 (low byte)	Channel 0 (high byte)	Channel 1 (low byte)	Channel 1 (high byte)

16-BIT STEREO

Figure 4-6-2 Wavedata formats

Steps

Open and run WAVEVIEW.VBP, and use the File Open menu item to load a file into the wavefile viewer. The Zoom In and Zoom Out command buttons are used to increase and decrease wavefile magnification. When a wavefile is first loaded, the entire wavefile is visible but has much of its detail compressed. Use Zoom In and Zoom Out to get a better view of the data. When you've zoomed all the way in, there will be one pixel per sample, and you won't be able to see all of the wavefile at once. Use the horizontal scroll bar to adjust the zoomed-in section.

1. Create a new project named WAVEVIEW.VBP. Use the File Add menu item to add the CMMCHUNK.CLS and CMMIOFIL.CLS files to WAVEVIEW.

2. Add the following method to CMMIOFIL.CLS. This ReadFile method takes two arguments: buffer and count. The buffer argument specifies where the data

should be stored, either in a string or in the memory location given by the Long value of buffer. The count argument specifies the number of bytes to read.

```
Public Function ReadFile(buffer As Variant, count As Long) As Long
    Dim s As String
    Dim l As Long
    '
    ' Bail if file not open
    '
    If (hmmio = 0) Then
        ReadFile = 0
        Exit Function
    End If
    '
    ' Use either a string or a long variable
    '
    Select Case VarType(buffer)
        Case vbString
            s = buffer
            ReadFile = mmioRead(hmmio, ByVal s, count)
            buffer = s
        Case vbLong
            l = buffer
            ReadFile = mmioRead(hmmio, ByVal l, count)
        Case Else
            Err.Raise _
                vbObjectError + 1, _
                "VBHT.CMmioFile", _
                "Invalid buffer argument passed to ReadFile."
    End Select
End Function
```

3. Use the Insert Class Module menu item to add a new class module named CWAVFIL.CLS. Name it CWaveFile, and add the following code:

```
Option Explicit

Private Declare Function GlobalAlloc Lib "KERNEL32" _
    (ByVal wFlags As Integer, ByVal dwBytes As Long) As Long
Private Declare Function GlobalFree Lib "KERNEL32" _
    (ByVal hMem As Long) As Integer
Private Declare Function GlobalLock Lib "KERNEL32" _
    (ByVal hMem As Long) As Long
Private Declare Function GlobalUnlock Lib "KERNEL32" _
    (ByVal hMem As Long) As Integer
Private Declare Function GlobalReAlloc Lib "KERNEL32" _
    (ByVal hMem As Long, ByVal dwBytes As Long, ⇒
        ByVal wFlags As Integer) As Long
Private Declare Sub CopyMemory Lib "KERNEL32" Alias "RtlMoveMemory" ⇒
    (dst As Any, src As Any, ByVal dwBytes As Long)

Private Const GMEM_MOVEABLE = &H2
Private Const GMEM_ZEROINIT = &H40
Private Const GMEM_SHARE = &H2000
```

4. Add the following declarations to CWaveFile:

```
Private m_filename    As String
Private m_errmsg      As String
Private m_oWave       As CMmioFile
Private m_format      As PCMWAVEFORMAT
Private m_hData       As Long
Private m_lpData      As Long
Private m_lpHeader    As Long
Private m_hHeader     As Long
Private m_dwLength    As Long
```

5. Add the following code as CWaveFile's Class_Initialize subroutine. Crucial variables are initialized so that the code will always be working from a known state.

```
''''''''''''''''''''''''''''''''''''''''''''''''''''''''''''''''
' Class initialization/deinitialization
''''''''''''''''''''''''''''''''''''''''''''''''''''''''''''''''
Private Sub Class_Initialize()
    m_hData = 0
    m_lpData = 0
    m_dwLength = 0
End Sub
```

6. Add the following code as CWaveFile's Class_Terminate subroutine. When a wavefile is loaded, memory is allocated and the variable m_hData gets the handle. So, when m_hData is not zero, the memory is unlocked and freed.

```
Private Sub Class_Terminate()
    If (m_hData  0) Then
        Call GlobalUnlock(m_hData)
        Call GlobalFree(m_hData)
    End If
End Sub
```

7. Add the following Property Get procedure to CWaveFile. The Length property returns the length in bytes of the data portion of the loaded wavefile.

```
'====================================================
' Properties
'====================================================
Public Property Get Length() As Long
    Length = m_dwLength
End Property
```

8. Add the following Property Let procedure to CWaveFile. Although this procedure is not used in this How-To, it will be useful later and is included here as the counterpart to Get Length. When wavefiles are loaded into an instance of CWaveFile, Windows, memory is used; this is required for making calls to Windows API functions such as mmioRead. Windows provides the function GlobalReAlloc so that the size of an allocated block can be changed.

```
Public Property Let Length(dwLen As Long)
    If (m_dwLength <> dwLen) Then
        m_hData = GlobalReAlloc(m_hData, dwLen, GMEM_MOVEABLE)
        m_lpData = GlobalLock(m_hData)
    End If
    m_dwLength = dwLen
End Property
```

9. Add the following Property Get procedure to CWaveFile. It is often necessary to have the address of the wavefile's data so that it can be passed to other API functions. The Get Data property procedure returns a pointer to CWaveFile's buffer.

```
Public Property Get Data() As Long
    Data = m_lpData
End Property
```

10. Add the following Property Get procedure to CWaveFile. The Channels property tells you whether a wavefile has one or two channels.

```
Public Property Get Channels() As Integer
    Channels = m_format.wf.nChannels
End Property
```

11. Add the following Property Get procedure to CWaveFile. An important piece of information stored in a wavefile's fmt chunk is the sample rate for the wavefile. SamplesPerSecond returns the samples per second.

```
Public Property Get SamplesPerSecond() As Integer
    SamplesPerSecond = m_format.wf.nSamplesPerSec
End Property
```

12. Add the following Property Get procedure to CWaveFile. Another important piece of information stored in the fmt chunk is the number of bits per sample. This will be 8 or 16 for virtually all sound cards you are likely to encounter.

```
Public Property Get BitsPerSample() As Integer
    BitsPerSample = m_format.wBitsPerSample
End Property
```

13. Add the following Property Get procedure to CWaveFile. When a file is loaded by an instance of CWaveFile, the file name is saved in m_filename. Filename provides a way to retrieve a wavefile's name.

```
Public Property Get Filename() As String
    Filename = m_filename
End Property
```

14. Add the following Property Let procedure to CWaveFile. When a filename is set, CWaveFile's WaveLoad method is used to locate and load the wavefile format information and data.

```
Public Property Let Filename(fname As String)
    '
    ' Survive any errors that might occur in WaveLoad
    '
    On Error Resume Next
    m_filename = fname
    If (Me.WaveLoad(fname) = False) Then
        '
        ' Whoops ... not good, re-raise error for caller
        '
        Err.Raise Err.Number
    End If
End Property
```

15. Add the following Property Get procedure to CWaveFile. Descriptive error messages are saved in m_errmsg whenever an error occurs. The user of a CWaveFile object can retrieve the last error message by getting the ErrorMsg property.

```
Public Property Get ErrorMsg() As String
    ErrorMsg = m_errmsg
End Property
```

16. Add the following method to CWaveFile.

WaveLoad is where the fun really starts. The first thing that happens is creation of an instance of CMmiofile. CWaveFile is a special type of CMmioFile and inherits functionality from CMmioFile by embedding an instance of it. The new instance of CMmioFile is put to good use immediately when its OpenFile method opens the file given by the Filename argument.

Wavefiles have a WAVE chunk, which contains at least an fmt chunk and a data chunk. CMmioFile's Descend method is used to search for and descend into first the WAVE chunk and then the fmt chunk. Once the fmt chunk is located, the header information is read into a temporary buffer and then copied to the m_format variable for future use. (Having to allocate a temporary buffer as a string, read the data into the string, and then copy the data to the intended variable is one of those annoying tasks you have to do to work with a language that doesn't support pointers.) Once the fmt chunk has been located and read, it's time to find the actual wavedata. A wavefile may have one or more chunks between the fmt chunk and the data chunk, so a Do Loop is used to scan through the chunks until the data chunk is located. Once the data chunk is located, it's a simple matter to allocate a buffer using GlobalAlloc and read the data into it using CWaveFile's Read method.

```
'====================================================
' Methods
'====================================================
Private Function WaveLoad(Filename As String) As Boolean
    Dim parent      As New CMMChunkInfo
    Dim subchunk    As New CMMChunkInfo
    Dim wRtn        As Integer
```

438

```
Dim dwRtn          As Long
Dim buffer         As String

Set m_oWave = New CMmioFile
'
' Bail on errors
'
On Error GoTo ErrorExit
'
' Open wave file
'
m_oWave.OpenFile Filename, MMIO_READ
If Err Then
    Err.Raise Err, Err.Source, Err.Description
End If
'
' Look for RIFF(WAVE)
'
parent.fccType = "WAVE"
wRtn = m_oWave.Descend(parent, MMIO_FINDRIFF)
'
' Find wave m_format chunk
'
subchunk.ID = "fmt "
wRtn = m_oWave.Descend(subchunk, MMIO_FINDCHUNK, parent)
'
' Read m_format from chunk
'
buffer = String(Len(m_format), 0)
wRtn = m_oWave.ReadFile(buffer, Len(buffer))
CopyMemory m_format, ByVal buffer, Len(buffer)
If (m_format.wf.wFormatTag   WAVE_FORMAT_PCM) Then
    Err.Raise 2, _
                "MMIOTEST.CWaveFile", _
                "Wave file is not PCM"
End If
'
' Move up and out of m_format chunk
'
If (m_oWave.Ascend(subchunk) = False) Then
    Err.Raise 3, _
                "MMIOTEST.CWaveFile", _
                "Could not Ascend from Format Chunk"
End If
'
' Find data chunk
'
Do
    subchunk.ID = "data"
    If (m_oWave.Descend(subchunk, MMIO_FINDCHUNK, parent) = False) Then
        Err.Raise 4, _
                    "MMIOTEST.CWaveFile", _
                    "Could not find Data Chunk"
    End If
    If (subchunk.ID = "data") Then
```

Continued on next page

439

Continued from previous page

```
            Exit Do
        Else
            '
            ' Move up and out of format chunk
            '
            If (m_oWave.Ascend(subchunk) = False) Then
                Err.Raise 3, _
                    "MMIOTEST.CWaveFile", _
                    "Could not Ascend from Chunk"
            End If
        End If
    Loop
    '
    ' Check to see that there is really data in the chunk
    '
    If (subchunk.size = O&) Then
        Err.Raise 5, _
                    "MMIOTEST.CWaveFile", _
                    "Wave file has no wave data"
    End If
    m_dwLength = subchunk.size
    '
    ' Allocate memory for wave data
    '
    m_hData = GlobalAlloc(GMEM_MOVEABLE Or GMEM_SHARE, subchunk.size)
    If (m_hData = 0) Then
        Err.Raise 6, _
                    "MMIOTEST.CWaveFile", _
                    "GlobalAlloc failed"
    End If
    m_lpData = GlobalLock(m_hData)
    If (m_lpData = 0) Then
        Err.Raise 7, _
                    "MMIOTEST.CWaveFile", _
                    "GlobalLock failed"
    End If
    '
    ' Read the waveform data subchunk.
    '
    dwRtn = m_oWave.ReadFile(m_lpData, subchunk.size)
    If (dwRtn <> subchunk.size) Then
        wRtn = GlobalUnlock(m_hData)
        Err.Raise 8, _
                    "MMIOTEST.CWaveFile", _
                    "Could not read file"
    End If
    wRtn = GlobalUnlock(m_hData)

NormalExit:
    WaveLoad = True
    m_errmsg = ""
    Exit Function
ErrorExit:
    WaveLoad = False
    m_errmsg = Err.Description
```

440

```
    Err.Raise Err.Number
End Function
```

17. Use the Insert Class Module menu item to add a new class module named CWaveFileDisplay to WAVEVIEW. Add the following code to CWaveFileDisplay.

```
Option Explicit
'
' property variables
'
Private m_cWave        As CWaveFile
Private m_scale        As Integer
Private m_oCanvas      As Control
Private m_zoom         As Integer
Private m_offset       As Long
'
' internal variables
'
Private m_fWaveSet     As Boolean
Private m_fCanvasSet   As Boolean

Private Declare Sub CopyMemory Lib "KERNEL32" Alias "RtlMoveMemory" ⇒
   (dst As Any, src As Any, ByVal dwBytes As Long)
```

18. Add the following Property Get procedure to CWaveFileDisplay. The number of bytes per pixel depends on the canvas width, wavefile data length, and the zoom factor. In this code, the zoom factor (m_zoom) doubles the magnification each time m_zoom is incremented.

```
'=================================================
' Properties
'=================================================
Public Property Get BytesPerPixel() As Integer
   '
   ' Make sure we really belong in here
   '
   If (Not ValidContents) Then
      BytesPerPixel = 0
      Exit Property
   End If
   BytesPerPixel = (m_cWave.Length \ m_oCanvas.ScaleWidth) \ (2 ^ m_zoom)
   If (BytesPerPixel <= 0) Then
      BytesPerPixel = 1
   End If
End Property
```

19. Add the following Property Set procedure to CWaveFileDisplay. Canvas is used to specify the control that will be used for displaying a wavefile's data. Canvas must be set before any drawing can occur, and the flag m_fCanvasSet is used to indicate that Canvas has been set.

```
Public Property Set Canvas(aControl As Control)
    Set m_oCanvas = aControl
    m_fCanvasSet = True
End Property
```

20. Add the following Property Set procedure to CWaveFileDisplay. As with Canvas, the Wave code keeps track of whether a CWaveFile object has been assigned. Obviously, drawing would be difficult without a wavefile to display.

```
Public Property Set Wave(aWave As CWaveFile)
    Set m_cWave = aWave
    m_fWaveSet = True
End Property
```

21. Add the following Property Let procedure to CWaveFileDisplay. First, zoom is constrained to values greater than or equal to zero. Then zoom is further constrained so that the number of pixels per sample will never be less than one. Both of these constraints simplify the drawing code, but restrict the flexibility of the class.

```
Public Property Let Zoom(z As Integer)
    '
    ' Bail if we're not ready to use zoom
    '
    If (Not ValidContents()) Then
        Exit Property
    End If
    '
    ' We don't allow negative zooms!
    '
    If (z < 0) Then
        z = 0
    ElseIf ((m_cWave.Length \ m_oCanvas.ScaleWidth) \ (2 ^ z) > 0) Then
        m_zoom = z
    End If
End Property
```

22. Add the following Property Get procedure to CWaveFileDisplay. Having CWaveFileDisplay tracking the zoom makes it easier to use Zoom, since it helps to minimize the amount of information that the calling program needs to maintain.

```
Public Property Get Zoom() As Integer
    Zoom = m_zoom
End Property
```

23. Add the following Property Get procedure to CWaveFileDisplay. An application with zoom needs to also have a scroll bar to control what part of a wavefile's data is being displayed. Computing the correct range for a scroll bar is an appropriate part of the CWaveFileDisplay, since it depends on data and assumptions contained within the class.

```
Public Property Get ScrollRange() As Long
    Dim temp As Long
    '
    ' Got to have lots of valid variables before we
    ' can be in here!
    '
    If (Not ValidContents()) Then
        Exit Property
    End If

    temp = (m_cWave.Length / Me.BytesPerPixel) - m_oCanvas.ScaleWidth
    If (temp < 0) Then
        ScrollRange = 0
    Else
        ScrollRange = temp
    End If
End Property
```

24. Add the following Property Let procedure to CWaveFileDisplay. When a wavefile's display is zoomed in, we need to specify what part of the wavefile to display. Offset sets the number of wavefile bytes to skip before starting to draw the waveform.

```
Public Property Let Offset(o As Long)
    m_offset = o
End Property
```

25. Add the following Property Get procedure to CWaveFileDisplay.

```
Public Property Get Offset() As Long
    offset = m_offset
End Property
```

26. Add the following code as CWaveFileDisplay's Paint method. First, the ValidContents method checks to see if it is even possible to paint a waveform. Next, the four combinations of bits per sample and the number of channels are checked, and the appropriate paint routine is called.

```
'=================================================
' Methods
'=================================================
Public Sub Paint()
    '
    ' Can't paint if there's no wavefile or canvas!
    '
    If (Not ValidContents()) Then
        Exit Sub
    End If
    '
    ' 8 bit format?
    '
    If (m_cWave.BitsPerSample = 8) Then
```

Continued on next page

Continued from previous page

```
      '
      ' Is it one channel or two?
      '
      If (m_cWave.Channels = 1) Then
          DisplayMono8
      Else
          DisplayStereo8
      End If
   '
   ' How about 16 bit format?
   '
   ElseIf (m_cWave.BitsPerSample = 16) Then
      '
      ' Ok ... one channel or two?
      '
      If (m_cWave.Channels = 1) Then
          DisplayMono16
      Else
          DisplayStereo16
      End If
   Else
      MsgBox "Invalid format, only 8 and 16 bit stereo or mono PCM supported"
   End If
End Sub
```

27. Add the following Private subroutine to CWaveFileDisplay. A number of variables must be initialized before the drawing routine can really get rolling. First, we get the number of bytes in the wavefile's data chunk, as well as a pointer to the data itself. Next, wSamplesPerPixel is initialized with the return value from BytesPerPixel, and yScale is set so that the maximum sample value will plot at the top of the canvas. After setting the canvas's starting CurrentX and CurrentY values, the array b is dimensioned to hold all of the wavefile's data and CopyMemory is used to copy the data from memory that has been GlobalAlloc'd by m_cWave.

   With everything set up, drawing the waveform is easy. The variable x ranges from zero to the canvas's width. For each value of x, a wavefile sample is used to give the y coordinate for a line drawn from the current location. The variable wSamplesPerPixel skips the appropriate number of samples for the current zoom factor, and the variable m_offset takes the wavedata start position specified in a call to the Offset property procedure.

```
Private Sub DisplayMono8()
   Dim x                   As Integer
   Dim b()                 As Byte
   Dim dwLen               As Long
   Dim lpData              As Long
   Dim wSamplesPerPixel    As Integer
   Dim yScale              As Single
   '
   ' Get length of wavefile and address in memory
```

```
'
dwLen = m_cWave.Length
lpData = m_cWave.Data
'
' In 8 bit mono there is one byte per sample
'
wSamplesPerPixel = Me.BytesPerPixel
'
' Set yScale to number of twips per increment
'
yScale = m_oCanvas.ScaleHeight / (2 ^ 8)
'
' Set starting location for first line
'
m_oCanvas.CurrentX = 0
m_oCanvas.CurrentY = m_oCanvas.ScaleHeight / 2
'
' Get actual wave data
'
ReDim b(dwLen)
CopyMemory b(0), ByVal lpData, dwLen
'
' Plot data on canvas
'
For x = 0 To m_oCanvas.ScaleWidth - 1 Step 1
    m_oCanvas.Line -(x, b((x * wSamplesPerPixel) + m_offset) * yScale)
Next
End Sub
```

28. Add the following private subroutine to CWaveFileDisplay. This routine is similar to the one in step 27, except that it displays 8-bit stereo instead of 8-bit mono wavefiles. There are three major differences in displaying stereo instead of mono data. First, the number of bytes per sample is doubled. The computation of wSamplesPerPixel takes account of this by dividing BytesPerPixel by two. Also, since one waveform will be displayed on the top half of the canvas and the other on the bottom half, yScale is half of what it is when displaying mono data. And finally, there are two loops; one draws the upper waveform, and the other draws the bottom.

```
Private Sub DisplayStereo8()
    Dim x                 As Long
    Dim b()               As Byte
    Dim dwLen             As Long
    Dim lpData            As Long
    Dim wSamplesPerPixel  As Integer
    Dim yScale            As Single
    Dim i                 As Long
    '
    ' Get length of wavefile and address in memory
    '
    dwLen = m_cWave.Length
    lpData = m_cWave.Data
    '
```

Continued on next page

Continued from previous page

```
' There are two bytes per sample in 8 bit stereo
'
wSamplesPerPixel = Me.BytesPerPixel / 2
'
' Set scale so a full range value maps to half the
' canvas height
'
yScale = m_oCanvas.ScaleHeight / (2 ^ 9)
'
' Set position for first line
'
m_oCanvas.CurrentX = 0
m_oCanvas.CurrentY = m_oCanvas.ScaleHeight / 4
'
' Get wave data
'
ReDim b(dwLen)
CopyMemory  b(0), ByVal lpData, dwLen
'
' Draw left channel on top half of canvas
'
For x = 0 To m_oCanvas.ScaleWidth - 1 Step 1
    i = (x * 2 * wSamplesPerPixel) + (m_offset * 2)
    m_oCanvas.Line -(x, b(i) * yScale)
Next
'
' Get set for right channel
'
m_oCanvas.CurrentX = 0
m_oCanvas.CurrentY = m_oCanvas.ScaleHeight * 3 / 4
'
' Draw right channel on bottom half of canvas
'
For x = 0 To m_oCanvas.ScaleWidth - 1 Step 1
    i = (x * 2 * wSamplesPerPixel) + (m_offset * 2)
    m_oCanvas.Line -(x, b(i + 1) * yScale + m_oCanvas.ScaleHeight / 2)
Next
End Sub
```

29. Add the following private subroutine to CWaveFileDisplay. Displaying 16-bit
    mono wavefiles is a lot like displaying 8-bit mono files except for a couple of dif-
    ferences. Two bytes are used for each sample, so wSamplesPerPixel is half of what
    it would be for an 8-bit file. Also, since the range of values is 0 to 65536 instead
    of 0 to 255, the yScale variable must be computed appropriately.

```
Private Sub DisplayMono16()
    Dim x                   As Integer
    Dim b()                 As Integer
    Dim dwLen               As Long
    Dim lpData              As Long
    Dim wSamplesPerPixel    As Integer
    Dim yScale              As Single
    Dim i                   As Long
```

```
'
' Get length of wavefile and address in memory
'
dwLen = m_cWave.Length
lpData = m_cWave.Data
'
' Two bytes per sample
'
wSamplesPerPixel = Me.BytesPerPixel / 2
'
' Set scale for 0 - 65535
'
yScale = m_oCanvas.ScaleHeight / (2 ^ 16)
'
' Set start of first line
'
m_oCanvas.CurrentX = 0
m_oCanvas.CurrentY = m_oCanvas.ScaleHeight / 2
'
' Get wave data
'
ReDim b(dwLen)
CopyMemory b(0), ByVal lpData, dwLen
'
' Draw waveform on canvas
'
For x = 0 To m_oCanvas.ScaleWidth - 1 Step 1
    i = (x * wSamplesPerPixel) + (m_offset * 2)
    m_oCanvas.Line -(x, (b(i) + 2 ^ 15) * yScale)
Next
End Sub
```

30. Add the following private subroutine to CWaveFileDisplay. This subroutine is a lot like a combination of DisplayMono16 and DisplayStereo8. In fact, it would be possible to combine the routines, although a little extra housekeeping would be required.

```
Private Sub DisplayStereo16()
    Dim x                As Long
    Dim b()              As Integer
    Dim dwLen            As Long
    Dim lpData           As Long
    Dim wSamplesPerPixel As Integer
    Dim yScale           As Single
    Dim i                As Long
    '
    ' Get length of wavefile and address in memory
    '
    dwLen = m_cWave.Length
    lpData = m_cWave.Data
    '
    ' Four bytes per sample
    '
    wSamplesPerPixel = Me.BytesPerPixel / 4
```

Continued on next page

Continued from previous page

```
'
' Two channels with range 0 - 65535
'
yScale = m_oCanvas.ScaleHeight / (2 ^ 17)
'
' Set start position for left channel
'
m_oCanvas.CurrentX = 0
m_oCanvas.CurrentY = m_oCanvas.ScaleHeight / 4
'
' Get wavedata
'
ReDim b(dwLen)
CopyMemory b(0), ByVal lpData, dwLen
'
' Draw left channel
'
For x = 0 To m_oCanvas.ScaleWidth - 1 Step 1
    i = (x * 2 * wSamplesPerPixel) + (m_offset * 2)
    m_oCanvas.Line -(x, (b(i) + 2 ^ 15) * yScale)
Next
'
' Position for right channel
'
m_oCanvas.CurrentX = 0
m_oCanvas.CurrentY = m_oCanvas.ScaleHeight * 3 / 4
CopyMemory
End Sub
```

31. Add the following private function to CWaveFileDisplay., allowing it to draw when a valid wavefile exists and there is a canvas on which to draw. The variables m_fWaveSet and m_fCanvasSet are set by the appropriate Property routines.

```
Private Function ValidContents() As Boolean
    ValidContents = (m_fWaveSet And m_fCanvasSet)
End Function
```

32. Use the File Add menu item to add the class module CSCROLL.CLS from How-To 3.13. CSCROLL.CLS defines the CHugeScroll class, which gives us a handy way to use scroll bars that require values greater than 32767. (If you haven't looked at How-To 3.13 yet, you'll need to study it to understand how CHugeScroll works, but it isn't required for understanding this How-To.)

33. Select WAVEVIEW's Form1, and then add objects with properties and settings as shown in Table 4-6-1.

Table 4-6-1 Objects, properties, and settings for Form1

OBJECT	PROPERTY	SETTING
Form	Caption	"WaveView"
	Name	Form1
HScrollBar	Name	HScroll1

OBJECT	PROPERTY	SETTING
PictureBox	BackColor	&H00C0C0C0&
	ForeColor	&H00C00000&
	Name	Picture1
	ScaleMode	3 'Pixel
CommandButton	Caption	"Zoom In"
	Name	Command1
CommandButton	Caption	"Zoom Out"
	Name	Command2
CommonDialog	CancelError	-1 'True
	DefaultExt	"*.wav"
	DialogTitle	"Open Wave File"
	Filter	"Wave Files (*.wav)|*.wav|"
	Name	CommonDialog1

34. Add the following code to the General Declarations section of Form1. Substantial functionality can be added to a program with very little work, once you've collected the right set of class modules. The three object variables declared here do most of the work and don't require any additional variables or flags for tracking state or other information.

```
Option Explicit

Dim WaveFile     As New CWaveFile
Dim Display      As New CWaveFileDisplay
Dim HScroll      As New CHugeScroll
```

35. Add the following code as the FileOpen menu item's Click event procedure. After the user selects a wavefile, WaveFile's Filename property is set to CommonDialog1's Filename property. This initiates a number of actions involving both CWaveFile and its contained CMmioFile object. If a valid wavefile has been selected, the WaveFile object is assigned to Display's Wave property. Information about the wavefile is displayed in the form's caption, and Picture1.Refresh causes a Paint event to be fired for Picture1. When Picture1 recieves the Paint event, it invokes Display's Paint method and the wavefile is displayed.

```
Private Sub FileOpen_Click()
    Dim s As String
    '
    ' Catch press of cancel button
    '
    On Error Resume Next
    CommonDialog1.Action = 1
    If (Err) Then
        '
```

Continued on next page

Continued from previous page

```
        ' Canceled ... we're outta here
        '
        Exit Sub
    End If
    '
    ' Wavefile name ... setting property loads file
    '
    WaveFile.Filename = CommonDialog1.Filename
    If (Err) Then
        '
        ' Bad juju ... wavefile load failed
        '
        MsgBox WaveFile.ErrorMsg
    End If
    '
    ' Give Display thing a copy of the wavefile
    '
    Set Display.Wave = WaveFile
    '
    ' Put something like '8 Bit Stereo' in the title bar
    '
    s = WaveFile.BitsPerSample & " Bit "
    If (WaveFile.Channels = 1) Then
        s = s + "Mono"
    Else
        s = s + "Stereo"
    End If
    Me.Caption = s
    '
    ' Reset zoom and offset
    '
    Display.Zoom = 0
    Display.offset = 0
    HScroll.Max = Display.ScrollRange
    HScroll.Value = 0
    '
    ' Redisplay
    '
    Picture1.Refresh
End Sub
```

36. Add the following code as Form1's Form_Load event procedure. Display's Canvas property is set to Picture1, and the CHugeScroll object HScroll is initialized.

```
Private Sub Form_Load()
    '
    ' Set display's canvas
    '
    Set Display.Canvas = Picture1
    '
    ' Encapsulate HScroll1 in a CHugeScroll object
    '
    Set HScroll.Client = HScroll1
End Sub
```

37. Add the following code as Form1's Form_Resize event procedure. If the form is not minimized, this routine arranges all of the controls on the form. The Zoom command buttons are placed in the lower-left corner of the form. The Picture control is sized so that it occupies most of the rest of the form, except for space required for the horizontal scroll bar.

```
Private Sub Form_Resize()
    Dim perx As Single
    Dim pery As Single
    '
    ' Bail if we're minimized
    '
    If (Me.WindowState = 1) Then
        Exit Sub
    End If
    '
    ' Get scale factors handy place (and with short names!)
    '
    perx = Screen.TwipsPerPixelX
        pery = Screen.TwipsPerPixelY
        '
        ' Move command buttons to bottom of form
        '
        Command1.top = Form1.ScaleHeight - Command1.Height - (5 * pery)
        Command2.top = Command1.top
        '
        ' Fill most of the rest of the form with Picture1
        '
        Picture1.top = 5 * pery
        Picture1.left = 5 * perx
        Picture1.Height = Command1.top - HScroll1.Height - (10 * pery)
        Picture1.Width = Form1.ScaleWidth - (10 * perx)
        '
        ' But leave space for HScroll1
        '
        HScroll1.top = Picture1.top + Picture1.Height - pery
        HScroll1.left = Picture1.left
        HScroll1.Width = Picture1.Width
    HScroll.LargeChange = (Picture1.ScaleWidth * 4) \ 5
    Display.offset = 0
    HScroll.Value = 0
    Picture1.Refresh
End Sub
```

38. Add the following code as HScroll1's HScroll_Change event procedure. The CHugeScroll object, HScroll, causes Change events to fire under certain circumstances. Fortunately, it exposes the property Recursing, which will be True whenever HScroll1's Change event is fired because of something HScroll is doing. When Recursing is True, we simply skip the Change event. When the user has caused the Change event, HScroll's Change method is called, and the resulting value (HScroll.Value) is used to set the display offset. Finally Picture1's Refresh method is used to cause the wavefile to be redrawn.

```
Private Sub HScroll1_Change()
    '
    ' Avoid recursive calls caused by HScroll
    '
    If (HScroll.Recursing) Then
        Exit Sub
    End If
    '
    ' Let the CHugeScroll know what's happened
    '
    HScroll.Change
    '
    ' Change offset into wave file
    '
    Display.offset = HScroll.Value
    '
    ' Redisplay
    '
    Picture1.Refresh
End Sub
```

39. Add the following code as Command1's Click event procedure. First, the Display object's Zoom property is incremented. Then HScroll's Max property is set to reflect the new ScrollRange. Unfortunately, setting HScroll's Max property does not cause the Value property to be recomputed as it should, and so a redundant assignment of the current value forces the recomputation.

```
Private Sub Command1_Click()
    '
    ' Zoom In ... increment zoom level
    '
    Display.Zoom = Display.Zoom + 1
    '
    ' Set scrollbar range
    '
    HScroll.Max = Display.ScrollRange
    '
    ' Compensate for the fact that setting max does
    ' not recompute Value
    '
    HScroll.Value = HScroll.Value
    '
    ' Set display offset
    '
    Display.offset = HScroll.Value
    '
    ' Update display
    '
    Picture1.Refresh
End Sub
```

40. Add the following code as Command2's Click event procedure. The only difference between this routine and that in Command1_Click (step 39) is that zoom is decremented instead of incremented.

```
Private Sub Command2_Click()
    '
    ' Zoom out ... decrement zoom level
    '
    Display.Zoom = Display.Zoom - 1
    '
    ' Set scrollbar range
    '
    HScroll.Max = Display.ScrollRange
    '
    ' Compensate for fact that setting max doesn't
    ' recompute the scrollbar's value
    '
    HScroll.Value = HScroll.Value
    '
    ' Set offset and redisplay
    '
    Display.offset = HScroll.Value
    Picture1.Refresh
End Sub
```

41. Add the following code as Picture1's Paint event procedure. This simply invokes Display's Paint method.

```
Private Sub Picture1_Paint()
    Display.Paint
End Sub
```

42. Add the following code as the FileExit menu item's Click event procedure:

```
Private Sub FileExit_Click()
    End
End Sub
```

How It Works

The five class modules used in this project build a wavefile viewer that is deceptively simple if you only look at the code in Form1. Behind the scenes in the various class modules, there's a lot of action—beginning when you assign a filename to WaveFile, an instance of the CWaveFile class. WaveFile almost immediately turns part of the work over to its contained object, which is a member of CMmioFile where the file is opened. Then WaveFile finds the wavefile data and reads it (again using functionality contained in CMmioFile) into a buffer allocated using the Windows API function GlobalAlloc.

Later, when Picture1's Paint event procedure is fired, the Display's Paint method is invoked. Display is an instance of CWaveFileDisplay, a class that can draw a waveform when it's given a CWaveFile object and something on which to draw. Inside CWaveFileDisplay's Paint method, CWaveFile's properties are examined to determine which wavefile-plotting routine to use, and the approriate routine is used to draw the waveform on Picture1. CWaveFileDisplay also takes care of a couple of typical tasks: zooming in and out, and displaying a selected part of a zoomed-in wavefile.

Comments

This How-To makes significant use of class modules. In fact, the code in any one of the five class modules employed here is quite a bit more substantial than the code required in Form1 to display a wavefile. Once you've built a suitable collection of classes, it becomes easy to add a lot of handy, trick features to your programs. For instance, you could easily modify this How-To to have a small PictureBox in the lower-right of the form, always displaying a miniature version of the entire waveform. Then, by adding SelectionStart and SelectionEnd properties to CWaveFileDisplay, you could highlight in the miniature picture the part of the wavefile currently displayed in Picture1. Then you'd be all set to add a few mouse-related methods to CWaveFileDisplay. Next thing you know you'll be cutting and pasting wavefilesections!

4.7 How do I...
Play Wavefiles Using Low-Level API Calls?

COMPLEXITY: INTERMEDIATE
COMPATIBILITY: VB4 ONLY

Problem

The high-level API functions for playing wavefiles, such as sndPlaySound, work well enough when I just want to play an existing wavefile and don't need to know when it has finished. But sndPlaySound doesn't always give me the control I need, or let me know when a wavefile has finished playing. The *Multimedia Programmer's Guide* describes low-level API functions such as waveOutPlay, which provide notification when a file has finished playing. Also, since the wavefile must be loaded into memory before it is played, it will be possible to modify the wavefile data (to add echo, for instance). How can I play wavefiles using the Windows low-level API functions?

Technique

Accomplishing these elements is going to be a lot easier than you might expect. The previous How-To's in this chapter have developed powerful class modules, providing almost everything you need to play wavefiles. CMMChunkInfo, CMmioFile, and CWaveFile take care of opening wavefiles and loading the waveform data. All that remains is to add a means to play the wavefile. This How-To develops a new class named CWaveOut that can play the wave data contained in an instance of CWaveFile.

Steps

Open and run PLAYLOW.VBP, and you will see the form shown in Figure 4-7-1. Use the File Open menu item to select a wavefile to play. Then click on the Play button,

Figure 4-7-1 The PlayLow project

and the wavefile will be played. Meanwhile, the Play button will be disabled, and re-enabled when the play is completed.

1. Create a new project named PLAYLOW.VBP, and use the File Add menu item to add the classes and modules shown in Table 4-7-1. The class modules (files with a CLS extension) can be found in the VBHT\CLASSES directory, and WINMM32.BAS can be found in VBHT\MODULES.

Table 4-7-1 Classes and modules for Form1

FILE NAME	CLASS	PURPOSE
CMMCHUNK.CLS	CMMChunkInfo	Support for CMmioFile
CMMIOFIL.CLS	CMmioFile	Multimedia file access
CWAVEFIL.CLS	CWaveFile	Wavefile access
WINMM32.BAS	None	API declarations

2. Use the Insert Class Module menu item to create a new class module. Set the new module's Name property to CWaveOut.

3. Add the following code to CWaveOut. After the usual collection of Windows API calls required to handle memory allocation, a number of private variables are declared.

```
Option Explicit

Private Declare Function GlobalAlloc Lib "KERNEL32" _
    (ByVal wFlags As Integer, ByVal dwBytes As Long) As Long
Private Declare Function GlobalFree Lib "KERNEL32" _
    (ByVal hMem As Long) As Integer
Private Declare Function GlobalLock Lib "KERNEL32" _
    (ByVal hMem As Long) As Long
Private Declare Function GlobalUnlock Lib "KERNEL32" _
    (ByVal hMem As Long) As Integer
Private Declare Function GlobalReAlloc Lib "KERNEL32" _
```

Continued on next page

Continued from previous page

```
   (ByVal hMem As Long, ByVal dwBytes As Long, ByVal wFlags ⇒
         As Integer) As Long
Private Declare Sub CopyMemory Lib "KERNEL32" Alias "RtlMoveMemory" ⇒
      (dst As Any, src As Any, ByVal dwBytes As Long)


Private Const GMEM_MOVEABLE = &H2
Private Const GMEM_ZEROINIT = &H40
Private Const GMEM_SHARE = &H2000


Private m_filename    As String
Private m_errmsg      As String
Private m_oWave       As CMmioFile
Private m_format      As PCMWAVEFORMAT
Private m_hData       As Long
Private m_lpData      As Long
Private m_lpHeader    As Long
Private m_hHeader     As Long
Private m_dwLength    As Long
```

4. Add the following Property Set function to CWaveOut. CWaveOut objects can play the wavedata contained in a CWaveFile object. A copy of the passed CWaveFile object, aWaveFile, is stored in m_wave. Later calls to WaveOpen, WavePlay, and so on, will use the stored object so that it does not need to be passed as an argument. Wavefiles have an fmt chunk, which describes the format of the wavefile's data. This information is copied into the Windows data structure m_wave, an instance of PCMWAVEFORMAT, so that it can easily be passed to Windows API functions.

```
Public Property Set Wavefile(aWaveFile As CWaveFile)
   '
   ' Keep a reference to the CWaveFile object passed in
   '
   Set m_wave = aWaveFile
   '
   ' Set the Windows data structure PCMWAVEFORMAT using
   ' the values contained in the wavefile
   '
   m_format.wf.wFormatTag = m_wave.FormatTag
   m_format.wf.nChannels = m_wave.Channels
   m_format.wf.nSamplesPerSec = m_wave.SamplesPerSecond
   m_format.wf.nAvgBytesPerSec = m_wave.AvgBytesPerSecond
   m_format.wf.nBlockAlign = m_wave.BlockAlign
   m_format.wBitsPerSample = m_wave.BitsPerSample
End Property
```

5. Add the following code as CWaveOut's WaveOpen method. WaveOpen uses the Windows API function waveOutOpen to open a wave output device for playing the wavefile contained by m_wave. waveOutOpen requires quite a few parameters. The first parameter, m_hWaveOut, receives a handle to the opened wave output device if the call to waveOutOpen succeeds. The second parameter, WAVE_MAPPER, tells Windows to select the first available wave output device

that is capable of playing a wavefile in the format specified by the third parameter, m_format.wf. The fourth and sixth parameters tell Windows to send messages when wave output-related events occur, such as wavefile play completion. The sixth parameter, CALLBACK_WINDOW, is what tells Windows to send messages, and the fourth parameter, hWndNotify, is the window to which the messages will be sent. The fifth parameter is zero because it is used only when the sixth parameter is CALLBACK_FUNCTION.

```
Public Function WaveOpen(hWndNotify As Integer) As Boolean
    Dim wRtn As Integer

    On Error GoTo ErrorExit
    '
    ' Open the default wave output device for the data we have
    '
    wRtn = waveOutOpen(m_hWaveOut, WAVE_MAPPER, m_format.wf, ⇒
        hWndNotify, 0&, CALLBACK_WINDOW)
    If (wRtn <> 0) Then
        Err.Raise 8, _
                "MMIOTEST.CWaveOut", _
                "Could not open wave device, error:" & Str(wRtn)
    End If
NormalExit:
    m_errmsg = ""
    WaveOpen = True
    Exit Function
ErrorExit:
    m_errmsg = Err.Description
    WaveOpen = False
End Function
```

6. Add the following code as CWaveOut's WavePlay method. Before you can play a wavefile using the Windows API function waveOutWrite, you must first initialize and "prepare" a *waveheader data structure*. The waveheader, m_waveheader, specifies the wavefile data's memory address and the length of the wavedata. Windows requires that waveheaders be allocated using GlobalAlloc with the GMEM_MOVEABLE and GMEM_SHARE flags set. The GMEM_MOVEABLE flag tells Windows that it is OK to move a block of memory as required to optimize memory usage; and the GMEM_SHARE flag allows other processes to access the memory. The Windows API function waveOutPrepareHeader performs the actual preparation of a correctly initialized waveheader. After all the preparation, playing a wavefile is really easy. All you do is call waveOutWrite, passing the wave output device's handle, the address of your waveheader, and the length of the waveheader data structure.

```
Public Function WavePlay() As Boolean
    Dim wRtn As Integer
    '
    ' Get the buffer address and size into waveheader
    '
```

Continued on next page

Continued from previous page

```
    m_waveHeader.lpData = m_wave.Data
    m_waveHeader.dwBufferLength = m_wave.Length
    '
    ' Now make a GlobalAlloced copy of the waveheader
    '
    m_hWaveHeader = GlobalAlloc(GMEM_MOVEABLE Or GMEM_SHARE, ⇒
        Len(m_waveHeader))
    m_lpWaveHeader = GlobalLock(m_hWaveHeader)
    CopyMemory ByVal m_lpWaveHeader, m_waveHeader, Len(m_waveHeader)
    '
    ' Prepare the header for playing
    '
    wRtn = waveOutPrepareHeader(m_hWaveOut, ByVal m_lpWaveHeader, ⇒
        Len(m_waveHeader))
    If (wRtn <> 0) Then
        Err.Raise 10, _
                 "MMIOTEST.CWaveFile", _
                 "Could not prepare header, error: " & Str(wRtn)
    End If
    wRtn = waveOutWrite(m_hWaveOut, ByVal m_lpWaveHeader, ⇒
        Len(m_waveHeader))
    If (wRtn <> 0) Then
        Err.Raise 11, _
                 "MMIOTEST.CWaveFile", _
                 "Could not write to wave device, error:" & Str(wRtn)
    End If
NormalExit:
    m_errmsg = ""
    WavePlay = True
    Exit Function
ErrorExit:
    m_errmsg = Err.Description
    WavePlay = False
End Function
```

7. Add the following code as CWaveOut's WaveClose method, which resets the wave output device (terminating any play in progress), frees resources, and closes the wave output device.

```
Public Sub WaveClose()
    Dim wRtn As Integer
    '
    ' Reset wave out device
    '
    wRtn = waveOutReset(m_hWaveOut)
    '
    ' Unprepare header and free memory
    '
    wRtn = waveOutUnprepareHeader(m_hWaveOut, m_lpWaveHeader, ⇒
        Len(m_waveHeader))
    wRtn = GlobalUnlock(m_hWaveHeader)
    wRtn = GlobalFree(m_hWaveHeader)
    '
    ' Close wave out device
```

```
    '
    wRtn = waveOutClose(m_hWaveOut)
End Sub
```

8. Select Form1, and add objects with properties and settings as shown in Table 4-7-2. You don't need to be too particular about the arrangement of the controls, since they are arranged during the Form_Resize event.

Table 4-7-2 Object, properties, and settings for Form1

OBJECT	PROPERTY	SETTING
Form	BackColor	&H00C0C0C0&
	Caption	"PlayLow"
	FillStyle	0 'Solid
	Name	Form1
MsgHook	Name	MsgHook1
CommandButton	Caption	"Play"
	Name	Command1
CommonDialog	CancelError	-1 'True
	DefaultExt	"wav"
	DialogTitle	"Open Wave File"
	Filter	"Waves (*.wav)|*.wav|"
	Name	CommonDialog1
Label	Alignment	2 'Center
	BackStyle	0 'Transparent
	Caption	"Low-Level Wavefile Player"
	FontName	"Arial"
	FontSize	24
	ForeColor	&H000000FF&
	Index	0
	Name	Label1
Label	Alignment	2 'Center
	BackColor	&H00000080&
	BackStyle	0 'Transparent
	Caption	"Low-Level Wavefile Player"
	FontName	"Arial"
	FontSize	24
	ForeColor	&H00808080&
	Index	1
	Name	Label1

9. Use the Menu Editor to add the menu shown in Table 4-7-3 to Form1.

Table 4-7-3 Form1's menu

MENU NAME	CAPTION
FileMenu	"&File"
...FileOpen	"&Open..."
...FileSep1	"-"
...FileExit	"E&xit"

10. Add the following code to the General declarations section of Form1:

```
Option Explicit
'
' Objects directly used in this form
'
Dim Wavefile As New CWaveFile
Dim waveout  As New CWaveOut
```

11. Add the following code as Form1's Load event procedure. Visual Basic doesn't allow you to directly intercept Windows messages. Instead, it decides which Windows messages you need and calls event procedures as the messages arrive. For instance, when VB intercepts a WM_PAINT message, it calls the Paint event procedure belonging to the window to which WM_PAINT was sent. But sometimes, as in this case, you really need to intercept a Windows message that VB doesn't support. When a wavefile finishes playing, the Multimedia system can send a WOM_DONE message to your form. The MsgHook control allows interception of the message and reaction to it. To use the MsgHook control, you set only two properties: hWnd and Message. The hWnd parameter tells MsgHook which window you want to hook, and the array Message specifies which messages to intercept. In this project only one message, WOM_DONE, is intercepted, but in other projects you can intercept additional messages by setting more than one element of the Message array to True.

```
Private Sub Form_Load()
    '
    ' Initialize MsgHook control
    '
    MsgHook1.HwndHook = Me.hWnd
    '
    ' We're only interested in the Wave Output Message Done
    '
    MsgHook1.Message(WOM_DONE) = True
End Sub
```

12. Add the following code as Form1's Resize event procedure. This code arranges the command button and the two labels whenever Form1's Resize event procedure is called. When you have only a few controls to position and size, it's a simple matter to do it in code. With forms that have many controls, however, it's much easier to use a custom control, or the class module CStretch from How-To 2.9.

```
Private Sub Form_Resize()
    '
    ' Put play button near bottom center of form
    '
    Command1.top = Form1.ScaleHeight - (Command1.Height + 10 * ⇒
        Screen.TwipsPerPixelY)
    Command1.left = (Form1.ScaleWidth - Command1.Width) \ 2
    '
    ' Center first between top of button and top of form
    '
    Label1(0).top = (Command1.top - Label1(0).Height) \ 2
    Label1(0).left = (Form1.ScaleWidth - Label1(0).Width) \ 2
    '
    ' Offset second label (shadow) to create 3-d effect
    '
    Label1(1).top = Label1(0).top + 1 * Screen.TwipsPerPixelY
        Label1(1).left = Label1(0).left + 1 * Screen.TwipsPerPixelX
End Sub
```

13. Add the following code as the FileOpen menu item's Click event procedure. After the user selects a file, Wavefile's Filename property is set equal to CommonDialog1's Filename property. Setting a CWaveFile object's Filename property causes it to open the wavefile and load the file's wavedata into memory. Then the initialized CWaveFile object is assigned to waveout's Wavefile property.

```
Private Sub FileOpen_Click()
    '
    ' CommonDiaglog1's CancelError is True so an
    ' error will be generated if the user clicks on
    ' the dialog's Cancel button
    '
    On Error Resume Next
    CommonDialog1.action = 1
    If (Err) Then
        '
        ' User must have changed his mind ... outta here
        '
        Exit Sub
    End If
    '
    ' Got a file to use ... assign name to wavefile thing
    '
    Wavefile.Filename = CommonDialog1.Filename
    '
    ' Assign new wavefile to waveout's wavefile property
    '
    Set waveout.Wavefile = Wavefile
End Sub
```

14. Add the following code as Command1's Click event procedure. When Command1 is clicked, it's time to start playing the wavefile. First, however, Command1 is disabled, since attempting to play a wavefile while it is already being played will cause errors. Next, the wave output device is opened using

CWaveOut's WaveOpen method. The Form's hWnd is passed to WaveOpen, so that notification messages (such as WOM_DONE) will be sent to Form1. Finally, the wavefile play is started by calling the WavePlay method.

```
Private Sub Command1_Click()
    '
    ' Don't let the user try to play two files
    ' at the same time ... it won't work.
    '
    Command1.Enabled = False
    '
    ' Open the waveout device
    '
    waveout.WaveOpen Me.hWnd
    '
    ' Play the wavefile
    '
    waveout.WavePlay
End Sub
```

15. Add the following code as MsgHook1's Message event procedure. Windows (actually, the Multimedia subsystem in Windows) sends a WOM_DONE message when a wavefile finishes playing on a device opened using the CALLBACK_WINDOW flag. During Form_Load, MsgHook1 was set up to intercept WOM_DONE messages sent to Form1. When the message is sent, MsgHook1's Message event procedure is fired.

```
Private Sub MsgHook1_Message(ByVal msg As Long, ByVal wp As Long, ⇒
    ByVal lp As Long, result As Long)
    '
    ' Wavefile done playing ... enable command  button
    '
    Command1.Enabled = True
    '
    ' Close waveout device
    '
    waveout.WaveClose
End Sub
```

16. Add the following code as the FileExit menu item's Click event procedure.

```
Private Sub FileExit_Click()
    End
End Sub
```

How It Works

During Form_Load, a MsgHook control is initialized, so that MsgHook_Message will be called whenever a WOM_DONE message is received by Form1. The Multimedia subsystem in Windows sends a WOM_DONE message when a wavefile finishes playing.

After the form has loaded, the Resize event procedure is called. Here the few controls used in this How-To are resized. The most notable part of the user interface for this How-To is the shadow effect created for the text displayed on Form1. Using two labels (with the BackStyle property set to Transparent) facilitates the creation of a shadow effect. All you need to do is make two identical copies of a label, and set the Forecolor of each to obtain the text and shadow colors you want. Then, by offsetting the bottom label (the one with the shadow color) by some number of pixels, you can create the illusion of a shadow.

Once a file is chosen and the Play button is clicked, CWaveOut handles the details of opening the wave output device and playing the wavefile. After the play completes, WOM_DONE is handled in the MsgHook_Message event procedure, and the code reinitializes so that it is ready to replay the same file or a new user-selected file.

Comments

This How-To managed to scavenge a lot of functionality from existing classes—the CMMChunkInfo, CMmioFile, and CWaveFile classes made it quite simple. The only task to be done was writing some code to play wavefiles. With that wavefile-playing code encapsulated in a new class, CWaveOut, it will be available for use in later How-To's, and projects of your own.

4.8 How do I...
Change a Wavefile's Volume?

COMPLEXITY: INTERMEDIATE

COMPATIBILITY: VB4 ONLY

Problem

Some sound cards don't provide control over playback volume, but I want to allow the user of my program to set that volume. Also, I'm working on a wavefile editor that I can use to record and edit wavefiles. I can't find anything in the Visual Basic documentation or in the Windows API documents that allows for modifying a wavefile's volume. Can I write a program using Visual Basic to do this?

Technique

A wavefile's data chunk contains a number of samples. Each sample corresponds to the distance a speaker must be moved in order to create the part of the wavefile's sound represented by the sample. For instance, an 8-bit mono wavefile contains a number of bytes, each of which is one sample. For a file with a sample rate of 11.025 kHz, and containing 1 second's worth of data, there will be 11,025 bytes in the file's data chunk. When the file is played back, the sound card converts each byte into a voltage that controls the speaker's position for 1/11,025th of a second. As each byte is converted, the voltage changes and the speaker moves in and out.

If you supply bytes representing a sine wave, a pure tone will be produced, corresponding to the rapidity with which the speaker changes from its low (or farthest-in) position to its high (or farthest-out) position. The magnitude of the change between the high and low positions is the volume. When the change between the high and low positions is small, the volume is low, when the change is large, the volume is high.

Armed with this background information changing a wavefile's volume is fairly easy. First you need to get the wavefile's data. This How-To uses classes that were built in previous How-To's to get at the wavefile data. Then all you need to do is modify each byte so that it either increases or decreases the change in the speaker's previous position, depending upon whether you want to increase or decrease the volume.

Steps

Open and run WAVOLUME.VBP, and use the File Open menu item to load DING.WAV from your Windows directory. Figure 4-8-1 shows how WaveVolume will look after you've loaded DING.WAV. Click on the Play button to play the wavefile. Click on the + button a few times, and then click on the Play button again, and the volume will increase noticeably.

1. Create a new project named WAVOLUME.VBP. Use the File Add menu item to add the classes and modules shown in Table 4-8-1 to WAVOLUME.VBP. The class modules (files with a CLS extension) are in the VBHT\CLASSES directory, and MMSYSTEM.BAS is in VBHT\MODULES. As you can see, we've accumulated a handy collection of class modules.

Table 4-8-1 Classes and modules for Form1

FILE NAME	CLASS	PURPOSE
CMMCHUNK.CLS	CMMChunkInfo	Support for CMmioFile
CMMIOFIL.CLS	CMmioFile	Multimedia file access
CWAVEFIL.CLS	CWaveFile	Wavefile access
CWAVEDSP.CLS	CWaveFileDisplay	Displays wavefiles
CWAVEOUT.CLS	CWaveOut	Plays CWaveFile objects
MMSYSTEM.BAS	None	API declarations

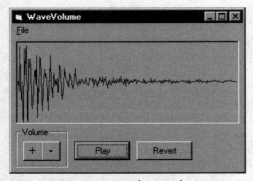

Figure 4-8-1 WaveVolume with DING.WAV loaded

2. Use the Insert Class Module menu item to add a new class module to WAVOLUME.VBP. Set the class's Name property to CWaveEffects, and add the following code:

```
'
' Windows API functions
'
Private Declare Sub CopyMemory Lib "KERNEL32" Alias "RtlMoveMemory" ⇒
     (dst As Any, src As Any, ByVal dwBytes As Long)
'
' Wavefile object
'
Private m_oWave    As New CWaveFile
```

3. Add the following code to CWaveEffects. Instances of CWaveEffects operate on the contents of an instance of CWaveFile. The Wave Property procedures are used to assign and examine the CWaveFile object to work with.

```
Public Property Set Wave(aWaveFile As CWaveFile)
    Set m_oWave = aWaveFile
End Property

Public Property Get Wave() As CWaveFile
    wavefile = m_oWave
End Property
```

4. Add the following public subroutine to CWaveEffects. This ChangeVolume routine first checks to see if the passed percentage is zero. Only if a non-zero percentage was passed will there be something to do. There will be two cases to handle, 8-bit data and 16-bit data. It would be possible to handle both in a single routine, but the routine would be large, overly complex, and potentially somewhat slower. The ChangeVolume method lets the user pass a percentage such as 110 or 155.5, which is converted to an actual percentage as it is passed to the appropriate subroutine.

```
Public Sub ChangeVolume(pct As Single)
    '
    ' No need to change anything if the percent change
    ' is zero!
    '
    If (pct = 0) Then
        Exit Sub
            End If
                '
                ' Otherwise dispatch to correct routine, convert
                ' to real percentage from value passed in
                '
                If (m_oWave.BitsPerSample = 8) Then
                    ChangeVol8 pct / 100
                ElseIf (m_oWave.BitsPerSample = 16) Then
                    ChangeVol16 pct / 100
                Else
```

Continued on next page

Continued from previous page

```
        MsgBox "Invalid m_format, only 8 and 16 bit stereo or ⇒
                mono PCM supported"
    End If
End Sub
```

5. Add the following Private subroutine to CWaveEffects. This subroutine is called when an 8-bit wavefile's volume is being changed. First, the b array is sized so that it can hold the wavefile's data, and the Windows API function CopyMemory is used to copy m_oWave's data to the array. Then each byte of the array is scaled by the passed percentage, and the modified data is copied back to m_oWave data using CopyMemory.

An important thing to know about 8-bit wave data is that its midpoint (or zero) is at 128. So when the sound card converts the 8-bit sample to a voltage, the speaker will be positioned at the midpoint of its motion range. That's the reason 128 is subtracted from each byte as it is read from the array, and added to the byte when it is put back. If values less than 128 were not moved into the negative range before multiplication by pct, they would move in the same direction along a number line as the values greater than 128. This would simply shift the waveform up in the range without affecting the magnitude of the change between high and low samples. Also, because the samples in an 8-bit file are restricted to values between 0 and 255, it is necessary to clip the result of multiplying a given sample by pct, so that it falls within that range when it is placed back in the array.

```
Private Sub ChangeVol8(pct As Single)
    Dim i    As Long
    Dim v    As Long
    Dim b() As Byte
    '
    ' Get wavefile data
    '
    ReDim b(m_oWave.Length)
    CopyMemory b(0), ByVal m_oWave.Data, m_oWave.Length
    '
    ' Scale each sample by pct
    '
    For i = 0 To m_oWave.Length
        v = (b(i) - 128) * pct
        '
        ' Make sure value doesn't get out of range
        '
        If (v > 127) Then
            v = 127
        ElseIf (v < -128) Then
            v = -128
        End If
        b(i) = CByte(v + 128)
    Next
    '
    ' Copy scaled wavedata back
    '
    CopyMemory ByVal m_oWave.Data, b(0), m_oWave.Length
End Sub
```

6. Add the following code to CWaveEffects. The process of changing the volume of a 16-bit wavefile is nearly identical to that for an 8-bit wavefile. Aside from the fact that an integer array is used as the workspace instead of a byte array, there is only one significant difference: 16-bit wave samples have their midpoint at zero, so there is no need to move the midpoint before multiplying by pct.

```
Private Sub ChangeVol16(pct As Single)
    Dim i    As Long
    Dim v    As Long
    Dim b() As Integer
    '
    ' Get wavefile data
    '
    ReDim b(m_oWave.Length / 2)
    CopyMemory b(0), ByVal m_oWave.Data, m_oWave.Length
    '
    ' For each sample
    '
    For i = 0 To m_oWave.Length / 2
        v = b(i) * pct
        '
        ' Make sure the data doesn't get out of range
        '
        If (v > 32767) Then
            v = 32767
        ElseIf (v < -32768) Then
            v = -32768
        End If
        b(i) = CInt(v)
    Next
    '
    ' Copy scaled data back
    '
    CopyMemory ByVal m_oWave.Data, b(0), m_oWave.Length
End Sub
```

7. Select Form1, and add objects with properties and settings as shown in Table 4-8-2.

Table 4-8-2 Objects, properties, and settings for Form1

OBJECT	PROPERTY	SETTING
Form	Caption	"WaveVolume"
	Name	Form1
CommandButton	Caption	"Play"
	Enabled	0 'False
	Name	Command3
CommandButton	Caption	"Revert"
	Enabled	0 'False

Continued on next page

Continued from previous page

OBJECT	PROPERTY	SETTING
	Name	Command4
MsgHook	Name	MsgHook1
PictureBox	BackColor	&H00C0C0C0&
	ForeColor	&H00C00000&
	Name	Picture1
	ScaleMode	3 'Pixel
CommonDialog	CancelError	-1 'True
	DefaultExt	"*.wav"
	DialogTitle	"Open Wave File"
	Filter	"Wave Files (*.wav)|*.wav"
	Name	CommonDialog1
Frame	Caption	"Volume"
	Name	Frame1

8. Create the controls, with properties and settings as shown in Table 4-8-3, as children of Frame1. To do this, click on the control's toolbar button; then create and size the control by clicking on Frame1 and dragging the sizing rectangle.

Table 4-8-3 Objects, properties, and settings for Frame1

OBJECT	PROPERTY	SETTING
CommandButton	Caption	"+"
	FontName	"Times New Roman"
	FontSize	13.5
	Name	Command1
	TabStop	0 'False
CommandButton	Caption	"–"
	FontName	"Times New Roman"
	FontSize	14.25
	Name	Command2
	TabStop	0 'False

9. Add the menu shown in Table 4-8-4 to Form1.

Table 4-8-4 Form1's menu

MENU NAME	CAPTION
FileMenu	"&File"
...FileOpen	"&Open..."
...FileSep1	"-"
...FileExit	"E&xit"

10. Add the following code to the General declarations section of Form1. This How-To directly uses objects of four different classes. The CWaveFile class uses two classes of its own, bringing the total number of class objects to 6.

```
Option Explicit

Dim Wavefile    As New CWaveFile
Dim Display     As New CWaveFileDisplay
Dim WaveFX      As New CWaveEffects
Dim WavePlayer  As New CWaveOut
```

11. Add the following code as Form1's Form_Load event procedure. We want to be able to see, as well as hear, the changes made to a waveform. The object Display, an instance of CWaveDisplay, takes care of this for us. The MsgHook control is initialized so that the message sent when a wavefile play finishes, WOM_DONE, can be intercepted.

```
Private Sub Form_Load()
    '
    ' Set display's canvas
    '
    Set Display.Canvas = Picture1
    '
    ' Get set for WaveOutputMessage_Done!
    '
    MsgHook1.HwndHook = Me.hWnd
    MsgHook1.Message(WOM_DONE) = True
End Sub
```

12. Add the following code as Form1's Form_Resize event procedure. This routine repositions Form1's controls so that most of Form1's screen space is occupied by Picture1.

```
Private Sub Form_Resize()
    Dim perx As Single
    Dim pery As Single
    '
    ' Bail if we're minimized
    '
    If (Me.WindowState = 1) Then
        Exit Sub
    End If
    '
    ' Get scale factors handy place (and with short names!)
    '
    perx = Screen.TwipsPerPixelX
    pery = Screen.TwipsPerPixelY
    '
    ' Move command buttons to bottom of form
    '
    Frame1.top = Form1.ScaleHeight - Frame1.Height - (5 * pery)
    Command3.top = Frame1.top + Command1.top
```

Continued on next page

Continued from previous page

```
    Command4.top = Command3.top
    '
    ' Fill most of the rest of the form with Picture1
    '
    Picture1.top = 5 * pery
    Picture1.left = 5 * perx
    Picture1.Height = Frame1.top - (10 * pery)
    Picture1.Width = Form1.ScaleWidth - (10 * perx)
    Display.offset = 0
    Picture1.Refresh
End Sub
```

13. Add the following code as Command1's Click event procedure. The CWaveEffects ChangeVolume is used to increase the wavefile's volume by 10 percent. Picture1.Refresh is used to generate a Picture1.Paint event, causing the wavefile to be redisplayed.

```
Private Sub Command1_Click()
    '
    ' Set volume to 110 percent of current volume
    '
    WaveFX.ChangeVolume 110
    Picture1.Refresh
End Sub
```

14. Add the following code as Command2's Click event procedure. The volume is changed to 90 percent of its current level.

```
Private Sub Command2_Click()
    '
    ' Set volume to 90 percent of current volume
    '
    WaveFX.ChangeVolume 90
    Picture1.Refresh
End Sub
```

15. Add the following code as Command3's Click event procedure. This routine is called when the user clicks on the Play command button. First we make sure that the user doesn't try to play a wavefile while it is already playing; disabling the command button takes care of this. Then the WavePlayer object (an instance of CWaveFile) is used to play the wavefile contained by the object variable named Wavefile. WavePlayer gets a reference to Wavefile in the FileOpen menu item's Click event procedure.

```
Private Sub Command3_Click()
    '
    ' Don't allow any attempt to start a play before
    ' the current play finishes
    '
    Command3.Enabled = False
    WavePlayer.WaveOpen Me.hWnd
    WavePlayer.WavePlay
End Sub
```

16. Add the following code as MsgHook1's Message event procedure. When a wavefile finishes playing, the WOM_DONE message is sent to Form1 and intercepted by MsgHook1, which then fires the Message event. Since the wavefile has finished playing, the Play button is re-enabled and the wave output device is closed.

```
Private Sub MsgHook1_Message(ByVal msg As Long, ByVal wp As Long, ⇒
    ByVal lp As Long, result As Long)
    '
    ' Play completed, renable Play button and close
    ' the waveout device
    '
    Command3.Enabled = True
    WavePlayer.WaveClose
End Sub
```

17. Add the following code as Command4's Click event procedure. After cranking the volume up and down a few times, you might want to restore the original wavefile—especially if clipping of high and/or low values has introduced audible artifacts into the wavefile. Clicking on the Revert button fires this event, and the wavefile is restored by simply reloading it.

```
Private Sub Command4_Click()
    '
    ' Restore (revert to) original wavefile
    '
    Wavefile.Filename = CommonDialog1.Filename
    Picture1.Refresh
End Sub
```

18. Add the following code as the FileOpen menu item's Click event procedure. After getting a file from the user and loading it into the Wavefile object, the Play and Command buttons are enabled. Then the fun begins: three objects (Display, WaveFX, and WavePlayer) receive and store a reference to the Wavefile object. It's important to be aware that these are references to a single object, and not separate copies of the Wavefile object. Changes made to the Wavefile referenced by one object will be visible from other objects.

```
Private Sub FileOpen_Click()
    Dim s As String
    '
    ' Catch press of cancel button
    '
    On Error Resume Next
    CommonDialog1.Action = 1
    If (Err) Then
        '
        ' Canceled ... we're outta here
        '
        Exit Sub
    End If
    '
```

Continued on next page

Continued from previous page

```
    ' Wavefile name ... setting property loads file
    '
    Wavefile.Filename = CommonDialog1.Filename
    If (Err) Then
        '
        ' Bad juju ... wavefile load failed
        '
        MsgBox Wavefile.ErrorMsg
    End If
    '
    ' Play and Revert are now both valid
    '
    Command3.Enabled = True
    Command4.Enabled = True
    '
    ' Give Display thing a copy of the wavefile
    '
    Set Display.Wave = Wavefile
    Set WaveFX.Wave = Wavefile
    Set WavePlayer.Wavefile = Wavefile
    '
    ' Reset zoom and offset
    '
    Display.Zoom = 0
    Display.offset = 0
    '
    ' Redisplay
    '
    Picture1.Refresh
End Sub
```

19. Add the following code as the FileExit menu item's Click event procedure:

```
Private Sub FileExit_Click()
    End
End Sub
```

20. Add the following code as Picture1's Paint event procedure. Because class module instances cannot have event procedures, it is necessary to call event-related methods from within other objects' event procedures, as is done here.

```
Private Sub Picture1_Paint()
    '
    ' Redraw waveform
    '
    Display.Paint
End Sub
```

How It Works

If you ignore the implementation details of the five previously developed class modules, this How-To is pretty straightforward. The new class, CWaveEffects, has a Wavefile property to which you can assign an instance of CWaveFile. In the FileOpen menu's Click event procedure, an instance of CWaveFile loads a wavefile, and the instance of CWaveFile is assigned to an instance of CWaveEffects named WaveFX. In the menu's Click event procedure, the same CWaveFile object is assigned to the Wavefile property of Display and to WavePlayer. Since all three objects (WaveFX, Display, and WavePlayer) have all stored a reference to the same CWaveFile object, using the CWaveEffects ChangeVolume method automatically changes the waveform drawn by Display, and the volume of the wavefile when played using WavePlayer.

Comments

In addition to taking advantage of a number of previously developed class modules, this How-To adds yet another class module that you can use in your projects. As it exists now, CWaveEffects isn't very impressive, but subsequent How-To's will improve the utility of the CWaveEffects class by adding new effects. How-To 4.9 adds the ability to merge wavefiles, How-To 4.10 lets you reverse a wavefile.

4.9 How do I...
Merge Two Wavefiles?

COMPLEXITY: INTERMEDIATE
COMPATIBILITY: VB4 ONLY

Problem

Sometimes I need to play more than one wavefile at a time. Most users have only one wave output device, so multiple wavefiles must be merged somehow before they can be played together. One way to do this was shown in How-To 4.5, and that technique works well in many situations—especially when the order in which wavefiles are played can only be determined at run time. However, what I really want to do here is simply build a composite wavefile. Can I make the wavefile editor program, for instance, merge two wavefiles and save them on disk? What do I have to do to merge two wavefiles using Visual Basic code?

Technique

This project is similar in many respects to the one in How-To 4.8. In that wave volume project, a number of class modules from other How-To's were used and a new class named CWaveEffects was created. Here the CWaveEffects class is extended by adding a Merge method.

Steps

Open and run WAVMERGE.VBP. Use the Open command button to load DING.WAV and RINGOUT.WAV from your Windows directory. Figure 4-9-1 shows WaveMerge after RINGOUT. WAV and DING.WAV have been opened. Then click on the Play

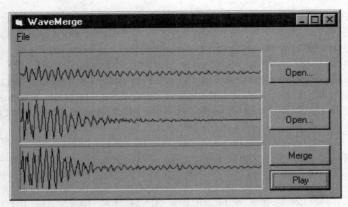

Figure 4-9-1 WaveMerge with RINGOUT.WAV and DING.WAV merged

button and you will hear the merged files play. You can load and merge additional wavefiles using the second Open button on the form. When you load a wavefile using the top Open button the loaded wavefile is also copied to the CWaveFile device whose data is displayed in the bottom picture. You merge multiple wavefiles by using the lower Open button and the Merge button many times. When the resulting wavefile gets totally out of hand, you can start over again by loading a file using the upper Open button. You can have some fun playing with various wavefiles using this How-To.

1. Create a new project named WAVMERGE.VBP, and use the File Add menu item to add the classes and modules shown in Table 4-9-1. The class modules (files with a CLS extension) are in the VBHT\CLASSES directory, and WINMM32.BAS is in VBHT\MODULES.

Table 4-9-1 Classes and modules for Form1

FILE NAME	CLASS	PURPOSE
CMMCHUNK.CLS	CMMChunkInfo	Support for CMmioFile
CMMIOFIL.CLS	CMmioFile	Multimedia file access
CWAVEFIL.CLS	CWaveFile	Wavefile access
CWAVEDSP.CLS	CWaveFileDisplay	Displays wavefiles
CWAVEOUT.CLS	CWaveOut	Plays CWaveFile objects
CBORDR3D.CLS	CBorder3D	Adds 3D effects to controls
WINMM32.BAS	None	API declarations

2. Copy the file CWAVEEFF.CLS from How-To 4.8 to this project's directory, and use the File Add menu item to add this class to the project.

3. Add the following public subroutine to CWaveEffects (CWAVEEFF.CLS). The Merge method has two arguments, an instance of CWaveFile and a Long. The CWaveEffects object has a variable named m_oWave, which holds an instance of CWaveFile. The Merge method merges the data from aWave with m_oWave, and leaves the result in m_oWave. The other argument, offset, is used to specify an offset (in milliseconds) into m_oWave's data, where the merge of data from aWave should begin. It is important to note that the foregoing code assumes that both wavefiles are either 8-bit or 16-bit, and that both files are either mono or stereo and that their sample rate is the same. Strange sounds will result if that is not the case, so you should probably add some sanity checking to this code before you use it for any serious work.

```
Public Sub Merge(aWave As CWaveFile, offset As Long)
    '
    ' Dispatch to correct routine
    '
    If (m_oWave.BitsPerSample = 8) Then
        Merge8 aWave, offset
        ElseIf (m_oWave.BitsPerSample = 16) Then
            Merge16 aWave, offset
    Else
        MsgBox "Invalid m_format, only 8 and 16 bit stereo or mono ⇒
            PCM supported"
    End If
End Sub
```

4. Add the following subroutine to CWaveEffects. This subroutine is called when an 8-bit file is being merged. First, the offset argument is used to compute the number of samples into m_oWave's wavefile data where we want to merge aWave's first sample. The result is stored in doff. The length of aWave's wavefile data (or the data + doff) may well be greater than the length of the destination wavefile, m_oWave. The code checks for this case; when it occurs, a number of things are done.

First, the variable srcRemains is assigned the number of samples from aWave that will remain after the last sample in m_oWave has accepted a merge. These samples will later be copied directly to m_oWave; however, to make this work, m_oWave's data buffer needs to be expanded. This is easily accomplished by simply assigning a new value to m_oWave's Length property. The Length property procedure takes care of expanding the buffer without destroying existing wavefile data. The length of m_oWave's buffer before it is expanded is saved in lim, so we will know when to stop merging samples from aWave and start copying them. If m_oWave's buffer is greater in size than that of aWave's buffer plus doff, things are much simpler. The variable lim is set to the length of aWave's data buffer, and srcRemains is set to zero. Next, two arrays are ReDimed, and the wavefile data from m_oWave and aWave are copied to the buffers.

Finally, it's time to do some merging. Successive samples are first adjusted so that the midpoint of the sample is at zero instead of 128, as required by the waveout device. Then the two samples are added together. The resulting sample is clipped for high and low range values, and converted back to the 128 midpoint format as in m_oWave's buffer. Finally, any samples remaining in aWave are simply copied to m_oWave.

```
Private Sub Merge8(aWave As CWaveFile, offset As Long)
    Dim i            As Long
    Dim lim          As Long
    Dim d()          As Byte
    Dim s()          As Byte
    Dim v            As Integer
    Dim doff         As Long
    Dim srcRemains   As Long
    '
    ' Convert millisecond offset to number of samples
    '
    doff = (m_oWave.SamplesPerSecond / 1000) * offset

    ' Check to see if destination is too small
    '
    If (m_oWave.Length < aWave.Length + doff) Then
        '
        ' Yep ... there will be bytes remaining from aWave
        ' find out how many
        '
        srcRemains = (aWave.Length + doff) - m_oWave.Length
        '
        ' Stop merging when m_oWave's current Length is reached
        '
        lim = m_oWave.Length
        '
        ' Make room in m_oWave for remaining samples
        '
        m_oWave.Length = aWave.Length + doff
    Else
        '
        ' aWave is shorter than m_oWave ... this is easy
        '
        lim = aWave.Length
        srcRemains = 0
    End If
    '
    ' Allocate arrays to work with
    '
    ReDim d(m_oWave.Length)
    ReDim s(aWave.Length)
    '
    ' Copy wave data to working arrays
    '
    CopyMemory d(0), ByVal m_oWave.Data, m_oWave.Length
    CopyMemory s(0), ByVal aWave.Data, aWave.Length
```

```
'
' Merge bytes upto lim
'
For i = 0 To lim - 1
    v = ((d(i + doff) - 128) + (s(i) - 128))
    '
    ' Clip to valid range of values
    '
    If (v > 127) Then
        v = 127
    ElseIf (v < -128) Then
        v = -128
    End If
    d(i + doff) = CByte(v + 128)
Next
'
' Copy any remaining samples from aWave
'
If (srcRemains <> 0) Then
    CopyMemory d(i), s(i), srcRemains
End If
'
' Put modified data into m_oWave
'
    CopyMemory ByVal m_oWave.Data, d(0), m_oWave.Length
End Sub
```

5. Add the following subroutine to CWaveEffects. This subroutine is nearly identical to the one in step 4. The only significant difference is that this routine deals with arrays of integers instead of bytes, since the data samples contain 16 bits instead of 8.

```
Private Sub Merge16(aWave As CWaveFile, offset As Long)
    Dim i           As Long
    Dim v           As Long
    Dim d()         As Integer
    Dim s()         As Integer
    Dim lim         As Long
    Dim doff        As Long
    Dim srcRemains As Long
    '
    ' Convert millisecond offset to number of samples
    '
    doff = (m_oWave.SamplesPerSecond / 1000) * offset
    '
    ' Check to see if destination is too small
    '
    If (m_oWave.Length < aWave.Length + doff * 2) Then
        '
        ' Yep ... there will be bytes remaining from aWave
        ' find out how many
        '
        srcRemains = (aWave.Length + doff * 2)
        '
```

Continued on next page

Continued from previous page

```
      ' Stop merging when m_oWave's current Length is reached

      lim = m_oWave.Length / 2
      '
      ' Make room in m_oWave for remaining bytes
      '
      m_oWave.Length = aWave.Length + doff * 2
   Else
      '
      ' aWave is shorter than m_oWave ... this is easy
      '
      lim = aWave.Length / 2
      srcRemains = 0
   End If
   '
   ' Allocate arrays to work with
   '
   ReDim d(m_oWave.Length / 2)
   ReDim s(aWave.Length / 2)
   '
   ' Copy wave data to working arrays
   '
   CopyMemory d(0), ByVal m_oWave.Data, m_oWave.Length
   CopyMemory s(0), ByVal aWave.Data, aWave.Length
   '
   ' Merge samples upto lim
   '
   For i = 0 To lim - 1
      v = CLng(d(i + doff)) + CLng(s(i))
      '
      ' Clip to valid range of values
      '
      If (v > 32767) Then
         v = 32767
      ElseIf (v < -32768) Then
         v = -32768
      End If
      d(i + doff) = CInt(v)
   Next
   '
   ' Copy any remaining samples from aWave
   '
   If (srcRemains <> 0) Then
      CopyMemory d(i), s(i), srcRemains
   End If
   '
   ' Put modified data into m_oWave
   '
   CopyMemory ByVal m_oWave.Data, d(0), m_oWave.Length
End Sub
```

6. Select Form1, and add objects with properties and settings as shown in Table 4-9-2.

Table 4-9-2 Objects, properties, and settings for Form1

OBJECT	PROPERTY	SETTING
Form	BackColor	&H00C0C0C0&
	Caption	"WaveMerge"
	Name	Form1
CommandButton	Caption	"Open..."
	Name	Command1
CommandButton	Caption	"Open..."
	Name	Command2
CommandButton	Caption	"Merge"
	Name	Command3
CommandButton	Caption	"Play"
	Enabled	'False
	Name	Command4
MsgHook	Name	MsgHook1
PictureBox	BackColor	&H00C0C0C0&
	BorderStyle	0 'None
	ForeColor	&H00C00000&
	Index	0
	Name	Picture1
	ScaleMode	3 'Pixel
PictureBox	BackColor	&H00C0C0C0&
	BorderStyle	0 'None
	ForeColor	&H00C00000&
	Index	1
	Name	Picture1
	ScaleMode	3 'Pixel
PictureBox	BackColor	&H00C0C0C0&
	BorderStyle	0 'None
	ForeColor	&H00C00000&
	Index	2
	Name	Picture1
	ScaleMode	3 'Pixel
CommonDialog	CancelError	-1 'True
	DefaultExt	"*.wav"
	DialogTitle	"Open Wave File"
	Filter	"Wave Files (*.wav)|*.wav|"
	Name	CommonDialog1

7. Add the file menu with menu names and captions shown in Table 4-9-3.

Table 4-9-3 Form1's menu

MENU NAME	CAPTION
FileMenu	"&File"
...FileExit	"E&xit"

8. Add the following code to the General declarations section of Form1. This How-To directly uses objects from five classes, and the CWaveFile class also uses two other classes. These classes contribute substantial functionality to the program, yet require little work from the programmer using them. Love those components!

```
Option Explicit

Dim Borders(3)     As New CBorder3D
Dim WaveFile(3)    As New CWaveFile
Dim Display(3)     As New CWaveFileDisplay
Dim WaveFX         As New CWaveEffects
Dim WavePlayer     As New CWaveOut
```

9. Add the following code as Form1's Form_Load event procedure. First the three PictureBoxes are assigned to the Display and Borders objects, and the Border style for each is set to sunken. Then the MsgHook control is initialized so that the Multimedia message WOM_DONE will be intercepted.

```
Private Sub Form_Load()
   Dim i As Integer
   '
   ' Setup display and border objects
   '
   For i = 0 To 2
      Set Display(i).Canvas = Picture1(i)
      Set Borders(i).Client = Picture1(i)
      Set Borders(i).Canvas = Me
      Borders(i).Style3D = 1
   Next
   '
   ' Setup to receive the WOM_DONE message when
   ' a wavefile finishes playing
   '
   MsgHook1.HwndHook = Me.hWnd
   MsgHook1.Message(WOM_DONE) = True
End Sub
```

10. Add the following code as Form1's Form_Resize event procedure. First the three picture boxes are evenly spaced, and their width set so that they use most of the form's space. Then the command buttons are arranged in the space remaining on the right side of the PictureBoxes.

```
Private Sub Form_Resize()
    Dim i               As Integer
    Dim perx            As Single
    Dim pery            As Single
    Dim borderWidth     As Integer
    Dim pictureSep      As Integer
    '
    ' Bail if we're minimized
    '
    If (Me.WindowState = 1) Then
        Exit Sub
    End If
    '
    ' Get scale factors handy place (and with short names!)
    '
    perx = Screen.TwipsPerPixelX
    pery = Screen.TwipsPerPixelY
    '
    ' Set width of border and space between pictures
    '
    borderWidth = 10 * perx
    pictureSep = 6 * perx
    '
    ' Locate top picture first
    '
    Picture1(0).Top = borderWidth
    Picture1(0).Left = borderWidth
    Picture1(0).Height = (Form1.ScaleHeight - (2 * borderWidth + 2 * ⇒
        pictureSep)) \ 3
    Picture1(0).Width = Form1.ScaleWidth - (3 * borderWidth + ⇒
        Command1.Width)
    '
    ' Base size of the remaining two pictures on the first one
    '
    For i = 1 To 2
        Picture1(i).Move _
            Picture1(i - 1).Left, _
            Picture1(i - 1).Top + Picture1(i - 1).Height + pictureSep, _
            Picture1(i - 1).Width, _
            Picture1(i - 1).Height
    Next
    '
    ' Position command buttons next to appropriate
    ' pictures
    '
    Command1.Left = Picture1(0).Left + Picture1(0).Width + borderWidth
    Command1.Top = Picture1(0).Top + (Picture1(0).Height - ⇒
        Command1.Height) / 2
    Command2.Left = Command1.Left
    Command2.Top = Command1.Top + Picture1(0).Height + pictureSep
    Command3.Left = Command1.Left
    Command3.Top = Picture1(2).Top
    Command4.Left = Command3.Left
    Command4.Top = Command3.Top + Command3.Height + pictureSep
    '
```

Continued on next page

Continued from previous page

```
    ' Cause a repaint
    '
    Form1.Refresh
End Sub
```

11. Add the following code as Picture1's Paint event procedure. First the picture is cleared, and then a wavefile (if one is loaded) is drawn on the picture by a Display object. Then a 3D border is drawn around the control by invoking CBorder3D's Refresh method.

```
Private Sub Picture1_Paint(Index As Integer)
    Picture1(Index).Cls
    Display(Index).Paint
    Borders(Index).Refresh
End Sub
```

12. Add the following code as Command1's Click event procedure. First, the GetWavefile subroutine that is shared with Command2 is called. The zero passed to GetWavefile specifies that the wavefile should be stored in WaveFile(0), and displayed using Display(0). After GetWavefile works, the saved filename is loaded into the WaveFile object displayed on the bottom PictureBox and the WaveFile object is loaded into the corresponding Display object. Then the WaveFX object and WavePlayer object, as well, get copies of the WaveFile object.

```
Private Sub Command1_Click()
    GetWavefile 0
    WaveFile(2).Filename = CommonDialog1.Filename
    Set Display(2).Wave = WaveFile(2)
    Set WaveFX.Wave = WaveFile(2)
    Set WavePlayer.WaveFile = WaveFile(2)
    Picture1(2).Refresh
    Command3.Enabled = True
End Sub
```

13. Add the following code as Command2's Click event procedure. GetWavefile is called to load a wavefile for Picture1(1).

```
Private Sub Command2_Click()
    GetWavefile 1
End Sub
```

14. Add the following private subroutine to Form1. After the user selects a filename, it is assigned to WaveFile(i).Filename. This results in the wavefile being loaded into memory. Then a reference to the WaveFile object is assigned to Display(i)'s Wave property. The wave form is displayed by evoking a Picture1_Paint event via its Refresh method.

```
Private Sub GetWavefile(i As Integer)
    Dim s As String
    '
    ' Catch press of cancel button
```

482

```
'
On Error Resume Next
CommonDialog1.Action = 1
If (Err) Then
    '
    ' Canceled ... we're outta here
    '
    Exit Sub
End If
'
' Wavefile name ... setting property loads file
'
WaveFile(i).Filename = CommonDialog1.Filename
If (Err) Then
    '
    ' Bad juju ... wavefile load failed
    '
    MsgBox WaveFile.ErrorMsg
End If
'
' Give Display thing a copy of the wavefile
'
Set Display(i).Wave = WaveFile(i)
'
' Redisplay
'
Picture1(i).Refresh
End Sub
```

15. Add the following code as Command3's Click event procedure. This is the Merge button's event procedure. Merging two wavefiles can take some time, so the mouse pointer is changed to an hourglass before the merge is invoked, using the WaveFX.Merge method.

```
Private Sub Command3_Click()
    Screen.MousePointer = vb Hourglass
    WaveFX.Merge WaveFile(1), 0
    Picture1(2).Refresh
    Screen.MousePointer = vb Default
    Command4.Enabled = True
End Sub
```

16. Add the following code as Command4's Click event procedure. The WavePlayer object takes care of playing the wavefile *only after* the top Open button and the Merge button have been disabled. It is very important to make sure the user cannot do anything that might result in deallocating the wavefile buffer being played. Loading a new wavefile into WaveFile(2) (which is the wavefile object that actually gets played) will cause a major GPF and the system will most likely have to be completely rebooted.

```
Private Sub Command4_Click()
    Command1.Enabled = False
```

Continued on next page

Continued from previous page

```
    Command4.Enabled = False
    WavePlayer.WaveOpen Me.hWnd
    WavePlayer.WavePlay
End Sub
```

17. Add the following code as MsgHook1's Message event procedure. The top Open button and the Play button are enabled, and the WavePlayer is closed.

```
Private Sub MsgHook1_Message(msg As Integer, wParam As Integer, ⇒
    lParam As Long, Action As Integer, result As Long)
    '
    ' Wavefile done, enable Play button, close waveout
    ' device
    '
    Command1.Enabled = True
    Command4.Enabled = True
    WavePlayer.WaveClose
End Sub
```

18. Add the following code as the FileExit menu item's Click event procedure:

```
Private Sub FileExit_Click()
    End
End Sub
```

How It Works

When the form loads the objects in each of the Display and Borders, object arrays are initialized with a reference to the corresponding element of the Picture1 control array.

When the top Open button is clicked, the user is prompted for a wavefile name, and that wavefile is assigned to WaveFile(0)'s Filename property. WaveFile(0), an instance of CWaveFile, in turn opens an instance of CMmioFile, and reads the file's header and data chunks. Also, when the top Open button is clicked, the destination WaveFile object (array element 2) loads a copy of the same file. The bottom Open button simply loads a wavefile for WaveFile(1). Later, when the Merge button is clicked, WaveFile(1) is merged with the contents of WaveFile(2) and can be played using the Play command button, which uses an instance of the CWaveOut class to play the merged wavefiles.

It's crucial to watch out, when you're working with wavefiles in memory, not to delete a wavefile while it is being played. If you do, unless you get lucky and hit a nice timing window at the end of the play, you will certainly get a GPF and most likely have to reboot your system. Recall that wavefile data is loaded into memory by CWaveFile using GlobalAlloc, and that when a new wavefile name is loaded into an instance of CWaveFile, the previously allocated buffer is simply released using GlobalFree. When memory being accessed by the Multimedia system is suddenly freed, the GPF occurs the next time the Multimedia system accesses that memory.

Comments

This How-To gives you a start toward building a useable and complete wavefile merge capability. However, there are a number of things that remain to be done. First, the Merge method doesn't check to see if both wavefiles have the same sample size and sample rate; this part of the code needs to be improved.

A full-featured Merge method must decide how to handle a number of cases. For instance, it is reasonable to merge an 8-bit mono file with a 16-bit stereo file. In this case you would want to first scale each 8-bit sample up, so that its values are in the 32,767 to –32,768 range, and then merge the result with both channels of the 16-bit file.

4.10 How do I...

Make a Drum Machine?

COMPLEXITY: ADVANCED
COMPATIBILITY: VB4 ONLY

Problem

I'd like to write a drum machine program so that I can create percussion tracks for games and multimedia programs. Eventually, I'd like to be able to set the volume for each track, compose multiple tracks and merge them into a single wavefile, and perhaps add other special effects. But first, I need to write a relatively simple, multitrack drum machine. Can I do this using Visual Basic?

Technique

The CWaveMix class module, first shown in How-To 4.7, provides the basic machinery required to write a drum machine. CWaveMix makes it easy to play as many as eight wavefiles simultaneously. Once you've mastered the fundamentals of playing multiple wavefiles, as shown in How-To 4.7, most of the remaining work is in creating a user interface suitable for editing the percussion tracks.

An important component used in this project is the HiTime custom control. Visual Basic's timer simply doesn't have the resolution required to handle the precision timing required by music. The VB Timer lets you set millisecond values for the Interval property, but in reality it only uses multiples of 55 milliseconds. The HiTime control, on the other hand, lets you set values as small as 1 millisecond for the timer interval, and it will then fire events every millisecond. You need to be somewhat careful with HiTime, since it is possible to fire events with such rapidity that VB will not have time to do anything but service those events. If this happens while you're developing a program, just use Ctrl-Break to interrupt Visual Basic.

Steps

Open and run DRUMS.VBP, and use the program's File Open menu item to load the drum track file named FOO.DRM into the editor. The program will look like Figure 4-10-1. Click on the Play command button to hear the tracks play once. If you cannot hear anything, check to be sure that your sound card is correctly configured (and make sure the speakers are plugged in!). If you still don't hear anything, try running How-To 4.7, and use the information in that directory to configure WAVEMIX.DLL so that it will work with your card.

There are a couple of controls in this project you can play with; both are useful for creating drum tracks. Try the Loop check box first. When it is checked and you press the Play command button, the tracks will play continuously, as if they are on a tape loop. Playing a track over and over again lets you fiddle around with starting and stopping instruments on various beats. You can also enable and disable entire tracks by either checking or unchecking the check box next to each track. Also, you can change the instrument used for each track by using the combo boxes on the left side of the form. You can even change instruments while the drum machine is playing.

1. Create a new project named DRUMS.VBP. Use the File Add menu item to add CWAVEMIX.CLS and WAVEMIX.BAS from the VBHT\CHAP4\4.7 project directory.

2. Select Form1, and add objects with properties and settings as shown in Table 4-10-1. The layout of the controls on Form1 doesn't need to be too precise, but the parent child relationship between some of the objects is important, so a few key items are used during Form_Load to arrange the rest of the controls. The left edges of the combo boxes are not changed during Form_Load, so you should line these up during design. The location of Picture1's top-left corner is crucial. The Top property of Picture1 is used to set the Top property of the first combo box,

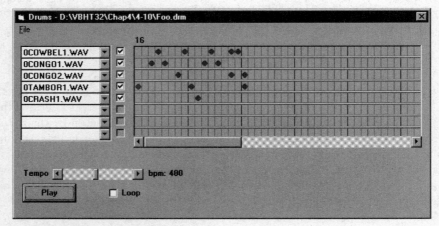

Figure 4-10-1 The Drum Machine

and the Left property is not changed at all during Form_Load. The other controls should be arranged as shown in Figure 4-10-2.

Table 4-10-1 Objects, properties, and settings for Form1

OBJECT	PROPERTY	SETTING
Form	BackColor	&H00C0C0C0&
	Caption	"Form1"
	Name	Form1
HiTime	Interval	0
	Name	HiTime1
CheckBox	BackColor	&H00C0C0C0&
	Caption	"Loop"
	Name	Check2
HScrollBar	LargeChange	10
	Max	250
	Min	16
	Name	HScroll2
CheckBox	BackColor	&H00C0C0C0&
	Caption	""
	Enabled	0 'False
	Name	Check1
CommandButton	Caption	"Play"
	Enabled	0 'False
	Name	Command1
ComboBox	Index	0
	Name	Combo1
	Sorted	-1 'True
	Style	2 'Dropdown List
ComboBox	Index	1
	Name	Combo1
	Sorted	-1 'True
	Style	2 'Dropdown List
ComboBox	Index	2
	Name	Combo1
	Sorted	-1 'True
	Style	2 'Dropdown List
ComboBox	Index	3
	Name	Combo1
	Sorted	-1 'True
	Style	2 'Dropdown List

Continued on next page

Continued from previous page

OBJECT	PROPERTY	SETTING
ComboBox	Index	4
	Name	Combo1
	Sorted	-1 'True
	Style	2 'Dropdown List
ComboBox	Index	5
	Name	Combo1
	Sorted	-1 'True
	Style	2 'Dropdown List
ComboBox	Index	6
	Name	Combo1
	Sorted	-1 'True
	Style	2 'Dropdown List
ComboBox	Index	7
	Name	Combo1
	Sorted	-1 'True
	Style	2 'Dropdown List
HScrollBar	Name	HScroll1
PictureBox	BackColor	&H00808080&
	Name	Picture1

3. To Picture1, add the controls with properties and settings as shown in Table 4-10-2. Be sure to create these controls on Picture1, not Form1. The arrangement of the controls on Picture1 is not terribly critical, since they are all resized and positioned during the Form_Load event.

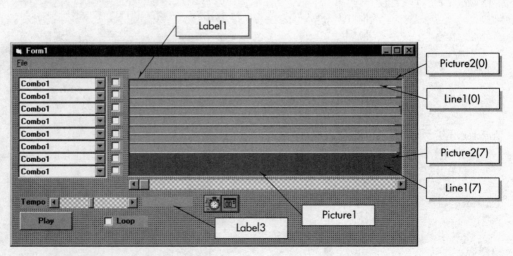

Figure 4-10-2 Layout of controls for Form1

Table 4-10-2 Objects, settings, and properties for Picture1

OBJECT	PROPERTY	SETTING
PictureBox	AutoRedraw	-1 'True
	BackColor	&H00C0C0C0&
	BorderStyle	0 'None
	FillColor	&H00C0C0C0&
	FillStyle	0 'Solid
	Index	0
	Name	Picture2
PictureBox	AutoRedraw	-1 'True
	BackColor	&H00C0C0C0&
	BorderStyle	0 'None
	FillColor	&H00C0C0C0&
	FillStyle	0 'Solid
	Index	1
	Name	Picture2
PictureBox	AutoRedraw	-1 'True
	BackColor	&H00C0C0C0&
	BorderStyle	0 'None
	FillColor	&H00C0C0C0&
	FillStyle	0 'Solid
	Index	2
	Name	Picture2
PictureBox	AutoRedraw	-1 'True
	BackColor	&H00C0C0C0&
	BorderStyle	0 'None
	FillColor	&H00C0C0C0&
	FillStyle	0 'Solid
	Index	3
	Name	Picture2
PictureBox	AutoRedraw	-1 'True
	BackColor	&H00C0C0C0&
	BorderStyle	0 'None
	FillColor	&H00C0C0C0&
	FillStyle	0 'Solid
	Index	4
	Name	Picture2
PictureBox	AutoRedraw	-1 'True
	BackColor	&H00C0C0C0&
	BorderStyle	0 'None

Continued on next page

Continued from previous page

OBJECT	PROPERTY	SETTING
	FillColor	&H00C0C0C0&
	FillStyle	0 'Solid
	Index	5
	Name	Picture2
PictureBox	AutoRedraw	-1 'True
	Index	5
	BackColor	&H00C0C0C0&
	BorderStyle	0 'None
	FillColor	&H00C0C0C0&
	FillStyle	0 'Solid
	Index	6
	Name	Picture2
PictureBox	AutoRedraw	-1 'True
	BackColor	&H00C0C0C0&
	BorderStyle	0 'None
	FillColor	&H00C0C0C0&
	FillStyle	0 'Solid
	Index	7
	Name	Picture2
Line	BorderColor	&H00FFFFFF&
	Index	0
	Name	Line1
Line	BorderColor	&H00FFFFFF&
	Index	1
	Name	Line1
Line	BorderColor	&H00FFFFFF&
	Index	2
	Name	Line1
Line	BorderColor	&H00FFFFFF&
	Index	3
	Name	Line1
Line	BorderColor	&H00FFFFFF&
	Index	4
	Name	Line1
Line	BorderColor	&H00FFFFFF&
	Index	5
	Name	Line1
Line	BorderColor	&H00FFFFFF&
	Index	6

OBJECT	PROPERTY	SETTING
	Name	Line1
Line	BorderColor	&H00FFFFFF&
	Index	7
	Name	Line1

4. Add the following code to the General declarations section of Form1. The user-defined type named Track contains all the information needed to play one track. The maximum number of tracks that CWaveMix can handle is defined by the constant MAX_WAVES in WAVEMIX.BAS; the value of MAX_WAVES is currently eight. Any array of Track data structures named Tracks has room for eight tracks, one for each of the possible wave mixer channels. The WaveMixer array is used to hold references to CWaveMix objects, and as with Tracks, there is one element for each possible wave mixer.

```
Option Explicit
'
' Track data structure
'
Private Type Track
    Wavefile    As String
    Playable    As Integer
    InUse       As Integer
    PlayPointer As Integer
    Whacks(100) As Integer
End Type
'
' Arrays for tracks and wave mixer channels
'
Private Tracks(MAX_WAVES)     As Track
Private WaveMixer(MAX_WAVES) As CWaveMix
```

5. Add the following declarations to the General declarations section of Form1. Two variables, MouseUpX and MouseUpBeat, are used to track the location of Picture2's Mouse_Click events. The variable named freq is set in HScroll2's Change event procedure and is used to set the interval of the HiTime control when tracks are being played. Each grid cell on the Picture2 controls corresponds to one beat. When tracks are being played, beat increments each time HiTime's Timer event routine is called, and all tracks that need an instrument played during that beat are activated.

```
'
' Location that a MouseUp event was fired for Picture2
'
Private MouseUpX      As Long
Private MouseUpBeat   As Integer
'
' Timer freq, current beat when playing
'
```

Continued on next page

Continued from previous page

```
Private freq As Integer
Private beat As Long
'
' Keeps track of current file name (when there is one)
'
Private CurrentFile As String
'
' Width in twips of each beat on the grid
'
Private TwipsPerWhack As Long
```

6. Add the following code as the Form_Load event procedure for Form1. After
   doing some minor initialization, the Combo1 controls are loaded with the names
   of all wavefiles in the current directory. This is the set of instruments from which
   the user can choose. Then all of the Picture2 and Line1 controls are arranged so
   that they create a visual workspace for each track.

```
Private Sub Form_Load()
    Dim s As String
    Dim i As Integer
    '
    ' Initialize TwipsPerWhack
    '
    TwipsPerWhack = 10 * Screen.TwipsPerPixelX
    '
    ' Get list of wave files into combo boxes
    '
    ChDir App.Path
    s = Dir("*.wav", 0)
    Do While s <> ""
        For i = 0 To MAX_WAVES - 1
            Combo1(i).AddItem s
        Next
        s = Dir
    Loop
    '
    ' Arange controls on form
    '
    For i = 0 To MAX_WAVES - 1
        If (i = 0) Then
            Picture2(i).Top = 0
        Else
            Picture2(i).Top = Line1(i - 1).Y1 + (3 * Screen.TwipsPerPixelY)
        End If
        Picture2(i).Height = 14 * Screen.TwipsPerPixelY
        Picture2(i).Width = 100 * 10 * Screen.TwipsPerPixelX
        Combo1(i).Top = Picture1.Top + Picture2(i).Top
        Check1(i).Top = Combo1(i).Top
        Picture2(i).Left = 0
        Line1(i).X1 = 0
        Line1(i).X2 = Picture2(0).Width
        Line1(i).Y1 = Picture2(i).Top + Picture2(i).Height + ⇒
            Screen.TwipsPerPixelY
```

```
      Line1(i).Y2 = Picture2(i).Top + Picture2(i).Height + ⇒
         Screen.TwipsPerPixelY
      DrawGrid (i)
   Next
   Picture1.Height = Line1(7).Y2
   HScroll1.Top = Picture1.Top + Picture1.Height - Screen.TwipsPerPixelX
   HScroll1.Left = Picture1.Left
   HScroll1.SmallChange = 10 * Screen.TwipsPerPixelX
   '
   ' Set initial timing value
   '
   HScroll2.Value = 125
   HScroll2_Change
End Sub
```

7. Add the following code as Form1's Resize event procedure. Picture1 is sized to
   occupy as much vertical space as possible, and HScroll1's Width property is set to
   match Picture1's new width. Then HScroll1's Max and LargeChange values are
   adjusted to accommodate Picture1's width.

```
Private Sub Form_Resize()
   '
   ' Adjust width of Picture1 to fit form
   '
   Picture1.Width = (Form1.ScaleWidth - Picture1.Left - (10 * ⇒
         Screen.TwipsPerPixelX))
   HScroll1.Width = Picture1.Width
   '
   ' Reset scrollbar max to reflect new difference
   ' between width of picture1 and picture2
   '
   HScroll1.Max = Picture2(0).Width - Picture1.Width
   HScroll1.LargeChange = (Picture1.Width * 3) / 4
End Sub
```

8. Add the following code as Combo1's Click event procedure. Each track has a corresponding element in the Combo1 control array. A track's combo box is used to
   select the instrument played by that track. When a filename is chosen, the track's
   Wavefile element is using the selected combo box item. It is possible to change
   instruments on the fly while a track is playing. When this happens, the InitTrack
   subroutine is called to make an immediate change to the instrument being
   played. The last line of the Click event procedure calls the SetTrackPlayableState
   subroutine, to mark the track's data structure as either playable or not playable.
   See step 10 for details on what makes a track playable.

```
Private Sub Combo1_Click(Index As Integer)
   '
   ' Check to see if a filename is selected
   '
   If (Combo1(Index).ListIndex <> -1) Then
      '
      ' Ok ... file selected, set name in Track data
```

Continued on next page

Continued from previous page

```
    ' structure
    '
    Tracks(Index).Wavefile = _
        Combo1(Index).List(Combo1(Index).ListIndex)
    '
    ' Turn on checkbox so track can be enabled
    '
    Check1(Index).Enabled = True
    If (Tracks(Index).Playable And Command1.Caption = "Stop") Then
        InitTrack Index
    End If
Else
    '
    ' Not a filename, set tracks element to null
    ' & disallow enabling the track
    '
    Tracks(Index).Wavefile = ""
    Check1(Index).Value = 0
    Check1(Index).Enabled = False
End If
SetTrackPlayableState Index
End Sub
```

9. Add the following code as Check1's Click event procedure. Check1_Click first calls SetTrackPlayableState to modify the track's Playable flag. If the track is then playable, and if tracks are being played, the InitTrack subroutine is used to enable the track and start it playing right away.

```
Private Sub Check1_Click(Index As Integer)
    SetTrackPlayableState Index
    If (Tracks(Index).Playable = True) Then
        '
        ' Are we playing right now?
        '
        If (Command1.Caption = "Stop") Then
            '
            ' Yep, set up track
            '
            InitTrack Index
        End If
    End If
End Sub
```

10. Add the following subroutine to Form1. SetTrackPlayableState is called whenever a Check1 or Combo1 control changes. A track is playable if it has a filename, and if the corresponding Check1 control is checked. Also, during this subroutine a track is checked as to whether it is playable; then the Play command button is enabled. If the track is not playable, all of the tracks are checked to see if any are playable, and the Play command button is enabled appropriately.

```
Private Sub SetTrackPlayableState(Index As Integer)
    Dim t As Integer
    '
```

```
' A track is playable if its checkbox is checked and there
' is a wave filename
'
If (Check1(Index).Value = 1 And Tracks(Index).Wavefile <> "") Then
    Tracks(Index).Playable = True
            Command1.Enabled = True
Else
    Tracks(Index).Playable = False
        '
        ' Enable/Disable Play button
    '
    For t = 0 To MAX_WAVES - 1
        If (Tracks(t).Playable) Then
            '
            ' Found a playable track ... enable Play button
            '
            Command1.Enabled = True
            Exit Sub
        End If
    Next
    '
    ' No playable tracks ... disable Command1
    '
    Command1.Enabled = False
    End If
End Sub
```

11. Add the following code as Picture2's Click event procedure. During the MouseUp event procedure (see step 13), the center of the grid cell within which the MouseUp event occurred is computed and stored in MouseUpX. Also, the beat number (grid cell number) is computed and stored in MouseUpBeat. The WhackedAt function is called to determine whether the selected grid cell currently has a beat or not. If it does, the beat is deleted; if it does not have a beat, one is added. The net effect is that mouse clicks in a grid cell toggle the beat for that cell.

```
Private Sub Picture2_Click(Index As Integer)
    '
    ' Clicked on picture2, insert whack or delete whack?
    '
    If (WhackedAt(Index, MouseUpBeat)) Then
        DeleteWhack Index, MouseUpX, MouseUpBeat
    Else
        InsertWhack Index, MouseUpX, MouseUpBeat
    End If
End Sub
```

12. Add the following code as Picture2's MouseMove event procedure. As the mouse moves over the Picture2 controls, Label2's caption is set to the beat number (grid cell) currently under the mouse pointer.

```
Private Sub Picture2_MouseMove(Index As Integer, Button As Integer, ⇒
    Shift As Integer, x As Single, Y As Single)
    '
```

Continued on next page

Continued from previous page

```
    ' Mouse moving around over some picture2 ... update
    ' beat number indicator
    '
    Label1.Caption = Int(x / Int(10 * Screen.TwipsPerPixelX))
End Sub
```

13. Add the following code as Picture2's MouseUp event procedure. Since the Mouse_Click event procedure receives no information about where the mouse click occurred, it is necessary to save the information passed to the MouseUp event procedure.

```
Private Sub Picture2_MouseUp(Index As Integer, Button As Integer, ⇒
      Shift As Integer, x As Single, Y As Single)
    '
    ' Mouse button released ... make note of what beat
    ' it was over
    '
    MouseUpBeat = Int(x / TwipsPerWhack)
    '
    ' And set MouseUpX to center of grid cell for this beat
    '
    MouseUpX = (MouseUpBeat * TwipsPerWhack) + (TwipsPerWhack / 2)
End Sub
```

14. Add the following function to Form1. This WhackedAt function is called whenever it is necessary to determine whether a track's instrument should be "whacked" on a given beat.

```
Private Function WhackedAt(Index As Integer, beat As Integer)
    Dim i As Integer
    '
    ' Search track to see if there's an event at 'x'
    '
    For i = 0 To 99
        '
        ' Take an early exit if we're beyond the number of
        ' events in this track
        '
        If (i + 1 > Tracks(Index).InUse) Then
            WhackedAt = False
            Exit Function
        End If
        '
        ' Otherwise check to see if we've got this one
        '
        If (Tracks(Index).Whacks(i) = beat) Then
            WhackedAt = True
            Exit Function
        ElseIf (Tracks(Index).Whacks(i) > beat) Then
            WhackedAt = False
            Exit Function
        End If
    Next
End Function
```

15. Add the following subroutine to Form1. This InsertWhack routine is called when an instrument needs to be marked for whacking on a given beat. The passed argument x gives the center of the grid cell that corresponds to the track given by the argument track. The beat argument specifies when the instrument should be whacked. Beats are stored in ascending order in each track's Whacks. A simple insertion sort is used to insert the new beat at the correct place in Whacks.

```
Private Sub InsertWhack(track As Integer, x As Long, beat As Integer)
    Dim i As Integer
    Dim cx As Single
    Dim cy As Single
    Dim radius As Single
    '
    ' Calculate values for drawing circle
    '
    cx = x
    cy = Picture2(track).Height / 2
    radius = 4 * Screen.TwipsPerPixelX
    '
    ' Set fill color to red
    '
    Picture2(track).FillColor = RGB(255, 0, 0)
    '
    ' Scan from end of events looking for place to insert
    '
    i = Tracks(track).InUse
    Tracks(track).InUse = Tracks(track).InUse + 1
    Do While (i > 0)
        If (beat > Tracks(track).Whacks(i - 1)) Then
            Tracks(track).Whacks(i) = beat
            Picture2(track).Circle (cx, cy), radius, RGB(255, 0, 0)
            Exit Sub
        End If
        Tracks(track).Whacks(i) = Tracks(track).Whacks(i - 1)
        i = i - 1
    Loop
    Tracks(track).Whacks(i) = beat
    Picture2(track).Circle (cx, cy), radius, RGB(255, 0, 0)
End Sub
```

16. Add the following subroutine to Form1. Deleting a whack at a given beat is a straightforward task. The correct whack is located using a linear search, and then the remaining whacks are moved down to fill the space previously occupied by the current beat.

```
Private Sub DeleteWhack(track As Integer, x As Long, beat As Integer)
    Dim i As Integer
    Dim cx As Single
    Dim cy As Single
    Dim radius As Single
    '
    ' Calculate values for circle drawing
    '
```

Continued on next page

Continued from previous page

```
      cx = x
      cy = Picture2(track).Height / 2
      radius = 4 * Screen.TwipsPerPixelX
      '
      ' Set the fill color to grey
      '
      Picture2(Index).FillColor = RGB(192, 192, 192)
      '
      ' Find index of event to delete
      '
      For i = 0 To Tracks(track).InUse
         If (Tracks(track).Whacks(i) = beat) Then
            Exit For
         End If
      Next
      '
      ' Now move the rest of the events down to fill in hole
      '
      Do While i < Tracks(track).InUse - 1
         Tracks(track).Whacks(i) = Tracks(track).Whacks(i + 1)
         i = i + 1
      Loop
      Tracks(track).InUse = Tracks(track).InUse - 1
      Picture2(track).Circle (cx, cy), radius, Picture2(track).BackColor
End Sub
```

17. Add the following code as Command1's Click event procedure. Command1 is used to start the tracks playing and to stop them. The first thing that Command1_Click does, then, is check to see if the tracks are playing; and, if so, they will be stopped. Stopping the tracks in the middle of play is a little tricky. Between the time when the user clicks on Command1 and VB actually calls the Command1_Click event subroutine, there may be timer messages queued for HiTime1. After HiTime1 is disabled, DoEvents is used to process any events that became pending after Commnd1 was clicked. After DoEvents is called, all of the CWaveMix objects are destroyed. If DoEvents was not used to process timer messages after the timer was disabled, you would sooner or later hit a timing window that allowed HiTimer events to be processed after the CWaveMix objects were destroyed. This would cause a run-time error by trying to access previously destroyed objects.

```
Private Sub Command1_Click()
   Dim i        As Integer
   Dim fPlay    As Boolean
   '
   ' Currently playing?
   '
   If (Command1.Caption = "Stop") Then
      '
      ' Yep, change caption from Stop
      '
      Command1.Caption = "Play"
      '
      ' Turn off timer
```

```
        '
        HiTime1.Enabled = False
        '
        ' Eat any timer events that may have occurred
        ' recently!
        '
        DoEvents
        '
        ' Destroy all of the wave mixer's channels
        '
        For i = 0 To MAX_WAVES - 1
            Set WaveMixer(i) = Nothing
        Next
        '
        ' Bail
        '
        Exit Sub
    End If
    '
    ' Attempt to start a play, assume there are no tracks
    ' available to play
    '
    fPlay = False
    '
    ' Now for each track
    '
    For i = 0 To MAX_WAVES - 1
        '
        ' Is the track playable?
        '
        If (Tracks(i).Playable <> False) Then
            '
            ' Initialize track for playing
            '
            InitTrack i
            '
            ' Found at least one playable track
            '
            fPlay = True
        End If
    Next
    '
    ' Ok ... any tracks to play?
    '
    If (fPlay = True) Then
        '
        ' Yes, start timer and change command1's caption
        ' to Stop
        '
        beat = 0
        HiTime1.Interval = freq
        HiTime1.Enabled = True
        Command1.Caption = "Stop"
    End If
End Sub
```

18. Add the following subroutine to Form1. This InitTrack routine prepares a track for playing by creating a new CWaveMix object, opening it, opening a wavefile for the object, and setting the track's PlayPointer to zero.

```
Private Sub InitTrack(t As Integer)
    '
    ' Create wavemixer channel
    '
    Set WaveMixer(t) = New CWaveMix
    '
    ' Open the channel
    '
    WaveMixer(t).OpenChannel WMIX_OPENSINGLE
    '
    ' Load the selected wavefile
    '
    WaveMixer(t).OpenWave Tracks(t).Wavefile, WMIX_FILE
    '
    ' Initialize the track's beat pointer
    '
    Tracks(t).PlayPointer = 0
End Sub
```

19. Add the following as the FileNew menu's Click event procedure. All tracks are reset, and the grid for each is cleared.

```
Private Sub FileNew_Click()
    Dim t As Integer
    '
    ' New file, reset everything
    '
    For t = 0 To MAX_WAVES - 1
        Tracks(t).Playable = False
        Tracks(t).InUse = 0
        Tracks(t).Wavefile = ""
        Combo1(t).ListIndex = -1
        Check1(t).Value = 0
        Check1(t).Enabled = False
        DrawGrid (t)
    Next
    CurrentFile = ""
End Sub
```

20. Add the following as the FileOpen menu's Click event procedure. FileOpen can be used to load a previously saved set of tracks. The CommonDialog CancelError property is set to True, so that an error is generated if the user clicks on the dialog's Cancel button. Trapping this error makes this click easy to detect. Once a file has been selected, its frequency when it was saved is read into the freq variable. Then each track is read, whacks are drawn on the track, and the track's combo box ListIndex property is set so that the combo box displays the correct file name for the track.

```
Private Sub FileOpen_Click()
    Dim t        As Integer
    Dim i        As Integer
    Dim l        As Integer
    Dim cx       As Single
    Dim cy       As Single
    Dim radius   As Single
    '
    ' Get name of file to open
    '
    CommonDialog1.DialogTitle = "Open Drum Tracks"
    CommonDialog1.CancelError = True
    On Error Resume Next
    CommonDialog1.Action = 1
    If (Err) Then
        '
        ' Whoops ... canceled, bail out
        '
        Exit Sub
    End If
    On Error GoTo 0
    '
    ' cy is center of circles to draw for each whack
    '
    cy = Picture2(0).Height / 2
    '
    ' Radius of circles
    '
    radius = 4 * Screen.TwipsPerPixelX
    '
    ' Open the selected file
    '
    Open CommonDialog1.FileName For Binary As #1
    '
    ' Read the timer frequency (beats per minute)
    '
    Get #1, , freq
    '
    ' For each track
    '
    For t = 0 To MAX_WAVES - 1
        '
        ' Read Track
        '
        Get #1, , Tracks(t)
        '
        ' Draw grid for track (also clears picture2(t)
        '
        DrawGrid (t)
        '
        ' Set checkbox according to the track's Playable
        ' status
        '
        If (Tracks(t).Playable = True) Then
            Check1(t).Value = 1
```

Continued on next page

Continued from previous page

```
        Else
            Check1(t).Value = 0
        End If
        '
        ' Set fill color to red
        '
        Picture2(t).FillColor = RGB(255, 0, 0)
        '
        ' Draw a circle for each drum whack
        '
        For i = 0 To Tracks(t).InUse - 1
            Picture2(t).Circle (Tracks(t).Whacks(i) * TwipsPerWhack + ⇒
                TwipsPerWhack \ 2, cy), radius, RGB(255, 0, 0)
        Next
        '
        ' Find wave filename in combobox
        '
        For l = 0 To Combo1(t).ListCount - 1
            If (Combo1(t).List(l) = Tracks(t).Wavefile) Then
                Combo1(t).ListIndex = l
                Exit For
            End If
        Next
    Next
    '
    ' Finish up
    '
    Close #1
    CurrentFile = CommonDialog1.FileName
    Form1.Caption = "Drums - " & CurrentFile
End Sub
```

21. Add the following as the FileSave menu's Click event procedure. If no filename was previously specified for the current tracks (after loading the program or using the File New menu item), then FileSaveAs_Click is called to prompt the user for a filename before saving. If a filename already exists, then the SaveFile subroutine is called to save the tracks to disk.

```
Private Sub FileSave_Click()
    '
    ' Trap attempt to save file without name
    '
    If (CurrentFile = "") Then
        '
        ' Use SaveAs when that happens
        '
        FileSaveAs_Click
    Else
        '
        ' Already had a filename ... just save the file
        '
        SaveFile
    End If
End Sub
```

22. Add the following code as the FileSaveAs menu's Click event procedure. After getting a filename from the user, the SaveFile subroutine is called to save the tracks in the specified file.

```
Private Sub FileSaveAs_Click()
    '
    ' Init common dialog control
    '
    CommonDialog1.DialogTitle = "Save Drumtrack As"
    CommonDialog1.CancelError = True
    On Error Resume Next
    CommonDialog1.Action = 2
    If (Err) Then
        '
        ' Canceled ... we're outta here
        '
        Exit Sub
    End If
    On Error GoTo 0
    CurrentFile = CommonDialog1.FileName
    SaveFile
    Form1.Caption = "Drums - " & CurrentFile
End Sub
```

23. Add the following subroutine to Form1. This SaveFile routine writes the current tracks and the rate at which beats occur, to the file given by CurrentFile. Writing the tracks to disk is easy: We write first the contents of freq, and then each track's data structure.

```
Private Sub SaveFile()
    Dim i As Integer
    '
    ' Open the file
    '
    Open CurrentFile For Binary As #1
    freq = HScroll2.Value
    '
    ' Write frequency (beats per minute)
    '
    Put #1, , freq
    '
    ' Write each track
    '
    For i = 0 To MAX_WAVES - 1
        Put #1, , Tracks(i)
    Next
    '
    ' Close file
    '
    Close #1
End Sub
```

24. Add the following subroutine to Form1. DrawGrid first clears and then redraws a series of vertical lines on a track's Picture2 control.

```
Private Sub DrawGrid(t As Integer)
    Dim x    As Integer
    Dim h    As Integer
    '
    ' Clear existing whacks
    '
    Picture2(t).Cls
    h = Picture2(t).Height
    '
    ' Draw vertical lines to make a grid
    '
    For x = TwipsPerWhack To Picture2(t).Width Step TwipsPerWhack
        If (x Mod (TwipsPerWhack * 8)  0) Then
            Picture2(t).Line (x, 0)-(x, h), RGB(128, 128, 128)
        Else
            Picture2(t).Line (x, 0)-(x, h), RGB(32, 32, 32)
        End If
    Next
End Sub
```

25. Add the following code as the FileExit menu's Click event procedure.

```
Private Sub FileExit_Click()
    Unload Me
End Sub
```

26. Add the following code as HiTime1's Timer event procedure. This is where the tracks actually get played. (Bet you thought you'd never find it!) Recall from the InsertWhack routine that instruments are whacked on a given beat, and that the beat numbers are stored in ascending order in each track's Whacks array. While HiTime1 is enabled, it generates Timer events at the rate given by freq. Each time the HiTime1_Timer routine is called, we compare the value stored in each track's Whacks array, at the position given by the track's PlayPointer, to the current beat (the value of the beat variable). If the beat is greater than or equal to the element pointed to by PlayPointer, then it's time to give the instrument a whack. CWaveMix's PlayWave method causes a wavemix channel to play. When there are no more whacks to play for any track, then it's time to check the Loop check box. If Loop is checked, each track's PlayPointer is reset to zero, beat is reset to zero, and the sequence starts over again. If Loop is not checked, then the tier is disabled and all the wave mixer channels are destroyed.

```
Private Sub HiTime1_Timer()
    Dim i        As Integer
    Dim wRtn     As Integer
    Dim foundOne As Integer
    '
    ' foundOne will still be false if there are no more events to play
    '
```

```
foundOne = False
'
' Check each track to see if there's anything to play
'
For i = 0 To MAX_WAVES - 1
    '
    ' If the track is playable and there's something left to play
    '
    If (Tracks(i).Playable = True And Tracks(i).InUse > ⇒
      Tracks(i).PlayPointer) Then
        '
        ' Still playing!
        '
        foundOne = True
        '
        ' Time to play this track's next whack?
        '
        If (Tracks(i).Whacks(Tracks(i).PlayPointer) <= beat) Then
            '
            ' Yes ... do it
            '
            WaveMixer(i).PlayWave WMIX_QUEUEWAVE Or WMIX_HIGHPRIORITY, 0
            Tracks(i).PlayPointer = Tracks(i).PlayPointer + 1
        End If
    End If
Next
'
' Increment current position
'
beat = beat + 1
'
' We're at the end of all the tracks when foundOne is False
'
If (foundOne = False) Then
    '
    ' Are we looping?
    '
    If (Check2.Value = 0) Then
        '
        ' Not looping ... turn off timer
        '
        HiTime1.Enabled = False
        '
        ' Change command1's caption and free all the
        ' wavemixer channels
        '
        Command1.Caption = "Play"
        For i = 0 To MAX_WAVES - 1
            Set WaveMixer(i) = Nothing
        Next
    Else
        '
        ' Loop is checked
        '
        For i = 0 To MAX_WAVES - 1
```

Continued on next page

Continued from previous page

```
            '
            ' Restart each playable track
            '
            If (Tracks(i).Playable = True) Then
                Tracks(i).PlayPointer = 0
            End If
        Next
        beat = 0
        HiTime1_Timer
    End If
End If
'
' This catches changes to the tempo scrollbar
'
HiTime1.Interval = freq
End Sub
```

27. Add the following code as HScroll1's Change event procedure. Whenever the form is resized (and during form load), HScroll1's Max property is set to the difference in size between the Picture1 and Picture2 controls. This makes the scroll bar's Max property equal to the maximum amount we want to move the Picture2 controls to the left, to display the rightmost grid cells. Setting the Picture2 control's Left property to the negation of HScroll1's value will move the right side of the pictures off the left side of Picture1. Because the Picture2 controls are children of Picture1, the parts of the Picture2 controls that are not inside of Picture1's area are not displayed.

```
Private Sub HScroll1_Change()
    Dim t As Integer
    '
    ' Scroll track grids according to HScroll1's value
    '
    For t = 0 To MAX_WAVES - 1
        Picture2(t).Left = -HScroll1.Value
    Next
End Sub
```

28. Add the following event procedures to Form1. Whenever the Frequency scroll bar changes, ChangeFrequency is called.

```
Private Sub HScroll2_Change()
    ChangeFrequency
End Sub
Private Sub HScroll2_Scroll()
    ChangeFrequency
End Sub
```

29. Add the following subroutine to Form1. ChangeFrequency is called whenever the value of HScroll2 changes. The variable freq is updated, and the resulting beats-per-minute value is displayed in Label3.

```
Sub ChangeFrequency()
    '
    ' Get new value for HiTime1
    '
    freq = HScroll2.Value
    Label3.Caption = "bpm:" & Str(Int(60000 / freq))
End Sub
```

How It Works

At heart, the operation of DRUMS is fairly simple—although it might be difficult to see the simplicity through all the code required to handle the track editor. Each track has an instrument name, an array named Whacks that contains beat numbers, and a PlayPointer that is an index into the Whacks array. When a track is being played, the beat variable increments each time the HiTimer's Timer event procedure is called. In addition, during each call into the Timer event procedure, the beat number stored at Tracks(t).Whacks(Tracks(t).PlayPointer is compared to the current beat. If the stored beat number is greater than or equal to beat, then it's time to play the instrument's sound.

Comments

This project can be improved in a number of ways. Adding volume control to each of the channels would be a nice touch. This will require the use of memory files. Also, you'll need to change the volume of the wavefile directly, since the WAVEMIX DLL doesn't support volume changes. See How-To 4.8 for help in this area.

Once you've got the volume under control, you might want to add the ability to merge a group of tracks into a single wavefile and save it to disk. It would be much more efficient to play a single, precomposed wavefile than to always use WAVEMIX in your finished application. Besides the efficiency issue, you can have a lot of fun by merging a set of tracks and then using the merged wavefile as one of the instruments during a further mix.

5

GRAPHICS

5

GRAPHICS

How do I...

If you've ever wondered how to use color palettes or create animations using Visual Basic you're going to love this chapter.

How-To's 5.1, 5.3, 5.4, 5.5, and 5.6 lead you through the development of some clever class modules you can use to develop color palettes in your Visual Basic applications. Along the way you'll learn how to read bitmap (.DIB) files, create stunning visual effects with color cycling and palette animation, add titles that gradually appear on a form or picture, and create a really smooth transition between pictures.

Everything you ever wanted to know about using WinG, Microsoft's powerful and fast new graphics API, is covered in How-To's 5.7, 5.8, and 5.9. After covering the fundamentals in How-To's 5.7 and 5.8, as well as developing a suite of powerful class modules for using WinG, you will see in How-To 5.9 how to create a complete action-packed space game using Visual Basic. The features and performance of games you can develop using the techniques shown in How-To 5.9 will rival what can be done using C and C++. By the time you get through How-To 5.9, you will have developed six powerful class modules that you can use over and over again.

The following table lists the class modules developed here in this chapter. If you haven't yet "got religion" when it comes to using class modules, you will have by the time you finish working through this chapter.

FILENAME	CLASS	PURPOSE
CDIB.CLS	CDib	Device-independent bitmap class
CPALETTE.CLS	CPalette	Palette functionality
CWGSPRIT.CLS	CWinGSprite	WinG Sprites
CWINGBIT.CLS	CWinGBitmap	WinG bitmaps
CWINGDC.CLS	CWinGDC	WinG device contexts
CWINGSTA.CLS	CWinGStage	WinG background stage

Many of the techniques in this chapter use one or more Windows API calls to accomplish their magic, including the following:

WINDOWS API	HOW-TO'S
AnimatePalette	5.3
BitBlt	5.1, 5.9
CreatePalette	5.1, 5.3
DeleteDC	5.7
DeleteObject	5.1, 5.3
GetDeviceCaps	5.1, 5.3
GetPaletteEntries	5.1
GetSystemPaletteEntries	5.3
GetSystemPaletteUse	5.3
hmemcpy	5.1, 5.2, 5.3, 5.7
hread	5.2, 5.6
hwrite	5.6
IntersectRect	5.9
lclose	5.2, 5.6
lcreate	5.6
LineTo	5.9
lopen	5.2, 5.6

WINDOWS API	HOW-TO'S
lread	5.2
MoveTo	5.9
PatBlt	5.7
RealizePalette	5.1, 5.3, 5.4, 5.5, 5.7, 5.8, 5.9
SelectObject	5.7
SelectPalette	5,1, 5.3, 5.7, 5.8, 5.9
SetPaletteEntries	5.1
StretchBlt	5.1, 5.6
UnionRect	5.7

5.1   Cycle PictureBox Colors

Windows programs can achieve some interesting graphical effects by rapidly changing a bitmap's colors in a way that colors appear to move across the image; this technique is referred to as *color cycling*. This How-To will begin the task of building a complete CPalette class by implementing the class framework and adding methods to support color cycling. The How-To itself will then create a really cool visual effect, using the color-cycling methods to rapidly change the colors used in a fractal image.

5.2   Read .DIB Files

Almost every .BMP file you're likely to run across is actually a device-independent bitmap (.DIB). These files have a color palette that specifies how the bitmap's pixels should be mapped to colors. In contrast, device-dependent bitmaps (those that *don't* have a palette) almost always cause problems because you can only display them using the current system colors. In How-To 5.2, a class named CDib will be created and used to read and display information about a .DIB file. The CDib class is a fundamental tool if you intend to do anything fancy with bitmaps and is used in most of the other How-To's of this chapter.

5.3   Fill Backgrounds with a Smooth Color Transition

Backgrounds with a smooth transition from one color to another—like the blue-to-black transition used in many setup programs—create an attractive backdrop for dialog boxes, status indicators, and other elements of an interface. Color transitions are used frequently in multimedia applications and in games. In this How-To, the CPalette class will be enhanced so that you can easily create a range of colors for filling the background. We will also add true palette animation to the class and use it to change the background colors without repainting the form.

5.4   Fade Text Titles In and Out

In this How-To you will learn how to use palette animation to create titles that gradually appear and disappear. You can use this technique to add sparkling highlights and all sorts of graphical techniques to the text in your applications.

5.5   Use Palette Animation

In this How-To (which could be called Mitch's Madness, in honor of the programmer) you'll see three different dazzling graphical effects. The first technique involves palette animation and fractals, with some charming extras thrown in. The second technique will show you how to quickly animate colors to create the effect of moving into a tunnel. And in the third technique you'll learn how to create a beautiful night sky filled with twinkling stars.

5.6   Fade between Pictures

Most multimedia authoring tools make it easy to create a smooth transition in which one picture fades in as the other fades out. This effect is similar to what can be accomplished with a pair of good slide projectors. In How-To 5.6 you'll see how to create a special type of .DIB file and a pair of color palettes that can later be used in a program to create a rapid and smooth transition between two completely different pictures.

5.7   Create Sprites Using WinG

Many games are based on sprite animation. A sprite is an irregularly shaped bitmap that can be moved over a background, without flickering and without destroying the background. Developers at Microsoft wrote a set of DLLs, collectively referred to as WinG, and Microsoft has made these DLLs widely available for free. In this How-To you will develop the first of a suite of class modules that will give you a good start at building powerful WinG applications using Visual Basic.

5.8   Create a Scrolling Background Using WinG

A game without a scrolling background is. . .well, just an old-fashioned sort of game! In How-To 5.8, the WinG class module suite is expanded to create a fast, smoothly scrolling background. And you will learn how to use a relatively small number of ray-traced frames to create a realistic-looking spaceship that you can fly around the scrolling universe.

5.9   Create a Game

Ever wondered if Visual Basic could be used to write a commercial-quality game? Stop wondering—it can be done! The space shoot'em-up game developed in How-To 5.9 may be somewhat simplistic, but it will clearly show that a high-quality action game can be written in Visual Basic. How-To 5.9 has all the essentials. You look out through the windows of a spaceship that you can pilot around the galaxy, and there are lots of (stupid!) enemy ships to track down and shoot. When you hit an enemy ship, it explodes in a ball of flame. The game also has excellent sound effects: a continous background music track, laser sounds, and realistic explosions.

5.1 How do I...
Cycle PictureBox Colors?

COMPLEXITY: INTERMEDIATE
COMPATIBILITY: VB4 ONLY

Problem

I've seen programs that achieve clever graphical effects by rapidly changing a bitmap's colors in a way to make the colors appear to move across the image. I read somewhere that the best way to accomplish this so-called *color cycling* is to modify a picture's color palette, but I don't see any direct way to modify palettes using Visual Basic. How can I add modify a PictureBox's palette to add color cycling to my Visual Basic programs?

Technique

Despite what you may have heard, color palettes aren't mysterious or difficult to work with. Color palettes are used with graphics devices that can display a large number of colors, but can only display a limited number simultaneously. Most graphics controllers in today's machines can display at least 2^{18} distinct colors, but from this large set of colors it is only possible to display 256 at any one time. A color palette provides a way to select the 256 colors you want to display.

As with other graphics objects in Windows, palettes are referenced by a handle; palette handles are called hPals. When a palette is created using the Windows API function CreatePalette, an hPal is returned. Whenever you want to modify the palette, you pass the hPal (and other arguments) to a Windows API function.

A Picture control's Picture property has a few properties itself—including one named hPal. By using the Picture.hPal property, you can retrieve a handle to the palette used by a Picture control. To modify a palette's colors, you first retrieve the palette colors using the Window API function GetPaletteEntries. After you have modified the colors, you call SetPaletteEntries so that Windows will begin using the new palette colors.

Steps

Open and run CYCLECLR.VBP, and you will see a form similar to that in Figure 5-1-1. Click on the Start command button, and you will see the PictureBox colors cycle in such a way that the colors seem to move inward. Click on the Out option button to reverse the direction in which the colors move. As you will see later, this effect is easy to achieve, once you know how to handle palettes.

1. Create a new project named CYCLECLR.VBP, and use the Insert Class Module menu item to add a new Class module to the project. Set the new class's Name

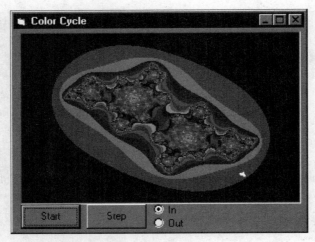

Figure 5-1-1 The CYCLECLR project

property to CPalette, and add the following code to the General section
of Cpalette:

```
Option Explicit
'
' API functions
'
Private Declare Sub CopyMemory Lib "Kernel32" Alias "RtlMoveMemory" ⇒
(dst As Any, src As Any, ByVal SIZE As Long)
'
' Palette handle
'
Private m_hPal            As Long'
' Logical palette structure
'
Private m_logPalette     As LOGPALETTE
```

2. Add the following code to the General section of Cpalette. You have to be careful when you're using palettes and other Windows GDI resources. If you don't free up the resources when you're finished with them, they will be lost to the rest of the system. And if you forget often enough, you will get the dreaded "Out of System Resources" message. So, the first thing that happens in this Let procedure is a check to see if there is currently a palette handle in m_hPal. If so, the palette is freed by calling the Windows API function DeleteObject.

   After the current palette is released Let hPal creates a new palette that is a copy of the palette passed in as the pal argument. Again, precision handling is required when you're using Windows GDI resources directly. Instead of simply assigning the pal to m_hPal, an entirely new palette is created. This is necessary because there is no way of knowing what will happen to the palette referenced by pal after the call to Let hPal has finished. In fact, the palette could be immediately destroyed by a call to DeleteObject. Therefore, Let hPal first initializes m_logPalette's palette header and then uses the Windows API function GetPaletteEntries to get the colors from pal's palette. Finally, a new palette is created using the Windows API function CreatePalette, and the handle to this new palette is saved in m_hPal.

```
Public Property Get hPal() As Integer
    hPal = m_hPal
End Property
```

3. Add the following code as CPalette's hPal Property Let procedure:

```
Public Property Let hPal(pal As Integer)
    '
    ' Delete current palette if any
    '
    If (m_hPal  0) Then
        DeleteObject (m_hPal)
    End If
    '
    ' Initialize palette header
    '
    m_logPalette.version = &H300
    m_logPalette.nEntries = 256
    '
    ' Get color table from palette
    '
    Call GetPaletteEntries(pal, 0, 256, m_logPalette.aEntries(0))
    '
    ' Create our own palette using caller's colors
    '
    m_hPal = CreatePalette(m_logPalette)
End Property
```

4. Add the following code to the General section of CPalette. The SetRgbColors method is used to set a range of color entries in the palette. After calling the Windows API function SetPaletteEntries, the logical palette structure m_logPalette is updated with the current colors.

```
Public Sub SetRgbColors(iStart As Integer, iColors As Integer, aRgb() ⇒
    As Long)
    Call SetPaletteEntries(m_hPal, iStart, iColors, aRgb(iStart))
    CopyMemory m_logPalette.aEntries(iStart), aRgb(iStart), 4 * iColors
End Sub
```

5. Add the following function to the General section of CPalette. GetRgbColors retrieves palette entries by calling the Windows API function GetPaletteEntries, and updates the logical palette m_logPalette.

```
Public Function GetRgbColors(iStart As Integer, iColors As Integer, ⇒
    aRgb() As Long) As Boolean
    Call GetPaletteEntries(m_hPal, iStart, iColors, aRgb(iStart))
    CopyMemory m_logPalette.aEntries(iStart), aRgb(iStart), 4 * iColors
End Function
```

6. Add the following code to the Class section of CPalette. Initializing the values of important variables helps to prevent unexpected bugs. In the first release of VB4, Boolean variables are for the most part always set to false (zero), and other variables are cleared to zero, so it is not strictly necessary to initialize m_hPal when a new CPalette object is created. However, when it comes to variable initialization, it's better to be safe than sorry. And you *would* be sorry if some future version of VB handles variable initialization differently.

```
Sub Class_Initialize()
    m_hPal = 0
End Sub
```

7. Use the Insert Module menu item to add a new module to CYCLECLR.VBP, set the module's name to GDI, and then add the following code to the General section of the new module:

```
Option Explicit
'==========================================================
'                  WINDOWS API FUNCTIONS
'==========================================================
Declare Function GetDC Lib "Use32r" (ByVal hWnd As Long) As Long
Declare Function ReleaseDC Lib "User32" (ByVal hWnd As Long, ⇒
    ByVal hDC As Long) As Long
Declare Function DeleteObject Lib "GDI32" (ByVal hObject As Long) As Long
Declare Function GetDeviceCaps Lib "GDI32" (ByVal hDC As Long, ⇒
    ByVal nIndex As Long) As Long
Declare Function GetSystemPaletteUse Lib "GDI32" (ByVal hDC As Long) ⇒
    As Long
Declare Function CreatePalette Lib "GDI32" (lpLogPalette As LOGPALETTE) ⇒
    As Long
Declare Function SelectPalette Lib "GDI32" (ByVal hDC As Long, ⇒
    ByVal hPalette As Long, ByVal bForceBackground As Long) As Long
Declare Function RealizePalette Lib "GDI32" (ByVal hDC As Long) As Long
Declare Function GetSystemPaletteEntries Lib "GDI32" (ByVal hDC ⇒
    As Long, ByVal wStartIndex As Long, ByVal wNumEntries As Long, ⇒
    lpPaletteEntries As Any) As Long
Declare Function GetPaletteEntries Lib "GDI32" (ByVal hPalette As Long, ⇒
    ByVal wStartIndex As Long, ByVal wNumEntries As Long, lpPaletteEntries ⇒
    As Any) As Long
Declare Function SetPaletteEntries Lib "GDI32" (ByVal hPalette As Long, ⇒
    ByVal wStartIndex As Long, ByVal wNumEntries As Long, lpPaletteEntries ⇒
    As Any) As Long
Declare Sub AnimatePalette Lib "GDI32" (ByVal hPalette As Long, ByVal ⇒
    wStartIndex As Long, ByVal wNumEntries As Long, lpPaletteColors As Any)
Declare Function PatBlt Lib "GDI32" (ByVal hDC As Long, As Long, ⇒
    ByVal Y As Long, ByVal nWidth As Long, ByVal x ByVal nHeight ⇒
    As Long, ByVal dwRop As Long) As Long
Declare Function BitBlt Lib "GDI32" (ByVal hDestDC As Long, ByVal x ⇒
    As Long, ByVal Y As Long, ByVal nWidth As Long, ByVal nHeight ⇒
    As Long, ByVal hSrcDC As Long, ByVal XSrc As Long, ByVal YSrc ⇒
    As Long, ByVal dwRop As Long) As Long
Declare Function CreateCompatibleBitmap Lib "GDI32" (ByVal hDC As Long, ⇒
    ByVal nWidth As Long, ByVal nHeight As Long) As Long
```

```
Declare Function CreateCompatibleDC Lib "GDI32" (ByVal hDC As Long) ⇒
    As Long
Declare Function SetPixel Lib "GDI32" (ByVal hDC As Long, ByVal x ⇒
    As Long, ByVal Y As Long, ByVal crColor As Long) As Long
Declare Function SelectObject Lib "GDI32" (ByVal hDC As Long, ByVal hObject ⇒
    As Long) As Long
Declare Function DeleteDC Lib "GDI32" (ByVal hDC As Long) As Long
Declare Function UnionRect Lib "User32" (lpDestRect As RECT, lpSrc1Rect ⇒
    As RECT, lpSrc2Rect As RECT) As Long
'
'
' Constants for GetDeviceCaps
Global Const RASTERCAPS = 38        '  Bitblt capabilities
Global Const RC_PALETTE = &H100     '  supports a palette
'
' Bitblt mode
'
Global Const SRCCOPY = &HCC0020 ' (DWORD) dest = source
'
' Possible return from GetSystemPaletteUse
'
Global Const SYSPAL_NOSTATIC = 2
'
' Used with GetDeviceCaps to retrieve the number of colors
' a device supports
'
Global Const NUMCOLORS = 24         '  Number of colors the device supports
'
' Palette flags
'
Global Const PC_RESERVED = &H1   '  palette index used for animation
Global Const PC_NOCOLLAPSE = &H4 '  do not match color to system palette
'
' Structure of one palette entry
'
Type PALETTEENTRY
    peRed    As Byte
    peGreen  As Byte
    peBlue   As Byte
    peFlags  As Byte
End Type
'
' Logical palette structure
'
Type LOGPALETTE
    version          As Integer
    nEntries         As Integer
    aEntries(256)    As PALETTEENTRY
End Type
'
' RGB structure
'
Type RGBQUAD
    rgbBlue As Byte
    rgbGreen As Byte
```

Continued on next page

Continued from previous page

```
    rgbRed As Byte
    rgbReserved As Byte
End Type
'
' Palette entry flags
'
Global Const DIB_RGB_COLORS = 0  '  color table in RGBTriples
Global Const DIB_PAL_COLORS = 1  '  color table in palette indices
'
' ROP code for blackness
'
Global Const BLACKNESS = &H42&
'
' Windows rectangle structure
'
Type RECT
    left As Long
    top As Long
    right As Long
    bottom As Long
End Type
```

8. Select Form1. Then create objects and set their properties as shown in Table 5-1-1.

Table 5-1-1 Objects, properties, and settings for Form1

OBJECT	PROPERTY	SETTING
Form1Caption	"Color Cycle"	
	Name	Form1
PictureBox	Name	Picture1
OptionButton	Caption	"In"
	Index	0
	Name	Option1
OptionButton	Caption	"Out"
	Index	1
	Name	Option1
CommandButton	Caption	"Start"
	Name	Command1
CommandButton	Caption	"Step"
	Name	Command2
Timer1	Enabled	0 'False
	Interval	55

9. Add the following code to the General Declarations section of Form1.

```
Option Explicit
'
' CPalette object
'
```

```
Private pal As CPalette
'
' Array of rgb quads used for cycling
'
Private rgbquads(256)    As Long
```

10. Add the following code to Form1's Form_Load subroutine. The first thing Form_Load does is check to see if your systems graphics card uses palettes. The color-cycling technique demonstrated in this How-To requires a graphics card that uses palettes. If your graphics card uses palettes, Form_Load loads a picture into Picture1, creates an instance of CPalette and stores it in the variable pal, and assigns Picture1's hPal to pal.hPal. Finally the RGBQUAD color table is retrieved from pal using CPalette's GetRgbColors method.

```
Private Sub Form_Load()
Dim msg  As String
    Dim i     As Integer
    '
    ' Check to see if the graphics card supports palettes
    '
    If (Not DeviceUsesPalette(Picture1.hDC)) Then
        msg = "The graphics card you are using does not " & Chr$(13) & _
              "support color palettes."
        MsgBox msg, vbInformation
        End
    End If
    '
    ' Load a nice picture to use for color cycling
    '
    Picture1.Picture = LoadPicture(App.Path + "\fract001.dib")
    '
    ' Create new instance of CPalette
    '
    Set pal = New CPalette
    '
    ' Use Picture1's palette
    '
    pal.hPal = Picture1.Picture.hPal
' Select palette into Picture
    '
    Picture1.picture.hPal = pal.hPal
    dwrtn = SelectPalette(Picture1.hDC, Picture1.picture.hPal, False)
    dwrtn = RealizePalette(Picture1.hDC)
    Call pal.GetRgbColors(0, 256, rgbquads)
End Sub
```

11. Add the following code to the Timer event routine of Timer1. This is where the color cycling actually takes place. The value of Option1(0) determines whether the colors will move in toward the center of the fractal, or out from the center. To get the colors to move in, the rgbquads array is rotated to the right; for outward movement, the array is rotated to the left.

After the array has been rotated, pal's colors are set using CPalette's SetRgbColors method. Then pal's hPal property can be selected into Picture1's device context. And finally, the moment you've been waiting for—the Window's API function RealizePalette is used to copy the palette from Picture1's device context into the system palette. When this is done, Windows updates the graphics card's palette registers, and the screen colors change instantly.

```
Private Sub Timer1_Timer()
    Dim i                 As Integer
    '
    ' Which way do we want to shuffle the colors?
    '
    If (Option1(0).Value = True) Then
        '
        ' In Option selected, rotate right
        '
        rgbquads(0) = rgbquads(255)
        For i = 255 To 1 Step -1
            rgbquads(i) = rgbquads(i - 1)
        Next
    Else
        '
        ' Out option selected, rotate left
        '
        rgbquads(255) = rgbquads(0)
        For i = 0 To 254
            rgbquads(i) = rgbquads(i + 1)
        Next
    End If
    '
    ' Set rotated colors
    '
    pal.SetRgbColors 0, 256, rgbquads
    '
    ' Change palette, this changes the display without a repaint
    '
    Call RealizePalette(Picture1.hDC)
End Sub
```

12. Add the following code to Command1's Click event subroutine. This subroutine turns the timer on and off, and so controls whether color cycling takes place. Also, the Step command button is enabled while the timer is not running, and disabled while the timer is running.

```
Private Sub Command1_Click()
    If (Timer1.Enabled = True) Then
        '
        ' Timer's on, turn it off and enable Step button
        '
        Timer1.Enabled = False
        Command1.Caption = "Start"
        Command2.Enabled = True
    Else
        '
```

```
                ' Timer's off, turn it on and disable Step button
                '
                Timer1.Enabled = True
                Command1.Caption = "Stop"
                Command2.Enabled = False
        End If
End Sub
```

13. Add the following code to Command2's Click event procedure. The Click event causes a single palette cycle to occur by calling the Timer's event procedure.

```
Private Sub Command2_Click()
    '
    ' Simply call timer subroutine to step
    '
    Timer1_Timer
End Sub
```

14. Add the following function to the General Declarations section of Form1. This function, called during Form_Load, uses the Windows API function GetDeviceCaps to get the RASTERCAPS flags for a device context. The bit wise AND of GetDeviceCaps's return value and RC_PALETTE tells you whether a device uses color palettes or not. If the result of the GetDeviceCaps return value and RC_PALETTE is not zero, then the device uses palettes.

```
Private Function DeviceUsesPalette(hDC As Integer) As Boolean
    Dim wRtn As Integer
    '
    ' Get device capabilities
    '
    wRtn = GetDeviceCaps(hDC, RASTERCAPS)
    '
    ' Return True if the device uses palettes
    '
    DeviceUsesPalette = (wRtn And RC_PALETTE)  0
End Function
```

How It Works

When CYCLECLR loads, Form1's Form_Load routine loads a fractal into Picture1's Picture property. When you use LoadPicture to load a .DIB file into a Picture property, Visual Basic reads the color table, creates a palette using the colors, and assigns the palette to the hPal property of the picture. The Form_Load routine gets the value of Picture1's Picture.hPal property and stores it in an instance of CPalette for use during color cycling.

CPalette serves as a handy container for an hPal and the functions that can manipulate it. After Form_Load assigns Picture1's hPal to pal, an instance of CPalette, pal's GetRgbColors member function is used to retrieve the palette's color table. Then, each time the Timer's event procedure is called, the color table, rgbquads, is rotated either to the right or the left as specified by Option1(0)'s value. After the color table has been changed, pal's SetRgbColors member function is used to change the pal.hPal palette. Finally, the Windows API functions SelectPalette and RealizePalette are used to select pal.hPal's palette into Picture1's device context and update the system palette.

Comments

In addition to demonstrating a simple color-cycling technique, this How-To shows that you can have some fun with color palettes without getting a degree from Microsoft University! You can start with this How-To and construct a number of useful palette manipulation tools. For instance, gradually reducing the intensity of a palette's colors by subtracting some constant value (like &H040404) from each of the rgbquad entries will cause a picture to fade to black.

5.2 How do I...
Read .DIB Files?

COMPLEXITY: INTERMEDIATE
COMPATIBILITY: VB4 ONLY

Problem

Device Independent Bitmaps (.DIB files or DIBs) are used extensively in Windows, especially in programs that include Multimedia features. I know that the primary difference between a Device Dependent Bitmap (DDB) and a DIB is that the DIB has a color table providing data necessary to build the correct palette for displaying the actual bitmap part of the DIB. I'd also like to be able to use the WinG graphics routines in my program. WinG uses DIBs and requires me to supply the bitmap and palette portions of a DIB separately. How can I read DIBs using Visual Basic?

Technique

Reading DIBs is mostly a matter of paying attention to the details of the .DIB file format. A .DIB file has three sections: a file header, bitmap information, and the bitmap data. Figure 5-2-1 illustrates these three sections, their sizes, and the names of the user-defined types the Windows API uses when reading and writing each section of a DIB.

The first section, BITMAPFILEHEADER, has two fields that are important when reading a DIB. The first field, bfType, will always contain the value &H4D42—a magic cookie indicating that the file being read may be a DIB. The second field, bfSize, will always contain 14, the number of bytes in a BITMAPFILEHEADER. You may encounter some files with a .BMP extension that have a bfSize of 12. These are OS/2 DIBs, not valid Windows 3.0 DIBs. If you try to load the file 256COLOR.BMP from your Windows directory, the code in this How-To will reject it as an invalid file, because it is an OS/2 DIB.

The second section of a DIB contains a BITMAPINFO data structure, the first field of which is another data structure, BITMAPINFOHEADER. A number of fields in BITMAPINFOHEADER are important to verify that a file is in fact a DIB, and you will see how these fields are used in the CDib class. After the BITMAPINFOHEADER data structure comes the DIB's color table. Color tables can vary in size from no colors to 256 colors. The size of a color table for a DIB is calculated using data from BITMAPINFOHEADER. Only DIBs having 8 or fewer bits per pixel have a color table. DIBs using more than 8 bits per pixel explicitly give an RGB color for each pixel and so do not need a color table.

The third section of a DIB file contains the bitmap data itself. The size of this section, of course, depends upon the number of pixels in the bitmap.

The majority of the code in this How-To is centered around creating a robust and useful class module named CDib. The code in CDib takes care of verifying that a file is in fact a DIB, and loads the color table and bitmap data into memory. How-To 3.6 will show you how to enhance the CDib class so that you can write DIB files as well as read them.

Steps

Open and run READDIB.VBP (see Figure 5-2-2), and use the File Open menu item to open a bitmap. If the bitmap you selected is a DIB, a second form will open and

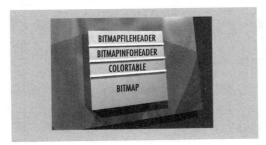

Figure 5-2-1 Format of a .DIB file

Figure 5-2-2 The READDIB project

display the DIB. If the bitmap you selected is not a DIB or if it is an OS/2 DIB, an error message will be displayed by the CDib class.

1. Create a new project named READDIB.VBP. Use the Insert Class menu item to create a new class module, and set the module's name to CDib. Add the following code to the General Declarations section of Cdib. CDib uses Windows API functions built into KERNEL.DLL to read a DIB. This isn't strictly necessary, but there is a major advantage to this approach: speed. DIBs can be huge; many hundreds of kilobytes can easily be used by a 24-bit-per-pixel DIB. The Windows API function hread was designed to read huge chunks of data from the disk with a single call. CDib uses hread to read the bitmap into memory, so the performance of this crucial part of the code is as good as you can get from Windows.

```
Option Explicit
'
' Windows API functions used in CDib
'
Private Declare Function lopen Lib "Kernel32" Alias "_lopen" ⇒
(ByVal lpPathName As String, ByVal iReadWrite As Integer) As Integer
Private Declare Function lread Lib "Kernel32" Alias "_lread" (ByVal ⇒
hfile As Integer, lpBuffer As Any, ByVal wBytes As Integer) As Integer
Private Declare Function lclose Lib "Kernel32" Alias "_lclose" ⇒
(ByVal hfile As Integer) As Integer
Private Declare Function hread Lib "Kernel32" Alias "_hread" ⇒
(ByVal hfile As Integer, Buffer As Any, ByVal n As Long) As Long'
' Windows constants and data structures used in CDib
'
Private Const OPEN_READ = 0        ' used with lopen
```

2. Add the following code to the General section of CDib. These user-defined types and constants define the contents of a DIB.

```
Private Type BITMAPFILEHEADER
    bfType As Integer
    bfSize As Long
    bfReserved1 As Integer
    bfReserved2 As Integer
    bfOffBits As Long
End Type

Private Type BITMAPINFOHEADER
    biSize As Long
    biWidth As Long
    biHeight As Long
    biPlanes As Integer
    biBitCount As Integer
    biCompression As Long
    biSizeImage As Long
    biXPelsPerMeter As Long
    biYPelsPerMeter As Long
    biClrUsed As Long
    biClrImportant As Long
End Type
```

```
'
' Constants for BITMAPINFOHEADER.biCompression
'
Private Const BI_RGB = 0&
Private Const BI_RLE4 = 2&
Private Const BI_RLE8 = 1&

Private Type BITMAPINFO
    bmiHeader       As BITMAPINFOHEADER
    bmiColors(256) As Long
End Type
```

3. Add the following code to the General section of CDib. Each instance of CDib has its own BITMAPINFO, BITMAPFILEHEADER, and bitmap bytes. Also, m_hfile since it is used by a number of subroutines and functions when a DIB is being loaded, is defined as global to the CDib class.

```
'
' CDib's private variables
'
Private m_bminfo   As BITMAPINFO
Private m_fheader  As BITMAPFILEHEADER
Private m_bytes()  As Byte
Private m_hfile    As Long
```

4. Add the following code to the General section of CDib. BitsPerPixel provides access to the BITMAPINFOHEADER's biBitCount field, and tells you how many bits are required to represent the color of one pixel in the DIB. Typical values for this field are 2, 4, 8, and 24, for monochrome, 16-color, 256-color, and true color, respectively.

```
'
' Get number of bits per pixel
'
Public Property Get BitsPerPixel() As Long
    BitsPerPixel = m_bminfo.bmiHeader.biBitCount
End Property
```

5. Add the following code to the General section of CDib. ColorsUsed returns the number of colors used by a DIB. The BITMAPINFOHEADER field biClrUsed does not always provide the number of colors used in a DIB. If biClrUsed is non-zero, then it provides the number of colors used in a DIB. If biClUsed is zero, then you need to use the number of bits per pixel to determine how many colors a DIB uses.

```
'
' Get number of colors in color table
'
Public Property Get ColorsUsed() As Long
    Dim dwClrUsed As Long
    '
    ' If biClrUsed is non-zero then it gives the number of
    ' colors used
    '
```

Continued on next page

Continued from previous page

```
    dwClrUsed = m_bminfo.bmiHeader.biClrUsed
    If (dwClrUsed  0) Then
        NumColors = dwClrUsed
        Exit Property
    End If
    '
    ' Otherwise calculate the number of colors in the color table based on
    ' the number of bits per pixel for the DIB.
    '
    Select Case BitsPerPixel
        Case 1
            NumColors = 2
        Case 4
            NumColors = 16
        Case 8
            NumColors = 256
        Case Else
            NumColors = 0
    End Select
End Property
```

6. Add the following code to the General section of CDib. Width returns the width, in pixels, of the bitmap.

```
'
' Width of bitmap image
'
Public Property Get Width() As Integer
    Width = m_bminfo.bmiHeader.biWidth
End Property
```

7. Add the following code to the General section of CDib. Height returns the height of the bitmap.

```
'
' Height of bitmap image
'
Public Property Get Height() As Integer
    Height = m_bminfo.bmiHeader.biHeight
End Property
```

8. Add the following code to the General section of CDib. ByteWidth returns the number of bytes used by one row of the bitmap. Each row of a DIB is rounded up in size to the nearest 4-byte boundary, so this Property procedure needs to do some calculation in order to return the correct value. The expression (CLng(m_bminfo.bmiHeader.biBitCount) * CLng(m_bminfo.bmiHeader.biWidth) calculates the number of bits used in one row. Adding 31 to that and then masking off the lower 5 bits with &HFFE0 rounds the number of bits per row up to the nearest long integer (4-byte) value. Finally, dividing by 8 gives the total number of bytes used per row in the bitmap.

```
'
' Number of bytes in one row
'
Public Property Get ByteWidth() As Long
```

```
With m_bmInfo.bmiHeader
    ByteWidth = ((CLng(.biBitCount) * CLng(.biWidth) + 31&) ⇒
        And &HFFE0)\8
End With
End Property
```

9. Add the following code to the General section of CDib. The BitmapSize property procedure returns the total number of bytes used in the bitmap of a DIB.

```
'
' Total number of bytes in bitmap
'
Public Property Get BitmapSize() As Long
    BitmapSize = CLng(m_bminfo.bmiHeader.biHeight) * ByteWidth
End Property
```

10. Add the following code to the General section of CDib. ReadDib first tries to open a file using the Windows API function, lopen. If lopen succeeds, then lread is used to read the BITMAPFILEHEADER data structure. Lread returns the number of bytes actually read from a file, so checking to see if Len(m_fheader)'s worth of bytes have been read gives a first check on the validity of the file. If the file is too small to be a DIB then ReadDib returns False. After reading m_fheader from the file, ReadBmInfo and ReadBits are called. Both of these functions do more validity checking and may return a False if the file is not a useable DIB.

```
'
' Read a DIB file from disk
'
Public Function ReadDib(filename As String) As Boolean
    '
    ' Open file, display error on failure
    '
    m_hfile = lopen(filename, OPEN_READ)
    If (m_hfile = 0) Then
        MsgBox "Could not open " & filename & "."
        ReadDib = False
        Exit Function
    End If
    '
    ' Avoid messy Else code by assuming failure
    '
    ReadDib = False
    If (lread(m_hfile, m_fheader, Len(m_fheader)) = Len(m_fheader)) Then
        If (ReadBmInfo() = True) Then
            If (ReadBits() = True) Then
                '
                ' Got a good one
                '
                ReadDib = True
            End If
        End If
    End If
    Call lclose(m_hfile)
End Function
```

11. Add the following code to the General section of CDib. ReadBmInfo first tries to read sufficient bytes from the file to fill the BITMAPINFOHEADER structure. If the file is too small to supply the required number of bytes, an error message is displayed and the function returns False. Next, the function ValidateHeader is called to verify that the bmiHeader contains valid data, and returns False if bmiHeader is not valid. Finally, ReadBmInfo checks to see if the DIB has a color table and, if so, reads it from the file.

```
'
' Read bitmap info header and color table
Private Function ReadBmInfo() As Boolean
    Dim colorTableSize As Long
    '
    ' Read header, return error if read fails
    '
    If (lread(m_hfile, m_bminfo.bmiHeader.biSize, Len(m_bminfo.bmiHeader)) ⇒
        () Len(m_bminfo.bmiHeader))
Then
        ReadBmInfo = False
        MsgBox "Could not read bminfo."
        Exit Function
    End If
    '
    ' Check the header, bail if it's not valid
    '
    If (ValidateHeader = False) Then
        ReadBmInfo = False
        Exit Function
    End If
    '
    ' Looks like a valid header
    '
    colorTableSize = ColorsUsed * Len(colorTableSize)
    '
    ' No color table if bits per pixel > 8
    '
    If (BitsPerPixel <= 8) Then
        '
        ' Read color table, return result of read as value of function
        '
        If (lread(m_hfile, m_bminfo.bmiColors(0), () colorTableSize) ⇒
            colorTableSize) Then
            MsgBox "Could not read color table."
            ReadBmInfo = False
        Else
            ReadBmInfo = True
        End If
    Else
        ReadBmInfo = True
    End If
End Function
```

12. Add the following code to the General section of CDib. ValidateHeader first checks the "magic cookie" that should be in the BITMAPFILEHEADER's bfType field. A valid DIB has the two ASCII characters B and M stored in the integer field bfType. Because Intel processors store integers with the least significant byte first, the characters look like MB when accessed as an integer. The hex value 4D42 is the ASCII equivalent of the two characters MB. As one final check, ValidateHeader examines some of the other fields in m_bminfo to make sure they are reasonable. There is no sure way to know whether a file is actually a DIB, but checking a number of different fields makes it extremely unlikely that some other type of file will slip through.

```
Private Function ValidateHeader() As Boolean
    '
    ' First look for magic-cookie "BM"
    '
    If (m_fheader.bfType  &h4d42) Then
        '
        ' Woops, no cookie
        '
        ValidateHeader = False
        MsgBox "Invalid value for bfType."
        Exit Function
    End If
    '
    ' Check header for consistency
    '
    With m_bminfo.bmiHeader
        If ((.biSize = Len(m_bminfo.bmiHeader)) And _
            (.biPlanes = 1) And _
            ((.biBitCount = 1) Or _
            (.biBitCount = 4) Or _
            (.biBitCount = 8) Or _
            (.biBitCount = 24)) And _
            ((.biCompression = BI_RGB) Or _
            (.biCompression = BI_RLE4 And .biBitCount = 4) Or _
            (.biCompression = BI_RLE8 And .biBitCount = 8))) Then
            '
            ' Header looks good
            '
            ValidateHeader = True
        Else
            '
            ' Header is bad
            '
            MsgBox "Invalid bmiHeader."
            ValidateHeader = False
        End If
    End With
End Function
```

13. Add the following code as CDib's ReadBits method, which reads the actual bitmap values from a .DIB file.

531

```
Private Function ReadBits() As Boolean
    Dim byteCount As Long
    Dim bytesRead As Long
    '
    ' Get size in bytes of bitmap and resize array
    '
    byteCount = BitmapSize
    ReDim m_bytes(byteCount)
    '
    ' Read the data bytes
    '
    bytesRead = hread(m_hfile, m_bytes(0), byteCount)
    If (bytesRead () byteCount) Then
        MsgBox "Could not read all bytes."
        ReadBits = False
    Else
        ReadBits = True
    End If
End Function
```

14. Select Form1, and add the objects with properties and settings shown in Table 5-2-1.

Table 5-2-1 Objects, properties, and settings for Form1

OBJECT	PROPERTY	SETTING
Form	Caption	"ReadDIB"
	Name	Form1
Frame	Name	Frame1
CommonDialog	CancelError	-1 'True
	Filter	"Bitmaps (*.bmp,*.dib)|*.bmp;*.dib|"
	Name	CommonDialog1

15. Add the the labels shown in Table 5-2-2 to Form1's Frame1.

Table 5-2-2 Objects, properties, and settings for Form1's Frame1

LABEL	PROPERTY	SETTING
Label	Caption	"Height:"
	Index	0
	Name	Label1
Label	Caption	"Width:"
	Index	1
	Name	Label1
Label	Caption	"Color Table Size:"
	Index	2
	Name	Label1

LABEL	PROPERTY	SETTING
Label	Caption	"Bitmap Size:"
	Index	3
	Name	Label1
Label	Caption	"Total Size:"
	Index	4
	Name	Label1
Label	Caption	""
	Index	5
	Name	Label1
Label	Caption	""
	Index	6
	Name	Label1
Label	Caption	""
	Index	7
	Name	Label1
Label	Caption	""
	Index	8
	Name	Label1
Label	Caption	""
	Index	9
	Name	Label1

16. Use the Tools Menu Editor menu item to create the menu shown in Table 5-2-3.

Table 5-2-3 Form1's menu

MENU	CAPTION
FileMenu	"&File"
...FileOpen	"&Open..."
...FileSep1	"-"
...FileExit	"E&xit"

17. Add the following code to the File Open menu's Click event procedure. The first order of business is to use the CommonDialogs control so the user can select a file. Since the CancelError property of CommonDialog1 is set to True, an error will be generated if the user clicks on the Cancel button instead of selecting a file. When a file is selected, CDib's ReadDib method is called, and returns True if the file selected was a DIB. Once a valid DIB file has been selected, it is displayed on Form2, with information about the DIB displayed on Form1.

```
Option Explicit

Private Sub FileOpen_Click()
    Dim dib As New CDib
    '
    ' Get file to open
    '
    On Error Resume Next
    CommonDialog1.Show Open
    If (Err) Then
        '
        ' Bail if Cancel used
        '
        Exit Sub
    End If
    On Error GoTo 0
    '
    ' Read dib and display dib and dib info if valid
    '
    If (dib.ReadDib(CommonDialog1.filename) = True) Then
        '
        ' Display dib on Form2
        '
        Form2.DisplayDib CommonDialog1.filename, dib
        Form2.Show
        '
        ' Display information about the dib
        '
        Label1(5).Caption = CStr(dib.Height)
        Label1(6).Caption = CStr(dib.Width)
        Label1(7).Caption = CStr(dib.NumColors * 4)
        Label1(8).Caption = CStr(dib.BitmapSize)
        '
        ' Only dibs with 8 or less bits per pixel use a color table
        '
        If (dib.BitsPerPixel <= 8) Then
            Label1(9).Caption = CStr(54 + dib.NumColors * 4 + dib.BitmapSize)
        Else
            Label1(9).Caption = CStr(54 + dib.BitmapSize)
        End If
    End If
End Sub
```

18. Add the following code to the File Exit menu's Click event procedure:

```
Private Sub FileExit_Click()
    '
    ' We're done ... unload forms
    '
    Unload Form2
    Unload Me
End Sub
```

19. Use the Insert Form menu item to add a new form to your project. Create the objects with property settings as shown in Table 5-2-4.

Table 5-2-4 Objects, properties, and settings for Form2

OBJECT	PROPERTY	SETTING
Form	AutoRedraw	-1 'True
	Name	Form2
	Caption	"DisplayDIB"
Image	Name	Image1
	Stretch	-1 'True

20. Add the following code to the General Declarations section of Form2:

```
Option Explicit
```

21. Add the following subroutine to the General Declarations section of Form2.
    DisplayDib first uses LoadPicture to read the DIB from disk, convert it to a
    Picture object, and assign it to the Picture property of Image1. Then the form is
    resized so that its width/height ratio is the same as the DIB's width/height ratio.
    Finally, the form is made visible (it is not visible when first loaded).

```
Public Sub DisplayDib(fname As String, dib As CDib)
    '
    ' Load dib into Image1
    '
    Image1.Picture = LoadPicture(fname)
    '
    ' Set initial form height
    '
    Me.Height = 200 * Screen.TwipsPerPixelY
    '
    ' Scale form width to match dib's width/height ratio
    '
    Me.Width = (200 * (dib.Width / dib.Height)) * Screen.TwipsPerPixelX
    '
    ' Make sure this form is visible
    '
    Me.Show
End Sub
```

22. Add the following code to Form2's Resize event procedure. Image1 is positioned
    so that it fills the entire client area of Form2. Image1's Stretch property is set to
    True, so the DIB will be stretched to fill the client area of Form2.

```
Private Sub Form_Resize()
    '
    ' Fill form with image
    '
    Image1.Move 0, 0, Me.ScaleWidth, Me.ScaleHeight
End Sub
```

How It Works

Using CDib's ReadDib function to load a DIB is as easy as using LoadPicture—at least from the perspective of the programmer using CDib. Behind the simple interface are a number of calls to Windows API functions, and some bit-twiddling.

ReadDib starts by trying to read a BITMAPFILEHEADER. There isn't a lot of useful information in the file header, so ReadDib simply checks to see that it was able to read the correct number of bytes from disk to fill the m_fheader variable. After the file header has been read, ReadDib calls ReadBmInfo and ReadBits to read the rest of the DIB.

ReadBmInfo first tries to read the BITMAPINFO data structure from disk, storing it in the m_bminfo variable. Then ValidateHeader is called to see if the header information makes sense. If ValidateHeader returns True, ReadBmInfo proceeds to determine if the DIB has a color table, and how large it is. Then the color table is read from the disk. This leaves the file positioned so that the first byte of the next read will be the first byte of the bitmap.

After ReadBmInfo returns True, ReadBits is called to read the bitmap bits from the file. CDib's BitmapSize property procedure is used to determine the number of bytes in the bitmap. Then the Byte array, m_bytes, is ReDimed to the correct size for holding the bitmap data. The bytes are then read from the disk.

Comments

This READDIB How-To demonstrates how to read and validate a DIB, using Windows API calls. The CDib class is not very useful as it is; for instance, there is no way to access the bitmap bytes or color information. However, class modules make it easy to add more functionality when required.

5.3 How do I...
Fill Backgrounds with a Smooth Color Transition?

COMPLEXITY: ADVANCED
COMPATIBILITY: VB4 ONLY

Problem

Backgrounds with a smooth color transition from one color to another—like the blue-to-black transition used in many setup programs—create an attractive backdrop for dialog boxes, status indicators, and other user interface elements. Color transitions are also used frequently in multimedia applications and in games. I've tried to create this kind of smooth transition using a form's ForeColor property, but for some reason Visual Basic creates dithered colors instead of the pure colors I've seen in other programs. Is there a way to create smooth color transitions in Visual Basic?

Technique

Visual Basic normally uses only the standard 16 VGA colors when painting. Other colors must be simulated by dithering. To create a smooth transition from one color to another, you must create a palette containing the colors you want to use. Then you arrange for the control on which you'll be painting—a Form or PictureBox, for instance—to use the palette you've created.

In this How-To you will add powerful new capabilities to the CPalette class started in How-To 5.1. CPalette comprises all of the functionality you're likely to need, and if it falls short for some future project you can easily extend it without breaking programs that use CPalette current functionality.

About Palettes

You've probably heard a lot of grumbling about palettes, and it's all true. Palettes are one of those things you can't live with, and you can't live without. Color palettes have their origins in hardware, and so reflect the limitations that component costs impose on hardware architectures.

Most VGA cards are capable of displaying at least 2^{18} colors, but not all at the same time. The cost of video RAM chips is the source of the problem. Each pixel that gets displayed on the screen requires its own complement of memory bits on the video card. To display any given number of pixels on a card that has 24 bits per pixel instead of the more common 8 bits per pixel, the required amount of Video RAM triples. To keep the cost of video cards relatively low yet still provide the ability to display colors from a broad spectrum, hardware designers have settled on the idea of using a palette. A palette is simply a lookup table built out of hardware. On VGA cards, an 8-bit value is used as an index into a table (palette) of 24-bit values, and the 24-bit value at the indexed location is the actual color value to be displayed.

Internally, Windows maintains what is called the System Palette, which is a copy of the VGA's hardware palette. An active application can modify the System Palette and change the set of colors available. The System Palette has 256 entries, one for each of the VGA's 256 color registers, in its hardware palette. Windows reserves the first 10 and the last 10 colors, so that it can always have the 16 normal VGA colors plus 4 others for painting menus, scroll bars, buttons, and so on. The other 236 palette entries are for us to have fun with!

Steps

Open and run GRADFILL.VBP, and you will see the program shown in Figure 5-3-1. There are six scroll bars on the form, arranged in two groups of three. The group on the left controls the color of the form's top line, and the group on the right controls the color of the form's bottom line. The lines between the top and bottom lines are colored so that there is a smooth color transition from top to bottom. Play around with the scroll bars, and you may be amazed to see the range of colors your video card is capable of displaying.

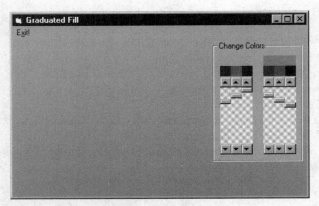

Figure 5-3-1 GRADFILL doing its thing

1. Create a new project named GRADFILL.VBP. Use the File Add menu item to add CPALETTE.CLS from How-To 5.1 to GRADFILL. In this How-To, we will implement some new capabilities in CPalette.

2. Add the following code to CPalette. This little two-liner is where all the action takes place. The Windows API function AnimatePalette replaces the hardware palette register values with values passed in the array aRgb. When the hardware palette's color table is changed, the colors on your screen change to the new colors immediately (well, within a 30th of a second, to be precise). You do not need to repaint at all for the new colors to be displayed, so this is the fastest way possible to change a picture's colors. Notice that CopyMemory is used here to keep the logical palette structure current. Whenever the palette is changed, the code in CPalette makes sure that the logical palette structure gets updated, too.

```
Public Sub Animate(iStart As Integer, iColors As Integer, aRgb() As Long)
    AnimatePalette m_hPal, iStart, iColors, aRgb(iStart)
CopyMemory m_logPalette.aEntries(iStart), aRgb(iStart), 4 * iColors
End Sub
```

3. Add the following code to the General section of CPalette. Some Windows API functions, such as AnimatePalette, require that a palette be created with certain flags set. The ReCreate method deletes the existing palette and creates a new palette, using the Windows API function CreatePalette. Any flags that have been changed in m_logPalette's color table will be correctly set in the newly created palette. The flags that you might want to set in a palette will be described in Step 5.

```
'=========================================================
' Methods
'=========================================================
Public Sub ReCreate()
    '
    ' Delete old palette handle, if it exists
```

```
'
If (m_hPal () 0) Then
    DeleteObject (m_hPal)
End If
'
' Create a new palette
'
m_hPal = CreatePalette(m_logPalette)
End Sub
```

4. Add the following code to CPalette. FadeEntries creates a wash (a smooth transition from one color to the next) in a group of palette entries. The rgbStart and rgbStop arguments give the start and stop values for the wash. The firstEntry argument is the index of the first palette entry to be modified (it is assigned the value rgbStart). And the steps argument specifies the number of steps to use between (inclusively) the rgbStart and rgbStop colors. When this subroutine finishes the internal copy of the logical palette, m_logPalette, will have the step number of entries—starting with firstEntry modified so that they contain a wash between rgbStart and rgbStop. It is important to notice that FadeEntries does not update the actual palette referenced by m_hPal. You must call either SetRgbColors or Animate before the wash takes effect.

```
Public Sub FadeEntries(rgbStart As Long, rgbStop As Long, ⇒
    firstEntry as integer, steps As Integer)
    Dim stepsize As Long
    Dim i         As Long
    Dim rStep     As Single
    Dim gStep     As Single
    Dim bStep     As Single
    Dim r         As Single
    Dim g         As Single
    Dim b         As Single
    '
    ' Calculate size of step for each of red, green, and blue
    ' color components
    '
    rStep = ((rgbStop And &hff&) - (rgbStart And &hff&)) / steps
    gStep = (((rgbStop And &hff00&) - (rgbStart And &hff00&)) / steps)
    / &h100&
    bStep = (((rgbStop And &hff0000) - (rgbStart And &hff0000)) / ⇒
        steps) / &h10000
    '
    ' Get starting red, green, and blue
    '
    r = CByte(rgbStart And &hff)
    g = CByte(((rgbStart And &hff00&) \ &h100&) And &hff)
    b = CByte(((rgbStart And &hff0000) \ &h10000) And &hff)
    '
    ' Fill palette entries
    '
    For i = 0 To steps - 1
        m_logPalette.aEntries(firstEntry + i).peRed = CByte(r)
```

Continued on next page

Continued from previous page

```
        m_logPalette.aEntries(firstEntry + i).peGreen = CByte(g)
        m_logPalette.aEntries(firstEntry + i).peBlue = CByte(b)
        r = r + rStep
        g = g + gStep
        b = b + bStep
    Next
End Sub
```

5. Add the following code to CPalette. Each of the 256 palette entries has 4 bytes. Three of the bytes specify a color, and the fourth byte is for various flags that may be set. There are three possible values for each palette entry's flags byte.

➤ The PC_EXPLICIT flag specifies that the low-order words (aEntries.peRed and aEntries.peGreen) are a hardware palette index. This flag allows an application to show the contents of the hardware palette.

➤ The PC_NOCOLLAPSE flag specifies that the color will be mapped to an unused slot in the system palette. If there are no unused slots, the color will be mapped to the closest color already in the system palette.

➤ The third flag value, PC_RESERVED, is used for palette animation. Setting this flag for a palette entry prevents other applications from using the slot or referencing the color in that slot. This leaves your application free to change the color using AnimatePalette, without affecting the colors displayed by other applications. Only palette entries marked with the PC_RESERVED flag may be changed by calling AnimatePalette.

```
Public Sub SetFlags(first As Integer, count As Integer, flags As Integer)
    '
    ' Set specified number of palette flags
    '
    Do While (count > 0)
        count = count - 1
        m_logPalette.aEntries(first + count).peFlags = flags
    Loop
End Sub
```

6. Add the following code to CPalette. CreateIdentityPalette is so named because it creates a palette that is identical to the system palette in the first 10 and last 10 palette entries. Always use identity palettes when you're doing graphics in Windows, because it allows Windows to optimize BitBlt's and other graphics functions. As long as you leave the first 10 and last 10 palette entries alone, you won't have to worry about this much, since CPalette creates identity palettes automatically.

```
Public Function CreateIdentityPalette(aRgb() As Long, nColors As Integer) ⇒
    As Integer
    Dim i            As Integer
    Dim hdcScreen    As Integer
```

```
'
' Initialize palette header
'
m_logPalette.version = &h300
m_logPalette.nEntries = 256
'
' Get screen device context
'
hdcScreen = GetDC(0)

' SYSPAL_NOSTATIC, copy the color table into a PALETTEENTRY
'
If (GetSystemPaletteUse(hdcScreen) = SYSPAL_NOSTATIC) Then
    '
    ' Fill in the palette with the given values, marking each
    ' as PC_NOCOLLAPSE
    '
    For i = 0 To nColors - 1
        m_logPalette.aEntries(i).peFlags = (aRgb(i) \ &h1000000) And
        &hff
        m_logPalette.aEntries(i).peRed = (aRgb(i) \ 65536) And &hff
        m_logPalette.aEntries(i).peGreen = (aRgb(i) \ 256) And &hff
        m_logPalette.aEntries(i).peBlue = aRgb(i) And &hff
    Next
    '
    ' Mark any unused entries PC_NOCOLLAPSE
    '
    Do While i < 256
        m_logPalette.aEntries(i).peFlags = PC_NOCOLLAPSE
        i = i + 1
    Loop
    '
    ' Make sure the last entry is white
    '
    m_logPalette.aEntries(255).peRed = 255
    m_logPalette.aEntries(255).peGreen = 255
    m_logPalette.aEntries(255).peBlue = 255
    m_logPalette.aEntries(255).peFlags = 0
    '
    ' And the first is black
    '
    m_logPalette.aEntries(0).peRed = 0
    m_logPalette.aEntries(0).peGreen = 0
    m_logPalette.aEntries(0).peBlue = 0
    m_logPalette.aEntries(0).peFlags = 0
Else
    '
    ' SYSPAL_STATIC, get the twenty static colors into, then fill
    ' in the empty spaces with the given color table
    '
    Dim nStaticColors As Integer
    Dim nUsableColors As Integer
    '
    ' Get the static colors from the system palette
    '
```

Continued on next page

Continued from previous page

```
    nStaticColors = GetDeviceCaps(hdcScreen, NUMCOLORS)
    GetSystemPaletteEntries hdcScreen, 0, 256,
    m_logPalette.aEntries(0)
    '
    ' Set the peFlags of the lower static colors to zero
    '
    nStaticColors = nStaticColors / 2

    For i = 0 To nStaticColors - 1
        m_logPalette.aEntries(i).peFlags = 0
    Next
    '
    ' Fill in the entries from the given color table
    '
    nUsableColors = nColors - nStaticColors
    Do While (i < nUsableColors)
        m_logPalette.aEntries(i).peFlags = (aRgb(i) \ &h1000000) And &hff
        m_logPalette.aEntries(i).peRed = (aRgb(i) \ &h10000) And &hff
        m_logPalette.aEntries(i).peGreen = (aRgb(i) \ &h100) And &hff
        m_logPalette.aEntries(i).peBlue = aRgb(i) And &hff
        i = i + 1
    Loop
    '
    ' Mark any empty entries as PC_NOCOLLAPSE
    '
    Do While (i < 256 - nStaticColors)
        m_logPalette.aEntries(i).peFlags = PC_NOCOLLAPSE
    Loop
    '
    ' Set the peFlags of the upper static colors to zero
    '
    For i = 256 - nStaticColors To 255
        m_logPalette.aEntries(i).peFlags = 0
    Next
End If
'
' Remember to release the DC!
'
ReleaseDC 0, hdcScreen
'
' Return the palette

m_hPal = CreatePalette(m_logPalette)
CreateIdentityPalette = m_hPal
End Function
```

7. Replace the Class_Initialize procedure in CPalette with the code shown below.
   When a new instance of CPalette is created an identity palette is created containing all black entries (except for the first 10 and last 10, of course) and its handle
   is saved in m_hPal.

```
'=======================================================
' Class Initialize/Terminate
'=======================================================
```

```
Sub Class_Initialize()
    Dim rgbs(256) As Long
    Dim i As Integer
    '
    ' Initialize all colors to zero
    '
    For i = 0 To 256
        rgbs(i) = PC_NOCOLLAPSE * &h100000
    Next
    '
    ' Create an identity palette
    '
    m_hPal = CreateIdentityPalette(rgbs, 256)
End Sub
```

8. Use the File Add menu item to add VBHT\MODULES\GDI.BAS to the project. GDI.BAS has declarations for Windows API functions, constants, and data structures used in Chapter 5.

9. Select Form1, and add the objects and properties with settings as shown in Table 5-3-1.

Table 5-3-1 Objects, properties, and settings for Form1

OBJECT	PROPERTY	SETTING
Form	Caption	"Graduated Fill"
	Name	Form1
	Picture	"RAINBOW.DIB"
Frame	BackColor	&H00C0C0C0&
	Caption	"Change Colors"
	Name	Frame1

10. Now add the objects and properties with settings as shown in Table 5-3-2 to Frame1. For each object you're adding to Frame1, first click on the appropriate toolbar button, and then create the object on Frame1 by dragging on Frame1. This will ensure that the controls are created as children of Frame1, not Form1. The placement of these controls on Frame1 is important to the display's sense when the program runs. Figure 5-3-2 shows how the controls should be arranged.

Table 5-3-2 Objects, properties, and settings for Frame1

OBJECT	PROPERTY	SETTING
PictureBox	BorderStyle	0 'None
	Index	0
	Name	Picture1
	Picture	"RAINBOW.DIB"

Continued on next page

Continued from previous page

OBJECT	PROPERTY	SETTING
PictureBox	BorderStyle	0 'None
	Index	1
	Name	Picture1
	Picture	"RAINBOW.DIB"
PictureBox	BorderStyle	0 'None
	Index	2
	Name	Picture1
	Picture	"RAINBOW.DIB"
PictureBox	BorderStyle	0 'None
	Index	3
	Name	Picture1
	Picture	"RAINBOW.DIB"
VScrollBar	Index	0
	LargeChange	16
	Name	VScroll1
	SmallChange	4
VScrollBar	Index	1
	LargeChange	16
	Name	VScroll1
	SmallChange	4
VScrollBar	Index	2
	LargeChange	16
	Name	VScroll1
	SmallChange	4
VScrollBar	Index	3
	LargeChange	16
	Name	VScroll1
	SmallChange	4
VScrollBar	Index	4
	LargeChange	16
	Name	VScroll1
	SmallChange	4
VScrollBar	Index	5
	LargeChange	16
	Name	VScroll1
	SmallChange	4

11. Using the menu editor, add the menu shown in Table 5-3-3 to Form1.

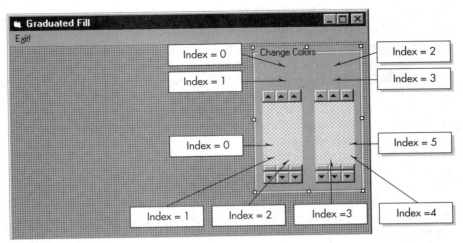

Figure 5-3-2 Arrangement of controls on Frame1

Table 5-3-3 Menu for Form1

MENU NAME	CAPTION
ExitMenu	"E&xit!"

12. Add the following code to the General Declarations section of Form1. Three variables are declared after the usual Option Explicit. The first variable, rgbquads, is an array used when setting and retrieving color palette entries. The second variable, fSkipScrollChange, prevents execution of code within VScroll1's Change event when the scroll bar's values are being changed within the program. And the third variable, pal, holds an object of the CPalette class.

```
Option Explicit
'
' Copy of palette colors
'
Private rgbquads(256)        As Long
'
' Used to skip color selector scollbar events when
' changing between display of text and background
' colors
'
Private fSkipScrollChange    As Boolean
'
' The magic palette thing
'
Private pal As CPalette
```

13. Add the following code to Form1's Load procedure. This is the moment you've been waiting for! The first order of business is to create an instance of the

CPalette class and assign it to the object variable named pal. Next, the pal object's FadeEntries member function is used to create a fade from blue to black, using palette entries 10 through 73. There will be 64 distinct shades of blue in this range of palette entries. Eight elements of the rgbquads array are then initialized with the start and end colors that will be displayed. The four PictureBoxes you created on Frame1 are used to display the individual scroll bar-selected colors, and the composite color chosen by each set of three scroll bars. Picture1(0) displays the color selected by VScroll1(0, 1, and 2), and one-third of Picture1(1) is used to display the red, green, or blue component of the composite color, as selected by the scroll bars. Pictures(2 and 3) serve the same purpose for the end-color selection scroll bars, VScroll(3, 4, and 5). One palette entry is used for the color selected by each scroll bar, and one palette is used for each of the two composite colors, so a total of eight palette entries are used for the color selectors. The member function SetRgbColors is used to copy the eight rgbquad entries to the palette.

Now that all the colors have been initialized, it is necessary to reserve these entries for animation using the PC_RESERVED flag. For this sample program, all of the available 236 palette entries are reserved. In a real program, however, you should only reserve the entries you absolutely must use. After the entries are marked, a call to pal's ReCreate member function creates a new palette using the colors built with FadeEntries and through explicit assignment via SetRgbColors. Since all of these entries have been marked for animation with PC_RESERVED, it is possible to change the colors displayed without any repainting of the form, and without the attendant flicker.

Now that a suitable palette has been built, it is assigned to Form1's Picture.hPal property; and the Windows API call RealizePalette is used so that the system palette (and VGA hardware registers) will be changed to reflect the new palette values. Then, finally, the scroll bar values are adjusted by a call to SetScrollBars to accurately reflect the current color selections.

```
Private Sub Form_Load()
    Dim i As Integer
    Dim j As Integer
    '
    ' Create new palette thing
    '
    Set pal = New CPalette
    '
    ' Create 64 shades of blue
    '
    pal.FadeEntries RGB(255, 0, 0), RGB(0, 0, 0), 10, 64
    '
    ' Create palette entries for color selection scrollbar
    ' display
    '
    ' First four are for start value
    '
    rgbquads(100) = RGB(255, 0, 0)
```

```
rgbquads(101) = RGB(0, 0, 0)
rgbquads(102) = RGB(0, 0, 0)
rgbquads(103) = RGB(255, 0, 0)
'
' Second four are for end value
'
rgbquads(104) = RGB(0, 0, 0)
rgbquads(105) = RGB(0, 0, 0)
rgbquads(106) = RGB(0, 0, 0)
rgbquads(107) = RGB(0, 0, 0)
'
' Get these colors into our palette
'
pal.SetRgbColors 100, 8, rgbquads
'
' Reserve all palette entries
'
pal.SetFlags 10, 236, PC_RESERVED
'
' Create a new palette
'
pal.ReCreate
'
' Select palette into form1
'
Form1.picture.hPal = pal.hPal
For i = 0 To 3
    Picture1(i).picture = Form1.picture
    Picture1(i).picture.hPal = pal.hPal
Next
'
' Realize palette to update system palette
'
Call RealizePalette(Form1.hdc)
'
' Make scrollbars reflect current color values
'
SetScrollBars
End Sub
```

14. Add a Paint event procedure to Form1 and include the following code. When the form is first displayed, and later if it is uncovered or resized, the Paint procedure is called. Since there are 64 colors in our palette that fade from one color to another, the form is painted with 64 bands (or swaths) of color. Form_Paint uses a new trick you might not have seen before: specifying colors by palette index number instead of RGB color. Normally you assign 3-byte RGB values to ForeColor (and other color properties) to select a color. However, color properties are 4-byte values, and when the upper byte is set to 1, the meaning of the other three bytes changes. Setting the upper byte to a 1 tells Windows that the least significant byte of the 4-byte value is actually a palette index rather than the red part of an RGB color. Using a palette index instead of an RGB color lets you directly specify what palette entry to use. Later you can change the color value at

that palette index (using AnimatePalette), and whatever was drawn with the index will instantly change color.

```
Private Sub Form_Paint()
    Dim i          As Integer
    Dim height     As Integer
    '
    ' Our palette has 64 colors, so paint 64 swaths
    '
    height = Form1.ScaleHeight / 64
    For i = 0 To 63
        '
        ' Use palette index color 10 + swath number
        '
        Form1.ForeColor = &h100000a + i
        Form1.Line (0, i * height)-(Form1.ScaleWidth, i * height ⇒
            + height), , BF
    Next
End Sub
```

15. Add a Paint event procedure for Picture1 as shown below. There are two groups of three scroll bars on Frame1. The left group is used to control the transition's start color, and the right group controls the end color. Above each group of scoll bars are two PictureBoxes. The PictureBox closest to the top of the scroll bars is used to display the color selected by each individual scroll bar, and the PictureBox immediately above that is used to display the RGB color selected by the three scroll bars. The Picture1_Paint subroutine paints the PictureBoxes with appropriate palette index colors, so that the start and stop values will be displayed as the scroll bars change value.

```
Private Sub Picture1_Paint(index As Integer)
    Dim third As Single
    Dim i As Integer
    '
    ' Width of each individual scrollbar's color indicator
    '
    third = Picture1(1).ScaleWidth / 3
    '
    ' Paint composite start color
    '
    Picture1(0).ForeColor = &h1000000 + 103
    Picture1(0).Line (0, 0)-(Picture1(0).ScaleWidth,
    Picture1(0).ScaleHeight), , BF
    '
    ' Paint color for each start color scrollbar
    '
    For i = 0 To 2
        Picture1(1).ForeColor = &h1000000 + 100 + i
        Picture1(1).Line (i * third, 0)-(i * third + third,
        Picture1(1).ScaleHeight), , BF
    Next
    '
    ' Paint composite stop color
    '
```

```
    Picture1(2).ForeColor = &h1000000 + 107
    Picture1(2).Line (0, 0)-(Picture1(2).ScaleWidth,
    Picture1(2).ScaleHeight), , BF
    '
    ' Paint color for each stop color scrollbar
    '
    For i = 0 To 2
        Picture1(3).ForeColor = &h1000000 + 104 + i
        Picture1(3).Line (i * third, 0)-(i * third + third, ⇒
            Picture1(3).ScaleHeight), , BF
    Next
End Sub
```

16. Add the following subroutine to Form1. The ChangeColors subroutine is called whenever a scroll bar's value changes. During Form_Load the scroll bar is set by the program, and this causes the scroll bar Change event to fire. The variable fSkipScrollChange is used to exit the ChangeColors subroutine immediately if the program is changing the scroll bars. When the scroll bar values really do require an update of the palette, a new transition is created by calling FadeEntries and then Animate. And the palette entries used by the color selector are also changed to reflect the new scroll bar values.

```
Private Sub ChangeColors()
    Dim offset As Integer
    Dim rgbs(256) As Long
    Dim i As Integer
    '
    ' Bail if program is changing the scrollbar values
    '
    If (fSkipScrollChange) Then
        Exit Sub
    End If
    '
    ' Pick up value of each scrollbar
    '
    For i = 0 To 5
        rgbs(i) = VScroll1(i).Value
    Next
    '
    ' Create new fade based on current scrollbar values
    '
    pal.FadeEntries RGB(rgbs(0), rgbs(1), rgbs(2)), RGB(rgbs(3),
    rgbs(4), rgbs(5)), 10, 64
    '
    ' Get colors from CPalette object
    '
    pal.GetRgbColors 10, 64, rgbquads
    '
    ' Animate palette using new colors
    '
    pal.Animate 10, 64, rgbquads
    '
    ' Calculate new start color values
    '
```

Continued on next page

Continued from previous page

```
      rgbs(100) = RGB(VScroll1(0).Value, 0, 0) + &h1000000
      rgbs(101) = RGB(0, VScroll1(1).Value, 0) + &h1000000
      rgbs(102) = RGB(0, 0, VScroll1(2).Value) + &h1000000
      rgbs(103) = RGB(VScroll1(0).Value, VScroll1(1), VScroll1(2)) + &h1000000
      '
      ' Calculate new end color values
      '
      rgbs(104) = RGB(VScroll1(3).Value, 0, 0) + &h1000000
      rgbs(105) = RGB(0, VScroll1(4).Value, 0) + &h1000000
      rgbs(106) = RGB(0, 0, VScroll1(5).Value) + &h1000000
      rgbs(107) = RGB(VScroll1(3).Value, VScroll1(4), VScroll1(5)) + &h1000000
      '
      ' Animate these into palette also
      '
      pal.Animate 100, 8, rgbs
End Sub
```

17. Add the following Private subroutine to the General Declarations section of Form1. The SetScrollBars subroutine is called during Form_Load and calculates the correct position for each of the scroll bar thumbs, given the current palette contents. The fSkipScrollBarChange flag is set while this happens, so that scroll bar events will be ignored.

```
Private Sub SetScrollBars()
      Dim rgbs(256) As Long
      '
      ' Get colors 10 thru 73
      '
      pal.GetRgbColors 10, 64, rgbs
      '
      ' Ignore scrollbar change events while we change
      ' the scrollbar values
      '
      fSkipScrollChange = True
      '
      ' Set thumbs for start colors
      '
      VScroll1(0).Value = rgbs(10) And &hff
      VScroll1(1).Value = (rgbs(10) \ &h100) And &hff
      VScroll1(2).Value = (rgbs(10) \ &h10000) And &hff
      '
      ' Set thumbs for end colors
      '
      VScroll1(3).Value = rgbs(73) And &hff
      VScroll1(4).Value = (rgbs(73) \ &h100) And &hff
      VScroll1(5).Value = (rgbs(73) \ &h10000) And &hff
      '
      ' Ok ... we'll take scroll events now
      '
      fSkipScrollChange = False
End Sub
```

18. Add the following subroutines to Form1. Whenever a scroll bar's value changes the ChangeColors subroutine is called, ChangeColors modifies the palette. The new set of colors set by the scroll bars is instantly activated by calling pal's Animate member function.

```
Private Sub VScroll1_Change(index As Integer)
    ChangeColors
End Sub

Private Sub VScroll1_Scroll(index As Integer)
    ChangeColors index
End Sub
```

19. And, last but not least, add the following subroutine to Form1. When the Exit! menu item is selected, the program ends.

```
Private Sub ExitMenu_Click()
    End
End Sub
```

How It Works

When you're using a 256-color display, the color for each pixel is specified by a byte containing a number between 0 and 255. VGA cards running in 256-color mode have one byte for each pixel displayed on your monitor. The actual color displayed for a given pixel is determined when the VGA card uses the corresponding byte as an index into its palette registers. The output of each palette register is (usually) a 24-bit value with 8 bits each for the red, green, and blue components. Each of the 8-bit values is fed into digital-to-analog converters, which control the intensity of your monitor's red, green, and blue guns. As the guns' electron streams sweep across each line of the monitor, a new byte is used as an index and a new intensity for each of the guns may result.

In Windows, a bitmap must be selected into a device context (DC) before it can be displayed. You can also select a palette into a DC; if you don't select a palette, you get the default palette containing only the 20 static colors. Among the optimizations that occur inside Windows, when you display a bitmap Windows looks at the palette selected into the same DC and determines which system palette entry best matches the DC's palette entry. Windows then stores the 1-byte index of that palette entry in the VGA's video RAM.

When you use palette index numbers instead of RGB color numbers, Windows ignores the usual color-matching result and stores the palette index without color matching. Later, if you change the actual RGB value for a given palette index, anything that was painted previously with the old RGB value will change color automatically. The GRADFILL project takes advantage of this behavior by using only palette indexes to specify colors. When the Form_Paint procedure is called, 64 bands of color are painted on the form. Since the colors are palette indexes, later calls to Animate will automatically change the colors displayed.

Comments

This How-To deploys a powerful class, CPalette, which you can use to create all sorts of interesting visual effects. In How-To 5.4 you will observe the use of palette animation to create a typical fade in/fade out graphical effect. Then, How-To 5.5 demonstrates a number of clever effects you can achieve using CPalette.

5.4 How do I...
Fade Text Titles In and Out?

COMPLEXITY: INTERMEDIATE
COMPATIBILITY: VB4 ONLY

Problem

I'd like to have titles and other text gradually appear on a form or in a PictureBox. I've seen this done in other programs where, for instance, blue letters gradually appear on a black background. When I try this, it's too slow and sometimes I get flicker. How can I get text to gradually appear without these annoying visual side-effects?

Technique

The best way to get the fade in/fade out effect you want is to use palette animation. By rapidly changing a palette entry's color, you can easily create the illusion of text appearing out of nowhere. Beginning with Visual Basic 4.0, it's a lot easier to accomplish this sort of effect than it was before. Prior versions of Visual Basic made it nearly impossible to do superior palette animations.

In this How-To you will use the CPalette class module introduced in How-To 5.3 to handle palette animation. Throw in a timer and a Form1.Print statement or two, and you'll have professional-looking text fades in no time.

Steps

Open and run FADETEXT.VBP, and you will see a form with a single command button and a blank form. Click on the command button. Text gradually appears on the form, and then you will see something like Figure 5-4-1. Click on the command button again, and the text will fade away.

1. Create a new project named FADETEXT.VBP, and add the files CPALETTE.CLS and GDI.BAS from How-To 5.3. CPALETTE.CLS and GDI.BAS provide the tools you'll be using to do text fades. If you haven't yet looked at How-To 5.3, you should probably do so now, since it will be a lot easier to understand this How-To.

Figure 5-4-1 The FADETEXT project after the first click on Command1

2. Add the following method to CPalette. The Clone method is used to make an identical copy of a CPalette object.

```
Public Function Clone() As CPalette
    Dim rgbs(256)    As Long
    Dim newpal       As New CPalette
    '
    ' Get colors from current palette
    '
    GetRgbColors 0, 256, rgbs()
    '
    ' Set colors for new palette
    '
    newpal.SetRgbColors 0, 256, rgbs()
    '
    ' Return new palette
    '
    Set Clone = newpal
End Function
```

3. Add to Form 1, the objects and properties with settings as shown in Table 5-4-1.

Table 5-4-1 Objects, properties, and settings for Form1

OBJECT	PROPERTY	SETTING
Form	Caption	"Fade Text"
	FontName	"Times New Roman"
	FontSize	27.75
	Name	Form1
	Picture	"RAINBOW.DIB"
Timer	Enabled	0 'False
	Interval	1

Continued on next page

OBJECT	PROPERTY	SETTING
	Name	Timer1
CommandButton	Caption	"Fade In"
	Name	Command1

4. Use the menu editor to add the menu shown in Table 5-4-2 to Form1.

Table 5-4-2 Form1's menu

MENU NAME	CAPTION
ExitMenu	"E&xit!"

5. Add the following code to the General Declarations section of Form1. This project uses four form-scoped variables. The first, rgbquads, is used initially as a workspace when constructing the palette for this project, and then later serves to hold a copy of the actual colors used in the project's palette. The second variable, quad, is used as an index into the rgbquads array. Later you will see how the indexing accomplishes the fade in/out effect. The third variable, direction, keeps track of whether the fade is in or out. When direction is positive, text gradually appears on the form, and when it is negative, the text gradually disappears. The fourth variable, pal, contains an instance of the CPalette class. Pal, as you might expect, plays a central role in the palette animation performed by this How-To.

```
Option Explicit
'
' Copy of palette colors
'
Private rgbquads(256)        As Long
'
' Index into rgbquads ... used during palette animation
'
Private quad As Integer
'
' Direction of fade, either +1 or -1
'
Private direction As Integer
'
' The magic palette thing
'
Private pal As CPalette
```

6. Create a Form_Load subroutine that contains the code shown below. The first thing that Form_Load does is create two instances of the CPalette class. The first instance is stored in the form-level variable named pal; the second instance is created by cloning a copy of pal using the CPalette Clone method. Clone creates a second palette identical to the Palette object whose Clone method was invoked, pal in this case. Unlike pal, the second palette (stored in the object variable

named p) will be destroyed when Form_Load returns. The Class_Terminate function in CPalette takes care of freeing any resources allocated. After the temporary CPalette object p is created, a 64-color fade from gray to blue is placed in p's palette indexes 101 through 164 by invoking p.FadeEntries. Next p.GetRgbColors is used to copy the fade colors from p's palette into the rgbquads array. The first color in the fade (at index 101) is assigned to the 100th palette entry; this will be the color used to draw Form1's text.

```
Private Sub Form_Load()
Dim p As CPalette
    '
    ' Create new palette thing
    '
    Set pal = New CPalette
    '
    ' Create a temporary palette thing
    '
    Set p = pal.Clone
    '
    ' Create 64 shades of color for text
    '
    p.FadeEntries RGB(192, 192, 192), RGB(255, 0, 0), 101, 64
    '
    ' Get colors
    '
    p.GetRgbColors 100, 65, rgbquads
    '
    ' Set current color at index 100
    '
    rgbquads(100) = rgbquads(101)
    pal.SetRgbColors 100, 1, rgbquads
    '
    ' Reserve a palette entry
    '
    pal.SetFlags 100, 1, PC_RESERVED
    '
    ' Create a new palette
    '
    pal.ReCreate
    '
    ' Select palette into Form1
    '
    Form1.picture.hPal = pal.hPal
    '
    ' Realize palette to update system palette
    '
    Call RealizePalette(Form1.hdc)
    '
    ' Initialize for fade in
    '
    direction = 1
End Sub
```

7. Add a Form_Paint procedure to Form1 as shown below. Most of the code in Form_Paint is typical "print something on a form" code. The only trick here is the value assigned to Form1's ForeColor property. Setting the most significant byte of the long integer value to a 1 tells Windows to use a palette index rather than an RGB value when painting on the form. The least significant byte gives the palette index to use—in this case, we're using the color in palette entry 100 (a 64 in hex) when painting the form. As you will see later, CPalette's Animate method is used to change the color for palette entry 100.

```
Private Sub Form_Paint()
    '
    ' Put text on form
    '
    Form1.ForeColor = &h1000064
    Form1.CurrentX = (Form1.ScaleWidth / 2) - (Form1.TextWidth("Visual ⇒
        Basic 4.0") / 2)
    Form1.CurrentY = Form1.TextHeight("Visual Basic 4.0")
    Form1.Print "Visual Basic 4.0"
    Form1.CurrentX = (Form1.ScaleWidth / 2) - (Form1.TextWidth("How-To") / 2)
    Form1.Print "How-To"
End Sub
```

8. Now add the Timer event procedure shown below to Timer1. This is where the fade in/fade out actually happens. Earlier, in the Form_Load event, rgbquads (101 to 164) were loaded with a wash containing colors from gray to blue. The variable quad is used as an index into the rgbquads array, and on each timer event the value of quad is either incremented or decremented (depending upon whether direction is positive or negative). If text is fading away, direction is negative, and after 64 Timer events, quad will also become negative. Similarly, when direction is positive, text is fading in after enough Timer events, quad will be incremented beyond the range of values required to do the fade. Whenever quad becomes less than zero or greater than 64, the current fade is finished, so the timer is disabled and Command1 is re-enabled. Also, Command1's caption is changed to indicate what will happen the next time it is clicked and quad and direction are reinitialized. As quad increments through the values 0 to 63, the rgbquad indexed by quad is assigned to rgbquad(100), and pal.Animate is used to put the new color in the palette.

```
Private Sub Timer1_Timer()
    '
    ' Change current quad
    '
    quad = (quad + direction)
    If (quad < 0 Or quad > 63) Then
        '
        ' We're done, disable timer and enable command
        '
        Timer1.Enabled = False
```

```
        Command1.Enabled = True
        '
        ' Switch directions
        '
        direction = -direction
        If (direction < 0) Then
            '
            ' Direction now less than zero, fade out
            '
            Command1.Caption = "Fade Out"
            quad = 64
        Else
            '
            ' Direction now greater than zero, fade in
            '
            quad = -1
            Command1.Caption = "Fade In"
        End If
        Exit Sub
    End If
    '
    ' Get appropriate color from rgbquads
    '
    rgbquads(100) = rgbquads(quad + 101) Or &h1000000
    '
    ' Animate it into the palette
    '
    pal.Animate 100, 1, rgbquads
End Sub
```

9. Add the following code as the Click event procedure for Command1. There's not much to do here. First Timer1 is enabled—Timer1's Timer event procedure is where the fun stuff happens—and Command1 is disabled, so the user won't be able to start a fade while another one is in progress.

```
Private Sub Command1_Click()
    '
    ' Start timer, disable command till fade done
    '
    Timer1.Enabled = True
    Command1.Enabled = False
End Sub
```

10. Add the following code as the Resize event procedure for Form1. When the form is resized, this subroutine keeps the command button in the lower-left corner of the form and uses the Form's Refresh method to force a repaint of the Form.

```
Private Sub Form_Resize()
    '
    ' Keep command button in the lower left corner
    '
    Command1.Top = Form1.ScaleHeight - (Command1.Height + 10 * ⇒
        Screen.TwipsPerPixelY)
```

Continued on next page

557

Continued from previous page

```
    Command1.Left = 10 * Screen.TwipsPerPixelX
    '
    ' Erase and repaint the form
    '
    Me.Refresh
End Sub
```

11. Finally add an ExitMenu_Click event procedure to end the program.

```
Private Sub ExitMenu_Click()
    '
    ' Th-th-th-that's all folks
    '
    End
End Sub
```

How It Works

The first things that happen when FADETEXT loads are creation and initialization of a palette and some RGB color values to use for fading text. During Form_Load, pal is initialized and then immediately cloned using CPalette's Clone method. The wash from gray to blue is created in the cloned palette and not in pal because the intent is to get the wash colors into the rgbquads array, rather than to change the palette used by Form1 so that it contains the wash.

Next, the single palette entry at index 100 has its color set to the first color in the wash, and the entry is reserved for animation by setting the PC_RESERVED flag and invoking CPalette's ReCreate method. After Form_Load exits, Form_Paint is called, where text is painted on the screen. After the first Form_Paint, the text will not be visible because its color is gray, the same as Form1's background.

Once Form_Paint is called you're ready to roll. When Command1 is clicked, Timer1's Enable property is set to True. Each time Timer1's Timer event is fired, the next color (or previous color, depending on whether text is fading in or out) in the rgbquad's wash is assigned to rgbquad(100). Also, pal's Animate method is used to place the new color in the System Palette and in the VGA card's palette registers. After 64 ticks of the timer, the last color in the wash has been selected and the text is either fully visible or fully invisible, so the timer is disabled and variables are initialized for the next Command1_Click event.

Comments

This How-To shows how simple palette animation can be with the resourceful CPalette class and Visual Basic 4.0. Also demonstrated is a way to animate over a large range of color values using only a single palette entry. This will be a valuable technique as you use more and more palette entries and they become scarce.

If you're interested in special graphics and palette animation, you will want to check out the next How-To, 5.5. In this one, CPalette shows off some excellent palette tricks.

5.5 How do I...
Use Palette Animation?

COMPLEXITY: ADVANCED
COMPATIBILITY: VB4 ONLY

Problem

Games, graphics programs, and multimedia titles use palette animation to create all sorts of interesting special effects. I'd like to know how I can use palette animation to add some pizazz to my Visual Basic programs.

Technique

In this How-To you'll learn how to create three different interesting graphical effects using palette animation. One display uses color cycling and a bitmap; another involves painting a number of progressively smaller rectangles with palette-index colors and then cycling the colors; and the third effect creates a sky filled with twinkling stars.

Each of the three graphical effects in this How-To relies upon the CPalette class module described in How-To's 5.3 and 5.4. It is not mandatory that you read those previous How-To's, but if you do, you'll have a deeper understanding of how the CPalette class module works.

Steps

Load and run PALANIM.VBP. PALANIM initially displays a fractal image, like that shown in Figure 5-5-1. In the lower-right corner of the form is a frame containing command buttons, option buttons, and some scroll bars.

The left command button—the caption is Cycle when the form first loads—is used to start and stop the color cycling. The other command button—named Random when the form first loads—enables a timer that makes random changes to the bitmap's palette when the timer's event occurs.

The three scroll bars can be used to directly set the colors for palette entries 10 through 73 (that's a total of 64 palette entries). The three scroll bars on the left control the red, green, and blue components of palette entry 10, and the three scroll bars on the right control the red, green, and blue components of palette entry 73. Each time the scroll bars are changed, a fade is created in the palette entries that lie between the colors selected for palette entries 10 and 73.

The three option buttons in the lower-left corner of the frame are used to select the type of effect to display. When the form first loads, the Bitmap option button is enabled. Clicking on the Rectangles or Stars option buttons displays other graphical effects.

Probably the best way to see the various graphical effects in this project is to first click on the Cycle button. You will then see the bitmap's colors cycle from one color to another. Next, click on the Rectangles option button to see how cycling the same set of colors can create an interesting effect in a set of nested rectangles. Then check

559

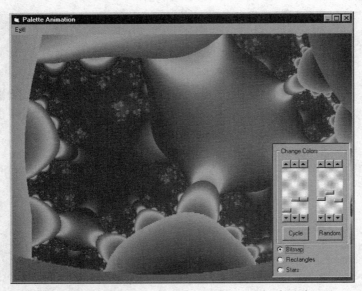

Figure 5-5-1 PALANIM with a fractal bitmap displayed

out the Stars option which creates a random star field and uses color cycling to create a twinkling effect. Once you've seen the basic color-cycling techniques in action, you can randomly change the palette by clicking on the Random command button, and set a range of colors using the scroll bars.

There's one more tool you might like to try out when you're running the PALANIM project. Included in the project directory is a program called MYPAL.EXE, which always displays the contents of the System Palette. Run MYPAL, and size it so it fits somewhere on the bottom or top edges of your screen; you will then be able to see palette changes as they occur.

1. Create a new project named PALANIM.VBP. Use the File Add menu item to add VBHT\CLASSES\CPALETTE.CLS and VBHT\MODULES\GDI.BAS to the project.

2. Select Form1, and add the objects with properties and settings shown in Table 5-5-1.

Table 5-5-1 Objects, properties, and settings for Form1

OBJECT	PROPERTY	SETTING
Form	Caption	"Palette Animation "
	FillStyle	0 'Solid
	FontName	"Arial"
	FontSize	15.75
	Name	Form1

OBJECT	PROPERTY	SETTING
PictureBox	BackColor	&H00C0C0C0&
	Name	Picture1
Timer	Enabled	0 'False
	Interval	1000
	Name	Timer1
Timer	Enabled	0 'False
	Interval	1
	Name	Timer2
Timer	Enabled	-1 'True
	Interval	10000
	Name	Timer 3

3. To Picture1, add the objects with properties and settings shown in Table 5-5-2. Be sure to create these objects on Picture1, not on Form1.

Table 5-5-2 Objects, properties and settings for Picture1

OBJECT	PROPERTY	SETTING
Frame	BackColor	&H00C0C0C0&
	Caption	"Change Colors"
	ClipControls	0 'False
	Name	Frame1
OptionButton	BackColor	&H00C0C0C0&
	Caption	"Bitmap"
	Name	Option1
OptionButton	BackColor	&H00C0C0C0&
	Caption	"Rectangles"
	Name	Option2
OptionButton	BackColor	&H00C0C0C0&
	Caption	"Stars"
	Name	Option3

4. To Frame1, add the objects with properties and settings shown in Table 5-5-3. Be sure to create these objects on Frame1, not on Picture1 or Form1.

Table 5-5-3 Objects, properties, and settings for Frame1

OBJECT	PROPERTY	SETTING
VScrollBar	Index	0
	Max	0
	Min	255

Continued on next page

Continued from previous page

OBJECT	PROPERTY	SETTING
	Name	VScroll1
VScrollBar	Index	1
	Max	0
	Min	255
	Name	VScroll1
VScrollBar	Index	2
	Max	0
	Min	255
	Name	VScroll1
VScrollBar	Index	3
	Max	0
	Min	255
	Name	VScroll1
VScrollBar	Index	4
	Max	0
	Min	255
	Name	VScroll1
VScrollBar	Index	5
	Max	0
	Min	255
	Name	VScroll1
CommandButton	Caption	"Random"
	Name	Command1
CommandButton	Caption	"Cycle"
	Name	Command2

5. Use the menu editor to create a menu for Form1, as shown in Table 5-5-4.

Table 5-5-4 Form1's menu

MENU NAME	CAPTION
ExitMenu	"E&xit!"

6. Add the following code to the General Declarations section of Form1. This project uses three form-level variables. Rgbquads holds a working copy of the palette. The fSkpScrollChange variable prevents any action in the scroll bar Change event unless the event results from changes made by the user. Pal is an object variable and holds an instance of the CPalette class.

```
Option Explicit
'
' Copy of palette colors
'
```

```
Private rgbquads(256)          As Long
'
' Used to skip color selector scollbar events when
' changing between display of text and background
' colors
'
Private fSkipScrollChange   As Boolean
'
' The magic palette thing
'
Private pal As CPalette
```

7. Add a Form_Load subroutine as shown below. During Form_Load, a bitmap is loaded into Form1's Picture property, and the bitmap's palette is assigned to the hPal property of a newly created instance of CPalette. Except for the system-reserved (static) entries, all of the palette entries are marked "reserved," and a new palette is created using the ReCreate method. A new palette is needed to activate the PC_RESERVED flags, and ReCreate is a handy way to create a new palette while discarding the old one. Finally, the palette is selected into Form1's Picture and activated by calling the Windows API function RealizePalette.

```
Private Sub Form_Load()
    Dim i As Integer
    Dim j As Integer
Dim temp As CPalette
    '
    ' Start random number sequence
    '
    Randomize
    '
    ' Load the fractal bitmap
    '
    Form1.Picture = LoadPicture("fract001.bmp")
    '
    ' Create new palette thing
    '
    Set pal = New CPalette
    '
    ' Get palette used by the fractal
    '
    pal.hPal = Form1.Picture.hPal
    '
    ' Reserve all palette entries
    '
    pal.SetFlags 10, 236, PC_RESERVED
    '
    ' Create a new palette
    '
    pal.ReCreate
    '
    ' Select palette into form1
    '
    Form1.picture.hPal = pal.hPal
    '
```

Continued on next page

Continued from previous page

```
' Realize palette to update system palette
'
Call RealizePalette(Form1.hdc)
'
' Get working copy of palette entries
'
pal.GetRgbColors 10, 236, rgbquads
'
' Set initial scrollbar values
'
SetScrollBars
End Sub
```

8. Add the Private subroutine SetScrollBars, as shown below. This subroutine is only called during Form_Load. It sets the scroll bar thumbs so that they reflect the RGB values of palette entries 10 and 73.

```
Private Sub SetScrollBars()
    Dim rgbs(256) As Long
    '
    ' Get colors for entries 10 through 73
    '
    pal.GetRgbColors 10, 64, rgbs
    '
    ' Avoid executing code when scroll bar values change
    '
    fSkipScrollChange = True
    '
    ' Set the scrollbars using the rgb values for palette entries
    ' 10 and 73
    '
    VScroll1(0).Value = rgbs(10) And &hff
    VScroll1(1).Value = (rgbs(10) \ &h100) And &hff
    VScroll1(2).Value = (rgbs(10) \ &h10000) And &hff

    VScroll1(3).Value = rgbs(73) And &hff
    VScroll1(4).Value = (rgbs(73) \ &h100) And &hff
    VScroll1(5).Value = (rgbs(73) \ &h10000) And &hff
    '
    ' Ok ... we'll take scroll bar events now
    '
    fSkipScrollChange = False
End Sub
```

9. Add the following Click event procedure for Command1. Command1 is used to enable and disable Timer1. When Timer1's Timer event routine is called, a random change is made to the palette. Each time that Command1's Click subroutine is called, the state of Timer1's enable is toggled, and the resulting value of the Enabled property is used to determine the caption for Command1. When the timer has been enabled (and the caption changed to Stop) an initial call to ChangeRndColors is made. This ensures that the palette begins to change right

away, so that the user knows something is happening in response to clicking on the command button.

```
Private Sub Command1_Click()
    '
    ' Toggel Timer1's Enabled property
    '
    Timer1.Enabled = Not (Timer1.Enabled)
    '
    ' Update Command1's caption so that it indicates
    ' what will happen the next time it is clicked
    '
    If Timer1.Enabled Then
        '
        ' Make an initial change so user knows something
        ' is happening
        '
        ChangeRndColors
        Timer1.Interval = (Rnd * 500) + 125
        Command1.Caption = "Stop"
    Else
        Command1.Caption = "Random"
    End If
End Sub
```

10. Add the following Timer1_Timer event procedure to Form1. As described in step 9, Timer1 makes random changes to the palette. The ChangeRndColors subroutine is called to make the changes.

```
Private Sub Timer1_Timer()
    ChangeRndColors
End Sub
```

11. Add the following subroutine to Form1. ChangeRndColors is used to randomly change part of the palette. First a starting entry is picked, and a number of entries to change. Then the current values at the start and end of the range are copied into the rgbs array. Next, a random choice is made to modify either the first or second color in the range. The chosen color is then modified by setting each of the red, green, and blue components to a random value between 0 and 255. Finally, a fade is created over the chosen range, using the new start and end color values. The changed entries are activated using pal's Animate method.

```
Private Sub ChangeRndColors()
    Dim fadelength As Integer
    Dim fadestart  As Integer
    Dim offset     As Integer
    Dim rgbs(6)    As Byte
    Dim i          As Integer
    '
    ' Pick a random number of entries to change
    '
    fadelength = (Rnd * 63) + 1
```

Continued on next page

Continued from previous page

```
'
' Start somewhere between the first entry that
' can be animated and the last entry that still
' allows room for the chosen length
'
fadestart = 10 + Rnd * (236 - fadelength)
'
' Get current rgbs from the start and end positions
'
rgbs(0) = rgbquads(fadestart) And &hff
rgbs(0) = (rgbquads(fadestart) \ &h100) And &hff
rgbs(0) = (rgbquads(fadestart) \ &h10000) And &hff

rgbs(0) = rgbquads(fadestart + fadelength - 1) And &hff
rgbs(0) = (rgbquads(fadestart + fadelength - 1) \ &h100) And &hff
rgbs(0) = (rgbquads(fadestart + fadelength - 1) \ &h10000) And &hff

' Modify either start of range's value or end
' of range ... choose at random
'
If Rnd > 0.5 Then
   offset = 3
Else
   offset = 0
End If
'
' Modify either start or end value
'
For i = 0 To 2
   rgbs(offset + i) = Int(Rnd * 256)
Next
'
' Create a fade
'
pal.FadeEntries RGB(rgbs(0), rgbs(1), rgbs(2)), RGB(rgbs(3), rgbs(4), ⇒
   rgbs(5)), fadestart, fadelength
'
' Get the fade colors
'
pal.GetRgbColors fadestart, fadelength, rgbquads
'
' Animate the new colors
'
pal.Animate fadestart, fadelength, rgbquads
End Sub
```

12. Add the following Command2_Click event procedure to Form1. Command2's Click event procedure toggles Timer2's Enabled property, and then it changes its own caption to indicate what will happen the next time Command2 is clicked.

```
Private Sub Command2_Click()
   '
   ' Toggle Timer2's Enabled property
   '
```

```
      Timer2.Enabled = Not (Timer2.Enabled)
      '
      ' Update Command2's Caption so that it indicates
      ' what will happen the next time it is clicked
      '
      If Timer2.Enabled Then
          Command2.Caption = "Stop"
      Else
          Command2.Caption = "Cycle"
      End If
  End Sub
```

13. Add the following Timer2_Timer event procedure to Form1, to accommodate the color cycling. When Timer2's Timer event is fired, palette entries 11 through 246 are rotated so that each color moves to the next higher entry—except for the last entry, which becomes the new first entry. If you use MYPAL to watch what happens to the palette during color cycling, you will see that this is a rotate-right operation.

```
Private Sub Timer2_Timer()
    Dim i          As Integer
    Dim first      As Long
    '
    ' Save highest palette entry
    '
    first = rgbquads(245)
    '
    ' Move all palette entries up on entry
    '
    For i = 245 To 11 Step -1
        rgbquads(i) = rgbquads(i - 1)
    Next
    '
    ' Previous highest is now the lowest
    '
    rgbquads(10) = first
    '
    ' Animate the new palette colors
    '
    pal.Animate 10, 236, rgbquads
End Sub
```

14. Add the following subroutines. Whenever a scroll bar changes, the ChangeColors subroutine is called.

```
Private Sub VScroll1_Change(index As Integer)
    ChangeColors
End Sub

Private Sub VScroll1_Scroll(index As Integer)
    ChangeColors
End Sub
```

15. Add the following ChangeColors subroutine to Form1's code. The scroll bar values are used to set the start and end RGB values, for a fade of palette entries 10 through 73.

```
Private Sub ChangeColors()
    Dim offset   As Integer
    Dim rgbs(6) As Byte
    Dim i        As Integer
    '
    ' Bail outta here if the scrollbar change was made
    ' by the SetScrollBars routine
    '
    If (fSkipScrollChange) Then
        Exit Sub
    End If
    '
    ' Get scrollbar values
    '
    For i = 0 To 5
        rgbs(i) = VScroll1(i).Value
    Next
    '
    ' Create new wash using the new scrollbar values
    '
    pal.FadeEntries RGB(rgbs(0), rgbs(1), rgbs(2)), RGB(rgbs(3), rgbs(4), ⇒
        rgbs(5)), 10, 64
    '
    ' Retrieve the colors
    '
    pal.GetRgbColors 10, 64, rgbquads
    '
    ' And use Animate to make them active
    '
    pal.Animate 10, 64, rgbquads
End Sub
```

16. Next, add the Timer3_Timer event procedure, which is used to randomize the interval used by Timer1. Timer1, as shown previously, randomly changes a section of the palette every time its Timer event procedure is called. Timer3 introduces still more spontaneity into the display by periodically altering the frequency of Timer1.

```
Private Sub Timer3_Timer()
    '
    ' Alter the interval at between calls to changeRndColor
    '
    Timer1.Interval = (Rnd * 500) + 125
End Sub
```

17. Add the following Option1_Click event procedure to Form1's code. Option1 redisplays the bitmap by causing the form to repaint itself.

```
Private Sub Option1_Click()
    '
    ' Redraw bitmap
```

```
    '
    Form1.Refresh
End Sub
```

18. Add the following Option2_Click event procedure to Form1. This event procedure fills the form with progressively smaller rectangles, each having a different palette index color.

```
Private Sub Option2_Click()
    Dim i          As Integer
    Dim nboxes     As Integer
    Dim xmid       As Single
    Dim ymid       As Single
    Dim dx         As Single
    Dim dy         As Single
    Dim ulx        As Single
    Dim uly        As Single
    Dim lrx        As Single
    Dim lry        As Single
    '
    ' Number of boxes to draw
    '
    nboxes = 200
    '
    ' Screen midpoint
    '
    xmid = Form1.ScaleWidth / 2
    ymid = Form1.ScaleHeight / 2
    '
    ' dx and dy give amount to change width and height
    ' between rectangles
    '
    dx = xmid / nboxes
    dy = ymid / nboxes
    '
    ' Set start values for upper left x and y (ulx, uly)
    ' and lower right x and y (lrx, lry)
    '
    ulx = 0
    uly = 0
    lrx = Form1.ScaleWidth
    lry = Form1.ScaleHeight
    '
    ' Start with palette index 200
    '
    i = 210
    '
    ' Draw progressively smaller boxes on the form
    '
    Do While (uly < lry)
        Form1.ForeColor = &h1000000 + i
        Form1.Line (ulx, uly)-(lrx, lry), , BF
        ulx = ulx + dx
        uly = uly + dy
        lrx = lrx - dx
```

Continued on next page

Continued from previous page

```
        lry = lry - dy
        i = i - 1
    Loop
    '
    ' Put some text in the center
    '
    Form1.CurrentX = xmid - (Form1.TextWidth("VISUAL") / 2)
    Form1.CurrentY = ymid - (Form1.TextHeight("VISUAL") / 2)
    Form1.ForeColor = &h100000a + 90
    Form1.Print "VISUAL"
End Sub
```

19. Add the Option3_Click event procdure to Form1. When the user clicks on the Stars option, Option3_Click (the scatter subroutine) is called to draw the stars.

```
Private Sub Option3_Click()
    scatter 1
End Sub
```

20. Add the following subroutine to Form1. Scatter first clears Form1 to black and then creates randomly distributed pixels with colors from palette indices 10 through 127.

```
Private Sub scatter(n As Integer)
    Dim x     As Integer
    Dim y     As Integer
    Dim c     As Integer
    Dim pw    As Integer
    Dim ph    As Integer
    Dim i     As Integer
    Dim j     As Integer
    '
    ' Fill form with black
    '
    Form1.ForeColor = 0
    Form1.Line (0, 0)-(Form1.Width, Form1.Height), , BF
    pw = Form1.Width
    ph = Form1.Height
    '
    ' Scatter some pixels on the form
    '
    For j = 10 To 127
        For i = 0 To n
            x = Int(Rnd * pw)
            y = Int(Rnd * ph)
            Form1.Pset (x, y), &h1000000 + j
        Next i
    Next j
End Sub
```

21. Add the ExitMenu_Click subroutine.

```
Private Sub ExitMenu_Click()
    End
End Sub
```

How It Works

During Form_Load, a CPalette object is created and stored in the variable named pal, and the bitmap FRACT001.BMP is loaded into Form1's Picture property. Loading a device-independent bitmap (DIB) such as FRACT001.BMP into a Picture object also loads the DIB's palette and makes it accessible through the picture's hPal property. After the bitmap has been loaded, the palette handle is assigned to pal's hPal property, and the palette entries in pal's hPal are marked with the PC_RESERVED flag. Palette entries marked with PC_RESERVED when the palette is created can be animated using the Windows API function AnimatePalette. Because the initial load of FRACT001.BMP did not result in the PC_RESERVED flags being set, pal's ReCreate method is used to re-create pal's palette using the PC_RESERVED flags set during Form_Load.

Once the form has been loaded and a suitable palette created, the user can click on various controls to change the display. Clicking on the Cycle button starts Timer2. Every time the Timer2_Timer event procedure is called, the entire reserved range of the palette (entries 10 through 245) is rotated. This causes an immediate change to all of the colors displayed on Form1. Clicking on the Random button adds substantial variety to the display by enabling Timer1. Each time Timer1's Timer event procedure is called, some randomly chosen section of the palette is changed. And, to stir things up even more, the user can change the scroll bars to directly set the colors used in part of the palette.

The option buttons select three different types of graphical displays, all of which use and are altered by the existing palette. Clicking on the Bitmap button displays FRACT001.BMP. Clicking on the Rectangles button causes a sequence of nested rectangles to be drawn on Form1. By placing progressively smaller rectangles over each previously drawn rectangle, a series of bands parallel to the form's edges are drawn. You may have noticed that the rectangles are drawn so that the largest rectangle uses the highest-numbered palette index, and the smallest rectangle uses the lowest-numbered rectangle. During color cycling colors cycle from the lowest-numbered palette entry toward the highest, creating the illusion of movement into the center of the form as the colors move outward on the form. Clicking on the Stars button switches the display to a random set of pixels on a black background. The pixels use the same palette as the bitmap and rectangles, and if color cycling is turned on, the rapidly changing pixel colors create a twinkling effect.

Comments

Again, as in How-To's 5.3 and 5.4, this PALANIM project demonstrates some of the power of the CPalette class module. Palette animation can be used to add all sorts of special effects to your programs. In How-To 5.6, you'll see a clever way to smoothly transition from one bitmap to the next, using palette animation.

5.6 How do I...
Fade between Pictures?

COMPLEXITY: ADVANCED
COMPATIBILITY: VB4 ONLY

Problem

Most multimedia authoring tools make it easy to create a smooth transition between pictures, where one picture fades in as the other fades out. This effect is similar to what can be accomplished with a pair of good slide projectors, and I'd like to create this effect in my Visual Basic programs. Is there a way to create a fade between two pictures using Visual Basic only?

Technique

The idea in this How-To is fairly simple: palette animation can be used to change the colors of pixels being displayed, and if a pixel in one picture is gradually changed so that it has the same color as the corresponding pixel in another picture, then the transition has been accomplished for a single pixel. The tricky part is coming up with an efficient technique for changing tens of thousands of pixels at once.

The technique deployed in this project involves computing a new bitmap and a pair of color tables from two device-independent bitmaps (DIB), and saving the computed information so that the transition can occur quickly at run time.

Perhaps the best way to approach understanding the algorithm used in this How-To is to take a look at a highly simplified example. Figure 5-6-1 shows two DIBs and their palettes. The palettes contain only two entries (in real DIBs you will almost always be working with palettes that contain many more colors). Each of the DIBs has 16 bytes in its bitmap, and the value of each byte is an index into the color palette for that bitmap. When Dib 1 is displayed on the screen, you will see four rows of four pixels each. The first and third rows will be blue, and the second and fourth rows yellow. Similarly, when Dib 2 is displayed, the first and second rows will be green and the third and fourth rows red.

Now consider what the screen would look like if you displayed an image that is faded halfway between Dib1 and Dib2. There would be four rows, each a different color. The first row would be blue-green, the second row yellow-green, the third row purple, and the fourth row orange.

This illustrates an important limitation of the technique used in this How-To: the number of palette entries required to display a merged DIB may be as many as the number of colors in the first DIB multiplied by the number of colors in the second DIB. The exact number of palette entries required is equal to the number of different pairs of colors found by examining each pair of corresponding pixels in the two merged DIBs. Since the merged DIB's palette can hold no more than 256 colors, it may be necessary to modify the colors used by a pair of DIBs, *before* they can be

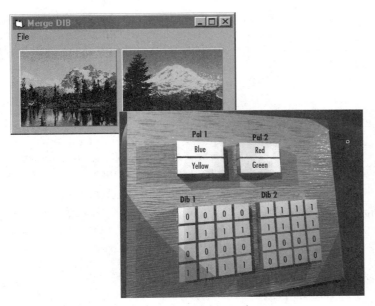

Figure 5-6-1 Two simple DIBs and their palettes

merged. As you will see later, the program automatically detects when color reduction is required, so that you can modify the DIBs.

Figure 5-6-2 shows the contents of the merged DIB's bitmap and three palettes that are created by invoking CMergeDib's Create method. When the merged DIB is first displayed, it will look exactly like the original Dib1, (rows 1 and 3 blue and rows 2 and 4 yellow). However, if the merged DIB's palette is changed so that it

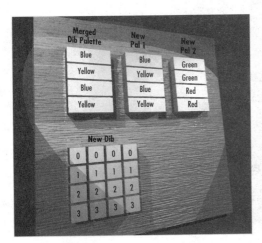

Figure 5-6-2 Merged DIB and palettes

contains the palette entries from NewPal2, then the displayed bitmap will look like the original Dib2. Given the three palettes and the merged DIB, it's fairly easy to fade between the two pictures. For instance, to create a 50 percent fade between Dib1 and Dib2, you simply assign to each entry of the merged DIB's palette the sum of half of the corresponding entries from NewPal1 and NewPal2.

Steps

Open and run MERGDIB.VBP, and use the File Load File menu item to load the merged DIB named MTNRAIN.MBM. Use the scroll bar to control the amount of fade between the two pictures in MTNRAIN.MBM. With the scroll bar's thumb halfway between the Min and Max values, you should see a picture similar to that displayed in Figure 5-6-3.

1. Create a new project named MERGDIB.VBP. Use the File Add menu item to add the classes and modules shown in Table 5-6-1 to MERGDIB.VBP. The class modules (files with a .CLS extension) are stored in the VBHT\CLASSES directory, and GDI.BAS is in VBHT\MODULES.

Table 5-6-1 Classes and modules for Form1

FILENAME	CLASS	PURPOSE
CDIB.CLS	CDib	Device-independent bitmap class
CPALETTE.CLS	CPalette	Palette functionality
CBORDR3D.CLS	CBorder3D	Adds 3D effects to controls
GDI.BAS	N/A	Windows API declarations

Figure 5-6-3 Merged DIBs

2. Use the Insert Class Module menu item to add a new class to MERGDIB. Set the new class's name to CMergeDib. Add the following code to CMergeDib's General Declarations section. When two DIBs are merged, the resulting DIB is stored in m_oMerged, an instance of the CDib class. Also, the number of colors in the resulting color tables is saved in m_mergedColors, and the color tables themselves are saved in m_primaryQuads and m_secondaryQuads.

```
Option Explicit

Private m_oMerged                As CDib
Private m_mergedColors           As Integer
Private m_primaryQuads(256)      As Long
Private m_secondaryQuads(256)    As Long

Private Declare Function lopen Lib "Kernel32" Alias "_lopen" ⇒
(ByVal lpPathName As String, ByVal iReadWrite As Integer) As Integer
Private Declare Function lread Lib "Kernel32" Alias "_lread" ⇒
(ByVal hfile As Integer, lpBuffer As Any, ByVal wBytes As Integer) ⇒
As Integer
Private Declare Function lclose Lib "Kernel32" Alias "_lclose" ⇒
(ByVal hfile As Integer) As Integer
Private Declare Function hread Lib "Kernel32" Alias "_hread" ⇒
(ByVal hfile As Integer, buffer As Any, ByVal n As Long) As Long
Private Declare Function hwrite Lib "Kernel32" Alias "_hwrite" ⇒
(ByVal hfile As Integer, buffer As Any, ByVal n As Long) As Long
Private Declare Function lcreate Lib "Kernel32" Alias "_lcreat" ⇒
(ByVal lpPathName As String, ByVal iReadWrite As Integer) As Long

Private Const OPEN_READ = 0

Private Const UnusedEntry = 255
```

3. Add the following function to CMergeDib. The pal function returns an instance of CMergeDib's m_oMerged.pal object.

```
Public Function pal() As CPalette
    Set pal = m_oMerged.pal
End Function
```

4. Add the following function to CMergeDib. The DIB function provides access to the CDib part of a merged DIB.

```
Public Function dib() As CDib
    Set dib = m_oMerged
End Function
```

5. Add the following subroutine to CMergeDib. The SaveAs function saves to the specified file everything that's needed to re-create an instance of CMergeDib. The first thing that happens in SaveAs is a call to the Windows API function lcreate. The lcreate function will truncate an existing file to zero bytes if it already exists, so there is no need to delete the file (if it exists!) first. Next, a magic cookie is

written to the file. Many Windows file types use these magic cookies to help veri-fy that a file is of the type indicated by its extension. Bitmap files, for instance, have BM for their magic cookie, and .EXE files have MZ (the initials of the devel-oper at Microsoft who invented the EXE header format). After the magic cookie, the color tables are written to the file and m_oMerged's StoreInFile method is called to store the DIB in the file.

```
Public Sub SaveAs(filename As String)
    Dim s         As String
    Dim hfile     As Integer
    '
    ' Create new file ... error message on failures
    '
    hfile = lcreate(filename, 0)
    If (hfile = -1) Then
        MsgBox "Could not create " & filename
        Exit Sub
    End If
    '
    ' Write MergeDib as a 'magic cookie'
    '
    s = "MergeDib"
    Call hwrite(hfile, ByVal s, Len(s))
    '
    ' Save number of colors in merge
    '
    Call hwrite(hfile, m_mergedColors, Len(m_mergedColors))
    '
    ' Write rgb quad tables
    '
    Call hwrite(hfile, m_primaryQuads(0), 1024)
    Call hwrite(hfile, m_secondaryQuads(0), 1024)
    '
    ' Write dib to file and close it
    '
    m_oMerged.StoreInFile (hfile)
    Call lclose(hfile)
End Sub
```

6. Add the following code to CMergeDib. This ReadFromFile function is simply the inverse of the SaveAs function in step 5. After verifying the file type by checking the magic cookie, the color tables and DIB are read from the file.

```
Public Function ReadFromFile(filename As String) As Boolean
    Dim s As String * 8
    Dim hfile As Integer
    '
    ' Open file ... error message on failures
    '
    hfile = lopen(filename, OPEN_READ)
    If (hfile = -1) Then
        MsgBox "Could not open " & filename
        ReadFromFile = False
```

```
        Call lclose(hfile)
        Exit Function
    End If
    '
    ' Read 'magic cookie' from file
    '
    Call hread(hfile, ByVal s, Len(s))
    If (s () "MergeDib") Then
        '
        ' Woops ... not a merged dib file
        '
        MsgBox "Invalid File Format"
        ReadFromFile = False
        Exit Function
    End If
    '
    ' Read number of colors in merge
    '
    Call hread(hfile, m_mergedColors, Len(m_mergedColors))
    '
    ' Read rgb color tables
    '
    Call hread(hfile, m_primaryQuads(0), 1024)
    Call hread(hfile, m_secondaryQuads(0), 1024)
    '
    ' Create a new dib
    '
    Set m_oMerged = New CDib
    '
    ' Read dib from disk and close the file
    '
    m_oMerged.ReadFromFile (hfile)
    ReadFromFile = True
    Call lclose(hfile)
End Function
```

7. Add the following subroutine to CMergeDib. This Create routine is used to create a new merged DIB from two instances of CDib, as described in the foregoing Techniques section. One aspect of this algorithm not described previously is the way in which the pixel values of the new DIB are derived. A 256-by-256 array named MergeMap tracks each unique combination of colors seen in corresponding pixels of the two source DIBs. For each pair of pixel values in the two DIBs, the pixel values are used as indices into the MergeMap array. If the value stored at that location in MergeMap is 255, then the pixel value pair hasn't been seen before, so a new palette entry is allocated in each of the three output palettes, and the newly used palette index is stored in MergeMap and as the value of the new DIBs pixel. When a value other than 255 is found in the MergeMap, it is simply assigned as the pixel value of the new DIB.

```
Public Sub Create(primary As CDib, secondary As CDib)
    Dim MergeMap(256, 256)   As Byte
    Dim r, c                 As Integer
```

Continued on next page

Continued from previous page

```
    Dim X, Y                    As Integer
    Dim paletteIndex            As Integer
    Dim i                       As Integer
    Dim primaryPixel            As Byte
    Dim secondaryPixel          As Byte
    Dim mergePixel              As Byte
    Dim mapValue                As Byte
    Dim oldPriQuads(256)        As Long
    Dim oldSecQuads(256)        As Long
    Dim mergeQuads(256)         As Long
    '
    ' Hourglass ... we're going to need this!
    '
    Screen.MousePointer = 11
    '
    ' Create merged dib
    '
    Set m_oMerged = primary.Clone
    '
    ' Mark color map as all unused
    '
    For r = 0 To 255
        For c = 0 To 255
            MergeMap(r, c) = UnusedEntry
        Next
    Next
    '
    ' Get current colors
    '
    primary.pal.GetRgbColors 0, 256, oldPriQuads
    secondary.pal.GetRgbColors 0, 256, oldSecQuads
    m_oMerged.pal.GetRgbColors 0, 256, mergeQuads
    '
    ' Skip reserved entries
    '
    paletteIndex = 10
    '
    ' For each row
    '
    For Y = 0 To primary.Height - 1
        '
        ' For each pixel in row
        '
        For X = 0 To primary.Width - 1
            '
            ' Get primary and secondary pixel values
            '
            primaryPixel = primary.Pixel(X, Y)
            secondaryPixel = secondary.Pixel(X, Y)
            '
            ' Get current map value
            '
            mapValue = MergeMap(primaryPixel, secondaryPixel)
            '
            ' Map entry been assigned?
            '
```

```
            If (mapValue = UnusedEntry) Then
                '
                ' New combination of primary and secondary
                '
                MergeMap(primaryPixel, secondaryPixel) =
                CByte(paletteIndex)
                '
                ' Write new pixel value to bitmap
                '
                m_oMerged.Pixel(X, Y) = CByte(paletteIndex)
                '
                ' Make a new palette entry for the primary dib
                '
                m_primaryQuads(paletteIndex) = oldPriQuads(primaryPixel)
                '
                ' Make a new palette entry for the secondary dib
                '
                m_secondaryQuads(paletteIndex) = oldSecQuads(secondaryPixel)
                '
                ' Make a new palette entry for the merged dib
                '
                mergeQuads(paletteIndex) = m_primaryQuads(paletteIndex) +
                &H1000000
                '
                ' Increment palette index
                '
                paletteIndex = paletteIndex + 1
                If (paletteIndex > 255) Then
                    MsgBox "Too many colors in bitmaps"
                    GoTo bail
                End If
            Else
                '
                ' Primary/secondary combination already allocated
                ' use map value as pixel value
                '
                m_oMerged.Pixel(X, Y) = mapValue
            End If
        Next
        '
        ' Let other things happen
        '
        DoEvents
    Next
bail:
    '
    ' We're done
    '
    m_mergedColors = paletteIndex - 10
    m_oMerged.pal.SetRgbColors 10, m_mergedColors, mergeQuads
    m_oMerged.ColorsUsed = m_mergedColors + 10
    m_oMerged.SetPaletteUsage m_oMerged.pal, DIB_PAL_COLORS
    Screen.MousePointer = 0
End Sub
```

8. Add the following code as CMergeDib's Merge method. It takes two parameters: val and range. Together, val and range specify how much of each of the original DIBs will be displayed. The ratio of the displayed original Dib1 to Dib2 is given by the formula (range-val) / range, so if val is 100 and range is 1,000, then 900/1,000th of Dib1 will be displayed and 1/100th of Dib2 will be displayed. Using values such as 100, 1,000, or even 10,000 makes it easy to think of the val parameter as "the percentage of Dib2 to display." For instance, when val is 250 and range is 1,000, then 75 percent of Dib1 and 25 percent of Dib2 will be displayed. Finally, after the palette is adjusted, m_oMerged's Animate method is used to activate the new palette colors.

```
Public Sub Merge(val As Long, range As Long)
    Dim i As Integer
    Dim mQuads(256) As Long
    Dim r, g, b       As Long
    '
    ' Create composite rgb values from two color tables
    '
    For i = 10 To m_mergedColors + 9
        b = ((((m_secondaryQuads(i) \ &H10000) And &HFF) * val) +
    (((m_primaryQuads(i) \ &H10000) And &HFF) * (range - val))) \ range
        g = ((((m_secondaryQuads(i) \ &H100) And &HFF) * val) +
    (((m_primaryQuads(i) \ &H100) And &HFF) * (range - val))) \ range
        r = (((m_secondaryQuads(i) And &HFF) * val) +
    ((m_primaryQuads(i) And &HFF) * (range - val))) \ range
        mQuads(i) = (b * &H10000) + (g * &H100) + r + &H1000000
    Next
    '
    ' Activate new palette colors
    '
    m_oMerged.pal.Animate 10, m_mergedColors, mQuads
End Sub
```

9. Select Form1, and add the objects with properties and settings as shown in Table 5-6-1.

Table 5-6-1 Objects, properties, and settings for Form1

OBJECT	PROPERTY	SETTING
Form	Caption	"Merge DIB"
	Name	Form1
Image	Name	Image2
	Stretch	-1 'True
Image	Name	Image1
	Stretch	-1 'True
CommonDialog	CancelError	-1 'True
	DefaultExt	"dib"

OBJECT	PROPERTY	SETTING
	Filter	"Bitmaps (*.bmp,*.dib)|*.bmp;*.dib"
	Name	CommonDialog1

10. Use the menu editor to create a menu for Form1. Create the menu items listed in Table 5-6-2.

Table 5-6-2 Form1's menu

MENU	NAME
FileMenu Caption	"&File"
...FileOpenPrimary	"Open &Primary..."
...FileOpenSecondary	"Open &Secondary..."
...FileSep1	"-"
...FileLoadFile	"&Load File..."
...FileSaveAs	"Sa&ve As..."
...FileSep2	"-"
...FileExit	"E&xit"

11. Add the following code to the General Declarations section of Form1. Form1 uses two image controls to display the contents of two DIBs, which are referenced by m_primary and m_secondary objects. Also, to spiff up the screen a little, two 3D border objects are used, one for each CDib.

```
Option Explicit

Dim m_priBorder As New CBorder3D
Dim m_secBorder As New CBorder3D
Dim m_primary   As CDib
Dim m_secondary As CDib
```

12. Add the following code as Form1's brief Form_Load event procedure. All that's needed is for the two 3D border objects to be initialized so that the image controls appear slightly raised above the form's background.

```
Private Sub Form_Load()
    '
    ' Setup 3D border for Image1
    '
    Set m_priBorder.Canvas = Form1
    Set m_priBorder.Client = Image1
    m_priBorder.Style3D = 2
    '
    ' Setup 3D border for Image2
    '
    Set m_secBorder.Canvas = Form1
    Set m_secBorder.Client = Image2
    m_secBorder.Style3D = 2
End Sub
```

13. Add the following code as the File Load File menu item's FileLoadFile_Click event procedure, used to load and display a previously saved merged DIB. The default behavior of this program is to save merged DIB with a filename extension of .MBM, so the Common Dialog control is initialized to present only .MBM files. When the user selects an .MBM file, the CMergeDib method ReadFromFile is used to load the file into the CMergeDib instance named merged. Finally, merged is assigned to Form2's MergedDib property.

It is important to note that after the assignment to MergedDib, there are two references to the CMergeDib object that is referenced by merged. The first reference is maintained by merged, and the second is maintained by Form2. When FileLoadFile exits and merged is destroyed, a reference to a valid CMergeDib object remains in Form2, and so the merged DIB is not destroyed along with the variable merged.

```
Private Sub FileLoadFile_Click()
    Dim merged As New CMergeDib
    '
    ' Get setup for MBM files
    '
    CommonDialog1.Filter = "Merged Dib(*.mbm)|*.mbm"
    CommonDialog1.DialogTitle = "Load Merged Dib"
    On Error Resume Next
    CommonDialog1.ShowOpen
    If (Err) Then
        '
        ' User canceled ... we're outta here
        '
        Exit Sub
    End If
    On Error GoTo 0
    '
    ' Read merged dib
    '
    merged.ReadFromFile (CommonDialog1.filename)
    '
    ' Assign to Form2's MergedDib property
    '
    Set Form2.MergedDib = merged
End Sub
```

14. Add the following code as the File Open Primary menu item's Click event procedure. Two bitmaps are required to create a merged bitmap; in this program they are the Primary and Secondary bitmaps. The FileOpenPrimary_Click event procedure first allows the user to select the primary bitmap. Then, assuming that a file was actually chosen, the CheckMerge subroutine is called to merge the DIBs if two equal-sized DIBs have been selected.

```
Private Sub FileOpenPrimary_Click()
    '
    ' Get file to open
    '
```

```
    On Error Resume Next
    CommonDialog1.Filter = "Bitmaps (*.bmp,*.dib)|*.bmp;*.dib|"
    CommonDialog1.Action = 1
    CommonDialog1.DialogTitle = "Open Primary Dib"
    If (Err) Then
        '
        ' Bail if Cancel used
        '
        Exit Sub
    End If
    On Error GoTo 0
    Set m_primary = New CDib
    '
    ' Read dib and display dib and dib info if valid
    '
    If (m_primary.ReadDIB(CommonDialog1.filename) = True) Then
        Image1.Picture = LoadPicture(CommonDialog1.filename)
    End If
    CheckMerge
End Sub
```

15. Add the following code as the File Open Secondary menu item's Click event procedure. This subroutine is identical to the one in step 14, except that m_secondary and Image2 are used instead of m_primary and Image1.

```
Private Sub FileOpenSecondary_Click()
    '
    ' Get file to open
    '
    On Error Resume Next
    CommonDialog1.Filter = "Bitmaps (*.bmp,*.dib)|*.bmp;*.dib|"
    CommonDialog1.DialogTitle = "Open Secondary Dib"
    CommonDialog1.Action = 1
    If (Err) Then
        '
        ' Bail if Cancel used
        '
        Exit Sub
    End If
    On Error GoTo 0
    Set m_secondary = New CDib
    '
    ' Read dib and display dib and dib info if valid
    '
    If (m_secondary.ReadDIB(CommonDialog1.filename) = True) Then
        Image2.Picture = LoadPicture(CommonDialog1.filename)
    End If
    CheckMerge
End Sub
```

16. Add the following subroutine to Form1. This CheckMerge subroutine first checks to see if DIBs have been assigned to both of the CDib objects (m_primary and m_secondary). If so, their sizes are compared to see if they are equal. CMergeDib's Create method only works with bitmaps that have identical height

and width. If two equal-sized bitmaps have been selected, then Form2's Merge method is used to create and display the merged bitmap.

```
Private Sub CheckMerge()
    If (Not m_primary Is Nothing And Not m_secondary Is Nothing) Then
        If (m_primary.Width = m_secondary.Width And m_primary.Height =
        m_secondary.Height) Then
            Form2.Merge m_primary, m_secondary
        Else
            MsgBox "Can't merge bitmaps of different sizes"
        End If
    End If
End Sub
```

17. Add the following code as the File Save As menu item's Click event procedure. This subroutine first prompts the user for an .MBM filename, and saves the merged DIB by using Form2.MergeDib's SaveAs method.

```
Private Sub FileSaveAs_Click()
    '
    ' Get set to save MBM file
    '
    CommonDialog1.Filter = "Merged Dib(*.mbm)|*.mbm"
    CommonDialog1.DialogTitle = "Save Merged Dib As"
    On Error Resume Next
    CommonDialog1.Action = 2
    If (Err) Then
        '
        ' Woops ... Cancel button used
        '
        Exit Sub
    End If
    On Error GoTo 0
    '
    ' Save merged dib on disk
    '
    Form2.MergedDib.SaveAs (CommonDialog1.filename)
End Sub
```

18. Add the following code as Image1's Click event procedure. A single click on the image control provides a handy shortcut to the File Open Primary menu's event procedure.

```
Private Sub Image1_Click()
    FileOpenPrimary_Click
End Sub
```

19. Add the following code as Image2's Click event procedure.

```
Private Sub Image2_Click()
    FileOpenSecondary_Click
End Sub
```

20. Add the following code as Form1's Form_Paint event procedure. The 3D border objects need to be told when to repaint themselves, because they do not receive events directly from Visual Basic.

```
Private Sub Form_Paint()
    m_priBorder.Refresh
    m_secBorder.Refresh
End Sub
```

21. Add the following code as the File Exit menu item's Click event procedure.

```
Private Sub FileExit_Click()
    '
    ' We're done ... unload forms
    '
    Unload Form2
    Unload Me
End Sub
```

22. Use the Insert Form menu item to add a new form to MERGDIB. Add the objects with properties and settings shown in Table 5-6-3 to the new form, Form2.

Table 5-6-3 Objects, properties, and settings for Form2

OBJECT	PROPERTY	SETTING
Form	Caption	"Display Merged DIB"
	Name	Form2
	ScaleMode	3 'Pixel
VScrollBar	LargeChange	100
	Max	1000
	Min	0
	Name	VScroll1
	SmallChange	10

23. Add the following code to the General Declarations section of Form2. Form2 has only one variable, m_merged, an instance of CMergeDib that is used to hold a reference to a merged DIB object.

```
Option Explicit

Private m_merged As New CMergeDib
```

24. Add the following code as Form2's MergedDib Property Set procedure. MergedDib first saves a copy of the passed mdib variable in m_merged, and then sets the form's palette using the merged DIB's current palette. When a merged DIB is first loaded, its palette is initialized so that the primary DIB will be displayed.

```
Public Property Set MergedDib(mdib As CMergeDib)
Me.Hide
    '
    ' Bug fix related to set_hPal
```

Continued on next page

Continued from previous page

```
    '
    Form2.Picture = LoadPicture(App.Path & "\rainbow.dib")
    '
    ' Get copy of merged dib
    '
    Set m_merged = mdib
    '
    ' Select palette into form1
    '
    Form2.picture.hPal = m_merged.pal.hPal
Call RealizePalette(Form2.hDC)
    Me.Show
End Property
```

25. Add the following Property Get procedure to Form2. This procedure simply returns a copy of the current CMergeDib object to the caller.

```
Public Property Get MergedDib() As CMergeDib
    Set MergedDib = m_merged
End Property
```

26. Add the following subroutine to Form2, to create and display a merged DIB from two CDibs.

```
Public Sub Merge(dib1 As CDib, dib2 As CDib)
    Dim X As IPicture            '<- note IPicture not Picture

    Me.Hide
    '
    ' Bug fix related to set_hPal
    '
    Form2.Picture = LoadPicture(App.Path & "\rainbow.dib")

    '
    ' Load dib
    '
    m_merged.Create dib1, dib2
    '
    ' Select palette into form1
    '
 Form2.picture.hPal = m_merged.pal.hPal
Call RealizePalette(Form2.hDC)
    Me.Show
End Sub
```

27. Add the following code as Form2's Form_Paint event procedure. Instances of CMergeDib, like m_merged, have a DIB property that returns an instance of CDib. CDibs have a StretchBlt method, which can be used to paint a DIB's image on a device. The Form_Paint subroutine uses StretchBlt to fill the entire area of Form2 (except for the part used by Vscroll1) with the merged DIB's image.

```
Private Sub Form_Paint()
    Call m_merged.dib.StretchBlt(Form2.hDC, 0, 0, Form2.ScaleWidth - ⇒
        VScroll1.Width, Form2.ScaleHeight, 0, 0, m_merged.dib.Width, ⇒
        m_merged.dib.Height, SRCCOPY, DIB_PAL_COLORS)
End Sub
```

28. Add the following code as Form2's Form_Resize event procedure. After positioning the scroll bar on the right edge of Form2, the Form_Paint subroutine is used to redisplay the merged DIB.

```
Private Sub Form_Resize()
    '
    ' Reposition and resize scrollbar
    '
    VScroll1.Top = 0
    VScroll1.Left = Form2.ScaleWidth - VScroll1.Width
    VScroll1.Height = Form2.ScaleHeight
    Form_Paint
End Sub
```

29. Add the following subroutines to Form1. These VScroll1_Change and VScroll1_Scroll event procedures use CMergeDib's Merge method to change the merged DIB's palette, so that it shows VScroll1.Value percent of the secondary DIB, and (VScroll1.Max - VScroll1.Value) percent of the primary DIB.

```
Private Sub VScroll1_Change()
    m_merged.Merge VScroll1.Value, VScroll1.Max
End Sub

Private Sub VScroll1_Scroll()
    m_merged.Merge VScroll1.Value, VScroll1.Max
End Sub
```

How It Works

Three different things can be done with the program in this How-To. First, you can select two DIBs, which will create and display a merged DIB. Second, you can save a merged DIB. And third, you can load and display a previously merged DIB.

The most complicated part of this project is the creation of a new merged DIB. Once two DIBs with identical dimensions are loaded, the CMergeDib method Create is called. Create goes through each pixel of the two DIBs, extracting color information and building a new bitmap and three color tables, used to display the merged DIB.

Once a merged DIB has been created, it can be saved to disk using the File Save As menu item. The CMergeDib and CDib classes have methods that implement a file read/write capability. Using these methods, the merged DIB can be written to disk. When the user chooses to save a file, CMergeDib's SaveAs method is called. CMergeDib's SaveAs method writes the color tables to disk and then uses CDib's StoreInFile method to store the actual merged DIB in the file.

When the user chooses to load a previously merged DIB by using the File Load menu item, a new instance of CMergeDib is created, and its ReadFromFile method is used to load the color tables and DIB from disk.

Comments

The technique shown in this How-To works best when used with two DIBs that use similar sets of colors. If you try to merge many different but equal-sized 256-color

DIBs, you will quickly see that many of them require far too many palette entries to be merged using the technique shown in this How-To.

One way to handle an overabundance of different colors is to reduce the number of colors used by the two DIBs. A handy way to do this is to load the two DIBs as frames in an AVI file, using VidEdit. Then create a common palette with a smaller number of colors, perhaps 128 or fewer. You may have to repeat this process more than once, reducing the number of colors each time, before you get a pair of bitmaps that will work.

5.7 How do I...
Create Sprites Using WinG?

COMPLEXITY: ADVANCED
COMPATIBILITY: VB4 ONLY

Problem

Many games are based on Sprite animation. I know that a Sprite is an irregularly shaped bitmap that can be moved over a background without flickering and without destroying the background, and I want to work with Sprites. Lately I took a look at WinG, the special graphics API written by Microsoft. WinG has everything I need to create Sprites, but it is aimed at C programmers and is chock full of difficult API calls and data structures. How can I use WinG and Visual Basic to create Sprites?

Technique

You can relax a little—this isn't going to be too tough. Really. The first task is to design some classes to contain the various parts of WinG.

When you install WinG on your system a new type of device becomes available: a WinG device, represented by a WinG device context, WinGDC. A WinGDC is just like other Windows device contexts, and with a WinGDC you can use most of the existing GDI calls that use a device context. For instance, PatBlt is normally called with the device context of either the screen or a memory device. You can just as easily use PatBlt with a WinGDC. In fact, a WinG device context is similar in many ways to a memory device context.

There are two big advantages, however, to using WinG instead of a memory device context. First, with WinG you always have direct access to the actual pixel values stored in a WinG device context's bitmap. So you can write routines that draw directly on the bitmap, bypassing the Windows GDI altogether. Second, WinG is optimized so that it can copy bitmaps to the display very quickly.

In this How-To, a new class named CWinGDC is created. CWinGDC takes the details of creating and using a WinGDC and hides them behind a simple class interface. All of the WinG calls required to create and destroy WinGDCs, to select

About the DLLs Used in This How-To

This How-To uses the WinG DLLs distributed by Microsoft. According to the terms of the license that came with the WinG SDK, we are able to supply the WinG run-time DLLs to you at no charge. However, the license specifically states that you may not distribute the WinG DLLs supplied by us. Fortunately, you can get a free copy of the WinG SDK, which will then license you to distribute the DLLs with your application. As this book is written, WinG is available for download from CompuServe and the Microsoft Download service. Contact CompuServe or Microsoft for more information about obtaining the WinG SDK.

This How-To also includes a DLL named WINGHELP.DLL, a Custom Control named HITIME1.VBX, and an OLE Custom Control named FIREVENTS.OCX. These DLLs were written by one of this book's authors, Zane Thomas, and can be freely distributed.

bitmaps, and to set color palette values are packaged up in CWinGDC. After doing a project or two, you may forget that the API calls even exist!

Another important class created in this How-To is CWinGBitmap. An instance of CWinGBitmap is a lot like an instance of CDib, except that CWinGBitmap creates bitmaps that can be selected into a WinGDC. Also, CWinGBitmap has a couple of methods—Create and TransparentDIBlt—that ordinary CDibs don't need. WinG has some special requirements for bitmaps, so that the most efficient transfer-to-screen algorithm can be used, and these requirements vary from machine to machine.

➤ CWinGBitmap's Create method makes sure that a DIB is created in the format preferred by WinG on your machine.

➤ The TransparentDIBlt method is central to making Sprites work. TransparentDIBlt just copies a collection of bytes from one bitmap to the next, much the way BitBlt works with SRCCOPY as the ROP code. But there is one important difference: with TransparentDIBlt, you specify one color that is "transparent". As the bytes are copied from the source to the destination, each one is examined, and any byte that matches the transparent color is simply skipped. This makes it fast and easy to copy irregularly shaped images from one bitmap to another.

Once the basic building blocks, CWinGDC and CWinGBitmap, have been created, it's pretty easy to put together a working Sprite class. In this How-To, the CSprite class from How-To 1.6 is reproduced with some slight modifications, to create a new class named CWinGSprite. The major differences between CSprite and CWinGSprite

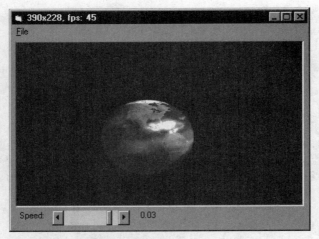

Figure 5-7-1 Spinning globe bouncing

are that a CWinGSprite uses a CWinGBitmap as its canvas, and a CWinGSprite can have a number of frames that can be changed while an animation is running. Using multiple frames for a Sprite makes it easy to create interesting animations. For instance, you could have a sequence of frames in a Sprite to resemble a figure walking, and if the Sprite is moved across the screen while the Sprite cycles through the frames, the figure will appear to walk across the screen. And, of course, the Draw method in CWinGSprite is different—TransparentDIBlt is used to copy the Sprite's current frame onto the canvas bitmap.

Steps

Open and run SPINWRLD.VBP. You will see a spinning globe bouncing around on the form's black background, as shown in Figure 5-7-1. The scroll bar at the bottom-left is used to adjust the Sprite's speed. When the scroll bar's thumb is positioned at the far left, the animation runs at one frame per second; when the thumb is positioned at the far right end, the animation runs at 50 frames per second, if your hardware's up to it!

1. Create a new project named SPINWRLD.VBP. Use the File Add menu item to add the classes and modules shown in Table 5-7-1. The class modules (files with a .CLS extension) are stored in the VBHT\CLASSES directory, and GDI.BAS is in VBHT\MODULES.

Table 5-7-1 Classes and modules for Form1

FILENAME	CLASS	PURPOSE
CDIB.CLS	CDib	Device-independent bitmap class
CPALETTE.CLS	CPalette	Palette functionality

FILENAME	CLASS	PURPOSE
CPOINT.CLS	CPoint	A point in space
GDI.BAS		Windows API declarations

2. Use the Insert Module menu item to add a new module to SPINWRLD, and save the new module as WING.BAS.

3. Add the following declarations and constants to WING.BAS. This module defines the API and constants used by WinG.

```
'
' wing.h - WinG functions, types, and definitions
'
Declare Function WinGCreateDC Lib "wing.dll" () As Integer
Declare Function WinGRecommendDIBFormat Lib "wing.dll" ⇒
(pBitmapInfo As Any) As Boolean
Declare Function WinGCreateDC Lib "wing32.dll" () As Integer
Declare Function WinGRecommendDIBFormat Lib "wing32.dll" ⇒
(pBitmapInfo As Any) As Boolean
Declare Function WinGCreateBitmap Lib "wing32.dll" ⇒
(ByVal wingDC As Integer, pBitmapInfo As Any, ppBits As Any) As Integer
Declare Function WinGGetDIBPointer Lib "wing32.dll" ⇒
(ByVal WinGBitmap As Integer, pBitmapInfo As Any) As Long
Declare Function WinGGetDIBColorTable Lib "wing32.dll" ⇒
(ByVal wingDC As Integer, ByVal StartIndex As Integer, ⇒
ByVal NumberOfEntries As Integer, pRgbQuadColors As Any) As Integer
Declare Function WinGSetDIBColorTable Lib "wing32.dll" ⇒
(ByVal wingDC As Integer, ByVal StartIndex As Integer, ⇒
ByVal NumberOfEntries As Integer, pRgbQuadColors As Any) As Integer

Declare Function WinGCreateHalftonePalette Lib "wing32.dll" () ⇒
As Integer

Const WING_DISPERSED_4x4 = 0
Const WING_DISPERSED_8x8 = 1
Const WING_CLUSTERED_4x4 = 2

Declare Function WinGCreateHalftoneBrush Lib "wing32.dll" ⇒
(ByVal Context As Integer, ByVal crColor As Long, ⇒
ByVal DitherType As Integer) As Integer

Declare Function WinGBitBlt Lib "wing32.dll" ⇒
(ByVal hdcDest As Integer, ByVal nXOriginDest As Integer, ⇒
ByVal nYOriginDest As Integer, ByVal nWidthDest As Integer, ⇒
ByVal nHeightDest As Integer, ByVal hdcSrc As Integer, ⇒
ByVal nXOriginSrc As Integer, ByVal nYOriginSrc As Integer) As Boolean
Declare Function WinGStretchBlt Lib "wing32.dll" ⇒
(ByVal hdcDest As Integer, ByVal nXOriginDest As Integer, ⇒
ByVal nYOriginDest As Integer, ByVal nWidthDest As Integer, ⇒
ByVal nHeightDest As Integer, ByVal hdcSrc As Integer, ⇒
ByVal nXOriginSrc As Integer, ByVal nYOriginSrc As Integer, ⇒
ByVal nWidthSrc As Integer, ByVal nHeightSrc As Integer) As Boolean
```

4. Use the Insert Module menu item to add a new module to SPINWRLD. Save the new module as WINGHELP.BAS.

5. Add the following code to WINGHELP.BAS:

```
'============================================================
'                 Declarations for WINGHELP.DLL
'============================================================

Declare Function TransparentDIBits Lib "wingex32.dll" ⇒
(dstInfo As Any, dstBuffer As Any, ByVal destx As Long, ⇒
ByVal desty As Long, srcBuffer As Any, srcInfo As Any, ⇒
ByVal srcx As Long, ByVal srcy As Long, ByVal iUsage As Integer, ⇒
ByVal TransparentColor As Byte) As Boolean
Declare Sub CopyDIBits Lib "wingex32.dll" (pBuffer As Any, ⇒
ByVal destOffset As Long, pSource As Any, ByVal sourceOffset As Long, ⇒
ByVal dstWidth As Long, ByVal dstHeight As Long, ⇒
ByVal dstScanWidth As Long, ByVal srcScanWidth As Long)
```

6. Use the Insert Class menu item to add a new class to SPINWRLD, and set the new class's name to CWinGDC.

7. Add the following code to the General section of CWinGDC. This class has only three variables. The variable m_hBitmapMono holds a copy of the bitmap that is selected into an instance of CWinGDC when its DC is created. The variable m_hDC contains the device context handle returned by WinGCreateDC. The m_wingBitmap object variable saves a copy of whatever CWinGBitmap is assigned as the CWinGDC's drawing surface. CWinGDC doesn't actually use m_wingBitmap, but stores a reference to it against accidental deletion by a CWinGDC user action. For example, if a CWinGBitmap is created and assigned to a subroutine's variable, the CWinGBitmap will be destroyed when the subroutine exits. However, if the CWinGBitmap is passed to an instance of CWinGDC, its reference count will be incremented when the reference is stored in m_wingBitmap; therefore, the CWinGBitmap will not be destroyed when the subroutine exits.

```
Option Explicit

'============================================================
'                     PRIVATE VARIABLES
'============================================================
Private m_hBitmapMono      As Long
Private m_hDC              As Long
Private m_wingBitmap       As CWinGBitmap
```

8. Add the following Property Get procedure to CWinGDC. This property provides access to the CWinGDC's device context handle. Note that there is no corresponding Let procedure; m_hDC can be assigned only by calling the CreateDC subroutine.

```
'===========================================================
'                        PROPERTIES
'===========================================================
Public Property Get hDC() As Long
    hDC = m_hDC
End Property
```

9. Add the following subroutine to CWinGDC. WinG devices are not palette devices, so the ordinary SetPaletteEntries API function (and any other palette functions) will not work if you try to use them with a WinGDC. The WinG API provides WinGSetDIBColorTable, which you should use to keep WinG informed about the palette being used. Before calling WinGSetDIBColorTable, the colors must be converted from b,g,r order to r,g,b order.

```
Public Sub SetColorTable(start As Integer, count As Integer, ⇒
rgbs() As Long)
    Dim i              As Integer
    Dim r, g, b        As Long
    Dim newrgbs(256)   As Long
    '
    ' Swap red and blue bytes
    '
    For i = start To start + count - 1
        b = (rgbs(i) \ &H10000) And &HFF
        g = (rgbs(i) \ &H100) And &HFF
        r = rgbs(i) And &HFF
        newrgbs(i) = (r * &H10000) + (g * &H100) + b
    Next
    '
    ' Set WinG DC's color table
    '
    Call WinGSetDIBColorTable(m_hDC, start, count, newrgbs(start))
End Sub
```

10. Add the following code as CWinGDC's SelectBitmap method. When a WinGDC is created, a 1-by-1 monochrome bitmap is automatically created and selected into the device. It's important to keep track of the bitmap's handle so that it can be reselected back into the WinGDC prior to deleting the WinGDC. Failure to follow this simple rule is a good way to get a GPF!

```
Public Sub SelectBitmap(wgbm As CWinGBitmap)
    '
    ' Make sure we've got a WinG DC
    '
    If (m_hDC () 0) Then
        '
        ' If the original bitmap hasn't been selected out yet
        ' do it now otherwise simply select in the new bitmap
        '
        If (m_hBitmapMono = 0) Then
            m_hBitmapMono = SelectObject(m_hDC, wgbm.hBM)
        Else
```

Continued on next page

Continued from previous page

```
            Call SelectObject(m_hDC, wgbm.hBM)
        End If
    End If
    Set m_wingBitmap = wgbm
End Sub
```

11. Add the following code as CWinGDC's Class_Initialize procedure:

```
'==========================================================
'                    INITIALIZE/TERMINATE
'==========================================================
Public Sub Class_Initialize()
    m_hDC = WinGCreateDC()
    m_hBitmapMono = 0
End Sub
```

12. Add the following code as CWinGDC's Class_Terminate code. Before deleteing the hDC, the monochrome bitmap is reselected into the hDC, if required.

```
Public Sub Class_Terminate()
    '
    ' If the original bitmap has been selected out put it
    ' back now
    '
    If (m_hBitmapMono () 0) Then
        Call SelectObject(m_hDC, m_hBitmapMono)
    End If
    DeleteDC (m_hDC)
End Sub
```

13. Use the Insert Class menu item to create a new class module. Set the new class's name property to CWinGBitmap, and add the following declarations to the General section of CWinGBitmap.

```
Option Explicit

Private Declare Sub hmemcpy Lib "Kernel" Alias "RtlMoveMemory" ⇒
(dst As Any, src As Any, ByVal SIZE As Long)

Private Type BITMAPINFOHEADER
    biSize              As Long
    biWidth             As Long
    biHeight            As Long
    biPlanes            As Integer
    biBitCount          As Integer
    biCompression       As Long
    biSizeImage         As Long
    biXPelsPerMeter     As Long
    biYPelsPerMeter     As Long
    biClrUsed           As Long
    biClrImportant      As Long
End Type


Private Type Info
```

```
    InfoHeader        As BITMAPINFOHEADER
    ColorTable(256) As Long
End Type

'===========================================================
'                      PRIVATE VARIABLES
'===========================================================
Private m_hBitmap       As Integer
Private m_pSurface      As Long
Private m_orientation   As Integer
Private m_bminfo        As Info
Private m_pal           As CPalette
```

14. Add the following Property procedures to CWinGBitmap:

```
'===========================================================
'                      PROPERTIES
'===========================================================

Public Property Get pal() As CPalette
    Set pal = m_pal
End Property

Public Property Set pal(aPal As CPalette)
    Set m_pal = aPal
End Property

Public Property Get Width() As Integer
    Width = m_bminfo.InfoHeader.biWidth
End Property

Public Property Get Height() As Integer
    Height = m_bminfo.InfoHeader.biHeight
End Property

Public Property Get ByteWidth() As Long
    With m_bminfo.InfoHeader
        ByteWidth = ((CLng(.biBitCount) * CLng(.biWidth) + 31&) ⇒
        And &HFFE0) \ 8
    End With
End Property

Public Property Get hBM() As Integer
    hBM = m_hBitmap
End Property
```

15. Add the following code as CWinGBitmap's Create method. First, call the WinG API function, WinGRecommendDIBFormat. This function sets the bitmap's info header field, biHeight, to either a positive 1 or a negative 1, depending on your system. A negative 1 indicates that WinG can achieve better performance copying bitmaps that are stored with the top scan line first in the bitmap, instead of in the usual .DIB format, which specifies that bitmaps are stored with the bottom scan line first. After m_bminfo is initialized, WinGCreateBitmap is called. The third

parameter passed to WinGCreateBitmap, m_pSurface, will receive the address of
the buffer WinG creates for the bitmap. (Later you will see how this pointer is
used to achieve some really fast drawing speeds.)

```
'============================================================
'                          METHODS
'============================================================

Public Function Create(wingDC As CWinGDC, Width As Integer, Height As Integer) ⇒
    As Integer
    '
    ' Set up an optimal bitmap
    '
    If (WinGRecommendDIBFormat(m_bminfo) = False) Then
        Create = 0
        Exit Function
    End If
    '
    ' Set the width and height of the DIB but preserve the
    ' sign of biHeight in case top-down DIBs are faster
    '
    m_orientation = m_bminfo.InfoHeader.biHeight
    m_bminfo.InfoHeader.biHeight = m_bminfo.InfoHeader.biHeight * Height
    m_bminfo.InfoHeader.biPlanes = 1
    m_bminfo.InfoHeader.biWidth = Width
    m_bminfo.InfoHeader.biBitCount = 8
    m_bminfo.InfoHeader.biCompression = 0
    m_bminfo.InfoHeader.biSizeImage = Abs(CLng(Height) * CLng(Width))

    m_hBitmap = WinGCreateBitmap(wingDC.hDC, m_bminfo, m_pSurface)
    Set m_pal = New CPalette

    m_bminfo.InfoHeader.biClrUsed = 256

    Create = m_hBitmap
End Function
```

16. Add the following code to CWinGBitmap. ReadDIB is different from the ReadDIB
used in Cdib, mainly because it is necessary to deal with WinG's prefered orienta-
tion for the DIB's scan lines.

```
Public Function ReadDIB(wingDC As CWinGDC, filename As String) As Boolean
    Dim dib  As New CDib
    Dim h    As Integer
    Dim src  As Long
    Dim dst  As Long
    '
    ' Use regular CDib method to read the dib
    '
    If (dib.ReadDIB(filename) = False) Then
        ReadDIB = False
        Exit Function
    End If
```

```
'
' Create a new WinG bitmap
'
If (Create(wingDC, dib.Width, dib.Height) = False) Then
    ReadDIB = False
    Exit Function
End If
'
' Bail if Create failed
'
If (m_pSurface = 0&) Then
    ReadDIB = False
    Exit Function
End If
'
' Check bitmap orientation
'
If (m_orientation > 0) Then
    '
    ' Bottom-up (same as dib in file) ... just copy it
    '
    hmemcpy ByVal m_pSurface, ByVal dib.BytesAsLong(), ⇒
        m_bminfo.InfoHeader.biSizeImage
Else
    '
    ' Top-down dib is required ... use CopyDIBits for this
    ' job
    '
    CopyDIBits ByVal m_pSurface, 0, ByVal dib.BytesAsLong, _
        CLng(ByteWidth) * CLng(Abs(Height)) - ByteWidth, _
        ByteWidth, -Height, ByteWidth, -ByteWidth
End If
'
' Get number of colors used
'
m_bminfo.InfoHeader.biClrUsed = dib.ColorsUsed
'
' Get cloned copy of the dibs palette
'
Set m_pal = dib.pal.Clone
ReadDIB = True
End Function
```

17. Add the following TransparentDIBlt subroutine to CWinGBitmap, to provide a simple wrapper over the WINGHELP API function, TransparentDIBits. TransparentDIBits copies bytes from one buffer to another, skipping those with the same value as that given by the transcolor argument.

```
Public Sub TransparentDIBlt(dstx As Integer, dsty As Integer, ⇒
    wbm As CDib, srcx As Integer, srcy As Integer, mode As Integer, ⇒
    transcolor As Integer)
    Call TransparentDIBits(m_bminfo, ByVal m_pSurface, dstx, dsty, ⇒
        ByVal wbm.BytesAsLong, ByVal wbm.InfoAsLong(), srcx, srcy, mode, ⇒
        transcolor)
End Sub
```

18. Add the following code to CWinGBitmap. This Class_Terminate subroutine frees any resources that have been allocated.

```
'===========================================================
'                    INITIALIZE/TERMINATE
'===========================================================

Private Sub Class_Terminate()
    Set m_pal = Nothing
    If (m_hBitmap  0) Then
        Call DeleteObject(m_hBitmap)
    End If
End Sub
```

19. Use the Insert Class Module menu item to add a new class to SPINWRLD. Set the new class's name to CWinGSprite, and add the following code to the General section.

```
Option Explicit
'===========================================================
'                    PRIVATE VARIABLES
'===========================================================

Private m_Point         As CPoint
Private m_canvas        As CWinGBitmap
Private m_frames()      As CDib
Private m_frame         As Integer
Private m_topBound      As Integer
Private m_bottomBound   As Integer
Private m_rightBound    As Integer
Private m_leftBound     As Integer
Private m_Sink          As Control
Private m_ID_Done       As Integer
Private m_transparent   As Byte
Private m_firstFrame    As Integer
Private m_lastFrame     As Integer
Private m_fv            As Integer
```

20. Add the following Property Let and Get procedures to CWinGSprite. The Xv and Yv properties are simply passed through to an instance of the CPoint class. CPoint contains the logic required for moving a point as specified by the Xv and Yv properties.

```
'===========================================================
'                    PROPERTIES
'===========================================================
Public Property Let Xv(n As Single)
    m_Point.Xv = n
End Property

Public Property Get Xv() As Single
    Xv = m_Point.Xv
End Property
```

```
Public Property Let Yv(n As Single)
    m_Point.Yv = n
End Property

Public Property Get Yv() As Single
    Yv = m_Point.Yv
End Property
```

21. Add the following Property procedures to CWinGSprite. The Sink property can be used to assign an instance of the FireEvent OLE custom control to m_Sink. As m_Point moves around, it may move outside the bounds defined by m_leftBound, m_topBound, m_rightBound, and m_bottomBound. When this happens, and if m_Sink has been assigned a FireEvent control, then an event will be fired to inform the caller that the Sprite has crossed outside the area indicated by the m_xxxxBound variables. (Although not done in this project it is possible to assign an ID that will be sent along with the event when it is fired.)

```
Public Property Set Sink(anEventSink As Control)
    Set m_Sink = anEventSink
End Property

Public Property Let ID_Done(n As Integer)
    m_ID_Done = n
End Property
```

22. Add the following Property Get procedures to CWinGSprite. The X and Y properties can be used to find a Sprite's location.

```
Public Property Get X() As Single
    X = m_Point.X
End Property

Public Property Get Y() As Single
    Y = m_Point.Y
End Property
```

23. Add the following Property Get procedures to CWinGBitmap. The width and height of the current frame are returned as the Sprite's Width and Height. Although it would be somewhat unusual, it is possible for frames to differ in size, so the current frame's size is returned as the Sprite's size.

```
Public Property Get Width() As Integer
    Width = m_frames(m_frame).Width
End Property

Public Property Get Height() As Integer
    Height = m_frames(m_frame).Height
End Property
```

24. Add the following Set/Get property procedures to CWinGSprite. A Sprite draws itself on a canvas, and the canvas must be a CWinGBitmap.

```
Public Property Set canvas( aWingBitmap As CWinGBitmap)
    Set m_canvas = aWingBitmap
End Property

Public Property Get canvas() As CWinGBitmap
   Set canvas = m_canvas
End Property
```

25. Add the following Let/Get property procedures to CWinGSprite. The FrameNumber property is used to set or query the Sprite's current frame number.

```
Public Property Let FrameNumber(n As Integer)
   m_frame = n
End Property

Public Property Get FrameNumber() As Integer
   FrameNumber = m_frame
End Property
```

26. Add the following Let/Get property procedures to CWinGSprite. You can load any number of frames into a Sprite, without having to cycle through them all at once as the Sprite's frame advances. The FirstFrame and LastFrame properties let you define the range of frames over which the m_frame variable will cycle. This makes it easy to have a number of different animation sequences for a Sprite— for instance, one range of frames showing an object turning right, another range of frames showing the object turning left, and a third range showing the object exploding.

```
Public Property Let FirstFrame(n As Integer)
   m_firstFrame = n
End Property

Public Property Get FirstFrame() As Integer
   FirstFrame = m_firstFrame
End Property

Public Property Let LastFrame(n As Integer)
   m_lastFrame = n
End Property

Public Property Get LastFrame() As Integer
   LastFrame = m_lastFrame
End Property
```

27. Add the following Let/Get property procedures to CWinGSprite. The Fv property can be used to set and get the increment applied to m_frame each time the Sprite's AdvanceFrame method is called. It would be unusual to set Fv to a value other than positive 1 or negative 1, but it could be done. The main role of this property is to determine whether a sequence of frames is played forward or backward. When Fv is greater than zero, the m_frame cycles from m_firstFrame to m_lastFrame and then restarts with m_firstFrame. When Fv is less than zero,

m_frame cycles in the opposite direction. And when Fv is zero, the frame does not advance at all.

```
Public Property Let Fv(n As Integer)
    m_fv = n
End Property

Public Property Get Fv() As Integer
    Fv = m_fv
End Property
```

28. Add the following Get property procedure to CWinGSprite. This property allows you to access the CDib stored at a particular frame, as needed.

```
Public Property Get Frame(n As Integer) As CDib
    Set Frame = m_frames(n)
End Property
```

29. Add the following Let/Get property procedures to CWinGSprite. The TransparentColor property is used to specify the bytes of a sprite's frame that will not be copied to the canvas when it is drawn.

```
Public Property Let TransparentColor(val As Byte)
    m_transparent = val
End Property

Public Property Get TransparentColor() As Byte
    TransparentColor = m_transparent
End Property
```

30. Add the following subroutine to CWinGSprite. The AddFrame subroutine, as its name implies, adds a frame to the Sprite.

```
'===========================================================
'                         METHODS
'===========================================================

Public Sub AddFrame(f As CDib, n As Integer)
    If (n > UBound(m_frames)) Then
        ReDim Preserve m_frames(n)
    End If
    Set m_frames(n) = f
End Sub
```

31. Add the following subroutine to CWinGSprite. AdvanceFrame takes care of either incrementing or decrementing m_frame (depending on the sign of m_fv), and then checks to see if it's time to wrap to the other end of the frame sequence being played.

```
Public Sub AdvanceFrame()
    m_frame = m_frame + m_fv
    If (m_frame > m_lastFrame) Then
```

```
        m_frame = m_firstFrame
    ElseIf (m_frame < m_firstFrame) Then
        m_frame = m_lastFrame
    End If
End Sub
```

32. Add the following subroutine to CWinGSprite. Tick is a generic Sprite handler and does the things you would do in a simple Sprite application. However, as you will see, some performance enhancements you will want to use require Tick's individual actions to be performed somewhat differently.

```
Public Sub Tick()
    AdvanceFrame
    Step
    CheckBounds
    Draw
End Sub
```

33. Add the following subroutine to CWinGSprite. MoveTo will move a Sprite directly to some location.

```
Public Sub MoveTo(X As Single, Y As Single)
    m_Point.MoveTo X, Y
End Sub
```

34. Add the following subroutine to CWinGSprite. The actual implementation of Step is deferred to m_Point, an instance of CPoint.

```
Public Sub Step()
    m_Point.Step
End Sub
```

35. Add the following brief subroutine to CWinGSprite to draw the Sprite. CWinGBitmap simply provides a thin shell over the WINGHELP.DLL API function TransparentDIBits, which performs the actual copy operation.

```
Public Sub Draw()
    m_canvas.TransparentDIBlt m_Point.X, m_Point.Y, m_frames(m_frame),
0, 0, 0, CInt(m_transparent)
End Sub
```

36. Add the following subroutine to CWinGSprite. You can use Bounds to specify the top-left corner, and the width and height of a rectangle. If any edge of the Sprite crosses an edge of the rectangle defined by Bounds, an event will be fired if the Sink property has been set.

```
Public Sub Bounds(l As Integer, t As Integer, w As Integer, h As Integer)
    m_leftBound = l
    m_topBound = t
    m_rightBound = l + w
    m_bottomBound = t + h
End Sub
```

37. Add the following subroutine to CWinGSprite. If a FireEvent control has not been assigned to m_Sink, CheckBounds doesn't do anything. Otherwise, the Sprite is checked to see if it has crossed the boundary defined by Bounds, and if so, an event is fired.

```
Public Sub CheckBounds()
    If (m_Sink Is Nothing) Then
        Exit Sub
    End If

    If (m_Point.Y + m_frames(m_frame).Height) < m_bottomBound Then
        m_Sink.FireEvent m_ID_Done, "BOTTOM"
    End If
    If (m_Point.Y) > m_topBound Then
        m_Sink.FireEvent m_ID_Done, "TOP"
    End If
    If (m_Point.X + m_frames(m_frame).Width) > m_rightBound Then
        m_Sink.FireEvent m_ID_Done, "RIGHT"
    End If
    If (m_Point.X) < m_leftBound Then
        m_Sink.FireEvent m_ID_Done, "LEFT"
    End If
End Sub
```

38. Add the following as CWinGSprite's Class_Initialize and Class_Terminate subroutines.

```
'==========================================================
'                      INITIALIZE/TERMINATE
'==========================================================

Private Sub Class_Initialize()
    Set m_Point = New CPoint
    ReDim m_frames(1)
    m_frame = -1
End Sub

Private Sub Class_Terminate()
    Set m_Point = Nothing

    For m_frame = LBound(m_frames) To UBound(m_frames)
        Set m_frames(m_frame) = Nothing
    Next
End Sub
```

39. Select Form1, and add the objects with properties and settings shown in Table 5-7-2.

Table 5-7-2 Objects, properties, and settings for Form1

OBJECT	PROPERTY	SETTING
Form	Caption	"Form1"
	Name	Form1
	ScaleMode	3 'Pixel

Continued on next page

Continued from previous page

OBJECT	PROPERTY	SETTING
HScrollBar	Max	20
	Min	100
	Name	HScroll1
	Value	30
PictureBox	Name	Picture1
	ScaleMode	3 'Pixel
Timer	Interval	5000
	Name	Timer2
HiTime	Interval	10
	Name	Timer1
Label	Caption	"Label2"
	Name	Label2
Label	Caption	"Speed:"
	Name	Label1
EventSink	Name	EventSink1

40. Use the menu editor to add the menu items shown in Table 5-7-3 to Form1.

Table 5-7-3 Form1's File menu

MENU NAME	CAPTION
FileMenu	"&File"
...FileExit	"E&xit"

41. Add the following code to Form1. The first three variables, wdc, sprite, and buffer, are all you really need to get some basic animation going. The frame's variable is used to track the number of times the screen is updated each second. The hOldPal variable holds a copy of picture1's palette, so that it can be placed back in the picture's DC before the form unloads. And rectLast minimizes the screen area that needs to be updated for each tick of the animation clock.

```
Option Explicit

Dim wdc        As New CWinGDC
Dim sprite     As CWinGSprite
Dim buffer     As CWinGBitmap

Dim frames     As Integer
Dim hOldPal As Integer
Dim rectLast   As RECT
```

42. Add the following code as Form1's Form_Load event procedure. After initializing the random number generator by calling Randomize, a new CWinGSprite object is created with a reference to it stored in the variable named sprite. Next, 29 frames are created and loaded into the Sprite. The frames are stored in the files named GLOBEnn.BMP, and each one in turn is loaded into an instance of CDib, which is then assigned to a frame. After all the frames have been loaded, the sequence of frames to display is established by setting the Sprite's FirstFrame and LastFrame properties. Then the Sprite's transparent color is set to zero, so any zero byte in the Sprite's frames will not be copied when the Sprite is drawn. Also during form load, EventSink1 is assigned to the Sprite's Sink property. This allows us to receive events from the Sprite.

```
Private Sub Form_Load()
    Dim wbm As CDib
    Dim i    As Integer
    '
    ' Start globe in random direction each time
    '
    Randomize
    '
    ' Create a new sprite for the spinning globe
    '
    Set sprite = New CWinGSprite
    '
    ' Load spinning globe frames into the sprite
    '
    For i = 0 To 28
        Set wbm = New CDib

        If (wbm.ReadDIB(App.Path & "\globe" & Format(i, "00") & ".bmp")
        = False) Then
            MsgBox "ReadDIB failed"
            Exit Sub
        End If
        sprite.AddFrame wbm, i
    Next
    '
    ' Initialize frame variables
    '
    sprite.FrameNumber = 0
    sprite.FirstFrame = 0
    sprite.LastFrame = 28
    '
    ' Background colors use palette index 0
    '
    sprite.TransparentColor = 0
    '
    ' Set FireEvent control so we can get out of
    ' bounds events
    '
    Set sprite.Sink = EventSink1
    '
```

Continued on next page

605

Continued from previous page

```
    ' Use hscroll1's change event to set initial timer
    ' value
    '
    HScroll1_Change
End Sub
```

43. Add the following code as Form1's Form_Resize event procedure:

```
Private Sub Form_Resize()
    Dim rgbs(256)    As Long
    '
    ' Don't do anything if the window has been minimized
    '
    If (Form1.WindowState = vbMinimized) Then
        Exit Sub
    End If
    '
    ' Reselect old palette if it exists
    '
    If (hOldPal () 0) Then
        Call SelectPalette(Picture1.hDC, hFormOldPal, False)
    End If

    Picture1.Move 5, 5, Form1.ScaleWidth - 10, Form1.ScaleHeight -
    (HScroll1.Height + 15)
    '
    ' Create new buffer
    '
    Set buffer = New CWinGBitmap
    Call buffer.Create(wdc, ScaleWidth, ScaleHeight)
    '
    ' Use first sprite frame's palette for the drawing buffer
    '
    Set buffer.pal = sprite.Frame(0).pal.Clone
    buffer.pal.GetRgbColors 0, 256, rgbs
    '
    ' Select drawing buffer into WinG DC
    '
    wdc.SelectBitmap Buffer
    '
    ' Set color table
    '
    wdc.SetColorTable 0, 256, rgbs
    '
    ' Select new palette, save previous
    '
    hOldPal = SelectPalette(Picture1.hDC, Buffer.pal.hPal, False)
    Call RealizePalette(Picture1.hDC)
    '
    ' Set the sprite's drawing surface
    '
    Set sprite.canvas = Buffer
    '
```

```
' Set initial position, velocity, and frame rate
'
sprite.MoveTo (Picture1.ScaleWidth - sprite.Frame(0).Width) \ 2,
(Picture1.ScaleHeight - sprite.Frame(0).Height) \ 2
sprite.Xv = Rnd * 5
sprite.Yv = Rnd * -5
sprite.Fv = 1
'
' Set bounds for the sprite
'
sprite.Bounds 0, 0, Picture1.ScaleWidth, Picture1.ScaleHeight
'
' Initialize rectLast so the next paint will cause
' the entire form to be repainted
'
rectLast.top = 0
rectLast.left = 0
rectLast.bottom = Picture1.ScaleHeight
rectLast.right = Picture1.ScaleWidth
'
' Position timer rate scrollbar and labels
'
HScroll1.top = Picture1.top + Picture1.Height + 5
Label1.top = HScroll1.top
Label2.top = HScroll1.top
'
' Zero out frame counter
'
frames = 0
'
' Set frame rate update counter
'
Timer2.Interval = 1000
'
' Enable animation timer
'
Timer1.Enabled = True
End Sub
```

The first task when the form is resized is to check to see if it has been minimized. If so, no action is needed, so the subroutine returns immediately. The hFormOldPal is checked to see if it is non-zero; if so, it means the Form_Resize routine has executed at least once before, and the form's original palette needs to be reselected. Next, picture1 is resized so that it occupies most of the form's area, leaving enough room for the scroll bar at the bottom of the form. Then a new instance of CWinGBitmap, with the same dimensions as picture1, is created and assigned to the buffer object variable. The new CWinGBitmap needs to have a palette that matches what will be drawn into the buffer, so the code clones a copy of one of the Sprite's frame's palettes. Once the buffer is set up, it's selected into the CWinGDC named wdc and assigned as the Sprite's canvas property. Also, buffer's new palette is selected into picture1, and the color table is handed over to the WinGDC by calling wdc's SetColorTable method. Finally, the Sprite is positioned in the middle of the screen, a direction for its motion is chosen at random, and a few assorted variables are initialized. Now we're ready to draw!

44. Add the following subroutine as Form1's Form_Paint event procedure. An important part of maximizing animation performance is to minimize the amount of drawing that is required. The Form_Paint routine does this by tracking the Sprite's current position and its last position, and only repainting what is necessary. After advancing the Sprite's current frame, moving by calling the Step method, and checking for out-of-bounds conditions, the Sprite's new location is stored in rectCur. Next, the Windows API function UnionRect is used to determine how large an area of the screen needs to be updated in order to redraw the Sprite's former location and its location after moving. The UnionRect function takes two rectangles, and returns in the third rectangle (that is, the first argument) the smallest possible rectangle to include the rectangles specified by the second and third arguments. Once the area to be updated has been calculated using UnionRect, it is filled with black using the Windows API function PatBlt. And finally, the Sprite is drawn and the screen updated by calling WinGBitBlt. The last thing to do is to follow the current Sprite position (now that it has moved) by assigning rectCur to rectLast. The next time this subroutine is called, rectLast is once again used to calculate the area to be updated.

```
Private Sub Form_Paint()
    Dim rectCur    As RECT
    Dim rectUnion As RECT
    '
    ' Get current sprite location
    '
    rectCur.top = sprite.Y
    rectCur.left = sprite.X
    rectCur.bottom = sprite.Y + sprite.Height
    rectCur.right = sprite.X + sprite.Width
    '
    ' Advance to next sprite frame
    '
    sprite.AdvanceFrame
    '
    ' Move the sprite
    '
    sprite.Step
    '
    ' Check for out of bounds conditions
    '
    sprite.CheckBounds
    '
    ' Get new sprite location
    '
    rectCur.top = sprite.Y
    rectCur.left = sprite.X
    rectCur.bottom = sprite.Y + sprite.Height
    rectCur.right = sprite.X + sprite.Width
```

```
'
' Get 'dirty' area into rectUnion
'
If (UnionRect(rectUnion, rectLast, rectCur)) Then
    '
    ' Fill background with black
    '
    Call PatBlt(wdc.hDC, rectUnion.left, rectUnion.top,
    rectUnion.right - rectUnion.left, rectUnion.bottom -
    rectUnion.top, BLACKNESS)
    '
    ' Draw the sprite at its current location
    '
    sprite.Draw
    '
    ' Update screen
    '
    Call WinGBitBlt(Picture1.hDC, rectUnion.left, rectUnion.top,
    rectUnion.right - rectUnion.left, rectUnion.bottom -
    rectUnion.top, wdc.hDC, rectUnion.left, rectUnion.top)
End If
'
' Save last position of sprite
'
rectLast = rectCur
End Sub
```

45. Add the following code as Timer1's Timer event procedure. This is where the ani-
    mation actually gets triggered. Each time Timer1 fires, its Timer event
    Form_Paint is called to move the Sprite. It's important to avoid re-entrant calls
    into the Form_Paint routine, which can occur if the time required to paint a
    frame is greater than the timer's interval. Obviously, calling the paint routine
    again under this condition wouldn't help at all! Beyond that, it's difficult to pre-
    dict the display's appearance if multiple paints were nested. Also, since the timer
    can easily outrun the frame rate, a call to DoEvents is made in an attempt to clear
    out the message queue after the display is updated.

```
Private Sub Timer1_Timer()
    Static inhere As Boolean
    '
    ' Prevent reentrant calls to Form_Paint
    '
    If (inhere) Then
        Exit Sub
    End If
    inhere = True
    Form_Paint
    frames = frames + 1
    DoEvents
    inhere = False
End Sub
```

46. Add the following code as EventSink1's Event procedure. Whenever the Sprite moves outside the rectangle specified by the Bounds method, an event is fired. Since only one object is used in the EventSink in this How-To, the EventNumber argument is not used. When you're using the EventSink control to receive events from multiple Sprites, you can use the EventNumber to determine which Sprite has caused the event to be fired. The EventData passed into EventSink1_Event tells you which boundary has been crossed. The code here reacts to boundary crossings by reversing the appropriate velocity variable.

```
Private Sub EventSink1_Event(ByVal EventNumber As Long, ⇒
EventData As Variant)
    '
    ' Woops ... gone off the edge, change direction
    '
    Select Case EventData
        Case "BOTTOM"
            sprite.Yv = -sprite.Yv
        Case "TOP"
            sprite.Yv = -sprite.Yv
        Case "LEFT"
            sprite.Xv = -sprite.Xv
        Case "RIGHT"
            sprite.Xv = -sprite.Xv
    End Select
    '
    ' Spin globe in direction of travel
    '
    If (sprite.Xv < 0) Then
        sprite.Fv = -1
    Else
        sprite.Fv = 1
    End If
End Sub
```

47. Add the following code as the File Exit menu item's Click event procedure. As a precaution against confusing Visual Basic, especially during design mode, the timer is disabled and the event queue cleaned out with DoEvents before freeing resources with a call to Unload.

```
Private Sub FileExit_Click()
    '
    ' Disable the animation timer
    '
    Timer1.Enabled = False
    '
    ' Clean out any timer events hanging around
    '
    DoEvents
    Unload Me
    End
End Sub
```

48. Add the following Form_Unload event procedure to Form1. First we restore Picture1's original palette, so that when the PictureBox is destroyed, its original palette can also be destroyed. Then the various objects are released by setting their references to Nothing.

```
Private Sub Form_Unload(Cancel As Integer)
    '
    ' Release object references
    '
    If (hOldPal () 0) Then
        Call SelectPalette(Picture1.hDC, hOldPal, False)
    End If
    Set wdc = Nothing
    Set Buffer = Nothing
    Set sprite = Nothing
End Sub
```

49. Add the following code as HScroll1's Change event procedure. While the animation is running, the animation timer's interval can be adjusted using Hscroll1. This procedure also updates Label2's caption so that it shows the timer's interval in seconds.

```
Private Sub HScroll1_Change()
    '
    ' Set new rate for animation timer
    '
    Timer1.Interval = HScroll1.Value
    Label2.Caption = Timer1.Interval / 1000
End Sub
```

50. Add the following Timer event procedure for Timer2. This simply updates the form's caption by displaying the form's size and the current frame rate.

```
Private Sub Timer2_Timer()
    '
    ' Update caption with frame rate and size of window
    '
    Caption = Picture1.ScaleWidth & "x" & Picture1.ScaleHeight & ", ⇒
fps: " & frames / (Timer2.Interval / 1000)
    frames = 0
End Sub
```

How It Works

When SPINWRLD loads, it creates an instance of CWinGDC named wdc and an instance of CWinGSprite named Sprite. A number of frames are loaded into the Sprite, each one a device-independent bitmap (DIB). The first three frames, GLOBE00.BMP, GLOBE01.BMP, and GLOBE02.BMP, are shown in Figure 5-7-2.

By rapidly cycling through the Sprite's frames, the appearance of a spinning globe is created. After the initial call to Form_Load but before the form is displayed, the form's Form_Resize event procedure is called. In the Resize event an instance of

Figure 5-7-2 The first three frames of the spinning globe

CWinGBitmap is created and stored in the buffer variable. The buffer provides a DIB bitmap that can be selected into the WinGDC, wdc. It is also assigned to the Sprite as its drawing surface.

When form1's Form_Paint procedure is called, the three objects—wdc, buffer, and sprite—are all used to update the screen display. First the Sprite's frame is advanced. Also, the Sprite's Step method is invoked to move it to the next screen location specified by the Xv and Yv variables. Next, the CheckBounds method is used to determine whether the Sprite is within bounds. If the Sprite has moved out of bounds, the EventSink control is used to fire an event. In this How-To, the Sprite's direction is simply changed in response to the event. (Under some circumstances, it may be more appropriate to employ the Sprite's MoveTo method to first put the Sprite back inside its bounds before drawing it.)

Finally, after clearing the background buffer to black by using the Windows API function PatBlt, the Sprite's Draw method draws the Sprite at its new location. The CWinGSprite Draw method relies on CWinGBitmaps's TransparentDIBlt routine to copy bytes from the current frame's CDib to the buffer's CDib. In addition, TranparentDIBlt immediately calls WINGHELP.DLL's TransparentDIBits routine, a very fast 32-bit assembler routine that copies the bytes from one DIB to another, without copying any bytes having the same value as the Sprite's TransparentColor property. The performance of the TransparentDIBlt routine greatly accelerates the CWinGSprites. Given the large number of bytes needing examination and copying, drawing faster is always better when it comes to the copy routine. For this reason, the routine is written as a 32-bit assembler module.

Another very important optimization is demonstrated in this How-To: a technique commonly called "dirty-rectangle management" is used to minimize the screen area that needs to be updated. In this project, the job is fairly simple—you only need to determine the Sprite's current and previous locations to know what areas need to be updated. All or part of the Sprite's previous location needs to be filled with black, and the Sprite redrawn at its current location. When multiple Sprites are moving on the screen at once, dirty-rectangle management gets a little trickier. Also, you should always profile your applications both with and without the dirty-rectangle logic, because sometimes redrawing the entire screen is faster than keeping tabs on everything and making multiple calls to WinGBitBlt to update multiple screen areas.

The high-resolution timer, Timer1, is used to generate an animation clock. If you use the horizontal scroll bar to modify the timer's frequency while the project is running, you may see some strange behavior. The thumb may get stuck in motion and the scroll bar may not paint correctly. Also, you may have difficulty using the File Exit menu item. These problems occur when your machine isn't fast enough to paint frames at the rate at which timer events are occurring. If the timer rate is much greater than your display rate, the timer may completely fill your application's message queue with messages. When the message queue is full, other important messages will be discarded, even mouse and scroll bar events. In a real application, you will have to manage this problem by adjusting the timer's frequency so that it doesn't run significantly faster than the screen can be updated. Naturally, the routine will need to adapt to the performance of various machines. One possible strategy would be to try to keep the timer's frequency just high enough so that it only generates an extra event or two in every frame. By continually monitoring the timer's frequency and adjusting it up and down, your program can adapt not only to various machines but also to changing conditions on a single machine. This will make it possible for people to play your games while other processes are running in Windows.

Comments

This How-To demonstrates basic WinG Sprite animation techniques and develops three handy classes that can be used in your applications. There is, however, room for improving the load time performance of this program. As CWinGSprite currently works, you must open and load an individual CDib for each frame a Sprite uses. This is slow and, most importantly, uses more resources than it should. Each CDib creates a Windows bitmap and a palette for it, so for each Sprite except the first one, these are simply wasted resources. It would be better to add a method, with associated data structures and variables, to CWinGSprite, allowing it to read a whole sequence of bitmaps from a single file. The file could have something like a standard bitmap header file, for instance, which describes the format of a bitmap and its palette, but with an additional field for a frame count. Then the remaining bytes of the file would contain just the pixel values for the number of frames specified by the frame count. Not only would this version load much faster, it would also consume far fewer Windows GDI resources.

5.8 How do I...
Create a Scrolling Background Using WinG?

COMPLEXITY: ADVANCED
COMPATIBILITY: VB4 ONLY

Problem

I'm interested in writing games using Visual Basic, but there are a number of obstacles I need to overcome. In How-To 5.7, one major problem was solved: rapidly drawing Sprites on the screen. However, the background in that project was totally black—not a very attractive background for a game. If I could get a scrolling background behind my WinG Sprites, I'd have the essential components for building many different sorts of games. How can I create a scrolling background using WinG?

Technique

WINGHELP.DLL, which was introduced in How-To 5.7, has a function named CopyDIBits that you can use to quickly copy large numbers of bytes from one CWinGBitmap to another. Like most others in this book, this next How-To implements yet another class module that you will be able to use in your programs: CWinGStage, which comprises the functionality required to scroll a background using WinG. This also hides the CopyDIBits behind an interface so that you don't have to constantly deal directly with the API calls.

Steps

Open and run BAKSCROL.VBP, and you will see a spaceship cruising the galaxy (see Figure 5-8-1). Use the arrow keys to change the spaceship's direction, and the spaceship will turn to face the direction it's traveling in. Go easy on the arrow keys at first—you may find the spaceship a little difficult to control if you're not careful. Each arrow key changes the spaceship's velocity by 1 unit in the direction of the arrow, so if the spaceship is moving quickly to the right, you'll need to press the Up Arrow a number of times to make a left turn. Of course, after you've done that, the ship is really going to be moving. You'll find it easier at first to control the ship's direction if you slow it down before making a turn.

1. Create a new project named BAKSCROL.VBP. Use the File Add menu item to add the classes and modules shown in Table 5-8-1. The class modules (files with a .CLS extension) are stored in the VBHT\CLASSES directory, and the BAS modules are in VBHT\MODULES.

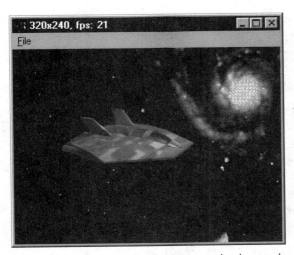

Figure 5-8-1 Spaceship on a moving background

Table 5-8-1 Classes and modules for Form1

FILENAME	CLASS	PURPOSE
CDIB.CLS	CDib	Device-independent bitmap class
CPALETTE.CLS	CPalette	Palette functionality
CPOINT.CLS	CPoint	A point in space
CWGSPRIT.CLS	CWinGSprite	WinG sprites
CWINGBIT.CLS	CWinGBitmap	WinG bitmaps
CWINGDC.CLS	CWinGDC	WinG device contexts
WING.BAS		WinG API declarations
WINGHELP.BAS		WINGHELP.DLL declarations
GDI.BAS		Windows API declarations

2. Use the Insert Class Module menu item to add a new class module to BAKSCROL.VBP, and set the new class's name to CWinGStage.

3. Add the following code to CWinGStage. This class uses four private variables to keep track of things. The m_background variable holds a reference to the CWinGBitmap being used as a background. The m_buffer variable holds a reference to the buffer upon which the background is drawn. The variables m_bx and m_by specify the coordinate of the background's pixel that will be drawn at location 0,0 in the buffer's bitmap. Positive changes to the value of m_bx move the background to the left, and positive changes to the value of m_by move the background up.

```
Option Explicit

Private m_background   As CWinGBitmap
```

Continued on next page

Continued from previous page

```
Private m_buffer      As CWinGBitmap
Private m_bx          As Integer
Private m_by          As Integer
```

4. Add the following Property Set/Get procedures to CWinGStage, to access the m_background property.

```
Public Property Set Background(bground As CWinGBitmap)
    Set m_background = bground
End Property

Public Property Get Background() As CWinGBitmap
    Set Background = m_background
End Property
```

5. Add the following Property Set/Get procedures to CWinGStage, to access the m_buffer property.

```
Public Property Set Buffer(buf As CWinGBitmap)
    Set m_buffer = buf
End Property

Public Property Get Buffer() As CWinGBitmap
    Set Buffer = m_buffer
End Property
```

6. Add the following Property Let/Get procedures to CWinGStage. The bx and by properties let you set the background's location relative to the buffer.

```
Public Property Let bx(val As Integer)
    m_bx = val
End Property

Public Property Get bx() As Integer
    bx = m_bx
End Property

Public Property Let by(val As Integer)
    m_by = val
End Property

Public Property Get by() As Integer
    by = m_by
End Property
```

7. Add the following subroutine to CWinGStage. This is where the action takes place. The first task is to check the m_bx and m_by variables and modify them if they are out of range for the background's dimensions. Next, the DivideHoriz and DivideVert variables are set to either True or False, depending upon whether the background will need to be wrapped to fill the buffer. When the current value of m_bx together with the width of the buffer are greater than the width of the background image, the image is split vertically and two copy operations are

required to fill the background. Likewise, whenever m_by together with the height of the buffer are greater than the height of the background, the image is split horizontally. Next, the subroutine checks to see if neither a vertical nor a horizontal split is required. When this is the case, CopyDIBits is used to quickly fill the buffer with a part of the background image. When either DivideVert or DivideHorz is True, two CopyDIBit calls are required to fill the background image. When both DivideVert and DivideHorz are True, four calls to CopyDIBit are required. (Keep this in mind when designing animations that are performance-sensitive; it is somewhat faster to copy bitmaps that scroll only vertically or horizontally.)

```
Public Sub Render()
    Dim DivideHoriz As Integer, DivideVert As Integer

    If m_bx > m_background.Width Then
        m_bx = m_bx - m_background.Width
    ElseIf m_bx < 0 Then
        m_bx = m_bx + m_background.Width
    End If

    If m_by > Abs(m_background.Height) Then
        m_by = m_by - Abs(m_background.Height)
    ElseIf m_by < 0 Then
        m_by = m_by + Abs(m_background.Height)
    End If

    DivideHoriz = False
    DivideVert = False

    If (m_bx + m_buffer.Width) > m_background.Width Then
        DivideVert = True
    End If

    If (m_by + Abs(m_buffer.Height)) > Abs(m_background.Height) Then
        DivideHoriz = True
    End If

    If Not (DivideVert Or DivideHoriz) Then
        '
        ' No splits ... copy entire background
        '
        CopyDIBits _
            ByVal m_buffer.m_pSurface, _
            0, _
            ByVal m_background.m_pSurface, _
            (m_by * m_background.ByteWidth) + m_bx, _
            m_buffer.Width, Abs(m_buffer.Height), _
            m_buffer.ByteWidth, m_background.ByteWidth
    ElseIf DivideVert And (Not DivideHoriz) Then
        '
        ' Left side
        '
        CopyDIBits _
```

Continued on next page

Continued from previous page

```
            ByVal m_buffer.m_pSurface, _
            0, _
            ByVal m_background.m_pSurface, _
            (m_by * m_background.ByteWidth) + m_bx, _
            m_background.Width - m_bx, Abs(m_buffer.Height), _
            m_buffer.ByteWidth, m_background.ByteWidth
        '
        ' Right side
        '
        CopyDIBits _
            ByVal m_buffer.m_pSurface, _
            (m_background.Width - m_bx), _
            ByVal m_background.m_pSurface, _
            (m_by * m_background.ByteWidth) + 0, _
            m_buffer.Width - (m_background.Width - m_bx), _
            Abs(m_buffer.Height), _
            Abs(m_buffer.ByteWidth), m_background.ByteWidth
    ElseIf (Not DivideVert) And DivideHoriz Then
        '
        ' Top side
        '
        CopyDIBits _
            ByVal m_buffer.m_pSurface, _
            0, _
            ByVal m_background.m_pSurface, _
            (m_by * m_background.ByteWidth) + m_bx, _
            m_buffer.Width, Abs(m_background.Height) - m_by, _
            m_buffer.ByteWidth, m_background.ByteWidth
        '
        ' Bottom side
        '
        CopyDIBits _
            ByVal m_buffer.m_pSurface, _
            (Abs(m_background.Height) - m_by) * m_buffer.ByteWidth, _
            ByVal m_background.m_pSurface, _
            m_bx, _
            m_buffer.Width, Abs(m_buffer.Height) -
            (Abs(m_background.Height) - m_by), _
            m_buffer.ByteWidth, m_background.ByteWidth
    ElseIf DivideVert And DivideHoriz Then
        '
        ' Top-left
        '
        CopyDIBits _
            ByVal m_buffer.m_pSurface, _
            0, _
            ByVal m_background.m_pSurface, _
            (m_by * m_background.ByteWidth) + m_bx, _
            m_background.Width - m_bx, Abs(m_background.Height) - m_by, _
            m_buffer.ByteWidth, m_background.ByteWidth
        '
        ' Top-right
        '
        CopyDIBits _
            ByVal m_buffer.m_pSurface, _
```

```
        (m_background.Width - m_bx), _
        ByVal m_background.m_pSurface, _
        (m_by * m_background.ByteWidth), _
        m_buffer.Width - (m_background.Width - m_bx),
        Abs(m_background.Height) - m_by, _
        Abs(m_buffer.ByteWidth), m_background.ByteWidth
    '
    ' Bottom-left
    '
    CopyDIBits _
        ByVal m_buffer.m_pSurface, _
        (Abs(m_background.Height) - m_by) * m_buffer.ByteWidth, _
        ByVal m_background.m_pSurface, _
        m_bx, _
        m_background.Width - m_bx, Abs(m_buffer.Height) -
        (Abs(m_background.Height) - m_by), _
        m_buffer.ByteWidth, m_background.ByteWidth
    '
    ' Bottom-right
    '
    CopyDIBits _
        ByVal m_buffer.m_pSurface, _
        (Abs(m_background.Height) - m_by) * m_buffer.ByteWidth +
        (m_background.Width - m_bx), _
        ByVal m_background.m_pSurface, _
        0, _
        m_buffer.Width - (m_background.Width - m_bx), _
        Abs(m_buffer.Height) - (Abs(m_background.Height) - m_by), _
        m_buffer.ByteWidth, m_background.ByteWidth
    End If
End Sub
```

8. Select Form1, and add the objects with properties and settings as shown in Table 5-8-2.

Table 5-8-2 Objects, properties, and settings for Form1

OBJECT	PROPERTY	SETTING
Form	Caption	"Form1"
	KeyPreview	-1 'True
	MouseIcon	"CROSHAIR.ICO"
	MousePointer	13 'Custom
	Name	Form1
	ScaleMode	3 'Pixel
Timer	Interval	5000
	Name	Timer2
HiTime	Interval	50
	Name	Timer1

9. Use the menu editor to create a new menu for Form1. Add the menu items shown in Table 5-8-3.

Table 5-8-3 Form1's menu

MENU	CAPTION
FileMenu	"&File"
...FileExit	"E&xit"

10. Add the following code to Form1's General Declaration section:

```
Option Explicit

Dim wdc         As New CWinGDC
Dim stage       As New CWinGStage
Dim sprite      As New CWinGSprite
Dim Background  As New CWinGBitmap
Dim Buffer      As CWinGBitmap

Dim dx          As Integer
Dim dy          As Integer
Dim frames      As Integer
Dim hFormOldPal As Long
```

11. Add the following code as Form1's Form_Load event procedure. First,
    Form_Load reads the background from disk by calling background's ReadDIB
    method. Then a Sprite is created, and the spaceship's 30 frames are loaded into
    the Sprite and its frame-related properties are initialized.

```
Private Sub Form_Load()
    Dim wbm  As New CDib
    Dim i    As Integer
    '
    ' Load background bitmap ... bail on errors
    '
    If (Background.ReadDIB(wdc, App.Path & "\backdrop.bmp") = False) Then
        MsgBox "ReadDIB failed"
        End
    End If
    Set stage.Background = Background
    '
    ' Load the sprite with frames
    '
    For i = 0 To 29
        Set wbm = New CDib

        If (wbm.ReadDIB(App.Path & "\ship" & Format(i, "00") & ".bmp") = ⇒
        False) Then
            MsgBox "ReadDIB failed"
            Exit Sub
        End If
        sprite.AddFrame wbm, i
    Next
    '
    ' Get set for action
    '
```

```
    sprite.FrameNumber = 0
    sprite.FirstFrame = 0
    sprite.LastFrame = 29
    sprite.TransparentColor = 0
End Sub
```

12. Add the following code as Form1's Form_Resize event procedure. Each time the form is resized, the CWinGBitmap object stored in Form1's buffer variable is re-created with a bitmap of exactly the right size for the form. Then the buffer bitmap's palette is set by cloning a copy of the background's palette, and the color table is retrieved and passed on to the WinG device context. Then, after initializing the sprite and stage objects, the animation timer, Timer1, is enabled and things really start to happen!

```
Private Sub Form_Resize()
    Dim rgbs(256)   As Long
    '
    ' Get outta here if the window is minimized!
    '
    If (Form1.WindowState = 1) Then
        Exit Sub
    End If
    '
    ' Reselect the form's old palette if we've been here
    ' before
    '
    If (hFormOldPal () 0) Then
        Call SelectPalette(Form1.hDC, hFormOldPal, False)
    End If
    '
    ' Create a buffer
    '
    Set Buffer = New CWinGBitmap
    Call Buffer.Create(wdc, ScaleWidth, ScaleHeight)
    '
    ' Select the buffer into our CWinGDC object
    '
    wdc.SelectBitmap Buffer
    '
    ' Clone a copy of the background palette
    '
    Set Buffer.pal = Background.pal.Clone
    '
    ' Load color table into wdc
    '
    Buffer.pal.GetRgbColors 0, 256, rgbs
    wdc.SetColorTable 0, 256, rgbs
    '
    ' Select the palette into form1
    '
    hFormOldPal = SelectPalette(Form1.hDC, Buffer.pal.hPal, False)
    Call RealizePalette(Form1.hDC)
    '
```

Continued on next page

Continued from previous page

```
    ' Initialize the sprite
    '
    Set sprite.canvas = Buffer
    sprite.MoveTo (Me.ScaleWidth - sprite.Width) \ 2, (Me.ScaleHeight - ⇒
                    sprite.Height) \ 2
    '
    ' Initialize the stage
    '
    Set stage.Buffer = Buffer
    '
    ' Set initial background velocity
    '
    dx = 2
    dy = 2
    '
    ' Call KeyDown to compute correct frame for the ship
    '
    Form_KeyDown 0, 0
    '
    ' Paint the first frame
    Form_Paint
    '
    ' Get set to count the frame rate
    '
    frames = 0
    Timer1.Enabled = True
    '
    ' Turn on the animation timer
    '
    Timer2.Interval = 1000
End Sub
```

13. Add the following code as Form1's Form_Paint subroutine, to handle the anima-
    tion. First the background image is rendered, and then the Sprite Draw method is
    used to draw the Sprite on top of the background. Remember that the
    CWinGBitmap stored in the buffer variable has been assigned to the stage, sprite,
    and wdc objects. These three objects share the buffer's bitmap, so any changes
    made to it by one object will be visible from within the other objects. When
    WinGBitBlt copies wdc's image to Form1, all the changes just made to the buffer
    will be displayed.

```
Private Sub Form_Paint()
    '
    ' Copy background to buffer
    '
    stage.Render
    '
    ' Draw the sprite over the background
    '
    sprite.Draw
    '
    ' Copy the whole works to the screen
    '
```

```
Call WinGBitBlt(Form1.hDC, 0, 0, Me.ScaleWidth, Me.ScaleHeight, ⇒
   wdc.hDC, 0, 0)
End Sub
```

14. Add the following code as Form1's Form_KeyDown event procedure. This procedure recognizes five keys: the four arrow keys and the spacebar. The arrow keys control the background's direction of movement (and its speed); and the spacebar turns the animation timer on and off. This subroutine then calculates the correct Sprite frame to display. We want the ship to appear to be moving in a direction opposite to that of the background; that is, if the background is moving to the left, the spaceship would face right and look like it is flying to the right. When the background is moving only vertically or horizontally, it is possible to directly pick the correct frame by examining the dx and dy variables. In fact, it's desirable to do this, to avoid later divide-by-zero errors. When the background is not moving in a strictly horizontal or vertical direction, Visual Basic's Atn function determines which frame to use. This calculation returns a value for frames in the first quadrant only. The resulting frame number is adjusted by examining the signs of the dx and dy variables.

```
Private Sub Form_KeyDown(KeyCode As Integer, Shift As Integer)
    '
    ' Deal with keyboard action
    '
    Select Case KeyCode
        '
        ' Left arrow
        '
        Case 37
            dx = dx - 1
        '
        ' Up arrow
        Case 38
            dy = dy - 1
        '
        ' Right arrow
        '
        Case 39
            dx = dx + 1
        '
        ' Down arrow
        '
        Case 40
            dy = dy + 1
        '
        ' Space key
        '
        Case 32
            Timer1.Enabled = Not Timer1.Enabled
    End Select
    '
    ' Decide which sprite frame to use, check special
```

Continued on next page

Continued from previous page

```
    ' cases first (either dx or dy equal to zero)
    '
    If (dx = 0) Then
        If (dy < 0) Then
            sprite.FrameNumber = 23
        Else
            sprite.FrameNumber = 8
        End If
    ElseIf (dy = 0) Then
        If (dx < 0) Then
            sprite.FrameNumber = 15
        Else
            sprite.FrameNumber = 0
        End If
    Else
        '
        ' Not a special case ... calculate frame number
        ' from dy/dx
        '
        sprite.FrameNumber = Abs((Atn(dy / dx))) * (180 / 3.141592) \ 12
        '
        ' Deal with quadrants 2, 3, and 4
        '
        If (dx < 0 And dy > 0) Then
            sprite.FrameNumber = 15 - sprite.FrameNumber
        ElseIf (dx < 0 And dy < 0) Then
            sprite.FrameNumber = 15 + sprite.FrameNumber
        ElseIf (dx > 0 And dy < 0) Then
            sprite.FrameNumber = 30 - sprite.FrameNumber
            If sprite.FrameNumber = 30 Then
                sprite.FrameNumber = 0
            End If
        End If
    End If
End Sub
```

15. Add the following code as Form1's Form_Unload event procedure Timer1 is disabled, and the event queue is emptied by calling DoEvents. Then the form's original palette is reselected. And finally, all of the object variable references are released.

```
Private Sub Form_Unload(Cancel As Integer)
    '
    ' Turn off timer and clean out event queue
    '
    Timer1.Enabled = False
    DoEvents
    '
    ' Reselect previous palette, if required
    '
    If (hFormOldPal () 0) Then
        Call SelectPalette(Form1.hDC, hFormOldPal, False)
    End If
    '
    ' Release all objects
```

```
    '
    Set wdc = Nothing
    Set stage = Nothing
    Set Background = Nothing
    Set sprite = Nothing
    Set Buffer = Nothing
End Sub
```

16. Add the following Timer event procedure for Timer1, which drives the animation. The Timer event routine first increments the stage's background offsets and then calls the Form_Paint subroutine to update the screen.

```
Private Sub Timer1_Timer()
    Static inhere As Boolean
    '
    ' Prevent reentrant calls
    '
    If (inhere) Then
        Exit Sub
    End If
    inhere = True
    '
    ' Move background
    '
    stage.bx = stage.bx + dx
    stage.by = stage.by + dy
    '
    ' Repaint the screen
    '
    Form_Paint
    frames = frames + 1
    DoEvents
    inhere = False
End Sub
```

17. Add the following code as Timer2's Timer event procedure. This displays the form size and animation rates in the form's caption, so that you can easily see the impact of various form sizes on animation speed.

```
Private Sub Timer2_Timer()
    Me.Caption = Form1.ScaleWidth & "x" & Form1.ScaleHeight & ", fps: "
& frames / (Timer2.Interval / 1000)
    frames = 0
End Sub
```

18. Add the following code as the File Exit menu item's Click event procedure. The Form_Unload routine is invoked to make sure that resources get released, and then the program simply ends.

```
Private Sub FileExit_Click()
    Unload Me
    End
End Sub
```

How It Works

Form1's code in this project is quite similar to the code in Form1of How-To 5.7. The main difference in the Form_Paint routine in this How-To is that the entire form is repainted for each frame. This is necessary since the background is moving constantly.

The scrolling effect is achieved by using an instance of the CWinGStage class. During Form_Load, the background image BACKDROP.BMP is loaded and assigned as the stage's Background property. During Form_Resize, the CWinGBitmap stored in the variable named buffer is also assigned to the stage. Then, when stage's Render method is called, the background is copied to the buffer.

There are four different cases that need to be handled when copying the background:

➤ The first case is the easiest—when a rectangle the size of the buffer can be copied directly from the background given the current values of m_bx and m_by. A single call to CopyDIBits gets the job done.

➤ The second case is when the value of m_bx becomes large enough so that m_bx plus the width of Form1 are greater than the width of the background image. When this happens, Form1.Width columns are copied from the current column selected by m_bx, and the remaining columns are copied from the start of the background image. This creates a circular effect in the horizontal direction. The bitmap has effectively been rolled into a cylinder around the y-axis.

➤ The third case is similar to the second case, except this one occurs when the rows of pixels are insufficient to fill the buffer, given the current value of m_by. By filling the remainder of the buffer with rows from the top of the background bitmap, we roll the bitmap around the x-axis, creating what is effectively a cylinder around the x-axis.

➤ The fourth case combines both the second and third cases. When the values of m_bx and m_by are both so large that the buffer cannot be entirely filled, it's necessary to use four CopyDIBits to fill the entire buffer.

Comments

WinG makes it really easy to create excellent animation effects using Visual Basic. When you're evaluating the performance of WinG applications, and especially when you're comparing their speed to that of DOS games, it's important to remember that even at low resolution (640x480), Windows screens display four times as many pixels as are typically used by a DOS-based game. DOS games almost always use a screen resolution of 320x240. On the positive side, the appearance of images at the higher pixel resolution is very good. Though DOS games always look a bit grainy, the exact same image displayed at a 640x480 or higher resolution can look very realistic.

5.9 How do I...
Create a Game?

COMPLEXITY: ADVANCED
COMPATIBILITY: VB4 ONLY

Problem

I would like to write a video game with some interesting graphics and sound. The class modules from Chapters 4 and 5 seem to have everything I need, but I can't quite figure out how to put everything together to make an exciting, action-oriented game. Is it possible to create a VB game that rivals the features found in DOS games?

Technique

All the pieces you need have been developed in this chapter and the previous one (Chapter 4, "Sounds"). In this How-To, eight different classes from previous How-To's will be used to create an action-oriented space game—complete with moving background, enemy ships that move around in space, plus explosions and other sound effects. The game is shown in Figure 5-9-1.

Two timers are used to drive the action. One serves as the fundamental animation timer, driving the background scrolling and ship movement. Another timer is used to randomly re-create ships after you've blown them up, and to randomly change the ship's directions from time to time.

A third timer updates the form's caption with the form size and frame rate. This information is useful when you're testing various approaches to solving animation problems, providing an easy way to monitor the program's performance.

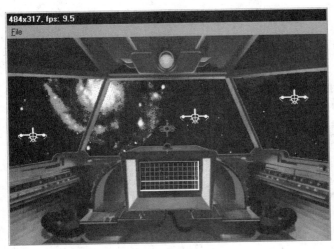

Figure 5-9-1 Space game in action

627

Steps

Open and run GAME.VBP. Use the arrow keys to move around in space. When an enemy ship comes into your sights, fire your laser by pressing the Spacebar. In the bottom-center part of the cockpit, you will see a grid showing the location of your ship and the enemy ships. Your ship's location is indicated by crosshair, and each enemy ship is indicated by a red dot.

1. Create a new project named GAME.VBP, and use the File Add menu item to add the classes and modules shown in Table 5-9-1. The class modules (files with a .CLS extension) are stored in the VBHT\CLASSES directory, and the BAS modules are in VBHT\MODULES.

Table 5-9-1 Classes and modules for Form1

FILENAME	CLASS	PURPOSE
CDIB.CLS	CDib	Device-independent bitmap class
CPALETTE.CLS	CPalette	Palette functionality
CPOINT.CLS	CPoint	A point in space
CWGSPRIT.CLS	CWinGSprite	WinG sprites
CWINGBIT.CLS	CWinGBitmap	WinG bitmaps
CWINGDC.CLS	CWinGDC	WinG device contexts
CWINGSTA.CLS	CWinGStage	WinG background stage
CWAVEMIX.CLS	CWaveMix	Provides multiple wavefile playing
WAVEMIX.BAS		CWaveMix declarations
WING.BAS		WinG API declarations
WINGHELP.BAS		WINGHELP.DLL declarations
GDI.BAS		Windows API declarations

2. To Form1, add the objects with properties and settings shown in Table 5-9-2.

Table 5-9-2 Objects, properties, and settings for Form1

OBJECT	PROPERTY	SETTING
Form	BorderStyle	3 'Fixed Double
	Caption	"Form1"
	ControlBox	0 'False
	KeyPreview	-1 'True
	MaxButton	0 'False
	MinButton	0 'False
	Name	Form1
	ScaleMode	3 'Pixel

OBJECT	PROPERTY	SETTING
Timer	Interval	1
	Name	Timer1
Timer	Interval	2000
	Name	Timer2
Timer	Interval	1000
	Name	Timer3
PictureBox	AutoRedraw	-1 'True
	AutoSize	-1 'True
	Name	picBlip
	Picture	"BLIP.BMP"
	Visible	0 'False
PictureBox	BackColor	&H00000000&
	Name	picScope
	ScaleMode	3 'Pixel
PictureBox	AutoRedraw	-1 'True
	BackColor	&H00000000&
	Name	picScopeWork
	Picture	"GRID.BMP"
	ScaleMode	3 'Pixel
	Visible	0 'False

3. Use the menu editor to create a menu for Form1, and add the menu shown in Table 5-9-3.

Table 5-9-3 Menu for Form1

MENU	CAPTION
FileMenu	&File
...FileExit	E&xit

4. Add the following code to the General Declarations section of Form1:

```
Option Explicit
'
' Change this to change the maximum number of enemy ships
'
Private Const NumEnemies = 4
'
' Animation objects
'
Dim wdc         As New CWinGDC
Dim stage       As New CWinGStage
Dim fg          As New CWinGSprite
Dim Background  As New CWinGBitmap
```

Continued on next page

Continued from previous page

```
Dim Buffer          As CWinGBitmap
'
' Enemy ship sprites
'
Dim enemies(NumEnemies) As New CWinGSprite
'
' Sounds
'
Dim music           As CWaveMix
Dim laser           As CWaveMix
Dim explosion       As CWaveMix
'
' Miscellaneous variables
'
Dim dx              As Integer
Dim dy              As Integer
Dim frames          As Integer
Dim hFormOldPal     As Long
Dim rgbs(256)       As Long
```

The constant named NumEnemies defines the maximum number of enemy
ships that will be created. You can change this number by modifying
NumEnemies. After the NumEnemies declaration, a number of Class object variables are declared. The first group creates objects used for the animation; a WinG
device context; a stage for animating the background; a Sprite to hold the cockpit
image; a background for the game; and the drawing buffer. Next, an array of
Sprites named enemies is declared, along with some CWaveMix channels for the
various sound effects. Finally, a few miscellaneous variables are declared for tracking the background velocity, the number of frames per second, and so forth.

5. Add the following code as Form1's Form_Load event procedure, which calls the
   LoadGraphics and LoadSounds subroutines discussed in steps 6 and 7.

```
Private Sub Form_Load()
    LoadGraphics
    LoadSounds
End Sub
```

6. Add the following subroutine to Form1. Here, a WinGDC is created by using
   wdc's CreateDC method. Then the background is loaded from disk with the
   CWinGBitmap ReadDIB method. The enemy ships have seven frames, and the
   bitmaps for the frames are stored in SHIP00.BMP through SHIP06.BMP. The
   bitmaps are loaded into the temporary CDib named wbm, and then a reference to
   each frame is stored in each of the enemy ships. Once the enemy ship frames are
   loaded, the frame number and transparent color are set for each of the enemy
   ships. Finally, the cockpit bitmap is loaded and stored in the CWinGSprite
   named fg.

```
Private Sub LoadGraphics()
    Dim wbm As CDib
    Dim e   As Integer
    Dim f   As Integer
```

```
'
' Start enemy ships in different positions each run
'
Randomize
'
' Create WinG device context
'
wdc.CreateDC
'
' Get background bitmap
'
If (Background.ReadDIB(wdc, App.Path & "\backdrop.bmp") = False) Then
    MsgBox "ReadDIB failed, program aborted"
    End
End If
'
' Load enemy ship frames
'
For f = 0 To 6
    Set wbm = New CDib
    If (wbm.ReadDIB(App.Path & "\ship" & Format(f, "00") & ".bmp") = ⇒
    False) Then
        MsgBox "ReadDIB failed, program aborted"
        Unload Me
        End
    End If

    For e = 0 To NumEnemies - 1
        enemies(e).AddFrame wbm, f
    Next
Next
'
' Set frame number and transparent color for enemy ships
'
For e = 0 To NumEnemies - 1
    enemies(e).FrameNumber = 0
    enemies(e).TransparentColor = 253
Next
'
' Load cockpit bitmap
'
Set wbm = New CDib
If (wbm.ReadDIB(App.Path & "\cockpit.bmp") = False) Then
    MsgBox "ReadDIB failed"
    Exit Sub
End If
'
' Add cockpit as foreground bitmap
'
fg.AddFrame wbm, 0
fg.FrameNumber = 0
fg.TransparentColor = 253
fg.MoveTo 0, 0
End Sub
```

631

7. Add the following subroutine to Form1. Here, the three CWaveMix objects are created, and their sounds are loaded from disk using CWaveMix's OpenWave method. The background music, music1.wav, is started right away with the CWaveMix PlayWave method, specifying a −1 as the loop count causes the wavefile to be played continuously. The other sounds are played as required during the game.

```
Private Sub LoadSounds()
    '
    ' Background music
    '
    Set music = New CWaveMix
    music.OpenChannel (WMIX_OPENSINGLE)
    music.OpenWave App.Path & "\music1.wav", WMIX_FILE
    music.PlayWave WMIX_QUEUEWAVE, -1
    '
    ' Start background music playing
    '
    music.Pump
    '
    ' Laser
    '
    Set laser = New CWaveMix
    laser.OpenChannel (WMIX_OPENSINGLE)
    laser.OpenWave App.Path & "\laser1.wav", WMIX_FILE
    '
    ' Explosion
    '
    Set explosion = New CWaveMix
    explosion.OpenChannel (WMIX_OPENSINGLE)
    explosion.OpenWave App.Path & "\explode1.wav", WMIX_FILE
End Sub
```

8. Add the following code as Form1's Resize event procedure. During resize the drawing buffer is created and stored in the CWinGBitmap object named Buffer. Then Buffer's Create method is used to make a bitmap with the same size as the Form's client area. Buffer serves as drawing surface for the foreground, background, and the enemy ship Sprites. Since Buffer is also selected as wdc's bitmap, it's easy to blast a new frame to the screen after the frame has been drawn.

```
Private Sub Form_Resize()
    Dim e As Integer
    '
    ' Outta here if window is minimized
    '
    If (Form1.WindowState = 1) Then
        Exit Sub
    End If
    '
    ' Reselect previous form palette if required
    '
    If (hFormOldPal () 0) Then
```

```
        Call SelectPalette(Form1.hDC, hFormOldPal, False)
End If
'
' Create new buffer bitmap
'
Set Buffer = New CWinGBitmap
Call Buffer.Create(wdc, Me.ScaleWidth, Me.ScaleHeight)
'
' Setup as WinGDC's buffer
'
wdc.SelectBitmap Buffer
'
' Get palette and colors
'
Set Buffer.pal = Background.pal.Clone
Buffer.pal.GetRgbColors 0, 256, rgbs
Buffer.pal.Animate 0, 256, rgbs
'
' Assign color table to WinGDC
'
wdc.SetColorTable 0, 256, rgbs
'
' Select palette into form
'
hFormOldPal = SelectPalette(Form1.hDC, Buffer.pal.hPal, False)
'
' Initialize location and direction of enemies
'
For e = 0 To NumEnemies - 1
    Set enemies(e).canvas = Buffer
    enemies(e).MoveTo Background.Width * Rnd, Abs(Background.Height) * ⇒
        Rnd
    enemies(e).Xv = 6 * Rnd
    enemies(e).Yv = 6 * Rnd
Next
'
' Load drawing surface and background into the stage
'
Set stage.Buffer = Buffer
Set stage.Background = Background
'
' Set initial stage location
'
stage.bx = 0
stage.by = 0
'
' Set foreground (cockpit) drawing surface
'
Set fg.canvas = Buffer
'
' Initialize frames/second counter
'
frames = 0
'
' Display form dimensions
```

Continued on next page

Continued from previous page

```
    '
    Me.Caption = Form1.ScaleWidth & "x" & Form1.ScaleHeight
    '
    ' Start animation timer
    '
    Timer1.Enabled = True
End Sub
```

9. Add the following code as Form1's Form_Paint event procedure. Form_Paint immediately calls the Paint subroutine, passing True as an argument. This causes the entire form to be repainted, which the appropriate action when Form_Paint is fired.

```
Private Sub Form_Paint()
    '
    ' Repaint entire screen
    '
    Paint True
End Sub
```

10. Add the following subroutine to Form1, Paint is called from both Form_Paint and Timer1_Timer. The argument named "all" determines whether the entire form is painted or just the portion that changes during animation. Form_Paint always passes True, and Timer1_Timer always passes False. First stage's Render method is called, to fill the Buffer with part of the background image. The displayed part of the background is determined by the stage's bx and by properties. Next, each of the enemy ship Sprites is examined; if it is visible, it is moved. The enemy ships' velocities are incremented directly, not by calling the Step method, because it is necessary to keep the ships moving along with the background. Subtracting the background velocity, given by dx and dy, from the Sprite's velocity compensates for the fact that the background is moving. After moving a ship, its AdvanceFrame method is called. Normally, the ship's Fv is zero and there is no change in the ship's appearance; however, when a ship is exploding, Fv will be one (it will be cycling up to frame 6). When frame 6 is reached, the ship is drawn onto the background one last time, and then its Visible property is set to False. In most cases, however, the ship is checked to see if it is within the animation area, and if so, it is drawn into the buffer. After all of the ships have been moved, the cockpit (stored in the variable fg) is drawn over everything else in the buffer. Because of the transparent color that matches the color in COCKPIT.BMP's windows, the background and ships show through the windows.

Next, it's time to actually update the screen with either a full-form update or a partial update. When the argument all is True, the full-form update is used; this is necessary whenever the form receives a Form_Paint event. The other case, all = False, is used during normal animation. When all is False, only the middle part of the buffer is copied to the screen using WinGBitBlt. Look at the second WinGBitBlt in the code below; you will see that the second, third, fourth, and fifth arguments are 0, 72, Me.ScaleWidth, and 120 respectively. These arguments define a rectangle to BitBlt to. The upper-left corner is at x = 0, y = 72; the rectangle's width is the same as Form1; and the rectangle's height is 120. The last two arguments, also 0 and 72, specify the starting location in Buffer from which bits are copied.

After the background, ships, and foreground have been updated on the screen, the scope (or long-range scanner, if you prefer) needs to be updated. This is done by first calling ClearScope, then calling ShowLocationOnScope, and finally plotting the location of each visible enemy ship.

Finally, CWaveMix's Pump method is called to make sure the sounds keep playing. It's important to call Pump whenever you're working on a lengthy task, so that the wave mixer gets enough cpu cycles to keep all of the channels playing.

```
Private Sub Paint(all As Boolean)
    Dim e As Integer
    '
    ' Draw background on buffer
    '
    stage.Render
    '
    ' Move and draw enemy ships
    '
    For e = 0 To NumEnemies - 1
        If (enemies(e).Visible = True) Then
            enemies(e).MoveTo enemies(e).X + enemies(e).Xv - dx,
            enemies(e).Y + enemies(e).Yv - dy
            If (enemies(e).X > Background.Width) Then
                enemies(e).MoveTo 0, enemies(e).Y
            End If
            If (enemies(e).Y > Abs(Background.Height)) Then
                enemies(e).MoveTo enemies(e).X, 0
            End If
            enemies(e).AdvanceFrame
            '
            ' If ship has just finished exploding draw it and then
            ' make it invisible
            '
            If (enemies(e).FrameNumber = 6) Then
                enemies(e).Draw
                enemies(e).Visible = False
            '
            ' Otherwise only draw enemies which might be visible
            ' through cockpit windows
            '
            ElseIf (enemies(e).X < Buffer.Width And enemies(e).Y <
            Abs(Buffer.Height)) Then
                enemies(e).Draw
            End If
        End If
    Next
    '
    ' Draw foreground over everything else
```

Continued on next page

Continued from previous page

```
'
fg.Draw
'
' If we need to repaint the entire scene make sure the palette
' is still realized and then blt the whole thing, otherwise
' we only need to blt the middle band
'
If (all = True) Then
    Call RealizePalette(Form1.hDC)
    Call WinGBitBlt(Form1.hDC, 0, 0, Me.ScaleWidth, Me.ScaleHeight,
    wdc.hDC, 0, 0)
Else
    Call WinGBitBlt(Form1.hDC, 0, 72, Me.ScaleWidth, 120, wdc.hDC, 0, 72)
End If
'
' Clear the long-range view
'
ClearScope
'
' Draw crosshair to show current location in space
'
ShowLocationOnScope
'
' Draw enemy ships on the scope
'
For e = 0 To NumEnemies - 1
    If (enemies(e).Visible) Then
        ShowEnemyOnScope e
    End If
Next
'
' Keep the music playing!
'
music.Pump
End Sub
```

11. Add the following subroutine to Form1. ShowEnemyOnScope is called by the Paint routine for each visible enemy ship. This ship's location is scaled and stored in the variables X and Y. This location is then used as the destination for BitBlt to place a 3x3 bitmap on the scope's PictureBox.

```
Private Sub ShowEnemyOnScope(e As Integer)
    Dim X As Integer
    Dim Y As Integer
    '
    ' Calculate enemy position scaled to size of picScope
    '
    X = picScope.ScaleWidth * (stage.bx + enemies(e).X) /
    Background.Width
    Y = picScope.ScaleHeight * (stage.by + enemies(e).Y) /
    Abs(Background.Height)

    If X > picScope.ScaleWidth Then
        X = X - picScope.ScaleWidth
```

```
      End If

      If Y > picScope.ScaleHeight Then
          Y = Y - picScope.ScaleHeight
      End If
      '
      ' Copy a blip to the scope
      '
      Call BitBlt(picScope.hDC, X, Y, 3, 3, picBlip.hDC, 0, 0, SRCCOPY)
End Sub
```

12. Add the following subroutine to Form1. This ShowLocationOnScope routine draws one horizontal line and one vertical line on the scope. The intersection of the two lines is the location in space of your ship.

```
Private Sub ShowLocationOnScope()
    Dim X As Integer
    Dim Y As Integer
    '
    ' Calculate center of crosshair
    '
    X = picScope.ScaleWidth * ((stage.bx + (Buffer.Width / 2)) /
    Background.Width)
    Y = picScope.ScaleHeight * ((stage.by + (Abs(Buffer.Height) / 2)) /
    Abs(Background.Height))
    If X > picScope.ScaleWidth Then
        X = X - picScope.ScaleWidth
    End If
    If Y > picScope.ScaleHeight Then
        Y = Y - picScope.ScaleHeight
    End If
    '
    ' Draw crosshair
    '
    picScope.ForeColor = RGB(255, 255, 255)
    Call MoveTo(picScope.hDC, X, 0)
    Call LineTo(picScope.hDC, X, picScope.ScaleHeight)
    Call MoveTo(picScope.hDC, 0, Y)
    Call LineTo(picScope.hDC, picScope.ScaleWidth, Y)
End Sub
```

13. Add the following subroutine to Form1. ClearScope simply copies the grid pattern from the invisible PictureBox, picScopeWork, onto picScope. After this subroutine is called, the enemy ship locations and the crosshairs can be updated on the scope.

```
Private Sub ClearScope()
    Call BitBlt(picScope.hDC, 0, 0, picScope.Width, picScope.Height, ⇒
        picScopeWork.hDC, 0, 0, SRCCOPY)
End Sub
```

14. Add the following code as Form1's Form_KeyDown event procedure. Five keys are managed in this How-To: the four arrow keys and the Spacebar. The arrow

keys control the scrolling direction of the background, and hence the apparent motion of the user's ship. The Spacebar is used to shoot at enemy ships.

```
Private Sub Form_KeyDown(KeyCode As Integer, Shift As Integer)
    Select Case KeyCode
        '
        ' Right arrow
        '
        Case 37
            dx = dx - 1
        '
        ' Down arrow
        '
        Case 38
            dy = dy - 1
        '
        ' Left arrow
        '
        Case 39
            dx = dx + 1
        '
        ' Up arrow
        '
        Case 40
            dy = dy + 1
        '
        ' Spacebar
        '
        Case 32
            Shoot
    End Select
End Sub
```

15. Add the following subroutine to Form1. To begin, we want to make some noise! The laser channel is started, with a Pump thrown in for good measure. Then, after filling a Windows RECT structure with the dimensions of the cockpit's sight, a loop is entered to check for an intersection between the sight's rectangle and that of enemy ships. When we find an enemy ship's rectangle that intersects with the sight of the ship's frame, variables are set so that the ship will cycle through its explosion frames, and the explosion sound is played.

```
Private Sub Shoot()
    Dim rectSight As RECT
    Dim rectEnemy As RECT
    Dim rectTemp As RECT
    Dim e As Integer
    '
    ' Make shooting sound
    '
    Laser.PlayWave WMIX_QUEUEWAVE, 0
    Laser.Pump
    '
    ' Figure out where the sight is
```

```
'
rectSight.left = fg.Width \ 2 - 16
rectSight.top = fg.Height \ 2 - 16
rectSight.right = rectSight.left + 16
rectSight.bottom = rectSight.top + 16
'
' Scan enemies looking for a kill
'
For e = 0 To NumEnemies - 1
    rectEnemy.left = enemies(e).X
    rectEnemy.top = enemies(e).Y
    rectEnemy.right = rectEnemy.left + enemies(e).Width
    rectEnemy.bottom = rectEnemy.top + enemies(e).Height
    If (IntersectRect(rectTemp, rectSight, rectEnemy)) Then
        '
        ' Got one! Start explosion animation and make some noise.
        '
        enemies(e).FrameNumber = 2
        enemies(e).FirstFrame = 2
        enemies(e).LastFrame = 6
        enemies(e).Fv = 1
        explosion.PlayWave WMIX_CLEARQUEUE, 0
        explosion.Pump
    End If
    Next
End Sub
```

16. Add the following code as Timer1's Timer event procedure, which drives the animation. After incrementing the background position by the amount specified in dx and dy, the Paint subroutine is called to move the enemy ships and redraw the screen. Then the frame counter is incremented so that frames per second can be calculated and displayed.

```
Private Sub Timer1_Timer()
    Static inhere As Boolean
    '
    ' Prevent reentrant calls
    '
    If (inhere) Then
        Exit Sub
    End If
    inhere = True
    '
    ' Move background
    '
    stage.bx = stage.bx + dx
    stage.by = stage.by + dy
    '
    ' Paint the middle section of the form
    '
    Paint False
    '
    ' Increment frames/second counter
    '
```

Continued on next page

Continued from previous page

```
    frames = frames + 1
    '
    ' Give time up for other events
    '
    DoEvents
    inhere = False
End Sub
```

17. Add the following code as Timer2's Timer event subroutine, which studies the performance of the animation routines. Timer2 fires its event every 2 seconds, and the current value of frames is then used to calculate and display the frames per second in the form's caption.

```
Private Sub Timer2_Timer()
    '
    ' Display form size and frames/second
    '
    Me.Caption = Form1.ScaleWidth & "x" & Form1.ScaleHeight & ", fps: "
    & frames / (Timer2.Interval / 1000)
    frames = 0
End Sub
```

18. Add the following code as Timer3's Timer event procedure, which resurrects dead enemy ships and adds a little spontaneity to their movements.

```
Private Sub Timer3_Timer()
    Dim e As Integer
    '
    ' Restart a dead enemy every once in a while
    '
    If (Rnd > 0.5) Then
        For e = 0 To NumEnemies - 1
            If (enemies(e).Visible = False) Then
                enemies(e).Visible = True
                enemies(e).FirstFrame = 0
                enemies(e).LastFrame = 0
                enemies(e).FrameNumber = 0
                enemies(e).MoveTo Rnd * Background.Width, Rnd *
                Background.Height
                enemies(e).Fv = 0
                Exit For
            End If
        Next
    End If
    '
    ' Change directions once in a while too
    '
    e = Int(Rnd * NumEnemies)
    If (enemies(e).Visible = True) Then
        enemies(e).Xv = Rnd * 6
        enemies(e).Yv = Rnd * 6
    End If
End Sub
```

19. Add the following code as the File Exit menu item's Click event procedure. First the form is unloaded to free all objects, and then the program simply ends.

```
Private Sub FileExit_Click()
    Unload Me
    End
End Sub
```

20. Add the following code as Form1's Form_Unload event procedure. First the animation timer, Timer1, is disabled, and the message queue cleaned out. This guarantees that no timer events will be serviced while objects are being freed. (Although not strictly necessary, this procedure is a good idea. You never know when someone's going to put a DoEvents in one of the class modules.) Next, all of the objects are released by setting them to Nothing, and the wave channels are all closed.

```
Private Sub Form_Unload(Cancel As Integer)
    Dim e As Integer
    '
    ' Turn off timer
    '
    Timer1.Enabled = False
    '
    ' Clean out message queue
    '
    DoEvents
    '
    ' Free everything!
    '
    Set wdc = Nothing
    Set stage = Nothing
    Set fg = Nothing
    Set Background = Nothing
    Set Buffer = Nothing
    For e = 0 To NumEnemies - 1
        Set enemies(e) = Nothing
    Next
    music.CloseWave
    music.CloseChannel 0
    Set music = Nothing
    laser.CloseWave
    laser.CloseChannel 0
    Set laser = Nothing
    explosion.CloseWave
    explosion.CloseChannel 0
    Set explosion = Nothing
End Sub
```

How It Works

Behind the scenes in this project are eight class modules, each of which comprises functionality that is important in a game. The wdc, Buffer, Background, and stage objects (all members of the CWinG family of classes) provide the essentials: a scrolling background, and a fast way to update the screen. Each time the Timer1 event procedure is called, the stage is scrolled and part of the background is copied to the buffer by calling the stage's Render method. Then each visible enemy ship is moved and drawn on top of the buffer's new contents. Finally, the foreground is copied over the background and the enemy ships. The enemy ships and the foreground take advantage of WINGHELP's routines to leave holes (transparent regions) when copying a bitmap.

This How-To also puts the CWaveMix class to good use. Background music plays continually on one channel, while two other channels are used for laser sounds and explosions. As the form loads, the background music is started by calling the PlayWave method, and a loop count argument of −1 is used so that the wavefile will be played repeatedly without any further attention.

Comments

This How-To is deceptively simple. The code in Form1, though not trivial, is dwarfed by that in the various class modules used. The ability to easily create complex applications by fastening together class objects, along with a little extra logic, is one of the main benefits of object-oriented programming. The game in this How-To is a convincing demonstration of the power of this approach.

There are many ways to improve the game's speed. Perhaps most surprising is the amount of time required to update the scope. You can comment out the scope-updating part of the code at the end of the Paint routine, and get about a 25 percent increase in the number of frames per second. You can add a lot more enemy ships before you've absorbed that 25 percent increase in speed! It's probably best to modify the scope routine to work in a way similar to the way the stage, background, and buffer work.

Another area that could be optimized is the drawing of the background and foreground images. Most of the time, the Paint routine is called only when the middle section of the form gets painted, so it doesn't make much sense to draw the complete buffer. The code could be modified to take account of this fact.

6

OBJECT LINKING
AND EMBEDDING

6

OBJECT LINKING AND EMBEDDING

How do I...

Object linking and embedding (OLE) technology is clearly the future of Windows, and is of great importance to developers. In this chapter we'll show you the basics of controlling other applications' objects programmatically, and how to register object applications or OLE Automation servers. The last three How-To's explore the capabilities and limitations of Automation servers.

Many of the How To's in this chapter employ one or more Windows API calls, as listed here:

WINDOWS API	HOW-TO'S
EnableWindow	6.4
FindWindow	6.4
SendMessage	6.5
SetWindowLong	6.4

6.1 Browse Program Manager Groups and Items

When you need to look through the properties for a lot of Program Manager items at one time, using Program Manager's File Properties menu item to review the items is a tedious and repetitive task. This How-To will show you how you can pull this information into a Visual Basic program so that you can create your own efficient user interface.

6.2 Perform Background Operations with an In-Process OLE Server

OLE automation servers are ideal for performing background processing, because they exist in the background to start with. Automation servers with no visible interface can still benefit from Visual Basic controls and forms. This How-To is centered around a state-machine-style function that is started periodically by a timer on an invisible form. For this usage, a timer needs to be created for each object instantiated by client applications. To achieve this, the class's initialization procedure creates a new form with a timer, set to a private object variable of the class. To demonstrate a lengthy server process, the program in this How-To finds all prime numbers between upper and lower limits specified by the user.

6.3 Build an OLE Object Viewer

More and more business applications are being developed to provide specialized, selective access to data stored in the formats of popular commercial spreadsheets, word processors, and databases. These front-end applications often need to allow users to select the type of object displayed in a window. VB's OLE control does not allow programmatic manipulation of other applications' objects, but it excels at giving users run-time access to these objects. The Viewer application in this How-To will demonstrate object linking and embedding, along with in-place activation of objects. It will show how to provide menu negotiation, resulting in a menu bar that shows menu items of the VB-created application and the one supplying the object, simultaneously.

6.4 Assemble Documents with Word for Windows 6.0

Thanks to the inclusion of Visual Basic for Applications in the Visual Basic 4.0 development package, we can programmatically control applications that expose their objects. Word for Windows 6.0 exposes the WordBasic object, which will be used in this How-To to assemble a document.

6.5 Transfer Data and Send Notifications between VB Applications, Using an Automation Server

To control the size and memory signature of applications, many developers and teams divide tasks into a suite of communicating applications. This modular approach also provides alternatives to distribution, when users' needs vary widely. In earlier versions of Visual Basic, a significant obstacle to this type of development has been communicating data among the related applications. Several solutions have been used, none of which was particularly elegant. Sending information to a starting application with a command-line argument is obviously limited. DDE can be used in some situations, but is somewhat error prone. Creating global memory blocks and letting all applications access them is complicated in VB. Perhaps the best solution has been to package information in a user-defined variable and then include the address of that data structure as an argument to the Windows SendMessage or PostMessage functions, along with a message interception custom control. In Windows 3.1, the only problem with this technique was the fact that the slightest error in coding caused General Protection Faults. Also, this technique is not useable in 32-bit applications. As demonstrated by this How-To, using an Automation server allows interapplication communication with no custom controls or API functions.

6.1 How do I...
Browse Program Manager Groups and Items?

COMPLEXITY: INTERMEDIATE
COMPATIBILITY: VB4 ONLY

Problem

Sometimes I need to look through the properties for a lot of Program Manager items at one time. It's tedious to have to keep going in and out of Program Manager's File Properties menu to review the items. Is there a way to pull this information into a Visual Basic program so that I can create my own user interface that is more efficient?

Technique

Program Manager provides a dynamic data exchange (DDE) interface through which other programs can send commands to control Program Manager's processing. Using the powers of DDE, we can tell Program Manager to do such things as create new groups, add items to the groups, and even close itself down. Upon command, it will also deliver detailed information about each of its groups and their associated items. These information delivery commands are used in this How To. We'll create a Cpmdde class file to encapsulate the complexity of sending DDE commands to Program Manager and parsing the information returned by Program Manager.

Information from Program Manager's File Properties dialog box is all available through this DDE interface, but the icon is only available indirectly. Program Manager returns the name of the icon executable file and the selected icon index number, so we'll use the CIconExec class file that was developed for How-To 7.11 to extract the icon and display it in our new program.

Steps

Open and run PMBROWSE.VBP, as shown in action in Figure 6-1-1. You'll see all the Program Manager groups in a list box on the left, in alphabetical order with a count of the number of groups displayed above the list. The first group name is highlighted, and all of its items are displayed alphabetically in a list box to the right. In the list of items, the first description is highlighted, and above it is a count of the number of items in the list. Below the two list boxes is a framed set of details for the highlighted item. If an icon is associated with the item, it is displayed to the left of the icon executable filename.

Try selecting various groups and items to see how quickly this user interface lets you browse item properties. (It's definitely faster than going in and out of Program

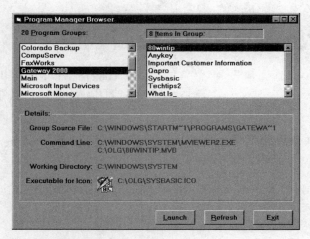

Figure 6-1-1 Program Manager Browser in action

648

Manager's File Properties menu and dialog box.) Try launching any item, and you'll find that it will launch minimized if that's the way it's specified in Program Manager. Go to Program Manager and add an item to a group. When you select that group, the new item will appear. Then go back to Program Manager and add a new group. It will appear as soon as you click the Refresh button on the Program Manager Browser.

1. Create a new project called PMBROWSE.VBP. Create a form with the controls as shown in Figure 6-1-2. Note the placement of the GroupsText and ItemsText text boxes, which are invisible at run time. Set form objects and properties as shown in Table 6-1-1, and save the form as PMBROWSE.FRM.

Table 6-1-1 PMBROWSE.FRM form properties

OBJECT	PROPERTY	SETTING
Form	Name	BrowserForm
	Caption	"Program Manager Browser"
	ScaleWidth	3 'Pixel
TextBox	Name	GroupsText
	Visible	0 'False
Label	Name	ProgramGroupsLabel
	BackStyle	0 'Transparent
	Caption	"&Program Groups:"
TextBox	Name	ItemsText
	Visible	0 'False
Label	Name	ItemsLabel
	BackStyle	0 'Transparent
	Caption	"&Items in Group:"
ListBox	Name	GroupList
	Sorted	-1 'True
Frame	Name	DetailsFrame
	Caption	"Details:"
Label	Name	Label
	Alignment	1 'Right Justify
	BackStyle	0 'Transparent
	Caption	"Group Source File:"
	Index	0
Label	Name	Label
	Alignment	1 'Right Justify
	BackStyle	0 'Transparent
	Caption	"Command Line:"
	Index	1

Continued on next page

Continued from previous page

OBJECT	PROPERTY	SETTING
Label	Name	Label
	Alignment	1 'Right Justify
	BackStyle	0 'Transparent
	Caption	"Working Directory:"
	Index	2
Label	Name	Label
	Alignment	1 'Right Justify
	BackStyle	0 'Transparent
	Caption	"Executable for Icon:"
	Index	3
Label	Name	GroupSourceFileLabel
	BackStyle	0 'Transparent
	Caption	"group source file"
	Forecolor	Red
Label	Name	CommandLineLabel
	BackStyle	0 'Transparent
	Caption	"command line"
	Forecolor	Red
Label	Name	WorkingDirectoryLabel
	BackStyle	0 'Transparent
	Caption	"working directory"
	Forecolor	Red
Label	Name	ExecForIconLabel
	BackStyle	0 'Transparent
	Caption	"icon executable file"
	Forecolor	Red
PictureBox	Name	IconPicBox
	AutoRedraw	-1 'True
	ScaleWidth	3 'Pixel
CommandButton	Name	LaunchButton
	Caption	"Launch"
CommandButton	Name	RefreshButton
	Caption	"Refresh"
CommandButton	Name	ExitButton
	Caption	"Exit"

2. Use the File Add menu item to add the file named EXECICON.CLS to PMBROWSE.VBP.

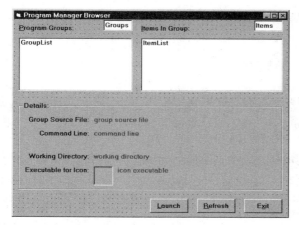

Figure 6-1-2 BrowserForm during design

3. Place the following code at the beginning of the PMBROWSE.FRM. These variables define class files to handle dynamic data exchange (DDE) with Program Manager and to extract an icon from an executable—specifically, the icon associated with an item in a Program Manager group. A variable is also set to keep track of the currently selected item.

```
Option Explicit
'
' Class files for Program Manager DDE and for extracting icons
' from an executable. Also variable for currently selected item.
'
Private m_ProgMan As New Cpmdde
Private m_IconExtract As New CExecIcons
Private m_ItemIndex As Integer
```

4. Place the following code in the Form_Load event procedure. This subroutine adjusts the IconPicBox to display a borderless icon and sets it as the container for the IconExtract class object. The routine also sets containers for DDE group and item information retrieved by the ProgManDDE class object. It centers and then fills the form by triggering the RefreshButton's Click event.

```
Private Sub Form_Load()
    '
    ' Adjust the height and width of the icon PictureBox to fit
    ' one icon. Clear the border style and set it as the container
    ' for the IconExtract class file.
    '
    IconPicBox.Height _
        = IconPicBox.Height * (32 / IconPicBox.ScaleHeight)
    IconPicBox.Width _
        = IconPicBox.Width * (32 / IconPicBox.ScaleWidth)
    IconPicBox.BorderStyle = vbBSNone
```

Continued on next page

Continued from previous page

```
    Set m_IconExtract.Container = IconPicBox
    '
    ' Set the GroupsText and ItemsText TextBoxes as containers for
    ' the ProgManDDE class file. The class file will direct
    ' ProgMan's DDE values to these boxes.
    '
    Set m_ProgMan.GroupsContainer = GroupsText
    Set m_ProgMan.ItemsContainer = ItemsText
    '
    ' "Click" the refresh button to fill form. Then center it.
    '
    RefreshButton_Click
    Move (Screen.Width - Width) \ 2, (Screen.Height - Height) \ 2
End Sub
```

5. Place the following code in the RefreshButton_Change event procedure. This routine triggers the ProgManDDE object's Refresh method to refresh the set of Program Manager groups that will be accessible via the object. The ProgManDDE class provides a GroupCount property and an indexed GroupName property, which are used to retrieve the updated set of groups and add them into the GroupList list box. This subroutine also displays the number of groups in a label above the list, and highlights the first group name in the list. Highlighting the group name triggers the GroupList_Click event procedure.

```
Private Sub RefreshButton_Click()
    '
    ' This takes some time so change mouse pointer to hourglass.
    '
    MousePointer = vbHourglass
    '
    ' Refresh the DDE group info from ProgMan. Then clear the
    ' group list, and re-add the ProgMan group names. Because
    ' they're added in alpha sort sequence, save the actual index
    ' in the GroupList's ItemData field for later use.
    '
    m_ProgMan.Refresh
    GroupList.Clear
    Dim i As Integer
    For i = 0 To m_ProgMan.GroupCount - 1
        GroupList.AddItem m_ProgMan.GroupName(i)
        GroupList.ItemData(GroupList.NewIndex) = i
    Next i
    '
    ' Show in the label how many groups are in the list and
    ' highlight the first group in the list.
    '
    ProgramGroupsLabel.Caption _
        = Str$(m_ProgMan.GroupCount) & " &Program Groups:"
    If m_ProgMan.GroupCount > 0 Then
        GroupList.ListIndex = 0
    End If
    '
    ' Work is done. Return mouse pointer to default.
```

```
    '
    MousePointer = vbDefault
End Sub
```

6. Place the following code in the GroupList_Click event procedure. This subroutine sets the ProgManDDE object's GroupIndex equal to the index of the currently selected group name. Then it retrieves, via ProgManDDE, a source file name for the group and descriptions for the items in the group. It adds the descriptions into the ItemList list box, displays the number of items in a label above the list, and highlights the first description in the list. Highlighting a description in the list triggers the ItemList_Click event procedure.

```
Private Sub GroupList_Click()
    '
    ' This takes some time so change mouse pointer to hourglass.
    '
    MousePointer = vbHourglass
    '
    ' Remove the previously selected group's items and display the
    ' source file name for the group just selected. Then add each
    ' of the items in the newly selected group to the ItemList.
    ' Because they're added in alpha sort sequence, save the
    ' actual index in the ItemList's ItemData field for later use.
    '
    ItemList.Clear
    Set m_ProgMan.GroupIndex _
        = GroupList.ItemData(GroupList.ListIndex)
    GroupSourceFileLabel.Caption = m_ProgMan.SourceFile
    Dim i As Integer
    For i = 0 To m_ProgMan.ItemCount - 1
        ItemList.AddItem m_ProgMan.ItemDescription(i)
        ItemList.ItemData(ItemList.NewIndex) = i
    Next i
    '
    ' Label the ItemList with the number of items in the list and
    ' highlight the first item in the list. Clear the item details
    ' if there are no items in the list.
    '
    ItemsLabel.Caption _
        = Str$(m_ProgMan.ItemCount) & " &Items In Group:"
    If m_ProgMan.ItemCount > 0 Then
        ItemList.ListIndex = 0
    Else
        CommandLineLabel.Caption = ""
        WorkingDirectoryLabel.Caption = ""
        ExecForIconLabel.Caption = ""
        IconPicBox.Cls
    End If
    '
    ' Work is done. Return mouse pointer to default.
    '
    MousePointer = vbDefault
End Sub
```

7. Place the following code in the ItemList_Click event procedure. This subroutine accesses the ProgManDDE object to retrieve details about the selected item. It displays details such as command line and working directory in labels on the form. If an icon executable file is specified, the IconExtract object is used to get a count of icons in the file and to retrieve the icon specified as one of the ProgManDDE item details. When an icon is available for display, the icon executable file label is shifted to the right to accommodate the icon display.

```
Private Sub ItemList_Click()
    '
    ' Set an ItemIndex variable based on the ItemData value stored
    ' in the item that was just clicked. Use it to get the
    ' corresponding item details from the ProgManDDE class file.
    '
    m_ItemIndex = ItemList.ItemData(ItemList.ListIndex)
    CommandLineLabel.Caption _
        = m_ProgMan.CommandLine(m_ItemIndex)
    WorkingDirectoryLabel.Caption _
        = m_ProgMan.WorkingDirectory(m_ItemIndex)
    ExecForIconLabel.Caption _
        = m_ProgMan.IconExecutable(m_ItemIndex)
    '
    ' Compare the icons in the executable to the IconIndex set by
    ' ProgMan. If in range, show the icon to the right of the
    ' file providing the icon. Otherwise, show only the file name.
    '
    Dim NumIcons As Integer
    Dim IconExec As String
    Dim IconIndex As Integer
    IconExec = ExecForIconLabel.Caption
    ElseIf IconExec = Then NumIcons = 0
        NumIcons = m_IconExtract.CountIcons(IconExec)
    End If
    IconIndex _
        = m_ProgMan.IconIndex(m_ItemIndex)
    If IconIndex "" NumIcons Then
        IconPicBox.Visible = True
        ExecForIconLabel.Left = IconPicBox.Left + 500
        m_IconExtract.ShowIcons IconExec, IconIndex + 1
    Else
        IconPicBox.Cls
        IconPicBox.Visible = False
        ExecForIconLabel.Left = IconPicBox.Left
    End If
End Sub
```

8. Place the following code in the GroupList_GotFocus event procedure, to put a border around the label above the GroupList list box. This lets the user know visually that the GroupList has the focus.

```
Private Sub GroupList_GotFocus()
    '
    ' Put border around corresponding label to indicate focus is
```

```
' here.
'
    ProgramGroupsLabel.BorderStyle = vbFixedSingle
End Sub
```

9. Place the following code in the GroupList_LostFocus event procedure, to remove the border from around the label above the GroupList list box. This lets the user know visually that the GroupList no longer has the focus.

```
Private Sub GroupList_LostFocus()
    '
    ' Remove border from corresponding label to indicate focus is
    ' no longer here.
    '
    ProgramGroupsLabel.BorderStyle = vbBSNone
End Sub
```

10. Place the following code in the ItemList_GotFocus event procedure, to put a border around the label above the ItemList list box. This lets the user know visually that the ItemList has the focus.

```
Private Sub ItemList_GotFocus()
    '
    ' Put border around corresponding label to indicate focus is
    ' here
    '
    ItemsLabel.BorderStyle = vbFixedSingle
End Sub
```

11. Place the following code in the ItemList_LostFocus event procedure, to remove the border from around the label above the ItemList list box. This lets the user know visually that the ItemList no longer has the focus.

```
Private Sub ItemList_LostFocus()
    '
    ' Remove border from corresponding label to indicate focus is no
    ' longer here.
    '
    ItemsLabel.BorderStyle = vbBSNone
End Sub
```

12. Place the following code in the LaunchButton_Click event procedure. This procedure first changes to the selected item's working directory, if one is specified. Then it uses the Shell command to launch whatever is specified for the item's command line, starting it minimized with no focus if the ProgManDDE minimized flag is set for the item. Launching without focus is consistent with the way Program Manager launches minimized items.

```
Private Sub LaunchButton_Click()
    Const cMinimizedNoFocus As Integer = 6
    Const cNormalFocus As Integer = 1
```

Continued on next page

Continued from previous page

```
    '
    ' Change to the item's working directory before launching it.
    ' Launch it minimized with no focus if the minimize flag is
    ' set that way. Otherwise launch it normal with focus.
    '
    'On Error Resume Next
    If WorkingDirectoryLabel <> "" Then
        ChDir WorkingDirectoryLabel
        If Err.Number <> 0 Then MsgBox "ChDir Error"
    End If
    If m_ProgMan.MinimizeFlag(m_ItemIndex) Then
        Shell CommandLineLabel, cMinimizedNoFocus
    Else
        Shell CommandLineLabel, cNormalFocus
    End If
    '
    ' Capture and provide a message about any error launching the
    ' item.
    '
    If Err.Number = 0 Then Exit Sub
    Select Case Err.Number
        Case 5
            MsgBox "Can't Launch Application. Invalid program name."
        Case 7
            MsgBox "Can't Launch Application. Out of Memory."
        Case 53
            MsgBox "Can't Launch Application. Program not found."
        Case 76
            MsgBox "Can't Launch Application. Path not found."
        Case Else
            MsgBox "Can't Launch Application. Unknown error " _
                & Err.Number & "."
    End Select
End Sub
```

13. Place the following code in the ExitButton_Click event procedure:

```
Private Sub ExitButton_Click()
    '
    ' All done.
    '
    End
End Sub
```

14. Use the Insert Class Module menu item to add a new class module named Cpmdde. Put the following code at the beginning of the file. This code creates user-defined types for storing the Program Manager group and item details.

```
Option Explicit
'
' User defined type for storing all the DDE item information for
' each of the items in the selected group.
'
Private Type DDEItem
```

```
        Description As String
        CommandLine As String
        WorkingDirectory As String
        IconExecutable As String
        HPosInGroup As Integer
        VPosInGroup As Integer
        IconIndex As Integer
        ShortCutKey As Integer
        MinimizeFlag As Boolean
End Type
'
' User defined type for storing all the DDE group information
' for the selected group.
'
Private Type DDEGroup
    Name As String
    SourceFile As String
    ItemCount As Integer
    SequNum As Integer
    Items() As DDEItem
End Type
```

15. Add this code next, to set the private variables for the class module:

```
'
' TextBoxes on form used to receive DDE data from ProgMan.
'
Private m_DDEGroups As Object
Private m_DDEItems As Object
'
' Store a count of the number of groups and store all their
' names.
'
Private m_GroupCount As Integer
Private m_GroupName() As String
'
' Store parsed DDE info about the selected group and keep track
' of the currently selected group and item.
'
Private m_DDEGroup As DDEGroup
Private m_GroupIndex As Integer
Private m_ItemIndex As Integer
```

16. Add the following code to the General section of Cpmdde. The Set
    GroupsContainer property gets and stores the current object to be used for
    retrieving group information via DDE from Program Manager. Only a label or text
    box can be used to capture the DDE string.

```
Public Property Set GroupsContainer(GroupsText As Object)
    '
    ' Set Label or TextBox control for DDE Link to get list of
    ' ProgMan groups.
    '
    If TypeOf GroupsText Is Label _
```

Continued on next page

Continued from previous page

```
    Or TypeOf GroupsText Is TextBox Then
        Set m_DDEGroups = GroupsText
    Else
        MsgBox "Items container must be a Label or TextBox."
    End If
End Property
```

17. Add the following code to the General section of Cpmdde. The Get GroupsContainer property returns the current DDE group's container object to the calling program.

```
Public Property Get GroupsContainer() As Object
    '
    ' Return current GroupsContainer object to calling program.
    '
    GroupsContainer = m_DDEGroups
End Property
```

18. Add the following code to the General section of Cpmdde. The Set ItemsContainer property gets and stores the current object to be used for retreiving item information for one group via DDE from Program Manager. Only a label or text box can be used to capture the DDE string.

```
Public Property Set ItemsContainer(ItemsText As Object)
    '
    ' Set Label or TextBox control for DDE Link to get group and
    ' item info for selected group
    '
    If TypeOf ItemsText Is Label _
    Or TypeOf ItemsText Is TextBox Then
        Set m_DDEItems = ItemsText
    Else
        MsgBox "Items container must be a Label or TextBox."
    End If
End Property
```

19. Add the following code to the General section of Cpmdde. The Get ItemsContainer property returns the current DDE group item's container object to the calling program.

```
Public Property Get ItemsContainer() As Object
    '
    ' Return current ItemsContainer object to calling program.
    '
    ItemsContainer = m_DDEItems
End Property
```

20. Add the following public subroutine to the General section of Cpmdde. The Refresh subroutine provides the calling program with a method for refreshing the set of Program Manager groups. This subroutine executes two private routines: the first one executes a DDE link with Program Manager to get a current list of

groups. The second one extracts the group names from the DDE string returned by Program Manager.

```
Public Sub Refresh()
    '
    ' Perform DDELink to refresh groups and parse out the group
    ' names.
    '
    DDELinkForGroups
    ExtractGroupNames
End SubEnd Sub
```

21. Add the following private subroutine to the General section of Cpmdde. DDELinkForGroups sets various link properties for the m_DDEGroups object, which is the group's container label or text file. It performs the LinkRequest method for the object. This method triggers the filling of the container with a DDE string containing a current list of all the Program Manager groups. To close out the DDE channel when done, it sets the LinkMode back to None.

```
Private Sub DDELinkForGroups()
    '
    ' DDE Link to fill Label or TextBox object with list Progman
    ' Groups.
    '
    m_DDEGroups.LinkTopic = "Progman|progman"
    m_DDEGroups.LinkItem = "Groups"
    m_DDEGroups.LinkMode = vbLinkManual
    m_DDEGroups.LinkRequest
    m_DDEGroups.LinkMode = vbLinkNone
End Sub
```

22. Add the following private subroutine to the General section of Cpmdde. ExtractGroupNames parses through the DDE string of Program Manager groups, extracting the actual group names and storing them in a private array variable called m_GroupName(). The total number of names found in the DDE string is stored in a private variable called m_GroupCount.

```
Private Sub ExtractGroupNames()
    '
    ' Initialize a TextSegment variable with list of ProgMan
    ' groups from DDE LinkRequest.
    '
    Dim TextSegment As String
    TextSegment = m_DDEGroups.Text
    '
    ' Each group name ends with a carriage return and line feed
    '
    Dim CarriageReturnPos As Integer
    Dim i As Integer
    i = 0
    Do While Len(TextSegment) > 0
        ReDim Preserve m_GroupName(i)
```

Continued on next page

Continued from previous page

```
        CarriageReturnPos = InStr(TextSegment, Chr(13))
        m_GroupName(i) = Mid(TextSegment, 1, CarriageReturnPos - 1)
        TextSegment = Mid(TextSegment, CarriageReturnPos + 2)
        i = i + 1
    Loop
    m_GroupCount = i
End Sub
```

23. Add the following code to the General section of Cpmdde. The Get GroupCount property returns the current count of the number of Program Manager groups to the calling program.

```
Public Property Get GroupCount() As Integer
    '
    ' Return count of groups passed back in DDE Link for groups.
    '
    GroupCount = m_GroupCount
End Property
```

24. Add the following code to the General section of Cpmdde. The Get GroupName property returns the name of the Program Manager group corresponding to the index requested by the calling program. But first, it verifies that the requested index is within range for the current number of groups.

```
Public Property Get GroupName(Index As Integer) As String
    '
    ' Return group name for selected group.
    '
    If Index < 0 Or Index > m_GroupCount - 1 Then
        MsgBox "Index out of range."
    Else
        GroupName = m_GroupName(Index)
    End If
End Property
```

25. Add the following code to the General section of Cpmdde. The Let GroupIndex property gets the desired value from the calling program and stores it as a private variable. Then the routine performs two private subroutines: the first subroutine executes a DDE link with Program Manager to get current additional information about the group, including the items in the group. The second subroutine extracts the group information from the DDE string returned by Program Manager.

```
Public Property Let GroupIndex(PickGroup As Integer)
    '
    ' Set group index for selected group. Then perform DDELink to
    ' get info about the group and the items in the group. Finally
    ' parse out the group and item information.
    '
    If PickGroup > m_GroupCount - 1 _
    Or PickGroup < 0 Then
```

```
            MsgBox "Error. GroupIndex = " & PickGroup _
                  & "Out of valid range of 0 to " & m_GroupCount - 1
         Else
            m_GroupIndex = PickGroup
            DDELinkForGroupItems
            ExtractGroupAndItemInfo
         End If
End Property
```

26. Add the following private subroutine to the General section of Cpmdde. DDELinkForGroupItems sets various link properties for the m_DDEItems object, which is the item's container label or text file, and executes a DDE request to fill the container with a DDE string containing a current set of group information about the requested Program Manager group. When the routine is done, it sets the LinkMode back to None to close the DDE channel.

```
Public Sub DDELinkForGroupItems()
    '
    ' DDE to fill ItemsText TextBox with list of group and
    ' items details for the selected Progman group.
    '
    m_DDEItems.LinkTopic = "Progman|progman"
    m_DDEItems.LinkItem = m_GroupName(m_GroupIndex)
    m_DDEItems.LinkMode = vbLinkManual
    m_DDEItems.LinkRequest
    m_DDEItems.LinkMode = vbLinkNone
End Sub
```

27. Add the following private subroutine to the General section of Cpmdde. ExtractGroupAndItemInfo parses through the DDE string of Program Manager group information. First it extracts basic information about the group, including the name of the source file for the group and a count of the number of items in the group. Then it extracts information about each item in the group. This item information includes such details as the item's command line and a filename for extracting an icon for the item. All the information is stored in a private variable called m_DDEGroup, which is based on a user-defined type comprising the many elements needed to store group item information in an item array, as well as the basic information available for the group.

```
Public Sub ExtractGroupAndItemInfo()
    '
    ' Initialize a TextSegment variable with data from DDE'
    ' LinkRequest. It starts with info about the requested group,
    ' delimited by commas and ending with a carriage return and
    ' line feed. It continues with information about each item in
    ' the group. Data for each item is also delimited by commas
    ' and ended with a carriage return and line feed.
    '
    Dim CommaPos As Integer
    Dim CarriageReturnPos As Integer
    Dim TextSegment As String
```

Continued on next page

Continued from previous page

```vb
TextSegment = m_DDEItems.Text
'
' Name (drop quotes from each end)
CommaPos = InStr(TextSegment, Chr(44))
m_DDEGroup.Name = Mid(TextSegment, 2, CommaPos - 3)
TextSegment = Mid(TextSegment, CommaPos + 1)
'
' Source file
CommaPos = InStr(TextSegment, Chr(44))
m_DDEGroup.SourceFile = Mid(TextSegment, 1, CommaPos - 1)
TextSegment = Mid(TextSegment, CommaPos + 1)
'
' Item count
CommaPos = InStr(TextSegment, Chr(44))
m_DDEGroup.ItemCount = Mid(TextSegment, 1, CommaPos - 1)
TextSegment = Mid(TextSegment, CommaPos + 1)
'
' Sequence number ends with carriage return and line feed
CarriageReturnPos = InStr(TextSegment, Chr(13))
m_DDEGroup.SequNum _
    = Mid(TextSegment, 1, CarriageReturnPos - 1)
TextSegment = Mid(TextSegment, CarriageReturnPos + 2)
'
' For each item in group, pull out individual item values
' drop it from the text segment.

Dim i As Integer
For i = 0 To m_DDEGroup.ItemCount - 1
    ReDim Preserve m_DDEGroup.Items(i)
    '
    ' Description (Drop quotes from each end)
    CommaPos = InStr(TextSegment, Chr(44))
    m_DDEGroup.Items(i).Description _
        = Mid(TextSegment, 2, CommaPos - 3)
    TextSegment = Mid(TextSegment, CommaPos + 1)
    '
    ' CommaPosndLine (Drop quotes from each end)
    CommaPos = InStr(TextSegment, Chr(44))
    m_DDEGroup.Items(i).CommandLine _
        = Mid(TextSegment, 2, CommaPos - 3)
    TextSegment = Mid(TextSegment, CommaPos + 1)
    '
    ' Working Directory
    CommaPos = InStr(TextSegment, Chr(44))
    m_DDEGroup.Items(i).WorkingDirectory _
        = Mid(TextSegment, 1, CommaPos - 1)
    TextSegment = Mid(TextSegment, CommaPos + 1)
    '
    ' Icon Executable
    CommaPos = InStr(TextSegment, Chr(44))
    m_DDEGroup.Items(i).IconExecutable _
        = Mid(TextSegment, 1, CommaPos - 1)
    TextSegment = Mid(TextSegment, CommaPos + 1)
    '
```

```
      ' Horizontal Position in Group
      CommaPos = InStr(TextSegment, Chr(44))
      m_DDEGroup.Items(i).HPosInGroup _
          = Mid(TextSegment, 1, CommaPos - 1)
      TextSegment = Mid(TextSegment, CommaPos + 1)
      '
      ' Vertical Position in Group
      CommaPos = InStr(TextSegment, Chr(44))
      m_DDEGroup.Items(i).VPosInGroup _
          = Mid(TextSegment, 1, CommaPos - 1)
      TextSegment = Mid(TextSegment, CommaPos + 1)
      '
      ' IconIndex
      CommaPos = InStr(TextSegment, Chr(44))
      m_DDEGroup.Items(i).IconIndex _
          = Mid(TextSegment, 1, CommaPos - 1)
      TextSegment = Mid(TextSegment, CommaPos + 1)
      '
      ' Numeric value for ShortCutKey
      CommaPos = InStr(TextSegment, Chr(44))
      m_DDEGroup.Items(i).ShortCutKey _
          = Mid(TextSegment, 1, CommaPos - 1)
      TextSegment = Mid(TextSegment, CommaPos + 1)
      '
      ' Minimize Flag (ends with carriage return and line feed)
      CarriageReturnPos = InStr(TextSegment, Chr(13))
      m_DDEGroup.Items(i).MinimizeFlag _
          = Mid(TextSegment, 1, CarriageReturnPos - 1)
      TextSegment = Mid(TextSegment, CarriageReturnPos + 2)
   Next i
End Sub
```

28. Add the following code to the General section of Cpmdde. The Get SourceFile
    property returns the current value to the calling program.

```
Public Property Get SourceFile() As String
   '
   ' Return source file name for selected group.
   '
   SourceFile = m_DDEGroup.SourceFile
End Property
```

29. Add the following code to the General section of Cpmdde. The Get ItemCount
    property returns the current value to the calling program.

```
Public Property Get ItemCount() As Integer
   '
   ' Return count of items passed back in DDE Link for items in
   ' group.
   '
   ItemCount = m_DDEGroup.ItemCount
End Property
```

663

30. Add the following code to the General section of Cpmdde. The Get SequNum property returns the current value to the calling program.

```
Public Property Get SequNum() As Integer
    '
    ' Return the sequence number for the selected group.
    '
 SequNum = m_DDEGroup.SequNum
End Property
```

31. Add the following code to the General section of Cpmdde. The Let ItemIndex property gets the ItemIndex from the calling program, storing it as the index to be used when the calling program requests specific item information.

```
Public Property Let ItemIndex(PickItem As Integer)
    '
    ' Set selected item in selected group.
    '
    If PickItem > m_DDEGroup.ItemCount - 1 _
    Or PickItem < 0 Then
        MsgBox "Error. ItemIndex = " & PickItem _
            & "Out of valid range of 0 to " _
            & m_DDEGroup.ItemCount - 1
    Else
        m_ItemIndex = PickItem
    End If
End Property
```

32. Add the following code to the General section of Cpmdde. The Get ItemIndex property returns the value of the current item index to the calling program.

```
Public Property Get ItemIndex() As Integer
    '
    ' Return selected item of selected group.
    '
    ItemIndex = m_ItemIndex
End Property
```

33. Add the following code to the General section of Cpmdde. The Get ItemDescription property returns the item description for the requested item index to the calling program.

```
Public Property Get ItemDescription(ItemIndex As Integer) _
    As String
    '
    ' Return item description for selected item in selected group.
    '
    ItemDescription = m_DDEGroup.Items(ItemIndex).Description
End Property
```

34. Add the following code to the General section of Cpmdde. The Get
    CommandLine property returns the command line for the requested item index
    to the calling program.

```
Public Property Get CommandLine(ItemIndex As Integer) As String
    '
    ' Return command line for selected item in selected group.
    '
    CommandLine = m_DDEGroup.Items(ItemIndex).CommandLine
End Property
```

35. Add the following code to the General section of Cpmdde. The Get
    WorkingDirectory property returns the working directory for the requested item
    index to the calling program.

```
Public Property Get WorkingDirectory(ItemIndex As Integer) _
    As String
    '
    ' Return working directory for selected item in selected group.
    '
    WorkingDirectory _
        = m_DDEGroup.Items(ItemIndex).WorkingDirectory
End Property
```

36. Add the following code to the General section of Cpmdde. The Get
    IconExecutable property returns the icon executable file for the requested item
    index to the calling program.

```
Public Property Get IconExecutable(ItemIndex As Integer) _
    As String
    '
    ' Return icon executable file name for selected item in
    ' selected group.
    '
    IconExecutable = m_DDEGroup.Items(ItemIndex).IconExecutable
End Property
```

37. Add the following code to the General section of Cpmdde. The Get HPosInGroup
    property returns a number for the requested item index to the calling program.
    The number represents the horizontal position that is used to display the item's
    icon in the Program Manager group.

```
Public Property Get HPosInGroup(ItemIndex As Integer) As Integer
    '
    ' Return horizontal position of selected item in selected
    ' group.
    '
    HPosInGroup = m_DDEGroup.Items(ItemIndex).HPosInGroup
End Property
```

38. Add the following code to the General section of Cpmdde. The Get VPosInGroup property returns a number for the requested item index to the calling program. This number represents the vertical position that is used to display the item's icon in the Program Manager group.

```
Public Property Get VPosInGroup(ItemIndex As Integer) As Integer
    '
    ' Return vertical position of selected item in selected group.
    '
    VPosInGroup = m_DDEGroup.Items(ItemIndex).VPosInGroup
End Property
```

39. Add the following code to the General section of Cpmdde. The Get IconIndex property returns a number for the requested item index to the calling program. This number represents an index for retrieving an icon from the icon executable file for this item.

```
Public Property Get IconIndex(ItemIndex As Integer) As Integer
    '
    ' Return icon index for selected item in selected group.
    '
    IconIndex = m_DDEGroup.Items(ItemIndex).IconIndex
End Property
```

40. Add the following code to the General section of Cpmdde. The Get ShortCutKey property returns a number for the requested item index to the calling program. This number represents a short cut key for launching the item from Program Manager.

```
Public Property Get ShortCutKey(ItemIndex As Integer) As Integer
    '
    ' Return short cut key for selected item in selected group.
    '
    ShortCutKey = m_DDEGroup.Items(ItemIndex).ShortCutKey
End Property
```

41. Add the following code to the General section of Cpmdde. The Get MinimizeFlag property returns a Boolean value for the requested item index to the calling program. This minimize flag indicates whether or not Program Manager should launch the item in a minimized state.

```
Public Property Get MinimizeFlag(ItemIndex As Integer) As Boolean
    '
    ' Return minimize flag for selected item in selected group.
    '
    MinimizeFlag = m_DDEGroup.Items(ItemIndex).MinimizeFlag
End Property
```

How It Works

The project in this How-To uses dynamic data exchange (DDE) to get information from the Program Manager. The complexity of conversing with Program Manager and parsing out the returned information is encapsulated into a new class file called Cpmdde.

When a Visual Basic program initiates a DDE conversation, the VB program is considered to be the destination application. As such, VB must provide a label or text box to establish the link. The Label and TextBox controls have properties for specifying the link (LinkTopic, LinkItem, and LinkMode). Because class files don't have their own controls, the calling program sets container controls for the Cpmdde class file to use.

The LinkTopic property specifies the link application and topic, separated by a vertical bar or "pipe" character (ANSI character code 124). In our Browser example, this property is set to "Progman|progman". A LinkItem set to "Groups" tells Program Manager to fill the GroupsText text box with information about all its groups. A LinkItem set to an exact group name tells Program Manager to fill the ItemsText text box with information about the group, including a list of all the group's items. In both cases, the LinkMode is set to None at design time and to Manual just before initiating the LinkRequest. The LinkRequest triggers the conversation itself. Immediately after the LinkRequest completes, the LinkMode is set back to None to terminate the conversation.

When Program Manager gets a "Groups" request, it returns a text string filled with the names of each of the groups, separated by carriage return and line feed characters. Cpmdde parses through the text string, pulling out the group names, counting them, and storing them in an array. When Program Manager gets a request for information about a specific group, it returns a more complex text string. This text string starts with comma-delimited information about the group, and continues with comma-delimited information about each item in the group. Each set of information is terminated by a carriage return and line feed. Cpmdde parses through this information, as well, storing the group and item information, and making the group and item information available to the calling program through Get properties.

As in How-To 7.11, the CExecIcon class file hides the work necessary to extract an icon, given a filename and an icon index in the file.

Comments

This How-To only scratches the surface of managing DDE communications with Program Manager. Upon command, Program Manager will also add, delete, and display groups; add, delete, and replace items; and even shut itself down.

6.2 How do I...
Perform Background Operations with an In-Process OLE Server

COMPLEXITY: INTERMEDIATE
COMPATIBILITY: VB4 ONLY

Problem

I would like to be able to use an automation server DLL to perform background operations so that the client application is freed up for other activities in the meantime. The client application should not be responsible for determining when the OLE server yields.

Technique

With preemptive multitasking operating systems such as Windows 95 and Windows NT, it isn't necessary to design your application to yield system time to other apps. The operating system ensures that each running app gets its share of execution time. However, this doesn't help for situations where your application must pause during a long calculation to accept keystrokes or other user input.

OLE servers are ideal for encapsulating activities that involve long calculations. The operating system ensures that out-of-process OLE servers yield to their clients, because the servers run in separate process spaces. But out-of-process servers may be unacceptably slow when the activity involves a lot of communication with their clients. In-process OLE servers do not have to communicate with their clients across process boundaries, so they run much faster. For the same reason though, you must control the yielding of the server to its client in the server's code.

In order to yield, an OLE automation server can begin and periodically resume its calculations based on an event generated by its own timer. In this How-To, the server contains an invisible form with a timer control. Calculations proceed for a specified number of operations and then the values needed to resume calculating are stored in static variables. If a second calculation is requested before completion of the current one, the original data is deleted and the new calculation begins. The calculation function has a parameter that controls whether it will resume or restart when called.

Steps

Open and run the PRIMES.VBP automation server application (as shown in Figure 6-2-1). Compile it as a DLL, causing it to become registered in your system. Run the CLIENT.EXE application. The client application finds all prime numbers between an upper and lower limit of long values. If you enter large values, for example 100,000 and 101,000, the calculation will take quite a while. The application is not tied-up

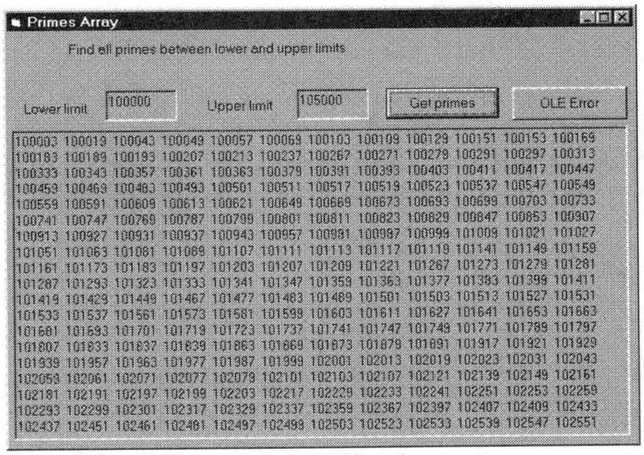

Figure 6-2-1 The PRIMES program, running

during the calculation. During this period you can enter new values of the upper and lower limits, and request a new calculation. The calculation process is reentrant, so the original calculation will be discarded and the new values will be used. The OLE Error button demonstrates the server's response to a request for two primes calculator objects from the client.

1. Create a new project called PRIMES.VBP. In the Project Options dialog, set the project's Startup form to Sub Main, its Project Name to Primes, its application description to Primes Calculator, and its Startup Mode to object application.

2. Insert a new class module named CCalcPrimes. Save it as PRIMES.CLS. Set its Instancing property to 2-Creatable MultiUse and its Public property to True.

3. Add the following declarations to PRIMES.CLS.

```
Option Explicit
'
Public m_TimerForm As Object
'
Private m_Up As Long
Private m_Low As Long
```

4. Add the following subroutine to PRIMES.CLS. This is the method available to the client, which initiates the main calculation.

```
Public Sub Calculate()
    '
    m_TimerForm.TimerLow = m_Low
    m_TimerForm.TimerUp = m_Up
    '
    GetPrimesBetween m_Low, m_Up, _
```

Continued on next page

Continued from previous page

```
        Starting:=True
    m_TimerForm.Timer1.Enabled = True
    '
End Sub
```

5. Add the following property procedure to PRIMES.CLS, representing the lower limit of the values between which the prime numbers will be found.

```
Public Property Let LowerLimit(Low As Long)
    m_Low = Low
End Property
```

6. Add the following property procedure to PRIMES.CLS, representing the upper limit for the primes.

```
Public Property Let UpperLimit(Up As Long)
    m_Up = Up
End Property
```

7. Add the following Property Set procedure to PRIMES.CLS. It allows the OLE server to generate an event in the client—a notification that the server has completed its activity. In this case the server's calculation results are displayed directly by the server.

```
Public Property Set ResultsBox(List As Object)
    '
    Set g_ResultsBox = List
End
```

8. Add the following Property Get procedure to PRIMES.CLS. It allows the user access to the prime numbers array, or returns Null if the calculation is not finished.

```
Public Property Get PrimeArray() As Variant
    '
    'The client application can check for a Null value,
    '(but doesn't need to) indicating the server is
    'still calculating.
    '
    PrimeArray = GetPrimesBetween(m_Low, m_Up, _
    Starting:=False)
    '
End Property
```

9. Add the following initialization procedure to PRIMES.CLS. It creates a form with a timer for each instance of the CCalcPrimes Class.

```
Private Sub Class_Initialize()
    '
    If g_PrevInst Then
        Err.Raise Number:=vbObjectError + 512, Description:= _
        "You can use only one instance of the primes " & _
```

```
          "calculator object per project."
      End If
      '
      g_PrevInst = True
      Set m_TimerForm = New Form1
      Load m_TimerForm
      '
End Sub
```

10. Add the following termination procedure to PRIMES.CLS to destroy the forms used by the calculator objects.

```
Private Sub Class_Terminate()
    '
    g_PrevInst = False
    g_CalcObjDestroyed = True
    Unload m_TimerForm
    Set m_TimerForm = Nothing
    Debug.Print "Terminating CalcPrimes object"
    '
End Sub
```

11. Insert a new standard module named ModMain. Save it as MAIN.BAS.

12. Place the following declaration in MAIN.BAS:

```
Option Explicit
'
Public g_ResultsBox As Object
Public g_CalcObjDestroyed As Integer
Public g_PrevInst As Integer
```

13. Place the following empty Sub Main procedure in MAIN.BAS.

```
Sub Main()
End Sub
```

14. Place the following function in MAIN.BAS. It is declared as Public to be available within the class module and the form module. Because it is in a standard module it will not appear in an automation object browser.

```
Public Function GetPrimesBetween(ByVal Low As Long, _
 ByVal Up As Long, _
 ByVal Starting As Boolean) As Variant
    '
    Dim L1 As Long
    Static EndVal As Long
    Static Current As Long
    Static Done As Boolean
    Static PrimesOf() As Long
    '
    'The GRAIN constant determines how many cycles are executed
    'before yielding. A sofisticated server could make this
```

Continued on next page

Continued from previous page

```
    'available as a property.
    '
    Const GRAIN = 40
    '
    'This process is reentrant. Only clear the array
    'if the previous calculation is finished or you
    'are starting a new calculation.
    '
    On Error GoTo ERRHAN:
    '
    If Starting = False And Done = True Then
        '
        'If done calculating but not beginning a new
        'calculation then return the array of primes.
        '
        GetPrimesBetween = PrimesOf
        Exit Function
    ElseIf Starting = True Then
        '
        'Redim the PrimesOf array and begin calculating.
        '
        Done = False
        ReDim PrimesOf(0)
        Current = Low
        If Current < 1 Then Current = 1
        EndVal = Up
        GetPrimesBetween = Null
    ElseIf Starting = False And Done = False Then
        '
        'If not done, return Null and continue calculating.
        '
        GetPrimesBetween = Null
    End If
    '
    For L1 = Current To Current + GRAIN
        If IsPrime(L1) Then
            ReDim Preserve PrimesOf(UBound(PrimesOf) + 1)
            PrimesOf(UBound(PrimesOf)) = L1
        End If
        If L1 = EndVal Then
            GetPrimesBetween = PrimesOf
            Done = True
            '
            FillResultsBox PrimesOf
            Exit Function
        End If
        '
    Next L1
    Current = Current + GRAIN + 1
    '
    Exit Function
    '
ERRHAN:
```

```
    If g_CalcObjDestroyed Then
        '
        'Normal mid-calculation termination.
        '
    Else
        Err.Raise Number:=vbObjectError + 513, Description:= _
        "Primes calculation failed."
        '
    End If
    Exit Function
    '
End Function
```

15. Place the following helper function in MAIN.BAS:

```
Public Function IsPrime(ByVal Num As Long) As Boolean
    '
    Dim L1 As Long
    If Num < 3 Then IsPrime = False: Exit Function
    For L1 = 2 To Num - 1
        If Num Mod L1 = 0 Then
            IsPrime = False
            Exit Function
        End If
    Next L1
    IsPrime = True
    '
End Function
```

16. Place the following function in MAIN.BAS to send the calculation results back to the client. Some control of the client must be passed to the server to allow the server to generate an event in the client. In this case, rather than notifying the client through a textbox_change event, the results are written to the textbox directly by the server. Alternatively, they could have been supplied in an array contained in a variant return value of a CCalcPrimes class method.

```
Private Sub FillResultsBox(PrimesArray() As Long)
    Dim L1 As Long
    Dim ResStr As String
    '
    For L1 = 1 To UBound(PrimesArray)
        ResStr = ResStr & PrimesArray(L1) & " "
    Next L1
    '
    g_ResultsBox.TEXT = ResStr
    '
End Sub
```

17. Add a new form to the project and save it as FORM1.FRM. Add the objects and properties shown in Table 6-2-1.

Table 6-2-1 Form1's objects and properties

OBJECT	PROPERTY	SETTING
Form	Name	Form1
	Visible	False
Timer	Name	Timer1
	Enabled	False
	Interval	50

18. Add the following declarations to FORM1.FRM.

```
Option Explicit
'
Public TimerLow As Long
Public TimerUp As Long
Public ParentIndex As Integer
```

19. Add the following subroutine to FRMTIMER.FRM to resume background calculation within the automation server.

```
Private Sub Timer1_Timer()
    '
    Static BeenHere As Boolean
    '
    'Testing the return value for null (which indicates it is
    'still calculating) also executes the function for
    'another cycle.
    '
    If Not IsNull(GetPrimesBetween(TimerLow, TimerUp, _
      Starting:=Not (BeenHere))) Then
        BeenHere = False
        Timer1.Enabled = False
        Exit Sub
    End If
    If Not BeenHere Then
        BeenHere = True
    End If
    '
End Sub
```

20. Using the Tools|Options menu in VB, set the Project Description to Primes Calculator and the Project Name to Primes. It is not necessary to set the StartMode to Object Server, as this option only applies to running within the VB environment.

21. Using the Make OLE file option in VB's File menu, compile this project as PRIMES.DLL.

22. Create a new project called CLIENT.VBP. Add a new form and save it as CLIENT.FRM. Add the objects and properties shown in Table 6-2-2.

Table 6-2-2 FrmNotify's objects and properties

OBJECT	PROPERTY	SETTING
Form	Name	Form1
	Caption	"Primes Array"
TextBox	Name	Text1
TextBox	Name	Text2
CommandButton	Name	Command1
	Caption	"Get primes"
CommandButton	Name	Command2
	Caption	"OLE Error"
Label	Name	Label1
	Caption	"Lower limit"
Label	Name	Label2
	Caption	"Upper limit"
Label	Name	Label3
TextBox	Name	txtResults
	MultiLine	True

23. Add the following declarations to CLIENT.FRM.

```
Option Explicit
'
Public PrimesCalculator As New CCalcPrimes
```

24. Clicking the Command Button sets properties of PrimesCalculator, this form's instance of the CCalcPrimes class. Add the following declarations to CLIENT.FRM.

```
Private Sub Command1_Click()
    '
    On Error GoTo ERRHANDLER
    '
    Label3 = "Calculation in progress."
    txtResults.TEXT = ""
    Refresh
    If IsNumeric(Text1) And IsNumeric(Text2) Then
        If Val(Text2) - Val(Text1) < 0 Then
            MsgBox "Upper limit must be greater"
        Else
            PrimesCalculator.UpperLimit = Val(Text2)
            PrimesCalculator.LowerLimit = Val(Text1)
            '
```

Continued on next page

Continued from previous page

```
                    'Pass a client control into the server, so the
                    'server can generate an event in the client.
                    '
                    Set PrimesCalculator.ResultsBox = txtResults
                    PrimesCalculator.Calculate
                    '
                    'Completion of the server can be detected by
                    'txtResults's Change event. The entire result
                    'array could just as easily have been returned to
                    'the client in a variant property.
                    '
            End If
            '
        Else
            MsgBox "The values must be integers or longs."
        End If
        '
        Exit Sub
        '
ERRHANDLER:
        '
        MsgBox Err.Description
        Exit Sub
        '
End Sub
```

25. Add the following procedure to CLIENT.FRM. It demonstrates handling of a server error by the client.

```
Private Sub Command2_Click()
        '
        "Cause an OLE error"
        'Only one instance
        Dim Test1 As New CCalcPrimes
        Dim Test2 As New CCalcPrimes
        '
        On Error GoTo ERRHANDLER
        '
        Test1.UpperLimit = 100
        Test2.UpperLimit = 200
        '
        Exit Sub
        '
ERRHANDLER:
        '
        Err.Clear
        Exit Sub
        '
End Sub
```

26. Add the following Form_Load procedure to initialize CLIENT.FRM.

```
Private Sub Form_Load()
```

```
    '
    Label3 = "Find all primes between lower and upper limits"
    '
End Sub
```

27. The client needs a means of determining when the server has finished its calculation. Allowing the server to cause an event in the client prevents needing to poll the server for completion. Add the following procedure to CLIENT.FRM.

```
Private Sub txtResults_Change()
    '
    Label3 = "Find all primes between lower and upper limits"
    '
End Sub
```

How It Works

The automation server supplies clients with CCalcPrimes class objects. After setting upper and lower limit property values for objects of this class, the client application begins calculating by using the served object's Calculate method. Rather than periodically polling the server to see if it has finished calculating, we pass one of the client's controls to the server as a property. When the server has finished its calculations, it generates an event in the textbox control received from the client, filling the textbox with results in the process.

The calculation function was constructed to be versatile and generic. It is called by the Calculate method to start calculation, and by the timer to resume. If any use of the function results in completion of calculating the primes array (which is a static array in the function) an internal Done flag is set. Then all future calls without the Starting argument return the array of primes.

Comments

Because Visual Basic has no provision for static class variables, all class data variables must be declared in a standard module. By using a reentrant calculation function with several static variables, the number of Public variables can be greatly reduced. Several are still needed to communicate to the invisible form, however.

This project also demonstrates a circuitous workaround for VB4's lack of provision to manually control the reference count of objects. All of the subroutines in the server's standard module would ideally be placed in the class module. This would require that the timer form call a function in the class module, and would thus require the timer form to have a "Parent" object property containing a reference to its owning CCalcPrimes object. Such child-parent circular references between objects in VB effectively prevent the client from terminating objects it created, because setting the served object to Nothing in the client application would not cause the timer form to release its reference to that object.

In out-of-process OLE servers, the Instancing property of a class can be set to Single Use, thereby forcing each instance of a server to handle only one object. The Single Use setting cannot be used with an in-process server though. The primes calculator server prevents a client from instantiating a second CCalcPrimes object rather heavy-handedly: by raising an error to the client. Another way of dealing with the fact that code in the server's standard module is shared by all instances of the related class is to store an array of object indexes and arrays of all the values held in this How-To by static variables of the GetPrimesBetween function. Needless to say, all this would be much easier if VB provided static class variables and programmer control of object reference count.

6.3 How do I...
Build an OLE Object Viewer?

COMPLEXITY: EASY
COMPATIBILITY: VB4 ONLY

Problem

I would like to be able to allow users to view any type of document or file in an OLE container. How can I do this?

Technique

The OLE control is ideal for allowing users to select the class of an object while an application is running. The OLE control provides methods to display system dialogs for inserting an embedded or linked object of all classes available on the user's system. It also provides CreateEmbed and CreateLink methods to the developer for programmatically carrying out these actions.

Steps

Open and run the VIEWER.VBP application (see Figure 6-3-1). It uses an MDI form with an empty OLE control on a child form that is loaded with the application. Closing the child form results in the MDI form's menu being displayed, providing a menu item to load a new child form. Select Insert object from the child form's View Object menu. With the Insert Object dialog open, if the Create New option is selected, you will see a list of all object types supported by your system. If the Create from file option is selected, you will be able to select any file for insertion. If the file is one of the registered object types, it will be displayed within the OLE container. If not it will appear simply as an icon.

Double-clicking on the OLE control will activate the object and the menu of the application that originated it. Note that the child form's Viewer Window menu is retained.

Use the Insert Object dialog to create a new, empty word processor document. With the document activated in the OLE control, drag the icon of a document of that

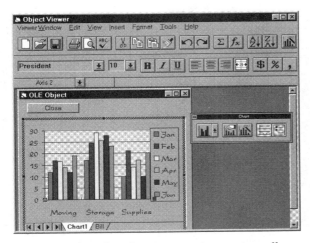

Figure 6-3-1 The Object Viewer showing its stuff

type from Windows File Manager over the OLE control and release it. The document will be displayed in the container.

You can also copy the contents of the clipboard into the OLE container by selecting Copy Clipboard from the child form's menu. The Create Embed and Create Link menu items also allow insertion of objects, but via the standard Open-File dialog box.

1. Create a new project called VIEWER.VBP. Add an MDIForm with the objects and properties listed in Table 6-3-1. Save the MDIForm as MDIFORM1.FRM.

Table 6-3-1 MDIForm1's objects and properties

OBJECT	PROPERTY	SETTING
MDIForm	Name	MDIForm1
	Caption	"Object Viewer"
PictureBox	Name	Picture1
	Align	Align Right
ListBox	Name	List1
ListBox	Name	List2
ListBox	Name	List3
CommonDialog	Name	CommonDialog1
	Cancelerror	True
	Filter	"*.*|*.*"
Label	Name	Label1
	Caption	"Verbs"

Continued on next page

Continued from previous page

OBJECT	PROPERTY	SETTING
Label	Name	Label2
	Caption	"Accept formats"
Label	Name	lblUpdate
	Name	Label3
	Caption	"Get formats"
Label	Name	lblClass
Label	Name	lblObjPtr

2. Using the Menu Design window, give MDIForm1a menu with the characteristics listed in Table 6-3-2.

Table 6-3-2 Viewer project MDI form menu values

CAPTION	NAME
"Viewer &Window"	"mnuWin"
"&New"	"mnuNew"

3. Add the following declaration to MDIFORM1.FRM:

```
Option Explicit
```

4. Add the following event procedure to MDIFORM1.FRM to allow the user to close an activated OLE object by clicking on the MDIForm background:

```
Private Sub MDIForm_Click()
     Me.ActiveForm.OLE1.Close
End Sub
```

5. Add the following procedure to MDIFORM1.FRM to load a child form with an empty OLE control:

```
Private Sub mnuNew_Click()
   Dim NewForm As New Form1
     Load NewForm
End Sub
```

6. Add a new form to the project and save it as FORM1.FRM. Add the objects and properties as listed in Table 6-3-3.

Table 6-3-3 Form1's objects and properties

OBJECT	PROPERTY	SETTING
Form	Name	Form1
	Caption	"OLE Object"

OBJECT	PROPERTY	SETTING
	MDIChild	True
CommandButton	Name	Command1
	Caption	"Close"
OLE	Name	OLE1
	AutoActivate	Automatic
	OLEDropAllowed	True
	OLETypeAllowed	'Either

7. Using the Menu Design window, give MDIForm1a menu with the characteristics listed in Table 6-3-4.

Table 6-3-4 Viewer project Form1 menu values

CAPTION	NAME	NEGOTIATE POSITION
"Viewer &Window"	mnuWin	Left
"&New"	mnuNew	
"&View Object"	mnuBrowse	
"&Insert Object"	mnuInsert	
"&Paste Clipboard"	mnuClip	
"Create &Embed"	mnuEmbed	
"Create &Link"	mnuLink	

8. Add the following declaration to FORM1.FRM:

```
Option Explicit
```

9. Add the following procedure to FORM1.FRM to fill the child form with the OLE control:

```
Private Sub Form_Resize()
      OLE1.Move 100, 500, Width - 300, Height - 1000
End Sub
```

10. Add the following procedure to FORM1.FRM to show the Insert Object dialog and record the characteristics of the OLE object accessed:

```
Private Sub mnuInsert_Click()
    Dim i As Integer
    Dim s1 As String
    OLE1.InsertObjDlg
    ShowOLEDetails
End Sub
```

11. Add the following procedure to FORM1.FRM to paste the contents of the clipboard into the OLE control.

```
Private Sub mnuClip_Click()
    Dim s1 As String
    If OLE1.PasteOK Then
        OLE1.PasteSpecialDlg
        ShowOLEDetails
    Else
        s1 = "Content of the clipboard is in an incorrect "
        s1 = s1 & "clipboard format. To paste into the OLE "
        s1 = s1 & "container, the clipboard must contain "
        s1 = s1 & "data of a class that is registered in your "
        s1 = s1 & "system registry."
        MsgBox s1
    End If
End Sub
```

12. Add the following procedure to FORM1.FRM. It demonstrates programmatic control of object embedding.

```
Private Sub mnuEmbed_Click()
    Dim s1 As String
    On Error GoTo EMBEDERR
    MDIForm1.CommonDialog1.ShowOpen
    OLE1.CreateEmbed MDIForm1.CommonDialog1.FileName
    ShowOLEDetails
EMBEDERR:
    Exit Sub
End Sub
```

13. Add the following procedure to FORM1.FRM. It demonstrates programmatic control of object linking.

```
Private Sub mnuLink_Click()
    Dim s1 As String
    On Error GoTo LINKERR
    MDIForm1.CommonDialog1.ShowOpen
    OLE1.CreateLink MDIForm1.CommonDialog1.FileName
    ShowOLEDetails
LINKERR:
    Exit Sub
End Sub
```

14. Add the following procedure to FORM1.FRM to load a new child form containing the OLE control.

```
Private Sub mnuNew_Click()
    Dim NewForm As New Form1
    Load NewForm
End Sub
```

15. The following subroutine demonstrates access to a number of characteristics about the OLE object contained in the OLE control. Note that these characteristics are accessed directly through the OLE control.

```
Private Sub ShowOLEDetails()
    Dim i As Integer
    Dim s1 As String

    MDIForm1.List1.Clear
    MDIForm1.List2.Clear
    MDIForm1.List3.Clear

    With OLE1
        For i = 1 To .ObjectVerbsCount - 1
            If .ObjectVerbs(i) = .ObjectVerbs(0) Then
                s1 = "(default) "
            Else
                s1 = CStr(i) & ": "
            End If
                MDIForm1.List1.AddItem s1 & .ObjectVerbs(i)
        Next i
        '
        'Tolerate errors due to unrecognized formats.
        '
        On Error Resume Next
        '
        For i = 0 To .ObjectAcceptFormatsCount - 1
            MDIForm1.List2.AddItem .ObjectAcceptFormats(i)
            If .Format = .ObjectAcceptFormats(i) Then
                MDIForm1.List1.ListIndex = i
            End If
        Next i
        For i = 0 To .ObjectGetFormatsCount - 1
            MDIForm1.List3.AddItem .ObjectGetFormats(i)
        Next i
        MDIForm1.lblObjPtr = "lpOleObject: H" & Hex(.LpOleObject)
        MDIForm1.lblClass = "Class: " & .Class
        Select Case .UpdateOptions
            Case 0
                s1 = "Automatic"
            Case 1
                s1 = "Frozen"
            Case 2
                s1 = "Manual"
        End Select
        MDIForm1.lblUpdate = "Update type: " & s1
    End With
End Sub
```

16. Add the following subroutine to FORM1.FRM. Because the OLE control's OLEDropAllowed property is set to True, its Paste method can be used when items from the File Manager are dropped on the control.

```
Private Sub OLE1_DragDrop(Source As Control, X As Single, _
     Y As Single)
   OLE1.Paste
End Sub
```

17. Add the following subroutine to FORM1.FRM allowing the user to close the OLE object.

```
Private Sub Command1_Click()
   If Not OLE1.Class = vbNullString Then OLE1.Close
End Sub
```

How It Works

The OLE control provides simple, high-level access to OLE objects. Methods of the OLE control directly open the system dialogs for inserting embedded or linked objects, or for pasting from the clipboard. The Insert Object and Paste Clipboard menu items simply call these methods. Once an OLE object has been created, the ShowOLEDetails sub obtains characteristics of the object via property values of OLE control. The CreateEmbed and CreateLink methods, accessed from the other menu items, allow easy programmatic creation of objects without explicitly identifying the object's class.

Comments

The OLE control is particularly suited for business applications that act simultaneously as front ends to a number of common commercial applications such as word processors and databases.

6.4 How do I...
Assemble Documents with Word for Windows 6.0?

COMPLEXITY: ADVANCED
COMPATIBILITY: VB4 ONLY
REQUIRES: WORD FOR WINDOWS 6.0

Problem

Word for Windows 6.0 provides lots of options and power for assembling documents, but none of them provides an elegant user interface for data entry. Visual Basic lets me look up data in a database and lets me create great-looking data entry forms. How can I combine the best of Word for Windows 6.0 and the best of Visual Basic 4.0, to create an awesome document-assembly application?

Technique

The project in this How-To takes a document-centric approach to document assembly. Users can work within Word for Windows 6.0 to create a new document based on a template. That template, which is programmed using Word Basic, drives the document assembly process. The Visual Basic application merely delivers data entry forms when requested by the document template.

To make this approach work, Word communicates with Visual Basic using dynamic data exchange (DDE). Visual Basic returns data to Word using OLE Automation. Since OLE Automation is the intended replacement for DDE, why not use it for all the communications? Unfortunately, Word for Windows cannot use OLE Automation to access objects in other applications. However, other applications that support OLE Automation—including Visual Basic 4.0—can use OLE Automation to access the Word Basic object. In other words, Word for Windows can act as an OLE Automation Server for another application, but it cannot act as an OLE Automation Client.

Steps

Figure 6-4-1 shows the document assembly project at work. To try it out, copy CONTRACT.DOT from the directory where you installed this How-To into your Word for Windows 6.0 \TEMPLATE subdirectory. You may need to modify the template before running it, so start Word for Windows and open up CONTRACT.DOT. Choose ToolsMacro, select the CONTRACT.DOT AutoNew macro, and click Edit.

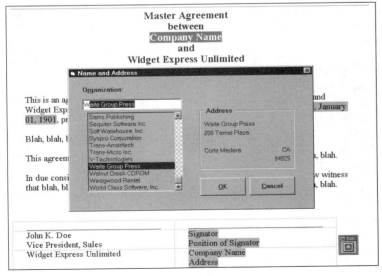

Figure 6-4-1 The document assembler in action

Near the top of the macro, change

```
ChDir "c:\vb4ht\chap6\6.4"
```

to the subdirectory where you installed this How-To. Choose the Win32 subdirectory or the Win16 subdirectory depending on your operating system. Save and close the template, and you're ready to assemble a document. Use the executable created through this project.

Begin Document Assembly

In Word for Windows, select File|New, and choose Contract from the list of templates. You'll see a welcome box appear, asking you to wait while the data is retrieved from the database, and reminding you to Tab from field to field. (Tabbing is the way Word for Windows controls data entry in a protected document with form fields—that is, a Form.)

Name and Address Data-Entry

After some time (more about that later), the document changes to a full-screen display, and a Name and Address data-entry form appears on top of the document. Click on the Word document and notice that it is locked until you click Cancel or select a name and click OK. More about that later, too.

For now, just choose a name and click OK. Watch how fields in the document that you're assembling are updated with the organization name, address, city, state, and zip code.

Document Dates Data-Entry

Press Tab to move to the next form field that's enabled for input. A Document Dates data entry form appears which you can use to enter Effective and Expiration dates. These dates are required when assembling almost any sort of contract. If you experiment with data entry here, you'll see that the data-entry application makes sure you enter valid dates in a range acceptable to Word, and that the effective date is earlier than the expiration date.

Signature Data-Entry

Click OK when you've entered a set of dates, and watch the dates appear in the document. Then press Tab to move to the next form field. A Company Signator data entry form appears. Use it to enter the name and title of the person designated to sign the contract for the organization. When you click OK, you'll see your entries appear in appropriate places in the document.

Finish Document Assembly

Press Tab one more time, and you'll see a message box telling you that the document is ready to edit, print, or save. At this point, the document is unprotected,

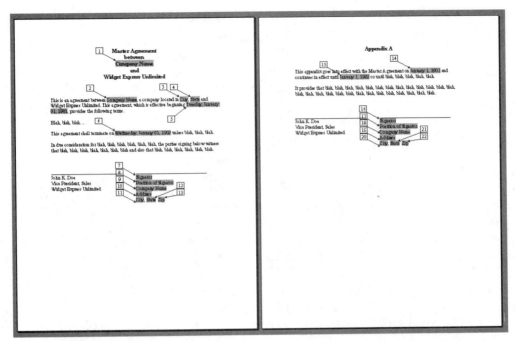

Figure 6-4-2 The CONTRACT.DOT document template, with form fields identified by number

allowing you to change text (even the form fields). The automated document-assembly process is complete.

Follow these steps to build this document assembler yourself.

1. Create a Word for Windows 6.0 template called CONTRACT.DOT. Enter text as shown in Figure 6-4-2 which also identifies the template's form fields. Using Figure 6-4-2 as a guide, set form fields and properties as shown in Table 6-4-1, and save the template.

Table 6-4-1 Fields and properties for CONTRACT.DOT form

FIELD NUMBER	PROPERTY	SETTING
1	Bookmark	CompanyName1
	DefaultText	Company Name
	EntryMacro	GetNameAndAddress
	Fill-inEnabled	Yes

Continued on next page

Continued from previous page

FIELD NUMBER	PROPERTY	SETTING
	Type	Regular Text
2	Bookmark	CompanyName2
	DefaultText	Company Name
	Fill-inEnabled	No
	Type	Regular Text
3	Bookmark	City1
	DefaultText	City
	Fill-inEnabled	No
	Type	Regular Text
4	Bookmark	State1
	DefaultText	State
	Fill-inEnabled	No
	Type	Regular Text
5	Bookmark	EffectiveDate1
	DateFormat	dddd, MMMM dd, yyyy
	DefaultDate	Tuesday, January 01, 1901
	EntryMacro	GetDates
	Fill-inEnabled	Yes
	Type	Date
6	Bookmark	ExpirationDate1
	DateFormat	dddd, MMMM dd, yyyy
	DefaultDate	Wednesday, January 02, 1901
	Fill-inEnabled	No
	Type	Date
7	Bookmark	Signator1
	DefaultText	Signator
	EntryMacro	GetSignatorInfo
	Fill-inEnabled	Yes
	Type	Regular Text
8	Bookmark	Position1
	DefaultText	Position of Signator
	Fill-inEnabled	No
	Type	Regular Text
9	Bookmark	CompanyName3
	DefaultText	Company Name
	Fill-inEnabled	No
	Type	Regular Text
10	Bookmark	Address1
	DefaultText	Address

FIELD NUMBER	PROPERTY	SETTING
	Fill-inEnabled	No
	Type	Regular Text
11	Bookmark	City2
	DefaultText	City
	Fill-inEnabled	No
	Type	Regular Text
12	Bookmark	State2
	DefaultText	State
	Fill-inEnabled	No
	Type	Regular Text
13	Bookmark	Zip1
	DefaultText	Zip
	Fill-inEnabled	No
	Type	Regular Text
14	Bookmark	EffectiveDate2
	DateFormat	MMMM d, yyyy
	DefaultDate	Tuesday, January 01, 1901
	Fill-inEnabled	No
	Type	Date
15	Bookmark	ExpirationDate2
	DateFormat	MMMM d, yyyy
	DefaultDate	Wednesday, January 02, 1901
	Fill-inEnabled	No
	Type	Date
16	Bookmark	Signator2
	DefaultText	Signator
	Fill-inEnabled	No
	Type	Regular Text
17	Bookmark	Position2
	DefaultText	Position of Signator
	Fill-inEnabled	No
	Type	Regular Text
18	Bookmark	CompanyName4
	DefaultText	Company Name
	Fill-inEnabled	No
	Type	Regular Text
19	Bookmark	Address2
	DefaultText	Address
	Fill-inEnabled	No

Continued on next page

Continued from previous page

FIELD NUMBER	PROPERTY	SETTING
	Type	Regular Text
20	Bookmark	City3
	DefaultText	City
	Fill-inEnabled	No
	Type	Regular Text
21	Bookmark	State3
	DefaultText	State
	Fill-inEnabled	No
	Type	Regular Text
22	Bookmark	Zip2
	DefaultText	Zip
	Fill-inEnabled	No
	Type	Regular Text

2. Create the following Word Basic macro and name it AutoNew:

```
Sub MAIN
'
' Launch VB Document Assembly program unless it's already run
' ning which it could be during a test run.
'
Message$ = "Welcome to document assembly for this contract. "
Message$ = Message$ + Chr$(13) + Chr$(10) + Chr$(13) + Chr$(10)
Message$ = Message$ + "Please be patient while names and "
Message$ = Message$ + "addresses " + Chr$(13) + Chr$(10)
Message$ = Message$ + "are retrieved from the database. "
Message$ = Message$ + Chr$(13) + Chr$(10) + Chr$(13) + Chr$(10)
Message$ = Message$ + "Also, remember to use the tab key to move"
Message$ = Message$ + Chr$(13) + Chr$(10)
Message$ = Message$ + " to each form field."
MsgBox Message$
If Not AppIsRunning("Document Assembly Transaction Center") Then
    ChDir "c:\vb4ht\chap6\6.4"
    Shell "DOCASMBY.EXE Word"
End If
'
' Take over the entire screen and protect the form.
'
ScreenUpdating 0
ViewNormal
ViewZoom .ZoomPercent = 100
ToggleFull
ScreenUpdating 1
DocMaximize 1
If CommandValid("ToolsUnprotectDocument") = 0 Then
    ToolsProtectDocument .DocumentPassword = "", .Type = 2
End If
'
```

```
' Initialize VB form status variables. Then perform routine
' to show VB Name and Address form.
'
NameAndAddressForm$ = "Not Done"
DocumentDatesForm$ = "Not Done"
SignatorForm$ = "Not Done"
GetNameAndAddress
End Sub
```

An AutoNew macro automatically runs every time a new document is created
from the template. This procedure displays a message box containing basic information and instructions. Then it launches the executable for our sample program.
It uses as much screen real estate as possible for displaying the new document. It
also protects the form document so that users can only Tab to the fill-in-enabled
form fields. This template is designed to show three separate Visual Basic forms
from our sample application, so it initializes variables to indicate that data entry
is incomplete for each of these forms. At the startup of a Word form document,
the cursor is located at the beginning of the first fill-in enabled form field—
Company Name in our example. So the last thing this macro does is to perform
the Word Basic macro, GetNameAndAddress, which is the On Entry macro associated with the Company Name form field. It is triggered automatically when the
user tabs to the Company Name form field.

3. Create the following WordBasic macro and name it GetNameAndAddress.
   Assuming the document assembly processing is not yet complete, this procedure
   sets parameters to request a data entry form for entering name and address information. Then it triggers another macro that carries the request forward to our
   Visual Basic program. If document assembly is complete, a different macro is triggered to do some wrap-up processing.

```
Sub MAIN
    '
    ' If data gathering complete for all of the forms, then
    ' perform the WrapUp subroutine. Otherwise request the
    ' NameAndAddressForm from Visual Basic.
    '
    If DocAssembly.IsDone = 0 Then
        MyApplication$ = "DocAsmby"
        MyTopic$ = "TransactionCenterForm"
        MyCommand$ = "NameAndAddressForm"
        Call DocAssembly.FormRequest(MyApplication$, MyTopic$, MyCommand$)
    Else
        DocAssembly.WrapUp
    End If
End Sub
```

4. Create the following WordBasic macro and name it GetDates. Assuming the document assembly processing is not yet complete, this procedure sets parameters to
   request a data entry form for entering document dates. Then it triggers another

macro that carries the request forward to our Visual Basic program. If document assembly is complete, a different macro is triggered to do some wrap-up processing.

```
Sub MAIN
    '
    ' If data gathering complete for all of the forms, then
    ' perform the WrapUp subroutine. Otherwise request the
    ' DocumentDatesForm from Visual Basic.
    '
    If DocAssembly.IsDone = 0 Then
        MyApplication$ = "DocAsmby"
        MyTopic$ = "TransactionCenterForm"
        MyCommand$ = "DocumentDatesForm"
        Call DocAssembly.FormRequest(MyApplication$, MyTopic$, MyCommand$)
    Else
        DocAssembly.WrapUp
    End If
End Sub
```

5. Create the following WordBasic macro and name it GetSignatorInfo. Assuming the document assembly processing is not yet complete, this procedure sets parameters to request a data entry form for entering information about the document signer. Then it triggers another macro that carries the request forward to our Visual Basic program. If document assembly is complete, a different macro is triggered to do some wrap-up processing.

```
Sub MAIN
    '
    ' If data gathering complete for all of the forms, then
    ' perform the WrapUp subroutine. Otherwise request the
    ' SignatorForm from Visual Basic.
    '
    If DocAssembly.IsDone = 0 Then
        MyApplication$ = "DocAsmby"
        MyTopic$ = "TransactionCenterForm"
        MyCommand$ = "SignatorForm"
        Call DocAssembly.FormRequest(MyApplication$, MyTopic$, MyCommand$)
    Else
        DocAssembly.WrapUp
    End If
End Sub
```

6. Create the following WordBasic macro and name it DocAssembly. It provides a space for creating three general document-assembly functions, which will be described in steps 7 through 9.

```
Sub MAIN
End Sub
```

7. Place the following WordBasic subroutine immediately following the MAIN subroutine in the DocAssembly macro. This procedure sends a DDE request to the hidden Visual Basic TransactionCenterForm. MyCommand$ tells which data entry form should be displayed by the TransactionCenterForm. This routine also

ensures there is only one attempt to send the ShutDown request—after all, there's no point in sending a DDE request to a program you've just told to shut down!

```
Sub     FormRequest(MyApplication$, MyTopic$, MyCommand$)
        '
        ' Send form request, but don't send ShutDown request more
        ' than once.
        '
        On Error Resume Next
        If AppIsRunning("Document Assembly Transaction Center") Then
                If ShutDownStatus$ <> "Sent" Then
                        MyChanNum = DDEInitiate(MyApplication$, MyTopic$)
                        DDEExecute MyChanNum, MyCommand$
                        DDETerminate MyChanNum
                End If
        End If
        If MyCommand$ = "ShutDown" Then
                ShutDownStatus$ = "Sent"
        End If
End Sub
```

8. Place the following Word Basic subroutine immediately following the FormRequest subroutine in the DocAssembly macro. When data has been entered on all three of the Visual Basic data entry forms, this wrap-up procedure requests that the Visual Basic program be shut down and unprotects the document to allow user edits.

```
Sub WrapUp
        '
        ' When done, unprotect document for further editing and
        ' send DDE message to shutdown VB Document Assembly program.
        '
        ToolsUnprotectDocument
        MsgBox "Document is ready to edit, print, or save!"
        MyApplication$ = "DocAsmby"
        MyTopic$ = "TransactionCenterForm"
        MyCommand$ = "ShutDown"
        Call FormRequest(MyApplication$, MyTopic$, MyCommand$)
End Sub
```

9. Place the following WordBasic subroutine immediately following the WrapUp subroutine in the DocAssembly macro. This function checks variables to see if data entry via Visual Basic forms is complete for all of the forms. When all three forms are complete, it sets IsDone to True (-1).

```
Function IsDone
        '
        ' Set ISDone when data has been entered at least once for
        ' each of the data entry forms.
        '
        IsDone = 0
        If GetDocumentVar$("NameAndAddressForm") = "Done" Then
                If GetDocumentVar$("DocumentDatesForm") = "Done" Then
                        If GetDocumentVar$("SignatorForm") = "Done" Then
                                IsDone = - 1
```

Continued on next page

Continued from previous page

```
                        End If
                End If
        End If
End Function
```

10. Create a new project called DOCASMBY.VBP. Create a form and place controls as shown in Figure 6-4-3. Set form objects and properties as shown in Table 6-4-2, and save the form as TRANSCTR.VBP.

Table 6-4-2 TRANSCTR.FRM form properties

OBJECT	PROPERTY	SETTING
Form	Name	TransCenterForm
	Caption	"Document Assembly Transaction Center"
	LinkMode	1 'Source
	LinkTopic	"TransactionCenterForm"
Frame	Name	Frame1
	Caption	"Show Form"
OptionButton	Name	ShowOption
	Caption	"&Dates"
	Index	0
OptionButton	Name	ShowOption
	Caption	"&Name and Address"
	Index	1
OptionButton	Name	ShowOption
	Caption	"&Signator"
	Index	2
CommandButton	Name	OKButton
	Caption	"&OK"

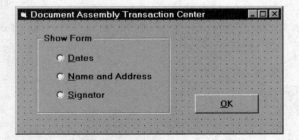

Figure 6-4-3 Document Assembly Transaction Center form

11. Place the following code at the beginning of the TRANSCTR.FRM. This variable stores the last command string sent via DDE by Word for Windows.

```
Option Explicit
'
' Variable to save the last LinkExecute command string set by
' Word for Windows.
'
Private LastLinkExecCmd As String
```

12. Place the following code in the Form_Load event procedure. This subroutine loads and hides each of the other application forms. So that it's easier to test the application stand-alone (without the Word for Windows interface), this procedure is programmed to stay visible when started without a command line argument.

```
Private Sub Form_Load()
    '
    ' Perform routines to load and hide the forms so they're
    ' ready when called for.
    '
    HideForm NameAndAddressForm
    HideForm DocumentDatesForm
    HideForm SignatorForm
    '
    ' When this program is started without a command line
    ' argument, show the transaction center form which allows
    ' picking other forms for testing.
    '
    If Command = "" Then
        Me.Visible = True
    Else
        Me.Visible = False
    End If
End Sub
```

13. Place the following code in the Form_LinkExecute event procedure. During a normal run, the document-assembly program is started by Word for Windows, and this subroutine is triggered when Word sends the form a command string via DDE. The command string indicates which form should be displayed for data capture, and the Form_LinkExecute routine acts as a transaction router by showing the requested form. When Word sends a request to shut down, nothing happens immediately, but the request is saved and acted upon as soon as Word follows with a command to terminate the DDE conversation.

```
Private Sub Form_LinkExecute(cmdStr As String, Cancel As Integer)
    '
    ' Save the command string sent by Word for Windows. Then show
    ' the form requested by Word. Skip the ShutDown command. It
    ' will be processed after Word sends the DDE terminate
    ' command. If Word sends an unexpected command string, set the
    ' Cancel parameter to let Word know the command string was not
```

Continued on next page

Continued from previous page

```
    ' acceptable.
    '
    LastLinkExecCmd = cmdStr
    Cancel = False
    Select Case cmdStr
    Case "NameAndAddressForm"
        ShowForm NameAndAddressForm
    Case "DocumentDatesForm"
        ShowForm DocumentDatesForm
    Case "SignatorForm"
        ShowForm SignatorForm
    Case "ShutDown"
    Case Else
        Cancel = True
    End Select
End Sub
```

14. Place the following code in the Form_LinkClose event procedure. Word for Windows follows up every LinkExecute command string with a command to terminate the DDE conversation, and the termination command triggers this subroutine. Normally, Form_Link Close has nothing to do; however, as soon as Word terminates the conversation after sending a command to shut down, this procedure releases all resources and reactivates Word before ending the program.

```
Private Sub Form_LinkClose()
    '
    ' Every time Word sends a command string via LinkExecute, it
    ' follows with a DDE terminate command which triggers this
    ' event procedure. If the last command string sent was to
    ' "ShutDown", this routine clears out everything and ends.
    '
    If LastLinkExecCmd = "ShutDown" Then
        Unload NameAndAddressForm
        Unload DocumentDatesForm
        Unload SignatorForm
        Unload Me
        Activate Word
        End
    End If
End Sub
```

15. Place the following code in the OKButton_Click event procedure. The OK button can only be clicked when this form is visible and therefore running as a stand alone test transaction center. This makes it easy to do concentrated testing of the other forms. When the OK button is clicked, this procedure shows (makes visible) the selected form.

```
Private Sub OKButton_Click()
    '
    ' This routine is only triggered in test when this form is
    ' visible and no communications are happening with Word.
    ' It loads a selected form for testing.
```

```
'
If ShowOption(0) = True Then
    ShowForm DocumentDatesForm
ElseIf ShowOption(1) = True Then
    ShowForm NameAndAddressForm
Else
    ShowForm SignatorForm
End If
End Sub
```

16. Use the File Add menu item to add the file named ADDRESS.FRM to DOCASM-BY.VBP. Set its ShowInTask Bar property to False. This form is developed in How-To 8.1, and you can add the code shown here in bold to the start of the module, in the Option Explicit section. A variable is created for storing the data entry field, NameEdit.

```
Option Explicit
'
' Declare QCombo class file. Save NameEdit text box value so it
' can be restored if cancel is pressed.
'
Dim QCombo As New CQCombo
Dim OrigNameEdit As String
```

17. Create a new Form_Activate event procedure, and add the following code to it. This form remains hidden until called for by Word. Each time it's made visible, the Form_Activate event is triggered. This procedure saves the text value in the data entry field, NameEdit, so it can be restored if the user selects a different name and then clicks the Cancel button.

```
Private Sub Form_Activate()
    '
    ' Save the value in the NameEdit text box every time the form
    ' activates so it can be restored if the cancel button is
    ' pressed.
    '
    OrigNameEdit = NameEdit
    NameEdit.SetFocus
End Sub
```

18. Add the line shown in bold to the NameEdit_GotFocus event procedure to set the Text value to the selected NameEdit value.

```
Private Sub NameEdit_Got Focus()
    '
    ' On first entry, synchronize organization list,
    ' address display, and edit control displays.
    '
    If Not Len(QCombo.EditControl.TEXT) Then
    MailingAddress.Recordset.FindFirst "OrgID="
                    & QCombo.RowSource.Recordset("OrgID")
```

Continued on next page

Continued from previous page

```
    QCombo.DisplayEdit QCombo.RowSource.Recordset("Name")
    QCombo.QList.TEXT=NameEdit
    End if
End Sub
```

19. Replace the OKButton_Click event procedure with the following code. Normally, this application is communicating with Word and needs to return data to Word when the OK button is clicked. After performing the ReturnDataToWord subroutine, it activates Word and hides itself.

```
Private Sub OKButton_Click()
    '
    'Return form values to Word, activate Word, and hide the form
    'so it can be reactivated quickly if it's reselected.
    '
    ReturnDataToWord Me
    ActivateWord
    HideForm Me
End Sub
```

20. Create a new public subroutine called SendValuesToWord, and place in it the following code. This subroutine is actually called from a common routine in the common module, VBWORD.BAS, that we'll examine later (step 52). When called, this procedure sends selected input and database lookup fields to the corresponding form fields located in the document being assembled in Word for Windows.

```
Public Sub SendValuesToWord()
    '
    ' This routine is triggered from within the ReturnDataToWord
    ' subroutine.
    '
    Dim AddressLines As String
    SendValueToWord "CompanyName1", NameDisplay.Caption
    SendValueToWord "CompanyName2", NameDisplay.Caption
    SendValueToWord "CompanyName3", NameDisplay.Caption
    SendValueToWord "CompanyName4", NameDisplay.Caption
    If AddressLine1 <> "" And AddressLine2 <> "" Then
        AddressLines = AddressLine1.Caption & Chr(11) & AddressLine2.Caption
    Else
        AddressLines = AddressLine1.Caption & AddressLine2.Caption
    End If
    SendValueToWord "Address1", AddressLines
    SendValueToWord "Address2", AddressLines
    SendValueToWord "City1", CityName.Caption
    SendValueToWord "City2", CityName.Caption
    SendValueToWord "City3", CityName.Caption
    SendValueToWord "State1", State.Caption
    SendValueToWord "State2", State.Caption
    SendValueToWord "State3", State.Caption
    SendValueToWord "Zip1", Zip.Caption
    SendValueToWord "Zip2", Zip.Caption
End Sub
```

21. Replace the CancelButton_Click event procedure with the following code. When the Cancel button is clicked, this subroutine restores the NameEdit value that was saved when the form activated. Then it synchronizes the other controls to match, before activating Word and hiding itself.

```
Private Sub CancelButton_Click()
    '
    ' Reset the text and list box settings to what they were when
    ' the form activated. Hide the form and let Word know the
    ' input was canceled.
    '
    NameEdit = OrigNameEdit
    QCombo.QList.Text = NameEdit
    QCombo.Synchronize
    MailingAddress.Recordset.FindFirst "OrgID = " _
                            & QCombo.RowSource.Recordset("OrgID")
    ActivateWord
    HideForm Me
End Sub
```

22. Use the File Add menu item to add the file named QCOMBO.CLS to DOCASM-BY.VBP. This class file, developed in How-To 8.1, supports the ADDRESS.FRM and requires no changes for this How-To.

23. Create a new form with controls arranged as shown in Figure 6-4-4. Set form objects and properties as shown in Table 6-4-3, and save the form as DOC-DATES.FRM.

Table 6-4-3 DOCDATES.FRM form properties

OBJECT	PROPERTY	SETTING
Form	Name	DocumentDatesForm
	Caption	"Document Dates"
	ShowInTaskBar	0 False
Label	Name	Label1
	Caption	"Effective Date:"
	Index	0
TextBox	Name	EffectiveDate
Label	Name	Label1
	Caption	"Expiration Date:"
	Index	1
TextBox	Name	ExpirationDate
CommandButton	Name	OKButton
	Caption	"&OK"
CommandButton	Name	CancelButton
	Caption	"&Cancel"

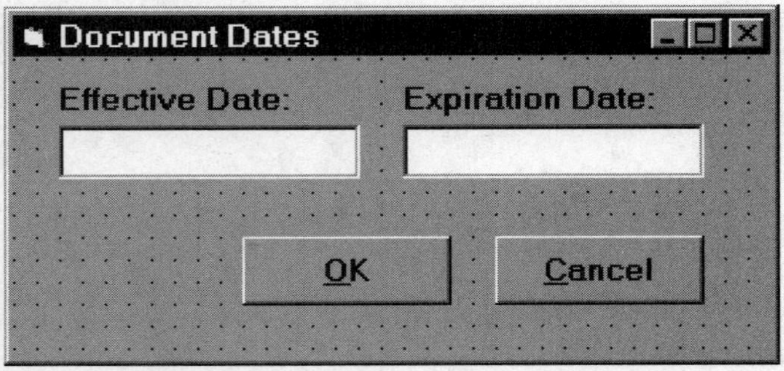

Figure 6-4-4 Document Dates data-entry form

24. Place the following code at the beginning of the DOCDATES.FRM. Variables are created to store the Effective and Expiration data entry fields. Also, a Dates object is created based on the CDates class filename.

```
Option Explicit
'
' Variables to save dates for restoration if Cancel clicked.
' Set Dates as object referece to CDates class file.
'
Dim OrigEffectiveDate As String
Dim OrigExpirationDate As String
Dim Dates As New CDates
```

25. Add the following code to the General section of the DocDatesForm, to center the form when it is loaded:

```
Private Sub Form_Load()
    '
    ' Center the form.
    '
    Move (Screen.Width - Width) \ 2, (Screen.Height - Height) \ 2
End Sub
```

26. Place the following code in the Form_Activate event procedure. This form remains hidden until called for by Word. Each time it's made visible, the Form_Activate event is triggered. This procedure saves the Effective and Expiration dates so they can be restored if the user enters new values and then clicks the Cancel button.

```
Private Sub Form_Activate()
    '
    ' Save the effective and expiration dates every time the form
    ' activates so they can be restored if the cancel button is
    ' pressed. Start with focus at the first text field.
    '
    OrigEffectiveDate = EffectiveDate
```

```
    OrigExpirationDate = ExpirationDate
    EffectiveDate.SetFocus
End Sub
```

27. Place the following code in the EffectiveDate_GotFocus event procedure, to high-
    light the value in the text box when it gets the focus:

```
Private Sub EffectiveDate_GotFocus()
    '
    ' Highlight the text for easy replacement when the field gets
    ' the focus.
    '
    HighlightText EffectiveDate
End Sub
```

28. Place the following code in the EffectiveDate_LostFocus event procedure. (You
    may want to review How-To 3.13 for the trials and tribulations of dealing with
    lost focus events.) Assuming the lost focus wasn't triggered by a click on the
    Cancel button, this subroutine executes a ValidDate function to confirm that the
    value input was, in fact, a valid date.

```
Private Sub EffectiveDate_LostFocus()
    '
    ' If the Cancel button was just clicked, don't bother checking
    ' for valid data.
    '
    If Me.ActiveControl.Name = "CancelButton" Then
        Exit Sub
    End If
    '
    ' Common routine will validate and format the data or reset
    ' focus to the date field if it's not valid.
    '
    If Not ValidDate(EffectiveDate) Then
        MsgBox "Word handles dates from 1/1/1901 through 12/31/4095", _
            0, "Date Validation"
    End If
End Sub
```

29. Place the following code in the ExpirationDate_GotFocus event procedure, to
    highlight the value in the text box when it gets the focus:

```
Private Sub ExpirationDate_GotFocus()
    '
    ' Highlight the text for easy replacement when the field gets
    ' the focus.
    '
    HighlightText ExpirationDate
End Sub
```

30. Place the following code in the ExpirationDate_LostFocus event procedure. This
    subroutine makes sure the lost focus wasn't triggered by a click on the Cancel

button. It also avoids a recursive loop as noted in the commented code. (If you skipped the prior advice to review How-To 3.13 regarding lost focus, please do it now!) For a "legitimate" lost-focus event, this subroutine executes a ValidDate function to confirm that the value input was, in fact, a valid date.

```
Private Sub ExpirationDate_LostFocus()
    '
    ' If the Cancel button was just clicked, don't bother checking
    ' for valid data.
    '
    If Me.ActiveControl.Name = "CancelButton" Then
        Exit Sub
    End If
    '
    ' To keep from getting in a recursive loop started by tabbing
    ' here from an invalid effective date, don't try to validate
    ' expiration date until you know that effective date is valid.
    '
    If Not ValidDate(EffectiveDate) Then
        EffectiveDate.SetFocus
        Exit Sub
    End If
    '
    ' Common routine will validate and format the data or reset
    ' focus to the date field if it's not valid.
    '
    If Not ValidDate(ExpirationDate) Then
        MsgBox "Word handles dates from 1/1/1901 through " _
            & "12/31/4095", 0, "Date Validation"
    End If
End Sub
```

31. Create a HighlightText subroutine and place the following code in it. This procedure highlights the value in whatever control is passed to it. Of course, this will not be meaningful for every type of control, but in this form we're only passing in TextBox controls.

```
Private Sub HighlightText(ThisControl As Control)
    '
    ' Highlight the entire selection for the control.
    '
    ThisControl.SelStart = 0
    ThisControl.SelLength = Len(ThisControl)
End Sub
```

32. Create a ValidDate function and place the following code in it. This procedure ensures that the control contains a date in the range that Word for Windows can handle. If the date is invalid, focus is returned to the control and the value is highlighted. A special note: Word for Windows 6.0's documentation implies that it handles a date as early as 12/30/1899; in fact, it chokes on any value less than 1/1/1901.

```
Private Function ValidDate(ThisControl As Control) _
    As Boolean
    '
    ' If the control's default value is a date in the range that
    ' Word can handle, format it. Otherwise return focus to the
    ' control.
    '
    If IsDate(ThisControl) Then
        If CDate(ThisControl) >= CDate("1/1/1901") _
        And CDate(ThisControl) <= CDate("12/31/4095") Then
            ThisControl = Format$(ThisControl, "mm/dd/yyyy")
            ValidDate = True
            Exit Function
        End If
    End If
    ThisControl.SetFocus
    HighlightText ThisControl
    ValidDate = False
End Function
```

33. Place the following code in the OKButton_Click event procedure. First, it calls a class module's Dates.Compare function to make sure the Effective date is earlier than the Expiration date, and to return focus to the EffectiveDate text box if it's not. Normally, this application is communicating with Word for Windows. If the dates cross-check correctly, and when the program is communicating with Word, it needs to return the dates to Word when the OK button is clicked. After performing the ReturnDataToWord subroutine, it reactivates Word and hides itself.

```
Private Sub OKButton_Click()
    '
    ' Cross check dates and return focus to effective date if
    ' necessary.
    '
    If Not Dates.Compare(EffectiveDate, ExpirationDate, "LT") Then
        MsgBox "Effective date not less than Expiration Date", _
            0, "Date Validation"
        EffectiveDate.SetFocus
        Exit Sub
    End If
    '
    ' Return form values to Word, activate Word, and hide the Form
    ' so it can be reactivated quickly if it's reselected.
    '
    ReturnDataToWord Me
    ActivateWord
    HideForm Me
End Sub
```

34. Create a new public subroutine called SendValuesToWord, and place in it the following code. Like its corresponding routine in the NameAndAddressForm, this subroutine is actually called from a common routine in the common module, VBWORD.BAS (see step 52). When called, this procedure sends the Effective and

Expiration dates to the corresponding form fields located in the document being assembled in Word for Windows.

```
Public Sub SendValuesToWord()
    '
    ' This routine is triggered from within the ReturnDataToWord
    ' subroutine.
    '
    SendValueToWord "EffectiveDate1", EffectiveDate.Text
    SendValueToWord "EffectiveDate2", EffectiveDate.Text
    SendValueToWord "ExpirationDate1", ExpirationDate.Text
    SendValueToWord "ExpirationDate2", ExpirationDate.Text
End Sub
```

35. Place the following code in the CancelButton_Click event procedure. When the Cancel button is clicked, this subroutine restores the Effective and Expiration dates to the values that were saved when the form activated. Then it reactivates Word and hides itself.

```
Private Sub CancelButton_Click()
    '
    ' Reset the effective and expiration dates to what they were
    ' when the form activated. Hide the form and let Word know the
    ' input was canceled.
    '
    EffectiveDate = OrigEffectiveDate
    ExpirationDate = OrigExpirationDate
    ActivateWord
    HideForm Me
End Sub
```

36. Place the following code in the Form_Unload event procedure, to release all resources associated with the form when it is unloaded.

```
Private Sub Form_Unload(Cancel As Integer)
    '
    ' Release resources.
    '
    Set Dates = Nothing
    Set DocumentDatesForm = Nothing
End Sub
```

37. Use the File Add menu item to add the file named DATES.CLS to DOCASMBY.VBP. The routine used in this class file is explained in How-To 9.2. It supports the DOCDATES.FRM and requires no changes for this How-To.

38. Create a new form with controls arranged as shown in Figure 6-4-5. Set form objects and properties as shown in Table 6-4-4, and save the form as SIGNER.FRM.

Table 6-4-4 SIGNER.FRM form properties

OBJECT	PROPERTY	SETTING
Form	Name	SignatorForm
	Caption	"Company Signator"
	ShowInTaskBar	0 'False
Label	Name	Label1
	Caption	"Signator:"
	Index	0
TextBox	Name	SignatorText
Label	Name	Label1
	Caption	"Position:"
	Index	1
TextBox	Name	PositionText
CommandButton	Name	OKButton
	Caption	"&OK"
CommandButton	Name	CancelButton
	Caption	"&Cancel"

39. Place the following code at the beginning of the SIGNER.FRM. Variables are created to store the data entry fields.

```
Option Explicit
'
' Variables to save signer and title for restoration if Cancel
' clicked.
'
Dim OrigSignator As String
Dim OrigPosition As String
```

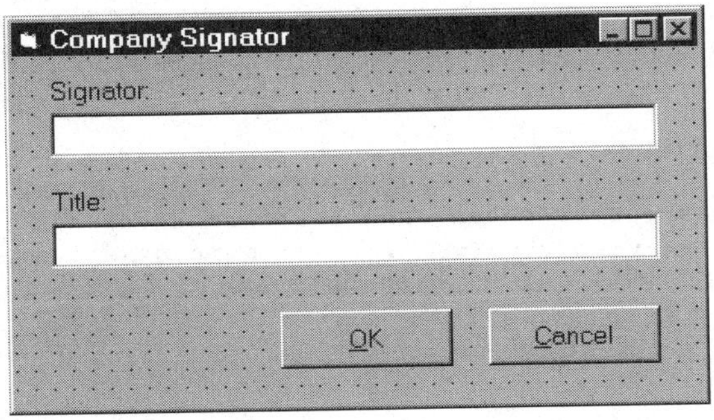

Figure 6-4-5 Company Signator data-entry form

40. Add the following code to the General section of the SignerForm, to center the form when it is loaded.

```
Private Sub Form_Load()
    '
    ' Center the form.
    '
    Move (Screen.Width - Width) \ 2, (Screen.Height - Height) \ 2
End Sub
```

41. Place the following code in the Form_Activate event procedure. This form remains hidden until called for by Word. Each time it's made visible, the Form_Activate event is triggered. This procedure saves the Signator and Position text box values so they can be restored if the user enters new values and then clicks the Cancel button.

```
Private Sub Form_Activate()
    '
    ' Save the signer and title every time the form activates so
    ' they can be restored if the cancel button is pressed. Start
    ' with focus at the first text field.
    '
    OrigSignator = SignatorText
    OrigPosition = PositionText
    SignatorText.SetFocus
End Sub
```

42. Place the following code in the SignatorText_GotFocus event procedure, to highlight the value in the text box when it gets the focus:

```
Private Sub SignatorText_GotFocus()
    '
    ' Highlight the text for easy replacement when the field gets
    ' the focus.
    '
    Call HighlightText(SignatorText)
End Sub
```

43. Place the following code in the SignatorText_LostFocus event procedure. Assuming the lost focus wasn't triggered by a click on the Cancel button, this subroutine executes a common ValidateText subroutine.

```
Private Sub SignatorText_LostFocus()
    '
    ' If the Cancel button was just clicked, don't bother checking
    ' for valid data. Otherwise validate the text which returns
    ' focus to the text box if nothing has been entered.
    '
    If Me.ActiveControl.Name = "CancelButton" Then
        Exit Sub
    End If
    ValidateText SignatorText
End Sub
```

44. Place the following code in the PositionText_GotFocus event procedure, to highlight the value in the text box when it gets the focus:

```
Private Sub PositionText_GotFocus()
    '
    ' Highlight the text for easy replacement when the field gets
    ' the focus.
    '
    HighlightText PositionText
End Sub
```

45. Place the following code in the PositionText_LostFocus event procedure. This subroutine makes sure the lost focus wasn't triggered by a click on the Cancel button. It also avoids a recursive loop, as noted in the commented code. For a "legitimate" lost focus event, this subroutine will execute a common ValidText subroutine.

```
Private Sub PositionText_LostFocus()
    '
    ' If the Cancel button was just clicked, don't bother checking
    ' for valid data.
    '
    If Me.ActiveControl.Name = "CancelButton" Then
        Exit Sub
    End If
    '
    ' To keep from getting in a recursive loop started by tabbing
    ' here from an empty signator field, don't try to validate
    ' position field until you know that signator field is valid.
    '
    If SignatorText = "" Then
        SignatorText.SetFocus
    Else
        ValidateText PositionText
    End If
End Sub
```

46. Create a HighlightText subroutine and place the following code in it. This procedure highlights the value in whatever control is passed to it.

```
Private Sub HighlightText(ThisControl As Control)
    '
    ' Highlight the entire selection for the control.
    '
    ThisControl.SelStart = 0
    ThisControl.SelLength = Len(ThisControl)
End Sub
```

47. Create a ValidateText subroutine and place the following code in it. This procedure checks to see that some text was entered; if not, focus returns the control in question.

```
Sub ValidateText(ThisControl As Control)
    '
    ' If the control's default value is not set, pop up a
    ' message box about the problem and return focus to the
    ' control.
    '
    If ThisControl.Text = "" Then
        MsgBox "Please enter text in this box", _
            0, "Text Validation"
        ThisControl.SetFocus
    End If
End Sub
```

48. Place the following code in the OKButton_Click event procedure. This procedure first makes sure that both text fields are filled in, returning focus to one or the other if necessary. Normally, this application is communicating with Word for Windows. When it is, it needs to return the Signator and Position values to Word when the OK button is clicked. After performing the ReturnDataToWord subroutine, it reactivates Word and hides itself.

```
Private Sub OKButton_Click()
    '
    ' Make sure both the signer and the title fields are filled in
    ' before continuing.
    '
    If SignatorText = "" Then
        MsgBox "Signator must be entered.", 0, "Text Validation"
        SignatorText.SetFocus
        Exit Sub
    End If
    If PositionText = "" Then
        MsgBox "Position must be entered.", 0, "Text Validation"
        PositionText.SetFocus
        Exit Sub
    End If
    '
    ' Return values to Word, activate Word, and hide the form
    ' so it can be reactivated quickly if it's reselected.
    '
    ReturnDataToWord Me
    ActivateWord
    HideForm Me
End Sub
```

49. Create a new public subroutine called SendValuesToWord, and place in it the following code. Like the corresponding routines in the NameAndAddressForm and the DocumentDatesForm, this subroutine is actually called from a common routine in the common module, VBWORD.BAS (see step 52). When called, this procedure sends the Signator and Position values to the corresponding form fields located in the document being assembled in Word for Windows.

```
Public Sub SendValuesToWord()
    '
    ' This routine is triggered from within the ReturnDataToWord
    ' subroutine.
    '
    SendValueToWord "Signator1", SignatorText.Text
    SendValueToWord "Signator2", SignatorText.Text
    SendValueToWord "Position1", PositionText.Text
    SendValueToWord "Position2", PositionText.Text
End Sub
```

50. Place the following code in the CancelButton_Click event procedure. When the Cancel button is clicked, this subroutine restores the Signator and Position values to the values that were saved when the form activated. Then it reactivates Word and hides itself.

```
Private Sub CancelButton_Click()
    '
    ' Reset the Signator and Position text boxes to what they were
    ' when the form activated. Hide the form and let Word know the
    ' input was canceled.
    '
    SignatorText = OrigSignator
    PositionText = OrigPosition
    ActivateWord
    HideForm Me
End Sub
```

51. Place the following code in the Form_Unload event procedure, to release resources associated with the form when the form is unloaded:

```
Private Sub Form_Unload(Cancel As Integer)
    '
    ' Release resources.
    '
    Set SignatorForm = Nothing
End Sub
```

52. Use the Insert Module menu item to create a new code module and save it as VBWORD.BAS. This module is for routines of general use to document assembly applications where Word for Windows and Visual Basic are communicating.

```
Option Explicit
'
' Establish an object for OLE Automation using Word Basic.
'
Public objWordBasic As Object
```

53. Add the following variable, constant, and declarations to the General Declarations section of VBWORD.BAS to provide the functions needed to make this application's data entry forms modal to Word for Windows.

```
'
' Declare Variables, Constants, and Windows API functions
' needed to make this application's forms owned by
' Word for Windows and modal to Word.
'
Private WinWordhWnd As Long
Private Const GWL_HWNDPARENT=(-8)
#If Win32 Then
    Declare Function FindWindow Lib "user32"_
        Alias "FindWindowA"_
        (ByVal lpClassName As String,_
        ByVal lpWindowName As String)
    As Long
    Declare Function SetWindowLong Lib "user32"_
        Alias "SetWindowLongA"_
        (ByVal hWnd As Long,_
        ByVal nIndex As Long,_
        ByVal dwNewLong As Long)_
    As Long
    Declare Function Enable Window Lib "user32"_
        (ByVal hWnd As Long,_
        ByVal fEnable As Long)_
#Else
    Declare Function FindWindow Lib "User"_
        (ByVal lpClassName As Any,_
        ByVal lpWindowName As Any)_
    As Integer
    Declare Function SetWindowLong Lib "User"_
        (ByVal hWnd As Integer,_
        ByVal nIndex As Integer_
        By Val dwNewLong As Long)_
    As Long
    Declare Function EnableWindow Lib "User"_
        (ByVal hWnd As Integer,_
        ByVal aBOOL As Integer)_
    As Integer
#End If
```

54. Create a ShowForm subroutine by adding the following code to the General section of VBWord. When Word for Windows is controlling document assembly in a normal (nontesting) way, it passes "Word" as a command-line argument when it launches this Visual Basic application. This is the normal situation and it tells the subroutine to make Word the "owner" of the Visual Basic application and to disable Word. This has the effect of making the Form Modal to Word.

```
Public Sub ShowForm(AnyForm As Form)
    '
    ' If there is no command line argument, this program
    ' is running in pure VB test mode, and the Word-specific
    ' portions of this routine should be skipped.
    '
    If Command = "" Then
        AnyForm.Show
        Exit Sub
```

```
      End If
      '
      ' Show the form after making it the child of Word for Windows.
      ' Make the form modal to WinWord by disabling WinWord while
      ' the form is in control.
      '
      WinWordhWnd = FindWindow("OpusApp",vbNullString)
      SetWindowLong AnyForm.hWnd, GWL_HWNDPARENT, WinWordhWnd
      AnyForm.Show
      EnableWindow WinWordhWnd, False
End Sub
```

55. Create a HideForm subroutine by adding the following code to the General section of VBWord. When appropriate, this subroutine removes Word's ownership of the form before hiding it.

```
Public Sub HideForm(AnyForm As Form)
      '
      ' If there is no command line argument, this program
      ' is running in pure VB test mode, and the Word-specific
      ' portion of this routine should be skipped.
      '
      If Command = "" Then
         AnyForm.Show
         Exit Sub
      End If
      '
      ' Remove child/parent relationship between form and Word
      ' for Windows before hiding the form.
      '
      SetWindowLong AnyForm.hWnd, GWL_HWNDPARENT, 0
      AnyForm.Hide
End Sub
```

56. Create a CreateWordBasicObject subroutine by adding the following code to the General section of VBWord, to create an OLE Automation object for the Word for Windows Word.Basic object. This one simple line is all it takes for Visual Basic to obtain access to nearly all of the Word Basic commands available in Word for Windows 6.0.

```
Public Sub CreateWordBasicObject()
      '
      ' Create the OLE Automation object, Word Basic.
      '
      Set objWordBasic = CreateObject("Word.Basic")
End Sub
```

57. Create a ReturnDataToWord subroutine by adding the following code to the General section of VBWord. This subroutine is executed from each of the data entry forms when the OK button is clicked. It performs the SendValuesToWord routine found in the form being processed. These commonly named routines are actually coded to take the values unique to the data values on each form and

return them as form fields in Word. After returning values, the routine sets a Word variable to indicate that data entry is complete for that form.

```
Public Sub ReturnDataToWord(AnyForm, Status As String)
    '
    ' If the command line argument doesn't begin with "Word ",
    ' program is running in pure VB test mode, and this routine
    ' should be skipped.
    '
    If Command = "" Then Exit Sub
    '
    ' Send form's unique values to Word then set a variable
    ' in the Word document to indicate that this Form's portion
    ' of the data collection is done.
    '
    CreateWordBasicObject
    AnyForm.SendValuesToWord
    Dim DocVar As String
    DocVar = Screen.ActiveForm.Name
    objWordBasic.SetDocumentVar$ DocVar, "Done"
    EndWordBasicObject
End Sub
```

58. Create an ActivateWord subroutine by adding the following code to the General section of VBWord. This subroutine re-enables Word for Windows before reactivating it. This allows the user to continue assembling the document.

```
Sub ActivateWord()
    '
    ' If the command line argument doesn't begin with "Word",
    ' program is running in pure VB test mode, and this routine
    ' should be skipped.
    '
    If Command = "" Then Exit Sub
    '
    ' Before activating Word, Reenable it. It gets disabled to make
    ' this application's forms function as modal to Word when they
    ' are visible).
    '
    EnableWindow WinWordhWnd, True
    CreateWordBasicObject
    If objWordBasic,DocMaximize() = True Then
        AppActivate "Microsoft Word - " + objWordBasic.[WindowName$]()
    Else
        AppActivate "Microsoft Word"
    End If
    EndWordBasicObject
End Sub
```

59. Create a SendValuesToWord subroutine by adding the following code to the General section of VBWord. This subroutine is executed by each of the data entry forms—once for each Word form field requiring data. SetFormResult is a

command new to Word for Windows 6.0. As its name implies, it is used to set the form field value in a protected Word form document.

```
Public Sub SendValuesToWord(WordFieldName As String, _
                            WordFieldValue As Variant)
    '
    ' Each form that sends values to Word has a routine called
    ' SendValuesToWord. It executes this routine as many times
    ' as is needed to send it's values to every corresponding Word
    ' field.
    '
    objWordBasic.SetFormResult WordFieldName, WordFieldValue
End Sub
```

60. Create an EndWordBasicObject subroutine by adding the following code to the General section of VBWord. This simply releases resources when the Word.Basic OLE automation object is not in use.

```
Public Sub EndWordBasicObject()
    '
    ' Destroy the OLE Automation object, Word Basic.
    '
    Set objWordBasic = Nothing
End Sub
```

How It Works

In this How-To you saw how to use Word Basic to drive a document-assembly process from within a document template in Word for Windows 6.0. The document template in this example is designed to protect the standard text in a sample contractual agreement. Until the document is completely assembled, the template allows data entry only in unprotected form fields. When you create a new document based on a protected form template, it will have the same protection as the template.

Sending Commands to Visual Basic

An AutoExec macro is associated with the sample contract template. The macro launches the corresponding Visual Basic application which will run hidden until the template requests a data entry form. The AutoExec macro triggers the first request to show a form by executing another Word Basic macro, GetNameAndAddress.

GetNameAndAddress sets DDE parameters for the application, topic, and command. Specifically, it sets the application to DocAsmby, the name of the hidden Visual Basic application; it sets the topic to TransactionCenterForm, the value of the LinkTopic property for a Visual Basic form that controls display of the data entry forms; and it sets the command string to NameAndAddressForm, the desired data entry form. The Word Basic command, DDEExecute, is required to send a command string via DDE to another application. This command triggers the TransactionCenterForm's LinkExecute event procedure.

Handling Commands from Word for Windows

In the transaction center's LinkExecute procedure is a Case statement that checks the DDE command string to see what work Word is requesting—in this case, the Name and Address data entry form.

Making Forms Modal to Word

The Visual Basic ShowForm subroutine shows that form in a way that makes it modal to the entire Word for Windows Application. The sequence is crucial to making this work. First, Word is made the parent of the Form using the FindWindow and SetWindowLong Windows API functions. Next, the form is made visible. Finally, Word is disabled using the Windows API function, EnableWindow. The ActivateWord and HideForm functions must also do their work in a specific sequence to correctly undo the modality of the Form with respect to Word.

Returning Data to Word for Windows

When the data entry form's OK button is clicked, it needs to send the data back to the Word document. Since Word for Windows 6.0 exposes most of the Word Basic functionality in an OLE Automation object, that provides the easiest mechanism to return the data. The Word Basic SetFormResult command is used to set Word form fields based on their corresponding data-entry form values. After setting the Word form fields each sets a Word variable to indicate its work is done, and reactivates the Word application before hiding itself.

You may be wondering what WordBasic commands are not available to OLE Automation. Unavailable commands include: control structures (for example, If. . . Then. . . Else), declaration (for example, DIM), custom dialog box statements, statements requiring array variable arguments, and the FileExit statement.

Tabbing in Fill-In Forms

Our sample contract template in Word has three form fields that are set to Fill-in-Enabled. In a protected document such as this one, the user can tab to a form field only if it is enabled for fill-in. Tabbing out of the first fill-in enabled field, bookmarked CompanyName1, takes us to the next enabled field, which is the first Effective Date field in the document. Its bookmark name is EffectiveDate1, and GetDates is its Entry macro. GetDates works very much like GetNameAndAddress, requesting the Document Dates data entry form. Likewise, the Document Dates form works much like the Name and Address form, setting Effective and Expiration dates in the document before hiding itself and reactivating Word. Tabbing again takes us to the last enabled field, bookmarked Signator1, and the process continues with the Signator data entry form.

Terminating Visual Basic

The Entry macro for each enabled field checks variables that are set by Visual Basic to indicate which data entry forms have been completed. When all are done, the document template sends a DDE command string to Visual Basic, telling it to shut itself down. As soon as Word follows with the DDE conversation termination command, the Visual Basic application clears out all resources from memory, and ends.

Testing Options

One final note about testing: it is sometimes helpful to test this application without Word for Windows. To overcome this, a command-line argument is introduced. The document template normally starts DOCASMBY.EXE with a command-line argument set to "Word"; but for testing, the application can be started by running the DOCASMBY.VBP project from within the Visual Basic development environment. This is done by leaving the command-line argument empty to provide a way to test the forms separately without testing the interface with Word for Windows. In that case, the transaction center form makes itself visible and allows you to select each of the data entry forms for testing.

Comments

The initial loading of database information into the hidden Name and Address form takes a long time, though once it's loaded the response time to display the form is fairly good. How-To 2.1 provides a technique for using a splash screen to distract the user's attention during a long startup process. It could be nicely applied in an application such as this one.

Our sample application has its data mapped in code to various form fields in the document template. For example, the organization name is returned to four form fields in the document template. If you're going to build more than one document assembly template, a more generic approach would be better. You could create a database to associate Word document-assembly templates and their form fields with Visual Basic applications and their data-entry form fields. This would take additional database access code, and processing would slow down a bit, but it would mean that any number of document-assembly templates could reuse any number of data entry forms. Document templates could be changed to include additional references to existing data-entry fields, without requiring changes to the data entry forms themselves.

In this How-To, forms are made Modal to the entire Word for Windows application. Better yet would be to make them modal to Word's active child window (the document being assembled).

6.5 How do I...
Transfer Data and Send Notifications between VB Applications, Using an Automation Server?

COMPLEXITY: INTERMEDIATE
COMPATIBILITY: VB4 ONLY

Problem

I would like to build a suite of VB applications with separate executable files. The applications need to send data back and forth between them. DDE runs too slowly and is error prone. How can I transfer data quickly and safely, and notify the recipient that data is waiting for it? I would like to be able to use an automation server to dispatch the data, without the need for the applications to continuously check for new data.

Technique

The introduction of OLE automation has greatly simplified transferring data between applications. One approach would be to make each application an object application that provided several public properties that could be set directly by another application. A more robust method involves using an automation server to control packaging, temporarily storing and transmitting data contained in data objects.

Steps

Open and run DATASTOR.VBP. Start a new instance of Visual Basic and open CLIENT.VBP. From the Tools menu, add a reference to the DataServer demo. Run the application. Click the New client command button to create a few instances of the client form. Enter some text in the text window of an instance of the Client (as shown in Figure 6-5-1) and add it to the outgoing data. You can repeat this process several times, and then click the button to send all outgoing data. At this point the data is transferred to temporary storage in the automation server. Any instance of the Client that was designated as a recipient of data will have now had its check box checked, indicating that the server is holding data for that Client. If additional data items were transmitted, the button to read the next item will be enabled.

1. Create a new project called DATASTOR.VBP. In the Project Options dialog, set the project's Startup form to Sub Main, its Project Name to DataServer, its application description to DataServer demo, and its Startup mode to object application.

2. Insert a new class module named CDataDispatcher. Save it as DISPATCH.CLS. Set its Instancing property to 2 - Creatable MultiUse, and its Public property to True.

3. Add the following declarations to DISPATCH.CLS.

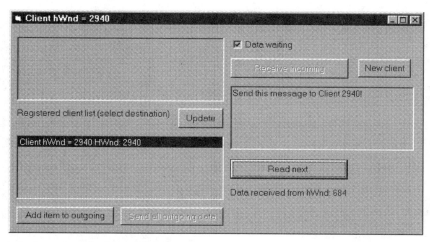

Figure 6-5-1 The CLIENT program

```
Option Explicit
'
Private Declare Function SendMessage Lib "user32" Alias _
  "SendMessageA" (ByVal hwnd As Long, ByVal wMsg As Long, _
  ByVal wParam As Integer, ByVal lParam As Long) As Long
'
Private m_IncomingDataItems As New Collection
Private m_OutgoingDataItems As New Collection
Private m_HWnd As Long
```

4. Add the following subroutine to DISPATCH.CLS. This method is used by client applications to receive incoming data from the automation server. It adds data items to the applications data collection and removes them from the server's collection of temporarily stored data.

```
Public Sub ReceiveIncomingData(hwnd As Integer)
    Dim DataItem As CDataItem, i As Integer
    '
    ' Move the data item from the server's collection to
    ' the user's Incoming collection. Note that the user's
    ' incoming collection is maintained by the dispatcher;
    ' the user can only access it through a property array
    ' and the methods provided by the dispatcher.
    '
    i = 1
    Do While i <= g_ServerDataItems.Count
        If g_ServerDataItems(i).ReceiverHWnd = hwnd Then
            '
            ' Add data item to the app's data item collection
            '
            m_IncomingDataItems.Add g_ServerDataItems(i)
            '
```

Continued on next page

717

Continued from previous page

```
                    ' Remove transmitted items from the server's collection
                    '
                g_ServerDataItems.Remove i
                i = i - 1
            End If
            i = i + 1
    Loop
    '
End Sub
```

5. Add the following method to the DISPATCH.CLS. It operates essentially as the reverse of the above method, removing objects from the client's outgoing collection, and adding them to the m_ServerDataItems temporary storage collection of the automation server.

```
Public Function SendOutgoingData()
    Dim DataItem As CDataItem
    Dim i As Integer, lv As Long
    '
    For Each DataItem In m_OutgoingDataItems
        '
        ' Notify the recipient.
        '
        lv = SendMessage(DataItem.ReceiverHWnd, &H800, 0, 0)
        '
        ' Add it to the server's message collection.
        '
        g_ServerDataItems.Add DataItem
        '
        ' The argument of the Remove method is always 1 in
        ' this case, since all previous items have been
        ' removed; it is an unconditional removal.
        '
        m_OutgoingDataItems.Remove 1
    Next
    '
End Function
```

6. Add the following Property Get procedure to DISPATCH.CLS. This procedure is implemented as a property array, and is used in conjunction with the OutgoingCount property.

```
Public Property Get OutgoingDataItems(Index As Integer) As CDataItem
    '
    ' Allow user access through this property array only.
    '
    If Index > m_OutgoingDataItems.Count Then Exit Property
    OutgoingDataItems = m_OutgoingDataItems(Index)
End Property
```

7. Add the following Property Get procedure to DISPATCH.CLS. This procedure allows the user to add data objects created by the Sender client application to the private m_OutgoingDataItems collection.

```
Public Sub AddToOutgoing(DataItem As CDataItem)
    '
    m_OutgoingDataItems.Add DataItem
End Sub
```

8. The user's Receiver application will access received data items via the ReceivedDataItems property array. Add the following Property Get procedure to DISPATCH.CLS to return a data item object specified by a numerical index.

```
Public Property Get ReceivedDataItems(Index As Integer) As CDataItem
    '
    If Index > m_IncomingDataItems.Count Then Exit Property
    Set ReceivedDataItems = m_IncomingDataItems(Index)
End Property
```

9. The user's Receiver application should be able to remove received data items. Add the following Property Get procedure to DISPATCH.CLS to remove items from the underlying private m_IncomingDataItems collection. Note that this sub does not destroy objects; it merely removes them.

```
Public Sub RemoveFromReceived(DataItem As CDataItem)
    '
    ' Allow user to remove received items.
    '
    ' The user must independently destroy the object by
    ' setting it equal to Nothing if she desires.
    ' This sub merely removes it from the Incoming collection
    '
    Dim i As Integer
    For i = 1 To m_IncomingDataItems.Count
        If m_IncomingDataItems(i) Is DataItem Then
            m_IncomingDataItems.Remove i
            '
            ' You must exit the For loop, since you have
            ' changed the collection Count. Otherwise the index
            ' (i) will exceed the number of items in the collection.
            '
            Exit For
        End If
    Next
End Sub
```

9. Add the following Property Get routine to DISPATCH.CLS to return the number of items in the private m_IncomingDataItems collection.

```
Public Property Get ReceivedCount() As Integer
    '
    ReceivedCount = m_IncomingDataItems.Count
End Property
```

10. Add the following similar routine to DISPATCH.CLS to return the number of items in the private m_OutgoingDataItems collection. Like the above property, this will be read-only.

719

```
Public Property Get OutgoingCount() As Integer
    '
    OutgoingCount = m_OutgoingDataItems.Count
End Property
```

11. Add the following function to DISPATCH.CLS. Running this demo in design mode results in all instances of the Client running in the same application, but in general, clients will need to register themselves, so that the server can identify (in this case through unique window handles) all of the potential recipients.

```
Public Sub RegisterClient(Caption As String, hwnd As Long)
    Dim Client As New CClient
    '
    m_HWnd = hwnd
    Client.hwnd = hwnd
    Client.Caption = Caption
    g_Clients.Add Client, CStr(hwnd)
    '
End Sub
```

12. Add the following function into DISPATCH.CLS. Ideally, you would like this to be a Property Get procedure with an associated Property Set procedure, allowing "Item" to be the default method of an exposed Clients collection, however, Visual Basic 4.0 does not allow optional parameters in property procedures.

```
Public Function Clients(Optional Key As Variant) As Variant
    '
    ' This kludge, to give the Client's collection a fake
    ' default method (item), only works if you use it to
    ' return (not set) a vaule.
    '
    If IsMissing(Key) Then
        Set Clients = g_Clients
    Else
        Set Clients = g_Clients(Key)
    End If
    '
End Function
```

13. Add the following function into DISPATCH.CLS, returning the number of clients registered with the dispatcher.

```
Public Property Get ClientsCount() As Integer
    '
    ClientsCount = g_Clients.Count
End Property
```

14. Add code for the object termination event, to remove the associated client object from the global collection of client objects.

```
Private Sub Class_Terminate()
    '
```

```
' Remove the associated client from Client's collection.
'
g_Clients.Remove CStr(m_HWnd)
'
End Sub
```

15. Insert a new class module named CDataItem. Save it as DATAITEM.CLS. Set its Instancing property to 2 - Creatable MultiUse and its Public property to True.

16. Add the following declarations to DATAITEM.CLS.

```
Option Explicit
'
Private m_DataDetail As Variant
Private m_SenderHWnd As Long
Private m_ReceiverHWnd As Long
```

17. Objects of the CDataItem class will have three public properties: DataDetail, ReceiverHWnd, and SenderHWnd. These properties will allow controlled access to the underlying private variables. Add the following Property Get procedure to DATAITEM.CLS to access the private value of m_DataDetail.

```
Public Property Get DataDetail() As Variant
    '
        DataDetail = m_DataDetail
End Property
```

18. Add this corresponding Property Let procedure to DATAITEM.CLS to set the private value of m_DataDetail.

```
Public Property Let DataDetail(Data1 As Variant)
    '
        m_DataDetail = Data1
End Property
```

19. The Window handle of the recipient is used to embed a destination in the data packages. Add the following Property Get procedure to DATAITEM.CLS to return the hWnd.

```
Public Property Let ReceiverHWnd(hWnd1 As Variant)
    '
        ReceiverHWnd = m_ReceiverHWnd
End Property
```

20. Add this corresponding Property Let procedure to DATAITEM.CLS to set the hWnd property of the data item.

```
Public Property Let ReceiverHWnd(hWnd1 As Variant)
    '
        m_ReceiverHWnd = hWnd1
End Property
```

21. The sender of a data package also will record its hWnd value in the SenderHWnd property of the data item. This Property Get procedure returns the private value of an object of the CDataItem class.

```
Public Property Get SenderHWnd() As Variant
    '
    SenderHWnd = m_SenderHWnd
End Property
```

22. Add this corresponding Property Let procedure to DATAITEM.CLS to record the sender's hWnd.

```
Public Property Let SenderHWnd(hWnd1 As Variant)
    '
    m_SenderHWnd = hWnd1
End Property
```

23. There is no good way to limit the number of instances of a public class provided by the automation server. For this reason the central data storage object, the private m_ServerDataItems collection resides in a standard module. This collection object is declared as public, to allow all instances of the automation server's classes to have direct access to it. It will not appear in the Object Browser, however. Enter the following declaration in a module named ServeStatic and save it as DATASERV.BAS. The Sub Main procedure is necessary for the application to run as an object server with no forms.

```
Option Explicit
'
Public g_ServerDataItems As New Collection
Public g_Clients As New Collection
'
Sub Main()
    '
End Sub
```

24. Insert a new class module named CClient. Save it as CCLIENT.CLS. Set its Public property to True and its Instancing property to 0 - Not Creatable.

25. Add the following declarations to CCLIENT.CLS.

```
Option Explicit
'
Private m_Caption As String
Private m_HWnd As Long
```

26. Add the following Property Get procedure to CCLIENT.CLS, to allow a client to obtain the captions of other clients.

```
Public Property Get Caption() As String
    '
    Caption = m_Caption
End Property
```

27. Add the following Property Let procedure to CCLIENT.CLS, to allow a client to register its caption with the server.

```
Public Property Let Caption(Capt As String)
    '
    m_Caption = Capt
End Property
```

28. Add the following Property Get procedure to CCLIENT.CLS, to allow a client to obtain the windows handle of other clients.

```
Public Property Get hwnd() As Long
    '
    hwnd = m_HWnd
End Property
```

29. Add the following Property Let procedure to CCLIENT.CLS, to allow a client to register the handle with the server.

```
Public Property Let hwnd(Handle As Long)
    '
    m_HWnd = Handle
End Property
```

30. To build the Client, start a new instance of Visual Basic. Create a new form and add the controls and property settings shown in Table 6-5-1.

Table 6-5-1 Client's objects and properties

OBJECT	PROPERTY	SETTING
Form	Name	Form1
CheckBox	Name	Check1
	Caption	"Data waiting"
CommandButton	Name	cmdNew
	Caption	"New client"
CommandButton	Name	cmdAdd
	Caption	"Add item to outgoing"
CommandButton	Caption	"Send all outgoing data"
	Enabled	0 'False
	Name	CmdSend
CommandButton	Caption	"Read next"
	Name	cmdReadNext
CommandButton	Caption	"Receive incoming"
	Name	cmdReceive
CommandButton	Caption	"Update"
	Name	cmdUpdate

Continued on next page

Continued from previous page

OBJECT	PROPERTY	SETTING
TextBox	Name	txtIncoming
TextBox	Name	txtOutgoing
ListBox	Name	List1
Label	Name	Label1
Label	Name	Label2
	Caption	"Registered client list (select destination)"
Msghook	Name	Msghook1

31. Add the following declarations to Form1's code.

```
Option Explicit
'
Public Dispatcher As New CDataDispatcher
```

32. Add the following code to the Click event procedure of CmdAdd. This code adds a data object that the user has created to the outgoing data array. Note that the user does not directly create the outgoing collection. It is owned by the automation server and is accessed via methods supplied by the client's dispatcher object.

```
Private Sub cmdAdd_Click()
    Dim AppData As New CDataItem
    Dim s1 As String
    '
    AppData.DataDetail = txtOutgoing.Text
    s1 = List1.List(List1.ListIndex)
    s1 = Mid(s1, InStr(s1, ": ") + 2)
    AppData.ReceiverHWnd = CLng(s1)
    AppData.SenderHWnd = Me.hwnd
    '
    ' Add this message to the outgoing collection.
    ' User does not have direct access to the data collections
    ' and must use methods provided by the dispatcher.
    '
    Dispatcher.AddToOutgoing AppData
    CmdSend.Enabled = True
    txtOutgoing = ""
    '
End Sub
```

33. Add the following code to the Click event procedure of CmdSend. It also uses methods supplied by the client's dispatcher object.

```
'
Private Sub cmdSend_Click()
    '
    ' Send the data in the Outgoing collection.
    '
    Dispatcher.SendOutgoingData
    CmdSend.Enabled = False
End Sub
```

34. Add the following code to the Load event of Form1, to display the hWnd of the Sender.

```
Private Sub Form_Load()
    '
    ' Generate a random caption to differentiate
    ' instances of the client for this How To.
    '
    Caption = "Client hWnd = " & Me.hwnd
    '
    Dispatcher.RegisterClient Me.Caption, Me.hwnd
    ListClients
    List1.ListIndex = 0
    '
    ' Use of MsgHook is not mandatory, but it allows
    ' the server to send a notification directly to
    ' a client, causing an event in the client.
    '
    Msghook1.HwndHook = Me.hwnd
    Msghook1.Message(&H800) = True
    '
End Sub
```

35. Add the following code to the Click event procedure of CmdReceive.

```
Private Sub cmdReceive_Click()
    '
    Dispatcher.ReceiveIncomingData Me.hwnd
    If Dispatcher.ReceivedCount Then
        cmdReadNext.Enabled = True
        cmdReadNext.Value = True
    End If
    cmdReceive.Enabled = False
    '
End Sub
```

36. Add the following code to the Click event procedure of CmdReadNext.

```
Private Sub cmdReadNext_Click()
    Static Count As Integer
    '
    If Count < Dispatcher.ReceivedCount Then
        Count = Count + 1
            txtIncoming = Dispatcher.ReceivedDataItems(Count).DataDetail
        Label1 = "Data received from hWnd: " & _
            Dispatcher.ReceivedDataItems(Count).SenderHWnd
        If Count = Dispatcher.ReceivedCount Then
            cmdReadNext.Enabled = False
            Check1.Value = 0
        End If
    Else
        cmdReadNext.Enabled = False
    End If
    '
End Sub
```

37. Add the following code to the Click event procedure of cmdUpdate.

```
Private Sub cmdUpdate_Click()
    '
    ListClients
End Sub
```

38. Add the following code to the Click event procedure of cmdNew, to create multiple instances of the Client, to demonstrate data transmission.

```
Private Sub cmdNew_Click()
    Dim A As Form1
    '
    Set A = New Form1
    A.Show
End Sub
```

39. Add the following subroutine to poll the server for all registered clients.

```
Private Sub ListClients()
    Dim Client As CClient
    '
    ' At least one client (Me) will always be listed.
    '
    List1.Clear
    For Each Client In Dispatcher.Clients
        List1.AddItem Client.Caption & " HWnd: " & Client.hwnd
    Next
End Sub
```

40. Add the following code to the MsgHook event indicating receipt of a Windows message from the server, indicating that the Client has data waiting for it.

```
Private Sub Msghook1_Message(msg As Long, wp As Long, lp As Long, _
        action As Integer, result As Long)
    '
    ' Interpret receipt of message &H800 as notification
    ' that you have mail waiting.
    '
    Check1.Value = vbChecked
    cmdReceive.Enabled = True
    '
End Sub
```

How It Works

Visual Basic does not allow creation of static class variables, so an automation server must store data needed by all objects of the class in a standard module. By using an automation server to store a collection of DataItem objects in a standard module, all applications can access the data. The Sender application can be closed after sending a package of data, but before the Receiver has received it. Since the data actually resides in the server, the Receiver will still be able to receive the data package. This project demonstrates unlimited data transfer capability. Note that the MsgHook control intercepts Windows messages sent by the server indicating that data is waiting, but the Windows message itself does not contain or point to any details of the message.

Comments

This project could be used as a starting point for a suite of communicating applications or applets, as they are sometimes called. Some of the applets might be configured to send and receive data. Because the DataDetail property of CDataItem is a variant (which can contain an object), arrays and objects could be passed as data. To allow objects to be passed, Property Set procedures would need to be added to the Dispatcher's methods. For more flexibility, a series of descriptive properties could be added to the CDataItem class.

7

SYSTEM SERVICES

7

SYSTEM SERVICES

How do I...

Every program needs to make use of the system. In this chapter we show you how to do just that. You'll find lots of specific information for getting at some of those elusive elements of the system, and some pointers for delving into the depths on your own.

A few of the How-To's in this chapter make use of a DLL that provides access to DOS interrupts. It's called VBINTR.DLL, and it's free. Using interrupts allows you to get to information not provided by Windows—drive information, SHARE status, and so on. A word of warning here is warranted, VBINTR.DLL is like a blow torch. Used properly, it's a great tool; used improperly, it can do damage to your system. So be careful!

Many of the techniques in this chapter use one or more Windows API calls to make it all work. You will encounter the following Windows API calls:

WINDOWS API	HOW-TO'S
BringWindowToTop	7.4
CloseHandle	7.8
ClosePrinter	7.1
CreateFile	7.8
DestroyIcon	7.9
DrawIcon	7.9
EndDocPrinter	7.1
EndPagePrinter	7.1
ExtractIcon	7.9
GetDesktopWindow	7.3, 7.4
GetDriveType	7.6
GetModuleFileName	7.5
GetPrivateProfileString	7.2
GetProfileString	7.1, 7.2
GetVersion	7.10
GetWindow	7.3, 7.4
GetWindowsDirectory	7.2
GetWindowText	7.4
GetWindowWord	7.3, 7.5, 7.9
GetWindowThreadProcessId	7.3
IsWindow	7.3
LocalFileTimeToFileTime	7.8
OpenPrinter	7.1
SendMessage	7.2
SetFileTimeWrite	7.8
SetFocus	7.4
ShowWindow	7.3
StartDocPrinter	7.1
StartPagePrinter	7.1
SystemTimeToFileTime	7.8
WritePrinter	7.1
WritePrivateProfileString	7.2
WriteProfileString	7.2

7.1 Submit a File to the Print Spooler

Often, it's necessary to submit files directly to the print spooler for spooling to a user-selected printer. However, because they're not always text files, they can't be opened up, read line-by-line, and printed to the Printer object. This How-To shows how to use API calls to overcome this and submit a file directly to the print spooler.

7.2 Manipulate .INI Files

There are many different ways to store information in an .INI file, including using custom controls. The variety of possibilities can be confusing. This How-To will aleviate some of that confusion by demonstrating ways to efficiently manage and use .INI files. To make it easier, a module of code is included for you to copy directly into your own programs.

7.3 Get an hWnd from a Process Handle (hProcess)

When running another program using a Shell command, it's sometimes necessary to manipulate the other window. Using the task ID passed back by Shell results in fails and occasional GPF's. This How-To shows a technique to find the required window handle without the usual pitfalls.

7.4 Get an hWnd from a Partial Title

Sometimes it's necessary to activate another application when you don't know the full title of the required window. The technique in this How-To shows how to traverse the windows in the system to find the one you need.

7.5 Determine Whether a Project Is Compiled

It's important to know whether an application is compiled or running in the Visual Basic development environment. When compiled, data files will be assumed to be in the application directory. But when under development, they typically have several versions each stored in their own project directory. These should all look to one centralized location for test data. This How-To will show you how to tell whether you're working from the design environment or running an .EXE program.

7.6 Determine a Drive's Type

Often, you will want to allow the user to do different things or show different pictures or icons depending on what type of drive they're accessing. Sometimes, you'll want to give them some information about the drive File Manager and other desktop shells by showing different bitmaps on their buttons for different drive types. This How-To will show you how to do this using VBINTR.DLL to determine a drive's type.

7.7   Check for a File's Existence

When your program's actions are based on whether a file exists (such as a configuration file, user info file, etc.), you need to figure this out beforehand. This How-To will demonstrate how.

7.8   Set a File's Date and Time

When you need to change a file's date and time, in the past you've been out of luck. Visual Basic documentation and its help file show you only how to read the time stamp. However, this How-To will show you how to write a file's time/date stamp using VBINTR.DLL.

7.9   View Icons in Executable Files

It's obvious that executable files contain icons because Program Manager gives the option to browse them when it sets program item properties. This How-To demonstrates how to extract and view these icons.

7.10 Detect Which OS Is Running

Modern, professional-looking About boxes can contain system information, including the current version of the operating system. Using API calls doesn't always return the values you need. In this How-To, you will watch a program that digs into the system and determines the name and version of the operating system.

7.1 How do I...
Submit a File to the Print Spooler?

COMPLEXITY: INTERMEDIATE
COMPATIBILITY: VB4 ONLY

Problem

I'd like to submit files directly to the print spooler for spooling to a user-selected printer. Since they're not text files, I can't simply open them up, read them line by line, and print them to the Printer object. Visual Basic's File Copy command won't accept a port, the way the DOS Copy command does, and I don't want to open a DOS box and use a batch file. Is there an API that I can use?

Technique

This How-To demonstrates the techniques necessary to submit binary data directly to the print spooler in either Windows NT or Windows 95. A specific series of API calls is required to open the printer and put it in document page mode, ready to accept "RAW" data. For this example, a disk file is read and submitted in 16K chunks; however, a memory buffer would work just as well.

To make this project a useful utility, a list of available printers is built using the new Printers collection and offered as choices for directing the output. In a working application, it is the programmer's responsibility to ensure that the spooled file is already formatted in the appropriate printer language for the selected printer. This demo may be used with pure text files and printers that accept such input, or with files "printed to disk" from another application, as long as the same printer is targeted as was when the file was created.

Steps

Open and run SPOOL.VBP. Your default printer will be listed in the drop-down list box, as shown in Figure 7-1-1. If you'd prefer, you can choose any other available printer. Select a file either by typing in its name, or pressing the File button and choosing the file from the dialog box. This can be either a simple text file, or one "printed to disk" from another application.

Press the Print button to submit the file to the selected printer. If it's a very small file, most likely you won't even detect that it's been processed. To slow down the chain of events, take your printer off line, and then make Print Manager visible after submitting a file. You'll see the submitted job listed under the chosen printer, and eventually get a printer time-out error.

Building SPOOL.FRM

1. Start a new project, name the initial form frmSpool, save it as SPOOL.FRM, and save the project as SPOOL.VBP. Place the controls, and set the properties listed in Table 7-1-1.

Figure 7-1-1 SPOOL.VBP in action

Table 7-1-1 Objects and their properties on frmSpool

OBJECT	PROPERTY	SETTING
Form	Name	frmSpool
	BorderStyle	4 - Fixed ToolWindow
	Caption	"Submit File to Print Spooler"
	MaxButton	False
Label	Name	Label1
	AutoSize	True
	Caption	"File to Submit:"
TextBox	Name	txtFile
	Text	"txtFile"
Label	Name	Label2
	AutoSize	True
	Caption	"Available Printers:"
ComboBox	Name	Combo1
	Style	2 - Dropdown List
CommandButton	Name	cmdFile
	Caption	"&File"
CommandButton	Name	cmdPrint
	Caption	"&Print"
CommandButton	Name	cmdExit
	Caption	"E&xit"
CommonDialog	Name	CommonDialog1
	CancelError	True
	DialogTitle	"Select File to Print"

2. Add the following code to the Declarations section of frmSpool. This declares an object variable to use with the CBorder3D class module, which was developed in How-To 3.4 in Chapter 3.

```
Option Explicit
'
' Declare an object variable for CBorder3D
'
Private Frm3D As New CBorder3D
```

3. Insert the following code in the Form_Initialize event of frmSpool. This is just a check to ensure that at least one printer is installed. There is no reason to continue the demonstration if not.

```
Private Sub Form_Initialize()
    '
    ' Make sure there are printers installed!
    ' No point in proceeding if not.
    '
```

```
        If Printers.Count = 0 Then
            MsgBox "No printers are installed. Can't continue.", _
                    vbCritical, "Fatal Error"
            End
        End If
End Sub
```

4. Insert the following code in the Form_Load event of frmSpool. The new Printers collection is first cycled, and the device name and port of each printer is added to Combo1. Then, the SelectDefaultPrinter routine is called to highlight the current default printer from the list. This special approach is more useful, because if your program changes the current printer in use, it's no longer possible to retrieve the current system default printer using the Printers collection. Finally, the contents of the text box are cleared, the form is sized and positioned, and another routine is called to set up a 3D border effect.

```
Private Sub Form_Load()
    Dim prn As Printer
    '
    ' Fill combo box with available printers, and
    ' select default printer.
    '
    For Each prn In Printers
        Combo1.AddItem prn.DeviceName & " on " & prn.Port
    Next prn
    '
    ' Select default printer.
    '
    SelectDefaultPrinter Combo1
    '
    ' Size and position form; clear textbox.
    '
    Me.Width = txtFile.Width + txtFile.Left * 2 + _
                (Me.Width - Me.ScaleWidth)
    Me.Height = cmdFile.Top + cmdFile.Height + Label1.Top + _
                (Me.Height - Me.ScaleHeight)
    Me.Move (Screen.Width - Me.Width) \ 2, _
                (Screen.Height - Me.Height) \ 2
    txtFile = ""
    '
    ' Create 3D border effect for form.
    '
    Call Setup3D
End Sub
```

5. Add a private routine called Setup3D to frmSpool, and place the following code in it. This sequence of instructions defines a 3D object that paints a sunken border around the edge of the form.

```
Private Sub Setup3D()
    '
    ' Called from Form_Load
```

Continued on next page

Continued from previous page

```
    ' Styles supported by CBorder3D
    '
    Const StyleNone = 0
    Const StyleSunken = 1
    Const StyleRaised = 2
    Const StyleFramed = 3
    Const StyleDouble = 4
    Const StyleWithin = 5
    Const StyleCustomFramed = 6
    Const StyleCustomDouble = 7
    Const StyleCustomWithin = 8
    '
    ' Setup 3D border effect around edge of form
    '
    Set Frm3D.Canvas = Me
    Frm3D.Style3D = StyleCustomWithin
    Frm3D.BevelOuter = StyleSunken
    Frm3D.BevelWidth = 2
    Frm3D.Left = 0
    Frm3D.Top = 3 * Screen.TwipsPerPixelY
    Frm3D.Width = Me.ScaleWidth
    Frm3D.Height = Me.ScaleHeight - Frm3D.Top
End Sub
```

6. Insert a call to refresh the 3D object in the Form_Paint event of frmSpool.

```
Private Sub Form_Paint()
    '
    ' Refresh 3D border around form.
    '
    Frm3D.Refresh
End Sub
```

7. Insert the following code in the cmdFile_Click event of frmSpool. Here, the common dialog custom control is used to query for a file to spool.

```
Private Sub cmdFile_Click()
    '
    ' Set dialog properties
    '
    CommonDialog1.Flags = FileMustExist Or HideReadOnly
    CommonDialog1.Filter = "Print Files (*.prn)|*.PRN|AllFiles (*.*)|*.*"
    '
    ' Get filename. Allow user to cancel.
    '
    On Error Resume Next
    CommonDialog1.ShowOpen
    If Err = 0 Then
        '
        ' Place selected filename into textbox.
        '
        txtFile = CommonDialog1.FileName
    End If
End Sub
```

8. Insert the following code in the cmdPrint_Click event of frmSpool. First, the existence of the file is tested, in case the user typed in a bad filename or didn't select one at all. Next, each element of the Printers collection is compared to the selection in Combo1. When a match is found, its name and the submitted file's name are passed to the SpoolFileNow routine.

```
Private Sub cmdPrint_Click()
    Dim Submit As String
    Dim prn As Printer
    '
    ' Warn user if file doesn't exist.
    '
    Submit = UCase(Trim(txtFile))
    If Not IsFile(Submit) Then
        MsgBox "Can't find file: " & Submit, vbExclamation, "Error"
        Exit Sub
    End If
    '
    ' Submit file to spooler after extracting name.
    '
    For Each prn In Printers
        If InStr(Combo1, prn.DeviceName) = 1 _
            And Right(Combo1, Len(prn.Port)) = prn.Port Then
                Call SpoolFileNow(Submit, prn.DeviceName)
                Exit For
        End If
    Next prn
End Sub
```

9. Insert an Unload Me line in the cmdExit_Click event of frmSpool, to exit the applet when this button is pressed.

```
Private Sub cmdExit_Click()
    '
    ' All Done
    '
    Set Frm3D = Nothing
    Unload Me
End Sub
```

Building SPOOL.BAS, a Module of Support Routines

10. Using the Insert Module menu item, add a new code module to the project. Name the module MSpool and save it as SPOOL.BAS. Place the following code in the Declarations section, to declare the required Win32 API calls and an associated private data structure.

```
Option Explicit
'
' Win32 API Calls
'
```

Continued on next page

Continued from previous page

```
Private Declare Function GetProfileString Lib "kernel32" Alias ⇒
    "GetProfileStringA" (ByVal lpAppName As String, ByVal lpKeyName ⇒
    As Any, ByVal lpDefault As String, ByVal lpReturnedString As String, ⇒
    ByVal nSize As Long) As Long
Private Declare Function OpenPrinter Lib "winspool.drv" Alias ⇒
    "OpenPrinterA" (ByVal pPrinterName As String, phPrinter As Long, ⇒
    pDefault As Any) As Long
Private Declare Function StartDocPrinter Lib "winspool.drv" Alias ⇒
    "StartDocPrinterA" (ByVal hPrinter As Long, ByVal Level As Long, ⇒
    pDocInfo As DOC_INFO_1) As Long
Private Declare Function StartPagePrinter Lib "winspool.drv" ⇒
    (ByVal hPrinter As Long) As Long
Private Declare Function WritePrinter Lib "winspool.drv" (ByVal hPrinter ⇒
    As Long, pBuf As Any, ByVal cdBuf As Long, pcWritten As Long) As Long
Private Declare Function EndPagePrinter Lib "winspool.drv" ⇒
    (ByVal hPrinter As Long) As Long
Private Declare Function EndDocPrinter Lib "winspool.drv" ⇒
    (ByVal hPrinter As Long) As Long
Private Declare Function ClosePrinter Lib "winspool.drv" ⇒
    (ByVal hPrinter As Long) As Long
'
' Structure required by StartDocPrinter
'
Private Type DOC_INFO_1
    pDocName As String
    pOutputFile As String
    pDatatype As String
End Type
```

11. To MSpool, add a public routine called SelectDefaultPrinter, and insert the following code in it. Here, each item in the drop-down list is compared against the current default printer as extracted from WIN.INI. If a match is found, that list index is selected and the procedure exits.

```
Public Sub SelectDefaultPrinter(Lst As ComboBox)
    Dim sRet As String
    Dim nRet As Integer
    Dim i As Integer
    '
    ' Look for default printer in WIN.INI
    '
    sRet = Space(255)
    nRet = GetProfileString("Windows", ByVal "device", "", _
                            sRet, Len(sRet))
    '
    ' Truncate default printer name.
    '
    If nRet Then
        sRet = UCase(Left(sRet, InStr(sRet, ",") - 1))
        '
        ' Cycle list looking for matching entry.
        '
        For i = 0 To Lst.ListCount
            If Left(UCase(Lst.List(i)), Len(sRet)) = sRet Then
```

```
        '
        ' Found it. Set index and bail.
        '
            Lst.ListIndex = i
            Exit For
        End If
      Next i
   End If
End Sub
```

12. To MSpool, add a public routine called SpoolFileNow, and insert the following code in it. This routine performs the actual submission to the print spooler. One element of the DOC_INFO_1 structure is a job title for the submission, typically a combination of the names of the application and the file, which will be displayed in the spooler status window. In this example, the selected file is appended to letters representing the title of this book. The selected printer is then opened, and placed in document page mode, which prepares it to accept "RAW" binary data.

   The file to be spooled is then opened, and read into a byte array buffer in 16K chunks. A byte array was chosen to avoid the messy conversion issues related to using Unicode strings, and to provide optimum performance. As each chunk is read, it is written to the printer. As it is most likely that the file is not an even multiple of 16K, one last read and write must be made with the remaining bytes. All that remains to do is to close the printer. One interesting thing to note is that spooling will begin immediately with the first WritePrinter call. You can observe this by stepping through the code line-by-line.

```
Public Sub SpoolFileNow(sFile As String, PrnName As String)
   Dim hPrinter As Long
   Dim Buffer() As Byte
   Dim hFile As Integer
   Dim Written As Long
   Dim di As DOC_INFO_1
   Dim i As Long
   Const BufSize% = 16384
   '
   ' Extract filename from passed spec, and build job name.
   ' Fill remainder of DOC_INFO_1 structure.
   '
   If InStr(sFile, "\") Then
      For i = Len(sFile) To 1 Step -1
         If Mid(sFile, i, 1) = "\" Then Exit For
            di.pDocName = Mid(sFile, i, 1) & di.pDocName
      Next i
   Else
      di.pDocName = sFile
   End If
   di.pDocName = "VB4HT: " & di.pDocName
   di.pOutputFile = vbNullString
   di.pDatatype = "RAW"
   '
   ' Open printer for output to obtain handle.
```

Continued on next page

Continued from previous page

```
   ' Set it up to begin recieving raw data.
   '
   Call OpenPrinter(PrnName, hPrinter, vbNullString)
   Call StartDocPrinter(hPrinter, 1, di)
   Call StartPagePrinter(hPrinter)
   '
   ' Open file and pump it to the printer.
   '
   hFile = FreeFile
   Open sFile For Binary Access Read As hFile
      '
      ' Read in 16K buffers and spool.
      '
      ReDim Buffer(1 To BufSize) As Byte
      For i = 1 To LOF(hFile) \ BufSize
         Get #hFile, , Buffer
         Call WritePrinter(hPrinter, Buffer(1), BufSize, Written)
      Next i
      '
      ' Get last chunk of file if it doesn't
      ' fit evenly into a 16K buffer.
      '
      If LOF(hFile) Mod BufSize Then
         ReDim Buffer(1 To (LOF(hFile) Mod BufSize)) As Byte
         Get #hFile, , Buffer
         Call WritePrinter(hPrinter, Buffer(1), UBound(Buffer), Written)
      End If
   Close #hFile
   '
   ' Shut down spooling process.
   '
   Call EndPagePrinter(hPrinter)
   Call EndDocPrinter(hPrinter)
   Call ClosePrinter(hPrinter)
End Sub
```

13. To MSpool, add a public function called IsFile, and insert the following code in it. IsFile uses Visual Basic's GetAttr function and a process of elimination to test the passed filespec. Error trapping catches invalid filenames, and if no error is generated the passed string represents either a file or a directory. To rule out a directory, the retrieved attribute is compared against the attribute for directories. If the directory attribute bit is not set, then the string represents a valid, existing file.

```
Public Function IsFile(SpecIn As String) As Boolean
   Dim Attr As Byte
   '
   ' Guard against bad SpecIn by ignoring errors.
   '
   On Error Resume Next
   '
   ' Get attribute of SpecIn.
   '
   Attr = GetAttr(SpecIn)
   If Err = 0 Then
```

```
    '
    ' No error, so something was found.
    ' If Directory attribute set, then not a file.
    '
    If (Attr And vbDirectory) = vbDirectory Then
        IsFile = False
    Else
        IsFile = True
    End If
  End If
End Function
```

How It Works

Both Windows NT and Windows 95 provide print spooling functions in the WIN-SPOOL.DRV driver. Using these functions, you can bypass the installed printer driver, and submit binary data directly to any installed printer—local or remote. As the job spools, its progress is visible in the spooler status window (Print Manager in Windows NT).

With just a printer device name, you can use OpenPrinter to obtain a handle for writing to it. Calling StartDocPrinter, the spooler is instructed to regard the forthcoming data as "RAW," rather than as instructions to the driver. The StartPagePrinter function opens the pathway for the data to begin flowing. Oddly, this call only seems to be required when printing to local printers under Windows 95. If the printer is remote, or the application is running in Windows NT, it would not seem necessary. But, it doesn't interfere in these situations, and is required in one other, so it's best left there.

After the spooler has been prepared, the file is read into a byte array buffer in chunks, then written out to the spooler. The size of these chunks is somewhat arbitrary, and 16K was chosen simply because it's an even multiple of the size of most disk system's storage allocation units. You could just as easily read the entire file into a single byte array, and submit it all at once. This approach may not be faster though, especially in situations of low RAM or large files. After the file has been completely submitted to the spooler, the process of opening the printer is reversed and the printer is closed.

Comments

Files submitted in this manner to the spooler must already be formatted appropriately for the device to which they are targeted. In fact, for this reason, these calls are typically only used by device drivers. This method is nevertheless a good way to offload the process of sending bytes out to a printer, taking advantage of the background-processing the print spooler offers. The demo applet in this How-To will likely prove to be a useful utility, even as simple as it is. A typical use for it might be to reprint a sheet of labels. Perhaps you have designed disk labels in a graphics program. By printing those to a disk file, you can spool off several sheets whenever you run low.

7.2 How do I...
Manipulate .INI Files?

COMPLEXITY: INTERMEDIATE
COMPATIBILITY: VB4 ONLY

Problem

I want my application to store some information in an .INI file. I've seen a lot written about this technique, and I've even tried a few custom controls that handle .INI files. At this point, I'm a little confused—there are so many different ways to handle them. What's a nice, simple way to handle these files?

Technique

IniEdit, the project in this How-To, relies on a few API calls to manage the .INI files: GetProfileString, WriteProfileString, GetPrivateProfileStirng, and WritePrivateProfileString. Using these four functions, we can accomplish practically anything. Figure 7-2-1 shows the INI File Editor in action.

Curiously, Windows treats WIN.INI differently from all other .INI files. GetProfileString and WriteProfileString handle WIN.INI, and GetPrivateProfileString and WritePrivateProfileString are for all other .INI files. A nuisance, perhaps, but we just have to remember which one we're dealing with.

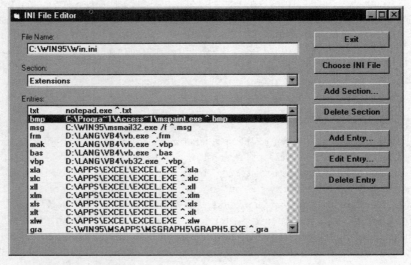

Figure 7-2-1 INI File Editor running

744

We read the .INI file three ways—two through the API, and one on our own. The first way we read the file is one entry at a time, as shown in Figure 7-2-2. This is how most programs use it to get the values of the data stored in the file.

The second way we read the .INI file is by reading an entire section at once (seen in Figure 7-2-3). This allows us to see everything within a section. With applications such as our INI File Editor, it's important to know everything that's in the file. The third way we read the .INI file is by parsing it ourselves. To get the list of sections in an .INI file, you have to open it and scan through the file.

When it comes to writing to an INI file, we use only the API calls, and write a single entry at a time. This is done very easily through the WriteProfileString and WritePrivateProfileString functions.

WriteProfileString and WritePrivateProfileString also allow us to delete entries and sections from .INI files.

Steps

Make a copy of an .INI file that you can play with. Open and run INIEDIT.VBP. Click on Choose INI File, and select the copy that you made. Play with the various controls and observe the program at work. Then follow these steps to see how this program was put together.

1. Create a new project called INIEDIT. Select Form1 and name it IniEdit. Save the form as INIEDIT.FRM and save the project as INIEDIT.VBP. Select the form, and add objects and set their properties as listed in Table 7-2-1.

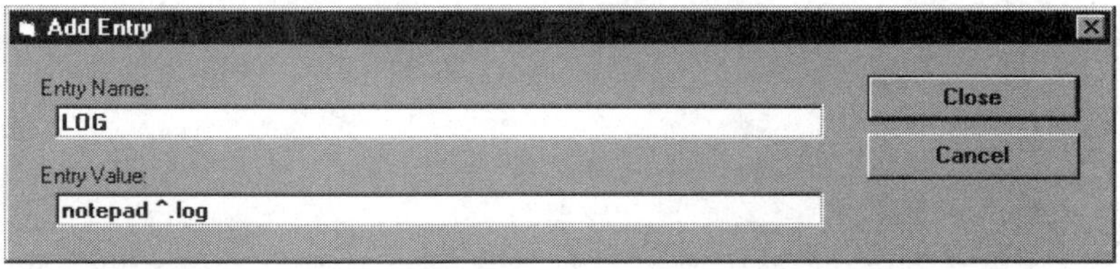

Figure 7-2-2 Adding an entry

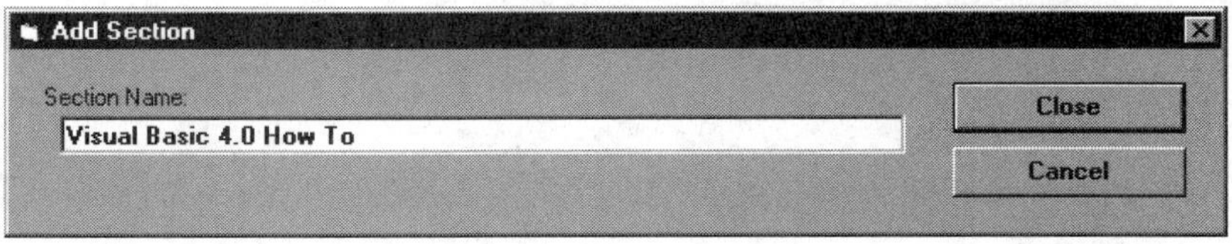

Figure 7-2-3 Adding a section

745

Table 7-2-1 Objects, properties, and settings for IniEdit

OBJECT	PROPERTY	SETTING
Form	Name	IniEdit
	Caption	"INI File Editor"
	Height	5745
	Left	1035
	Top	1170
	Width	8910
CommandButton	Name	btnEditEntry
	Caption	"Edit Entry"
	Enabled	0 'False
	Height	375
	Left	6840
	Top	3000
	Width	1695
CommandButton	Name	btnDeleteEntry
	Caption	"Delete Entry"
	Enabled	0 'False
	Height	375
	Left	6840
	Top	3480
	Width	1695
CommandButton	Name	btnDeleteSection
	Caption	"Delete Section"
	Enabled	0 'False
	Height	375
	Left	6840
	Top	1920
	Width	1695
CommandButton	Name	btnAddEntry
	Caption	"Add Entry"
	Enabled	0 'False
	Height	375
	Left	6840
	Top	2520
	Width	1695
ListBox	Name	lstEntries
	Height	3150
	Left	360
	Top	1920

OBJECT	PROPERTY	SETTING
	Width	6135
CommandButton	Name	btnAddSection
	Caption	"Add Section"
	Enabled	0 'False
	Height	375
	Left	6840
	Top	1440
	Width	1695
ComboBox	Name	cmbSections
	Height	300
	Left	360
	Sorted	-1 'True
	Style	2 'Dropdown List
	Top	1200
	Width	6135
CommandButton	Name	btnChooseIniFile
	Caption	"Choose INI File"
	Height	375
	Left	6840
	Top	840
	Width	1695
CommandButton	Name	btnExit
	Cancel	-1 'True
	Caption	"Exit"
	Height	375
	Left	6840
	Top	240
	Width	1695
TextBox	Name	txtFilename
	Height	285
	Left	360
	ReadOnly	-1 'True
	TabStop	0 'False
	Top	480
	Width	6135
Label	Name	Label3
	Caption	"Entries:"
	Height	255
	Left	240

Continued on next page

Continued from previous page

OBJECT	PROPERTY	SETTING
	Top	1680
	Width	2295
Label	Name	Label2
	Caption	"Section:"
	Height	255
	Left	240
	Top	960
	Width	2295
CommonDialog	Name	CommonDialog1
	Left	8040
	Top	4080
Label	Name	Label1
	Caption	"File Name:"
	Height	255
	Left	240
	Top	240
	Width	2295

2. Add the following code to the General Declarations section of IniEdit. Always use Option Explicit; it will save you many hours of frustration.

```
Option Explicit
```

3. Add the following code to the General Declarations section of IniEdit. This sub-routine loads the sections of the selected .INI file into the Sections combo box.

```
Private Sub LoadSections(Filename As String)
    Dim NumSections As Integer
    Dim I As Integer
    Dim Sections() As String
    '
    ' if we're dealing with WIN.INI, use WIN.INI
    ' functions
    '
    If IsWinIni(Filename) Then
        WinIniRegister ""
        NumSections = WinGetSectionsEx(Sections())
    Else
        ' otherwise, use private INI file functions
        PrivIniRegister "", Filename
        NumSections = PrivGetSectionsEx(Sections())
    End If
    '
    ' load up sections combo box
    '
    cmbSections.Clear
```

```
      For I = 0 To NumSections - 1
          cmbSections.AddItem Sections(I)
      Next I
  End Sub
```

4. Add the following code to the General Declarations section of IniEdit. This function loads the Entries list box. It installs the entries and values found in the .INI file, using the section selected in the Sections combo box.

```
Private Sub LoadEntries(Filename As String, Section As String)
    Dim NumEntries As Integer
    Dim I As Integer
Dim Entries() As String
    '
    ' if we're dealing with WIN.INI, use WIN.INI
    ' functions
    '
    If IsWinIni(Filename) Then
        WinIniRegister Section
        NumEntries = WinGetSectEntriesEx(Entries())
    Else
        '
        ' otherwise, use private INI file functions
        '
        PrivIniRegister Section, Filename
        NumEntries = PrivGetSectEntriesEx(Entries())
    End If
    '
    ' load up entries list box
    '
    lstEntries.Clear
For I = 0 To NumEntries - 1
        lstEntries.AddItem Entries(0, I) & Chr(9) & Entries(1, I)
    Next I
End Sub
```

5. Add the following code to the Click event handlers for the Add Entry button. This function uses the AddEntry function on the Entry form to add a new entry. When it's done, it loads the entry list.

```
Private Sub btnAddEntry_Click()
    Entry.AddEntry txtFilename, cmbSections.Text
    '
    ' update entries list box
    '
    LoadEntries txtFilename, cmbSections.Text
End Sub
```

6. Add the following code to the Click handler for the Add Section button. This function calls the AddSection function on the Section form. If it adds a new section, the Sections combo box and the entries list are reloaded.

```
Private Sub btnAddSection_Click()
    Dim NewSectionName
    '
```

Continued on next page

Continued from previous page

```
   ' get new section name
   '
   NewSectionName = Section.AddSection(txtFilename, cmbSections)
   '
   ' if there's a new section to add, add it
   '
   If NewSectionName () "" Then
       '
       ' add to the combo, but not to the INI file
       ' yet. A section with no entries is pointless
       '
       cmbSections.AddItem NewSectionName
       cmbSections.ListIndex = cmbSections.NewIndex
       '
       ' clear entries list and make appropriate
       ' changes to buttons
       '
       lstEntries.Clear
       btnAddEntry.Enabled = True
       btnAddSection.Enabled = True
       btnDeleteEntry.Enabled = False
       btnEditEntry.Enabled = False
       btnDeleteSection.Enabled = True
   End If
End Sub
```

7. Add the following code to Click event of the Choose INI File button. It uses the File Open common dialog to select an .INI file. Then the Sections combo box and the Entries list box are loaded with the data from the .INI file.

```
Private Sub btnChooseIniFile_Click()
   Dim Filename As String
   '
   ' get a new INI file name
   '
   CommonDialog1.Filter = "INI Files(*.INI)|*.INI"
   CommonDialog1.Flags = &H1804 ' vbOFNFileMustExist Or _
       vbOFNPathMustExist Or vbOFNHideReadOnly
   CommonDialog1.Filename = ""
   CommonDialog1.ShowOpen
   '
   ' if the user didn't press cancel
   '
   Filename = CommonDialog1.Filename
   If Len(Filename) () 0 Then
       '
       ' display the filename
       '
       txtFilename = Filename
       '
       ' reset everything
       '
       cmbSections.Clear
       lstEntries.Clear
```

```
'
' load the sections combo box
'
LoadSections Filename
'
' if there are sections in this INI file,
' load up the entries list box for the
' first section
'
If cmbSections.ListCount > 0 Then
    cmbSections.ListIndex = 0
    LoadEntries Filename, cmbSections.Text
    btnDeleteSection.Enabled = True
End If
'
' enable buttons
'
btnAddSection.Enabled = True
btnAddEntry.Enabled = True
    End If
End Sub
```

8. Add this routine to the Delete Entry button to confirm that the user wishes to delete the entry in question. If the user confirms, the entry is deleted and the Entries list box is reloaded.

```
Private Sub btnDeleteEntry_Click()
    Dim EntryName As String
    '
    ' extract entry name
    '
    EntryName = lstEntries.List(lstEntries.ListIndex)
    If InStr(EntryName, Chr(9)) Then
        EntryName = Left(EntryName, InStr(EntryName, Chr(9)) - 1)
    End If
    '
    ' confirm the deletion
    '
    If (MsgBox("Are you sure you want to delete the " & EntryName & _
            " entry from this INI file?", vbYesNo) = vbYes) Then
        '
        ' delete entry
        '
        If IsWinIni(txtFilename) Then
            WinIniRegister cmbSections.Text
            WinDeleteEntry EntryName
        Else
            '
            ' otherwise, use private INI file functions
            '
            PrivIniRegister cmbSections.Text, txtFilename
            PrivDeleteEntry EntryName
        End If
```

Continued on next page

Continued from previous page

```
    '
    ' reset entries list
    '
    lstEntries.Clear
    btnDeleteEntry.Enabled = False
    btnEditEntry.Enabled = False
    '
    ' load up the entries list box for the section
    '
    LoadEntries txtFilename, cmbSections.Text
    btnDeleteSection.Enabled = False
    End If
End Sub
```

9. Add this subroutine to the Click event for the Delete Section button, to confirm that the user wishes to delete the section. If so, the routine calls into INI.BAS to delete the section. Then both the Sections combo box and the Entries list box are reloaded.

```
Private Sub btnDeleteSection_Click()
    '
    ' confirm the deletion
    '
    If (MsgBox("Are you sure you want to delete the " & _
            cmbSections.Text & " section from this INI file?", _
            vbYesNo) = vbYes) Then
        '
        ' delete section
        '
        If IsWinIni(txtFilename) Then
            WinIniRegister cmbSections.Text
            WinDeleteSection
        Else
            '
            ' otherwise, use private INI file functions
            '
            PrivIniRegister cmbSections.Text, txtFilename
            PrivDeleteSection
        End If
        '
        ' reset everything
        '
        cmbSections.Clear
        lstEntries.Clear
        btnDeleteEntry.Enabled = False
        btnEditEntry.Enabled = False
        '
        ' load the sections combo box
        '
        LoadSections txtFilename
        '
        ' if there are sections in this INI file,
        ' load up the entries list box for the
        ' first section
```

```
        '
        If cmbSections.ListCount > 0 Then
            cmbSections.ListIndex = 0
            LoadEntries txtFilename, cmbSections.Text
        Else
            btnDeleteSection.Enabled = False
        End If
    End If
End Sub
```

10. Add the following code to the Click handler for the Edit Entry button, to call the EditEntry function in the Entry form. When it comes back, changed or not, the Entries list box is updated using the LoadEntries function.

```
Private Sub btnEditEntry_Click()
    Dim EntryName As String
    '
    ' extract entry name
    '
    EntryName = lstEntries.List(lstEntries.ListIndex)
    If InStr(EntryName, Chr(9)) Then
        EntryName = Left(EntryName, InStr(EntryName, Chr(9)) - 1)
    End If
    '
    ' edit this entry
    '
    Entry.EditEntry txtFilename, cmbSections.Text, EntryName
    '
    ' update entries list box
    '
    LoadEntries txtFilename, cmbSections.Text
End Sub
```

11. Add the following code to the Click event for the Exit button. This makes the program exit when the user presses the button.

```
Private Sub btnExit_Click()
    '
    ' get out
    '
    End
End Sub
```

12. Add the following routine to the Sections combo box's Click event handler, to load the Entries list box with the newly selected section.

```
Private Sub cmbSections_Click()
    '
    ' update entries list box
    '
    LoadEntries txtFilename, cmbSections.Text
End Sub
```

13. Add the following code to Form's Unload handler. This ensures that the program exits.

```
Private Sub Form_Unload(Cancel As Integer)
    '
    ' make sure the program exits
    '
    End
End Sub
```

14. Add the following code to Click event handler for the Entries list box. This enables/disables the Delete and Edit Entry buttons.

```
Private Sub lstEntries_Click()
    '
    ' an entry is selected, allow it to be deleted
    '
    If Not btnDeleteEntry.Enabled Then
        btnDeleteEntry.Enabled = True
    End If
    '
    ' ... or edited
    '
    If Not btnEditEntry.Enabled Then
        btnEditEntry.Enabled = True
    End If
End Sub
```

15. Add the following code to the DblClick event routine for the Entries list box. This subroutine causes the Edit Entry form to come up when the user double-clicks on an entry.

```
Private Sub lstEntries_DblClick()
    btnEditEntry_Click
End Sub
```

The .INI File Management Module (INI.BAS)

16. Create a new module, name it INI, and save it as INI.BAS. Add the following code which defines all of the API calls used, some constants used by those API calls, and some variables used by this module.

```
Option Explicit
'
' Declare Windows API calls
'
Declare Function GetProfileString Lib "Kernel" Alias "GetProfileString" ⇒
    (ByVal lpAppName As String, _
```

```
        ByVal lpKeyName As Any, ByVal lpDefault As String, _
        ByVal lpReturnedString As String, ByVal nSize As Integer) As Integer
Declare Function WriteProfileString Lib "Kernel" Alias _
        "WriteProfileString" (ByVal lpAppName As Any, _
        ByVal lpKeyName As Any, ByVal lpString As Any) As Integer
Declare Function GetPrivateProfileString Lib "Kernel" _
        Alias "GetPrivateProfileString" (ByVal lpAppName As String, _
        ByVal lpKeyName As Any, ByVal lpDefault As String, _
        ByVal lpReturnedString As String, ByVal nSize As Integer, _
        ByVal lpFileName As String) As Integer
Declare Function WritePrivateProfileStringDelEntry Lib "kernel32" _
        Alias "WritePrivateProfileStringA" (ByVal lpApplicationName As String, ⇒
        ByVal lpKeyName As Any, ByVal lpValue As Long, ByVal lpFileName ⇒
        As String) As Long
Declare Function WritePrivateProfileStringDelSect Lib "kernel32" _
        Alias "WritePrivateProfileStringA" (ByVal lpApplicationName As String, ⇒
        ByVal lpKey As Long, ByVal lpValue As Long, ByVal lpFileName ⇒
        As String) As Long
Declare Function WriteProfileString Lib "kernel32" Alias "WriteProfileStringA" ⇒
        (ByVal lpszSection As String, ByVal lpszKeyName As String, ⇒
        ByVal lpszString As String) As Long
Declare Function SendMessage Lib "user32" Alias "SendMessageA" ⇒
        (ByVal hwnd As Long, ByVal wMsg As Long, ByVal wParam As Integer, ⇒
        ByVal lParam As Long) As Long
Declare Function SendMessageString Lib "user32" Alias "SendMessageA" _
        (ByVal hwnd As Long, ByVal wMsg As Long, ByVal wParam As Integer, ⇒
        ByVal lpstr As String) As Long
Declare Function GetWindowsDirectory Lib "Kernel" Alias "GetWindowsDirectory" ⇒
        (ByVal lpBuffer As String, ByVal nSize As Integer) As Integer
'
' Module-level variables for [Section] and Ini file names
'
Dim CurSectionName As String ' Current section in private Ini file
Dim CurIniFileName As String ' Fully qualified path/name of current
                             ' private Ini file
Dim CurWinSection As String  ' Current section in Win.Ini
Dim WinInitFlag As Integer   ' Flag to indicate that Win.Ini section
                             ' is initialized
Dim PrivInitFlag As Integer  ' Flag to indicate that Private.Ini
                             ' is initialized
'
' Buffer sizes
'
Const MaxSectionBuffer = 4096
Const MaxEntryBuffer = 255
'
' WIN.INI change message constants
'
Const HWND_BROADCAST = &HFFFF
Const WM_WININICHANGE = &H1A
```

17. Add the following code to INI. This function extracts the filename from a full filespec. Optionally, it can remove any filename extension.

```
'
' get name from full filename/path
'
Private Function ExtractName(sSpecIn As String, _
        BaseOnly As Boolean) As String
    Dim sSpecOut As String
    Dim nCnt As Integer
    Dim nDot As Integer
    '
    On Local Error Resume Next
    '
    ' strip path from front
    '
    If InStr(sSpecIn, "\") Then
        For nCnt = Len(sSpecIn) To 1 Step -1
            If Mid$(sSpecIn, nCnt, 1) = "\" Then
                sSpecOut = Mid$(sSpecIn, nCnt + 1)
                Exit For
            End If
        Next nCnt
    ElseIf InStr(sSpecIn, ":") = 2 Then
        sSpecOut = Mid$(sSpecIn, 3)
    Else
        sSpecOut = sSpecIn
    End If
    '
    ' if we're looking for only the base filename,
    ' strip out any extension
    '
    If BaseOnly Then
        nDot = InStr(sSpecOut, ".")
        If nDot Then
            sSpecOut = Left$(sSpecOut, nDot - 1)
        End If
    End If
    '
    ' return to caller
    '
    ExtractName = UCase$(sSpecOut)
End Function
```

18. Add the following function to INI, to extract the path from a full filespec.

```
'
' get path from full filename/path
'
Private Function ExtractPath(sSpecIn As String) As String
    Dim nCnt As Integer
    Dim sSpecOut As String

    On Local Error Resume Next
```

```
'
' strip filename from back
'
If InStr(sSpecIn, "\") Then
    For nCnt = Len(sSpecIn) To 1 Step -1
        If Mid$(sSpecIn, nCnt, 1) = "\" Then
            sSpecOut = Left$(sSpecIn, nCnt)
            Exit For
        End If
    Next nCnt
ElseIf InStr(sSpecIn, ":") = 2 Then
    sSpecOut = CurDir$(sSpecIn)
    If Len(sSpecOut) = 0 Then
        sSpecOut = CurDir$
    End If
Else
    sSpecOut = CurDir$
End If
'
' make sure we terminate with a \
'
If Right$(sSpecOut, 1) () "\" Then
    sSpecOut = sSpecOut + "\"
End If
'
' return to caller
'
ExtractPath = UCase$(sSpecOut)
End Function
```

19. Add the following code to the INI module. This function returns True if the file-name has passed points to the WIN.INI file.

```
Public Function IsWinIni(Filename As String) As Boolean
    '
    ' check base of filename
    '
    IsWinIni = (ExtractName(Filename, True) = "WIN")
End Function
```

20. Add the following subroutine to the INI module, to clear the specified entry from a private .INI file.

```
Public Sub PrivClearEntry(sEntryName As String)
    '
    ' get out if not initialized
    '
    If Not PrivInitFlag Then
        PrivIniNotReg
        Exit Sub
    End If
    '
    ' Clears a specific entry in Private.Ini
    '
```

Continued on next page

Continued from previous page

```
    WritePrivateProfileStringDelEntry CurSectionName, sEntryName, O&, ⇒
        CurIniFileName
End Sub
```

21. Add the following subroutine to INI. This function deletes the specified entry from the selected private .INI file.

```
Public Sub PrivDeleteEntry(sEntryName As String)
    '
    ' get out if not initialized
    '
    If Not PrivInitFlag Then
        PrivIniNotReg
        Exit Sub
    End If
    '
    ' Deletes a specific entry in Private.Ini
    '
    WritePrivateProfileStringDelEntry CurSectionName, sEntryName, O&,⇒
        CurIniFileName
End Sub
```

22. Add the following code to the INI module. This function deletes the entire selected section from a private .INI file.

```
Public Sub PrivDeleteSection()
    '
    ' get out if not initialized
    '
    If Not PrivInitFlag Then
        PrivIniNotReg
        Exit Sub
    End If
    '
    ' Deletes an *entire* [Section] and all its Entries
    ' in Private.Ini
    '
    WritePrivateProfileStringDelEntry CurSectionName, sEntryName, O&, ⇒
        CurIniFileName
    '
    ' Now Private.Ini needs to be reinitialized
    '
    CurSectionName = ""
    PrivInitFlag = False
End Sub
```

23. Add the following code to the INI module. This function retrieves an entire section from a private .INI file.

```
Public Function PrivGetSectEntries() As String
    Dim sTemp As String * MaxSectionBuffer
    Dim ListSize As Integer
    '
    ' get out if not initialized
    '
```

```
    If Not PrivInitFlag Then
        PrivIniNotReg
        Exit Function
    End If
    '
    ' Retrieves all Entries in a [Section] of Private.Ini
    ' Entries null terminated; last entry double-terminated
    '
    ListSize = IniGetPrivateProfileString(CurSectionName, 0&, "", _
        sTemp, Len(sTemp), CurIniFileName)
    PrivGetSectEntries = Left$(sTemp, ListSize + 1)
End Function
```

24. Add the following function to INI. This function uses PrivGetSectEntries to retrieve and parse an entire section from a private .INI file. It returns the number of entries found, and passes the entry names and values back into the array that is passed in.

```
Public Function PrivGetSectEntriesEx(sTable() As String) As Integer
    Dim TempStr As String
    Dim NumEntries As Integer
    Dim NullOffset As Integer
    '
    ' get out if not initialized
    '
    If Not PrivInitFlag Then
        PrivIniNotReg
        Exit Function
    End If
    '
    ' Retrieves all Entries in a [Section] of Private.Ini
    ' Entries null terminated; last entry double-terminated
    '
    TempStr = PrivGetSectEntries
    '
    ' Parse entries into first dimension of table
    ' and retrieve values into second dimension
    '
    NumEntries = 0
    Do While Asc(TempStr)  0
        ReDim Preserve sTable(0 To 1, 0 To NumEntries)
        NullOffset = InStr(TempStr, Chr$(0))
        sTable(0, NumEntries) = Left$(TempStr, NullOffset - 1)
        sTable(1, NumEntries) = PrivGetString(sTable(0, _
            NumEntries), "")
        TempStr = Mid$(TempStr, NullOffset + 1)
        NumEntries = NumEntries + 1
    Loop
    '
    ' return count
    '
    PrivGetSectEntriesEx = NumEntries
End Function
```

25. Add the following function to INI.BAS, to retrieve all of the section names from a private .INI file.

```
Public Function PrivGetSections() As String
    Dim sRet As String
    Dim sBuff As String
    Dim hFile As Integer
    '
    ' get out if not initialized
    '
    If Not PrivInitFlag Then
        PrivIniNotReg
        Exit Function
    End If
    '
    ' Extract all [Section] lines
    '
    hFile = FreeFile
    Open CurIniFileName For Input As hFile
    Do While Not EOF(hFile)
        Line Input #hFile, sBuff
        sBuff = StripComment$(sBuff)
        If InStr(sBuff, "[") = 1 And InStr(sBuff, "]") = _
                Len(sBuff) Then
            sRet = sRet + Mid$(sBuff, 2, Len(sBuff) - 2) + Chr$(0)
        End If
    Loop
    Close hFile
    '
    '   Assign return value
    '
    If Len(sRet) Then
        PrivGetSections = sRet + Chr$(0)
    Else
        PrivGetSections = String$(2, 0)
    End If
End Function
```

26. Add the following code to the INI module. This function uses PrivGetSections to retrieve and parse the list of sections in a private .INI file.

```
Public Function PrivGetSectionsEx(sTable() As String) As Integer
    '
    ' Get "normal" list of all [Section]'s
    '
    Dim sSect As String
    sSect = PrivGetSections$()
    If Len(sSect) = 0 Then
        PrivGetSectionsEx = 0
        Exit Function
    End If
    '
    'Parse [Section]'s into table
    '
```

```
    Dim nEntries As Integer
    Dim nNull As Integer
    '
    Do While Asc(sSect)
        ReDim Preserve sTable(0 To nEntries)
        nNull = InStr(sSect, Chr$(0))
        sTable(nEntries) = Left$(sSect, nNull - 1)
        sSect = Mid$(sSect, nNull + 1)
        nEntries = nEntries + 1
    Loop
    '
    ' Make function assignment
    '
    PrivGetSectionsEx = nEntries
End Function
```

27. Add the following function to INI.BAS, to retrieve the specified entry value from a private .INI file.

```
Public Function PrivGetString(sEntryName As String, _
    ByVal sDefaultValue As String) As String
    '
    ' get out if not initialized
    '
    If Not PrivInitFlag Then
        PrivIniNotReg
        Exit Function
    End If
    '
    ' Retrieves Specific Entry from Private.Ini
    '
    Dim sTemp As String * MaxEntryBuffer
    Dim nRetVal As Integer
    nRetVal = IniGetPrivateProfileString(CurSectionName, _
        sEntryName, sDefaultValue, sTemp, Len(sTemp), CurIniFileName)
    If nRetVal Then
        PrivGetString = Left$(sTemp, nRetVal)
    Else
        PrivGetString = ""
    End If
End Function
```

28. Add the following code to INI. This function forces the Windows .INI file manager to flush its cache for the current private .INI file.

```
Public Sub PrivIniFlushCache()
    '
    ' get out if not initialized
    '
    If Not PrivInitFlag Then
        PrivIniNotReg
        Exit Sub
    End If
```

Continued on next page

Continued from previous page

```
    '
    ' To improve performance, Windows keeps a cached version of the
    ' most-recently accessed initialization file. If that filename is
    ' specified and the other three parameters are NULL, Windows
    ' flushes the cache
    '
    WritePrivateProfileString 0&, 0&, 0&, CurIniFileName
End Sub
```

29. Add the following code to the INI module. This function will be called only when this module is not correctly used by the programmer.

```
Private Sub PrivIniNotReg()
    '
    ' Warn *PROGRAMMER* that there's a logic error!
    '
    MsgBox "[Section] and FileName Not Registered in Private.Ini!", _
        vbCritical, "INI Logic Error"
End Sub
```

30. Add the following subroutine to INI. Use this function to select the filename and section that you wish to work with.

```
Public Sub PrivIniRegister(sSectionName As String, _
    sIniFileName As String)
    '
    ' Store module-level values for future reference
    '
    CurSectionName = Trim$(sSectionName)
    CurIniFileName = Trim$(sIniFileName)
    PrivInitFlag = True
End Sub
```

31. Add the following code to the INI module. This function writes the specified value into a private .INI file.

```
Public Sub PrivIniWrite(SectionName As String, _
    FileName As String, EntryName As String, _
    ByVal NewVal As String)
    '
    ' One-shot write to Private.Ini
    '
    WritePrivateProfileString SectionName$, EntryName$, _
        NewVal$, IniFileName$
End Sub
```

32. Add the following function to INI.BAS. This function writes the specified value into the currently selected private .INI file.

```
Public Function PrivPutString(sEntryName As String, _
    ByVal sValue As String) As Integer
    '
    ' get out if not initialized
    '
```

```
    If Not PrivInitFlag Then
        PrivIniNotReg
        Exit Function
    End If
    '
    ' Write a string to Private.Ini
    '
    PrivPutString = IniWritePrivateProfileString(CurSectionName, _
        sEntryName, sValue, CurIniFileName)
End Function
```

33. Put this function in INI.BAS, to check for the existence of the currently selected section in a private .INI file.

```
Public Function PrivSectExist() As Integer
    '
    ' Retrieve list of all [Section]'s
    '
    Dim sSect As String
    sSect = PrivGetSections$()
    '
    ' if there are no sections, this one doesn't exist
    '
    If Len(sSect) = 0 Then
        PrivSectExist = False
        Exit Function
    End If
    '
    ' Check for existence registered [Section]
    '
    sSect = Chr$(0) + UCase$(sSect)
    If InStr(sSect, Chr$(0) + UCase$(CurSectionName) + Chr$(0)) Then
        PrivSectExist = True
    Else
        PrivSectExist = False
    End If
End Function
```

34. Add the following code to INI.BAS. This function strips an INI comment from a string.

```
Private Function StripComment(ByVal StrIn As String) As String
    Dim nRet As Integer
    '
    ' Check for comment
    '
    nRet = InStr(StrIn, ";")
    '
    ' Remove it if present
    '
    If nRet = 1 Then
        '
        ' Whole string is a comment
        '
```

Continued on next page

Continued from previous page

```
        StripComment = ""
        Exit Function
    ElseIf nRet > 1 Then
        '
        ' Strip comment
        '
        StrIn = Left$(StrIn, nRet - 1)
    End If
    '
    ' Trim any trailing space
    '
    StripComment = Trim$(StrIn)
End Function
```

35. Add the following subroutine to the INI module, to clear the specified entry from WIN.INI.

```
Public Sub WinClearEntry(sEntryName As String)
    '
    ' Get out if not initialized
    '
    If Not WinInitFlag Then
        WinIniNotReg
        Exit Sub
    End If
    '
    ' Sets a specific entry in Win.Ini to Nothing or Blank
    '
    WritePrivateProfileStringDelEntry CurWinSection, sEntryName, ⇒
        0&, "WIN.INI"
    WinIniChanged
End Sub
```

36. Add the following subroutine to INI, to delete the specified entry from WIN.INI.

```
Public Sub WinDeleteEntry(sEntryName As String)
    '
    ' Get out if not initialized
    '
    If Not WinInitFlag Then
        WinIniNotReg
        Exit Sub
    End If
    '
    ' Deletes a specific entry in Win.Ini
    '
    WritePrivateProfileStringDelEntry CurWinSection, sEntryName, ⇒
        0&, "WIN.INI"
    WinIniChanged
End Sub
```

37. Add the following code to the INI module, to delete the entire selected section from WIN.INI.

```
Sub WinDeleteSection()
```

```
'
' Get out if not initialized
'
If Not WinInitFlag Then
    WinIniNotReg
    Exit Sub
End If
'
' Deletes an *entire* [Section] and all its Entries in Win.Ini
'
WritePrivateProfileStringDelSect CurWinSection, 0&, 0&, "WIN.INI"
'
' Now Win.Ini needs to be reinitialized
'
CurWinSection = ""
WinInitFlag = False
WinIniChanged
End Sub
```

38. Add the following function to the INI module, to retrieve an entire section from WIN.INI.

```
Public Function WinGetSectEntries() As String
    '
    ' Get out if not initialized
    '
    If Not WinInitFlag Then
        WinIniNotReg
        Exit Function
    End If
    '
    ' Retrieves all Entries in a [Section] of Win.Ini
    ' Entries null terminated; last entry double-terminated
    '
    Dim sTemp As String * MaxSectionBuffer
    Dim nRetVal As Integer
    nRetVal = IniGetProfileString(CurWinSection, 0&, "", sTemp, _
        Len(sTemp))
    WinGetSectEntries = Left$(sTemp, nRetVal + 1)
End Function
```

39. Add the following function to INI. This function uses WinGetSectEntries to retrieve and parse an entire section from WIN.INI. It returns the number of entries found, and passes the entry names and values back into the array that is passed in.

```
Public Function WinGetSectEntriesEx(sTable() As String) As Integer
    '
    ' Get out if not initialized
    '
    If Not WinInitFlag Then
        WinIniNotReg
        Exit Function
    End If
    '
```

Continued on next page

Continued from previous page

```
    'Retrieves all Entries in a [Section] of Win.Ini
    'Entries nul terminated; last entry double-terminated
    '
    Dim sBuff As String * MaxSectionBuffer
    Dim sTemp As String
    Dim nRetVal As Integer
    nRetVal = IniGetProfileString(CurWinSection, 0&, "", sBuff, _
        Len(sBuff))
    sTemp = Left$(sBuff, nRetVal + 1)
    '
    ' Parse entries into first dimension of table
    ' and retrieve values into second dimension
    '
    Dim nEntries As Integer
    Dim nNull As Integer
    Do While Asc(sTemp)
        ReDim Preserve sTable(0 To 1, 0 To nEntries)
        nNull = InStr(sTemp, Chr$(0))
        sTable(0, nEntries) = Left$(sTemp, nNull - 1)
        sTable(1, nEntries) = WinGetString(sTable(0, nEntries), "")
        sTemp = Mid$(sTemp, nNull + 1)
        nEntries = nEntries + 1
    Loop
    '
    ' Make final assignment
    '
    WinGetSectEntriesEx = nEntries
End Function
```

40. Add the following function to INI.BAS, to retrieve all of the section names from WIN.INI.

```
Public Function WinGetSections() As String
    Dim sWinIni As String
    Dim sRet As String
    Dim sBuff As String
    Dim hFile As Integer
    Dim nRet As Integer
    '
    ' Find Win.Ini
    '
    sBuff = String$(MaxEntryBuffer, 0)
    nRet = IniGetWindowsDirectory(sBuff, MaxEntryBuffer)
    sWinIni = Left$(sBuff, nRet) + "\Win.Ini"
    '
    ' Extract all [Section] lines
    '
    hFile = FreeFile
    Open sWinIni For Input As hFile
    Do While Not EOF(hFile)
        Line Input #hFile, sBuff
        sBuff = StripComment$(sBuff)
        If InStr(sBuff, "[") = 1 And InStr(sBuff, "]") = _
            Len(sBuff) Then
```

```
            sRet = sRet + Mid$(sBuff, 2, Len(sBuff) - 2) + Chr$(0)
        End If
    Loop
    Close hFile
    '
    ' Assign return value
    '
    If Len(sRet) Then
        WinGetSections = sRet + Chr$(0)
    Else
        WinGetSections = String$(2, 0)
    End If
End Function
```

41. Add the following code to the INI module. This function uses WinGetSections to retrieve and parse the list of sections in WIN.INI.

```
Public Function WinGetSectionsEx(sTable() As String) As Integer
    '
    ' Get "normal" list of all [Section]'s
    '
    Dim sSect As String
    sSect = WinGetSections$()
    If Len(sSect) = 0 Then
        WinGetSectionsEx = 0
        Exit Function
    End If
    '
    ' Parse [Section]'s into table
    '
    Dim nEntries As Integer
    Dim nNull As Integer
    Do While Asc(sSect)
        ReDim Preserve sTable(0 To nEntries)
        nNull = InStr(sSect, Chr$(0))
        sTable(nEntries) = Left$(sSect, nNull - 1)
        sSect = Mid$(sSect, nNull + 1)
        nEntries = nEntries + 1
    Loop
    '
    ' Make function assignment
    '
    WinGetSectionsEx = nEntries
End Function
```

42. Add the following function to INI.BAS, to retrieve the specified entry value from WIN.INI.

```
Public Function WinGetString(sEntryName As String, _
        ByVal sDefaultValue As String) As String
    '
    ' Get out if not initialized
    '
    If Not WinInitFlag Then
        WinIniNotReg
```

Continued on next page

Continued from previous page

```
        Exit Function
    End If
    '
    ' Retrieves Specific Entry from Win.Ini
    '
    Dim sTemp As String * MaxEntryBuffer
    Dim nRetVal As Integer
    nRetVal = IniGetProfileString(CurWinSection, sEntryName, _
        sDefaultValue, sTemp, Len(sTemp))
    If nRetVal Then
        WinGetString = Left$(sTemp, nRetVal)
    End If
End Function
```

43. Add the following code to INI. This function notifies all other applications that WIN.INI has changed.

```
Private Sub WinIniChanged()
    '
    ' Notify all other applications that Win.Ini has been changed
    '
    SendMessageString HWND_BROADCAST, WM_WININICHANGE, 0, _
        ByVal CurWinSection
End Sub
```

44. Add the following code to INI. This function forces the Windows .INI file manager to flush its cached version of WIN.INI.

```
Public Sub WinIniFlushCache()
    '
    ' Windows keeps a cached version of WIN.INI to improve
    ' performance. If all three parameters are NULL, Windows flushes
    ' the cache.
    '
    WriteProfileString 0&, 0&, 0&
End Sub
```

45. Add the following code to the INI module. This function will be called only when this module is not correctly used by the programmer.

```
Private Sub WinIniNotReg()
    '
    ' Warn *PROGRAMMER* that there's a logic error!
    '
    MsgBox "[Section] Not Registered in Win.Ini!", 16, _
        "IniFile Logic Error"
End Sub
```

46. Add the following subroutine to INI. Use this function to select the filename and section that you wish to work with.

```
Public Sub WinIniRegister(sSectionName As String)
    '
    ' Store module-level for future reference
    '
    CurWinSection = Trim$(sSectionName)
    WinInitFlag = True
End Sub
```

47. Add the following function to INI.BAS. This function writes the value specified to WIN.INI.

```
Public Function WinPutString(sEntryName As String, _
    ByVal sValue As String) As Integer
    '
    ' Get out if not initialized
    '
    If Not WinInitFlag Then
        WinIniNotReg
        Exit Function
    End If
    '
    ' Write a string to Win.Ini
    '
    WinPutString = IniWriteProfileString(CurWinSection, _
        sEntryName, sValue)
    WinIniChanged
End Function
```

48. Put this function in INI.BAS, to check for the existence of the currently selected section in WIN.INI.

```
Public Function WinSectExist() As Integer
    '
    ' Retrieve list of all [Section]'s
    '
    Dim sSect As String
    sSect = WinGetSections$()
    If Len(sSect) = 0 Then
        WinSectExist = False
        Exit Function
    End If
    '
    ' Check for existence registered [Section]
    '
    sSect = Chr$(0) + UCase$(sSect)
    If InStr(sSect, Chr$(0) + UCase$(CurWinSection) + Chr$(0)) Then
        WinSectExist = True
    Else
        WinSectExist = False
    End If
End Function
```

The Entry Form (ENTRY.FRM)

49. Create a new form. Name it Entry and save it as ENTRY.FRM. Select the form, and add objects with properties set as in Table 7-2-2.

Table 7-2-2 Objects, properties, and settings for Entry

OBJECT	PROPERTY	SETTING
Form	Name	Entry
	BorderStyle	3 'Fixed Double
	Caption	"Entry"
	Height	2145
	Left	1515
	LockControls	-1 'True
	Top	2760
	Width	8895
TextBox	Name	txtEntryValue
	Height	285
	Left	360
	Top	1200
	Width	6135
TextBox	Name	txtEntryName
	Height	285
	Left	360
	Top	480
	Width	6135
CommandButton	Name	btnClose
	Caption	"Close"
	Default	-1 'True
	Enabled	0 'False
	Height	375
	Left	6840
	Top	240
	Width	1695
CommandButton	Name	btnCancel
	Cancel	-1 'True
	Caption	"Cancel"
	Height	375
	Left	6840
	Top	720
	Width	1695

OBJECT	PROPERTY	SETTING
Label	Name	Label2
	Caption	"Entry Value:"
	Height	255
	Left	240
	Top	960
	Width	2295
Label	Name	Label1
	Caption	"Entry Name:"
	Height	255
	Left	240
	Top	240
	Width	2295

50. Add the following code to the General Declarations section of Entry:

```
Option Explicit
'
' cancel button pressed?
'
Dim fCancel As Boolean
```

51. Continue adding code to the General Declarations section of Entry, as follows. This function displays the Entry form, with a caption of "Add Entry." After accepting the user's input, this function adds the entry and its value to the currently selected .INI file and section.

```
Public Function AddEntry(Filename As String, _
    SectionName As String) As Boolean
    '
    ' functions don't take string parms from controls
    '
    Dim EntryName As String
    Dim EntryValue As String
    '
    ' show form with appropriate caption
    '
    fCancel = False
    txtEntryName.ReadOnly = False
    Me.Caption = "Add Entry"
    Me.Show 1
    '
    ' if the name is blank, get out
    '
    txtEntryName = Trim(txtEntryName)
    If txtEntryName = "" Or fCancel Then
        AddEntry = False
        Exit Function
    End If
```

Continued on next page

Continued from previous page

```
    '
    ' is it WIN.INI?  If so, use those funcs
    '
    EntryName = txtEntryName
    EntryValue = txtEntryValue
    If IsWinIni(Filename) Then
        WinIniRegister SectionName
        WinPutString EntryName, EntryValue
        WinIniFlushCache
    Else
        '
        ' otherwise, use private INI file functions
        '
        PrivIniRegister SectionName, Filename
        PrivPutString EntryName, EntryValue
        PrivIniFlushCache
    End If
    '
    ' function worked
    '
    AddEntry = True
End Function
```

52. Add the following code to the General Declarations section of Entry. This function displays the Entry form with a caption of "Edit Entry." It allows the user to change the value of an entry.

```
Public Function EditEntry(Filename As String, _
    SectionName As String, EntryName As String) As Boolean
    '
    ' functions don't take string parms from controls
    '
    Dim EntryValue As String
    '
    fCancel = False
    txtEntryName.ReadOnly = True
    btnClose.Enabled = True
    '
    ' is it WIN.INI?  If so, use those funcs to get value
    '
    If IsWinIni(Filename) Then
        WinIniRegister SectionName
        EntryValue = WinGetString(EntryName, "")
    Else
        '
        ' otherwise, use private INI file functions
        '
        PrivIniRegister SectionName, Filename
        EntryValue = PrivGetString(EntryName, "")
    End If
    '
    ' show form with appropriate caption
    '
    Me.Caption = "Edit Entry"
```

```
    txtEntryName = EntryName
    txtEntryValue = EntryValue
    Me.Show 1
    EntryValue = Trim(txtEntryValue)
    '
    ' if cancelled, get out
    '
    If fCancel Then
        EditEntry = False
        Exit Function
    End If
    '
    ' is it WIN.INI?  If so, use those funcs
    '
    txtEntryValue = Trim(txtEntryValue)
    EntryValue = txtEntryValue
    If IsWinIni(Filename) Then
        WinIniRegister SectionName
        WinPutString EntryName, EntryValue
        WinIniFlushCache
    Else
        '
        ' otherwise, use private INI file functions
        '
        PrivIniRegister SectionName, Filename
        PrivPutString EntryName, EntryValue
        PrivIniFlushCache
    End If
    '
    ' function worked
    '
    EditEntry = True
End Function
```

53. Add the following code to the Click event handler of the Cancel button. This function sets the Cancel flag and then hides the form. This causes the AddEntry or EditEntry functions to abort.

```
Private Sub btnCancel_Click()
    txtEntryName = ""
    txtEntryValue = ""
    fCancel = True
    Me.Hide
End Sub
```

54. Add the following code to the Click event handler of the Close button. This function hides the form and causes the AddEntry or EditEntry functions to finish their tasks.

```
Private Sub btnClose_Click()
    fCancel = False
    Me.Hide
End Sub
```

55. Add the following code to the Change event subroutine of txtEntryName, to enable/disable the Close button.

```
Private Sub txtEntryName_Change()
    '
    ' enable Close button
    '
    btnClose.Enabled = Len(txtEntryName) () 0
End Sub
```

56. Add the following code to the Change event subroutine of txtEntryValue, to enable/disable the Close button.

```
Private Sub txtEntryValue_Change()
    '
    ' enable Close button
    '
    btnClose.Enabled = Len(txtEntryName)  0
End Sub
```

The Section Form (SECTION.FRM)

57. Create a new form. Name it Section and save it as SECTION.FRM. Select the form and add objects with properties set as in Table 7-2-3.

Table 7-2-3 Objects, properties, and settings for Section

OBJECT	PROPERTY	SETTING
Form	Name	Section
	BorderStyle	3 'Fixed Double
	Caption	"Add Section"
	Height	1755
	Left	1350
	LockControls	-1 'True
	Top	1650
	Width	8910
CommandButton	Name	btnCancel
	Cancel	-1 'True
	Caption	"Cancel"
	Height	375
	Left	6840
	Top	720
	Width	1695
TextBox	Name	txtSectionName
	Height	285

OBJECT	PROPERTY	SETTING
	Left	360
	Top	480
	Width	6135
CommandButton	Name	btnClose
	Caption	"Close"
	Default	-1 'True
	Enabled	0 'False
	Height	375
	Left	6840
	Top	240
	Width	1695
Label	Name	Label1
	Caption	"Section Name:"
	Height	255
	Left	240
	Top	240
	Width	2295

58. Add the following code to the General Declarations section of Section:

```
Option Explicit
```

59. Continue adding code to the General Declarations section of Section. This next function adds a section to the current .INI file. (If the section is already present, it isn't added.)

```
Public Function AddSection(Filename As String, _
    SectionList As Object) As String
  Dim fExist As Boolean

  Do
     Me.Show 1
     '
     ' if the name is blank, get out
     '
     txtSectionName = Trim(txtSectionName)
     If txtSectionName = "" Then
        Exit Do
     End If
     '
     ' is it WIN.INI?  If so, use those funcs
     '
     If IsWinIni(Filename) Then
        WinIniRegister txtSectionName
        fExist = WinSectExist()
     Else
```

Continued on next page

Continued from previous page

```
            ' otherwise, use private INI file functions
            PrivIniRegister txtSectionName, Filename
            fExist = PrivSectExist()
        End If
        '
        ' if the section exists, display error to user
        '
        If fExist Then
            MsgBox "The " & txtSectionName & _
                " section already exists.", vbOK And vbExclamation, _
                "Add Section"
            txtSectionName = ""
        End If
    Loop While fExist
    '
    ' return new section name to caller
    '
    AddSection = txtSectionName
End Function
```

60. Add the following code to the Click event handler of the Cancel button. This subroutine makes the form hide, which starts the second half of the AddSection function.

```
Private Sub btnCancel_Click()
    txtSectionName = ""
    Me.Hide
End Sub
```

61. Add the following code to the Click event handler of the Close button. This subroutine causes the form to hide, which starts the second half of the AddSection function.

```
Private Sub btnClose_Click()
    Me.Hide
End Sub
```

62. Add the following code to the Change event handler of txtSectionName, to enable/disable the Close button whenever the text changes.

```
Private Sub txtSectionName_Change()
    btnClose.Enabled = (Len(txtSectionName) > 0)
End Sub
```

How It Works

IniEdit shows the user two lists gathered from an .INI file selected by the user. The lists are of the sections in the .INI file and of entries/values in the current section. Whenever the user changes one of the lists by adding, removing, or editing one of its elements, the lists are reloaded from the .INI file so that the user always sees the latest data. This also means that our program doesn't have to keep track of everything in memory—that's what the .INI file is for.

IniEdit works by using the INI API wrapper functions in INI.BAS, which provide high-level access to .INI files. These functions allow the VB program to retrieve the list of sections, the list of entries in a given section, and the value of one of the entries. The program can then write to that entry, delete that entry, or delete an entire section.

INI.BAS generates the list of sections in an .INI file by parsing the .INI file itself. It scans the file for lines that look like "[Section Name]." It stores the list and passes it back to IniEdit (or whatever program is calling it).

The list of entries in a section is generated by calling one of the INI API functions (either GetProfileString or GetPrivateProfileString). These functions have an option that allow you to retrieve the data for an entire section. INI.BAS does this, parsing the data and putting it into a format that VB programmers can deal with easily.

Getting the value of an entry is straightforward. Once again, GetProfileString and GetPrivateProfileString are used to retrieve the data. (This is probably the most common usage of these functions.) Writing an entry's value is just as simple, with the WriteProfileString and WritePrivateProfileString functions. (This is their most common use.)

Deleting an entry requires giving WriteProfileString or WritePrivateProfileString a NULL pointer for the entry value. This is accomplished by passing a 0& to the function. Deleting an entire section is similar to deleting an entry, except the NULL is passed as both the entry name and the entry value.

INI.BAS also handles flushing the INI cache. The INI API functions keep the data cached for higher performance. Unfortunately, however, they don't always write often enough, so flushing is suggested after writing.

Lastly, INI.BAS notifies other applications when WIN.INI is updated. The WM_WININICHANGED message is broadcast to all application windows.

Comments

A couple of notes about INI file use. First off, don't put your applications information in WIN.INI. This is considered very bad form. It makes it hard for people to remove your application from the system.

Second, don't use INI files as if they are databases. They're great, easy-to-use, etc. But, they perform poorly. And, thrashing an INI file will fragment your hard drive quicker than a hammer will. Keep relatively static data in the INI file. If you need to store data that changes frequently, keep it in a separate file.

7.3 How do I...
Get an hWnd from a Process Handle (hProcess)?

COMPLEXITY: INTERMEDIATE
COMPATIBILITY: VB3 AND VB4

Problem

After I run another program using the Shell command, I want to manipulate the other window. I try to use the process ID passed back by Shell, but it always fails and sometimes generates a GPF. What is this ID used for? How can I use it to manipulate the program I started?

Technique

The terminology used in the VB documentation to describe the Shell command is misleading. The documentation says Shell returns a "task identifier," so you might presume that Shell returns a task ID. In reality, the "task identifier" returned by Shell is really a process handle (hProcess).

GETHWND, the project in this How-To (shown in Figure 7-3-1), finds the window handle associated with the instance handle, by searching all the windows in the

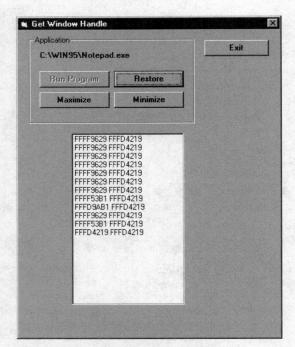

Figure 7-3-1 GETHWND project in action

system for one that has an instance handle matching the one returned by Shell. This window handle can then be used to manipulate the application (move the window, minimize/maximize, and so forth).

Steps

Open and run the GETHWND.VBP project. Click on the Run Program button and find an .EXE file to run (such as Write). Then play with the other three buttons: Restore, Maximize, and Minimize.

1. Create a new project called GETHWND.VBP Select Form1, and add objects with properties set as shown in Table 7-3-1.

Table 7-3-1 Objects, properties, and settings for Form1

OBJECT	PROPERTY	SETTING
Form	Name	GetHwnd
	BorderStyle	3 'Fixed Double
	Caption	"Get Window Handle"
	Height	2820
	Left	1335
	Top	1365
	Width	6015
Frame	Name	Frame1
	Caption	"Application"
	Height	2055
	Left	240
	Top	120
	Width	3735
CommandButton	Name	btnExit
	Caption	"Exit"
	Height	375
	Left	4200
	Top	240
	Width	1455
CommandButton	in Frame1	
	Name	btnMinimize
	Caption	"Minimize"
	Enabled	0 'False
	Height	375
	Left	1920
	Top	1320
	Width	1575

Continued on next page

Continued from previous page

OBJECT	PROPERTY	SETTING
CommandButton	in Frame1	
	Name	btnMaximize
	Caption	"Maximize"
	Enabled	0 'False
	Height	375
	Left	240
	Top	1320
	Width	1575
CommandButton	in Frame1	
	Name	btnRestore
	Caption	"Restore"
	Enabled	0 'False
	Height	375
	Left	1920
	Top	840
	Width	1575
CommandButton	in Frame1	
	Name	btnRunProgram
	Caption	"Run Program"
	Height	375
	Left	240
	Top	840
	Width	1575
CommonDialog	Name	CommonDialog1
	Left	4200
	Top	1680
	Filter	"EXE Files (*.EXE)|*.EXE"
	Flags	4096
Label	in Frame1	
	Name	lblFilename
	Caption	"None"
	Height	255
	Left	240
	Top	360
	Width	3375
Timer	Name	Timer1
	Enabled	0 'False
	Interval	1000
	Left	4680
	Top	1680

2. Add this code to the General Declarations section of Form1. This code defines all of the API calls used and the constants needed in this program. It also defines hInstProgram and hWndProgram. The global variable hInstProgram holds the instance handle for the program that the user runs (this is zero if there's no program running). And hWndProgram holds the window handle for hInstProgram.

```
Option Explicit
'
' declare API calls
'
Private Declare Function GetWindowThreadProcessId Lib "user32" ⇒
    (ByVal hWnd As Long, lpdwProcessId As Long) As Long
Private Declare Function GetWindow Lib "user32" (ByVal hWnd As Long, ⇒
    ByVal wCmd As Long) As Long
Private Declare Function IsWindow Lib "user32" (ByVal hWnd As Long) ⇒
    As Long
Private Declare Function GetDesktopWindow Lib "user32" () As Long
Private Declare Function ShowWindow Lib "user32" (ByVal hWnd As Long, _
    ByVal nCmdShow As Long) As Long
'
' declare constants used by the API calls
'
Private Const GW_HWNDNEXT = 2
Private Const GW_CHILD = 5
Private Const SW_MAXIMIZE = 3
Private Const SW_MINIMIZE = 6
Private Const SW_RESTORE = 9
'
' global variables
'
Dim hProcessProgram As Long
Dim hWndProgram As Long
```

3. Add this code to the General Declarations section of Form1. This function does the majority of the work when finding a window that uses the process handle in question. It checks all the immediate children of hWndStart; each child, if it isn't the window we're looking for, searches all of its children.

```
Private Function GetWindowHandleLow(ByVal hWndStart As Integer, _
    hProcess As Integer) As Integer
    Dim hWnd As Integer
    Dim hWndReturn As Integer
    Dim hProcessCur As Integer
    '
    ' Get first child
    '
    hWnd = GetWindow(hWndStart, GW_CHILD)
    '
    ' Loop through all children
    '
    Do Until hWnd = 0
        '
        ' Get the window's process handle
```

Continued on next page

Continued from previous page

```
        '
        GetWindowThreadProcessId hWnd, hProcessCur
        '
        ' if the process handle matches, return the
        ' window's handle
        '
        If hProcessCur = hProcess Then
            GetWindowHandleLow = hWnd
            Exit Function
        End If
        '
        ' Search all of the children of this window
        '
        hWndReturn = GetWindowHandleLow(hWnd, hProcess)
        '
        ' return handle to caller if non-zero
        '
        If hWndReturn () 0 Then
            GetWindowHandleLow = hWndReturn
            Exit Function
        End If
        '
        ' No match, get the next window
        '
        hWnd = GetWindow(hWnd, GW_HWNDNEXT)
    Loop
    '
    ' return window handle not found
    '
    GetWindowHandleLow = 0
End Function
```

4. Add this code to the General Declarations section of Form1. This is the entry point for searching for a window with a specific process handle (hProcess). The function calls GetWindowHandleLow and tells it to start the search at the desktop.

```
Private Function GetWindowHandle(hProcess As Integer) As Integer
    '
    ' recursively collect all of the window handles
    ' to search for the instance handle (hProcess).
    ' return to caller (0 if not found)
    '
    GetWindowHandle = GetWindowHandleLow(GetDesktopWindow, hProcess)
End Function
```

5. Add this code to the General Declarations section of Form1:

```
Private Sub btnExit_Click()
    '
    ' get out
    '
    End
End Sub
```

6. Add this code to the General Declarations section of Form1. This code enables or disables the buttons. If a program is started by the user, the Run Program button is disabled and the Restore, Maximize, and Minimize buttons are enabled. If no other program is running, however, then the Run Program is enabled and the other three buttons are disabled.

```
Private Sub EnableButtons()
    '
    ' if we're running a program
    '
    If hProcessProgram <> 0 Then
        '
        ' enable window management buttons and
        ' disable run program button
        '
        btnRunProgram.Enabled = False
        btnRestore.Enabled = True
        btnMaximize.Enabled = True
        btnMinimize.Enabled = True
    Else
        '
        ' otherwise, enable run program button
        ' and disable program management buttons
        '
        btnRunProgram.Enabled = True
        btnRestore.Enabled = False
        btnMaximize.Enabled = False
        btnMinimize.Enabled = False
    End If
End Sub
```

7. Add this code to the General Declarations section of Form1, to maximize the program run by the user, if it is running.

```
Private Sub btnMaximize_Click()
    '
    ' if we're running, maximize the window
    '
    If hWndProgram <> 0 Then
        ShowWindow hWndProgram, SW_MAXIMIZE
        btnMaximize.SetFocus
    End If
End Sub
```

8. Add this code to the General Declarations section of Form1, to minimize (iconize) the program run by the user, if it is running.

```
Private Sub btnMinimize_Click()
    '
    ' if we're running, minimize the window
    '
    If hWndProgram <> 0 Then
        ShowWindow hWndProgram, SW_MINIMIZE
```

Continued on next page

Continued from previous page

```
        btnMinimize.SetFocus
    End If
End Sub
```

9. Add this code to the General Declarations section of Form1, to restore the program run by the user to its normal size, if it is running.

```
Private Sub btnRestore_Click()
    '
    ' if we're running, restore the window
    ' to normal size
    '
    If hWndProgram <> 0 Then
        ShowWindow hWndProgram, SW_RESTORE
        btnRestore.SetFocus
    End If
End Sub
```

10. Add the following code to the General Declarations section of Form1. This subroutine runs another program, selected by the user. It displays a File Open dialog box (from the Common Dialogs control) that forces the user to select an .EXE file. The executable file is run using the Shell() function, saving the process handle returned. The buttons are enabled/disabled to reflect the program running. If the program sucessfully runs, the filename label is changed to show the path and filename, and the timer is started to periodically verify that the program is still running. This could also be accomplished by sitting in a loop with a DoEvents, but the timer method allows us to do other processing while waiting for the program to end.

```
Private Sub btnRunProgram_Click()
    '
    ' get a program's name and run it
    '
    CommonDialog1.ShowOpen
    hProcessProgram = Shell(CommonDialog1.FileName, vbNormalNoFocus)
    '
    ' enable/disable the buttons based on the result
    '
    EnableButtons
    '
    ' if we've got a program running
    '
    If hProcessProgram () 0 Then
        '
        ' set the filename to the currently running
        ' program
        '
        lblFilename = CommonDialog1.FileName
        '
        ' get the program's window handle and start
        ' the timer to detect when the window exits
```

```
        '
        hWndProgram = GetWindowHandle(hProcessProgram)
        Timer1.Enabled = True
    Else
        '
        ' otherwise, tell the user
        '
        lblFilename = "None"
    End If
End Sub
```

11. Add this code to the General Declarations section of Form1. The timer is enabled while another program is running. Every second, it checks to see if that program is still running. If the program has stopped, everything is reset for the next time. Also, a message box appears, telling the user that the program is no longer running.

```
Private Sub Timer1_Timer()
    '
    ' if we're no longer running
    '
    If IsWindow(hWndProgram) = 0 Then
        '
        ' stop the timer, disable the buttons,
        ' and get ready for the next go 'round
        '
        Timer1.Enabled = False
        hProcessProgram = 0
        hWndProgram = 0
        EnableButtons
        lblFilename = "None"
        '
        ' tell the user the program stopped
        '
        MsgBox "The program has exited.", vbInformation
    End If
End Sub
```

How It Works

GETHWND finds a window handle from a process handle (like Shell passes back). GETHWND also lets the user change the size of the window it finds (but, this is secondary). GETHWND finds the window by recursively scanning all of the windows through the GetWindow() API call. Every window's siblings and then all of its children are scanned. This is to ensure that the highest window with the process handle is selected.

When scanning the windows, GETHWND uses the GetWindowThreadProcessID() API call to get the process handle (hProcess) for that window. The program determines whether the correct window has been found by comparing the instance handle for that window with the instance handle returned by Shell.

Comments

This technique has many uses. The window handle is the key to many other actions performed in another window.

7.4 How do I...
Get an hWnd from a Partial Title?

COMPLEXITY: INTERMEDIATE
COMPATIBILITY: VB4 ONLY

Problem

Sometimes I want to activate another application, whose full title I don't always know. How can I find the window using only a partial title?

Technique

GETHANDL (shown running in Figure 7-4-1) searches all of the windows in the system. For each window it gets the text associated with that window (through the GetWindowText() function) and compares that text to the partial title it's looking for. All windows that match are added to GETHANDL's list box.

Steps

1. Create a new project called GETHANDL.VBP. Select Form1, and add objects with properties set as shown in Table 7-4-1.

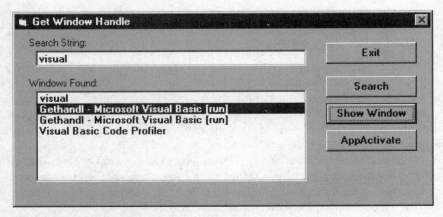

Figure 7-4-1 The GETHANDL project in action

Table 7-4-1 Objects, properties, and settings for Form1

OBJECT	PROPERTY	SETTING
Form	Name	GetHandle
	BorderStyle	3 'Fixed Double
	Caption	"Get Window Handle"
	Height	3510
	Left	1320
	Top	1365
	Width	7335
CommandButton	Name	btnAppActivate
	Caption	"AppActivate"
	Enabled	0 'False
	Height	375
	Left	5400
	Top	1800
	Width	1575
CommandButton	Name	btnExit
	Cancel	-1 'True
	Caption	"Exit"
	Height	375
	Left	5400
	Top	240
	Width	1575
CommandButton	Name	btnSearch
	Caption	"Search"
	Default	-1 'True
	Enabled	0 'False
	Height	375
	Left	5400
	Top	840
	Width	1575
CommandButton	Name	btnShowWindow
	Caption	"Show Window"
	Enabled	0 'False
	Height	375
	Left	5400
	Top	1320
	Width	1575
Label	Name	Label1
	Caption	"Search String:"

Continued on next page

Continued from previous page

OBJECT	PROPERTY	SETTING
	Height	255
	Left	240
	Top	120
	Width	1575
Label	Name	Label2
	Caption	"Windows Found:"
	Height	255
	Left	240
	Top	840
	Width	1575
ListBox	Name	List1
	Height	1785
	Left	360
	Top	1080
	Width	4695
TextBox	Name	txtSearchString
	Height	285
	Left	360
	Top	360
	Width	4695

2. Add this code to the General Declarations section of Form1, to define all of the API calls used and constants needed in this program.

```
Option Explicit
'
' declare API calls
'
Private Declare Function GetDesktopWindow Lib "user32" () As Long
Private Declare Function GetWindowText Lib "user32" Alias "GetWindowTextA" ⇒
    (ByVal hWnd As Long, ByVal lpString As String, ByVal cch As Long) ⇒
    As Long
Private Declare Function GetWindow Lib "user32" (ByVal hWnd As Long, ⇒
    ByVal wCmd As Long) As Long
Private Declare Function BringWindowToTop Lib "user32" (ByVal hWnd ⇒
    As Long) As Boolean
'
' declare constants used by GetWindow()
'
Private Const GW_HWNDNEXT = 2
Private Const GW_CHILD = 5
```

3. Add this code to the General Declarations section of Form1. This function gets the text from a window based on its window handle (hWnd). It does this by calling GetWindowText().

```
Private Function VBGetWindowText(hWnd As Long) As String
    Dim WindowText As String
    Dim StrLen As Integer
    '
    ' allocate space for and get the window text
    ' for the window specified
    '
    WindowText = Space(255)
    StrLen = GetWindowText(hWnd, WindowText, 255)
    WindowText = Left(WindowText, StrLen)
    '
    ' return the text
    '
    VBGetWindowText = WindowText
End Function
```

4. Add this subroutine to the General Declarations section of Form1. GetWindowsLow recursively searches the windows in the system. It looks for windows that have text matching the text passed in WindowText. When it finds a window with a match, it is added to hWndArray().

```
Private Sub GetWindowsLow(hWndArray() As Long, _
        ByVal hWndStart As Long, WindowText As String)
    Dim hWnd As Long
    Dim CurWindowText As String
    Dim CurClassName As String
    Dim StrLen As Integer
    '
    ' Get first child
    '
    hWnd = GetWindow(hWndStart, GW_CHILD)
    '
    ' Loop through all children
    '
    Do Until hWnd = 0
        '
        ' Search all of the children of this window
        '
        GetWindowsLow hWndArray(), hWnd, WindowText
        '
        ' Get the window text
        '
        CurWindowText = VBGetWindowText(hWnd)
        '
        ' check for matching window names
        '
        If (UCase$(CurWindowText) Like WindowText) Then
            Dim NumFound
```

Continued on next page

Continued from previous page

```
                '
                ' make the array of windows found, one bigger
                '
                NumFound = UBound(hWndArray) + 1
                ReDim Preserve hWndArray(0 To NumFound)
                '
                ' add this window handle to the list of
                ' windows found
                '
                hWndArray(NumFound) = hWnd
            End If
            '
            ' Get the next window
            '
            hWnd = GetWindow(hWnd, GW_HWNDNEXT)
        Loop
    End Sub
```

5. Add this function to the General Declarations section of Form1, to start the search for the windows. This function initializes the window handle array, passes in the text to search for, surrounded by asterisks (for the Like comparator). Then GetWindowsLow is called, which returns the number of window handles found.

```
Private Function GetWindows(hWndArray() As Long, _
    WindowText As String) As Integer
  ReDim hWndArray(0 To 0)
  '
  ' recursively collect all of the window handles
  ' that match the current name. Note the use
  ' of asterisks before and after the window title.
  ' this is so that the Like comparison will work
  ' properly.
  '
  GetWindowsLow hWndArray, GetDesktopWindow, _
    UCase$("*" & WindowText & "*")
  '
  ' return number of windows found
  '
  GetWindows = UBound(hWndArray)
End Function
```

6. Add this code to the General Declarations section of Form1, to activate the application selected in the list box.

```
Private Sub btnAppActivate_Click()
  '
  ' activate the item selected in the list
  '
  If List1.ListIndex () -1 Then
    AppActivate List1.List(List1.ListIndex)
  End If
End Sub
```

7. Add this subroutine to the General Declarations section of Form1, to ensure that the program exits.

```
Private Sub btnExit_Click()
    '
    ' get out
    '
    End
End Sub
```

8. Add this subroutine to the General Declarations section of Form1. This code searches the windows in the system for the string specified in the Search String edit box. If no windows are found, it says so in a message box. If windows are found, the list box is filled with the windows' titles and the window handles are placed in the ItemData for each list item.

```
Private Sub btnSearch_Click()
    Dim hWnds() As Long
    Dim I As Integer
    Dim NumWindows As Integer
    '
    ' tell the user it's going to be a little time
    '
    MousePointer = 11
    '
    ' initialize
    '
    List1.Clear
    btnSetFocus.Enabled = False
    btnAppActivate.Enabled = False
    '
    ' get all of the window handles
    '
    NumWindows = GetWindows(hWnds(), txtSearchString.Text)
    '
    ' if no windows found, tell user
    '
    If NumWindows = 0 Then
        MsgBox "Sorry. No windows found.", vbExclamation, "Search"
    Else
        '
        ' since there are windows found, show them
        ' in the list box with their titles
        '
        For I = 1 To NumWindows
            List1.AddItem VBGetWindowText(hWnds(I)) & " (" _
                & Hex$(hWnds(I)) & ")"
            List1.ItemData(List1.NewIndex) = hWnds(I)
        Next I
    End If
    '
    ' back to normal
    '
    MousePointer = 0
End Sub
```

9. Add this code to the General Declarations section of Form1. This function attempts to set the focus to the window handle specified by the item currently selected in the list box.

```
Private Sub btnSetFocus_Click()
    '
    ' if an item s selected in the list
    '
    If List1.ListIndex () -1 Then
        BringWindowToTop List1.ItemData(List1.ListIndex)
    End If
End Sub
```

10. Add this code to the General Declarations section of Form1. This function enables or disables the Set Focus and AppActivate buttons. If an item is selected in the list box, the buttons are enabled; otherwise, they're disabled.

```
Private Sub List1_Click()
    '
    ' enable the set focus and app activate
    ' buttons if an item is selected in the list
    '
    btnSetFocus.Enabled = (List1.ListIndex () -1)
    btnAppActivate.Enabled = (List1.ListIndex () -1)
End Sub
```

11. Add this subroutine to the General Declarations section of Form1. This function enables or disables the Search button based on the search string. If the search string is empty, the button is disabled; otherwise, it's enabled.

```
Private Sub txtSearchString_Change()
    '
    ' enabled the search button if the search string
    ' is not empty
    '
    btnSearch.Enabled = (Len(txtSearchString) > 0)
End Sub
```

How It Works

GETHANDL searches all the windows in the system for a partial title. It recursively scans all of the windows through the GetWindow() API call. For every window, all of the children and then all of the siblings are scanned.

When it's checking a window, GETHANDL gets the text associated with that window and uses the Like operator to see if there's a match. All matches and their window handles are added to the list box on the form. The user can select one of these items and try out either the BringWindowToTop() API call or use VB's built-in AppActivate command (using the text from the window).

Not all windows can be activated. Nor will all windows accept the focus. (Toolbars and such tend to behave like this.)

Comments

The technique in this How-To can be used for more than just setting the focus to another window or application. Many API calls require a window handle to do their job. Using this technique, you can find those needed handles.

7.5 How do I...
Determine Whether a Project Is Compiled?

COMPLEXITY: EASY
COMPATIBILITY: VB3 AND VB4

Problem

I need to know whether my application is compiled or is running in the Visual Basic development environment. When compiled, data files are assumed to be in the application directory; but when under development, I typically have several versions of each application stored in project directories. All of these versions should look to one centralized location for test data. How do I determine whether the currently executing instance is actually compiled?

Technique

This How-To uses the GetModuleFilename API call to retrieve the name of the currently running program. If the application is not compiled, the Visual Basic integrated development environment (IDE) .EXE filename will be returned. If it is compiled, the actual .EXE filename is returned. Because the method for getting this information is slightly different under Win32 than in Win16, this project uses conditional compilation to include the correct code for the targeted operating system.

Steps

Open and run VBEXE.VBP within the Visual Basic IDE. The main form appears centered on screen with the text "VB IDE" on it. Close the project, using its system menu.

Select Make EXE File from the File menu. If you are running the 16-bit version of VB4 under Windows, use the filename VBEXE16.EXE as the executable name. If you are running the 32-bit version of VB4, use VBEXE32.EXE. In File Manager or Explorer, double-click on the newly created executable (or select Run from the File menu) to start it.

Now, the text "Compiled" EXE is displayed across the form, as shown in Figure 7-5-1. Before closing the compiled instance, switch back to Visual Basic and run another instance of VBEXE.VBP. This version correctly identifies itself as running within the IDE.

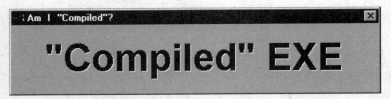

Figure 7-5-1 VBEXE32.EXE when executed

Building a Test Form

1. Create a new project called VBEXE.VBP. Create a new form with the properties listed in Table 7-5-1, and save it as VBEXE.FRM.

Table 7-5-1 Properties of VBEXE.FRM

OBJECT	PROPERTY	SETTING
Form	Name	Form1
	BorderStyle	3 - Fixed Dialog
	Caption	"Am I Compiled?"
	Font.Name	Arial
	Font.Bold	True
	Font.Size	36

2. Add the following code to the Declarations section of Form1. A string variable is used to hold the message printed on the form.

```
Option Explicit
'
' Variable to hold type of program
'
Dim vbType As String
```

3. Insert the following code in the Form_Load event of Form1. A call is placed to the routine vbCompiled in the module VBEXE.BAS, and the string vbType is assigned based on the results. The form is then sized to fit the result string, and centered on screen.

```
Private Sub Form_Load()
    '
    ' Determine whether compiled or not
    '
    If vbCompiled(Me.hWnd) Then
        vbType = """Compiled""" EXE"
    Else
        vbType = "VB IDE"
    End If
    '
    ' Size and center form
    '
    Me.Move (Screen.Width - Me.Width) \ 2, _
```

794

```
        (Screen.Height - Me.Height) \ 2, _
        Me.TextWidth(vbType) * 1.25, _
        Me.TextHeight(vbType) * 2
End Sub
```

4. Insert the following code in the Form_Paint event of Form1. The vbType string is printed twice in the center of the form—first, in the color used for 3D highlights, and then offset by one pixel to the left and up in the color used for dark 3D shadows. This technique makes the text look sunken.

```
Private Sub Form_Paint()
    '
    ' Position and print highlight text
    '
    CurrentX = (Me.ScaleWidth - Me.TextWidth(vbType)) \ 2
    CurrentY = (Me.ScaleHeight - Me.TextHeight(vbType)) \ 2
    Me.ForeColor = vb3DHighLight
    Me.Print vbType
    '
    ' Position and print foreground text
    '
    CurrentX = (Me.ScaleWidth - Me.TextWidth(vbType)) \ 2 _
               - Screen.TwipsPerPixelX
    CurrentY = (Me.ScaleHeight - Me.TextHeight(vbType)) \ 2 _
               - Screen.TwipsPerPixelY
    Me.ForeColor = vb3DDKShadow
    Me.Print vbType
End Sub
```

Functions to Determine Compilation State

5. Add a new code module to the project, and save it as VBEXE.BAS. Add the ever-present Option Explicit to the Declarations section. Figure 7-5-2 shows the

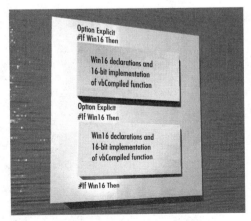

Figure 7-5-2 Conditional compilation code organization in VBEXE.BAS

general layout of VBEXE.BAS. There are two functions, each with the same name, but blocked off by conditional compilation directives to determine which one is included in the executable and which is used within the IDE.

6. Add the following code block to the General section of VBEXE.BAS. This block is delimited by a test of the built-in Win16 conditional compilation argument. Within the block are declarations for the two Win16 API calls used, the definition of a Win16 API constant value, and the 16-bit implementation of the function vbCompiled.

```
' **************************************************
' Win16-specific declarations and code
' **************************************************
#If Win16 Then
    '
    ' Win16 API calls used to get executing filename
    '
    Private Declare Function GetModuleFileName Lib "Kernel" (ByVal hModule ⇒
        hModule As Integer, ByVal lpFilename As String, ByVal nSize ⇒
        As Integer) As Integer
    Private Declare Function GetWindowWord Lib "User" (ByVal hWnd ⇒
        As Integer, ByVal nIndex As Integer) As Integer
    '
    ' Window field offsets for GetWindowWord()
    '
    Private Const GWW_HINSTANCE = -6

    Function vbCompiled(hWndMain As Integer) As Boolean
        Dim hInst As Integer
        Dim nRtn As Integer
        Dim Buffer As String
        '
        ' Get instance associated with main form
        '
        hInst = GetWindowWord(hWndMain, GWW_HINSTANCE)
        '
        ' Create buffer for filename and retrieve
        '
        Buffer = Space$(128)
        nRtn = GetModuleFileName(hInst, Buffer, Len(Buffer))
        Buffer = Left(Buffer, nRtn)
        '
        ' Compare module filename with known VB environment name
        '
        If Right(Buffer, 7) = "\VB.EXE" Then
            vbCompiled = False
        Else
            vbCompiled = True
        End If
    End Function
#End If
```

7. Add the following code block to the General section of VBEXE.BAS. This block is delimited by a test of the built-in conditional compilation argument Win32.

Within the block is a declaration for the single Win32 API call used, and the 32-bit implementation of the function vbCompiled. Notice that the hWnd argument to vbCompiled is optional in this implementation, due to differences in the way GetModuleFilename operates in Win16 and Win32 operating systems. Also, the buffer for the returned filename is twice as long as the Win16 implementation to accommodate the long filenames supported under Win32.

```
' *********************************************
' Win32-specific declarations and code
' *********************************************
#If Win32 Then
    '
    ' Win32 API call used to get executing filename
    '
    Private Declare Function GetModuleFileNameA Lib "kernel32" (ByVal _
        hModule As Long, ByVal lpFilename As String, ByVal nSize As Long) _
        As Long

    Function vbCompiled(Optional hWndMain As Variant) As Boolean
        Dim nRtn As Long
        Dim Buffer As String
        '
        ' Create buffer for filename and retrieve
        '
        Buffer = Space$(256)
        nRtn = GetModuleFileNameA(0&, Buffer, Len(Buffer))
        Buffer = UCase(Left(Buffer, nRtn))
        '
        ' Compare module filename with known VB environment name
        '
        If Right(Buffer, 9) = "\VB32.EXE" Then
            vbCompiled = False
        Else
            vbCompiled = True
        End If
    End Function
#End If
```

How It Works

In the Win16 implementation, the window handle (hWnd) of the main form must be passed in to vbCompiled. For the Win16 GetModuleFilename function to work, it needs to receive either a module handle (hModule) or an instance handle (hInst). The Win32 GetModuleFilename will return the filename of the process that started the current thread, if it's passed a NULL pointer rather than a specific hModule or hInst. This allows greater freedom, since no windows need be created before determining whether the application is compiled or running in the IDE. To maintain compatibility with source code elsewhere in the project, the hWnd for the main form is left as an optional parameter to vbCompiled in its 32-bit implementation.

Under Win16, the hInst can be retrieved by passing the hWnd of a form to the GetWindowWord API function. This is accompanied by the GWW_HINSTANCE index into the data that GetWindowWord is capable of returning. As discussed above, the hInst is a required parameter for GetModuleFilename under Win16.

Notice that GetModuleFilename has an A appended to its name in the Win32 declaration and call. Many Win32 API calls support both Unicode and ANSI usage, and have two distinct names. Appending A tells Win32 to use the ANSI version; appending W (wide characters) indicates Unicode usage. If Visual Basic doesn't recognize or can't find a Win32 API function definition, appending this character is the first thing to try. Odds are high that you're dealing with a dual-use API call.

When the filename of the current executable is returned, the null termination is stripped off, and the end of it is compared to "known" names for the Visual Basic IDE–VB.EXE or VB32.EXE, depending on implementation. Though hard-coding such information is generally a bad idea, it will not cause problems in this case unless you rename either of the two Visual Basic executables, or name your final project the same as Visual Basic. In either case, you would be knowingly disrupting the detection scheme and could alter it to fit your situation.

To use the VBEXE.BAS module in Visual Basic 3, remove the conditional compilation directives (#If, #End If) and the 32-bit version of the vbCompiled function.

Comments

This How-To demonstrates how to determine whether a project is running as a compiled executable or under the Visual Basic IDE. This fact can be useful for a number of purposes—one of the more common is finding data files. Often compiled projects will look first to their own application directory; projects under development may be pointed toward a common data directory. Determining where to send debugging information can be based on whether Visual Basic's Debug window is present. If compiled, debugging output would need to be directed to either a file or another application. Another use would be for finer error-checking or bounds-checking while developing an application. You may want to explicitly test a number of conditions for validity while in the IDE, without slowing down the user of your finished application with such tests.

7.6 How do I...
Determine a Drive's Type?

COMPLEXITY: EASY
COMPATIBILITY: VB4 ONLY

Problem

Sometimes I want to allow particular user actions or display particular pictures/icons depending on what type of drive is being accessed. Sometimes I just want to supply a little information about the drive. File Manager and other desktop shells show bitmaps on their buttons representing different drive types. I really like this small detail. How can I determine a drive's type in my own application?

Technique

DRIVETYP.VBP (shown running in Figure 7-6-1) uses the Windows API to determine the type of a particular drive (hard drive, floppy, network, CD-ROM, etc). It uses the GetDriveType API call to figure out what kind of drive is being accessed.

Figure 7-6-1 The DRIVETYP project

Steps

1. Create a new project called DRIVETYP.VBP. Select Form1, and add objects and set properties as in Table 7-6-1.

Table 7-6-1 Objects, properties, and settings for Form1

OBJECT	PROPERTY	SETTING
Form	BorderStyle	3 'Fixed Double
	Caption	"Drive Type"
	Height	2010
	Left	1200
	Top	1290
	Width	3975
DriveListBox	Name	Drive1
	Height	315
	Left	360
	Top	480
	Width	3255
Label	Name	Label1
	Caption	"Drive:"
	Height	255
	Left	240
	Top	240

Continued on next page

Continued from previous page

OBJECT	PROPERTY	SETTING
	Width	2655
Label	Name	Label2
	Caption	"Drive Type:"
	Height	255
	Left	240
	Top	960
	Width	2655
Label	Name	lblDriveType
	Caption	"lblDriveType"
	Height	255
	Left	360
	Top	1200
	Width	3255

2. Add the following code to the General Declarations section of Form1. This defines the GetDriveType API call and the constants returned by GetDriveType.

```
Option Explicit
'
' declare API functions
'
Private Declare Function GetDriveType Lib "Kernel" _
   (ByVal nDrive As Integer) As Integer
'
' declare API constants
'
Const DRIVE_REMOVABLE = 2
Const DRIVE_FIXED = 3
Const DRIVE_REMOTE = 4
Const DRIVE_CDROM = 5
Const DRIVE_RAMDISK = 6
```

3. Add the following code to the General Declarations section of Form1. This LoadDriveType function works by checking the Windows API call, GetDriveType.

```
Private Sub LoadDriveType()
'
   ' hourglass cursor
   '
   MousePointer = 11
   '
   ' get the drive type of the currently selected
   ' drive and handle accordingly
   '
   Select Case GetDriveType(UCase(Left(Drive1.Drive, 1)) & ":\")
      Case DRIVE_REMOVABLE
```

```
            lblDriveType = "Floppy Drive"
        Case DRIVE_FIXED
            lblDriveType = "Hard Drive"
        Case DRIVE_REMOTE
            lblDriveType = "Network Drive"
        Case DRIVE_CDROM
            lblDriveType = "CD-ROM Drive"
        Case DRIVE_RAMDISK
            lblDriveType = "RAM Disk"
        Case 0
            lblDriveType = "Could not determine drive type."
        Case 1
            lblDriveType = "Drive does not exist."
        Case Else
            lblDriveType = "Unknown or Illegal Drive"
    End Select
    '
    ' normal cursor
    '
    MousePointer = 0
End Sub
```

4. Add the following code to the General Declarations section of Form1. This loads the Drive Type label with the current drive type when the Drive combo box changes.

```
Private Sub Drive1_Change()
    '
    ' load the drive type label when the drive combo
    ' changes
    '
    LoadDriveType
End Sub
```

5. Add the following code to the General Declarations section of Form1. This loads the Drive Type label at start-up.

```
Private Sub Form_Load()
    '
    ' load the drive type label on startup
    '
    LoadDriveType
End Sub
```

How It Works

This program determines the drive type by calling GetDriveType, a Windows API call, to determine the drive type: removable, fixed, remote, CD-ROM, or RAM Disk.

Comments

The Win32 API is rich with this kind of information. Take a peek at it.

7.7 How do I...
Check for a File's Existence?

COMPLEXITY: EASY
COMPATIBILITY: VB3 AND VB4

Problem

My program needs to know if a file (such as a configuration file, user info file, etc.) exists, in order to determine the next action. So, I need to have this information long before I open the file. How do I determine if a file exists?

Technique

FEXIST (shown running in Figure 7-7-1) works by using the error handler to catch nonexistent files. In trying to determine the existence of a file, FEXIST first sets up the error handler. If an error occurs during the process, FEXIST presumes the file doesn't exist. Once the error handler is set up, FEXIST attempts to get the attributes of the file. The attributes are then checked; if they reflect that the filename is a directory, FEXIST presumes the file doesn't exist (you can't have a directory with the same name as a file). In either case, FEXIST displays the result of its test to the user in a label on the form.

Steps

Open and run FEXIST.VBP. Type a filename into the Filename box and press the "File Exist?" button. Try different file names.

1. Start a new project, name the initial form FileExist, save the initial form as FEXIST.FRM, and save the project as FEXIST.VBP. Place the controls, and set the properties, listed in Table 7-7-1.

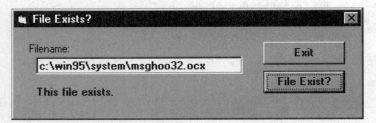

Figure 7-7-1 FEXIST in action

Table 7-7-1 Objects and their properties on Form1

OBJECT	PROPERTY	SETTING
Form	Name	FileExist
	BorderStyle	3 'Fixed Double
	Caption	"File Exists?"
	Height	1890
	Left	1035
	Top	1170
	Width	5790
CommandButton	Name	btnExit
	Cancel	-1 'True
	Caption	"Exit"
	Height	375
	Left	4080
	Top	240
	Width	1335
CommandButton	Name	btnFileExist
	Caption	"File Exist?"
	Default	-1 'True
	Height	375
	Left	4080
	Top	720
	Width	1335
Label	Name	Label1
	Caption	"Filename:"
	Height	255
	Left	240
	Top	240
	Width	1575
Label	Name	lblFileExist
	Caption	"lblFileExist"
	Height	255
	Left	360
	Top	960
	Width	3375
TextBox	Name	txtFilename
	Height	285
	Left	360
	Text	"txtFilename"
	Top	480
	Width	3375

2. Add the following code to the Declarations section of FileExist. This ensures that every variable is explicitly declared. No program should be without Option Explicit!

```
Option Explicit
```

3. Add the following code to the Declarations section of Form1. This function determines whether or not a given file exists. Wildcard characters are not accepted (the function specifically checks and rejects filenames that have them). It determines if the file is present by using the GetAttr function. If an error occurs while the function is getting the file's attributes, then the file isn't present and the error-handling code gets executed. If the file is present, the function returns True; otherwise, it returns False.

```
Function FileExists(Filename As String) As Boolean
    Dim TempAttr As Integer
    '
    ' if the filename is empty or if there are wildcards
    ' in the filename, then the file does not exist
    '
    If (Len(Filename) = 0) Or (InStr(Filename, "*") > 0) Or _
            (InStr(Filename, "?") > 0) Then
        FileExists = False
        Exit Function
    End If
    '
    ' if an error happens, we know the file doesn't
    ' exist
    '
    On Error GoTo ErrorFileExist
    '
    ' try to get the attributes of the file, if
    ' we can't (i.e., there's an error) then
    ' the file doesn't exist
    '
    TempAttr = GetAttr(Filename)
    '
    ' we got this far, so check to see if it's a
    ' directory, if not, it's a file
    '
    FileExists = ((TempAttr And vbDirectory) = 0)
    GoTo ExitFileExist

ErrorFileExist:
    '
    ' since we got here, obviously there's a problem
    ' and the file couldn't be opened. return
    ' not exist ...
    '
    FileExists = False
    Resume ExitFileExist
```

```
ExitFileExist:
    '
    ' get rid of error handling
    '
    On Error GoTo 0
End Function
```

4. Add the following code to the Click event handler of btnExit. This causes the program to exit when the user presses the Exit button.

```
Private Sub btnExit_Click()
    '
    ' get out
    '
    End
End Sub
```

5. Add the following code to the Click event subroutine for btnFileExist. This function checks to see if the filename specified in the txtFilename text box exists. The file's status is displayed to the user in the lblFileExist label.

```
Private Sub btnFileExist_Click()
    '
    ' check for the existence of the file
    '
    If Not FileExists(txtFilename) Then
        '
        ' if it doesn't exist, tell the user
        '
        lblFileExist = "This file does not exist."
    Else
        '
        ' if it's there, tell the user
        '
        lblFileExist = "This file exists."
    End If
End Sub
```

6. Add the following code to the Load event handler of Form1, to ensure that all of the controls are initialized properly.

```
Private Sub Form_Load()
    '
    ' clear the filename edit box and the file exist
    ' feedback label
    '
    txtFilename = ""
    lblFileExist = ""
End Sub
```

How It Works

FEXIST uses the combination of On Error Goto and the GetAttr function to determine if a file exists. FEXIST accomplishes this by setting up the On Error code. If an error occurs, it's presumed that the file doesn't exist, so the error-handling code merely returns that fact. If there's no error, then the code passes through to another check. GetAttr also returns valid data for directories. Then we have to ensure that we're not looking at a directory. If we are, this means the file doesn't exist. Once we're past all of these checks, we can safely assume that the file exists and let the user know.

Comments

There are probably as many ways to check for a file as there are programmers. However, this is the only one you should use!

7.8 How do I...
Set a File's Date and Time?

COMPLEXITY: INTERMEDIATE
COMPATIBILITY: VB4 ONLY

Problem

I need to be able to change a file's date and time. I've looked all through the VB documentation and the help file and can only find instructions for reading the time stamp. What do I do?

Technique

Setting the time stamp on a file used to be mildly annoying. It wasn't supported in the Windows API, so one had to use DOS interrupts to do this. Win32 (Windows 95 and Windows NT) makes this task much easier.

Setting a file's date/time stamp is simple: Just open the file, set the time stamp, and close the file. There's a little bit more to it than that, however: you have to convert the time from the human readable form to a UTC (Coordinated Universal Time). This is the number of 100 nanosecond intervals since January 1, 1901. Fortunately, there are functions in the API to do all of the conversions for us.

Steps

Open and run FILEDT.VBP (shown running in Figure 7-8-1). Use the Directory list and the Drive combo box to navigate your disks. Find a file that is safe to fiddle with. Select it in the Files list box, change the date or time and press the Set Time Stamp button. You have just changed the date and time on that file. Use the DOS Dir command or the File Manager to verify that there is a new time stamp, and then change it back if you like.

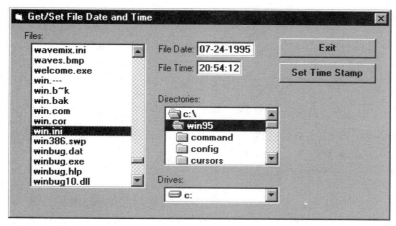

Figure 7-8-1 FILEDT showing the date/time stamp of WIN.INI

1. Start a new project, name the initial form FileDT, save it as FILEDT.FRM, and save the project as FILEDT.VBP. Place the controls and set the properties listed in Table 7-8-1.

Table 7-8-1 Objects and their properties on FileDT

OBJECT	PROPERTY	SETTING
Form	Name	FileDT
	BorderStyle	3 'Fixed Double
	Caption	"Get/Set File Date and Time"
	Height	4110
	Left	1035
	Top	1170
	Width	7215
CommandButton	Name	btnSetTimeStamp
	Caption	"Set Time Stamp"
	Enabled	0 'False
	Height	375
	Left	5040
	Top	720
	Width	1815
TextBox	Name	txtTime
	Height	285
	Left	3480
	Text	"txtTime"
	Top	675

Continued on next page

Continued from previous page

OBJECT	PROPERTY	SETTING
	Width	855
TextBox	Name	txtDate
	Height	285
	Left	3480
	Text	"txtDate"
	Top	315
	Width	1095
DriveListBox	Name	cmbDrive
	Height	315
	Left	2880
	Top	3120
	Width	2175
DirListBox	Name	lstDirectory
	Height	1155
	Left	2880
	Top	1560
	Width	2175
FileListBox	Name	lstFile
	Height	2955
	Left	360
	Top	360
	Width	2175
CommandButton	Name	btnExit
	Caption	"Exit"
	Height	375
	Left	5040
	Top	240
	Width	1815
Label	Name	Label5
	Caption	"File Time:"
	Height	255
	Left	2760
	Top	720
	Width	855
Label	Name	Label4
	Caption	"File Date:"
	Height	255
	Left	2760
	Top	360

OBJECT	PROPERTY	SETTING
	Width	855
Label	Name	Label3
	Caption	"Drives:"
	Height	255
	Left	2760
	Top	2880
	Width	1695
Label	Name	Label2
	Caption	"Files:"
	Height	255
	Left	240
	Top	120
	Width	1695
Label	Name	Label1
	Caption	"Directories:"
	Height	255
	Left	2760
	Top	1320
	Width	1695

2. Add the following code, as usual, to the Declarations section of FileDT, to ensure that every variable is explicitly declared.

```
Option Explicit
'
' time structure definitions
'
Private Type FILETIME
    dwLowDateTime As Long
    dwHighDateTime As Long
End Type
'
Private Type SYSTEMTIME
    wYear As Integer
    wMonth As Integer
    wDayOfWeek As Integer
    wDay As Integer
    wHour As Integer
    wMinute As Integer
    wSecond As Integer
    wMilliseconds As Integer
End Type
'
' Declarations for API calls
'
Private Const GENERIC_WRITE = &H40000000
```

Continued on next page

Continued from previous page

```
Private Const OPEN_EXISTING = 3
Private Const FILE_SHARE_READ = &H1
Private Const FILE_SHARE_WRITE = &H2
'
Private Declare Function SetFileTimeWrite Lib "kernel32" Alias "SetFileTime" _
    (ByVal hFile As Long, ByVal NullP As Long, ByVal NullP2 As Long, _
    lpLastWriteTime As FILETIME) As Long
Private Declare Function SystemTimeToFileTime Lib "kernel32" _
    (lpSystemTime As SYSTEMTIME, lpFileTime As FILETIME) As Long
Private Declare Function CreateFile Lib "kernel32" Alias "CreateFileA" _
    (ByVal lpFileName As String, ByVal dwDesiredAccess As Long, ⇒
    ByVal dwShareMode As Long, ByVal lpSecurityAttributes As Long, ⇒
    ByVal dwCreationDisposition As Long, ByVal dwFlagsAndAttributes ⇒
    As Long, ByVal hTemplateFile As Long) As Long
Private Declare Function CloseHandle Lib "kernel32" (ByVal hObject ⇒
    As Long) As Long
Private Declare Function LocalFileTimeToFileTime Lib "kernel32" _
    (lpLocalFileTime As FILETIME, lpFileTime As FILETIME) As Long
```

3. Add the following code to the Declarations section of FileDT, to set the time stamp of a file. This function works by opening the file and using the Win32 file time API to set the time stamp. It takes the time stamp passed in as a variant and converts it to the format required by FileSetTime.

```
Function FileSetTimeStamp(Filename As String, _
    TimeStamp As Variant) As Boolean
Dim SysTime As SYSTEMTIME
    Dim LocalFTime As FILETIME
    Dim FTime As FILETIME
    Dim FileHandle As Long
    '
    ' break down time into its components
    '
    SysTime.wYear = Year(TimeStamp)
    SysTime.wMonth = Month(TimeStamp)
    SysTime.wDay = Day(TimeStamp)
    SysTime.wDayOfWeek = WeekDay(TimeStamp) - 1
    SysTime.wHour = Hour(TimeStamp)
    SysTime.wMinute = Minute(TimeStamp)
    SysTime.wSecond = Second(TimeStamp)
    SysTime.wMilliseconds = 0
    '
    ' attempt to convert the time to local time
    '
    If SystemTimeToFileTime(SysTime, LocalFTime) = False Then
        FileSetTimeStamp = False
        Exit Function
    End If
    '
    ' convert from local time to UTC
    '
    If LocalFileTimeToFileTime(LocalFTime, FTime) = False Then
```

```
      FileSetTimeStamp = False
      Exit Function
   End If
   '
   ' attempt to set file's time stamp
   '
   FileHandle = CreateFile(Filename, GENERIC_WRITE, FILE_SHARE_READ Or ⇒
FILE_SHARE_WRITE, ByVal 0&, OPEN_EXISTING, 0, 0)
   '
   ' check for errors
   '
   If FileHandle = -1 Then
      FileSetTimeStamp = False
      Exit Function
   End If
   '
   ' actually set the time of the file
   '
   If SetFileTimeWrite(FileHandle, ByVal 0&, ByVal 0&, FTime) = ⇒
False Then
      FileSetTimeStamp = False
      CloseHandle FileHandle
      Exit Function
   End If
   '
   '
   ' Close file and return OK
   '
   CloseHandle FileHandle
   FileSetTimeStamp = True
End Function
```

4. Add the following code to the Click event handler of btnExit. This causes the program to exit when the user presses the Exit button.

```
Private Sub btnExit_Click()
   '
   ' exit the program
   '
   End
End Sub
```

5. Add the following code to the Click event handler of btnSetTimeStamp, to set the currently selected file's date and time from the two edit boxes. The first thing this function does is double-check the validity and format of the data entered. If the data is poorly formatted or contains bad values, a message box is displayed, and the function exits without changing the file's date and time. If the data is well formed, then the various elements (hour, minute, second, and so on) are extracted. The elements are put together in a variant using the DateSerial and TimeSerial functions. Finally, FileSetTimeStamp is called to do the real work. If this fails, the user is informed with a message box.

```
Private Sub btnSetTimeStamp_Click()
    Dim TimeStamp As Variant
    Dim TempFilename As String
    Dim Hour As Integer
    Dim Minute As Integer
    Dim Second As Integer
    Dim Year As Integer
    Dim Month As Integer
    Dim Day As Integer
    '
    ' check date input, allow for 2 and 4 digit years
    '
    If ((Len(txtDate) () 8) And (Len(txtDate) () 10)) Or _
            (Mid(txtDate, 3, 1) () "-") Or _
            (Mid(txtDate, 6, 1) () "-") Then
        MsgBox "The date field should be formatted like: DD-MM-YY or _
            DD-MM-YYYY", vbInformation
        Exit Sub
    End If
    '
    ' check time input
    '
    If (Len(txtTime) () 8) Or (Mid(txtTime, 3, 1)   ":") Or _
            (Mid(txtTime, 6, 1) () ":") Then
        MsgBox "The time field should be formatted like: HH:MM:SS", _
            vbInformation
        Exit Sub
    End If
    '
    ' break time down
    '
    Hour = Val(Mid(txtTime, 1, 2))
    Minute = Val(Mid(txtTime, 4, 2))
    Second = Val(Mid(txtTime, 7, 2))
    '
    ' double check time components
    '
    If (Hour < 0) Or (Hour >= 24) Then
        MsgBox "The hour component should be between 0 and 23, _
            inclusive.", vbInformation
        Exit Sub
    End If
    '
    If (Minute < 0) Or (Minute >= 60) Then
        MsgBox "The minute component should be between 0 and 59, _
            inclusive.", vbInformation
        Exit Sub
    End If
    '
    If (Second < 0) Or (Second >= 60) Then
        MsgBox "The second component should be between 0 and 59, _
            inclusive.", vbInformation
        Exit Sub
    End If
    '
```

```
' break date down
'
Month = Val(Mid(txtDate, 1, 2))
Day = Val(Mid(txtDate, 4, 2))
Year = Val(Mid(txtDate, 7))
'
' double check date components
'
If (Month < 1) Or (Month > 12) Then
    MsgBox "The month component should be between 1 and 12, _
        inclusive.", vbInformation
    Exit Sub
End If
'
If (Day < 1) Or (Day > 31) Then
    MsgBox "The day component should be between 1 and 31, _
        inclusive.", vbInformation
    Exit Sub
End If
'
If (Year < 0) Or ((Year >= 100) And (Year <= 1980)) Then
    MsgBox "The year component (" & Year & ")is invalid.", _
        vbInformation
    Exit Sub
End If
'
' adjust for two-digit years
'
If (Year < 80) Then
    Year = Year + 2000
ElseIf (Year < 100) Then
    Year = Year + 1900
End If
'
' compute the time stamp from the components
' broken out of the user's input
'
TimeStamp = DateSerial(Year, Month, Day) + _
    TimeSerial(Hour, Minute, Second)
'
' generate the full filename with path
'
If Right(lstFile.Path, 1) = "\" Then
    TempFilename = lstFile.Path & lstFile.Filename
Else
    TempFilename = lstFile.Path & "\" & lstFile.Filename
End If
'
'
' set the file's time stamp with the new date
' and time, check for errors
'
If Not FileSetTimeStamp(TempFilename, TimeStamp) Then
    '
    ' if we get an error, let the user know
    '
```

Continued on next page

Continued from previous page

```
        MsgBox "Failed to set the time stamp of file " & _
            lstFile.Filename, vbCritical
        Exit Sub
    Else
        '
        ' load the file's date and time again, which
        ' formats it nicely
        '
        lstFile_Click
    End If
End Sub
```

6. Add the following code to the Load event handler of FileDT. This code clears the time and date text boxes when the program loads.

```
Private Sub Form_Load()
    '
    ' clear the labels when the program starts
    '
    txtDate.Text = ""
    txtTime.Text = ""
End Sub
```

7. Add the following code to the Change event section of lstDirectory. When the user changes the directory, this function updates the File list box. Since there's no selection in the list box at this point, the Set Time Stamp button is disabled.

```
Private Sub lstDirectory_Change()
    '
    ' disable the set time stamp button, since the
    ' file list box will not have anything selected
    '
    btnSetTimeStamp.Enabled = False
    '
    ' update the file list path to reflect the
    ' change of directory
    '
    lstFile.Path = lstDirectory.Path
End Sub
```

8. Add the following code to the Change event handler of cmbDrive. When the user changes the drive, this function updates the Directory list box's path and uses the new path from the Directory list box to update the File list box. Since the File list box will have no selection, the Set Time Stamp button is disabled.

```
Private Sub cmbDrive_Change()
    '
    ' disable the set time stamp button, since the
    ' file list box will not have anything selected
    '
    btnSetTimeStamp.Enabled = False
    '
```

```
' update the paths to reflect the drive change
'
lstDirectory.Path = cmbDrive.Drive
lstFile.Path = lstDirectory.Path
End Sub
```

9. Add the following code to the Click event handler for lstFile. This function gets the date and time of the file that is clicked on. It does this by calling FileDateTime, and passing in the full path and filename of the selected file. The time stamp (passed back as a variant) is used to fill in the File Date and File Time edit boxes.

```
Private Sub lstFile_Click()
    Dim TimeStamp As Variant
    Dim TempFilename As String
    '
    ' enabled the set time stamp button so the user
    ' can change the date and time for the file
    ' they just selected
    '
    btnSetTimeStamp.Enabled = True
    '
    ' generate the full filename with path
    '
    If Right(lstFile.Path, 1) = "\" Then
        TempFilename = lstFile.Path & lstFile.Filename
    Else
        TempFilename = lstFile.Path & "\" & lstFile.Filename
    End If
'
    ' get the time stamp
    '
    TimeStamp = FileDateTime(TempFilename)
    '
    ' display the selected file's date and time
    '
    txtTime.Text = Format$(TimeStamp, "HH:MM:SS")
    txtDate.Text = Format$(TimeStamp, "mm-dd-yyyy")
End Sub
```

10. Add the following code to the PathChange event handler for lstFile. When the File list box's path changes, the selection is cleared. This function makes sure the time and date fields are also cleared.

```
Private Sub lstFile_PathChange()
    '
    ' clear the date and time fields when the
    ' user changes the current path
    '
    txtTime.Text = ""
    txtDate.Text = ""
End Sub
```

How It Works

FILEDT lets the user select a file. It partially simulates a File Open dialog box to allow changing the directory and drive. When the user clicks on one of the files in the File list box, FILEDT gets the file's date and time (using FileDateTime) and puts them in the edit boxes on the form.

The user can then edit the date and time in the edit boxes and change the file's date and time by pressing the Set Time Stamp button. This button, when pressed, verifies the date and time in the edit boxes (checking for good format and good numbers). If everything is acceptable, FILEDT then calls FileSetTimeStamp with the file's full name and path, and the VB-formatted time and date.

FileSetTimeStamp uses the FileSetTime function to set the time stamp. It takes the time stamp passed into and converts to the format that Win32 likes (using SystemTimeToFileTime and LocalFileTimeToFileTime). It then opens the file and gets the file handle. Then, using the file handle, it sets the new time and date stamps. Finally, it closes the file. If any errors occur along the way, FileSetTimeStamp exits, returning an error.

Comments

The program in this How-To takes the mystery out of changing a file's date and time.

7.9 How do I...
View Icons in Executable Files?

COMPLEXITY: INTERMEDIATE
COMPATIBILITY: VB4 ONLY

Problem

I know executable files can contain icons because Program Manager gives me an option to browse them when I'm setting program item properties. Is there a way to use Visual Basic to view these icons?

Technique

This is no problem using Visual Basic and a set of Windows API routines. The API function, ExtractIcon, has two uses: it will return a count of the number of icons in a file when you set an index parameter to zero. Otherwise, it will extract the icon for the requested index and return its icon handle. By getting a count first, we can make sure we don't try to extract icons that aren't there.

ExtractIcon needs to know the instance handle for the application. We can get that instance handle from the GetWindowWord API function by passing it the window handle for our form.

After extracting an icon, we pass its handle to the DrawIcon API function, along with the device context handle for the control where the icon should be drawn. And we'll need to specify x and y control coordinates for where to start drawing the icon. As soon as the icon is painted into the control, we'll need to use the API function, DestroyIcon, to destroy the extracted icon, removing it from memory.

For this How-To, we'll be displaying extracted icons in a picture box and scrolling through them using a horizontal scroll bar. We'll encapsulate the extraction, painting, and scrolling routines into a class file, which we'll access by making an object instance of the class called CExecIcon. We'll set Container and HScroll properties for the object, and we'll perform CountIcons and ShowIcons methods for the object. A file property is specified with each method. An icon number property is also specified with the ShowIcons method, to indicate which icon index should be shown. Setting the icon number property to zero tells the ShowIcons method to show all icons.

This project uses relatively standard techniques for imitating the behavior of the Common File Open dialog box. One exception is noteworthy, however. When another pattern is selected in the combo box below the file list, the Windows Common File Open dialog puts the pattern into the text box above the file list. It does this whether or not there was already a file in the text box. Program Manager's Browse Item Icons dialog box behaves differently. If there is already a file in the text box, the filename is not replaced with the new pattern. That way, any icons displayed for the currently selected file can continue to be displayed. This How-To follows Program Manager's convention because it makes sense for this use.

Steps

Open and run EXECICON.VBP. Select various .EXE, .DLL, and .ICO files, and take a look at the icon(s) embedded in them. When you're ready, follow these steps to see how it works:

1. Create a new project called EXECICON.VBP. Create a form with controls like the one shown in action in Figure 7-9-1. Set form objects and properties as shown in Table 7-9-1, and save the form as EXECICON.FRM.

Table 7-9-1 EXECICON.FRM form properties

OBJECT	PROPERTY	SETTING
Form	Name	ExecIconForm
	Caption	"Executable Icon Viewer"
	ScaleWidth	3 'Pixel
Frame	Name	IconFrame
	Caption	""
PictureBox	Name	IconPicBox
	AutoRedraw	-1 'True
	ScaleWidth	3 'Pixel
HScrollBar	Name	Hscroll1

Continued on next page

CHAPTER 7: SYSTEM SERVICES

Continued from previous page

OBJECT	PROPERTY	SETTING
Label	Name	Label4
	Caption	"File &Name:"
TextBox	Name	IconFile
FileListBox	Name	FileList
Label	Name	Label5
	Caption	"List Files of &Type:"
ComboBox	Name	FileTypesCombo
	List	Icon Files
		Programs (*.exe)
		Libraries (*.dll)
		Icons (*.ico)
		All Files (*.*)
	Style	2 'Dropdowown List
Label	Name	Label3
	Caption	&Directories:
Label	Name	PathNameLabel
	Caption	"Path Name"
DirListBox	Name	Directory
Label	Name	Label2
	Caption	"Dri&ves:"
DriveListBox	Name	Drive
CommandButton	Name	Command1
	Caption	"Exit"

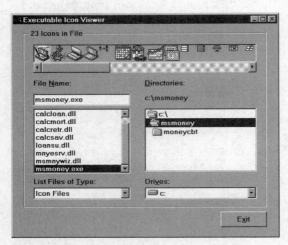

Figure 7-9-1 Executable File Icon Viewer in action

2. Place the following code at the beginning of EXECICON.FRM. Visual Basic supports 32x32-pixel icons, the norm for Windows. The numeric constants for the file-list patterns correspond to index values for the equivalent text in the FileTypesCombo ComboBox. IconExtract is set as a new object of the class, CExecIcons.

```
Option Explicit
'
' Constant values for pixel width and height of icon.
'
Private Const cIconPixelWidth As Integer = 32
Private Const cIconPixelHeight As Integer = 32
'
' Constant values for file list pattern.
'
Private Const cIconFiles As Integer = 0
Private Const cPrograms As Integer = 1
Private Const cLibraries As Integer = 2
Private Const cIcons As Integer = 3
Private Const cAllFiles As Integer = 4
'
' Extract icons class file.
'
Dim IconExtract As New CExecIcons
```

3. Place the following code in the Form_Load event procedure. This subroutine fine-tunes the height of the IconPicBox and adjusts its scroll bar as needed for displaying and scrolling through 32x32-pixel icons. Then it sets these objects as the container and scroll bar to be used by the IconExtract class object, for displaying icons found in files. It also defaults to listing all icon files, displays the initial directory path, and centers the form.

```
Private Sub Form_Load()
    '
    ' Set the height of the Icon viewer picture box to the height
    ' of exactly one icon and adjust top of the horizontal scroll
    ' bar to line up under it. Set the small scroll to one icon
    ' at a time and the large scroll to 5 icons at a time. Then
    ' tell the CExecIcons class file to use these objects.
    '
    IconPicBox.Height _
        = IconPicBox.Height _
        * (cIconPixelHeight / IconPicBox.ScaleHeight)
    HScroll1.Top = IconPicBox.Top + IconPicBox.Height
    HScroll1.SmallChange = cIconPixelWidth
    HScroll1.LargeChange = cIconPixelWidth * 5
    Set IconExtract.Container = IconPicBox
    Set IconExtract.HScroll = HScroll1
    '
    ' Default the file types selection to all icon files and
    ' display the initial directory path. Center the form.
    '
    FileTypesCombo.ListIndex = cIconFiles
```

Continued on next page

Continued from previous page

```
    PathNameLabel = Directory.Path
    Move (Screen.Width - Width) \ 2, (Screen.Height - Height) \ 2
End Sub
```

4. Place the following code in the Drive_Change event procedure. When the user changes the drive, this routine sets the current path for that drive, triggering the Directory_Change event procedures.

```
Private Sub Drive_Change()
    '
    ' Update the directory path to match the drive path
    '
    Directory.Path = Drive.Drive
End Sub
```

5. Place the following code in the Directory_Change event procedure. This procedure sets the file list path to reflect the new directory path, and displays the directory path in a label above the directory list.

```
Private Sub Directory_Change()
    '
    ' Update file list path to match directory.
    '
    FileList.Path = Directory.Path
    PathNameLabel = Directory.Path
End Sub
```

6. Place the following code in the Directory_KeyUp event procedure. The Directory list box can be navigated with arrow keys. This routine lets the user press Enter to set a new directory path.

```
Private Sub Directory_KeyUp(KeyCode As Integer, Shift As Integer)
    '
    ' When enter key is pressed set the directory path to the
    ' highlighted directory.
    '
    If KeyCode = vbKeyReturn Then
        Directory.Path = Directory.List(Directory.ListIndex)
    End If
End Sub
```

7. Place the following code in the FileTypesCombo_Click event procedure. This procedure sets the pattern for the FileList list box. If there is not already a file in the IconFile text box, the pattern is also displayed there. This logic makes the pattern selection work the same way it works in Program Manager's icon-selection dialog box.

```
Private Sub FileTypesCombo_Click()
    '
    ' Set the FileList pattern based on the combo box that offers
    ' a choice of appropriate file types.
    '
    Select Case FileTypesCombo.ListIndex
```

```
        Case cIconFiles
            FileList.Pattern = "*.ico;*.exe;*.dll"
        Case cPrograms
            FileList.Pattern = "*.exe"
        Case cLibraries
            FileList.Pattern = "*.dll"
        Case cIcons
            FileList.Pattern = "*.ico"
        Case Else
            FileList.Pattern = "*.*"
    End Select
    '
    ' If there is no file name in the IconFile TextBox, then show
    ' the FileList pattern in the box.
    '
    If IconFile = "" Or Left(IconFile, 1) = "*" Then
        IconFile = FileList.Pattern
    End If
End Sub
```

8. Place the following code in the FileList_Click event procedure. This subroutine sets the name of the file in the IconFile text box to match the newly selected file. Changing the text box triggers the IconFile_Change event described in step 9.

```
Private Sub FileList_Click()
    '
    ' Set the IconFile text to match the highlighted file in the
    ' file list
    '
    IconFile = FileList.List(FileList.ListIndex)
End Sub
```

9. Place the following code in the IconFile_Change event procedure. This procedure builds a fully qualified filename and gets from the IconExtract object a count of the number of icons in the file. It clears the IconPicBox if there are no icons in the file. Otherwise, it performs the ShowIcons method for the object, requesting that all icons be displayed in the object's container, the IconPicBox. Finally, it updates and refreshes the IconFrame to indicate the number of icons in the file.

```
Private Sub IconFile_Change()
    Const cShowAll As Integer = 0
    Dim NumIcons As Integer
    Dim IconExec As String
    '
    ' If the IconFile TextBox has a file name in it, concatinate
    ' it to the path and save the pathed file name in a variable.
    '
    If IconFile = "" Or Left(IconFile, 1) = "*" Then
        Exit Sub
    Else
        If InStr(Len(FileList.Path), FileList.Path, "\") Then
            IconExec = FileList.Path & IconFile
        Else
```

Continued on next page

Continued from previous page

```
                IconExec = FileList.Path & "\" & IconFile
        End If
    End If
    '
    ' Get from the CExecIcons class file a count of the number of
    ' icons embedded in this file. If there are one or more icons
    ' in the file, have the class file show them. Otherwise clear
    ' the PictureBox.
    '
    NumIcons = IconExtract.CountIcons(IconExec)
    If NumIcons > 0 Then
        IconExtract.ShowIcons IconExec, cShowAll
    Else
        IconPicBox.Cls
    End If
    '
    ' Set the IconFrame caption to reflect the number of icons in
    ' the file.
    '
    If NumIcons = 1 Then
        IconFrame.Caption = "1 Icon in File"
    ElseIf NumIcons > 1 Then
        IconFrame.Caption = Str(NumIcons) & " Icons in File"
    Else
        IconFrame.Caption = "No Icons in File"
    End If
    IconFrame.Refresh
End Sub
```

10. Place the following code in the HScroll1_Change event procedure. This sub-routine just passes to the CExecIcon class object the fact that the scroll bar has been changed.

```
Private Sub HScroll1_Change()
    '
    ' Let the CExecIcons class file know that the horizontal
    ' scroll bar was scrolled.
    '
    IconExtract.HScroll_Change
End Sub
```

11. Use the Insert Class menu item to create a new class module and save it as EXE-CICON.CLS. Name it CExecIcon and put the following code at the beginning of the file. This code defines the constant, variables, and Windows API functions needed to extract icons from executable files and to draw them into a picture box. The code defines each of the class property variables and other class file variables.

```
Option Explicit
'
' Constant, variables, and declares for extracting icons from
' executables and for drawing them into a picture box.
'
Private Const GWW_HINSTANCE = (-6)
#If Win32 Then
    Private m_hInst As Long
```

```
    Private Declare Function GetWindowWord Lib "user 32"_
        (ByVal hWnd As Long,_
        ByVal nIndex As Long)_
      As Long
    Private Declare Function ExtractIcon Lib "shell32" _
      Alias "ExtractIconA" _
        (ByVal hInst As Long, _
        ByVal lpszExeFileName As String, _
        ByVal nIconIndex As Long) _
      As Long
    Private Declare Function DestroyIcon Lib "user32" _
        (ByVal hIcon As Long) _
      As Long
    Private Declare Function DrawIcon Lib "user32" _
        (ByVal hDC As Long, _
        ByVal X As Long, _
        ByVal Y As Long, _
        ByVal hIcon As Long) _
      As Long
#Else
    Private m_hInst As Integer
    Private Declare Function GetWindowWord Lib "User" _
        (ByVal hWnd As Integer, ByVal nOffset As Integer) _
      As Integer
    Private Declare Function ExtractIcon Lib "Shell" _
        (ByVal hInst As Integer, ByVal lpszFileName As String, _
        ByVal nIconIndex As Integer) As Integer
    Private Declare Function DestroyIcon Lib "User" _
        (ByVal hIcon As Integer) _
      As Integer
    Private Declare Function DrawIcon Lib "User" _
        (ByVal hDC As Integer, _
        ByVal X As Integer, ByVal Y As Integer, _
        ByVal hIcon As Integer) _
      As Integer
#End If
```

12. Add this code next, to set the private variables for the class object.

```
'
' Private variables for container and associated scrolling. Also
' for current file and count of icons it contains.
'
Private m_Container As Object
Private m_HScroll As Object
Private m_ShowHScroll As Boolean
Private m_IconExec As String
Private m_IconCount As Integer
```

13. Add the following code to the Initialization section of CExecIcon. This is the initialization subroutine for the CExecIcon class. It sets up the class to work without a scroll bar if necessary.

```
Private Sub Class_Initialize()
    '
```

Continued on next page

Continued from previous page

```
    ' This variable will be changed to true if the calling program
    ' set a horizontal scroll bar object.
    '
    m_ShowHScroll = False
End Sub
```

14. Add the following code to the General section of CExecIcon. The Set procedure for the Container property gets and stores the current container object from the calling program, making sure it is a PictureBox control. It also uses the window handle of the control's parent form to retrieve and store the instance handle for the application. The instance handle will be passed to the Windows API function that extracts icons from a file.

```
Public Property Set Container(PB As Object)
    '
    ' If the container is a PictureBox, get the handle of its
    ' parent form for use in getting the instance handle of the
    ' application. The instance handle is needed in the draw icon
    ' process.
    '
    If TypeOf PB Is PictureBox Then
        Set m_Container = PB
        m_hInst _
            = GetWindowWord mContainer.Parent.hWnd(GWW_HINSTANCE)
    Else
        MsgBox "Container is not a valid PictureBox"
    End If
End Property
```

15. Add the following code to the General section of CExecIcon. The Get procedure for the Container property returns the current container object to the calling program.

```
Public Property Get Container() As Object
    '
    ' Return the current PictureBox to the calling program.
    '
    Set Container = m_Container
End Property
```

16. Add the following code to the General section of CExecIcon. The Set procedure for the HScroll property gets and stores the current scroll-bar object from the calling program. If it is a valid HScrollBar control, scrolling values are initialized and the m_ShowHScroll flag is set to true.

```
Public Property Set HScroll(HS As Object)
    '
    ' If its a valid HScrollBar object, initialize the associated
    ' variables.
    '
    If TypeOf HS Is HScrollBar Then
        Set m_HScroll = HS
        m_HScroll.Min = 0
```

```
        m_HScroll.Max = 0
        m_HScroll.Value = 0
        m_ShowHScroll = True
    Else
        MsgBox "Scrolling Object is not a valid horizontal " _
            & "scroll bar"
    End If
End Property
```

17. Add the following code to the General section of CExecIcon. The Get procedure for the HScroll property returns the current scroll-bar object to the calling program.

```
Public Property Get HScroll() As Object
    '
    ' Return the current HScrollBar object to the calling program.
    '
    Set HScroll = m_HScroll
End Property
```

18. Add the following public function to the General section of CExecIcon. It returns a count of the number of icons found in the requested file.

```
Public Function CountIcons(IconExec As String) As Integer
    '
    ' Return an IconCount for the designated file. But don't
    ' store it globally until the file itself is stored globally
    ' in the ShowIcons subroutine.
    '
    Dim ICount As Integer
    ICount = ExtractIcon(m_hInst, IconExec, -1)
    CountIcons = ICount
End Function
```

19. Add the following public subroutine to the General section of CExecIcon, to provide the ShowIcons method for the class object. Before clearing the container and resetting the scroll bar, the routine validates the requested number of icons to display (0 for all) against the number of icons found in the file. Then, if exactly one icon is requested for display, it is painted into the container and the routine exits. If all icons are requested for display, it paints as many as will fit into the container, starting with the first one. The scroll bar maximum is adjusted to allow scrolling through exactly as many icons as are in the file.

```
Public Sub ShowIcons(Iexec As String, Inum As Integer)
    '
    ' Store the file and a count of the number of embedded icons.
    ' Exit the subroutine if there are no icons in the file or if
    ' and invalid icon number is passed in.
    '
    m_IconExec = Iexec
    m_IconCount = CountIcons(m_IconExec)
    If m_IconCount < 1 Then
```

Continued on next page

Continued from previous page

```
        MsgBox "No icons found in file: " & m_IconExec
        Exit Sub
    End If
    Dim IconNum As Integer
    IconNum = Inum
    If IconNum < 0 Or IconNum > m_IconCount Then
        MsgBox "Icon number " & IconNum & " is not between 0 and " _
            & m_IconCount
        Exit Sub
    End If
    '
    ' To prep for showing a set of icons, clear the container and,
    ' if a horizontal scroll bar is in use, initialize its values.
    '
    m_Container.Cls
    If m_ShowHScroll Then
        m_HScroll.Value = 0
        m_HScroll.Max = 0
    End If
    '
    ' When the icon number is set to a number, paint that icon
    ' into the picture box, otherwise paint as many as will fit.
    '
    If IconNum > 0 Then
        PaintIcons IconNum - 1
        Exit Sub
    Else
        PaintIcons 0, m_IconCount - 1
    End If
    '
    ' When multiple icons are to be painted into a scrolling
    ' PictureBox, set the scroll max to 0 if they'll all fit.
    ' Otherwise set it to scroll to the last icon in the set.
    '
    If Not m_ShowHScroll Then Exit Sub
    m_IconCount * 32 > (m_Container.ScaleWidth \ 32) * 32 Then
    m_HScroll.Max _
        = m_IconCount * 32
        - (m_Container.ScaleWidth \ 32) * 32
    Else
        m_HScroll.Max = 0
    End If
End Sub
```

20. Add the following private subroutine to the General section of CExecIcon. This routine paints one or more icons into the container object. An index number for the starting icon is required, but it is optional for the ending icon. First, this routine needs to compute a limit for the number of icons to paint into the container. If only one is requested, that's all that gets painted. Otherwise, the maximum number of icons is limited to what will fit in the container, but not to exceed the number requested. For each icon to be painted, the routine extracts it from the file using the ExtractIcon Windows API function. Then it uses the DrawIcon API function to paint the icon into the container, aligned to the left edge of the con-

tainer or to the previously drawn icon, and aligned to the top of the container.
Finally, it destroys the extracted icon using the DestroyIcon API.

```
Private Sub PaintIcons(i As Integer, Optional c As Variant)
    '
    ' Limit the number of icons to paint to a single icon if the
    ' calling routine didn't set a limit. Otherwise limit it to
    ' the number requested or the number that will fit in the
    ' container, whichever is less.
    '
    Dim IconLimit As Integer
    If IsMissing(c) Then
        IconLimit = i
    Else
        If c > m_Container.ScaleWidth \ 32 Then
            IconLimit = i + m_Container.ScaleWidth \ 32
        Else
            IconLimit = c
        End If
    End If
    '
    ' And finally, paint one or more icons into the container!
    ' For each icon to be painted, extract the icon handle. Then
    ' draw it into the container starting at the left (0) edge of
    ' the container and always aligning at the top (0) edge.
    '
    Dim IconIndex As Long
    Dim hIcon As Long
    For IconIndex = i To IconLimit
        hIcon = ExtractIcon(m_hInst, m_IconExec, IconIndex)
        DrawIcon m_Container.hDC, (IconIndex - i) * 32, 0, hIcon
        DestroyIcon hIcon
    Next IconIndex
End Sub
```

21. Add the following subroutine to the General section of CExecIcon. This subroutine would normally be triggered by the client scroll bar's Change routine. The code clears the container and requests that the PaintIcons subroutine repaint the container, starting at an icon index equivalent to the current value of the scroll bar, and ending at the last icon in the file. Remember that the PaintIcons subroutine will, for efficiency, limit the number painted to what will actually fit in the container. Note that this routine will not be triggered when only one icon is requested, because in that case the scroll bar maximum is set to 0.

```
Public Sub HScroll_Change()
    '
    ' Clear the container. Then paint the icons in starting at the
    ' first icon that corresponds to the position of the scrollbar.
    '
    m_Container.Cls
    PaintIcons m_HScroll.Value \ 32, m_IconCount
End Sub
```

How It Works

The project in this How-To allows the user to choose a file from any directory on any drive, and to display any and all icons embedded in the file.

Events for DriveListBox, DirectoryListBox, and FileListBox are programmed to work in concert for selecting a file. A drop-down list-style ComboBox provides patterns for the types of files that are likely to have embedded icons in them. Specifically, patterns are supplied for executable files (*.exe), library files (*.dll), icon files (*.ico), and icon files in general (*.ico;*.exe;*.dll).

When the user selects a file, the program uses the CExecIcon class file's CountIcons method to find out if the file has any embedded icons. If it does, the ShowIcons method is used to get the icons displayed in a scrolling PictureBox.

The CExecIcon class file hides all the muss and fuss of counting, extracting, and displaying these icons. Give it the full path to a file, and it can tell you how many icons, if any, are in the file. Tell it what PictureBox to paint the icons into, and give it a horizontal scroll bar if scrolling is desired, and it can paint your choice of one or all icons into the PictureBox. It'll handle the scrolling for you, as well.

The ExtractIcon API function is used both to find out how many icons are in a file and to extract an individual icon. The DrawIcon is used to paint an extracted icon into the container PictureBox's device context. Knowing that Visual Basic handles only 32x32-pixel icons makes it easy for the class file to calculate where in the device context to paint the icons. It loops through each of the icons to be painted, putting each one just to the right of the prior one. For efficiency, it only paints as many icons as are needed to show in the PictureBox—even if it's a scrolling PictureBox. When the scroll bar value is changed, the class figures out which icon should be leftmost in the PictureBox. Then it displays icons from that icon to the last one in the file, or to the last one that will show, whichever is less.

Comments

You may notice that both the form and the class file get a count of the number of icons in the file, to keep from attempting to extract icons that aren't there. This is not redundant; it's just a good example of defensive programming. Class-file routines should not have to process invalid requests. Likewise, calling programs should do their best not to make invalid requests.

7.10 How do I...
Detect Which OS Is Running?

COMPLEXITY: EASY
COMPATIBILITY: VB4 ONLY

Problem

I want every aspect of my application to look professional, including the About box. Modern About boxes contain a good deal of system information, including the current version of the operating system. I tried using a couple of API calls, but they either didn't tell me everything, or they seemed to return the wrong value. How do I figure out what operating system is running and its version number?

Technique

All flavors of Windows will tell you about themselves, if you ask them the right questions. In this project, we're trying to figure out two things: the system's version and the system's name. Figure 7-10-1 shows GETOSVER in action.

Determining the version number is pretty straightforward. The GetVersionEx() API call does all of the work.

Getting the name of the operating system is just a matter of interpreting the data returned by GetVersion() and GetVersionEx(). If the high bit of the number returned by GetVersion() is zero, then we're running on Windows NT. Otherwise, we're running on Windows or Windows 95. We determine which by the version number.

Steps

1. Create a new project called GETOSVER.VBP. Select Form1, and add objects with properties set as in Table 7-10-1.

Figure 7-10-1 GETOSVER's display

Table 7-10-1 Objects, properties, and settings for Form1

OBJECT	PROPERTY	SETTING
Form	BorderStyle	3 'Fixed Double
	Caption	"Get OS Version"
	Height	1395
	Left	1020
	Top	1275
	Width	6270
Label	Name	Label1
	Height	255
	Left	480
	Top	480
	Width	5415
Label	Name	Label2
	Caption	"System Version:"
	Height	255
	Left	240
	Top	240
	Width	1935

2. Add the following to the General section of Form1. This portion of the code defines all of the API calls used and their constants. Notice that, once again, we're using Option Explicit. Always use this in your code. It'll save you a lot of time trying to track down misspelled variable names.

```
Option Explicit
'
' definitions for getting the Windows version
'
Private Type OSVERSIONINFO
   dwOSVersionInfoSize As Long
   dwMajorVersion As Long
   dwMinorVersion As Long
   dwBuildNumber As Long
   dwPlatformId As Long
   szCSDVersion As String * 128      ' Maintenance string for PSS usage
End Type
'
Private Declare Function GetVersion Lib "kernel32" () As Long
Private Declare Function GetVersionEx Lib "kernel32" Alias _
   "GetVersionExA" (lpVersionInformation As OSVERSIONINFO) As Long
```

3. Add the following code to the General Declarations section of Form1. This function gets the current version number and name of Windows and returns it as a string.

```
Private Function GetWindowsVersion() As String
    Dim OSName As String
    Dim APIName As String
    Dim OSVI As OSVERSIONINFO
    Dim WinVer As Long
    '
    ' get version number for system
    '
    OSVI.dwOSVersionInfoSize = 148
    GetVersionEx OSVI
    WinVer = GetVersion()
    '
    ' format version number
    '
    If WinVer & &H8000000 Then
        If OSVI.dwMajorVersion >= 4 Then
            OSName = "Windows 95"
            APIName = "Win32"
        ElseIf OSVI.dwMinorVersion = 95 Then
            OSName = "Windows 95"
            APIName = "Win16"
        Else
            OSName = "Windows"
            APIName = "Win32s"
        End If
    Else
        OSName = "Windows NT"
        APIName = "Win32"
    End If
    '
    ' final formatting and return string
    '
    GetWindowsVersion = OSName & " v" & OSVI.dwMajorVersion & "." _
        & Format(OSVI.dwMinorVersion, "00") & " running " & APIName
End Function
```

4. Add the following code to the General Declarations section of Form1. This function gets the system and version strings, concatenates them, and then puts them into a label for the user to see.

```
Private Sub Form_Load()
    '
    ' get  the operating system name and version
    ' and show it to the user
    '
    Label1.Caption = GetWindowsSystem()
End Sub
```

How It Works

GETOSVER works by using the two Win32 API system version calls to get information about the current system. It finds out what version is running by calling GetVersionEx().

Figuring out the system name takes a little deduction. If the high bit of the version number returned by GetVersion() is zero, then we are running on Windows NT (and Win32). Otherwise, we're running on either Windows 3.X or Windows 95.

This is easily determined from the version number returned from GetVersionEx(). If the version number is 4.00 or greater, then we're running Windows 95 and Win32. If the version number is 3.95, then we're running Windows 95 and Win16. If it's less, then we're running Windows 3.X and Win16.

Comments

The techniques shown here can be used to determine other information about the current system, such as the current processor, what networks are running, and so forth.

8

DATABASE

8

DATABASE

How do I...

Many Visual Basic applications require that data be stored and manipulated. Though the text and binary file handling available in Visual Basic is fine for small or simple applications, most applications will need to use the data access objects (DAOs) to manipulate database files. This chapter makes use of the controls and DAOs provided with Visual Basic Professional Edition.

The ability to use DAOs was introduced in Visual Basic 3.0. These objects function in conjunction with the JET Engine, Microsoft's database engine. That helps to shield the programmer from the specifics of a particular database system. This is similar to the way Windows provides printer drivers so you don't need to know all the control codes for the printers in your system. Although all of the How-To's in this chapter deal with Access database files, you can easily adapt the techniques presented here to dBase, FoxPro, and other database files.

8.1   Create a Quicken-Style ComboBox for Data Lookup

Visual Basic 4.0 provides new list controls that bind to database tables. The new DBList and DBCombo controls provide more capabilities than their data unaware counterparts, but you still need to do a bit of programming to bring out their best functionality. This How-To will show you how to create a Visual Basic class to control a DBList, using a text box to mimic the way a Quicken-style combo box selects a matching item in the list as the user types.

8.2   Create a Selection List from a Lookup Table

The DBList and DBCombo controls contain most of the features of their data unaware counterparts, but they do not support multiple selections. In this case you have to take a step backward to move ahead. This How-To will give you an example of adding database capabilities to the data unaware ListBox control. The user can select multiple items from the list box, and the selections will be updated in the associated database table.

8.3   Display Tables and Fields in an Access Database

Microsoft has been guiding Visual Basic along a particular path with regard to database applications. When the JET Engine was added in Version 3.0, Visual Basic was tied tightly to Access database files. Unfortunately, only rudimentary handling of Access tables and fields was provided with the Professional Edition of Visual Basic. This How-To will show how to extract the definitions of tables and fields from an Access database (.MDB) file. It will also demonstrate the usefulness of the Outline control for displaying hierarchical data. This control is generally used to display directories and files but has many other uses. The Outline control is used again in How-To's 8.5 and 8.6.

8.4   Build a Better Data Control

Visual Basic's data control provides a powerful way for users to browse through database records. Clicking on one of the data control's buttons causes all bound controls to display a selected record without any additional coding. As with Visual Basic's other controls, you can add code to improve the data control's operation. In this How-To a set of command buttons will be used to control a hidden data control. The controls bound to the data control don't know that it is being manipulated by a program rather than the user's mouse clicks. In addition to the movement buttons provided by the data control, the Better Data control adds the ability to mark and return to specific records. It also disables buttons that would allow a user to move beyond the beginning or end of the database table.

8.5   Display Values from Any Access Database

This How-To will take the structure of Access tables a step further and show you how to display the data in those tables. Once again, as in How-To 8.3, a data control will be manipulated under program control. This time the DatabaseName and RecordSource properties are changed as the user selects a database file and table in an Outline control. Extra versatility will be provided by a text box that accepts search criteria to filter the data display. The value of the text box is added as a WHERE clause to the SQL statement for the Data control.

8.6   Create a Database from a Text File Description

During the design and implementation phases of your projects, you may need to redefine the structure of your database files many times. There's always that one field you forgot, or those other fields that should be moved to a different table. Access allows you to change the structure of tables at any time, but Visual Basic does not. This How-To will give you a way to define your database in a text file and use that file to create a database file. You define the tables, fields, indexes, and relations in a text-based schema file. If you need to change the structure of the database, you simply change the schema file and re-create the database. Unfortunately, you cannot change the format of a table and keep the data intact. How-To 8.7 will help solve this problem.

8.7   Import Text Records into a Database

Once you have a database created, there are two ways of getting data into it. One method is to create forms and have the user type in the data. This is fine for capturing data as it is received—but if you have existing data you need to use the other method: load it all at once. Most applications allow you to export data as a text file. This How-To will demonstrate Visual Basic's ability to read that text file just as if it were another database table. All you need to do is define the text file for Visual Basic, and the rest is automatic. Loading the data becomes a simple matter of reading from the text file, copying each field to the database record, computing any fields that require special attention, and adding the new record to the database.

   If you need to change your database definition, you can write a routine to put the data out as a text file, change the database schema, re-create the database file using the techniques in How-To 8.6, and then reload the data, altering the input to match the new schema.

8.8   Find Incorrectly Spelled Names in a Database

Though it's not a foolproof method, How-To 8.8 employs the Soundex algorithm, which generates a code based on the sound of a name to help you find misspellings. Names that sound alike or even similar will likely have the same Soundex code. You can also employ Soundex in creating applications that require the user to search by name. Instead of showing a list of identical names, the application can display a list of similar names. The user is then protected from the problem of various spellings for some names (Smith, Smythe, and Smyth, for example).

8.1 How do I...
Create a Quicken-Style ComboBox for Data Lookup?

COMPLEXITY: INTERMEDIATE
COMPATIBILITY: VB4 ONLY

Problem

I like the combo boxes used in Quicken. They let me select a row with a minimum of keystrokes while reminding me of what I've entered. How can I provide a combo box of this style in my Visual Basic application?

Technique

Visual Basic 4.0 provides the new bound controls, DBList and DBCombo. They work directly with the standard data controls to access external database information. As you'd expect, a DBCombo box simply combines an edit control with a DBList box. Both the DBCombo and DBList controls provide for the automatic fill of a list box and the automatic update of a table field. Depending on the situation, the programmer may use either or both of these capabilities with a given bound control.

The new DBCombo control supports an extended search mode. Although this mode provides some of the features we're looking for, the DBCombo box doesn't highlight the current selection candidate. And, unlike the Quicken-style combo box, it doesn't fill the edit control with the full text of the selection candidate.

In this How-To, we use the automatic fill capability of the DBList control. Our project mimics the Quicken style by providing a CQCombo class to coordinate a DBList control with an enhanced edit control. The current selection is always displayed in the list, and it's enhanced to distinguish the characters keyed in by the user from the rest of the selection. For this example, the QCombo box displays a lookup table containing a list of organizations having addresses on file. When the user selects an organization, the code behind the Name and Address form finds and displays the mailing address.

Steps

Open and run ADDRESS.VBP. In the Name and Address form, notice that the list displays the organizations in alphabetical order. The first organization is highlighted in both the list and the edit control. The mailing address of the selected organization appears in the frame to the right.

With the focus in the edit control, press P (upper- or lowercase) and observe the results. The first organization with a name beginning with P is highlighted in the list box. This name also appears in the edit control, but there the first character (the one keyed by the user) is *not* highlighted. The mailing address of the new organization appears.

Slowly Press O and then, after a slight pause, press W, observing the behavior of the form as it reaches the point illustrated in Figure 8-1-1. Now press X, a letter that doesn't cause another match. The computer beeps, drops the X, and returns the form to the way it looked before.

Backspace a few times and see what happens. Move the cursor to the list box and click on one organization name, then another. Press M and then I, and notice that the focus is still in the edit control. When you are done experimenting, click the OK button to close the form.

1. Create a new project called ADDRESS.VBP, and create a new form called ADDRESS.FRM. Place the controls on the form as shown in Figure 8-1-2. Then set all the properties listed in Table 8-1-1.

   The two invisible data controls establish connections with the Access database VBHT.MDB, which is located in the same subdirectory as the project files. Visual Basic makes it very convenient to establish a simple connection with a table. You may also choose to supply your own SQL statement, or name a query in an Access database. The data controls on this form illustrate both of those more advanced techniques.

   Pay special attention to the DBList control. Its *automatic fill* capability relieves you of having to build and maintain the list of items displayed. To use the automatic fill capability, you simply click on the RowSource property and then choose a data control from the drop-down list. In this example, you click on the

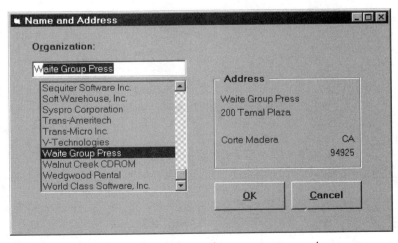

Figure 8-1-1 The Quicken-style ComboBox in action on the SelectAddress form

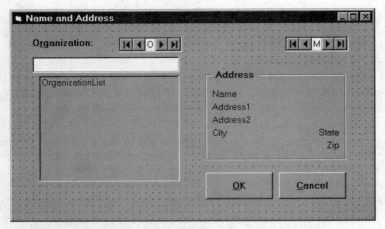

Figure 8-1-2 The SelectAddress form during design

Organization entry. Next, you move the pointer to the ListField property and click. From the list of available fields, choose the Name field.

Table 8-1-1 ADDRESS.FRM objects and properties

OBJECT	PROPERTY	SETTING
Form	Name	SelectAddress
	Caption	"Name and Address"
Data	Name	Organization
	Connect	"Access"
	ReadOnly	-1 'True
	RecordsetType	1 'Dynaset
	RecordSource	"SELECT * FROM tblOrganization ORDER BY Name;"
	Visible	False
Data	Name	MailingAddress
	Connect	"Access"
	ReadOnly	-1 'True
	RecordsetType	1 'Dynaset
	RecordSource	"qselMailingAddress"
	Visible	False
Label	Name	Label1
	Caption	"O&rganization:"
TextBox	Name	NameEdit
	TabIndex	0

OBJECT	PROPERTY	SETTING
DBList	Name	OrganizationList
	TabIndex	1
	ListField	"Name"
	RowSource	Organization
CommandButton	Name	OKButton
	Caption	"&OK"
	TabIndex	2
CommandButton	Name	CancelButton
	Caption	"&Cancel"
	TabIndex	3
Frame	Name	Address
	Caption	"Address"
Label	Name	NameDisplay
	DataField	"Name"
	DataSource	"MailingAddress"
Label	Name	AddressLine1
	DataField	"Address1"
	DataSource	"MailingAddress"
Label	Name	AddressLine2
	DataField	"Address2"
	DataSource	"MailingAddress"
Label	Name	CityName
	DataField	"City"
	DataSource	"MailingAddress"
Label	Name	State
	DataField	"St"
	DataSource	"MailingAddress"
Label	Name	Zip
	DataField	"ZipCode"
	DataSource	"MailingAddress"

2. Place the following code at the beginning of ADDRESS.FRM. The QCombo object is established as an instance of the CQCombo class.

```
Option Explicit
'
' Declare QCombo class file.
'
Dim QCombo As New CQCombo
```

841

3. Place the following code in the Form_Load event procedure, to establish pointers to the sample database. It also sets the properties of the QCombo box. These properties identify the text box used as the edit control, the DBList for displaying the organization list, and the Data control identifying the source of the list items.

```
Private Sub Form_Load()
    '
    'Establish database pointers.
    '
    Organization.DatabaseName
        = App.Path _
            & IIF(Right$ (App.Path, 1) <> "\", "\", "") _
            & "VBHT.MDB"
    MailingAddress.DatabaseName
        =App.Path _
            & IIF(Right$(App.Path, 1) "\", "\", "")
            & "VBHT.MDB"
    '
    ' Tell the QCombo class which TextBox, DBList, and Data to use.
    '
    Set QCombo.EditControl = NameEdit
    Set QCombo.QList = OrganizationList
    Set QCombo.RowSource = Organization
    '
    ' Center form.
    '
    Move (Screen.Width - Width) \ 2, (Screen.Height - Height) \ 2
End Sub
```

4. Place the following code in the NameEdit_GotFocus event procedure. If the edit control is empty, as it will be when the form is loaded, this code synchronizes the QCombo box with the mailing address display. It first sets the mailing address equal to the first record in the QCombo RowSource, and then uses the DisplayEdit method to initialize the QCombo box. Note that the OrgID field is used to link the organization name with the organization address. Visual Basic handles this behind the scenes, and the OrgID field never appears on the form at all.

```
Private Sub NameEdit_GotFocus()
    '
    ' On first entry, synchronize organization list,
    ' address display, and edit control displays.
    '
    If Not Len(QCombo.EditControl.Text) Then
        MailingAddress.Recordset.FindFirst "OrgID = " _
                                & QCombo.RowSource.Recordset("OrgID")
        QCombo.DisplayEdit QCombo.RowSource.Recordset("Name")
    End If
End Sub
```

5. Place the following code in the NameEdit_Click event procedure. This code allows the user to highlight the full selection.

```
Private Sub NameEdit_Click()
    '
```

```
' Allow the user to highlight the selection by clicking on the
' edit control.
'
QCombo.Highlight
End Sub
```

6. Place the following code in the NameEdit_Keypress event procedure. To process each keystroke in the edit control, we pass the keystroke to the EditKey method for the QCombo box. (This method does most of the work of making the QCombo box behave like Quicken, as you will see in step 20.) After the work with the keystroke is done, the keypress value is cleared to suppress any further action with it, and the new mailing address record is located and set. Because the MailingAddress data control is the DataSource for all labels in the address frame, the labels will automatically display the new values.

```
Private Sub NameEdit_KeyPress(KeyAscii As Integer)
    '
    ' Let QCombo handle keypress. Then suppress value and display
    ' address of organization selected.
    '
    QCombo.EditKey KeyAscii
    KeyAscii = 0
    MailingAddress.Recordset.FindFirst "OrgID = " _
                            & QCombo.RowSource.Recordset("OrgID")
End Sub
```

7. Place the following subroutine in the OrganizationList_GotFocus event procedure. This code lets the user see an address by clicking on a name in the list box. The Synchronize method sets the edit control and current record to match the user's selection, as well as placing the focus back on the edit control. The Synchronize method returns control to subroutine, which finds the corresponding mailing address record. This causes the display of the new address information.

```
Private Sub OrganizationList_GotFocus()
    '
    ' Accept selection when user clicks on list box entry. (Note
    ' that the Synchronize method sets the focus back to the
    ' edit control.) Display the corresponding address.
    '
    QCombo.Synchronize
    MailingAddress.Recordset.FindFirst "OrgID = " _
                            & QCombo.RowSource.Recordset("OrgID")
End Sub
```

8. Place the following code in the OKButton_Click event procedure. The Unload statement unloads the form and triggers the Unload event. Clicking OK accepts the address displayed for later use in a larger process.

```
Private Sub OKButton_Click()
    '
    ' Unload form and exit.
    '
```

Continued on next page

Continued from previous page

```
    Unload Me
    End
End Sub
```

9. Place the following code in the CancelButton _Click event procedure. This allows exit from the form, without displaying the address. See How-To 6.4 for a way the Cancel button supports a larger process.

```
Private Sub CancelButton_Click()
    '
    ' Provide cancel button to provide convenient exit for
    ' application that calls form.
    '
    Call OKButton_Click
End Sub
```

10. Place the following code in the Form_Unload event procedure. This code disconnects the form from system resources, so those resources can be released.

```
Private Sub Form_Unload(Cancel As Integer)
    '
    ' Release resources.
    '
    Set NameAndAddress = Nothing
End Sub
```

11. Use the Insert Class menu item to create a new class module and save it as QCOMBO.CLS. Name it CQCombo, and put the following code at the beginning of the file. This code sets the private variables for the class object.

```
Option Explicit
'
' Private variables for use with the edit control and list box.
'
Private m_Edit As Object
Private m_QList As Object
Private m_RowSource As Object
Private m_Field As String
Private m_Keyed As String
```

12. Add the following code to the General section of CQCombo. The Set property for EditControl gets, validates, and stores the TextBox object that will be used as the edit control. Look at step 3 to see how the EditControl property is set in this project.

```
Public Property Set EditControl(TB As Object)
    '
    ' Make sure object is a text box and, if so, initialize.
    '
    If TypeOf TB Is TextBox Then
        Set m_Edit = TB
```

```
    Else
        MsgBox "EditControl is not a valid TextBox."
    End If
End Property
```

13. Add the following code to the General section of CQCombo. The Get property for EditControl returns the current edit control object to the calling program. Look at step 4 to see how the get EditControl property is used in this project.

```
Public Property Get EditControl() As Object
    '
    ' Return the current TextBox to the caller.
    '
    Set EditControl = m_Edit
End Property
```

14. Add the following code to the General section of CQCombo. The Set property for QList gets, validates, and stores the DBList object that will be used as the list box. Then the m_Field variable is initialized with the name of the field that will be displayed in the list box. This name is needed later to construct RecordSet.FindFirst criteria strings.

```
Public Property Set QList(QL As Object)
    '
    ' Make sure object is a DBList box and, if so, initialize.
    '
    If TypeOf QL Is DBList Then
        Set m_QList = QL
        m_Field = m_QList.ListField
    Else
        MsgBox "QList is not a valid DBList."
    End If
End Property
```

15. Add the following code to the General section of CQCombo. The Get property for QList returns the current DBList object to the calling program.

```
Public Property Get QList() As Object
    '
    ' Return the current DBList to the caller.
    '
    Set QList = m_QList
End Property
```

16. Add the following code to the General section of CQCombo. The Set property for RowSource gets, validates, and stores the data object that will be used as the RowSource for the list box. Look at step 3 to see how the RowSource property is set in this project.

```
Public Property Set RowSource(RS As Object)
    '
    ' Make sure object is a Data control and, if so, initialize.
    '
```

Continued on next page

Continued from previous page

```
    If TypeOf RS Is Data Then
        Set m_RowSource = RS
    Else
        MsgBox "RowSource is not a valid Data control."
    End If
End Property
```

17. Add the following code to the General section of CQCombo. The Get property for RowSource returns the current data object to the calling program. Look at step 4 to see two examples of how the get RowSource property is used in this project.

```
Public Property Get RowSource() As Object
    '
    ' Return the current Data control to the caller.
    '
    Set RowSource = m_RowSource
End Property
```

18. Add the following public subroutine to the General section of CQCombo. It provides the DisplayEdit method for the class object. Look at step 4 to see how the DisplayEdit method is used in this project.

```
Public Sub DisplayEdit(Etext As String)
    '
    ' Initialize edit control and list to the same entry and
    ' highlight text.
    '
    m_Edit.Text = Etext
    Call Highlight
End Sub
```

19. Add the following public subroutine to the General section of CQCombo. It provides the Highlight method for the class object. Look at steps 5 and 18 to see examples of how the Highlight method is used in this project.

```
Public Sub Highlight()
    '
    ' Highlight the full edit control text.
    '
    m_Edit.SelStart = 0
    m_Edit.SelLength = Len(m_Edit.Text)
End Sub
```

20. Add the following public subroutine to the General section of CQCombo, to provide the EditKey method for the class object. The EditKey method is the workhorse of the class, and it's the heart of providing Quicken-like functionality. It is used every time the user presses a character key while the focus is in the edit control text box. Look again at step 6 to see how the EditKey method is used in this project.

```
Public Sub EditKey(Kascii As Integer)
    '
    ' Preserve keystrokes, clearing them after edit control
    ' is clicked.
    '
    If m_Edit.SelLength = Len(m_Edit.Text) Then m_Keyed = ""
    '
    ' Remove last keystroke if backspace pressed and at least
    ' one keystroke saved; otherwise, add new keystroke.
    '
    If Kascii = vbKeyBack And Len(m_Keyed) Then
        m_Keyed = Left(m_Keyed, Len(m_Keyed) - 1)
    Else
        m_Keyed = m_Keyed & Chr(Kascii)
    End If
    '
    ' Look for first entry beginning with the characters
    ' saved. If none found, restore the controls to the previous
    ' state.
    '
    m_RowSource.Recordset.FindFirst m_Field & " Like """ _
                                    & m_Keyed & "*"""
    If m_RowSource.Recordset.NoMatch Then
        m_Keyed = Left(m_Keyed, Len(m_Keyed) - 1)
        m_RowSource.Recordset.FindFirst m_Field & " Like """ _
                                        & m_Keyed & "*"""
        Beep
    End If
    '
    ' Display the record found, synchronize controls,
    ' and highlight the edit text not actually keyed.
    '
    m_QList.Text = m_RowSource.Recordset(m_Field)
    m_Edit.Text = m_QList.Text
    m_Edit.SelStart = Len(m_Keyed)
    m_Edit.SelLength = Len(m_Edit.Text) - (Len(m_Keyed))
End Sub
```

EditKey uses the m_Keyed variable to track the user's keystrokes. It starts by clearing out the previous keystrokes when the entire selection is highlighted, before the user enters a character. Users have come to expect this behavior of Windows applications when selecting some text and then entering a character.

Next, EditKey checks for a Backspace entry. If one is found, the previous character (if there was one) is removed. If the user entered something other than a Backspace, that character is added to the end of m_Keyed. The m_Keyed string is then used to construct a criteria string for use with the FindFirst method. FindFirst looks for the first list item beginning with the characters entered by the user so far. If it doesn't find a match, the last keystroke is removed from m_Keyed, and the current record is reset to its previous state.

Finally, KeyEdit sets the edit control to display the current selection in the list box. The portion of the text keyed in by the user, stored in the m_Keyed variable, is displayed normally, and the portion of the text completing the selection is highlighted. Then, EditKey returns to the caller for another keystroke.

21. Add the following public subroutine to the General section of CQCombo to provide a Synchronize method for the class object. Synchronize is used whenever the user clicks on an item in the list box. The subroutine sets the current selection and the edit control text to reflect the user's choice and then returns the focus to the edit control. Look at step 7 to see how the Synchronize method is used in this project.

```
Public Sub Synchronize()
    '
    ' If the user selects an item by clicking in the QList
    ' box, set the current record accordingly, display the
    ' new item in the edit control, and set the focus back
    ' to the edit control.
    '
    m_RowSource.Recordset.FindFirst m_Field & " = """ _
                                  & m_QList.Text & """"
    m_Edit.Text = m_QList.Text
    Call Highlight
    m_Edit.SetFocus
End Sub
```

How It Works

This SelectAddress form allows the user to select and display database information using a Quicken-style combo box to make the selections.

Two data controls are used to establish connections with the Access database. One supplies a lookup table to provide the automatic fill data for a DBList bound control. The other data control supplies the source for database information displayed as a result of the user's selections. The form itself contains code to associate the selection and the display, based on a common field with unique values.

The CQCombo class associates a DBList bound control and a text box, which work together to provide the Quicken-style combo box behavior. The operational details are hidden within the methods of the class.

Comments

VB4's new bound controls provide automatic fill of a list box as well as automatic update of a table field. The automatic fill capability, used in this How-To, frees you from having to write code to build a display list. The automatic update capability (not needed for this project) comes into play when you want the user to select a field value for one table from a separate lookup table.

The syntax of the criteria statement used with the RecordSet.FindFirst method can be tricky because of the need to embed quotation marks within the string. In this How-To you saw some examples of statements that work.

8.2 How do I...
Create a Selection List from a Lookup Table?

COMPLEXITY: INTERMEDIATE
COMPATIBILITY: VB4 ONLY

Problem

I often need to select a number of rows from my database for further processing—for example, to generate mailing labels for customers in several cities. The extended multiple selections provided by the regular ListBox and FileListBox controls work just the way I want, but the MultiSelect property doesn't exist for the DBList control. How can I create the selection list I need?

Technique

The DBList control comes in handy when you want to deal with a single record at a time. In this How-To, though, we need to tie a table to a regular ListBox through Visual Basic code, to get the extended multiple-selection capability that we need. Of course, it means losing the automatic fill in the DBList control, but you can't have everything. We'll just have to write a little code to load the list.

Because multiple selection will be useful in many database applications, it is encapsulated in a separate class named CDbMulti, which is the basis of the program in this How-To.

The table we use in this How-To is a simple one, with just two fields in each record: a city name string ("strCity") and a Boolean selection flag ("ysnSelected"). The flag preserves the selections made on the Visual Basic form so they can be used in subsequent processes. The upshot of this is that our code must also clean up any previous selections that may be remaining before it gets down to the business at hand, as well as clean up after itself whenever the user cancels the selection process.

To show that the database reflects the user's selections we also use a DBList control. Just by refreshing the data control used by the DBList, we cause it to display the information we need.

Steps

Open and run CITIES.VBP. The Select Cities form appears (Figure 8-2-1). Notice that the list displays the cities in alphabetical order. Click on a city to highlight it. Then press the Shift key while clicking on another city. All the cities between the two you've clicked are also highlighted. Click the Select button, and all the highlighted cities appear in the Selected list. This means their selection flags have been turned on in the database. Note: If you can't select multiple entries, make sure the List1 Multi-Select property is still set to 2 (Extended). In early beta releases, Visual Basic 4.0 exhibited a tendency to change this property to 0.

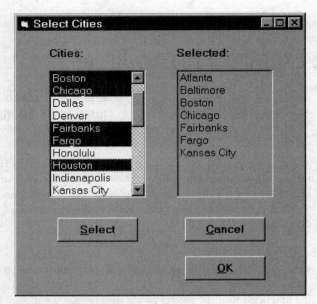

Figure 8-2-1 Multiple database selections in action on the Select Cities form

Go back to the Cities list. Press and hold Ctrl, and double-click on a city that is not right next to a city you've already selected. This new city is highlighted and added to the Selection list. This How-To uses a double-click as an alternative to the Select button. Now Ctrl-double-click on a city that is currently highlighted. The highlight disappears, and the city is removed from the Selection list.

Continue to experiment, if you wish, to verify that the extended multiple-selection features are available. When you are done, click the OK button to close the form.

1. Create a new project called CITIES.VBP, and a new form called CITIES.FRM. Place the controls on the form as shown in Figure 8-2-2, and then set all the properties listed in Table 8-2-1.

    The two invisible data controls establish connections with the Access database, VBHT.MDB. In this case, we use a simple SQL statement to establish each RecordSource. For the Data1 object, we use a snapshot record set. We only use it to load the list, and we aren't interested in any changes throughout the process. Take a look at the WHERE clause for the Data2 object. This restricts the second list, the DBList, to database records that are marked as selected.

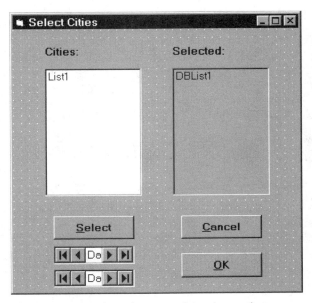

Figure 8-2-2 The Select Cities form during design

Table 8-2-1 CITIES.FRM objects and properties

OBJECT	PROPERTY	SETTING
Form	Name	Form1
	Caption	"Select Cities"
Data	Name	Data1
	Connect	"Access"
	ReadOnly	-1 'True
	RecordsetType	2 'Snapshot
	RecordSource	"SELECT * FROM tselCity
		ORDER BY strCity;"
	Visible	False
Data	Name	Data2
	Connect	"Access"
	ReadOnly	-1 'False
	RecordsetType	1 'Dynaset
	RecordSource	"SELECT * FROM tselCity
		WHERE ysnSelected = True
		ORDER BY strCity;"
	Visible	False

Continued on next page

Continued from previous page

OBJECT	PROPERTY	SETTING
Label	Name	Label1
	Caption	"Cities:"
Label	Name	Label2
	Caption	"Selected:"
ListBox	Name	List1
	DataField	"strCity"
	DataSource	"Data1"
	MultiSelect	2 'Extended
	Sorted	0 'False
	TabIndex	0
DBList	Name	DBList1
	Listfield	"strCity"
	RowSource	"Data2"
CommandButton	Name	SelectButton
	Caption	"&Select"
	TabIndex	1
CommandButton	Name	CancelButton
	Caption	"&Cancel"
	TabIndex	2
CommandButton	Name	OKButton
	Caption	"&OK"
	TabIndex	3

2. Place the following code at the beginning of CITIES.FRM. The DbMulti object is established as an instance of the CDbMulti class.

```
Option Explicit
'
' Declare CDbMulti class.
'
Dim DbMulti As New CDbMulti
```

3. Place the following code in the Form_Load event procedure to establish pointers to the sample database. It also sets the DbMulti class properties that identify the ListBox and Data controls to be used for the multiple selections, and for the name of the flag field used to mark the selections in the database table. Then it centers the form.

```
Private Sub Form_Load()
    '
    ' Establish database pointers
    Data1.Database Name = App.Path & _
        IIF (Right$(App.Path, 1) <> "\", "\", "") & _
        "VBHT.MDB"
```

```
    Data2.DatabaseName = App.Path & _
        IIF (Right$(App.Path, 1) <> "\", "\", "") & _
        "VBHT.MDB
    '
    ' Set DbMulti properties.
    '
    Set DbMulti.Lookup = List1
    Set DbMulti.LookupData = Data1
    DbMulti.LookupFlagFieldName = "ysnSelected"
    '
    ' Center form.
    '
    Move (Screen.Width - Width) \ 2, _
        (Screen.Height - Height) \ 2
End Sub
```

4. Place the following code in the Data1_Reposition event procedure. The DbMulti class needs to open the database and clean out any extraneous selection flags. It also needs to use the AddItem method to build the list for the ListBox. It can't do those things at form load time, because the connection has not yet been established with the database. However, the Reposition event fires when the first record is made current for the data control, so we make use of that event to trigger our initial cleanup. When that job finishes, we refresh the data control for the DBList control, to make sure it displays a clean slate.

```
Private Sub Data1_Reposition()
    '
    ' When first current record is established,
    ' have class prepare table to synchronize
    ' with selections.
    '
    Static TablePrepared As Boolean
    If Not TablePrepared Then
        DbMulti.PrepareTable
        TablePrepared = True
        Data2.Refresh
    End If
End Sub
```

5. Place the following code in the List1_DblClick event procedure. This code sets the selection flags in the database for each record highlighted in the ListBox, and turns off the selection flags for all the other records. Then it refreshes the other list to display the results.

```
Private Sub List1_DblClick()
    '
    ' Mark database rows selected. Then redisplay
    ' the selections in the selection list box.
    '
    DbMulti.Mark
    Data2.Refresh
End Sub
```

6. Place the following code in the SelectButton_Click event procedure. Note that this duplicates the double-click processing added in step 5.

```
Private Sub SelectButton_Click()
    '
    ' Mark database rows selected. Then redisplay
    ' the selections in the selection list box.
    '
    DbMulti.Mark
    Data2.Refresh
End Sub
```

7. Place the following code in the CancelButton_Click event procedure. This code first removes any selection flags that have been set, and then exits by calling the OKButton subroutine.

```
Private Sub CancelButton_Click()
    '
    ' Remove all selections from table,
    ' clear display, and exit.
    '
    DbMulti.ClearSelections
    Call OKButton_Click
End Sub
```

8. Place the following code in the OKButton_Click event procedure. The Unload statement unloads the form. Setting Form1 to Nothing disconnects the form from system resources, so those resources can be released. Clicking OK accepts the marked selections for later use in a larger process, such as a mailing label print process.

```
Private Sub OKButton_Click()
    '
    ' Unload form, retaining any row selections in the
    ' database.
    '
    Unload Me
    Set Form1 = Nothing
    Set DbMulti = Nothing
    End
End Sub
```

9. Use the Insert Class menu item to create a new class module, and save it as DBMULTI.CLS. Name it CDbMulti, and put the following code at the beginning of the file. This code sets the private variables for the class object.

```
Option Explicit
'
' Private variables for lists and command buttons.
'
Private m_Lookup As Object
Private m_LookupData As Object
'
```

```
Private m_Db As Database
Private m_LookupTable As Recordset
'
Private m_LookupTableName As String
Private m_LookupFlagFieldName As String
Private m_LookupListFieldName As String
Private m_LookupTableOpen As Boolean
```

10. Add the following code to the General section of CDbMulti. The Set property for Lookup gets, validates, and stores the ListBox object that will be used for the multiple-selection display. Look at step 3 to see how the Lookup property is set in this project. After storing the object, this code also stores the name of the DataField for the ListBox. This name is needed so we can match up the database records with the selections made in the ListBox. See step 16 for an example.

```
Public Property Set Lookup(LB As Object)
    '
    ' Make sure object is a ListBox and, if so, initialize.
    '
    If TypeOf LB Is ListBox Then
        Set m_Lookup = LB
        m_LookupListFieldName = m_Lookup.DataField
    Else
        MsgBox "Lookup is not a valid ListBox."
    End If
End Property
```

11. Add the following code to the General section of CDbMulti. The Get property for Lookup returns the current ListBox object to the calling program.

```
Public Property Get Lookup() As Object
    '
    ' Return the current ListBox to the caller.
    '
    Set Lookup = m_Lookup
End Property
```

12. Add the following code to the General section of CDbMulti. The Set property for LookupData gets, validates, and stores the data control object that will be used to initialize the list. Look at step 3 to see how the LookupData property is set in this project.

```
Public Property Set LookupData(DC As Object)
    '
    ' Make sure object is a Data control and, if so, initialize.
    ' Save name of the table for the lookup recordset. Extract it
    ' from the SQL statement if necessary. Clear the database
    ' open flag.
    '
    If TypeOf DC Is Data Then
        Set m_LookupData = DC
```

Continued on next page

Continued from previous page

```
        m_LookupTableName = m_LookupData.RecordSource
        If InStr(m_LookupTableName, " ") Then
            m_LookupTableName = NextWord(m_LookupTableName, "FROM")
        End If
        m_LookupTableOpen = False
    Else
        MsgBox "LookupData is not a valid Data control."
    End If
End Property
```

Having stored the object, the code uses its RecordSource property to find the name of the lookup table. It accepts a string with no embedded spaces as the table name; otherwise, it assumes the string contains a SQL command and extracts the table name from the string. In step 1 we set the RecordSource for Data1 to

```
SELECT * FROM tselCity ORDER BY strCity;
```

The code here in step 12 looks for the next word after FROM and stores it as the table name. In this case, we get tselCity, which is the name of the table we need. Then we make sure the object knows that the database has not yet been initialized.

13. Add the following code to the General section of CDbMulti. The Get routine for the property LookupData returns the current data control object to the calling program.

```
Public Property Get LookupData() As Object
    '
    ' Return the current LookupData to the caller.
    '
    Set LookupData = m_LookupData
End Property
```

14. Add the following code to the General section of CDbMulti. The Let routine for the property LookupFlagFieldName stores the name of the field which we will set to True or False, to indicate whether each record in the lookup table was selected. See step 16 for an example.

```
Public Property Let LookupFlagFieldName(LF As String)
    '
    ' Save lookup flag field name. This field indicates whether a
    ' row has been selected or not.
    '
    m_LookupFlagFieldName = LF
End Property
```

15. Add the following code to the General section of CDbMulti. The Get routine for the property LookupFlagFieldName returns the name of the current flag field to the calling program.

```
Public Property Get LookupFlagFieldName() As String
    '
    ' Return the current LookupFlagFieldName to the caller.
    '
    LookupFlagFieldName = m_LookupFlagFieldName
End Property
```

16. Add the following code to the General section of CDbMulti. Here, the m_LookupTableOpen flag makes sure this procedure is executed only once. Take special notice of the first Set statement after the flag is tested. This statement illustrates how Visual Basic 4.0 ties data-access objects to form controls, a very powerful capability. Subsequent code opens a table in the same database connected to the lookup data control, and tells the object to use the primary index. Then the procedure loops through all the records in the lookup table, adding them to the list via AddItem and setting each flag to False.

```
Public Sub PrepareTable()
    '
    ' If necessary, open lookup table, build selection list,
    ' and deselect all lookup table records.
    '
    If Not m_LookupTableOpen Then
        Set m_Db = m_LookupData.Database
        Set m_LookupTable = m_Db.OpenRecordset(m_LookupTableName, _
                                                dbOpenTable)

        m_LookupTable.Index = "PrimaryKey"
        '
        Do While Not m_LookupTable.EOF
            m_Lookup.AddItem m_LookupTable(m_LookupListFieldName)
            m_LookupTable.Edit
            m_LookupTable(m_LookupFlagFieldName) = False
            m_LookupTable.Update
            m_LookupTable.MoveNext
        Loop
        '
        m_LookupTableOpen = True
        m_Lookup.Refresh
    End If
End Sub
```

17. Add the following code to the General section of CDbMulti. This code marks the selection flags True or False, using the lookup table opened in step 16. It does this by looping through the lookup list and using the Seek method to find the lookup record matching the lookup item. Note that the Edit and Update methods are both required.

```
Public Sub Mark()
    '
    ' Mark selection flag field with true or false, depending upon
    ' whether or not the row was selected.
    '
    Dim i As Integer
```

Continued on next page

Continued from previous page

```
    For i = 0 To m_Lookup.ListCount - 1
        m_LookupTable.Seek "=", m_Lookup.List(i)
        m_LookupTable.Edit
        If m_Lookup.Selected(i) Then
            m_LookupTable(m_LookupFlagFieldName) = True
        Else
            m_LookupTable(m_LookupFlagFieldName) = False
        End If
        m_LookupTable.Update
    Next i
End Sub
```

18. Add the following public subroutine to the General section of CDbMulti. This loop sets the selection flags on all the lookup records to False. In contrast to the loop in step 17, which goes through all the list items, this one goes through all the table records.

```
Public Sub ClearSelections()
    '
    ' Set the selection flag to false on all the lookup rows.
    '
    m_LookupTable.MoveFirst
    Do While Not m_LookupTable.EOF
        m_LookupTable.Edit
        m_LookupTable(m_LookupFlagFieldName) = False
        m_LookupTable.Update
        m_LookupTable.MoveNext
    Loop
End Sub
```

19. Add the following public subroutine to the General section of CDbMulti. Here we provide a function useful in parsing SQL strings, returning the word following the word provided. See step 12 for an example of this function in action. (This function could be coded more compactly, but this format lets you see how the Visual Basic string-manipulation functions work.)

```
Private Function NextWord(Source As String, ForeWord As String) _
                                                            As String
    '
    ' Match one word in a source string and return the next word.
    '
    Dim start As Integer, length As Integer, workstring As String
    '
    start = InStr(1, Source, ForeWord & " ", 1) + Len(ForeWord) + 1
    workstring = LTrim(Mid(Source, start))
    length = InStr(workstring, " ") - 1
    NextWord = Left(workstring, length)
End Function
```

How It Works

The program in this How-To allows the user to make multiple selections from a lookup table, to be used in further processing.

The CDbMulti class takes the multiple selections from an associated ListBox, and provides the VB4 data-access logic needed to update the selection flags in the associated table. String-manipulation functions extract information needed from an SQL command.

The Cities form uses an instance of the CDbMulti class to accept multiple selections of cities for use by another process, such as printing mailing labels. A separate DBList control uses the automatic fill capability to display the database results from each selection. The Refresh method on the associated Data control triggers the redisplay of the database results.

Comments

Just because powerful new bound controls are now available in VB4, the regular Visual Basic controls should not be overlooked. Sometimes, as in this How-To, the older functionality fills the bill—especially when it is combined with new data-access capabilities.

8.3 How do I...
Display Tables and Fields in an Access Database?

COMPLEXITY: INTERMEDIATE
COMPATIBILITY: VB4 ONLY

Problem

Sometimes I want to track down a particular Access table, but I can't remember what database it's in or exactly what it's named. When that happens, I really need to see a list of the field names in several tables, to make sure I identify the correct table. Access and the Visual Basic Data Manager both let me look in only one database table at a time. That's just too tedious—isn't there an easier way?

Technique

The program in this How-To makes Access database information easily accessible on a single form by marrying the DriveListBox, DirListBox, and FileListBox controls to an outline control. Drive, directory, and file list boxes are coordinated to provide a selection of Access databases. When the user chooses a database from the file list, the outline control is filled with database information obtained using the Database and TableDef data-access objects.

The outline control provides a convenient way to organize database information, making it easy to explore multiple tables and fields in a database. We organize the outline by placing the database name at the top. Then table names are indented one level; field names are indented one level from table names; and field specifications are indented one level from field names.

Steps

Open and run DBFIELDS.VBP. Choose a path with one or more Access databases, and watch the .MDA and .MDB filenames appear in the Select: list. Click or double-click on one of these files to select it, and notice that the name of the database appears in the Structure outline list, preceded by a plus (+) sign. Click on the plus sign; it changes to a minus (–) sign, and the outline expands to list the names of the tables in the database. Click on the plus sign in front of one of the tables, and watch the outline expand to list the names of the fields for that table. Click on the plus sign in front of another table in the database, and watch the outline expand again, this time listing the names of the fields for that table. Each field is preceded by a plus sign, as well. Click on one or more of the field plus signs to see basic information about the field, including type and size.

You can click on any minus sign to collapse the outline and hide all the subordinate information.

1. Create a new project called DBFIELDS.VBP. Create a form, and add controls in a layout like that shown in action in Figure 8-3-1. Set form objects and properties as shown in Table 8-3-1, and save the form as DBFIELDS.FRM.

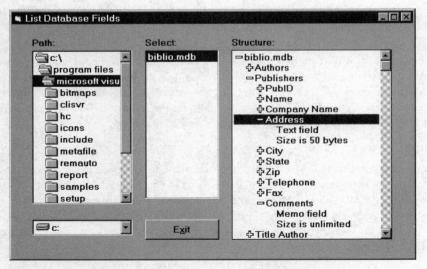

Figure 8-3-1 Displaying Access database tables and fields

Table 8-3-1 DBFIELDS.FRM form properties

OBJECT	PROPERTY	SETTING
Form	Name	DBFieldsForm
	Caption	"List Database Fields"
Label	Name	Label1
	BackStyle	0 'Transparent
	Caption	"Path:"
DirListBox	Name	Dir1
DriveListBox	Name	Drive1
Label	Name	Label2
	BackStyle	0 'Transparent
	Caption	"Select:"
FileListBox	Name	File1
Label	Name	Label3
	BackStyle	0 'Transparent
	Caption	"Structure:"
Outline	Name	Outline1
	Style	2 'Plus/Minus and Text

2. Place the following code at the beginning of DBFIELDS.FRM:

```
Option Explicit
'
' Define private constants
'
Private Const DbLvl As Integer = 1
Private Const TblLvl As Integer = 2
Private Const FldLvl As Integer = 3
Private Const FldPropLvl As Integer = 4
'
' Define private variables
'
Private Db As Database
Private TDef As Tabledef, Fld As Field
Private DbPath As String
Private DbName As String
Private TblName As String
Private FldName As String
```

3. Place the following code in the Form_Load event procedure. This subroutine centers the form. Then it initializes the drive letter, directory path, and database path to match the path of the application. It sets the file pattern to allow only .MDA and .MDB files to be displayed in the file list.

```
Private Sub Form_Load()
    '
    ' Center the form, initialize the paths to the application path,
    ' and set the file pattern to display databases only.
    '
```

Continued on next page

861

Continued from previous page

```
    Outline1.BackColor = File1.BackColor
    Me.Move (Screen.Width - Me.Width) \ 2, _
            (Screen.Height - Me.Height) \ 2
    Drive1.Drive = App.Path
    Dir1.Path = App.Path
    File1.Pattern = "*.mdb;*.mda"
End Sub
```

4. Place the following code in the Drive1_Change event procedure. When the drive changes, this subroutine sets the directory path to match the current path for the drive. A common error occurs here when no diskette is in drive A. When that happens, the drive is reset to the drive letter in the current directory path.

```
Private Sub Drive1_Change()
    '
    ' When drive changes, synchronize directory path.
    ' Handle floppy disk errors, etc.
    '
    On Error GoTo Drive1_Err
    Dir1.Path = Drive1.Drive
    '
Drive1_Done:
    On Error GoTo 0
    Exit Sub
    '
Drive1_Err:
    Drive1.Drive = Dir1.Path
    Resume Drive1_Done:
End Sub
```

5. Place the following code in the Dir1_Change event procedure. This subroutine sets the file and database paths to match the directory path, whenever the directory path changes.

```
Private Sub Dir1_Change()
    '
    ' When directory path changes, synchronize file list and save.
    '
    File1.Path = Dir1.Path
    DbPath = Dir1.Path & IIF (Right$(Dir1.Path, 1) <> "\", "\", "")
End Sub
```

6. Place the following code in the Dir1_LostFocus event procedure. When the directory list box loses focus, the directory path is set to the directory currently selected in the list. The directory path changes automatically with a click event, but not when the Up Arrow and Down Arrow keys are used to move to another directory in the list. This routine makes sure the directory path gets changed to the current selection when the directory list loses focus.

```
Private Sub Dir1_LostFocus()
    '
    ' Set directory path to final selection.
    '
    Dir1.Path = Dir1.List(Dir1.ListIndex)
End Sub
```

7. Place the following code in the File1_Click event procedure. This subroutine verifies that the file name is valid before setting the database name variable and before setting the focus to the outline control, which displays the database.

```
Private Sub File1_Click()
    '
    ' When user clicks on a valid file name, build the outline.
    '
    If Len(File1.FileName) > 4 Then
        DbName = File1.FileName
        Outline1.SetFocus
    End If
End Sub
```

8. Place the following code in the File1_DblClick event procedure, to make sure a double-click is handled just like a click for selecting the desired database file.

```
Private Sub File1_DblClick()
    '
    ' Treat double click as click.
    '
    Call File1_Click
End Sub
```

9. Place the following code in the Outline1_GotFocus event procedure. This subroutine first determines if the requested database has changed from the one currently displayed in the outline. If so, the subroutine closes the current database, clears the outline, and sets a flag to indicate that the work of filling the outline is incomplete. It then prepares to fill the outline with information about the newly requested database, by opening that database and setting an object variable reference for it.

    The database name is added as the first outline entry, with no indent. Then the program loops through each table definition in the database's TableDefs collection. It skips the system tables and adds table name lines in the outline, indented one level from the database name. Field objects for attached tables and other remote tables are contained in their local databases, so they aren't available here. These tables are identified by non-zero attribute fields. On the outline, they appear as "leaf" items, without a plus or minus sign.

    For each local table name added to the outline, however, we do have access to field information. The code loops through each field definition in the Fields collection. It adds field name lines to the outline, indented one level from the table name. Indented another level, it adds two property "leaf" lines—one for the type of the field, and one for the size of the field.

```
Private Sub Outline1_GotFocus()
    '
    ' Build the outline from the TableDefs and Fields in the selected
    ' database.
    '
```

Continued on next page

Continued from previous page

```
    Dim i As Integer
    Dim TName As String
    Static OutlineDone As Boolean
    '
    ' If new database, clear outline.
    '
    If Outline1.ListCount Then
        If (DbName <> Outline1.List(0)) Then
            Outline1.Clear
            Db.Close
            OutlineDone = False
        End If
    End If
    '
    ' If valid new database name, open database and start outline.
    '
    If Len(DbName) > 4 And Not OutlineDone Then
        Screen.MousePointer = vbHourglass
        Set Db = OpenDatabase(DbPath & DbName)
        '
        ' Index 0 is the database, and gets the 1st indentation level.
        '
        Outline1.AddItem DbName, 0
        Outline1.Indent(0) = DbLvl
        i = 1
        '
        ' For each TableDef that is not for a system table,
        ' add the table name at the 2nd level.
        '
        For Each TDef In Db.TableDefs
            If (TDef.Attributes And dbSystemObject) = 0 Then
                Outline1.AddItem TDef.Name, i
                Outline1.Indent(i) = TblLvl
                i = i + 1
                If TDef.Attributes = 0 Then
                    '
                    ' For each field in the TableDef, add the name at the
                    ' 3rd level.
                    '
                    For Each Fld In TDef.Fields
                        Outline1.AddItem Fld.Name, i
                        Outline1.Indent(i) = FldLvl
                        i = i + 1
                        '
                        ' At the 4th level, add the type and size of
                        ' each field.
                        '
                        Select Case Fld.Type
                        Case dbBoolean
                            TName = "Yes/no"
                        Case dbByte
                            TName = "Byte"
                        Case dbInteger
                            TName = "Integer"
                        Case dbLong
```

```
                    If Fld.Attributes And dbAutoIncrField Then
                        TName = "Counter"
                    Else
                        TName = "Long integer"
                    End If
                Case dbCurrency
                    TName = "Currency"
                Case dbSingle
                    TName = "Single"
                Case dbDouble
                    TName = "Double"
                Case dbDate
                    TName = "Date/time"
                Case dbText
                    TName = "Text"
                Case dbLongBinary
                    TName = "OLE Object"
                Case dbMemo
                    TName = "Memo"
                Case Else
                    TName = "Code" & Str$(Fld.Type)
                End Select
                '
                Outline1.AddItem TName & " field", i
                Outline1.Indent(i) = FldPropLvl
                i = i + 1
                '
                If TName = "Memo" Then
                    Outline1.AddItem "Size is unlimited", i
                Else
                    If Fld.Size = 1 Then
                        Outline1.AddItem "Size is 1 byte", i
                    Else
                        Outline1.AddItem "Size is " & Fld.Size _
                                         & " bytes", i
                    End If
                End If
                Outline1.Indent(i) = FldPropLvl
                i = i + 1
            Next Fld
        End If
      End If
    Next TDef
    OutlineDone = True
    Screen.MousePointer = vbNormal
  End If
End Sub
```

10. Place the following code in the ExitCommand_Click event procedure. This sub-routine releases resources and ends the program.

```
Private Sub ExitButton_Click()
    '
    ' Release resources and quit.
    '
```

Continued on next page

Continued from previous page

```
    Unload Me
    Set DBFieldsForm = Nothing
    End
End Sub
```

How It Works

The project in this How-To uses the built-in hierarchical display features of an outline control to expose the table and field structure of an Access database selected by the user.

In Visual Basic 4.0 you can manipulate data access objects in code to obtain the information you need to modify already existing form controls at run time. In this How-To we use that capability to open any Access database chosen by the user. From the database object, the program obtains a collection of table definitions, and from each table definition object, it obtains a collection of field objects. These objects provide all the information needed to build the outline.

Comments

This How-To displays only a few of the database specification properties that are available using the Database TableDefs collection and the TableDef Fields collection. Other field properties that could be displayed include, for example, DefaultValue and ValidationText.

8.4 How do I...
Build a Better Data Control?

COMPLEXITY: INTERMEDIATE
COMPATIBILITY: VB4 ONLY

Problem

The combination of Visual Basic 4.0's data control and bound controls makes certain tasks much easier. Unfortunately, the data control does not support many of the enhanced features of data access objects. Is it possible to make use of features such as Bookmarks and the new Move methods without giving up the functionality of the data control? Also, is it possible to disable buttons that should not be pressed? For example, if the user is looking at the last record in the table, I want the Next and Last buttons to be disabled.

Technique

Data controls can include operations other than just buttons to press. In this example you will create a class that manipulates a hidden data control. Using command buttons, you will present the user with an extended data control, the Better Data Contol, that provides added functionality.

Steps

Open and run DATACTL.VBP. This better data control consists of six VCR-style buttons and two bookmark buttons. Four of the VCR buttons are equivalent to their data control counterparts. The two new buttons, << and >>, move the record pointer several records at a time. The number of records can be changed (it is set to 20 for this example). The buttons will automatically be enabled or disabled based on the location of the current record. The Set Bookmark button allows you to mark a record and return to it by pressing the Go To Bookmark button.

1. Create a new project named DATACTL.VBP. Create a new form with a data control, text boxes, and a control array of command buttons, using the properties in Table 8-4-1. Save the form as FORM1.FRM. When finished, it should look like Figure 8-4-1.

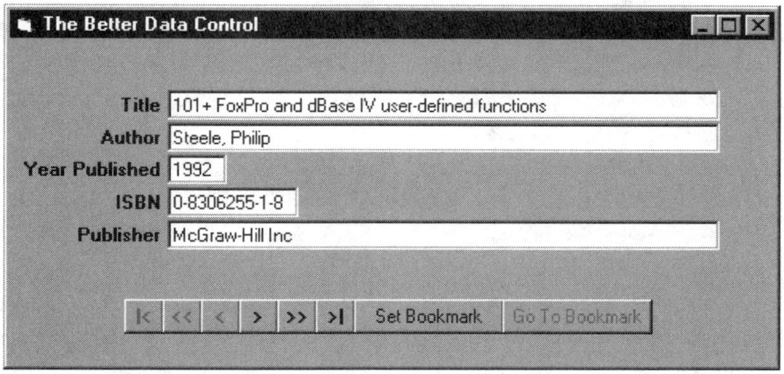

Figure 8-4-1 The DataCtl project

Table 8-4-1 Objects and properties for Form1

OBJECT	PROPERTY	SETTING
Form	Name	Form1
	Caption	"The Better Data Control"
	BackColor	&HC0C0C0&
Data	Name	Data1
	DatabaseName	C:\VB\BIBLIO.MDB
	RecordSource	All Titles
	Visible	False
Label	Name	Label1

Continued on next page

Continued from previous page

OBJECT	PROPERTY	SETTING
	Caption	Title
	BackStyle	0 - Transparent
	AutoSize	True
TextBox	Name	Text1
	DataField	Title
	DataSource	Data1
Label	Name	Label2
	Caption	"Author"
	BackStyle	0 - Transparent
	AutoSize	True
TextBox	Name	Text2
	DataField	Author
	DataSource	Data1
Label	Name	Label3
	Caption	"Year Published"
	BackStyle	0 - Transparent
	AutoSize	True
TextBox	Name	Text3
	DataField	Year Published
	DataSource	Data1
Label	Name	Label4
	Caption	"ISBN"
	BackStyle	0 - Transparent
	AutoSize	True
TextBox	Name	Text4
	DataField	ISBN
	DataSource	Data1
Label	Name	Label5
	Caption	"Publisher"
	BackStyle	0 - Transparent
	AutoSize	True
TextBox	Name	Text5
	DataField	Company Name
	DataSource	Data1
CommandButton	Caption	I<
	Name	Command1
	Index	0
CommandButton	Caption	<<
	Name	Command1

OBJECT	PROPERTY	SETTING
	Index	1
CommandButton	Caption	<
	Name	Command1
	Index	2
CommandButton	Caption	>
	Name	Command1
	Index	3
CommandButton	Caption	>>
	Name	Command1
	Index	4
CommandButton	Caption	>|
	Name	Command1
	Index	5
CommandButton	Caption	"Set Bookmark"
	Name	Command1
	Index	6
CommandButton	Caption	"Go To Bookmark"
	Name	Command1
	Index	7

2. Use the Insert Class Module menu item to add a new class to your project. Open your new class module in the project window, and then use the properties window to set the module's name to cDataCtl and set the Creatable property to True.

3. Add the following code to the General section of cDataCtl. This defines the constants and properties for the cDataCtl class.

```
' cDataCtl - The Better Data Control Class
'
' This class is used to manipulate a data control on any form.
'
'*** Constants - All start with bdc prefix.
'
' Indexes of the data control buttons
'
Const bdcFirst = 0
Const bdcPageUp = 1
Const bdcPrevious = 2
Const bdcNext = 3
Const bdcPageDn = 4
Const bdcLast = 5
Const bdcSetBookmark = 6
Const bdcGoToBookmark = 7
'
'*** Public properties
```

Continued on next page

Continued from previous page

```
'
' Amount used for page scrolling.
'
Public ScrollByAmount As Integer
'
' Name of button control array.
'
Public Buttons As String
'
'*** Private properties
'
' User's data form.
'
Private UserForm As Form
'
' User's data control.
'
Private DataCtl As Data
'
' Holder for Set Bookmark button.
'
Private MyBookmark As String

Public Property Set TheDataCtl(UserDataCtl As Control)
    '
    ' This allows the user to set the DataCtl property to
    ' point to the data control on the user's form.
    '
    Set DataCtl = UserDataCtl
    DataCtl.Refresh
    '
    ' Move to last and then first records to establish
    ' the record count. Show the hourglass since this could
    ' take a few seconds depending on the recordset.
    '
    Screen.MousePointer = vbHourglass
    DataCtl.Recordset.MoveLast
    DataCtl.Recordset.MoveFirst
    Screen.MousePointer = vbDefault
End Property

Public Property Set TheForm(UserDataForm As Form)
    '
    ' This allows the user to set the UserForm property to
    ' point to the form containing the better data control buttons.
    '
    Set UserForm = UserDataForm
End Property
```

4. Add the following code to the General section of the cDataCtl class. This ProcessButtons subroutine is where most of the work is done. Each Case statement provides the functionality for one of the eight buttons of the Better Data Control. The buttons are enabled and disabled based on our current location in the record set.

```
Public Sub ProcessButtons(ButtonIndex As Integer)
    '
    ' This sub directly manipulates the user's data contol
    ' according to the value of ButtonIndex.
    '
    Dim Ds As Recordset
    '
    ' First check to see if the DataCtl and UserForm objects
    ' are defined and the name of the button control array is
    ' set. Ignore requests if not. You may wish to put error
    ' reporting code here.
    '
    If (DataCtl Is Nothing) Or (UserForm Is Nothing) _
        Or (Buttons = "") Then
        Exit Sub
    End If


    '
    ' Make Ds refer to the better data control's recordset
    '
    Set Ds = DataCtl.Recordset
    '
    ' If there are no records or just one record do not enable
    ' the buttons.
    '
    If Ds.RecordCount <= 1 Then
        DisableUpButtons
        DisableDownButtons
        DisableBookmark
        Exit Sub
    End If
    '
    ' Choose the proper action depending on the button pressed.
    '
    Select Case ButtonIndex
        Case bdcFirst
            '
            ' Move to the first record and only
            ' allow movement downwards in the file.
            '
            Ds.MoveFirst
            DisableUpButtons
            EnableDownButtons

        Case bdcPageUp
            '
            ' Move backward by the number of records
            ' specified by ScrollAmount.
            '
            Ds.Move -ScrollByAmount
            '
            ' Check to see if we went off the
            ' beginning of the file.
            '
            If Ds.BOF Then
```

Continued on next page

Continued from previous page

```
            '
            ' We went past the beginning. Move to
            ' the first record.
            '
            Ds.MoveFirst
            DisableUpButtons
        Else
            '
            ' If we are at the first record in the
            ' file, disable the upward movement
            ' buttons.
            '
            If Ds.AbsolutePosition = 0 Then
                DisableUpButtons
            Else
                EnableUpButtons
            End If
        End If
        EnableDownButtons

    Case bdcPrevious
        '
        ' Move back one record.
        '
        Ds.MovePrevious
        '
        ' If we are at the first record, disable
        ' the upward movement buttons.
        '
        If Ds.AbsolutePosition = 0 Then
            DisableUpButtons
        Else
            EnableUpButtons
        End If
        EnableDownButtons

    Case bdcNext
        '
        ' Move forward one record
        '
        Ds.MoveNext
        '
        ' If we are at the last record, disable
        ' the downward movement buttons.
        '
        If Ds.AbsolutePosition = Ds.RecordCount - 1 Then
            DisableDownButtons
        Else
            EnableDownButtons
        End If
        EnableUpButtons

    Case bdcPageDn
        '
        ' Move forward by the number of records
```

```
   ' specified by ScrollAmount.
   '
   Ds.Move ScrollByAmount
   '
   ' Check to see if we went off the
   ' end of the file.
   '
   If Ds.EOF Then
      '
      ' We went past the end. Move to
      ' the last record.
      '
      Ds.MoveLast
      DisableDownButtons
   Else
      '
      ' If we are at the last record in the
      ' file, disable the upward movement
      ' buttons.
      '
      If Ds.AbsolutePosition = Ds.RecordCount - 1 Then
         DisableDownButtons
      Else
         EnableDownButtons
      End If
   End If
   EnableUpButtons

Case bdcLast
   '
   ' Move to the last record and only
   ' allow movement upwards in the file.
   '
   Ds.MoveLast
   EnableUpButtons
   DisableDownButtons

Case bdcSetBookmark
   MyBookmark = Ds.Bookmark

Case bdcGoToBookmark
   '
   ' Only move if there is a bookmark saved.
   '
   If MyBookmark <> "" Then
      Ds.Bookmark = MyBookmark
      '
      ' If we are at the first record, disable
      ' the upward movement buttons.
      '
      If Ds.AbsolutePosition = 0 Then
         DisableUpButtons
      Else
         EnableUpButtons
      End If
      '
```

Continued on next page

Continued from previous page

```
                    ' If we are at the last record, disable
                    ' the downward movement buttons.
                    '
                    If Ds.AbsolutePosition = Ds.RecordCount - 1 Then
                        DisableDownButtons
                    Else
                        EnableDownButtons
                    End If
            End If
        End Select
    '
    ' If there is no saved bookmark disable the
    ' Go To Bookmark button.
    '
    If MyBookmark = "" Then
        UserForm.Controls(Buttons)(bdcGoToBookmark).Enabled = False
    Else
        UserForm.Controls(Buttons)(bdcGoToBookmark).Enabled = True
    End If
    '
    ' Deallocate the Ds object
    '
    Set Ds = Nothing
End Sub
```

5. Add the following code to the General section of the cDataCtl class. These sub-routines disable and enable groups of Better Data Control buttons.

```
Private Sub DisableUpButtons()
    '
    ' Disable the First, Page Up and Previous buttons.
    '
    UserForm.Controls(Buttons)(bdcFirst).Enabled = False
    UserForm.Controls(Buttons)(bdcPageUp).Enabled = False
    UserForm.Controls(Buttons)(bdcPrevious).Enabled = False
End Sub

Private Sub DisableDownButtons()
    '
    ' Disable the Next, Page Down and Last buttons.
    '
    UserForm.Controls(Buttons)(bdcNext).Enabled = False
    UserForm.Controls(Buttons)(bdcPageDn).Enabled = False
    UserForm.Controls(Buttons)(bdcLast).Enabled = False
End Sub

Private Sub DisableBookmark()
    '
    ' Disable the Set Bookmark and Go To Bookmark buttons.
    '
    UserForm.Controls(Buttons)(bdcSetBookmark).Enabled = False
    UserForm.Controls(Buttons)(bdcGoToBookmark).Enabled = False
End Sub

Private Sub EnableUpButtons()
```

```
'
' Enable the First, Page Up and Previous buttons.
'
    UserForm.Controls(Buttons)(bdcFirst).Enabled = True
    UserForm.Controls(Buttons)(bdcPageUp).Enabled = True
    UserForm.Controls(Buttons)(bdcPrevious).Enabled = True
End Sub

Private Sub EnableDownButtons()
'
' Enable the Next, Page Down and Last buttons.
'
    UserForm.Controls(Buttons)(bdcNext).Enabled = True
    UserForm.Controls(Buttons)(bdcPageDn).Enabled = True
    UserForm.Controls(Buttons)(bdcLast).Enabled = True
End Sub

Private Sub EnableBookmark()
'
'Enable the Set Bookmark and Go To Bookmark buttons.
'
    UserForm.Controls(Buttons)(bdcSetBookmark).Enabled = True
    UserForm.Controls(Buttons)(bdcGoToBookmark).Enabled = True
End Sub
```

6. Add the following code to the Class section of cDataCtl, to provide default values for the properties.

```
Private Sub Class_Initialize()
'
' This sub gets called when an instance of the cDataCtl
' class is created. It clears the DataCtl and UserForm
' objects and the Bookmark and Buttons properties and
' sets the default ScrollByAmount of 10 records.
'
    Set DataCtl = Nothing
    Set UserForm = Nothing
    Buttons = ""
    MyBookmark = ""
    ScrollByAmount = 10
End Sub
```

7. Add the following code to the Declarations section of the form:

```
'
' Declare object of class cDataCtl.
'
Private MyDataCtl As cDataCtl
```

8. Add the following code to the Form_Load event, to create a cDataCtl object and attach our ordinary data control to it.

```
Private Sub Form_Load()
'
' Intantiate the cDataCtl class, set its properties and
' move to the firt record so the buttons can be enabled
```

Continued on next page

Continued from previous page

```
    ' or disabled as necessary.
    '
    Set MyDataCtl = New cDataCtl
    With MyDataCtl
       Set .TheDataCtl = Data1
       Set .TheForm = Form1
       .Buttons = "Command1"
       .ProcessButtons 0
    End With
End Sub
```

9. Add the following code to the Command button's Click event. This code will handle all eight buttons by passing the Index value to the ProcessButtons method in cDataCtl.

```
Private Sub Command1_Click(Index As Integer)
    '
    'Click Event for all Better Data Control buttons.
    '
    MyDataCtl.ProcessButtons Index
End Sub
```

How It Works

The cDataCtl class contains all we need to manipulate data controls on any form, since each instance of a class contains its own set of properties. Our form, Form1, simply instantiates the class, sets a few properties, and tells cDataCtl which button was pressed.

The properties we have to set are a pointer to the data control we wish to manipulate (DataCtl); a pointer to the form containing the Better Data Control buttons (UserForm); the name of the control array of command buttons (Buttons); and the number of records forward or backward we want to move when we press the Page Up (<<) and Page Down (>>) buttons (ScrollByAmount). This is done in the Form_Load event for Form1.

Notice how the DataCtl and UserForm properties are set indirectly using Property Set routines (for TheDataCtl and TheForm, respectively). This is only necessary if a property is a reference to an object.

The data control (Data1) is set up normally—except for the Visible property, which is set False, making the data control invisible at run time. Data1 is still going to be manipulating our data, so we have to set the DatabaseName and RecordSource properties accordingly. This example uses the BIBLIO.MDB database file; be sure to enter the proper path for your particular machine in the DatabaseName property.

The buttons on Form1 that replace the data control are defined as a control array (Command1). The need for a control array is evident in the Command1_Click event. This single click event handles all eight buttons by passing an index value representing the button that was pressed. This index is passed along to the ProcessButtons subroutine in the cDataCtl class. Thus, all eight buttons are handled with one line of code. The bulk of the processing takes place in the cDataCtl class. This is as it should be—it allows more than one form to use the cDataCtl class at one time, each with its own instance of the class.

The ProcessButtons subroutine contains most of the code in the cDataCtl class. It handles the operation of all of the Better Data Control buttons and uses the ButtonIndex parameter to indicate which button was pressed. Notice that the first thing ProcessButtons does is check to see that we initialized the DataCtl, UserForm, and Buttons properties. For this example, we will simply ignore requests if any of these have not been initialized.

The Better Data Control is designed to provide two enhancements. First, we offer additional buttons for paging through records and using bookmarks. These, as well as the original buttons, are handled individually by each Case statement in ProcessButtons. The second enhancement is to disable buttons that should not be pressed based on the location of the current record in the record set. This feature requires a bit of trickery. The first thing ProcessButtons does is check for the two specific cases when we will want all of the buttons disabled: an empty record set and a record set containing only one record. If either of these conditions exists, the buttons are all disabled by calling subroutines that disable groups of buttons at a time.

Calling these subroutines avoids a lot of duplicated code. There are two sets of subroutines: one disables the buttons and the other enables them. Since the subroutines are all very similar, we'll look at only one set in detail, DisableUpButtons.

Although control arrays are very handy, there is no easy way to pass a control array as a parameter. The statement

```
UserForm.Controls(Buttons)(bdcFirst).Enabled = False
```

demonstrates the trick necessary to access the control array of buttons on Form1. In Visual Basic 4.0, references to controls using the Controls collection can use names as well as index numbers. We set the UserForm property to point to Form1, and the Buttons property to the name of the button control array, Command1. Thus, the above statement is equivalent to this:

```
Form1.Controls("Command1")(bdcFirst).Enabled = False
```

giving the cDataCtl class access to all eight of the Better Data Control buttons.

Back in the ProcessButtons subroutine, each Case statement handles a single button. The appropriate commands are passed to the data control.

A check is then made to determine if the current record is at the top or bottom of the file depending on the direction of travel. If it is at one end or the other, the appropiate buttons are disabled.

The first six cases handle the six VCR buttons. The last two cases handle bookmarks. Each record in a record set can be identified by a unique bookmark. (Visual Basic allows bookmarks to be stored in strings.) A bookmark may then be restored, causing the data control to return to the associated record.

The Set Bookmark button saves the bookmark of the current record in the private property MyBookmark. The Go To Bookmark button restores the current record pointer to the record indicated by MyBookmark. Notice that MyBookmark is first checked to see if a Set Bookmark was executed. If it was, MyBookmark will not be an empty string.

All that's needed to initialize the state of the buttons is to call the ProcessButtons method in Form1's Form_Load Event, passing it a 0 to tell it to execute a MoveFirst.

Comments

This example does not include support for adding or deleting records. You can add buttons for these functions as you would for Visual Basic's data control.

8.5 How do I...
Display Values from Any Access Database?

COMPLEXITY: INTERMEDIATE
COMPATIBILITY: VB4 ONLY

Problem

My PC subdirectories contain a number of .MDB and .MDA files. I know those files are Access databases used for sample applications. How can I use Visual Basic to get a fast look at the information stored in those database fields? And is there a way to use wildcards to restrict the displayed information to just values of interest to my application?

Technique

Visual Basic 4.0 lets you modify a DBList control and an associated Data control at run time. As we saw in How-To 8.3, visibility into the structure of the databases is also provided. The project in this How-To extends the one in How-To 8.3 to allow the user to display actual values from any application field in any local database table. This is accomplished by building a SQL statement corresponding to the user's selection. How-To 8.5 uses this SQL statement, plus the names of the field and table selected by the user, to modify the Data and DBList controls at run time.

The SQL statement includes a WHERE clause that makes use of any pattern, including a powerful set of wildcards. The * wildcard matches zero or more characters and the standard ? wildcard matches any single character. The # wildcard matches any single digit.

Placing a list of characters in brackets is another way to construct a search pattern. For example, the pattern [A-C2]*[!X-Z] matches any string that begins with A, B, C, or 2 and does not end with X, Y, or Z. This technique adds considerable power to the search capabilities.

Steps

Open and run DBDSPLAY.VBP. In the Display Database Fields form, double-click on your Visual Basic directory to display its database files. Then click or double-click on BIBLIO.MDB, the sample database provided.

When the hourglass disappears, click on the plus sign in front of biblio.mdb and click again on the plus sign in front of Authors. This expands the outline to display the fields in the Authors table. Double-click on the text portion of the Author field name. This causes the DBList control to list all the authors in the table. The asterisk in the text box above the list indicates that all items were selected. Next, type *mi* in the text box and double-click. The new display will include only author names containing the letter combination *mi*. See Figure 8-5-1 for an example of the Display Database Fields form in action.

Let's try something more exotic. Key in a pattern of ?an*[!s-z]. Check the display; it will include only names with *an* as the second and third letters, and that don't end with a letter from *s* through *z*.

Continue to experiment as you like with different fields, tables, and databases. When you are done, click the Exit button to close the form.

1. Create a new project called DBDSPLAY.VBP, and create a new form called DBDSPLAY.FRM. Place controls on the form as shown in Figure 8-5-2, and set properties as listed in Table 8-5-1. Notice that the invisible data control does not have a DatabaseName or RecordSource property, and the DBList control

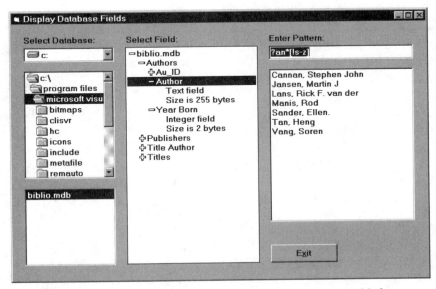

Figure 8-5-1 Field displays in action on the Display Database Fields form

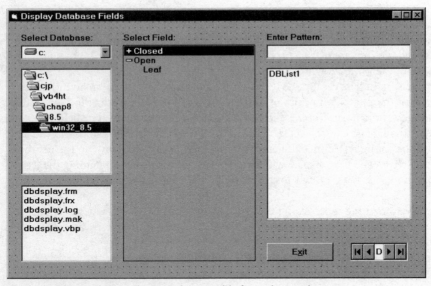

Figure 8-5-2 The Display Database Fields form during design

does not have a ListField property. These will be provided at run time when the user chooses what to display.

Table 8-5-1 DBDSPLAY.FRM objects and properties

OBJECT	PROPERTY	SETTING
Form	Name	Form1
	Caption	"Display Database Fields"
DriveListBox	Name	Drive1
	TabIndex	2
DirListBox	Name	Dir1
	TabIndex	0
FileListBox	Name	Drive1
	TabIndex	1
Outline	Name	Outline1
	TabIndex	3
	Style	2 'Plus/minus and text
Data	Name	Data1
	Connect	"Access"
	DatabaseName	""
	ReadOnly	0 'False
	RecordsetType	1 'Dynaset

OBJECT	PROPERTY	SETTING
	RecordSource	""
	Visible	0 'False
TextBox	Name	Text1
	TabIndex	4
DBList	Name	DBList1
	TabIndex	5
	ListField	""
	RowSource	"Data1"
CommandButton	Name	ExitButton
	Caption	"E&xit"
	TabIndex	6
Label	Name	Label1
	Caption	"Select Database:"
Label	Name	Label2
	Caption	"Select Field:"
Label	Name	Label3
	Caption	"Enter Pattern:"

2. Place the following code at the beginning of DBDSPLAY.FRM to define the module-level constants and variables needed.

```
Option Explicit
'
' Define private constants & variables
'
Private Const DbLvl As Integer = 1
Private Const TblLvl As Integer = 2
Private Const FldLvl As Integer = 3
Private Const FldPropLvl As Integer = 4
'
Private Ws As Workspace, Db As Database
Private TDef As Tabledef, Fld As Field
Private DbPath As String
Private DbName As String
Private TblName As String
Private FldName As String
```

3. Add the code shown in bold to the following event procedures. These routines perform the functions as discussed in How-To 8.3. They have been modified, though, to establish a relationship between the database and a default workspace object.

In the data-access object model, the top object in the hierarchy is the JET database engine, the DBEngine. This object contains a collection of workspaces, and each workspace contains a collection of databases. Each workspace establishes a security context that determines what operations may be performed upon an

open database within that workspace. Multiple databases may be opened within
each workspace.

```
Private Sub Form_Load()
    '
    ' Center the form, initialize the paths to the application path,
    ' and set the file pattern to display databases only.
    '
    Outline1.BackColor = DBList1.BackColor
    Me.Move (Screen.Width - Me.Width) \ 2, _
            (Screen.Height - Me.Height) \ 2
    Drive1.Drive = App.Path
    Dir1.Path = App.Path
    File1.Pattern = "*.mdb;*.mda"
    Set Ws = DBEngine.Workspaces(0)
End Sub

Private Sub Drive1_Change()
    '
    ' When drive changes, synchronize directory path.
    ' Handle floppy disk errors, etc.
    '
    On Error GoTo Drive1_Err
    Dir1.Path = Drive1.Drive
    '
Drive1_Done:
    On Error GoTo 0
    Exit Sub
    '
Drive1_Err:
    Drive1.Drive = Dir1.Path
    Resume Drive1_Done:
End Sub

Private Sub Dir1_Change()
    '
    ' When directory path changes, synchronize file list and save.
    '
    File1.Path = Dir1.Path
    DbPath = Dir1.Path IIf (Right$(Dir1.Path, 1) <> "\", "")
End Sub

Private Sub Dir1_LostFocus()
    '
    ' Set directory path to final selection.
    '
    Dir1.Path = Dir1.List(Dir1.ListIndex)
End Sub

Private Sub File1_Click()
    '
    ' When user clicks on a valid file name, build the outline.
    '
    If Len(File1.FileName) > 4 Then
        DbName = File1.FileName
```

```
        Outline1.SetFocus
    End If
End Sub

Private Sub File1_DblClick()
    '
    ' Treat double click as click.
    '
    Call File1_Click
End Sub

Private Sub Outline1_GotFocus()
    '
    ' Build the outline from the TableDefs and Fields in the selected
    ' database.
    '
    Dim i As Integer
    Dim TName As String
    Static OutlineDone As Boolean
    '
    ' If new database, clear outline.
    '
    If Outline1.ListCount Then
        If (DbName <> Outline1.List(0)) Then
            Outline1.Clear
            Db.Close
            OutlineDone = False
        End If
    End If
    '
    ' If valid new database name, open database and start outline.
    '
    If Len(DbName) > 4 And Not OutlineDone Then
        Screen.MousePointer = vbHourglass
        Set Db = Ws.OpenDatabase(DbPath & DbName)
        '
        ' Index 0 is the database, and gets the 1st indentation level.
        '
        Outline1.AddItem DbName, 0
        Outline1.Indent(0) = DbLvl
        i = 1
        '
        ' For each TableDef that is not for a system table,
        ' add the table name at the 2nd level.
        '
        For Each TDef In Db.TableDefs
            If (TDef.Attributes And dbSystemObject) = 0 Then
                Outline1.AddItem TDef.Name, i
                Outline1.Indent(i) = TblLvl
                i = i + 1
                If TDef.Attributes = 0 Then
                    '
                    ' For each field in a local TableDef, add the name at
                    ' the 3rd level.
                    '
```

Continued on next page

Continued from previous page

```
For Each Fld In TDef.Fields
    Outline1.AddItem Fld.Name, i
    Outline1.Indent(i) = FldLvl
    i = i + 1
    '
    ' At the 4th level, add the type and size of
    ' each field.
    '
    Select Case Fld.Type
    Case dbBoolean
        TName = "Yes/no"
    Case dbByte
        TName = "Byte"
    Case dbInteger
        TName = "Integer"
    Case dbLong
        If Fld.Attributes And dbAutoIncrField Then
            TName = "Counter"
        Else
            TName = "Long integer"
        End If
    Case dbCurrency
        TName = "Currency"
    Case dbSingle
        TName = "Single"
    Case dbDouble
        TName = "Double"
    Case dbDate
        TName = "Date/time"
    Case dbText
        TName = "Text"
    Case dbLongBinary
        TName = "OLE Object"
    Case dbMemo
        TName = "Memo"
    Case Else
        TName = "Code" & Str$(Fld.Type)
    End Select
    '
    Outline1.AddItem TName & " field", i
    Outline1.Indent(i) = FldPropLvl
    i = i + 1
    '
    If TName = "Memo" Then
        Outline1.AddItem "Size is unlimited", i
    Else
        If Fld.Size = 1 Then
            Outline1.AddItem "Size is 1 byte", i
        Else
            Outline1.AddItem "Size is " & Fld.Size & _
                            " bytes", i
        End If
    End If
    Outline1.Indent(i) = FldPropLvl
    i = i + 1
```

```
              Next Fld
           End If
        End If
     Next TDef
     OutlineDone = True
     Screen.MousePointer = vbNormal
   End If
End Sub
```

4. Place the following code in the Outline1_DblClick event procedure. Visual Basic triggers this event when the user double-clicks on the text portion of an item, but not when the double-click is on the plus or minus sign (or on any other graphical hot spot). As with any list control, the ListIndex property identifies the item selected.

   The indentation level of the item determines whether it is a database (level 1), a table (level 2), a field (level 3), or a field property (level 4). If the user double-clicks a database or a table, we can't identify a particular field to display. So we just expand the item if it is collapsed and wait for another event. If the user double-clicks a field or a field property, though, we're in business.

```
Private Sub Outline1_DblClick()
   '
   ' Check to see that the user clicked a field name or a property
   ' of a field. If so, find the table name (parent) and perform
   ' field display logic. If not, expand the item if it is
   ' collapsed.
   '
   Dim i As Integer
   i = Outline1.ListIndex
   Select Case Outline1.Indent(i)
   Case DbLvl, TblLvl
      If Not Outline1.Expand(i) Then
         Outline1.Expand(i) = True
      End If
   Case FldLvl
      FldName = Outline1.List(i)
      TblName = Outline1.List(ParentItem(i))
      Text1.Text = "*"
      Call ConnectTable
   Case FldPropLvl
      i = ParentItem(i)
      FldName = Outline1.List(i)
      TblName = Outline1.List(ParentItem(i))
      Text1.Text = "*"
      Call ConnectTable
   End Select
End Sub
```

5. Place the following code in the Text1_DblClick event procedure. This code causes the display of a subset of the field values corresponding to the pattern entered by the user.

```
Private Sub Text1_DblClick()
    '
    ' On a double click of the text box, display fields corresponding
    ' to the new pattern.
    '
    Call ConnectTable
End Sub
```

6. Place the following code in the ExitButton_Click event procedure, to release resources and exit the application.

```
Private Sub ExitButton_Click()
    '
    ' Release resources and quit.
    '
    Unload Me
    Set Form1 = Nothing
    End
End Sub
```

7. Place the following function in the General section, to return the index of an item's parent. This is needed to identify the table name for a particular field, and also to identify the field name whenever the user double-clicks a field property.

```
Private Function ParentItem(Idx As Integer) As Integer
    '
    ' For a given list item index, return the index of its parent.
    '
    Dim Lvl As Integer
    Lvl = Outline1.Indent(Idx)
    If Lvl > 0 Then
        Lvl = Lvl - 1
        Do Until Outline1.Indent(Idx) = Lvl
            Idx = Idx - 1
        Loop
    End If
    ParentItem = Idx
End Function
```

8. Place the following subroutine in the General section. This code fills in the information missing from the Data and DBList controls, and refreshes both of them. Then it highlights the pattern text (by selecting it) and places the focus in the text box. During these operations, the mouse pointer changes to the hourglass.

```
Private Sub ConnectTable()
    '
    ' Provide database file and SQL statement to the Data control,
    ' and provide the field name to the DBList control. Then refresh
    ' both controls, highlight the text pattern, and move the focus.
    '
    Screen.MousePointer = vbHourglass
    Data1.DatabaseName = DbPath & DbName
    Data1.RecordSource = "SELECT [" & FldName & _
```

```
                         "] FROM [" & TblName & _
                         "] WHERE [" & FldName & _
                         "] LIKE """ & Text1.Text & _
                         """" ORDER BY [" & FldName & "];"
    On Error GoTo ErrorHandler
    Data1.Refresh
    DBList1.Refresh
    DBList1.ListField = FldName
    Text1.SelStart = 0
    Text1.SelLength = Len(Text1.Text)
    Text1.SetFocus
    Screen.MousePointer = vbNormal
Exit Sub
ErrorHandler
    If Err.Number = 3117 Then
        MsgBox "Can't Display a Memo or OLE Object"
    Else
        MsgBox "Can't Display the Data"
    End If
    Err.Clear
    Screen.MousePointer = vbNormal
End Sub
```

How It Works

The form in this How-To allows the user to go from database to database, examining the values of various table fields in each database. It works by using Visual Basic code to control the displays, based on user's choices.

The database name comes from the database filename chosen by the user and is the same name that is used to build the outline of tables and fields. By putting the database name into the Data1.DatabaseName property, we allow the data control to connect with the database at run time.

The field name comes from the user's choice of a field or field property on the outline. By putting the field name into the DBList1.ListField property, we tell the DBList control what field to display when the Refresh method executes.

The heart of this code is the statement that builds the SQL statement for the Data1.RecordSource property at run time. The SQL statement pulls together the table name, the field name, and the pattern in the text box to tell the data control exactly what dynaset to create. The SQL statement is a string that looks like

```
SELECT [Author] FROM [Authors] WHERE [Author] Like "?an*[!s-z]"
ORDER BY [Author]
```

In this example, the field name is Author, the table name is Authors, and the pattern in the text box is ?an*[!s-z]. The brackets around the table and field names are used to hold together names that may include spaces, which are permitted in Access.

Having filled in all the information needed, the code uses the Refresh methods on the Data control and the DBList. This creates the dynaset specified and displays the results on the form.

Comments

The example in this How-To opens up a world of possibilities in Visual Basic 4.0. You can open multiple databases within a workspace, obtain detailed information from the collections within the data access object hierarchy, and construct and execute SQL statements based on the information obtained.

One interesting programming point comes up regarding the following statement in the Outline1_GotFocus event procedure:

```
If (TDef.Attributes And dbSystemObject) = 0 Then
```

Here the And operator does a bit comparison between the table definition attributes field and the dbSystemObject internal constant. The dbSystemObject has a value in hexadecimal of 80 00 00 02, so 2 bits are set on; and the test above will fail if either of those 2 bits is set in the Tdef.Attributes field. And, in fact, a system object will have one or the other of those attribute bits set.

But what if you need to test *for* a system object? Because the high-order bit identifies a negative number (decimal $-2,147,483,648$), you need a test like the following:

```
If (TDef.Attributes And dbSystemObject) <> 0 Then
```

It is not sufficient to use > 0 because this will not catch the objects identified by the high-order attribute bit.

8.6 How do I...
Create a Database from a Text File Description?

COMPLEXITY: INTERMEDIATE
COMPATIBILITY: VB4 ONLY

Problem

The Data Access Guide shows how to create a database using data access objects. Unfortunately, the example shown there requires that all of the database elements be hard-coded. The applications I design, however, contain several tables, and I often need to change the structure of my tables during the development process. Changing this code each time is not practical. I'd like to save a text file containing a description of my database and edit the description whenever I have to make changes to the database. Can I write a program to re-create my database from the text file description?

Technique

The Professional Edition of Visual Basic 4.0 provides the data access objects necessary to define as well as work with databases. This How-To demonstrates how to create a database and define its tables, fields, indexes, and relationships.

Instead of writing a new program for each database you need to create, in this project you will use a text file to hold the database description. You can create this text file using any text editor that can save simple ASCII files. The following schema demonstrates the format for such a text file:

```
'
' Schema  file comments work just like Visual Basic comments.
' Groups of items are enclosed in parens "()" and items within
' the parens are separated by commas ",".
'
' First define the database name
'
Database VbHowTo.mdb
(
    '
    ' A table definition begins with a keyword Table followed by the
    ' table's name.
    '
    Table Order
    (
        '
        ' Each table has one or more fields
        '
        ' A field definition begins with the keyword Field followed by
        ' the field's name and, in parens, the field's type and
        ' attributes
        '
        ' Valid field types are:
        '        Boolean    Byte      Integer     Long
        '        Currency   Single    Double      Date
        '        Binary     Text      LongBinary  Memo
        '
        Field OrderNr (Long, Counter)
        Field Class (Byte)
        Field Credit (Boolean)
        Field CustomerNr (Long)
        Field CouponAmt (Currency)
        Field Discount (Single)
        '
        ' Tables can also have indexes
        '
        ' An index definition begins with the keyword Index followed by
        ' the index's name and, in parens, a list of fields and,
        ' optionally, the keywords to indicate a Unique key or a
        ' Primary key. Only one Primary key is allowed per table.
        '
        ' Each field must begin with a "+" or "-" indicating
        ' ascending or descending collating order for the field.
        '
        Index CustomerOrder
        (
            +CustomerNr,
            +OrderNr,
            Unique
        )
```

Continued on next page

Continued from previous page

```
      Index PrimaryKey
      (
         +OrderNr,
         Primary
      )
   )
   Table OrderItem
   (
      Field OrderNr (Long)
      Field LineNr (Long, Counter)
      Field Complete (Boolean)
      Field ProductDesc (Text 20)
      Field Zip (Text 9)
      Field Picture (LongBinary)
      Field Notes (Memo)
      Index PrimaryKey
      (
         +OrderNr,
         +LineNr,
         Primary
      )
      Index Reverse
      (
         +OrderNr,
         -LineNr,
         Unique
      )
      Index Product
      (
         +ProductDesc
      )
   )
'
'
' A relation definition consists of the keyword Relation followed
' by the name of the relation and, in parens, the following:
'      1. The keyword PrimaryTable followed by a table name
'      2. The keyword ForeignTable followed by a table name
'      3. In parens, pairs of field names that comprise the
'         relation.
'      4. Any attributes to be applied to the relation.
'
Relation Relation1
(
   PrimaryTable (Order)
   Foreigntable (OrderItem)
   (OrderNr, OrderNr)
   RelationLeft,
   UpdateCascade,
   DeleteCascade
)
)
```

Note: The fields shown above are for illustration only and are not intended to represent realistic data. Figure 8-6-1 shows the result of loading the above schema.

Steps

Open and run DBCREATE.VBP. Use the File Open menu item to open the sample schema DBCREATE.SCH. The outline displays the definition of your database. Click the closed file folders to open additional levels of the outline. To collapse a line's subordinate levels, click the open file folders. After you've loaded a schema, you can create the new database by selecting the File Create Database menu item. When finished, your form should look like Figure 8-6-1.

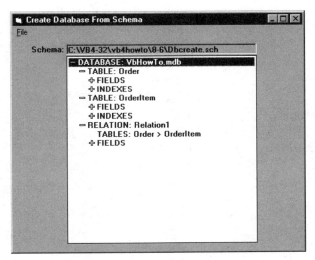

Figure 8-6-1 The DBCreate project

1. Create a new project named DBCREATE.VBP, and add the properties shown in Table 8-6-1 to Form1.

Table 8-6-1 Objects and properties for Form1

OBJECT	PROPERTY	SETTING
Form	Caption	"Create Database From Schema"
	Name	Form1
	BackColor	&H00C0C0C0&
Outline	Name	Outline1
	Style	Plus/Minus and Text
	BackColor	&H00FFFFFF&
CommonDialog	Name	CMDialog1
	DefaultExt	"*.sch"
	DialogTitle	"Open Schema"
	Filter	"Schema (*.sch)|*.sch"

Continued on next page

Continued from previous page

OBJECT	PROPERTY	SETTING
Label	Name	Label1
	Caption	"Schema:"
	Alignment	Right Justify
	BackStyle	Transparent
Label	Name	SchemaName
	Caption	""

2. Use the menu design window to create the menu shown in Table 8-6-2.

Table 8-6-2 Form1's menu

MENU NAME	CAPTION	ENABLED
FileMenu	"&File"	True
—FileOpenSchema	"&Open Schema..."	True
—Sep1	"-"	True
—FileCreate Database	"&Create Database"	False
—Sep2	"-"	True
—FileExit	"E&xit"	True

3. Add the following code to the General Declarations section of Form1. This defines a COutline class that provides better functionality for the outline control, and a CSchema class that will load and process a database schema.

```
Option Explicit
'
' Define classes.
'
Private MyOutline As cOutline
Private MySchema As CSchema
```

4. Add the following code to the Form_Load event, to create instances of the COutline and CSchema classes.

```
Private Sub Form_Load()
    '
    ' Instantiate MyOutline class
    '
    Set MyOutline = New COutline
    Set MyOutline.OutlineCtl = Outline1
End Sub
```

5. Add the following code to the FileOpenSchema_Click event. Selecting this menu item pops up a File Open dialog and tells the CSchema class to load a schema. Once a valid schema is loaded, Outline1 is filled to display the structure of the proposed database.

```
Private Sub FileOpenSchema_Click()
    '
    ' Open and load a schema.
    '
    Dim FileNum As Integer
    Dim result As Boolean
    Dim t As Integer
    Dim f As Integer
    Dim i As Integer
    Dim indf As Integer
    Dim r As Integer
    Dim rf As Integer
    Dim IndexAttribute As String
    Dim IndexField As String
    '
    ' Create a new CSchema class
    '
    If Not MySchema Is Nothing Then
        Set MySchema = Nothing
    End If
    Outline1.Clear
    SchemaName.Caption = ""
    Set MySchema = New CSchema
    '
    ' Get a filenumber to use.
    '
    FileNum = FreeFile
    '
    ' Get the schema filename from the user.
    '
    CMDialog1.FileName = ""
    CMDialog1.InitDir = App.Path
    CMDialog1.ShowOpen
    If (CMDialog1.FileName = "") Then
        Exit Sub
    End If
    '
    ' Open the schema file.
    '
    Open CMDialog1.FileName For Input As FileNum
    '
    ' Zap the schema outline contents.
    '
    SchemaName.Caption = ""
    Outline1.Clear
    '
    ' Tell MySchema the file handle.
    '
    MySchema.FileNum = FileNum
    '
    ' Go parse the schema.
    '
    Screen.MousePointer = vbHourglass
    result = MySchema.ParseSchema()
    Screen.MousePointer = vbNormal
```

Continued on next page

Continued from previous page

```
'
' Close the schema file.
'
Close FileNum
'
' Disable the Create Database menu item.
'
FileCreateDatabase.Enabled = False
'
' If we got a useable schema build the schema outline.
'
If result Then
    Screen.MousePointer = vbHourglass
    SchemaName.Caption = CMDialog1.FileName
    SchemaName.Refresh
    MyOutline.AddItemToOutline 1, "DATABASE: " & MySchema.dbName
    MyOutline.ExpandOutlineToLevel 1
    For t = 0 To MySchema.dbTablesCount - 1
        '
        ' Add a table.
        '
        MyOutline.AddItemToOutline 2, "TABLE: " _
                                    & MySchema.TableName(t)
        '
        ' Add the table's fields.
        '
        If MySchema.TableFieldCount(t) > 0 Then
            MyOutline.AddItemToOutline 3, "FIELDS"
            For f = 0 To MySchema.TableFieldCount(t) - 1
                MyOutline.AddItemToOutline 4, _
                                    MySchema.FieldName(t, f)
            Next f
        End If
        '
        ' Add the table's indexes
        '
        If MySchema.TableIndexCount(t) > 0 Then
            MyOutline.AddItemToOutline 3, "INDEXES"
            For i = 0 To MySchema.TableIndexCount(t) - 1
                IndexAttribute = ""
                If MySchema.IndexPrimary(t, i) Then
                    IndexAttribute = " (Primary, Unique)"
                Else
                    If MySchema.IndexUnique(t, i) Then
                        IndexAttribute = " (Unique)"
                    End If
                End If
                MyOutline.AddItemToOutline 4, _
                                    MySchema.IndexName(t, i) _
                                    & IndexAttribute
                For indf = 0 To MySchema.IndexFieldCount(t, i) - 1
                    IndexField = MySchema.IndexFieldName(t, i, indf)
                    If (MySchema.IndexFieldAttributes(t, i, indf) _
                        And dbDescending) Then
                        IndexField = IndexField & " (Descending)"
                    End If
```

```
                    MyOutline.AddItemToOutline 5, IndexField
                Next indf
            Next
        End If
    Next t
    '
    ' Add the database's relations
    '
    For r = 0 To MySchema.dbRelationsCount - 1
        '
        ' Add a relation.
        '
        MyOutline.AddItemToOutline 2, "RELATION: " _
                                    & MySchema.RelName(r)
        '
        ' Add primary and foreign tables
        '
        MyOutline.AddItemToOutline 3, "TABLES: " _
                                    & MySchema.RelPrimaryTable(r) _
                                    & " > " _
                                    & MySchema.RelForeignTable(r)
        '
        ' Add the relation's fields.
        '
        If MySchema.RelFieldCount(r) > 0 Then
            MyOutline.AddItemToOutline 3, "FIELDS"
            For rf = 0 To MySchema.RelFieldCount(r) - 1
                MyOutline.AddItemToOutline 4, _
                                    MySchema.RelFieldName(r, rf) _
                                    & " > " & _
                                    MySchema.RelForeignName(r, rf)
            Next rf
        End If
    Next r
    '
    ' Start the outline open as far as the
    ' Fields/Indexes level and highlight the
    ' database name.
    '
    MyOutline.ExpandOutlineToLevel 2
    Outline1.ListIndex = 0
    '
    ' Enable the Create Database menu item.
    '
    FileCreateDatabase.Enabled = True
    Screen.MousePointer = vbNormal
    End If
End Sub
```

6. Add the following code to the FileCreateDatabase_Click event. This calls the CSchema class to generate the database.

```
Private Sub FileCreateDatabase_Click()
    '
    ' Create the database from the loaded schema.
```

Continued on next page

Continued from previous page

```
    '
    MySchema.CreateDatabase
End Sub
```

7. Add the following code to the FileExit_Click event. Selecting this menu item terminates the DBCreate project.

```
Private Sub FileExit_Click()
    '
    ' Exit the DBCreate project.
    '
    End
End Sub
```

The COutline Class

8. Use the Insert Class Module menu item to add a new class to your project, the
   COutline class. Open your new class module in the project window. Use the properties window to set the module's name to COutline, and set the Creatable property to True. This class is used to improve the interface to the outline control.

9. Add the following code to the General section of COutline. This defines the
   m_OutlineCtl property, which gets set to point to the outline control on Form1.

```
Option Explicit
'
' COutline - Methods to assist the VB4 Outline Control
'
' Pointer to the outline control to be assisted.
'
Private m_OutlineCtl As Control

Public Property Set OutlineCtl(NewOutlineCtl As Control)
    '
    ' Set the OutlineControl property.
    '
    Set m_OutlineCtl = NewOutlineCtl
End Property
```

10. Add the following code to the General section of COutline. This method simpli-
    fies the addition of items to the outline, by setting the indent level and text at the
    same time.

```
Public Sub AddItemToOutline(ItemIndent As Integer, ItemText As String)
    '
    ' Add an item to an outline at a given level
    ' and using a given picture type.
    '
    m_OutlineCtl.AddItem ItemText
    m_OutlineCtl.Indent(m_OutlineCtl.ListCount - 1) = ItemIndent
End Sub
```

11. Add the following code to the General section of COutline. This method, which expands all levels up to and including a given level, is used by the DBCreate project to expand the outline out to the Fields/Indexes level when initially shown.

```
Public Sub ExpandOutlineToLevel(Level As Integer)
    '
    ' Expand all levels up to and including a given level.
    '
    Dim x As Integer
    '
    ' Cycle through all lines and expand any that have a level less
    ' than or equal to the target level.
    '
    For x = 0 To m_OutlineCtl.ListCount - 1
        If m_OutlineCtl.HasSubItems(x) Then
            m_OutlineCtl.Expand(x) = (m_OutlineCtl.Indent(x) <= Level)
        End If
    Next x
End Sub
```

The CParser Class

12. Use the Insert Class Module menu item to add a new class to your project, the CParser class. Open your new class module in the project window. Use the properties window to set the module's name to CParser, and set the Creatable property to True. This class is a generalized parser that divides a file into tokens. Each token is a word or symbol delimited by spaces, tabs, commas, or any control character with an ASCII value less than a space (32). The CParser class may be used for any project that requires separating a file into tokens.

13. Add the following code to the General section of CParser, to define the properties used in the cParser class. The public property FileNum must be set to an open file handle before any parsing takes place.

```
Option Explicit
'
' CParser - General Purpose Text Parser
'
'
' Input file handle.
'
Public FileNum As Integer
'
' Source line number, useful when printing error messages.
'
Public CurLineNumber As Integer
'
' Used during parsing as a single char pushback buffer.
'
Private m_SavedChar As String
'
' Source line.
```

Continued on next page

Continued from previous page

```
'
Private m_CurLine As String
'
' Current position in source line.
'
Private m_CurLineIndex As Integer
'
' String of delimiter characters.
'
Private m_Delim As String
'
' String of whitespace characters > space character.
'
Private m_WhiteChars As String
```

14. Add the following method to the General section of the CParser class, to return the next token in the file. If the FileNum property was not set or an end of file condition exists, an empty string ("") is returned.

```
Public Function GetToken() As String
    '
    ' Get the next token in the file.
    '
    Dim Token As String
    Dim Char  As String
    '
    ' Check for valid FileNum
    '
    If FileNum ≤ 0 Then
        GetToken = ""
        Exit Function
    End If
    '
    ' Skip leading whitespace.
    '
    SkipWhitespace
    '
    ' Get the next character.
    '
    Char = GetChar()
    '
    ' Skip comment lines.
    '
    Do While Char = "'"
        FlushLine
        Char = GetChar()
    Loop
    '
    ' The '(' and ')' characters are  tokens.
    '
    If Char = "(" Or Char = ")" Then
        GetToken = Char
    Else
        '
        ' Any string of characters followed by a delimeter
```

```
    ' character is a token.
    '
    Do While Char <> "" And InStr(m_Delim, Char) = 0
        Token = Token & Char
        Char = GetChar()
    Loop
    '
    ' Push the character following the token back onto
    ' the character stream.
    '
    UngetChar (Char)
    GetToken = Token
    End If
End Function
```

15. Add the following code to the General section of the CParser class. Use this method when you expect a particular token to be next in the file. The method gets a token, compares it against a given string, and returns True or False based on the comparison.

```
Public Function ExpectToken(Expected As String) As Boolean
    '
    ' Get a token and see if it matches a given token.
    '
    Dim i As Integer
    Dim Token As String
    '
    ' Get the next token.
    '
    Token = UCase(GetToken())
    '
    ' If no token is returned we've reached the end-of-file.
    '
    If Token = "" Then
        MsgBox "Unexpected end of file"
        ExpectToken = False
    '
    ' Got a token, see if it was what we expected.
    '
    ElseIf Expected <> Token Then
        MsgBox "Expected " & Expected & " at line " _
              & Str(CurLineNumber)
        ExpectToken = False
    Else
        ExpectToken = True
    End If
End Function
```

16. Add the following code to the General section of the CParser class. This method skips characters until the end of the current line is reached.

```
Private Sub FlushLine()
    '
    ' Advance to the end of the current line. The next
    ' call to GetChar will cause a new line to be read.
```

Continued on next page

Continued from previous page

```
    '
    m_SavedChar = ""
    m_CurLineIndex = Len(m_CurLine) + 1
End Sub
```

17. Add the following code to the General section of the CParser class. This method returns the next non-whitespace character in the file. (See step 19 for a definition of whitespace characters.)

```
Private Function GetChar() As String
    '
    ' If a character has been pushed back return it.
    '
    If m_SavedChar <> "" Then
        GetChar = m_SavedChar
        m_SavedChar = ""
        Exit Function
    End If
    '
    ' If the current line is empty read a new one.
    '
    If m_CurLine = "" Or m_CurLineIndex ≤ Len(m_CurLine) Then
        If Not GetLine() Then
            GetChar = ""
            Exit Function
        End If
    End If
    '
    ' Return the next char from the current line.
    '
    GetChar = Mia$(m_CurLine, m_CurLineIndex, 1)
    m_CurLineIndex = m_CurLineIndex + 1
End Function
```

18. Add the following code to the General section of the CParser class. This method reads the next line in the input file into a buffer, m_CurLine, and moves to the first non-whitespace character on the line. (See step 19 for a definition of whitespace characters).

```
Private Function GetLine()
    '
    ' Read the next line from the input file.
    '
    Do While Not EOF(FileNum) _
            And (m_CurLine = "" Or m_CurLineIndex > Len(m_CurLine))
        Line Input #FileNum, m_CurLine
        CurLineNumber = CurLineNumber + 1
        m_CurLineIndex = 1
        '
        ' Trim leading spaces, tabs, and other meaningless
        ' chars from the line.
        '
        Do While m_CurLineIndex ≤ Len(m_CurLine) _
```

```
              And (Mid$(m_CurLine, m_CurLineIndex, 1) ≤ " " _
              Or InStr(m_WhiteChars, Mid$(m_CurLine, _
                     m_CurLineIndex, 1)) > 0)
          m_CurLineIndex = m_CurLineIndex + 1
      Loop
   Loop
   GetLine = Not m_CurLine = ""
End Function
```

19. Add the following code to the General section of the CParser class. This method skips over whitespace characters. Whitespace characters either have ASCII codes with values less than a space (32), or are in the m_WhiteChars string. The m_WhiteChars string is currently initialized to a comma (","). See the CParser's Class_Initialize event (step 21) for more information.

```
Private Sub SkipWhitespace()
   '
   ' Skip over any characters < space or in m_WhiteChars.
   '
   Dim Char As String
   '
   ' Skip characters until either eof (Char = "") or
   ' we've got a non-whitespace character.
   '
   Char = GetChar()
   Do While Char <> "" And (Char <= " " _
            Or InStr(m_WhiteChars, Char) > 0)
      Char = GetChar()
   Loop
   '
   ' Put the first non-whitespace character back in
   ' the input stream.
   '
   UngetChar (Char)
End Sub
```

20. Add the following code to the General section of the CParser class. As CParser looks for characters, it is sometimes necessary to look ahead one character before the stopping point can be determined. The method used here puts the extra character aside in the m_SavedChar property, and the GetChar method checks this property before reading further in the file.

```
Private Sub UngetChar(Char As String)
   '
   ' Push char back onto input stream.
   '
   m_SavedChar = Char
End Sub
```

21. Add the following routine to the Class section of the CParser class, to initialize properties and define the delimiters and whitespace characters for the class. If you need to change the delimiters or whitespace character lists, do it here. The

delimiters are the space, single quote, open and close parentheses, comma, and tab characters. The only whitespace character that is set is the comma. CParser automatically considers any character with an ASCII code less than or equal to a space (32) to be a whitespace character.

```
Private Sub Class_Initialize()
    '
    ' Initialize the CParser class
    '
    FileNum = 0
    m_SavedChar = ""
    m_CurLine = ""
    m_CurLineIndex = 0
    CurLineNumber = 0
    '
    ' Set the delimiter characters and whitespace
    ' characters. If you need to change them do it here.
    '
    m_Delim = " '()," & Chr$(9)
    m_WhiteChars = ","
End Sub
```

The CSchema Class

22. Use the Insert Class Module menu item to add a new class, the CSchema class, to your project. Open your new class module in the project window. Then use the properties window to set the module's name to CSchema and set the Creatable property to True. This class parses a text description of a database file into its component fields, indexes, and relationships. Once a schema is parsed, the database CSchema can create the database file and define its structure.

23. Add the following code to the General section of the CSchema class, to set up the user-defined types and properties that hold the database definition.

```
'
' CSchema - Database schema processing class
'
'
' Arbitrary limits on data structure sizes.
'
Private Const MaxIndexesPerTable = 10
Private Const MaxFieldsPerTable = 32
Private Const MaxFieldsPerIndex = 32
Private Const MaxTablesPerDatabase = 32
Private Const MaxRelationsPerDatabase = 32
'
' Information retrieved when parsing a Field statement.
'
Private Type FieldDesc
    Name            As String
    Type            As Integer
    Size            As Integer
```

```
        Attributes        As Long
        Required          As Boolean
        AllowZeroLength   As Boolean
        Updatable         As Boolean
        ForeignName       As String
    End Type
    '
    ' Information retrieved when parsing an Index statement.
    '
    Private Type IndexDesc
        Name                      As String
        fieldCount                As Integer
        Fields(MaxFieldsPerIndex) As FieldDesc
        Unique                    As Boolean
        Primary                   As Boolean
    End Type
    '
    ' Information retrieved when parsing a Table statement.
    '
    Private Type TableDesc
        Name                       As String
        fieldCount                 As Integer
        Fields(MaxFieldsPerTable)  As FieldDesc
        indexCount                 As Integer
        Indexes(MaxIndexesPerTable) As IndexDesc
    End Type
    '
    ' Information retrieved when parsing a Relation statement
    '
    Private Type RelationDesc
        Name As String
        PrimaryTable As String
        ForeignTable As String
        fieldCount As Integer
        Fields(MaxFieldsPerTable) As FieldDesc
        Attributes As Long
    End Type
    '
    ' Name of database.
    '
    Public dbName As String
    '
    ' Number of tables in the database.
    '
    Public dbTablesCount As Integer
    '
    ' Number of relations in the database.
    '
    Public dbRelationsCount As Integer
    '
    ' Structures to hold the schema.
    '
    Private dbTables(MaxTablesPerDatabase) As TableDesc
    Private dbRelations(MaxRelationsPerDatabase) As RelationDesc
    '
```

Continued on next page

903

Continued from previous page

```
' Used to keep track of the current position in
' various arrays.
'
Private m_tblIndex As Integer
Private m_fldIndex As Integer
Private m_indIndex As Integer
Private m_ifldIndex As Integer
Private m_relIndex As Integer
Private m_rfldIndex As Integer
```

24. Add the following code to the General section of the CSchema class. This defines an object of the CParser class, and a Property Let routine that will pass along the file handle (FileNum) when it is set by the caller.

```
'
' The parser object used to extract data from the
' schema file.
'
Private m_Parser As CParser
'
' Set the parser's FileNum property when the schema's
' FileNum property is set.
'
Public Property Let FileNum(NewFileNum As Integer)
  m_Parser.FileNum = NewFileNum
End Property
```

25. Add the following code to the General section of the CSchema class. These Property Gets provide external access to the schema. The Form1 code that builds the schema outline uses these routines to access the data. By using Property Gets, we reduce the complexity of the code as compared with the code that actually retrieves the data. This is especially apparent in the Property Gets for index field information.

```
'
' Property Gets for the Table type.
'
Public Property Get TableName(TableNr As Integer) As String
    TableName = dbTables(TableNr).Name
End Property

Public Property Get TableFieldCount(TableNr As Integer) As Integer
    TableFieldCount = dbTables(TableNr).fieldCount
End Property

Public Property Get TableIndexCount(TableNr As Integer) As Integer
    TableIndexCount = dbTables(TableNr).indexCount
End Property
'
' Property Gets for the Field type.
'
Public Property Get FieldName(TableNr As Integer, _
                              FieldNr As Integer) As String
```

```
      FieldName = dbTables(TableNr).Fields(FieldNr).Name
End Property

Public Property Get FieldType(TableNr As Integer, _
                              FieldNr As Integer) As Integer
    FieldType = dbTables(TableNr).Fields(FieldNr).Type
End Property

Public Property Get FieldSize(TableNr As Integer, _
                              FieldNr As Integer) As Integer
    FieldSize = dbTables(TableNr).Fields(FieldNr).Size
End Property

Public Property Get FieldAttributes(TableNr As Integer, _
                                    FieldNr As Integer) As Integer
    FieldAttributes = dbTables(TableNr).Fields(FieldNr).Attributes
End Property

Public Property Get FieldRequired(TableNr As Integer, _
                                  FieldNr As Integer) As Boolean
    FieldRequired = dbTables(TableNr).Fields(FieldNr).Required
End Property

Public Property Get FieldAllowZeroLength(TableNr As Integer, _
                                         FieldNr As Integer) As Boolean
    FieldAllowZeroLength = _
        dbTables(TableNr).Fields(FieldNr).AllowZeroLength
End Property

Public Property Get FieldUpdatable(TableNr As Integer, _
                                   FieldNr As Integer) As Boolean
    FieldUpdatable = dbTables(TableNr).Fields(FieldNr).Updatable
End Property
'
' Property Gets for the Index type.
'
Public Property Get IndexName(TableNr As Integer, _
                              IndexNr As Integer) As String
    IndexName = dbTables(TableNr).Indexes(IndexNr).Name
End Property

Public Property Get IndexFieldCount(TableNr As Integer, _
                                    IndexNr As Integer) As Integer
    IndexFieldCount = dbTables(TableNr).Indexes(IndexNr).fieldCount
End Property

Public Property Get IndexUnique(TableNr As Integer, _
                                IndexNr As Integer) As Boolean
    IndexUnique = dbTables(TableNr).Indexes(IndexNr).Unique
End Property

Public Property Get IndexPrimary(TableNr As Integer, _
                                 IndexNr As Integer) As Boolean
    IndexPrimary = dbTables(TableNr).Indexes(IndexNr).Primary
End Property
```

Continued on next page

Continued from previous page

```
Public Property Get IndexFieldName(TableNr As Integer, _
                                   IndexNr As Integer, _
                                   FieldNr As Integer) As String
    IndexFieldName = _
        dbTables(TableNr).Indexes(IndexNr).Fields(FieldNr).Name
End Property

Public Property Get IndexFieldAttributes(TableNr As Integer, _
                                         IndexNr As Integer, _
                                         FieldNr As Integer) As String
    IndexFieldAttributes = _
        dbTables(TableNr).Indexes(IndexNr).Fields(FieldNr).Attributes
End Property
'
' Property Gets for the Relations type.
'
Public Property Get RelName(RelationNr As Integer) As String
    RelName = dbRelations(RelationNr).Name
End Property

Public Property Get RelPrimaryTable(RelationNr As Integer) As String
    RelPrimaryTable = dbRelations(RelationNr).PrimaryTable
End Property

Public Property Get RelForeignTable(RelationNr As Integer) As String
    RelForeignTable = dbRelations(RelationNr).ForeignTable
End Property

Public Property Get RelFieldCount(RelationNr As Integer) As Integer
    RelFieldCount = dbRelations(RelationNr).fieldCount
End Property

Public Property Get RelFieldName(RelationNr As Integer, _
                                 FieldNr As Integer) As String
    RelFieldName = dbRelations(RelationNr).Fields(FieldNr).Name
End Property

Public Property Get RelForeignName(RelationNr As Integer, _
                                   FieldNr As Integer) As String
    RelForeignName = _
        dbRelations(RelationNr).Fields(FieldNr).ForeignName
End Property

Public Property Get RelAttributes(RelationNr As Integer) As Long
    RelAttributes = dbRelations(RelationNr).Attributes
End Property
```

26. Add the following method to the General section of the CSchema class, to load the schema into the dbTables structure. This method is called when the user selects the Load Schema menu item and chooses a schema file. If any errors occur during the parsing process, a message box pops up describing the error, and execution terminates. If all is successful, the loaded schema can be used to create a database file using CSchema's CreateDatabase method.

```
Public Function ParseSchema() As Boolean
    '
    ' Parse a database schema.
    '
    Dim Token As String
    Dim result As Boolean
    '
    ' Reset the table index .
    '
    m_tblIndex = 0
    '
    ' The first thing we expect in the source file (excluding
    ' whitespace and comments) is the DATABASE statement.
    '
    If (m_Parser.ExpectToken("DATABASE") = False) Then
        ParseSchema = False
        Exit Function
    End If
    '
    ' Assume that the next token contains a valid database name.
    '
    dbName = m_Parser.GetToken()
    '
    ' No tables or relations are defined yet.
    '
    dbTablesCount = 0
    dbRelationsCount = 0
    '
    ' Next we expect to see an open paren.
    '
    If Not m_Parser.ExpectToken("(") Then
        ParseSchema = False
        Exit Function
    End If
    '
    ' Assume success.
    '
    result = True
    '
    ' We now expect to see zero or more Table statements.
    '
    Do While Token <> ")" And result
        Token = UCase(m_Parser.GetToken())
        Select Case Token
            Case "TABLE"
                result = ParseTable()
            Case "RELATION"
                result = ParseRelation()
            Case ")"
            Case Else
                MsgBox "Error at line " _
                        & Format(m_Parser.CurLineNumber) _
                        & ". Expected either 'Table' or ')', got '" _
                        & Token & ".'"
                result = False
```

Continued on next page

907

Continued from previous page

```
        End Select
    Loop
    '
    ' If there were no parsing errors save the number
    ' of tables parsed in dbTablesCount and the number of
    ' relations parsed in dbRelationsCount.
    '
    If result Then
        dbTablesCount = m_tblIndex
        dbRelationsCount = m_relIndex
    End If
    ParseSchema = result
End Function
```

27. Add the following code to the General section of the CSchema class. This method loads a table definition.

```
Private Function ParseTable() As Boolean
    '
    ' Parse a table entry.
    '
    Dim Token       As String
    Dim result      As Boolean
    '
    ' Assume that the next token is a valid table name.
    '
    dbTables(m_tblIndex).Name = m_Parser.GetToken()
    dbTables(m_tblIndex).fieldCount = 0
    '
    ' We expect to see an open paren next.
    '
    If Not m_Parser.ExpectToken("(") Then
        ParseTable = False
        Exit Function
    End If
    '
    ' Assume success for the rest of the table parse.
    '
    result = True
    m_fldIndex = 0
    m_indIndex = 0
    '
    ' Each table contains zero or more Field or Index
    ' statements.
    '
    Do While Token <> ")" And result
        Token = UCase(m_Parser.GetToken())
        Select Case Token
            Case ")"
            Case "FIELD"
                result = ParseField()
                If (result = True) Then
                    m_fldIndex = m_fldIndex + 1
                End If
            Case "INDEX"
```

```
            result = ParseIndex()
            If (result = True) Then
                m_indIndex = m_indIndex + 1
            End If
        Case Else
            MsgBox "Error at line " _
                    & Format(m_Parser.CurLineNumber) _
                    & ". Expected either 'Field' or ')', got '" _
                    & Token & "'."
            result = False
    End Select
Loop
'
' If the parse was without error update the database
' tables information.
'
If result Then
    dbTables(m_tblIndex).fieldCount = m_fldIndex
    dbTables(m_tblIndex).indexCount = m_indIndex
    m_tblIndex = m_tblIndex + 1
End If

ParseTable = result
End Function
```

28. Add the following code to the General section of the CSchema class. This method loads the fields for a table.

```
Private Function ParseField() As Boolean
    '
    ' Parse a field entry.
    '
    Dim Token As String
    Dim result As Boolean
    Dim fldSize As Integer
    Dim fldType As Integer
    Dim fldAttrib As Long
    Dim fldRequired As Boolean
    Dim fldAllowZeroLength As Boolean
    Dim fldUpdatable As Boolean
    '
    ' The next token is assumed to be a valid field name.
    '
    With dbTables(m_tblIndex).Fields(m_fldIndex)
        .Name = m_Parser.GetToken()
    End With
    '
    ' Field names must be followed by an open paren.
    '
    If Not m_Parser.ExpectToken("(") Then
        ParseField = False
        Exit Function
    End If
    '
    ' Get the field type.
    '
```

Continued on next page

Continued from previous page

```
    result = True
    Token = UCase(m_Parser.GetToken())
    Select Case Token
        Case "BOOLEAN"
            fldType = dbBoolean
            fldSize = 1
        Case "BYTE"
            fldType = dbByte
            fldSize = 1
        Case "INTEGER"
            fldType = dbInteger
            fldSize = 2
        Case "LONG"
            fldType = dbLong
            fldSize = 4
        Case "CURRENCY"
            fldType = dbCurrency
            fldSize = 8
        Case "SINGLE"
            fldType = dbSingle
            fldSize = 4
        Case "DOUBLE"
            fldType = dbDouble
            fldSize = 8
        Case "DATE"
            fldType = dbDate
            fldSize = 8
        Case "BINARY"
            fldType = dbLongBinary
            fldSize = 0
        Case "TEXT"
            Token = m_Parser.GetToken()
            fldType = dbText
            fldSize = Val(Token)
        Case "LONGBINARY"
            fldType = dbLongBinary
            fldSize = 0
        Case "MEMO"
            fldType = dbMemo
            fldSize = 0
        Case Else
            MsgBox "Invalid field type '" & Token & "', line " _
                & Format(m_Parser.CurLineNumber) & "."
            result = False
    End Select

    Do While result And Token <> ")"
        '
        ' Didn't get a close paren, so we should have a field
        ' attribute.
        '
        Token = UCase(m_Parser.GetToken())
        Select Case Token
            Case "FIXED"
                fldAttrib = fldAttrib Or dbFixedField
```

```
            Case "COUNTER"
                fldAttrib = fldAttrib Or dbAutoIncrField
            Case "REQUIRED"
                fldRequired = True
            Case "ALLOWNULL"
                fldAllowZeroLength = True
            Case "UPDATABLE"
                fldUpdatable = True
            Case ")"
            Case Else
                MsgBox "Invalid Field Attribute: " & Token _
                        & " in line" & Str(m_Parser.CurLineNumber) & "."
                result = False
        End Select
    Loop
    '
    ' Save definition of this field.
    '
    If result Then
        With dbTables(m_tblIndex).Fields(m_fldIndex)
            .Size = fldSize
            .Type = fldType
            .Required = fldRequired
            .AllowZeroLength = fldAllowZeroLength
            .Updatable = fldUpdatable
            .Attributes = fldAttrib
        End With
    End If
    ParseField = result
End Function
```

29. Add the following code to the General section of the CSchema class. This method loads the indexes for a table.

```
Private Function ParseIndex() As Boolean
    '
    ' parse an index entry.
    '
    Dim Token       As String
    Dim result      As Boolean
    Dim fieldCount  As Integer
    '
    ' The next token is assumed to be a valid index name.
    '
    With dbTables(m_tblIndex).Indexes(m_indIndex)
        .Name = m_Parser.GetToken()
    End With
    '
    ' We expect an open paren to follow the index name.
    '
    If Not m_Parser.ExpectToken("(") Then
        ParseIndex = False
        Exit Function
    End If
    '
```

Continued on next page

Continued from previous page

```
' Assume that all goes well.
'
result = True
'
' The next tokens are either fields (indicated by a
' leading '+' or '-'), an index attribute or a ')'.
' Multiple fields are listed consecutively. The
' attribute should be the last item before the
' closing ')'.
'
m_ifldIndex = 0
fieldCount = 0
Do While result And Token <> ")"
    Token = m_Parser.GetToken()
    Select Case Mid$(Token, 1, 1)
        Case "+"
            With dbTables(m_tblIndex).Indexes(m_indIndex)
                .Fields(m_ifldIndex).Name = Mid$(Token, 2)
                .Fields(m_ifldIndex).Attributes = 0
            End With
            m_ifldIndex = m_ifldIndex + 1
            fieldCount = fieldCount + 1
        Case "-"
            With dbTables(m_tblIndex).Indexes(m_indIndex)
                .Fields(m_ifldIndex).Name = Mid$(Token, 2)
                .Fields(m_ifldIndex).Attributes = dbDescending
            End With
            m_ifldIndex = m_ifldIndex + 1
            fieldCount = fieldCount + 1
        Case ")"
        Case Else
            Select Case UCase(Token)
                Case "UNIQUE"
                    With dbTables(m_tblIndex).Indexes(m_indIndex)
                        .Unique = True
                    End With
                Case "PRIMARY"
                    With dbTables(m_tblIndex).Indexes(m_indIndex)
                        .Primary = True
                        .Unique = True
                    End With
                Case Else
                    MsgBox "Invalid token '" & Token _
                            & "'. Line number" _
                            & Str(m_Parser.CurLineNumber)
                    result = False
            End Select
            '
            ' One index attribute is allowed. It must be
            ' followed by a close paren.
            '
            Token = m_Parser.GetToken()
            If (Token <> ")") Then
                MsgBox "Invalid token '" & Token _
                        & "'. Line number" _
```

```
                        & Str(m_Parser.CurLineNumber) _
                        & ". Expected token ')'."
                result = False
            End If
        End Select
    Loop

    dbTables(m_tblIndex).Indexes(m_indIndex).fieldCount = fieldCount
    ParseIndex = result
End Function
```

30. Add the following code to the General section of the CSchema class. This method loads the relations for a table.

```
Private Function ParseRelation() As Boolean
    '
    ' Parse a relationship entry.
    '
    Dim Token        As String
    Dim fldAttrib    As Long
    Dim result       As Boolean
    '
    ' Assume that the next token is a valid table name.
    '
    dbRelations(m_relIndex).Name = m_Parser.GetToken()
    dbRelations(m_relIndex).fieldCount = 0
    '
    ' We expect to see an open paren next.
    '
    If Not m_Parser.ExpectToken("(") Then
        ParseRelation = False
        Exit Function
    End If
    '
    ' Assume success for the rest of the table parse.
    '
    result = True
    m_rfldIndex = 0
    '
    ' We expect to see a PrimaryTable token.
    '
    If Not m_Parser.ExpectToken("PRIMARYTABLE") Then
        ParseRelation = False
        Exit Function
    Else
        '
        ' Process primary table name.
        '
        If Not m_Parser.ExpectToken("(") Then
            ParseRelation = False
            Exit Function
        End If
        dbRelations(m_relIndex).PrimaryTable = m_Parser.GetToken()
        If Not m_Parser.ExpectToken(")") Then
            ParseRelation = False
```

Continued on next page

Continued from previous page

```
            Exit Function
        End If
    End If
    '
    ' We expect to see a ForeignTable token.
    '
    If Not m_Parser.ExpectToken("FOREIGNTABLE") Then
        ParseRelation = False
        Exit Function
    Else
        '
        ' Process primary table name.
        '
        If Not m_Parser.ExpectToken("(") Then
            ParseRelation = False
            Exit Function
        End If
        dbRelations(m_relIndex).ForeignTable = m_Parser.GetToken()
        If Not m_Parser.ExpectToken(")") Then
            ParseRelation = False
            Exit Function
        End If
    End If
    '
    ' Now there should be an open paren followed by a pair of
    ' field names or attribute keywords.
    '
    Do While result And Token <> ")"
        '
        ' Didn't get a close paren, so we should have a
        ' pair of fields or an attribute.
        '
        Token = UCase(m_Parser.GetToken())
        Select Case Token
            Case "("
                With dbRelations(m_relIndex).Fields(m_rfldIndex)
                    .Name = m_Parser.GetToken()
                    .ForeignName = m_Parser.GetToken()
                End With
                If Not m_Parser.ExpectToken(")") Then
                    ParseRelation = False
                    Exit Function
                End If
                m_rfldIndex = m_rfldIndex + 1
            Case "UNIQUE"
                fldAttrib = fldAttrib Or dbRelationUnique
            Case "DONTENFORCE"
                fldAttrib = fldAttrib Or dbRelationDontEnforce
            Case "RELATIONLEFT"
                fldAttrib = fldAttrib Or dbRelationLeft
            Case "RELATIONRIGHT"
                fldAttrib = fldAttrib Or dbRelationRight
            Case "UPDATECASCADE"
                fldAttrib = fldAttrib Or dbRelationUpdateCascade
            Case "DELETECASCADE"
                fldAttrib = fldAttrib Or dbRelationDeleteCascade
```

```
            Case ")"
            Case Else
               MsgBox "Invalid Relation Attribute: " & Token _
                      & " in line" & Str(m_Parser.CurLineNumber) & "."
               result = False
         End Select
   Loop
   '
   ' If the parse was without error update the database
   ' relations information.
   '
   If result Then
      dbRelations(m_relIndex).Attributes = fldAttrib
      dbRelations(m_relIndex).fieldCount = m_rfldIndex
      m_relIndex = m_relIndex + 1
   End If

   ParseRelation = result
End Function
```

31. Add the following method to the General section of the CSchema class, to create a database from the loaded schema. This method is called when the user selects the Create Database menu item, and is used to create a new database. If this method should fail because of an invalid filename or an already existing file, an error box pops up and the database is not created. (Code to prompt the user and possibly correct these errors could be added.) Once a database is created, the tables, fields, indexes, and relationships are added.

```
Public Sub CreateDatabase()
   '
   ' Create a database file from the loaded schema.
   '
   Dim db As Database
   Dim tbl As TableDef
   Dim fld As Field
   Dim idx As Index
   Dim rel As Relation
   Dim t As Integer
   Dim f As Integer
   Dim i As Integer
   Dim r As Integer
   '
   ' This will take a while so turn the mouse pointer into
   ' an hourglass.
   '
   Screen.MousePointer = vbHourglass
   '
   ' Trap errors from CreateDatabase.
   '
   On Error Resume Next
   Set db = DBEngine(0).CreateDatabase(dbName, dbLangGeneral)
   If Err Then
      MsgBox "Could not create " & dbName & ". " & Error
```

Continued on next page

915

Continued from previous page

```
        Screen.MousePointer = vbNormal
        Exit Sub
    End If
    On Error GoTo 0
    '
    ' Create Tables.
    '
    For t = 0 To dbTablesCount - 1
        Set tbl = db.CreateTableDef(dbTables(t).Name)
        '
        ' Add fields.
        '
        For f = 0 To dbTables(t).fieldCount - 1
            Set fld = tbl.CreateField(dbTables(t).Fields(f).Name, _
                                      dbTables(t).Fields(f).Type)
            fld.Size = dbTables(t).Fields(f).Size
            fld.Attributes = dbTables(t).Fields(f).Attributes
            tbl.Fields.Append fld
        Next f
        '
        ' Add indexes.
        '
        For i = 0 To dbTables(t).indexCount - 1
            With dbTables(t).Indexes(i)
                Set idx = tbl.CreateIndex(.Name)
                idx.Primary = .Primary
                idx.Unique = .Unique
                For f = 0 To .fieldCount - 1
                    Set fld = tbl.CreateField(.Fields(f).Name)
                    fld.Attributes = .Fields(f).Attributes
                    idx.Fields.Append fld
                Next f
                tbl.Indexes.Append idx
            End With
        Next i
        db.TableDefs.Append tbl
    Next t
    '
    ' Add relations.
    '
    If dbRelationsCount > 0 Then
        For r = 0 To dbRelationsCount - 1
            Set rel = db.CreateRelation(dbRelations(r).Name, _
                                        dbRelations(r).PrimaryTable, _
                                        dbRelations(r).ForeignTable, _
                                        dbRelations(r).Attributes)
            For f = 0 To dbRelations(r).fieldCount - 1
                Set fld = rel.CreateField(dbRelations(r).Fields(f).Name)
                fld.ForeignName = dbRelations(r).Fields(f).ForeignName
                rel.Fields.Append fld
            Next f
        Next r
        db.Relations.Append rel
    End If
    '
```

```
    ' All done. Let the user know.
    '
    MsgBox "Database " & dbName & " created. "
    Screen.MousePointer = vbNormal
End Sub
```

32. Add the following code to the Class section of the CSchema class. This initializes the CParser class object used by the parsing routines.

```
Private Sub Class_Initialize()
    '
    ' Instantiate a new parser class.
    '
    Set m_Parser = New cParser
End Sub
```

How It Works

Two major functions are required to create a database file using this project: parsing the schema and creating the database. Each of these functions has been placed in its own class—CParser and CSchema, respectively.

CParser is a token-extracting class. It requires the file handle of an open text file, and returns each token within the file or verifies that the next token matches a given string. A token is defined as either an open or close parenthesis, or any string of non-blank characters delimited by spaces, commas, or tabs. The public method, GetToken, returns the next token in the file each time it is called.

Normally, the calling routine (in this case a routine in the CSchema class) is responsible for validating the token that is returned. However, you can use the ExpectToken method to have CParser get the next token and compare it against any string you pass. For example, the first token in a schema file must be the string, Database. Rather than using GetToken and then comparing the result, ExpectToken is used to indicate whether or not the token is present.

The CSchema class is responsible for making sense out of the tokens returned and compared by the CParser class. The schema has a specific syntax, which is checked step by step as the schema is parsed. The first token has to be Database, followed by a token that is assumed to be a database name. (Code could be added at this point to validate the database name. No such validation is done in this example.) The next token found must be an open parenthesis; the next is the string Table; then the table name, and so on. Each of CSchema's parsing routines handles one piece of the puzzle. ParseSchema calls ParseTable, which in turn calls ParseField, then ParseIndex. Finally, ParseSchema calls ParseRelation. If the schema file adheres to the schema syntax, the result is placed in the dbTables and dbRelations structures.

The dbTables and dbRelations structures are private properties in CSchema. Property Get routines are provided for each of the variables within the structure, so that an external routine can access the schema. Form1 uses these routines to build an outline of the schema. You can click on the plus and minus symbols in the outline to expand and collapse parts of the outline.

When you select the Create Database menu item, CSchema is called to do the actual creation using the loaded schema.

Visual Basic versions prior to 4.0 required that field and index objects be created individually for each field and index. This is no longer the case. When an object is appended to a collection, it is copied into the collection and the original object can be reused. CSchema takes advantage of this and reuses objects in the loops within CreateDatabase.

An additional class, the COutline class, is included with this project to make working with the outline control easier. This class provides methods to set the text and indent level of a line with one call, and expand the outline to a desired level. These routines could have been added to the code in Form1, but placing them in a class lets you use them easily in other projects. If you think of any additional functionality you wish to add to the outline control, simply add it to the COutline class. Just remember to instantiate one COutline class for each outline control on a form, and set its OutlineCtl property to refer to the specific outline control.

Comments

This project provides a general means of creating database files. By adding this code to other projects, you can forget about having to write code to create specific database files.

Since the major functionality has been placed in reuseable classes you can add enhancements as needed. For example, you might add code to validate field and index names as they are encountered, as well as to check that the field names appearing in the index field list match the fields added to the table. You might also add the ability to create other database objects, such as QueryDefs, to CSchema.

8.7 How do I...
Import Text Records into a Database?

COMPLEXITY: INTERMEDIATE
COMPATIBILITY: VB4 ONLY

Problem

Many of my Visual Basic applications need to import data from other sources. Some of that data resides in applications that have the ability to export the data as text files; other data is already in text files. How can I read these text files and import the data to my database?

Technique

Visual Basic 4.0 Professional Edition includes an installable ISAM driver for reading and writing text files. This driver allows you to use the standard data access objects to work with the text file as if you were working with a database object. You then simply read from one record set and add records to another.

In the mailing list example of this How-To, you will import data from three text files into a database. All three of these text files contain records in CommaDelimited format. This means each field varies in length and is separated by a comma.

The database schema, LOADTEXT.SCH, is as follows:

```
'
' Sample database schema for LOADTEXT.VBP
'
Database loadtext.mdb
(
    Table Organizations
    (
        Field ID (Long, Counter)
        Field Name (Text 40)
        Field Street_Address (Text 40)
        Field City (Text 20)
        Field State (Text 2)
        Field Zip (Text 9)
        Index OrgIdIndex
        (
            +ID,
            Primary
        )
        Index OrgNameIndex
        (
            +Name,
            Unique
        )
    )
    Table Members
    (
        Field ID (Long, Counter)
        Field Name (Text 20)
        Index MemberIdIndex
        (
            +ID,
            Primary
        )
        Index MemberNameIndex
        (
            +Name,
            Unique
        )
    )
    Table OrganizationMembers
    (
        Field Organization_ID (Long)
        Field Member_ID (Long)
        Index MemberOrganizationIndex
        (
            +Member_ID,
            +Organization_ID,
```

Continued on next page

919

Continued from previous page

```
          Primary
      )
      Index MemberIndex
      (
          +Member_ID
      )
      Index OrganizationIndex
      (
          +Organization_ID
      )
   )
)
```

The three text files containing the data to import are: ORGS.TXT, MEMBERS.TXT, and MEMBSHIP.TXT.

ORGS.TXT consists of records containing the names and addresses of the organizations on the mailing list. The format of the records is as follows:

```
1000 Friends of Washington,1224 Fourth Ave.,Seattle,WA,98101
```

MEMBERS.TXT is simply a list of names, one name per line, as follows:

```
Eleanor Bauxdale
```

MEMBSHIP.TXT contains records for the members of each organization in the database. There are two fields in each record of this file, one for the member's name and one for the name of the organization. Some people may be members of more than one organization. When the data is imported to the OrganizationMembers table, these names will be replaced by the associated IDs. The records in MEMBSHIP.TXT have the following format:

```
Eleanor Bauxdale,Washington State Audobon Society
Eleanor Bauxdale,1000 Friends of Washington
```

In order for Visual Basic to recognize these text files, you have to place some entries in your VB.INI file. Visual Basic uses these entries to locate the dynamic link library, MSTXT2016.DLL, that parses text files and defines some default characteristics of text files. The VB.INI file is typically located in the WINDOWS directory on the drive where Windows is located.

Be sure that the following entry is in the [Installable ISAMs] section of VB.INI:

```
Text=C:\WINDOWS\SYSTEM\MSTX2016.DLL
```

This entry tells Visual Basic that MSTXT2016.DLL resides in your C:\WINDOWS\SYSTEM. If the DLL is located elsewhere, you need to change the directory path of this Text-statement to match.

The following entries must appear in a [Text ISAM] section of VB.INI. If the section doesn't exist, you must create it. Here is an example of this section:

```
[Text ISAM]
Extensions=none,asc,csv,tab,txt
ColNameHeader=False
Format=TabDelimited
MaxScanRows=25
CharacterSet=OEM
```

These settings are typical for [Text ISAM] section; for more information regarding the meanings of these entries, see the Visual Basic Data Access Guide.

Setting Up a SCHEMA.INI File

Unlike database files, text files do not contain descriptions of their fields. Visual Basic has to be told the structure of the text file before it can be parsed and read. You need to create a SCHEMA.INI file to describe each of your text files. It is convenient to place the SCHEMA.INI file in the application directory, so that each application can have its own SCHEMA.INI file.

The SCHEMA.INI file used for this How-To is as follows:

```
[orgs.txt]
ColNameHeader=False
Format=Delimited(,)
MaxScanRows=25
CharacterSet=OEM
Col1=Name Char
Col2=Street_Address Char
Col3=City Char
Col4=State Char
Col5=Zip Char

[members.txt]
ColNameHeader=False
Format=Delimited(,)
MaxScanRows=25
CharacterSet=OEM
Col1=Name Char

[membship.txt]
ColNameHeader=False
Format=Delimited(,)
MaxScanRows=25
CharacterSet=OEM
Col1=Name Char
Col2=Organization Char
```

Each section in the SCHEMA.INI file describes a single text file. The Visual Basic Data Access Guide describes all of the entries in detail. The important entries for this example are the Format and Col*n* entries.

The Format entry defines how fields are separated. This example uses commas to separate the fields. Other frequently used formats are CSVDelimited, TabDelimited, and FixedLength. Like CommaDelimited format, the CSVDelimited format uses commas to separate the fields, along with quotes around text fields. This format allows commas to be embedded in the text data. TabDelimited text files are commonly used with spreadsheets, where columns of numbers are separated by tab characters. The FixedLength format requires that individual fields be the same size in each record. For example, the Name field would always be 20 characters long. If a name is shorter than 20 characters, it is padded with spaces. Most applications that export data have a function that can place its data into one of these formats.

The Col*n* entries describe each field in a record (Col1, Col2, etc.). The general format is

```
Coln=FieldName Format
```

You use the FieldName when referencing the field in Visual Basic. The FieldName is followed by the format of the field. All of our fields are of type Char. If the text file is a FixedLength type, the format includes the length of the field.

Error Handling

One additional consideration when importing data is the problem of errors occurring during the import. If an error occurs, you want to reject the entire import, otherwise, the database could become corrupt. Visual Basic provides a feature called *transaction processing* to handle these problems. All updates occurring between BeginTrans and EndTrans statements are handled as if they were one update. If anything goes wrong during the import, you can use the Rollback statement to abort the entire update. The Rollback statement returns the database to its state prior to the execution of the last BeginTrans statement.

Steps

Before running the LoadText project, you will need to create the sample database LOADTEXT.MDB, using the DBCreate program from How-To 8.6. After LOADTEXT.MDB has been created, open and run LOADTEXT.VBP. The running form should look like Figure 8-7-1.

Select the File Import menu item to load the database. When you execute LoadText, if the current directory is not the same as the project directory, the program will not find the database file, LOADTEXT.MDB, or the text files, ORGS.TXT, MEMBERS.TXT, and MEMBSHIP.TXT. When this happens, the program displays a dialog box that you can use to select the appropriate file in the project directory.

As described in the Technique section above, be sure that the VB.INI file has been updated and that the SCHEMA.INI file is in the project directory.

1. Create a new project named LOADTEXT.VBP. Add the objects and properties shown in Table 8-7-1 to Form1.

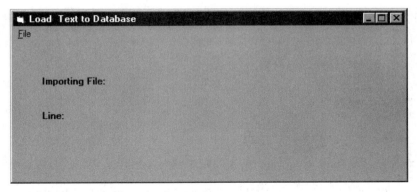

Figure 8-7-1 The form for the LoadText project

Table 8-7-1 Objects and properties for Form1

OBJECT	PROPERTY	SETTING
Form	Name	Form1
	Caption	"Load Text to Database"
CommonDialog	Name	CMDialog1
	DialogTitle	Import Text
	DefaultExt	"*.txt"
	Filter	"Text Files (*.txt)|*.txt"
Label	Name	LineLabel
	Caption	""
Label	Name	Label3
	Caption	"Line:"
Label	Name	FileNameLabel
	Caption	""
Label	Name	Label1
	Caption	"Importing File:"

2. Use the menu design window to create the menu for Form1 as shown in Table 8-7-2.

Table 8-7-2 Menu for Form1

MENU NAME	CAPTION
FileMenu	"&File"
—FileImport	"&Import"
—FileSep1	"-"
—FileExit	"E&xit"

3. Add the following code to the General Declarations section of Form1:

```
Option Explicit
'
' Variables to hold database objects
'
Private dbIn As Database
Private dbOut As Database
Private RecordsetIn As Recordset
'
' Application path
'
Private AppPath As String
```

4. Add the following code to the General section of Form1. This function returns the application path and makes sure that there is a backslash (\) at the end, so a filename can be appended to it.

```
Private Function GetAppPath() As String
    If Right$(App.Path, 1) = "\" Then
        GetAppPath = App.Path
    Else
        GetAppPath = App.Path & "\"
    End If
End Function
```

5. Add the following code to the General section of Form1. This function opens the ORGS.TXT file, reads the data, and adds new records to the Organizations table.

```
Private Function ImportOrgs() As Boolean
    Dim tbl As Recordset
    '
    ' Organization source file has 5 fields:
    '     Name
    '     Street address
    '     City
    '     State
    '     Zip
    '
    ' Open source text file
    '
    If OpenTextFile(GetAppPath()&"orgs.txt") Then
        LineLabel.Caption = ""
        LineLabel.Refresh
        '
        ' Open table to modify
        '
        Set tbl = dbOut.OpenRecordset("Organizations", dbOpenTable)
        '
        ' Start transaction
        '
        DBEngine.Workspaces(0).BeginTrans
        On Error GoTo ImportOrgs_Error
        '
```

```
    ' Read each line from source file
    '
    RecordsetIn.MoveFirst
    Do While Not RecordsetIn.EOF
        '
        ' Create new record
        '
        tbl.AddNew
        tbl("Name") = RecordsetIn("Name")
        tbl("Street_Address") = RecordsetIn("Street_Address")
        tbl("City") = RecordsetIn("City")
        tbl("State") = RecordsetIn("State")
        tbl("Zip") = RecordsetIn("Zip")
        tbl.Update
        LineLabel.Caption = RecordsetIn("Name")
        LineLabel.Refresh
        RecordsetIn.MoveNext
    Loop
    '
    ' All done commit changes
    '
    DBEngine.Workspaces(0).CommitTrans
    On Error GoTo 0
    RecordsetIn.Close
    ImportOrgs = True
  End If
  Exit Function
'
' Handle import errors
'
ImportOrgs_Error:
    '
    ' Woops...error in source file, abort transaction
    '
    MsgBox "Error " & Err & " - " & Error$(Err)
    On Error GoTo 0
    DBEngine.Workspaces(0).Rollback
    RecordsetIn.Close
    ImportOrgs = False
End Function
```

6. Add the following code to the General section of Form1. This function imports data from MEMBERS.TXT into the Members table.

```
Private Function ImportMembers() As Boolean
  Dim tbl As Recordset
  '
  ' Members source file has only one field: Name
  '
  ' Open source file
  '
  If OpenTextFile(GetAppPath()&"members.txt") Then
      LineLabel.Caption = ""
      LineLabel.Refresh
      '
```

Continued on next page

Continued from previous page

```
            ' Open table to load
            '
            Set tbl = dbOut.OpenRecordset("Members", dbOpenTable)
            '
            ' Start transaction
            '
            DBEngine.Workspaces(0).BeginTrans
            On Error GoTo ImportMembers_Error
            '
            ' Read each line from source file
            '
            RecordsetIn.MoveFirst
            Do While Not RecordsetIn.EOF
                '
                ' Create new record
                '
                tbl.AddNew
                tbl("Name") = RecordsetIn("Name")
                tbl.Update
                LineLabel.Caption = RecordsetIn("Name")
                LineLabel.Refresh
                RecordsetIn.MoveNext
            Loop
            '
            ' All done commit changes
            '
            DBEngine.Workspaces(0).CommitTrans
            On Error GoTo 0
            RecordsetIn.Close
            ImportMembers = True
        End If
        Exit Function
'
' Handle import errors
'
ImportMembers_Error:
    '
    ' Woops...error in source file, abort transaction
    '
    MsgBox "Error " & Err & " - " & Error$(Err)
    On Error GoTo 0
    DBEngine.Workspaces(0).Rollback
    If Not RecordsetIn Is Nothing Then
        RecordsetIn.Close
        Set RecordsetIn = Nothing
    End If
    ImportMembers = False
End Function
```

7. Add the following code to the General section of Form1. This function imports the data in MEMBSHIP.TXT into the OrganizationMember table. Unlike the other two tables (Organizations and Members), the OrganizationMember table doesn't accept data directly from the MEMBSHIP.TXT file. Rather, the input data is used

to look up the ID fields from the Member and Organization tables using the Seek methods. The IDs are then entered into the OrganizationMember record.

```
Private Function CreateRelations() As Boolean
    Dim tbl As Recordset
    Dim members As Recordset
    Dim orgs As Recordset
    '
    ' Each line of 'membship.txt' has two fields:
    '    Member name
    '    Organization name
    '
    ' Open source file
    '
    If OpenTextFile(GetAppPath()&"membship.txt") Then
        LineLabel.Caption = ""
        LineLabel.Refresh
        '
        ' Open table to load
        '
        Set tbl = dbOut.OpenRecordset("OrganizationMembers", dbOpenTable)
        '
        ' Open organization and members tables for lookup
        '
        Set orgs = dbOut.OpenRecordset("Organizations", dbOpenTable)
        orgs.Index = "OrgNameIndex"
        Set members = dbOut.OpenRecordset("Members", dbOpenTable)
        members.Index = "MemberNameIndex"
        '
        ' Start transaction
        '
        DBEngine.Workspaces(0).BeginTrans
        On Error GoTo CreateRelations_Error
        '
        ' Read each line from source file
        '
        RecordsetIn.MoveFirst
        Do While Not RecordsetIn.EOF
            '
            ' Lookup Organization ID
            '
            orgs.Seek "=", RecordsetIn("Organization")
            '
            ' Lookup Member Name
            '
            members.Seek "=", RecordsetIn("Name")
            '
            ' Create new record
            '
            tbl.AddNew
            tbl("Organization_ID") = orgs("ID")
            tbl("Member_ID") = members("ID")
            tbl.Update
            LineLabel.Caption = RecordsetIn("Organization") _
                             & "/" & RecordsetIn("Name")
```

Continued on next page

Continued from previous page

```
        LineLabel.Refresh
        RecordsetIn.MoveNext
    Loop
    '
    ' All done commit changes
    '
    DBEngine.Workspaces(0).CommitTrans
    On Error GoTo 0
    RecordsetIn.Close
    CreateRelations = True
    End If
    Exit Function
'
' Handle import errors
'
CreateRelations_Error:
    '
    ' Woops...error in source file, abort transaction
    '
    MsgBox "Error " & Err & " - " & Error$(Err)
    On Error GoTo 0
    DBEngine.Workspaces(0).Rollback
    RecordsetIn.Close
    CreateRelations = False
End Function
```

8. Add the following code to the General section of Form1, to open the LOADTEXT.MDB database. If the operation fails, the user is prompted to choose another file or cancel the operation.

```
Private Function OpenDB(Filename As String) As Boolean
    Dim FilenameToTry As String
    Dim MsgRtn As Integer
    Dim Finished As Boolean
    '
    ' Assume success
    '
    OpenDB = True
    FilenameToTry = Filename
    Finished = False
    Do While Not Finished
        '
        ' If a filename is needed prompt for it
        '
        If FilenameToTry = "" Then
            FilenameToTry = PromptForFilename(FilenameToTry, _
                        "Open Database", _
                        "Access Files (*.mdb)|*.mdb", "*.mdb")
            If FilenameToTry = "" Then
                OpenDB = False
                Finished = True
            End If
        End If
        '
```

```
   ' Open the database.
   '
   If Not Finished Then
       On Error Resume Next
       Set dbOut = DBEngine.Workspace(0).OpenDatabase(FilenameToTry)
       If Err Then
           '
           ' Couldn't open file on first try ... path may be wrong
           ' let user try with Open Dialog
           '
           MsgRtn = MsgBox("Error " & Err & " - " & Error$(Err) _
                           & Chr$(13) & Chr$(10) _
                           & "Do you want to try another file?", _
                           vbCritical + vbYesNo, _
                           "DATABASE OPEN ERROR")
           On Error GoTo 0
           FilenameToTry = ""
           If MsgRtn <> vbYes Then
               OpenDB = False
               Finished = True
           End If
       Else
           Finished = True
       End If
   End If
Loop
End Function
```

9. Add the following code to the General section of Form1, to open a text file. If the operation fails, the user is prompted to choose another file or cancel the operation.

```
Private Function OpenTextFile(Filename As String) As Boolean
    Dim FilenameToTry As String
    Dim FilePath As String
    Dim TableIn As String
    Dim MsgRtn As Integer
    Dim Finished As Boolean
    Dim x As Integer
    '
    ' Assume success
    '
    OpenTextFile = True
    FilenameToTry = Filename
    Finished = False
    Do While Not Finished
        '
        ' If a filename is needed prompt for it
        '
        If FilenameToTry = "" Then
            FilenameToTry = PromptForFilename(Filename, _
                            "Open Text File", _
                            "Text Files (*.txt)|*.txt", "*.txt")
            If FilenameToTry = "" Then
                OpenTextFile = False
                Finished = True
```

Continued on next page

Continued from previous page

```
            End If
        End If
    '
    ' Open the text file.
    '
    If Not Finished Then
        For x = Len(FilenameToTry) To 1 Step -1
            If Mid$(FilenameToTry, x, 1) = "\" Then
                Exit For
            End If
        Next x
        If x > 0 Then
            FilePath = Mid$(FilenameToTry, 1, x)
        Else
            FilePath = "."
        End If
        TableIn = Mid$(FilenameToTry, x + 1)

        FileNameLabel.Caption = FilenameToTry
        Set dbIn = DBEngine.Workspaces(0).OpenDatabase(FilePath, _
                    False, False, "TEXT")
        On Error Resume Next
        Set RecordsetIn = dbIn.OpenRecordset(TableIn)
        If Err Then
            '
            ' Error opening text file. See if user wants to try
            ' again.
            '
            MsgRtn = MsgBox("Error " & Err & " - " & Error$(Err) _
                        & Chr$(13) & Chr$(10) _
                        & "Do you want to try another file?", _
                        vbCritical + vbYesNo, _
                        "TEXT FILE OPEN ERROR")
            On Error GoTo 0
            FilenameToTry = ""
            If MsgRtn <> vbYes Then
                OpenTextFile = False
                Finished = True
            End If
        Else
            On Error GoTo 0
            Finished = True
        End If
    End If
    Loop
End Function
```

10. Add the following code to the General section of Form1. This function prompts the user to select a file and returns the filename chosen. If the user cancels the selection, an empty string ("") is returned.

```
Private Function PromptForFilename(Filename As String, _
                Title As String, Filter As String, _
                DefExt As String) As String
```

```
'
' Load properties
'
CMDialog1.DialogTitle = Title
CMDialog1.Filter = Filter
CMDialog1.DefaultExt = DefExt
CMDialog1.Filename = Filename
'
' Set CancelError = True so that we can tell if the
' user is giving up
'
CMDialog1.CancelError = True
On Error Resume Next
CMDialog1.ShowOpen
If Err Then
    '
    ' No file specified
    '
    PromptForFilename = ""
Else
    '
    ' File specified, return name as value of this function
    '
    PromptForFilename = CMDialog1.Filename
End If
On Error GoTo 0
End Function
```

11. Add the following code to the FileImport_Click event of Form1. This routine is executed when the user selects the File Import menu item. It calls OpenDB to open LOADTEXT.MDB, and then calls ImportOrgs, ImportMembers, and CreateRelations. If any of the import routines fail, the database is restored using the Rollback statement.

```
Private Sub FileImport_Click()
    Dim Success As Boolean
    '
    ' Change mouse pointer to hourglass.
    '
    Screen.MousePointer = vbHourglass
    '
    ' Open database.
    '
    If OpenDB(AppPath & "loadtext.mdb") Then
        '
        ' Database opened, start a transaction. The subsequent
        ' table modifications are contained within their own
        ' transactions.
        '
        DBEngine.Workspaces(0).BeginTrans
        '
        ' Import Organization data.
        '
        Success = ImportOrgs()
```

Continued on next page

Continued from previous page

```
        If Success Then
            '
            ' Import Member data.
            '
            Success = ImportMembers()
        End If
        If Success Then
            '
            ' Import Relations.
            '
            Success = CreateRelations()
        End If
        '
        ' If the entire import completed successfully then commit
        ' the changes otherwise roll the database back to its prior
        ' state
        '
        If Success Then
            DBEngine.Workspaces(0).CommitTrans
        Else
            DBEngine.Workspaces(0).Rollback
        End If
    End If
    '
    ' Restore mouse pointer to normal
    '
    Screen.MousePointer = vbNormal
    If Success Then
        MsgBox "Data imported."
    Else
        MsgBox "Data import failed."
    End If
    FileNameLabel = ""
    LineLabel = ""
End Sub
```

12. Add the following code to the Form_Load event for Form1:

```
Private Sub Form_Load()
    '
    ' Get the application path
    '
    AppPath = GetAppPath()
End Sub
```

13. Add the following code to the FileExit_Click event for Form1. This gets executed when the File Exit menu item is selected, and simply ends the program.

```
Private Sub FileExit_Click()
    End
End Sub
```

How It Works

When the user selects the File Import menu item, the FileImport_Click event opens the database and begins a transaction. Next, the functions ImportOrgs, ImportMembers, and CreateRelations are called.

ImportOrgs, ImportMembers, and CreateRelations are almost identical in structure. They each open an input text file and loop through its records. The text file operates just like a record set attached to a database. As far as your program is concerned, there is no difference except that you can't delete or update data in a text file.

The Organizations and Members tables each have a counter field, ID. This field gets set to a unique number automatically by Visual Basic whenever a record is added. The remaining fields are set from their equivalent fields in the respective text files.

The OrganizationMembers table relates members to their organizations. Instead of holding the names of the members and organizations, this table stores the ID fields from the related records in the Organizations and Members tables. This allows one person to be a member of several organizations and one organization to have several members.

Comments

You can use the routines in this How-To as the basis for future import routines you need. By altering the SCHEMA.INI file, you can import files in any of the standard text file formats. None of the program code will change because all of the text files look the same to the program.

This example does some error checking with regard to Visual Basic and Data Access errors. There is no error checking, however, devoted to integrity of the data. For example, the lookups that take place in CreateRelations assume that the matching records will be in the Organizations and Members tables. You can add additional error checking to abort the import if inconsistencies are found in the data.

8.8 How do I...
Find Incorrectly Spelled Names in a Database?

COMPLEXITY: INTERMEDIATE
COMPATIBILITY: VB4 ONLY

Problem

In user interface design today, there is a trend away from using codes to locate records in a database. In my applications I want the user to be able to find names using list boxes rather than ID codes. In many cases, the names I want to search are not part of the primary key; therefore, little error checking is done when the name is entered. This presents a problem, because these names are more likely to be entered incorrectly. How can I locate records in a database where the names I'm searching for or the search entries themselves may be spelled incorrectly?

Technique

You're probably wishing there was a way to convert names to strings that would make misspelled names or names with alternate spellings appear equal. Well, you're in luck: such an algorithm does exist. It is called Soundex, because it attempts to create a code based on the sound of the name rather than its spelling.

According to Donald Knuth, in his classic *The Art of Programming, Vol. 3, Searching and Sorting,* the Soundex algorithm was originally developed by Margaret K. Odell and Robert C. Russell [cf. U.S. Patents 1261167 (1918), 1435663 (1922)]. This algorithm changes a string containing a person's last name into a string containing a letter followed by three numeric characters. The characters of the resulting string will often be the same for similar sounding names. For example, the Soundex codes for Smith, Smythe, and Smyth are all S530.

Steps

Before running the Soundex project, you will need to create a sample database, SOUNDEX.MDB, using the DBCreate program from How-To 8.6. The schema file, SOUNDEX.SCH, is loaded by the DBCreate program, and the SOUNDEX.MDB file is then created. Create the schema file, SOUNDEX.SCH, as follows:

```
'
' Sample database schema for SOUNDEX.VBP
'
Database soundex.mdb
(
    Table Names
    (
        Field ID (Long, Counter)
        Field LastName (Text 20)
        Field FirstName (Text 20)
        Field Soundex (Text 4)
        Index IdIndex
        (
            +ID,
            Primary
        )
        Index SoundexIndex
        (
            +Soundex
        )
    )
)
```

The Soundex project imports a list of names to the SOUNDEX.MDB database. As described in How-To 8.7, be sure that your VB.INI file is updated then create a SCHEMA.INI file to define the NAMES.TXT file, as follows:

```
[names.txt]
ColNameHeader=False
Format=Delimited(,)
MaxScanRows=25
CharacterSet=OEM
Col1=LastName Char
Col2=FirstName Char
```

This file is used to import the names in the NAMES.TXT file into the database using the technique demonstrated in How-To 8.7.

With these fundamentals set up, you can now open and run SOUNDEX.VBP. The running program looks like Figure 8-8-1. The first time you run Soundex, it loads the names in NAMES.TXT when the program starts, so it may take a number of seconds for the form to load.

All the names in the database will be displayed in the list box on the right. Enter a name in the Last Name text box and click on the Search button. Try names that match those in the list box, as well as similar names and misspelled names. Each time you press the Search button, the database is searched for similar names having the same Soundex code as the code for the name you entered. All matching names are displayed in the list box on the left side.

1. Create a new project named SOUNDEX.VBP. Enter the objects and properties shown in Table 8-8-1 to Form1.

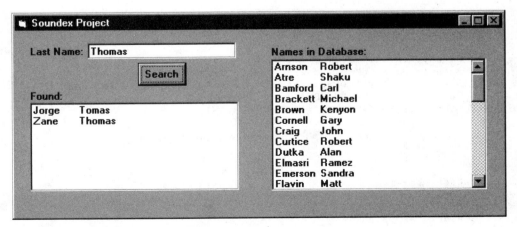

Figure 8-8-1 The Soundex project in action

Table 8-8-1 Objects and properties for Form1

OBJECT	PROPERTY	SETTING
Form	Name	Form1
	Caption	"Soundex Project"
	BackColor	&H00C0C0C0&
Label	Name	Label1
	Caption	"Last Name:"
	BackStyle	0-Transparent
TextBox	Name	Text1
	Text	""
CommandButton	Name	Command3D1
	Caption	"Search"
Label	Name	Label2
	Caption	"Names in Database:"
ListBox	Name	List1
	TabStop	False
Label	Name	Label3
	Caption	"Found:"
ListBox	Name	List2
	Sorted	True
	TabStop	False
CommonDialog	Name	CMDialog1

2. Create a new module named SOUNDEX.BAS, and add the following code to the General Declarations section.

```
'
' Windows API functions and constants
'
Declare Function GetDialogBaseUnits Lib "User" () As Long
Declare Function SendMessage Lib "User" (ByVal hWnd As Integer, ByVal
wMsg As Integer, ByVal wParam As Integer, lParam As Any) As Long
Public Const WM_USER = &H400
Public Const LB_SETTABSTOPS = (WM_USER + 19)
```

3. Add the following code to the General Declarations section of Form1.

```
Option Explicit
'
' Database objects.
'
Private db As Database
Private dbIn As Database
Private RecordsetIn As Recordset
'
' Soundex class.
'
```

```
Private Soundex As CSoundex
'
' Application path.
'
Private AppPath As String
```

4. Add the following code to the Form_Load event. This routine instantiates the CSoundex class and calls CreateDatabase to import the Names table.

```
Private Sub Form_Load()
    AppPath = GetAppPath()
    '
    ' Display form right away since opening the
    ' database will take a while
    '
    Form1.Show
    Form1.Refresh
    '
    ' Set pointer to hourglass
    '
    Screen.MousePointer = vbHourglass
    '
    ' Instantiate a CSoundex class object
    '
    Set Soundex = New CSoundex
    '
    ' Import the name records
    '
    CreateDatabase
    '
    ' Load records into list box
    '
    LoadListOfAllRecords
    '
    ' We're done ... return mouse pointer to normal
    '
    Screen.MousePointer = vbNormal
End Sub
```

5. Add the following code to the General section of Form1. This function, initially used in How-To 8.7, returns the application path and appends a backslash character, if necessary.

```
Private Function GetAppPath() As String
    '
    ' Get the application path and put a "\" on the
    ' end if necessary.
    '
    If Right$(App.Path, 1) = "\" Then
        GetAppPath = App.Path
    Else
        GetAppPath = App.Path & "\"
    End If
End Function
```

6. Add the following code to the General section of Form1. This routine loads List2 with a list of all names in the database.

```
Private Sub LoadListOfAllRecords()
    Dim snap As Recordset
    Dim tabstop As Long
    Dim wRtn As Integer
    '
    ' Create two columns in the list box
    '
    tabstop = 4 * 20
    wRtn = SendMessage(list2.hWnd, LB_SETTABSTOPS, 1, tabstop)
    '
    ' Get a dynaset containing all of the records in
    ' the Names table
    '
    Set snap = db.OpenRecordset("Names", dbOpenSnapshot)
    If snap.RecordCount > 0 Then
        snap.MoveFirst
        '
        ' Add each record in the dynaset to list2
        '
        Do While (snap.EOF = False)
            list2.AddItem snap("LastName") & Chr$(9) _
                          & snap("FirstName")
            snap.MoveNext
        Loop
    End If
End Sub
```

7. Add the following code to the General section of Form1. This routine opens the SOUNDEX.MDB database, deletes any records already in the Names table, and imports data from the NAMES.TXT file.

```
Private Sub CreateDatabase()
    Dim Success As Boolean
    '
    ' Change mouse pointer to hourglass.
    '
    Screen.MousePointer = vbHourglass
    '
    ' Open database.
    '
    If OpenDB(AppPath & "soundex.mdb") Then
        '
        'Run action query to delete existing
        'data in the Names table
        '
        db.Execute "DELETE FROM Names"
        '
        ' Database opened, start a transaction. The subsequent
        ' table modifications are contained within their own
        ' transactions.
        '
```

```
        DBEngine.Workspaces(0).BeginTrans
        '
        ' Import Names data.
        '
        Success = ImportNames()
        '
        ' If the entire import completed successfully then commit
        ' the changes otherwise roll the database back to its prior
        ' state
        '
        If Success Then
            DBEngine.Workspaces(0).CommitTrans
        Else
            DBEngine.Workspaces(0).Rollback
        End If
    End If
    '
    ' Restore mouse pointer to normal
    '
    Screen.MousePointer = vbNormal
    If Not Success Then
        MsgBox "Data import failed."
        End
    End If
End Sub
```

8. Add the following code to the General section of Form1. This routine is similar to the import routines in How-To 8.7. It imports the names to the database and assigns the Soundex codes to the records.

```
Private Function ImportNames() As Boolean
    Dim tbl As Recordset
    '
    ' Import the Name table
    '
    ' Open source file
    '
    If OpenTextFile("names.txt") Then
        '
        ' Open table to load
        '
        Set tbl = db.OpenRecordset("Names", dbOpenTable)
        '
        ' Start transaction
        '
        DBEngine.Workspaces(0).BeginTrans
        On Error GoTo ImportNames_Error
        '
        ' Read each line from source file
        '
        RecordsetIn.MoveFirst
        Do While Not RecordsetIn.EOF
            '
            ' Create new record
            '
```

Continued on next page

Continued from previous page

```
            tbl.AddNew
            tbl("LastName") = RecordsetIn("LastName")
            tbl("FirstName") = RecordsetIn("FirstName")
            tbl("Soundex") = _
                    Soundex.MakeSoundex(RecordsetIn("LastName"))
            tbl.Update
            RecordsetIn.MoveNext
        Loop
        '
        ' All done commit changes
        '
        DBEngine.Workspaces(0).CommitTrans
        On Error GoTo 0
        RecordsetIn.Close
        ImportNames = True
    End If
    Exit Function
'
' Handle import errors
'
ImportNames_Error:
    '
    ' Woops...error in source file, abort transaction
    '
    MsgBox "Error " & Err & " - " & Error$(Err)
    On Error GoTo 0
    DBEngine.Workspaces(0).Rollback
    If Not RecordsetIn Is Nothing Then
        RecordsetIn.Close
        Set RecordsetIn = Nothing
    End If
    ImportNames = False
End Function
```

9. Add the following code to the Command1_Click event. This routine is executed when the Search button is pressed. It loads List1 with a list of records with Soundex codes that match the Soundex code of the entry in Text1.

```
Private Sub Command1_Click()
    Dim snap    As Recordset
    Dim tabstop As Long
    Dim wRtn    As Integer
    Dim Criteria As String
    '
    ' Clear search results list box
    '
    list1.Clear
    '
    ' Set tab stops
    '
    tabstop = 4 * 20
    wRtn = SendMessage(list1.hWnd, LB_SETTABSTOPS, 1, tabstop)

    ' Create a snapshot containing records that match the soundex
```

```
' code for the name entered in text1.
'
Criteria = "WHERE Soundex = " & "'" _
           & Soundex.MakeSoundex(CStr(text1.Text)) & "'"
Set snap = db.OpenRecordset("SELECT * FROM Names " & Criteria, _
                            dbOpenSnapshot)
If snap.RecordCount > 0 Then
    snap.MoveFirst
    '
    ' Add result set to List1
    '
    Do While (snap.EOF = False)
        List1.AddItem snap("FirstName") & Chr$(9) _
                      & snap("LastName")
        snap.MoveNext
    Loop
Else
    MsgBox "No matching name found."
End If
End Sub
```

10. Add the following code to the General section of Form1. (Note: these routines are identical to the corresponding routines in How-To 8.7.)

```
Private Function OpenDB(Filename As String) As Boolean
    Dim FilenameToTry As String
    Dim MsgRtn As Integer
    Dim Finished As Boolean
    '
    ' Assume success
    '
    OpenDB = True
    FilenameToTry = Filename
    Finished = False
    Do While Not Finished
        '
        ' If a filename is needed prompt for it
        '
        If FilenameToTry = "" Then
            FilenameToTry = PromptForFilename(FilenameToTry, _
                            "Open Database", _
                            "Access Files (*.mdb)|*.mdb", "*.mdb")
            If FilenameToTry = "" Then
                OpenDB = False
                Finished = True
            End If
        End If
        '
        ' Open the database.
        '
        If Not Finished Then
            On Error Resume Next
            Set db = DBEngine.Workspaces(0).OpenDatabase(FilenameToTry)
            If Err Then
                '
```

Continued on next page

Continued from previous page

```
                ' Couldn't open file on first try ... path may be wrong
                ' let user try with Open Dialog
                '
                MsgRtn = MsgBox("Error " & Err & " - " & Error$(Err) _
                                & Chr$(13) & Chr$(10) _
                                & "Do you want to try another file?", _
                                vbCritical + vbYesNo, _
                                "DATABASE OPEN ERROR")
                On Error GoTo 0
                FilenameToTry = ""
                If MsgRtn <> vbYes Then
                    OpenDB = False
                    Finished = True
                End If
            Else
                Finished = True
            End If
        End If
    Loop
End Function

Private Function OpenTextFile(Filename As String) As Boolean
    Dim FilenameToTry As String
    Dim FilePath As String
    Dim TableIn As String
    Dim MsgRtn As Integer
    Dim Finished As Boolean
    Dim x As Integer
    '
    ' Assume success
    '
    OpenTextFile = True
    FilenameToTry = AppPath & Filename
    Finished = False
    Do While Not Finished
        '
        ' If a filename is needed prompt for it
        '
        If FilenameToTry = "" Then
            FilenameToTry = PromptForFilename(Filename, _
                            "Open Text File", _
                            "Text Files (*.txt)|*.txt", "*.txt")
            If FilenameToTry = "" Then
                OpenTextFile = False
                Finished = True
            End If
        End If
        '
        ' Open the text file.
        '
        If Not Finished Then
            For x = Len(FilenameToTry) To 1 Step -1
                If Mid$(FilenameToTry, x, 1) = "\" Then
                    Exit For
                End If
```

```
            Next x
            If x > 0 Then
               FilePath = Mid$(FilenameToTry, 1, x)
            Else
               FilePath = "."
            End If
            TableIn = Mid$(FilenameToTry, x + 1)

            Set dbIn = DBEngine.Workspaces(0).OpenDatabase(FilePath, _
                                                 False, False, "TEXT")

            On Error Resume Next
            Set RecordsetIn = dbIn.OpenRecordset(TableIn)
            If Err Then
                '
                ' Error opening text file. See if user wants to try again.
                '
                MsgRtn = MsgBox("Error " & Err & " - " & Error$(Err) _
                             & Chr$(13) & Chr$(10) _
                             & "Do you want to try another file?", _
                             vbCritical + vbYesNo, _
                             "TEXT FILE OPEN ERROR")

                On Error GoTo 0
                FilenameToTry = ""
                If MsgRtn <> vbYes Then
                    OpenTextFile = False
                    Finished = True
                End If
            Else
                On Error GoTo 0
                Finished = True
            End If
        End If
    Loop
End Function

Private Function PromptForFilename(Filename As String, _
                 Title As String, Filter As String, _
                 DefExt As String) As String
    '
    ' Load properties
    '
    CMDialog1.DialogTitle = Title
    CMDialog1.Filter = Filter
    CMDialog1.DefaultExt = DefExt
    CMDialog1.Filename = Filename
    '
    ' Set CancelError = True so that we can tell if the
    ' user is giving up
    '
    CMDialog1.CancelError = True
    On Error Resume Next
    CMDialog1.ShowOpen
    If Err Then
        '
        ' No file specified
```

Continued on next page

943

Continued from previous page

```
    '
    PromptForFilename = ""
  Else
    '
    ' File specified, return name as value of this function
    '
    PromptForFilename = CMDialog1.Filename
  End If
  On Error GoTo 0
End Function
```

The CSoundex Class

11. Use the Insert Class Module menu item to add a new class, CSoundex, to your project. Open your new class module in the project window. Use the properties window to set the module's name to CSoundex, and set the Creatable property to True. This class creates the Soundex code for a given string.

12. Add the following code to the General Declarations section of the CSoundex class, to declare an array that will hold a digit for each letter in the alphabet.

```
Option Explicit
'
' Array of codes. One for each letter of the alphabet.
' "A" is index 0, "Z" is index 25.
'
Private Codes(25) As Byte
```

13. Add the following code to the Class_Initialize event of the CSoundex class:

```
Private Sub Class_Initialize()
    '
    ' Substitution codes for A-Z (0-25)
    '
    Codes(0) = 0
    Codes(1) = 1
    Codes(2) = 2
    Codes(3) = 3
    Codes(4) = 0
    Codes(5) = 1
    Codes(6) = 2
    Codes(7) = 0
    Codes(8) = 0
    Codes(9) = 2
    Codes(10) = 2
    Codes(11) = 4
    Codes(12) = 5
    Codes(13) = 5
    Codes(14) = 0
    Codes(15) = 1
    Codes(16) = 2
    Codes(17) = 6
    Codes(18) = 2
```

```
        Codes(19) = 3
        Codes(20) = 0
        Codes(21) = 1
        Codes(22) = 0
        Codes(23) = 2
        Codes(24) = 0
        Codes(25) = 2
End Sub
```

14. Add the following code to the General section of the CSoundex class. This is the function that creates a Soundex code from a given string.

```
Public Function MakeSoundex(From As String) As String
    '
    ' Create a soundex code for a given string
    '
    Dim PrevCode As Byte
    Dim CurrentCode As Byte
    Dim i As Integer
    Dim j As Integer
    Dim CurrentChar As Integer
    Dim Soundx As String
    Dim A As Byte
    Dim Z As Byte

    If (Len(From) = 0) Then
        MakeSoundex = ""
        Exit Function
    End If

    Z = Asc("Z")
    A = Asc("A")
    '
    ' Start with the first letter of the string.
    '
    Soundx = UCase$(Left$(From, 1))
    '
    ' Hold the code for the first character.
    '
    PrevCode = Codes(Asc(Left$(Soundx, 1)) - Asc("A"))
    '
    ' Process each letter until the string is exhausted
    ' or the soundex string is 4 characters long.
    '
    i = 2
    Do While (i <= Len(From)) And Len(Soundx) < 4
        CurrentChar = Asc(UCase$(Mid$(From, i, 1)))
        If (CurrentChar >= A And CurrentChar <= Z) Then
            '
            ' Get the code for the current character.
            '
            CurrentCode = Codes(CurrentChar - A)
            '
            ' If the code is not 0 and not equal to the
            ' previous code, add it to the soundex string.
```

Continued on next page

Continued from previous page

```
            '
            If (CurrentCode <> 0) Then
                If (CurrentCode <> PrevCode) Then
                    Soundx = Soundx & Format$(CurrentCode)
                End If
            End If
            '
            ' Hold the code for the current character.
            '
            PrevCode = CurrentCode
        End If
        i = i + 1
    Loop
    '
    ' Pad the soundex string if it is less than 4 characters long.
    '
    Soundx = Left$(Soundx & "0000", 4)
    '
    ' Return the soundex code.
    '
    MakeSoundex = Soundx
End Function
```

How the Soundex Algorithm Works

The Soundex algorithm returns a four-character string that is constructed according to the following rules:

a)   Retain the first letter of the name, and drop all other occurrences of A, E, H, I, O, U, W, and Y.

b)   Assign the following numbers to the remaining letters:

B, F, P, V	1
C, G, J, K, Q, S, X, Z	2
D, T	3
L	4
M, N	5
R	6

c)   Retain only one occurrence of duplicate adjacent codes.

d)   If the result is less than four characters long, add enough trailing zeros to make the result four characters long. Or, if the result is longer than four characters, retain only the first four.

   The Codes array holds the numeric codes associated with the letters in the alphabet. The letters A, E, H, I, O, U, W, and Y are assigned a value of zero. If a zero is encountered during the Soundex conversion, the letter is skipped.

How It Works

When records are added to the Names table, the Soundex code for the person's last name is computed and stored in the Soundex field of the record. An index exists based on the Soundex field, so records can be accessed quickly by the Soundex codes. When the user presses the Search button, the Soundex code for the string in Text1 is computed, and any names with matching Soundex codes are added to the Found list.

Comments

The Soundex code is not 100 percent accurate in finding misspellings. If the first letter is wrong, the Soundex codes will not match. For example, Anderson and Endleson sound similar, but their codes will start with A and E, respectively; this obscures the similarity. Remember that Soundex is a tool, not a cure-all.

9

TIPS AND TRICKS

9

TIPS AND TRICKS

How do I...

What programmer doesn't have a bag of tricks? In this chapter, we offer you some neat tips and tricks from ours. Use them to make your programming life easier.

Many of the techniques in this chapter use one or more Windows API calls as follows:

WINDOWS API	HOW-TO'S
BringWindowToTop	9.6
CreateProcess	9.6
FindWindow	9.6
GetLastError	9.6

Continued on next page

Continued from previous page

WINDOWS API	HOW-TO'S
GetParent	9.6
GetProfileString	9.7
GetSystemDirectory	9.6
GetWindow	9.6
GetWindowPlacement	9.6
GetWindowRect	9.6
GetWindowsDirectory	9.6
GetWindowText	9.6
GetWindowThreadProcessId	9.6
IsIconic	9.6
IsWindow	9.6
IsWindowVisible	9.6
IsZoomed	9.6
MoveWindow	9.6
RegCloseKey	9.3
RegCreateKey	9.3
RegOpenKey	9.3
RegQueryValue	9.3
RegSetValueEx	9.3
SendMessage	9.6
SetForegroundWindow	9.6
SetWindowLong	9.6
SetWindowPlacement	9.6
SetWindowText	9.6
ShowWindow	9.6
SystemParametersInfo	9.3
WaitForInputIdle	9.6
WinExec	9.6

9.1 Return an Ordinal Number for Any Number

If you ever need to refer to an ordinal number in a text string—for example, popping up a special message such as "Congratulations on your 50th wedding anniversary"—this How-To will show you how to do it.

9.2 Return an Anniversary Description for Any Set of Dates

Want to send custom messages to people on their special days? Once you've recorded birth dates, wedding dates, job start dates, etc. for friends and family, you can quickly compute how old they'll be on their next birthdays, how many years they'll have been married or on the job, and so forth. This How-To will demonstrate all of this and more.

9.3   Set the Desktop Wallpaper

You may have developed some software that produces graphics that are updated and displayed to the user in the background (such as current sales and current market information). This type of information is relatively static, so it may be suitable to put it on the desktop, as the wallpaper. This How-To will show you how to easily change the wallpapar from your VB code.

9.4   Generate an Interval Series of Dates

The How-To will give you a way to generate any interval series of dates based on certain options. For instance, you may have created a program to schedule meetings and want to offer a wide variety of scheduling options, from daily through biannually. You might also offer the flexibility of scheduling either a fixed number of meetings or a set of meetings within a date range.

9.5   Use Dir$ to Recursively Search a Directory Tree

Yes, there is a way to use the Dir function recursively. This How-To will demonstrate searching an entire disk or directory tree, gathering all the files or directories into a structure that can be manipulated.

9.6   Use Notepad as a Debugging Window

This How-To shows you a way to output debugging information both while working in the Visual Basic development environment and when running as a compiled executable. It's a simple unified approach; the output statements don't require additional tests, and the output can be turned on remotely — at a client site. The output can optionally be saved to a file. This How-To shows you how to use Notepad for this sort of reporting.

9.7   Parse a String into Its Elements

This How-To will give you a general-purpose string parsing function. You can use it to parse a string into its separate elements—for example, the command-line parameters that are passed to an application, or a null-separated string returned from one of the Windows Profile functions, or lines of text from a tab-delimited data file.

9.8   Manipulate Bits, Bytes, Words, and Dwords

In this How-To you will see all of the following neatly packaged into a BAS file: pack a dword (double word, represented with long values in Visual Basic) with two words (integers in Visual Basic); evaluate the high byte of the low word of a dword; set, clear, or toggle bits within a word; and other such numeric manipulations. These are not very easy to do within Visual Basic, considering VB's lack of unsigned integers and shift operators. With these manipulation routines, you won't have to worry about overflow or sign-bit problems.

9.1 How do I...
Return an Ordinal Number for Any Number?

COMPLEXITY: EASY
COMPATIBILITY: VB3 OR VB4

Problem

Sometimes I want to refer to an ordinal number in a text string. For example, I may want to pop up a special message such as "Congratulations on your 50th wedding anniversary." Is there a common routine that I could use to calculate any ordinal number?

Technique

A public function in a standard module provides an ordinal number when passed any long integer value, calling upon a private function to compute the ordinal suffix. Once you examine the translation of some numbers to their ordinal equivalents, you'll see that there's not much of a trick to the process. Every number ending in 4 through 9 is suffixed with *th*. A number ending in 1 is usually suffixed with *st*. A number ending in 2 is usually suffixed with *nd,* and a number ending in 3 is usually suffixed with *rd.* The only exceptions are 11, 12, and 13, which are each suffixed with *th*.

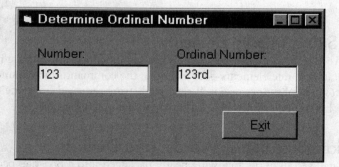

Figure 9-1-1 The ordinal number calculator in action

This simple project also gives you a handy technique for limiting the input in a text box to a long integer value. The KeyPress event checks every keystroke to ensure that no keystroke is accepted that would change the entry from being a long integer.

Steps

Open and run ORDINAL.VBP. Begin entering digits in the left-hand text box, and you'll see matching ordinal numbers in the right-hand text box. Here are the steps for setting up the ordinal number calculator.

1. Create a new project called ORDINAL.VBP. Create a form with controls arranged to approximate the one shown in Figure 9-1-1. Set the form objects and properties as shown in Table 9-1-1, and save the form as ORDINAL.FRM.

Table 9-1-1 ORDINAL.FRM form properties

OBJECT	PROPERTY	SETTING
Form	Name	OrdinalForm
	Caption	"Determine Ordinal Number"
Label	Name	Label1
	BackStyle	0 'Transparent
	Caption	"Number:"
TextBox	Name	NumberText
Label	Name	Label2
	BackStyle	0 'Transparent
	Caption	"Ordinal Number:"
Label	Name	OrdinalNumberLabel
	BorderStyle	1 'Fixed Single
CommandButton	Name	Command1
	Caption	"Exit"

2. Place the following code at the beginning of the ORDINAL.FRM. The FormLoad subroutine sets the BackColor of OrdinalNumberLabel control to make it look like a text box.

```
Option Explicit
'
Private Sub Form_Load()
    '
    ' Set Label BackColor to mimic a TextBox and Show
    ' the Form.
    '
    OrdinalNumberLabel.BackColor = NumberText.BackColor
    OrdinalForm.Show
End Sub
```

3. Place the following code in the NumberText_GotFocus event procedure. When the NumberText text box gets the focus, its value will be highlighted for easy replacement.

```
Private Sub NumberText_GotFocus()
    '
    ' Highlight for replacement the current value in the text box.
    '
    NumberText.SelStart = 0
    NumberText.SelLength = Len(NumberText)
End Sub
```

4. Place the following code in the NumberText_KeyPress event procedure. This subroutine checks the keys pressed; only numbers will be allowed. The number cannot exceed 2,147,483,647, the maximum value for a long integer. A keypress of zero (0) is accepted when it is embedded in a number, but not when it is the first number entered. A backspace is allowed to remove the previous character if there is one to remove. Any invalid keypress results in a beep, and the keypress is removed by setting its ASCII value to zero.

```
Private Sub NumberText_KeyPress(KeyAscii As Integer)
    '
    ' Allow the backspace key to do its thing.
    '
    If Len(NumberText) And KeyAscii = vbKeyBack Then Exit Sub
    '
    ' Otherwise, allow only numeric keys to be pressed. Prevent a
    ' number greater than a valid maximum Long value (2147483647)
    ' from being entered. Eat the invalid key press and beep.
    '
    If KeyAscii < vbKey0 _
    Or KeyAscii > vbKey9 _
    Or Val(NumberText) > 214748364 _
    Or (Val(NumberText) = 214748364 _
        And KeyAscii > vbKey7) _
    Or (Len(NumberText) = NumberText.SelLength _
        And KeyAscii = vbKey0) Then
        KeyAscii = 0
        Beep
    End If
End Sub
```

5. Place the following code in the NumberText_Change event procedure. This event is triggered by each keystroke that makes it past the KeyPress event. If the number is not numeric, the ordinal number is set to nothing. Otherwise, the entered number is passed to the OrdinalNumber function, and the ordinal number that is returned is used to set the OrdinalNumberLabel value.

```
Private Sub NumberText_Change()
    '
    ' Display the ordinal number for the entered number, clearing
    ' out the display if not numeric.
    '
    If IsNumeric(NumberText) Then
        OrdinalNumberLabel = OrdinalNumber(NumberText)
    Else
        OrdinalNumberLabel = ""
    End If
End Sub
```

6. Place the following code in the ExitCommand_Click event procedure to release resources and end the program:

```
Private Sub ExitCommand_Click()
    '
    ' When Exit button is clicked, release resources and end
    ' program.
    '
    Unload Me
    Set OrdinalForm = Nothing
    End
End Sub
```

7. Use the Insert Module menu item to create a new standard module and save it as ORDINAL.BAS. Name it OrdinalModule, and put the following code at the beginning of the file:

```
Option Explicit
```

8. Add a public function called OrdinalNumber to the OrdinalModule. This function receives a long integer value as a single argument. A private function, OrdinalSuffix, is called to compute the correct suffix for the number. Then OrdinalNumber concatenates the ordinal suffix to the number, returning the ordinal number as a string value.

```
Public Function OrdinalNumber(Nbr As Long) As String
    '
    ' Returns "1st", "2nd", "3rd", "4th", etc, depending on
    ' number.
    '
    OrdinalNumber = CStr(Nbr) & OrdinalSuffix(Nbr)
End Function
```

9. Add the private function OrdinalSuffix to the OrdinalModule. This function determines the correct ordinal suffix for a number that is received as a single argument. As the code illustrates, numbers ending in 4 through 9 are always

suffixed with *th*. Numbers ending in 1 are suffixed with *st* except 11, which is suffixed with *th*. Numbers ending in 2 are suffixed with *nd* except 12, which is suffixed with *th*. And finally, numbers ending in 3 are suffixed with *rd* except 13, which is suffixed with *th*.

```
Private Function OrdinalSuffix(Nbr As Long) As String
    '
    ' Determines appropriate suffix for number.
    '
    If Nbr >= 11 And Nbr <= 13 Then
        OrdinalSuffix = "th"
    ElseIf Nbr Mod 10 = 1 Then
        OrdinalSuffix = "st"
    ElseIf Nbr Mod 10 = 2 Then
        OrdinalSuffix = "nd"
    ElseIf Nbr Mod 10 = 3 Then
        OrdinalSuffix = "rd"
    Else
        OrdinalSuffix = "th"
    End If
End Function
```

How It Works

This program allows a number to be entered in one text box. A KeyPress event procedure accepts keystrokes representing only numbers between 1 and 2,147,483,647—the maximum value for a long integer. The program beeps and "swallows" invalid keystrokes.

Every time the entered number changes, a corresponding ordinal number is computed and displayed in a boxed label to the right of the long integer number.

A standard module provides the code for the OrdinalNumber function, making it easy to include the routine in any program that needs it. OrdinalNumber is a public function that accepts a long integer value as input and returns the equivalent ordinal number in a string. The OrdinalNumber function calls a private function, OrdinalSuffix, which determines the appropriate suffix. The string returned by the OrdinalNumber function is simply a concatenation of the number and its ordinal suffix.

Comments

Ordinal numbers are often written in text. For example, a contract may state, "This agreement shall expire on October 21st, 1995." How-To 9.2 makes use of the OrdinalNumber function from this project.

9.2 How do I...
Return an Anniversary Description for Any Set of Dates?

COMPLEXITY: EASY
COMPATIBILITY: VB4 ONLY

Problem

I've recorded birth dates, wedding dates, and job start dates for many of my friends and family. Now I'd like to be able to quickly compute how old they'll be on their next birthday, and how many years they'll have been married or on the job. I have in mind sending custom messages on birthdays and special anniversaries. How can I put Visual Basic to work to help me customize these messages?

Technique

The program in this How-To encapsulates a variety of date routines into a new class file called CDates. The external interface provides named functions or methods such as AnnivYears, Compare, DayOfWeek, and DayOfYear. Internally, the date routines take care of details such as checking to see that each date value is, in fact, a date before passing it to any of Visual Basic's built-in date functions. Visual Basic provides a multipurpose DatePart function that can return any one of a variety of values, based on the arguments passed to it. CDates hides the multipurpose complexity of this function, providing functions with simpler names, such as Year, Month, and Day.

The OrdinalNumber function developed in How-To 9.1 is put to use here, to compose an ordinal value for each birth date and anniversary date.

Messages are customized based on the type of anniversary (work, birthday, or wedding) and the dates involved. Messages are customized for event dates in the future, event dates equal to the current message date, and anniversary dates.

Steps

Open and run ANNIV.VBP. The form will load with today's date in the Message Date text box, with Work selected as the anniversary type, and with the cursor positioned to allow you to enter an anniversary date.

Experiment by entering anniversary dates in the past, present, and future. For each of these, try out the three anniversary-type selections to see how the anniversary message is affected. Notice that each keystroke affects the anniversary message, when you change either the anniversary date or the message date. Notice also that the anniversary message is cleared whenever one of the text boxes does not evaluate to a valid date (for instance, 3/15/).

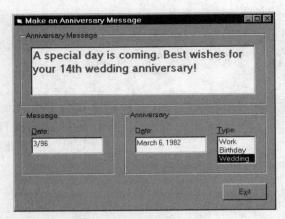

Figure 9-2-1 The Make an Anniversary
Message project in action

1. Create a new project called ANNIV.VBP. Create a form with controls arranged like
    the form shown in action in Figure 9-2-1. Set form objects and properties as
    shown in Table 9-2-1, and save the form as ANNIV.FRM.

Table 9-2-1 ANNIV.FRM form properties

OBJECT	PROPERTY	SETTING
Form	Name	AnniversaryForm
	Caption	"Make an Anniversary Message"
Frame	Name	AnnivMsgFrame
	Caption	"Anniversary Message"
TextBox	Name	AnnivMsgText
	Enabled	0 'False
	Font	MS Sans Serif
		Bold
		12 pt
Frame	Name	MsgDateFrame
	Caption	"Message"
Label	Name	MsgDateLabel
	Caption	"&Date:"
	TabIndex	0
TextBox	Name	MsgDateText
	TabIndex	1
Frame	Name	AnnivDateFrame
	Caption	"Anniversary"
Label	Name	AnnivDateLabel

OBJECT	PROPERTY	SETTING
	Caption	"D&ate:"
	TabIndex	2
TextBox	Name	AnnivDateText
	TabIndex	3
Label	Name	AnnivTypeLabel
	Caption	"&Type:"
	TabIndex	4
ListBox	Name	AnnivTypeList
	List	"Work"
		"Birthday"
		"Wedding"
	TabIndex	5
CommandButton	Name	Command1
	Caption	"Exit"
	TabIndex	6

2. Place the following code at the beginning of ANNIV.FRM, to create the object needed to access the date function in the CDates class file.

```
Option Explicit
'
' The dates class file provides various general date routines.
'
Dim Dates As New CDates
```

3. Place the following code in the Form_Load event procedure. This subroutine establishes default values for the message date and the type of anniversary. After centering and showing the form, it positions the cursor so the user can begin entering the anniversary date.

```
Private Sub Form_Load()
    '
    ' Default to first type of anniversary in list. Default to a
    ' message date of today's date. Center and show the form. Then
    ' set the focus to allow entry into the anniversary date text
    ' box.
    '
    AnnivTypeList.ListIndex = 0
    MsgDateText = Date
    Move (Screen.Width - Width) \ 2, (Screen.Height - Height) \ 2
    Show
    AnnivDateText.SetFocus
End Sub
```

4. Place the following code in the AnnivDateText_GotFocus event procedure. When the AnnivDateText text box gets the focus, its value is highlighted for easy replacement.

```
Private Sub AnnivDateText_GotFocus()
    '
    ' Highlight the text box when it gets the focus.
    '
    AnnivDateText.SelStart = 0
    AnnivDateText.SelLength = Len(AnnivDateText)
End Sub
```

5. Place the following code in the AnnivDateText_Change event procedure. This routine performs the common UpdateAnniversaryMessage subroutine whenever the user changes the anniversary date.

```
Private Sub AnnivDateText_Change()
    '
    ' Perform the routine to update the anniversary message when
    ' ever the anniversary date changes.
    '
    UpdateAnniversaryMessage
End Sub
```

6. Place the following code in the MsgDateText_GotFocus event procedure. When the MsgDateText text box gets the focus, its value is highlighted for easy replacement.

```
Private Sub MsgDateText_GotFocus()
    '
    ' Highlight the text box when it gets the focus.
    '
    MsgDateText.SelStart = 0
    MsgDateText.SelLength = Len(MsgDateText)
End Sub
```

7. Place the following code in the MsgDateText_Change event procedure. This routine performs the common UpdateAnniversaryMessage subroutine whenever the user changes the message date.

```
Private Sub MsgDateText_Change()
    '
    ' Perform the routine to update the anniversary message when
    ' ever the message date changes.
    '
    UpdateAnniversaryMessage
End Sub
```

8. Place the following code in the AnnivTypeList_Click event procedure. This routine performs the common UpdateAnniversaryMessage subroutine whenever the user clicks an entry in the anniversary-type list.

```
Private Sub AnnivTypeList_Click()
    '
    ' Perform the routine to update the anniversary message when
    ' ever the type of anniversary changes.
```

```
'
    UpdateAnniversaryMessage
End Sub
```

9. Add an UpdateAnniversaryMessage subroutine to the General Declarations section of the Anniversary form. This routine determines whether, relative to the message date, the anniversary date occurs in the future, in the past, or on the same date. It uses a Compare function in the Dates class file to make this determination. Depending on the date comparison, it performs the appropriate message creation subroutine or clears the message if one or both dates is invalid.

```
Private Sub UpdateAnniversaryMessage()
    '
    ' Perform the appropriate message create routine depending on
    ' whether the special date is a date in the past, the future,
    ' or "now" -- relative to the message date.
    '
    If Dates.Compare(AnnivDateText, MsgDateText, "LT") Then
        CreateAnniversaryMessage
    ElseIf Dates.Compare(AnnivDateText, MsgDateText, "EQ") Then
        CreateCurrentEventMessage
    ElseIf Dates.Compare(AnnivDateText, MsgDateText, "GT") Then
        CreateFutureEventMessage
    Else
        ' One or both of the values is not a valid date
        AnnivMsgText = ""
    End If
End Sub
```

10. Add a CreateAnniversaryMessage subroutine to the General Declarations section of the anniversary form. If the anniversary does not fall exactly on the month and day of the message date, this subroutine precedes the anniversary message with the sentence, "A special day is coming." The program assumes that the message will refer to the next anniversary, not the last one, even if the prior anniversary date is closer to the message date than the next one. No matter what, the subroutine goes on to compute the anniversary years using the AnnivYears function in the CDates class file, and converts it to an ordinal number of years using an Ordinal function from a standard module. (The Ordinal function is explained in How-To 9.1.) Finally, the subroutine prepares a custom anniversary message, depending on the selected anniversary type (work, birthday, or wedding).

```
Private Sub CreateAnniversaryMessage()
    Dim OrdinalAnniv As String
    '
    ' If the anniversary doesn't fall exactly on the day of the
    ' message, precede the message with an "...is coming" sentence.
    '
    If Dates.Month(AnnivDateText) = Dates.Month(MsgDateText) _
    And Dates.Day(AnnivDateText) = Dates.Day(MsgDateText) Then
        AnnivMsgText = ""
    Else
```

Continued on next page

Continued from previous page

```
            AnnivMsgText = "A special day is coming. "
        End If
        '
        ' Get the anniversary number of years expressed as an ordinal
        ' number.
        '
        OrdinalAnniv = OrdinalNumber(Dates.AnnivYears(AnnivDateText, _
                                                MsgDateText))
        '
        ' Prepare an anniversary message that's appropriate for the
        ' type of anniversary currently selected.
        '
        Select Case AnnivTypeList.ListIndex + 1
            Case 1
                AnnivMsgText = AnnivMsgText _
                                & "Congratulations on your " _
                                & OrdinalAnniv _
                                & " year on the job!"
            Case 2
                AnnivMsgText = AnnivMsgText _
                                & "Happy " _
                                & OrdinalAnniv _
                                & " birthday!"
            Case 3
                AnnivMsgText = AnnivMsgText _
                                & "Best wishes for your " _
                                & OrdinalAnniv _
                                & " wedding anniversary!"
        End Select
End Sub
```

11. Add a CreateCurrentEventMessage subroutine to the General Declarations section of the Anniversary form. This subroutine is performed when the anniversary month, day, and year exactly match the message date. A custom message is prepared, depending on the selected anniversary type (work, birthday, or wedding), to express good wishes for the special event to occur on that very day.

```
Private Sub CreateCurrentEventMessage()
    '
    ' Prepare a message that's appropriate for the type of
    ' special event happening today.
    '
    Select Case AnnivTypeList.ListIndex + 1
        Case 1
            AnnivMsgText _
                = "Congratulations, your new job starts today!"
        Case 2
            AnnivMsgText _
                = "This is a very special day. " _
                & "Congratulations on the birth of your child!"
        Case 3
            AnnivMsgText _
                = "You're getting married today. " _
                & "Congratulations and best wishes!"
```

```
     End Select
End Sub
```

12. Add a CreateFutureEventMessage subroutine to the General Declarations section of the Anniversary form. This subroutine is performed when the anniversary date is in the future with respect to the message date. A custom message is prepared, depending on the selected anniversary type (work, birthday, or wedding) to express good wishes for the special event coming up. A DayOfWeek function in the CDates class file is used to customize the message by including the day of the week in which the future event will occur.

```
Private Sub CreateFutureEventMessage()
    '
    ' Prepare a message that's appropriate for the type of
    ' special future event.
    '
    Select Case AnnivTypeList.ListIndex + 1
        Case 1
            AnnivMsgText _
                = "Your new job will start on " _
                & Dates.DayOfWeek(AnnivDateText) _
                & ", " _
                & AnnivDateText _
                & ". Good luck!"
        Case 2
            AnnivMsgText _
                = "The stork told us you're expecting a baby on " _
                & Dates.DayOfWeek(AnnivDateText) _
                & ", " _
                & AnnivDateText _
                & ". Congratulations!"
        Case 3
            AnnivMsgText _
                = "We hear you're planning to be married on " _
                & Dates.DayOfWeek(AnnivDateText) _
                & ", " _
                & AnnivDateText _
                & ". Congratulations and best wishes!"
    End Select
End Sub
```

13. Place the following code in the ExitCommand_Click event procedure. This subroutine releases resources and ends the program.

```
Private Sub ExitCommand_Click()
    '
    ' When the exit button is clicked, unload the form, release
    ' resources from memory, and end the program.
    '
    Unload Me
    Set Dates = Nothing
    Set AnniversaryForm = Nothing
    End
End Sub
```

14. Use the File Add menu item to add the file named ORDINAL.BAS to ANNIV.VBP. This standard module was developed in How-To 9.1, steps 7 through 9. It is used without modification here in this How-To.

15. Use the Insert Class menu item to create a new class module and save it as DATES.BAS. Name it CDates, and put the following code at the beginning of the file:

```
Option Explicit
```

16. Add a public function called Compare to the CDates class file. This function confirms that both input date values are in fact valid dates before performing a date compare per the requested Compare operation. Compare is returned as a Boolean value. It's set to True when the dates compare successfully based on the requested compare operation; otherwise, it's set to False.

```
Public Function Compare(Date1 As Variant, _
                        Date2 As Variant, _
                        CompareOperation As String) _
                    As Boolean
    '
    ' Initialize Compare to False.
    '
    Compare = False
    '
    ' Exit function if one or the other of the input values is
    ' not a valid date.
    '
    If Not IsDate(Date1) Or Not IsDate(Date2) Then
        Exit Function
    End If
    '
    ' If both values passed in are valid dates, convert them to
    ' date types and perform a date comparison per the requested
    ' compare operation. Return True if they satisfy the compare
    ' operation. Otherwise return False.
    '
    Select Case CompareOperation
        Case "<", "LT"
            If CVDate(Date1) < CVDate(Date2) Then
                Compare = True
            End If
        Case "<=", "LE"
            If CVDate(Date1) <= CVDate(Date2) Then
                Compare = True
            End If
        Case "=", "EQ"
            If CVDate(Date1) = CVDate(Date2) Then
                Compare = True
            End If
        Case "<>", "NE"
            If CVDate(Date1) <> CVDate(Date2) Then
                Compare = True
```

```
            End If
        Case ">", "GT"
            If CVDate(Date1) > CVDate(Date2) Then
                Compare = True
            End If
        Case ">=", "GE"
            If CVDate(Date1) >= CVDate(Date2) Then
                Compare = True
            End If
    End Select
End Function
```

17. Add a public function called AnnivYears to the CDates class file. This function uses the CDates Compare function to ensure that the compare date exceeds the anniversary date before calculating the anniversary number of years.

```
Public Function AnnivYears(AnnivDate As Date, _
                        CompareDate As Date) _
                As Integer
    '
    ' If dates are valid and special date is in the past,
    ' calculate current and Anniv year and day of year.
    ' If the coming anniversary is next year, add a year.
    '
    If Compare(CompareDate, AnnivDate, "GT") Then
        If DayofYear(AnnivDate) < DayofYear(CompareDate) Then
            AnnivYears = (Year(CompareDate) - Year(AnnivDate)) + 1
        Else
            AnnivYears = Year(CompareDate) - Year(AnnivDate)
        End If
    End If
End Function
```

18. Add a public function called DayOfWeek to the CDates class file. When a valid date is passed in, this function uses Visual Basic's WeekDay function to determine the input date's day number. It returns the name of the weekday if the input date is valid, or an empty value for the weekday name, otherwise. In this How-To, the DayOfWeek function is used to provide the day of the special event for future events.

```
Public Function DayOfWeek(AnyDate As Date) As String
    '
    ' Set day of week to nothing if the date is invalid.
    '
    If Not IsDate(AnyDate) Then
        DayOfWeek = ""
        Exit Function
    End If
    '
    ' Use the built in WeekDay function to determine the week day
    ' number. Set the spelled out DayOfWeek accordingly.
    '
    Select Case WeekDay(AnyDate)
```

Continued on next page

Continued from previous page

```
        Case vbSunday
            DayOfWeek = "Sunday"
        Case vbMonday
            DayOfWeek = "Monday"
        Case vbTuesday
            DayOfWeek = "Tuesday"
        Case vbWednesday
            DayOfWeek = "Wednesday"
        Case vbThursday
            DayOfWeek = "Thursday"
        Case vbFriday
            DayOfWeek = "Friday"
        Case vbSaturday
            DayOfWeek = "Saturday"
    End Select
End Function
```

19. Add a public function called DayOfYear to the CDates class file. When a valid date is passed in, this function uses Visual Basic's DatePart function to extract the day of the year from the input date. DayOfYear is used by the AnnivYears function in the CDates class file, but it is defined as a public function because it can be put to good use externally, as well.

```
Public Function DayofYear(AnyDate As Date) As Integer
    '
    ' Set DayOfYear to zero if the date is invalid.
    '
    If Not IsDate(AnyDate) Then
        DayofYear = 0
        Exit Function
    End If
    '
    ' Set the DayOfYear to the day number for the year otherwise.
    '
    DayofYear = DatePart("y", AnyDate)
End Function
```

20. Add a public function called Month to the CDates class file. When a valid date is passed in, this function uses Visual Basic's DatePart function to extract the month from the input date. This Month function is used by the CreateAnniversaryMessage function in the Anniversary form module.

```
Public Function Month(AnyDate As Date) As Integer
    '
    ' Set Month to zero if the date is invalid.
    '
    If Not IsDate(AnyDate) Then
        Month = 0
        Exit Function
    End If
    '
    ' Set the Month to the month number in the year otherwise.
```

```
'
    Month = DatePart("m", AnyDate)
End Function
```

21. Add a public function called Day to the CDates class file. When a valid date is passed in, this function uses Visual Basic's DatePart function to extract the day of the month from the input date. This Day function is used by the CreateAnniversaryMessage function in the Anniversary form module.

```
Public Function Day(AnyDate As Date) As Integer
    '
    ' Set Day to zero if the date is invalid.
    '
    If Not IsDate(AnyDate) Then
        Day = 0
        Exit Function
    End If
    '
    ' Set the Day to the day number in the month otherwise.
    '
    Day = DatePart("d", AnyDate)
End Function
```

22. Add a public function called Year to the CDates class file. When a valid date is passed in, this function uses Visual Basic's DatePart function to extract the year number from the input date. This Year function is used by the AnnivYears function in the CDates class file, but it is defined as a Public function because it can be put to good use externally as well.

```
Public Function Year(AnyDate As Date) As Integer
    '
    ' Set Year to zero if the date is invalid.
    '
    If Not IsDate(AnyDate) Then
        Year = 0
        Exit Function
    End If
    '
    ' Set the Year to the year number otherwise.
    '
    Year = DatePart("yyyy", AnyDate)
End Function
```

How It Works

The Anniversary form in this How-To allows the entry of two dates, a message date and an anniversary date. Unlike How-To 9.1, this one makes no attempt to limit the keystrokes to those that are valid for a date. In fact, Visual Basic recognizes dates in many forms, including 10/1/99, 10/01/1999, Oct 1, 1999, and October 01, 99, for example. The program compares the values in the two date text boxes and clears the anniversary message if none of the compares (<, =, or >) returns a True value. That will happen when one or both of the values is not a valid date.

When the anniversary date is less than the message date, we have a true anniversary on our hands, and the program generates the appropriate anniversary message. The message is appropriately varied depending on the type of anniversary—years on the job, birthday, or wedding anniversary. When the two dates are equal, the program generates a "Today is your special day" type of message. When the anniversary date is in the future, the program customizes the message for a future first day on the job, birth of a child, or planned wedding.

Comments

Start with the tool provided in How-To 9.1, for returning an ordinal number for any number. Mix it with How-To 9.2, for returning an anniversary description for any set of dates. What's left to do? Toss in a database of names, addresses, and special dates, and combine with OLE Automation to drive a print merge in Word for Windows. Those are the ingredients of a very handy utility for keeping up with all the special events in the lives of your friends, family, coworkers, and business associates.

9.3 How do I...
Set the Desktop Wallpaper?

COMPLEXITY: EASY
COMPATIBILITY: VB4 ONLY

Problem

I'm developing some software that produces graphics that are updated and displayed to the user in the background (such as current sales and market information). This type of information is relatively static, so I've decided to put it on the desktop, as the wallpaper. How can I change the wallpaper from within VB?

Technique

WALLPAPR uses the SystemParametersInfo API call to set the current desktop wallpaper. This function allows the programmer to just supply a filename to change the wallpaper. Tiling (or not) is handled by changing a setting in the registration database.

Steps

Open and run WALLPAPR.VBP (shown in Figure 9-3-1). Click on Choose Wallpaper and select a bitmap file. Select the Tile option before choosing. Or, get rid of the wallpaper by pressing the No Wallpaper button. Follow the steps below to see how this program was put together.

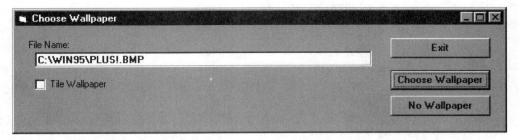

Figure 9-3-1 The WallPaper program, running

1. Create a new project called WALLPAPR. Select Form1 and name it WallPaper. Save the form as WALLPAPR.FRM, and save the project as WALLPAPR.VBP. Select the form, and add the objects with properties set as shown in Table 9-3-1.

Table 9-3-1 Objects, properties, and settings for WallPaper

OBJECT	PROPERTY	SETTING
Form	Name	Wallpaper
	Caption	"Choose Wallpaper"
	Height	2355
	Left	1035
	LockControls	-1 'True
	Top	1170
	Width	9015
CheckBox	Name	chkTile
	Caption	"Tile Wallpaper"
	Height	255
	Left	360
	Top	960
	Width	2895
CommandButton	Name	btnNoWallpaper
	Caption	"No Wallpaper"
	Height	375
	Left	6840
	Top	1320
	Width	1815
CommandButton	Name	btnChooseWallpaper
	Caption	"Choose Wallpaper"
	Height	375
	Left	6840

Continued on next page

Continued from previous page

OBJECT	PROPERTY	SETTING
	Top	840
	Width	1815
CommandButton	Name	btnExit
	Cancel	-1 'True
	Caption	"Exit"
	Height	375
	Left	6840
	Top	240
	Width	1815
TextBox	Name	txtFilename
	Height	285
	Left	360
	ReadOnly	-1 'True
	TabStop	0 'False
	Top	480
	Width	6135
CommonDialog	Name	CommonDialog1
	Left	6000
	Top	840
Label	Name	Label1
	Caption	"File Name:"
	Height	255
	Left	240
	Top	240
	Width	2295

2. Add the following code to the General Declarations section of Wallpaper, to define the API calls and constants used by this program. (Always use Option Explicit; it will save you many hours of frustration.)

```
Option Explicit
'
' declare wallpaper change function
'
Private Declare Function SystemParametersInfo Lib "user32" Alias _
    "SystemParametersInfoA" (ByVal uAction As Long, ByVal uParam As Long, _
    ByVal lpvParam As Any, ByVal fuWinIni As Long) As Long
'
' Declare registration database functions
'
Const REG_SZ = 1
Const HKEY_CURRENT_USER = &H80000001
Private Declare Function RegCloseKey Lib "advapi32.dll" (ByVal hKey As Long) As Long
```

```
Private Declare Function RegCreateKey Lib "advapi32.dll" Alias "RegCreateKeyA" _
    (ByVal hKey As Long, ByVal lpSubKey As String, phkResult As Long) As Long
Private Declare Function RegOpenKey Lib "advapi32.dll" Alias "RegOpenKeyA" _
    (ByVal hKey As Long, ByVal lpSubKey As String, phkResult As Long) As Long
Private Declare Function RegQueryValue Lib "advapi32.dll" Alias "RegQueryValueA" _
    (ByVal hKey As Long, ByVal lpSubKey As String, ByVal lpValue As String, _
    lpcbValue As Long) As Long
Private Declare Function RegSetValueEx Lib "advapi32.dll" Alias "RegSetValueExA" _
    (ByVal hKey As Long, ByVal lpValueName As String, ByVal Reserved As Long, _
    ByVal dwType As Long, ByVal lpData As String, ByVal cbData As Long) As Long
'
' declare API constants
'
Const SPI_SETDESKWALLPAPER = 20
Const SPIF_SENDWININICHANGE = &H2
Const SPIF_UPDATEINIFILE = &H1

Private Sub UpdateWinIni()
    SystemParametersInfo SPI_SETDESKWALLPAPER, 0, ByVal "", SPIF_SENDWININICHANGE
End Sub
```

3. Add the following code to the Click event routine of Choose Wallpaper. This code displays the Open File common dialog box. If the user chooses a .BMP file, that file is set as the wallpaper for the system.

```
Private Sub btnChooseWallpaper_Click()
    Dim Filename As String
    Dim Result As Integer
    '
    ' get a new bitmap for the wall paper
    '
    CommonDialog1.Filter = "BMP Files(*.BMP)|*.BMP"
    CommonDialog1.Flags = &H1804
    CommonDialog1.Filename = ""
    CommonDialog1.ShowOpen
    '
    ' if the user didn't press cancel
    '
    Filename = Trim(CommonDialog1.Filename)
    If Len(Filename) <> 0 Then

        ' user selected file, so show it as the wp
        '
        txtFilename = Filename
        Result = SystemParametersInfo(SPI_SETDESKWALLPAPER, 0, _
            ByVal Filename, SPIF_UPDATEINIFILE)
        UpdateWinIni
    End If
End Sub
```

4. Add the following code to the Click event for the Exit button:

```
Private Sub btnExit_Click()
    '
    ' get out
```

Continued on next page

Continued from previous page

```
    '
    End
End Sub
```

5. Add the following code to the No Wallpaper button's Click event. This code clears the existing desktop wallpaper and sets it to the default pattern found in WIN.INI.

```
Private Sub btnNoWallpaper_Click()
    '
    ' clear the wallpaper
    '
    SystemParametersInfo SPI_SETDESKWALLPAPER, 0, ByVal "", _
        SPIF_UPDATEINIFILE
    UpdateWinIni
End Sub
```

6. Add the following code to the form's Unload event routine, to ensure that the program exits.

```
Private Sub Form_Unload(Cancel As Integer)
    '
    ' make sure the program exits
    '
    End
End Sub
```

7. Add the following code to the Tiling check box's Click event. This subroutine turns tiling on or off depending on the value of the check box.

```
'
' Tile/center wall paper based on check box.
'
Private Sub chkTile_Click()
    Dim Ret As Long
    Dim KeyName As String
    Dim KeyValue As String
    Dim KeyHandle As Long
    Dim KeyValueLength As Long
    '
    ' make sure tiling is set properly
    '
    KeyValue = CStr(chkTile.VALUE)
    KeyName = "desktop\TileWallpaper"
    KeyValueLength = Len(KeyValue) + 1
    Ret = RegOpenKey(HKEY_CURRENT_USER, "Control Panel\desktop", KeyHandle)
    If Ret = 0 Then
        Ret = RegSetValueEx(KeyHandle, "TileWallpaper", 0, REG_SZ, _
            KeyValue, KeyValueLength)
        Ret = RegCloseKey(KeyHandle)
    End If
    UpdateWinIni
End Sub
```

How It Works

The Wallpaper program lets the user select the current desktop wallpaper, using the File Open common dialog. When the user selects a new bitmap file, SystemParametersInfo is called with the SPI_SETDESKWALLPAPER flag. This sets the current desktop wallpaper. The SPIF_UPDATEINIFILE and SPIF_SEND-WININICHANGE flags are also used to update the registration database settings.

When the user presses the No Wallpaper button, SystemParametersInfo is called to set the current wallpaper bitmap file to nothing.

Comments

You can use this program to update all kinds of interesting information. In sales-tracking programs, you can set the wallpaper for sales/marketing people to show graphs of the current sales to date, stock market programs can show yesterday's data; and football pool tracking software can display the latest playoff standings.

SystemParametersInfo is good for a lot of other things, too—lots of goodies to get and set. Take a peek at it in the Windows 95 API Help file.

9.4 How do I...
Generate an Interval Series of Dates?

COMPLEXITY: EASY
COMPATIBILITY: VB4 ONLY

Problem

I'm creating a program to schedule meetings, and I'd like to offer a wide variety of scheduling options, from daily through biannually. I'd also like to offer the flexibility of scheduling either a fixed number of meetings or a set of meetings within a date range. How can I generate an interval series of dates based on these kinds of options?

Technique

The project in this How-To extends the CDates class file developed in How-To 9.2. A ComputeSchedule method is added here, which accepts a schedule start date, frequency, and either a schedule end date or a number of dates to be scheduled. A Container property is added to the class file, as well. The Container can be set to either a ListBox or ComboBox control, and it provides the container to hold the schedule dates generated by the ComputeSchedule method.

Steps

Open and run SCHEDULE.VBP. The form will load with today's date in the Starting Date text box, with Biannually selected as the scheduling frequency, and with the cursor positioned to allow you to enter an end date.

Experiment by entering a variety of Ending dates, both before and after the Starting Date. Notice that when the end date precedes the start date, the start date is the only scheduled date. Also notice that nothing is scheduled if the end date is more than ten years after the start date. Try out each of the scheduling frequencies to see the resulting interval series of dates.

Tab from the Ending date text box to the OR Number text box, and enter a few different numbers. Then enter a start date with a day number of 31, choose a monthly, bimonthly or quarterly frequency, and create a schedule of ten or so dates. You'll see that the resulting end-of-the-month scheduled dates are valid for each month they fall into.

1. Create a new project called SCHEDULE.VBP. Create a form with controls laid out to approximate the one shown in action in Figure 9-4-1. Set form objects and properties as shown in Table 9-4-1, and save the form as SCHEDULE.FRM.

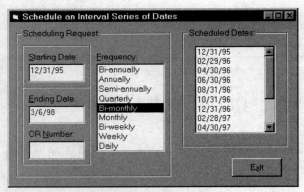

Figure 9-4-1 Schedule of dates in action

Table 9-4-1 SCHEDULE.FRM form properties

OBJECT	PROPERTY	SETTING
Form	Name	ScheduleForm
	Caption	"Generate an Interval Series of Dates"
Frame	Name	SchedRequFrame
	Caption	"Scheduling Request:"
Frame	Name	Frame1
Label	Name	StartDateLabel
	Caption	"&Starting Date:"
	TabIndex	0
TextBox	Name	StartDateText
	TabIndex	1
Frame	Name	Frame2

OBJECT	PROPERTY	SETTING
Label	Name	EndDateLabel
	Caption	"&Ending Date:"
	TabIndex	2
TextBox	Name	EndDateText
	TabIndex	3
Label	Name	NumberOfDatesLabel
	Caption	&Number of Dates:
	TabIndex	4
TextBox	Name	NumberOfDateText
	TabIndex	5
Label	Name	FrequencyLabel
	Caption	"&Frequency:"
	TabIndex	6
ListBox	Name	FrequencyList
	TabIndex	7
Frame	Name	ScheduleFrame
	Caption	"Scheduled Dates:"
ListBox	Name	SchedDatesList
CommandButton	Name	Command1
	Caption	"Exit"
	TabIndex	8

2. Place the following code at the beginning of the SCHEDULE.FRM, to create the object needed to access the date functions in the CDates class file:

```
Option Explicit
'
' The dates class file provides various general date routines.
' This form uses it to calculate a schedule of dates.
'
Dim Dates As New CDates
```

3. Place the following code in the Form_Load event procedure. This subroutine sets default values for the start date and scheduling frequency, and makes the SchedDatesList control the container for the CDates class file. Then, after centering and showing the form, it positions the cursor so the user can begin entering the end date.

```
Private Sub Form_Load()
    '
    ' Default to first frequency in list. Set the container for
    ' the scheduled dates. Default to a start date of today's
    ' date. Center and show the form. Then set the focus to allow
    ' entry into the end date text box.
    '
```

Continued on next page

Continued from previous page

```
    FrequencyList.ListIndex = 0
    Set Dates.Container = SchedDatesList
    StartDateText = Date
    Move (Screen.Width - Width) \ 2, (Screen.Height - Height) \ 2
    Show
    EndDateText.SetFocus
End Sub
```

4. Place the following code in the StartDateText_GotFocus event procedure. When the StartDateText text box gets the focus, its value is highlighted for easy replacement.

```
Private Sub StartDateText_GotFocus()
    '
    ' Highlight the text box when it gets the focus.
    '
    StartDateText.SelStart = 0
    StartDateText.SelLength = Len(StartDateText)
End Sub
```

5. Place the following code in the StartDateText_Change event procedure, to perform the common ComputeScheduleDates subroutine whenever the user changes the start date.

```
Private Sub StartDateText_Change()
    '
    ' Perform the routine to compute the schedule of dates when
    ' ever the start date changes.
    '
    ComputeScheduleDates
End Sub
```

6. Place the following code in the EndDateText_GotFocus event procedure. When the EndDateText text box gets the focus, its value is highlighted for easy replacement.

```
Private Sub EndDateText_GotFocus()
    '
    ' Highlight the text box when it gets the focus.
    '
    EndDateText.SelStart = 0
    EndDateText.SelLength = Len(EndDateText)
End Sub
```

7. Place the following code in the EndDateText_Change event procedure. Because the values for the end date and number of dates are mutually exclusive, this routine first makes sure there is a value in Ending Date. If it has a value, the routine clears out the value in the NbrOfDatesText text box before performing the common ComputeScheduleDates routine. It needs to trigger that subroutine whenever the user changes the end date.

```
Private Sub EndDateText_Change()
    '
    ' Unless the end date is being changed to nothing, clear out
    ' the number of dates text box because only one of these is
    ' used at a time. Then perform the routine to compute the
    ' schedule of dates whenever the end date changes.
    '
    If EndDateText <> "" Then
        NbrOfDatesText = ""
        ComputeScheduleDates
    End If
End Sub
```

8. Place the following code in the NbrOfDatesText_GotFocus event procedure. When the NbrOfDatesText text box gets the focus, its value is highlighted for easy replacement.

```
Private Sub NbrOfDatesText_GotFocus()
    '
    ' Highlight the text box when it gets the focus.
    '
    NbrOfDatesText.SelStart = 0
    NbrOfDatesText.SelLength = Len(NbrOfDatesText)
End Sub
```

9. Place the following code in the NbrOfDatesText _Change event procedure. Because the values for the end date and number of dates are mutually exclusive, this routine first makes sure there is a value in the Number of Dates text box. If it has a value, the routine clears out the value in the Ending Date text box before performing the common ComputeScheduleDates. It needs to trigger that subroutine whenever the user changes the number of dates.

```
Private Sub NbrOfDatesText_Change()
    '
    ' Unless the number of dates is being changed to nothing,
    ' clear out the end date text box because only one of these is
    ' used at a time. Then perform the routine to compute the
    ' schedule of dates whenever the end date changes.
    '
    If NbrOfDatesText <> "" Then
        EndDateText = ""
        ComputeScheduleDates
    End If
End Sub
```

10. Place the following code in the FrequencyList _Click event procedure, to perform the common ComputeScheduleDates subroutine whenever the user clicks an entry in the Frequency list.

```
Private Sub FrequencyList_Click()
    '
    ' Perform the routine to compute the schedule of dates when
```

Continued on next page

Continued from previous page

```
' ever the frequency changes.
'
ComputeScheduleDates
End Sub
```

11. Add a ComputeScheduleDates subroutine to the General Declarations section of the Schedule of Dates form. This routine first clears out the Scheduled Dates list to prepare it for receiving a new list of scheduled dates. Before developing an interval series of dates based on start and end dates, the subroutine first makes sure that there are no more than ten years between the dates. This is a simple way to guard against a lengthy processing time. Notice that ComputeSchedule, a function in the CDates class file, handles optional parameters. It accepts a start date and either an end date or a number of dates.

```
Private Sub ComputeScheduleDates()
    '
    ' Clear the scheduled dates list in preparation for new list.
    '
    SchedDatesList.Clear
    '
    ' If start and end dates are filled in and no more than 10
    ' years from start to end, compute the scheduled dates based
    ' on the start date, end date, and frequency. Set the mouse
    ' pointer to hourglass because this can take a long time.
    '
    If EndDateText <> "" Then
        If IsDate(StartDateText) _
        And IsDate(EndDateText) Then
            If DateAdd("yyyy", 10, CVDate(StartDateText)) _
                > CVDate(EndDateText) Then
                MousePointer = vbHourglass
                Dates.ComputeSchedule StartDateText, _
                                    FrequencyList.ListIndex, _
                                    EndDateText
            End If
        End If
    '
    ' If number of dates is filled in, compute the scheduled dates
    ' based on the start date, number of dates, and frequency. Set
    ' the mouse pointer to hourglass since this can take a long
    ' time.
    '
    ElseIf NbrOfDatesText <> "" Then
        MousePointer = vbHourglass
        Dates.ComputeSchedule StartDateText, _
                            FrequencyList.ListIndex, _
                            , _
                            NbrOfDatesText
    End If
    '
    ' Return the mouse pointer to normal when done.
    '
    MousePointer = vbDefault
End Sub
```

12. Place the following code in the ExitCommand_Click event procedure. This subroutine releases resources and ends the program.

```
Private Sub ExitCommand_Click()
    '
    ' When the exit button is clicked, unload the form, release
    ' resources from memory, and end the program.
    '
    Unload Me
    Set ScheduleForm = Nothing
    Set Dates = Nothing
    End
End Sub
```

13. Use the File Add menu item to add the file named DATES.CLS to SCHEDULE.VBP. This class file was developed in How-To 9.2, and additions will be made to it for this How-To. Begin by adding the following variables and constants immediately following the Option Explicit in the Declarations section of the file:

```
'
' Class file's private variables
'
Private m_Container As Object
Private m_ListCount As Integer
Private m_StartDate As Variant
Private m_EndDate As Variant
Private m_Frequency As Integer
Private m_NbrOfDates As Integer
Private m_Interval As String
Private m_NbrOfIntervals As Long
'
' Constants for schedule date intervals
'
Private Const consBiannually As Integer = 0
Private Const consAnnually As Integer = 1
Private Const consSemiannually As Integer = 2
Private Const consQuarterly As Integer = 3
Private Const consBimonthly As Integer = 4
Private Const consMonthly As Integer = 5
Private Const consBiweekly As Integer = 6
Private Const consWeekly As Integer = 7
Private Const consDaily As Integer = 8
```

14. Add the following code to the General section of CDates. This Set property for Container gets, validates, and stores the ListBox or ComboBox object that will be used as the container for the scheduled list of dates.

```
Public Property Set Container(AnyBox As Control)
    '
    ' If control must be a list box or a combo box, use it as the
    ' container for returning a list of dates.
    '
    If Not TypeOf AnyBox Is ListBox _
```

Continued on next page

981

Continued from previous page

```
    And Not TypeOf AnyBox Is ComboBox Then
        MsgBox "Dates container must be a list box or combo box.", _
            , "Dates"
        Exit Property
    End If
    Set m_Container = AnyBox
End Property
```

15. Add a public function called ComputeSchedule to the CDates class file. This function checks the validity of each of the input arguments. It performs a private subroutine, SetInterval, to compute interval variables from the frequency option requested. It makes sure that either an end date or a number of dates is passed in, not both. Then, depending on which argument is set, it performs a private subroutine to compute a schedule based on the requested end date or on the requested number of dates.

```
Public Sub ComputeSchedule(StartDate As Variant, _
                           Frequency As Integer, _
                           Optional EndDate As Variant, _
                           Optional NbrOfDates As Variant)
    '
    ' Validate and store each of the arguments. Depending on the
    ' option, either compute a schedule based on an end date, or
    ' compute a schedule based on the requested number of dates.
    '
    If IsDate(StartDate) Then
        m_StartDate = StartDate
    Else
        Exit Sub
    End If
    If IsNumeric(Frequency) And Frequency >= 0 Then
        m_Frequency = Frequency
        SetInterval
    Else
        Exit Sub
    End If
    If IsMissing(EndDate) And IsMissing(NbrOfDates) Then Exit Sub
    If Not IsMissing(EndDate) _
    And Not IsMissing(NbrOfDates) Then
        Exit Sub
    End If
    If Not IsMissing(EndDate) And IsDate(EndDate) Then
        m_EndDate = EndDate
        m_NbrOfDates = 1
        ComputeEndDateSchedule
    Else
        If Not IsMissing(NbrOfDates) _
        And IsNumeric(NbrOfDates) Then
            If CInt(NbrOfDates) > 0 Then
                m_NbrOfDates = CInt(NbrOfDates)
                ComputeNbrOfDatesSchedule
            End If
        End If
    End If
End Sub
```

16. Add a private subroutine called SetInterval to the CDates class file. This procedure sets the private variables, m_Interval and m_NbrOfIntervals, based on the frequency argument passed to the ComputeSchedule public subroutine. The interval type and number of interval values are set so that they are directly useable later as arguments to Visual Basic's DateAdd function.

```
Private Sub SetInterval()
    '
    ' Set the interval string and the number of intervals to
    ' based on the desired frequency.
    '
    Select Case m_Frequency
        Case consBiannually
            m_Interval = "yyyy"
            m_NbrOfIntervals = 2
        Case consAnnually
            m_Interval = "yyyy"
            m_NbrOfIntervals = 1
        Case consSemiannually
            m_Interval = "q"
            m_NbrOfIntervals = 2
        Case consQuarterly
            m_Interval = "q"
            m_NbrOfIntervals = 1
        Case consBimonthly
            m_Interval = "m"
            m_NbrOfIntervals = 2
        Case consMonthly
            m_Interval = "m"
            m_NbrOfIntervals = 1
        Case consBiweekly
            m_Interval = "ww"
            m_NbrOfIntervals = 2
        Case consWeekly
            m_Interval = "ww"
            m_NbrOfIntervals = 1
        Case consDaily
            m_Interval = "d"
            m_NbrOfIntervals = 1
    End Select
End Sub
```

17. Add this private subroutine called ComputeEndDateSchedule to the CDates class file:

```
Private Sub ComputeEndDateSchedule()
    Dim SchedDate As Variant
    Dim i As Integer
    '
    ' Compute scheduled dates based on the start date, interval
    ' type, and number of intervals == until the start date
    ' exceeds the end date.
    '
    SchedDate = m_StartDate
```

Continued on next page

Continued from previous page

```
    i = 1
    Do Until CVDate(SchedDate) > CVDate(m_EndDate)
        m_Container.AddItem SchedDate
        SchedDate = DateAdd(m_Interval, _
                            m_NbrOfIntervals * i, _
                            m_StartDate)
        i = i + 1
    Loop
End Sub
```

This routine adds items to the Container list box or combo box, starting with the start date, incrementing dates based on the requested frequency, and stopping at the last date that does not exceed the end date. Visual Basic's DateAdd function is used to increment the dates. Beginning with the start date, the date is incremented based on the interval string and number of intervals that correspond to the desired frequency. For example, if the desired frequency is bimonthly, the interval string is set to m, and the number of intervals is set to 2.

Notice that each scheduled date is computed based on the original start date, with the number of intervals extended by the number of times through the loop. This ensures that month-based increments continue to honor a starting date of the month (such as 31). The DateAdd function will automatically drop the day of the month down to a valid day number when necessary. But by basing each calculation on the original start date, the earlier day of the month won't be repeated in months where it's not necessary to go lower.

18. Add a private subroutine called ComputeNbrOfDatesSchedule to the CDates class file. This routine adds items to the Container list box or combo box, beginning with the start date, incrementing dates based on the requested frequency, and stopping once the requested number of dates is added. See the comments in step 17 regarding use of the DateAdd function, and for an explanation of why the start date is always incremented rather than incrementing each newly calculated date.

```
Private Sub ComputeNbrOfDatesSchedule()
    Dim SchedDate As Date
    Dim i As Integer
    '
    ' Compute scheduled dates based on the start date, interval
    ' type, and number of intervals, stopping when the number of
    ' computed dates exceeds the desired number of dates.
    '
    SchedDate = m_StartDate
    For i = 1 To m_NbrOfDates
        m_Container.AddItem SchedDate
    On Error Resume next
        SchedDate = DateAdd(m_Interval, _
                            m_NbrOfIntervals * i, _
                            m_StartDate)
    If Err.Number <> 0 Then Exit Sub
    Next i
End Sub
```

How It Works

The Schedule of Dates form in this How-To allows the entry of a schedule start date and either a schedule end date or a number of dates to schedule. As in How-To 9.2, this project makes no attempt to limit the keystrokes to those valid for a date, since Visual Basic recognizes dates in a variety of formats (10/1/99, 10/01/1999, Oct 1, 1999, October 01, 99, and so on). This How-To also allows the selection of a scheduling frequency from a list box. The list box limits the choice of frequencies to those supported by the new ComputeSchedule method in the CDates class file.

When a change is made to the EndDateText value, the NbrOfDatesText value is cleared—but only when the end date change did not result in clearing that value. That keeps the first keystroke in the EndDateText text box intact. Otherwise, clearing the NbrOfDatesText value would trigger a Change event that would clear the first keystroke from the EndDateText value. Similar checking is done to prevent losing the first keystroke in NbrOfDatesText.

The CDates ComputeSchedule method is triggered whenever a change is made to any of the scheduling "ingredients"—the start date, the end date, the number of dates to schedule, or the scheduling frequency. The CDates class file contains all the logic to translate any frequency option into the interval string and interval number that Visual Basic's DateAdd function understands. Also contained there is the looping for the desired number of dates or date range. A list box provides a convenient container for the interval series of dates that result from ComputeSchedule's computations.

Comments

A list box provides a convenient container for the interval series of dates, but it doesn't necessarily provide all the flexibility that may be needed by any program wanting to obtain a schedule of dates. A user-defined collection of dates or simply an array of dates might provide more flexibility.

9.5 How do I...
Use Dir$ to Recursively Search a Directory Tree?

COMPLEXITY: INTERMEDIATE
COMPATIBILITY: VB4 ONLY

Problem

I'd like to be able to search an entire disk or directory tree, gathering all the files or directories into a structure I can manipulate. The documentation and help file state that the Dir function can't be used recursively, but I know it's been done. What's the trick?

Technique

In this How-To you'll see a class module built, called CFiles, that uses the Dir function to recursively search an entire disk or directory tree. Every file found is stored within the class module and can be referenced by index. The CFiles class by default searches for files of all attributes, but allows the search to be narrowed down to files that match a given attribute mask. Starting paths and file specs are also optional, the defaults being the root of the current drive and *.*. Recursion is optional, and two types of searches are offered: for files or for directories. After the search is complete, files and their related information (size, date, time, attributes) may be retrieved individually, or CFiles also offers a DOS-like, Dir-style listing string as shown in Figure 9-5-1.

The Dir command requires a file specification to find the first matching file. After that, passing Dir a null string will return the next matching file until no more are found. If you attempt to recursively drop down into a found directory, however, there is no way to resume where you left off when you return. To get around this, CFiles stores a mini-array of all the subdirectories encountered in the current directory and processes each one in turn.

Steps

Open and run RECURSE.VBP. Enter a path in the text box near the top of the form, and press the Go! button. For experimentation, choose a directory without too many

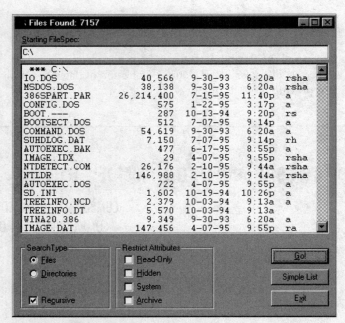

Figure 9-5-1 The CFiles demonstration project in action

files and subdirectories, because searching an entire large disk can take quite a while. Try turning on some of the attribute restrictions using the check boxes, and run a nonrecursive search on the root directory of your boot drive (where a wide variety of file attributes are often present). Pressing the Dir Style button transforms the simple list of all found files into a DOS-like listing of the files with all their related information. That button acts as a toggle between the two listing styles, without actually performing a new search. If more files are found than will fit in the list box (a distinct possibility under Win16), you'll be informed of how many were found and how many are displayed. Clicking on any entry in the list box places the path of that file or directory into the text box that indicates where to start the next search.

Building the CFiles Class Module

1. Create a new project called RECURSE.VBP, and use the Insert Class Module menu item to add a new class module to the project. Name it CFiles, and save the module as CFILES.CLS.

2. Add the following code to the General section of CFiles. This defines a structure, FileDataType, to hold the information found on directory searches. Internal property variables and constants used to define the search type of the class are declared. Also, two constants—which can be used to find all files, all directories, or all files and directories (when OR'd together)—are defined using the intrinsic Visual Basic constants for file attribute values.

```
Option Explicit
'
' Structure to hold data about files found.
'
Private Type FileDataType
    Name        As String
    Path        As String
    FullName    As String
    Length      As Long
    Stamp       As Double
    Attr        As Byte
End Type
'
' Member variables to hold property values
'
Private m_File() As FileDataType
Private m_Dir As String
Private m_Recurse As Boolean
Private m_Spec As String
Private m_Attr As Byte
Private m_Count As Long
Private m_Type As Integer
'
' Constants used to define SearchType property.
'
Const findFiles = 0
Const findDirs = 1
```

Continued on next page

Continued from previous page

```
'
' Constants to define increments used to size m_File array,
' and common file attribute masks.
'
Private Const ArraySize = 500
Private Const AllFiles = vbReadOnly + vbSystem + vbHidden + vbArchive
Private Const AllDirs = vbReadOnly + vbHidden + vbDirectory
```

3. Insert the following code in the Class_Initialize event of CFiles. Here, all the property variables are set to the default values.

```
Private Sub Class_Initialize()
    '
    ' Set default values for class members
    '
    m_Dir = Left(CurDir, 3)
    m_Recurse = True
    m_Spec = "*.*"
    m_Attr = vbNormal
    m_Count = 0
    m_Type = findFiles
End Sub
```

4. Add the following pair of property procedures to CFiles, to set and retrieve the SearchType property. This indicates whether to search for files or directories. The default setting produces a file search.

```
Public Property Let SearchType(NewVal As Integer)
    '
    ' Store desired search type - files or dirs
    '
    If NewVal = findFiles Or NewVal = findDirs Then
        m_Type = NewVal
    End If
End Property

Public Property Get SearchType() As Integer
    '
    ' Return current searching type
    '
    SearchType = m_Type
End Property
```

5. Add the following pair of property procedures to CFiles, to set and retrieve the SearchDir property. This indicates where to begin the next search. The default setting is the root directory of the current drive. The actual searching routines require that the passed directory be terminated with a backslash, so it's added here for convenience.

```
Public Property Let SearchDir(ByVal NewVal As String)
    '
    ' Set location to start file searches
    ' Append trailing backslash
```

```
    '
    NewVal = UCase(Trim(NewVal))
    If Right(NewVal, 1)  "\" Then
        NewVal = NewVal & "\"
    End If
    m_Dir = NewVal
End Property

Public Property Get SearchDir() As String
    '
    ' Return where file searches start
    '
    SearchDir = m_Dir
End Property
```

6. Add the following pair of property procedures to CFiles, to set and retrieve the SearchSpec property. This indicates the file specification to use with the next search. The default setting, *.*, retrieves all files.

```
Public Property Let SearchSpec(NewVal As String)
    '
    ' Store wildcard matching spec
    '
    m_Spec = UCase(Trim(NewVal))
End Property

Public Property Get SearchSpec() As String
    '
    ' Return wildcard matching spec
    '
    SearchSpec = m_Spec
End Property
```

7. Add the following pair of property procedures to CFiles, to set and retrieve the SearchAttr property. This acts as a mask against which the attribute bits of each found file are compared. If all the attribute bits in the mask are set for the found file, it is stored for future retrieval; otherwise, it's discarded and the search continues. By default, all files match the initial attribute mask of vbNormal.

```
Public Property Let SearchAttr(NewVal As Byte)
    '
    ' Store what attribute(s) to search for
    '
    m_Attr = NewVal
End Property

Public Property Get SearchAttr() As Byte
    '
    ' Return what attribute(s) to search for
    '
    SearchAttr = m_Attr
End Property
```

8. Add the following pair of property procedures to CFiles, to set and retrieve the Recurse property. This controls whether the next search will be recursive and search into every branch of the StartDir, or be restricted to just searching the StartDir. The default setting is True.

```
Public Property Let Recurse(NewVal As Boolean)
    '
    ' Store whether or not to recurse through tree
    '
    m_Recurse = NewVal
End Property

Public Property Get Recurse() As Boolean
    '
    ' Return whether recursion will be used
    '
    Recurse = m_Recurse
End Property
```

9. Add the following read-only property procedure to CFiles, to retrieve the value of the Count property. This returns the number of files or directories found during the last search. It can be used to determine if the last search was successful, and for looping through all finds.

```
Public Property Get Count() As Long
    '
    ' Note: Read-only
    ' Return number of files or directories found
    '
    Count = m_Count
End Property
```

10. Add the following read-only property procedure to CFiles, to retrieve the File property for a given index. Pass an index value between 0 and (Count −1) for the filename of the associated file.

```
Public Property Get File(Index As Long) As String
    '
    ' Note: Read-only
    ' Return specific found file name.
    '
    If Index >= 0 And Index < m_Count Then
        File = m_File(Index).Name
    End If
End Property
```

11. Add the following read-only property procedure to CFiles, to retrieve the Path property for a given index. Pass an index value between 0 and (Count −1) for the path of the associated file.

```
Public Property Get Path(Index As Long) As String
    '
```

```
    ' Note: Read-only
    ' Return specific found path name.
    '
    If Index >= 0 And Index < m_Count Then
       Path = m_File(Index).Path
    End If
End Property
```

12. Add the following read-only property procedure to CFiles, to retrieve the PathFile property for a given index. Pass an index value between 0 and (Count −1) for the fully qualified path and filename of the associated file. Since both these items are known at the time of the search, it proves more flexible to store them individually and concatenated. This arrangement consumes more memory in the array but allows much faster use of the data for activities such as filling list boxes.

```
Public Property Get PathFile(Index As Long) As String
    '
    ' Note: Read-only
    ' Return specific, fully-qualified, found file name.
    '
    If Index >= 0 And Index < m_Count Then
       PathFile = m_File(Index).FullName
    End If
End Property
```

13. Add the following read-only property procedure to CFiles, to retrieve the Length property for a given index. Pass an index value between 0 and (Count −1) for the number of bytes in the associated file.

```
Public Property Get Length(Index As Long) As Long
    '
    ' Note: Read-only
    ' Return specific found file size
    '
    If Index >= 0 And Index < m_Count Then
       Length = m_File(Index).Length
    End If
End Property
```

14. Add the following read-only property procedure to CFiles, to retrieve the Stamp property for a given index. Pass an index value between 0 and (Count −1) for a double precision value in which both the date and time stamp of the associated file are stored.

```
Public Property Get Stamp(Index As Long) As Double
    '
    ' Note: Read-only
    ' Return specific found file date
    '
    If Index >= 0 And Index < m_Count Then
       Stamp = m_File(Index).Stamp
    End If
End Property
```

15. Add the following read-only property procedure to CFiles, to retrieve the Attr property for a given index. Pass an index value between 0 and (Count −1) for a byte value in which both the combined attributes of the associated file are stored. To test for a specific attribute, AND the return value with the appropriate constant value. See the code in the DirEntry property for specific examples.

```
Public Property Get Attr(Index As Long) As Byte
    '
    ' Note: Read-only
    ' Return specific found file attributes
    '
    If Index >= 0 And Index < m_Count Then
        Attr = m_File(Index).Attr
    End If
End Property
```

16. Add the following read-only property procedure to CFiles, to retrieve the Attr property for a given index. Pass an index value between 0 and (Count −1) for a formatted string that contains similar data to what appears in either a DOS Dir listing or in File Manager. This string contains the filename, size, date, time, and attributes. Most of these can be set into the return string with one reference to the m_File array, but the attributes are a little more troublesome. Since DOS and Windows machines store all the attributes in separate bits within a single byte, each attribute of interest must be individually checked.

```
Public Property Get DirEntry(Index As Long) As String
    Dim ThisFile As String
    Dim AttrStr As String
    '
    ' Note: Read-only
    ' Return formatted (DIR-like) entry
    '
    If Index >= 0 And Index < m_Count Then
        '
        ' Build bulk of directory listing string
        '
        ThisFile = Space(52)
        LSet ThisFile = m_File(Index).Name
        Mid(ThisFile, 16, 12) = LPad(m_File(Index).Length, 12)
        Mid(ThisFile, 30, 8) = LPad(Format(m_File(Index).Stamp, _
            "m-dd-yy"), 8)
        Mid(ThisFile, 40, 6) = LPad(Format(m_File(Index).Stamp, _
            "h:mma/p"), 6)
        '
        ' Build attribute string and set into directory string
        '
        If (m_File(Index).Attr And vbDirectory) = vbDirectory Then
            AttrStr = AttrStr & "d"
        End If
        If (m_File(Index).Attr And vbReadOnly) = vbReadOnly Then
            AttrStr = AttrStr & "r"
        End If
```

```
        If (m_File(Index).Attr And vbSystem) = vbSystem Then
            AttrStr = AttrStr & "s"
        End If
        If (m_File(Index).Attr And vbHidden) = vbHidden Then
            AttrStr = AttrStr & "h"
        End If
        If (m_File(Index).Attr And vbArchive) = vbArchive Then
            AttrStr = AttrStr & "a"
        End If
        Mid(ThisFile, 48, Len(AttrStr)) = AttrStr
        '
        ' Return built-up string.
        '
        DirEntry = ThisFile
    End If
End Property
```

17. Add the following private function to CFiles. This LPad function supports the DirEntry property by formatting and left-padding numbers or strings passed to it, so they are returned at a given fixed width.

```
Private Function LPad(ValIn As Variant, WidthOut As Integer, Optional nDec ⇒
    As Variant) As String
    '
    ' Formatting function left pads with spaces, using specified
    ' number of decimal digits.
    '
    If IsNumeric(ValIn) Then
        If IsMissing(nDec) Then nDec = 0
        If nDec > 0 Then
            LPad = Right(Space(WidthOut) & Format(ValIn, "#,##0." _
                & String(nDec, "0")), WidthOut)
        Else
            LPad = Right(Space(WidthOut) & Format(ValIn, "#,##0"), _
                WidthOut)
        End If
    Else
        LPad = Right(Space(WidthOut) & ValIn, WidthOut)
    End If
End Function
```

18. Add the public Refresh method, with the following code, to CFiles. Here, after resetting the file counter to 0, the starting directory specification is checked for validity with a call to the private IsValid function. If a valid path has been specified, the m_File array is redimensioned to clear it of its previous contents. Since there's no way to know how large it must grow, m_File() is initially set to 500 elements, and it grows by that same amount whenever more elements are required. This is much more efficient than resizing the array as each new element is added. Based on the SearchType property, the appropriate searching routine is called, and then m_File is resized one more time so that it consumes no more memory than is necessary.

```
Public Sub Refresh()
    Dim StartDir As String
    '
    ' Reset counter, then check pathspec for validity.
    '
    m_Count = 0
    If IsValid Then
        '
        ' Call appropriate routine based on SearchType.
        '
        Screen.MousePointer = vbHourglass
        ReDim m_File(0 To ArraySize - 1) As FileDataType
        StartDir = m_Dir
        Select Case m_Type
            Case findFiles
                Call Me.GetAllFiles(StartDir)
            Case findDirs
                Call Me.GetAllDirs(StartDir)
        End Select
        '
        ' Reduce array to only use required entries.
        '
        If m_Count Then
            ReDim Preserve m_File(0 To m_Count - 1) As FileDataType
        End If
        Screen.MousePointer = vbDefault
    End If
End Sub
```

19. Add the private IsValid function to CFiles. IsValid checks the SearchDir property to determine whether it indeed exists. This is accomplished with a simple call to the Dir function with error trapping enabled. If an error occurs, it's assumed that the SearchDir property is invalid.

```
Private Function IsValid() As Boolean
    Dim Temp As String
    '
    ' Turn on error trapping to catch invalid pathspec
    '
    On Error Resume Next
    '
    ' Check path for validity using Dir
    '
    Temp = Dir(m_Dir & "*.*", AllFiles Or AllDirs)
    '
    ' If an error occured, the path is invalid
    '
    If Err Then
        IsValid = False
    Else
        IsValid = True
    End If
End Function
```

20. Add the private GetAllFiles method to CFiles. When SearchType is equal to findFiles, this routine is passed a starting directory, and does the actual recursive processing. All directories passed to GetAllFiles must be terminated with a back-slash so that the SearchSpec can be appended to them. Initially, a call to the Dir

function is made to find the first matching file, given the specified path and file-name, without regard to attributes. If one is found, a loop is entered that will repeatedly recall Dir until no more matches are made. Within the loop, the found file's attributes are retrieved and compared to the SearchAttr mask as the final test for a "hit." If this also matches, then the file's information is stored in the next available m_File array entry. When the array becomes full, it is expanded by another 500 entries.

After all matching files in the starting directory have been processed, a call is placed to GetDirs, which returns an array of all subdirectories at the current level. This array is used to recursively call GetAllFiles, thus traversing down the direc-tory tree. Since the CFiles class exposes the SearchSpec property, and this can be set to anything by the calling program, a second search just for subdirectories is required to ensure that none are missed on the first pass.

```
Private Sub GetAllFiles(StartDir As String)
    Dim SubDir() As String
    Dim Spec As String
    Dim ThisAttr As Byte
    Dim nDirs As Integer
    Dim i As Integer
    '
    ' StartDir must end in backslash
    '
    If Right(StartDir, 1) <> "\" Then
        StartDir = StartDir & "\"
    End If
    '
    ' Look for first matching file or directory
    '
    Spec = Dir(StartDir & m_Spec, AllFiles)
    '
    ' Loop until no more files or directories match
    '
    Do While Len(Spec)
        '
        ' Check file attributes for match
        '
        ThisAttr = GetAttr(StartDir & Spec)
        If (ThisAttr And m_Attr) = m_Attr Then
            '
            ' Found file matches the spec and attributes requested.
            '
            m_File(m_Count).Name = Spec
            m_File(m_Count).Path = StartDir
            m_File(m_Count).FullName = StartDir & Spec
            m_File(m_Count).Length = FileLen(m_File(m_Count).FullName)
            m_File(m_Count).Stamp = FileDateTime(m_File(m_Count). _
                FullName)
            m_File(m_Count).Attr = ThisAttr
            m_Count = m_Count + 1
            If m_Count Mod ArraySize = 0 Then
                '
                ' Expand array every (ArraySize) files
                '
                ReDim Preserve m_File(0 To m_Count + ArraySize - 1) _
```

Continued on next page

Continued from previous page

```
                    As FileDataType
        End If
    End If
    '
    ' Get next matching file or directory
    '
    Spec = Dir
Loop
'
' Call GetDirs to find all subdirectories in this directory.
' Required to allow matches against all directories for
' recursion, since all dirs must be found, not just m_Spec.
'
If m_Recurse Then
    '
    ' Get all subdirectories within StartDir
    '
    nDirs = Me.GetDirs(StartDir, SubDir())
    If nDirs Then
        '
        ' Loop through all found directories, calling for each.
        '
        For i = 0 To nDirs - 1
            Call Me.GetAllFiles(StartDir & SubDir(i))
        Next i
    End If
End If
End Sub
```

21. Add the private GetAllDirs method to CFiles. When SearchType is equal to findDirs, this routine is passed a starting directory, and does the actual recursive processing. All directories passed to GetAllDirs must be terminated with a back-slash so that the SearchSpec can be appended to them. Initially, a call to the private GetDirs function is made, which returns an array of all subdirectories at the current level. The relevant information for each found directory is stored in the m_File array, and the array is resized as required. GetAllDirs then calls itself for each subdirectory found at the current level, to recurse through the entire tree.

```
Private Sub GetAllDirs(StartDir As String)
    Dim SubDir() As String
    Dim nDirs As Integer
    Dim i As Integer
    '
    ' StartDir must end in backslash
    '
    If Right(StartDir, 1) <> "\" Then
        StartDir = StartDir & "\"
    End If
    '
    ' Get all subdirectories within StartDir
    '
    nDirs = Me.GetDirs(StartDir, SubDir())
    If nDirs Then
        '
        ' For each found subdirectory, store relevant data
        '
        For i = 0 To nDirs - 1
```

```
        m_File(m_Count).Name = SubDir(i)
        m_File(m_Count).Path = StartDir
        m_File(m_Count).FullName = StartDir & SubDir(i)
        m_File(m_Count).Stamp = FileDateTime(m_File(m_Count). _
           FullName)
        m_File(m_Count).Attr = GetAttr(m_File(m_Count).FullName)
        m_Count = m_Count + 1
        If m_Count Mod ArraySize = 0 Then
           '
           ' Expand array every (ArraySize) files
           '
           ReDim Preserve m_File(0 To m_Count + ArraySize - 1) _
              As FileDataType
        End If
     Next i
     '
     ' For each subdirectory found, call this routine again.
     '
     If m_Recurse Then
        For i = 0 To nDirs - 1
           Me.GetAllDirs StartDir & SubDir(i)
        Next i
     End If
   End If
End Sub
```

22. Add the private GetDirs function to CFiles.

```
Private Function GetDirs(DirSpec As String, SubDir() As String) As Integer
   ReDim SubDir(0) As String
   Dim Spec As String
   Dim ThisAttr As Byte
   Dim nDirs As Integer
   '
   ' Look for first matching file or directory
   '
   Spec = Dir(DirSpec & "*.*", AllDirs)
   '
   ' Loop until no more files or directories match
   '
   Do While Len(Spec)
      '
      ' Not interested in the dot or double-dot directory entries
      '
      If Not (InStr(Spec, ".")) = 1 Then
         '
         ' Check file attributes for match
         '
         ThisAttr = GetAttr(DirSpec & Spec)
         If ThisAttr And vbDirectory Then
            SubDir(nDirs) = Spec
            nDirs = nDirs + 1
            ReDim Preserve SubDir(0 To nDirs) As String
         End If
      End If
      '
      ' Find next match
      '
      Spec = Dir
```

Continued on next page

Continued from previous page

```
    Loop
    '
    ' Return number of directories found.
    '
    GetDirs = nDirs
End Function
```

This function is passed an empty string array, which it fills with the names of all subdirectories found within the passed DirSpec. (GetDir's actions are very similar to those in GetAllFiles.) An attempt is made to find the first match, using the Dir function with an attribute value that could include any possible settings for directory entries. If any subdirectories are found, a loop is entered, which will use the FindNext method of calling the Dir function to continue retrieving all matches to the original parameters. Two special cases, which exist in every subdirectory, are ignored—the dot and double-dot entries that are DOS pointers to the current and parent directory entries. Found subdirectories are then compared to the SearchAttr mask, in case the user wanted to find only hidden directories, for example. As each match is found, the return string array is increased in size to hold the new entry, and its information is stored. The function itself returns the total number of subdirectories contained in the SubDir array.

Building a Test Project for the CFiles Class Module

23. Add a new form to your project, name it frmRecurse, and save it as RECURSE.FRM. Place the controls and set the properties as listed in Table 9-5-1. Tables 9-5-2 and 9-5-3 list the controls that should be contained within Frame1 and Frame2, respectively. When you've completed setting it up, it should appear similar to Figure 9-5-2.

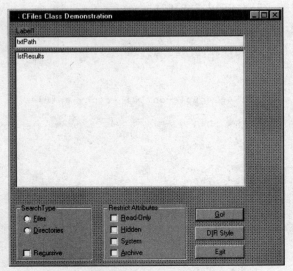

Figure 9-5-2 RECURSE.FRM at design time

Table 9-5-1 Objects and their properties on RECURSE.FRM

OBJECT	PROPERTY	SETTING
Form	Name	frmRecurse
	Caption	"CFiles Class Demonstration"
	Height	6700
	Width	7000
Label	Name	Label1
	AutoSize	True
Textbox	Name	txtPath
Listbox	Name	lstResults
Frame	Name	Frame1
	Caption	"Search Type"
Frame	Name	Frame2
	Caption	"Restrict Attributes"
CommandButton	Name	Command1
	Caption	"&Go!"
	Default	True
CommandButton	Name	Command2
	Caption	"D&IR Style"
CommandButton	Name	Command3
	Caption	"E&xit"

Table 9-5-2 Objects and their properties contained within Frame1

OBJECT	PROPERTY	SETTING
OptionButton	Name	optType
	Caption	"&Files"
	Index	0
OptionButton	Name	optType
	Caption	"&Directories"
	Index	1
CheckBox	Name	chkRecurse
	Caption	"Re&cursive"

Table 9-5-3 Objects and their properties contained within Frame2

OBJECT	PROPERTY	SETTING
CheckBox	Name	chkAttr
	Caption	"&Read-Only"
	Index	0

Continued on next page

Continued from previous page

OBJECT	PROPERTY	SETTING
CheckBox	Name	chkAttr
	Caption	"&Hidden"
	Index	1
CheckBox	Name	chkAttr
	Caption	"S&ystem"
	Index	2
CheckBox	Name	chkAttr
	Caption	"&Archive"
	Index	3

24. Using the File Add menu item, add the CStockFont class module, CSFONT.CLS, to the project. This module was developed in How-To 3.14, but if you haven't read it yet, don't worry—it isn't critical to understanding this demonstration. Just be aware that CStockFont allows use of fixed-width fonts in standard Visual Basic controls.

25. Add the following code to the Declarations section of frmRecurse. An object variable is declared, and a new instance created, of the CFiles class. The constants used by the CFiles SearchType property are defined. Several flags are required to track the current state of the demonstration. The constant values supported by CStockFont are imported for use with the list box.

```
Option Explicit
'
' Object variable for CFiles class
'
Dim fi As New CFiles
'
' Two search types offered by CFiles class
'
Const findFiles = 0
Const findDirs = 1
'
' Flags: List type to display.
'        Was last search recursive?
'
Private DirList As Boolean
Private DidRecurse As Boolean
'
' Values supported for StockFont property of CStockFont
'
Const sfOEM_FIXED = 0
Const sfANSI_VAR = 1
Const sfANSI_FIXED = 2
Const sfSYSTEM_VAR = 3
Const sfSYSTEM_FIXED = 4
Const sfDEVICE_DEFAULT = 5
```

26. Insert the following code in the Form_Load event of frmRecurse. This sets a starting directory to be displayed in the text box, and sets the initial state of several controls. Each attribute check box has the related attribute value assigned to its Tag property. The findfiles search type is enabled by checking that option button, and recursion by checking that check box.

```
Private Sub Form_Load()
    '
    ' Set and highlight starting path
    '
    If IsDirectory("C:\") Then
        txtPath = "C:\"
    Else
        txtPath = Left(CurDir, 3)
    End If
    txtPath.SelStart = 0
    txtPath.SelLength = Len(txtPath)
    '
    ' Assign respective constants to Attribute checkboxes
    '
    chkAttr(0).Tag = vbReadOnly
    chkAttr(1).Tag = vbHidden
    chkAttr(2).Tag = vbSystem
    chkAttr(3).Tag = vbArchive
    '
    ' Select findFiles as starting SearchType
    '
    optType(findFiles).Value = True
    '
    ' Turn on Recursion
    '
    chkRecurse = vbChecked
End Sub
```

27. Insert the following code in the Form_Resize event of frmRecurse. This form was designed to automatically adjust the position and size of all its controls whenever the form is resized. This allows the user to read very long entries, or view more entries in the list box by simply resizing the form.

```
Private Sub Form_Resize()
    Dim Offset As Integer
    '
    ' Adjust control placement to fit new form size.
    ' Ignore errors caused by the user making it too small.
    '
    If Me.WindowState <> vbMinimized Then
        Offset = lstResults.Left
        txtPath.Width = Me.ScaleWidth - Offset * 2
        Frame1.Top = Me.ScaleHeight - Frame1.Height - Offset
        Frame2.Move Frame1.Left + Frame1.Width + Offset, _
                    Me.ScaleHeight - Frame2.Height - Offset
        Command1.Move Me.ScaleWidth - Command1.Width - Offset, _
                    Frame1.Top + Offset
```

Continued on next page

Continued from previous page

```
        Command2.Move Me.ScaleWidth - Command2.Width - Offset, _
                   Command1.Top + Command1.Height + Offset
        Command3.Move Me.ScaleWidth - Command3.Width - Offset, _
                   Command2.Top + Command2.Height + Offset
        On Error Resume Next
        lstResults.Move Offset, lstResults.Top, txtPath.Width, _
                   Frame1.Top - Offset - lstResults.Top
    End If
End Sub
```

28. Insert the following code in the chkAttr_Click event of frmRecurse. Whenever the user toggles one of these check boxes, a new attribute mask is calculated by adding up the Tag properties of all checked check boxes. (In Form_Load, the related constant values for each attribute were loaded into the Tag of the appropriate check box.) This mask is then assigned to the SearchAttr property of the CFiles object.

```
Private Sub chkAttr_Click(Index As Integer)
    Dim i As Integer
    Dim NewAttr As Integer
    '
    ' Assemble file search attribute mask
    '
    For i = 0 To 3
        If chkAttr(i) = vbChecked Then
            NewAttr = NewAttr + chkAttr(i).Tag
        End If
    Next i
    '
    ' Assign SearchAttr property to CFiles object
    '
    fi.SearchAttr = NewAttr
End Sub
```

29. Insert the following code in the chkRecurse_Click event of frmRecurse. Each time the user toggles this check box, the Recurse property of the CFiles object is updated appropriately.

```
Private Sub chkRecurse_Click()
    '
    ' Assign Recurse property to CFiles object
    '
    fi.Recurse = chkRecurse
End Sub
```

30. Insert the following code in the optType_Click event of frmRecurse. Whenever the user clicks one of these option buttons, the SearchType property of the CFiles object is updated appropriately. The label above the text box is also changed to reflect upcoming search types.

```
Private Sub optType_Click(Index As Integer)
    '
```

```
' Assign SearchType property to CFiles object
'
fi.SearchType = Index
'
' Alter spec label to match SearchType
'
Select Case Index
    Case findFiles
        Label1 = "&Starting FileSpec:"
    Case findDirs
        Label1 = "&Starting Directory:"
End Select
End Sub
```

31. Insert the following code in the Command1_Click event of frmRecurse. This code is executed when the user wants the search to begin. The SearchDir property is set after extracting a path from the text box. If no path was entered, then the current directory is used by default. The SearchSpec is extracted from the text box, defaulting to *.* if no specification was entered. The form's caption is updated to let the user know the search is occurring, and the CFiles.Refresh method is invoked. Before leaving the routine, the value of the CFiles.Recurse property is stored for future reference (since the user can change it at any time, it's convenient to know what the last search was). Another routine is called to fill the list box with all the found files or directories.

```
Private Sub Command1_Click()
    Dim Spec As String
    '
    ' Extract just the path from txtPath and assign to
    ' SearchDir. If nothing entered in search path textbox,
    ' then use current directory.
    '
    If Len(txtPath) Then
        fi.SearchDir = ExtractPath(txtPath)
    Else
        txtPath = CurDir$
        fi.SearchDir = CurDir$
    End If
    '
    ' Extract the filespec from txtPath if present,
    ' otherwise use "*.*".
    '
    Spec = ExtractName(txtPath)
    If Len(Spec) Then
        fi.SearchSpec = Spec
    Else
        fi.SearchSpec = "*.*"
    End If
    '
    ' Call CFiles.Refresh method.
    '
    Me.Caption = "Searching..."
    fi.Refresh
```

Continued on next page

Continued from previous page

```
    '
    ' Remember if this search was recursive.
    ' Fill listbox with as many hits as will fit.
    '
    DidRecurse = fi.Recurse
    FillList
End Sub
```

32. Insert the following code in the Command2_Click event of frmRecurse. This but-
    ton toggles the list box display between a straight listing of the fully qualified file-
    names and a more Dir-like listing. The button's caption is altered, a flag is set,
    and the FillList routine is called.

```
Private Sub Command2_Click()
    '
    ' Toggle button caption, set flag, and fill list.
    '
    If DirList Then
        Command2.Caption = "D&IR Style"
        DirList = False
    Else
        Command2.Caption = "S&imple List"
        DirList = True
    End If
    FillList
End Sub
```

33. Insert a Me.Unload in the Command3_Click event to exit the demonstration.

```
Private Sub Command3_Click()
    '
    ' All done!
    '
    Unload Me
End Sub
```

34. Add FillList to frmRecurse as a private subroutine, and insert the following code
    in it:

```
Private Sub FillList()
    Dim i As Long
    Dim ThisDir As String
    Dim sfObj As New CStockFont
    '
    ' Update form caption to show number found.
    '
    If optType(findFiles) Then
        Me.Caption = "Files Found: " & fi.Count
    ElseIf optType(findDirs) Then
        Me.Caption = "Directories Found: " & fi.Count
    End If
    '
    ' Clear listbox and fill with as many hits as will fit.
```

```
    '
    lstResults.Clear
    If fi.Count Then
        '
        ' Set error handling jump in case list grows too big.
        ' Turn on hourglass cursor.
        '
        On Error GoTo ListTooBig
        Screen.MousePointer = vbHourglass
        If DirList Then
            ' Use fixed-width font to fill listbox with
            ' all hits, using a DIR style listing.
            '
            Set sfObj.Client = lstResults
            sfObj.StockFont = sfANSI_FIXED
            For i = 0 To fi.Count - 1
                '
                ' Keep track of current directory, output
                ' whenever it changes.
                '
                If DidRecurse Then
                    If fi.Path(i) <> ThisDir Then
                        ThisDir = fi.Path(i)
                        lstResults.AddItem " *** " & ThisDir
                        lstResults.ItemData(lstResults.NewIndex) = i
                    End If
                End If
                '
                ' Add to name and index to list.
                '
                lstResults.AddItem fi.DirEntry(i)
                lstResults.ItemData(lstResults.NewIndex) = i
            Next i
        Else
            '
            ' Fill listbox with simple listing of fully-qualified
            ' filespecs. Very fast, comparitively.
            '
            Set sfObj.Client = lstResults
            sfObj.StockFont = sfANSI_VAR
            For i = 0 To fi.Count - 1
                lstResults.AddItem fi.PathFile(i)
                lstResults.ItemData(lstResults.NewIndex) = i
            Next i
        End If
ListTooBig:
        If Err Then
            '
            ' Listbox ran out of memory. Display message
            ' and update caption, then cleanup.
            '
            MsgBox "Too many files to fit in Listbox!"
            Me.Caption = Me.Caption & " [" & lstResults.ListCount & " displayed]"
        End If
```

Continued on next page

1005

Continued from previous page

```
        Screen.MousePointer = vbDefault
    End If
End Sub
```

Here, all the files or directories found during the last search are updated in the list box. First, the form's caption is changed to reflect how many files were found. This also alerts the user that the search is done, and that the data is now being loaded into the list box. Then, the list box is cleared, and as many entries as will fit are loaded into it. Under Win16, it's a very real possibility that a single disk will contain more files than a list box can display, so error trapping is a necessity.

If the user has asked for the Dir-style listing, CStockFont is used to set a fixed-width stock font into the list box. This allows easy formatting of the tabular directory data. A loop begins, using the Count property of CFiles to cycle through every file found, and adding the return string from DirEntry to the list. If the search was recursive, a new line is added for each new directory so that it's clear where each file is actually located. For each line in the list box, the corresponding index into the CFiles array is stored in the list's ItemData property. This allows easy lookup when the user clicks on the list.

If the user has asked for a simple listing, CStockFont is used to set a variable-width stock font into the list box. For this listing style, the CFiles.PathFile property is used to fill the list, and the index is again used for the list's ItemData property.

If an error occurs using either style, it's assumed to have been caused by an out-of-memory condition within the list box's data space. In this case, the form's caption is again updated to reflect the number of files actually displayed.

35. Insert the following code in the lstResults_Click event. Whenever the user clicks on a list item, its ItemData property is used as an index into the CFiles array to retrieve the path of that particular file. The path is placed in the text box as a potential new starting path for the next search. (This demonstrates how simply data may be recalled from the CFiles class by tracking the index of interest.)

```
Private Sub lstResults_Click()
    '
    ' When user clicks on a file, put its path into txtPath.
    '
    If lstResults.ListCount Then
        txtPath = fi.Path(lstResults.ItemData(lstResults.ListIndex)) _
            & "*.*"
    End If
End Sub
```

One More Support Module

36. Add a new code module to the project, name it MFiles, and save it as MFILES.BAS. This module will contain four general-purpose, file- and path-related functions that you will find useful in many applications.

37. Add the public function ExtractName to the General section of MFiles. This function extracts the filename that appears at the end of an input string. If the optional parameter BaseOnly evaluates to True, the extension of the filename will be removed. This is useful for replicating a given base filename if you're using a different extension—when you're looking for an .INI file with the same base filename as your application, for instance.

```
Public Function ExtractName(SpecIn As String, Optional BaseOnly As Variant) ⇒
     As String
    Dim i As Integer
    Dim SpecOut As String
    '
    ' Ignore errors caused by strange SpecIn's,
    ' such as "C:"
    '
    On Error Resume Next
    '
    ' SpecIn could fall into one of four categories.
    '
    If IsDirectory(SpecIn) Then
        '
        ' Return null string
        '
        SpecOut = ""
    ElseIf InStr(SpecIn, "\") Then
        '
        ' Assume what follows last backslash is
        ' the filespec.
        '
        For i = Len(SpecIn) To 1 Step -1
            If Mid(SpecIn, i, 1) = "\" Then
                SpecOut = Mid(SpecIn, i + 1)
                Exit For
            End If
        Next i
    ElseIf InStr(SpecIn, ":") = 2 Then
        '
        ' A drive and filename were passed.
        '
        SpecOut = Mid(SpecIn, 3)
    Else
        '
        ' Just the filename was passed.
        '
        SpecOut = SpecIn
    End If
    '
    ' If user requested, remove the extension.
    ' Useful for appending a different extension.
    '
    If Not IsMissing(BaseOnly) Then
        If CBool(BaseOnly) Then
            i = InStr(SpecOut, ".")
            If i Then
```

Continued on next page

Continued from previous page

```
                SpecOut = Left(SpecOut, i - 1)
            End If
        End If
    End If
    '
    ' Return capitalized SpecOut
    '
    ExtractName = UCase(SpecOut)
End Function
```

ExtractName must deal with the many possible variations that an application may pass. The first test is to see if the string is actually a directory. If so, a null string is returned. Otherwise, if one or more backslashes are present in the string, everything beyond the last one is returned as the filename. If there are no backslashes, and the second character is a colon, the assumption is that a drive and filename were passed (such as, C:AUTOEXEC.BAT). If none of these tests are met, the final assumption is that a filename alone was passed in. Obviously, there will be cases where very strange input may return twisted filenames, so some caution must be taken to assure a bit of sanity in the SpecIn parameter. No validity checking is performed on the final SpecOut, but in most instances, ExtractName will return the desired results.

38. Add the public function ExtractPath to the General section of MFiles. ExtractPath operates on virtually the same assumptions used in ExtractName, but returns the path instead of the filename.

```
Public Function ExtractPath(SpecIn As String) As String
    Dim i As Integer
    Dim SpecOut As String
    '
    ' Ignore errors caused by strange SpecIn's,
    ' such as invalid drives.
    '
    On Local Error Resume Next
    '
    ' SpecIn could fall into one of four categories.
    '
    If IsDirectory(SpecIn) Then
        '
        ' Just return SpecIn
        '
        SpecOut = SpecIn
    ElseIf InStr(SpecIn, "\") Then
        '
        ' Assume what follows last backslash is
        ' the filespec. Remove it.
        '
        For i = Len(SpecIn) To 1 Step -1
            If Mid(SpecIn, i, 1) = "\" Then
                SpecOut = Left(SpecIn, i - 1)
                Exit For
            End If
```

```
       Next i
    ElseIf InStr(SpecIn, ":") = 2 Then
       '
       ' Get current directory on drive passed.
       '
       SpecOut = CurDir(SpecIn)
    Else
       '
       ' No backslashes or colons. Return null.
       '
       SpecOut = ""
    End If
    '
    ' Return capitalized SpecOut
    '
    ExtractPath = UCase(SpecOut)
End Function
```

39. Add the public function IsDirectory to the General section of MFiles. This function relies on Visual Basic's GetAttr function to test the Directory attribute of the passed-in SpecIn string. There are several special cases that first must be considered. All are valid directory references, but may or may not actually exist. Other cases will absolutely exist if IsDirectory returns True.

```
Public Function IsDirectory(SpecIn As String) As Boolean
    Dim Attr As Byte
    '
    ' Special cases: "C:", "..", "." all generate
    ' "Path not found" errors when passed to GetAttr.
    ' "D:\" may return an attribute value of 0 if
    ' it refers to a removeable drive.
    '
    Select Case Len(SpecIn)
       Case 1
          If SpecIn = "." Then
             IsDirectory = True
             Exit Function
          End If
       Case 2
          If SpecIn = ".." Or InStr(SpecIn, ":") = 2 Then
             IsDirectory = True
             Exit Function
          End If
       Case 3
          If InStr(SpecIn, ":\") = 2 Then
             IsDirectory = True
             Exit Function
          End If
    End Select
    '
    ' Guard against bad SpecIn by ignoring errors.
    ' Get attribute of SpecIn.
    '
    On Error Resume Next
```

Continued on next page

Continued from previous page

```
        Attr = GetAttr(SpecIn)
    On Error GoTo 0
    '
    ' Check for presence of Directory attribute.
    '
    If (Attr And vbDirectory) = vbDirectory Then
        IsDirectory = True
    End If
End Function
```

40. Add the public function IsFile to the General section of MFiles. IsFile can be used to test whether a file exists. It uses Visual Basic's GetAttr function to test the input SpecIn string (as IsDirectory does). If an error isn't generated, then either a file or directory with the passed name does indeed exist. To confirm it's a file, not a directory, the returned attribute byte is tested to see if the Directory bit is set.

```
Public Function IsFile(SpecIn As String) As Boolean
    Dim Attr As Byte
    '
    ' Guard against bad SpecIn by ignoring errors.
    '
    On Error Resume Next
    '
    ' Get attribute of SpecIn.
    '
    Attr = GetAttr(SpecIn)
    If Err = 0 Then
        '
        ' No error, so something was found.
        ' If Directory attribute set, then not a file.
        '
        If (Attr And vbDirectory) = vbDirectory Then
            IsFile = False
        Else
            IsFile = True
        End If
    End If
End Function
```

How It Works

The project in this How-To builds the CFiles class module, and uses it to fill and store an array of files and relevant information about them. CFiles defines a data structure that holds the file's name, path, size, date, time, and attributes. As a search is performed, the information is stored in an array of elements, using the defined structure for each file or directory that matches the filters set by the application. Individual entries may be retrieved by index, as either formatted strings or separate values.

An application may set many filters, such as where to begin the search, what file spec the files must match, what attributes the returned files must have, and whether to search for files or just directories. After a search is complete, the Count property may be used to cycle through the collected array of matching files. All stored information about each file is accessible through other exposed read-only properties: Name, Path, PathName (for a fully qualified name), Size, Stamp, and Attr.

The specifics of the CFiles class module operation are many, and are explained in detail in the discussion preceding each listed routine. In essence, the Dir function is used to retrieve the names of all files within a starting subdirectory. These files are then matched against the criteria set by the application. If a match is found, it is stored along with information about it, in a class array. After checking all the files within a directory, another search looks for all the subdirectories within that directory. For each subdirectory, the process is repeated recursively.

Unfortunately, if you've ever written a similar project using a truly compiled language such as QuickBasic or Visual Basic for DOS, this project demonstrates one of the true drawbacks to Visual Basic for Windows: reliance on interpreted pseudocode. Searching routines like the ones in CFiles absolutely must be as fast as possible, and this is an excellent example of why Visual Basic really needs a native language compiler.

Comments

The CFiles class offers a base upon which many useful utility-type functions can be added. One possible extension to the functionality of CFiles would be to add more search criteria, such as file date or size. This addition would be simple to implement; you'd need only to add new property procedures to set the newly defined SearchXXXX filter, and an additional test for this condition in the GetAllFiles routine. Another possibility would be to add Move, Rename, Delete, or other methods to act upon the found files.

The RECURSE project allows you to experiment with many of the variations for using CFiles. The RECURSE interface allows the user to set and retrieve virtually all the properties of a CFiles class object, and you can build in other new properties and methods as you develop them.

9.6 How do I...
Use Notepad as a Debugging Window?

COMPLEXITY: ADVANCED
COMPATIBILITY: VB4 ONLY

Problem

I often find that I need to produce debugging information while working in the Visual Basic development environment, as well as when running as a compiled executable. I know I could test whether the program is compiled or not, and redirect the output appropriately, but that's a lot of overhead. I'd prefer a simple unified approach so that the output statements don't require additional tests, and I'd also like to be able to turn on this output remotely, at a client site. This way, I wouldn't have to rely on a client's recollection of events, but rather on a solid report. I also want the option of saving the output to a file. Could I perhaps use a utility such as Notepad for this sort of reporting?

Technique

In this How-To we will develop a class module that provides an interface to the Windows Notepad, through a series of simple-to-call methods. Output may be of any length (though this is really only the case in Windows NT; under Windows 95, Notepad is still using a 16-bit edit control, which is limited in similar ways to 16-bit Visual Basic text boxes), appended to existing output, saved to a file, cleared from Notepad, and either visible or completely transparent to the user. An application using CDebug becomes the "owner" of Notepad; thus Notepad is hidden whenever the application is minimized and doesn't show up as a separate process in the Task List. As many instances of Notepad as necessary become available for debugging output.

The CDebug class uses a good number of API functions to find and control the appropriate instance of Notepad. Since Notepad may be visible and thus available for the user to edit or even close, we need to "find" it with nearly every call that uses its window handle (hWnd). Even if the stored hWnd is still valid to Windows, CDebug must confirm that another process hasn't inherited it after Notepad was shut down. If Notepad hasn't started or has been closed, a new instance is started with CreateProcess. You'll learn how to "walk the window list" looking for a particular top-level window with the thread handle (hInst) that CreateProcess returns, using FindWindow, GetWindow, and GetWindowThreadProcessId to retrieve its hWnd.

Communication with Notepad is entirely based on messages, using the SendMessage API. The hWnd for the multiline edit control (text box) that is Notepad's editing area is obtained, and a number of window messages are employed to instruct the edit control. Text may be replaced or retrieved; the caret is optionally positioned at the end of the latest output; and the modification flag is set when output is sent (so Notepad will prompt to save if the user tries closing it)—all done with SendMessage. Programmatic saving of the Notepad's contents is done internally to CDebug, to prevent messy dialog boxes from appearing and possibly confusing the user, and to provide absolute control to the programmer.

Steps

Open and run DEBUG.VBP. Press the Output Debugging Information button. Notice that the label along the top of the main form shows the number of characters in Notepad. Figure 9-6-1 shows the appearance of the main form after pressing the Output button several times. To make Notepad visible, press the Show button. Notepad comes up in a normal state with its caption changed to BugPad. As you produce more debugging data, the label on the main form tracks the total amount of text currently in Notepad. Turn on AutoScrolling by selecting the appropriate check box.

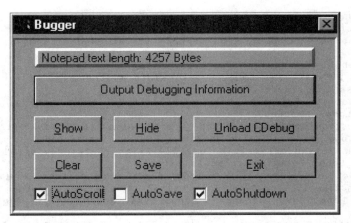

Figure 9-6-1 The Bugger program in action

Now, as you output more data, Notepad's window scrolls to keep up with you. Experiment with the Hide and Clear buttons; output can continue to be sent when Notepad is invisible. If the AutoShutdown check box is checked when you exit Bugger, Notepad will also be shut down, and with its contents saved if the AutoSave check box is also checked.

Creating the CDebug Class

1. Create a new project called DEBUG.VBP, and use the Insert Class Module menu item to add a new class module to the project. Name the module CDebug, and save the file as CDEBUG.CLS.

2. Add the following code to the General section, to declare and support the necessary Win32 API calls used by CDebug:

```
Option Explicit
'
' Win32 API declarations used in CDebug
'
Private Declare Function SendMessage Lib "user32" Alias "SendMessageA" _
    (ByVal hWnd As Long, ByVal wMsg As Long, ByVal wParam As Long, _
    ByVal lParam As Any) As Long
Private Declare Function WinExec Lib "kernel32" (ByVal lpCmdLine _
    As String, ByVal nCmdShow As Long) As Long
Private Declare Function FindWindow Lib "user32" Alias "FindWindowA" _
    (ByVal lpClassName As Any, ByVal lpWindowName As Any) As Long
Private Declare Function IsWindow Lib "user32" (ByVal hWnd As Long) As Long
Private Declare Function SetForegroundWindow Lib "user32" _
    (ByVal hWnd As Long) As Long
Private Declare Function ShowWindow Lib "user32" (ByVal hWnd As Long, _
    ByVal nCmdShow As Long) As Long
Private Declare Function GetWindowPlacement Lib "user32" (ByVal hWnd _
    As Long, lpwndpl As WINDOWPLACEMENT) As Long
```

Continued on next page

Continued from previous page

```
Private Declare Function SetWindowPlacement Lib "user32" (ByVal hWnd _
    As Long, lpwndpl As WINDOWPLACEMENT) As Long
Private Declare Sub GetWindowRect Lib "user32" (ByVal hWnd As Long, _
    lpRect As RECT)
Private Declare Sub MoveWindow Lib "user32" (ByVal hWnd As Long, _
    ByVal x As Long, ByVal Y As Long, ByVal nWidth As Long, _
    ByVal nHeight As Long, ByVal bRepaint As Long)
Private Declare Function GetWindow Lib "user32" (ByVal hWnd As Long, _
    ByVal wCmd As Long) As Long
Private Declare Function GetWindowText Lib "user32" Alias "GetWindowTextA" _
    (ByVal hWnd As Long, ByVal lpString As String, ByVal aint As Long) As Long
Private Declare Sub SetWindowText Lib "user32" Alias "SetWindowTextA" _
    (ByVal hWnd As Long, ByVal lpString As String)
Private Declare Function GetParent Lib "user32" (ByVal hWnd As Long) As Long
Private Declare Function SetWindowLong Lib "user32" Alias "SetWindowLongA" _
    (ByVal hWnd As Long, ByVal nIndex As Long, ByVal dwNewLong As Long) _
    As Long
Private Declare Function CreateProcess Lib "kernel32" Alias "CreateProcessA" _
    (ByVal lpApplicationName As String, ByVal lpCommandLine As String, _
    ByVal lpProcessAttributes As Any, ByVal lpThreadAttributes As Any, _
    ByVal bInheritHandles As Long, ByVal dwCreationFlags As Long, _
    ByVal lpEnvironment As Any, ByVal lpCurrentDriectory As Any, _
    lpStartupInfo As STARTUPINFO, lpProcessInformation _
    As PROCESS_INFORMATION) As Long
Private Declare Function GetLastError Lib "kernel32" () As Long
Private Declare Function WaitForInputIdle Lib "user32" (ByVal hProcess As Long, _
    ByVal dwMilliseconds As Long) As Long
Private Declare Function GetWindowThreadProcessId Lib "user32" _
    (ByVal hWnd As Long, lpdwProcessId As Long) As Long
Private Declare Function IsWindowVisible Lib "user32" (ByVal hWnd _
    As Long) As Long
Private Declare Sub BringWindowToTop Lib "user32" (ByVal hWnd As Long)
Private Declare Function IsIconic Lib "user32" (ByVal hWnd As Long) As Long
Private Declare Function IsZoomed Lib "user32" (ByVal hWnd As Long) As Long
'
' Structures used with CreateProcess
'
Private Type STARTUPINFO
    cb As Long
    lpReserved As String
    lpDesktop As String
    lpTitle As String
    dwX As Long
    dwY As Long
    dwXSize As Long
    dwYSize As Long
    dwXCountChars As Long
    dwYCountChars As Long
    dwFillAttribute As Long
    dwFlags As Long
    wShowWindow As Long
    cbReserved2 As Long
    lpReserved2 As Integer
    hStdInput As Long
    hStdOutput As Long
    hStdError As Long
```

```
End Type

Private Type SECURITY_ATTRIBUTES
    nLength As Long
    lpSecurityDescriptor As Long
    bInheritHandle As Long
End Type

Private Type PROCESS_INFORMATION
    hProcess As Long
    hThread As Long
    dwProcessID As Long
    dwThreadID As Long
End Type
'
' Types used with Set/GetWindowPlacement
'
Private Type POINTAPI
    x As Integer
    Y As Integer
End Type

Private Type RECT
    Left As Integer
    Top As Integer
    Right As Integer
    Bottom As Integer
End Type

Private Type WINDOWPLACEMENT
    Length As Integer
    flags As Integer
    showCmd As Integer
    ptMinPosition As POINTAPI
    ptMaxPosition As POINTAPI
    rcNormalPosition As RECT
End Type
'
' Constants used with SendMessage
'
Private Const WM_SETTEXT = &HC
Private Const WM_GETTEXT = &HD
Private Const WM_GETTEXTLENGTH = &HE
Private Const WM_CLOSE = &H10
Private Const EM_SETSEL = &HB1
Private Const EM_SCROLLCARET = &HB7
Private Const EM_GETMODIFY = &HB8
Private Const EM_SETMODIFY = &HB9
'
' Constants used with GetWindow
'
Private Const GW_CHILD = 5
Private Const GW_HWNDNEXT = 2
'
' Constant used with SetWindowLong
'
```

Continued on next page

Continued from previous page

```
Private Const GWL_HWNDPARENT = -8
'
' Constants used with ShowWindow & SetWindowPlacement
'
' ShowWindow() Commands
Private Const SW_HIDE = 0
Private Const SW_SHOWNORMAL = 1
Private Const SW_NORMAL = 1
Private Const SW_SHOWMINIMIZED = 2
Private Const SW_SHOWMAXIMIZED = 3
Private Const SW_MAXIMIZE = 3
Private Const SW_SHOWNOACTIVATE = 4
Private Const SW_SHOW = 5
Private Const SW_MINIMIZE = 6
Private Const SW_SHOWMINNOACTIVE = 7
Private Const SW_SHOWNA = 8
Private Const SW_RESTORE = 9
Private Const SW_SHOWDEFAULT = 10
Private Const SW_MAX = 10
'
' Constants used with CreateProcess
'
Private Const STARTF_USESHOWWINDOW = &H1
Private Const STARTF_USESIZE = &H2
Private Const STARTF_USEPOSITION = &H4
Private Const STARTF_USECOUNTCHARS = &H8
Private Const STARTF_USEFILLATTRIBUTE = &H10
Private Const STARTF_RUNFULLSCREEN = &H20        ' ignored for non-x86 platforms
Private Const STARTF_FORCEONFEEDBACK = &H40
Private Const STARTF_FORCEOFFFEEDBACK = &H80
Private Const STARTF_USESTDHANDLES = &H100
'
' Class member variables
'
Private m_hOwner As Long
Private m_hNotepad As Long
Private m_hProcess As Long
Private m_hThread As Long
Private m_Title As String
Private m_Visible As Boolean
Private m_WindowState As Long
Private m_AutoSave As Boolean
Private m_AutoShutdown As Boolean
Private m_AutoScroll As Boolean
Private m_SaveFile As String
Private m_Debugger As String
```

3. Add the following code to the General section of CDebug. This declares the variables used internally by the class to store property values and provide convenient string "constants."

```
'
' Class member variables
'
Private m_hOwner As Long
Private m_hNotepad As Long
```

```
Private m_hProcess As Long
Private m_hThread As Long
Private m_Title As String
Private m_Visible As Boolean
Private m_WindowState As Long
Private m_AutoSave As Boolean
Private m_AutoShutdown As Boolean
Private m_AutoScroll As Boolean
Private m_SaveFile As String
Private m_Debugger As String
```

4. Insert the following code into the Class_Initialize event of CDebug. Here, all the member variables are set to their default values. A quick search is also made for Notepad.exe, looking in both the Windows and System directories. If it's not found, an error is raised that must be handled by the calling application. One potential enhancement to this class would be to allow different editors to be "plugged in."

```
Private Sub Class_Initialize()
    Dim path As String
    Dim nRet As Long
    '
    ' Set defaults for properties
    '
    m_hOwner = 0
    m_hNotepad = 0
    m_Title = App.Title
    m_Visible = True
    m_WindowState = SW_SHOWMINNOACTIVE
    m_AutoShutdown = False
    m_AutoSave = False
    m_AutoScroll = False
    m_SaveFile = App.path & "\Debug.Txt"
    '
    ' Find where Notepad is installed, since
    ' CreateProcess requires a complete path.
    ' Try Windows directory first (where Win95
    ' installs Notepad).
    '
    path = Space(256)
    nRet = GetWindowsDirectory(path, Len(path))
    path = (Left(path, nRet)) & "\" & "notepad.exe"
    If Len(Dir(path)) Then
        m_Debugger = path
        Exit Sub
    End If
    '
    ' Next try system directory (NT sometimes
    ' installs Notepad there).
    '
    path = Space(256)
    nRet = GetSystemDirectory(path, Len(path))
    path = (Left(path, nRet)) & "\" & "notepad.exe"
    If Len(Dir(path)) Then
```

Continued on next page

Continued from previous page

```
        m_Debugger = path
        Exit Sub
    End If
    '
    ' Throw an error, since Notepad can't be found.
    '
    Err.Raise Number:=vbObjectError + 1, Source:="CDebug", _
                Description:="Can't find Notepad.Exe"
End Sub
```

5. Add the following hWnd property procedure, to allow applications to retrieve the window handle for the class's associated instance of Notepad. This property is provided as read-only, since altering an hWnd would serve no use. Unlike hWnd properties within typical Visual Basic applications, this CDebug.hWnd property should be used immediately after retrieval, because the user may shut down Notepad.

```
Public Property Get hWnd() As Long
    '
    ' Note: Read-only!
    ' Returns hWnd for current Notepad instance. WARNING: Use
    ' immediately, as it may change if user closes Notepad,
    ' and it is later reopened by more debug output.
    '
    hWnd = GetHWndDebug()
End Property
```

6. Add the following hWndDebug property procedure, to allow applications to retrieve the window handle for the multiline edit control (text box) in the class's associated instance of Notepad. This hWnd property is provided as read-only, since altering an hWnd would serve no use. As with the CDebug.hWnd property, this CDebug.hWndDebug property should be used immediately after retrieval because the user may shut down Notepad.

```
Public Property Get hWndDebug() As Integer
    '
    ' Note: Read-only!
    ' Returns hWnd for text entry area in the current Notepad
    ' instance.WARNING: Use immediately, as it may change if
    ' user closes Notepad, and it is later reopened by more
    ' debug output. The text area in Notepad is its main window's
    ' first child. Get handle to it, so we can manipulate it.
    '
    hWndDebug = GetWindow(GetHWndNotepad(), GW_CHILD)
End Property
```

7. Add the following private function, GetHWndDebug, to CDebug. This function retrieves the hWnd for the current instance of Notepad. It first calls the FindDebugWindow function to see if the previous instance is still running. If it isn't, a new instance is started. If the Owner property is set, that form becomes

the owner of this instance of Notepad. This means Notepad will be hidden whenever that form is minimized, and Notepad will always float over the form.

```
Private Function GetHWndDebug() As Long
    '
    ' See if existing instance of Notepad can be found.
    '
    If FindDebugWindow() Then
        GetHWndDebug = m_hNotepad
        Exit Function
    End If
    '
    ' If Notepad wasn't already started, or couldn't be found,
    ' fire up another instance and get its hWnd.
    '
    If m_Visible Then
        m_hNotepad = ExecDebugWindow(m_WindowState)
    Else
        m_hNotepad = ExecDebugWindow(SW_HIDE)
    End If
    '
    ' If desired (user passed form's hWnd), make application
    ' the owner of this instance of Notepad.
    '
    If m_hOwner Then
        Call SetWindowLong(m_hNotepad, GWL_HWNDPARENT, m_hOwner)
    End If
End Function
```

8. Add the private FindDebugWindow function to CDebug. Since Notepad may be visible and subject to closure by the user, its existence must be checked often. If an instance has already been opened, the first thing that's done is to see if any windows currently exist with that handle. If so, their caption is compared against the two possible captions (CDebug recaptions Notepad to reflect its current use). If a likely match was found, the function exits and returns the current handle.

   Some customization is then done to integrate Notepad into the calling application. Notepad's caption is altered to BugPad, followed by a title that the application can customize. Notepad's position is also fixed, using SetWindowPlacement, so that when it isn't either minimized or maximized it will occupy an area in the lower-right corner of the screen. Then the window handle is returned as the function result.

```
Private Function FindDebugWindow() As Long
    Dim Buffer As String
    '
    ' If Notepad's already been opened, try to find
    ' that instance.
    '
    If m_hNotepad Then
        '
        ' See if window still exists
        '
```

Continued on next page

Continued from previous page

```
        If IsWindow(m_hNotepad) Then
            '
            ' Make sure another window hasn't inherited
            ' the handle by checking caption.
            '
            Buffer = Space(80)
            Call GetWindowText(m_hNotepad, Buffer, Len(Buffer))
            If InStr(Buffer, "Notepad") Then
                '
                ' Got it!  Assign previously known handle,
                ' and re-assert caption
                '
                If Len(m_Title) Then
                    Call SetWindowText(m_hNotepad, """BugPad"" - " & m_Title)
                Else
                    Call SetWindowText(m_hNotepad, """BugPad""")
                End If
                FindDebugWindow = m_hNotepad
            ElseIf InStr(Buffer, """BugPad""") Then
                '
                ' Found it!  Assign previous handle.
                '
                FindDebugWindow = m_hNotepad
            End If
        End If
    End If
End Function
```

9. Add the private ExecDebugWindow function to CDebug. Believe it or not, this is what is required to start a new process in Win32! Most of this function simply prepares to make the CreateProcess call. Visual Basic's Shell was always simply a "wrapper" for the WinExec API, and in Win32 WinExec is similarly a "wrapper" for CreateProcess. This new function has a wealth of options available to it, and can be somewhat overwhelming when first investigated. An example of its usefulness is how Notepad can be positioned before launch with this call.

   After a new process is created in Win32, control is immediately returned to the calling application. In fact, this is often long before the new process has even had a chance to finish initializing. So, after the call to CreateProcess, another call is made to WaitForInputIdle, passing process handle for the new Notepad. This call won't return until the new process has finished its initialization, and is waiting for user input. If this wait wasn't imposed, we would start trying to communicate with a process that otherwise isn't fully in existence yet!

```
Private Function ExecDebugWindow(WindowState As Long) As Long
    Dim StartUp As STARTUPINFO
    Dim Security As SECURITY_ATTRIBUTES
    Dim Process As PROCESS_INFORMATION
    Dim DebugTitle As String
    '
    ' Set length of StartUp structure.
    '
    StartUp.cb = Len(StartUp)
```

```
    '
    ' Fill StartUp structure. lpReserved and lpDesktop are reserved,
    ' and *must* be set to NULL!  lpTitle only applies to console apps.
    ' VB automatically passes null pointer?
    '
    StartUp.lpReserved = vbNullString
    StartUp.lpDesktop = vbNullString
    StartUp.lpTitle = vbNullString

    ' Set new position and size info into StartUp structure.
    ' Requires STARTF_USEPOSITION and STARTF_USESIZE flags.
    '
    StartUp.dwX = (Screen.Width \ 4) \ Screen.TwipsPerPixelX
    StartUp.dwY = (Screen.Height - (Screen.Height \ 3)) \ Screen.TwipsPerPixelY
    StartUp.dwXSize = (Screen.Width \ Screen.TwipsPerPixelX) - StartUp.dwX
    StartUp.dwYSize = (Screen.Height \ Screen.TwipsPerPixelY) - StartUp.dwY
    '
    ' These StartUp parameters are ignored in GUI processes.
    '
    StartUp.dwXCountChars = 0
    StartUp.dwYCountChars = 0
    StartUp.dwFillAttribute = 0
    '
    ' Set appropriate StartUp flags.
    '
    StartUp.dwFlags = STARTF_USEPOSITION Or STARTF_USESIZE Or _
        STARTF_USESHOWWINDOW Or STARTF_FORCEONFEEDBACK
    '
    ' Set StartUp ShowWindow flag.
    '
    StartUp.wShowWindow = WindowState
    '
    ' More ignored (or console-only) StartUp parameters.
    '
    StartUp.cbReserved2 = 0
    StartUp.lpReserved2 = 0
    StartUp.hStdInput = 0
    StartUp.hStdOutput = 0
    StartUp.hStdError = 0
    '
    ' Call CreateProcess to start Notepad.
    '
    If CreateProcess(m_Debugger, vbNullString, 0&, 0&, 0&, 0&, 0&, 0&, _
        StartUp, Process) Then
        m_hProcess = Process.dwProcessID
        m_hThread = Process.dwThreadID
        Call WaitForInputIdle(Process.hProcess, 3000)
        ExecDebugWindow = GetHWndByThread()
    Else
        Debug.Print "Can't CreateProcess: "; GetLastError()
        m_hProcess = 0
        m_hThread = 0
        ExecDebugWindow = False
    End If
End Function
```

10. Add the private GetHWndByThread function to CDebug. This function is called by ExecDebugWindow to retrieve Notepad's hWnd following a successful CreateProcess. A GetWindow loop is used to "walk the window list," looking for another top-level window that has the same process handle as that returned for Notepad. (This is an extremely useful function and can be copied into many projects. With only slight modification, it could be used to find a partial title match for windows that have variable captions. Whatever you are searching for, just change the innermost condition to match, and you have a function that will find it!) When a match is found, that window's hWnd is returned.

```
Private Function GetHWndByThread() As Long
    Dim hWndTmp As Long
    Dim hProcTmp As Long
    Dim hThreadTmp As Long
    '
    ' Find first window in top-level window list
    '
    hWndTmp = FindWindow(0&, 0&)
    '
    ' Walk through list of top-level windows, checking the
    ' process and thread handles against client handles.
    '
    Do While hWndTmp
        '
        ' Only check windows that don't have parents
        '
        If GetParent(hWndTmp) = 0 Then
            hThreadTmp = GetWindowThreadProcessId(hWndTmp, hProcTmp)
            If m_hThread = hThreadTmp Then
                If m_hProcess = hProcTmp Then
                    '
                    ' Got it! Return window handle that matches desired
                    ' instance handle.
                    '
                    GetHWndByThread = hWndTmp
                    Exit Do
                End If
            End If
        End If
        '
        ' Haven't found it yet. Get next window in list.
        '
        hWndTmp = GetWindow(hWndTmp, GW_HWNDNEXT)
    Loop
End Function
```

11. Add the following pair of property procedures to set and retrieve the CDebug.Owner property. This is the handle of the Visual Basic form, which will assume ownership of new Notepad instances as they're spawned. Before accepting the value passed in as the new Owner, the Let procedure confirms that a window exists with that handle, and also whether it's a top-level window.

```
Public Property Let Owner(hWnd As Integer)
    '
    ' Store window handle to a form in user application
    ' which will be set as the owner of Notepad. Keeps
    ' Notepad floating over window, and hides Notepad when
    ' owner is minimized. Some validity checking is done
    ' to insure that a top-level window actually exists
    ' with this handle.
    '
    If IsWindow(hWnd) Then
        If GetParent(hWnd) = 0 Then
            m_hOwner = hWnd
        End If
    End If
End Property

Public Property Get Owner() As Integer
    '
    ' Return hWnd of Notepad's owner form
    '
    Owner = m_hOwner
End Property
```

12. Add the following pair of property procedures to set and retrieve the CDebug.Title property. This is the string that follows "BugPad" in Notepad's caption area.

```
Public Property Let Title(NewVal As String)
    '
    ' Store Title which is appended to Notepad caption
    '
    m_Title = NewVal
End Property

Public Property Get Title() As String
    '
    ' Return value for Title property
    '
    Title = m_Title
End Property
```

13. Add the following pair of property procedures to set and retrieve the CDebug.Visible property. This property is used to turn the display of Notepad on or off. Setting the Visible property triggers a call to either the CDebug.Show or CDebug.Hide method.

```
Public Property Let Visible(NewVal As Boolean)
    '
    ' Turn Notepad's visibility on or off
    '
    m_Visible = NewVal
    If m_Visible Then
        Me.Show
    Else
```

Continued on next page

Continued from previous page

```
        Me.Hide
    End If
End Property

Public Property Get Visible() As Boolean
    '
    ' Return visibility of Notepad
    '
    Visible = m_Visible
End Property
```

14. Add the following pair of property procedures to set and retrieve the CDebug.AutoSave property. If AutoSave is set to True when the CDebug class terminates, the contents of the currently associated Notepad is saved to the file that is set with the CDebug.SaveFile property.

```
Public Property Let AutoSave(NewVal As Boolean)
    '
    ' Store whether to save Notepad text when class
    ' is terminated.
    '
    m_AutoSave = NewVal
End Property

Public Property Get AutoSave() As Boolean
    '
    ' Return value for AutoSave property
    '
    AutoSave = m_AutoSave
End Property
```

15. Add the following pair of property procedures to set and retrieve the CDebug.AutoShutdown property. If AutoShutdown is set to True, the currently associated instance of Notepad is closed as the CDebug class terminates. If AutoShutdown is set to False, Notepad will be made visible, and the user can dispose of it and its contents as desired.

```
Public Property Let AutoShutdown(NewVal As Boolean)
    '
    ' Store whether to shutdown Notepad when class is
    ' terminated.
    '
    m_AutoShutdown = NewVal
End Property

Public Property Get AutoShutdown() As Boolean
    '
    ' Return value for AutoShutdown property
    '
    AutoShutdown = m_AutoShutdown
End Property
```

16. Add the following pair of property procedures to set and retrieve the CDebug.AutoScroll property. If AutoScroll is set to True, and Notepad is visible, the caret will be advanced to the end of all output after each write, and the edit control will scroll to keep the caret in view (thus new output will remain visible).

```
Public Property Let AutoScroll(NewVal As Boolean)
    '
    ' Store whether to scroll Notepad to end of text
    ' with each modification.
    '
    m_AutoScroll = NewVal
End Property

Public Property Get AutoScroll() As Boolean
    '
    ' Return value for AutoScroll property
    '
    AutoScroll = m_AutoScroll
End Property
```

17. Add the following pair of property procedures to set and retrieve the CDebug.SaveFile property. This property determines where contents of Notepad are stored whenever the Save method is executed, or when an AutoSave occurs.

```
Public Property Let SaveFile(NewVal As String)
    '
    ' Store name of file to Save to.
    '
    m_SaveFile = NewVal
End Property

Public Property Get SaveFile() As String
    '
    ' Return name of file Saves are written to.
    '
    SaveFile = m_SaveFile
End Property
```

18. Add the following property procedure to set the CDebug.Text property. When setting the Text property, all existing text in Notepad is first cleared. Then the passed text is set into it, using the Clear and Output methods of CDebug.

```
Public Property Let Text(NewVal As String)
    '
    ' Clear existing text, then display new text.
    '
    Me.Clear
    Me.Output NewVal
End Property
```

19. Add the following property procedure to retrieve the CDebug.Text property. This is where things start to get interesting! The hWndDebug property is retrieved to

get a handle to the text area in the current Notepad. Then SendMessage is used to request the total byte count in that control, and a properly sized buffer is created. SendMessage is again used to retrieve the text. Finally, the terminating null character is stripped off, and the text is returned.

```
Public Property Get Text() As String
    Dim nLen As Long
    Dim hDebugTxt As Long
    Dim Buffer As String
    '
    ' If an instance has not already been opened, return null
    '
    If m_hNotepad = 0 Then
        Text = ""
        Exit Property
    End If
    '
    ' Get handle to text entry area in Notepad
    '
    hDebugTxt = Me.hWndDebug
    '
    ' Retrieve the current length of existing text in Notepad.
    '
    nLen = SendMessage(hDebugTxt, WM_GETTEXTLENGTH, 0, 0&)
    If nLen Then
        '
        ' Allow for null termination, and create a buffer
        ' that will hold existing text.
        '
        nLen = nLen + 1
        Buffer = Space(nLen)
        '
        ' Retrieve existing text from Notepad into buffer.
        '
        Call SendMessage(hDebugTxt, WM_GETTEXT, nLen, Buffer)
        '
        ' Strip null termination
        '
        Buffer = Left(Buffer, nLen - 1)
    End If
    '
    ' Return results or null string (if nothing in Notepad).
    '
    Text = Buffer
End Property
```

20. Add the following property procedure to retrieve the read-only value of the CDebug.Length property. Again, SendMessage is used to query the edit control in Notepad. This is a useful property to check occasionally, to ensure saving the output contents before Notepad fills up. The CDebug class uses a built-in limit of 32K characters, because SendMessage starts breaking down at that point in Win16—even though Notepad itself can accept more text than that.

```
Public Property Get Length() As Long
    Dim hDebugTxt As Integer
    '
    ' Note: Read-only!
    ' Retrieve the current length of existing text in Notepad,
    ' if an instance has already been opened
    '
    If m_hNotepad Then
        Length = SendMessage(Me.hWndDebug, WM_GETTEXTLENGTH, 0, 0&)
    Else
        Length = 0
    End If
End Property
```

> Note: The 16-bit version of Notepad runs out of memory at seemingly random times. During development of this project, Notepad would display an error message when its text reached points as low as 28K, but sometimes not until it had over 43K characters. You will want to avoid this by watching the Length property fairly conscientiously, because the error message (shown in Figure 9-6-2) is somewhat confusing. No matter how many applications are closed, no more memory will become available to Notepad's edit control.

21. Add the following public Output method to CDebug. Output appends a text string to the existing contents in Notepad. If the Optional parameter Cr is present and evaluates to True, Output will append a carriage return/line feed pair to the end of the passed text string. The new text is transferred to Notepad by sending its edit control an EM_SETTEXT message along with the replacement text string. If the AutoScroll property is set, the EM_SETSEL message moves the caret to the very end of the text, and the EM_SCROLLCARET message scrolls the window so the caret is visible. Finally, the modification flag in Notepad is set with the EM_SETMODIFY message, so that the user will be queried about whether to save if the applet is closed.

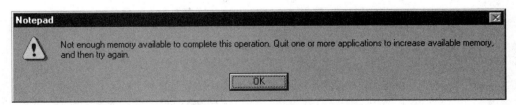

Figure 9-6-2 Notepad's enigmatic error message when full

```
Public Sub Output(ByVal dText As String, Optional Cr As Variant)
    Dim hDebugTxt As Long
    '
    ' Append a carriage return if desired.
    '
    If Not IsMissing(Cr) Then
        If CBool(Cr) Then
            dText = dText & vbCrLf
        End If
    End If
    '
    ' Append to existing (if any) text in Notepad, and
    ' Null terminate text to be output.
    '
    dText = Me.Text & dText & vbNullChar
    '
    ' Get handle to text entry area in Notepad
    '
    hDebugTxt = Me.hWndDebug
    '
    ' Send modified text back to Notepad, replacing what was there.
    '
    Call SendMessage(hDebugTxt, WM_SETTEXT, 0, dText)
    '
    ' Move Notepad caret to end of text.
    '
    If m_AutoScroll Then
        Call SendMessage(hDebugTxt, EM_SETSEL, Len(dText), Len(dText))
        Call SendMessage(hDebugTxt, EM_SCROLLCARET, 0, 0&)
    End If
    '
    ' Set the modification flag in Notepad, so it will ask
    ' whether to save if the user tries shutting it down.
    '
    Call SendMessage(hDebugTxt, EM_SETMODIFY, True, 0&)
End Sub
```

22. Add the following public Clear method to CDebug. Clear sends the WM_SET-TEXT with a null string to Notepad's edit control. This message erases whatever was there.

```
Public Sub Clear()
    '
    ' Don't do anything if no instances have been opened, else
    ' clear text area by setting a zero-length string into it.
    '
    If m_hNotepad Then
        Call SendMessage(Me.hWndDebug, WM_SETTEXT, 0, "")
    End If
End Sub
```

23. Add the following public Save method to CDebug. Save writes the contents of Notepad's edit control to the file named by the SaveFile property. After saving the debugging output, an EM_SETMODIFY message is used to clear the modification

flag. Notepad uses this flag to determine whether to ask the user about saving as Notepad shuts down.

```
Public Sub Save()
    Dim hFile As Integer
    '
    ' If there's text in Notepad, open a new copy of m_SaveFile,
    ' retrieve text from Notepad, and output to m_SaveFile. By
    ' opening for Output, an existing file with this name is
    ' effectively deleted.
    '
    If Me.Length Then
        On Error Resume Next
            hFile = FreeFile
            Open m_SaveFile For Output As hFile
            Print #hFile, Me.Text;
            Close hFile
        On Error GoTo 0
        '
        ' Clear modify flag in Notepad.
        '
        Call SendMessage(Me.hWndDebug, EM_SETMODIFY, False, 0&)
    End If
End Sub
```

> Note: Several shortcuts are taken in the Save method, and proper use of this method requires the programmer's diligence. If a file exists with the same name as what is about to be used, the existing file will effectively be erased by opening it in the Output mode. While opening, writing to, and closing the file, errors are ignored. The programmer must ensure that valid file specs are passed, space is available, and nothing of value is overwritten. Because these are fairly typical functions, we did not duplicate them in this class. The recommended use of Save, in the case where multiple files are required, would be to increment a counter, which is appended to the output filespec with each successive save.

24. Add the following Show and Hide pair of public methods to CDebug; these are fairly self-explanatory. Show uses ShowWindow to make Notepad visible and restore it to its normal window state. This call is documented to always activate the specified window, but that doesn't necessarily happen—hence the call to SetForegroundWindow. If you only want to make Notepad visible without transferring focus to it, do so by setting the class' Visible property to True. The EM_SETSEL message isn't acted upon by invisible windows, so when AutoScroll is set, this message is resent to move the caret to the end of the output text. The Hide method just has to place a call to ShowWindow and update the tracking variable.

```
Public Sub Show()
    '
    ' Show Notepad, and make it the active window.
    '
    m_WindowState = SW_SHOWNORMAL
    Call ShowWindow(Me.hWnd, SW_SHOWNORMAL)
    Call SetForegroundWindow(m_hNotepad)
    '
    ' Move cursor to end of text if AutoScroll is set
    ' and Notepad was previously invisible.
    '
    If m_AutoScroll = True And m_Visible = False Then
        Call SendMessage(Me.hWndDebug, EM_SETSEL, Me.Length, Me.Length)
        Call SendMessage(Me.hWndDebug, EM_SCROLLCARET, 0, 0&)
    End If
    m_Visible = True
End Sub
Public Sub Hide()
    '
    ' If an instance of Notepad has been started, hide it.
    '
    If m_hNotepad Then
        Call ShowWindow(Me.hWnd, SW_HIDE)
        m_Visible = False
    End If
End Sub
```

25. Add the following public Move method to CDebug. Move acts just like Visual
Basic's Move method, except that it accepts named arguments. This method
allows you to position the Notepad window anywhere on screen with one simple
call. If Notepad is invisible, it is first shown in its normal window state (neither
minimized nor maximized). The GetWindowRect API fills a rectangle structure
with the coordinates that Notepad occupies; then the right and bottom coordinates are converted to represent the width and height of the window. For each
parameter received, its value is placed into the modified rectangle structure, and
then Notepad is resized with a call to MoveWindow.

```
Public Sub Move(Optional Left, Optional Top, Optional Width, Optional Height)
    Dim rc As RECT
    '
    ' Make sure Notepad isn't minimized, is visible, and
    ' get current coordinates
    '
    m_Visible = True
    Call ShowWindow(Me.hWnd, SW_SHOWNORMAL)
    Call GetWindowRect(m_hNotepad, rc)
    '
    ' Convert Right and Bottom coords to Width and Height.
    '
    rc.Right = rc.Right - rc.Left
    rc.Bottom = rc.Bottom - rc.Top
    '
```

```
    ' Set new coordinate(s) into redefined rectangle structure
    '
    If Not IsMissing(Left) Then
        rc.Left = CInt(Left)
    End If
    If Not IsMissing(Top) Then
        rc.Top = CInt(Top)
    End If
    If Not IsMissing(Width) Then
        rc.Right = CInt(Width)
    End If
    If Not IsMissing(Height) Then
        rc.Bottom = CInt(Height)
    End If
    '
    ' Move Notepad to new coordinates
    '
    Call MoveWindow(m_hNotepad, rc.Left, rc.Top, rc.Right, rc.Bottom, True)
End Sub
```

26. Add a public Shutdown method to CDebug, which allows programmatic shutdown of the Notepad applet. First, the IsWindow API call looks for a window with the stored handle to Notepad. If that doesn't exist, there's no need to load another instance just so it can be closed. If the window exists and AutoSave is enabled, the Save method is invoked. AutoShutdown eliminates the need to prompt the user about saving, because either the Save method (or AutoSave) has already been invoked, or displaying the data on screen was sufficient. So the Notepad's Modify flag is cleared if AutoSave is True, and no questions are asked. Sending a WM_CLOSE message instructs Notepad to shut itself down.

```
Public Sub Shutdown()
    '
    ' If an instance has been opened, try to close it.
    '
    If IsWindow(m_hNotepad) Then
        '
        ' Save debugging text in Notepad if AutoSave in force.
        '
        If m_AutoSave Then
            Me.Save
        End If
        '
        ' Clear the modify flag so Save warning doesn't popup,
        ' if AutoShutdown is in effect.
        '
        If m_AutoShutdown Then
            Call SendMessage(GetWindow(m_hNotepad, GW_CHILD), _
                EM_SETMODIFY, False, O&)
        End If
        Call SendMessage(m_hNotepad, WM_CLOSE, O, O&)
    End If
End Sub
```

27. Insert the following code in the Class_Terminate event of CDebug. The Terminate event occurs when objects that were set to an instance of a class are then set to Nothing. Use of this practice is recommended with CDebug, as saving and shutting down Notepad is done from here. In the case where the Shutdown method is not called, and AutoShutdown is not enabled or the user canceled a shutdown, Notepad is made visible (as an icon) so the user can still interact with it. Otherwise, only special utilities, such as WPS could extract Notepad from memory; and even then, there'd be no practical way to get at the data it contained.

```
Private Sub Class_Terminate()
    '
    ' Save debugging text in Notepad if AutoSave in force.
    '
    If m_AutoSave Then
        Me.Save
    End If
    '
    ' Try shutting down Notepad if AutoShutdown in force.
    ' Otherwise, make sure it's visible so user can access it.
    ' Note class must be set to Nothing for this to execute!
    '
    If m_AutoShutdown Then
        Me.Shutdown
    End If
    '
    ' In case the user pressed Cancel on Save warning, or
    ' it wasn't closed, make sure Notepad is visible.
    '
    If IsWindow(m_hNotepad) Then
        Call ShowWindow(m_hNotepad, SW_SHOWMINNOACTIVE)
    End If
End Sub
```

Building a Test Project for the CDebug Class

28. Add a new form to your project, name it frmBugger, and save it as DEBUG.FRM. Place the controls and set the properties as listed in Table 9-6-1. It should look similar to Figure 9-6-1 when you're done.

Table 9-6-1 Objects and their properties on frmBugger

OBJECT	PROPERTY	SETTING
Form	Name	frmBugger
	BorderStyle	3 - Fixed Double
	Caption	"Bugger"
	MaxButton	False
Label	Name	Label1
CommandButton	Name	cmdOutput
	Caption	"Output Debugging Information"

OBJECT	PROPERTY	SETTING
CommandButton	Name	cmdDebug
	Index	0
	Caption	"&Show"
CommandButton	Name	cmdDebug
	Index	1
	Caption	"&Hide"
CommandButton	Name	cmdDebug
	Index	2
	Caption	"&Clear"
CommandButton	Name	cmdDebug
	Index	3
	Caption	"Sa&ve"
CommandButton	Name	cmdDebug
	Index	4
	Caption	"&Unload CDebug"
CommandButton	Name	cmdDebug
	Index	5
	Cancel	True
	Caption	"E&xit"
CheckBox	Name	chkScroll
	Caption	"AutoScroll"
	Value	0 - Unchecked
CheckBox	Name	chkSave
	Caption	"AutoSave"
	Value	0 - Unchecked
CheckBox	Name	chkShutdown
	Caption	"AutoShutdown"
	Value	1 - Checked

29. Add the CBorder3D class, developed in How-To 3.4, to the project. Save the project as DEBUG.VBP.

30. Add the following code to the Declarations section of frmBugger. One new CDebug object and two new CStyle3D objects are declared.

```
Option Explicit
'
' Declare a new instance of the CDebug object
'
Private dbg As New CDebug
'
' Object variables for Style3D effects.
'
```

Continued on next page

Continued from previous page

```
Private Obj3D1 As New CBorder3D
Private Obj3D2 As New CBorder3D
```

31. Insert the following code in the Form_Load event of frmBugger. Here, the
CDebug object is passed the values for several properties. This form is set to own
new instances of Notepad as they're opened. The caption of frmBugger is used as
additional information to be placed in Notepad's caption. Also, AutoShutdown is
enabled to match the design-time setting for the associated check box. For
debugging output, a series of random numbers will be generated, so Randomize
is used to reset the pointer into the random-number sequencer. Finally, a call is
made to initialize the CBorder3D objects, and the label is updated to indicate that
Notepad hasn't been loaded yet.

```
Private Sub Form_Load()
    '
    ' Set properties for CDebug object.
    '
    dbg.Owner = Me.hWnd
    dbg.Title = Me.Caption
    dbg.AutoShutdown = True
    '
    ' Sample output will be random series of numbers.
    '
    Randomize
    '
    ' Setup 3D border effects
    '
    Setup3D
    '
    ' Initialize Label1 display
    '
    Label1 = " Notepad not open."
End Sub
```

32. Add the following private routine to frmBugger. Setup3D is used to initialize the
two CBorder3D objects used to spruce up the form. (For complete information
on the capabilities of CBorder3D, see How-To 3.4.)

```
Private Sub Setup3D()
    '
    ' Called from Form_Load
    ' Styles supported by CBorder3D
    '
    Const StyleNone = 0
    Const StyleSunken = 1
    Const StyleRaised = 2
    Const StyleFramed = 3
    Const StyleDouble = 4
    Const StyleWithin = 5
    Const StyleCustomFramed = 6
    Const StyleCustomDouble = 7
    Const StyleCustomWithin = 8
    '
```

```
' Setup 3D border effect around edge of form
'
Set Obj3D1.Canvas = Me
Obj3D1.Style3D = StyleCustomWithin
Obj3D1.BevelOuter = StyleSunken
Obj3D1.BevelWidth = 2
Obj3D1.Left = 0
Obj3D1.Top = 3 * Screen.TwipsPerPixelY
Obj3D1.Width = Me.ScaleWidth
Obj3D1.Height = Me.ScaleHeight - Obj3D1.Top

' Setup 3D border effect around Label1
'
Set Obj3D2.Client = Label1
Set Obj3D2.Canvas = Me
Obj3D2.Style3D = StyleDouble
Obj3D2.BevelWidth = 3
End Sub
```

33. Insert the following code in the Form_Paint event, to refresh the CBorder3D objects whenever the form needs repainting.

```
Private Sub Form_Paint()
    '
    ' Refresh 3D objects
    '
    Obj3D1.Refresh
    Obj3D2.Refresh
End Sub
```

34. Insert the following code in the cmdDebug_Click event. This event illustrates the extreme simplicity of using the methods that CDebug exposes. For the five methods related to command buttons, only one line of code, with no parameters, is required. After one of the methods is invoked, the label is updated to reflect the number of characters currently in the associated Notepad.

```
Private Sub cmdDebug_Click(Index As Integer)
    '
    ' Act on button press
    '
    Select Case Index
        Case 0: dbg.Show
        Case 1: dbg.Hide
        Case 2: dbg.Clear
        Case 3: dbg.Save
        Case 4: dbg.Shutdown
        Case 5: Unload Me
    End Select
    '
    ' Update Label1 display
    '
    If Index < 4 Then
        Label1 = " Notepad text length: " & dbg.Length & " Bytes"
    ElseIf Index = 4
```

Continued on next page

Continued from previous page

```
        Label1 = " Notepad not open."
    End If
End Sub
```

35. Insert the following code in the cmdOutput_Click event. This event first produces the current date and time, and then generates a series of 100 random numbers, just to demonstrate CDebug's Output method. Figure 9-6-3 shows how the output appears in Notepad.

```
Private Sub cmdOutput_Click()
    Dim i As Integer
    Dim j As Integer
    Dim Bugs As String
    Dim BugLen As Long
    '
    ' Set mouse cursor to hourglass
    '
    Me.MousePointer = vbHourglass
    '
    ' Output date/time stamp
    '
    dbg.Output Format(Now, "long date") & ", "
    dbg.Output Format(Now, "long time"), True
    '
    ' Display 100 random numbers
    '
    For i = 1 To 10
        For j = 1 To 10
            Bugs = Bugs & Format(Rnd * 90 + 10, "0.000  ")
        Next j
        dbg.Output Bugs, True
        Bugs = ""
    Next i
    '
    ' Update Label1 display.
    '
    BugLen = dbg.Length
    Label1 = " Notepad text length: " & BugLen & " Bytes"
    '
    ' Set mouse cursor to default
    '
    Me.MousePointer = vbDefault
End Sub
```

36. Insert the following code to toggle the AutoSave, AutoScroll, and AutoShutdown properties of CDebug in the respective chkSave_Click, chkScroll_Click, and chkShutdown_Click events:

```
Private Sub chkSave_Click()
    '
    ' Set CDebug.AutoSave property
    '
    dbg.AutoSave = chkSave.Value
End Sub
```

```
Private Sub chkScroll_Click()
    '
    ' Set CDebug.AutoScroll property
    '
    dbg.AutoScroll = chkScroll.Value
End Sub

Private Sub chkShutdown_Click()
    '
    ' Set CDebug.AutoShutdown property
    '
    dbg.AutoShutdown = chkShutdown.Value
End Sub
```

37. Insert the following code in the Form_Unload event of frmBugger. Caution: It's very important to fire the Terminate event in CDebug by setting existing objects of that class to Nothing before exiting your applications. This allows CDebug to either save and shut down, or at least make visible, running instances of Notepad.

```
Private Sub Form_Unload(Cancel As Integer)
    '
    ' Terminate CDebug object and associated Notepad.
    '
    Set dbg = Nothing
End Sub
```

How It Works

CDebug works by sending a variety of messages to Notepad and its multiline edit control as CDebug's methods and properties are invoked. There's also some tricky sleuthing done to make sure that the current instance of Notepad still exists, since the user may have closed it if it was visible. After using CreateProcess to launch an instance of Notepad, a very interesting routine that will find a given window and return its window handle, based on its thread handle, is employed. CreateProcess

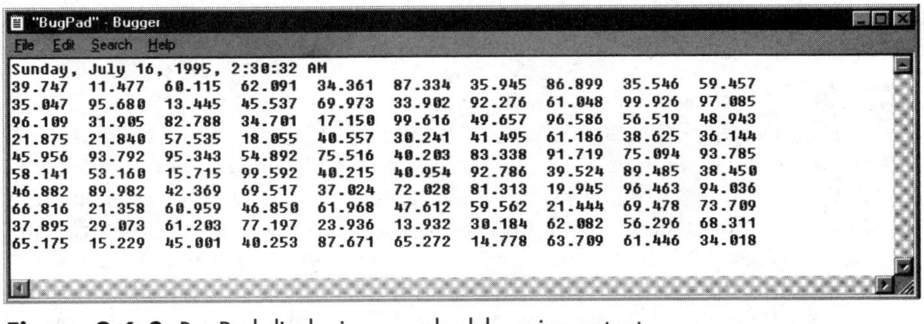

Figure 9-6-3 BugPad displaying sample debugging output

offers many benefits over Shell, including that windows may be initially invisible and that their initial positions may be set before launch. This is in contrast to Shell, with which the windows will always at least flash before they can be hidden and there is no control over positioning.

Window positioning, visibility, and the appearance of Notepad are controlled with a number of API calls. ShowWindow is used primarily to toggle visibility and window state. GetWindowRect and MoveWindow are used to reposition Notepad in CDebug's Move method. SetWindowText makes the caption of Notepad a little more interesting.

Communication with Notepad is carried out through the SendMessage API. The WM_GETTEXT and WM_SETTEXT messages receive and transmit text to the Notepad's multiline edit control; WM_GETTEXTLENGTH returns the size buffer required to retrieve the text. The EM_SETSEL message can be used to position the caret or alter the text selection within multiline edit controls. CDebug uses it to keep the latest output within view, by positioning the caret at the very end and scrolling with EM_SCROLLCARET so that it's visible. The EM_SETMODIFY and EM_GET-MODIFY messages set or clear the internal modification flag of edit controls and retrieve the current state of that flag. This flag tells Notepad whether text needs to be saved before exiting. The last message used is WM_CLOSE, which instructs Windows applications to initiate their own shutdown.

After dimensioning a New CDebug object instance, you may begin to send output to it immediately. If desired, a few properties such as Owner, AutoShutdown, AutoSave, and SaveFile may also be set. Notepad will be invisible, so if you want to observe the output as it occurs, you'll need to fire the Show method. For AutoShutdown to be effective, you must remember to set CDebug objects to Nothing before exiting your application.

Because there are at least three "flavors" of Notepad out there—a Win16 version that comes with Windows 3.x, a Win32 version that comes with Windows NT, and a hybrid that comes with Windows 95—it's best to take the precaution of carefully monitoring the length of your debug output as only the Win32 version is capable of unlimited (practically speaking) quantities of text. CDebug can pump data pretty fast to Notepad when there isn't much already there, but it does slow down considerably when the amount of text grows much beyond 20K or so. For these two reasons, the programmer must decide what level of risk or inconvenience is acceptable, and save the output as frequently as necessary if it begins to accumulate.

Comments

Using CDebug objects in your applications is extremely simple; nearly as easy as calling the Debug window's Print method within the Visual Basic development environment. Of course, there are many advantages to using CDebug—principally, that it can be called from compiled applications. Also, a much richer set of properties and methods becomes available. By exposing the Text property, you're free to output debugging information from perhaps dozens of routines, then read it back and manipulate it as a whole. You can save what's been output to a file, so remote users can send you accurate results if requested, or you can compare results of various runs. You may want to implement such debugging output based on command line switches or .INI file entries. (For instance, if /D were passed on the command line, debugging output would be enabled via a Boolean flag.) Due to the relatively great differences between controlling another application in Win16 and Win32, a separate project written just for 16-bit Visual Basic is included on the CD-ROM that comes with this book. It follows the same general approach, but the APIs were different enough that conditional compilation would not have been simple.

9.7 How do I...
Parse a String into Its Elements?

COMPLEXITY: EASY
COMPATIBILITY: VB3 AND VB4

Problem

I occasionally need to parse a string into its separate elements. Sometimes it's the command-line parameters that are passed to my application, or sometimes it's a null-separated string returned from one of the Windows Profile functions, or maybe lines of text from a tab-delimited data file. How would I write a general-purpose string parsing function?

Technique

In this How-To we construct a simple function that can be used in a variety of situations. It accepts a string to parse, and a dynamic array in which to return the results. Optionally, the desired delimiter may be passed, as well, but this will default to a space character if not specified.

The function, ParseString, passes once through the input string, searching for delimiter characters. When it finds one, a flag is set to indicate that the function is not currently "in" an element. Upon finding the next nondelimiter character, this flag is toggled, the return array is expanded to hold another element, and the current and following nondelimiter characters are appended to the new array element. ParseString returns the number of elements as the function result.

Steps

Open and run PARSE.VBP. It will look like Figure 9-7-1. The top list box is filled with the results of parsing the text box that appears in the middle of the form. As the program starts up, 250 random "words" are added to the text box, each with three to eight characters, with one or several spaces in between. You can control the number of words by changing it in the Words text box at the bottom of the form. Press the Random button to regenerate that number of new words. Press the Parse button to fill the list box with the individual words.

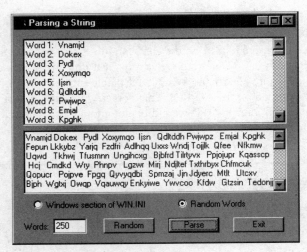

Figure 9-7-1 The Parser in action

You can also choose to view the contents of the [Windows] section of WIN.INI. One call to GetProfileString retrieves all the entries in this section. The API returns the name of each entry, separated by Chr(0) characters. These are parsed out, and a loop retrieves the contents of each.

1. Create a new project named PARSE.VBP. On Form1, arrange the controls and set the properties as listed in Table 9-7-1. (Control positioning isn't important; just arrange them in a pattern similar to Figure 9-7-1.)

Table 9-7-1 Objects and their properties on Form1

OBJECT	PROPERTY	SETTING
Form	Name	Form1
	Caption	"Parsing a String"
ListBox	Name	List1
TextBox	Name	Text1
	MultiLine	True
	ScrollBars	2 - Vertical
	Text	""
OptionButton	Name	Option1
	Caption	"Windows section of WIN.INI"
	Index	0
OptionButton	Name	Option1
	Caption	"Random Words"
	Index	1
	Value	True

1040

OBJECT	PROPERTY	SETTING
Label	Name	Label1
	AutoSize	True
	Caption	"Words:"
TextBox	Name	Text2
	Text	"250"
CommandButton	Name	cmdRandom
	Caption	"Random"
CommandButton	Name	cmdParse
	Caption	"Parse"
	Default	True
CommandButton	Name	cmdExit
	Cancel	True
	Caption	"Exit"

2. Place the following code in the Declarations section of Form1. Here, the GetProfileString function is declared, which is used to read WIN.INI under Win16 installations. Also, index constants for the option buttons are defined.

```
Option Explicit
'
' Win16 declaration to read WIN.INI
'
#If Win16 Then
    Private Declare Function GetProfileString Lib "Kernel" (ByVal lpAppName ⇒
        As String, ByVal lpKeyName As Any, ByVal lpDefault As String, _
        ByVal lpReturnedString As String, ByVal nSize As Integer) As Integer
#ElseIf Win32 Then
    Private Declare Function GetProfileString Lib "kernel32" Alias _
        "GetProfileStringA" (ByVal lpAppName As String, ByVal lpKeyName _
        As Any, ByVal lpDefault As String, ByVal lpReturnedString _
        As String, ByVal nSize As Long) As Long
#End If
'
' Index to option button command array.
'
Private Const oWindows = 0
Private Const oRandom = 1
```

3. Insert the following code in the Form_Load event of Form1. The random number generator is randomized, and the button that generates the random words is "clicked."

```
Private Sub Form_Load()
    '
    ' Jumble up the possible strings to parse, and
    ' load textbox with random words.
    '
    Randomize
```

Continued on next page

Continued from previous page

```
        cmdRandom_Click
End Sub
```

4. Insert the following code in the cmdRandom_Click event of Form1. This event generates a string consisting of as many "words" as Text2 indicates. Each "word" consists of random characters, the first one capitalized. A random number of spaces are inserted between words to make sure the parsing routine does its job.

```
Private Sub cmdRandom_Click()
    Dim Greek As String
    Dim i As Integer
    Dim j As Integer
    '
    ' Generate Val(Text2) random "words".
    '
    For i = 1 To Text2
        '
        ' Each word will be from 3 to 8 characters.
        '
        For j = 0 To Rnd * 5 + 2
            '
            ' If it's not the first character, use lower-
            ' case, otherwise use upper-case for first.
            '
            If j Then
                Greek = Greek & Chr(97 + (Rnd * 25))
            Else
                Greek = Greek & Chr(65 + (Rnd * 25))
            End If
        Next j
        '
        ' Add random spaces to separate words
        '
        Greek = Greek & Space(Rnd * 2 + 1)
    Next i
    '
    ' Assign to textbox
    '
    Text1 = Trim(Greek)
End Sub
```

5. Insert the following code in the cmdParse_Click event of Form1. If the Random Words radio button is selected, this event passes the text in Text1 to ParseString, as well as an empty dynamic array. The return result of ParseString is used as the To element in a For loop that adds each string element to List1. If the Windows section of WIN.INI radio button is selected, all entry names from the [Windows] section are retrieved with one call. This offers the opportunity to try ParseString with a delimiter other than the space character. After parsing, each entry is retrieved and the list box is filled.

```
Private Sub cmdParse_Click()
    Dim i As Integer
    Dim sRet As String
```

```
    Dim nLen As Integer
    Dim Words() As String
    '
    ' Clear list, check which option to do.
    '
    List1.Clear
    If Option1(oRandom) Then
        '
        ' Call parsing routine, fill list with random words.
        '
        For i = 0 To ParseString(Text1, Words()) - 1
            List1.AddItem "Word " & i + 1 & ":  " & Words(i)
        Next i
    Else
        '
        ' Fill list with [Windows] section of WIN.INI.
        ' First, retrieve list of all entries in section.
        '
        sRet = Space(2048)
        nLen = GetProfileString("Windows", 0&, "", sRet, Len(sRet))
        sRet = Left(sRet, nLen)
        For i = 0 To ParseString(sRet, Words(), Chr(0)) - 1
            '
            ' For each entry, retrieve value and add to list.
            '
            sRet = Space(128)
            nLen = GetProfileString("Windows", Words(i), "", _
                                    sRet, Len(sRet))
            sRet = Left(sRet, nLen)
            Words(i) = Words(i) & "=" & sRet
            List1.AddItem Words(i)
        Next i
    End If
End Sub
```

6. Insert the following code in the Option1_Click event of Form1. This just does a
   little visual housekeeping as the user chooses which type of test to run. If
   WIN.INI is being read, the controls that are used only with the random words
   will not be needed, so they're hidden or covered up.

```
Private Sub Option1_Click(Index As Integer)
    '
    ' Hide controls that only apply to random words.
    '
    Label1.Visible = Index
    Text2.Visible = Index
    cmdRandom.Visible = Index
    '
    ' Clear list and textbox.
    '
    List1.Clear
    Text1 = ""
    '
    ' Resize listbox, and show/hide textbox depending
    ' on chosen option.
```

Continued on next page

Continued from previous page

```
    '
    If Index = oWindows Then
        Text1.Visible = False
        List1.Height = List1.Height + Text1.Height
    Else
        List1.Height = List1.Height - Text1.Height
        Text1.Visible = True
    End If
End Sub
```

7. Unload Form1, and end the project from the cmdExit_Click event.

```
Private Sub cmdExit_Click()
    '
    ' All Done!
    '
    Unload Me
End Sub
```

8. Add a code module, using the Insert Module menu item, and save it as PARSE.BAS.

9. Add the ParseString function, containing the following code, to PARSE.BAS. ParseString first checks to see if the Delimiter parameter was received. If not, the space character becomes the default delimiter. As the passed string is processed, a flag is used to track whether the current position is within or in between elements. As each new element is entered, the array that was passed in is expanded to hold one more element. And as each nondelimiting character is processed, it's added to the current array element. When the function ends, the number of elements found is passed back in the return value.

```
Function ParseString(StrIn As String, StrOut() As String, Optional Delimiter ⇒
    As Variant) As Integer
    Dim InElement As Boolean
    Dim NumEls As Integer
    Dim nPos As Long
    Dim Char As String
    Dim Delimit As String
    '
    ' Check for specific delimiter, if missing use a space.
    '
    Delimit = " "
    If Not IsMissing(Delimiter) Then
        If Len(Delimiter) Then
            Delimit = Left(Delimiter, 1)
        End If
    End If
    '
    ' InElement serves as a flag to tell if we're currently
    ' processing an element or are in-between.
    '
    InElement = False
    '
```

```
' Process each character in string.
'
For nPos = 1 To Len(StrIn)
    '
    ' Extract current character
    '
    Char = Mid(StrIn, nPos, 1)
    If Char  Delimit Then
        '
        ' Non-space chars serve as separators.
        '
        If Not InElement Then
            '
            ' Set flag to indicate we're moving thru an element,
            ' increment argument counter, expand return array.
            '
            InElement = True
            NumEls = NumEls + 1
            ReDim Preserve StrOut(0 To NumEls - 1)
        End If
        '
        ' Append current character to current element.
        '
        StrOut(NumEls - 1) = StrOut(NumEls - 1) & Char
    Else
        '
        ' Set flag to indicate we're between arguments.
        '
        InElement = False
    End If
Next nPos
'
' Assign number of arguments as return value for function.
'
ParseString = NumEls
End Function
```

How It Works

The ParseString function is about as simple as they come. Yet, it can be somewhat daunting to write it the first time. It walks through an input string, one character at a time, keeping track of whether it is within or in between elements. Since functions can't return arrays directly, a dynamic array is passed into ParseString, which in turn fills it with the elements found in the input string. The programmer can specify which character should act as the delimiter, or can allow this option to default to the space character.

Comments

For a routine that's so basic, this one has a wide variety of applications. Though more so in the days of DOS, some programs still benefit by accepting command-line parameters. ParseString would be a fast way to separate those parameters and then act on them individually. Another use, shown here, is parsing a string returned by an API function that contains substrings separated by nulls. Tab-delimited data files would be another use. With slight modifications, you could create another routine that reads the standard CSV (comma-separated value) files, which uses commas between values and quotes around text.

The only modification necessary to use ParseString with Visual Basic 3 programs is to make the Delimiter parameter required—in which case you'd probably also want to change it to a String rather than a Variant.

9.8 How do I...
Manipulate Bits, Bytes, Words, and Dwords?

COMPLEXITY: EASY
COMPATIBILITY: VB3 AND VB4

Problem

I find that I often need to pack a dword (double word, represented with long values in Visual Basic) with two words (integers in Visual Basic); or evaluate the high byte of the low word of a dword; set, clear or toggle bits within a word; and other such numeric manipulations. These tasks just don't seem to be very easy within Visual Basic—especially considering VB's lack of unsigned integers and shift operators. What I need is a solid set of manipulation routines that I can trust to reliably work with bits, bytes, words, and dwords—without my having to worry about overflow or sign-bit problems.

Technique

In this How-To we will develop a code module that supports a wide array of routines to do numeric manipulation. An accompanying form module will exercise the routines and, hopefully, allay any fears over special conditions that are historically troublesome for the Basic language. Because Visual Basic supports only signed integers, this project includes a technique to treat numbers as unsigned.

Unsigned integers have a range of 0 to 65,535 (&h0 to &hFFFF), but Basic has always used the high bit to indicate the sign, thus shifting the range to −32,768 to 32,767. To allow support for the full unsigned range, a negative integer must be temporarily copied to a long, and then have 65,536 (&h10000) added to it. Likewise, if, after manipulation, a long that is serving as a temporary integer evaluates to greater than 32,767, then 65,536 is subtracted from it before assigning it back to the final integer result.

These tricks effectively deal with the sign-bit problem. As you get familiar with this sort of manipulation, you'll find that it also helps greatly to think in hexadecimal. In fact, most of the code is written that way for clarity. The central concept here is that the actual number being stored is just a series of bytes. Visual Basic chooses to interpret those in a signed manner. You, however, can choose to interpret them differently!

Steps

Open and run HILO.VBP. An interface form, similar to that shown in Figure 9-8-1, is displayed. The text box is used to enter values directly for manipulation. Enter any value (within the long integer range) of interest. By default, values are interpreted as hexadecimal, but selecting the Input Base/Decimal radio button changes that assumption. When you press the Calc button, the various words and bytes are extracted from the value you entered and are displayed in the labels in the center of the form. The entered value is also displayed in binary, as indicated by the cursor in Figure 9-8-1. You can use the mouse to toggle, set, and clear the individual bits by clicking, Shift-clicking, and Ctrl-clicking on any particular bit. Experiment with various values, especially those falling in the troublesome boundary or transition ranges where the sign toggles.

Building the Interface to HiLo

1. Create a new project named HILO.VBP, and save the initial form as HILO.FRM. From the File menu, select Add File, and incorporate CBORDR3D.CLS (which was developed in How-To 3.4). Add the controls and set their properties as listed in Tables 9-8-1, 9-8-2, and 9-8-3.

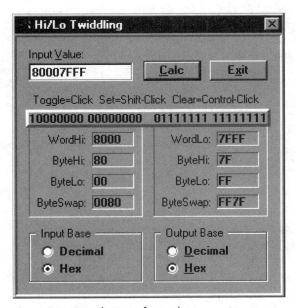

Figure 9-8-1 The HiLo form, demonstrating boundary conditions

Table 9-8-1 Objects and their properties on Form1

OBJECT	PROPERTY	SETTING
Form	Name	Form1
	BorderStyle	3 - Fixed Double
	Caption	"Hi/Lo Twiddling"
	MaxButton	False
Label	Name	lblEnter
	AutoSize	True
	Caption	"Enter &Value"
TextBox	Name	txtInput
	Font.Bold	True
CommandButton	Name	cmdVal
	Caption	"&Calc"
	Default	True
	Font.Bold	True
CommandButton	Name	cmdEnd
	Cancel	True
	Caption	"E&xit"
	Font.Bold	True
Label	Name	lblClick
	AutoSize	True
	Caption	"Toggle=Click Set=Shift-Click Clear=Control-Click"
Label	Name	lblBin
	Caption	lblBin
	Font.Bold	True
Label	Name	lblCaption
	AutoSize	True
	Alignment	1 - Right Justify
	Caption	"WordHi:"
	Index	0
Label	Name	lblVal
	Font.Bold	True
	Index	0
Label	Name	lblCaption
	AutoSize	True
	Alignment	1 - Right Justify
	Caption	"WordLo:"
	Index	1
Label	Name	lblVal
	Font.Bold	True

OBJECT	PROPERTY	SETTING
	Index	1
Label	Name	lblCaption
	AutoSize	True
	Alignment	1 - Right Justify
	Caption	"ByteHi:"
	Index	2
Label	Name	lblVal
	Font.Bold	True
	Index	2
Label	Name	lblCaption
	AutoSize	True
	Alignment	1 - Right Justify
	Caption	"ByteHi:"
	Index	3
Label	Name	lblVal
	Font.Bold	True
	Index	3
Label	Name	lblCaption
	AutoSize	True
	Alignment	1 - Right Justify
	Caption	"ByteLo:"
	Index	4
Label	Name	lblVal
	Font.Bold	True
	Index	4
Label	Name	lblCaption
	AutoSize	True
	Alignment	1 - Right Justify
	Caption	"ByteLo:"
	Index	5
Label	Name	lblVal
	Font.Bold	True
	Index	5
Label	Name	lblCaption
	AutoSize	True
	Alignment	1 - Right Justify
	Caption	"ByteSwap:"
	Index	6
Label	Name	lblVal

Continued on next page

Continued from previous page

OBJECT	PROPERTY	SETTING
	Font.Bold	True
	Index	6
Label	Name	lblCaption
	AutoSize	True
	Alignment	1 - Right Justify
	Caption	"ByteSwap:"
	Index	7
Label	Name	lblVal
	Font.Bold	True
	Index	7
Frame	Name	Frame1
	Caption	"Input Base"
Frame	Name	Frame2
	Caption	"Output Base"

Table 9-8-2 Objects and their properties contained within Frame1

OBJECT	PROPERTY	SETTING
OptionButton	Name	optInBase
	Caption	"Decimal"
	Index	0
	Value	False
OptionButton	Name	optInBase
	Caption	"Hex"
	Index	1
	Value	True

Table 9-8-3 Objects and their properties contained within Frame2

OBJECT	PROPERTY	SETTING
OptionButton	Name	optOutBase
	Caption	"Decimal"
	Index	0
	Value	False
OptionButton	Name	optOutBase
	Caption	"Hex"
	Index	1
	Value	True

2. Place the following code in the Declarations section of Form1. Other than the ever-present Option Explicit, constants are defined to reference the label and option button control arrays.

```
Option Explicit
'
' Label Index constants
'
Private Const lblWordHi = 0
Private Const lblWordLo = 1
Private Const lblWHByteHi = 2
Private Const lblWHByteLo = 3
Private Const lblWLByteHi = 4
Private Const lblWLByteLo = 5
Private Const lblWHByteSwap = 6
Private Const lblWLByteSwap = 7
'
' Option button Index constants
'
Private Const oDec = 0
Private Const oHex = 1
```

3. Insert the following code in the Form_Load event of Form1. Here, the display is initialized by calculating all relevant bits, bytes, and words for 0 (as if we didn't know!), and a call is made to place some 3D objects on the form.

```
Private Sub Form_Load()
    '
    ' Initialize input value and output display
    '
    txtInput = 0
    CalcVals
    '
    ' Initialize and draw 3D effects
    '
    Call Setup3D
End Sub
```

4. To Form1, add a private routine called CalcVals, and place the following code in it. This routine calls nearly every routine in the HILO.BAS module and places the results into the appropriate label controls. First, the value entered in the text box is evaluated by the GetInputVal function; then the output is formatted according to the selected output option button.

```
Private Sub CalcVals()
    Dim InVal As Long
    '
    ' Clean up input value
    '
    InVal = GetInputVal((optInBase(oHex)))
    '
    ' Display Hi/Lo Byte/Word values using a variety
    ' of routines from HiLo.
```

Continued on next page

Continued from previous page

```
    '
    If optOutBase(oHex) Then
        '
        ' Display values in hex.
        '
        lblVal(lblWordHi) = FmtHex(WordHi(InVal), 4)
        lblVal(lblWordLo) = FmtHex(WordLo(InVal), 4)
        lblVal(lblWHByteHi) = FmtHex(ByteHi(WordHi(InVal)), 2)
        lblVal(lblWHByteLo) = FmtHex(ByteLo(WordHi(InVal)), 2)
        lblVal(lblWLByteHi) = FmtHex(ByteHi(WordLo(InVal)), 2)
        lblVal(lblWLByteLo) = FmtHex(ByteLo(WordLo(InVal)), 2)
        lblVal(lblWHByteSwap) = FmtHex(ByteSwap(WordHi(InVal)), 4)
        lblVal(lblWLByteSwap) = FmtHex(ByteSwap(WordLo(InVal)), 4)
    ElseIf optOutBase(oDec) Then
        '
        ' Display values in decimal
        '
        lblVal(lblWordHi) = WordHi(InVal)
        lblVal(lblWordLo) = WordLo(InVal)
        lblVal(lblWHByteHi) = ByteHi(WordHi(InVal))
        lblVal(lblWHByteLo) = ByteLo(WordHi(InVal))
        lblVal(lblWLByteHi) = ByteHi(WordLo(InVal))
        lblVal(lblWLByteLo) = ByteLo(WordLo(InVal))
        lblVal(lblWHByteSwap) = ByteSwap(WordHi(InVal))
        lblVal(lblWLByteSwap) = ByteSwap(WordLo(InVal))
    End If
    '
    ' Display binary representation of InVal
    lblBin = FmtBin(WordHi(InVal)) & "    " & FmtBin(WordLo(InVal))
End Sub
```

5. To Form1, add a private function called GetInputVal, and place the following code in it. This function reads the text entered in txtInput and if necessary, reformats it so that Visual Basic's Val function can treat it as a hex value.

```
Private Function GetInputVal(UseHex As Boolean) As Long
    Dim tmpVal As String
    '
    ' Clean up input text, and determine value using
    ' current input number base.
    '
    tmpVal = UCase(Trim(txtInput))
    If UseHex Then
        '
        ' Convert to hex by adding prefix, and
        ' trimming if necessary. 8 digits max.
        '
        If InStr(tmpVal, "&H") <> 1 Then
            tmpVal = "&H" & Left(tmpVal, 8)
        End If
        '
        ' Make sure it's considered a Long by
        ' appending suffix.
        '
```

```
      If Len(tmpVal) <= 6 Then
          tmpVal = tmpVal & "&"
      End If
   End If
   GetInputVal = Val(tmpVal)
End Function
```

6. Insert the following code in the cmdVal_Click event of Form1. Pressing this button calls the CalcVals routine.

```
Private Sub cmdVal_Click()
   '
   ' Calculate new values
   '
   CalcVals
End Sub
```

7. Insert the following code in the cmdEnd_Click event of Form1. Pressing this button ends the demonstration.

```
Private Sub cmdEnd_Click()
   '
   ' Exit demonstration
   '
   Unload Me
End Sub
```

8. Insert the following code in the optInBase_Click event of Form1. These option buttons control how the input value is interpreted, either as decimal or hex. When one button is selected, the input value is read using the previous base, and then reformatted using the newly selected base.

```
Private Sub optInBase_Click(Index As Integer)
   Dim InVal As Long
   '
   ' Interpret the value in textbox, based upon number
   ' base that was previously in effect.
   '
   InVal = GetInputVal((Index + 1) Mod 2)
   '
   ' Place value back in textbox using new number base.
   '
   If Index = oHex Then
      txtInput = Hex(InVal)
   Else
      txtInput = InVal
   End If
End Sub
```

9. Insert the following code in the optOutBase_Click event of Form1. This set of option buttons control how the output labels are displayed, either as decimal or hex. To switch the display, only a call to CalcVals is required.

```
Private Sub optOutBase_Click(Index As Integer)
    '
    ' Recalculate output display values
    '
    CalcVals
End Sub
```

10. Insert the following code in the lblBin_MouseUp event of Form1. This event triggers the bit manipulations of the binary label. A normal click will toggle the selected bit. If the Q key is down, the bit will be cleared; and if the F key is depressed, the bit is set. To determine which bit was clicked on, the program cycles through, comparing the X mouse coordinate with the cumulative TextWidth at each position within the label. As soon as X is less, that bit is selected. The bit-manipulation routines in HILO.BAS only work with integer values. Therefore, if the selected bit is greater than 15, the bit number has 16 subtracted from it, to represent its position within the high word. The appropriate word is then extracted within the call to the appropriate bit routine. This all happens within a call to MakeLong, which puts the altered word and its partner back together again. This altered value is reentered into the text box, and a call to CalcVals updates the remainder of the display for the new value.

```
Private Sub lblBin_MouseUp(Button As Integer, Shift As Integer, ⇒
     X As Single, Y As Single)
    Dim InVal As Long
    Dim Bit As Integer
    Dim tmpVal As String
    Dim i As Integer
    '
    ' Interpret value in textbox
    '
    InVal = GetInputVal((optInBase(oHex)))
    '
    ' Grab binary representation, and "walk" through
    ' it bit-by-bit until X is less than the cummulative
    ' string length.
    '
    tmpVal = lblBin.Caption
    Bit = 31
    For i = 1 To Len(tmpVal)
        If X < TextWidth(Left(tmpVal, i)) Then
            Exit For
        End If
        If Mid(tmpVal, i, 1) <> " " Then
            '
            ' Decrement bit pointer, if not a space.
            '
            Bit = Bit - 1
        End If
    Next i
    '
    ' Alter bit clicked on by user. Control-Click clears it,
```

```
    ' Shift-Click sets it, and simple Click toggles it.
    '
    If Bit > 15 Then
        '
        ' Subtract 16 from Bit, since it will be used to
        ' alter extracted word.
        '
        Bit = Bit - 16
        '
        ' Use bit routines on extracted high word. Make a
        ' new long using unaltered low word.
        '
        If (Shift And vbCtrlMask) Then
            InVal = MakeLong(BitClear(WordHi(InVal), Bit), _
                WordLo(InVal))
        ElseIf (Shift And vbShiftMask) Then
            InVal = MakeLong(BitSet(WordHi(InVal), Bit), WordLo(InVal))
        Else
            InVal = MakeLong(BitToggle(WordHi(InVal), Bit), _
                WordLo(InVal))
        End If
    Else
        '
        ' Use bit routines on low word. Make a new long using
        ' unaltered high word.
        '
        If Shift And vbCtrlMask Then
            InVal = MakeLong(WordHi(InVal), BitClear(WordLo(InVal), _
                Bit))
        ElseIf Shift And vbShiftMask Then
            InVal = MakeLong(WordHi(InVal), BitSet(WordLo(InVal), Bit))
        Else
            InVal = MakeLong(WordHi(InVal), BitToggle(WordLo(InVal), _
                Bit))
        End If
    End If
    '
    ' Place new value back in textbox, calculate new display
    ' values based on altered bit.
    '
    If optInBase(oHex) Then
        txtInput = Hex$(InVal&)
    Else
        txtInput = Format$(InVal&)
    End If
    CalcVals
End Sub
```

11. If desired, add a private routine, called Setup3D, to Form1. Place the following optional code in Setup3D. In this additional example of the versatility of the CBorder3D class, a total of 12 objects are used to dress up the form. Since all the effects are static and the form is relatively small, AutoRedraw is turned on while the effects are first drawn, and then turned off again. This allows you to set up the effects once as the program begins, and forget about them from then on. They

will be drawn on a persistent bitmap image of the form, and Visual Basic will automatically refresh them whenever the form needs repainting.

```
Private Sub Setup3D()
    Dim i As Integer
    Dim Frm3D As CBorder3D
    Dim Bin3D As CBorder3D
    Dim Lab3D(0 To 7) As CBorder3D
    Dim Box3D(0 To 1) As CBorder3D
    '
    ' Called from Form_Load
    ' Styles supported by CBorder3D

    Const StyleNone = 0
    Const StyleSunken = 1
    Const StyleRaised = 2
    Const StyleFramed = 3
    Const StyleDouble = 4
    Const StyleWithin = 5
    Const StyleCustomFramed = 6
    Const StyleCustomDouble = 7
    Const StyleCustomWithin = 8
    '
    ' Setup 3D border effect around edge of form.
    '
    Set Frm3D = New CBorder3D
    Set Frm3D.Canvas = Me
    Frm3D.Style3D = StyleCustomWithin
    Frm3D.BevelOuter = StyleSunken
    Frm3D.BevelWidth = 2
    Frm3D.Left = 0
    Frm3D.Top = Screen.TwipsPerPixelY
    Frm3D.Width = Me.ScaleWidth
    Frm3D.Height = Me.ScaleHeight - Frm3D.Top
    '
    ' Setup 3D border effect around output labels.
    '
    For i = 0 To 7
        Set Lab3D(i) = New CBorder3D
        Set Lab3D(i).Client = lblVal(i)
        Lab3D(i).Style3D = StyleSunken
    Next i
    '
    ' Setup 3D border effect around binary label.
    '
    Set Bin3D = New CBorder3D
    Set Bin3D.Canvas = Me
    Set Bin3D.Client = lblBin
    Bin3D.Style3D = StyleDouble
    Bin3D.BevelWidth = 3
    '
    ' Setup 3D pseudo-frames around labels.
    '
    For i = 0 To 1
        Set Box3D(i) = New CBorder3D
```

```
            Set Box3D(i).Canvas = Me
            Box3D(i).Style3D = StyleCustomWithin
            Box3D(i).BevelOuter = StyleSunken
            Box3D(i).BevelWidth = 1
            Box3D(i).Top = lblBin.Top + lblBin.Height
            Box3D(i).Width = Frame1.Width
            Box3D(i).Height = lblVal(6).Top - Box3D(i).Top + _
                lblVal(0).Height * 1.7
        Next i
        Box3D(0).Left = Frame1.Left
        Box3D(1).Left = Frame2.Left
        '
        ' Since there are so many 3D objects, paint them
        ' only once with AutoRedraw turned on. They would
        ' work just fine the other way, but they are static
        ' and the form's small, so...
        '
        Me.Show
        Me.AutoRedraw = True
            For i = 0 To 1
                Box3D(i).Refresh
            Next i
            For i = 0 To 7
                Lab3D(i).Refresh
            Next i
            Bin3D.Refresh
            Frm3D.Refresh
        Me.AutoRedraw = False
End Sub
```

Building the HILO.BAS Module

12. Use the Insert Module menu item to add a new code module to the project; save it as HILO.BAS.

13. In the Declarations section, only Option Explicit is required. Most likely, you've seen countless discussions on the mechanics of binary operations. These won't be repeated here in detail, therefore. Instead we'll present a comprehensive set of functions that do the actual work you'd like to accomplish.

14. To HILO.BAS, add a public function called BitClear, and place the following code in it.

```
Public Function BitClear(WordIn As Integer, Bit As Integer) As Integer
    Dim tmpWord As Long
    '
    ' Clear the Nth Bit to 0 using a temp Long,
    ' and clear all bits of high word.
    '
    tmpWord = (WordIn And Not (2 ^ Bit))
    tmpWord = tmpWord And Not &HFFFF0000
    '
    ' Account for sign-bit
```

Continued on next page

Continued from previous page

```
    '
    If tmpWord > &H7FFF Then
        BitClear = tmpWord - &H10000
    Else
        BitClear = tmpWord
    End If
End Function
```

BitClear accepts a word (integer) to work with, and the bit number to clear. Here and in other bit routines, bits are numbered from 0 (least significant) to 15 (most significant). As with many of the routines in HILO.BAS, integers are temporarily converted to longs before manipulation. This allows sign-bit issues to be overcome by opening up the entire unsigned integer range. BitClear uses the binary Not operator to create a mask with all bits set except the one passed. This mask is then AND'd with the passed word, and the result is assigned to the temporary dword. Since the intermediate result is now contained within a long integer, the high word must be cleared using the same technique that was used to clear a single bit. As discussed earlier, if the result of the previous calculations is greater than 32,767 (&h7FFF), an overflow error will occur if we attempt to assign it to an integer. For Visual Basic to correctly store what we know to be the correct value, it must be converted to the negative number whose hex value is equivalent. Remember, if the high bit is set, Visual Basic interprets that as being a negative number. Subtracting 65,536 (&h10000) slides the value back into the range that Visual Basic considers valid, yet maintains the same hex representation.

15. To HILO.BAS, add a public function called BitSet, and place the following code in it. BitSet uses the same general strategy as BitClear, except that the mask used in this case has only the bit of interest set, and when it is OR'd with the input word, that bit is turned on in the intermediate result.

```
Public Function BitSet(WordIn As Integer, Bit As Integer) As Integer
    Dim tmpWord As Long
    '
    ' Set the Nth Bit to 1, using a temp Long,
    ' and clear all bits of high word.
    '
    tmpWord = (WordIn Or (2 ^ Bit))
    tmpWord = tmpWord And Not &HFFFF0000
    '
    ' Account for sign-bit
    '
    If tmpWord > &H7FFF Then
        BitSet = tmpWord - &H10000
    Else
        BitSet = tmpWord
    End If
End Function
```

16. To HILO.BAS, add a public function called BitToggle, and place the following code in it. BitToggle, too, works just like BitSet and BitClear, but this time the Xor operator is employed.

```
Public Function BitToggle(WordIn As Integer, Bit As Integer) As Integer
    Dim tmpWord As Long
    '
    ' Toggle the Nth Bit, 1->0 or 0->1, using a temp long,
    ' and clear all bits of high word
    '
    tmpWord = (WordIn Xor (2 ^ Bit))
    tmpWord = tmpWord And Not &HFFFF0000
    '
    ' Account for sign-bit
    '
    If tmpWord > &H7FFF Then
        BitToggle = tmpWord - &H10000
    Else
        BitToggle = tmpWord
    End If
End Function
```

17. To HILO.BAS, add a public function called BitValue, and place the following code in it. BitValue creates a mask with only the bit in question set. This mask is AND'd with the input value, which returns either the mask value if the bit is set or 0 if it's clear. This result is compared with 0 and the Boolean result is returned.

```
Public Function BitValue(WordIn As Integer, Bit As Integer) As Boolean
    '
    ' Return Nth power bit as true/false
    '
    BitValue = ((WordIn And (2 ^ Bit)) > 0)
End Function
```

18. To HILO.BAS, add a public function called ByteHi, and place the following code in it. If the passed word is interpreted by Visual Basic to be less than 0, then it is shifted up into the unsigned integer range by adding 65,536. The low byte is lopped off with an integer divide by 256 (&h100). This operation shifts the decimal point to the left by 8 bits. Since it uses integer math, the fractional portion is discarded.

```
Public Function ByteHi(WordIn As Integer) As Byte
    '
    ' Lop off low byte with divide. If less than
    ' zero, then account for sign bit (adding &h10000
    ' implicitly converts to Long before divide).
    '
    If WordIn < 0 Then
        ByteHi = (WordIn + &H10000) \ &H100
    Else
        ByteHi = WordIn \ &H100
    End If
End Function
```

19. To HILO.BAS, add a public function called ByteLo, and place the following code in it. ByteLo uses the AND operator to discard the high byte of an integer. Only the lower 8 bits of the mask are set (&hFF). AND'ing this with the input word keeps only those bits in the lower 8 that were originally set.

```
Public Function ByteLo(WordIn As Integer) As Byte
    '
    ' Mask off high byte and return low.
    '
    ByteLo = WordIn And &HFF
End Function
```

20. To HILO.BAS, add a public function called ByteSwap, and place the following code in it. ByteSwap could be reduced to two calls, one each to ByteHi and ByteLo, with one more line of code to combine the results. For efficiency, however, all manipulation is done in-line, rather than making the function calls. After each byte is extracted, the low byte is shifted left by 8 bits, and the sign bit is accounted for. Recombining the bytes is a simple matter of addition (or using the OR operator).

```
Public Function ByteSwap(WordIn As Integer) As Integer
    Dim ByteHi As Integer
    Dim ByteLo As Integer
    Dim NewHi As Long
    '
    ' Separate bytes using same strategy as in
    ' ByteHi and ByteLo functions. Faster to do
    ' it inline than to make function calls.
    '
    If WordIn < 0 Then
        ByteHi = (WordIn + &H10000) \ &H100
    Else
        ByteHi = WordIn \ &H100
    End If
    ByteLo = WordIn And &HFF
    '
    ' Shift low byte left by 8
    '
    NewHi = ByteLo * &H100&
    '
    ' Account for sign-bit
    '
    If NewHi > &H7FFF Then
        ByteLo = NewHi - &H10000
    Else
        ByteLo = NewHi
    End If
    '
    ' Place high byte in low position
    '
    ByteSwap = ByteLo + ByteHi
End Function
```

21. To HILO.BAS, add a public function called WordHi, and place the following code in it. WordHi masks the lower byte, and then uses an integer divide to shift the high byte right by 16 bits. In fact, the divide covers all cases but one: if the high word is equal to &h8000, the erroneous value &h8001 would be returned if the low byte isn't first masked off. When developing routines of this sort, &h8000 is the value to test first. More than any other, it can break an otherwise functional routine.

```
Public Function WordHi(LongIn As Long) As Integer
    '
    ' Mask off low word then do integer divide to
    ' shift right by 16.
    '
    WordHi = (LongIn And &HFFFF0000) \ &H10000
End Function
```

22. To HILO.BAS, add a public function called WordLo, and place the following code in it. To retrieve the value of the low word, the high word is masked off. However, if the low word alone would produce a value greater than 32,767, then it needs to be slid back into the signed integer range by subtracting 65,536.

```
Public Function WordLo(LongIn As Long) As Integer
    '
    ' Low word retrieved by masking off high word.
    ' If low word is too large, twiddle sign bit.
    '
    If (LongIn And &HFFFF&) > &H7FFF Then
        WordLo = (LongIn And &HFFFF&) - &H10000
    Else
        WordLo = LongIn And &HFFFF&
    End If
End Function
```

23. To HILO.BAS, add a public function called WordSwap, and place the following code in it. WordSwap uses the same logic as other functions within this module, but it makes sense to perform a function of this nature completely in-line, to avoid any unneccesary overhead in calling yet more functions.

```
Public Function WordSwap(LongIn As Long) As Long
    Dim WordLo As Variant
    Dim WordHi As Integer
    '
    ' Use the same logic as the WordLo and WordHi functions.
    '
    If (LongIn And &HFFFF&) > &H7FFF Then
        WordLo = (LongIn And &HFFFF&) - &H10000
    Else
        WordLo = LongIn And &HFFFF&
    End If
    WordHi = (LongIn And &HFFFF0000) \ &H10000
    '
    ' Ditto the MakeLong function. Note that WordLo needs
```

Continued on next page

Continued from previous page

```
' to be a Variant to avoid overflow when it's equal
' to &h8000.
'
    WordSwap = (WordLo * &H10000) + (WordHi And &HFFFF&)
End Function
```

24. To HILO.BAS, add a public function called MakeLong, and place the following code in it. MakeLong calls on the magic of Variant promotion. In all cases but one, WordHi could be passed in as an integer and the function would succeed. However, if WordHi is equal to &h8000 (there's that number again!), multiplying it by &h10000 overflows the long integer range. By turning WordHi into a Variant, the error is avoided, because the Variant is promoted to an 8-byte value when this condition is detected. Otherwise, the function is straightforward. WordHi is shifted left by 16 bits when multiplied by 65,536. To this is added WordLo, but only after masking potential bits in the high word of WordLo. As illogical as that sounds, it's required to circumvent the type coercion Visual Basic uses when doing math.

```
Public Function MakeLong(WordHi As Variant, WordLo As Integer) As Long
    '
    ' High word is coerced to a variant on call to allow
    ' it to overflow limits of multiplication which shifts
    ' it left.
    '
    MakeLong = (WordHi * &H10000) + (WordLo And &HFFFF&)
End Function
```

25. To HILO.BAS, add a public function called MakeWord, and place the following code in it. MakeWord first checks whether the high byte will send the new word beyond the signed integer range. To shift the high byte into position, it's multiplied by 256, and the low byte is added to this value to arrive at the new value. If need be, the final result must be slid back into range, by subtracting 65,536.

```
Public Function MakeWord(ByteHi As Byte, ByteLo As Byte) As Integer
    '
    ' If the high byte would push the final result out of the
    ' signed integer range, it must be slid back.
    '
    If ByteHi > &H7F Then
        MakeWord = ((ByteHi * &H100&) + ByteLo) - &H10000
    Else
        MakeWord = (ByteHi * &H100&) + ByteLo
    End If
End Function
```

26. To HILO.BAS, add a public function called FmtHex, and place the following code in it. FmtHex is a utility function that nicely formats a given value in hexadecimal, and pads it out to a prescribed length. Whenever hex displays are required, this is a very useful function.

```
Public Function FmtHex(InVal As Long, OutLen As Integer) As String
    '
    ' Left pad with zeros to OutLen
    '
    FmtHex = Right(String(OutLen, "0") & Hex(InVal), OutLen)
End Function
```

27. To HILO.BAS, add a public function called FmtBin, and place the following code in it. FmtBin accepts an integer, and formats it into a binary string by stepping through each bit mathematically. If a given bit is set, a 1 is placed in the output string; if the bit is clear, a 0 is added in. Reading a 16-bit binary value is somewhat difficult, so a space is inserted between the two bytes (a matter of preference, and you may want to remove that line of code).

```
Public Function FmtBin(InVal As Integer) As String
    Dim tmpRet As String
    Dim i As Integer
    Dim pos As Integer
    '
    ' Pad output string with all 0's
    '
    tmpRet = String(16, "0")
    '
    ' Cycle through each position inserting a 1 in
    ' return string if that bit is set.
    '
    For i = 15 To 0 Step -1
        pos = pos + 1
        If InVal And (2 ^ i) Then
            Mid(tmpRet, pos, 1) = "1"
        End If
    Next i
    '
    ' Add a space between bytes
    '
    FmtBin = Left(tmpRet, 8) + " " + Right(tmpRet, 8)
End Function
```

How It Works

The HILO demonstration project allows the user to enter any value within the long integer range, and press a button to manipulate and display the value, separated into its constituent elements. The user can also click on the individual bits within the calculated value, to toggle, set, or clear them. Interestingly, it takes nearly four times as much code (byte count, not lines) to demonstrate the manipulation routines than what is required for those routines themselves!

HILO.BAS contains a wide variety of routines that can do just about anything to a number when it comes to picking it apart, interpreting its components, or combining it with others. Bitwise manipulation is employed virtually throughout to turn bits on and off. Simple multiplication and integer division is used to shift values left or right. Subtraction and addition slide values in and out of signed integer ranges.

When you're doing this sort of math, the most important thing to recognize is that computers store bytes, not numbers. Visual Basic chooses to interpret a pair of two bytes as a signed integer, and four bytes as a signed long integer. Often, communication with other programs requires unsigned integers. Once you understand the true nature of the numbers Visual Basic uses, it's easy to transform them to the type of numbers other programs want to see.

Comments

When programming under Windows, the routines in HILO.BAS will most commonly come into play in your interactions with the API. For instance, the GetVersion call returns the DOS version in the high word, and the Windows version in the low word, with major and minor versions stored in the high and low bytes of each word. The GetViewportExt returns the X and Y extents of a device context's viewport, using the low word for X and the high word for Y. Coordinates of many types are also quite often packed into a long.

The routines in HILO.BAS are almost entirely transportable directly into Visual Basic 3.0, or Visual Basic for DOS, as well. The ones that make use of the new Byte and Boolean data types will need to be modified to use integers instead. The logic will be the same, since these new data types are used only for efficiency and consistency.

INDEX

NOTES

NOTES

NOTES

NOTES

NOTES

NOTES

NOTES

NOTES

NOTES

NOTES

Books have a substantial influence on the destruction of the forests of the Earth. For example, it takes 17 trees to produce one ton of paper. A first printing of 30,000 copies of a typical 480-page book consumes 108,000 pounds of paper, which will require 918 trees!

Waite Group Press™ is against the clear-cutting of forests and supports reforestation of the Pacific Northwest of the United States and Canada, where most of this paper comes from. As a publisher with several hundred thousand books sold each year, we feel an obligation to give back to the planet. We will therefore support organizations which seek to preserve the forests of planet Earth.

LIMITED WARRANTY

The following warranties shall be effective for 90 days from the date of purchase: (i) The Waite Group, Inc. warrants the enclosed disk to be free of defects in materials and workmanship under normal use; and (ii) The Waite Group, Inc. warrants that the programs, unless modified by the purchaser, will substantially perform the functions described in the documentation provided by The Waite Group, Inc. when operated on the designated hardware and operating system. The Waite Group, Inc. does not warrant that the programs will meet purchaser's requirements or that operation of a program will be uninterrupted or error-free. The program warranty does not cover any program that has been altered or changed in any way by anyone other than The Waite Group, Inc. The Waite Group, Inc. is not responsible for problems caused by changes in the operating characteristics of computer hardware or computer operating systems that are made after the release of the programs, nor for problems in the interaction of the programs with each other or other software.

THESE WARRANTIES ARE EXCLUSIVE AND IN LIEU OF ALL OTHER WARRANTIES OF MERCHANTABILITY OR FITNESS FOR A PARTICULAR PURPOSE OR OF ANY OTHER WARRANTY, WHETHER EXPRESS OR IMPLIED.

EXCLUSIVE REMEDY

The Waite Group, Inc. will replace any defective disk without charge if the defective disk is returned to The Waite Group, Inc. within 90 days from date of purchase.

This is Purchaser's sole and exclusive remedy for any breach of warranty or claim for contract, tort, or damages.

LIMITATION OF LIABILITY

THE WAITE GROUP, INC. AND THE AUTHORS OF THE PROGRAMS SHALL NOT IN ANY CASE BE LIABLE FOR SPECIAL, INCIDENTAL, CONSEQUENTIAL, INDIRECT, OR OTHER SIMILAR DAMAGES ARISING FROM ANY BREACH OF THESE WARRANTIES EVEN IF THE WAITE GROUP, INC. OR ITS AGENT HAS BEEN ADVISED OF THE POSSIBILITY OF SUCH DAMAGES.

THE LIABILITY FOR DAMAGES OF THE WAITE GROUP, INC. AND THE AUTHORS OF THE PROGRAMS UNDER THIS AGREEMENT SHALL IN NO EVENT EXCEED THE PURCHASE PRICE PAID.

COMPLETE AGREEMENT

This Agreement constitutes the complete agreement between The Waite Group, Inc. and the authors of the programs, and you, the purchaser.

Some states do not allow the exclusion or limitation of implied warranties or liability for incidental or consequential damages, so the above exclusions or limitations may not apply to you. This limited warranty gives you specific legal rights; you may have others, which vary from state to state.

SOFTWARE LICENSE AGREEMENT

Get the results you need from Visual Basic. Faster.

Visual Basic® Developer will keep you on top of Visual Basic—month after month.

Visual Basic Developer is the independent Visual Basic resource you've been waiting for! Pinnacle Publishing's monthly newsletter and companion disk will help you use Visual Basic faster and more effectively.

Every issue of *Visual Basic Developer* provides more than just tips and shortcuts— you get in-depth articles and step-by-step techniques that help you get the most out of Visual Basic and add-in tools. You'll learn easier, more efficient ways to:

- Create multi-user and client/server applications
- Write down modular, reusable code to save develpment time down the line
- Design more intuitive forms faster
- Link Visual Basic with many other applications via OLE 2.0 and DDE

This information comes from expert authors who know Visual Basic inside and out. They'll show you features you didn't know about, and they'll help you work around the tough spots in Visual Basic.

Companion disk with every issue

Each issue of *Visual Basic Developer* comes with a 3.5" companion disk at no additional cost. You'll find all the source code for that issue— plus programs, utilities, custom controls, demos, and other bonuses. You can put the concepts right to work!

Special offer: Save $50

Order today and you'll receive 12 monthly issues of *Visual Basic Developer*—plus compan ion disks—for just $129. That's $50 off the regular subscription rate! (Please mention off code BGB.)

100% money-back guarantee

"If you ever decide you're not satisfied with *Visual Basic Developer*, you can cancel your subscription and receive a full refund —whether you're in your first month or your last."

Susan Jameson Harker
Publisher

To begin your subscription to
Visual Basic Developer, call toll-free

800/788-1900

206/251-1900 ▲ Fax 206/251-5057

Pinnacle Publishing, Inc.
18000 72nd Avenue South, Suite 217 ▲ Kent, WA 9803

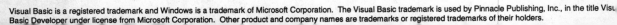

SATISFACTION REPORT CARD

Please fill out this card if you wish to know of future updates to
Visual Basic 4 How-To, **or to receive our catalog.**

First Name: _____ Last Name: _____

Address: _____

Street: _____

City: _____ State: _____ Zip: _____

Daytime Telephone: (_____) _____

E-mail address: _____

Date product was acquired: Month _____ Day _____ Year _____ Your Occupation: _____

Overall, how would you rate *Visual Basic 4 How-To?*

☐ Excellent   ☐ Very Good   ☐ Good
☐ Fair   ☐ Below Average ☐ Poor

What did you like MOST about this book? _____

_____

_____

What did you like LEAST about this book? _____

_____

Please describe any problems you may have encountered with installing or using the disk: _____

_____

How did you use this book (problem-solver, tutorial, reference...)?

_____

What is your level of computer expertise?

☐ New   ☐ Dabbler   ☐ Hacker
☐ Power User   ☐ Programmer   ☐ Experienced Professional

What computer languages are you familiar with? _____

Please describe your computer hardware:

Computer _____ Hard disk _____

5.25" disk drives _____ 3.5" disk drives _____

Video card _____ Monitor _____

Printer _____ Peripherals _____

Sound board _____ CD-ROM _____

Where did you buy this book?

☐ Bookstore (name): _____
☐ Discount store (name): _____
☐ Computer store (name): _____
☐ Catalog (name): _____
☐ Direct from WGP   ☐ Other _____

What price did you pay for this book? _____

What influenced your purchase of this book?

☐ Recommendation   ☐ Advertisement
☐ Magazine review   ☐ Store display
☐ Mailing   ☐ Book's format
☐ Reputation of Waite Group Press   ☐ Other

How many computer books do you buy each year? _____

How many other Waite Group books do you own? _____

What is your favorite Waite Group book? _____

_____

Is there any program or subject you would like to see Waite Group Press cover in a similar approach? _____

_____

Additional comments? _____

_____

Please send to: **Waite Group Press**
                        200 Tamal Plaza
                        Corte Madera, CA 94925

☐ **Check here for a free Waite Group catalog**

A Partial List of How-Tos Included in Visual Basic 4 How-To
HOW DO I...